新时代
汉英小词典

NEW AGE
Little Chinese-English
Dictionary

潘绍中　主编

商务印书馆
THE COMMERCIAL PRESS
2003年·北京

主　编：潘绍中

副主编：赫迎红

编　委：胡水娟

　　　　卜焕芳

　　　　梅　琼

　　　　吕　惠

　　　　陆晓红

前　言
Foreword

　　《新时代汉英小词典》是"新时代汉英词典系列"的小型本。它和已出版的大型本《新时代汉英大词典》(2000)和中型本《新时代汉英词典》(2002)一起，构成了"新时代汉英词典系列"的基本框架，希望可以满足广大读者的不同需要。

　　作为小型本，本书主要针对大中学生、中初级英语学习者和外籍汉语学习者的需要。综观当前图书市场，虽然已有一些此类小型本，但普遍为某个大中型辞书的简单压缩，容量小、信息量也小——一则小矣，但查找起来，往往找不到某些常用的词语，或者只有释义而无从了解其用法，颇有隔靴搔痒之感。可见小有小的难处。编好小型本的关键在于针对特定读者的实际需要，在保持较小篇幅的前提下涵盖他们日常所需的信息和知识，并尽可能地提供词语的用法。本书的编者都是多年从事英语教学的教师，深知中初级英语学习者的需要，因此在编辑本书过程中力求根据他们的需要做到以下几点：

　　一、在选条、释义等方面切实满足中初级读者的实际需要，如在选条上主要收录常用的字头与词条，其中既包括新近出现的基本社科、科技词汇，如："非典"（及其学名）、"冠状病毒"、"带宽"（当然还有"宽带"）、"转基因"（及有关搭配）、"原教旨主义"等，又保留了一些常用的书面词语和关于传统文化的词语，如"干支"、

"尧舜"、"魑魅魍魉"等。此外,一些在当代汉语中(尤其在中青年读者中)普遍使用的英语字词,如 DIY(自己动手做),SIM 卡(用户身份识别卡)等,则收录在正文后的"英文字母开头的词语"中。

二、鉴于汉语中成语较多,对英语学习者的表达和汉语学习者的理解来说都是个难题,本书收入了较为丰富的常见成语、俗语和谚语,或列为词条,如:"重蹈覆辙"、"欲盖弥彰"……或收为例证,如:"与时俱进"(列于"与"字下)、"不怕官,只怕管。"(收入"不怕"条下)……并附以简明、实用的释义。

三、另一个重点是抓住中初级英语学习者最需要解决的英语搭配问题,注意在释义和例证中说明用法。这样,有的释义即使省去了例证,读者仍然可以知道如何使用英语词语,如:"干涉"释为"interfere(in sth or with sb)"就不必再举例,而另外两个对应词"intervene"和"meddle"的搭配则通过例证予以说明。

上述三条保证了本书收录的字头、词条和固定搭配都比较适量而实用,作为一部小型词典,基本能够满足中初级读者的需要。

为了确保实现上述目标,本书大力控制篇幅,处处力求精简。例如:相对简单的常用词语不设条,而用作例证,以节省篇幅;在需用例证时多用短语,少用句子;在必须用句子时,力求短而精。又如:为避免重复,所收录的词条和例证一般都以第一个字为准,不重复出现。再如,删去不能单独为首使用的字、词,如将"尬"列入"尴尬"条,而不单独立条;不收"头角"为词条,但在"崭露头角"条和"露头角"例中可以查到其用法。同时,作为小型词典,本书也略去了姓氏和绝大多数的专名,等等。

　　以上这些想法说起来比较简单,但做起来并不容易。尤其因为受到篇幅的限制,尽管字斟句酌,仍常有捉襟见肘之感。好在书已编出来了,敬请广大读者和同行专家多提批评建议,以便今后修订时汲取、改进。

潘　绍　中

2003 年 6 月于北京

目 录
Contents

使 用 说 明

A Guide to the Use of the Dictionary

一、条目安排

1. 本书以收录现代汉语字、词为主,酌收少量有用的古旧和方言字、词。单字条目(即字头)有繁体、异体的,加圆括号附于正体之后;如繁、异体只适用于某些义项,则在其左上角加所适用的义项数码,如:"云(❶❷雲) yún"。

2. 本书字头按汉语拼音字母顺序排列;形音相同的,收为一个条目。同音异调的,按声调顺序排列(一般按音节分组排列);轻声放在非轻声的后面。同音同调的(即在同一音节组中),按笔画由少到多排列;笔画相同的,按起笔笔形"横(一)、竖(丨)、撇(丿)、点(丶)、折(乛)"顺序排列。

在同一字头下的多字条目(即词条),按其第二字参照上述字头排列原则排列;如第二字相同,则按第三字排列,以此类推。

3. 字头中,凡形同而音、义不同的,或形、义相同而音不相同,各有适用范围的,都分立条目。前者如:"奔 bēn"和"奔 bèn","奇 jī"和"奇 qí"。后者如:"绿 lǜ"和"绿 lù"。这两类条目用 *see also*("另见")相互连接。

4. 有些条目意义相关而需要参见,在英文释义后用 *see also*

（"另见"）引出，如：

申 shēn… ❷ 9th of the Earthly Branches　*see also* "干支" gānzhī

大寒 dàhán　Great Cold, 24th seasonal division point　*see also* "节气" jiéqì

其中，有的条目略去释义，直接用 *see*（"见"）引出相关条目，如：

乾 qián　❶ *see* "八卦" bāguà　❷ …

二、如何查找

1. 查找字头：请按第一部分第 2 条的说明查找。但有些字头不能单独使用，只用于一两个以其他字头开始的固定搭配，在本书中就不单独立条，如"尬"要查词条"尴尬"，"璃"可见词条"玻璃"、"琉璃"。

2. 查找词条：本书多字条目一律以第一个字为准。因此，一般只要按第一部分第 2 条的说明找到其所属的字头，即可"按图索骥"。其中，有些字头一般只用于某个词语，本书就直接用该词语为条，找到字头也就找到了该词语，如：

魑 chī　魑魅魍魉 chīmèi-wǎngliǎng　〈书〉demons and monsters; evil people of every description（"魅"、"魍"、"魉"三字不单独收录）

崔 cuī　崔巍 cuīwēi　*also* "崔嵬"〈书〉high; lofty; towering（"嵬"字不单独收录）

若有些词语仅用于以别的字头开始的搭配，在本书中也不单独立条,如"头角"不单立词条,可查"崭露头角"(词条);"露头角"(见"露"字下例证)。

3. 特殊结构:汉语中有一些成语或固定搭配,具有某种相同的、有一定含义的结构,在本书中往往归结为同一个词条,以节省篇幅。在这种情况下,要请读者仔细查找,如"一蹶不振"等成语和"一动不动"等固定用法,就要查"一…不…"条:

一…不… yī…bù… ❶ *used before antonymous verbs to indicate irreversible action or condition*:一病不起 take to one's bed and never leave it again; fall ill never to recover /一蹶不振 collapse after one setback; be unable to recover after one defeat or failure ❷ *used before a noun and a verb for emphasis*:一动不动 not move an inch; be perfectly still

其他如"不…不…"("不明不白","不上不下"……),"七…八…"("七拼八凑","七嘴八舌"……),"上…下…"("上行下效","上有政策,下有对策"……)等结构均照此处理。

4. 查找例证:查找做例证用的词语,一般仍要先从第一个字或词着手,如"热血沸腾"只用于"热血"下为例,"图文并茂"只在"图文"条下出现,"反攻倒算"要到"反攻"条下去找,不可反其道而行之。

在少数情况下也有采用本条目字、词在后的搭配作为例证的,但这只是因为前面的字、词没有单独成条,或没有收录这一例证,如:"鬻 yù 〈书〉sell:卖儿～女 sell one's children for survival"("卖儿"不成条,而"卖"字头下也未收此搭配)。又如:"营 yíng ❶ seek (profit, etc); pursue:非～利机构 non-profit institution ...".

5. 例证顺序：查找做例证用的词语，往往需要了解本书例证排列的顺序。凡是三个以下的例证，一般按先短语后句子，先直译后意译的顺序排列。

多于三个的例证，也按先短语后句子的顺序排列；但同是短语的，则按"本条目词语在后"，"本条目词语在前"，"本条目词语居中"的顺序排列；同类情况的，按字数由少及多排列；字数相等的，按拼音顺序排列，如：

花 huā　... ❷ anything resembling a flower；fireworks；cotton：放～ shoot off fireworks／挂～ get wounded (in battle)／～卷 steamed twisted roll／～炮 fireworks and firecrackers／冰～儿 ice flower／泪～儿 tears ...

三、关于释义

1. 本书中的汉语字、词义项，一般不以词类区分，但其英语释义，尽量使用词性相同的对应词；同一义项的对应词中，如有直译和意译之分，则通常先直译，后意译，有的还加上门类词，如：

夜叉 yèchā　*yaksha*, an evil spirit；〈喻〉hideous and ferocious person：母～ hideous woman；termagant (woman)

神出鬼没 shénchū-guǐmò　move about like a supernatural being；come and go like a shadow；appear and disappear mysteriously

2. 有些字、词无英语对应词，则采用说明的方式处理，如：

袄 ǎo　short Chinese-style coat or jacket

叹词、量词、助词、象声词等无英语对应词的,以斜体说明其用法,前面加门类词,如:

啊(呵) ā 〈叹〉*expressing surprise*, *etc*; …

3. 英语释义与汉语在词义或用法上不完全对应时,加圆括号用英语对释义加以限定或补充,如"女王 queen (as a monarch in her own right)"例中的括号说明它与做"王后"讲的 queen 不同。又如:

田 tián ❶ (cultivated) land; farmland; field (of ores, etc) …

筝 zhēng … ❷ (usu 风筝) kite

4. 其他方面需要加以说明的,同样放在圆括号内:

氧 yǎng (usu 氧气)〈化〉oxygen (O)

女士 nǚshì (polite form of address for a woman) lady; madam

非典 fēidiǎn (common name for 严重急性呼吸综合征) SARS (serious acute respiratory syndrome)

议会 yìhuì *also* "国会" (UK) Parliament; (US) Congress; (France) National Assembly; (Japan) Diet; (Germany) Reichstag; (Russia) Duma

5. 为了简省篇幅,有些释义中用圆括号标明两种意义相同或不同的译法,如词条"函购 purchase by mail (order)"表示:同一个意思可以说"purchase by mail",也可以说"purchase by mail order";而例证"支着儿 (watch a game of chess and) give advice to a player; kibitz"的前一释义则表示两个意思:"watch a game

of chess and give advice to a player"（即其原义,大体与 kibitz 相同）或"give advice to a player"（即原义、喻义均可）。

四、其他说明

1. 英语拼法：一般以英国拼法为准,不列其他拼法;有几种写法的,取其规范写法或常见写法,不列变体。

2. 汉语音译：一般按汉语拼音规定,如"元"译为 yuan,"北京"译为 Beijing……。音译是否用斜体则按英语惯例,如 yuan 不用斜体,而"角"的音译就要用斜体 *jiao*。

如某些词语已有约定俗成的英译,本书中一般仍予以沿用,如："孔子 Confucius","道教 Taoism","长江 Yangtze River","澳门 Macao"等。

其中,有些词语虽有常见的英译名,但存在这样那样的问题,就根据情况或共用,或加说明：

武术 wǔshù　　*wushu*；martial arts；kung fu …

珠穆朗玛峰 Zhūmùlǎngmǎfēng　　（shortened as 珠峰）Mount Qomolangma（known in the West as Mt Everest）

3. 释义和例证中的词和词组凡为名词的,开始的冠词均省去,以节省篇幅,如：

关（關）guān　…　❷ mountain pass；checkpoint；customs (house)：…　❸ barrier；critical juncture；crucial point …

关头 guāntóu　　juncture；moment：生死～ moment of life and death

释义中如有量词,则英文保留不定冠词。如：

　　批 pī　…　❹〈量〉batch；lot；group：刚到的一～货　a new lot of 'goods

　　4. 本书所用的英语缩略语，照当代英语一般惯例，凡可以不用省略号"."的，都不用，如：

AD（公元）　　BC（公元前）　　eg（例如）　　etc（等等）

ie（即）　esp（especially）　pl（plural）　sing（singular）

sb（somebody）　sth（something）　usu（usually）

HK（Hongkong）　UK（United Kingdom；Britain）

US（United States）

少数情况下，为避免误解仍保留省略号，如：

a. m.（上午）　　p. m.（下午）　　c.（circus 约）

cent.（世纪）　　v.（versus 对比）

附：门类词表

一、词类和修辞：

〈贬〉〈粗〉〈方〉〈副〉〈敬〉〈旧〉〈口〉〈连〉〈量〉〈谦〉〈书〉〈俗〉〈叹〉〈套〉〈婉〉〈象声〉〈谑〉〈谚〉〈喻〉〈助〉

二、百科：

〈地〉〈电〉〈动物〉〈法〉〈化〉〈建筑〉〈经〉〈军〉〈考古〉〈理〉〈迷信〉〈农〉〈生理〉〈史〉〈数〉〈体〉〈天文〉〈通信〉〈戏〉〈信息〉〈医〉〈语言〉〈乐〉〈哲〉〈植〉〈中药〉〈中医〉〈宗教〉

部 首 检 字 表

Radical Index

说　明

1. 本检字表收录本字典的全部单字字头,依据《汉字统一部首表(草案)》201部归类,并标出序号,其中201龠部没有相应的字头。字头归部与正文相应,以收字量较多的形体为主,收字量较少的形体有的不单立部,加括号附在主部首后面;有的单立部,检字表中前面加"△"号附在主部首后面,目录中在主部首下加括号列出,后标明页码,以便查检。

2. 部首次序按部首笔画数的多少排列,部首的其他形体也排列在内,加上括号标出。

3. 同一部首的字按部首以外笔画数的多少依次排列,同笔画的字按起笔笔形的一、丨、丿、丶、乛的次序排列,如第一笔笔形相同,则按第二笔,依次类推。

（一）部首目录

（部首右边的号码指检字表的页码）

一画								
		10 卜(⺊)	14	23 卩(㔾)	18	34 艹(艸)	22
		11 冂(冋)	14	24 阝(在左)	18	35 寸	23
1 一	11	12 亻	14	25 阝(在右)	18	36 廾	23
2 丨	11	(人入)	15	26 力	18	37 大	23
3 丿	11	13 八(丷)	15	27 厶	19	38 尢(尣)	23
4 丶	12	14 勹	16	28 又	19	39 弋	23
5 乛(乛乙乛乙)		15 儿	16	29 廴	19	40 小(⺌)	23
	12	16 匕	16			41 口	24
		17 几(凡)	16	三画		42 囗	25
二画		18 亠	16	30 干	19	43 山	26
6 十	12	19 冫	16	31 工	19	44 巾	26
7 厂(厂)	13	20 冖	17	32 土	19	45 彳	26
8 匚	13	21 讠(訁)	17	(士)	20	46 彡	27
9 刂	13	(言)		33 扌	20	47 夊	27
(刀⺈)	13	22 凵	17	(手龵)	21	(犬)	27

（二）检字表

（字右边的号码指本字典正文的页码）

1 一部

一 856

一画

二 193
丁 168
七 578

二画

三 637
干 236
　 240
于 893
亏 439
才 68
下 789
丈 925
与 896
万 897

三画

丰 218
井 397
开 415
夫 224
天 725
无 773
元 901
云 906
专 963
丏 235
廿 542
五 777

卅 636
不 58
友 889
屯 747
互 315

四画

末 526
未 764
击 341
正 934
　 936
世 675
本 35
可 424
丙 52
左 987
右 892
布 66
册 75
平 570
东 172
丝 698

五画

考 422
老 451
共 261
亘 253
吏 464
再 910
（亘）253
在 911
百 15
有 889
而 192

死 700
夷 865
尧 851

六画

严 842
甫 228
東 689
两 471
丽 464
（夾）234
　 354
　 357
来 445

七画

奉 223
武 779
忝 728
（長）82
　 924
（亞）840
其 580
（來）445
（東）172
画 321
事 676
（兩）471
亞 347

八画

奏 982
毒 177
（甚）658
甚 660
巷 296

　 803
東 362
歪 750
甭 37
昼 957

九画

泰 714
秦 601
恭 260
哥 247
孬 536
夏 792

十画

焉 841
（專）963
戛 357
爽 693
（畫）957

十一画

棘 348
（棗）914
（甦）357
（畫）321

十二画

（勘）796
赖 447

十三画

（爾）192

十四画

夐 885

十五画以上

矗 191
整 936
囊 536

2 丨部

二至三画

上 648
中 950
　 954
（弔）166
书 685

四画

卡 415
　 587
北 32
旧 402
帅 691
归 280
且 598
甲 357
由 886
史 673
央 847
冉 620
出 107

五画

师 668
曲 611
　 612

六画
县　796
串　115
七画
非　211
果　286
畅　86
八画以上
临　476
幽　886
(黟)　338

3
丿部
一画
匕　38
九　401
乃　532
二画
千　587
乞　582
川　113
义　869
及　345
久　401
么　507
丸　753
三画
午　779
壬　625
夭　850
币　40
爻　851
乏　198
丹　143
乌　772
四画
生　661

失　666
　　918
乍　609
丘　312
乎　455
乐　905
五画
年　541
朱　957
丢　171
乔　596
乒　570
乓　556
向　803
后　310
杀　642
丶 六画
我　771
兵　51
(兔)　744
希　783
龟　281
卵　493
系　352
　　787
七画
垂　118
乖　272
秉　52
卑　31
肴　851
八画
重　104
　　955
复　231
(帥)　691
九画
(烏)　772
(師)　668

十一至十二画
(喬)　596
粤　906
斌　679
(與)　896
　　897
十三画
舞　779
睾　245
孵　224

4
丶部
二画
丫　838
之　939
三画
丹　143
为　760
　　764
四画
主　958
半　21
必　40
永　883
五至六画
州　956
农　546
良　469
八画
亲　600
　　608
叛　556
举　406

5
乛(乀乛乚乙)部
乙　866

一画
刁　166
了　456
　　474
二画
子　380
也　854
飞　210
习　785
乡　798
三画
丑　107
以　867
予　893
　　896
孔　430
幻　325
四画
司　698
民　519
弗　224
(疋)　564
电　163
甩　691
发　195
　　199
五画
丞　95
买　500
六画
君　414
甫　883
七画
肃　705
承　95
函　293
八画
(飛)　210

癸　282
十画以上
乾　592
(肅)　705
(亂)　493
豫　900

6
十部
十　669
一至三画
千　587
午　779
升　661
古　266
四画
早　914
毕　40
协　811
五画
克　426
六画
卓　971
直　942
丧　640
衰　640
(協)　811
卖　501
七至八画
南　531
　　534
真　931
隼　709
索　711
九画
率　492
　　691

减	363
凛	477
凝	544

20
一 部

二至五画

冗	630
写	812
军	412
罕	293

七画以上

冠	276
	277
冢	954
冥	524
冤	900

21
讠(言)部

二画

订	170
计	350
讣	229
认	626
讥	341

三画

讧	310
讨	720
让	621
讪	646
讫	586
(託)	747
训	837
议	869
讯	837
记	350

四画

| 讲 | 369 |
| 讳 | 333 |

讴	550
讶	840
许	828
讹	189
论	494
讼	704
讽	222
设	654
访	208
诀	410

五画

证	938
评	572
诅	983
识	671
诈	918
诉	705
诊	933
诋	158
诌	956
(註)	961
(詠)	884
词	120
诏	928
译	871

六画

诓	438
试	677
诗	668
诘	381
(誇)	435
诙	329
诚	95
诛	957
话	322
诞	145
诟	264
诠	616
诡	282
询	836
诣	871
诤	938
该	234

详	801
诧	79
浑	335
诩	829

七画

诫	386
(誌)	946
诬	773
(誆)	34
语	896
诮	598
误	781
诰	247
诱	893
诲	333
诳	438
说	695
	696
(認)	626
诵	704

八画

请	608
诸	958
诺	549
读	178
诽	212
课	427
诿	764
谀	894
谁	656
(諭)	494
谂	660
调	167
	729
谄	82
谅	472
谆	969
谇	715
谊	871

九画

| 谋 | 528 |
| 谍 | 168 |

谎	328
谏	367
谐	812
谑	835
谒	856
谓	766
谕	899
(諡)	679
谗	80
(謅)	972
谙	6
谚	847
谛	162
谜	514
(諲)	831
(諄)	333

十画

(講)	369
(謀)	319
谢	813
谣	851
(謳)	956
谤	24
谥	679
谦	589

十一画

谨	389
(謳)	550
谩	503
谪	930
谬	524

十二画

潜	917
(譖)	671
谰	447
谱	577
(譜)	938
谲	412
(譏)	341

十三画

| (護) | 316 |

谴	592
(譯)	871
(譭)	332
谵	920
(議)	869

十四画

| (譎) | 930 |

十五画

| (讀) | 178 |

十六画

| 雠 | 107 |

十七画

谶	93
(讒)	80
(讓)	621

十九画

| (讚) | 912 |

△言 部

| 言 | 842 |

六画

誓	974
誊	722
誉	900

七画

| 誓 | 679 |

十二画以上

警	397
(譽)	900
譬	565
(讐)	106
	107

22
山 部

二至四画

| 凶 | 823 |

云　906
允　907

三画

去　613
台　713

四至五画

牟　528
县　796
矣　868

六画

叁　639
参　70
　　76
　　657

七至九画

垒　457
畚　36
能　539
(参)　70
　　76
　　657

28
又部

又　892

一画

叉　77
　　79

二画

友　889
反　202
劝　616
双　692

三画

圣　664
对　183
发　195
　　199

四至五画

戏　787
观　274
　　277
欢　323
鸡　342

六画

叔　686
艰　361

七画

叟　705
叙　829

八至九画

难　534
　　535
(隻)　940
叟　503

十一画以上

叠　168
聚　408
(雙)　692

29
廴部

(巡)　836
延　733
　　841
(廹)　574
建　366

30
干部

干　236
　　240
午　779
刊　419
平　570
旱　294

31
工部

工　254

二至三画

左　987
巧　597
(仝)　736
功　258
式　676
巩　260

四画

汞　260
　　261
攻　259

六画

项　803

32
土部

土　743

二画

去　613

三画

圩　761
　　827
圭　281
寺　702
在　911
地　154
　　159
场　83
　　85

四画

坛　715
坏　323
址　944
坚　360
坐　989
坎　420
坍　714
均　413

坞　780
坑　216
　　428
坊　206
　　207
块　436
坠　969

五画

坩　238
坯　562
坪　572
坦　716
坤　440
垃　443
幸　823
坨　748
坡　573

六画

型　822
垣　901
垮　435
城　96
垢　264
垛　188
垫　165
垠　875

七画

埂　254
埋　500
　　502
坝　835
埃　2

八画

堵　179
基　343
域　899
(堅)　360
堑　593
堆　182
埠　67
培　559

(堃)　440
(執)　941
堕　188

九画

堪　420
塔　712
堰　847
堙　875
堤　157
(場)　83
　　85
堡　28
(塊)　436
(報)　28
(塔)　830

十画

填　728
塌　712
(塢)　780
塘　718
塑　706
(塗)　743
塞　636
塞　636
塞　641
(塚)　954

十一画

墙　595
墟　828
墅　690
(塲)　83
塾　688
境　399
墒　648
(墊)　165
(鹽)　188
(墜)　969

十二画

(墳)　216
墩　185

增　917

十三画

(墼)　428
(壇)　715
塞　883
壁　42

十四画

墼　304
(壓)　838
(塲)　835
壕　296

十六画以上

(壞)　323
疆　369
壤　620
(壩)　12

△士部

士　674

一至四画

壬　625
吉　346
壮　967
壳　424
壳　598
志　946
声　663
(壯)　967

九画

喜　786
(殻)　598
(壺)　314

十至十二画

鼓　268
(穀)　267
(壽)　684
(賣)　501

十九画

鸞　873

33

扌部

一至二画

扎　909
　　917
打　130
　　131
扑　575
扒　11
　　552
扔　628

三画

扛　240
　　421
扣　433
扦　588
托　747
执　941
扩　441
扪　512
扫　640
　　641
扬　847

四画

扶　225
抚　228
技　351
抔　575
抠　431
扰　621
扡　190
拒　407
找　927
批　562
扯　90
抄　86
折　654
　　928

抓　929
　　963
扳　19
抢　493
扮　22
抢　595
抵　944
　　870
抛　557
投　740
抗　421
护　175
抉　316
抉　410
扭　545
抖

把　12
　　13
报　28
拟　540
抒　686

五画

抹　498
抹　526
抹　526
拓　712
　　749
拢　487
拔　11
抨　561
拣　362
拌　587
括　541
担　143
　　145
抻　90
押　838
抽　105
拐　273
拃　918
拖　747
拍　552
拆　79
拎　476
拥　883

抵　158
拘　404
抱　29
拄　960
拉　443
　　444
拦　447
拌　22
扛　436
拧　544
拧　544
　　545
振　521
拂　225
抽　970
招　925
披　562
拨　54
择　916
　　919
(拚)　568
抬　713
拇　529
拗　8
　　546

六画

拭　678
挂　271
持　100
拮　381
拷　422
拱　261
挎　435
挞　712
挟　812
挠　536
挡　148
拽　963
挺　734
括　442
拴　692
拾　673
挑　728
　　730

指　945
挣　935
　　939
挤　349
拼　568
挖　750
按　6
挥　329
挪　549
拯　936

七画

捞　450
捕　58
捂　779
振　933
(挾)　812
捎　652
　　653
捍　294
捏　543
捉　970
捆　441
捐　409
损　709
捌　11
捡　362
挫　128
捋　491
　　495
换　325
挽　754
捣　150
捅　738
挨　2
挨　2

八画

捧　561
(掛)　271
揶　854
措　128
描　518
捺　532
掎　350

掩 844　捷 383　排 553　掉 167　掳 489　捆 273　捶 118　推 744　掀 794
(捨) 654　(掄) 493　(採) 69　授 685　捻 542　掏 719　掐 587　掬 405　掠 493
掂 162　掖 853　接 378　掷 948　(捲) 409　(揸) 562　掸 145　控 431　掴 592
探 717　(掃) 640　641　据 408　掘 412　掺 80　掇 187

九画

揍 811　搂 982　揲 79　搭 130　振 840　(揀) 362　揩 419　(揹) 31　揽 448

提 157　722　(揚) 847　揖 864　揭 379　揣 113　揪 602　插 77　揪 400
(揑) 543　搜 704　(拋) 118　揄 895　援 902　搀 80　搁 247　249　搓 128
搂 487　楼 487　搅 375　揎 830　握 772　揞 54　揍 440　搔 640　揉 630

十画

摄 655　摸 524　搏 57　(搗) 712　搕 192　摆 17　携 812　(搞) 150　搬 19
摇 851　(搶) 595　搞 245　搪 718　搐 113　搛 362　搛 51

(搾) 919　(搁) 645　摊 715　操 640

十一画

(摳) 431　摽 49　(搜) 487　(搜) 487　摔 474　摭 497　(摳) 273　摧 126
摣 943　摘 919　摔 691　撇 568　撅 568　(摺) 929　(摻) 80

十二画

撑 542　(撓) 536　撅 812　(撻) 712　撕 700　撒 636　撒 636　撅 410
撩 473　撩 473　撲 575　撑 93　(撐) 93　撮 128　988　(揮) 145　(撫) 228
撬 598　播 55　撙 602　撸 488　(撚) 542

撞 968　撤 90　搏 987　(撈) 450　撺 126　撰 966　(撥) 54

十三画

擀 240　撼 295　擂 456　457　(捶) 436　(據) 408　(擄) 489　(擋) 148
操 74　(擇) 916　919　(撿) 362　(擔) 143　145　擅 646　擁 883　擗 565

十四画

(擡) 713　擤 822　(擬) 540　(擯) 441　擠 349　(擲) 948　(擯) 51　擦 68
(擰) 544　(擰) 544　(擠) 545　擢 972

十五画

(擾) 621　(擺) 17

十六画

攒 126　912　(攔) 487

十七画

(攔) 447　(撓) 80　攘 620

十八画

(攝) 655　(攤) 812　(擯) 126

十九画

(攪) 715

二十画以上

攫 412　攥 985　(攪) 375　(攤) 448　攮 536

△手扌 部

手 681

四至五画

拜 18

六画

挈 599　挚 948　拿 531　挛 493　拳 616

八画

掌 924　掣 90　掰 13

十三画

衡 307

十四画以上

(鑅) 899
衢 612

46
彡部

四画

形 821
杉 642
　 645
彤 737

五画

衫 645
参 70
　 76
　 657

六画

须 827

八画

彪 48
(参) 70
　 76
　 657

十一画以上

彰 924
影 881
(鬱) 897

47
犭部

二至三画

犰 610
犯 204
犷 280

四画

狂 438
犹 887

五画

狙 405
狎 789
狐 314
狗 263
狍 558
狞 544

六画

狭 789
狮 668
独 177
(狗) 837
狰 935
狡 374
狩 685
狱 898
狼 305

七画

(狹) 789
狸 459
猗 875
狼 449

八画

猜 68
猪 958
猎 475
猫 505
猖 82
猝 125
猕 514
猛 513

九画

猢 315
猩 820
猥 764
猬 766

猾 319
猴 310
(猶) 887

十画

猿 903
(獅) 668

十一画

(獄) 898
獐 924

十二画

獠 473

十三画

(獲) 339
獭 712
(獨) 177

十四画

(獷) 280
(獰) 544

十五画以上

(獵) 475
獾 323
(獼) 514

△犬部

犬 616

四至九画

(狀) 968
哭 433
臭 107
献 798

十二画以上

飙 48
器 586
(獸) 685
(獻) 798

48
夕部

夕 782

三画

舛 115
名 521
岁 708
多 186

八画以上

梦 513
够 264
夤 876
(夢) 513

49
夂部

二画

务 780

三画

各 250

九画以上

夆 34
夏 885

50
饣(食)部

二画

饥 341

三画

饧 821

四画

饪 628
饬 102
饭 204

五画

饯 366

饰 677
饱 25
饲 703
饴 865

六画

饵 193
饶 621
蚀 673
(餁) 628
饷 802
饸 303
饺 374
饼 52

七画

饽 55
饿 191
(餘) 893
馁 537

八画

(饊) 366
馄 335
(餶) 851
馅 798
馆 276

九画

(餬) 315
(餳) 821
(饜) 766
馈 440
馊 704
(餒) 440
馋 81

十画

馍 525
馏 484
　 485
馕 826
(饎) 245

十一画

馒 502

十二画		四画		康	468	六画		汇	332
(饶)	621	床	116	**十一画**		闱	281	汉	294
(馑)	966	库	435	(廣)	279	闻	769	(氾)	205
(饯)	341	庇	41	**十二画**		闽	521		
十三画以上		应	878			闾	491	**三画**	
(馓)	525		881	(廚)	111	阀	198	汗	294
(馋)	81	庐	489	(廟)	700	阁	248	污	772
馕	536	序	829	(廠)	519			江	368
				(廠)	85	**七画**		(汎)	205
△食部		**五画**		(廢)	213	阄	400	汲	346
		庞	557			阅	905	汐	783
食	673	店	165	**十四画以上**				汛	837
飨	802	庙	519	膺	879	**八画**		池	100
餐	71	府	228	鹰	879	阃	899	汝	632
(饗)	802	底	158	(廬)	489	阄	841	汤	717
饔	719	庖	558	(龐)	557	阅	788	汊	79
		庚	253	(廳)	732	阁	334		
51		废	213			阄	844	**四画**	
爿(爿)部				**53**		阄	82	汪	756
		六画		门(門)部				沐	530
三画		度	180	门	511	**九画**		沛	559
壮	967		187	(門)	511	阃	447	汰	714
妆	966	庭	733			阄	614	沤	551
(妝)	966			**一至三画**		阔	442	沥	465
		七画		闩	692	(闕)	762	沏	578
四画		席	785	闪	645	阄	618	沙	642
(牀)	116	座	990	闭	40			汽	586
状	968	唐	717	问	770	**十画**		沃	771
(狀)	968			闯	116	阄	303	沦	494
戕	593	**八画**				阄	617	泅	824
		庶	690	**四画**				泛	205
五画以上		庵	6	闰	634	**十一画**		沧	73
(將)	368	廊	449	(開)	415	(關)	273	沟	262
	370	康	421	闱	762			没	507
(牆)	595	庸	883	闲	794	**十二至**			526
				间	360	**十三画**		沪	316
52		**九画**			365	(闡)	82	(沈)	91
广部		(廄)	402	(閒)	360	(關)	565	沈	660
广	279	(廂)	801		794			沉	91
		(廁)	75	闷	511	**54**		沁	602
三画					512	氵部		(決)	410
庄	966	**十画**		**五画**		**二画**		**五画**	
庆	608	(廈)	643	闸	918	汀	732	沫	527
		廓	442	闹	537	汁	940	浅	592

（慘）	72	怂	703
		忽	313

十二画

懂	173
憬	397
（憚）	146
憔	597
懊	9
憧	104
（憐）	467
憎	917

十三画

（懍）	513
憷	113
懒	448
憾	295
懈	813
（憶）	869

十四画

（懦）	840
懦	549

十五画

懵	513

十六画以上

（懷）	322
（懺）	82
（懾）	655
（懼）	408

△心（小）部

心	814

三画

志	716
忘	758
忌	352

四画

态	714
忠	952

五画

怎	916
（怱）	122
怨	904
怒	547
息	142

六画

恚	333
恐	430
恶	190
	781
虑	492
恩	191
恋	469
恣	978
恕	690

七画

悬	831
患	326
悠	886
您	544

八画

（惡）	190
	781
惠	334
惑	340
惩	97
愈	34

九画

想	802
感	239
愚	895
愁	106
愿	589
愈	900
（愛）	3

十画

（態）	714

十一画

慧	334
（慙）	72
（慮）	492
（想）	587
（慈）	703
（慶）	608
慭	49
慜	292
慰	766

十二画

憩	587
（憑）	34
（憑）	572
（憲）	798

十三画

（懋）	428
（應）	878
（應）	881

十四画以上

（懿）	97
（懸）	831
（戀）	732
（戀）	469
戆	242
戆	968

56

宀部

二画

宁	544
	545
（穴）	630
它	712

三画

字	896
守	682
宅	919

字	978
安	4

四画

完	753
宋	704
宏	309
牢	451
灾	910

五画

宝	26
宗	978
定	170
宜	865
审	660
宙	957
官	275
宛	754
实	671

六画

宣	830
宦	325
宥	893
室	679
宫	260
宪	798
客	427

七画

害	291
宽	437
宵	805
宴	846
宾	50
宰	910
案	7

八画

寇	433
寅	876
寄	353
寂	353
宿	706

	826
	827
（宽）	900

九画

寒	293
富	232
寓	899
（甯）	544
	545
寐	510

十画

塞	636
塞	636
塞	641
寞	527
寝	602

十一画

寨	920
赛	637
（寬）	437
寡	271
察	79
蜜	515
（寧）	544
	545
瘩	781
（寢）	602
寥	473
（實）	671

十二画

寮	473
（寫）	812
（審）	660

十三画

（憲）	798
寰	324

十七画

（寶）	26

已	867
巳	10
包	24
导	149
异	870
忌	352

61

弓部

弓	256

一至三画

引	876
弘	308
弛	100

四画

张	923
弟	161

五画

弧	314
弥	513
弦	795
弩	547

六画

弭	515

七画

弸	260

八画

(張)	923
弹	146
	716

九画

弼	41
强	370
	594
	595
(發)	195

十一画

(彎)	50

十二画以上

(彈)	146
(彌)	513
(彎)	752

62

子(孑)部

子	973

二至三画

孕	907
存	127
孙	709

四画

李	461
李	461

五画

季	352
孤	265
孢	25
享	801
学	833

六至七画

孪	493
孩	290
(孫)	709

十三画以上

(學)	833
孺	632
孽	544
(孿)	493

63

中(屮)部

屯	747
(彝)	111
(孼)	544

64

女部

女	548

二画

奶	532
奴	547

三画

奸	359
如	631
妆	966
妄	758
妇	230
妃	211
好	297
	299
她	712
妈	498

四画

妍	843
妩	779
妓	352
妪	897
妙	519
妊	628
妖	850
妗	392
姊	974
妨	207
妒	180
妞	545

五画

妹	510
姑	265
(妬)	180
妻	578
姐	383
妯	956
姓	823
姗	645
妮	539
始	674

六画

娃	750

姥	455
要	850
	852
姨	865
(姪)	943
娟	875
妹	686
娇	373
(姙)	628
姣	373
姿	972
姘	569
姹	79
(姦)	359

七画

娱	894
娟	409
娥	189
娴	795
娘	542
娓	764
婀	189

八画

婊	49
娶	613
娼	82
(娻)	487
婴	879
婢	41
婚	334
婵	81
婆	573
婶	660
婉	755
(婦)	230

九画

媒	509
媪	8
嫂	641
(媿)	440
媚	510
婿	830

十画

媾	264
媳	786
媲	565
嫒	4
嫉	349
嫌	795
嫁	359
嫔	569
(嫋)	543

十一画

嫣	841
嫩	538
嫜	897
嫖	567
嫦	85
嫡	158

十二画

嬉	785
(嫺)	795
(嬃)	81
(嬈)	779
(嬌)	373

十三画

(嬡)	4
嬗	647

十四画

(嬪)	569

十五画以上

(嬙)	660
(嬾)	448
嬷	693

65

飞(飛)部

飞	210
(飛)	210

66

马(馬)部

马	499

字	页	字	页	字	页	字	页	字	页
枇	564	柒	578	梵	205	棺	276	榜	23
杵	112	染	620	梦	513	椰	449	(槡)	629
枚	508	柠	544	梗	254	椽	162	寨	920
斫	783	柳	355	梧	777	椭	749	槟	52
板	20	架	358	梢	652	(椫)	346	榨	919
采	69	树	689	(桿)	238	**九画**		榕	629
松	703	**六画**		梨	460	楔	811	榷	618
枪	593	框	439	梅	509	椿	119	**十一画**	
枫	221	榔	23	(梟)	804	楠	535	(椿)	967
枭	804	桂	283	检	362	禁	388	横	306
构	263	桔	382	梓	974		392		307
杭	295		406	梳	687	楂	79	樯	595
杰	381	栖	578	梯	722	楚	112	槽	74
枕	933	桎	948	梁	470	楷	419	(樞)	686
五画		柴	80	棂	479	(楊)	848	(標)	47
标	47	桌	970	桶	738	楫	349	(樓)	487
栈	922	档	148	梭	709	椴	182	樱	879
柑	238	桐	737	**八画**		槐	323	樊	202
荣	629	株	957	棒	23	槌	118	橡	804
枯	433	桥	597	棱	457	榆	895	樟	924
柿	948	桦	322	棋	581	(楼)	979	(樣)	849
柄	52	桁	306	椰	853	楼	487	(樑)	470
栿	486	栓	692	植	943	楦	833	橄	240
枢	402	桃	719	森	641	概	235	(橢)	749
柠	573	桅	762	焚	216	楹	881	(槳)	370
栋	174	桨	383	(棶)	174	楝	115	**十二画**	
相	799	格	247	椅	868	**十画**		(樹)	689
	803		248	(楼)	578	榛	932	橱	111
查	78	桊	370	棻	922	(構)	263	橛	412
柚	888	桩	967	椒	374	(楨)	242	(樸)	577
	893	校	376	棻	718	(榖)	267	橘	596
(枬)	273		809	棵	423	(樺)	322	(橋)	597
柞	990	核	303	棍	283	模	525	樵	618
柏	17		314	棘	348		528	橙	489
	56	样	849	(棗)	914	榍	249	橦	98
栎	466	桉	6	棰	118	槛	367	橘	406
枸	263	案	7	(棃)	460		420	(機)	341
栅	918	根	251	椎	969	榻	712	**十三画**	
柳	484	栩	829	集	348	榫	709	(隸)	465
柱	962	桑	640	棉	516	榭	813	(檔)	148
柿	678	**七画**		弑	679	(槍)	593	(櫚)	484
亲	600	械	813	棚	561	榴	484	檄	786
	608	彬	50	(棄)	586	橘	246		
栏	447			棕	979				

十二画以上		四画		杳	852	八画		十四画	
(戰)	922	武	779	昌	82	晴	607	(曠)	438
戴	143	肯	428	沓	131	替	724	十五画以上	
(戲)	787	齿	101		712	暑	688	曝	31
戳	120	些	810	(昇)	661	最	985		577
79		**五至九画**		明	522	晰	784	曦	785
比 部		歪	750	昏	334	量	470	(曬)	644
比	38	耻	101	易	871		472	**83**	
毕	40	(歲)	708	昂	8	暂	912	**贝(貝)部**	
昆	441	**十一画以上**				晶	395	贝	32
毗	564	(齒)	101	**五画**		智	949	(貝)	32
皆	378	整	936	春	118	景	397	**二至三画**	
毖	41	(歸)	280	昧	510	晾	473	贞	931
毙	41	**82**		是	678	普	577	负	229
琵	564	**日(日日)部**		冒	506	曾	76	坝	12
80		日	628	映	882		917	贡	261
瓦 部		日	904	星	819	**九画**		财	69
瓦	750	**一至二画**		昨	987	(會)	332	员	901
四画		旦	145	昵	540		436	**四画**	
瓮	770	旧	402	昭	926	暖	548	责	915
六画		早	914	**六画**		暗	7	贤	794
瓷	121	旮	234	(時)	670	暄	831	账	925
瓶	573	旭	829	耆	581	暇	789	货	339
九画		旬	836	晋	392	**十画**		质	947
甄	932	旨	944	晒	644	(暱)	540	贩	205
十三画		曳	855	晓	809	暮	530	贪	714
(甕)	770	**三画**		(晉)	392	(暢)	86	贫	569
81		旱	294	晃	328	(瞥)	84	贬	44
止 部		时	670	晁	328	暖	4	购	264
止	944	更	253	晌	648	**十一画**		贮	961
一至三画			254	晏	846	暴	30	贯	277
正	934	旷	438	晖	329	蝎	811	**五画**	
	936	**四画**		晕	906	**十二画**		贰	194
此	121	旺	758		908	(曉)	809	贱	366
步	66	昙	715	**七画**		(曇)	715	贲	35
		者	930	匙	101	曈	737	贴	731
		昔	783	晤	781	**十三画**		贵	283
				晨	92	曙	689	贷	142
				曼	503	(曖)	4	贸	507
				晦	333				
				晚	754				
				冕	517				
				(晝)	957				

皿（续）

盅 953
盆 560
盈 880

五画
盏 920
盐 844
监 361
　 366
盎 8
益 871

六画
盔 439
盛 97
　 665
盅 268
盘 555
盒 303
盗 152
盖 235

八画
(蓋) 235
(盞) 920
盟 513

九画
(監) 361
　 366
(盡) 389

十至十一画
(盤) 555
盥 277

十二画
(盪) 148

十八画以上
(蠱) 268
(鹽) 844
(豔) 846

115
钅(金)部

二画
针 931
钉 169
　 170

三画
(釬) 294
钍 744
(釦) 433
钎 588
钏 116
钓 166
钗 80

四画
钙 235
钚 67
钛 714
(鉅) 407
钝 185
钞 87
钟 953
钡 34
钢 241
　 242
钠 532
钤 590
钥 853
钦 600
钧 414
钨 773
钩 262
钮 546
(鈀) 552

五画
钱 591
钳 591
钴 268
钵 55
钹

钻 984
钴 984
铀 888
钾 357
铁 731
铂 56
铃 479
铄 697
铅 589
(鉤) 262
铆 506
(铇) 29
铊 748

六画
铐 423
铗 357
铙 536
铛 147
铝 491
铠 737
铡 419
铜 918
铢 958
铣 786
　 796
铤 734
铧 319
铨 616
铩 643
铬 251
铭 524
铮 935
铰 375
铱 864
铲 82
铳 105
铵 6
银 875

七画
铸 962
铺 576
　 577
(鋏) 357

链 469
铿 428
销 805
锁 711
(鐦) 294
锃 917
锄 111
锂 462
锅 284
锆 247
锈 827
锉 129
锋 222
锌 817
锐 634
锑 722
锒 449
锏 405

八画
(錶) 48
锗 930
错 129
锚 506
锛 35
(錢) 591
锡 784
锣 495
(銅) 241
　 242
(鍋) 284
锤 118
锥 969
锦 389
锨 794
锭 171
键 367
(録) 489
锯 408
锰 513
锔 973

九画
锲 599
锞 469

锶 700
锹 596
(鍾) 953
锻 182
(鎚) 118
锴 594
镀 180
镁 510
镂 488

十画
镄 544
(鏰) 319
镇 934
镉 250
(鐋) 419
镊 409
镍 544
(鎢) 773
(鍛) 643
(鎗) 593
镏 484
　 485
镐 246
镑 24
(鎌) 468
镕 630

十一画
(鏗) 428
镖 48
镗 718
(鏤) 488
镙 37
镜 400
(鏟) 82
镞 983
(鏇) 832
(鐯) 594

十二画
(鏜) 536
镣 475
(鐏) 409

（鐘）	953	（鑾）	367
镯	594	（镬）	493
镫	156	（鑿）	914

十三画

（鐵）	731
镭	457
（鐺）	147
锡	972
镰	468
（鋪）	827

十四画

（鑄）	962
（鑑）	367
（鑠）	439
镲	79

十五画

（鑼）	697
镶	445

十七画

（鑰）	853
镶	801

十八画以上

（鑷）	544
（鑼）	495
（钻）	984
（鑽）	984
镶	412

△金 部

金	387

五至六画

鉴	367
銮	493

十一画以上

鏖	8

116

生 部

生	661
星	819
（产）	81
（甦）	705
甥	664

117

矢 部

矢	673

二至六画

矣	868
知	940
矩	406
矫	375

七画

短	181
矬	128

八画以上

矮	3
雉	949
疑	866
（矯）	375

118

禾 部

禾	300

二画

利	465
秃	741
秀	826
私	698

三画

秆	238
和	302

	304
	313
	336
	339
（秈）	794
秉	52
季	352
委	763

四画

秕	39
秒	518
香	800
种	953
	955
秋	609
科	423

五画

秦	601
秣	527
秫	688
秤	98
乘	97
租	982
积	343
秧	847
秩	948
称	92
	93
秘	515

六画

秸	379
秽	333
移	865

七画

（稉）	395
酥	705
稍	652
	653
（稈）	238
程	97
稀	784

黍	688
税	695

八画

（稜）	457
	424
稚	949
稗	18
稠	626
稠	106
颖	881
（稟）	53

九画

（稭）	379
（種）	953
	955
（稱）	92
	93
	98
稳	769

十画

稽	344
	584
稷	353
稻	152
黎	460
稿	246
稼	359

十一画

（積）	343
穆	530
（穌）	421
麇	619

十二画

穗	709
黏	542

十三画

（穫）	339
（穢）	333

十四画

（穭）	549

（穩）	769

119

白 部

白	14

一至三画

百	15
皂	914
的	154
	157
	161

四画

皇	327
泉	616
皈	281

六画

皑	2
皎	375
（習）	785

七至九画

皓	300
皖	755
皙	784
碧	41
魄	575

十画

（皚）	2
（樂）	455
	905

120

瓜 部

瓜	271
瓢	567
瓤	620

121

鸟（鳥）部

鸟	543
（鳥）	543

考 422
孝 809
者 930

132
耳部

耳 193

二至三画
耶 853
取 613
耷 130

四画
耸 703
耽 144
(耻) 101

五画
职 943
聆 479
聊 473

六至九画
聒 284
联 467
(聖) 664
聘 570
聚 408
聪 122

十一画
(聲) 663
(聰) 122
(聾) 703
(聯) 467

十二画以上
(職) 943
(聽) 732

133
臣部

臣 90
卧 771

(臥) 771
臧 913
(豎) 689
(臨) 476
(覽) 448

134
西(覀)部

西 782

三至五画
要 850
　　 852
栗 466
贾 268
票 568

六画以上
粟 706
覆 233
(覉) 345

135
而部

耐 533
耍 690
斋 919

136
页(頁)部

页 855
(頁) 855

二至三画
顶 169
顷 608

三画
项 803
顺 695
须 827

四画
顽 754
顾 270

顿 185
颂 19
颂 704
预 898

五画
硕 698
颅 489
领 480
颇 573
颈 397

六画
颉 812
颊 357
颌 303
颍 424

七画
颐 866
(頰) 357
(頸) 397
频 569
颓 745

八画
颗 424

九画
题 723
颚 191
颜 844
额 189

十画
颠 162
(顢) 904
(類) 457

十二画
嚣 806
(顥) 270

十三画以上
颤 82

923
(顯) 795
(顰) 489
颥 616

137
至部

至 946
致 948
(臺) 713
臻 933

138
虍部

二至三画
虏 489
虐 549

五画
虚 827
(處) 111
　　 112

六至七画
虞 895
(虜) 489

九画
(膚) 224

十画以上
(盧) 489
(戯) 787
(虧) 439

△虎部

虎 315
彪 48
(號) 296
　　 299

139
虫部

虫 104

一至二画
虬 610
(虯) 610
虱 668

三画
虹 309
虾 788
虽 707
虻 251
蚁 868
虺 512
蚤 914
蚂 499
　　 500

四画
蚌 23
蚕 72
蚜 839
蚋 634
蚬 796
蚝 296
蚊 769

五画
蛀 292
萤 880
蛎 466
蛆 612
蚰 888
蛱 620
蚱 919
蚯 609
蛙 962
蛇 654
蛋 146
蛏 93

六画
蛙 750
蛊 609
蛰 930

A

ā

阿 ā 〈方〉used before a monosyllabic word to form a term of endearment or of kinship：～爸 dad /～方 A Fang　see also ē

阿斗 Ā Dǒu　weak-minded person; fool; sucker; 扶不起的～ weakling who is beyond help

阿飞 āfēi　young hooligan or street rowdy (usu in outlandish dress)

阿訇 āhōng　(Islam) ahung; imam

阿拉伯 Ālābó　Arab; Arabia; ～人 Arab /～语 Arabic (language) /～数字 Arabic numerals

阿猫阿狗 āmāo-āgǒu　〈方〉people of any description or of little importance; every man jack

阿门 āmén　〈宗教〉amen

阿Q Ā Qiū　also Ā Kiū Ah Q, a backward peasant who interprets his defeats as moral victories：一副～相 a complete likeness of Ah Q

阿司匹林 āsīpǐlín　aspirin

阿姨 āyí　❶ term of address for a woman of one's mother's generation; auntie ❷ nurse; nanny; housemaid; 幼儿园的～ kindergarten teacher

啊（呵） ā 〈叹〉expressing surprise, etc：～, 太阳出来了! Oh, the sun has come out!

á

啊（呵） á 〈叹〉used to ask a further question or request repetition of what was said：～? 你说什么来着? I beg your pardon?

ǎ

啊（呵） ǎ 〈叹〉expressing doubt：～? 这是怎么回事儿呀? Humph, what's all this about?

à

啊（呵） à 〈叹〉❶ expressing consent or understanding：～, 我明白了! Oh, I see. ❷ expressing surprise, etc：～, 这里怎么有一摊血! Why! There's a pool of blood here!

a

啊（呵） a 〈助〉❶ used at the end of a sentence：哥俩儿像不像～? Do the two brothers look like each other, eh? ❷ used after things enumerated：书、笔～、报纸～, 摆了一桌子。The desk is littered with books, pens, newspapers and what not.

āi

哎（嗳） āi 〈叹〉❶ used to convey surprise or dissatisfaction：～! 我又忘带眼镜了。Why, I forgot to bring my glasses again! ❷ *used as a reminder or warning*: ～，别把盘子碰掉了！Hey! Don't knock off the plate!

哎呀 āiyā *also* "唉呀（叹）❶ *see* 哎 ❶" ❷ *used to express complaints or impatience*: ～，丢了太可惜了。Ah, it's a pity to part with it.

哎哟 āiyō 〈叹〉*used to show astonishment or pain*: ～! 玻璃碎啦！Hey, the glass is broken. / ～! 好疼! Ouch! It hurts!

哀 āi ❶ grief; sorrow：～愁 lamentation; sorrow / ～号 cry piteously; wail; bemoan / ～求 *also* "哀告" beg or plead piteously; entreat; implore / ～恸 grieve; sorrow / ～痛 grief; sorrow / ～婉 sad and moving; pathetic ❷ mourning; condolences：～歌 mournful song; dirge; elegy / ～乐 funeral music ❸ feel compassion for; pity：~其不幸 have pity on sb for his or her misfortune

哀兵必胜 āibīngbìshèng an army burning with righteous indignation is bound to win; those who have burnt their boats have a good chance to triumph

哀悼 āidào grieve or mourn (over sb's death); lament (sb's death)：表示沉痛的～ express one's profound condolences

哀鸿遍野 āihóngbiànyě victims of a disaster can be found everywhere; the land is swarming with famished refugees

哀鸣 āimíng plaintive whine; wail; lament

哀伤 āishāng grieved; distressed; sad：哀而不伤 restrained grief; gentle sadness

哀思 āisī sad memories (of the deceased); grief; sorrow：寄托～ (do sth) as a token of one's remembrance

哀叹 āitàn sigh in sorrow; lament; bewail

哀怨 āiyuàn plaintive; sad; aggrieved：缠绵～ sentimental and plaintive

埃 āi dust：黄～ yellow dust

埃及 Āijí Egypt：～人 Egyptian

挨 āi ❶ in the order of; one after another：～个儿（口）one by one; in turn / ～家～户 from door to door; from house to house ❷ near; close or close to：～近 get close to; be near to / ～肩擦背 rub shoulders; be crowded together *see also* ái

唉 āi 〈叹〉❶ *indicating response*：～! All right. I'm coming! ❷ *sound of sighing sadly*：～, 我真倒霉! Ah! How unlucky I am!
see also ài

唉声叹气 āishēng-tànqì heave deep sighs; sigh in despair; moan and groan

ái

挨 ái ❶ suffer; endure; get (sth bad)：～饿 suffer from hunger; starve / ～骂 *also* "挨呲儿" be given a telling-off; get a scolding / ～整 be made to suffer; be in for criticism and denunciation / ～打受气 be bullied and beaten / ～了一记耳光 get a box on the ear ❷ drag out; pull through：～日子 drag out a miserable existence / ～过了一场大病 pull through a serious illness ❸ delay; put off
see also āi

皑（皚） ái 〈书〉pure or snow white：～～ 积雪 vast expanse of white snow

癌 ái (formerly pronounced yán) cancer; carcinoma：原发～ primary cancer / ～变 canceration / ～症 cancer; carcinoma / ～扩散 *also* "癌转移" spread of cancer; metastasis (of cancer) / ～细胞 cancer cell / 致～物质 carcinogen; carcinogenic substance

ǎi

嗳（嗳） ǎi 〈叹〉used to show dissent or displeasure：~，别开玩笑了。Come on, stop kidding, please. *see also* āi

矮 ǎi ❶ short（of stature）；low（in height）：~化 stunt；dwarf；〈喻〉lower / ~胖 short and stout；dumpy / ~小 short and small；undersized / ~子〈贬〉shorty；dwarf / ~墩墩 pudgy；dumpy；stocky / ~个儿 person of short stature；short person ❷ be lower（in status, etc）than；inferior to：比人~半截儿 much inferior to others

蔼 ǎi friendly；affable；amiable；然可亲 affable

霭 ǎi 〈书〉mist；haze：晨~ morning haze

ài

艾 ài ❶ also "艾蒿" Chinese mugwort；moxa ❷〈书〉halt；end：~~难言 speak haltingly（from embarrassment, etc）

艾滋病 àizībìng also "爱滋病" AIDS（acquired immune deficiency syndrome）：~病毒 HIV（human immunodeficiency virus）

唉 ài 〈叹〉used to express sadness or regret：~，真可惜！Oh, what a shame! *see also* āi

爱（愛） ài ❶ love；神 God of Love；Cupid / ~财如命 love money as if it were one's own life；love nothing better than money / ~美之心 love of beauty；desire to be well groomed / ~憎分明 be clear whom to love and whom to hate；boast clear-cut sentiments ❷ be fond of；like：~称 term of endearment；pet name / ~说长道短 delight in gossip ❸ treasure；cherish：~才如命 treasure talent as the apple of one's eye ❹ be apt to；be in the habit of：~发急 easily get into a temper / ~感冒 be liable to colds

爱…不… ài…bù… used before the same verb to express lack of concern or free choice：爱理不理 also "爱答不理" show indifference；be cool or standoffish / 爱信不信 believe it or not / 爱要不要 take it or leave it

爱不释手 àibùshìshǒu cannot tear oneself away from sth；can scarcely take one's eyes off sth

爱戴 àidài adore；love；hold in（high）esteem：深受~ be held in high esteem

爱抚 àifǔ have tender affection for；show loving care for；caress

爱国 àiguó love one's country；be patriotic：~心 patriotic sentiment / ~者 patriot / ~主义 patriotism / ~一家。All patriots belong to one family.

爱好 àihào ❶ love；be keen on or fond of：~者 lover（of art, etc）；enthusiast；fan ❷ activity one enjoys；hobby

爱护 àihù cherish；treasure；take good care of

爱克斯光 àikèsīguāng X-ray：照~ have an X-ray taken / ~照片 X-ray film；radiograph

爱怜 àilián tender affection；compassion：惹人~ arouse one's tender feelings

爱恋 àiliàn be in love with；feel deeply attached to：对亲人的~ attachment to one's kith and kin

爱面子 àimiànzi have a strong sense of "face"；care too much about "face"；be vain

爱莫能助 àimònéngzhù be willing but unable to help；not be in a position to help

爱慕 àimù ❶ yearn or long for：~虚

A

荣 be vain ❷ admire; adore; fall in love with

爱情 àiqíng　love (between man and woman): ～片 love film / ～专一 be constant in love

爱人 àirén　❶ husband or wife; spouse ❷ sweetheart

爱屋及乌 àiwūjíwū　〈书〉love for a person extends to everything associated with him or her; love me, love my dog

爱惜 àixī　cherish; treasure; use sparingly: ～光阴 make the best use of time / ～人才 value men of talent

爱心 àixīn　love; sympathy; compassion: 献出一片～ offer one's loving care

隘 ài　❶ pass; 险～ strategic pass ❷ narrow: ～谷 narrow gully; ravine / ～口 (mountain) pass

碍（礙） ài　hinder; obstruct; be in the way of: ～事 be in the way (usu in the negative) be of consequence; matter / ～眼 be offensive to the eye; be out of place / ～手～脚 be in the way; be a hindrance / ～情面 be afraid to hurt sb's feelings or to harm one's relations with sb / ～难从命.〈书〉I find it hard to comply with your wish.

嗳（嗳） ài　〈叹〉used to express regret, etc: ～，早知道就好了! Oh! If only I had known.　see also ǎi

媛（媛） ài　beloved or darling daughter

暧（暧） ài

暧昧 àimèi　❶ (of attitude, intention, etc) ambiguous; equivocal ❷ (of relationship, etc) shady; dubious; questionable

ān

安 ān　❶ peaceful; calm; content: ～适 serene and comfortable; contented / ～睡 be sound asleep; sleep soundly / ～闲 peaceful and carefree; leisurely; uneventful / ～邦定国 bring peace and stability to the country / ～贫乐道 find contentment in poverty and joy in one's principles; be happy to lead a simple and virtuous life / ～土重迁 be attached to one's native land and reluctant to leave it / ～于现状 be content with the status quo; rest on one's laurels ❷ safe; in good health: ～如磐石 as firm as a rock / 敬祝～康 (at the end of a letter) wishing you the best of health / 身心～泰 be sound in body and mind ❸ install; fix; place: ～电话 install a telephone / ～钉子 place an obstacle (for sb); place one's agent in a key position (to obstruct sb) / ～罪名 bring false charges (against sb); frame ❸ safe; ～营扎寨 pitch a camp; camp ❹ (short for 安培)〈电〉ampere

安步当车 ānbùdàngchē　walk over leisurely instead of riding in a carriage; go on foot rather than by car

安插 ānchā　❶ place or plant in a certain position; assign to a job: ～亲信 plant one's trusted follower (in a key position) ❷ insert (an extra item in a programme, etc); interpose (sth)

安定 āndìng　❶ (of life, etc) stable; calm; settled: 工作～ job security / 团结的政治局面 political stability and unity ❷ maintain; stabilize: ～人心 maintain public morale; reassure the public

安顿 āndùn　find a place for; arrange for; settle in: 把孩子～在幼儿园里 put or place a child in a kindergarten

安放 ānfàng　place; lay; put in a certain position: ～家具 put furniture in place; arrange furniture

安分 ānfèn　keep one's place; be law-abiding: ～守己 know and keep one's place; abide by the law and behave properly

安抚 ānfǔ appease; placate; pacify:~民，pacify the people; appease the public

安好 ānhǎo in good health; safe and sound;家中~如常。Everything is fine in the family as usual.

安家 ānjiā make one's home; settle down;~费 settling-in allowance; family allowance / ~落户 make one's home in a place; settle

安检 ānjiǎn (short for 安全检查) security check:过~ go through a security check

安静 ānjìng silent; quiet; calm:保持~ keep silent / ~下来 calm down

安居 ānjū settle down (in a place):~乐业 live and work in peace and contentment / ~工程 low-cost or affordable housing project

安拉 Ānlā (of Islam) Allah

安乐 ānlè peace and happiness:~死〈医〉mercy killing; painless death; euthanasia / ~窝〈喻〉cosy nest (for people)/~椅 armchair; easy chair

安理会 Ānlǐhuì (short for 安全理事会) Security Council (of the United Nations)

安眠 ānmián sleep peacefully:~药 sleeping pill

安民告示 ānmíngàoshi notice to reassure the public; advance information:出个~ keep people informed (about sth)

安宁 ānníng ❶ tranquil; peaceful;社会~ social tranquility ❷ calm; composed;使人不得~ disturbing; upsetting

安排 ānpái arrange; deal with in an orderly manner:~活动日程 work out a schedule / 把客人~在宾馆里 put guests up at a guesthouse

安琪儿 ānqí'ér angel

安全 ānquán safe; secure:~带 safety belt / ~阀〈电〉〈喻〉safety valve / ~感 sense of security / ~帽 safety helmet /

~门 emergency exit / ~期〈医〉safe period / ~套〈医〉condom / ~第一 (put) safety first

安然 ānrán ❶ safe:~无事 pass without mishap / ~无恙 escape unscathed; be safe and sound ❷ free from worry; at ease:~入睡 fall asleep peacefully

安身 ānshēn make one's home; take shelter:~立命 settle down in one's life and career

安神 ānshén soothe the nerves; relieve uneasiness of body and mind:~药〈中药〉sedative; tranquilizer

安生 ānshēng ❶ peaceful; restful:过~日子 live a peaceful life ❷ quiet; still:睡不~ cannot sleep soundly

安危 ānwēi safety (or danger):把个人的~置之度外 have no thought for one's own safety

安慰 ānwèi comfort; console; feel or make happy:~剂 placebo / ~奖 consolation prize / ~赛〈体〉consolation event or match

安稳 ānwěn ❶ smooth and steady:~着陆 land smoothly ❷ peaceful; calm; settled:一点都不~ (of a child, etc) restless

安息 ānxī ❶ also "安歇" rest; go to sleep; retire for the night ❷ rest in peace:老朋友，~吧! May you rest in peace, my old friend!

安详 ānxiáng serene; composed; unruffled:神态~ look unruffled

安心 ānxīn ❶ intend; mean:没安好心 harbour no good intentions; be up to no good ❷ be at ease; set one's mind at rest:~养病 recuperate patiently / ~本职工作 devote oneself to one's work

安逸 ānyì easy and comfortable:生活~ (lead an) easy life / 不得~ have no peace of mind

安葬 ānzàng bury (the dead):~仪式 burial ceremony

安之若素 ānzhīruòsù bear (hardship, etc) with equanimity; regard (wrongdoing, etc) with indifference: 粗茶淡饭, ~ lead a spartan life contentedly

安置 ānzhì find a place for; arrange for; resettle: ~费 settlement or placement allowance / ~下岗人员 find work for those who are laid off

安装 ānzhuāng install: ~费用 installation cost or charge

桉 ān also "桉树" eucalyptus

氨 ān 〈化〉ammonia; hydrogen nitride: ~水 ammonia water; aqua ammonia / ~基酸 amino-acid

庵(菴) ān ❶ 〈书〉hut: 茅~ thatched hut ❷ nunnery; Buddhist convent

谙 ān 〈书〉know well; be well-versed: ~达世情 be familiar with the ways of the world; be worldly-wise

鹌 ān

鹌鹑 ānchún 〈动物〉quail

鞍 ān saddle

鞍马 ānmǎ ❶ 〈体〉pommelled or side horse ❷ 〈书〉saddle and horse: ~顿 fatigued by a long journey; travel-worn / ~生涯 life on horseback — soldiering / 鞍前马后 run before or behind the master's horse; act as a faithful assistant or follower

ǎn

俺 ǎn 〈方〉❶ also "俺们" we (excluding those addressed): ~乡下人 we country folk ❷ my; I: ~家 my family or home / ~兄弟 my brother

铵 ǎn 〈化〉ammonium

àn

岸 àn bank; shore; coast: 靠~ (of a ship) come ashore

按 àn ❶ press; push down: ~铃 ring a bell / ~脉 feel or take the pulse / ~扣儿〈口〉snap fastener ❷ hold (back or down); keep a tight grip on; restrain: ~住性子 control one's temper ❸ according to; in accordance with: ~时 on schedule; on time / ~日 by the day; per day; per diem / ~劳分配 distribution according to work; to each according to his work / ~质论价 pricing by quality / ~人口平均收入 per capita income ❹ also "按语"; "案语" note; comment

按兵不动 ànbīngbùdòng hold one's troops where they are; take no action: ~, 坐观成败 hold back from the fray to see which side is going to win; sit on the fence

按部就班 ànbù-jiùbān follow the prescribed order; act in the conventional way; stick to the same old rut

按键 ànjiàn key (on a keyboard); push button: ~电话 push-phone

按揭 ànjiē (usu in real estate) mortgage: 首期~ down-payment / ~利率 mortgage (interest) rate

按理 ànlǐ also "按说" according to reason or principle; in the normal course of things; normally

按摩 ànmó massage: ~器 massager; masseur / ~师 massager; masseur; masseuse / ~院 massage parlour / ~疗法 massotherapy

按捺 ànnà also "按纳" restrain; check; control

按钮 ànniǔ push button: 按~ push a button / ~开关 push-button switch

按时 ànshí at an appointed time; on time: ~报到 report (for work, etc) at the appointed time / ~作息 keep regular hours

按图索骥 àntúsuǒjì look for a fine horse with the aid of its picture — try to locate sth by following up a clear clue; do sth mechanically

按照 ànzhào according to; in keeping with; in the light of

胺 àn 〈化〉amine

案 àn ❶ old-fashioned long narrow table; long board serving as a table or counter; ~ 板 kneading or chopping board ❷ 〈law〉case; ~ 犯 〈法〉the accused; offender; suspect / ~ 件 (law) case / ~ 由 main points of a case; brief; summary / ~ 值 value involved in an economic case / ~ 例 研究 case study ❸ record; file: 记录为 ~ be on record / ~ 卷 file folder; files; archives ❹ plan submitted for approval; proposal; 议 ~ draft resolution ❺ see “按❹” àn

案情 ànqíng (facts or details of a) case; 调查 ~ investigate a case / ~ 复杂 complicated case

案头 àntóu on the desk or table; ~ 日历 also “台历” desk calendar

案子 ànzi ❶ long board serving as a table or counter; 台球 ~ billiard table ❷〈口〉case; 审 ~ try a case

暗 àn ❶ dark; dim; dull; ~ 红 dark or dull red / ~ 室 (in photography) darkroom ❷ hidden; secret; covert; ~ 堡〈军〉bunker / ~ 娼 unlicensed prostitute / ~ 道 secret path, passage, or tunnel / ~ 火 smouldering fire / ~ 恋 be secretly in love (with sb) / ~ 流 undercurrent; latent trend / 心中 ~ 喜 feel a surge of inmost joy ❸ 〈书〉hazy; muddled; unclear; ~ 于知己 unclear about oneself; poor in knowing oneself

暗暗 àn'àn secretly; inwardly; to oneself; ~ 思忖 turn (sth) over in one's mind; think to oneself

暗藏 àncáng hide; conceal; ~ 枪支 illegally possess firearms; have a secret cache of firearms / ~ 的敌人 hidden enemy

暗淡 àndàn also “黯淡” dim; faint; gloomy; 星光 ~ dim starlight / 心情 ~ (be in a) dismal mood

暗渡陈仓 àndùchéncāng engage in sth covertly while making a feint in the open; (esp) carry on an illicit love affair

暗害 ànhài stab in the back; kill secretly; murder

暗号 ànhào secret signal or sign; 对 ~ check the signals / 回答 ~ (give the) countersign

暗箭 ànjiàn arrow shot from hiding; stab in the back; ~ 伤人 stab sb in the back; injure sb by underhand means

暗礁 ànjiāo submerged reef or rock; latent difficulty; concealed obstacle

暗杀 ànshā assassinate; ~ 者 assassin / ~ 事件 assassination

暗示 ànshì ❶ (drop a) hint; suggest ❷ suggestion; ~ 疗法 suggestion therapy

暗送秋波 ànsòngqiūbō make (sheep's) eyes (at sb) on the sly;〈喻〉make secret overtures (to sb)

暗算 ànsuàn plot against; lay a trap for; 险遭 ~ narrowly escape a plot or trap

暗无天日 ànwútiānrì complete darkness; total absence of justice; ~ 的社会 dark society

暗箱 ànxiāng ❶ (in photography) camera bellows ❷ in camera or secret; ~ 操作 operate (usu sth related to the public) in camera; do secretly

暗笑 ànxiào laugh in or up one's sleeve; sneer secretly; snigger

暗中 ànzhōng ❶ also “暗处” in the dark; 躲在 ~ 张望 hide in the dark and keep watch ❷ also “暗地里” in secret; on the sly; surreptitiously; ~ 打听 gather information in secret

暗自 ànzì to oneself; inwardly; secretly; ~ 庆幸 secretly congratulate oneself; consider oneself lucky

黯 àn dim; obscure; gloomy; ~ 黑 的夜晚 dark night

黯淡 àndàn　*see* "暗淡" àndàn

黯然 ànrán ❶ dim; faint; ~失色 be overshadowed or eclipsed; pale into insignificance ❷ dejected; low-spirited; downcast; ~神伤 feel dejected or depressed

āng

肮(骯) āng
肮脏 āngzāng　dirty; filthy; mean; ~话 dirty words

áng

昂 áng ❶ hold (one's head) high; ~然而入 walk in proudly / ~首阔步 stride along with one's chin up; stride proudly ahead ❷ high; soaring; expensive; ~贵 expensive; costly / 群情~扬。Public feeling ran high.

àng

盎 àng 〈书〉brimming; abundant; 生气~然 full of vigour
盎司 àngsī　*also* "盎斯" ounce

āo

凹 āo concave; hollow; sunken; ~镜 concave mirror / ~陷 hollow; depressed; sunken / ~版印刷 intaglio or gravure printing / ~凸不平 uneven; full of bumps and holes

熬 āo cook in water; boil; stew
see also áo

áo

遨 áo
遨游 áoyóu　roam; travel; ~太空 travel in space

嗷 áo 嗷嗷〈象声〉*used to indicate cries of pain or suffering*; ~待哺 (as of young birds or babies) cry piteously for food / 疼得~叫 howl with pain

熬 áo ❶ boil; decoct; ~药 decoct Chinese medicine (by boiling medicinal herbs) / ~粥 make gruel; cook porridge ❷ endure; suffer; ~煎 suffering; torture; torment / ~夜 stay up late; burn the midnight oil / ~日子 drag out a miserable existence / ~过难关 pull through hard times; tide over difficulties
see also āo

螯 áo pincers (of crustaceans); ~虾 crayfish; crawfish

翱 áo
翱翔 áoxiáng　soar; hover

廒 áo
廒战 áozhàn　fight hard; engage in fierce battle

ǎo

袄(襖) ǎo short Chinese-style coat or jacket; 夹~ lined jacket

媪 ǎo 〈书〉old woman; 翁~ old man and woman

ào

拗 ào disobedient; intractable; refractory; ~强 (of a person) obstinate; stubborn; intractable *see also* niù
拗口 àokǒu　hard to pronounce; awkward-sounding; ~令 tongue twister / 这句话读起来~。The sentence is quite a mouthful.

傲 ào proud; haughty; arrogant; ~骨 lofty and unyielding charac-

ter; innate pride / ～世 despise the world and its people; be extremely proud / ～视 turn up one's nose at; show disdain for; regard superciliously / ～然屹立 stand defiant and proud

傲慢 àomàn haughty; arrogant; impudent; ～无礼 arrogant and insolent

傲气 àoqì air of arrogance; haughtiness: 这人有一股～。The man exudes arrogance.

奥 ào ❶ profound; abstruse; ～秘 profound mystery or secret ❷ (Ào) (short for 奥林匹克 or 奥运会) Olympic (Games); 申～ bid for the hosting of the Olympic Games / ～委会 Olympic Committee

奥林匹克 Àolínpǐkè Olympic; ～运动会 Olympic Games; Olympics; Olympiad / 数学～竞赛 maths Olympics

奥妙 àomiào profundity; subtlety: 不解其中～ fail to understand the subtlety (of the situation, etc); not understand what is behind it

奥运 Àoyùn ❶ (short for 奥林匹克运动会) Olympiad; Olympics; Olympic Games: ～村 Olympic village / ～主办城市 Olympic host city ❷ (short for 奥林匹克运动) Olympic Movement: ～精神 spirit of the Olympic Movement

澳 Ào ❶ (short for 澳门) Macao: ～元 (Macao) *Pataca* / ～人治 ～。Macao people administer Macao. ❷ (short for 澳大利亚) Australia: ～抗 (short for 澳大利亚抗原) Australia antigen; HAA (hepatitis-associated antigen)

澳大利亚 Àodàlìyà Australia: ～人 Australian / ～元 (shortened as 澳元) Australian dollar

澳洲 Àozhōu ❶ Australia ❷ *also* "大洋洲" Oceania

懊 ào regretful; remorseful; annoyed

懊悔 àohuǐ feel remorseful; repent; regret: ～不已 (know) no end of regret

懊恼 àonǎo annoyed; vexed; upset: 为实验失败而～ be upset at the failure of an experiment

懊丧 àosàng upset; dejected; depressed: 神情～ look dejected; crestfallen

B

bā

八 bā (pronounced bá before words with tone 4) eight; eighth; octo—/ ～度〈乐〉octave / ～方支援 help from all directions or quarters / ～分音符〈乐〉eighth note; quaver / ～小时工作制 eight-hour day

八宝 bābǎo eight treasures or ingredients: ～菜 eight-treasure pickles; assorted soy sauce pickles / ～饭 eight-treasure rice pudding (containing red bean paste, nuts and seeds, preserved fruits, etc)

八成 bāchéng ❶ eighty per cent: ～熟 not quite well-done or ripe / ～新 mostly or practically new ❷ most probably or likely: 他病了。Most probably he is ill.

八哥儿 bāgēr 〈动物〉(crested) myna(h)

八股 bāgǔ eight-part essay prescribed for imperial civil service examinations; 〈喻〉stereotyped writing

八卦 bāguà Eight Trigrams (eight combinations of three whole or broken lines, called 乾、坤、坎、离、震、巽、艮、兑 and formerly used in divination): 摆～阵 present an eight-trigram battle array; apply mystifying tactics

八角 bājiǎo ❶〈植〉(star) anise; aniseed ❷ octagonal: ～帽 octagonal cap / ～形 octagon

八九不离十 bājiǔbùlíshí 〈口〉pretty close; very near; about right: 猜个～ make a very close guess; be not far off the mark

八路 Bālù ❶ also "八路军" Eighth Route Army (led by the CCP 1937-1945) ❷ Eighth Route Army man; revolutionary: 老～ veteran revolutionary / 土～ irregular guerrilla; rustic (revolutionary)

八面玲珑 bāmiànlínglóng be able to get along well with everybody; be all things to all people; be smooth and slick

八仙桌 bāxiānzhuō big square table around which two people can sit at each side; (square) table for eight

八月 bāyuè ❶ August ❷ eighth month of the lunar year: ～节 Mid-Autumn Festival (15th day of the 8th lunar month)

八字 bāzì ❶ (like) the character 八 splayed: ～步 measured gait with the toes pointing outwards / ～胡 splayed moustache / ～脚 splayfoot / ～没一撇 nothing tangible is in sight; be up in the air ❷ the Eight Characters (representing the year, month, day and hour of a person's birth, used as basis for fortune-telling); horoscope: 问一～ consult a fortune-teller (about one's horoscope)

巴 bā ❶ hope earnestly; wait anxiously: ～望 hope in real earnest ❷ see "扒"❶ bā ❸ bus: 大～ bus / 小～ minibus ❹ (Bā) area generally equivalent to present Chongqing

巴不得 bābude 〈口〉be only too

anxious (to do sth); earnestly wish; be eager (to do sth)/～不去 would rather not go /～的事 just what one has been looking for

巴结 bājie fawn on; curry favour with; toady to

巴黎 Bālí Paris, capital of France;～人 Parisian

巴儿狗 bārgǒu *also* "哈巴狗"; "叭儿狗" pekinese; lapdog;〈喻〉syco-phant

巴士 bāshì 〈方〉bus: 小～ minibus; minivan /～站 bus stop

巴西 Bāxī Brazil;～木〈植〉brazilwood /～人 Brazilian

巴掌 bāzhang palm; hand;～大块地 tiniest lot (of land) / 打了一～ give (sb) a slap in the face / 一个～拍不响 〈俗〉you can't clap with one hand — it takes two to quarrel or cooperate

扒 bā ❶ hold on to; stick or cling to:～锅 (of cooked food) stick to the pot /～车 jump onto a train or bus (usu stealthily) ❷ dig up; rake; pull down:～房 pull down a house /～土 rake earth ❸ strip, take or peel off; skin:～皮 strip the skin off; exploit or punish harshly

see also pá

扒拉 bāla push lightly; remove:～开人群 push one's way through a crowd /～算盘珠 click the beads of an abacus; calculate

芭 bā

芭蕉 bājiāo 〈植〉*bajiao* banana; plantain

芭蕾 bālěi *also* "芭蕾舞" ballet;～演员 ballet dancer; ballerina

吧 bā ❶ *also* "叭"〈象声〉*snap-ping or cracking sound*:～的一声,碗摔碎了。The bowl fell crashing to the ground. ❷ (short for 酒吧) bar:～女 barmaid; bar girl /～台 bar

see also ba

吧嗒 bādā ❶〈象声〉patter; splat-ter; 雨点~~地打在玻璃窗上。Big raindrops pattered on the windows. ❷ (bādā) *also* "吧唧" smack one's lips; draw or drag at a pipe, etc:～一口烟 have a puff (at a pipe, etc)

疤 bā scar; sth like a scar:～痕 cic-atrix; scar /～瘌脸 scarred face

捌 bā eight (used for the numeral 八 to avoid mistakes or alter-ations)

笆 bā bamboo- or wicker-basket-ry:～斗 round-bottomed bamboo or wicker basket

bá

拔 bá ❶ draw; tug; pull out or up:～除 remove; pull out; eradi-cate /～河〈体〉(have a) tug of war /～牙 extract a tooth; have a tooth ex-tracted /～营〈军〉strike or break camp /～钉子 pull out a nail;〈喻〉re-move an obstacle ❷ suck out; draw (out):～毒〈中医〉draw out pus or poison ❸ choose; select; promote ❹ stand out; surpass:～地而起 (of a mountain, building, etc) stand tall and erect; rise straight from the ground ❺ 〈方〉cool (sth) in water

拔刀相助 bádāoxiāngzhù unsheathe one's sword and go to sb's rescue (for the sake of justice); take up the cudgels against an injustice

拔火罐 báhuǒguàn *also* "拔罐子" 〈中医〉cupping

拔尖 bájiān ❶〈口〉top-notch; tip-top:～人才 top-notch talent; outstand-ing person ❷ push oneself to the front; be pushy

拔苗助长 bámiáozhùzhǎng *also* "揠苗助长" try to help the shoots grow by pulling them upward — spoil things by excessive enthusiasm; haste makes waste

拔丝 básī　candied floss：～山药 hot-candied yam

拔腿 bátuǐ　❶ start to run：～就跑 dash off at once；take to one's heels immediately ❷ get away or extricate oneself (from work，etc)

跋 bá　❶ cross mountains：～前踬后 can neither go ahead nor retreat；be caught in a dilemma ❷ postscript：～文 also 跋语 postscript；epilogue

跋扈 báhù　domineering；bossy

跋涉 báshè　trudge；trek；长途～ trek over a long distance；make a long arduous journey

bǎ

把 bǎ　❶ hold；grasp；control：～舵 hold the rudder or helm；steer / ～着手 hold sb by the hand；hold sb's hand / ～揽大权 monopolize all power；keep all power in one's own hands ❷〈口〉guard；watch：～风 keep watch (for sb)；be on the lookout ❸ handlebar (of a bicycle，etc) ❹〈量〉a) used of sth with a handle：一～剪刀 a pair of scissors / 一～雨伞 an umbrella b) used of sth one can pick up with one hand：一～儿花 a bunch of flowers / 一～泥土 a handful of earth c) used of certain abstract things：加一劲 put in an extra effort d) used of the motion of a hand or an arm：擦～脸 and wash one's face / 帮我一～。Lend me a hand，please! ❺〈介〉used before a noun a) when it is the receiver of the action of the ensuing verb：～花浇一浇 water flowers b) to show that sth undesirable has happened：～我吓坏了。I was scared stiff. ❻ added to such measure words as 个，百，千，万 or 里，丈，斤 to indicate an approximate number：个～月 a month or so / 斤～肉 around half a kilo of meat ❼ referring

to a relationship of sworn brotherhood：～兄弟 sworn brothers / 拜～子 become sworn brothers

see also bà

把柄 bǎbǐng　handle；excuse；grounds：给人～ give sb a handle (against one)

把持 bǎchí　dominate；control；monopolize：～一个部门 control or dominate a department

把关 bǎguān　❶ guard a pass ❷ check and guarantee the quality or standard (of sth)：层层～ make checks at all levels / 把政治关 ensure political soundness

把门 bǎmén　also "把大门" ❶ guard the entrance；keep guard at the door or gate：这人嘴上缺个～的。The man has got a big mouth. ❷〈体〉be a goalkeeper

把守 bǎshǒu　guard；defend

把手 bǎshou　handle；knob；handlebar

把握 bǎwò　❶ hold；grasp；seize：～时机 grasp an opportunity；seize the right time / ～自己的命运 be master of one's own destiny ❷ (usu used after 有 or 无) assurance；certainty：有绝对～ be absolutely certain (about sth)；be dead sure (of sth)

把戏 bǎxì　acrobatics；jugglery；trick：变～ play a (jugglery) trick；juggle；conjure / 戳穿～ show up sb's trick or ploy

靶 bǎ　target：打～ (do) shooting or target practice / 环～ round target / 中～ hit the target / 移动～ moving target / ～场 shooting or firing range / ～心 bull's eye

bà

坝(壩) bà　❶ dam；dike；embankment：～顶 dam crest / ～基 base of a dam ❷ (usu used in place names) flatland；plain：川～

子 West Sichuan Plain

把 bà ❶ handle; grip:枪~儿 rifle butt / 印~子 (handle of an) official seal; political power ❷ 〈植〉 stem; peduncle; petiole

see also bǎ

爸 bà also "爸爸" 〈口〉 pa; dad; daddy

耙 bà harrow:圆盘~ disc harrow / ~地 harrow a field *see also* pá

罢(罷) bà ❶ stop; cease:~课 (of students) boycott classes; students' strike / ~赛 refuse to participate in a competition; (of athletes) go on strike / ~市 (of business people) suspend business as a protest; shopkeepers' strike / 欲~不能 find it hard to stop ❷ dismiss; relieve; remove from office:~官 dismiss (an official) from office / ~职 remove from a position; dismiss from office ❸ complete; finish: 吃~饭 after eating one's meal; after the meal

罢黜 bàchù 〈书〉 ❶ remove from office; dismiss ❷ ban; banish; reject

罢工 bàgōng strike; go or be on strike:总~ general strike / 静坐~ sit-down strike; sit-in / 声援~ (hold a) sympathetic strike / ~者 striker / ~纠察线 picket line

罢了 bàle ❶〈助〉just; merely; only:说说~ only a casual remark; lip service ❷ (bàliǎo) let it pass; leave it at that:这事难道就这样~? How can it be that at that?

罢免 bàmiǎn recall; remove; dismiss:~权 (right of) recall; right to remove (sb) from office

罢手 bàshǒu call it quits; give up; stop:就此~ call it quits then and there

罢休 bàxiū give up; stop:不达目的绝不~ not stop until the goal is achieved

霸 bà ❶ also "霸王" tyrant; despot ❷ hegemonic power; hegem-

ony:争~ contend for hegemony; vie for supremacy / 海上~主 maritime overlord ❸ dominate; lord it over:~气 arbitrary or peremptory air; domineering manner / 各~一方 each lording it over his locality

霸道 bàdào ❶ rule by force; despotic rule or government ❷ overbearing; domineering; high-handed

霸权 bàquán hegemony; supremacy:~主义 hegemonism / 争夺世界~ struggle or contend for world supremacy

霸占 bàzhàn forcibly occupy; seize:~良家妇女 seize a woman of a good family and force her to be one's sex slave / ~他人财产 come into unlawful possession of sb's property

ba

吧(罷) ba 〈助〉 ❶ *used at the end of a sentence to indicate* a) *suggestion, request, or command*:快点儿~。Hurry up, will you? b) *agreement or approval*:好~,我答应你了。OK, you have my word. c) *surmise or probability*:你就是李先生~? You are Mr Li, I suppose. ❷ *used in a sentence to indicate a pause after a supposition, concession, or condition*:就算你完全正确~,也该谦虚点儿。Even if you are entirely correct, you should be a bit more modest. *see also* bā

bāi

掰 bāi break or snap off with the fingers and thumb; break up:~两半儿 break (sth) in two / ~腕子 (have a) wrist wrestling contest / ~着手指算 count on one's fingers / 他俩就这么~了。So they've broken with each other.

bái

白 bái ❶ white; bright; light: ～布 white cloth; calico / ～桦〈植〉white birch / ～嫩 (of complexion) fair and delicate / ～旗 white flag / ～熊 white or polar bear / ～杨〈植〉white poplar / ～皮书 white paper or book / ～发苍苍 grey-haired; hoaryhaired / ～面书生 pale-faced young scholar / 东方发～。It dawns in the east. ❷ White (as a symbol of counter-revolution): ～区 White area ❸ clear: 真相大～。The whole truth is out. ❹ plain; blank; pure: ～饭 plain cooked rice; cooked rice with nothing to go with it / ～开水 also "白水" plain boiled water / 交～卷 hand in an unanswered examination paper; fail to do one's job; lay an egg ❺ in vain; for nothing: ～free of charge: ～吃 get a free meal / ～饶 get or give (sth extra) free of charge; throw in free / ～说 speak in vain; waste one's breath / ～跑一趟 make a fruitless trip ❻ state; explain: 辩～ offer an explanation; plead innocence ❼ spoken part (in opera, etc); (of) spoken language; vernacular: 对～ dialogue / 半文半～ half classical, half vernacular ❽ (of Chinese characters) wrongly written or mispronounced: 把字念～了 mispronounce a word ❾ give a supercilious or unfriendly look: 他～了我一眼。He gave me a cold stare.

白皑皑 bái'ái'ái (of snow, frost, etc) pure white

白白 báibái in vain; to no purpose; for nothing: ～放过时机 let an opportunity slip through one's fingers

白班儿 báibānr 〈口〉day shift: 上～ be on day shift

白璧 báibì white jade; sth perfect; paragon: ～微瑕 speck in white jade—slight blemish on sth otherwise perfect

白菜 báicài Chinese cabbage

白痴 báichī idiocy; idiot

白搭 báidā 〈口〉no use; no good; in vain: 功夫全～了。Everything was in vain.

白癜风 báidiànfēng 〈医〉vitiligo

白费 báifèi waste; be of no avail: ～蜡〈口〉useless; in vain; for nothing / ～唇舌 waste one's breath / ～心思 rack one's brains for nothing

白宫 Báigōng (US) White House, official residence of the president in Washington, DC; American administration: 入主～ win the presidency

白果 báiguǒ also "银杏"〈植〉ginkgo (nut)

白喉 báihóu 〈医〉diphtheria

白花花 báihuāhuā shining white: ～的银子 gleaming silver (coins) / ～的胡子 hoary beard

白话 báihuà ❶ unrealizable or unfounded statement: 空口说～ make empty promises; pay lip service ❷ vernacular: ～诗 free verse in vernacular Chinese / ～文 (writing in) vernacular Chinese

白金 báijīn (common term for 铂) platinum

白净 báijing also "白皙" (of skin, complexion, etc) fair and clear

白酒 báijiǔ liquor usually distilled from sorghum or maize; spirit: 低度～ low-proof liquor

白兰地 báilándì brandy: ～加苏打水 brandy and soda

白兰瓜 báilánguā honeydew, Lanzhou, or Wallace melon

白鲢 báilián 〈动物〉silver carp

白领 báilǐng white-collar: ～犯罪 white-collar crime / ～工作 white-collar job / ～阶层 white-collar employees

白露 báilù White Dew—15th seasonal division point see also "节气" jiéqì

白茫茫 báimángmáng vast expanse of whiteness (of mist, snow, floodwater, etc)

白蒙蒙 báiméngméng （of mist, smoke, etc) whitish and indistinct

白米 báimǐ （polished）rice；～饭 cooked white rice

白面 báimiàn （wheat）flour：～馒头 steamed wheat flour bun

白面儿 báimiànr heroin；抽～ smoke or take heroin；be addicted to heroin

白描 báimiáo ❶ line-drawing in the traditional ink and brush style ❷ simple, straightforward style of writing

白内障 báinèizhàng 〈医〉cataract：～摘除术 cataract extraction

白热 báirè also "白炽"white heat；incandescence：～灯 tungsten or incandescent lamp / 白热化 turn white-hot；reach a crisis or climax

白人 báirén white person；Caucasian

白刃 báirèn naked sword or knife；bayonet：～战 bayonet charge；hand-to-hand fighting

白日 báirì ❶ sun ❷ daytime：大天～（in）broad daylight / ～做梦 daydream；indulge in wishful thinking

白色 báisè ❶ white：～人种 White or Caucasian race／～收入 white or legal income／～污染 white (ie plastics) pollution ❷ White (as a symbol of reaction)：～恐怖 White terror／～政权 White regime

白食 báishí free food or meal；吃～的 one who is prone to live off other people；hanger-on；parasite

白手 báishǒu with bare hands：～夺刀 seize the opponent's sword with bare hands／～起家 start from scratch；be self-made

白薯 báishǔ （popular term for 甘薯）sweet potato；烤～ baked sweet potato

白糖 báitáng （refined）white sugar；绵～ refined white sugar／白砂糖 white granulated sugar

白天 báitiān daytime；day：～黑夜 day and night／大～抢银行 rob a bank in broad daylight

白条 báitiáo unofficial receipt；IOU：打～ give an IOU (instead of paying cash)

白头偕老 báitóuxiélǎo also "白头到老"（of a married couple）live together to a ripe old age

白细胞 báixìbāo also "白血球"〈生理〉white blood cell or corpuscle；leucocyte：～数 leukocyte count

白雪公主 Báixuěgōngzhǔ Snow White；pure, lovely girl

白血病 báixuèbìng leukaemia：～患者 leukaemic

白眼 báiyǎn supercilious or scornful look：遭人～ be slighted or cold-shouldered／看人～ look upon sb with scorn；show disdain towards sb

白衣 báiyī white frock (as a doctor's uniform, etc)：～天使 nurse／～战士 medical worker；doctor or nurse

白蚁 báiyǐ 〈动物〉termite；white ant：～巢 termitary

白银 báiyín （popular name for 银）silver

白纸黑字 báizhǐ-hēizì （written）in black and white：～难以抵赖。What is in black and white can hardly be denied.

白种 báizhǒng white or Caucasian race：～人 white (person)；Caucasian

白昼 báizhòu daytime；daylight；day

白字 báizì wrongly written or mispronounced character；尽念～ tend to mispronounce characters／～连篇 (of an essay, etc) teem with wrongly written characters

bǎi

百 bǎi ❶ hundred：～儿八十〈口〉about one hundred；a hundred or so／～米赛跑 100-metre dash or sprint ❷ numerous；all kinds of：～宝箱 treasure box or trove／～读不厌 never get bored even if one reads sth for the hundredth time; be worth reading again and again / ~花争妍 all flowers vie for beauty; the flowers are a riot of colours / ~里挑一 one in a hundred; cream of the crop; pick

百般 bǎibān ❶ in every possible way; by every means; ~庇护 shield (sb) by every means / ~温柔 be as tender as tender can be; be all tenderness / ~无奈 have no alternative whatsoever; cannot help it ❷ all kinds of; numerous; ~痛苦 all kinds of suffering or pain

百倍 bǎibèi hundred times; hundredfold; 身价~ increase one's importance hundredfold; rise dramatically in social status / ~努力 work a hundred times harder; make redoubled efforts

百尺竿头, 更进一步 bǎichǐgāntóu, gèngjìnyībù work for even greater success; forge further ahead

百发百中 bǎifābǎizhòng shoot with unfailing precision; act with absolute certainty; do without fail

百废待举 bǎifèidàijǔ a host of neglected tasks cry out for attention; a thousand and one things wait to be done

百分 bǎifēn per cent; percent; ~比 percentage / ~点 percentage point / ~数 percentage / ~制 hundred-point or percentage system / ~分之一 hundred percent; entirely; absolutely

百感交集 bǎigǎnjiāojí a multitude of sentiments well up in one's heart; all sorts of feelings or thoughts crowd in upon one

百合 bǎihé 〈植〉lily (bulb)

百花齐放 bǎihuāqífàng a hundred flowers blooming at the same time — free development and flourishing of different varieties and styles of art and literature; ~, 百家争鸣 let a hundred flowers blossom and a hundred schools of thought contend

百货 bǎihuò general merchandise; 日用~ articles of everyday or daily use / ~商店 department or general store

百科全书 bǎikē quánshū encyclopaedia

百孔千疮 bǎikǒng-qiānchuāng also "千疮百孔" honeycombed with gaping wounds; afflicted with all disorders

百灵 bǎilíng also "百灵鸟" lark

百年 bǎinián ❶ hundred years; century; many years; ~不遇 not likely to happen once in a century; once in a blue moon; extremely rare / ~大业 cause that lasts a hundred years; work of enduring significance / ~纪念 centenary; centennial / ~树人 It takes a hundred years to make education bear fruit. ❷ lifetime; human span; ~之后 〈婉〉after sb is gone or passes away

百思不解 bǎisībùjiě fail to understand sth after thinking it over a hundred times; not have a clue though one has pondered long over the matter

百万 bǎiwàn million; mega-; ~吨 megaton / ~富翁 millionaire / ~雄师 a million bold warriors; a mighty army (of one million)

百闻不如一见 bǎiwénbùrúyíjiàn 〈谚〉seeing is believing

百无 bǎiwú none whatever; not in the least; ~禁忌 nothing is taboo; speak or act with no restrictions whatever / ~聊赖 not know what to do with oneself; languish in boredom

百姓 bǎixìng common or ordinary people; civilians; the populace

百叶窗 bǎiyèchuāng also "百页窗" shutter; (Venetian) blind; louvre

百依百顺 bǎiyī-bǎishùn all obedience; docile; 对她~ comply with every whim of hers

百战百胜 bǎizhànbǎishèng also "百战不殆" fight a hundred battles and always emerge the victor; be ever-victorious

百折不挠 bǎizhébùnáo also "百折不回" show no sign of weakness despite repeated setbacks; be indomitable

佰 bǎi hundred (used on cheques, receipts, etc to avoid mistakes or alterations)

柏 bǎi cypress; cedar *see also* bó

柏油 bǎiyóu asphalt; tar; pitch;～路 asphalt or tarmac road

摆(擺) bǎi ❶ put; lay; place;～花 arrange flowers / ～宴 host a banquet; feast / ～擂台 set up a stage for contest and invite challengers; take on challengers one by one / ～正二者的关系 put the two in a correct relationship with each other ❷ put on; assume; show off;～阔 flaunt or show off one's wealth; go in for ostentation / ～架子 put on airs; play hard-to-get / ～谱儿〈方〉keep up appearances; show off; throw one's weight about / ～威风 give oneself airs; put on airs; throw one's weight about / ～老资格 strike the pose of an elder; flaunt one's seniority ❸ sway; swing; wave;～手 shake one's hand in disapproval; wave one's hand; beckon ❹〈理〉pendulum;～轮 balance wheel (of a mechanical watch or clock); balance ❺ set forth; state; speak;～条件 lay down terms; offer conditions / ～事实,讲道理 present the facts and reason things out / 把问题～到桌面上来 place the cards on the table; bring the issue out into the open

摆布 bǎibù order about; manipulate; have at one's mercy;任人～ allow oneself to be dictated to; be at sb's mercy

摆动 bǎidòng sway; wave; swing;～手中的鲜花 wave the flowers in one's hand

摆渡 bǎidù ferry across (a river, etc); ferryboat

摆弄 bǎinòng ❶ move (sth) back and forth; fiddle with (sth) ❷ order (sb) about; manipulate; twist (sb) round one's little finger

摆平 bǎipíng ❶ treat equally; strike a balance; be even-handed or impartial ❷〈方〉punish or fix (sb); settle (sth)

摆设 bǎishè ❶ furnish and decorate ❷ (bǎisher) ornaments; furnishings;〈喻〉figurehead;小～ knickknacks

摆脱 bǎituō shake off; break away from; free or extricate oneself from;～贫困 shake off poverty / ～困境 extricate oneself from a predicament; resolve a dilemma

摆样子 bǎiyàngzi (do) for show;桌上放了几本书～。A few books were placed on the desk for show.

摆子 bǎizi〈方〉malaria;打～ suffer from malaria

bài

败 bài ❶ be defeated; lose;～兵 defeated army; routed troops / ～将 defeated general; vanquished foe; loser (in a match or game) / ～诉 lose a lawsuit / ～下阵来 lose a battle or contest / 主队以零比三～于客队。The host team lost to the visiting team nil to 3. ❷ defeat; beat;大～对手 thoroughly trounce the opponent ❸ fail;此事难成易～。The matter is difficult of success but liable to failure. ❹ spoil; ruin;～胃口 spoil one's appetite / 事情就～在他手里。It was he who bungled the whole business. ❺ counteract; relieve;～火〈中医〉relieve internal heat or inflammation ❻ decay; wither;～草 withered grass / ～谢 wither and fall

败北 bàiběi〈书〉suffer defeat; lose a battle or war

败笔 bàibǐ faulty stroke in calligraphy

or painting; faulty expression in writing; flaw or fault in an otherwise perfect work

败坏 bàihuài　ruin; undermine; corrupt: ～声誉 discredit (sb) / defame (sb) / ～社会风气 corrupt social values; ruin social morals

败家 bàijiā　cause the decline of a family; dissipate a family fortune: ～子 spendthrift; wastrel; prodigal

败局 bàijú　lost game; losing battle: 挽回～ reverse a defeat; retrieve a bad situation / ～已定。The game is lost.

败类 bàilèi　scum or dregs of a community; degenerate: 民族～ national traitors; dregs or scum of a nation

败露 bàilù　(of a plot, conspiracy, etc) fall through and stand exposed; be brought to light

败落 bàiluò　decline (in wealth and position): 家道～。The family is on the decline.

败退 bàituì　retreat in defeat; evacuate after defeat

败兴 bàixìng　dampen (sb's) enthusiasm; spoil (sb's) pleasure or interest; disappoint: ～而归 come back disappointed / 让人～的家伙 spoilsport

败血症 bàixuèzhèng　〈医〉septicaemia

败仗 bàizhàng　lost battle; defeat: 打～ be defeated in battle; suffer a defeat

拜 bài　❶ do obeisance (to sb): ～佛 worship Buddha ❷ extend greetings; congratulate: ～寿 offer birthday felicitations (usu to an elderly person) ❸ make a courtesy call; visit: ～客 call on people; pay visits / ～街坊 visit one's neighbours (on moving into a neighbourhood) ❹ perform a ceremony to confer an official title or establish a relationship: ～将 be appointed commander (by the emperor, etc) / ～师 acknowledge sb as one's teacher or master / ～把子 become sworn brothers ❺ 〈敬〉used before some verbs: ～读 peruse with reverence; have the pleasure of reading / ～领 accept with thanks / ～谢 bow one's thanks; thank

拜拜 bàibài　(say) bye-bye: 钱一到手,他就跟你～了。As soon as he gets hold of your money, he'll walk out on you.

拜倒 bàidǎo　〈贬〉prostrate oneself; fall on one's knees; grovel: ～在石榴裙下 be infatuated with a woman

拜访 bàifǎng　pay a visit; call on: 专程～ make a special or exclusive visit

拜会 bàihuì　(often used on diplomatic occasions) pay a call on; call on: 告别～ (pay a) farewell call (on sb) / 礼节性～ courtesy call

拜见 bàijiàn　also "拜望" pay a formal visit; call to pay one's respects

拜金主义 bàijīn zhǔyì　money worship; Mammonism: ～者 Mammonist

拜年 bàinián　pay a New Year call; send New Year greetings; wish a Happy New Year: 电话～ send New Year greetings over the phone / 拜个早年 extend one's New Year greetings ahead of time / 拜个晚年 extend one's New Year greetings after the event

拜堂 bàitáng　also "拜天地" (of bride and groom) make formal bows to the groom's parents and / or to heaven and earth at a traditional wedding ceremony; perform the wedding ceremony

拜托 bàituō　〈敬〉ask a favour of; entrust; request: 这件事就～给您了。I would like to leave this matter with you.

拜谒 bàiyè　pay a formal visit; call to pay respects; pay homage (at a monument, mausoleum, etc)

稗 bài　❶ also "稗子"〈植〉barnyard grass or millet ❷〈书〉insignificant; unofficial: ～史 unofficial history; private record of events / ～官野史 unofficial history; book of anecdotes

bān

扳 bān ❶ pull; turn:～弓 pull or draw a bow / ～着指头数 count on one's fingers ❷ win back what has been lost:～本〈方〉win back one's lost wagers / ～平 equalize the score; manage to draw a match

扳机 bānjī trigger:扣～ pull the trigger; trigger (a gun)

扳手 bānshou ❶ also "扳子" spanner; wrench ❷ lever (on a machine)

班 bān ❶ class; team; (theatrical) troupe;〈军〉squad:～长 class monitor or president;〈军〉squad leader; (work) team leader / ～主任 teacher in overall charge of a class; class adviser or counsellor ❷ shift; duty:交～ hand over to the next shift ❸ regularly-run; scheduled:～车 shuttle service or bus / ～机 regular air service; airliner; flight ❹〈量〉a) a group of people:一～青年 a group of youths b) number of runs in transport:末～车 last bus or train / 每日三～ three buses or trains a day

班次 bāncì ❶ (order of) classes or grades at school ❷ number of runs or flights

班底 bāndǐ key members of an organization; cast; setup

班房 bānfáng 〈口〉jail; prison

班门弄斧 bānménnòngfǔ display one's learning or parade one's skill in the presence of an expert; teach your grandmother to suck eggs

班师 bānshī 〈书〉order troops to withdraw from the front; (of troops) return (triumphantly) from the front

班子 bānzi ❶〈旧〉theatrical troupe ❷ group or team organized for a given task; task group; cast:搭～ organize one's team; put together a cast

般 bān sort; kind; way:狮子～怒吼 roar like an angry lion / 闪电～的攻击 lightning attack; blitz

般配 bānpèi be well matched (as in marriage); match

颁 bān promulgate; issue; publish:～奖 hand out or give an award / ～布宪法 promulgate a constitution / ～部～文件 papers issued by a ministry

颁发 bānfā ❶ issue; promulgate:～禁令 issue a ban (on sth) ❷ award; confer:～勋章 confer or award a medal

斑 bān spot; speck; stripe:～点 spot; speckle; dot / 泪痕～ tear-stained

斑白 bānbái also "班白" grizzled; greying:须发～ (have) hoary hair and beard

斑驳 bānbó also "班驳"〈书〉mottled; motley; patched:～陆离 variegated; of different colours; multi-coloured

斑斓 bānlán gorgeous; bright-coloured; multi-coloured:五彩～ a riot of colour

斑马 bānmǎ 〈动物〉zebra:～线 zebra or pedestrian crossing; crosswalk

斑纹 bānwén stripe; streak; scaling:大理石的～ streaks in marble

搬 bān ❶ move (usu sth heavy or big); carry; remove:～兵 call in reinforcements; ask for help / 把桌子～走 move or carry a table away / ～上舞台 present or put on the stage ❷ apply indiscriminately; copy mechanically; imitate:～书本 imitate what is written in books

搬家 bānjiā move (house); move from one place to another; migrate:～公司 house-moving company / 脑袋～have one's head cut off; get killed

搬弄 bānnòng ❶ move (sth) about; fiddle or mess with (sth) ❷ show off; display ❸ instigate; stir up trouble:

是非 sow dissension; tell tales

搬迁 bānqiān　move house; relocate: ～户 people or families to be relocated; relocated household or person

搬运 bānyùn　carry; transport; ～费 shifting charge; removal expense; portage / ～工 porter (at a railway station); docker; stevedore

瘢
瘢 bān　also "瘢痕" scar; cicatrix

癍
癍 bān　abnormal pigmentary deposit on the skin; fleck

bǎn

板
板 bǎn　❶ board; plank; plate: ～报〈口〉blackboard newspaper or bulletin / ～材 (as raw material) board; slab; sheet / ～刷 scrubbing brush; brush eraser / ～条箱 crate / ～上钉钉 be final and irreversible ❷〈乐〉clappers; accented beat; time; 快～ allegro / 慢～ lento ❸ hard; stiff; rigid; ～滞 stiff; dull / ～着脸不说话 look stern or grave and say nothing / 这块地发～。The soil here is too hard (for growing crops).

板凳 bǎndèng　wooden bench or stool: ～队员〈体〉understudy who sits in reserve

板胡 bǎnhú　banhu, a Chinese two-stringed fiddle

板结 bǎnjié　harden; crust: 土壤～ surface crusting (of soil)

板块 bǎnkuài　〈地〉plate: ～结构 plate or raft tectonics / ～运动 plate movement or motion

板栗 bǎnlì　Chinese chestnut

板球 bǎnqiú　〈体〉cricket

板鸭 bǎnyā　pressed or dried salted duck

板牙 bǎnyá　〈方〉❶ front tooth; incisor ❷ molar

板眼 bǎnyǎn　measure in traditional Chinese music; 〈喻〉orderliness;

method; 一板三眼 one accented beat followed by three unaccented ones; four-four time / 办事有板有眼 be methodical in doing things

板子 bǎnzi　❶ board; plank ❷ bamboo or birch for corporal punishment; cane; 挨～ get caned / 〈喻〉be criticized

版
版 bǎn　❶ printing plate; block: 套～ process or colour plate / ～式 format (of a book, etc) ❷ edition: 本 edition ❸ page (of a newspaper, etc): ～面 space of a whole page; layout of a printed sheet; typeface

版画 bǎnhuà　engraving; etching

版权 bǎnquán　copyright: ～页 copyright page / ～所有 all rights reserved / ～作品 copyrighted work

版税 bǎnshuì　royalty (on books)

版图 bǎntú　domain; territory: 划入～ be included as part of a country's territory

bàn

办(辦)
办(辦) bàn　❶ do; handle; manage: ～案 handle a case / ～护照 apply for or process a passport / ～手续 go through the formalities / ～私事 attend to private affairs / 要我让步～不到。It would be impossible to make me give in. ❷ set up; run: ～报 run a newspaper / ～教育 undertake educational work ❸ purchase; get sth ready: ～货 make purchases (usu for a company or enterprise); buy goods / ～酒席 prepare a feast; cater ❹ punish; bring to justice: ～罪 punish (sb) for his or her crime

办法 bànfǎ　way; measure; approach

办公 bàngōng　handle official business; work (usu in an office): ～费 administrative or running expenses / ～厅 (usu higher than 办公室) general office / ～桌 desk; bureau / ～大楼 office building / ～时间 office or business hours

办公室 bàngōngshì ❶ office：～终端〈信息〉office terminal ❷ administrative department of a unit：厂部～ general office of the factory management

办理 bànlǐ handle；do；transact：～零售、批发业务 handle both retail and wholesale business / 请酌情～。Please do as you see fit.

办事 bànshì handle affairs；act；work：～处 office；agency / ～员 office clerk；assistant / ～公道 be fair and square in what one does；act fair and square / ～拖拉 be dilatory in one's work / 办实事 do sth practical

办学 bànxué run a school：～方针 guiding principle for a school

半 bàn ❶ half；semi-；partly：～费 (at) half the fee or price / ～圆 semicircle / ～边天 half the sky；〈喻〉womenfolk / ～成品 semi-finished article or product / ～决赛〈体〉semifinals / ～透明 translucent；semi-transparent / ～文盲 semi-literate / 月刊 semi-monthly；fortnightly / ～殖民地 semi-colony / 封建社会 semifeudal society / ～熟练劳动 semi-skilled labour ❷ in the middle；halfway：～山腰 halfway up a hill ❸ very little；the least bit：～点 the least bit / 不值～文钱 not worth a farthing

半…半… bàn…bàn… used before two antonyms to indicate that two opposing qualities or states exist simultaneously：半工半读 part work，part study；work-study programme / 半饥半饱 half full；underfed / 半推半就 (yield) with seeming reluctance / 半信半疑 half believing，half doubting；not quite convinced；doubtful / 半真半假 half genuine and half sham；partly true，partly false / 半开玩笑半正经 half joking，half serious

半…不… bàn…bù… used in the same way as 半…半… but often in a

derogatory sense：半生不熟 underdone；half-cooked / 半死不活 more dead than alive；half dead / 半文不白 (sth) half literary，half vernacular / 半新不旧 not new though not worn-out

半场 bànchǎng 〈体〉❶ half a game：上～ first half of a game ❷ half court：～紧逼 half-court press

半导体 bàndǎotǐ semiconductor：～材料 semiconducting or semiconductor material / ～收音机 transistor radio or receiver

半岛 bàndǎo peninsula

半价 bànjià half price：～票 also "半票" half-price ticket；half fare / ～出售 sell at half price

半截 bànjié half or a section of sth；half the way：话说了～ leave half of one's words unsaid / ～入土 with one foot in the grave

半斤八两 bànjīn-bāliǎng six of one and half a dozen of the other；the pot calling the kettle black

半径 bànjìng radius

半空 bànkōng ❶ in mid-air；in the air ❷ half-empty；not full

半路 bànlù also "半道儿" halfway (through)；on the way；in midcourse：～出家 turn a Buddhist later in life；〈喻〉change to a new profession for which one has received no previous training / ～夫妻 couple married halfway through life (usu after a previous marriage)

半瓶醋 bànpíngcù 〈喻〉smatterer；dabbler

半球 bànqiú hemisphere：东～ Eastern Hemisphere

半身 bànshēn half one's body：～像 half-length photo or portrait；bust / ～不遂〈医〉hemiplegia；hemiparalysis

半生 bànshēng also "半辈子" half a lifetime：前～ first half of one's life / 大～ (for the) greater part of one's life

半数 bànshù　half the number；half；超过～ more than half

半天 bàntiān　also "半晌" ❶ half (a) day；前～ morning ❷ (quite) a long time

半途 bàntú　〈书〉halfway；midway；～拆伙 part company halfway / ～而废 leave off unfinished；give up or quit halfway

半脱产 bàntuōchǎn　partly excused from work or relieved of one's duties；～干部 part-time functionary / ～学习 study half the day while working the other half

半夜 bànyè　❶ half of a night；后～ also "下半夜" after midnight；in the small hours of the morning ❷ midnight；～三更 in the depth of night；late at night

半自动 bànzìdòng　semi-automatic；auto-manual；～步枪 semi-automatic rifle / ～交换台〈通信〉auto-manual or semi-automatic exchange

扮 bàn　❶ play the part of；disguise oneself as：～戏 (of actors, etc) make up；act in a play /～(演)反面人物 play the part of a villain ❷ put on (an expression)：～鬼脸 make grimaces or faces

扮相 bànxiàng　❶ how an actor or actress looks in costume and makeup；stage appearance：她的～和唱功都很好。Both her stage appearance and singing are excellent. ❷ how one looks in makeup：我这副～如何？How do I look in this makeup?

伴 bàn　❶ companion；partner：搭个～儿 join sb on a trip；travel together ❷ accompany：郎 (at a wedding) best man / ～娘 (at a wedding) maid of honour；bridesmaid

伴唱 bànchàng　vocal accompaniment：为舞蹈～ accompany a dance by singing

伴侣 bànlǚ　companion；mate；partner

伴随 bànsuí　accompany；follow；～着

欢快的乐曲跳舞 dance to the accompaniment of lively music

伴舞 bànwǔ　❶ be a dancing partner ❷ accompany (a singer, etc) with dance

伴奏 bànzòu　accompany (with musical instruments)：吉他～ guitar accompaniment / ～者 accompanist

拌 bàn　❶ mix；stir：～和 mix；blend；stir / ～种〈农〉seed dressing /～黄瓜丝 shredded cucumber salad ❷ quarrel；bicker：～了几句 have some words (with sb)

拌嘴 bànzuǐ　bicker；squabble；quarrel：小两口容易～，也容易和好。The young couple fall out as easily as they make up.

绊 bàn　(cause to) stumble；trip (over)：～了一跤 stumble over sth / ～手～脚 cumbersome；in the way / 让零七碎八的事～住了 get bogged down in trifles

绊脚石 bànjiǎoshí　stumbling block；obstacle：进步的～ obstacle to progress

绊子 bànzi　also "绊儿" trip：使～ trip up

瓣 bàn　❶ petal ❷ segment or section (of a tangerine, etc)；clove (of garlic)；piece：掰成两～儿 break into two pieces / 切成八～儿 cut (sth) in eight ❸ valve；lamella：鳃～ gill lamella

bāng

邦 bāng　nation；state；country：～交 diplomatic relations (between two countries) / ～联 confederated states；confederation；confederacy / 民为～本。The people are the foundation of a country.

帮(幫) bāng　❶ help；assist；～办 assist in managing or doing (sth) / ～工 (work as a) farm hand or journeyman / ～手 assistant；

helper / ～佣（work as a）servant or maid / ～补家用 help cover part of family expenses / ～教失足青少年 help and educate delinquent youths / 一个五十、一百的 contribute fifty or a hundred yuan ❷ side (of sth); rim; outer rind or leaf：菜～（子）outer leaves (as of cabbage) / 船～（子）side of a ship; gunwale / 鞋～（子）upper (of a shoe) ❸ gang; clique; secret society：～会 secret society; underworld gang / ～伙 gang; band; ring / ～主 head or chief of a gang ❹〈量〉used with people：一～（子）小朋友 a group of children

帮忙 bāngmáng　help; give or lend a hand; do a favour：帮倒忙 be a hindrance rather than a help; do more harm than good / 帮了大忙 be a great help; give a lot of help / 你能帮我一点忙吗? Can you do me a favour?

帮派 bāngpài　faction：～活动 factional activities; factionalism / ～体系 factionalist setup

帮腔 bāngqiāng ❶〈戏〉vocal accompaniment ❷ chime in (with); speak in support of sb

帮闲 bāngxián（serve as a) hireling; hack：～文人 hack writer

帮凶 bāngxiōng（serve as an) accomplice; accessory; cat's paw

帮助 bāngzhù　help; assist; aid：互相～ help each other / 无私的～ disinterested help or aid

梆 bāng ❶ watchman's bamboo or wooden clapper ❷〈象声〉sound of striking or knocking on wood：把桌子捶得～～响 keep thumping the table

梆硬 bāngyìng　very hard or stiff：～的土地 very hard soil

梆子 bāngzi ❶ see "梆❶" ❷ also "梆子腔" general term for local operas in Shaanxi, Shanxi, Hebei, Shandong, etc performed to the accompaniment of bangzi, clappers made of jujube wood

浜 bāng〈方〉creek; brook

bǎng

绑 bǎng ❶ tie (up); bind; truss (up)：～带 bandage; puttee / ～缚 truss or tie up; bind / ～腿 leg wrappings; puttee / ～扎 tie or bind up; wrap or bundle up ❷ used as follows：～匪 kidnapper / ～架 kidnap; abduct / ～票 hold or kidnap for ransom

榜 bǎng ❶ list of names posted up; announcement; notice：出～ put up a notice / ～上无名 not on the list of successful candidates ❷ horizontal inscribed board

榜首 bǎngshǒu　first on a published list or a contest：跃居～ come from behind to capture the championship or first place

榜样 bǎngyàng　good example; (role) model：学习的～ a role model to emulate / ～的力量是无穷的。A fine example is the best teacher.

膀 bǎng ❶ shoulder; (upper) arm：～臂 reliable assistant; right-hand man / ～大腰圆 broad-shouldered and solidly-built; hefty ❷ wing：光着～子 stripped to the waist (of a bird)：鸭～ duck wings
see also pāng;páng

bàng

蚌 bàng　freshwater mussel; clam

棒 bàng ❶ stick; club; cudgel：～操〈体〉club exercise / ～糖 lollipop; lollypop; sucker / ～打不回头〈口〉stubborn; pigheaded ❷〈口〉terrific; topping; superb：身体真～ in wonderful health / 干得～极了 do a terrific or swell job

棒球 bàngqiú baseball:～棒 baseball bat /～场 baseball field; diamond /～投手 pitcher /～击球手 batter /～接球手 catcher

棒子 bàngzi ❶ stick; club; cudgel ❷〈方〉(ear of) maize; corn; corncob:～面 cornmeal; corn flour

傍 bàng ❶ draw near; be close to:～依 be close to; be near ❷ (of time) towards; nearing:～晚 towards evening; at nightfall; at dusk /～午 towards noon ❸〈方〉follow; lean on; leech on to:～大款 (of a girl) leech on to a moneybags; find a sugar daddy

谤 bàng 〈书〉slander; defame; vilify:～毁 calumniate; slander /～议 calumny; slanderous comment

磅 bàng ❶ pound (about 0.4536 kilogramme) ❷ (weigh on the) scales:～秤 platform scale or balance /把东西～一～ weigh sth on the scales see also páng

镑 bàng pound (as currency unit):英～ pound sterling

bāo

包 bāo ❶ wrap; cover; surround:～书 wrap up a book in a piece of paper; put a jacket or cover on a book ❷ bundle; parcel; pack:行李～ luggage pack ❸ bag; sack; yurt:帆布～ canvas bag; kit bag ❹〈量〉used of bundled or packaged things:两一面粉 two bags or sacks of flour ❺ swelling; protuberance; lump:背上起了个～ have a swelling in the back ❻ include; embrace; contain:～藏祸心 harbour evil intentions /～孕危机 be fraught with danger /～蕴深意 be pregnant with meaning ❼ undertake (an assignment, etc) completely; be responsible for (the whole job):任务～给你了。The job now is entirely your responsi-

bility. ❽ guarantee; assure:～票 also "保票"warranty; guarantee /～退～换 guarantee return or change of faulty goods /～治百病 guarantee to cure all diseases; promise to be a cure-all /～你满意。I bet you'll like it. ❾ hire; charter:～场 (make a) block booking (for a film show, etc); exclusive session /～车 charter a car or bus; chartered car or bus /～房 rent a hotel room for a period of time; hotel room thus rented /～机 charter a plane; chartered plane /～二奶〈口〉keep a woman (as mistress)

包办 bāobàn ❶ take sole charge of; undertake completely:～宴席 offer catering service ❷ monopolize; arrange arbitrarily:～代替 push others aside and boss the show /～婚姻 arranged marriage or match

包庇 bāobì shield; cover up

包产 bāochǎn fix (farm) output quotas; undertake full responsibilities for such quotas:～田 contracted land with fixed production output /～到户 contracting output quotas to each (farm) household

包抄 bāochāo outflank (the enemy); envelop

包打天下 bāodǎtiānxià boss the show; run a business or affair all by oneself

包袱 bāofu ❶ cloth-wrapper; bundle wrapped in a cloth ❷ load (on one's mind); burden; hindrance

包干 bāogān undertake to do a job until it is completed:财务～ be responsible for one's own finances /分片～ divide a task into different portions and assign each to an individual or group

包工 bāogōng contract for a job:～头 labour contractor /～包料 contract for labour and materials

包裹 bāoguǒ ❶ wrap or bind up ❷ bundle; package; parcel:～单 postal parcel form or notification

包含 bāohán　contain; include; imply

包涵 bāohan　〈套〉excuse; forgive;照顾不周，请多～。Please forgive me for my inadequate hospitality.

包括 bāokuò　include; consist of; comprise

包揽 bāolǎn　take on entirely; monopolize (all work):一一切 put all under one's charge; monopolize all

包罗 bāoluó　cover; embrace; include:～万象 all-embracing; kaleidoscopic /～无遗 embrace all; be all-inclusive

包皮 bāopí　〈生理〉prepuce; foreskin

包容 bāoróng　❶ tolerant; magnanimous ❷ contain; hold

包围 bāowéi　surround; encircle; hem in:～圈 ring of encirclement

包厢 bāoxiāng　box (in a theatre or concert hall)

包销 bāoxiāo　❶ have exclusive selling rights:～权 exclusive selling rights ❷ 〈经〉underwrite (bonds, etc)

包扎 bāozā　dress; wrap or bind up:～所 dressing or first-aid station /～伤口 dress a wound

包装 bāozhuāng　pack; package:～材料 packaging; wrapping /～与推出新歌手〈喻〉packaging and promotion of a new singer

包子 bāozi　steamed stuffed bun; 肉～ meat-filled bun

苞 bāo　❶ bud ❷ 〈书〉luxuriant; profuse

孢 bāo　also "孢子" spore

胞 bāo　❶ also "胞衣" afterbirth; placenta ❷ born of the same parents:～兄弟 full brothers

炮 bāo　❶ quick-fry; sauté ❷ dry by heat　see also páo; pào

剥 bāo　peel; shell; skin:～豆 shell beans /～橘子 peel an orange　see also bō

龅 bāo

龅牙 bāoyá　bucktooth

煲 bāo　〈方〉❶ cooking pot; boiler; 沙～ earthen pot; casserole ❷ cook with boiler or cooker:～粥 cook porridge in a boiler

褒(襃) bāo　praise; commend; extol:～词 complimentary word /～奖 praise and honour; commend and award /～扬 praise; commend /～义 commendatory sense; laudatory or complimentary meaning /～善贬恶 praise virtue and censure vice

褒贬 bāobiǎn　❶ comment; pass judgement on:妄加～ make improper comments or presumptuous observations ❷ (bāobian) criticize; condemn; speak ill of:～得一文不值 condemn as worthless

báo

雹 báo　also "雹子" hail; hailstone

薄 báo　❶ thin; flimsy:～板 sheet (metal) /～饼 thin pancake; wafer ❷ coldly; shabbily:待人不～ treat sb quite generously ❸ weak; thin; light:酒味太～。The wine tastes insipid. ❹ infertile; poor:～田 also "薄地" infertile land; poor soil　see also bó; bò

bǎo

饱 bǎo　❶ eat one's fill; be full or replete:～餐 eat one's fill; 〈喻〉feast one's eyes (on beauty, etc) /～读经书 be well-read or -versed in the classics /～受凌辱 suffer untold humiliations and insults /～学之士 man of learning; learned scholar /～汉不知饿汉饥〈俗〉the well-fed don't know how the starving suffer; you can't feel for the starving with a full belly / ～食终日，无所用心 eat three square meals a day without doing any useful work—live like a parasite ❷ satisfy: 一～眼福 enjoy the view or sight to one's heart's content

饱尝 bǎocháng　experience; suffer; endure: ～艰辛 endure or experience all hardships

饱和 bǎohé　saturation: 市场～ saturated market / ～点 saturation point / ～轰炸〈军〉 saturation or carpet bombing / ～脂肪酸 saturated fatty acid

饱经 bǎojīng　experience to the full; have one's fill of: ～风霜 having experienced the hardships of life; weather-beaten / ～忧患 having had one's fill of trials and tribulations; long-suffering

饱满 bǎomǎn　❶ plump; rounded: 颗粒～ plump or full ears ❷ full of: be filled with: 精力～ full of vim and vigour

宝（寶） bǎo　❶ treasure; valuables; riches; ～爱〈书〉value; treasure / ～盒 jewel casket; treasure box; magical box / ～物 treasure ❷〈敬〉your: ～号 your firm or company; your name / ～眷 your wife and children; your family

宝宝 bǎobao　*term of endearment for a baby*: 好～ darling baby / ～装 infant clothes

宝贝 bǎobèi　❶ treasure; treasured object ❷ darling; dear; baby: 好～儿，听话。Darling, be a good child. ❸〈讽〉queer fish; crank; good-for-nothing: 你那个～兄弟 that good-for-nothing brother of yours

宝刀 bǎodāo　fine sword: ～不老 the man may be old, but not his sword—maintain one's vigour and skill in old age

宝贵 bǎoguì　❶ valuable; precious: ～

的贡献 significant contribution ❷ value; treasure; set store by: 最可～的遗产 most valued heritage

宝剑 bǎojiàn　double-edged sword

宝库 bǎokù　treasure house; treasury

宝石 bǎoshí　precious stone; gem; jewel: 红～ ruby / 蓝～ sapphire / 绿～ emerald / ～商 jeweller

宝塔 bǎotǎ　pagoda; dagoba

宝藏 bǎozàng　precious (mineral) deposit; treasure: 发掘民间艺术的～ explore the treasure-house of folk arts

宝座 bǎozuò　throne; treasured position or post

保 bǎo　❶ protect; defend; keep: ～暖 keep warm / ～国安民 defend the country and ensure a peaceful life for the people / ～住总经理的职位 keep one's position as general manager ❷ guarantee; insure; ensure: ～举 *also*"保荐"(guarantee and) recommend / ～媒 serve as a go-between (for marriage) / ～胎 prevent miscarriage; retain the fetus / ～质期 date stamping; use-by date / ～价包裹 insured parcel / ～命哲学〈贬〉survival mentality ❸ bail: 作～ stand bail or guarantor / ～外就医〈法〉receive medical treatment on bail / ～外执行〈法〉serve (part of one's) prison term outside prison on bail / ～值储蓄 inflation-adjusted savings deposit

保安 bǎo'ān　❶ ensure public security: ～公司 security company ❷ (ensure) safety (for personnel engaged in production, etc.): ～制度 safety rules ❸ security (personnel); guard

保本 bǎoběn　protect against possible loss; keep the capital intact; break even

保镖 bǎobiāo　(serve as) armed escort; bodyguard

保不住 bǎobuzhù　*also*"保不定"；"保不齐" more likely than not; most likely; may well: 他～会反对这事。He is very likely to oppose it.

保藏 bǎocáng keep in store; preserve: 由女主人～ in the mistress' safekeeping

保持 bǎochí keep; maintain; preserve: ～接触 stay or keep in touch (with sb); maintain contact / ～警惕 maintain vigilance; be on one's guard / ～距离 keep at a distance / ～镇静 keep one's head; keep cool / ～中立 maintain a neutral position; remain neutral; sit on the fence / ～世界记录 hold a world record / ～优良传统 carry on or keep up a fine tradition

保存 bǎocún preserve; keep; save: 完整地～ keep (sth) intact / ～程序〈信息〉save routine / ～精力 preserve one's strength

保单 bǎodān warrant; warranty; insurance policy

保管 bǎoguǎn ❶ take care of; store; manage: ～费 storage charges or fees / ～好自己的物品 take good care of one's belongings ❷ certainly; surely: ～你马上成功。You are sure to succeed.

保护 bǎohù protect; safeguard; preserve: 受到法律～ be under the protection of the law / ～国 protectorate / ～价 protective price (for the producer) / ～人 guardian; custodian; patron / ～伞〈贬〉protective umbrella; shield; cover / ～色〈动物〉protective coloration / ～关税 protective duty or tariff / ～主义 protectionism / ～国家利益 protect the national interests

保驾 bǎojià (often used jocularly) escort or guard (sb important, as the emperor): 你有老李～, 怕什么。What do you have to fear with Lao Li to escort you?

保健 bǎojiàn health protection or care: ～操 setting-up or fitness exercises / ～站 health centre; community clinic / ～按摩 keep-fit or therapeutic

massage / ～食品 health food

保龄球 bǎolíngqiú also "地滚球" bowling; bowling ball: ～场 bowling alley

保留 bǎoliú retain; keep; reserve: ～地 reservation / ～剧目 repertory (item); repertoire / ～自己的观点 keep or reserve one's own views

保密 bǎomì keep confidential; maintain secrecy: ～电话 secure telephone / ～条例 security regulations / ～文件 classified or confidential document / ～观念强 be security-conscious / 这事要绝对～。This must be kept under wraps.

保姆 bǎomǔ domestic childcare nurse; baby-sitter; housemaid

保全 bǎoquán save from damage; preserve; maintain: ～工 maintenance worker / ～面子 save face

保释 bǎoshì〈法〉release on bail; bail: 不准～ refuse bail / 准予～ allow bail

保守 bǎoshǒu ❶ guard; keep safe; secure: ～机密 guard or keep a secret ❷ conservative: ～党 Conservative Party / ～疗法〈医〉conservative or non-operative treatment

保税 bǎoshuì〈经〉keep in bond: ～区 bonded zone or area / ～仓库 bonded warehouse

保送 bǎosòng recommend for admission to a higher level school: ～生 recommended school graduate (for study in college)

保卫 bǎowèi defend; safeguard; protect: ～科 security section / ～部门 public security organ or department / ～国家主权 safeguard state sovereignty

保温 bǎowēn heat protection or insulation: ～杯 miniature thermos flask; thermos mug / ～层〈建筑〉(thermal) insulating layer / ～材料 thermal insulation material

保鲜 bǎoxiān keep fresh: ～剂 antistaling agent / ～膜 clingfilm; plastic wrap

保险 bǎoxiǎn ❶ insurance; 养老～ endowment insurance / ～单 insurance policy (form) / ～费 insurance premium or expense / ～金额 insured amount ❷ safe; secure; reliable; ～带 safety belt / ～栓 safety (catch) (on a gun, etc) / ～丝〈电〉(fuse) wire / ～箱 *also* "保险柜" safe; strongbox / ～刀片 safety razor / 为了～起见 to be on the safe side ❸ guarantee; be sure to; ～得第一 be sure or bound to win first place

保修 bǎoxiū guarantee repair or maintenance service for a commodity sold; ～单 warranty / ～期 period of guaranteed service / ～一年 a year's guarantee

保养 bǎoyǎng ❶ take good care of (one's health); preserve; ～得宜 well-preserved ❷ service; maintenance; upkeep; 定期～ regular servicing or maintenance; routine check-up / ～得很差 poorly maintained

保佑 bǎoyòu bless and protect; 上帝～你。May God bless you.

保育 bǎoyù childcare or welfare; ～员 childcare worker; nurse / ～院 nursery school

保障 bǎozhàng ensure; guarantee; safeguard; 缺少必要的～ lack necessary assurance or guarantee / ～制度 safeguard system / 依法～人身自由 ensure freedom of the person according to law

保真 bǎozhēn 〈通信〉fidelity; 高～ high fidelity; hi-fi / ～度 fidelity

保证 bǎozhèng guarantee; assure; guarantee; ～金 earnest money; cash deposit; 〈法〉bail / ～人 *also* "保人" guarantor; surety; 〈法〉bail / ～书 guarantee; written pledge / 一家人的生活有了～。The livelihood of the family is assured.

保重 bǎozhòng look after or take care of oneself; 多多～。Take good care of yourself.

鸹 bǎo *also* "鸹母"; "老鸹" procuress; madam; brothel keeper

葆 bǎo 〈书〉preserve; maintain; nurture; 永～青春 maintain one's youth or youthful look; keep alive the youthful spirit

堡 bǎo fort; fortress

堡垒 bǎolěi fortress; stronghold; fort; 顽固～ stronghold of conservatism; stubborn fellow; stick-in-the-mud

bào

报（報） bào ❶ tell; report; announce; ～案 report a case (to the police, etc) / ～分 call the score / ～批 submit (a request, etc) to a higher authority for approval / ～丧 announce sb's death; give obituary notice; herald misfortune / ～户口 apply for permanent or temporary residence; register one's domicile ❷ reciprocate; respond; reply; ～以嘘声 greet (sb) with boos and catcalls; hiss (sb) ❸ repay; requite; revenge; ～恩 repay sb's kindness ❹ sth that transmits information — newspaper, periodical, etc; ～界 the press; press circles; journalists / ～社 newspaper office; headquarters of a newspaper / ～摊 news-stand; news stall / ～刊杂志 newspapers and magazines / ～章文字 journalese

报表 bàobiǎo forms or tables for reporting statistics; report forms

报仇 bàochóu revenge; avenge; pay off old scores; ～雪耻 take revenge and wipe out a humiliation / 报私仇 wage a private vendetta (against sb); settle personal scores (with sb)

报酬 bàochóu reward; remuneration;

B

报答 bàodá　*also* "报偿" repay; requite: ~ 知遇之恩 repay sb for his generous recognition of one's talent

报到 bàodào　report for duty; check in; register

报道 bàodào　*also* "报导" report; cover: 现场 ~ cover (sth) live / 据官方 ~ according to official sources

报废 bàofèi　discard (as useless or worn out); scrap: ~ 零件 scrapped parts

报复 bàofù　retaliate (against sb); make reprisal: ~ 行为 vindictive act; act of reprisal / ~ 心很强 be revengeful or vindictive

报告 bàogào　❶ report; announce; make known: ~ 人 lecturer; speaker; rapporteur (at a conference, etc) / ~ 文学 reportage / 成绩 ~ 单 school report ❷ speech; lecture; report: 作 ~ make a speech; give a lecture

报关 bàoguān　declare at customs; make a customs declaration: ~ 单 customs declaration (form); entry

报国 bàoguó　dedicate oneself to the service of one's country: 以身 ~ lay down one's life for one's country

报价 bàojià　〈经〉quoted price; quotation; offer

报警 bàojǐng　report to the police, etc; give an alarm: ~ 器 alarm; warning device / 报匪警 report a robbery

报考 bàokǎo　enter oneself for an examination: ~ 北大 apply for study at Peking University

报名 bàomíng　enter one's name; sign (up): ~ 单 entry form / ~ 参军 sign up to join the army

报幕 bàomù　announce items of a (theatrical) programme: ~ 员 announcer

报时 bàoshí　give the correct time: ~ 器 chronopher / ~ 台 (telephone) time inquiry service

报数 bàoshù　number or count off: 一二 ~ ! Count off by twos!

报税 bàoshuì　declare dutiable goods; make a statement of taxable revenue; submit tax forms

报销 bàoxiāo　❶ submit an expense account; reimburse: ~ 单据 bills for reimbursement / ~ 差旅费 reimburse one's travelling expenses ❷ discard; write off; wipe out: 旧车该 ~ 了。The old car should be scrapped. / 一上午的时间全 ~ 了。The whole morning was wasted.

报效 bàoxiào　render service to repay kindness: ~ 祖国 serve one's country

报信 bàoxìn　pass a message to; inform; tip off

报应 bàoyìng　〈宗教〉divine retribution; judgement

报账 bàozhàng　submit an expense account; render an account

报纸 bàozhǐ　❶ newspaper: 订 ~ subscribe to a newspaper ❷ newsprint: 白 ~ newsprint

刨（鉋） bào　❶ plane; planer; planing machine: ~ 床 planer; planing machine ❷ plane (smooth); shave: ~ 花 (wood) shavings

see also páo

抱 bào　❶ hold, carry or clasp in the arms; embrace; hug: ~ 孩子 carry a child in one's arms / ~ 成一团 hang or gang together ❷ have one's first child or grandchild; adopt (a child): ~ 养的孩子 foster or adoptive child / 快 ~ 孙子了 will soon be a grandmother or grandfather ❸ cherish; harbour; feel: ~ 屈 *also* "抱委屈" feel wronged or aggrieved / 不 ~ 成见 not be prejudiced ❹ hatch (eggs); brood: ~ 小鸡儿 hatch (out) chickens

抱病 bàobìng　be ill; be in poor health: ~ 坚持工作 go on working despite poor health

抱残守缺 bàocán-shǒuquē stick to old-fashioned ideas and refuse to change; be a stick-in-the-mud

抱粗腿 bàocūtuǐ 〈口〉throw oneself under the protection of the mighty; latch on to the rich and powerful

抱负 bàofù aspiration; ambition; ideal

抱恨 bàohèn also "抱憾" be overwhelmed with remorse; ~ 终天 the bitter cud of repentance / ~ 终天 be harassed by lifelong remorse; be eaten up with eternal sorrow

抱歉 bàoqiàn be sorry; regret: ~, 让你久等了。Sorry to have kept you waiting.

抱头 bàotóu clasp one's or each other's head; ~ 鼠窜 clasp one's head and run away like a rat; turn tail and flee helter-skelter / ~ 痛哭 weep in each other's arms; cry on each other's shoulders

抱薪救火 bàoxīnjiùhuǒ carry faggots to put out a fire — take counterproductive measures; defeat one's own purpose

抱怨 bàoyuàn complain; grumble; grouse: 爱 ~ 的人 grumbler; grouser

豹 bào leopard; panther: 未窥全 ~ 〈喻〉have not obtained a complete picture of the overall situation / ~ 死留皮, 人死留名。As a leopard leaves his skin at death, so a man leaves his reputation when he dies.

鲍 bào

鲍鱼 bàoyú ❶ abalone ❷〈书〉salted fish

暴 bào ❶ sudden and fierce; precipitate; headlong: ~ 富 become rich suddenly; strike it rich / ~ 怒 fly into a rage; flare up / ~ 雨 torrential rain / ~ 涨 rise suddenly and sharply; (of prices, etc) soar / ~ 风雪 snowstorm; blizzard / ~ 饮 ~ 食 immoderate

eating and drinking ❷ cruel; savage; tyrannical; ~ 君 tyrant; despot / ~ 民 rioters; mob / ~ 晒 exposed to the (scorching) sun / ~ 徒 rioter; ruffian; thug / ~ 行 atrocity; outrage; ferocity / ~ 政 tyranny; despotic rule / ~ 虐无道 rule brutally in defiance of justice and morality ❸ hot-tempered; short-tempered; impetuous: ~ 烈 violent; fierce; fiery / ~ 性子 violent temper; fiery or impetuous temperament ❹ (make) stand out; protrude; bulge: 青筋 ~ 突 bulging blue veins ❺ spoil; ruin: ~ 珍天物 be recklessly wasteful of Nature's bounties

暴病 bàobìng sudden attack of disease: ~ 而死 die of a sudden illness

暴跌 bàodiē fall steeply; drop; slump: 股市 ~。The stock market crashed.

暴动 bàodòng insurrection; rebellion; uprising

暴发 bàofā ❶ occur abruptly; break out: ~ 性感染〈医〉fulminating infection / 山洪 ~。Mountain torrents rushed down. ❷ suddenly become rich or rise to an important position: ~ 户 nouveau riche; upstart

暴风雨 bàofēngyǔ storm; tempest: 遇上 ~ be caught in a storm / ~ 般的掌声 thunderous or tumultuous applause

暴力 bàolì violence; force: ~ 犯罪 violent crime / ~ 镜头 scene of violence

暴利 bàolì exorbitant profit; windfall; bonanza: 牟取 ~ seek exorbitant profits; profiteer / ~ 税 windfall tax

暴露 bàolù expose; reveal; lay bare: ~ 矛盾 expose a contradiction / ~ 身份 reveal or betray one's identity / ~ 文学 literature of exposure; muck-raking literature / ~ 原形 unmask one's true colours; be exposed for what one is

暴乱 bàoluàn riot; rebellion; revolt

暴跳如雷 bàotiàorúléi fly into a violent temper; be in a towering rage

暴躁 bàozào hot-tempered; irascible; irritable: 脾气 ~ hot-tempered; irascible by nature

曝 bào

曝光 bàoguāng　also "暴光" ❶ (in photography) exposure: ~ 表 exposure meter / ~ 不够 underexposed ❷ lay bare; expose: 让丑闻在电视上 ~ expose a scandal on TV

see also pù

爆 bào

爆 bào ❶ explode; burst: ~ 裂 crack; burst; split / ~ 米花 popcorn; pop rice ❷ appear or occur unexpectedly: ~ 冷门 (there is an) unexpected turn of events; surprise; upset / ~ 出特大新闻。Sensational news cropped up. ❸ quick-fry; quick-boil; pop: ~ 炒 quick-fry and stir

爆发 bàofā　erupt; break out: ~ 点 flash point / ~ 力〈体〉explosive force

爆满 bàomǎn　(of a theatre, etc) be filled to capacity; be packed

爆破 bàopò　blow up; demolish; blast: 定向 ~ guided demolition or blast / ~ 音 also "爆发音"〈语言〉explosive; plosive

爆炸 bàozhà　explode; dynamite; blast: ~ 物 explosives / ~ 性局势 explosive situation / ~ 性新闻 sensational news

爆竹 bàozhú　also "爆仗""炮仗" firecrackers: 放 ~ let off firecrackers

bēi

杯(盃) bēi

杯(盃) bēi ❶ cup; glass; mug: 两 ~ 牛奶 two glasses of milk / ~ 中物 wine; liquor ❷ (prize) cup; trophy: 世界 ~ World Cup

杯弓蛇影 bēigōngshéyǐng　be jittery with imaginary fears; be extremely nervous and suspicious

杯水车薪 bēishuǐ-chēxīn　utterly inadequate action or measure; drop in the bucket

卑 bēi

卑 bēi ❶ low-lying; of low rank; low: ~ 湿 low-lying and damp / ~ 不足道 not worth mentioning; negligible; insignificant ❷ of low character; inferior in quality: ~ 怯 base and cowardly; dastardly / ~ 视 despise; look down upon; think little of ❸ humble; modest: ~ 恭 humble and respectful / ~ 职〈旧〉your humble subordinate; I

卑鄙 bēibǐ　base; mean; contemptible: ~ 勾当 dirty deal

卑躬屈膝 bēigōng-qūxī　also "卑躬屈节" bow and scrape; cringe

卑贱 bēijiàn ❶〈旧〉of humble origin or status ❷ lowly; menial

卑劣 bēiliè　base; mean; despicable

卑微 bēiwēi　petty and low: 出身 ~ come from a lowly family

卑下 bēixià ❶ (of character) base; lowly ❷ (of status) low; humble

背(揹) bēi

背(揹) bēi ❶ carry on the back: ~ 包 (carry a) backpack; knapsack; blanket roll / ~ 带 braces; suspenders; (of a knapsack) straps / ~ 负 carry on the back; bear / ~ 头 swept-back hair ❷ bear; shoulder: ~ 包袱 have a weight or load on one's mind; take on a mental burden / ~ 黑锅〈口〉be unjustly blamed; be made a scapegoat (for sb) / ~ 了一身债 be saddled with debts; be heavily in debt

see also bèi

悲 bēi

悲 bēi ❶ sad; sorrowful; melancholy: ~ 怆〈书〉sorrowful; melancholy / ~ 悼 mourn; grieve (over sb's death) / ~ 酸 sad and depressed; aggrieved; bitter / ~ 欢离合 joys and sorrows, partings and reunions — vicissitudes of life / ~ 喜交集 (have) grief mingled with joy ❷ compassion; pity: 大慈大 ~ be immensely compassionate and merciful

悲哀 bēi'āi　sad; grieved; sorrowful

悲惨 bēicǎn　miserable; tragic; traumatic

悲愤 bēifèn　grief and indignation

悲歌 bēigē　❶ sing with solemn fervour ❷ sad, stirring song

悲观 bēiguān　pessimistic: ～失望 become pessimistic and lose heart; be disheartened / ～主义 pessimism

悲剧 bēijù　tragedy; misfortune; adversity: 悲喜剧 tragic-comedy

悲凉 bēiliáng　desolate; forlorn; disconsolate

悲伤 bēishāng　sad; sorrowful; mournful: ～到极点 overwhelmed by sorrow; grief-ridden

悲天悯人 bēitiān-mǐnrén　feel indignant at the depraved state of society and the misery of the people; be deeply concerned for the country and people

悲痛 bēitòng　grieved; sorrowful: 深感～ be deeply grieved; be filled with sorrow

悲壮 bēizhuàng　solemn and stirring; moving and tragic

碑 bēi　upright stone tablet; stele: ～记 also "碑志" record of events inscribed on a stone tablet / ～帖 rubbings from a stone inscription (used as a model for calligraphy) / ～文 also "碑铭" inscription on a tablet

běi

北 běi　❶ north: ～边 also "北面" northern part; north / ～风 north wind; Boreas / ～国〈书〉northern part of the country / ～美〈short for 北美洲〉North America / ～上 go up north / ～半球 Northern Hemisphere / ～温带 north temperate zone / ～南对话 North-South dialogue ❷〈书〉be defeated: 三战皆～ lose three battles in succession

北冰洋 Běibīngyáng　Arctic Ocean

北斗星 běidǒuxīng　Big Dipper; Plough

北方 běifāng　❶ north: 飞向～ fly north or northward ❷ northern part of the country, esp north of the Yellow River: ～话 northern dialect / ～人 northerner

北回归线 běihuíguīxiàn　〈地〉Tropic of Cancer

北极 běijí　North or Arctic Pole: ～光〈天文〉northern lights; aurora borealis / ～圈 Arctic circle / ～熊 Polar bear / ～地区 the Arctic (regions)

北京 Běijīng　(formerly spelt Peking) Beijing: ～话 Beijing dialect; mandarin / ～人 native of Beijing; Beijinger / ～猿人 Peking Man

北纬 běiwěi　north or northern latitude: ～38度 38th parallel of north latitude

北约 Běiyuē　(short for 北大西洋公约组织) NATO (North Atlantic Treaty Organization, 1949—)

bèi

贝(貝) bèi　❶〈generic term〉mollusc; shellfish; scallop: 鲜～ fresh scallop / ～壳 shell / 雕画～ shell carving picture; shell mosaic ❷ cowrie

贝雷帽 bèiléimào　beret: 蓝色～ the Blue Berets (UN peace-keeping force)

备(備) bèi　❶ be equipped with; possess; have: 德才兼～ have both ability and moral integrity ❷ prepare; get ready: ～份〈信息〉back-up (file) / ～考 (of an appendix, note, etc) for reference / ～课 (of a teacher or student) prepare one's lessons / ～战 prepare or get ready for war; be prepared against war / 存档～查 keep on file for future reference ❸〈书〉fully; in every possible way: 尝艰辛 experience untold hardships and difficulties / 颂扬～至 praise (sb) profusely; shower praise (on sb)

备案 bèi'àn enter (a case) in the records; put on record or file

备忘录 bèiwànglù ❶ memorandum; aide-memoire ❷ memorandum book

备用 bèiyòng reserve; alternate; spare;～件 also "备件" spare part; copy /～方案 alternative scheme / 备而不用 have ready just in case; keep for possible future use

备注 bèizhù remarks (for additional information, etc);～栏 remarks column

背 bèi ❶ back of the body or of an object; dorsum;～脊 back of the human body /～鳍〈动物〉dorsal fin /～疼 (have a) backache / 刀儿 back of a knife ❷ with the back towards; away (from sb or sth);～光 (do sth) with one's back to the light; (stand) in one's own light /～靠～ back to back; through an intermediary; not to sb's face /～着人 behind sb's back /～着手 with one's hands behind one's back ❸ also "背诵" recite or repeat from memory; learn by heart ❹ act contrary to; violate; break;～约 break an agreement; go back on one's word /～理 also "悖理" unreasonable; irrational / 走～运 have a run of bad luck; be down on one's luck ❺ out of the way; remote;～静 quiet and secluded; out of the way /～角处 unnoticed corner; quiet place ❻〈口〉unlucky; down on one's luck ❼ hard of hearing

see also bēi

背道而驰 bèidào'érchí run in the opposite direction; run counter (to sth); be diametrically opposed

背地里 bèidìlǐ behind sb's back; privately; on the sly

背风 bèifēng out of the wind; lee-ward;～处 lee or sheltered side

背后 bèihòu ❶ behind; at the back; in the rear ❷ behind sb's back; behind the scenes;～捣鬼 plot or scheme behind the scenes /～下毒手 stab sb in the back

背井离乡 bèijǐng-líxiāng leave one's native place (esp against one's will);受尽～之苦 suffer all the hardships of a displaced person

背景 bèijǐng stage setting; backdrop; background;时代～ background of the age / 以大海为～ be set against the sea /～音乐 background or environment music; muzak

背离 bèilí deviate or depart from;～公报的精神 deviate or depart from the spirit of the communiqué

背面 bèimiàn back; reverse or wrong side;请阅～ please turn over (PTO); see overleaf or the reverse side

背叛 bèipàn betray; forsake

背弃 bèiqì abandon; desert; renounce;～信仰 abandon one's belief; renounce one's faith

背时 bèishí also "悖时" ❶ behind the times; out-of-date; outmoded ❷ unlucky; unfortunate.～鬼 one who brings ill luck

背书 bèishū ❶ recite a lesson from memory ❷〈经〉〈喻〉endorse; support; stand by

背水一战 bèishuǐyīzhàn also "背城借一" make a last-ditch stand; fight to win or die; fight to the last ditch

背心 bèixīn sleeveless garment; waistcoat; vest;汗～ singlet; gym vest / 西服～ waistcoat; vest

背信弃义 bèixìn-qìyì faithless; perfidious;～的行径 breach of faith; perfidy

背阴 bèiyīn in the shade; shady;～处 shady spot

背影 bèiyǐng view of sb's back; figure viewed from behind;父亲逐渐走远

的～ father's receding figure

钡 bèi barium (Ba) / ～餐检查〈医〉barium meal examination

倍 bèi ❶ times; -fold: 2 的 3～是 6. Three times two is six. ❷ double; redouble: ～增 double; redouble; multiply

倍加 bèijiā all the more; doubly: ～努力 redouble one's efforts / ～小心 be all the more careful; be doubly careful

倍数 bèishù ❶〈数〉multiple ❷ times

悖(誖) bèi〈书〉❶ be contrary to; go against: ～论 paradox / 有～常理 contrary to common sense ❷ perverse; erroneous: ～谬 also "背谬" absurd; preposterous ❸ puzzled; confused; muddle-headed

被 bèi ❶ quilt: ～里 underneath side of a quilt / ～面 outside cover of a quilt / ～褥 bedding; bedclothes / ～罩 quilt slip or case ❷〈书〉cover: ～覆 cover ❸〈介〉used in a passive structure to introduce the doer: ～雷声惊醒 be woken up by a thunderclap ❹〈助〉used to form a passive verbal phrase or a noun phrase containing one: ～捕 be arrested; be under arrest / ～俘 be captured; be taken prisoner / ～害人〈法〉injured party; victim / ～保护人 protégé; ward / ～剥削者 the exploited / ～选举权 right to stand for election

被单 bèidān ❶ (bed) sheet ❷ quilt cover

被动 bèidòng passive: ～挨打 be in a passive position where one has to take beatings / ～吸烟 passive or secondary smoking / ～语态〈语言〉passive voice / 变～为主动 regain the initiative

被告 bèigào〈法〉defendant; the accused: ～席 defendant's seat; dock

被迫 bèipò be forced or coerced; be compelled or constrained: 出于～ under coercion / ～辍学 drop out of school against one's will

被套 bèitào ❶ bedding bag ❷ (bag-shaped) quilt case or slip ❸ cotton wadding for a quilt

被窝儿 bèiwōr quilt folded to sleep in; 钻进～里 crawl into bed

被子 bèizi quilt: 叠～ fold up a quilt; make the bed / 缝～ stitch or make a quilt

辈 bèi ❶ (in a family or clan) generation; seniority: ～出 emerge generation after generation; come forth in large numbers / ～分 seniority in the family or clan generational hierarchy ❷〈书〉people of a certain kind; the like: 无能之～ incompetents; people without ability ❸ usu "辈子" all one's life; lifetime

惫(憊) bèi exhausted; fatigued: ～倦〈书〉be tired and drowsy

焙 bèi bake over a slow fire: ～茶 prepare and cure tea / ～烧 bake (ores, etc); roast

蓓 bèi

蓓蕾 bèilěi bud: ～初放 be in bud

bei

呗 bei〈助〉❶ used to show that sth is self-evident: 学生的任务就是学习～. The task for the students is of course to study. ❷ used to express reluctant agreement or concession: 去就去～. Well, if I must (go), I must.

bēn

奔 bēn run quickly; dash; rush: 夜～ run away or flee under the cover of night / ～流 flow at great speed; pour / ～丧 hasten home (from afar) to attend to the funeral of a deceased elderly relative / ～赴灾区 hasten to the stricken area / ～跑如飞 run swiftly; race along　*see also* **bèn**

奔波 bēnbō　dash or rush about; hurry back and forth

奔驰 bēnchí　(of vehicles, horses, etc)'s speed; gallop; dash

奔放 bēnfàng　(of style of writing, etc) bold and unrestrained; uninhibited

奔忙 bēnmáng　bustle or dash about

奔腾 bēnténg ❶ (of horses, etc) gallop ❷ (of a river, etc) surge forward; roll on in waves

奔走 bēnzǒu　run around; rush or bustle about; ~呼号 go about campaigning (for a cause); canvass support / ~相告 rush about spreading the (exciting) news

贲 bēn

贲门 bēnmén　〈生理〉cardia (of the stomach)

锛 bēn ❶ (cut or shape with an) adze ❷ dent (edge of a knife, etc)

běn

本 běn ❶ root or stem of a plant; foundation; origin; ~干 (of a tree, etc) trunk / ~源 origin; source ❷ capital; principal; ~息 principal and interest ❸ original; initial; ~相 true features or colours / ~业 original or primary occupation; previous line of business / ~义 (of a word) original or primary meaning; literal sense ❹ one's own; native; this; ~店 this shop / ~职 one's job or duty / ~命年 year of one's symbolic animal (生肖) *see also* "干支" gānzhī / ~族语 native language; mother tongue ❺ current; this; present; ~题 current theme; point at issue; subject under discussion / ~世纪 this century; the present century ❻ *also* "本着" in line with; in accordance or conformity with; in the light of ❼

book; edition; script; 书 ~ book ❽ 〈量〉*used of books, scripts, etc*; 头~ first part (of a serialized drama, etc) / 两~账 two account-books

本部 běnbù　main or central part; headquarters; 学院 ~ major campus of a college

本埠 běnbù　this town or city; ~邮件 local mail

本地 běndì　local; ~人 native; local / ~特产 local speciality

本分 běnfèn ❶ one's job or duty ❷ contented and law-abiding; decent; 守 ~ keep one's place; never go beyond what is proper

本国 běnguó　(of) one's own country; ~语 native language; mother tongue / ~产品 home or domestic product

本行 běnháng　one's own profession, work or special line; 熟悉 ~ 业务 be well versed in one's line of work

本家 běnjiā　member of the same clan; relative with the same surname

本届 běnjiè　current; this year's; ~新生 this year's freshmen / ~党委会 current Party committee

本科 běnkē　regular undergraduate programme; ~生 (regular) college student; undergraduate

本来 běnlái ❶ original; initial; ~面目 true features; objective reality; truth / ~可以避免的事故 accident that could have been avoided ❷ naturally; as a matter of course; it goes without saying

本领 běnlǐng　*also* "本事" skill; ability; capability

本末 běnmò ❶ course of an event from beginning to end; ins and outs; 故事~ whole story; synopsis ❷ the fundamental and the incidental; ~倒置 place the non-essential before the fundamental; put the cart before the horse

本能 běnnéng　instinct; 出于 ~ by instinct / ~行为 instinctive behaviour

本钱 běnqián ❶ also "本金" capital; principal ❷ asset; ability

本人 běnrén ❶ I; me; myself ❷ oneself; in person; 求见市长～ ask to see the mayor himself

本色 běnsè ❶ inherent quality; distinctive characteristic; true feature ❷ (běnshǎi) natural colour; ~布 grey or white cloth

本身 běnshēn oneself; in oneself

本事 běnshì ❶ source material; original story;《莎氏乐府》 *Tales from Shakespeare* ❷ (běnshi) see "本领"

本土 běntǔ ❶ native country or land; 〈农〉 native soil; 本乡～ native land; home village / ~文化 indigenous or native culture

本位 běnwèi ❶ 〈经〉 standard; 金～ gold standard / ～货币 also "本币" standard or basic unit of a national currency ❷ department or unit one works in; one's post; ~主义 departmental egoism; departmentalism

本文 běnwén ❶ this text or article ❷ original (text)

本性 běnxìng innate nature; inherent quality; ~善良 be kind-hearted; have a heart of gold

本意 běnyì also "本心" original intention or idea; motive

本质 běnzhì essence; nature; innate character; intrinsic quality; ~上 essentially; basically; fundamentally / ~方面 essential aspect

本子 běnzi ❶ book; notebook; exercise-book; 改～ go over students' papers; correct students' homework ❷ 〈口〉 license; diploma; certificate; 考～ take tests for a driver's license

苯 běn 〈化〉 benzene; benzol

畚 běn 〈方〉 ❶ also "畚箕" bamboo or wicker scoop; dustpan ❷ scoop with a dustpan

bèn

奔 bèn ❶ make straight for; head for; go straight to; ~月 head for the moon / ~五十了 be getting on for fifty ❷ go about (sth); be after; ~钱 be after money / ~材料 be busy collecting data; go about procuring raw materials / ~头儿 sth to strive for or look forward to; prospect

see also bēn

奔命 bènmìng 〈口〉 be in a desperate hurry; 为生活～ hustle-bustle to make ends meet

笨 bèn ❶ stupid; foolish; clumsy; 脑子～ slow-witted; dull-witted; dumb / ~蛋 〈粗〉 blockhead; fool; idiot / ~手～脚 be clumsy (with one's hands and feet); all one's fingers are thumbs ❷ cumbersome; awkward; unwieldy; ~活儿 heavy unskilled work

笨鸟先飞 bènniǎoxiānfēi 〈谦〉 a clumsy bird must start flying before others; the slow must start working early

笨头笨脑 bèntóu-bènnǎo ❶ (of people) slow; slow-witted ❷ (of things) clumsy; cumbersome

笨重 bènzhòng ❶ heavy; cumbersome; unwieldy ❷ hard and strenuous

笨拙 bènzhuō clumsy; awkward; stupid; 笨口拙舌 clumsy in speech; inarticulate

bēng

崩 bēng ❶ collapse; crumble; ~塌 also "崩坍" (of a cliff, building, etc) collapse; crumble ❷ burst; crack; split; ~裂 burst or break apart; crack (open) / 他们早就~了。They fell out long ago. ❸ be hit by sth bursting; hit and smash ❹ 〈口〉 shoot; execute ❺ (of an emperor) die; pass away

崩溃 bēngkuì collapse; crumble; fall apart:防线～ crumbling or collapse of a defence line

绷(繃) bēng ❶ stretch tight; strain; (of a dress, etc) be tight or taut:～带 bandage ❷ baste; tack; pin:～子 embroidery frame; hoop; frame matting (for a bed) ❸ be barely able to subsist; manage with difficulty:～场面 (be barely able to) keep up appearances ❹ frame matting (for a bed)
see also bēng; bèng

嘣 bēng 〈象声〉*sound of sth beating, snapping, or bursting*:～的一声 with a snap / 心里～～直跳 with one's heart pounding or thumping incessantly

béng

甭 béng 〈方〉*don't (need to)*:～惦记着他。Don't worry about him. / 你～管。Keep off.

běng

绷(繃) běng ❶ pull (a long face) ❷ strain (oneself):～着劲 strain one's muscles (with bated breath)
see also bēng; bèng

bèng

泵 bèng pump:～房 pump house / ～站 pumping station

迸 bèng spurt; spout; blurt out:～飞 fly about / ～射 spew; spout; squirt / ～出一句话来 blurt out a few words

迸发 bèngfā burst forth or out:～一阵掌声。There was an outburst of applause.

迸裂 bèngliè split; burst (open):脑浆～ have one's brains dashed out

绷(繃) bèng ❶ split open; crack ❷ 〈口〉*used to intensify monosyllabic adjectives like* 硬,亮,*etc*:～亮 exceedingly bright / ～脆 very crisp
see also bēng; běng

镚 bèng *also* "镚儿";"镚子" small coin

蹦 bèng leap; jump; spring:～～跳跳 bounce and jump; prance about / ～跶不了几天 be on one's last legs

bī

逼 bī ❶ force; compel; drive:～和 (in a game) force the opponent to a draw / ～死 hound sb to death / ～供信 obtain confessions by extortion and establish them as evidence / ～良为娼 force a girl of virtue to be a prostitute; force an honest person to do sth dishonest ❷ press for; extort:～债 press for debt repayment; dun ❸ press or drive on towards; advance on; close in on:～近 press on towards; approach; draw near / ～肖 〈书〉bear a close resemblance to; be the very image of

逼供 bīgòng extort a confession; try to force sb to confess

逼迫 bīpò force; compel; coerce:在形势～下改变看法 have to change one's mind under the circumstances

逼人 bīrén pressing; threatening:～的眼光 threatening or piercing eyes / 寒气～。There is a nip in the air.

逼上梁山 bīshàngliángshān have no alternative but to join the rebels; be compelled to act desperately

逼真 bīzhēn ❶ lifelike; true to life ❷ (see or hear) distinctly; clearly

bí

荸

荸 bí

荸荠 bíqi water chestnut

鼻

鼻 bí nose：～尖 tip of the nose /
～梁 bridge of the nose / ～炎
〈医〉rhinitis / ～子 *also* "鼻头" nose：
被打得～青脸肿 be badly battered；be
beaten black and blue

鼻孔 bíkǒng nostril：～朝天 look
down one's nose at people；be stuck-up；
一个～出气 be hand in glove (with one
another)

鼻儿 bír hole in a utensil, etc for sth
to be inserted into；eye：针～ eye of a
needle / 门～ bolt staple

鼻涕 bítì nasal mucus；snivel：流～
have a running nose

鼻息 bíxī breath：～均匀 (have) regular and even breathing / ～如雷 snore
like thunder

鼻烟 bíyān snuff：～壶 snuff bottle

鼻音 bíyīn 〈语言〉nasal sound：说话
带～ speak with a twang / 鼻化音 na-
salized sound

鼻祖 bízǔ earliest ancestor or prece-
dent；originator (of a tradition, etc)；
founder

bǐ

匕

匕 bǐ (usu 匕首) dagger

比

比 bǐ ❶ compare；contrast；emu-
late：～美 compare favourably
with；rival / ～拼 fight or struggle (in
a competition, etc) / ～本事 have a
contest of skill / ～上不足，～下有余
better than some, though not as good
as others；fair to middling ❷ gesture；
gesticulate；direct (a gun, etc) towards
❸ draw an analogy；liken or compare
to；model after：～附〈书〉draw a

forced analogy；make a farfetched comparison / 把祖国～作母亲 compare
one's country to one's mother / ～着
葫芦画瓢 draw a dipper with a gourd as
a model；imitate ❹ ratio；proportion；
relation：～率 ratio；rate / ～值 specific
value；ratio；rate / 一～十 one to ten
❺〈介〉than；(superior or inferior)
to：我考得～他好。I did better in the
exam than he did. ❻〈书〉be next to；
be close together；～邻 (next-door)
neighbour / ～肩 shoulder to shoulder；
be as good as

比比 bǐbǐ 〈书〉❶ frequently；repeat-
edly：～失利 suffer frequent setbacks
❷ everywhere；all over：～皆是 be
seen or found everywhere

比方 bǐfang ❶ draw an analogy (between)；take for instance or example：
打个～ by way of analogy；for in-
stance；for example ❷ if；suppose：～
明天下雨,怎么办? What if it rains tomorrow?

比分 bǐfēn 〈体〉score：～接近。It was
a close game.

比画 bǐhua *also* "比划" gesture；ges-
ticulate：边说边～ gesticulate as one
speaks

比基尼 bǐjīní *also* "比基尼泳装"；
"三点式" bikini

比价 bǐjià price ratio or comparison；
rate of exchange；parity

比较 bǐjiào ❶ compare；contrast：～
级〈语言〉comparative (degree) / ～起
来 by comparison；in contrast ❷ than：
生活～以前有了提高 be better off than
before ❸ comparatively；relatively；
rather：～方便 quite convenient

比例 bǐlì ❶ proportion；scale：～尺
scale / ～图 scale map / ～失调 be out
of proportion ❷ ratio

比目鱼 bǐmùyú flatfish；flounder

比拟 bǐnǐ compare；draw a parallel or
analogy；match：不可～ beyond com-
pare；incomparable；matchless

比如 bǐrú for example; for instance; such as

比萨饼 bǐsàbǐng pizza:~屋 pizza hut

比赛 bǐsài match; contest; game:~规则 rules of the game / ~项目 event

比试 bǐshi ❶ have a competition or contest:~高低 have a contest to see who is the stronger ❷ measure with one's hand or arm; make a gesture of measuring

比特 bǐtè 〈信息〉bit

比翼 bǐyì (fly) wing to wing:~鸟 pair of love birds; devoted couple / ~双飞 fly side by side;〈喻〉keep each other company and help each other to make progress

比喻 bǐyù metaphor; analogy; figure of speech:~义 figurative meaning or sense

比照 bǐzhào ❶ after the model of; in the light of; according to ❷ contrast (two things, etc)

比重 bǐzhòng proportion;〈理〉specific gravity

彼 bǐ that; those; the other:~岸〈书〉(of a river, etc) the other side ❷ the other party; one's opponent

彼此 bǐcǐ ❶ each other; one another:~和睦相处 live in peace and amity together ❷〈套〉*used usu in duplication to indicate that all concerned are about the same*:别客气，论辛苦，大家～～。Come on, we are actually on the same par in terms of effort.

秕(粃) bǐ (of grain) not plump; blighted:~谷 *also* "秕子" blighted grains / 视为~糠 regard as worthless

笔(筆) bǐ ❶ pen; pencil; writing brush: ~ 尖 nib; tip of a writing brush or pencil / ~心 *also* "笔芯" pencil lead; refill (for a ballpoint pen) ❷ technique of writing, calligraphy or drawing:~力 vig-

our of strokes (in calligraphy or drawing):（of writing) vigour of style ❸ write:~供 written confession / ~名 pen name; pseudonym / ~试 written examination / ~误 (make) a slip of the pen / ~译 written translation / ~者 this author or writer / ~底生花 write beautifully or brilliantly / ~耕不辍 never give up writing / ~下留情 be charitable in one's written criticism / ~底下有功夫 write well; be versed in the art of writing ❹ stroke in Chinese painting or calligraphy; hand:~画 *also* "笔划"(number of) strokes of a Chinese character / ~顺 order of strokes observed in calligraphy ❺〈量〉*used to indicate sums of money, business, etc*:一~生意 a deal or transaction / 写得一好字 write a good hand

笔触 bǐchù brush or pen stroke; brushwork (in Chinese painting and calligraphy); style of drawing or writing

笔调 bǐdiào (of writing) tone; style:~明快 lucid and lively style

笔法 bǐfǎ technique of writing, calligraphy or drawing:~细腻 exquisitely-written

笔锋 bǐfēng vigour of style in writing or painting; stroke; touch:~犀利 write in a pungent style

笔杆子 bǐgǎnzi ❶ shaft of a pen or writing brush; pen-holder ❷ ability to write or wield the pen; effective writer

笔记 bǐjì note-taking; notes:记~ take notes / ~本 notebook / ~本电脑 notebook computer (NB); laptop

笔迹 bǐjì handwriting:对～ identify sb's hand or handwriting

笔录 bǐlù ❶ put down (in writing) ❷ notes; records:口供～ transcript of testimony or confession

笔墨 bǐmò pen and ink; words; writing:~官司 written polemic; battle of words / ~生涯 writing or literary career / ~之交 literary friend

笔挺 bǐtǐng ❶ very straight; bolt upright ❷ well-ironed; trim：～的西装 immaculate Western-style suit

笔头儿 bǐtóur 〈口〉❶ nib; pen point ❷ ability to write; writing skill：～好 write well

笔直 bǐzhí perfectly straight; straight as a ramrod; bolt upright

鄙 bǐ ❶ low; mean; vulgar：～贱〈书〉humble; lowly /～俗 vulgar; philistine ❷〈谦〉I; my：～见 also "鄙意" in my humble opinion; I beg to observe /～人 your humble servant; I ❸〈书〉despise; disdain; scorn：～称 derogatory term; pejorative appellation / 神情—夷 (with a) scornful expression

鄙薄 bǐbó ❶〈书〉look down on; despise; scorn ❷〈谦〉shallow and meagre

鄙陋 bǐlòu shallow; ignorant：～平庸 之辈 ignorant and mediocre people

鄙弃 bǐqì disdain; spurn; loathe：～其 为人 disdain or despise sb as a person

鄙视 bǐshì despise; belittle; look down upon

bì

币(幣) bì money; currency：外～ foreign currency /～值 currency value /～制 currency or monetary system

必 bì ❶ certainly; surely; necessarily：～不可少 absolutely necessary; indispensable; essential ❷ must; ought to; have to：～修课 required or obligatory course /～由之路 road or route that one must take; only way

必定 bìdìng ❶ be bound or sure to; must：这消息你听了～高兴。You will surely be delighted at the news. ❷ be resolved to：我明天～去。I'll be there tomorrow.

必恭必敬 bìgōng-bìjìng also "毕恭毕敬" reverent and respectful; extremely deferential

必然 bìrán inevitable; necessary; certain：～性 necessity; inevitability; certainty /～趋势 inexorable trend /～胜利 be bound or certain to succeed

必须 bìxū must; be necessary or imperative：～谦虚谨慎。It is imperative to remain modest and prudent.

必需 bìxū needed; essential; necessary：～品 daily necessities; necessaries

必要 bìyào required; necessary; essential：～性 necessity /～条件 essential condition; prerequisite

毕(畢) bì ❶ finish; complete; conclude：～命 die (usu a sudden or violent death) / ～其功于一役 accomplish the whole task at one stroke ❷〈书〉fully; altogether; completely：～肖 resemble closely; be the very image of; be true to life

毕恭毕敬 bìgōng-bìjìng see "必恭必敬" bìgōng-bìjìng

毕竟 bìjìng after all; when all is said and done; in the final analysis

毕生 bìshēng all one's life; lifetime：～为之奋斗 devote all one's life (to a cause)

毕业 bìyè graduate; finish school：～班 graduating class /～生 graduate / ～典礼 graduation (ceremony); commencement /～证书 diploma; graduation certificate

闭 bì ❶ shut; close：～嘴 shut up; be tongue-tied /～音节〈语言〉closed syllable /～卷考试 closed-book examination ❷ stop up; obstruct：～住气 hold one's breath ❸ stop; end：～市 close shop; suspend business

闭关自守 bìguān-zìshǒu close the country to, or seclude oneself from the outside world

闭路 bìlù closed circuit：～电流 closed current /～电视 closed-circuit TV

闭门 bìmén close the door (to sb)；shut oneself up：～思过 shut oneself up and ponder over one's mistakes; introspection behind closed doors / ～造车 work in isolation without reference to actual need; shut oneself off from reality

闭幕 bìmù ❶ the curtain falls; lower the curtain ❷ close; conclude; ～词 closing address or speech / ～式 closing ceremony

闭塞 bìsè ❶ stop up; block; 鼻孔～ (have a) stuffy nose / 闭目塞听 shut one's eyes and stop up one's ears — be out of touch with reality ❷ out-of-the-way; inaccessible; 交通～ difficult of access ❸ unenlightened; backward; 消息～ ill-informed

庇 bì shelter; shield; protect; ～佑 〈书〉bless; prosper

庇护 bìhù ❶ shelter; shield; take under one's wing ❷〈法〉asylum; 给予～ grant or give asylum / ～所 sanctuary; asylum

怭 bì 〈书〉caution

哔(嗶) bì

哔叽 bìjī (a fabric) serge

陛 bì 〈书〉flight of steps leading to a palace hall

陛下 bìxià 〈敬〉Your, His or Her Majesty; 两位～ Their Majesties / 女王～ Her Majesty the Queen

毙(斃) bì die; kill; 〈口〉shoot; ～命 meet violent death; get killed / ～伤甚重 suffer or inflict exceedingly heavy casualties

敝 bì ❶〈书〉shabby; worn-out; ragged; ～旧 old and shabby; worn-out; dilapidated / ～帚自珍 value one's own old broom — cherish sth of little value simply because it is one's own ❷〈谦〉my; our; this; ～人 your humble servant; I / ～同乡 my fellow townsman ❸〈书〉decline; worsen

婢 bì slave or servant girl

笓(篦) bì 〈书〉bamboo or wicker fence; faggot shelter; ～路蓝缕 drive a faggot cart and wear threadbare clothes (to reclaim a mountain wilderness) — endure great hardships in pioneer work

愎 bì wilful; self-willed

弼 bì 〈书〉assist

蓖 bì

蓖麻 bìmá also "大麻子"〈植〉castor-oil plant; ～蚕 castor silkworm / ～油 castor oil / ～子 castor bean

痹(痺) bì also "痹症"〈中医〉rheumatism

滗(潷) bì decant; strain; drain; 把油～掉 drain off the fat / 把汤～出去 decant the soup

裨 bì 〈书〉benefit; advantage; 于事无～. It won't help matters. see also pí

裨益 bìyì 〈书〉benefit; advantage; profit; 大有～ be of great help; be very beneficial

辟 bì 〈书〉❶ monarch; sovereign ❷ ward off; keep away; remove; ～谷 (of a Taoist) refrain from or live without eating grain / ～邪 exorcise evil spirits; ward off baneful influences see also pì

碧 bì 〈书〉❶ green jade ❷ bluish green; blue; ～蓝 bluish green; blue; turquoise / ～绿 dark green / 玉～ jasper, a kind of greenish jade / 波万顷 vast expanse of blue waves / 草如茵 carpet of green grass / ～空如洗 cloudless blue sky / ～血丹心 absolute or boundless loyalty

蔽 bì cover; shelter; hide; ～障 shelter; obstacle / ～塞 ill-informed; out of the way

算

算子 bìzi grate; grating; grid：炉 ~ fire grate / 铁 ~ metal grille; grating

弊 bì ❶ fraud; abuse; malpractice：~ 政 harmful or pernicious policies; corrupt politics / ~ 绝风清 have evil practices eliminated and public morals perfected; clean up social morals ❷ disadvantage; harm：~ 少利多。 The advantages outweigh the disadvantages.

弊病 bìbìng ❶ see "弊端" ❷ drawback; disadvantage

弊端 bìduān malpractice; abuse; corrupt practice：消除 ~ eliminate corrupt practices

笓 bì comb：~ 头 comb one's hair / ~ 子 double-edged, fine-toothed comb

壁 bì ❶ wall; sth resembling a wall：~ 报 wall newspaper / ~ 橱 also "壁柜" built-in wardrobe; closet / ~ 灯 wall lamp; bracket light / ~ 画 mural (painting); fresco / ~ 炉 fireplace / ~ 毯 tapestry / ~ 纸 wallpaper / ~ 钟 wall or bracket clock ❷ cliff ❸ rampart; breastwork

壁虎 bìhǔ 〈动物〉gecko; house lizard

壁垒 bìlěi rampart; barrier; line of demarcation：关税 ~ tariff barrier / ~ 森严 closely guarded; strongly fortified / ~ 分明 diametrically opposed; sharply divided

壁立 bìlì (of cliffs, etc) stand like a wall; rise steeply

壁球 bìqiú squash：~ 拍 squash racket

避 bì ❶ avoid; evade; shun：~ 世 escape from or shun the bustling world; live the life of a recluse / ~ 邪 〈迷信〉ward off evil spirits / 不 ~ 艰险 be undaunted by danger and hardship ❷ prevent; keep away; repel：~ 雷针 lightning rod / ~ 瘟散 〈中药〉fever-preventing powder

避风 bìfēng ❶ take shelter from the wind：~ 处 (in the) lee / ~ 港 haven;

harbour; shelter ❷ also "避风头" lie low; stay away from trouble

避讳 bìhuì ❶ avoid a taboo ❷ (bìhui) taboo ❸ (bìhui) evade; dodge：~ 提起 往事 avoid touching on past memories

避免 bìmiǎn avoid; refrain from; avert：~ 损失 avoid losses / ~ 主观性 guard against subjectivity; never be subjective

避难 bìnàn take refuge; seek asylum：要求政治 ~ ask for or seek political asylum / ~ 国 country of refuge / ~ 所 refuge; sanctuary; haven

避让 bìràng avoid; make way for

避实就虚 bìshí-jiùxū ❶ steer clear of the enemy's main strength and strike him where he is weak ❷ avoid the essential and concrete, and deal only with the trivial and abstract

避暑 bìshǔ ❶ be away for the summer; vacation at a summer resort：~ 胜地 summer resort ❷ prevent sunstroke：~ 药 medicine for preventing sunstroke

避嫌 bìxián avoid doing anything that may arouse suspicion; avoid suspicion (usu by staying away)

避孕 bìyùn contraception：~ 环 intra-uterine contraceptive ring / ~ 套 condom / ~ 丸 contraceptive pill; the pill / ~ 用品 contraceptives

避重就轻 bìzhòng-jiùqīng avoid the important and dwell on the trivial; keep silent about major charges while admitting minor ones：~ 的自我批评 skin-deep self-criticism

臂 bì arm：~ 膀 arm / ~ 力 strength of the arm / ~ 纱 black armband (as a sign of mourning) / ~ 章 armband (used to indicate one's rank or position)

璧 bì round flat piece of jade with a hole in the middle

璧还 bìhuán also "璧赵"〈敬〉return (sth borrowed) with thanks; decline (a gift) with thanks

biān

边(邊) biān ❶ side; margin; brim: 正方形的 ~ side of a square / ~ 锋〈体〉wing (forward) / ~ 线〈体〉sideline / ~ 角料 leftover bits and pieces ❷ (as an ornament) hem; border; edge: 衬衣的 ~ hem of a shirt / ~ 幅〈喻〉one's dress or appearance ❸ boundary; border; bound: ~ 民 border inhabitant; frontiersman / ~ 卡 border checkpoint or check-post / ~ 塞 frontier (fortress or pass) / ~ 远 remote; outlying ❹ party; side: 双 ~ bipartite ❺ (bian) *suffix of a word of direction*: 东 ~ east / 里 ~ inside

边…边… biān…biān… *used before two verbs respectively to indicate simultaneous actions*: 边吃边谈 talk while eating; talk over dinner / 边干边学 learn while working; train on the job

边防 biānfáng frontier or border defence: ~ 军 *also* "边防部队" frontier or border guards / ~ 站 frontier station; border check-post / ~ 检查 frontier inspection; border check

边际 biānjì ❶ limit; bound; boundary: 不着 ~〈喻〉neither here nor there / 无边无际 boundless; limitless ❷〈经〉marginal: ~ 成本 marginal cost

边疆 biānjiāng *also* "边陲" border (area); frontier (region)

边界 biānjiè boundary; border: ~ 线 boundary line / ~ 现状 status quo on the border

边境 biānjìng border (area); frontier: ~ 地区 (shortened as 边区) border area / ~ 贸易 (shortened as 边贸) frontier or border trade

边缘 biānyuán ❶ *also* "边沿" edge; verge; brink ❷ marginal; borderline: ~ 学科 borderline discipline / ~ 科学 frontier science

编 biān ❶ weave; plait: ~ 辫子 plait one's hair ❷ group; arrange: ~ 班 group or organize into classes ❸ edit; compile; compose: ~ 发 edit and release (news, etc) / ~ 后 (editorial) afterword / ~ 舞 choreograph; choreographer ❹ fabricate; invent; make or cook up: ~ 凑 concoct; cook up / 爱 ~ 瞎话 be prone to tell lies ❺ copy; book; volume: 上 ~ Book I; Volume I ❻ stipulated strength or size; establishment: ~ 余人员 redundant staff

编导 biāndǎo ❶ write and direct (a play, etc) ❷ playwright-director; scenarist-director (of a film); choreographer-director (of a dance)

编队 biānduì ❶ form into columns; organize into teams ❷〈军〉formation (of ships or aircraft)

编号 biānhào ❶ number; give车辆 ~ number the cars ❷ serial number

编辑 biānjí ❶ edit; compile: ~ 部 editorial department ❷ editor; compiler

编剧 biānjù ❶ write a play, scenario, etc ❷ playwright; screen-writer

编码 biānmǎ ❶〈信息〉code; encode: ~ 解码器 CODEC (coder / decoder) ❷ code (number)

编目 biānmù catalogue (books, etc); list

编年 biānnián annalistic; chronological: ~ 史 annals; chronicle

编排 biānpái arrange; lay out: 按音序 ~ arrange in phonetic order

编审 biānshěn ❶ edit (and finalize) ❷ (as a professional rank) senior editor; part ~ associate senior editor

编外 biānwài not on the regular payroll or permanent staff; irregular: 列入 ~ take off the regular payroll; treat as an irregular

编写 biānxiě compile; write; compose

编译 biānyì ❶ edit and translate ❷〈信息〉compile；～程序 compiling program or routine

编造 biānzào ❶ compile；draw up，work out；～预算 draw up a budget ❷ see "编❹"

编者 biānzhě editor；compiler；～按 editor's or editorial note

编织 biānzhī weave；knit；plait；～机 knitter；knitting-machine

编制 biānzhì ❶ work out；draw up；～计划 work out a plan ❷ authorized strength or size；establishment；压缩～cut down or reduce the staff；downsize / 战时～ wartime establishment

编钟 biānzhōng 〈乐〉chime or serial bells；carillon

编著 biānzhù also "编撰" compile；write

编纂 biānzuǎn compile（an encyclopaedia，etc）

煸 biān stir-fry

蝙 biān

蝙蝠 biānfú 〈动物〉bat；～衫 blouse or jacket with batwing sleeves / ～袖 batwing sleeve

鞭 biān ❶ also "鞭子" whip；lash；sth resembling a whip ❷ penis of certain animals used as medicine or cooked as food；牛～ ox's penis ❸ string of small firecrackers；～炮（string of small）firecrackers ❹〈书〉flog；whip；lash；～痕 welt；whip scar；lash mark / ～笞 flog；lash；castigate / ～挞 lash（out at）；〈喻〉castigate；criticize

鞭策 biāncè spur or urge on；encourage

鞭长莫及 biānchángmòjí beyond one's reach；too far away for one to be of help

鞭打 biāndǎ whip；lash；flog；～快牛 whip the willing horse；make the diligent work even more while letting the lazy alone

鞭辟入里 biānpìrùlǐ also "鞭辟近里" penetrating；trenchant；incisive

biǎn

贬 biǎn ❶ demote；relegate；～黜〈书〉demote；dismiss ❷ devalue；reduce；depreciate；～价出售 sell at a reduced price ❸ censure；belittle；play down；～损 also "贬抑" speak ill of；belittle；depreciate

贬斥 biǎnchì ❶〈书〉demote ❷ belittle and exclude；discriminate against

贬低 biǎndī belittle；play down

贬义 biǎnyì derogatory sense；pejorative meaning；～词 derogatory term；expression of censure

贬值 biǎnzhí （of a currency，etc）depreciate；devalue；～率 rate of depreciation or devaluation

扁 biǎn flat；压～ press flat；flatten / ～鼻子 flat nose / 把人看～了 belittle other people

扁担 biǎndan carrying or shoulder pole

扁豆 biǎndòu hyacinth bean；〈方〉kidney bean

扁桃体 biǎntáotǐ also "扁桃腺"〈生理〉tonsil；～炎〈医〉tonsillitis / ～肥大〈医〉hypertrophy of tonsils

匾 biǎn ❶ also "匾额" horizontal inscribed board ❷ silk banner embroidered with words of praise

褊 biǎn 〈书〉narrow；cramped；～急 narrow-minded and short-tempered

biàn

变（變） biàn ❶ change；vary；transform；～声（undergo）adolescent change of voice / ～

体 variant (of a character, etc) / ～样 change in appearance or shape; have a facelift / ～奏〈乐〉variation / ～压器〈电〉transformer / ～主意 change one's mind / ～成废墟 be reduced to ruins ❷ unexpected turn of events; ～兵 mutinous troops / ～乱 turmoil; social upheaval / ～生肘腋 (have an) incident occurring close at hand

变本加厉 biànběnjiālì worsen (rather than improve); become (further) aggravated; intensify

变电 biàndiàn power transformation and distribution; ～所 transformer house

变调 biàndiào ❶〈语言〉tonal modification;〈乐〉modulation ❷〈喻〉change to another tune; sing a different tune

变动 biàndòng (usu of social phenomena) change; alter; modify;人事 ～ personnel changes

变法 biànfǎ political or institutional reform

变法儿 biànfǎr〈口〉try different ways; try in a thousand and one ways

变革 biàngé change; transform;社会 ～ social change / ～自然 transform nature

变更 biàngēng change; alter; modify;作些 ～ make some modifications (in sth); modify

变故 biàngù unforeseen event; misfortune;突遭 ～ be overtaken by misfortune

变卦 biànguà (of sth already fixed) change; (of people) change one's mind; go back on one's word

变化 biànhuà change; vary; ～多端 most changeful; extremely varied / ～无常 fickle and unpredictable

变幻 biànhuàn change irregularly; fluctuate

变换 biànhuàn vary; alternate;季节 ～ alternation of the seasons / ～手法 change one's tactics

变节 biànjié betray one's country; recant one's faith; ～分子 renegade; turncoat; traitor

变脸 biànliǎn ❶ turn hostile;为了遗产～ fall out over a legacy ❷〈戏〉(abrupt) change of facial expression

变卖 biànmài sell off (property, etc)

变频 biànpín frequency conversion;～空调 variable frequency air-conditioner

变迁 biànqiān changes; vicissitudes

变色 biànsè ❶ change colour; discolour;～镜 sun-sensitive glasses / ～龙 chameleon ❷ change countenance; show signs of displeasure or anger

变数 biànshù also "变量" variable (factor)

变速 biànsù〈机〉speed change; gearshift;～杆 gearshift bar or lever / ～箱 gear box

变态 biàntài anomalous; abnormal; aberrant;心理 ～ psychological anomaly; aberrant personality / ～反应〈医〉allergy

变天 biàntiān ❶ change of weather (for the worse) ❷〈喻〉restoration of reactionary rule; comeback (of evil forces)

变通 biàntōng be flexible; make changes according to specific conditions; stretch a point; ～办法 accommodation; modus vivendi

变戏法 biànxìfǎ conjure; juggle; do by sleight of hand

变相 biànxiàng in disguised form; covert;～体罚 corporal punishment in disguise

变心 biànxīn transfer one's affection to another person; break faith

变形 biànxíng ❶ be out of shape; become deformed or distorted ❷ change from one shape into another; ～虫 amoeba / ～金刚 anamorphic king kong

变性 biànxìng change sex by surgical means;～人 transsexual / ～手术

transsexual operation

变异 biànyì　variation：~性 variability

变质 biànzhì　go bad；deteriorate；〈喻〉degenerate

变种 biànzhǒng　mutation；variety；variant

便 biàn ❶ convenient；handy；easy：得~请来一叙。Drop round and have a chat when you're free. ❷ informal；plain；simple：~函 short informal letter / ~门 side (or wicket-) door / ~桥 temporary or makeshift bridge / ~条 also "便笺" (informal) note / ~鞋 cloth shoes；slippers / ~宴 also "便酌" informal dinner ❸ relieve oneself；piss or shit；urine or stool：~池 urinal；toilet bowl / ~溺 relieve oneself；excrement / ~血 have blood in one's stool ❹〈副〉used in the same way as 就 but more formal：一点~通 understand the moment you drop a hint ❺〈连〉indicating a hypothetical concession：你~不说，我们也知道。We know everything even though you don't tell us.

see also pián

便步 biànbù　walk at ease；stroll：~走！〈军〉At ease, march!

便车 biànchē　vehicle in which one gets a lift, or which carries sth for one on the side：搭乘~ get a lift；hitchhike

便当 biàndang　convenient；handy；easy：用起来~ easy to use；handy

便道 biàndào ❶ shortcut：抄~ take a shortcut ❷ pavement；sidewalk ❸ makeshift road

便饭 biànfàn ❶ daily food；simple meal；potluck ❷ also "便餐" informal dinner

便服 biànfú　also "便装" ❶ everyday clothes；informal or casual dress ❷ civilian clothes；civvies；mufti

便览 biànlǎn　brief guide：旅游~ tourist guide

便利 biànlì　convenience；facility；

ease：交通~ have good transport facilities；be conveniently located / ~群众 be convenient for the public / ~条件 favourable condition；advantage

便秘 biànmì　also "便闭"〈医〉constipation

便民 biànmín　for the benefit or convenience of the people：~措施 measure benefiting the people / ~商店 convenience store

便人 biànrén　sb who can conveniently do a job for one：请托~把书捎来。Please send me the book by someone who comes my way.

便士 biànshì　(UK) penny

便携式 biànxiéshì　portable：~电台 portable radio station / ~计算机 portable computer；laptop

便衣 biànyī　civilian or plain clothes；plainclothesman

便宜 biànyí　convenient；handy：~行事 act at one's discretion；act as one sees fit　*see also* piányi

便于 biànyú　be easy to or convenient for：~查找 convenient for retrieval / ~携带 easy to carry；portable

遍（徧） biàn ❶ all over；throughout；everywhere：~布 spread all over；be found everywhere / ~地 everywhere；all around；all over the place / ~及 reach everywhere；spread all over / ~体鳞伤 be covered with cuts and bruises；be a mass of bruises ❷〈量〉denoting an action from beginning to end：两~ twice

辨 biàn　differentiate；distinguish；discriminate：~风向〈喻〉try to find out which way the wind blows / 不~真伪 fail to distinguish between truth and falsehood；be unable to tell the true from the false / ~正不实之说 rectify or clarify an untrue story

辨别 biànbié　differentiate；distinguish；discriminate：~古董和复制品 distinguish or tell a genuine antique from a reproduction

辨认 biànrèn *also* "辨识" identify; recognize;无法～ beyond recognition

辨析 biànxī differentiate and analyse; discriminate; 词义的～ semantic discrimination and analysis

辨证 biànzhèng 〈中医〉 diagnose symptoms (of a disease);～论治 *also* "辨证施治" base diagnosis and treatment on an overall analysis of the illness and the patient's condition

辩(辯) biàn argue; debate; dispute;～才〈书〉eloquence / ～辞"辩词" explanation; argument; justification / ～诬 defend oneself against false charges; prove one's innocence / ～明事理 reason or argue things out

辩白 biànbái *also* "辨白" offer an explanation so as to remove misunderstanding or censure; try to justify oneself

辩驳 biànbó dispute; refute; rebut; 无可～ beyond all dispute; irrefutable

辩护 biànhù defend; argue; plead;～人〈法〉defender; counsel / ～士〈贬〉advocate; apologist

辩解 biànjiě try to defend (oneself); make an explanation or excuse; explain (sth) away

辩论 biànlùn argue; debate;一般性～ general debate

辩证 biànzhèng dialectical;～法 dialectics / ～唯物主义〈哲〉dialectical materialism

辫(辮) biàn braid; plait; sth resembling a braid;蒜～ braid of garlic / 草帽～ plaited wheat straw (for making hats) / 绳～ lace for tying a pigtail or ponytail

辫子 biànzi ❶ plait; braid; sth resembling a plait;梳～ wear one's hair in braids;〈喻〉sort out problems ❷ mistake or shortcoming that may be exploited by an opponent; handle; 揪～ seize on sb's mistake; capitalize on

sb's vulnerable point

biāo

标(標) biāo ❶〈书〉tip or top of a tree; outward sign ❷ mark; sign; object;～的 target; objective / ～牌 trade mark; logo; signboard ❸ make clear by writing or with a mark, tag or label;～界 delimit a boundary / ～音 mark with phonetic symbols; transcribe ❹ tender; bid;～底 bottom price of a bid / ～书 bidding papers

标榜 biāobǎng ❶ brag about; parade; flaunt;～公正 flaunt one's impartiality ❷ boost; excessively praise; 自我～ blow one's own trumpet; sing one's own praises

标本 biāoběn ❶ root cause and symptoms;～兼治 seek both a temporary solution and a permanent cure ❷ specimen; sample; representative

标兵 biāobīng parade guard; pacesetter; role model

标点 biāodiǎn punctuation;给古文～ punctuate a piece of classical writing / ～符号 punctuation (mark)

标定 biāodìng ❶ calibrate; demarcate;～边界线 demarcate a boundary (by setting up boundary markers) ❷ standard; normal

标杆 biāogān surveyor's pole;〈喻〉example for others to follow; model

标号 biāohào grade;高～水泥 high-grade cement

标记 biāojì sign; mark; symbol;作～ make a mark

标价 biāojià mark a price; marked or posted price

标明 biāomíng mark; indicate;～号码 write a number; number

标签 biāoqiān label; tag;贴～ stick a label (on sth); label

标枪 biāoqiāng javelin;～运动员

javelin-thrower

标题 biāotí　title；heading；headline：小～ subheading；crosshead / ～新闻 headline news / ～音乐 programme music

标新立异 biāoxīn-lìyì　do sth unconventional or unorthodox；create sth new and original

标语 biāoyǔ　slogan；poster：～牌 placard

标志 biāozhì　*also* "标识" ❶ sign；mark；hallmark：交通～ traffic signs / ～性建筑 landmark building ❷ indicate；mark；symbolize

标致 biāozhì　(usu of women) beautiful；pretty

标准 biāozhǔn　standard；criterion：合乎～ up to standard / ～化 standardization / ～像 official portrait / ～音 standard pronunciation

彪 biāo　〈书〉(like a) young tiger：～悍 intrepid；doughty；valiant / ～形大汉 tall and strong man；burly or husky fellow

彪炳千古 biāobǐngqiāngǔ　shine through the ages

膘（臕） biāo　(of an animal) brawn；fat：～肥 brawny and sturdy / ～情 how brawny or fat an animal is

飙 biāo　〈书〉hurricane；whirlwind：～车〈方〉drive at top speed；speed (for the thrill) / ～升 (of prices, etc) soar；skyrocket

镖 biāo　dart-like weapon：飞～ flying dart / ～局〈旧〉commercial firm providing armed escort

biǎo

表（❼錶） biǎo　❶ surface；outside：～层 surface (layer) / ～土 surface soil；topsoil ❷ relationship between children or grandchildren of a brother and a sister, or of

sisters：～兄弟 male cousins by such ties ❸ show；express；demonstrate：～功 boast of one's meritorious service；claim merit for oneself / ～一～心意 express one's appreciation ❹ table；example ❺ table；form；list：～报 statistical tables and reports / ～格 form；table ❻ meter；gauge：水～ water meter ❼ watch；clock：～带 watchband；watch strap / ～链 watch chain

表白 biǎobái　explain oneself；vindicate；profess：～诚意 profess or assert one's sincerity

表达 biǎodá　express；convey；voice：～力 expressiveness；power of expression / ～方式 mode of presentation；way of expression

表决 biǎojué　decide by vote；vote：付～ put to the vote；take a vote / ～权 (right to) vote / ～通过 adopt by a vote

表里 biǎolǐ　outside and inside；outward show and inner thoughts：～不一 think in one way and behave in another；be hypocritical

表露 biǎolù　show；reveal；express

表面 biǎomiàn　❶ surface；face：～化 become apparent；come to a head / ～张力〈理〉surface tension ❷ appearance；superficiality：～文章 mere show；ostentation / 从～看问题 take a superficial view of sth

表明 biǎomíng　make known or clear；indicate；declare

表皮 biǎopí　(in physiology) epidermis；cuticle

表情 biǎoqíng　expression；countenance；look：富于～ expressive / ～不自然 look awkward or affected

表示 biǎoshì　express；show；indicate：有悔改的～ show signs of repentance / ～慰问 convey one's sympathy or solicitude / ～异议 take exception (to)

表述 biǎoshù　present；convey；state

表率 biǎoshuài　example；model：起～

作用 play an exemplary role; serve as a role model

表态 biǎotài　make known one's position; declare where one stands; commit oneself

表现 biǎoxiàn ❶ show; display; manifest;～形式 mode of expression; manifestation ❷ behaviour; performance;～很好 acquit oneself very well ❸ show off;好～like to show off

表象 biǎoxiàng　idea; image; presentation

表演 biǎoyǎn ❶ perform; act; play;～唱 singing with action /～赛〈体〉exhibition match /～过火 overdo one's part; overact ❷ demonstrate;～新方法 demonstrate a new technique

表扬 biǎoyáng　praise; commend;值得～praiseworthy; commendable /信 commendatory letter

表语 biǎoyǔ〈语言〉predicative

表彰 biǎozhāng　cite (in dispatches); commend

biǎo

婊子 biǎozi　whore; prostitute

裱 biǎo ❶ also "裱褙" mount (a picture, etc) ❷ also "裱糊" paste paper on; paper (a wall, etc)

biào

摽 biào ❶ fasten together; tie fast ❷ be arm in arm; cling to one another; hang together ❸ emulate by straining every muscle; be at odds with:～着劲儿地讲排场 rival each other for extravagance

鳔 biào ❶ (of fish) swim or air bladder ❷ (glue with) fish glue

biē

瘪(癟) biē　see also bié

瘪三 biēsān〈方〉wretch; bum

憋 biē ❶ suppress; hold back; bottle up:～火 bottle up one's anger; be filled with pent-up anger /～气 hold one's breath; feel suffocated or depressed; feel injured and resentful /～在心里 keep (sth) to oneself ❷ suffocate; stifle; choke (with emotion, etc);～闷 be depressed or dejected /～屈 feel wronged; be depressed ❸〈方〉snap; break;保险丝～了。The fuse has blown.

鳖(鼈) biē　soft-shelled turtle

bié

别 bié ❶ leave; part; depart:久～重逢 meet after a long separation ❷ differentiate; distinguish:～其真伪 determine whether it's true or false ❸ classification; category:职～categories of occupations ❹ other; another:～处 another place; elsewhere /～号 informal name; sobriquet /～样 other; different (in style) /～无二致 exactly the same; not in the least different / 又当～论 be a different matter altogether; be another cup of tea ❺ fasten (with sth); stick in or insert:把剪报～在一起 clip newspaper cuttings together ❻〈副〉used to forbid, stop, or dissuade:～客气。Don't stand on ceremony. or Make yourself at home. ❼〈副〉usu followed by 是, indicating supposition:你怎么情绪不高,～是没考好吧？Why, you look depressed. Is it because you didn't do well in the exam? see also biè

别出心裁 biéchūxīncái　start sth unique or original; try to be different:～的设计 original design

别动队 biédòngduì　commando; special detachment; fifth column

别管 biéguǎn ❶ no matter (who,

what, etc）：～干什么，都要尽力。You must do your best whatever you take up. ❷ leave alone; never mind：～闲事。Mind your own business.

别具匠心 biéjùjiàngxīn　possess or show distinctive ingenuity：～的布局 remarkably ingenious layout

别具一格 biéjùyīgé　have a unique or distinctive style：～的韵味 a charm of one's own

别开生面 biékāishēngmiàn　develop a new style; be out of the common run：～的运动会 an entirely new sort of sports meet

别离 biélí　leave; part; depart

别名 biémíng　❶ also "别称" another or alternative name ❷ sobriquet; alias：史密斯，～辛普森 Smith alias Simpson

别人 biérén　❶ someone else：这里没有～。There is no one else here. ❷ (biéren) other people; others：吸收～的意见 incorporate other people's views

别树一帜 biéshùyīzhì　set up a new banner; found a new school of thought; have a style of one's own

别墅 biéshù　also "别业" villa

别说 biéshuō　let alone; not to speak of; to say nothing of

别提 biétí　〈口〉you can well imagine; just; simply：那里的风景就～多美了。The scenery there is simply wonderful.

别有用心 biéyǒu-yòngxīn　have ulterior motives; have an axe to grind

别针 biézhēn　❶ (safety) pin ❷ brooch

别致 biézhì　original; novel; exquisite

别字 biézì　also "白字" incorrectly written or mispronounced character

蹩 bié　〈方〉sprain (one's ankle or wrist)

蹩脚 biéjiǎo　〈方〉inferior; shoddy; poor

biě

瘪（癟） biě　shrivelled; shrunken; deflated：花生～ blighted peanuts / 车胎～了。The tyre is flat. *see also* biē

biè

别（彆） biè　〈方〉sway; bring round：～不过 be unable to sway sb; cannot make sb change his or her mind *see also* bié

别扭 bièniu　❶ awkward; contrary; difficult：脾气～ be of uncertain temper; be contrary / 心里～ feel awkward and uncomfortable; feel bad ❷ not see eye to eye; not get on well; 闹～ be at odds (with sb); fall out ❸ (of speech or writing) unnatural; awkward

bīn

宾（賓） bīn　❶ guest：～馆 guesthouse / ～朋 guests and friends / ～主 host and guest / ～至如归 (of a guesthouse, etc) be a home away from home / ～客盈门。One's house is filled with guests. ❷〈语言〉object：～格 objective case / ～语 object

彬 bīn

彬彬 bīnbīn　〈书〉urbane; refined：～有礼 affable and courteous; urbane; polite

傧（儐） bīn

傧相 bīnxiàng　attendant of the bride or bridegroom at a wedding：男～ best man / 女～ bridesmaid

滨（濱） bīn　❶ water's edge; bank; shore：湖～ lakeshore; lakeside ❷ be close to (a river,

etc）；border on：～海 border on the sea /
～江大道 riverside avenue

缤（繽） bīn

缤纷 bīnfēn 〈书〉in riotous profusion：落英～ profusion of falling petals

濒（瀕） bīn ❶ be close to（the sea, etc）；border on ❷ on the brink or verge of：～绝 on the verge of extinction；dying out / ～于崩溃 verge on collapse

濒临 bīnlín be close to；border on；be on the verge of：～黄海 border on the Yellow Sea / ～死亡 be at death's door

濒危 bīnwēi ❶ be in imminent danger：～动物 endangered species ❷ be critically ill；be dying

bìn

摈（擯） bìn 〈书〉discard；reject：～斥异己 get rid of or exclude those who differ from one / ～除糟粕 discard the dross / ～绝杂念 discard all distracting or selfish considerations / ～弃旧习 break with outmoded customs

殡（殯） bìn lay a coffin in a memorial hall；carry a coffin to the burial place：送～ take part in a funeral procession / ～车 also "灵车" hearse / ～葬 put a corpse in a coffin and carry it to the grave / ～仪馆 the undertaker's；funeral parlour or home

髌（髕） bìn also "膑"；"髌骨" kneecap；patella

鬓（鬢） bìn temples；hair over the temples：～发 hair over the temples / ～脚 also "鬓角"（hair over the）temples

bīng

冰（氷） bīng ❶ ice；sth resembling ice：～雹 hail；

hailstone；hailstorm / ～川 glacier / ～刀〈体〉（ice）skates / ～点〈理〉freezing point / ～雕 ice sculpture or carving / ～柜 freezer；refrigerator / ～炭 ice and fire — mutually exclusive / ～鞋 skating boots；skates / ～棍儿 also "冰棒" popsicle；ice lolly；ice-sucker / ～天雪地 world of ice and snow；expanse of ice-bound and snow-covered land ❷（make）feel cold ❸ put on ice；ice

冰冻 bīngdòng freeze：～食物 frozen food / ～三尺，非一日之寒 it takes more than one cold day to freeze three feet of ice；the trouble is deep-rooted；Rome was not built in a day

冰毒 bīngdú "ice", popular name for methamphetamine

冰冷 bīnglěng also "冰凉" ice-cold；icy；frosty

冰淇淋 bīngqílín also "冰激凌" ice cream；蛋卷～ ice cream cone / 三色～ ice cream with three flavours

冰球 bīngqiú 〈体〉❶ ice hockey ❷ puck

冰山 bīngshān ❶ ice-covered mountain ❷ iceberg：～的一角〈喻〉tip of an iceberg

冰上 bīngshàng （on）ice：～舞蹈 also "冰上芭蕾" ice dancing or ballet / ～运动 ice sports

冰霜 bīngshuāng ❶ moral integrity ❷ austere（manner）；stern（countenance）

冰糖 bīngtáng crystal sugar；rock candy；～葫芦 candied haws or other fruit on a stick

冰箱 bīngxiāng ❶ icebox ❷ refrigerator；fridge

冰镇 bīngzhèn ice；iced：～啤酒 iced beer

兵 bīng ❶ weapons；arms：～谏 exhortations（to a ruler）backed up by force of arms / ～器 arms and weapons；armament；weaponry / ～工厂 munitions factory；arsenal；ordnance / ~不血刃 (win victory) without bloodshed / ~戎相见 resort or appeal to arms ❷ (rank-and-file) soldier; troop(s); army; ~变 mutiny / ~士 rank-and-file soldier; private / ~营 military camp; barracks / ~种 branch of one of the services; sub-service / ~多将广 have vast military forces; boast abundant resources / ~临城下 have enemy troops at the city gate; be under siege ❸ war; military affairs; ~法 art of war; military strategy and tactics / ~书 book or treatise on the art of war / ~站 military depot; army service station ❹ (in chess) pawn

兵不厌诈 bīngbùyànzhà　nothing is too deceitful in war; all's fair in war

兵贵神速 bīngguìshénsù　speed is vital in war; swift movement is the best tactic

兵荒马乱 bīnghuāng-mǎluàn　chaos or turmoil of war; ~的年月 turbulent years of war

兵家 bīngjiā　❶〈史〉military strategist (school) ❷ military commander; ~必争之地 place of strategic importance; strategic point

兵来将挡，水来土掩 bīngláijiàngdǎng, shuǐláitǔyǎn　〈谚〉counter move for move and measure for measure; one move can always be countered by another

兵力 bīnglì　military strength; armed forces; ~分散 spread one's forces out (too thin) / ~部署 battle array; troop dispositions

兵马 bīngmǎ　troops and horses; military forces; ~俑 (考古) terra cotta warriors and horses / ~未动，粮草先行.〈谚〉Food and fodder should go ahead of troops and horses — preparations should always precede the main work.

兵强马壮 bīngqiáng-mǎzhuàng　well-trained soldiers with sturdy horses — superior (military) strength

兵团 bīngtuán　❶ military unit consisting of several armies; army group; 野战~ field army ❷ army unit above regimental level; armed force; corps; 地方~ local armed forces / 生产建设~ production and construction corps

兵役 bīngyì　military service; 服~ be conscripted for military service; serve in the armed forces

槟(檳)　bīng

槟榔 bīnglang　areca (nut); betel palm or nut

bǐng

丙 bǐng　3rd of the Heavenly Stems; third; ~级 third grade; grade C / ~肝 (short for 丙型肝炎) hepatitis C　see also "干支" gānzhī

秉 bǐng　〈书〉❶ hold; grasp; ~烛 hold a candle / ~笔直书 wield the pen to record the truth ❷ control; preside over; ~政 wield power; be in power ❸ conform with; act according to; ~承 also "禀承" take orders from; act in accordance with

秉公 bǐnggōng　justly; impartially; ~办理 act impartially / ~而论 in all conscience; speaking frankly; to tell the truth

秉性 bǐngxìng　nature; temperament; disposition; ~纯朴 simple and plain by nature

柄 bǐng　❶ handle (of sth); stem or stalk (of a plant); 伞~ umbrella handle / 叶~ leafstalk ❷ opportunity that may serve as evidence against sb; handle; 话~ subject for ridicule; handle

饼 bǐng　❶ round flat cake; ~干 biscuit; cracker / 玉米~子 cornmeal cake ❷ sth shaped like a cake; ~肥 fertilizer cake

炳 bǐng 〈书〉bright; splendid; remarkable

屏 bǐng ❶ hold (one's breath):~气 also "屏息" hold one's breath ❷ reject; get rid of; exclude:~除成见 overcome one's prejudices / ~退左右 dismiss one's attendants
see also píng

屏弃 bǐngqì also "摒弃" discard; throw away; get rid of:~前嫌 dismiss all previous ill will

禀(禀) bǐng ❶〈书〉report; petition:~报 also "禀告" report to one's superior or senior) / ~明原委 explain or make clear the facts; tell the whole story ❷ receive (orders, etc); be endowed with:~赋 also "秉赋" endowment; gift / ~性 nature; disposition

bìng

并(❶併、❷❹並) bìng combine; merge; incorporate:~购〈经〉take over (another company, etc) / ~力〈书〉make joint efforts; join forces / ~案处理 combine related cases and deal with them as a package ❷ side by side; simultaneously; equally:~进 progress abreast; run parallel / ~立 stand side by side; exist simultaneously ❸〈副〉used before a negative for emphasis, usu as a retort:他的法文~不好。His French is not good at all. ❹ and:讨论~通过 discuss and adopt (a plan, etc)

并存 bìngcún coexist:挑战与机遇~。Challenges and opportunities coexist.

并发 bìngfā occur or erupt simultaneously; be complicated by:~症〈医〉complication / ~感染〈医〉accompanying infection

并驾齐驱 bìngjià-qíqū run neck and neck; drive abreast; be on a par

并肩 bìngjiān shoulder to shoulder; side by side:~前进 advance shoulder to shoulder / ~努力 make concerted efforts

并举 bìngjǔ develop or undertake simultaneously

并列 bìngliè stand side by side; be juxtaposed:~句〈语言〉compound sentence / ~榜首 share first place

并排 bìngpái side by side; abreast

并且 bìngqiě ❶ and; also; as well as ❷ furthermore; moreover; in addition

并吞 bìngtūn swallow up; annex; merge

并行 bìngxíng walk side by side; do two or more things at the same time; run in a parallel manner:携手~ walk together hand in hand / ~不悖 run parallel; be compatible / ~处理〈信息〉parallel processing

并用 bìngyòng use or apply simultaneously:手脑~ use both one's hands and brains

并重 bìngzhòng lay equal stress on; pay equal attention to

病 bìng ❶ (suffer from) illness; (catch a) disease:~变 pathological change; pathology / ~床 hospital bed; sickbed / ~倒 come down with illness; be laid up or bedridden / ~故 also "病逝" (of an adult) die of illness / ~菌 pathogenic bacterium; germ / ~体 also "病躯" sick body; ailing health / ~友 ward mate; fellow-sufferer (of a given disease) / ~灶 focus (of infection) / ~症 disease; illness / ~虫害 plant diseases and insect pests / ~~歪歪 weak and unsteady from illness; in bad shape ❷ fault; defect; wrong:~句 faulty sentence

病包儿 bìngbāor also "病秧子"〈口〉person who is frequently ill; chronic invalid; valetudinarian

病从口入，祸从口出 bìngcóngkǒurù, huòcóngkǒuchū 〈谚〉illness is caused by eating and misfortune by speaking; beware of what you eat and what you say

病毒 bìngdú virus：杀～〈信息〉kill virus / ～病 virus disease

病房 bìngfáng ward (of a hospital); sickroom：查～ (of a doctor) make one's rounds / 隔离～ isolation ward

病根 bìnggēn ❶ incompletely-cured or lingering illness; old complaint ❷ root cause of trouble

病号 bìnghào sick person; patient; invalid：老～ valetudinarian; chronic invalid / 泡～ malinger

病急乱投医 bìngjíluàntóuyī 〈俗〉try any remedy when the situation is desperate; a drowning man will catch at a straw

病假 bìngjià sick leave：休～ be on sick leave / ～条 doctor's note or certificate for sick leave

病理 bìnglǐ pathology：～诊断 pathological diagnosis

病历 bìnglì also "病案" medical record：～卡 case history；～室 records room

病例 bìnglì case of illness：典型～ typical case / ～报告 case report

病魔 bìngmó (evil spirit of) illness; disease：战胜～ overcome a troublesome disease; recover one's health / ～缠身 be afflicted with a lingering illness

病情 bìngqíng state of one's illness; patient's condition：～公报 medical bulletin / ～严重 be gravely ill

病人 bìngrén patient; invalid：急诊～ emergency case / 门诊～ out-patient / 住院～ in-patient

病入膏肓 bìngrùgāohuāng the disease has attacked the vitals—be beyond cure; be incurably ill

病史 bìngshǐ medical or case history; clinical notes

病态 bìngtài sickly appearance; morbid state or sign：故作～ pretend to be ill; try to look ill / ～心理 morbid psychology or mentality

病退 bìngtuì retire (from work) or drop out (of school) for health reasons

病危 bìngwēi be critically or terminally ill：～通知 (of a patient) critical condition notice

病休 bìngxiū sick leave：医生让我一周。The doctor prescribed a week's rest for me.

病因 bìngyīn cause of a disease; root trouble

病院 bìngyuàn specialized hospital：精神～ mental hospital

摒 bìng get rid of; dismiss; brush aside：～绝 put a stop to; dismiss for good and all / ～之门外 keep sb out

摒弃 bìngqì see "屏弃" bǐngqì

bō

拨（撥） bō ❶ (with hand, stick, etc) stir; poke; turn：～灰 stir ashes; poke a fire / ～号 dial (a number) / ～正 set right; correct ❷ allocate; assign; appropriate：～兵 despatch troops / ～付 allot; transfer; pay / ～款 allocate or appropriate funds (for) ❸〈量〉group; batch：分两～走 go in two groups

拨打 bōdǎ dial (a phone); make a call：～国际长途 make an international call

拨乱反正 bōluàn-fǎnzhèng bring order out of chaos; set things to rights; set things right

拨弄 bōnòng ❶ move to and fro; fiddle with ❷ also "播弄" stir up; incite：～是非 sow discord; stir up trouble (as by gossip) ❸ also "播弄" order about; manipulate：任人～ allow oneself to be manipulated

拨冗 bōrǒng 〈套〉find time in the

midst of pressing affairs：请 ～ 一阅。Please find time to read it.

拨云见日 bōyúnjiànrì　dispel the clouds and see the sun shining through 一 restore justice; enlighten

波 bō ❶ wave；～长〈通信〉wavelength / ～段〈通信〉wave band / ～峰 wave crest / ～谷 trough ❷ unexpected turn of events

波动 bōdòng undulate; fluctuate; rise and fall；物价 ～ price fluctuations

波及 bōjí spread to; involve; affect；～全国 spread all over the country; affect the whole country

波澜 bōlán big waves; billows；～壮阔〈scene〉unfolding on a magnificent scale; momentous / ～起伏 one climax unfolds after another; full of twists and turns

波浪 bōlàng wave；～式〈move〉by ups and downs; wavy style (of hair)

波斯 Bōsī （former name for 伊朗）Persia；～猫 Persian cat / ～语 Persian (language)

波涛 bōtāo great waves; billows；～汹涌 rolling waves; roaring sea

波纹 bōwén ❶ ripple ❷ corrugation

波折 bōzhé twists and turns; setback

玻 bō

玻璃 bōli ❶ glass；～板 plate glass; glass top (as of a desk) / ～杯 glass / ～窗 window-pane / ～制品 glasswork ❷ sth that looks like glass; transparent plastic；～钢 glass-fibre reinforced plastic / ～胶 glass cement / ～纸 cellophane; glassine / ～纤维 glass fibre; fibre glass / ～天花板〈喻〉glass ceiling 一 invisible limit

钵（鉢） bō earthen bowl; alms bowl (of a Buddhist monk)

饽

饽饽 bōbo （方）❶ pastry；～铺 pastry

shop ❷ steamed bun or cake：玉米 ～ maize cake

剥 bō used only in compounds see also bāo

剥夺 bōduó ❶ expropriate; strip (by force)；被 ～ 阶级 expropriated classes ❷ deprive (by law)：～政治权利终身 deprive sb of his or her political rights for life

剥离 bōlí （of tissue, etc）peel or come off; strip (ore, etc)

剥落 bōluò peel or come off

剥蚀 bōshí erode; wear away

剥削 bōxuē exploit；～者 exploiter / ～阶级 exploiting class / ～制度 exploitation system / 被～者 the exploited

菠 bō

菠菜 bōcài spinach

菠萝 bōluó also "凤梨" pineapple；～蜜 jackfruit

播 bō ❶ spread; broadcast；～唱 broadcast singing; sing over the radio / ～出 also "播放" broadcast; transmit by radio / ～发 broadcast (news, etc) / ～讲 teach or narrate by radio or TV; broadcast / ～送 broadcast or transmit (music, programme, etc) ❷ sow (seeds)：春 ～ spring sowing / ～撒 also "撒播" scatter; broadcast; broadcast-sowing

播弄 bōnong see "拨弄❷❸" bōnong

播音 bōyīn transmit; broadcast; go or be on the air：～室 broadcasting studio / ～员 announcer / 结束 ～ go off the air

播种 bōzhǒng ❶ sow (seeds); seed；～机 seeder; planter; grain drill ❷ （bōzhòng）grow by sowing seeds; plant：～季节 sowing season / ～面积 sown or seeded area

bó

伯 bó ❶ also "伯伯"；"伯父" father's elder brother；(also used

to address a man of father's generation) uncle ❷ eldest (of brothers)；~仲叔季 eldest, second, third and youngest of brothers；order of seniority among brothers / ~仲之间 be much the same；be on a par ❸ *also* "伯爵" 〈史〉earl；count

伯母 bómǔ　wife of father's elder brother；(also used to address wife of father's friend or mother of one's friend) aunt

驳 bó ❶ refute；reject：~斥 rebut；refute；denounce / ~倒 demolish sb's argument；refute；outargue / ~回 reject；turn down；overrule / ~面子 offend sb's sensibilities；make sb lose face ❷〈书〉(of different sorts or colours) mixed：~杂 heterogeneous；mixed；multifarious ❸ transport by barge or lighter：~船 barge；lighter / ~运 transport by lighter；lighter

帛 bó〈书〉silks：~画 painting on silk

泊 bó　cast anchor；moor；berth：~岸 be berthed or moored alongside the shore / ~位 berth；berthing　*see also* pō

柏 bó　*see also* bǎi

柏林 Bólín　Berlin, capital of Germany

勃 bó　prosperous；thriving：~发 thrive；erupt / 朝气~ youthful and vigorous；full of youthful vitality

勃起 bóqǐ〈生理〉(have an) erection：~障碍〈医〉erectile disfunction (ED)

勃然 bórán ❶ vigorously：~兴起 (shortened as 勃兴) rise suddenly；grow vigorously ❷ suddenly：~变色 change colour all at once；turn pale with anger / ~大怒 fly into a rage

钹 bó〈乐〉cymbals

铂 bó　(commonly known as 白金)〈化〉platinum (Pt)

舶 bó　oceangoing ship：~来品 imported goods

脖 bó　neck；sth shaped like a neck：~颈 *also* "脖梗" back of the neck；nape / ~子 neck / ~领儿〈方〉collar (of a garment)

博 bó ❶ rich；abundant；extensive：~爱 universal love or brotherhood；fraternity / ~采众论 gather or adopt advice from all quarters / ~而不精 know sth of everything but not much about anything / ~览群书 read extensively；be widely read / ~闻强记 have both wide learning and a retentive memory ❷ be knowledgeable and well informed：~识 knowledgeable；learned / ~雅 learned and refined；well-educated ❸ win；gain：~得信任 win sb's confidence ❹ gamble：~弈〈书〉play chess；gamble / ~彩业 gambling or gaming industry

博大 bódà　extensive；rich：~精深 be both extensive and profound / 胸怀~ broad-minded；large-minded

博古通今 bógǔ-tōngjīn　be conversant with things past and present；be learned and well-informed

博览会 bólǎnhuì　fair；exposition

博取 bóqǔ　try to gain；court：~欢心 curry favour

博士 bóshì　(an academic degree) doctor：哲学~ Doctor of Philosophy (PhD) / ~后 (one engaged in) postdoctoral research / ~生 doctoral student；PhD candidate / ~论文 doctoral dissertation or thesis / ~学位 doctor's degree；doctorate / ~生导师 (shortened as 博导) supervisor for doctoral students

博物 bówù　(as a general name) natural science：~馆 museum / 故宫~ Palace Museum (in Beijing)

博学 bóxué　learned；erudite：~之士 learned scholar / ~多才 have both extensive knowledge and ability; be knowledgeable and talented

渤 bó

渤海 Bóhǎi　Bohai Sea; ～湾 Bohai Gulf

搏 bó

❶ wrestle; fight; struggle; ～斗 wrestle; fight; struggle / ～击 strike; fight with / ～杀 fight and kill; combat / 最后一～ make a last effort ❷ beat; throb; 心脏～动 throbbing or pulsation of the heart

箔 bó

❶ screen (of reeds, etc) ❷ silkworm tray ❸ foil; tinsel; 铝～ aluminium foil ❹ paper tinsel burnt as offerings to the dead

薄 bó

❶ thin; slight; meagre; ～礼〈谦〉 modest gift; small present / ～田 also "薄地" infertile or poor land / ～雾 (thin) mist; haze / ～葬 simple burial ❷ unkind; mean; frivolous; ～待 treat unkindly / ～情 also "薄幸" inconstant in love; fickle / 看我～面〈谦〉 on my humble account ❸ despise; belittle; slight; 厚此～彼 favour one and slight the other ❹〈书〉 approach; near; ～暮 (at) dusk; twilight *see also* báo; bò

薄利 bólì　small profit; ～多销 (aim at) small profits and good sales / ～行业 industry with marginal profits

薄命 bómìng　(usu of women) born under an unlucky star; ill-fated; unfortunate; 红颜～。Beautiful women are often ill-fated.

薄膜 bómó　❶ membrane ❷ (thin) film; 塑料～ plastic film

薄弱 bóruò　weak; frail; ～环节 weak link; vulnerable spot / 责任心～ (with) little sense of responsibility

bǒ

跛 bǒ

lame; limping; 走路有点～ walk with a slight limp / ～脚

also "瘸腿" lame; crippled / ～子 lame person; cripple / "～鸭" president (ie the outgoing one)

簸 bǒ

❶ winnow; fan; ～箩 winnowing or wicker basket ❷ toss up and down; ～荡不止 keep rocking or rolling *see also* bò

bò

薄 bò

see also báo; bó

薄荷 bòhe　〈植〉 mint; peppermint; ～脑 peppermint / ～糖 peppermint candy / ～油 peppermint oil

擘 bò

擘画 bòhuà　*also* "擘划"〈书〉 plan; arrange

簸 bò

see also bǒ

簸箕 bòji　❶ winnowing pan ❷ dustpan ❸ loop (of fingerprint pattern)

bū

逋 bū

〈书〉 flee; escape; abscond; ～逃薮 refuge or haven for fugitives

bǔ

卜 bǔ

❶ divination; fortune-telling; ～卦 divination by the Eight Trigrams / ～辞〈考古〉 oracle inscriptions ❷〈书〉 foretell; predict

补(補) bǔ

❶ mend; patch; repair; ～漏 stop leaks; plug loopholes / ～牙 have a tooth filled or stopped / ～衣 mend or patch clothes / 打～丁 put a patch on; patch up ❷ fill; make up; repay; ～差 make up the difference (in pay, etc) / ～发 supply again; reissue; pay retroactively / ～考 (take a) make-up examination /

~票 buy a ticket afterwards (on the train, etc) / ~税 pay a dodged or an overdue tax / ~休 take a deferred leave or holiday / ~语〈语言〉complement / ~足 bring up to full strength; make up a deficiency; supplement / ~nourish; build or tone up (one's health); ~酒 tonic wine / ~品 tonic (as food) / ~血 enrich the blood / ~药 tonic (as medicine) / ~身体 tone up one's body ❹〈书〉benefit; use:于事无~ not help matters

补报 bǔbào ❶ report after the event; make a supplementary report ❷ repay (a kindness)

补偿 bǔcháng compensate; make up:~损失 compensate (sb) for a loss; cover a damage

补充 bǔchōng replenish; supplement; add:~题 additional questions / ~给养 replenish the supply

补给 bǔjǐ〈军〉supply; provisions:~品 supplies / ~线 supply line / ~站 depot

补救 bǔjiù remedy:无可~ beyond or past remedy; irremediable / ~措施 remedial measure; remedy

补课 bǔkè ❶ make up a missed lesson ❷ do remedial work in one's studies; make up what is lacking or weak

补缺 bǔquē ❶ fill up a vacancy;~选举 (shortened as 补选) by-election / also "补阙" supply a deficiency

补台 bǔtái help strengthen sb's position; support; boost

补贴 bǔtiē subsidy; allowance:生活~ living allowance / ~出口 subsidize exports

补习 bǔxí take refresher or make-up lessons:~班 refresher class or course / ~学校 continuation school

补养 bǔyǎng take a tonic or nourishing food to build up one's health:~身体 tone up the body

补助 bǔzhù subsidy; allowance:~金 subsidy

捕 bǔ catch; seize; arrest: ~猎 catch (wild animals); hunt / ~杀 catch and kill / ~食 catch and feed on; prey on / ~捞季节 fishing season

捕风捉影 bǔfēng-zhuōyǐng speak or act on hearsay or unsubstantiated evidence

捕获 bǔhuò catch; capture; seize:当场~ catch sb red-handed / ~量 (of fishing) catch; haul

捕捉 bǔzhuō catch; seize: ~害虫 catch harmful insects / ~镜头 capture a scene (for a picture); catch a good shot

哺 bǔ feed (a baby); nurse:~养 nurse; raise; bring up / ~育 feed; nurture; raise

哺乳 bǔrǔ breast-feed; suckle; nurse: ~室 nursing room / ~动物 mammal

bù

不 bù ❶ not; no:~冻港 ice-free port / ~锈钢 stainless steel / ~白之冤 unrighted wrong; gross injustice / ~毛之地 barren land / ~名一文 penniless; broke / ~为所动 remain unmoved (esp under pressure or temptation) / ~及物动词〈语言〉intransitive verb / ~平等条约 unequal treaty / ~受欢迎的人 persona non grata ❷ used as a negative prefix before a noun or its equivalent to form an adjective:~法 lawless; illegal / ~道德 immoral / ~名誉 disreputable; disgraceful ❸ used as a negative reply to a question:"他去吗?" "~,他~去。" "Is he going?" "No, he isn't." ❹ used as a question tag:你喝茶~? Would you care for some tea? ❺ used between a verb and a complement to indicate negation:说~清楚 cannot say for certain; cannot explain ❻ used as part of *a duplicate structure to express indifference, etc*：难～难，这事都得办。This has to be done, whatever the difficulty。❼ (*used in collocation with* 就) either (... or)：这几天～是刮风，就是下雨。It's been either windy or rainy these days。❽〈方〉〈套〉needn't; don't;～谢。Don't mention it. or You are welcome。

不安 bù'ān ❶ not tranquil or peaceful; restless; uneasy：于心～ feel uneasy (about sth); have a guilty conscience ❷〈套〉*used to express regret or gratitude*：深感～ be very sorry

不败 bùbài undefeated; invincible：记录 unbeaten record / 立于～之地 be in an invincible position

不必 bùbì need not; not have to; not be necessary：～客气 need not stand on ceremony /～认真 take it easy

不变 bùbiàn unchanged; constant：～价格 constant or fixed price

不便 bùbiàn ❶ inconvenient; inappropriate; unsuitable：～细问 find it inappropriate to make further inquiries ❷ short of cash; hard up：一时～ be short of money or cash for the time being

不…不… bù…bù… ❶ *used with two synonyms or analogues for emphasis*：不干不净 unclean; filthy /不慌不忙 unhurriedly; leisurely /不明不白 unclear; dubious /不偏不倚 even-handed; impartial /不痛不痒 superficial; perfunctory; irrelevant /不闻不问 unconcerned; indifferent /不折不扣 hundred per cent; to the letter ❷ *used with two antonyms meaning "neither … nor …"*: a) *to indicate "just right"*：不卑不亢 neither haughty nor humble; neither supercilious nor obsequious /不多不少 neither too much nor too little; just the right amount or number b) *to indicate a dilemma*：不离不弃 be neither too close nor too distant; keep at arm's length /不伦不类 nondescript;

incongruous /不上不下 suspended in mid air; in a (pretty) fix ❸ not … without; not … unless：不破不立 no construction without destruction; no making without breaking /不经一事，不长一智 wisdom stems from experience; knowledge increases with practice /不在其位,不谋其政。One who holds no official position does not discuss official business。

不测 bùcè accident; mishap; contingency：以防～ in case of any contingency /～风云 unforeseen or unexpected misfortune

不曾 bùcéng not yet; never

不成 bùchéng ❶ *used for negation*：～材 *also "*不成器*"* good-for-nothing; worthless /～敬意〈套〉(of a present, etc) serve merely as a token of respect ❷ *used as a tag indicating interrogation, supposition, etc*：难道就这样算了～? How can we let it go at that? ❸ *see "*不行*"* ❶❷

不成文 bùchéngwén unwritten; customary：～法 unwritten or common law

不齿 bùchǐ〈书〉despise; hold in contempt：人人～ be held in contempt by all

不耻 bùchǐ not feel ashamed (to do sth); not regard sth as beneath one：～下问 not feel ashamed to seek advice from one's subordinates

不辞 bùcí ❶ without saying goodbye：～而别 leave without saying goodbye; depart suddenly without a word ❷ not refuse or shirk：～辛苦 make light of hardships; take pains

不错 bùcuò ❶ correct; right ❷ *also "*不赖*"*〈口〉not bad; pretty good

不打自招 bùdǎzìzhāo confess of one's own accord; disclose unintentionally; give oneself away

不大 bùdà〈口〉❶ not very; not too：～好 not too good ❷ not often：～在家 not often at home

不但 bùdàn （used in conjunction with 而且,反而,etc) not only：～无益,反而有害 do no good but harm

不当 bùdàng unsuitable；improper；inappropriate

不倒翁 bùdǎowēng tumbler；roly-poly；〈喻〉"survivor"

不到 bùdào also "不周" thoughtless；inadequate；照顾 ～ not be considerate enough / ～之处,请多原谅．Please forgive us for any inadequacies.

不到黄河心不死
bùdàohuánghéxīnbùsǐ 〈谚〉not stop until one reaches one's goal or comes to a dead end；refuse to give up until all hope is lost

不得 bùdé ❶ must or should not；not be allowed：～怠慢 must not be neglected / ～有误 (do sth) without fail ❷ cannot obtain；fail to get or do：～而知 unable to find out；(of sth) unknown / ～人心 be unpopular / ～要领 fail to get the nick of sth；(of sth) fail to get to the point (bude) can't (afford to)；mustn't：马虎 ～ can't afford to be careless / 哭笑～ not know whether to laugh or to cry

不得不 bùdébù have no choice or option but to；cannot but；have to

不得劲 bùdéjìn ❶ 〈口〉awkward；not handy ❷ 〈口〉be indisposed；not feel well ❸ 〈方〉embarrassed；uneasy

不得了 bùdéliǎo ❶ disastrous；terrible ❷ (often used after 得) extremely；exceedingly：热得～ be awfully hot

不得已 bùdéyǐ act against one's will；be compelled to；have no alternative but to：～ 而为之 have no alternative but to do sth；do sth against one's will / ～的办法 last resort

不登大雅之堂 bùdēngdàyǎzhītáng 〈书〉not appeal to refined tastes；be coarse and vulgar

不等 bùděng vary；differ：大小～ differ in size / ～号〈数〉sign of inequality

不迭 bùdié ❶ hastily；too late：后悔 ～ too late to regret ❷ incessantly；endlessly：叫苦～ complain incessantly

不定 bùdìng ❶ not for certain：他～来不来呢．It's not certain if he's coming at all. ❷ indefinite；indeterminate；uncertain：心神～ feel perturbed；be in a flutter / ～式〈语言〉infinitive / ～冠词〈语言〉indefinite article

不动产 bùdòngchǎn real estate；immovable property

不动声色 bùdòngshēngsè also "不露声色" maintain one's composure；stay calm and quiet

不端 bùduān (of behaviour, etc) improper；dishonourable

不断 bùduàn unceasing；continuous；constant：～努力 make sustained efforts

不对 bùduì ❶ also "不对头" incorrect；wrong ❷ no：～,我没有那么说．No, I didn't say that. ❸ also "不对头" amiss；abnormal；queer：菜的味道～．This dish doesn't taste right. ❹ also "不对劲" not in harmony；not on good terms

不…而… bù…ér… used to indicate a result achieved without the condition mentioned：不寒而栗 shiver all over though not cold；tremble with fear；shudder / 不欢而散 part in a foul mood；break up in discord / 不劳而获 reap without sowing / 不谋而合 happen to hold identical views / 不期而遇 meet by chance / 不宣而战 (start an) undeclared war / 不言而喻 it goes without saying；it is self-evident / 不翼而飞 vanish without a trace / 不约而同 (do sth) simultaneously without previous consultation / 不战而胜 win without a fight

不二 bù'èr uniform；one and only：～价 uniform price；no bargaining / ～法门 one and only way

不发达国家 bùfādá guójiā underdeveloped country：最～ least developed country (LDC)

不乏 bùfá no lack of；not rare：～其人。Such people are not rare.

不凡 bùfán extraordinary；out of the common run；unconventional

不妨 bùfáng there is no harm (in doing sth)；might or may as well (do sth)

不费吹灰之力 bùfèichuīhuīzhīlì be as easy as pie；be a cinch

不分 bùfēn not distinguish between；treat in the same way：～彼此 share everything with each other / ～胜负 draw；tie；come out even / ～青红皂白 without distinguishing between right and wrong；indiscriminately

不服 bùfú ❶ refuse to obey or comply；not give in：～老 refuse to bow to old age / ～软〈口〉not go soft；refuse to bend ❷ not used or accustomed to：～水土 not acclimatized (to a new place)

不符 bùfú not agree or square with；not conform to

不甘 bùgān not resign oneself to；be unwilling：～寂寞 be unwilling to live an obscure life；be eager for publicity / ～失败 not take one's defeat lying down

不敢 bùgǎn ❶ dare not；have no courage to：～问津 not dare even to inquire / ～恭维 could not offer compliments / ～越雷池一步 dare not overstep the limit ❷ also "不敢当"〈谦〉(in response to compliments) you flatter me

不公 bùgōng unjust；unfair；inequitable

不攻自破 bùgōngzìpò (of a lie, etc) collapse by itself

不共戴天 bùgòngdàitiān absolutely irreconcilable；inveterate：～之仇 inveterate hatred；deep-seated enmity / ～的敌人 sworn enemy

不苟 bùgǒu never deviating an inch

from what is proper；conscientious；careful：～言笑 reserved；reticent

不够 bùgòu not enough；inadequate；lacking：～本 sell at a loss / ～朋友 not much of a friend

不顾 bùgù disregard；ignore；act in spite of sth：～大局 ignore or disregard the overall interests / ～自身安危 have no thought of one's own safety

不管 bùguǎn no matter (what, how, etc)；regardless of：～怎样 in any case；anyway / ～三七二十一 cast all caution to the winds；act recklessly

不轨 bùguǐ act against the law or discipline：～行为 lawless or conspiratorial act

不过 bùguò ❶ used after an adjective to indicate the supreme degree：再好～ couldn't be better；superb ❷ only；merely；no more than：～如此 just so-so ❸ but；however；yet

不好意思 bùhǎoyìsi ❶ embarrassed；shy：～推辞 find it difficult to decline ❷〈套〉(used to convey an apology) I'm afraid；it's kind of you：～，我得先走一步了。I'm afraid I must be leaving now.

不合 bùhé ❶ not conform to；be out of keeping with：～情理 contrary to reason；unreasonable / ～时宜 inopportune ❷ out of harmony；on bad terms；at odds

不和 bùhé not get along well；be on bad terms；be at odds：制造～ sow discord

不及 bùjí ❶ not as good as；inferior to ❷ find it too late：后悔～ repent too late / 准备～ be caught unprepared

不计 bùjì not take into account；disregard；ignore：～成败 leave success or failure out of account / ～其数 countless；innumerable

不记名 bùjìmíng unnamed；blank：～股票〈经〉blank or bearer stock / ～投票 (by) secret ballot

不济 bùjì 〈口〉not good; bad:～事 no good; (of) no use; of no avail / 运气～ have bad luck; be out of luck

不假思索 bùjiǎsīsuǒ *also* "不加思索" without hesitation or thinking; readily

不简单 bùjiǎndān ❶ not simple; fairly complicated ❷ remarkable; marvellous

不见 bùjiàn ❶ not see or meet:～不散 not leave till we meet; be there or be square / ～经传 not authoritative; unknown / ～棺材不落泪〈喻〉cry only when one sees the coffin — refuse to give up, or remain unconvinced until faced with grim reality ❷ (followed by 了) not seen or found; missing

不见得 bùjiàndé not necessarily or likely:他～肯干。He may not want to do this.

不结盟 bùjiéméng nonalignment;～运动 nonaligned movement

不解 bùjiě ❶ fail to comprehend; not understand:～其意 fail to grasp sb's point / ～之谜 unsolved riddle; mystery ❷ indissoluble; irreconcilable:～之仇 irreconcilable enmity / ～之缘 indissoluble bond

不禁 bùjīn can't help (doing sth); can't refrain from

不仅 bùjǐn *also* "不光";"不只" ❶ not merely; not simply; not only:～如此 nor is this all; moreover ❷ *see* "不但"

不尽 bùjìn ❶ incomplete; not fully; not quite:～然 not exactly; not necessarily ❷ endless:感恩～ be filled with boundless gratitude

不近人情 bùjìnrénqíng alien to human nature; unfeeling; unreasonable

不景气 bùjǐngqì 〈经〉depression; recession; slump:～综合征 depression syndrome / 生意～。Business is slack.

不久 bùjiǔ soon; before long; not long after:～以前 not long ago; recently / ～的将来 in the near future /

～人世 won't be long for this world; one's days are numbered

不拘 bùjū ❶ not stick to; not confine oneself to:～一格 not stick to one pattern; not be confined to one form / ～小节 not bother about small matters; not be fettered by petty convention ❷ *see* "不论"

不堪 bùkān ❶ cannot bear or stand; (of sth) be not fit or proper:～回首 cannot bear to think of the past / ～设想 (of sth) too dreadful to contemplate / ～一击 cannot withstand a single blow; collapse at the first blow ❷ utterly; extremely:破烂～ very much tattered; worn to shreds

不可 bùkě ❶ cannot; should or must not;～救药 incorrigible; hopeless / ～理喻 cannot be persuaded by reasoned argument; be blind to reason / ～磨灭 indelible; ineffaceable / ～收拾 irremediable; out of hand / ～思议 inconceivable; mysterious / ～一世 flaunt one's superiority; be extremely arrogant / ～同日而语 cannot be mentioned in the same breath; be poles apart ❷ *used together with* 非 *to indicate what one is set to do*:非看～ must see; cannot miss

不可开交 bùkěkāijiāo (used after 得) be locked or tied up (in sth); 忙得～ be up to one's ears in work; be awfully busy

不可知论 bùkězhīlùn 〈哲〉agnosticism;～者 agnostic

不客气 bùkèqì ❶ blunt; impolite; rude:～地说 to put it bluntly ❷ 〈套〉(used in response to expressions of thanks) don't mention it; you are welcome; not at all ❸ 〈套〉*indicating polite refusal of an offer*:"抽支烟。" "～。" "Have a cigarette." "No, thanks."

不快 bùkuài ❶ be unhappy or displeased; be in low spirits ❷ *see* "不适"

不愧 bùkuì be worthy of; deserve the

title of

不力 bùlì not exert oneself; be ineffective or incompetent

不利 bùlì ❶ unfavourable; disadvantageous; harmful:～于团结 harmful or detrimental to unity ❷ unsuccessful:出师～ lose the first battle

不良 bùliáng bad; harmful; unhealthy:～影响 harmful or adverse effect / 发育～ physically underdeveloped

不了了之 bùliǎoliǎozhī let things take their natural course; end up by letting sth drop

不料 bùliào unexpectedly; to one's surprise:不出所料 as expected

不论 bùlùn no matter (who, how, etc); whether...or...; regardless of:～何人，他都能合得来。He can get along with anyone.

不落窠臼 bùluòkējiù 〈书〉not follow the beaten track; not be restricted by convention; be original

不满 bùmǎn resentful; discontented; dissatisfied:表示～ show displeasure or dissatisfaction

不免 bùmiǎn (of sth) unavoidable; inevitable; (of sb) cannot help (doing sth)

不明 bùmíng ❶ not clear; unknown; unidentified:～飞行物 also "飞碟" unidentified flying object (UFO); flying saucer ❷ fail to understand; not know; be unaware of:～真相 be unaware or ignorant of the facts; be kept in the dark / ～事理 lack common sense; be unreasonable

不能 bùnéng cannot; be unable to; must or should not:～自拔 be unable to extricate oneself (from sth) / ～不表示反对 cannot but voice one's opposition

不念旧恶 bùniànjiù'è forget (about) past grudges; let bygones be bygones

不怕 bùpà not be afraid of; not fear:～官,只怕管。〈俗〉Fear no officials,

except those who officiate over you.

不配 bùpèi ❶ be unworthy of or unqualified for; not deserve ❷ not match

不平 bùpíng ❶ uneven; not level; not smooth ❷ injustice; unfairness; grievance:～则鸣 where there is injustice, there is complaint; people will cry out against injustice ❸ indignant (about sth unjust); resentful

不起眼 bùqǐyǎn 〈方〉inconspicuous; negligible; unimportant

不巧 bùqiǎo ˙ unfortunately; as luck would have it:真～,他今天又不在家。Unfortunately, he's out again today.

不切实际 bùqièshíjì unrealistic; impractical; impracticable

不求 bùqiú not seek; be content:～甚解 not seek to understand thoroughly; be content with a superficial understanding / ～有功,但求无过 seek to make no mistakes rather than win any merits; be content with an indifferent lot

不屈 bùqū unyielding; unbending:～不挠 undaunted; unswerving

不然 bùrán ❶ not so:表面谦虚,其实～ be modest on the surface, but not so at heart ❷ (used at the beginning of a sentence to indicate disagreement) No ❸ also "不然的话" or (else); otherwise; if not

不忍 bùrěn cannot bear:～离去 cannot (bear to) tear oneself away / ～之心 compassion

不容 bùróng not tolerate; not allow or permit:～置喙 not allow others to butt in; admit of no interference / ～置疑 beyond doubt; undoubtedly

不如 bùrú ❶ be not so good as; be inferior to ❷ may or might as well (do sth); it would be better (to do)

不三不四 bùsānbùsì dubious; shady; unseemly:～的话 unseemly or frivolous remarks / ～的人 dubious character

不善 bùshàn ❶ bad; ill; evil:来者

~。They did not come with the best of intentions. ❷ *also* "不善于" not good at;~交际 not a good mixer

不胜 bùshèng ❶ cannot bear or stand;~其烦 be bored beyond endurance;(of sth) be too much bother /~枚举 be too numerous to be mentioned one by one; be far too many ❷ *used between two identical verbs to indicate inability to do or complete sth*:这种漏洞堵一堵。Such loopholes are too numerous to plug. ❸ (used of emotions) very; extremely; deeply

不失为 bùshīwéi can still serve as; may as well be accepted;这一个应急办法。This may serve as a contingency measure.

不识 bùshí not know; fail to understand;~相〔方〕not know what is the right thing to do; have no sense of propriety /~大体 fail to take the overall interest into account; ignore the larger issues /~时务 fail to appreciate the realities of the times; cannot read the trends of the times /~抬举 *also* "不识好歹" not know which side one's bread is buttered; fail to appreciate favours

不时 bùshí ❶ frequently; often; from time to time ❷ at any time; at an unexpected moment;以备~之需 provide for a rainy day

不是 búshì〔口〕❶ no; not;~味儿 not have the right taste; be fishy or wrong;(of sb) feel bad ❷ (bùshì) fault; blame;落~ get the blame / 赔~ apologize

不适 búshì indisposed; under the weather; out of sorts;:肠胃~ not feel well in the stomach

不爽 bùshuǎng ❶ not well; out of sorts; in low spirits ❷ without discrepancy; accurate;~分毫 correct in every detail

不速之客 bùsùzhīkè uninvited guest; unexpected visitor; gate-crasher

不通 bùtōng ❶ be blocked up, obstructed, or impassable;鼻子~ have a stuffy nose / 此路~. Not a through road. or No thoroughfare. ❷ illogical; unreadable; ungrammatical ❸ not know; not understand;~情理 be unreasonable; be perverse /~文墨 not know how to read and write; be illiterate

不同 bùtóng different; varying; distinct;国情~ different national conditions /~凡响 out of the common run; outstanding

不妥 bùtuǒ not proper; inappropriate;~之处,请予指正。Please feel free to point out the inadequacies.

不外 bùwài *also* "不外乎" not beyond the scope of; nothing more than; only

不问 bùwèn ❶ not distinguish; disregard; ignore;~地位高低 irrespective or regardless of status ❷ let off; let (sb) go unpunished

不无 bùwú not without;~可取之处 not without merit

不务正业 bùwùzhèngyè ignore one's proper occupation; do no decent work

不惜 bùxī not spare, stint, or scruple;~工本 spare no expenses /~代价 at all costs; at any cost

不下 bùxià ❶ *also* "不下于" no less or fewer than; not inferior to; as good as ❷ *used after a verb to indicate incompleteness or inefficacy*;放心~ cannot rest assured; be worried

不相上下 bùxiāngshàngxià more or less equal; about the same

不详 bùxiáng ❶ not clear; unknown ❷ not in detail; unspecified;语焉~ be mentioned briefly; not go into detail

不祥 bùxiáng ominous; inauspicious;~之兆 ill omen

不像话 bùxiànghuà *also* "不成话" ❶ unreasonable; absurd; ridiculous ❷ outrageous; shocking; scandalous;闹得太~了 make a shocking scene; go

B

much too far

不像样 bùxiàngyàng ❶ unpresentable; bad ~的文章 bad writing ❷ *used after* 得 *to indicate extremity*: 破得~ shabby beyond recognition; worn to shreds

不孝 bùxiào fail to practise filial piety; be unfilial

不肖 bùxiào （书）unworthy: ~子孙 unworthy descendants

不屑 bùxiè regard (sth) as unworthy; scorn: ~一顾 consider (sth) unworthy of serious consideration; (of sth) be beneath one's attention

不懈 bùxiè unremitting; untiring; indefatigable

不信任 bùxìnrèn no confidence: ~案 no-confidence motion / 投~票 cast a vote of no confidence

不兴 bùxīng ❶ outmoded; out of fashion; obsolete ❷ see "不许" ❸ *used in rhetorical questions*: 你就~说简单点儿吗? Can't you be brief?

不行 bùxíng ❶ be not permissible or allowed; be out of the question; won't do ❷ not work; not be equal to; be no good: 这个办法~. This method won't work. ❸ dying: 老人看来~了. The old man seems to be on his last legs. ❹ *used after* 得 *to indicate intensity*, *etc*: 困得~ be terribly drowsy

不省人事 bùxǐngrénshì be unconscious; lose consciousness; go into a coma

不幸 bùxìng unfortunate; ill-fated; sad; ~中之大幸 most fortunate aspect of an unfortunate business; silver lining of a black cloud / ~而言中. The prediction unfortunately proved true.

不修边幅 bùxiūbiānfú not care about one's appearance; be slovenly or untidy

不朽 bùxiǔ immortal; perpetual; eternal: 永垂~ earn eternal glory; go down in history

不许 bùxǔ not allow or permit; must

not; 小孩子~这样称呼大人. Children are not supposed to address adults in such a manner.

不学无术 bùxué-wúshù have neither learning nor ability; be an unmitigated ignoramus

不厌 bùyàn not mind (doing sth); not tire of: ~其烦 not mind taking great pains; be very patient

不一 bùyī vary; differ; 型号~ vary in type / ~而足 not just once but on numerous occasions; by no means rare

不依 bùyī ❶ not comply or obey; refuse ❷ not let off easily; not let sb get away with it: ~不饶 just wouldn't let sb off

不宜 bùyí not fit or suitable; inadvisable; 儿童~ (of movies, etc) not fit for children; X-rated

不遗余力 bùyíyúlì spare or stint no effort; do one's utmost

不已 bùyǐ (used after a verb) incessantly; continuously; unremittingly; 赞叹~ praise without end

不以为然 bùyǐwéirán object; take exception; disagree

不义之财 bùyìzhīcái ill-gotten or undeserved wealth; dishonest gains

不亦乐乎 bùyìlèhū (often used after 得) extremely; awfully; 累得~ be dog-tired from exhaustion

不用 bùyòng need not; be unnecessary; ~说 needless to say; evidently

不由 bùyóu can't help: ~自主 can't help oneself; act involuntarily / ~得你不信. You couldn't help believing it.

不育 bùyù sterile; infertile; barren; ~症 barrenness; sterility

不在 bùzài ❶ not be in; be out or absent ❷ (婉) (often used with 了) die; be dead

不在话下 bùzàihuàxià be not worth mentioning; to say nothing of

不择手段 bùzéshǒuduàn by fair means or foul; by hook or by crook;

unscrupulously

不怎么样 bùzěnmeyàng mediocre; indifferent; not as good as should be

不正之风 bùzhèngzhīfēng unhealthy social trend; evil social practice

不知 bùzhī not know; be unaware; ～不觉 before one knows it; unwittingly; unawares / ～好歹 not know what's good for one or which side one's bread is buttered / ～所措 be at a loss; be at one's wits' end / ～天高地厚 have an exaggerated notion of one's abilities; be too arrogant (to know what is good for one)

不值 bùzhí not worth; ～一驳 not worth refuting

不止 bùzhǐ ❶ incessantly; without end; 咳嗽～ cough incessantly ❷ not limited to; more than

不至于 bùzhìyú cannot go so far as; be unlikely; ～连这点道理也不明白 must have more sense than that

不置可否 bùzhìkěfǒu decline to comment; be noncommittal

不准 bùzhǔn not allow; forbid; prohibit; ～停车。No parking. / ～动手! Hands Off!

不着边际 bùzhuóbiānjì not to the point; irrelevant; neither here nor there

不足 bùzú ❶ not enough; insufficient; inadequate; ～之处 deficiency; inadequacy ❷ be not worth; cannot; should not; ～道 not worth mentioning; of no consequence / ～为奇 nothing remarkable; not at all surprising / ～为训 not to be taken as an example; not to be regarded as authoritative

布(❷-❹佈) bù ❶ cloth; ～店 cloth or piece-goods store; draper's / ～料 cotton dress material / ～匹 cloth; piece-goods / ～头 leftover material (from a bolt of cloth); odd bits of cloth ❷ declare; announce; proclaim; ～告 notice;

bulletin; proclamation ❸ spread; disseminate; cover; ～道〈宗教〉preach; evangelize ❹ dispose; arrange; deploy; ～防 deploy troops for defence; garrison (a town or fort) / ～设圈套 set or lay a trap / ～天下罗地网 cast a gigantic escape-proof net (for catching a fugitive criminal, etc)

布丁 bùdīng pudding

布谷鸟 bùgǔniǎo cuckoo

布景 bùjǐng setting; scenery; ～设计师 set designer

布局 bùjú ❶ overall arrangement; layout ❷ composition (of an article, painting, etc) ❸ opening moves (in a chess game)

布雷 bùléi lay mines; mine; 港口～ mine a harbour / ～区 minefield

布施 bùshī 〈书〉(to Buddhists or Taoists) give alms; donate ❶ alms; charities; 化～ beg alms

布艺 bùyì cloth decoration or upholstery; ～沙发 cloth-upholstered sofa

布置 bùzhì ❶ tidy up; arrange; decorate ❷ assign; make arrangements for; give instructions about

步 bù ❶ step; pace; ～测 measure by pace; pace out / ～法 (as in dancing or certain sports) footwork / ～子 step; pace / ～～为营 move with great care; be always on the alert / ～好棋 an excellent move ❷ stage; step; 考虑下一～ consider the next step (to take) ❸ condition; situation; state; 落到这一～ land oneself in such a plight; come to such a pass ❹ walk; go on foot; tread; ～人后尘 follow in sb's footsteps; trail along

步兵 bùbīng infantry; infantryman

步调 bùdiào pace; step; ～一致 take concerted action; make concerted efforts

步伐 bùfá step; pace; 跟上时代的～ keep pace with the times

步履 bùlǚ 〈书〉walk; ～蹒跚 hobble

along；limp

步枪 bùqiāng　rifle：～射程内 within rifle shot

步行 bùxíng　go on foot；walk：～街 pedestrian mall

步骤 bùzhòu　step；move；measure：有～地 step by step

怖 bù　fear；be afraid of：景象可～。It was a horrible sight.

钚 bù　〈化〉plutonium (Pu)：～弹〈军〉plutonium bomb

部 bù　❶ part；section：东～ eastern part / ～件 part；component ❷ unit；department；ministry：～颁标准 ministry-authorized standard / ～优产品 ministry-recognized quality product ❸〈军〉headquarters：连～ company headquarters ❹〈书〉command：～将 military officer under one's command ❺〈量〉*of movies, books, machines, etc*：一～电影 a film / 三～汽车 three cars

部队 bùduì　army (unit)；armed forces；troops：～生活 army life

部分 bùfen　part；section；portion：～地区 some areas；part of an area / ～解决 partial solution

部落 bùluò　tribe：～社会 tribal society

部门 bùmén　department；sector；branch：国有～ state-owned sector / 有关～ departments concerned

部首 bùshǒu　〈语言〉radicals (of characters)

部属 bùshǔ　❶ subordinate ❷ affiliated with a ministry：～院校 universities and colleges under various ministries

部署 bùshǔ　arrange；map or lay out；deploy：作战～ operational plan；battle dispositions / ～兵力 deploy troops

部位 bùwèi　（particularly of the human body）position；location：受伤～ location of an injury

部下 bùxià　troops under one's command；subordinate

部长 bùzhǎng　minister；(US) secretary：～助理 assistant minister / ～级会议 conference at ministerial level

埠 bù　❶ wharf；pier ❷ town or city with a port；(port) city：本～ this city

簿 bù　book：～籍 account books，registers，records，etc / ～记 bookkeeping；standard account book

C

cā

擦 cā ❶ rub; scratch; shred (vegetables, etc):～火柴 strike a match /～萝卜丝 shred a turnip ❷ rub or wipe (with rags, etc); towel; wipe; cleanse; clean /～洗 wipe or wash clean; scrub /～澡 rub oneself down (with a wet towel); take a sponge bath /～皮鞋 polish or shine shoes /～屁股〈喻〉clean up a mess ❸ apply:～药水 apply medicinal lotion ❹ approach; touch; brush past:～网球〈体〉net ball

擦边球 cābiānqiú 〈体〉edge or touch ball; 〈喻〉sth almost, but not quite, illegal:打～ sail close to the wind

嚓 cā 〈象声〉used of scraping sounds:外面响起～～的脚步声。Heavy steps were heard from outside.

cāi

猜 cāi ❶ guess; speculate:～测 guess; conjecture /～拳 also "划拳" (have a) finger-guessing game /～想 suppose; suspect; guess /～谜儿 guess (a riddle) ❷ suspect; be doubtful:～忌 be suspicious and jealous (of sb) /～疑 have suspicions (often groundless); distrust

cái

才(❸❹ 纔) cái ❶ ability; talent; gift:～分 inborn talent; natural gift /～略 ability and sagacity (in political and military affairs) /～女 talented woman; bluestocking /～气 literary talent /～高八斗 outstanding literary talent /～貌双全 both talented and good-looking; brilliant and handsome ❷ capable person; talent; person of a certain type ❸ 〈副〉used to indicate a) sth has just happened:会议～开始。The meeting has just begun. b) sth happens later than is expected:到半夜～停 not stop until midnight c) sth happens only on given conditions:只有齐心协力,～能完成任务。The task can only be completed when everybody works in close concert. d) sth is small, low or weak by comparison:我们班～十个人。There are only ten students in our class. ❹ 〈副〉used for emphatic assertion:我～不去呢! I definitely won't go!

才干 cáigàn ability; competence:～是锻炼出来的。Competence comes with practice.

才华 cáihuá literary or artistic talent; talent:～横溢 brimming with talent; brilliant

才能 cáinéng ability; talent; natural gift:管理～ managerial ability

才识 cáishí talent and insight:～过人 be gifted with unusual talent and insight

才思 cáisī (in writing) imaginative power; creativeness:～敏捷 have a facile imagination

才学 cáixué　talent and learning; scholarship:才疏学浅〈谦〉have little talent and learning

才智 cáizhì　ability and wisdom:施展 ～ give play to one's wisdom and creativeness

才子 cáizǐ　gifted scholar:～佳人 talented scholars and beautiful ladies (in traditional romances)

材 cái　❶ timber; (raw) material: ～质 texture or quality of material ❷ coffin ❸ ability; talent; aptitude

材料 cáiliào　❶ material; data:收集 ～ gather material; collect data / ～科学 materials science ❷ makings; stuff:他是搞科研的好～。He has good research potential.

财 cái　wealth; money:～宝 money and valuables; treasure / ～阀 financial magnate; plutocrat; tycoon / ～力 financial power or resources / ～路 means to acquire wealth / ～权 property right; financial control / ～团 financial group; consortium / ～物 property; belongings / ～主 rich man; moneybags / ～神(爷) God of Wealth; extremely rich person; person or institution in charge of money / ～大气粗 wealth breeds arrogance; money talks; be purse-proud

财产 cáichǎn　property:～权 property right / ～损失 property damage

财富 cáifù　wealth; riches:～分配 distribution of wealth / 宝贵的～ precious asset or treasure

财经 cáijīng　finance and economy:～纪律 financial and economic discipline

财会 cáikuài　book-keeping and accounting:～人员 book-keepers and accountants

财礼 cáilǐ　see "彩礼" cǎilǐ

财路 cáilù　means to acquire wealth:广开～ open or exploit all possible avenues for wealth

财贸 cáimào　finance and trade:～工

作 work in finance and trade

财迷 cáimí　❶ money-grubber; miser ❷ crazy for money; greedy; avaricious:～心窍 befuddled with a craving for money; crazy about making money

财务 cáiwù　financial affairs:～往来 financial transaction / ～总监 CFO (Chief Financial Officer)

财源 cáiyuán　financial resources:～茂盛 (have) abundant sources of revenue

财政 cáizhèng　public finance:～年度 fiscal year / ～拨款 budgetary appropriations / ～危机 financial or fiscal crisis

裁 cái　❶ cut (paper, etc) into parts:～剪衣服 cut out a garment ❷ reduce; cut back:～军 disarmament / ～员 lay off employees; reduce the staff; downsize ❸ judge; decide; control:～定〈法〉pass judgement; rule (on sth) / ～夺 (consider and) decide

裁缝 cáiféng　❶ make (a dress); tailor ❷ (cáifeng) tailor; dressmaker:～铺 tailor shop; tailor's

裁减 cáijiǎn　reduce; cut down; lay off:～支出 cut back on expenditure

裁决 cáijué　ruling; adjudication:依法 ～ adjudicate according to law

裁判 cáipàn　❶〈法〉judgement; ruling ❷〈体〉referee; umpire; judge:担任～ referee (a match) / ～长 head or chief judge; chief referee or umpire

cǎi

采(❶❷採) cǎi　❶ pick; gather; select:～编 gather and edit (news) / ～伐 cut or fell (trees) / ～风 collect folk songs / ～光〈建筑〉daylighting; lighting / ～暖 heating / ～信 recognize (evidence, etc) adopt / ～血〈医〉blood-collection; blood-taking / ～用 adopt; use;

employ / ～摘 pick; pluck ❷ mine; extract; ～掘 excavate / ～矿 mining ❸ spirit; complexion ❹ see "彩" cǎi

采办 cǎibàn　buy (a fairly large amount of goods); purchase

采访 cǎifǎng　(of a reporter) gather news; cover (an event, etc); interview (a person, etc); 接受～ give an interview (to a reporter)

采购 cǎigòu　❶ purchase (for an institution, etc); ～团 purchasing mission / ～图书 order books ❷ also "采购员" purchasing agent; payer

采集 cǎijí　gather; collect; ～小麦良种 seek out good strains of wheat

采煤 cǎiméi　coal mining, extraction or cutting; ～工人 coal miner

采纳 cǎinà　accept; adopt; 方案已被领导～。The plan won the approval of the leadership.

采取 cǎiqǔ　adopt; take; ～措施 adopt or take measures

采样 cǎiyàng　sample; spot check; 食品～检查 food spot check

彩(❷**綵**)　cǎi　❶ colour; ～带 colourful ribbon / ～电 (short for 彩色电视) colour TV (set) / ～虹 also "虹" rainbow / ～绘 coloured drawing or pattern / ～卷 colour film / ～扩 (short for 彩色扩印) make enlargements from colour film / ～排 (have a) dress rehearsal / ～霞 rosy or pink clouds / ～照 colour photo ❷ coloured silk ❸ cheer; applaud; 赢得一阵～声 draw a burst of cheers ❹ prize; ～民 lottery buyer / ～票 also "彩券" lottery ticket

彩礼 cǎilǐ　also "财礼" betrothal gift (from the prospective bridegroom to the bride's family)

彩色 cǎisè　(multi-) colour; ～玻璃 stained glass; end-of-day glass / ～铅笔 colour pencil; crayon

睬　cǎi　pay attention to; take notice of; 不～某人 ignore or cut sb

踩(**跴**)　cǎi　❶ step on; tread; ～水 tread water / ～高跷 walk on stilts / ～着点到 arrive on the dot 〈喻〉trample on; belittle: 既会捧人，也会～人 know well how to flatter or belittle others

cài

菜　cài　❶ vegetable; greens; ～农 vegetable grower; truck farmer / ～园 vegetable garden / ～市场 food (esp greengrocery) market ❷ dish; course; meal; ～刀 kitchen knife; chopper / ～牛 beef cattle / ～系 style of cooking; school of culinary art / ～看 cooked food; dishes

菜单 càidān　❶ menu; bill of fare ❷ 〈信息〉menu

菜花 càihuā　❶ cauliflower; 绿～ broccoli ❷ rape flower

菜篮子 càilánzi　vegetable basket; shopping basket for food; ～工程 "vegetable basket" project (for ensuring non-staple food supply)

菜谱 càipǔ　❶ menu; bill of fare ❷ cookery-book; cookbook

菜色 càisè　be pallid from hunger; look famished or emaciated

菜蔬 càishū　❶ vegetables; greens ❷ dishes at a meal

菜子 càizǐ　❶ vegetable seeds ❷ rapeseed; ～油 also "菜油" rapeseed or canola oil

cān

参(**參**)　cān　❶ join; take part in; participate in; ～军 join the army; enlist / ～评 be sent in for public appraisal or competitive selection / ～赛 take part in a competition / ～选 run in an election; enter a contest ❷ refer; consult; ～看 consult; see also / ～阅 see also; consult; refer to ❸ call to pay one's respects: ~谒 pay homage or respects to

see also cén; shēn。

参半 cānbàn half; fifty-fifty; 疑信~ half believing, half doubting

参观 cānguān visit; look around; ~团 visiting group / 欢迎~。 Visitors are welcome.

参加 cānjiā ❶ join; take part in; be a member of: ~工作 begin one's career / ~会议 attend a meeting / ~考试 sit for or take an exam / ~体育活动 go in for sports' ~作家协会 join the writers' union ❷ give advice, etc; 你~意见。 Please give your opinion about it.

参见 cānjiàn ❶ see also; cf ❷ pay one's respects to (a superior, etc)

参考 cānkǎo read; consult; refer to: ~书 reference book / ~书目 list of reference books; bibliography / 仅供~。 For your information only.

参谋 cānmóu ❶ staff officer; 作战~ operations staff (officer) / ~部 general staff / ~长 chief of staff ❷ give advice; advise; 请你给我~~。 I would like to have your advice.

参数 cānshù 〈数〉parameter

参天 cāntiān reaching to the sky; very tall: ~大楼 high-rise building; skyscraper

参议 cānyì ❶ take part in the planning or deliberation (of sth): ~员 senator; (Japan) councillor; ~院 senate; (Japan) House of Councillors ❷ adviser; counsellor

参与 cānyù *also* "参预" participate in; be involved in: ~决策 take part in decision-making / ~其间 have a finger in the pie / ~意识 sense of participation

参赞 cānzàn counsellor: 文化~ cultural counsellor or attaché

参展 cānzhǎn supply exhibits for or participate in an exhibition: ~作品

works on display (at an exhibition)

参战 cānzhàn enter or go to war: ~国 belligerent state

参照 cānzhào consult; refer to: ~物 object of reference / ~系 reference frame / 这办法可~实行。 This method may as well be tried elsewhere.

参政 cānzhèng participate in managing the state: ~党 participating party / ~议政 participate in the deliberation and administration of state affairs

餐 cān ❶ eat: ~车 restaurant or dining car; diner / ~馆 restaurant / ~具 tableware; dinner service or set / ~厅 dining room or hall; restaurant ❷ food; meal; 快~ fast food; snack

餐巾 cānjīn table napkin: ~纸 paper napkin; napkin paper

餐饮 cānyǐn food and drink: ~业 catering (trade)

餐桌 cānzhuō dining table: ~转盘 lazy Susan

cán

残(殘) cán ❶ incomplete; deficient; remnant: ~存 remnant; remaining; surviving / ~品 defective product / ~阳 setting sun / ~兵败将 remnants of a routed army / ~羹剩饭 leftovers of a meal / ~垣断壁 broken walls; ruins / ~渣余孽 remnants (of evil forces); dregs (of an old society) ❷ injure; damage; wreck; ~破 broken; dilapidated ❸ savage; barbarous; ferocious: ~杀 murder; massacre; slaughter

残暴 cánbào cruel and ferocious; brutal; savage

残废 cánfèi ❶ maimed; disabled; 残而不废 disabled but still useful to the community ❷ disabled or maimed person

残骸 cánhái ❶ dead body; carcass;

skeleton:死者的～ body of the dead ❷
remains; wreckage:失事飞机的～
wreckage of a crashed plane

残害 cánhài   brutally injure or kill;
slaughter;～生命 kill wantonly

残疾 cánjí   *also* "残障" deformity;
handicap;～人 handicapped person; the
handicapped / ～人奥运会（shortened
as 残运会）Paralympic Games; Para-
lympics

残局 cánjú   ❶ final phase of a game of
chess; endgame ❷ situation resulting
from a débâcle or social unrest:收拾～
clear up the mess; pick up the pieces

残酷 cánkù   cruel; brutal; ruthless;～
地杀害 kill in cold blood

残留 cánliú   remain; be left over;～量
residual amount / ～物 residue

残年 cánnián   ❶ evening of one's
life; declining years ❷ last days of the
year

残缺 cánquē   incomplete; fragmentary:
这书已一不全。The book has missing
pages.

残忍 cánrěn   cruel; brutal;～成性
brutal by nature

残生 cánshēng   ❶ one's remaining
years; old age ❷ surviving span of life:
幸保～ come out alive by sheer luck

残余 cányú   remnants; remains; sur-
vivals;封建～ vestiges of feudalism /
～势力 remnant forces

蚕（蠶） cán   silkworm:～蛾
silk moth / ～茧 silk-
worm cocoon / ～农 silkworm raiser;
sericulturist / ～丝 (natural) silk /
蛹 silkworm chrysalis

蚕豆 cándòu   broad bean

蚕食 cánshí   nibble;～鲸吞 seize (another country's territory, etc) by
piecemeal encroachment or wholesale
annexation / ～政策 policy of piecemeal
encroachment; nibbling policy

惭（慚） cán   feel ashamed;～
愧 be ashamed; feel

guilty

cǎn

惨（慘） cǎn   ❶ miserable; pitiful; tragic;～剧 trage-
dy; calamity / ～死 die a tragic death /
～笑 (give a) wan smile / ～状 miserable condition; pitiful sight / ～遭不幸
meet with a tragic death; be killed in an
accident ❷ extreme; terrible; exceeding;～败 (suffer a) crushing or disastrous defeat / ～祸 terrible disaster;
great calamity ❸ cruel; savage;～杀
murder; massacre; kill in cold blood /
～无人道 very cruel and inhuman

惨案 cǎn'àn   ❶ massacre:流血～
bloody massacre ❷ disastrous incident;
disaster

惨白 cǎnbái   ❶ (of light) dim; pale
❷ (of countenance) deathly pale

惨不忍睹 cǎnbùrěndǔ   too horrifying
to look at; so appalling that one could
not bear the sight

惨淡 cǎndàn   ❶ (of light) gloomy;
bleak; dim ❷ dreary; desolate; de-
pressed:生意～ slack business; depressed trade ❸ painstaking; laborious;～经营 keep an enterprise going by
painstaking effort

惨绝人寰 cǎnjuérénhuán   tragic beyond compare in this human world; exceedingly brutal or horrible

惨然 cǎnrán   saddened; grieved:心中
～ heartbroken; heart-sore

惨痛 cǎntòng   extremely grieved;
painful; bitter;～的教训 bitter lesson

惨重 cǎnzhòng   heavy; grievous; dis-
astrous:伤亡～ suffer grievous casualties / 付出～的代价 pay a heavy price

càn

灿（燦） càn   bright; resplendent; dazzling:黄～～

的油菜花 bright-yellow rape flowers

灿烂 cànlàn　magnificent; splendid; bright

粲 càn

粲然 cànrán　〈书〉❶ brilliant; bright; remarkable ❷ (with a) broad smile; smilingly: ～一笑 give a beaming smile; grin with delight

璨 càn　❶ beautiful jade ❷ see "粲" càn

cāng

仓(倉) cāng　warehouse; storehouse; barn: ～房 warehouse; storehouse / ～廪〈书〉granary / ～容 storage capacity

仓储 cāngchǔ　keep grain, etc, in a storehouse; put goods in storage: ～费用 storage cost or charge / ～式超市 warehouse-type supermarket; "big box"

仓促 cāngcù　also "仓猝""仓卒" hurriedly; hastily; suddenly: ～应战 accept battle hastily; put up a flurry of resistance / 时间～ be pressed for time

仓皇 cānghuáng　also "苍黄" in panic; in a flurry; flustered: ～失措 be scared out of one's wits; be panic-stricken

仓库 cāngkù　warehouse; storehouse: 清理～ check warehouse stocks / ～保管员 warehouseman

伧(傖) cāng　〈书〉rude; uncouth; boorish: ～父 also "伧夫" boor; bumpkin / ～俗 vulgar; uncouth; coarse

苍(蒼) cāng　❶ green; blue: ～翠 dark green; verdant / ～郁 verdant and luxuriant ❷ grey; ashy ❸〈书〉heaven; sky: ～穹 vault of heaven; the firmament

苍白 cāngbái　❶ pale; pallid; wan: 面色～ look pale ❷ feeble; weak; insuf-

ficient: ～无力的论据 feeble argument

苍苍 cāngcāng　❶ greyish white; ashen: 两鬓～ have greying temples ❷ deep-blue: 天色～。The sky is blue. ❸ luxuriant; endless; boundless

苍劲 cāngjìng　❶ old and strong: ～的青松 hardy, old, green pines ❷ (of calligraphy or painting) vigorous; bold

苍老 cānglǎo　❶ (of appearance, voice, etc) old; aged ❷ see "苍劲❷"

苍凉 cāngliáng　desolate; bleak; melancholy

苍茫 cāngmáng　❶ (of land, sea, etc) vast; boundless ❷ vast and indistinct: 暮色～。Dusk is gathering, stretching far into the distance.

苍生 cāngshēng　common people: 天下～ ordinary people across the land

苍天 cāngtiān　❶ blue sky ❷ also "上苍" Heaven

苍蝇 cāngying　fly: ～拍子 fly-swatter

沧(滄) cāng　(of water) dark blue

沧海 cānghǎi　the (deep blue) sea: ～桑田 (shortened as 沧桑) seas change into mulberry fields — constant changes in the world; vicissitudes of life / ～一粟 a drop in the ocean

舱(艙) cāng　cabin; hold; module: ～口 hatchway; hatch / ～位 cabin seat or berth; shipping space

cáng

藏 cáng　❶ hide; conceal: ～奸 conceal or harbour evil intentions / ～匿 hide; go into hiding; conceal / ～拙 hide one's incompetence by keeping quiet / ～猫儿〈口〉play hide-and-seek / ～龙卧虎 hidden dragons and crouching tigers — outstanding people who remain obscure to the undiscerning eye; unrecognized talents / ～身之所 hiding place; hideout / ～头露尾 tell part of

the truth but withhold the rest / ～污
纳垢 shelter evil people and uphold evil
practices ❷ collect; store;～品 collected article / ～书 collection of books;
library

see also zàng

cāo

操 cāo ❶ grasp; hold; wield;～
起扁担 grasp a carrying pole /
生杀大权 wield power of life and death
(over sb); have (sb) completely at
one's mercy ❷ do; act; operate;～办
attend to; arrange; handle /～之过急
act too hastily; make undue haste ❸
speak (a language or dialect);～本地口
音 speak with a local accent ❹ drill;
exercise;～场 sports or drill ground /
～练 drill; practise; train ❺ conduct;
behaviour;～守 personal integrity;
moral conduct /～行 behaviour or conduct (usu of a student)

操持 cāochí manage; handle; make
arrangements;～家务 manage household affairs

操刀 cāodāo hold a knife, cleaver,
scalpel, etc; be in command;～必割.
Having got hold of a knife, one must cut
— Do not lose an opportunity when
there is one.

操劳 cāoláo ❶ work hard;～过度
overwork or strain oneself ❷ take
care; look after

操切 cāoqiè hasty; rash; head-over-
heels;凡事不宜～. Never rush into
anything.

操心 cāoxīn worry; rack one's
brains; 没少～ take no end of pains;
spare no effort

操纵 cāozòng ❶ operate; control;～
杆 operating lever; control rod or stick /
～台 control panel or board ❷ rig; manipulate (market, etc)

操作 cāozuò operate; manipulate;～

程序 operation sequence /～系统 operating system (OS)

糙 cāo rough; coarse;～米 brown
or half-polished rice / 活儿～
sloppy work

cáo

嘈 cáo noise; din;～杂 noisy;
bustling

漕 cáo (usu 漕运) water transport
(esp of grain)

槽 cáo ❶ trough;～头 trough (in
a livestock shed); manger /～子
trough; groove ❷ groove; slot;开～
cut a groove or notch; slot /～牙
molar

cǎo

草(艸) cǎo ❶ grass; straw;
hay;～场 grazing land;
pasture /～丛 thick (growth of) grass /
～垛 haystack; hayrick /～寇 robber
in the green woods; bandit /～料 forage; fodder /～帽 straw hat /～皮
sod; turf /～坪 lawn /～鞋 straw
sandals /～药 medicinal herb; herbal
medicine /～食动物 plant-eating animal; herbivore ❷〈口〉female (of certain domestic animals or fowls);～鸡
hen ❸ careless; hasty; sloppy;～～了
事 rush through the work; get the
work done any old way ❹ (of calligraphy) cursive hand; running style;
handwritten form (of romanized letters);～字 character written in the cursive hand ❺ draft;～案 draft (of a
plan, law, etc) /～拟 draft; draw up /
～图 sketch (map); draft / 打～稿
work out a draft

草包 cǎobāo ❶ straw bag or sack ❷
idiot; blockhead; good-for-nothing

草本 cǎoběn herbaceous;～植物 herb

草创 cǎochuàng start (an enterprise,

etc）; take the initial step in a process：
～阶段 initial stage

草地 cǎodì ❶ lawn ❷ pasture ❸ grassland

草菅人命 cǎojiānrénmìng treat human life as if it were not worth a straw; make light of human life

草莽 cǎomǎng ❶ rank growth of grass; uncultivated land ❷〈喻〉greenwood; common stock：～英雄 hero of the bush; greenwood hero

草莓 cǎoméi strawberry

草木皆兵 cǎomùjiēbīng every bush and tree looks like an enemy soldier — be panic-stricken

草签 cǎoqiān initial：～文本 initialled text

草率 cǎoshuài careless; rash; perfunctory：～从事 act rashly or carelessly; do a sloppy or perfunctory job / ～下结论 draw hasty conclusions; jump to conclusions

草体 cǎotǐ ❶ also "草书"(in Chinese calligraphy）cursive hand; running style ❷ also "手写体" running hand of alphabet

草鱼 cǎoyú also "鲩" grass carp

草原 cǎoyuán grassland; prairie：～退化 grassland deterioration

草纸 cǎozhǐ toilet paper

cè

册 cè ❶ volume; book：～子 book; booklet / 装订成～ bind into book form ❷〈书〉confer a title：～封诸侯 confer hereditary titles of nobility ❸〈量〉copy; volume：分两～ be in two volumes

厕（廁） cè ❶ lavatory; toilet; restroom：～所 lavatory; toilet; WC ❷〈书〉be mixed up or involved in; mingle with：～身〈谦〉work（in a particular field or department）; be（with certain people）

侧 cè ❶ side; lateral：～记 side-lights（on an event, etc）/ ～门 side door or entrance / ～翼 flank（of an army, etc）/ ～影 silhouette; profile ❷ lean; incline：～目（而视）look askance at sb（with fear or indignation）/ ～卧 lie on one's side / ～泳 sidestroke

侧面 cèmiàn side aspect; flank；生活的一个～ a facet of life / ～像 profile / 从～了解 find out from indirect sources

侧身 cèshēn on one's side; sideways：～而入 enter sideways; sidle in

侧重 cèzhòng lay particular emphasis on; focus on; stress：～抓销售 devote oneself especially to sales / 有所～ have one's priorities（in one's work, etc）

测 cè ❶ survey; measure; test：～控 observe and control / ～算 measure and calculate / ～谎器 lie detector; polygraph / ～体温 take sb's temperature / ～其内心 find or ferret out what sb really thinks ❷ conjecture; infer; predict：～度 estimate; infer

测定 cèdìng determine（through measuring or testing）：～性能 test the performance（of sth）/ ～年代 date（sth）

测绘 cèhuì （surveying and）mapping; cartography：～员 surveyor; cartographer / ～卫星 cartographic satellite

测量 cèliáng survey; measure; gauge：～员 surveyor / ～仪器 surveying instrument

测试 cèshì test：～合格 pass a test / ～英语 give a test in English / ～中心 test(ing) centre

测验 cèyàn test；小～ quiz; quick test

测字 cèzì fortune-telling by analysing the component parts of a Chinese character; glyphomancy：～先生 fortune-teller; glyphomancer

恻 cè sorrowful; sad：～隐〈书〉compassion; pity

cè

策 cè ❶ plan; scheme; strategy：～士谋臣 counsellors and strategists ❷ (use a) riding-crop; hunting-crop：～励 encourage; spur on／～马急驰 whip a horse on with a crop

策动 cèdòng instigate; stir up：～政变 plot or engineer a coup d'état

策反 cèfǎn instigate or incite defections within the enemy camp

策划 cèhuà ❶ plan; plot; scheme：～阴谋 hatch a plot／～于密室 scheme behind closed doors ❷ (of a film, etc) plan and launch; scheme：～人 schemer

策略 cèlüè ❶ tactics; strategy：～上的失误 tactical error ❷ tactful：你这样做不～. It was not tactful of you to act as you did.

策应 cèyìng 〈军〉 support by taking coordinated action

策源地 cèyuándì source; place of origin：战争～ hotbed of war

cēn

参(參) cēn see also cān; shēn

参差 cēncī irregular; uneven：～不齐 not uniform; uneven

cén

岑 cén

岑寂 cénjì 〈书〉 quiet; solitary; lonely

涔 cén

涔涔 céncén 〈书〉 (of sweat, tears or rain) dripping; streaming

cēng

噌 cēng 〈象声〉 sound of friction, quick motion：麻雀～的一声飞上了屋顶. The sparrow flapped its wings and landed on the roof.

céng

层(層) céng ❶ one on top of another; overlapping layer or tier：～～ layer upon layer; tier upon tier: at each level／～峦叠嶂 range upon range of mountains／～见叠出 occur frequently; appear repeatedly ❷ 〈量〉 a) layer; tier; stratum：一～薄冰 a sheet of ice b) storey; floor：三～楼房 three-storey building c) item or part in a sequence：这话还有一～意思. This remark has another implication.

层出不穷 céngchūbùqióng emerge in an endless stream; come thick and fast; come out one after another

层次 céngcì ❶ level; gradation (in colour, quality, etc)：楼房～ storeys or floors of a building／高～人员 personnel of high calibre／这种地方～太低. This kind of place is of low class. ❷ arrangement or sequence of ideas：～分明 clear and coherent; well-organized

层面 céngmiàn level; scope：经济～ economic aspect

曾 céng 〈副〉 once：～用名 previous name／她～到过伦敦. She's been to London. see also zēng

曾几何时 céngjǐhéshí 〈书〉 before long; in a short space of time

曾经 céngjīng 〈副〉 once：我～有过这个疑问. I did have this doubt.

曾经沧海 céngjīngcānghǎi have sailed the seven seas; have experienced much：～难为水. 〈谚〉 One who has experienced much will never be thrilled by something petty.

cèng

蹭 cèng ❶ grind; scratch; be smeared with：～破了皮 get a scratch ❷ 〈方〉 get sth free; scrounge：～车 get a free ride ❸ dawdle; dillydally：

loiter:一步步地往前～ inch one's way forward; drag along

chā

叉 chā ❶ fork:～车 forklift /～鱼 spear fish /～子 fork /～烧肉 skewer-roasted pork / 两手～腰 with arms akimbo ❷ cross ("×"):打个～ put a cross (over sth) *see also* chá

杈 chā wooden fork; hay-fork pitchfork　*see also* chà

差 chā ❶ difference; discrepancy:～池 *also* "差迟" error; mistake; mishap /～价 price difference ❷ *also* "差数"〈数〉difference ❸〈书〉a little; somewhat; slightly:～强人意 passable; barely satisfactory *see also* chà; chāi; cī

差别 chābié difference; disparity:年龄～ disparity of age; difference in age

差错 chācuò ❶ error; mistake:工作出～ make mistakes in one's work ❷ mishap; trouble; accident:汽车中途出了～。The car broke down on the way.

差额 chā'é difference; balance; margin:～选举 multi-candidate election

差距 chājù gap; disparity; difference:找～ find out where one falls short / 有很大的～ have a long way to go

差异 chāyì difference; divergence; diversity:人们的思想有～。People vary in thinking.

差之毫厘,谬以千里 chāzhīháolí, miùyǐqiānlǐ *also* "失之毫厘,差以千里" an error the breadth of a single hair can lead you a thousand *li* astray; a small discrepancy often leads to an error of serious consequence

插 chā insert; interpose; stick in:～播 insert (an item) in a radio or TV programme; broadcast or televise impromptu /～队 cut in a line; jump the queue /～门 latch or bolt the door /～入 insert; plug in /～图 *also* "插画" illustration; plate /～叙 flashback /～页 inset; insert /～座 socket; outlet /～翅难飞 impossible to escape / 手～在兜里 with one's hands in one's pockets

插班 chābān join a class in the middle of a school year or a course:～生 midcourse student

插花 chāhuā ❶ intermingled; in between; by turn:～地 land belonging to one but enclosed in that of another ❷ flower arrangement; ikebana

插话 chāhuà ❶ interpose; interrupt; chip in ❷ digression; episode

插科打诨 chākē-dǎhùn (of an actor or actress) make impromptu comic gestures and remarks; jesting; buffoonery

插口 chākǒu ❶ socket; jack; spigot:电器～ socket for electric appliances ❷ *see* "插嘴"

插曲 chāqǔ ❶ song in a film or play;〈乐〉interlude ❷ episode; interlude:生活中的一个小～ an episode in one's life

插手 chāshǒu ❶ take part in; lend a hand:我想帮忙也插不上手。I want to help but do not know how. ❷ have a hand in; meddle in; interfere:样样事他都要～。He wants to have a finger in every pie.

插头 chātóu *also* "插销"〈电〉plug:三脚～ three-pin plug

插销 chāxiāo ❶ bolt; latch (of a door or window) ❷ *see* "插头"

插秧 chāyāng transplant rice seedlings or shoots:～机 rice transplanter

插足 chāzú ❶ get a foothold:无处～。There is no room (for sb). ❷ get involved in:第三者～ involvement of a third party (in a marriage, etc)

插嘴 chāzuǐ interrupt; chip in:插不上嘴 can't get a word in edgeways

喳 chā *see also* zhā

喳喳 chāchā ❶〈象声〉whispering sound ❷ (chācha) whisper

chá

茬 chá ❶ stubble：豆～儿 bean stubble ❷ crop：〈喻〉generation：～口 crops for rotation；soil on which a crop has been planted and harvested／二～韭菜 second crop of Chinese chives ❸ see "碴儿" chár

茶 chá ❶ tea (leaves)：～杯 teacup／～道 (esp in Japan) tea ceremony／～馆 tea-house／～壶 teapot；tea kettle／～几 tea table；teapoy／～具 tea set or service／～楼 tea-house (usu of two storeys)／～盘 tea tray／～树 tea plant or tree／～锈 tea stain／～园 tea garden or plantation ❷ certain drinks or liquid food：奶～ cream tea；杏仁～ almond paste ❸ tea-oil tree；camellia：～花 camellia (blossom)／～油 also "茶子油" tea (-seed) oil

茶点 chádiǎn　tea and pastries or cookies；refreshments

茶话会 cháhuàhuì　informal meeting or get-together over tea and refreshments；informal tea party

茶色 chásè　dark brown：～眼镜 dark brown sunglasses

茶水 cháshuǐ　tea or boiled water：供应～ supply tea

茶叶 cháyè　tea (leaves)：～罐 tea canister

茶余饭后 cháyú-fànhòu　also "茶余酒后" over a cup of tea or after a meal — at one's leisure：～的消遣 light entertainment

茶座 cházuò ❶ tea-house (usu outdoor)；tea stall ❷ seat in a teahouse or at a tea stall

查 chá ❶ check；look into；investigate：～房 go the rounds of the wards (in a hospital)；(in some hostels) make a routine check of the rooms／～禁 ban；prohibit／～考 examine；do research on／～扣 check and seize／～收 (often used in letter writing) please find (sth) enclosed／～验 check；examine／～夜 go the rounds at night；make a night patrol ❷ look up；consult：～电表 read the electricity metre／～词典 look up a word in the dictionary；consult a dictionary／～档案 look into the files／～找资料 look for and gather data

查办 chábàn　investigate and deal with according to law

查抄 cháchāo　make an inventory of a criminal's possessions and confiscate them

查处 cháchǔ　investigate and deal with accordingly

查点 chádiǎn　check the number or amount of；make an inventory of：～库存 take stock

查对 cháduì　check；verify：～原文 check the original text；check (a quotation or translation) against the original text

查访 cháfǎng　go around and make inquiries；investigate：～被盗名画的下落 try to track down a stolen famous painting

查封 cháfēng　seal up；close down：～黄色书刊 seal up and ban pornographic publications

查获 cháhuò　check and find；hunt down and seize；ferret out

查看 chákàn　look over；inspect；examine：～地图 look up (a place on) a map

查明 chámíng　also "查清" ascertain or prove through investigation；find out：～情况 ascertain the facts

查问 cháwèn　question；interrogate；inquire：～陌生人 challenge a stranger／～火车票价 find out the price of a train ticket

查询 cháxún　inquire about：～台 information desk

查阅 cháyuè　look up；consult：～历史文献 consult historical documents

查证 cházhèng　investigate and verify; check;～属实 be checked and found to be true; be verified

搽 chá　put on or rub into the skin; apply:～粉 powder (one's face) /～药水 apply liquid medicine

楂 chá ❶ short, bristly hair or beard; stubble; 胡子～ stubbly beard ❷ see "茬❶" chá

碴 chá　(方) be cut (by broken glass, etc)

碴儿 chár ❶ broken piece; fragment; sharp edge of broken glass, etc; 骨头～ bits of bones ❷ (cause of) quarrel; 找～ find fault or pick a quarrel with sb ❸ sth just said or mentioned; cue; 接～ take the cue

察 chá　examine; look into; scrutinize;～访 investigate through visit and observation /～觉 be conscious or aware of; perceive; sense /～看 inspect; examine; observe /～言观色 try to read sb's thoughts from his or her words and facial expressions; watch sb's mood

chǎ

叉 chǎ　part so as to form a fork; fork;～开双腿 open one's legs　see also chā

镲 chǎ　(popular term for 钹) cymbal;打～ strike a pair of cymbals

chà

汊 chà　branch or arm of a river; tributary

衩 chà　branch (of a tree)　see also chā

岔 chà ❶ branch:～口 fork (in a road) ❷ turn off; diverge; change (topic of conversation, etc) ❸ stagger:把两个会的时间～开 stagger

two meetings ❹ accident; mishap; mistake:出～儿 also "出岔子" go wrong; have an accident

岔路 chàlù　also "岔道儿" branch or side road; byroad;三～ fork in the road; junction of three roads

岔气 chàqì　feel a pain in the chest when breathing

刹 chà　Buddhist temple or monastery　see also shā

刹那 chànà　instant; split second;～间 in a flash; in the twinkling of an eye

衩 chà　slit or vent in the side of a garment

诧 chà　be surprised:～异 be astonished or amazed

差 chà ❶ differ:相～甚远 be extremely different; differ greatly (from each other) ❷ wrong; mistake: 判断之～ mistake in judgement ❸ be wanting; fall short of:～十分两点 ten (minutes) to two /还～一个人。There is one person short. ❹ not up to standard; poor; inferior:我的英语比她～。My English is not as good as hers.　see also chā; chāi

差不多 chàbuduō　also "差不离儿" almost; nearly; similar:我没有那么大的雄心,～就行了。I'm not that ambitious. I'm quite happy being average.

差点儿 chàdiǎnr ❶ not quite up to the mark; not good enough ❷ almost; nearly:～(没)哭出来 hold back one's tears with difficulty

差劲 chàjìn　no good; disappointing: 两队打得都很～。Neither of the two teams played well.

姹 chà　(书) beautiful:～紫嫣红 brilliant purples and reds; blaze of colours

chāi

拆 chāi ❶ (tear) open; take apart; undo:～封 break the seal /

~毛衣 unravel a sweater ❷ pull down; demolish; dismantle: ~除 pull down; dismantle; demolish / ~毁 tear down; demolish / ~卸 dismantle; disassemble; dismount / ~东墙,补西墙 〈俗〉resort to a makeshift solution; rob Peter to pay Paul

拆穿 chāichuān expose; uncover; unmask: ~谎言 nail a lie to the counter; give the lie to sth or sb / ~伪装 strip off sb's mask; unmask

拆借 chāijiè 〈经〉make or take out a short-term loan (usu at a daily interest)

拆迁 chāiqiān pull down old houses and resettle the inhabitants: ~户 household to be resettled / ~工程 resettlement project

拆散 chāisàn ❶ break apart: 把一套瓷器~包装 pack a set of china separately ❷ (chāisàn) break up: ~婚姻 break up a marriage

拆台 chāitái also "拆墙脚" pull the rug (out) from under sb; cut the ground from under sb's feet; undermine

拆洗 chāixǐ ❶ wash (padded coats, etc) after removing the padding or lining: ~被褥 unpick and wash bedding ❷ (of a machine) strip and clean: ~抽油烟机 strip a grease pump for cleaning

钗 chāi hairpin (formerly worn by women for adornment)

差 chāi ❶ send on an errand; dispatch ❷ job; official post: ~旅费 allowances for a business trip

see also chā/chà

差遣 chāiqiǎn send on an errand or mission; dispatch; assign: 听候~ be at sb's disposal; be at sb's beck and call

差使 chāishǐ ❶ send; assign; appoint: 受人~ (do sth) at sb's order or instigation ❷ (chāishi) 〈旧〉official post; commission: 派了一个好~ be assigned a good post

差事 chāishì errand; assignment

❷ *see* "差使❷"

差役 chāiyì 〈旧〉❶ corvée: 服~ do corvée ❷ runner or bailiff in a *yamen*

chái

柴 chái ❶ firewood: ~火 also "柴草" firewood; faggot / ~米油盐 firewood, rice, oil and salt — daily necessities ❷ 〈方〉bony; not fleshy: 又~又硬 (of meat, etc) dry and tough ❸ 〈方〉poor; shoddy; inferior

柴油 cháiyóu diesel oil: ~发动机 diesel motor

豺 chái also "豺狗" jackal

豺狼 cháiláng jackals and wolves — cruel and evil people: ~成性 wolfish; rapacious and ruthless / ~当道 jackals and wolves hold sway; evil people are in power

chān

掺(摻) chān *see* "搀❷" chān

搀(攙) chān ❶ help by the arm; support with one's hand: ~扶 support with one's hand ❷ also "掺" mix; adulterate: ~假 adulterate / ~杂 mix; mingle / ~水的酒 diluted liquor

搀和 chānhuo ❶ mix; mingle ❷ meddle; interfere; tamper: 别在这里瞎~。Please stop messing things up here.

chán

单(單) chán *see also* dān

单于 chányú 〈史〉king of the *Xiongnu* (匈奴)

谗(讒) chán accuse or slander (behind sb's back);

backbite∶～害 slander and harm; frame (sb); persecute / ～言 malicious, false accusation; calumniation

婵(嬋) chán

婵娟 chánjuān 〈书〉❶ (often used of women) lovely; graceful ❷ moon

馋(饞) chán greedy; glutton-

ous∶～嘴 gluttonous; glutton / ～涎欲滴 one's mouth waters; start drooling / 他看见人家打乒乓球就～得慌。His hand itches when he sees others playing table tennis.

禅(禪) chán 〈宗教〉❶ chan

— prolonged, intense meditation (for cleansing the mind)∶～定 lost in Buddhist meditation ❷ Buddhism; Buddhist; Chan∶～机 Buddhist allegorical word or gesture; subtleties of Buddhism / ～林 Buddhist monasteries or temples / ～师 (complimentary term of address for a Buddhist monk) master / ～宗 Chan sect of Buddhism (in China); (Japan) Zen *see also* shàn

孱 chán weak; frail∶～弱 〈书〉

weak; feeble; powerless

缠(纏) chán ❶ twine; wind∶

～绑 bind; tie up∶足〔旧〕 foot-binding ❷ entangle; plague; pester∶～手 thorny; troublesome; hard to deal with / ～住不放 fasten onto (sb or sth) like a leech

缠绵 chánmián ❶ (of illness, emotion, etc) lingering; abiding; harassing∶～病榻 be bedridden with a lingering or chronic disease ❷ touching; moving; sentimental∶～悱恻 sad and sentimental; mushy

缠绕 chánrào ❶ twine; wind∶～植物 twiner; climbing plant ❷ *also* "缠扰" bother; harass

缠身 chánshēn twine round one; be bogged down in; be tied up with∶疾病～ be pestered by illness; be laid up

with illness / 债务～ be debt-ridden

蝉(蟬) chán (popularly called

知了) cicada∶～蜕 cicada slough

蝉联 chánlián continue to hold a post or title∶～世界冠军 retain a world championship

潺 chán 〈象声〉 *sound of flowing

water*∶～～ 水声 murmuring or gurgling water

蟾 chán toad∶～蜍 *also* "癞蛤蟆"

toad / ～宫 〈书〉 moon

产(產) chǎn ❶ give birth to;

bear; breed∶～儿 newborn baby; product; outcome / ～房 delivery or lying-in room / ～妇 lying-in woman / ～卵 (of birds, insects, etc) lay eggs; (of fish, frogs, etc) spawn / ～前检查 prenatal or antenatal examination / ～休～假 be on or take maternity leave ❷ produce; yield∶～出 output / ～量 output; yield / ～销 production and marketing / ～值 value of output; output value / ～煤区 coal-mining area ❸ product; produce∶土～ local product ❹ property; estate∶～权 property right; title (to property)

产地 chǎndì place of production or origin∶柑橘～ citrus growing area / 原料～ source of raw materials

产科 chǎnkē obstetrical or maternity department; obstetrics∶～医生 obstetrician

产品 chǎnpǐn product; produce∶～开发 product development / ～性能 properties of a product

产生 chǎnshēng ❶ produce; cause; engender∶～纠纷 lead to or give rise to disputes / ～效力 be effective; come into effect; take effect / ～疑问 call into question; cast doubt; arouse suspicion / ～影响 exert an influence; have impact ❷ emerge; come into being; arise

产物 chǎnwù product; outcome; result：必然～ inevitable result or outcome / 辛勤劳动的～ fruit of hard work

产业 chǎnyè ❶ estate; property：祖上的～ ancestral property ❷ industrial：～革命 also "工业革命" Industrial Revolution / ～结构 set-up of production; industrial structure

诒 chǎn flatter; fawn on：～媚 flatter; toady to / ～谀邀宠 ingratiate oneself (with sb) by obsequious flattery

铲（鏟、剷） chǎn ❶ shovel：～车 forklift truck / ～子 shovel ❷ lift or move with a shovel; shovel：～除 root out; eliminate; eradicate / ～球（体）sliding tackle / ～土机 earth remover or shovel; bulldozer

阐（闡） chǎn explain; expatiate：～发 expound; elucidate / ～明 clarify; expound; make clear / ～释 explain; interpret / ～述 set forth; state; elaborate

chàn

忏（懺） chàn repent; be penitent

忏悔 chànhuǐ ❶ repent; be penitent：～自己的罪过 repent of one's sin ❷〈宗教〉confess：临终～ (make) deathbed confessions

颤 chàn quiver; tremble; vibrate：～动 quiver; vibrate / ～音〈语言〉〈乐〉trill; shake / ～悠 shake; quiver; flicker / ～巍巍 in a tottering manner; unsteadily / 吓得两腿～抖 shake in one's shoes　see also zhàn

chāng

伥（倀） chāng also "伥鬼" ghost of a man devoured by a tiger who helps the tiger to devour others

昌 chāng prosperous; flourishing：～明 thriving; well-developed / ～盛 prosperous; flourishing

菖 chāng

菖蒲 chāngpú 〈植〉calamus; sweet flag

猖 chāng ferocious; fierce; savage：～獗 ferocious and rampant; wild and unrestrained / ～狂 fierce; outrageous; wild

娼 chāng prostitute：～妇 whore；〈粗〉bitch / ～妓 prostitute; whore

鲳 chāng also "平鱼" silvery pomfret; butterfly

cháng

长（長） cháng ❶ long：～波 long wave / ～度 length / ～空 vast sky / ～裤 trousers; pants; slacks / ～跑 long-distance running; distance race / ～袍儿 also "长衫" Chinese long gown / ～舌妇 long-tongued or gossipy woman / ～筒袜 stockings / ～叹一声 heave a deep sigh / ～吁短叹 moan and groan; whine / ～治久安 long period of peace and stability ❷ strong point; forte：～项 sth one is good at; strong point; forte ❸ be strong in; be good at：～于演讲 be an eloquent speaker　see also zhǎng

长臂猿 chángbìyuán gibbon

长城 Chángchéng ❶ the Great Wall ❷ impregnable bulwark：国家的钢铁～ wall of bronze of a country

长处 chángchu strong point; merit; forte：发挥～ bring one's strengths into full play

长此以往 chángcǐyǐwǎng (usu used in a negative sense) if things go on like this

this; if things remain what they are

长笛 chángdí 〈乐〉flute

长短 chángduǎn ❶ length；~一句 *another name for ci poetry* (词) / ~正合适 just the right length / 长长短短 of uneven length ❷ accident；mishap：万一有个~ should anything untoward happen ❸ right and wrong；merits and demerits；good and bad：议论别人的~ gossip about people

长方形 chángfāngxíng *also* "矩形" rectangle；oblong

长工 chánggōng farm labourer hired by the year：打~ work as a farmhand by the year

长号 chánghào 〈乐〉trombone

长河 chánghé ❶ long or large river；(esp) the Yellow River ❷ endless flow：人类历史的~ long process of human history

长话 chánghuà ❶ (short for 长途电话) long-distance telephone call ❷ long talk or story：~短说 (to) make a long story short

长江 Chángjiāng the Yangtze River：~后浪推前浪。〈俗〉In the Yangtze River the waves behind drive on those before — the new will always push on the old.

长颈鹿 chángjǐnglù giraffe

长久 chángjiǔ prolonged；protracted；lasting：~以来 for a long time now；long since / ~之计 long-term plan；permanent solution

长眠 chángmián 〈婉〉eternal sleep；death：~地下 lie buried

长命 chángmìng long life：~锁 "long-life lock"，worn by a child as a mascot for longevity / 祝你~百岁！I wish you a long, long life!

长年 chángnián all the year round；from year to year；for a long time：~累月 year in, year out；over the years

长篇 chángpiān ❶ lengthy；long：~大论 lengthy speech or article / ~小说

novel ❷ long fiction；novel

长期 chángqī long-term；prolonged；protracted：~性 protracted nature / ~贷款 long-term loan / ~失业 chronically unemployed / ~存在的问题 long-standing problem

长驱直入 chángqū-zhírù (of an army) drive straight in

长生 chángshēng long life：~不老 immortal / ~不老药 elixir of life

长寿 chángshòu long life；longevity：~老人 person who lives to a ripe old age

长途 chángtú ❶ long (distance)：~电话 long-distance or trunk call ❷ long-distance call or bus：打~ make a trunk call / 坐~ take a long-distance bus

长线 chángxiàn ❶ overproduction；oversupply：~产品 product in excessive supply ❷ long-term：~投资 long-term investment

长效 chángxiào (of) enduring or lasting effect；long-acting：~肥料 long-lasting or slow-release fertilizer / ~胶囊〈药〉spansule

长袖善舞 chángxiùshànwǔ long sleeves lend grace to dancing；powerful backing ensures success；the wealthy know how to manoeuvre

长远 chángyuǎn long-term；long-range：~利益 long-term interest / 这不是~的办法。This is only a stopgap measure.

长征 chángzhēng ❶ expedition；long march ❷ Long March (of the Chinese Workers' and Peasants' Red Army, 1934-1935)

长足 chángzú 〈书〉by leaps and bounds；considerably：取得~的进步 make great strides forward

场(場、塲) cháng ❶ level open space；threshing ground：~院 threshing or sunning ground ❷〈量〉*used to indicate a process*：一～大雪 a heavy snowfall / 生了一～大病 have been very ill *see also* chǎng

肠(腸) cháng ❶ intestines：～癌 intestinal cancer / ～炎 enteritis / ～子 intestines / ～痉挛〈医〉intestinal spasm / ～粘连〈医〉intestinal adhesion ❷ sausage：～衣 casing for sausages

肠胃 chángwèi (intestines and) stomach；stomach：～不好 suffer from indigestion

尝(嘗,❷嚐) cháng ❶ taste (food)；try；〈嚐〉experience：～试 attempt；try / ～鲜 *also* "尝新" taste what is just in season；have delicious food / ～到甜头 come to know the good (of sth)；have a foretaste of the joy (of sth) ❷ ever；once；未～晤面 have never met before

常 cháng ❶ common；normal；usual：～会 regular meeting / ～例 common practice；normal procedure / ～人 ordinary person；man in the street / ～事 common occurrence；everyday experience / ～温 normal atmospheric temperature (between 15℃ and 25℃) ❷ constant；invariable：～数〈数〉constant / ～青树 evergreen (tree) ❸ often；frequently；usually：～客 frequent guest or customer / ～住人口 permanent population

常备 chángbèi be always on hand or available；constantly stand by：～军 standing army / ～药 household or common medicine / ～不懈 be always on the alert；be ever prepared

常常 chángcháng often；frequently；generally

常春藤 chángchūnténg 〈植〉Chinese ivy

常规 chángguī ❶ convention；routine；common practice：～武器 conventional weapon ❷〈医〉routine (test)；

～检查 routine physical check-up

常轨 chángguǐ normal practice or course：越出～ abnormal；irregular

常见 chángjiàn often seen；common；commonplace：～的现象 common phenomenon；commonplace

常理 chánglǐ common sense；customary practice：有悖～ contrary to common sense or social convention

常绿 chánglǜ evergreen：～灌木 evergreen shrub

常年 chángnián ❶ all the year round；over a long period of time ❷ average year：～降雨量 average annual rainfall

常情 chángqíng reason；common sense；human nature：不合～ contrary to reason；against common sense / 人之～。It is only human nature.

常任 chángrèn permanent；standing：～理事 standing member of a council

常设 chángshè permanent；standing：～机构 standing body；permanent organization

常识 chángshí common，general or elementary knowledge；common sense：科学～ ABC of science

常态 chángtài normalcy；normal behaviour or state of affairs：保持～ maintain one's bearing；remain one's normal self

常委 chángwěi ❶ *also* "常委会" (short for 常务委员会) standing committee：人大～ Standing Committee of the People's Congress ❷ (short for 常务委员) member of the standing committee：党委～ member of the Party standing committee

常务 chángwù ❶ standing；permanent；executive：～理事 executive council member / ～董事 managing director ❷ routine；day-to-day business

常言 chángyán saying；proverb：～道 as the saying goes / ～说得好 it is well said that …

常用 chángyòng　in common use; often used or quoted: ～词语 basic or everyday expression

常驻 chángzhù　resident; permanent; ～记者 resident correspondent / ～上海 be stationed in Shanghai

偿(償) cháng

❶ repay; redeem; compensate: ～付 pay back; reimburse / ～还 repay; redeem / ～清债务 clear off or settle one's debts / 杀人～命 pay with one's life for a murder; a life for a life ❷ meet the need of; fulfil; satisfy: 得～夙愿 have one's long-cherished wish realized

徜 cháng

徜徉 chángyáng　also "倘佯" 〈书〉stroll; saunter; amble: 在知识的海洋中～ sail in the vast ocean of knowledge

嫦 cháng

嫦娥 Cháng'é　Goddess of the Moon

chǎng

厂(廠) chǎng

❶ factory; mill; plant: ～房 factory building; workshop / ～家 factory; manufacturer / ～商 factory owner; factories and companies / ～长 factory director or manager / ～矿企业 factories, mines and other enterprises; industrial enterprises ❷ yard; depot: 木材～ timber yard

场(場、塲) chǎng

❶ place (for a specific activity); spot; 〈理〉field: 体育～ gymnasiums and stadiums; grounds ❷ 〈戏〉scene; stage: 第三幕第二～ Act III, Scene II / ～记 log (keeper); script holder / ～景 scene; scenery; sight ❸ 〈量〉used of a process: 一～恶梦 a nightmare

see also cháng

场次 chǎngcì　number of showings or performances of a film, play, etc: 演出一百多～ have a run of over a hundred performances

场地 chǎngdì　place; site: 比赛～ competition arena or ground

场合 chǎnghé　occasion; situation: 公开～ in public; openly / 正式～ (on) formal occasions

场面 chǎngmiàn　❶ scene: 感人～ moving scene ❷ spectacle; occasion; scene: ～话 polite platitudes for the occasion; unctuous words / ～上吃得开 know one's way about in social life; be a good socializer ❸ appearance; front; façade: 摆～ maintain an impressive façade; be ostentatious / 撑～ keep up appearances

场所 chǎngsuǒ　place (for an activity); venue; 娱乐～ place of entertainment / 强盗出没的～ bandit-infested area

敞 chǎng

❶ (of houses, etc) spacious; roomy; open: ～亮 bright and spacious; 〈喻〉clear-minded / ～快人 forthright fellow ❷ open; uncover: ～篷车 open car / ～胸露怀 with one's coat or shirt unbuttoned; bare one's chest

敞开 chǎngkāi　❶ open (wide): ～国门 open the country wide / ～思想 speak up; get everything off one's chest ❷ put no limit on; de-regulate; de-control: ～儿吃 〈口〉eat one's fill / ～供应 supply without limit; ensure an open-ended supply

氅 chǎng

（usu 大氅）cloak

chàng

怅(悵) chàng

disappointed; sorry: ～惘 anxious and in low spirits; listless / ～然若失 feel depressed and perplexed; feel sad and distracted

畅（暢）

chàng ❶ smooth; unimpeded;信息不一。 The flow of information is impeded. ❷ free; uninhibited;～谈 talk freely and cheerfully; talk frankly and eagerly /～饮 drink to one's heart's content /～游 make a delightful trip; have a good swim (in a river, etc) /～所欲言 speak without reservation; speak one's mind freely /～叙友情 relive an old friendship

畅达 chàngdá fluent; smooth;交通～ have an efficient transport network / 文辞～ (of writing) read smoothly

畅快 chàngkuài free from inhibitions; carefree; happy;精神～ feel relaxed /～地玩了一天 have a splendid time the whole day

畅通 chàngtōng unblocked; unimpeded;～无阻 pass unimpeded; go unhindered

畅想 chàngxiǎng give free rein to imagination; boldly visualize;～未来 imagine freely what the future holds in store

畅销 chàngxiāo be in great demand; sell well; have a ready market;～品 hot item; hot buy /～书 best-seller

倡

chàng initiate; advocate;～导 initiate; propose; promote

倡议 chàngyì propose;～书 (written) proposal /～者 initiator

唱

chàng ❶ sing; chant; call;～本 script of a ballad-singer /～碟 (gramophone) record; disc /～段 aria /～工 also "唱功" (art of) singing /～机 gramophone; phonograph /～腔 melodies in a Chinese opera /～双簧 give a two-man comic show;〈喻〉～主角 play the leading role /～空城计 play the empty-city stratagem — present a bold front to conceal a weak defence; have almost all the staff vacated / 一个～红脸, 一个～白脸。One coaxes, while the other bullies. or One plays the good cop while the other plays the bad cop. ❷ song or singing part of a Chinese opera;小～ ditty; popular tune

唱反调 chàngfǎndiào sing a different tune; sound or strike a discordant note

唱高调 chànggāodiào make high-sounding statements; indulge in high-flown rhetoric

唱歌 chànggē sing (a song);～跳舞 singing and dancing / 很会～ be a good singer

唱和 chànghè ❶ one sings a song and the others join in the chorus ❷ also "唱酬" when one writes a poem, the other comes up with another in reply, usu using the same rhyme sequence

唱名 chàngmíng ❶ roll call;～表决 vote by roll call ❷ also "唱名法"〈乐〉sol-fa; solmization

唱片 chàngpiàn gramophone or phonograph record;放～ play a gramophone record / 灌～ cut a disc; make a record

唱票 chàngpiào call out the names of candidates while counting ballots;～人 teller

唱戏 chàngxì 〈口〉sing in an opera; put on a theatrical performance;爱～ be fond of acting in an opera / 唱独角戏 put on a one-man show; go it alone / 唱对台戏 put on a rival show; enter into rivalry (against sb)

chāo

抄

chāo ❶ copy; transcribe;照～ make a verbatim transcription of; copy out /～本 hand-copied book or text; transcript /～件 copy; duplicate (of a document, etc) /～录 make a copy of; quote /～送 make a copy (of a document, etc) for; send a duplicate to /～写 copy; transcribe ❷ copy; plagiarize; lift;～别人的作业 copy from sb's homework ❸ search and confiscate; make a raid upon; ~ 获 search and seize; ferret out / ~ 家 search sb's home and confiscate his or her property; ransack sb's home / ~ 没 ransack and confiscate ❹ take (a shortcut); outflank; ~ 道 also "抄近道"; "抄近路" take a shortcut / ~ 后路 outflank and attack (the enemy) in the rear; turn the enemy's rear ❺ fold (one's arms) in the sleeves ❻ grab; snatch; make away with; ~ 肥自搂 〈方〉wangle extra income for oneself

抄袭 chāoxí ❶ plagiarize; copy; lift; ~ 行为 (an act of) plagiarism ❷ borrow indiscriminately; copy; ~ 别国的经验 copy foreign experience ❸ launch a surprise attack (on the enemy) by making a detour; ~ 敌军侧翼 outflank the enemy

钞 chāo paper money; banknote; ~ 票 banknote; paper money; bill / 破 ~ incur an expense

绰 chāo ❶ grab (what is conveniently near) ❷ see "焯"chāo

see also chuò

超 chāo ❶ exceed; surpass; overtake; ~ 产 overfulfil a production target or quota / ~ 车 overtake other vehicles on the road / ~ 假 overstay one's leave / ~ 员 exceed the designated number; be overloaded or overstaffed ❷ (used before adjectives) super-; ultra-; extra-; ~ 薄 ultra-thin / ~ 低温 ultra-low temperature / ~ 短裙 miniskirt / ~ 高频 ultra-high or super-high frequency / ~ 高压 super-high pressure; ultra-high voltage (UHV); extra-high tension / ~ 小型 subminiature / ~ 一流棋手 super chess (-)player ❸ transcend; go beyond; ~ 俗 be free from vulgarities; be unconventional / ~ 自然 transcending nature; supernatural

超编 chāobiān exceed the personnel

quota; be overstaffed ~ 人员 excess personnel; redundant staff

超常 chāocháng supernormal; extraordinary; ~ 儿童 supernormal child / ~ 发挥 give an unusually good performance; surpass or outperform oneself

超出 chāochū overstep; go beyond; exceed

超导 chāodǎo 〈理〉superconduction; ~ 体 superconductor / ~ 性 superconductivity / ~ 材料 superconducting material; superconductor

超额 chāo'é overfulfil a quota; exceed a norm; ~ 利润 excess profit; super-profit / ~ 征税 overtaxation

超负荷 chāofùhè overload; excess load; ~ 工作 be overloaded with work; work extra hard

超过 chāoguò overtake; surpass; exceed

超级 chāojí super; ~ 大国 superpower / ~ 名模 supermodel / ~ 市场 (shortened as 超市) supermarket

超龄 chāolíng overage; ~ 团员 overage League member

超期 chāoqī exceeding or beyond a fixed term of service; ~ 服役 extended service or active duty

超前 chāoqián ahead of the times; aiming at the future; ~ 教育 future-oriented education / ~ 消费 unduly high level of consumption; over-consumption / ~ 意识 foresight; far-sight

超群 chāoqún also "超绝" pre-eminent; head and shoulders above all others; 才 学 ~ be unequalled both in knowledge and talent

超然 chāorán aloof; detached; ~ 物外 be above worldly considerations; stay away from worldly affairs

超人 chāorén ❶ out of the common run; superhuman; 智 力 ~ endowed with superior intelligence ❷ superman

超生 chāoshēng (short for 超计划生育) have more children than the family planning policy allows：～子女 children born without family planning

超声波 chāoshēngbō　supersonic or ultrasonic wave：～疗法 ultrasonic therapy / ～传感器 *also* "声呐" sonar

超脱 chāotuō ❶ free from convention；unconventional；uninhibited ❷ be detached from；keep or stand aloof from；not get involved in：～日常事务 detach oneself from routine business

超音速 chāoyīnsù　supersonic speed：～喷气机 supersonic jet

超越 chāoyuè　overstep；transcend；surpass：～前人 surpass one's predecessors / ～自我 outdo oneself；transcend self

超载 chāozài〈交通〉overload：～渡轮 overcrowded or overloaded ferry

超支 chāozhī　overspend；overdraw；live beyond one's means：～账户 overdrawn account

超重 chāozhòng ❶〈理〉〈化〉superheavy：～氢 superheavy hydrogen；tritium ❷ overload；overweight：～行李 overweight or excess luggage

焯 chāo　(way of cooking) scald；parboil

cháo

巢 cháo　nest：鸟～ bird's nest；～居 dwell in trees / ～穴 lair；den；hideout

朝 cháo ❶ court；government：在～ be in power / ～廷 royal or imperial court / ～野〈旧〉government and populace；ruling party and opposition / ～政 court affairs；affairs of state / ～中有人好做官。〈俗〉You will have a bright official career if you have powerful backing in the government. ❷ dynasty；(emperor's) reign：～代 dynasty；reign / 乾隆～ reign of Qianlong；Qianlong period ❸ have an audience with (an emperor, etc)；make

a pilgrimage to：～拜 pay respects or homage to；worship / ～贡 present tribute (to an imperial court) / ～见 *also*"朝觐"；"朝谒" have an audience with；be received by (the emperor) / ～圣 pilgrimage；(Islam) hadj ❹ facing；towards：～阳 illuminated by the sun；sunny；facing south / ～人招手 wave at sb / 坐北～南 (of a house) have a southern exposure；face south *see also* zhāo

嘲 cháo　ridicule；deride；sneer：～讽 sneer at；ridicule；deride / ～弄 mock；poke fun at；ridicule / ～笑 laugh or jeer at；ridicule；deride

潮 cháo ❶ tide：～水 tidewater；flood water / ～头 crest of a tide；trend / ～汛 annual flood tide / 心事如～涌。A tide of feelings welled up in one's heart. ❷ social upsurge；current：工～ workers' movement；industrial unrest ❸ damp；moist：～气 moisture in the air；damp；humidity / ～润 (of air, etc) wet；damp；(of eyes) teary / ～呼呼 damp；dank；clammy ❹〈方〉of low or inferior quality；poor：～金 impure gold / 手～ poor in skill (esp in driving)

潮流 cháoliú ❶ tide；tidal current：～汹涌 surging tide ❷ trend (of social change)；current：跟上时代的～ keep abreast of the trend of the times；keep pace with the times

潮湿 cháoshī　moist；damp：东西～得发霉了。Things got mildewed from the damp.

潮汐 cháoxī　morning and evening tides；ocean tide：～能 tidal energy or power

chǎo

吵 chǎo ❶ make a noise：～嚷 make a racket；clamour (for sth) / ～得没法儿睡 can't go to sleep on account of the noise / 别—了！Stop that racket! or Be quiet! ❷ quarrel；squabble；wrangle；~翻 fall out（with each other）

吵架 chǎojià *also "吵嘴"* quarrel；squabble；bicker：为钱～ bicker over money matters

吵闹 chǎonào ❶ wrangle；kick up a row：为孩子的事～ wrangle over one's children ❷ din；hubbub

炒 chǎo ❶ (stir-)fry；sauté：~菜 stir-fry；stir-fried dish / ~饭 fried rice / ~锅 wok，Chinese pan for stir-frying / ~货 roasted seeds and nuts / ~勺 round-bottomed frying pan with a handle / ~米花 puffed rice ❷ speculate；promote：~股（short for 炒股票）speculate in stocks ❸ (方) sack；fire：~鱿鱼 give sb the sack；fire sb

炒冷饭 chǎolěngfàn heat leftover rice — rehash（the same old thing）；dish up the same old stuff

炒面 chǎomiàn ❶ *chow mein* — fried noodles ❷ parched flour

炒作 chǎozuò（of or through the media）promote；hype：过分～ (over-)hype / 通过媒体～，这本书销路大增。Media promotion made the book a bestseller.

chē

车（車） chē ❶ vehicle：~把 handle bar / ~灯 light or lamp on a vehicle / ~队 convoy；motorcade；transport pool（of an institution）/ ~费 *also "车钱"* fare / ~号 license number / ~祸 traffic or road accident / ~检 vehicle inspection / ~库 garage / ~牌 license or number plate / ~棚 bicycle（parking）shed / ~皮 railway wagon or carriage；freight truck / ~票 ticket / ~胎 *also "车带"* tyre / ~位 parking place（for a car）/

~厢 *also "车箱"* railway carriage / ~闸 brake（of a vehicle）/ ~照 *also "车本"* driving license / ~辙 rut / ~把势 *also "车把式"* cart-driver；carter / ~马费 travel or transport allowance / ~匪路霸 highway and railroad robbers ❷ axled machine or instrument：试～ trial or test run of a machine ❸（机）lathe；turn：~床 *also "旋床"* lathe；turning machine / ~工 lathe operator / ~个零件 lathe a machine part ❹ lift（water）by waterwheel
see also jū

车场 chēchǎng ❶ place where automobiles are parked，serviced and repaired；garage ❷（railway）marshalling yard；road transport or public transit pool

车次 chēcì ❶ train number ❷ motorcoach number（indicating order of departure）

车到山前必有路 chēdàoshānqián bìyǒulù 〈谚〉the cart will find its way round the hill when it gets there — things will eventually sort themselves out

车道 chēdào traffic lane：快～ speed lane / 慢～ normal lane / 六～的高速公路 six-lane expressway

车轱辘 chēgūlu（口）wheel（of a vehicle）：~话 repetitious，rambling talk

车间 chējiān workshop；shop：~主任 workshop director

车辆 chēliàng vehicle：来往～ vehicles going to and fro；traffic

车轮 chēlún wheel（of a vehicle）：~战 tactic of several people taking turns in fighting one opponent to tire him or her out — gruelling tactic

车水马龙 chēshuǐ-mǎlóng endless stream of horses and carriages — heavy traffic

车头 chētóu ❶ locomotive ❷ front part of a vehicle

车载斗量 chēzài-dǒuliáng be enough

to fill carts and measured by the *dou*— common and numerous

车站 chēzhàn　station; stop; depot:~站长 station-master

chě

扯　chě　❶ pull; drag:~平 pull (sth) straight;〈喻〉break even; even up / ~后腿〈喻〉hold back from action; be a drag on; be a hindrance to ❷ tear:~开 tear open / ~个口子 tear a hole (in sth) ❸ talk; chat; gossip:~淡〈方〉talk nonsense / ~谎 tell a lie; lie / ~皮 dispute over trifles; argue back and forth; wrangle / ~家常 chat about everyday family affairs; chitchat

chè

彻(徹)　chè　thorough; penetrating; complete:~悟 become fully conscious (of sth); come to fully realize / ~夜 all night; all through the night / ~头~尾 out and out; sheer; downright / 寒气~骨。The cold cut one to the marrow.

彻底 chèdǐ　*also* "澈底" thorough; thoroughgoing:~调查 investigate fully or thoroughly / ~解决 solve once and for all; find a radical solution

掣　chè　❶ pull; tug; drag:~肘 hold (sb) back by the elbow; impede; obstruct ❷ draw:~签 draw lots

撤　chè　❶ remove; take away:~编 disestablish; deactivate / ~除 remove; dismantle / ~岗 remove a guard or sentry; eliminate a post / ~换 (dismiss and) replace; recall / ~席 clear the table (after a feast) / ~资 cancel or withdraw one's investment ❷ withdraw; retreat:~防 withdraw a garrison; withdraw from a defended position / ~军 *also* "撤兵" withdraw troops; pull back troops / ~离 with-

draw from; evacuate; leave / ~退 withdraw; retreat / ~出伤员 evacuate the wounded

撤回 chèhuí　❶ recall; withdraw:~使馆人员 recall embassy personnel ❷ retract; revoke; withdraw:~起诉 (shortened as 撤诉) withdraw a charge; drop a lawsuit

撤销 chèxiāo　*also* "撤消" cancel; revoke; rescind:~处分 rescind or annul a penalty

撤职 chèzhí　remove from office; dismiss or discharge from post:~查办 discharge sb from office and prosecute him or her

澈　chè　(of water) clear; limpid

chēn

抻　chēn　pull out; stretch:~面 make noodles by drawing out the dough by hand; hand-pulled noodles

嗔　chēn　〈书〉❶ angry; displeased:~怒 get angry / 面带~色 look displeased or angry ❷ be annoyed (with sb); blame:~怪 blame; rebuke; upbraid

瞋　chēn　〈书〉stare angrily; glare

chén

臣　chén　official under a feudal ruler; subject:~服〈书〉submit oneself to; acknowledge allegiance to / ~民 subjects of a feudal ruler

尘(塵)　chén　❶ dust; dirt:~暴 *also* "沙暴" dust storm / ~肺〈医〉pneumoconiosis / ~封 covered with dust; neglected / ~垢 dust and filth; dirt / ~土 dust; dirt / ~雾 cloud of dust; dust and smoke / ~埃落定〈喻〉the dust settles; the situation stabilizes ❷ this mortal world; worldly affairs; ～世 also "尘寰" this world; mortal life / ～缘 earthly; worldly; human world / ～缘 predestined bond; human bondage

辰 chén ❶ 5th of the Earthly Branches *see also* "干支" gānzhī ❷ celestial bodies ❸ time; day; occasion; ～光〈方〉time

沉(沈) chén ❶ sink; subside; ～降〈of the ground, etc〉subside / ～冤 injustice of long standing; unrighted wrong / ～渣 dregs; scum; dross / ～底儿 sink to the bottom ❷〈usu of abstract matters〉keep down; lower; ～吟 recite or read in a low voice; ponder irresolutely / ～下脸来 put on a stern expression; pull a long face / ～下心来 settle down (to one's work) ❸ concentrate (on one's study, etc) ❸ (of degree) deep; profound; ～疴 grave and lingering illness; serious chronic illness / 心事～ have a heavy heart; be deeply troubled ❹ heavy; uncomfortable; ～郁 depressed; downcast; gloomy / ～甸甸 heavy / 担子～ heavy load or responsibility

沉淀 chéndiàn ❶ settle; precipitate; ～池 precipitating or sedimentation tank / ～物 sediment; precipitate ❷ *see* "沉积②"

沉浮 chénfú ❶ sink and swim; drift; 与世～ swim with the tide; drift along ❷ vicissitude

沉积 chénjī ❶ deposit; sediment; ～作用〈地〉deposition; sedimentation ❷ (usu of abstract matters) accumulation; accretion; 文化～ accretion of culture

沉寂 chénjì quiet; still; ～下来 quiet down; fall silent

沉浸 chénjìn be immersed or steeped in; be permeated with; 在悲痛中～ steeped in sorrow; be plunged into grief

沉静 chénjìng quiet; calm; serene; 性情～ quiet by temperament / ～的夜晚 silent night

沉沦 chénlún sink into (vice, etc); 不甘～ refuse to submit to degradation

沉闷 chénmèn ❶ (of atmosphere, etc) dull; oppressive; depressing ❷ (of a person) in low spirits; (of character) withdrawn; retiring

沉迷 chénmí *also* "沉湎"; "沉溺" indulge or wallow in; be given to; ～酒色 be excessively fond of wine and women; be addicted to drinking and womanizing

沉没 chénmò sink; 触礁～ be wrecked on a reef

沉默 chénmò ❶ taciturn; reticent; quiet; ～寡言 taciturn; reticent; of few words ❷ silent; speechless; 保持～ keep quiet; remain silent / ～权 right of silence

沉睡 chénshuì be fast or sound asleep; 从～中醒来 awake from a deep sleep

沉思 chénsī ponder; meditate; be lost in thought

沉痛 chéntòng ❶ deep feeling of grief or remorse ❷ deeply felt; bitter; ～的教训 bitter lesson

沉稳 chénwěn ❶ prudent; discreet; steady; ～持重 discreet and self-possessed ❷ sound; steady; 睡得～ sound asleep

沉陷 chénxiàn ❶ sink; cave in; subside ❷ get bogged down; be lost; ～于往事的回忆 be lost in memories of the past

沉重 chénzhòng ❶ heavy; ～的代价 high price ❷ serious; critical; 病情～ be very ill

沉住气 chénzhùqì keep calm or cool; be steady; be as cool as a cucumber; 沉得住气 be able to hold back one's excitement or anger

沉着 chénzhuó calm; cool-headed; steady; ～应战 meet an attack calmly accept a challenge with calm confidence

沉醉 chénzuì　become intoxicated; immerse oneself; ～于幸福的回忆中 be immersed in happy memories

忱 chén 〈书〉true sentiment; sincere or hearty feeling

陈(陳) chén ❶ lay out; put on display; ～放 put on display; lay out / ～兵百万 deploy a million troops ❷ state; explain; ～情 state one's case; explain oneself; make a plea / ～请 submit a request (for consideration) / ～诉 state; recite; make a plea / ～说利害 explain the advantages and disadvantages ❸ old; stale; ～醋 mature vinegar / ～迹 thing of the past; old traces / ～酒 also "陈酿" old or mellow wine / ～词滥调 cliché; stereotyped phrase; platitude / 不落～套 free from outmoded style or conventional techniques

陈陈相因 chénchénxiāngyīn　follow a set routine; do the same thing over and over again; stay in the same old groove or rut

陈腐 chénfǔ　old and decayed; stale; outworn; ～内容 stale in content

陈谷子烂芝麻 chéngǔzilànzhīma old millet and stale sesame — dull and uninteresting things of the past; old garbage

陈规 chénguī　outmoded convention; ～陋习 outmoded conventions and practices

陈旧 chénjiù　old; outmoded; old-fashioned

陈列 chénliè　display; exhibit; ～馆 exhibition hall / ～柜 show case / ～品 exhibit

陈年 chénnián　of many years' standing; ～老酒 old wine / ～老账 long-standing debt; old score

陈设 chénshè ❶ exhibit; display; set out ❷ furnishings; ～典雅 elegantly furnished

陈述 chénshù　state; explain; ～句 〈语言〉declarative sentence / ～理由 state one's reasons

晨 chén　morning; ～炊 preparing of breakfast / ～练 morning exercise or practice / ～曦 first rays of the morning sun / ～兴夜寐 get up early and retire late — work very hard / 寥若～星 as few as stars at dawn / 一日之计在于～。The whole day's work depends on a good start in the morning.

chèn

衬(襯) chèn ❶ line; place underneath; ～上一层布 put a piece of cloth underneath ❷ be worn underneath; cloth lining; liner; ～布 lining cloth / ～裤 underpants; pants / ～里 lining / ～领 detachable collar lining (of a coat) / ～裙 underskirt; petticoat / ～衫 also "衬衣" underwear; shirt; blouse ❸ also "衬托" serve as a foil to; set off

称(稱) chèn　fit; suit; match; ～身 be a good fit / ～愿 feel gratified (esp at the misfortune of a much-hated person) / ～职 qualified; competent　see also chēng

称心 chènxīn　find sth gratifying; give complete satisfaction; ～如意 after one's own heart; to one's heart's content

趁 chèn ❶ take advantage of; avail oneself of; ～便 when it is no extra trouble; when it is convenient / ～空 when one has time to spare; in one's leisure ❷ 〈方〉possess; ～钱 also "称钱" have lots of money; be rich

趁火打劫 chènhuǒdǎjié　plunder a burning house; take advantage of sb's misfortune; fish in troubled waters

趁机 chènjī　seize a chance or an opportunity (to do sth)

趁热打铁 chènrèdǎtiě 〈喻〉strike while the iron is hot; make hay while the sun shines

趁势 chènshì make the best of an opportunity when it arises；～引导 take an opportunity to offer guidance

趁早 chènzǎo as soon as possible; at an early date; before it is late

谶 chèn 〈书〉augury (in the form of a prediction or an omen)；～语 prophecy believed to have been fulfilled

chēng

称(稱) chēng ❶ call; style；～孤道寡 look upon oneself as the supreme leader; assume the airs of a leader / ～得起是个英雄 deserve the title of hero ❷ name；～号 title; name; designation ❸ say; state；～便 find sth to be a great convenience / ～病 claim to be ill; plead illness / ～奇 speak admiringly of; regard as amazing ❹ 〈书〉praise; commend；～赏 commend; praise; speak highly of / ～誉 sing the praises of; praise; acclaim / ～叹不已 praise profusely / 令人～羡 admirable; enviable ❺ weigh; measure；～一～ weigh; measure

see also chèn

称霸 chēngbà play the bully; seek or maintain hegemony; dominate：称王～ act like an overlord; lord it over (sb); domineer

称道 chēngdào speak approvingly of; commend; praise：无足～ be not worthy of praise; be of little consequence

称呼 chēnghu ❶ call; address ❷ form of address

称颂 chēngsòng praise; extol; eulogize：大加～ heap praises upon; extol or commend profusely

称谓 chēngwèi appellation; form of address; title；～语 term of address; appellation

称兄道弟 chēngxiōng-dàodì call each other brother; be pals or cronies; be on intimate terms

称雄 chēngxióng exercise control over (a region, etc); be dominant；画坛 be the leading light in painting circles

称赞 chēngzàn *also* "称许" praise; acclaim; commend

蛏(蟶) chēng *also* "蛏子" 〈动物〉razor clam

撑(撐) chēng ❶ prop up; support：～起身子 prop oneself up ❷ punt (a boat) ❸ hold out; keep up：～场面 *also* "撑门面" keep up appearances / ～不住笑了 can't help laughing ❹ open; unfurl：～开雨伞 open an umbrella ❺ fill to the point of bursting：～得慌 〈喻〉be bursting with idle energy

撑持 chēngchí prop or shore up; sustain：～不了多久 can't hold out much longer

撑竿跳 chēnggāntiào 〈体〉pole jump or vault：～运动员 pole-vaulter

撑腰 chēngyāo support; back up; bolster：～打气 bolster and pep up / 背后有人～ have sb behind one

瞠 chēng 〈书〉stare：～目结舌 stare tongue-tied; be amazed and speechless / ～乎其后 lag helplessly behind / ～然若失 feel dumbfounded; be at a loss

chéng

成 chéng ❶ accomplish; achieve; succeed；～行 go on a trip; set out ❷ become; grow or turn into；～风 become a common practice; be all the rage / ～林 (of trees) grow into a wood / ～书 (of a book) be written; appear in book form / ～灾 cause a disaster / ～问题 be a problem; be open to question or doubt ❸ become fully developed or grown: ～虫〈动物〉imago; adult ❹ established; ready-made; existing: ～规 established practice; set rule / ～命 order already issued; decision already announced / ～说 accepted theory or formulation / ～药 patent medicine ❺ in considerable numbers or amounts: ～批 group by group; (in) batches / ～天 all day long; all the time / ～千～万 also "成千上万" thousands upon thousands; myriad / ～群结队 in large numbers; in crowds / ～双～对 in pairs ❻ OK; all right: ～不～? Yes or no? / 什么都～。Anything will do. ❼ able; capable: 你真～,竟然把他说通了。It was really smart of you to bring him around. ❽ one tenth; ten per cent; percentage: 七～新 70% new

成败 chéngbài　success or failure: ～在此一举。Success or failure hinges on this final effort.

成本 chéngběn　cost: ～核算 cost calculation / ～价格 cost price / ～效益 cost effectiveness

成材 chéngcái　❶ grow into useful timber: ～林 standing or mature timber ❷ also "成才" become a useful person; make the grade

成分 chéngfèn　also "成份" ❶ composition; element; ingredient ❷ one's class status, original or current; one's profession

成功 chénggōng　success: 不～,便成仁 fulfil one's mission or die a martyr's death; succeed or die

成果 chéngguǒ　achievement; fruit; result: ～累累 an abundance of results

成活 chénghuó　survive: ～率 survival rate

成绩 chéngjì　result; achievement; success: ～单 school report; report card

成家 chéngjiā　❶ (of a man) get married: ～立业 get married and start

one's career ❷ become a recognized authority

成见 chéngjiàn　preconceived idea; bias; prejudice: 抱有～ have a bias or prejudice (against sb); be prejudiced or biased

成交 chéngjiāo　strike a bargain; conclude a transaction; clinch a deal: ～额 volume of business

成就 chéngjiù　achievement; accomplishment; attainment: ～感 sense of achievement / ～大业 accomplish a great task

成立 chénglì　❶ establish; found; set up: ～大会 inaugural meeting ❷ (of a theory, etc) be tenable; hold water

成龙配套 chénglóng-pèitào　form a complete set; complete a system or chain

成名 chéngmíng　establish one's reputation; make a name for oneself: ～作 work that establishes one's reputation

成年 chéngnián　❶ grow up; come of age: 未～ under age; minor ❷ adult; grown-up: ～人 adult ❸ also "成年累月" year in and year out; all the year round

成品 chéngpǐn　end or finished product: 半～ semi-finished product / ～粮 processed grain

成气候 chéngqìhòu　be hopeful or promising; make the grade: 成不了气候 will not get anywhere

成器 chéngqì　grow up to be a useful person: 不～的人 good-for-nothing; ne'er-do-well

成亲 chéngqīn　also "成婚" get married

成全 chéngquán　help sb (achieve sth); facilitate (sth): ～好事 help bring about a happy event

成人 chéngrén　❶ grow up; become full-grown ❷ adult; grown-up: ～教育 adult education

成人之美 chéngrénzhīměi　help sb

fulfil his or her wish; help sb in achieving sth desirable

成色 chéngsè ❶ percentage of gold, etc; relative purity:～高 contain a high percentage (of gold, etc) ❷ quality:～好 of good quality

成事 chéngshì succeed; accomplish sth:～不足,败事有余 be not able to accomplish anything but quite capable of ruining it; never make but always break

成熟 chéngshú ripe; mature:～期 〈农〉mature period / 不～的意见 tentative opinion; immature view

成套 chéngtào form a complete set:～设备 complete set of equipment; plant

成为 chéngwéi become; turn into

成文 chéngwén ❶ existing writings ❷ written:～法〈法〉written or statute law

成效 chéngxiào effect; result:～显著 produce a marked effect; achieve remarkable success

成心 chéngxīn intentionally; deliberately; on purpose

成形 chéngxíng develop a definite form; take shape;〈医〉have a normal shape

成性 chéngxìng 〈贬〉by nature; become second nature:侵略～ aggressive by nature

成衣 chéngyī ❶ tailoring:～铺 tailor's (shop) ❷ ready-made clothes

成因 chéngyīn cause (of formation); contributing factor

成语 chéngyǔ 〈语言〉set phrase; idiom

成员 chéngyuán member:～国 member state

成则为王,败则为寇 chéngzéwéiwáng,bàizéwéikòu *also* "成者为王,败者为寇" the winner is the king, the loser a bandit; losers are always in the wrong; nothing succeeds like success

成长 chéngzhǎng ❶ grow up; grow to maturity ❷ 〈方〉development; growth:～率 growth rate

成竹在胸 chéngzhúzàixiōng *see* "胸有成竹" xiōngyǒuchéngzhú

丞

丞 chéng 〈旧〉assistant (officer):～相〈史〉chief minister

呈

呈 chéng ❶ assume (form, colour, etc); manifest:～现 present (a certain appearance); appear; emerge ❷ submit; present:～报 report to (one's superior, etc) in writing; submit /～文 official document submitted to a superior; memorial; petition /～递国书 present one's credentials

诚

诚 chéng ❶ sincere; honest:～朴 simple and honest / 以～待人 treat people with sincerity ❷〈书〉actually; really:～非易事 no easy task

诚惶诚恐 chénghuáng-chéngkǒng in fear and trepidation; filled with awe; awe-stricken

诚恳 chéngkěn sincere; earnest:～地接受 accept in all sincerity

诚然 chéngrán (used to introduce a concession) to be sure; admittedly:问题～不少,但总有办法解决。 True, there are quite a lot of problems, but we can always find solutions.

诚实 chéngshí honest; dependable:～可靠 honest and dependable

诚心 chéngxīn ❶ sincere desire; wholeheartedness:一片～ sincere desire or wish; (in all) sincerity ❷ sincerely; earnestly:～诚意 earnestly and sincerely; in all sincerity

诚信 chéngxìn faith; honesty:以～为本 take honesty as cardinal principle

诚意 chéngyì good faith; sincerity:缺乏～ lacking in sincerity

诚挚 chéngzhì sincere; cordial

承

承 chéng ❶ hold; bear; carry:～载能力 bearing or carrying capacity ❷ undertake; contract (to do a job); accept (orders, etc):～当 take up; take on; bear / ～运 undertake to transport or carry / ～转 forward (sth to sb) / ～欢膝下 attend on one's parents at home ❸〈套〉be indebted (to sb for a kindness):多～照顾 be greatly indebted to sb for his or her kindness ❹ continue; carry on

承办 chéngbàn undertake; take up; ～单位 responsible organization; institution in charge

承包 chéngbāo contract:～商 contractor / ～田 land contracted by a farmer (for cultivation) / ～责任制 system of contracted responsibility; contract system

承保 chéngbǎo undertake or accept insurance; insure:～范围 insurance coverage

承担 chéngdān undertake; bear; assume:～风险 run risks / ～后果 take the consequences / ～义务 commit oneself (to sb or sth); make a commitment

承继 chéngjì also "过继" adopt; be adopted

承接 chéngjiē ❶ continue; carry on:～上页 continued from the preceding page ❷ also "承揽" undertake; take in; accept:～来料加工 undertake to process materials supplied

承蒙 chéngméng〈书〉〈敬〉be granted a favour; be indebted (to sb for a kindness):～惠顾 be grateful to sb for his or her patronage

承诺 chéngnuò promise; undertake; commit oneself (to do sth):～书 letter of undertaking (L / U); letter of commitment

承平 chéngpíng〈书〉peaceful; tranquil:～岁月 times or years of peace

承认 chéngrèn admit; recognize; concede:～失败 concede defeat / ～罪行 plead guilty

承上启下 chéngshàng-qǐxià also "承上起下" form a connecting link between the preceding and the following; serve as a link between what goes before and what comes after

承受 chéngshòu ❶ bear; endure:～能力 ability to sustain or forbear; tolerance; affordability (of a consumer, etc) ❷ inherit (a legacy, etc)

承袭 chéngxí ❶ adopt; follow (a tradition, etc) ❷ inherit (a peerage, etc):～皇位 succeed to the throne

承先启后 chéngxiān-qǐhòu also "承前启后" inherit the past and usher in the future; serve as a link between past and future

承重 chéngzhòng (load-) bearing:～墙〈建筑〉(load-) bearing wall / ～三吨 carry no more than three tons

承租 chéngzū contract to lease (a shop, house, etc):～人 lessee; tenant / ～合同 contract for leasing; lease

城 chéng ❶ (city) wall:～堡 castle; citadel / ～关 area just outside a city gate / ～墙 city wall / ～厢 city proper and area outside its gates ❷ city:县～ county town / ～邦 city-state / ～池〈书〉city / ～隍 town or city god / ～区 city proper / ～镇 cities and towns / ～里人 townspeople; city dweller / ～管部门 city management department ❸ (used for a large and plentiful shop) town;美食～ food town

城府 chéngfǔ〈书〉subtlety or astuteness of mind; sophistication:～深 subtle and astute; sophisticated

城门 chéngmén city gate:～失火，殃及池鱼 when the city gate is on fire, the fish in the moat will suffer — fall victim to what others do; be a scapegoat for sb else's wrongdoing

城市 chéngshì town; city:～化 urbanization / ～布局 city layout / ～规划 urban or town planning / ～建设 urban construction / ～居民 city dwellers; urban population

城下之盟 chéngxiàzhīméng treaty concluded with the enemy outside the city wall; terms accepted under duress or pressure

城乡 chéngxiāng　urban and rural areas; town and country; city and countryside; ～ 差别 difference between town and country / ～结合部 area joining town and country

乘 chéng ❶ ride:～船 go by boat / ～警 train police / ～客 passenger / ～员 crew (member); passenger ❷ also "趁" avail oneself of; take advantage of; tap:～便 when there is a chance; at one's convenience; on the side / ～势 tap the momentum of sth;〈喻〉avail oneself of a favourable situation or an opportune moment / ～人不备 take sb by surprise / ～胜前进 advance on the crest of a victory; push on in the flush of victory ❸ multiply:～方〈数〉involution; power / ～号〈数〉multiplication sign / ～数〈数〉multiplier / 2～4 等于 8。Two by four is eight.

乘法 chéngfǎ　〈数〉multiplication;～表 multiplication table

乘风破浪 chéngfēng-pòlàng　ride the wind and cleave the waves;〈喻〉ride on the crest of a wave

乘机 chéngjī　seize an opportunity (to do sth)

乘凉 chéngliáng　enjoy the cool; relax in a cool place

乘人之危 chéngrénzhīwēi　take advantage of sb's precarious position; hit sb when he or she is down

乘务 chéngwù　service on trains, etc:～员 attendant on a train; steward or stewardess; conductor or conductress / ～组 crew (of a train or plane)

乘兴 chéngxìng　while one is in high spirits or in a happy mood:～而来,败兴而归 set out cheerfully and return disappointed

乘虚 chéngxū　take advantage of a weak point or an opening in an opponent's defence; act when sb is off guard:～而入 sneak in while people are off guard; break through at a weak point

盛 chéng ❶ fill; ladle:～器 vessel; container / ～汤 ladle out soup ❷ hold; contain:车厢能～150 人。The compartment can hold 150 people.

see also shèng

程 chéng ❶ order; procedure ❷ (leg of a) journey

程度 chéngdù　level; extent; degree:～不齐 in varying degrees / 在一定～上 to a certain extent or degree

程控 chéngkòng　(short for 程序控制) program control:～机床 program-controlled machine tool

程式 chéngshì　form; pattern; formula:～化 stylization; formulism / ～动作 stylized movements

程序 chéngxù ❶ procedure; order; sequence:～问题 point of order / ～性动议 procedural motion ❷〈信息〉program:编～ write a program / ～员 programmer / ～语言 program language

惩(懲) chéng ❶ punish; penalize:～办 also "惩处";"惩治" punish; penalize / ～戒 punish or discipline as a warning / ～恶劝善 punish evil-doers and encourage good works / ～一做百 punish one to warn a hundred; make an example of sb ❷〈书〉guard against; warn:～前毖后 (help people) learn from past mistakes to avoid future ones

惩罚 chéngfá　punish; penalize:免于～ exempt from punishment

澄 chéng ❶ (of water, etc) clear; transparent; limpid ❷ clear up; clarify

see also dèng

澄清 chéngqīng ❶ clear; bright; ～的溪水 transparent brook ❷ purify; clear up; clarify；～吏治 stamp out political corruption／～误会 clear up misunderstanding
see also dèngqīng

橙

橙 chéng ❶ orange；～汁 orange juice／～子 orange (fruit) ❷ orange (colour)：～红 orange red／～黄 orange

chěng

逞

逞 chěng ❶ show off; flaunt；～能 show off or parade one's skill or ability／～强 flaunt one's superiority; exhibit one's power／～威风 show off one's power; swagger about ❷ carry out (an evil design)；succeed (in a scheme)；～凶 act violently; go berserk／阴谋得～ succeed in a plot ❸ indulge; give free rein；～性 act on impulse; be wayward or reckless

骋

骋 chěng 〈书〉 ❶ gallop ❷ give free rein：～怀 enjoy oneself to one's heart's content／～目远望 scan distant horizons

chèng

秤(稱)

秤(稱) chèng balance; steelyard；～锤 *also* "秤砣" sliding weight of a steelyard／～杆 arm or beam of a steelyard／～盘 pan of a steelyard／～星 gradation marked on the beam of a steelyard

chī

吃(喫)

吃(喫) chī ❶ eat; take or have (a meal, etc.)；dine；～儿 *also* "吃食"〈口〉food; eats／～相 table manners／～药 take medicine／～不服 not be used to (certain food)／～不上 cannot afford to eat；

cannot get (sth to eat)／～不下 can eat no more; have no appetite (for sth)／～得开〈喻〉be popular; will work／～独食〈喻〉have sth all to oneself; monopolize sth／～馆子 eat at a restaurant; eat or dine out／～后悔药〈俗〉cry over spilt milk; repent only too late／～请受礼 accept gifts and invitations to dinner／～香的喝辣的〈俗〉enjoy tasty food and drinks; live in clover ❷ live off or on; scrounge off：～大户 dine on the rich guy／～老本 live off one's past gains; rest on one's laurels／～利息 live on interest ❸ absorb; soak up; take in：宣纸～墨。Rice paper absorbs ink. ❹ annihilate; wipe out; take (a chessman) ❺ endure; suffer; get：～败仗 suffer a defeat; be defeated／～得消 can endure, bear, or stand (sth)／～耳光 get a slap across the face; get a box on the ears／～黄牌〈体〉get a yellow card; be booked／～苦头 suffer; come to grief／～罪不起 cannot afford to take the blame／不～那一套 be not going to put up with that ❻ feel; experience; consume：～劲 strenuous

吃饱 chībǎo eat one's fill; be full；吃不饱 have not enough to eat；〈喻〉operate under capacity／～了撑的〈俗〉be restless from overeating — have too much energy for one's own good

吃闭门羹 chībìméngēng find the door closed on one — be denied a reception; fail to see sb when one calls on him or her

吃不了兜着走 chībuliǎodōuzhezǒu〈俗〉get more than one bargained for; be left holding the bag; land oneself in serious trouble

吃穿 chīchuān food and clothing：够吃够穿 have enough to eat and wear

吃醋 chīcù be jealous (of sb)：吃干醋 be unduly or vicariously jealous

吃大锅饭 chīdàguōfàn eat from the

same big pot—get the same pay regardless of one's work; practice egalitarianism

吃饭 chīfàn ❶ eat rice or a meal:吃白饭 eat rice alone (without anything to go with it) / 吃干饭 eat rice without working for it; be a parasite / 吃偏饭 *also* "吃偏食" eat better-than-average meals in the mess; enjoy special privilege or treatment / 吃闲饭 be a loafer; lead an idle life / ~现成饭 eat meals prepared by sb else; benefit from other people's labour ❷ live; make a living:靠天~ live at the mercy of nature

吃官司 chīguānsi be prosecuted or sued; be punished by law; be imprisoned

吃喝 chīhē eat and drink; wine and dine:~风 (unhealthy) practice of feasting at public expense / ~不分 share food and drink; be cronies

吃紧 chījǐn ❶ tense; critical:银根~。 Money is tight. ❷ important; essential

吃惊 chījīng be surprised, amazed or shocked; be taken aback:令人~ amazing

吃苦 chīkǔ bear hardships; suffer:~耐劳 bear hardship and hard work; be inured to hardship and toil

吃亏 chīkuī suffer losses; stand to lose; be at a disadvantage:吃哑巴亏 swallow a bitter pill in silence; have to keep one's grievances to oneself / 吃小亏占大便宜 take small losses for the sake of big gains; the best gain is to lose first / ~在于经验不足 suffer for lack of experience

吃里爬外 chīlǐ-páwài eat sb's food and cater to his enemy; live on one person while secretly serving another; betray one's own side

吃力 chīlì requiring much effort; laborious; strenuous:~不讨好 spare no pains but get no pains; do a thankless job

吃奶 chīnǎi (of a baby) suck at its mother's breast; take milk from its mother:~的婴儿 sucking baby / 使出~的力气 use all one's strength; strain every nerve; make every effort

吃软不吃硬 chīruǎnbùchīyìng be susceptible to persuasion rather than coercion; yield to soft rather than hard tactics

吃水 chīshuǐ ❶ 〈方〉 drinking water ❷ absorb water; be absorbent ❸ draught; draft:~两米 have a draught of two metres

吃素 chīsù ❶ be a vegetarian; be on a vegetarian diet ❷ (usu used in the negative) not killing; not effective (as a weapon):小心点,他的拳头可不是~的。 Mind you, his fists are not for decorative purposes.

吃透 chītòu understand thoroughly; have a thorough grasp of:吃不透 fail to understand correctly or thoroughly; cannot quite see; be not sure

吃香 chīxiāng 〈口〉 be in great demand; be much sought after; be popular

吃小灶 chīxiǎozào eat at a small mess where better food is prepared—enjoy special privilege:给困难学生~ give problem students special tutorials

吃一堑,长一智 chīyīqiàn, zhǎngyīzhì 〈谚〉 a fall into the pit, a gain in your wit

吃斋 chīzhāi abstain from meat and fish; be a vegetarian:吃长斋 (of a Buddhist, etc) be on a vegetarian diet all the year round

吃着碗里看着锅里 chīzhewǎnlǐkànzheguōlǐ 〈俗〉 keep looking at the pot while eating from one's bowl—never be contented with what one has but always covet more; be insatiably greedy

吃重 chīzhòng ❶ heavy (responsibility); arduous (task); strenuous ❷ (loading) capacity；～5 吨 have a loading capacity of five tons

哧 chī 〈象声〉 *sound of giggling or tearing*：～～地笑 titter；giggle

哧溜 chīliū *also* "嗤溜"〈象声〉 *sound of slipping or sliding*：～一下滑倒 slip and fall with a thump

嗒 chī 〈书〉 beat with a whip，etc；flog

嗤 chī sneer；～笑 jeer or laugh at／～之以鼻 give a snort of contempt；look down one's nose at；despise

痴(癡) chī ❶ silly；idiotic；stupid；～傻 feebleminded；idiotic ❷ be infatuated or crazy；～狂 infatuation；obsession／～梦 daydream；illusion／～醉 fascinated (as if drunk)；infatuated；spellbound／～男怨女 pining lovers (usu those who for some reason cannot get married)

痴呆 chīdāi silly；idiotic；deranged：～症〈医〉 dementia／儿童 mentally retarded children

痴迷 chīmí infatuated；obsessed；crazy：～不悟 be too infatuated or obsessed to shake free／～于声色 wallow in sensual pleasure

痴情 chīqíng deep passionate love；sentimental attachment or longing；obsession：～女子 foolishly or mawkishly sentimental girl；infatuated girl

痴人 chīrén idiot；fool：～说梦 idiot's daydream；idiotic nonsense

痴想 chīxiǎng ❶ be lost in thought or reverie ❷ wishful thinking；daydreaming；illusion

痴心 chīxīn infatuation；obsession；adoring love：～妄想 illusion；wishful thinking；daydreaming

魑 chī

魑魅魍魉 chīmèi-wǎngliǎng 〈书〉 demons and monsters；evil people of every description

chí

池 chí ❶ pond；pool：～塘 pond／～盐 lake salt／～沼 large pool or pond／～子 pond；pool；pool in a bathhouse ❷ place that resembles a pool：～汤 pool in a bathhouse；bath／～浴 bath in a common bathing pool ❸ 〈书〉 moat：城～ city

弛 chí 〈书〉 loosen；relax；slacken

驰 chí ❶ gallop；rush (to do sth)；(of one's thoughts，etc) reach or go out to：～骋 gallop；fight bravely (in battle)；play a prominent and active role／～念 think about (people far away)；concern oneself with (distant events)／～援 rush to the rescue／～目远眺 look far into the distance；look as far as the eye can see ❷ promulgate；spread：～名 (be) well known；famous；renowned

迟(遲) chí ❶ slow；tardy：～缓 slow；tardy；sluggish／～～不表态 be slow or reluctant to commit oneself ❷ late；delayed；belated：～到 be late (for sth)／～暮 dusk；evening；old age／～延 delay；procrastinate；retard／～早 sooner or later

迟钝 chídùn slow (-witted)；obtuse：思想～ be slow in thinking；think slowly

迟疑 chíyí be indecisive；hesitate：～不决 remain undecided；hesitate irresolutely

迟滞 chízhì ❶ slow；sluggish；stagnant ❷ dull；slow；listless：目光～ dull expression；glazed eyes ❸ slow down；hold up：～至今 have been delayed to the present

持 chí ❶ hold；grasp：～笔 hold or wield a pen／～股公司〈经〉

holding company / ～论公允 hold a fair and reasonable view; be fair in judgement or criticism / ～之有故 be well-grounded in one's views; hold valid arguments / ～不同政见 be a dissident / ～敌对态度 take or adopt a hostile attitude ❷ hold onto; uphold; maintain ❸ manage; run; handle: ～家 manage household affairs; keep house / ～身 conduct oneself

持久 chíjiǔ　lasting; enduring; protracted: ～力 staying power; endurance; stamina / ～战 protracted warfare / ～和平 lasting peace

持平 chípíng ❶ unbiased; fair; impartial: ～之论 unbiased view ❷ even; balanced; equal: 物价～。 Prices remain steady.

持续 chíxù　continuous; sustained; steady: ～努力 (make) sustained efforts / ～增长 sustainable growth

持之以恒 chízhīyǐhéng　pursue a matter with determination; persevere; persist

持重 chízhòng　prudent; circumspect; discreet: 为人～ be the soul of discretion

匙

chí spoon: 茶～ teaspoon

踟

chí

踟蹰 chíchú　also "踟躇" 〈书〉 hesitate; waver: ～不前 hesitate to move forward; stand still irresolutely

chǐ

尺

chǐ ❶ *chi*, unit of length equalling one third of a metre ❷ rule or ruler for measuring or drawing; instrument like a ruler: 钢～ steel rule

尺寸 chǐcùn ❶ (small or little as) *chi* or *cun*; jot; iota: 无～之功 without the least contribution ❷ (chǐcun) measurement; dimension; size: 量～

take (sb's) measurements

尺牍 chǐdú　correspondence; letters; letter-writing

尺度 chǐdù　yardstick; measure; standard: 放宽～ lower a standard; stretch a criterion

尺短寸长 chǐduǎn-cùncháng （short for 尺有所短，寸有所长） a foot may prove short while an inch may prove long — everyone has his strong and weak points

尺码 chǐmǎ ❶ (of shoes, etc) size ❷ 〈口〉 standard; yardstick

呎

chǐ　(now written as 英尺) foot (as a measurement of length)

齿（齒）

chǐ ❶ tooth: ～龈 (tooth) gum / ～间留香 (of food, etc) leave an unforgettable taste in one's mouth / 令人～冷 〈书〉 lay oneself open to scorn ❷ tooth-like part of an object; tooth: 梳～儿 teeth of a comb ❸ 〈书〉 age; 同～ of the same age ❹ 〈书〉 mention; speak of: 不足～数 not worth mentioning

齿轮 chǐlún　gear; toothed or cog wheel: ～箱 gear box / ～传动 gear drive

侈

chí 〈书〉 ❶ wasteful; extravagant ❷ exaggerate: ～谈 talk glibly about; prate or prattle about; speak high-sounding words

耻（恥）

chǐ　shame; humiliation; ignominy: ～辱 shame; disgrace; humiliation / ～笑 sneer at; mock / ～于人后 be ashamed to lag behind

褫

chǐ 〈书〉 dismiss; divest: ～夺政治权利 deprive (sb) of his or her political rights

chì

叱

chì 〈书〉 denounce loudly; roundly rebuke; shout at: ～呵 also "呵叱" shout or bawl at; yell / ～

令 shout an order (at sb); order loudly / ～责 scold; upbraid; rebuke / ～问 interrogate angrily; question loudly / ～咤风云 shaking heaven and earth; enormously powerful; all-conquering

斥 chì ❶ scold; reprimand; denounce; ～责 reprimand; rebuke; denounce / ～为邪说 denounce as heresy ❷ repel; exclude; dismiss; ～力 〈理〉 repulsion / ～退〈旧〉 dismiss; expel ❸ 〈书〉 pay; spend; ～资 pay the expenses; spend money

赤 chì ❶ a kind of red slightly lighter than vermilion; red; ～潮 *also* "红潮" red tide / ～红 crimson; flushed / ～陶 terracotta / ～小豆 red or adzuki bean ❷ revolutionary; Communist; ～色政权 Red power; revolutionary regime ❸ loyal; devoted; pure; ～诚 *also* "赤忱" absolute sincerity / ～金 pure or solid gold ❹ bare; ～背 naked to the waist; barebacked / ～脚 bare-footed; barefoot / ～裸 naked; totally unsheltered / ～贫 extreme or dire poverty; destitution / ～条条 stark naked / ～身露体 without a stitch on; stark naked / ～手空拳 barehanded; unarmed; with bare fists ❺ empty; ～地千里 vast expanse of barren land; scene of utter desolation

赤膊 chìbó　be naked to the waist; 打～ be stripped to the waist; barebacked / ～上阵 go into action stripped to the waist; 〈贬〉 throw away all disguise and come out into the open

赤胆忠心 chìdǎn-zhōngxīn　absolute loyalty; utter devotion; complete dedication

赤道 chìdào　equator; ～洋流 equatorial current / ～无风带 doldrums

赤裸裸 chìluǒluǒ ❶ naked; 全身～的 stark naked ❷ 〈喻〉 naked; undisguised; open; ～的强盗逻辑 out-and-out gangster logic

赤子 chìzǐ　〈书〉 newborn baby; 海外～ overseas compatriot / ～之心 complete innocence; unquestioning trust

赤字 chìzì　deficit; red ink; 出现～ run into red ink; result in a deficit / ～预算 deficit budget or budgeting

饬 chì ❶ 〈书〉 put in order; readjust; rectify ❷ (of higher authorities) order: ～令遵行 order sb to conform (with the rules, etc)

炽(熾) chì burning; flaming; ablaze; ～烈 flaming; blazing; fierce / ～情 passion; ardent emotion / ～热 white-hot; ardent; fervent

翅 chì ❶ (usu 翅膀) wing; wing-like object or part of an object; 鸡～ chicken wings ❷ shark's fin; ～席 shark's fin banquet

敕(勅) chì imperial edict; ～建 build by imperial edict / ～令 (issue an) imperial edict / ～命 decree by imperial edict

chōng

冲(❶❷衝) chōng ❶ thoroughfare; important place; ～要 strategically important (place); 〈喻〉 key (official) position ❷ charge; rush; clash; offend (a senior, deity, etc) / ～力 impulsive force; thrust; momentum ❸ pour (boiling) water on; ～茶 make tea / ～服 take (medicine) after mixing with water, etc / ～剂 〈中药〉 instant herbal mixture ❹ rinse; wash away; flush; ～垮 *also* "冲塌" (of floodwater, etc) cause to collapse; burst; break down / ～散 break up; scatter; disperse / ～澡 take a shower ❺ offset; cancel out; ～账 write off an item when balancing the accounts; reverse an entry
see also chòng

冲冲 chōngchōng　*used as a suffix to indicate excitement*: 急～ in a tearing hurry

冲刺 chōngcì 〈体〉spurt; sprint: ~
速度 spurting speed

冲淡 chōngdàn dilute; water down;
weaken

冲动 chōngdòng ❶ impulse: 艺术~
artistic impulse ❷ get excited; be impetuous; act rashly

冲锋 chōngfēng charge; assault: ~号
bugle call (to charge) / ~枪 assault
rifle; sub-machine gun / ~陷阵 charge
ahead in battle; fight bravely (for a
cause, etc)

冲昏头脑 chōnghūntóunǎo turn sb's
head; be or get carried away: 胜利~be
dizzy with success

冲击 chōngjī ❶ (of waves, etc) lash;
beat against; (of soldiers, etc) assault
❷ impact; shock; challenge: ~波
shock or blast wave / ~力 force of impact / 受到新思想的~be challenged
by new ideas

冲积 chōngjī 〈地〉alluviation: ~平原
alluvial plain

冲浪 chōnglàng 〈体〉〈信息〉surf: ~
板 surfboard / 网上~surf the Internet

冲破 chōngpò break through;
breach: ~禁区 break into a forbidden
zone; 〈喻〉do sth regarded as out of
bounds

冲刷 chōngshuā wash down or off;
scour (a utensil, etc)

冲天 chōngtiān towering; soaring: 怒
气~be in a towering rage; fume with
anger

冲突 chōngtū conflict; clash; contradict: 前后~self-contradictory

冲洗 chōngxǐ ❶ wash (down or
away); rinse ❷ develop (film)

冲撞 chōngzhuàng ❶ hit; strike;
ram ❷ offend; give offence to

充

充 chōng ❶ sufficient; full: ~盈
〈书〉plentiful; full (and round)
well-developed ❷ fill; stuff; ~塞 fill
up; cram / ~溢 be full to the brim;

overflow; be permeated ❸ serve or act
as: ~任 fill the post or / ❹ pretend to be; pose or pass
as; 以次~好 pass inferior stuff off as
quality goods

充斥 chōngchì flood; congest; be full
of: ~市场 flood the market / ~烟味
be full of smoke

充当 chōngdāng serve or act as; play
the part of: ~工具 be a pawn or tool;
act as a cat's paw

充电 chōngdiàn ❶ charge (a battery,
etc); recharge: ~器 battery charger ❷
〈喻〉retrain or enrich oneself

充耳不闻 chōng'ěrbùwén refuse to
hear; turn a deaf ear to

充分 chōngfèn full; ample; sufficient

充公 chōnggōng confiscate

充饥 chōngjī allay or appease one's
hunger

充满 chōngmǎn be full of; be filled or
imbued with

充沛 chōngpèi plentiful; abundant;
full

充其量 chōngqíliàng at most; at best

充实 chōngshí (make) substantial;
rich: 内容~rich in content / ~基层
strengthen organizations at the grass-
roots level

充数 chōngshù make up the number
or amount; serve as a stopgap; pass
muster

充血 chōngxuè congestion of blood:
~的眼睛 bloodshot eyes

充裕 chōngyù plentiful; abundant;
ample: 时间~plenty of time; ample
time

充足 chōngzú adequate; sufficient;
ample

忡

忡 chōng

忡忡 chōngchōng in an unhappy
mood; laden with anxiety

舂

舂 chōng pound; pestle: ~米 husk
rice with mortar and pestle

憧 chōng

憧憧 chōngchōng　flickering; moving: 烛影～ flickering shadows of candle-light

憧憬 chōngjǐng　long for; look forward to

chóng

虫(蟲) chóng ❶ insect; worm:～害 insect pest ❷〈贬〉used of certain sorts of people:懒～〈口〉lazybones; idler

虫牙 chóngyá (popular term for 龋齿) carious or decayed tooth

重 chóng ❶ repeat; duplicate:～样 of the same style or form ❷ again; once more:～播 rebroadcast or retransmit (a TV programme, etc); sow or seed (a field) for a second time /～犯 repeat (an error, etc); have a relapse /～提 bring up again; hark back (to sth) /～现 (of sth) reappear; reproduce (sth) /～演 restage; re-enact /～操旧业 resume one's old trade or job /～施故伎 play the same old trick; repeat a stock trick /～振军威 make an army's might felt once again /～打锣鼓另开张〈俗〉make a fresh start ❸〈量〉layer; tier: 多～关卡 numerous checkpoints

see also zhòng

重重 chóngchóng　layer upon layer; ring upon ring:～阻力 multiple obstacles

重蹈覆辙 chóngdǎofùzhé　follow the same old disastrous road or course; meet with the same fate

重叠 chóngdié　one on top of another; overlapping:机构～ overlapping organizations

重返 chóngfǎn　return (to); go back (to)

重逢 chóngféng　meet again; have a reunion; reunite

重复 chóngfù　repeat; duplicate:～税 double taxation /～建设 build redundant projects; duplicate similar projects

重婚 chónghūn　〈法〉bigamy

重见天日 chóngjiàntiānrì　see the light of day again; be delivered from oppression or persecution

重起炉灶 chóngqǐlúzào　set up a new stove or kitchen — start afresh; begin all over again

重申 chóngshēn　reaffirm; reiterate

重孙 chóngsūn　great-grandson

重孙女 chóngsūnnǚ　great-granddaughter

重弹老调 chóngtánlǎodiào　harp on the same string; sing the same old tune; repeat a platitude

重温 chóngwēn　review; relive:～旧梦 revive an old dream; relive an old experience

重新 chóngxīn　again; once more; afresh:～上台 regain power /～做人 begin a new life; turn over a new leaf

重修旧好 chóngxiūjiùhǎo　also "重归于好" renew cordial relations; become reconciled; bury the hatchet

重阳 Chóngyáng　also "重九" Double Ninth Festival (9th day of the 9th lunar month)

重洋 chóngyáng　seas and oceans:远渡～ travel across the oceans

重整旗鼓 chóngzhěngqígǔ　also "重振旗鼓" rally one's forces after a defeat; start all over again

崇 chóng ❶ high; lofty; sublime:～高 lofty; sublime; noble /～山峻岭 high mountains and lofty ridges ❷ esteem; worship; respect:～拜 worship; adore; admire /～敬 esteem; respect; revere /～尚 uphold; advocate /～信 believe in (a religion); trust (a person) /～洋媚外 worship things foreign and fawn on foreigners

chǒng

宠(寵) chǒng favour; dote on; indulge; ~ 爱 make a pet of; dote on / ~ 儿 favourite; pet; darling / ~ 物 pet / ~ 信 〈贬〉 cherish excessive fondness for and place undue trust in / ~ 辱不惊 keep one's head cool whether bestowed with favour or subjected to humiliation; be neither carried away by success nor upset by failure / 这孩子给 ~ 坏了。The child is spoiled.

chòng

冲(衝) chòng ❶ vigorous; blunt; (of smell) strong; ~ 劲儿 drive and vigour / 说话 ~ speak bluntly ❷ 〈口〉 facing; towards; ~ 人笑了笑 smile to sb ❸ 〈口〉 on the strength or basis of; because of; ~ 你的面子 out of respect for you ❹ 〈机〉 punching; ~ 床 punch (press); punching machine

see also chōng

铳 chòng blunderbuss; shotgun; 鸟 ~ fowling piece

chōu

抽 chōu ❶ take out (from sth); take a part from a whole; draw; ~ 税 levy or impose a tax; tax / ~ 屉 drawer / ~ 头 take a percentage or cut (of sth) / ~ 血 draw blood (for a test, etc) / ~ 逃资金 withdraw capital secretly or illegally / ~ 油烟机 grease pump; hood fan; range hood ❷ (of plants) put forth (buds, etc); ~ 穗 head; ear / ~ 芽 bud; sprout ❸ obtain by drawing; breathe; draw; ~ 支烟 smoke a cigarette / ~ 烟斗 draw or pull at a pipe; smoke a pipe ❹ shrink; ~ 缩 shrink; contract ❺ lash; whip; thrash; ~ 打 lash; whip; beat / ~ 球 〈体〉 drive

抽查 chōuchá (make a) selective examination; (make a) spot check or test; sample; ~ 合格 pass a spot check

抽搐 chōuchù 〈医〉 twitch; tic

抽调 chōudiào transfer personnel or material; second; 被 ~ 去基层工作 be transferred or seconded to a grassroots unit

抽风 chōufēng ❶ 〈医〉 convulsion ❷ do sth abnormal or perverse; be out of one's mind ❸ pump (in or out) air; ~ 机 air pump

抽奖 chōujiǎng draw lots (for prizes); draw a winning number (for lottery, etc); ~ 活动 prize-drawing event / 抽了个头奖 win first prize (in a sweepstake)

抽筋 chōujīn ❶ pull out a tendon; ~ 剥皮 skin sb and pull out his tendons; practise extremely cruel exploitation and oppression ❷ cramp; 腿 ~ 儿 have a cramp in the leg

抽空 chōukòng find time (to do sth); 抽不出空 have no time to spare

抽冷子 chōulěngzi *also* "瞅冷子" do sth when people are off guard

抽泣 chōuqì *also* "抽噎" sob

抽签 chōuqiān draw or cast lots; ~ 决定 decide by lot

抽身 chōushēn leave (one's work, etc); get away; 及早 ~ quit as soon as possible; get away at the first chance

抽水 chōushuǐ ❶ pump water; ~ 机 water pump / ~ 站 pumping station / ~ 马桶 flush toilet; water closet ❷ (of cloth) shrink

抽象 chōuxiàng abstract; general; vague; ~ 思维 abstract thought; abstraction

抽样 chōuyàng (of statistics) sample; sampling; ~ 调查 sample survey; sampling

chóu

仇(讐) chóu ❶ enemy; foe; ～敌 enemy; foe / ～人 *also* "仇家" (personal) enemy ❷ hatred; enmity; grudge; ～恨 hatred; enmity; hostility / ～杀 murder in revenge; kill in a feud / ～视 look upon with hostility; to regard as an enemy / ～深似海 entertain a hatred as great as the ocean

俦(儔) chóu 〈书〉❶ companion ❷ likes; peers

惆 chóu 〈书〉disappointed; aggrieved; ～怅 melancholy; disconsolate; sad

绸 chóu silk (fabric); ～子 silk fabric / ～缎 silks and satins
绸缪 chóumóu 〈书〉❶ sentimentally attached; 情意～ be deeply in love ❷ *see* "未雨绸缪" wèiyǔchóumóu

畴(疇) chóu 〈书〉❶ farmland ❷ kind; division
畴昔 chóuxī *also* "畴日" 〈书〉in former times; of yore

酬 chóu ❶ repay (a kindness); reward; ～劳 reward (sb for his or her service); recompense / ～谢 reward / 开业～宾 sales at the opening of a business; opening sales ❷ payment; remuneration; ～报 reward; recompense; remuneration / ～金 payment for service; monetary reward; remuneration ❸ social intercourse; socializing; ～对 respond; reply; retort / ～应 *also* "酬酢" socializing ❹ fulfil; realize; 壮志未～身先死 die without fulfilling one's noble aspirations
酬答 chóudá ❶ reward (sb for his or her kindness) ❷ *also* "酬和" respond with a poem or speech; 赋诗～ write a poem in response

稠 chóu thick; dense; ～密 dense; thick / ～人广众 big crowd or gathering; large audience

愁 chóu ❶ be worried or anxious; ～苦 anxiety; distress / ～闷 feel gloomy; be in low spirits / ～绪〈书〉gloomy mood / ～容满面 look deeply worried; have sorrow written all over one's face / 别～坏了身体。Don't let anxiety wear you down. ❷ melancholy; sadness; sorrow; 乡～ homesickness
愁肠 chóucháng pent-up feelings of sadness; ～百结 have anxiety gnawing at one's heart; be weighed down with anxiety / ～寸断 be eaten up with deep sorrow
愁眉 chóuméi knitted brows; worried look; ～不展 look downcast; knit one's brows / ～苦脸 have a worried look; look miserable

筹(籌) chóu ❶ (usu 筹码) chip; counter ❷ prepare; plan; raise; ～款 raise money or funds / ～算 calculate / ～组 prepare and form / ～资办学 raise funds for schools ❸ resource; way; means; ～略 tactics; strategy
筹办 chóubàn make preparations or arrangements (for sth)
筹备 chóubèi prepare; arrange; ～组 preparatory team; planning group
筹措 chóucuò *also* "筹集" raise (money or funds)
筹划 chóuhuà plan and prepare; ～有方 be good at planning
筹建 chóujiàn prepare to construct or establish; 开始～ begin preparations (for the construction of sth)

踌(躊) chóu
踌躇 chóuchú *also* "踌蹰" ❶ hesitate; shilly-shally; ～不决 hesitating and irresolute; indecisive / ～不前 hesitate to move forward; be indecisive ❷〈书〉be self-satisfied; be filled with pride; ～满志 enormously proud of one's success; puffed up with pride

雠（讎）chóu ❶ compare texts; collate; text collation ❷ see "仇" chóu

chǒu

丑（❷❸醜）chǒu ❶ 2nd of the Earthly Branches see also "干支" gānzhī ❷ ugly; unsightly; hideous; ～恶 ugly; hideous; wicked / ～化 discredit; smear; vilify / ～话 vulgar or coarse language; blunt words / ～陋 ugly; hideous / ～八怪〈口〉very ugly person; monster ❸ disgraceful; scandalous; unpleasant; ～剧 farce / ～事 disgraceful affair; scandal / ～闻 scandal / ～表功 brag shamelessly about one's deeds; claim an undeserved merit ❹〈戏〉clown; comedian; ～角 clown; buffoon; ignoble role

丑态 chǒutài ugly or ludicrous performance; buffoonery; ～百出 cut a despicable figure; put on an abominable show; reveal all one's hideous features

瞅 chǒu〈方〉look at; ～见 see; have or catch a glimpse (of sth or sb) / ～空儿 seek an opportunity; find time

chòu

臭 chòu ❶ smelly; foul; stinking; ～烘烘 foul; stinking / ～气冲天 stink to the sky ❷ disgusting; disgraceful; ～美 show off one's smartness; feel immensely pleased with oneself / 摆～架子 put on disgusting airs ❸ inferior; poor; bad; ～球〈口〉lousy pass or shot (in a ball game); rotten game

see also xiù

臭虫 chòuchóng bedbug

臭豆腐 chòudòufu strong-smelling fermented bean curd

臭骂 chòumà curse roundly; scold angrily; give a good dressing down

臭名 chòumíng bad reputation; notoriety; ～远扬 be notorious far and wide / ～昭著 also "臭名昭彰" of ill repute; notorious

臭味相投 chòuwèixiāngtóu〈贬〉be birds of a feather; be two of a kind

臭氧 chòuyǎng〈化〉ozone; ～层 ozone layer; ozonosphere / ～空洞 hole in the ozonosphere

chū

出（❿齣）chū ❶ go or come out; ～访 go abroad on an official visit; visit (foreign countries) / ～嫁 (of a woman) get married; marry / ～借 lend; loan / ～门 go or be out; be away from home; go on a journey / ～洋 go abroad / ～院 leave hospital; be released from hospital / ～走 also "出奔" (be forced to) leave; flee; run away / ～污泥而不染 emerge unsullied from the filth — remain undefiled in spite of general corruption ❷ come; arrive; ～操 drill; do exercises / ～道 embark on one's career; become known ❸ exceed; go beyond; ～轨 be derailed; go off the rails / ～〈响〉overstep the bounds / 不～三年 within three years ❹ issue; offer; pay (out); ～钱 offer or pay money / ～布告 post an announcement; put up a notice / ～点子 also "出主意" offer advice; make suggestions ❺ produce; yield; emerge; ～活 yield good results in work; be efficient / ～错 make mistakes; go wrong / ～毛病 go wrong; (of a machine, etc) be out of order; break down ❻ publish (a book, etc); ～榜 publish a list (of successful candidates, etc) ❼ put forth; vent; ～芽 sprout; germinate / ～疹子 have measles ❽ (usu 出饭) (of rice, etc) rise well (with cooking) ❾ (chu) *used after a verb to indicate direction or completion of an action*: 拿～证件 produce one's papers ❿〈量〉*used of drama, chapter in a romance, etc*: 一～戏 a play; an opera

出版 chūbǎn publish; come off the press: ～权 right of publication / ～社 publishing house / ～物 publication / ～者 publisher

出殡 chūbìn carry a coffin to the cemetery; hold a funeral procession

出兵 chūbīng dispatch or send troops

出差 chūchāi be away on official business; go on a business trip: ～费 allowance for a business trip

出产 chūchǎn produce; manufacture: ～丰富 rich in (agricultural) produce

出厂 chūchǎng (of products) leave the factory: ～价 producer or ex-factory price / ～日期 date of production or manufacture

出场 chūchǎng come on the stage; appear on the scene; enter the arena or sports ground: ～费 appearance fee / ～名单 list of players for a game

出超 chūchāo favourable balance of trade

出丑 chūchǒu make a fool of oneself; cut a sorry figure

出处 chūchù *also* "出典" source (of a quotation); chapter and verse (for an allusion)

出动 chūdòng set off; go or send into action; dispatch

出尔反尔 chū'ěr-fǎn'ěr go back on one's word; contradict oneself

出发 chūfā ❶ set off; start (off); leave ❷ start or proceed from: 从全局～ (proceed) from the overall interests (of a group) / ～点 intention; purpose; point of departure

出风头 chūfēngtou seek the limelight; be in the limelight; get a lot of publicity

出格 chūgé *also* "出圈儿" exceed what is proper; overstep the bounds; go too far

出国 chūguó go abroad: ～热 craze for going abroad / ～访问 visit foreign countries

出海 chūhǎi put (out) to sea: ～捕鱼 go fishing on the sea

出汗 chūhàn sweat; perspire: 出了一身汗 break into a sweat; sweat all over

出乎意料 chūhūyìliào unexpected; unforeseen; contrary to one's expectations: ～的快 sooner or faster than expected

出击 chūjī launch an attack; hit or strike out; make a sally

出家 chūjiā become a monk or nun: ～人 Buddhist or Taoist priest; monk; nun

出境 chūjìng leave the country or a certain district, etc; exit: ～签证 exit visa

出局 chūjú ❶ (in cricket) bowl out; (in baseball or soft ball) strike out or be put out ❷ be eliminated (from the next round of games, or from a competitive market)

出具 chūjù write; issue: ～证明 issue a certificate

出口 chūkǒu ❶ speak; utter: ～伤人 speak bitingly / ～成章. Words flow from one's mouth as from the pen of a master. ❷ export: ～商 exporter / ～补贴 export subsidy / ～贸易 export trade / ～商品 export commodities or goods / ～退税 tax refund or rebate on exports ❸ exit; way out

出来 chūlái ❶ come or go out ❷ appear; emerge ❸ (chulai) *used after certain verbs to indicate* a) *direction of motion from inside*: 从兜里拿～ produce from one's pocket b) *completion of an action*: 把计划订～ work out a plan c) *change from a hidden or ambiguous state to certainty*: 打听～ find out

出类拔萃 chūlèi-bácuì stand out from one's fellows; be out of the ordinary: ～的人物 outstanding figure; the best and the brightest

出力 chūlì put forth one's strength; exert oneself; make efforts

出笼 chūlóng be just out of the steamer; 〈贬〉come out into the open; appear

出路 chūlù way out; outlet

出马 chūmǎ go into action; take charge: 亲自～ take personal charge (of sth); attend personally to sth)

出卖 chūmài ❶ see "出售" ❷ sell out; betray; barter away (principles, etc)

出面 chūmiàn act in a given capacity or on behalf of an organization: 以个人名义～ appear in a personal capacity; act in one's own name

出名 chūmíng ❶ famous; well-known; celebrated ❷ use the name of; lend one's name (to an occasion or enterprise)

出没 chūmò appear and disappear; haunt: 有老虎～ haunted by tigers

出谋划策 chūmóu-huàcè give (evil) counsel; make (evil) designs: 背后～ plot behind the scenes

出纳 chūnà ❶ receive and pay out (money, etc); receive and lend (books, etc) ❷ also "出纳员" cashier; teller

出品 chūpǐn produce; manufacture; make: ～人 producer / 本地的～ local product

出其不意 chūqíbùyì take sb by surprise; catch sb unawares or off guard

出奇 chūqí unusually; extraordinarily: 冷得～ exceedingly cold

出奇制胜 chūqízhìshèng win by making a surprise move; make a surprise attack

出气 chūqì vent one's spleen; give

vent to one's anger; take it out (on sb): ～筒 (方) person on whom to vent one's anger; punching bag

出勤 chūqín turn out for work: ～率 (rate of) attendance / 出全勤 never miss a day of work

出去 chūqù ❶ go or get out: ～透透气 go out for a breath of air ❷ (chuqu) *used after a verb to indicate outward movement*: 从屋里溜～ sneak out of a room

出让 chūràng sell articles of one's own (usu not for profit or as a business)

出人头地 chūréntóudì rise head and shoulders above others; stand out among one's fellows; become outstanding

出人意表 chūrényìbiǎo *also* "出人意料" go beyond all expectations; come as a surprise

出任 chūrèn take up the post of

出入 chūrù ❶ come in and go out: ～证 pass (identifying a staff member, etc) ❷ discrepancy; divergence; difference: 有～ not tally (with sth)

出色 chūsè outstanding; remarkable; splendid

出山 chūshān leave a hilly region; 〈喻〉enter politics as a government official; (leave some other work and) take up a post or some task

出身 chūshēn family background; class origin; previous experience or occupation

出神 chūshén be spellbound; be lost in thought: 看得～ watch spellbound

出神入化 chūshén-rùhuà reach the height or acme of perfection: ～的画笔 superb brushwork

出生 chūshēng be born: ～地 birthplace / ～率 birthrate / ～证 birth certificate

出生入死 chūshēng-rùsǐ go through fire and water; brave untold dangers

出师 chūshī ❶ also "出徒" finish one's apprenticeship ❷ 〈书〉launch a campaign：～不利 meet with initial setbacks; get off to a bad start

出示 chūshì show; produce：～黄牌〈体〉produce a yellow card

出世 chūshì ❶ come into the world; come into being or existence; be born ❷ renounce human society; stand aloof from the mortal world：～思想 otherworldly thoughts

出事 chūshì meet with a mishap; have an accident：飞机～ air crash

出手 chūshǒu ❶ get (hoarded goods, etc) off one's hands; dispose of; sell ❷ produce; offer：～大方 spend money liberally; be generous ❸ skill displayed in making opening moves：～不凡 make masterly opening moves（in *wushu*, etc）❹ begin to strike; come to blows：该～时就～。Strike when you must.

出售 chūshòu offer for sale; sell：汽车～。Car for sale.

出台 chūtái appear on the stage; make a debut; (of a programme, etc) become or make public：～亮相 strike a pose on the stage; be publicized

出庭 chūtíng appear in court; enter an appearance：～辩护 defend a case in court

出头 chūtóu ❶ extricate oneself from miserable circumstances：～之日(have) one's day ❷ appear or act (on behalf of sb)；take the lead：～露面 make a public appearance; be in the limelight ❸ a little over; odd：一百～ one hundred odd

出土 chūtǔ ❶ earth; excavate ❷ (of plants) come up out of the ground

出席 chūxí attend; be present：～人数 number of persons present; attendance

出息 chūxi promise; prospects; future：有～的青年 promising youth

出现 chūxiàn appear; arise; emerge

出线 chūxiàn 〈体〉become qualified

for the next round of competition：～权 qualification (for the next round)

出血 chūxiě ❶ 〈医〉haemorrhage; bleeding ❷ 〈方〉pay or cough up (money)

出言 chūyán speak; remark：～不逊 make impertinent or rude remarks

出洋相 chūyángxiàng cut a sorry figure; make an exhibition of oneself

出以公心 chūyǐgōngxīn keep the public interest in mind; act without any selfish consideration

出于 chūyú stem from; be motivated or dictated by; proceed from：～无奈 have no alternative (but to do sth) /～自愿 of one's own free will

出诊 chūzhěn (of a doctor) visit a patient at home; pay a home or house visit：～费 house visit charge; fee for a house visit

出征 chūzhēng go on an expedition; be sent to the front

出众 chūzhòng out of the common run; outstanding

出租 chūzū let; lease; rent or hire out：～车 taxi; cab; taxicab / 房屋～。House to let.

初 chū ❶ at the beginning of; in the early part of：～春 first month of spring; early spring /～叶 early years (of a century) / 清朝～年 in the early years of the Qing Dynasty ❷ first (in order); only just begun：～犯 first offender or offence /～稿 first draft /～恋 first love /～试 first try; preliminary examination /～战 first battle; prelude to major battle /～次见面 first meeting /～来乍到 newly arrived; new (to a job or place) ❸ elementary; rudimentary：～中 (short for 初级中学) junior secondary school /～学者 beginner /～等数学 elementary mathematics ❹ original：～衷 original intention

初步 chūbù tentative; initial; preliminary：～设想 tentative idea / ～繁荣昌盛 beginnings of prosperity

初出茅庐 chūchūmáolú　at the beginning of one's career; fledgling

初级 chūjí　primary; elementary; junior：～班 junior class; elementary course / ～产品 primary product / ～阶段 primary or preliminary stage / ～市场 primary market / ～人民法院 primary people's court

初露锋芒 chūlùfēngmáng　also "初露头角" show one's talent or ability for the first time; begin to distinguish oneself

初期 chūqī　initial stage; early days; 建国～(in the) early years of the People's Republic (of China)

初审 chūshěn　❶ preliminary check, examination or evaluation：～合格 pass the preliminary check ❷ preliminary or initial interrogation; first trial；〈法〉trial of first instance：～裁决 ruling of first instance / ～法院 trial court; court of first instance

初生牛犊不怕虎 chūshēngniúdúbùpàhǔ　〈俗〉newborn calves are not afraid of tigers — young people dare anything and fear nothing

chú

刍(芻) chú　❶〈书〉hay; fodder ❷〈谦〉my：～议 also "刍见" my (humble) opinion or suggestion

除 chú　❶ get rid of; eliminate; remove：～根 root out (weeds, etc); cure (a disease, etc) once and for all / ～害 get rid of a scourge; eliminate what is harmful / ～草剂 herbicide; weed-killer / ～恶务尽 one must be thorough in exterminating evil; evil must be rooted out ❷ except (for); in addition to ❸〈数〉divide：～法 division / ～号 division sign / ～数 divisor

除非 chúfēi　only when; only if;

unless：～他去，我才会去。I won't go unless he goes. ❷ see "除了❶"

除旧布新 chújiù-bùxīn　do away with the old, usher in the new; ring out the old, ring in the new

除了 chúle　❶ except (for)：～他我谁也不见。I'll see no one except him. ❷ besides; in addition to; apart from：获奖的～你还有两位。There are two other winners in addition to yourself. ❸ (used in coordination with 就是) either… or：这些日子～刮风，就是下雨。It has been either windy or rainy these days.

除名 chúmíng　expel; dismiss：被学校～ be expelled from school; be sent down

除外 chúwài　except; not counting or including：每天开放，节日～ be open every day except on holidays

除夕 chúxī　New Year's Eve

厨(廚) chú　❶ kitchen：下～ work in the kitchen; serve as a cook / ～房 kitchen / ～具 kitchen utensils ❷ cook; chef：～师 cook; chef

锄(鋤) chú　❶ hoe：～头〈方〉hoe; pickaxe ❷ work with a hoe; hoe：～地 weed or loosen the soil with a hoe ❸ uproot; eliminate; wipe out：～奸 ferret out traitors and spies

雏(雛) chú　young (bird)：～儿〈口〉young bird; fledgling / ～妓 child prostitute / ～形 embryonic form; embryo；〈建筑〉model

橱(櫥) chú　cabinet; closet：～窗 show or shop window; showcase; glass-fronted billboard / ～柜 cupboard; sideboard

chǔ

处(處) chǔ　❶〈书〉dwell; be situated; be in a certain condition：地～海滨 be situated on the coast / ～变不惊 keep presence of mind in the face of disaster / ～于逆境 be in adverse circumstances ❷ get along (with sb):容易～ easy to get along with ❸ manage; handle; deal with:～事精明 sharp and shrewd in handling matters ❹ punish; sentence:免于～刑 exempt sb from punishment

see also chù

处罚 chǔfá　punish; penalize

处方 chǔfāng　❶ write out a prescription; prescribe:～权 right of prescription ❷ prescription; recipe:开～ write out a prescription / ～药 prescription medicine / 非～药 over-the-counter (OTC) medicine

处分 chǔfèn　take disciplinary action against; punish:行政～ administrative disciplinary measure

处境 chǔjìng　unfavourable situation; plight; predicament

处决 chǔjué　❶ *also* "处死" put to death; execute ❷ deal with and settle

处理 chǔlǐ　❶ handle; deal with; dispose of ❷ punish; penalize:～从宽 lenient in meting out punishment ❸ sell at reduced prices:～品 shopworn or substandard goods sold at reduced prices / ～价格 bargain price ❹ treat by a special process:热～ heat treatment / 数据～〈信息〉data processing

处女 chǔnǚ　virgin; maiden;〈喻〉first effort or experience;老～ old maid; spinster / ～地 virgin land or soil / ～航 maiden voyage or flight / ～林 virgin forest / ～膜〈生理〉hymen; maidenhead / ～作 maiden work; first effort

处世 chǔshì　conduct oneself in society:～哲学 philosophy of life / 善于～ versed in the ways of the world; worldly-wise

处暑 chǔshǔ　Limit of Heat, 14th seasonal division point　*see also* "节气" jiéqì

处心积虑 chǔxīn-jīlǜ　rack one's brains (to do sth evil); scheme incessantly; bend every effort

处之泰然 chǔzhītàirán　take things calmly; remain unruffled

处置 chǔzhì　❶ handle; deal with; dispose of:～失当 mishandle sth ❷ *also* "处治" punish

杵 chǔ　❶ pestle:～臼 mortar and pestle ❷ wooden club used to pound clothes in washing ❸ poke (with sth long and slender):～了个窟窿 poke a hole (in sth)

础(礎) chǔ　plinth:～润知雨 a damp plinth predicts rain—sign that sth is going to happen

储(儲) chǔ　❶ store up; keep in reserve:～户 depositor / ～油构造 oil-bearing structure ❷ heir to the throne:～君 crown prince

储备 chǔbèi　store for use; lay up; reserve:黄金～ gold reserve / ～粮食 store up grain / ～银行 reserve bank

储藏 chǔcáng　❶ save and preserve; store; keep:～室 storeroom; room for storage ❷ deposit

储存 chǔcún　lay in or up; store; stockpile:战略～ strategic stockpile / ～文件〈信息〉save a file

储量 chǔliàng　reserves:可采～ recoverable or workable reserves

储蓄 chǔxù　deposit; savings:～额 total savings deposits / ～所 branch savings bank / ～实名制 (regulation for) opening savings deposits in real names

楚 chǔ　❶〈书〉pang; suffering ❷ clear; neat ❸ (Chǔ) name for the region covering Hunan and Hubei, esp Hubei

楚楚 chǔchǔ　❶ clear; tidy; neat ❷ graceful; delicate:～动人 delicate and attractive; lovely

chù

处(處) chù　❶ place:～～ everywhere; in all re-

spects / 〜所 place; location / 短〜
weak point; weakness ❷ division; office; department; 〜长 head of a department or office; division chief
see also chǔ

怵 chù 〈书〉fear; fright; 〜目惊心
be extremely nervous, afraid, or
shocked at the sight of sth

绌 chù 〈书〉inadequate; insufficient

畜 chù (domestic) animal; livestock; 〜力 animal power / 〜肥
animal manure　*see also* xù

畜生 chùsheng ❶ domestic animals
❷〈粗〉beast; swine; 简直是个〜!
What a beast!

搐 chù (usu 搐动) twitch;〈医〉
tic

触(觸) chù ❶ touch; contact; hit; 〜电 get an
electric shock / 〜雷 run into or hit a
mine / 〜礁 strike a reef or rock;
〈喻〉run into difficulty; be snarled /
〜觉 tactile or tactual sensation;
sense of touch ❷ move (sb); stir up
(sb's feelings); 〜怒 make angry;
infuriate; enrage / 〜到痛处 touch a
sore spot; touch sb to the quick

触动 chùdòng ❶ touch (slightly) ❷
collide (against sth); offend; affect;〜
既得利益 affect vested interests ❸
move; touch; stir up

触发 chùfā detonate by contact; touch
or spark off; trigger; 〜战争 spark
(off) a war / 〜乡思 cause nostalgia

触犯 chùfàn offend; violate; infringe;
〜法律 break or violate the law / 〜尊
hurt sb's pride

触及 chùjí touch (on); 〜要害 hit
home / 〜敏感问题 touch on a sensitive issue

触角 chùjiǎo *also* "触须"〈动物〉an-
tenna; feeler; tentacle

触景生情 chùjǐngshēngqíng the sight
strikes a chord in one's heart; the scene

brings back past memories

触类旁通 chùlèipángtōng　grasp a
typical example and you will master the
whole category; comprehend by analogy

触摸 chùmō stroke; touch;〜屏 touch
screen

触目 chùmù ❶ meet the eye; 〜惊心
startling; shocking ❷ eye-catching;
conspicuous

憷 chù flinch; feel nervous or
timid;〜头 *also* "怵头"〈方〉
shrink from difficulties; feel nervous or
timid / 〜见生人 be shy of strangers

黜 chù 〈书〉remove or dismiss sb
from office; reject; 〜免 dismiss
(a government official)

矗 chù 〈书〉stand tall and upright; 〜立 stand tall and upright; tower (over sth)

chuāi

揣 chuāi hide or carry in one's
clothes; tuck; 〜在怀里 hide
(sth) in the bosom　*see also* chuǎi

chuǎi

揣 chuǎi 〈书〉estimate; conjecture; surmise; 〜测 guess; suppose; conjecture / 〜度 make a rough
estimate of; appraise; estimate / 〜摩
also "揣摸" try to figure out; elicit by
careful study　*see also* chuāi

chuài

踹 chuài ❶ kick (with sole and
heel) ❷ trample; tread; step in

chuān

川 chuān ❶ river; 〜流不息 flow
past in an endless stream ❷ flat

land；plain ❸ (Chuān) *short for* Sichuan (四川)：～菜 food of Sichuan flavour；Sichuan cuisine／～剧 Sichuan opera

川资 chuānzī　travelling expenses

穿 chuān ❶ pierce；penetrate；～透 pass through；penetrate／甲弹〈军〉armour-piercing shell，bullet or projectile／～堂风 draught ❷ *used after certain verbs to indicate thoroughness or completeness*：磨～ wear through (shoes，etc)；grind through ❸ go or pass through；thread one's way；cross：～越 pass or cut across／乱～马路 jaywalk ❹ wear；put or have on；be dressed in：～孝 be in mourning／～衣镜 full-length mirror／～靴戴帽 *also* "穿鞋戴帽" pad (writing or speech) with stereotypes，esp at the beginning and end of it／～一条裤子 *also* "穿连裆裤" gang up with sb；work cheek by jowl

穿插 chuānchā ❶ alternate；arrange or do by turns ❷ insert；weave in；interweave ❸ thrust deep into the enemy forces

穿戴 chuāndài ❶ *also* "穿着" dress；apparel ❷ dress oneself：～整齐 be neatly dressed；dress neatly

穿孔 chuānkǒng　bore or punch a hole；perforate：胃～〈医〉gastric perforation

穿山甲 chuānshānjiǎ　〈动物〉pangolin；〈中药〉pangolin scales

穿梭 chuānsuō　shuttle back and forth：～外交 shuttle diplomacy

穿小鞋 chuānxiǎoxié　have things made difficult for one；be put to trouble deliberately

穿凿 chuānzáo　give a far-fetched or strained interpretation；read too much meaning into：～附会 give strained interpretations and draw far-fetched analogies — distort (the original，etc)

穿针 chuānzhēn　thread a needle：～引线 thread a needle；〈喻〉serve as go-between

chuán

传(傳) chuán ❶ pass (on)；transmit；teach：～球〈体〉pass／～热 transmit or conduct heat／～艺 teach a skill or trade／～种 propagate；reproduce／～感器 sensor／～家宝 family heirloom；cherished heritage／～声筒 megaphone；〈喻〉one who parrots another／～经送宝 pass on one's valuable experience／～宗接代 have a son to carry on one's family name；continue the lineage ❷ spread；circulate：～布 circulate；spread／～单 leaflet；handbill；propaganda sheet／～道〈宗教〉preach；〈旧〉propagate the doctrines of ancient sages／～颂 be eulogized everywhere；be on everybody's lips／～扬 spread(from mouth to mouth)／～阅 pass around or circulate for perusal／～为佳话 become a favourite topic；be handed down as a popular tale ❸ convey；express：～情 convey one's amorous feelings ❹〈法〉summon：～唤 summon；subpoena／～审 summon to court／～讯 summon for interrogation or trial；subpoena *see also* zhuàn

传播 chuánbō　spread widely；publicize；disseminate：～业 communication industry／～病菌 spread germs

传达 chuándá ❶ convey；transmit；relay：～报告 relay a report／～命令 convey or transmit an order ❷ reception and registration of callers：～室 reception or receptionist's office；janitor's room ❸ janitor

传导 chuándǎo　conduction；transmission：～神经 conducting nerve

传递 chuándì　transmit；deliver；pass on

传动 chuándòng　〈机〉transmission；

drive;～装置 gearing; transmission

传话 chuánhuà ❶ pass on a message; send word ❷ gossip (behind sb's back)

传教 chuánjiào 〈宗教〉do missionary work;～士 missionary

传令 chuánlìng　transmit or dispatch orders;～兵 messenger / ～嘉奖 cite sb in a dispatch

传媒 chuánméi 〔 short for 传播媒介〕 ❶ (mass) media ❷ medium or vehicle (for transmitting a disease)

传票 chuánpiào ❶〈法〉summons; subpoena;下 ～ issue a summons ❷ voucher;现 金 收 入 ～ cash receipt voucher

传奇 chuánqí　legend; romance;～人物 legendary figure; legend

传染 chuánrǎn　infect; be contagious; ～病 infectious or contagious disease / ～源 source of infection; infectious agent

传人 chuánrén 〈书〉disciple; off-spring:龙 的 ～ descendants of the dragon — the Chinese

传神 chuánshén　vivid; lifelike;～之笔 vivid touch (in writing or painting)

传世 chuánshì　be handed down from generation to generation;～之作 enduring work

传授 chuánshòu　pass on; impart; teach

传说 chuánshuō ❶ pass from mouth to mouth; circulate; it is said ❷ legend; tradition

传送 chuánsòng　convey; transmit; pass;～带 conveyor belt

传统 chuántǒng　tradition;～观念 traditional idea

传闻 chuánwén ❶ it is said or ru-moured; they say ❷ also "传言" hear-say; rumour; talk

传真 chuánzhēn 〈通信〉facsimile; fax;发 ～ send a fax / ～机 fax (ma-chine)

船 chuán　ship; boat; ～舶 ships; shipping / ～舱 ship's hold; cabin / ～厂 shipyard; dockyard / ～籍 nationality of a ship; registry / ～票 steamer; boat or ship ticket / ～身 body of a ship; hull / ～头 stem; bow / ～尾 stern / ～坞 dock; shipyard / ～员（ship's）crew; seaman; sailor / ～闸 (ship) lock / ～长 captain; skipper / ～只 vessels; shipping

椽 chuán　rafter;～子 also "椽条" rafter / 如～之笔 also "椽笔" 〈敬〉writing brush as big as a rafter— (your) magnificent writing

chuǎn

舛 chuǎn 〈书〉❶ (usu 舛错) er-ror ❷ accident; mishap;命途多 ～ suffer many a setback during one's life

喘 chuǎn ❶ breathe heavily; gasp for breath; pant:～气 breathe (deeply); pant; take a breather / ～不过气来 be out of breath ❷ 〈医〉asthma

喘息 chuǎnxī ❶ pant; gasp for breath;～未定 before regaining one's breath; before one has a chance to catch one's breath ❷ breather; breathing spell; respite

chuàn

串 chuàn ❶ string together; con-spire; gang up;～供 act in collu-sion to make each other's confessions tally (so as to cover up sth) ❷〈量〉string; bunch; cluster:一 ～ 葡萄 a cluster of grapes / 一 ～ 钥匙 a bunch of keys ❸ get things mixed up:～行 (in reading or typing) skip a line; confuse two lines / ～味 (of food, etc) absorb the peculiar smell of sth else; be taint-ed in flavour / ～秧儿 cross-breed hybridize ❹ go about; rove; ～游 roam; wander; loaf / ～门儿（口）call (on sb); drop in / ～亲戚 go visiting one's relatives ❺ play a part (in a play); act: ～演主角 act or take the lead

串讲 chuànjiǎng ❶ explain a text (esp in classical Chinese) sentence by sentence ❷ give a summing-up of a text after going over it paragraph by paragraph

串联 chuànlián also "串连" establish ties; contact; ～几个人办店 contact several others and start running a store together

串通 chuàntōng gang up; collaborate; collude; ～一气 work hand in glove; act in close collaboration

钏 chuàn bracelet

chuāng

创（創） chuāng wound; trauma;～痕 scar / ～伤 wound; trauma / ～巨痛深 badly injured and in great pain; in deep distress from severe trauma　see also chuàng

疮（瘡） chuāng ❶ sore; skin ulcer ❷ wound; 刀～ sword wound

疮疤 chuāngbā ❶ scar ❷ sore or tender spot; 揭人～ touch sb's sore spot; touch sb on the raw

疮痍 chuāngyí also "创痍"〈书〉 wound; devastation; ～满目 a scene of devastation meets the eye everywhere

窗 chuāng window;～户 window; casement / ～花 paper-cut for window decoration / ～框 window frame / ～帘 curtain; drape / ～台 also "窗沿" windowsill / ～明几净 with bright windows and clean tables; bright and clean

窗口 chuāngkǒu ❶ window; 站在～ stand by the window ❷ wicket; window;售票～ ticket window ❸ sth like a window; ～行业 service trades, etc, bearing directly on people's life — showcase trades / 发挥～作用 serve as a medium (for sth)

chuáng

床（牀） chuáng ❶ bed; ～单 (bed) sheet / ～垫 mattress / ～铺 bed; bunk / ～位 bed; bunk; berth / ～罩 bedspread; counterpane / ～头柜 bedside cabinet; night stand / ～上用品 bedclothes ❷ sth shaped like a bed; 苗～ seedbed ❸〈量〉 used of sth that covers a bed; 一～被子 a quilt

chuǎng

闯 chuǎng ❶ rush; dash; charge; ～红灯 jump a red light;〈喻〉 violate law and discipline; break down a barrier or limit ❷ go around (for a living, etc); be busy running about; temper oneself thus; ～荡 venture out into the world; try to make a living away from home / ～将 daring general; path-breaker / ～劲 spirit of a pathbreaker; pioneering spirit / ～练 go out into society to temper oneself; get tempered in the world / ～江湖 make a living wandering from place to place; go (into the world) and hew out one's career / ～新路 break a new path; blaze a trail ❸ get into or bring on (sth undesirable); ～祸 also "闯乱子" get into trouble; bring on a disaster

chuàng

创（創） chuàng start; create; achieve (for the first time); ～见 original idea; creative thinking / ～举 pioneering work or undertaking / ～利 make or earn a profit / ～收 generate or increase income / 纪录 break a record; create or register a new record / ～新说 found a new theory　*see also* chuāng

创办 chuàngbàn　establish; found; set up:～人 founder

创汇 chuànghuì　earn foreign exchange profit (from exports, etc):～产品 foreign-exchange-earning product / ～工业 export-oriented industry

创建 chuàngjiàn　found; establish:～新的学派 found a new school of thought

创刊 chuàngkān　start publication:～号 first issue (of a newspaper, etc)

创立 chuànglì　found; originate:～一所大学 found a university

创牌子 chuàngpáizi　*also* "闯牌子" (of an enterprise, etc) produce and establish a brand name; work hard to establish a name for oneself

创始 chuàngshǐ　originate; initiate:～人 founder / 联合国的～国 founding member of the United Nations

创新 chuàngxīn　bring forth new ideas; blaze new trails; innovate:～产品 innovative product / ～精神 pioneering or creative spirit

创业 chuàngyè　start an undertaking; do pioneering work:～资金 starting or venture capital

创议 chuàngyì　propose; initiate:好的～ good proposal

创意 chuàngyì ❶ create a new concept of art; break fresh ground in imaginative art ❷ originality; creativity:颇有～ rather original in concept

创造 chuàngzào　create; produce; bring about:～力 creative power or ability / ～性 creativeness; creativity / ～奇迹 work wonders; create miracles

创作 chuàngzuò　write; produce; create:～方法 mode of writing or creation

怆（愴） chuàng 〈书〉sorrowful:～然 look sad; seem sorrowful

chuī

吹 chuī ❶ blow; puff; play (wind instruments):～鼓手 trumpeter; bugler; apologist / ～冷风 blow cold wind over; throw cold water on / ～胡子瞪眼 froth at the mouth and glare with rage; fume ❷ (of wind) blow:门～开了。The door blew open. ❸ 〈口〉boast; brag; flatter:～喇叭; 抬轿子 pile downright flattery (on sb) ❹ *also* "吹台" 〈口〉break up; fall through; fizzle out

吹打 chuīdǎ ❶ play wind and percussion instruments:～乐 ensemble of Chinese wind and percussion instruments / 吹吹打打 pipe and drum; make an ostentatious show ❷ (of a rainstorm) hit; beat

吹风 chuīfēng ❶ be in a draught; catch a chill ❷ dry (hair, etc) with a blower:～机 hair dryer; blower ❸ brief in advance; give a cue; tip off:～会 (background) briefing

吹灰之力 chuīhuīzhīlì　just a small effort:不费～ (of sth) be as easy as pie; be a walkover

吹毛求疵 chuīmáoqiúcī　find fault (with); cavil (at); be nitpicking

吹牛 chuīniú　*also* "吹牛皮" boast; brag; talk big:～拍马 boast and flatter

吹拍 chuīpāi　flatter; toady (upon sb):又吹又拍 do one's utmost to flatter / 吹吹拍拍, 拉拉扯扯 resort to flattery and touting

吹捧 chuīpěng　flatter; lavish praise on; extol:互相～ flatter each other; blow each other's trumpet

吹嘘 chuīxū　lavish praise on (sb); boast

吹奏 chuīzòu　play (wind instruments)：～乐 wind music / ～乐队 (wind) band

炊 chuī cook a meal：～具 cooking utensils / ～烟 smoke from kitchen chimneys / ～事员 cook

chuí

垂 chuí ❶ hang down；droop：～钓 fish with a hook and line：go angling / ～柳 also "垂杨柳" weeping willow / ～帘听政 (of an empress or mother queen) attend to court affairs from behind a screen ❷〈书〉used of kind action from senior or high-up people：～怜 show sympathy (for sb in misfortune) / ～青 look upon with favour ❸〈书〉hand down；bequeath to posterity；go down in history：～范后世 set a shining example for posterity ❹〈书〉approach；near；verge on：～暮 near sunset；approaching old age / ～老 approach old age：～～老矣 approach old age；get on in years

垂手 chuíshǒu ❶ with hands down；easily：～可得 (can) obtain sth without lifting a finger；(of sth) be extremely easy to obtain ❷ with the hands at one's side；respectfully

垂死 chuísǐ dying；moribund：～挣扎 put up a desperate struggle；be in one's death throes

垂头丧气 chuítóu-sàngqì crestfallen；dejected；downcast

垂危 chuíwēi critically ill；at one's last gasp：生命～ dying；at one's last gasp

垂涎 chuíxián drool (at sight of food, etc)；salivate；covet：～三尺 drool with envy；be greedy or covetous

垂直 chuízhí perpendicular；vertical：～起落 vertical take-off and landing (VTOL) / ～相交 meet at right angles

捶（搥） chuí beat (with a stick or fist)；thump；

pound：～打 strike；beat；thump / ～腿 pound sb's leg (as in massage) / ～胸顿足 thump one's chest and stamp one's feet (with sorrow, etc)

棰 chuí 〈书〉❶ short wooden club；cudgel ❷ beat with a cudgel；whip；flog ❸ see "棰" chuí

槌 chuí mallet：木～ mallet / 鼓儿 drumstick

锤（鎚） chuí ❶ hammer；sth shaped like a hammer：秤～ steelyard weight / ～子 hammer ❷ hammer into shape；knock with a hammer

锤炼 chuíliàn ❶ temper (oneself, etc) ❷ polish；refine (writing, etc)

chūn

春 chūn ❶ spring：～饼 spring pancake / ～耕 spring ploughing / ～节 Spring Festival；Chinese New Year's Day / ～卷 spring roll (stuffed and fried) / ～联 Spring Festival couplets (pasted on gateposts or door panels) / ～笋 spring bamboo shoots / ～游 spring outing or excursion / ～运 (passenger) transport during the Spring Festival period / ～小麦 spring wheat ❷ a year's time；year ❸ love；lust：～宫 also "春画" pornographic picture / ～药 aphrodisiac ❹ vital energy；life：着手成～ bring the dying back to life

春分 chūnfēn Vernal Equinox, 4th seasonal division point see also "节气" jiéqì

春风 chūnfēng ❶ spring breeze：～化雨 life-giving spring breeze and rain—salutary influence of education / ～得意 be flushed with success；ride on the crest of success ❷ kind and pleasant countenance：～满面 beaming with satisfaction；radiant with happiness

春光 chūnguāng sights and sounds of

spring; spring scenery：～明媚 enchanting scene of spring

春寒 chūnhán　cold spell in spring；倒～ unexpected cold spell in spring / ～料峭。There is a nip in the cold spring air.

春季 chūnjì　spring；springtime；spring season

春梦 chūnmèng　spring dream；pipe dream

春秋 chūnqiū　❶ spring and autumn；year：～衫 jacket for spring or autumn wear / 苦度～ eke out a living year in and year out ❷ age：～鼎盛 be in the prime of life / ～已高 be advanced in years ❸〈Chūnqiū〉*Spring and Autumn Annals*；Spring and Autumn Period（770 BC-476 BC）；～笔法 euphemistical critical approach in writing

春色 chūnsè　❶ spring scenery ❷ joyful look

春宵 chūnxiāo　spring night；〈喻〉night of sexual bliss：～苦短。Nights are always too short for lovers.

春意 chūnyì　❶ breath or hint of spring：～盎然。Spring is very much in the air. ❷ *also*"春心" ardent desire for love；lust

椿 chūn　〈植〉❶ *also*"香椿" Chinese toon ❷ *also*"臭椿" tree of heaven

chún

纯 chún　❶ pure；unmixed；pure and simple：～度 purity；pureness / ～金 pure gold / ～利 net profit / ～棉 pure cotton / ～真 pure；true；sincere / ～种 purebred / ～收入 net income / ～文学 belles-lettres；serious literature / ～属污蔑 sheer slander / 目标～一 singleness of purpose；single-mindedness ❷ skilful；well versed；fluent：技艺不～ not skilful enough

纯粹 chúncuì　❶ pure；unadulterated：～的人 a man of gold ❷（usu followed by 是）solely；purely：这～是虚构。This is sheer fabrication.

纯洁 chúnjié　❶ pure and honest；innocent ❷ purify：～组织 purify an organization

纯净 chúnjìng　❶ pure；clean ❷ purify：～水 purified water

纯朴 chúnpǔ　*see*"淳朴"chúnpǔ

纯熟 chúnshú　skilful；practised；well-versed：小提琴拉得～ play the violin with dexterous skill

纯正 chúnzhèng　❶ pure；perfect：发音～ flawless pronunciation ❷ pure and upright：思想～ pure and sound in mind；ideologically sound

唇（脣）chún　lip：下～ lower lip / ～膏 lipstick / ～裂 *also*"兔唇"harelip；cleft lip

唇齿 chúnchǐ　lips and teeth：～相依 be as interdependent as lips and teeth / 唇亡齿寒 if the lips are gone, the teeth will be exposed to the cold；share a common lot

唇枪舌剑 chúnqiāng-shéjiàn　cross verbal swords；have a battle of words or heated argument

唇舌 chúnshé　words；argument；persuasion：颇费～ take a lot of persuading

淳 chún　〈书〉pure；honest：～美 pure and sweet

淳厚 chúnhòu　*also*"醇厚"simple and honest；simple and plain；unsophisticated

淳朴 chúnpǔ　*also*"纯朴"honest and simple；unsophisticated

醇 chún　❶ strong alcoholic drink；liquor；〈化〉alcohol：～化 alcoholize；〈喻〉refine；perfect ❷〈书〉pure；unadulterated；mellow：～酒 mellow and pure wine / ～香 pure and fragrant

醇厚 chúnhòu　❶（of taste, etc）pleasantly strong；pure and unadulterated ❷ see "淳厚" chúnhòu

chǔn

蠢 chǔn ❶ stupid; foolish; clumsy: ~笨 awkward; stupid; clumsy / ~材 also 蠢货 (粗) blockhead; dunce; idiot / ~话 stupid remark; foolish words / ~驴 also 蠢猪 (粗) silly ass; idiot / ~头 stupid-looking ❷ 〈书〉 wriggle; squirm: ~动 squirm; create disturbances; stir up trouble / ~~欲动 ready to make trouble; be restless and about to create disturbances

chuō

戳 chuō ❶ jab; poke; stab: ~一指头 poke sb with a finger ❷ 〈方〉 get sprained or blunted: ~了手腕子 sprain one's wrist ❸ 〈方〉 stand (sth) on end; stand erect also "戳子" stamp; seal: 盖~ stamp (sth)

戳穿 chuōchuān ❶ pierce; puncture ❷ lay bare; expose: ~西洋景 strip off the camouflage; give away the show

戳脊梁骨 chuōjǐliánggǔ　criticize sb behind his or her back; point an accusing finger at sb

chuò

啜 chuò 〈书〉 ❶ sip; suck: ~茗 sip tea ❷ (usu 啜泣) sob

绰 chuò 〈书〉 ample; spacious: ~~有余 enough and to spare; more than sufficient; more than enough see also chāo

绰号 chuòhào　nickname

绰约 chuòyuē 〈书〉 (of a girl) graceful: ~多姿 graceful and lovely

辍 chuò stop; cease: ~笔 stop writing or painting / ~学 discontinue one's studies; drop out of school

cī

刺 cī 〈象声〉 tearing or spluttering sound: ~~地冒出火星 keep spattering sparks　see also cì

刺棱 cīlēng 〈象声〉 sound of quick movement: 猫~一下跑了。Whew! The cat scampered away.

刺溜 cīliū 〈象声〉 sound of slipping or sliding: 一条蛇~从脚下窜过。A snake slid past underfoot.

呲 cī give a talking-to or dressing-down; scold: 挨~ get a scolding

疵 cī flaw; defect; blemish: ~品 defective or sub-standard product

cí

词 cí ❶ wording; words; language: 推敲一句 weigh one's words / ~不达意 The words fail to convey the idea. ❷ cí, classical poetry written to given tunes: ~牌 name of a cí tune ❸ 〈语言〉 word; character: ~典 also "辞典" dictionary; lexicon / ~法 morphology / ~根 root; radical / ~类 part of speech / ~素 morpheme / ~条 entry (in a dictionary) / ~头 prefix / ~序 word order / ~尾 suffix / ~性 part of speech / ~义 meaning or sense of a word / ~语 words and expressions; terms / ~源 origin of a word; etymology / ~缀 affix / ~组 word group; phrase

词汇 cíhuì　vocabulary; words and phrases: 基本~ basic vocabulary or word-stock / ~表 word list; vocabulary

词令 cílíng　see "辞令" cílíng

词讼 císòng also "辞讼" legal case or action: 诉诸~ resort to law; take legal action

词藻 cízǎo　see "辞藻" cízǎo

词章 cízhāng　see "辞章" cízhāng

祠 cí ancestral or memorial temple：～堂 memorial hall；ancestral temple

瓷 cí porcelain；china：～瓶 porcelain vase or bottle；〈电〉insulator / ～器 porcelain；chinaware / ～釉 porcelain glaze / ～砖 ceramic or glazed tile

瓷实 císhí 〈方〉solid；firm：肌肉～ strong-muscled；muscular / 睡得～ sleep soundly

辞(辭) cí ❶ take leave：～别 bid farewell (to)；take one's leave (of)；say goodbye (to) / ～世 pass away；die / ～岁 bid farewell to the outgoing year；celebrate New Year's Eve / ～旧迎新 bid farewell to the old and usher in the new；ring out the old year and ring in the new ❷ resign；hand in one's resignation：～呈 (letter of) resignation / ～官 resign one's government post ❸ dismiss；discharge：～退 dismiss；discharge ❹ decline；resign；evade：～工 ask for a discharge；resign / ～谢 decline with thanks；politely decline / ～让 politely decline or yield / ～职 hand in one's resignation ❺ diction；phraseology：～典 dictionary；lexicon / ～书 dictionary and other reference books ❻ genre of classical Chinese literature

辞令 cílìng also "词令" language appropriate to the occasion：外交～ diplomatic language / 不擅～ not good at speech

辞行 cíxíng say goodbye before setting out on a journey：不及～ have no time for farewell calls

辞藻 cízǎo also "词藻" diction；rhetoric：玩弄～ juggle with words

辞章 cízhāng also "词章" ❶ poetry and prose ❷ art of writing：讲究～ be particular about one's writing

慈 cí ❶ love；affection；kindness：～爱 loving；affectionate；kind / ～母 loving mother / ～祥 kindly ❷ mother：～命 mother's wish or instruction

慈悲 cíbēi mercy；benevolence；pity：～为怀 have mercy at heart / ～心肠 merciful heart

慈善 císhàn charitable；benevolent；philanthropic：～家 philanthropist / ～机构 charitable or philanthropic institution / ～事业 charities

磁 cí ❶ magnetism：～场 〈理〉magnetic field / ～带 (magnetic) tape / ～化 〈理〉magnetize / ～卡 magnetic card / ～力 magnetic force / ～疗 magneto therapy / ～盘 magnetic disk / ～铁 also 磁石"；"吸铁石" magnet / ～头 (magnetic) head / ～性 〈理〉magnetism / ～悬浮列车 mag-lev (short for "magnetic levitation" or magnetic suspension train ❷ see "瓷" cí

雌 cí female：～蜂 female or queen bee / ～性 female / ～激素 estrogen / ～雄未决。Victory hangs in the balance.

cǐ

此 cǐ ❶ this：～后 after that；hereafter / ～刻 (at) this moment；at present / ～前 previously / ～路不通！Not a Through Road! or No Thoroughfare! ❷ now；then；here：～间 (around) here

此起彼伏 cǐqǐ-bǐfú also "此伏彼起" rise here and subside there；rise one after another：～的歌声 undulating sound of singing

此时 cǐshí this moment；right now：～此地 here and now / ～不走，更待何时? Go while the going is good.

此外 cǐwài besides；in addition；moreover

此一时，彼一时 cǐyīshí, bǐyīshí things are different from what they were; circumstances or times have changed

此致 cǐzhì (used at the end of a letter) here I wish to convey：～敬礼 with best regards

cì

次 cì ❶ order; sequence：～第 one after another ❷ second; next：sub-：～日 (the) next day / ～长 vice-minister; under-secretary / ～大陆 subcontinent / ～生林 (of forest) second growth; secondary forest / 不～于任何人 second to none ❸ shoddy; second-rate; inferior：～品 also "次货" inferior or substandard product; shoddy or defective stuff ❹ 〈量〉time; occasion：四～ four times / 13～列车 No 13 train

次数 cìshù number of times; frequency：～不多 only a few times; seldom

次序 cìxù order; sequence：～井然 in apple-pie order

次要 cìyào less important; secondary; minor：～角色 secondary or supporting role / ～矛盾 secondary or minor contradiction

伺 cì see also sì

伺候 cìhou wait upon; serve：难～ hard to please

刺 cì ❶ prick; pierce; stab：～骨 piercing (to the bones); biting / 胸部被～ be stabbed in the chest ❷ assassinate：遇～ be attacked by an assassin; be assassinated / ～客 assassin ❸ make roundabout or secret inquiries; spy; pry：～探情报 collect secret information; gather intelligence ❹ sting; thorn; splinter：他说话带～儿。There is a sting in his remark.

see also cī

刺刺不休 cìcìbùxiū rattle or babble on

刺刀 cìdāo bayonet：拼～ bayonet-fighting / 上～ fix bayonets

刺耳 cì'ěr grating on the ear; jarring; harsh

刺激 cìjī ❶ stimulate; give play or incentive to：～消费 stimulate consumption / ～景气政策 pump-priming or reflationary policy ❷ provoke; irritate; upset：很受～ feel terribly upset; be stung to the quick

刺杀 cìshā ❶ assassinate ❷ bayonet charge：练～ practise bayonet charge

刺猬 cìwei 〈动物〉hedgehog

刺绣 cìxiù embroider

刺眼 cìyǎn ❶ dazzling ❷ offensive to the eye

刺痒 cìyang 〈口〉itchy; itch：背上～ feel itchy in the back

赐 cì ❶ (of a senior person) confer; bestow：～予 also "赐与" grant; bestow ❷ 〈敬〉grant; favour：～教 care to enlighten me with your instructions; be so kind as to give me your advice

cōng

匆（怱） cōng hastily; hurriedly：～促 also "匆猝" hastily; in a hurry / 来去～～ come and go in haste; rush to and fro

匆忙 cōngmáng hastily; in a hurry; in haste：～作出反应 make a hasty response / 不必如此～! Don't be in such a rush!

葱 cōng ❶ onion; scallion：～花 chopped green scallion / ～头 onion ❷ green：～翠 fresh or lush green; luxuriantly green / ～绿 pale yellowish or lush green; verdant

聪（聰） cōng ❶ 〈书〉faculty of hearing：失～ become deaf ❷ bright; clever; intelligent：～明 bright; keen; sharp-witted / ～慧 also

"聪颖" bright; intelligent

聪明 cōngmíng clever; bright; intelligent; ~才智 intelligence and ability / ~伶俐 bright and clever / ~反被~误 〈俗〉clever people may be their own victims; cleverness may overreach itself

cóng

从（從） cóng ❶ follow: ~师 study under sb; serve one's apprenticeship with sb ❷ comply or conform with; obey: ~命 comply with sb's request; do sb's bidding / ~俗 conform with convention; follow the fashion; swim with the tide ❸ join; be engaged in: ~艺 be engaged in performing arts *also* "从戎" join the army; enlist / ~政 go into politics; embark on a political career ❹ act in a certain way: ~缓 put sth off till a later time; be in no hurry (to do sth) / ~宽处理 treat sb with leniency / ~轻发落 let sb off lightly ❺ follower; attendant ❻ secondary; accessory: ~犯 〈法〉accessory (criminal) / ~句 〈语言〉subordinate clause ❼ *indicating relationship between cousins, etc, of the same paternal grand father, great-grand father, etc*: ~兄弟 cousins (of the same clan) ❽ from; since; by: ~今以后 from now on; in the future / ~大路走来 come by the main road ❾ *used to emphasize a negative*: ~不迟到 be never late

从长计议 cóngchángjìyì consider a matter carefully (before making a decision); (of sth) need further consideration or thought

从此 cóngcǐ from now or then on; henceforth; thereupon

从……到…… cóng…dào… from… to… 从古到今 from ancient times to the present / 从南到北 from the south to the north

从而 cóng'ér 〈连〉thus; thereby

从简 cóngjiǎn act according to the principle of simplicity: 婚事~ hold a wedding in a modest way / 一切~ dispense with all unnecessary formalities

从来 cónglái always; at all times; all along

从略 cónglüè be omitted: 其余~。 The details are omitted.

从前 cóngqián before; formerly; in the past

从容 cóngróng ❶ calm; leisurely: ~不迫 calm and unhurried; composed and steady / ~就义 go to death unflinchingly; meet one's death like a hero ❷ ample (time or money); plenty of: 手头~ be in easy circumstances; have plenty of cash

从善如流 cóngshànrúliú follow or accept good advice readily

从事 cóngshì ❶ go in for; be engaged in ❷ act; deal with: 鲁莽~ act rashly

从属 cóngshǔ subordinate; affiliated; dependent

从速 cóngsù as soon as possible; without delay: ~处理 deal with sth as soon as possible / 欲购~。 Take the opportunity and buy now.

从头 cóngtóu ❶ from the beginning ❷ once again; all over again

从小 cóngxiǎo from or since childhood; as a child

从心所欲 cóngxīnsuǒyù have one's own way; do as one pleases; act at will

从严 cóngyán be strict; maintain a high demand on: 从快~ take prompt and strict measures (to do sth); act promptly and sternly

从业 cóngyè be engaged; obtain employment; get a job: ~机会 job opportunities / ~人员 those employed in commerce or service trades

从优 cóngyōu give or offer preferential treatment: 价格~ offer preferential prices

从中 cóngzhōng out of; from among: ～渔利 profit from / ～作梗 place obstacles in the way; hinder sb (from carrying out a plan)

丛(叢) cóng ❶ crowd together; cluster: ～集 crowd together; collection / ～杂 motley (of things); jumbled ❷ clump; crowd; collection:人～ crowd of people / ～刊 series of books; collection / ～林 jungle; forest / ～书 set of books issued in the same format; series of books; collection

丛生 cóngshēng ❶ (of plants) grow thickly:荆棘～ overgrown with thorny bushes ❷ (of diseases, evils, etc) break out in profusion:险象～ riddled with danger

淙 cóng

淙淙 cóngcóng 〈象声〉 murmuring; gurgling; babbling:溪水～ babbling brook

còu

凑(湊) còu ❶ gather together; collect; pool:～集 gather together; collect (money) / ～份子 also "凑钱" pool money; club together (to do sth) ❷ it so happens; within easy reach / ～空儿 (do sth) while one is free ❸ move close to; press near:～近 come or draw close to / ～拢 move closer; draw together

凑合 còuhe ❶ assemble; collect; gather together ❷ knock together; improvise; 临时～ knock (sth) together on the spur of the moment ❸ make do: ～事儿 do sth half-heartedly; go through the motions / ～着用 make do with (sth) ❹ so-so; passable; not too bad

凑巧 còuqiǎo luckily; fortunately; as luck would have it: 说也～ as luck

would have it / 真不～ unfortunately

凑趣儿 còuqù ❶ join in (a game, etc) just to please others ❷ make a joke about; poke fun at:拿别人～ make fun of sb

凑热闹 còurènao ❶ join in the fun ❷ add to the trouble or confusion, esp by poking one's nose into others' business

凑数 còushù ❶ make up the number or amount:凑个整数 make up a round number ❷ serve as a stopgap; pass muster

cū

粗 cū ❶ (in diameter) wide; broad; thick: ～棍 thick stick / ～眉大眼 bushy eyebrows and big eyes; heavy features ❷ coarse; crude; rough: ～笨 clumsy; unwieldy; cumbersome / ～布 coarse cloth; handwoven cloth / ～活 heavy manual labour; unskilled work / ～粮 coarse food-grain / ～加工 crude or rough processing / ～茶淡饭 plain tea and simple food; homely meal ❸ gruff; husky:～声～气 deep, gruff voice ❹ careless; negligent:～疏 careless; neglectful; inattentive / ～中有细 be careful at critical junctures though usually careless ❺ rude; unpolished; vulgar: ～鄙 vulgar; coarse; sordid / ～话 vulgar language / ～人 blunt or rash person;〈谦〉uneducated or unlettered man ❻ roughly; slightly: ～具规模 be roughly in order or shape / ～通英文 know a little English

粗暴 cūbào rude; harsh; crude

粗糙 cūcāo ❶ rough; coarse; unrefined:皮肤～ rough skin ❷ crudely made or done; of poor workmanship: 工艺～ crude craftsmanship

粗放 cūfàng ❶ crude; careless;〈经〉extensive: ～经营 extensive manage-

粗犷 cūguǎng ❶ rough; rude; boorish ❷ straightforward and uninhibited; unconstrained and bold:风格～ free and bold style

粗劣 cūliè of poor quality; cheap; shoddy

粗鲁 cūlǔ also "粗卤" rude; coarse; boorish

粗略 cūlüè sketchy; rough:～的介绍 sketchy account (of sth) /～地读一遍 read through quickly; leaf through

粗浅 cūqiǎn shallow; superficial; simple:～的想法〈谦〉tentative idea

粗率 cūshuài rough and careless; thoughtless; ill-considered:表态～ take a position rashly or imprudently

粗细 cūxì ❶ (degree of) thickness:手指～ as thick as a finger ❷ degree of finish; quality of work

粗线条 cūxiàntiáo ❶ (in) thick lines; (in) rough outline:～的勾画 rough sketch ❷ (of a person) rough-and-ready; slapdash

粗心 cūxīn careless; thoughtless:～大意 careless; negligent

粗野 cūyě rough; boorish; uncouth:动作～ play rough (in a match)

粗枝大叶 cūzhī-dàyè ❶ crude and careless; sloppy; slapdash ❷ (in) rough sketch; (in) brief outline:～地说一说 sketch out the main points

粗制滥造 cūzhì-lànzào produce in a rough and slipshod way; turn out rough and slipshod work:～的翻译 shoddy translation /～的房子 jerry-built house

粗重 cūzhòng ❶ (of voice, etc) low but heavy; rough and loud ❷ big and strong; thick and heavy ❸ heavy and clumsy; bulky; (of work) strenuous

粗壮 cūzhuàng ❶ (of a person) sturdy; thickset; brawny ❷ (of a plant, etc) thick and strong; sturdy ❸

(of voice) deep and resonant

cù

促 cù ❶ (of time) short; urgent; hurried:～迫 urgent; pressing; in a hurry ❷ urge; promote; hurry:～成 help to bring about; facilitate /～进 promote; advance; accelerate /～请 urge and request /～使 impel; spur /～销 promote the sale of goods /～变因素 agent of change ❸〈书〉close to; near:～膝谈心 (sit close and) have a heart-to-heart talk

猝 cù also "卒"〈书〉sudden; abrupt; unexpected:～发 have a sudden attack (of some disease); (of an incident) occur abruptly /～然 abruptly; unexpectedly; suddenly /～死 sudden death /～不及防 be taken by surprise; be caught unprepared

醋 cù ❶ vinegar:陈～ mature vinegar /～精 vinegar concentrate /～酸 also "乙酸"〈化〉acetic acid ❷ jealousy (particularly in love affairs):～意 also "醋劲儿" (feeling of) jealousy /～坛子 also "醋罐子" person eaten up with jealousy; jealousy

簇 cù ❶ form a cluster; pile up:～生 (of a plant) grow in clusters; cluster /～拥 cluster or swarm round ❷〈量〉cluster; bunch:一～玫瑰 a bunch of roses

簇新 cùxīn brand new:一套～的衣服 a brand new suit

蹙 cù〈书〉❶ pressed; cramped:穷～ in dire straits ❷ knit (one's brows); frown

蹴 cù〈书〉❶ kick ❷ tread:～踏 tread; stamp

cuān

氽 cuān quick-boil:～丸子 quick-boiled meat balls with soup

撺（攛） cuān

撺掇 cuānduo　urge (sb to do sth); egg on; instigate

蹿（躥） cuān　❶ leap up or forward; ~ 蹦 leap; jump; bounce / ~ 红 become popular rapidly / ~ 升 (of prices, etc) soar; skyrocket / ~ 个儿 (of a child) grow rapidly within a relatively short time ❷〈方〉spurt; gush; ~ 血 gush blood / ~ 稀〈口〉have loose bowels; get the trots; have running stool

cuán

攒（欑） cuán　gather together; collect; assemble; ~ 聚 gather closely together / ~ 一台计算机 assemble a computer (out of parts bought separately)　see also zǎn

cuàn

窜（竄） cuàn　❶〈贬〉flee; scurry; scamper; ~ 犯 raid; make inroads into / ~ 扰 (intrude and) harass ❷ change (the wording in a text, etc); alter; ~ 改 alter; tamper with

篡 cuàn　usurp; seize illegally; ~ 夺 usurp; seize illegally / ~ 权 usurp power (usu political power) / ~ 位 usurp the throne

篡改 cuàngǎi　tamper with; falsify

cuī

崔 cuī

崔巍 cuīwēi　also "崔嵬"〈书〉high; lofty; towering

催 cuī　❶ urge; hurry; press; ~ 逼 press sb for sth / ~ 讨 press for repayment (of a loan) or payment (for sth) ❷ hasten; expedite; speed up; ~ 产 also "催生" expedite (child) delivery / ~ 促 urge; hasten; press / ~ 肥 fatten (livestock, etc) / ~ 化剂 catalyst; catalytic agent / ~ 泪弹 tear bomb; tear gas grenade

催眠 cuīmián　hypnotize; mesmerize; lull (sb to sleep); ~ 曲 lullaby; cradle-song / ~ 术 hypnotism; mesmerism / ~ 疗法 hypnotherapy

催命 cuīmìng　hasten sb on his or her way to death;〈喻〉persistently urge; continually press; ~ 鬼 person who keeps pressing for sth

摧 cuī　break; destroy; ~ 毁 destroy; smash; wreck / ~ 枯拉朽 destroy with overwhelming force

摧残 cuīcán　wreck; destroy; devastate; ~ 身体 ruin or wreck one's health / ~ 致死 persecute or torture to death

cuǐ

璀 cuǐ

璀璨 cuǐcàn　〈书〉lustrous; bright; resplendent

cuì

脆 cuì　❶ fragile; brittle; ~ 骨 cartilage; gristle (as food) / ~ 弱 fragile; frail; weak / ~ 性 brittleness; fragileness ❷ (of food) crisp; crunchy; ~ 枣 also "焦枣"〈方〉crisp dates ❸ (of voice, sound, etc) clear; crisp ❹〈方〉neat; tidy; crisp; 这事干得真~。The job was neatly done.

萃 cuì　〈书〉❶ come together; assemble; ~ 集 also "萃聚" gather together; assemble ❷ gathering; collection

萃取 cuìqǔ　〈化〉extraction; ~ 塔 extraction tower

啐 cuì　spit; expectorate; ~ 人 spit at sb

淬 cuì temper by dipping (hot metal) in water, etc; quench;～钢 chilled steel /～火 quench /～砺〈书〉temper oneself through severe trials

瘁 cuì 〈书〉overworked; exhausted

粹 cuì 〈书〉❶ pure ❷ essence; the best

翠 cuì ❶ (emerald) green;～绿 emerald or jade green; vivid green /～微 green mountain scenery; green hill ❷ (usu 翡翠鸟) kingfisher ❸ jadeite

cūn

村(❶邨) cūn ❶ village; populated place or area;～民 villager /～寨 (stockaded) village /～镇 villages and small towns /～庄 also "村落";"村子" village; hamlet /移民～ housing area for immigrants ❷ rustic; boorish;～话 coarse language

皴 cūn (of skin) chapped; cracked

cún

存 cún ❶ exist; live; survive;～世 survive; be extant /～续 continue; last ❷ store; save; keep;～底 keep the original draft on file; keep a file copy /～盘〈信息〉save /～货 goods in stock; existing stock; inventory /～案备查 (shortened as 存查) put on file for future reference /～而不论 leave the question open / 心～疑虑 have misgivings; worry ❸ deposit;～户 depositor /～折 deposit or account book; bankbook; passbook /～银行 deposit (money) in the bank ❹ leave (for safe keeping); check;～车 park vehicles (esp bicycles) /～放 leave (with sb); leave in sb's care /～行李 check one's luggage /～衣处 cloakroom; checkroom ❺ remain; stay; be in stock;～食 (suffer from) indigestion /～余 surplus; leftover; remainder

存储 cúnchǔ storage;～费 storage charge /～器 also "存贮器"〈信息〉memory (storage) /～容量〈信息〉storage or memory capacity

存档 cúndàng (place on) file; keep in the archives

存根 cúngēn counterfoil; stub; 支票～ cheque stub

存活 cúnhuó survive; exist;～率 survival rate

存款 cúnkuǎn deposit money in the bank;～单 also "存单" deposit receipt /～利率 deposit rate

存亡 cúnwáng live or die; survive or perish; 失踪者～未卜 The fate of those missing remains unknown.

存心 cúnxīn cherish certain intentions;～不良 cherish evil designs ❷ intentionally; deliberately; on purpose;～为难人 deliberately make things difficult for sb

存疑 cúnyí leave a question open; leave a matter for future consideration

存在 cúnzài exist; be; 难以～ can hardly exist /～主义〈哲〉existentialism /～决定意识〈哲〉Being determines consciousness.

cǔn

忖 cǔn turn over in one's mind; ponder; mull over;～度 speculate; conjecture; fathom /～量 gauge; consider; think over

cùn

寸 cùn ❶ cun, a unit of length (1/10 of a chi or 1/30 of a metre)

❷ very little，short or small；～功 small contribution；meagre achievement / ～刻 very short time / ～土必争 fight for every inch of land / 手无一铁（to-tally）unarmed / ～金难买寸光阴〈谚〉money can't buy time；time is more precious than gold

寸步 cùnbù　(usu in the negative) tiny step；single step；～不离 follow（sb）closely；keep close（to sb）/ ～不让 refuse to yield a single inch；not budge an inch / ～难行 be unable to move even a single step；be in an extremely difficult situation

寸草 cùncǎo　small grass；blade of grass；～不留 not leave even a blade of grass— completely destroy / ～不生 without even a blade of grass growing；barren

寸头 cùntóu　crew cut；留～ wear a crew cut / 理个～ have one's hair crew-cut

寸心 cùnxīn　❶（inner）heart；～如割 be cut up in one's innermost heart；be in acute agony ❷ feelings；聊表～ as a small token of friendship；just to show my appreciation

cuō

搓 cuō　rub or twist with the hands；scrub；～板 washboard / ～洗 scrub（clothes, etc）/ ～澡 give（sb）a rubdown with a damp towel；rub oneself down / ～手 wring one's hands（anxiously or impatiently）/ 麻绳 make cords by twisting hemp fibres between the palms

磋 cuō　consult；deliberate

磋商 cuōshāng　consult；exchange views；政治～ political consultation / 与某人～某事 consult with sb about sth

撮 cuō　gather；bring together；scoop up（with a dustpan, etc）；

～合 make a match；act as a match-maker or go-between ❷ extract；summarize；～要（make an）abstract；(outline) essential points ❸〈方〉have a meal；eat；请人一顿 invite sb for a meal ❹〈量〉*used to indicate a tiny number or amount*；一～盐 a pinch of salt / 一小～坏人 a handful of evil-doers *see also* zuǒ

蹉 cuō　fall；slip；(commit an) error

蹉跎 cuōtuó　idle away；let slip；waste (time)；～岁月 idle away one's time；let time slip by without achieving anything；wasted years

cuó

矬 cuó　❶〈方〉short；～子 shorty；dwarf ❷ lower one's body；crouch

痤 cuó

痤疮 cuóchuāng　〈医〉acne

cuò

挫 cuò　❶ defeat；frustrate；～败 frustrate；defeat ❷ subdue；lower；deflate；～人锐气 deflate sb's arrogance

挫伤 cuòshāng　❶〈医〉contusion；bruise ❷ deflate；dampen；discourage；～积极性 dampen sb's enthusiasm

挫折 cuòzhé　inhibit；check；frustrate；遭到重大～ suffer a major set-back

措 cuò　❶ arrange；manage；handle；～置失当 mishandle a problem；not deal with a question properly ❷ make plans（for sth）；map out；～办款项 raise funds

措辞 cuòcí　*also*"措词" wording；diction；～得当 appropriately worded

措施 cuòshī　measure；step

措手 cuòshǒu set one's hand to; set about; 难以～ difficult to handle or deal with / ～不及 be caught unprepared or unawares

锉 cuò (make smooth with a) file; ～平 file away rough edges

错 cuò ❶ interlocked and jagged; intermeshed; ～杂 mixed; heterogeneous; jumbled / ～综复杂 intricate; complex ❷ miss; alternate; stagger; ～过机会 miss an opportunity / ～开工作时间 stagger working hours ❸ wrong; mistaken; erroneous; ～案 misjudged case / ～处 fault; mistake; error / ～怪 blame wrongly; blame the wrong person / ～话 mistaken remarks; wrong words / ～账 account error / 有～就改。Correct a mistake once you have made it. ❹ (used in the negative) bad; poor; 生意不～。Business is not half bad.

错爱 cuò'ài 〈谦〉undeserved kindness; 承蒙如此～。I feel honoured by such favour.

错车 cuòchē give another vehicle the right of way

错觉 cuòjué wrong or false impression; misconception; illusion

错乱 cuòluàn in disorder or confusion; deranged; 思绪～ confused in mind

错落 cuòluò scattered here and there; strewn at random; ～有致 apparently scattered about but properly spaced; in graceful disorder

错位 cuòwèi ❶〈医〉mal-position; 关节～ joint mal-position ❷ misplacement; dislocation; 价值～ misplaced values

错误 cuòwù ❶ wrong; mistaken; erroneous ❷ mistake; error; blunder; ～百出 full of mistakes; error-ridden

错字 cuòzì wrongly written character; misprint; ～连篇 full of misprints or wrongly written characters / 错别字 wrongly written or misused character

D

dā

耷 dā *also* "耷拉" droop; hang down

搭 dā ❶ put or prop up; build; ～架子 set up a framework; get (sth) roughly into shape; 〈方〉put on airs ❷ join or mix together; hang or lay over; overlap; ～伴 join sb on a trip; travel together or in company with sb / ～线 make contact; act as a match-maker or go-between ❸ throw in more (people; money, etc); add; ～头 sth thrown in as an extra / ～载 (of boat or truck) take on additional passengers or goods; (of passengers or goods) be carried in (a vehicle) / ～工夫 put in a lot of time or work ❹ lift or carry together ❺ take (a vehicle); travel or go by; ～(乘)公共汽车 travel by bus; take a bus

搭车 dāchē ❶ go by bus, car, etc; hitchhike; 搭便车 get a lift (in sb's car) ❷ 〈喻〉get on board (with a policy, etc); follow suit (in doing sth); 禁止～涨价 ban unauthorized chain-reaction price rises

搭档 dādàng *also* "搭当" cooperate; work together; be partners; 老～ old partner or colleague / 跟人～ team up with sb

搭伙 dāhuǒ ❶ join as partner; work together; ～经商 be business partners ❷ have a meal arrangement (with a restaurant, at sb's house, etc)

搭界 dājiè border on; be adjacent to; 〈方〉have to do with (each other, etc)

搭救 dājiù rescue; save

搭配 dāpèi ❶ arrange; match; organize in pairs or groups; ～不好 ill-matched; poorly assorted / ～销售 tie-in sale; bundling ❷ 〈语言〉collocation

搭腔 dāqiāng *also* "答腔" ❶ *also* "搭茬儿" answer; respond ❷ 〈方〉talk to each other; be on speaking terms

搭桥 dāqiáo build a bridge; 〈喻〉act as a go-between; introduce; (心脏)～手术 〈医〉heart bypass surgery

搭讪 dāshàn *also* "搭赸" try to make conversation; accost; say sth to smooth over an awkward situation

搭手 dāshǒu give or lend a hand; help; 搭不上手 have no idea how to help

嗒 dā 〈象声〉马蹄～～ clatter of horses' hoofs / 挂钟的～～声 ticktocks of a wall clock *see also* tà

答 dā *used in the following phrases see also* dá

答理 dāli *also* "搭理" (usu used in the negative) acknowledge (sb's greeting, etc); respond; answer; 不爱～人 be stand-offish; be distant in manner

答应 dāying ❶ answer; reply; respond ❷ agree; promise; comply with

dá

打 dá 〈量〉dozen; 一～毛巾 a dozen face towels *see also* dǎ

达(達) dá ❶ go through to; reach; achieve; ～标

reach or attain the required standards；qualify／工作～且 work till dawn ❷ understand thoroughly；be understanding；～观 take (bad) things philosophically；be philosophical ❸ express；convey；communicate；～意 express or convey one's ideas ❹ eminent；prominent；distinguished；～官贵人 high officials

达成 dáchéng reach (agreement)；achieve；～一致 achieve unanimity or consensus

达到 dádào achieve；attain；reach；～标准 be up to standard／～要求 meet the requirements

沓 dá 〈量〉pile (of paper, etc)；pad；一～便笺 a note pad／一～钞票 a wad of banknotes *see also* tà

答 dá ❶ answer；reply；respond；～案 answer；solution；key／～卷 examination or test papers／～疑 answer questions／～非所问 give an irrelevant answer；sidestep a question（～记者问 press interview）❷ return (a visit, etc)；reciprocate；repay；～词 (give a) thank-you speech；reply／～礼 reciprocate sb's courtesy；return a salute *see also* dā

答辩 dábiàn reply (to a charge, query, etc)；～状 written reply (to a charge, etc)／～委员会 querying committee (for an oral defence)

答复 dáfù answer；reply；不予～ make no reply

答谢 dáxiè express appreciation (for sb's kindness or hospitality)；acknowledge；～词 speech of thanks；thank-you speech／～宴会 return banquet

dǎ

打 dǎ ❶ strike；hit；attack；～斗 fight；fistfight／～翻 overturn；

knock over／～骂 beat and scold；maltreat／～闹 act boisterously；be rowdy；quarrel and fight／～肿脸充胖子〈俗〉do sth beyond one's means in order to look impressive／杯子～了。The cup is broken. ❷ make (as in a smithy)；forge；build；～铁 forge iron；work as a blacksmith／～造 make (implements)；forge／～地基 lay the foundation／～家具 make furniture ❸ (of people) associate or deal with；～成一片 become one with；identify oneself with；mix with／～得火热 be on intimate terms；be cheek by jowl with sb ❹ tie up；pack；～结 tie a knot／～行李 pack one's luggage；pack up ❺ knit；weave；～补丁 patch up；mend／～毛衣 knit a sweater ❻ apply (sth to sth else)；draw；mark；～蜡 wax；polish／～问号 put a question mark (to sth)；question；doubt ❼ open (up)；dig；drill；～井 dig or sink a well／～眼 punch or bore a hole；drill ❽ raise；hold up；hoist；～伞 hold or put up an umbrella／～起精神 cheer up；pluck up courage ❾ send；dispatch；～电报 send a telegram／～入十八层地狱 banish to the lowest depths of hell；condemn to eternal damnation ❿ issue or receive a certificate, etc)；～保票 *also* "打包票" vouch for；guarantee／～病假条 get a doctor's certificate for sick leave ⓫ remove；get rid of；～虫 wipe out a pest；get rid of parasites／～杈 prune (a plant) ⓬ gather (in)；catch；draw；～柴 gather firewood／～鱼 catch fish；go fishing／～井水 draw water from a well／～粮食 gather in a grain crop；harvest or yield grain ⓭ buy；～酒 buy some liquor／～票 purchase or buy a ticket ⓮ work out；draw up；calculate；～底稿 prepare or make a first draft／～少了费用 underestimate the expenses ⓯ play；～球 play ball ⓰ label；charge；被～成特务

be labelled a spy **⑰** do; engage in; assume (an attitude) / ～头 take the lead (in sth) / ～官腔 mouth officialese; assume bureaucratic airs / ～拍子 beat time / ～下手 act as assistant (to sb) / ～杂儿 do odds and ends; do odd jobs / ～光棍儿〈口〉remain a bachelor; stay single **⑱** *used to indicate certain body movements*: ～榧子 snap one's fingers / ～手势 make gestures; gesticulate / ～躬作揖 bow and scrape **⑲** *used with another verb to form a new one*: ～滚 roll or toss about / ～滑 (of a vehicle) skid; (of a person) slip; (of a floor) be slippery / ～劫 rob; plunder; loot **⑳** from; since; ～那以后 since then / ～心眼里 from the bottom of one's heart *see also* dá

打靶 dǎbǎ　target or shooting practice: ～场 target or shooting range

打败 dǎbài　**❶** defeat (in war); vanquish; trounce **❷** suffer a defeat (in war or competition); be defeated

打扮 dǎban　**❶** make up; deck out: ～得花枝招展 be gorgeously dressed **❷** the way one is dressed

打包 dǎbāo　**❶** bale; pack: ～机 baler; bagging or packaging machine **❷** unpack: ～检验 unpack for check **❸** put leftovers into a "doggie bag" (after eating in a restaurant)

打抱不平 dǎbàobùpíng　intervene on behalf of an injured party; defend sb against an injustice

打草惊蛇 dǎcǎojīngshé　stir the grass and alarm the snake — act rashly and alert the enemy

打岔 dǎchà　interrupt; cut in

打场 dǎcháng　thresh grain (on a threshing ground)

打倒 dǎdǎo　**❶** attack and knock down; fell **❷** topple; overthrow: ～独裁统治! Down with the dictatorship!

打的 dǎdí　*also* "打车" take a taxi

打点 dǎdian　**❶** get (luggage, etc)

ready: ～行装 pack up for a trip; get ready for a journey **❷** bribe: 上下～ bribe everyone concerned (in a case)

打动 dǎdòng　move; touch

打赌 dǎdǔ　bet (money, etc, on sth); wager

打断 dǎduàn　**❶** break: ～脊梁骨 break one's backbone **❷** interrupt; cut short

打盹儿 dǎdǔnr　〈口〉*also* "打瞌睡" doze off; take a nap

打发 dǎfa　**❶** send; dispatch: ～孩子去上学 send a child to school **❷** dismiss; send away: 把来人～走 send a visitor away **❸** while away (one's time); kill time

打分 dǎfēn　give grades or marks; mark papers

打嗝儿 dǎgér　〈口〉hiccup; belch; burp

打工 dǎgōng　hire out for work; do manual work (for sb or temporarily): ～妹 casual female labourer (usu a rural girl working in a city)

打鼓 dǎgǔ　**❶** beat a drum **❷**〈口〉feel nervous

打官司 dǎguānsi　go to court or law; engage in a lawsuit: 打笔墨官司 engage in written polemics; fight a battle of words

打哈哈 dǎhāhā　tease; make fun of; crack a joke

打哈欠 dǎhāqian　*also* "打呵欠" yawn

打夯 dǎhāng　ram; tamp: ～机 rammer; tamper

打呼噜 dǎhūlu　*also* "打鼾" snore

打火 dǎhuǒ　strike sparks (from a flint) or a light: ～机 cigarette lighter / ～石 flint

打击 dǎjī　**❶**〈乐〉percussion: ～乐器 percussion instrument **❷** attack; strike; upset: ～犯罪 crack down on crime / ～报复 retaliate (against sb); take revenge (on sb)

打假 dǎjiǎ crack down on (production and sale of) counterfeit goods

打架 dǎjià come to blows; have a fistfight; scuffle; ～斗殴 fistfights and scuffles / 打群架 engage in a gang fight; scuffle

打交道 dǎjiāodao make or come into contact with; have dealings with; 不好～ hard to deal with

打搅 dǎjiǎo also "打扰" ❶ disturb; trouble; 请勿～。(sign on door) Do not disturb. ❷〈婉〉give trouble to; 实在～您了。Thank you for your hospitality.

打卡 dǎkǎ punch card; 上班～ punch in / ～购物 buy sth with one's credit card

打开 dǎkāi ❶ open; unfold; ～盖子 take off a lid / ～天窗说亮话〈俗〉not beat about the bush; speak frankly ❷ turn or switch on ❸ open up; widen; ～思路 broaden one's thinking / ～销路 develop new markets (for a product, etc)

打捞 dǎlāo get out of the water; salvage; ～船 rescue vessel; salvage ship

打雷 dǎléi thunder

打量 dǎliang ❶ measure with the eye; look up and down; size up ❷ think; suppose; reckon

打猎 dǎliè go hunting

打乱 dǎluàn disrupt; throw into confusion; upset; ～阵脚 throw into confusion; cut the ground from under sb's feet

打马虎眼 dǎmǎhuyǎn act dumb or feign ignorance (to fool sb); stall

打埋伏 dǎmáifu ❶ lie in ambush ❷ hold sth back for one's own use; 打了埋伏的预算 inflated budget

打牌 dǎpái play cards or mahjong; 〈喻〉exploit sth for one's own end; 打"民意"牌 play the "public opinion" card

打喷嚏 dǎpēntì sneeze

打破 dǎpò break; smash; ～常规 break free from convention / ～平衡 overturn the balance / ～沙锅问到底〈俗〉get to the bottom of things; acquaint oneself with every detail of a matter

打气 dǎqì ❶ inflate; pump up; ～筒 bicycle pump; inflator ❷ boost the morale; encourage; cheer up

打情骂俏 dǎqíng-màqiào tease (a lover, etc) by pretending to be displeased; flirt boisterously with a member of the opposite sex

打趣 dǎqù tease; banter; make fun of

打拳 dǎquán do Chinese shadowboxing; 打太极拳 practise tai chi chuan; 〈喻〉dodge and shirk; stall

打扫 dǎsǎo sweep; clean; ～卫生 have a general cleaning

打手 dǎshou hired roughneck or thug; hatchet man

打算盘 dǎsuànpan work or use an abacus; 〈喻〉calculate; 打错算盘 miscalculate / 打小算盘 be calculating in a petty manner; be petty and scheming / 打如意算盘 indulge in wishful thinking

打算 dǎsuan ❶ intend; plan; think of ❷ plans; consideration; calculation

打胎 dǎtāi have an (induced) abortion; ～药 abortive (medicine)

打听 dǎtīng ask or inquire about; ～情况 ask for information about sth

打通 dǎtōng get through; open up; ～电话 get a call through / ～隧道 through a tunnel / ～关节 grease the palms of those concerned

打退堂鼓 dǎtuìtánggǔ beat a retreat; back out; give up

打响 dǎxiǎng ❶ open fire; (as of a battle) start ❷ win initial success; 一炮～ succeed at the first attempt; get off to a flying start

打消 dǎxiāo give up (an idea, etc); dispel (a doubt, etc); cancel or drop (a plan, etc)

打印 dǎyìn ❶ type and print ❷〈信

息）print out：～机 printer

打游击 dǎyóujī ❶ wage guerrilla warfare ❷〈口〉(eat, sleep, etc) at no fixed place

打圆场 dǎyuánchǎng mediate a dispute；smooth things over

打战 dǎzhàn *also* "打颤" shiver；shudder；tremble

打仗 dǎzhàng go into battle；fight；打败仗 be defeated；suffer a defeat／打硬仗 fight a hard battle／打嘴仗 *also* "打口水仗" have a battle of words；quarrel

打招呼 dǎzhāohu ❶ greet；say hello ❷ notify；let (sb) know

打折扣 dǎzhékòu ❶ sell at a discount；give a discount ❷ fall short of a requirement, standard or promise；这些要求不能～。These requirements must be met to the letter.

打针 dǎzhēn give or have an injection；打预防针 give or have an inoculation；〈喻〉give or take a warning in advance

打主意 dǎzhǔyi think of a plan；evolve an idea；try to obtain；别打我的主意！Leave me out of your calculations.

打字 dǎzì typewrite；type；～稿 typescript／～机 typewriter／～员 typist

dà

大 dà ❶ big；great；major；～道 main road；〈喻〉road of justice；way to a bright future／～敌 formidable enemy；major obstacle or difficulty／～捷 resounding victory (of a major battle)／～业 great cause or undertaking／～志 high or lofty aim；exalted ambition；high aspirations／～家庭 extended or big family；community／～人物 great man；bigwig；VIP／～扫除 general or thorough cleaning／～步流星 with vigorous strides／～声说话

speak loudly／～政方针 guiding principles of fundamental importance；major policies ❷ to a great extent or degree；greatly；fully：～吃一惊 be greatly surprised／～打出手 attack brutally；come to blows／～动干戈 go to war；go all out；make a lot of fuss／～失所望 greatly disappointed；to one's great disappointment／～为改观 change greatly or considerably／～白于天下 be brought to light／不～出门 seldom go out ❸ age；seniority；the eldest：～哥 eldest brother (also used as a polite form of address for a man about one's own age)／～姐 eldest sister (also used as a polite form of address for a woman about one's own age)／～少爷 eldest or spoilt son (of a rich family)；young master；spendthrift／你多～了？How old are you？❹ further on or back in time：～后天 third day from today；three days later／～前天 three days ago ❺ *used before a phrase of time for emphasis*：～白天 in broad daylight／～过节的还加班呢！Why, you're working even on a festival！❻〈敬〉your, etc：～札 your letter

see also dài

大白菜 dàbáicài Chinese cabbage

大半 dàbàn ❶ more than half；greater part；most：～年 better part of a year；over six months ❷ very likely；most probably

大本营 dàběnyíng ❶〈军〉general or supreme headquarters；〈喻〉centre；stronghold ❷ base camp

大便 dàbiàn defecate；have a bowel movement；shit：～不通 (suffer from) constipation

大伯 dàbó father's elder brother；uncle (also used as a polite form of address for an elderly man)

大不列颠 Dàbùlièdiān Great Britain (comprising England, Wales and Scotland)

大不了 dàbùliǎo ❶ at (the) worst; if the worst comes to the worst:～从头开始。We could start all over again at the worst. ❷ (mostly used in the negative) alarming; serious: 没什么～的。That's no big deal.

大材小用 dàcáixiǎoyòng waste one's talent on a petty job; assign trivial tasks to talented people

大肠 dàcháng 〈生理〉large intestines

大臣 dàchén (in a monarchy) minister; secretary

大葱 dàcōng large green Chinese onion

大…大… dà…dà… used before a noun, a verb or an adjective to indicate great scale or magnitude:大操大办 go in for ostentation and extravagance / 大吹大擂 make a big fanfare; boast excessively / 大慈大悲 be infinitely merciful or compassionate / 大模大样 in an ostentatious manner; with a swagger / 大起大落 great ups and downs; violent fluctuations / 大是大非 major issue of cardinal principle; major question of right and wrong / 大摇大摆 walk with a swagger / 大鱼大肉 plenty of meat and fish; rich food

大大 dàdà greatly; enormously; tremendously:～出乎意料 quite contrary to one's expectations

大大咧咧 dàda-liēliē (of a person) careless; happy-go-lucky

大胆 dàdǎn bold; daring; audacious:～向前 go or forge ahead bravely

大刀阔斧 dàdāo-kuòfǔ bold and resolute; drastic

大道理 dàdàoli major or general principle; great truth:讲～talk in generalities; talk platitudes

大地 dàdì ❶ earth; land; world:～母亲 Mother Earth ❷ of the earth; ground; terrestrial:～折射 terrestrial refraction

大典 dàdiǎn ❶ grand ceremony:开国～ founding ceremony (of a state) ❷ body of classical writings; canon:《永乐～》Yongle Canon (1403-1408)

大动脉 dàdòngmài 〈生理〉〈喻〉main artery; aorta

大豆 dàdòu soybean; soya bean

大度 dàdù magnanimous; generous; large-minded:～包容 magnanimous and tolerant

大队 dàduì ❶ military unit corresponding to the battalion or regiment; (in the air force) group ❷ brigade:消防～ fire brigade ❸ large body or contingent:～人马 large contingent of troops; large body of marchers, etc

大多 dàduō also "大都" for the most part; mostly; largely

大多数 dàduōshù great or vast majority; bulk:在～情况下 in most cases

大发雷霆 dàfāléitíng fly into a rage; be furious; bawl angrily

大凡 dàfán (used at the beginning of a sentence) generally (speaking); in most cases

大方 dàfang ❶ generous (with money); liberal; open-handed ❷ natural and poised; easy; in good taste:举止～ carry oneself with ease and confidence; have an easy manner / 样式～ tasteful in style

大放厥词 dàfàngjuécí talk a lot of nonsense; spout a stream of empty rhetoric

大粪 dàfèn human excrement; night soil

大风大浪 dàfēng-dàlàng strong wind and big waves; 〈喻〉social upheaval; storm and stress

大幅度 dàfúdù by a big margin; substantially; drastically

大副 dàfù (on a ship) first mate; chief officer

大腹便便 dàfùpiánpián potbellied; paunchy

大概 dàgài ❶ general (idea); broad

(outline)；approximate：说个～ give a brief account（of sth）❷ probably；most likely；presumably

大纲 dàgāng　outline；précis：教学～ teaching programme；syllabus

大哥大 dàgēdà〈口〉❶ mobile or cellular phone ❷ boss；big-wig

大公无私 dàgōng-wúsī ❶ selfless；unselfish ❷ just and fair；perfectly impartial

大功告成 dàgōnggàochéng　be crowned with success；come off with flying colours；be brought to a successful conclusion

大褂 dàguà　unlined long Chinese-style gown；robe

大规模 dàguīmó　large-scale；extensive；massive：～杀伤性武器 weapon of mass destruction

大锅饭 dàguōfàn　cooked rice in a big pot—a meal prepared for many；〈喻〉equalitarian distribution of income

大海捞针 dàhǎilāozhēn　see“海底捞针”hǎidǐlāozhēn in“海底”

大寒 dàhán　Great Cold，24th seasonal division point　see also“节气”jiéqi

大好 dàhǎo　excellent；superb：～ 河山 beautiful rivers and mountains of a country；one's beloved motherland

大号 dàhào ❶〈敬〉your（given）name ❷ large size（L）

大合唱 dàhéchàng　cantata；chorus

大河 dàhé ❶ great river ❷ the Yellow River

大亨 dàhēng　big shot；tycoon；magnate

大红 dàhóng　bright red；scarlet：～大紫 bright red and purple；〈喻〉（of people）at the height of influence or popularity

大户 dàhù ❶〈旧〉wealthy and influential family；rich family with ancient lineage ❷ unit or individual occupying a prominent place in a given field：用电～

large consumer of power

大话 dàhuà　big talk；boast；bragging：少说～。Stop bragging.

大会 dàhuì ❶ plenary session；general meeting；conference ❷ mass meeting or rally

大伙儿 dàhuǒr　also“大家伙儿”〈口〉we all；you all；everybody

大惑不解 dàhuòbùjiě　be extremely puzzled；be baffled or bewildered；be all at sea

大吉 dàjí ❶ extremely lucky；very auspicious：祝你新年～大利。Wish you every luck in the New Year. ❷ used after a verb to add a touch of humour：关门～ close down；shut down for good

大计 dàjì　major issue；programme of lasting importance：共商～ come together to discuss matters of vital importance

大家 dàjiā ❶ great master；authority：～手笔 work of a master；master-stroke ❷ well-known ancient family；distinguished family of long standing：～风范 manners of good breeding／ 闺秀 daughter from a family of good social standing ❸ all；everybody；everyone：～ 来出主意。Let's put our heads together.

大江 dàjiāng ❶ great river ❷ the Yangtze River

大奖 dàjiǎng　big award or prize；top prize：～ 赛 prize-giving competition；〈体〉Grand Prix

大将 dàjiàng ❶〈军〉senior general ❷ general（officer）：～ 风度 poise of a great general；qualities of a great commander ❸ person of special importance or ability

大街 dàjiē　(main) street；avenue：～ 小巷 streets and lanes

大惊小怪 dàjīng-xiǎoguài　be alarmed at sth apparently normal；make much fuss about nothing

大局 dàjú overall situation；overall (public) interest：～已定。The outcome is irreversible.

大举 dàjǔ carry out (a military operation) on a large scale：～反攻 launch an all-out counter-offensive

大军 dàjūn ❶ main forces；huge army：～压境 with a large enemy army gathering on the border ❷ large contingent：文艺～ ranks of writers and artists

大卡 dàkǎ〈理〉kilocalorie；large calorie (Cal)

大快人心 dàkuàirénxīn affording general satisfaction；most gratifying to the people

大款 dàkuǎn〈口〉moneybags (used as a singular noun)；fat cat；upstart：傍～ (of a girl) find a sugar daddy

大老粗 dàlǎocū uncouth fellow；uneducated person；rough and ready fellow

大理石 dàlǐshí marble

大力 dàlì energetic or great effort：出～ exert oneself；do a great deal ／ ～发展高科技 devote major efforts to developing hi-tech industries

大梁 dàliáng ❶〈建筑〉girder；roof beam；ridgepole ❷〈喻〉most important part of work；backbone：挑～ play a central role in the work；be the mainstay

大量 dàliàng ❶ large number；great quantity：～时间 lots of time ／ ～消耗体力 consume one's strength considerably ❷ see "大度"

大龄青年 dàlíngqīngnián unmarried man or woman of the age group between 28 and 35

大陆 dàlù ❶ contin-ent；mainland：～架 continental shelf ／ ～性气候 continental climate ❷ also "中国大陆" (China's) mainland

大路 dàlù ❶ high road；main street ❷ cheap and in great demand：～货 run-of-the-mill or low-end goods

大略 dàlüè ❶ see "大概❶" ❷ great vision and talent：胸怀～ be a man with great vision

大妈 dàmā also "大娘" wife of father's elder brother；aunt (also used as an affectionate or respectful form of address for an elderly woman)

大麻 dàmá ❶ hemp：～籽 hempseed ❷ marijuana；hashish；cannabis

大麦 dàmài barley：～茶 barley water

大门 dàmén street or front door；gate：〈体〉goal：看～儿的〈口〉doorkeeper；gate-keeper

大米 dàmǐ (husked) rice

大名 dàmíng ❶ formal personal name；official name ❷〈敬〉your (given) name：请问尊姓～？ May I know your name, please？ ❸ great or famous name：～鼎鼎 famous；well-known；celebrated

大拇指 dàmúzhǐ thumb

大男子主义 dànánzǐzhǔyì male chauvinism：～思想严重 be very male-chauvinistic

大难 dànàn catastrophe；disaster；calamity：～临头 be faced with imminent disaster；be in immediate danger

大脑 dànǎo〈生理〉cerebrum：～皮层 cerebral cortex；pallium

大逆不道 dànìbùdào high treason；treason and heresy；greatest outrage：视为～ regard (sb) as a traitor or heretic；consider (sth) to be treason or heresy

大年 dànián ❶ good year；year of bumper harvest；(of fruit trees) on-year：今年是苹果～。We've had a bumper crop of apples this year. ❷ lunar New Year's Day；Spring Festival：过～ celebrate the (lunar) New Year's Day ／ ～初一 lunar New Year's Day

大排档 dàpáidàng〈方〉street stall of a restaurant；cheap, popular eating-place (often on the sidewalk)

大牌 dàpái 〈口〉big-name（pop singer，film star，etc）；extremely famous：～球星 super ball-player

大炮 dàpào ❶ big gun；artillery；cannon ❷〈口〉one who speaks boastfully or forcefully；blunt person：放～ shoot one's mouth off；talk big

大篷车 dàpéngchē ❶（covered）wagon ❷ covered truck or lorry；caravan（for goods，etc）

大批 dàpī large quantities，amounts or numbers：～生产 large-batch or mass production；large-scale manufacture

大片 dàpiàn big-budget film；blockbuster

大屏幕 dàpíngmù large screen：～电视 large-screen television

大气 dàqì ❶ atmosphere；air：～层 atmospheric layer；atmospheric / ～压 atmospheric or barometric pressure；atmosphere（atm）❷ heavy breathing：吓得连～也不敢出 catch or hold one's breath in fear

大气候 dàqìhòu macro-climate；〈喻〉overall situation in the country or world；general political climate（for sth）

大气磅礴 dàqìpángbó （of literary works，etc）of great momentum or power；of immense sweep

大器 dàqì treasure；〈喻〉great talent：必成～ certain to become a prominent figure；be promising / ～晚成 great vessels take years to build；great minds mature slowly

大千世界 dàqiānshìjiè boundless universe；vast world：～，无奇不有。Anything is possible under the sun.

大庆 dàqìng grand celebration；（usu of every fifth or tenth）birthday or anniversary

大权 dàquán power or authority over major issues：～旁落 lose one's power（to others）

大人 dàrén ❶〈敬〉used as a respect-

ful form of address for a person of an elder generation：母亲～（used at the beginning of a letter）Dear Mother ❷（dàren）〈旧〉Your or His Excellency：总督～ His Excellency the Governor ❸（dàren）adult；grown-up

大嫂 dàsǎo ❶ eldest brother's wife；sister-in-law ❷（polite form of address for a married woman about one's own age）elder sister

大厦 dàshà large building；mansion：～将倾 the great building is about to collapse—the whole situation is beyond remedy

大赦 dàshè amnesty；general pardon

大婶儿 dàshěnr 〈口〉wife of father's younger brother；aunt（also used as a polite form of address for a married woman about one's mother's age）

大声疾呼 dàshēngjíhū raise a cry of warning；raise a hue and cry；make a passionate appeal（for a cause，etc）

大师 dàshī ❶（great）master：艺术～ leading artist ❷〈宗教〉Great Master，courtesy title for a Buddhist monk：班禅～ Panchen Lama

大师傅 dàshifu 〈口〉cook；chef

大使 dàshǐ ambassador：特命全权～ ambassador extraordinary and plenipotentiary / ～馆 embassy / ～级会谈 talks at ambassadorial level

大事 dàshì ❶ great or major event；important matter；major issue：国家～ state affair / ～记 record or chronicle of major events / 出～了！Something terrible has happened. ❷ overall situation：～不好。A disaster is imminent. ❸ in a big way：～宣传 play up；make a big thing of（an announcement，etc）

大势 dàshì general trend of events；main course of development：～所趋 trend of the times；general trend / ～已去。The game is up.

大手笔 dàshǒubǐ ❶（work of a）great master ❷（often ironical）bold stroke; lavish style; extravagance

大手大脚 dàshǒu-dàjiǎo be lavish, extravagant or wasteful (with money)

大叔 dàshū 〈口〉 younger brother of one's father; uncle (also used as a polite form of address for a man somewhat younger than one's father)

大暑 dàshǔ Great Heat, 12th seasonal division point *see also* "节气" jiéqi

大水 dàshuǐ flood; 发～ (of a river, etc) overflow the banks; be in spate; flood / ～冲了龙王庙。〈俗〉 The flood inundates the temple of the Dragon King — people on the same side fight each other by mistake.

大肆 dàsì without restraint; wantonly; viciously: ～挥霍 spend without restraint; squander / ～吹嘘 preach and trumpet; boast wildly

大蒜 dàsuàn garlic: 一头～ a head of garlic

大…特… dà…tè… *used each before the same verb, expressing magnitude and depth*: 大错特错 completely mistaken; absolutely wrong / 大书特书 record in letters of gold; write volumes (about sth); write repeatedly and elaborately

大提琴 dàtíqín violoncello; cello

大体 dàtǐ ❶ cardinal principle; general interest: 不识～ fail to keep the general interest in mind; be petty-minded ❷ generally; more or less: 认识～一致 have a similar opinion

大厅 dàtīng (big) hall; lobby (of a hotel, etc)

大庭广众 dàtíng-guǎngzhòng (before a) big crowd; (on a) public occasion: 在～之中丢丑 cut a sorry figure in the public eye; behave shamelessly in public

大同 dàtóng ❶ great harmony — ideal or perfect society: ～世界 ideal world ❷ identical view; consensus on major issues: ～小异 largely identical despite minor differences

大头 dàtóu ❶ larger or thicker end (of sth); major part: ～针 pin / 抓住～ grasp major issues ❷ *also* "冤大头" sucker: 拿～ treat as a sucker; make a sucker of

大头菜 dàtóucài rutabaga (pickled as food)

大团圆 dàtuányuán ❶ happy family reunion ❷ happy ending: 以～结局 end in happiness

大腿 dàtuǐ thigh; leg

大腕 dàwàn top-notch artist; star; heavyweight: ～夫妇 power couple

大王 dàwáng ❶ king; magnate; tycoon ❷ person of a certain outstanding talent; master: 足球～ ace footballer

大西洋 Dàxīyáng Atlantic (Ocean)

大喜 dàxǐ ❶ great rejoicing or happiness: ～过望 be delighted that things are better than one expected; be overjoyed ❷ marriage: 选定～的日子 choose one's wedding day

大显 dàxiǎn display fully; give full play to: ～身手 display one's prowess or abilities fully; cut a dashing figure; distinguish oneself / ～神通 give full play to one's remarkable skill or prowess

大相径庭 dàxiāngjìngtíng widely divergent; totally different; poles apart

大小 dàxiǎo ❶ big or small; size: 一般～ be of the same size / ～是笔生意。 That was a transaction all right, however small it was. ❷ seniors and juniors; adults and children: 没大没小 disregard differences in seniority; be impolite to one's elders / 一家～ the whole family (including both adults and children)

大写 dàxiě ❶ capital form of a Chinese numeral: ～金额 amount in words ❷ capitalization: ～字母 capital letters

大兴 dàxīng go in for in a big way: ～土木 go in for large-scale construction;

get busy building

大猩猩 dàxīngxing　gorilla

大型 dàxíng　large-scale; large; full-length;～客机 jumbo /～管弦乐队 grand orchestra

大修 dàxiū　major or general repair; overhaul

大选 dàxuǎn　general election;总统～ presidential election

大学 dàxué　university; college;～学院 university college /～预科 preparatory course for college

大学生 dàxuéshēng　university or college student;一年级～ freshman / 二年级～ sophomore /三年级～ junior / 四年级～ senior

大雪 dàxuě　❶ heavy snow;～纷飞。 It's snowing thick and fast. ❷ (dàxuě) Great Snow, 21st seasonal division point　see also "节气" jiéqi

大牙 dàyá　❶ molar ❷ front tooth;叫人笑掉～ make people split their sides with laughter; make a laughing stock of oneself

大烟 dàyān　opium;～鬼 opium addict; heavy smoker

大言不惭 dàyánbùcán　brag unblushingly; boast unashamedly;～地自我吹嘘 brag about oneself without batting an eyelid

大雁 dàyàn　wild goose

大洋 dàyáng　❶ ocean;～洲 Oceania /～彼岸 on the other side of the ocean; beyond the ocean ❷〈旧〉silver dollar

大爷 dàyé　arrogant and self-willed man who does not do a stroke of work;～脾气 rude, wilful temperament ❷ (dàye)〈口〉father's elder brother; uncle (also used as a respectful address for a man around one's father's age or older)

大衣 dàyī　overcoat; topcoat; greatcoat

大义 dàyì　cardinal principles of righteousness; righteous cause;～凛然 be fearless with justice on one's side; be firm and stern in upholding justice /～灭亲 place righteousness above family loyalty

大意 dàyì　❶ general idea; main points; gist ❷ (dàyi) careless; negligent; inattentive;～出了错 make a mistake out of carelessness or negligence

大有 dàyǒu　plenty; a great deal; of a great amount;～人在 there are plenty of such people; such people are by no means rare /～文章 there is sth behind all this; there is more to it than meets the eye /～作为 there is plenty of scope for one's talents; be able to develop one's ability to the full

大雨 dàyǔ　heavy rain;～倾盆。It rained cats and dogs.

大院 dàyuàn　courtyard; compound;大杂院儿 residential compound occupied by several families

大约 dàyuē　❶ approximately; about ❷ probably

大战 dàzhàn　(wage a) great war or battle;棉花～ fierce competition for cotton; cotton war

大张旗鼓 dàzhāngqígǔ　on a grand scale; in a big way; with a great fanfare;～地开展反腐败斗争 launch a great campaign against corruption

大丈夫 dàzhàngfu　true or real man;～能屈能伸。A great man knows when to yield and when not.

大致 dàzhì　also "大抵" ❶ in the main; on the whole; by and large;～相似 similar on the whole; largely alike ❷ roughly; approximately; more or less;～不会错 be approximately right

大智若愚 dàzhìruòyú　a man of great wisdom often appears slow-witted

大众 dàzhòng　common people; the public; broad masses of people;～化 popularize; do or make in a popular style /～传媒 mass (communication)

media / ～文化 mass culture

大专 dàzhuān ❶ universities and polytechnics；～院校 universities and polytechnics；institutions of higher education or learning ❷ junior college (as distinct from 中专)：～生 junior college student / ～文凭 associate degree

大自然 dàzìrán nature；Mother Nature：回归～ (go) back to nature

大宗 dàzōng ❶ large amount or quantity：～款项 large amount of money；large sum / ～交易 block trading ❷ staple：出口以电机为～。Electrical machinery is the staple export product.

大作 dàzuò ❶〈敬〉your celebrated work，book，article，etc ❷ erupt；upheave：狂风～。A strong wind suddenly rose.

dāi

呆 dāi ❶ slow-witted；dull；dumb：～子 idiot；simpleton；blockhead / ～头～脑 dull and stupid；stupid-looking ❷ blank；dumbstruck：～若木鸡 dumb as a post；transfixed (with fear or amazement) ❸ see "待" dāi

呆板 dāibǎn stiff；rigid；inflexible

呆滞 dāizhì ❶ dull；inert；lifeless：表情～ vacant expression ❷ sluggish；stagnant；slack：～商品 unsaleable commodity；drug on the market

呆账 dāizhàng bad debt or loan

待 dāi also "呆" stay：～着不动 stay put；stand still / 他～会儿就来。It won't be long before he comes. see also dài

dǎi

歹 dǎi bad；evil；vicious：～毒 vicious；malicious / ～徒 also "歹人" scoundrel；thug；thief / ～意 mal-

ice；malicious or evil intent

逮 dǎi capture；catch：猫～老鼠 (like a) cat catching mice see also dài

傣 dǎi Dai or Tai nationality，living in Yunnan Province

dài

大 dài see also dà

大夫 dàifu doctor；physician

代 dài ❶ take the place of；act as：～笔 write on sb's behalf / ～号 code name / ～码 code / ～言人 spokesman；mouthpiece / ～用品 substitute；ersatz / ～总理 acting premier / ～人受过 bear the blame for sb；be a whipping boy ❷ historical period or era；dynasty；〈地〉era：古～ ancient times ❸ generation：～沟 gap between two generations；generation gap

代办 dàibàn ❶ do sth for sb；act on sb's behalf ❷ chargé d'affaires

代表 dàibiǎo ❶ deputy；delegate；representative：～团 delegation；mission；deputation / ～大会 ，congress；representative assembly / ～队 team of contestants (representing a school，country，etc) / ～权 (right of) representation / ～性 representativeness / ～作 representative work / ～全体同学讲话 speak in the name or on behalf of all the students

代价 dàijià price；cost：不惜～ be prepared to pay any price；(do sth) at any cost

代课 dàikè take over a class or stand in for an absent teacher；be a substitute (teacher)

代劳 dàiláo ask sb to do sth for one or act on one's behalf；do or take care of sth for sb：可否请你～？May I leave this to your care?

代理 dàilǐ ❶ act for a person in a responsible position or engage in certain activities on behalf of one's client; serve as an agent; ~权 power of attorney; attorneyship / ~人〈法〉procurator; attorney / ~商 commercial agent; factor

代名词 dàimíngcí ❶ another name; synonym ❷ also "代词" pronoun

代培 dàipéi train students for an organization

代数 dàishù algebra

代替 dàitì replace; substitute for; take the place of; 可以互相~ be interchangeable

代销 dàixiāo be commissioned to sell sth (usu as a sideline); act as a commission agent

代谢 dàixiè ❶ change; supersession; 四时~ change of the seasons ❷ also "代谢作用" metabolism

带(帶) dài ❶ belt; band; tape; 鞋~ shoestrings; shoelaces / 汽车外~ car tyre ❷ zone; area; belt ❸ leucorrhoea; whites ❹ take; bring; carry; ~话 take or give a message ❺ do in passing or by the way; do incidentally; 随手把门~上 close the door after one ❻ bear; contain; have; ~菌 carry pathogenic bacteria / ~刺儿 prickly; 〈喻〉with a touch of sarcasm / ~电作业 live-wire work / ~病参加比赛 take part in a competition despite one's illness ❼ lead; bring up; ~兵 lead troops; be a commander / ~队 lead a group of people / ~孩子 look after children / ~徒弟 take on or train an apprentice

带动 dàidòng drive; operate; give impetus to; 柴油机~的汽艇 boat driven by a diesel engine / ~全局 promote work as a whole

带劲 dàijìn ❶ energetic; forceful; 工作~ work like a horse ❷ interesting; wonderful; exciting

带宽 dàikuān 〈通信〉bandwidth

带领 dàilǐng ❶ take to a place; guide; ~游客参观 show tourists around ❷ lead; direct; ~学生做试验 direct students in an experiment

带路 dàilù show or lead the way; serve as a guide; ~人 guide; leader

带头 dàitóu take the lead or initiative; set an example; ~人 leader; forerunner / 起~作用 play a leading role

带鱼 dàiyú cutlass fish; hairtail

带子 dàizi ❶ belt; band; ribbon ❷ 〈口〉videotape; (cassette) tape

殆 dài ❶ danger ❷ almost; nearly; 挥霍~尽 squander almost all

贷 dài 〈书〉 loan; credit; ~方〈经〉credit (side); creditor / ~笔钱 borrow a sum of money; get a loan / ~学金 student loan

贷款 dàikuǎn extend or grant credit; get or obtain a loan; ~人 borrower (of a loan); lender; creditor / ~购物 purchase on credit / ~利率 loan interest rate

待 dài ❶ treat; entertain; 在家~客 entertain guests at home ❷ wait for; await; ~命 await orders ❸ 售 ready for sale; yet to be sold / 未完~续 (usu used at the end of an instalment of a long article, etc) to be continued ❸ need; require; 自不~言 this goes without saying; be taken for granted

see also dāi

待人 dàirén treat people; conduct oneself towards others; ~接物 the way one gets along with people

待业 dàiyè wait for employment; unemployed; ~人员 unemployed people

待遇 dàiyù ❶ treatment; 政治~ political status or treatment ❷ remuneration; pay; 生活~ material benefits

怠 dài idle; lax; slack; ~工 go slow; slow down; work-to-rule

怠慢 dàimàn ❶ slight; cold-shoulder; neglect ❷〈套〉(used by a host to show modesty) fail to give proper attention (to one's guests):真对不起，太～了。I am sorry to have been a poor host.

袋 dài ❶ bag; sack; pocket:~鼠 kangaroo / ~装 packed in a bag / ~子 bag; sack ❷〈量〉:一一白糖 a bag or packet of sugar / 抽一一烟 smoke a pipe

逮 dài〈书〉reach:力所不～ beyond one's reach or power　*see also* dǎi

逮捕 dàibǔ arrest; apprehend; take into custody:~证 arrest warrant / ~归案 bring to book or justice

戴 dài ❶ put on; wear; don:~孝 *also* "带孝" wear mourning (for a parent, etc); be in mourning / ~罪立功 *also* "带罪立功" atone for one's offence by rendering good service; redeem oneself by doing good deeds ❷ respect; esteem; support:爱～ love and esteem

戴帽子 dàimàozi wear a hat;〈喻〉branded as; bear the label of:戴高帽子 wear a dunce's cap;〈喻〉praise (sb) unctuously; flatter / 戴绿帽子 be a cuckold; have an unfaithful wife

dān

丹 dān ❶ red; cinnabar:~心 red or loyal heart; loyalty / ~顶鹤 red-crowned crane ❷ (of Chinese medicine) pellet; powder

丹青 dānqīng〈书〉red and black colours;〈喻〉painting:~手 painter / ~妙笔 touch of a great painter

丹田 dāntián pubic region:气沉～ inhale a deep breath

担(擔) dān ❶ carry on a shoulder pole;~架 stretcher; litter ❷ take on; undertake; shoulder:~纲 play the leading role; star; be the mainstay / ~风险 run risks / ~责任 shoulder responsibility; take the blame / ～惊受怕 feel alarmed; get scared
see also dàn

担保 dānbǎo assure; guarantee; vouch for:~金 bail; bond / ~人 guarantor; guarantee

担待 dāndài ❶ forgive; excuse:请多～。Please forgive me (for my thoughtlessness). ❷ accept responsibility:不～ cannot accept responsibility (for sth)

担当 dāndāng *also* "担负" take on; assume; undertake:~重任 take on heavy responsibilities

担搁 dānge　*see* "耽搁" dānge

担任 dānrèn assume the office of; hold the post of; act as:~校长 be principal of a school

担心 dānxīn worry; feel anxious; fear:~他的安全 be concerned about his safety

担忧 dānyōu worry (about); be anxious

单(單) dān ❶ one; single; simple:~词 (individual) word / ~打(体)singles / ~利(经)simple interest / ～程票 single or one way ticket / ～方面 one-sided; unilateral / ～相思 unrequited or unreturned love / ～眼皮 single-layer eyelids / ～亲家庭 single-parent family ❷ odd (number):~号 odd number (of a ticket, etc) ❸ only; alone:~说这点吧 Let's take up this point alone. ❹ thin; weak:~弱 delicate; frail; fragile ❺ (of clothes) unlined or unpadded:~衫 unlined jacket ❻ list; bill:价目～ price list
see also chán

单边 dānbiān unilateral:~贸易 one-way or unilateral trade / ～主义 unilateralism

单薄 dānbó ❶ (of clothing) thin:你穿得太～了。You should put on warmer clothes. ❷ delicate；frail；身体～ in delicate health；frail ❸ insubstantial；flimsy；weak；内容～ thin in content

单纯 dānchún ❶ simple；pure；思想～ unsophisticated ❷ alone；purely；merely

单刀直入 dāndāozhírù come straight to the point；speak without mincing one's words；put (a question) point-blank

单调 dāndiào monotonous；dull；drab；～的情节 insipid plot

单独 dāndú on one's own；by oneself；independent；～核算 independent accounting

单干 dāngàn work by oneself；do (sth) single-handed；go it alone；～户 peasant family farming on its own；self-employed person；loner

单杠 dāngàng 〈体〉horizontal bar (gymnastics)

单轨 dānguǐ ❶ also "单线" single track；～制（喻）single-track or uniform system ❷ monorail；～火车 monorail train

单价 dānjià unit price；每公斤～ per kilo price

单间儿 dānjiānr ❶ one-room housing ❷ single room (as in a hotel)；separate room (as in a restaurant)

单据 dānjù receipt；bill；凭～报销 be reimbursed by receipts

单枪匹马 dānqiāng-pǐmǎ single-handed；all by oneself；alone

单人 dānrén one person；single；individual；～床 single bed／～舞 solo dance

单身 dānshēn ❶ unmarried；single；～汉 bachelor／～女子 single woman；spinster／～宿舍 bachelor quarters；single dorm ❷ not be with one's family；live alone

单数 dānshù ❶ odd number ❷ 〈语言〉singular number

单位 dānwèi ❶ unit (as a standard of measurement)；～面积产量（shortened as 单产）yield per unit area；per unit

yield ❷ unit (as an organization, a department, etc)；事业～ (non-profit-making) institution／～犯罪〈法〉institutional crime

单线 dānxiàn ❶ single line, wire or track ❷ one-way (contact)；single-line (link)；～联系 have single-line contact (with sb)

单项 dānxiàng 〈体〉individual event；～比赛 individual competition

单行 dānxíng ❶ specific (to a particular situation or place)；separate；special；～本 separate edition；collection (of newspaper articles, etc)；offprint／～条例 regulations to be implemented separately；specific regulations ❷ one-way；unidirectional；～线 one-way traffic or road

单一 dānyī single；unitary；～汇率 unitary rate；single exchange rate／～价格 single or uniform price／～经济 single-product economy

单元 dānyuán unit (of textbook, housing, etc)；～楼 apartment building；block of flats

单子 dānzi ❶ list；bill；form ❷ cloth sheet

耽 dān ❶ delay；～误 delay；hold up；spoil through delay ❷〈书〉abandon oneself to；indulge in；～溺 be immersed (in sth evil)

耽搁 dānge also "担搁" ❶ stop over；stay；途中～三天 stop over for three days on the way ❷ delay；procrastinate；spoil through delay

殚（殫） dān〈书〉devote；exhaust；～精竭虑 devote all one's knowledge and experience；dedicate oneself without reserve；rack one's brains

dǎn

胆（膽） dǎn ❶〈生理〉gall bladder；～囊 gall bladder / ～石〈医〉gallstone / ～汁 bile ❷ courage; guts; bravery; ～敢 dare; have the audacity to / ～力 courage and resolution; boldness and sweep / ～略 courage and resourcefulness; bold vision / ～识 courage and insight; boldness and vision ❸ bladder-like inner container; 保温瓶～ glass liner of a thermos

胆大 dǎndà bold; audacious; ～包天 audacious in the extreme / ～妄为 bold and reckless; devil-may-care / ～心细 bold but cautious; courageous and wise

胆固醇 dǎngùchún cholesterol

胆寒 dǎnhán terrified; struck with terror; awestricken

胆量 dǎnliàng courage; guts; pluck; 有～ have plenty of guts

胆怯 dǎnqiè timid; cowardly; 从不～ one's courage never fails one; never flinch

胆小 dǎnxiǎo timid; cowardly; ～鬼 coward / ～怕事 timid and overcautious / ～如鼠 as timid as a mouse; chicken-hearted

胆战心惊 dǎnzhàn-xīnjīng tremble with fear; be scared out of one's wits; be terror-stricken; 成天～地过日子 live in perpetual fear

胆子 dǎnzi boldness; courage; nerve; ～大 bold; courageous / ～小 timid

掸(撣) dǎn brush lightly; whisk; ～子 duster

dàn

旦 dàn ❶〈书〉dawn; daybreak ❷ day; 元～ New Year's Day ❸ also "旦角"〈戏〉female role in Chinese traditional opera

旦夕 dànxī 〈书〉morning and evening; short while; ～祸福 anyone may be lucky one moment and unlucky the next; fortune is fickle / ～之间 in a short while; overnight

但 dàn ❶ merely; only; just; ～求无过 merely wish to be free from error / ～说无妨。Just speak out what is on your mind. ❷ but; yet; nevertheless; 忙是忙，～不觉得累。Busy as I am, I don't feel tired.

但是 dànshì but; still; yet; 他虽然年过七十，～精力仍很健旺。Though over 70, he's still full of vitality.

但愿 dànyuàn if only; I wish; ～如此。If only it were so. / ～他健康长寿。I wish him good health and a long life.

担(擔) dàn ❶ also "担子" carrying pole and the load on it; load; burden; 挑重～ shoulder heavy tasks; take on difficult jobs ❷ dan, a unit of weight (= 50 kilograms) ❸〈量〉used of things carried on a shoulder pole; 两～柴 four bundles of firewood

see also dān

诞 dàn ❶ birth; ～辰 birthday / ～生 be born; come into existence; emerge ❷ birthday; 50 华～ fiftieth birthday or anniversary

淡 dàn ❶ thin; (of colour) light; ～红 pink / ～妆 in light make-up; dressed up in a quiet, good taste / 天高云～。The sky is clear and the clouds are thin. ❷ tasteless; weak; 酒 weak wine / ～水 fresh or sweet water / 这菜太～。The dish wants a pinch of salt. ❸ indifferent; cool; ～于名利 be indifferent to fame and wealth; care little about fame and fortune / ～地笑了一笑 give a faint smile ❹ dull; slack; ～月 slack month

淡泊 dànbó *also* "澹泊"〈书〉not hanker after fame and fortune

淡薄 dànbó ❶ thin; light; ～的烟雾 thin mist ❷ weak; mild; 酒味～。The wine is weak. ❸ (of emotion, interest, etc) become weak or cool; flag ❹ faint; dim; hazy; 记忆已经～。My memory has become blurred.

淡化 dànhuà ❶ become faint or unimportant; give less prominence to; weaken:家族观念～ weakening of clannish concepts ❷ desalinate:海水～ desalination of sea water

淡季 dànjì　slack or dull season; off season:旅游～ slack season for tourism

淡漠 dànmò ❶ indifferent; unconcerned; apathetic:表情～ look indifferent; appear apathetic ❷ see "淡薄❹"

淡然 dànrán　〈书〉unconcerned; casual; indifferent:～处之 treat sth with (an air of) complete indifference

淡忘 dànwàng　(of sth) fade from one's memory; (of a person) forget:～的往事 bygone, forgotten matter

淡雅 dànyǎ　simple and elegant; quietly elegant:色调～ quietly elegant colour

悼(憚) dàn　〈书〉fear; dread

弹(彈) dàn ❶ ball; pellet; bullet; shell; bomb;～痕 bullet or shell hole / ～壳 cartridge or shell case; bombshell / ～片 shell fragment or splinter; shrapnel / ～头 bullet; projectile nose; warhead / ～尽粮绝 run out of ammunition and provisions / ～无虚发。Every shot hits the target.

see also tán

弹道 dàndào　trajectory; ballistic path:～导弹 ballistic missile

弹弓 dàngōng　catapult; slingshot

弹丸 dànwán ❶ ball; pellet; shot ❷〈书〉(of land) tiny; small and narrow:～之地 small bit of land; tiny place

弹药 dànyào　ammunition:～库 ammunition depot

弹子 dànzi ❶ pellet shot from a catapult ❷ marble:～游戏 game of marbles ❸〈方〉billiards

蛋 dàn ❶ egg:下～ lay eggs / ～糕 cake / ～鸡 layer; laying hen / ～

壳 eggshell / ～花汤 egg-drop soup ❷ egg-shaped thing; ball

蛋白 dànbái ❶ also "蛋清" egg white; albumen ❷ protein:～酶〈化〉protease; proteinase / ～质 protein

蛋黄 dànhuáng　yolk:～酱 mayonnaise

蛋卷 dànjuǎn　egg roll:～冰淇淋 ice-cream cone

氮 dàn　〈化〉nitrogen (N):～肥 nitrogenous fertilizer / ～气 nitrogen (gas)

dāng

当(當) dāng ❶ equal; match:～量 equivalent (weight) / 得失相～。The gain equals the loss. ❷ ought to; should; must:断则断 decide when a decision is called for ❸ just at (a time or place); facing:～门而立 stand against the door / ～机立断 make a prompt decision; act promptly ❹ serve, act or work as; be:～兵 serve in the army; enlist / ～差〈旧〉work as a petty official in a *yamen*; be a servant / ～一天和尚撞一天钟〈俗〉go on tolling the bell as long as one is a monk—take a passive attitude towards one's work ❺ deserve; accept:～之无愧 fully deserve (a title, an honour, etc); be worthy of ❻ manage; be in charge of; direct:～政 be in power or office ❼〈象声〉sound made by striking metals:～～的钟声 tolling of a bell

see also dàng

当班 dāngbān　be on duty; be on a shift

当场 dāngchǎng　on the spot; then and there:～抓住 catch (sb) red-handed

当初 dāngchū　at the beginning; originally; initially

当代 dāngdài　present age; contemporary era：～文豪 literary giant of our time

当道 dāngdào ❶ in the middle of the road：～站立 stand in the way ❷ be in power；hold sway：坏人～，好人遭殃。When scoundrels are in power, good people suffer.

当地 dāngdì in the locality；local：～时间 local time

当归 dāngguī 〈中药〉Chinese angelica

当即 dāngjí right away；at once；immediately

当家 dāngjiā run a household；call the roost：～作主 be master in one's own house or of one's own affairs

当今 dāngjīn now；at present；nowadays：～社会 present-day society

当局 dāngjú the authorities ❷ be involved (in a game, etc)：～者迷，旁观者清〈俗〉the spectators see the chess game better than the players；an outsider sees things more clearly than one involved

当空 dāngkōng high above in the sky；红日～。A blazing sun hangs in the sky.

当面 dāngmiàn to sb's face；in sb's presence：～对质 confront sb (with facts, questions, etc)；challenge sb face to face

当年 dāngnián ❶ in those years；formerly：精力不减～ as energetic as ever ❷ in the prime of life：正～ be in one's prime　see also "当❹" dàng

当前 dāngqián ❶ before or facing one：大敌～ be confronted by a formidable foe ❷ present；current：～利益 immediate interests

当权 dāngquán hold or wield power；be in power：～派 person or people in power；powers that be

当然 dāngrán ❶ it is only natural；it is as it should be：～应该如此。That is just as it should be. ❷ certainly；of course；to be sure：我们～会去。We

will certainly go there. ❸ natural：～继承〈法〉natural succession / ～成员 ex officio member

当仁不让 dāngrénbùràng not pass on to others what one is called upon to do；feel duty-bound to shoulder a responsibility：他～地接受了委派。He accepted the assignment as his due.

当时 dāngshí ❶ then；at that time ❷ just at the right time；in season　see also "当❹" dàng

当事人 dāngshìrén person or party concerned；interested party；litigant

当头 dāngtóu ❶ right overhead；right on the head；head-on：～一棒 head-on blow；surprise attack ❷ facing or confronting one；imminent：国难～ when disaster threatens a nation；when a nation is confronted with a crisis ❸ put in the first place；give priority to：他总是怕字～。Fear pre-dominates whatever he does.

当务之急 dāngwùzhījí burning issue or pressing matter of the moment；top priority

当先 dāngxiān in the van；in the front ranks；at the head：事事～ take the lead in everything one does

当心 dāngxīn ❶ be careful；beware；watch out：～扒手。Beware of pickpockets. ❷ middle of the chest；middle or centre of sth：～一拳 hit (sb) in the chest

当选 dāngxuǎn be elected；win an election：～总统 be elected president；president-elect

当中 dāngzhōng ❶ in the middle or centre of；among；in the midst of

当众 dāngzhòng in the presence of all；in public：～表态 make clear one's position in public；take a public stance

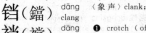

铛（鐺） dāng 〈象声〉clank；clang

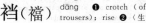

裆（襠） dāng ❶ crotch (of trousers)；rise ❷ 〈生

理）crotch

dǎng

挡（擋） dǎng ❶ keep or ward off; shelter or shield (sb) against or from sth; block; ～板 board; guard; baffle / ～驾〈婉〉put off (a visitor) with some excuse; decline to see (a guest); deny admittance / ～箭牌 shield; excuse; pretext / ～风玻璃 (of a car, etc) windshield; windscreen ❷ fender; blind; 窗—子 window blind or shade ❸ gear; 换—change gear

党（黨） dǎng ❶（political）party; ～报 party newspaper or organ / ～费 party membership due / ～风 conduct of party members; work style of a political party / ～魁〈贬〉party boss or chieftain / ～龄 party standing / ～徒〈贬〉member of a clique or a political party; henchman / ～员 party member / ～章 party constitution / ～纪国法 party discipline and state laws ❷ the Party (ie the Communist Party of China); ～委 Party committee / ～支部 Party branch / 中央 Central Committee of the Party; Party Centre / ～外人士 non-Party personage ❸ clique; faction; gang; ～羽 member of a clique; adherent; henchman

党籍 dǎngjí　party membership; 开除～expel (sb) from a party

党派 dǎngpài　political parties and groups; party groupings; ～关系 party affiliation / ～之争 partisan struggle or strife

党同伐异 dǎngtóng-fáyì　gang up with those who are of the same faction and attack those who are not; be (narrowly) partisan

党性 dǎngxìng　party spirit or character; ～强 have a solid party character; be a staunch party member

党政 dǎngzhèng　Party and government; ～不分 failure to distinguish between the Party and government functions

dàng

当（當） dàng ❶ proper; right; appropriate; 处理得～ handle properly ❷ be equal to; match; 一个钱～两个钱花 make one cent do the job of two — be frugal or economical ❸ treat (as); take (for); regard; 不～回事儿 treat lightly; make light of / 被人～做小偷 be taken for a thief / 我～你走了。I thought you had left. ❹ that very (day, year, etc); ～年 the same year; that very year / ～时 right away; at once; immediately ❺ pawn; pledge; sth pawned; ～铺 pawnshop / ～手饰 pawn one's jewellery; put one's jewellery in pawn

see also dāng

当天 dàngtiān　same day; that very day; ～往返 one-day round trip / ～有效 good for the date stipulated

当真 dàngzhēn　❶ take seriously ❷ really (true); 此话～? Is it really true?

荡（蕩，❶-❸盪） dàng ❶ swing; sway; wave; ～舟 row a boat ❷ loaf; loiter; 闲～ lounge around ❸ rinse; clear away; sweep off; ～涤〈书〉cleanse; clean up; wash away / ～平 mop up and quell; suppress and wipe out / ～然无存〈书〉all gone; with nothing left ❹ debauched; licentious; ～妇 dissolute woman; woman of loose morals; prostitute ❺ shallow lake; marsh; 芦苇～ reed marsh

荡漾 dàngyàng　ripple; undulate; 碧波～ rippling waves / ～着春意 overflow with a sense of spring; be filled with ardent desire

档（檔） dàng ❶ shelves (for files); files; archives;

查～ consult the files / 归～ place on file；file (a document) ❷ grade；分～出售 sell goods by different grades

档案 dàng'àn　files；archives；record；～柜 filing cabinet

档次 dàngcì　grading；grade；拉开工资～ widen the gap between salary grades / ～不高 not of a high grade；of low grade or taste

档子 dàngzi 〈方〉〈量〉 *used before an event or issue*：不是一～事 not the same thing

dāo

刀 dāo ❶ knife；sword；any cutting tool；～具 *also* "刃具" cutting or knife tool；cutter；tool bit / ～片 razor blade / ～鞘 sheath；scabbard / ～把儿 *also* "刀柄" handle of a knife；hilt of a sword / ～耕火种 slash-and-burn farming or cultivation ❷ sth shaped like a knife；冰～ ice skates ❸ 〈量〉(usu a hundred) sheets (of paper)

刀光剑影 dāoguāng-jiànyǐng　glint and flash of cold steel—fierce fighting

刀枪 dāoqiāng　sword and spear；weapons；～不入 (of a person) invulnerable to swords and spears；〈喻〉proof against criticism or admonition

刀刃 dāorèn　*also* "刀口" edge of a knife or cutting tool；blade；〈喻〉crucial point；好钢用在～上 use the best steel to make the best blade—use resources where they are needed most

刀山火海 dāoshān-huǒhǎi　mountain of swords and sea of flames—immense dangers and difficulties；most severe trials

刀子 dāozi 〈口〉small knife；pocketknife；～嘴，豆腐心〈俗〉(have) a sharp tongue but a soft heart / 软～杀人 kill with an invisible knife—harm a person imperceptibly

叨 dāo　*see also* dáo；tāo

叨叨 dāodao　*also* "叨唠" talk on and on；chatter away；babble

dáo

叨 dáo　*see also* dāo；tāo

叨咕 dáogu　chatter in a whisper；murmur away

dǎo

导（導） dǎo ❶ lead；guide；direct；～播 organize and direct the broadcast of a radio or TV programme；producer of a radio or TV programme / ～言 preamble；foreword；introduction / ～语 synopsis (of a long article, etc) / ～购小姐 shopping guide；sales girl ❷ transmit；conduct；～热 heat conduction or transmission / ～体 conductor / ～尿〈医〉catheterization

导弹 dǎodàn　guided missile；～部队 missile force；missilemen / ～发射器 missile launcher / ～防御系统 missile defence system

导电 dǎodiàn　electric conduction；～体 electric conductor / ～性 electric conductivity；conductance

导管 dǎoguǎn ❶ conduit；pipe；duct ❷ vessel；trachea；duct ❸〈医〉catheter；插入～ catheterize

导航 dǎoháng　navigation；为船舶navigate or pilot a ship / ～灯 range light / ～仪 avigraph；navigator / ～员 navigator；pilot

导火线 dǎohuǒxiàn　(blasting) fuse；〈喻〉apparently insignificant incident leading to a big conflict

导论 dǎolùn　introductory remarks；introduction；survey

导师 dǎoshī ❶ tutor；adviser；

supervisor ❷ guide of a great cause;
teacher; mentor; 革命～ prophet or
mentor of a revolution

导线 dǎoxiàn 〈电〉lead; (conducting)
wire

导向 dǎoxiàng guidance; orientation;
direction; 市场～ market-oriented / 舆
论～ orientation of the media; media
guidance of public opinion

导演 dǎoyǎn ❶ direct (a film, play,
etc) ❷ director

导游 dǎoyóu ❶ conduct a sightseeing
tour; guide a tour; ～图 tourist map ❷
tour guide

导致 dǎozhì lead to; bring about;
cause; ～失眠 cause sleeplessness or insomnia / 骄傲～失败。Pride goes before a fall.

岛(島) dǎo island; ～国 is-
land country / ～屿
islands (and islets)

捣(搗) dǎo ❶ pound (with a
pestle, etc); beat; at-
tack; ～毁 smash up; demolish;
destroy / ～烂 pound (sth) into pulp
❷ disturb; make trouble for

捣蛋 dǎodàn 〈口〉make trouble; ～鬼
〈谑〉mischievous imp; trouble-maker

捣鬼 dǎoguǐ play tricks; do mischief
(in secret)

捣乱 dǎoluàn make trouble; create a
disturbance; disturb; ～分子 trouble-
maker

倒 dǎo ❶ fall; tumble down; col-
lapse; ～伏 (of crops) lodging /
～毙街头 drop or fall dead in the
streets ❷ fall or bring down; fail; ～闭
close down; go bankrupt / ～台 fall
from power; fail ❸ spoil (appetite); ～
胃口 spoil one's appetite; kill one's
interest ❹ change; exchange; ～ 班
change shifts; work in shifts / ～ 车
change trains or buses / ～换 rotate;
replace; exchange / ～休 (of workers,
etc) exchange working days and holi-

days; stagger holidays ❺ sell or rent
out (a business, etc); speculate;
profiteer; ～汇 deal illegally or speculate in foreign exchange / ～爷〈口〉
speculator; profiteer

see also dào

倒戈 dǎogē change sides in a war;
turn one's coat; transfer one's allegiance; 临阵～ change sides on the
battlefield; defect in battle

倒卖 dǎomài resell at a (high) profit;
speculate; 倒买～ (engage in) speculative buying and selling

倒霉 dǎoméi *also* "倒楣" have bad
luck; be out of luck or down on one's
luck; be unlucky; ～透了! What lousy
luck!

倒手 dǎoshǒu ❶ shift or move from
one hand to the other ❷ (of merchandise, etc) change hands

倒腾 dǎoteng *also* "捣腾"〈口〉❶
move; replace; rearrange; 把化肥～到
地里去 carry fertilizer to the fields ❷
buy and sell; deal or trade in

祷(禱) dǎo ❶ pray; 告
pray; say one's prayers /
～文 prayer ❷ (used in correspondence) long or hope for; 盼～
earnestly hope

蹈 dǎo ❶〈书〉tread; step; ～险
tread into danger; take risks ❷
move up and down; skip

dào

到 dào ❶ arrive; reach; up to; ～
顶 reach the top or limit; leave
no room for improvement ❷ leave; go
to; 我要～上海去了。I'm leaving for
Shanghai. ❸ *used as the complement
of a verb indicating the result of an*

action:看~他了吗? Did you see him? / 能说的我都说 ~ 了。I've said all I could. ❹ considerate; thoughtful; thorough;不~之处请原谅 I hope you will forgive me if I have not been thoughtful enough.

到场 dàochǎng　turn or show up; be present:~作证 attend as a witness

到处 dàochù　everywhere; at all places:这事不要 ~ 乱传。Don't bandy it about.

到达 dàodá　reach; arrive (at or in); get to:火车应于晚上 10 点~。The train is due at 10 p. m.

到底 dàodǐ　❶ to the end; in the end; at last:拼 ~ fight to the bitter end / 说 ~ in the final analysis ❷ 〈副〉used in an interrogative sentence for emphasis:你~想干什么? What on earth are you up to? ❸ after all; when all is said and done:~还是这主意行。It's this idea that works after all.

到家 dàojiā　❶ arrive home ❷ be perfect or excellent:我的功夫还不 ~。My skill is still far from perfect.

到来 dàolái　arrival (of sb); advent (of sth)

到期 dàoqī　become due; expire; mature:~利息 interest due.

到手 dàoshǒu　have in one's hands; take possession of; get hold of

到头来 dàotóulái　(usu used in a bad sense) in the end; finally:~没有好下场 come to no good end

到位 dàowèi　reach the designated place; be in place or position:传球 ~ pass the ball well / 资金不 ~。The capital is not in place.

到职 dàozhí　also "到任" assume office; take up one's post

倒 dào　❶ turn upside down or front-side back; reverse; move backwards:~带 rewind a cassette; reverse / ~ 灌 (of river or sea water) flow from a lower to a higher level; flow backwards / ~ 流 〈喻〉flow backwards; reverse flow / ~ 叙 flashback / 挂 ~ 了 hang (sth) upside down ❷ tip; dump; pour:~茶 pour or serve tea / ~ 垃圾 dump rubbish; empty garbage ❸ also "倒是"〈副〉used to indicate contrast, concession, or impatience:她 ~ 不是这个意思。Actually, this is not what she meant. / 东西是贵, ~ 还值得买。It is expensive but worth the money. / 你 ~ 说句话呀! Say something, will you!

see also dǎo

倒背如流 dàobèirúliú　can recite (sth) backwards fluently — know (sth) thoroughly by heart

倒彩 dàocǎi　booing; hooting; catcall:喝 ~ jeer at or boo sb; make catcalls

倒车 dàochē　back a car; back up:开历史~ turn back the wheel of history; put the clock back

倒打一耙 dàodǎyīpá　make unfounded countercharges; put the blame on one's victim; recriminate

倒挂 dàoguà　❶ hang upside down ❷ be contrary to the natural order of things; be in an inverted order:购销价格 ~ inverted purchasing and selling prices

倒计时 dàojìshí　countdown:进入~。The countdown (to sth) begins.

倒立 dàolì　❶ stand upside down:树影~水中。The tree is reflected upside down in the water. ❷ 〈体〉handstand:~行走 walk on one's hands

倒数 dàoshǔ　count in reverse order:~第二名 last but one on a list / ~第五行 fifth line from the bottom (of the page)

倒贴 dàotiē　lose money (instead of making a profit); pay (instead of receiving):~抛售 dump (goods) at a loss

倒退 dàotuì　go backwards; fall back; retrogress:~一步 fall or take one step back

倒行逆施 dàoxíng-nìshī　try to put the clock back; go against the historical trend; act perversely

倒影 dàoyǐng　inverted image; inverted reflection in water

倒置 dàozhì　place upside down; invert: 请勿～。This end up.

倒装 dàozhuāng　〈语言〉inversion; inverted order: ～句 inverted sentence

盗 dào ❶ steal; rob; burglarize: ～墓 rob a grave; commit grave robbery / ～印 print illegally; pirate (a book, etc) / ～用 embezzle; usurp ❷ thief; robber; burglar: ～匪 bandit; robber / ～贼 thief; robber

盗版 dàobǎn　illegal copy; pirate copy: ～书 pirated book / ～行为 piracy

盗汗 dàohàn　〈医〉night sweat: 出～ perspire during sleep

盗窃 dàoqiè　steal; burgle: ～案 case of theft or burglary / ～犯 thief; burglar / ～罪 robbery; theft; larceny

悼 dào　mourn; grieve: ～词 also "悼辞" memorial speech (at a funeral); funeral oration / ～念死者 grieve for the deceased; express one's condolences upon sb's death

道 dào ❶ course; road; way: ～路 road; way; path / 为人之～ way to conduct oneself ❷ morality; virtue; justice: ～高一尺, 魔高一丈〈俗〉as virtue rises one foot, vice rises ten; while the priest climbs a foot, the devil climbs ten ❸ method; technique; skill: ～～儿多 full of ideas; resourceful ❹ doctrine; principle: ～不同, 不相与谋。There is little common ground for understanding between people of different principles. ❺ Taoism; Taoist: ～姑 Taoist nun / ～观 Taoist temple / ～家 Taoist school; Taoists / ～袍 Taoist robe / ～士 Taoist priest ❻ line: 细～ thin lines ❼ say; speak; express: 白 also "念白" spoken parts in a trad-

itional opera / ～别 say goodbye; bid farewell; take leave / ～喜 also "道贺" congratulate (sb on sth) ❽ suppose; think: 我～是纯棉的呢。I thought it was pure cotton. ❾〈量〉**a)** of rivers and certain long and narrow things: 一～闪电 a flash of lightning **b)** of doors, walls, etc: 设两～岗 post double lines of sentries **c)** of orders, questions, etc: 一～命令 an order **d)** indicating steps or times: 还有一～手续 have one more formality to go through

道德 dàodé　morality; morals; ethics: ～规范 moral standards or criteria; code of ethics / ～品质 moral character or qualities

道教 Dàojiào　〈宗教〉Taoism

道具 dàojù　stage property; prop

道理 dàoli ❶ truth; principle; hows and whys: 针灸的～ principles or theories of acupuncture ❷ reason; argument: 这话有～。This is reasonable.

道貌岸然 dàomào'ànrán　appear as if one were a person of high morals; be sanctimonious

道破 dàopò　point out frankly; reveal; lay bare: 一语～其中奥妙 unveil the mystery with one remark

道歉 dàoqiàn　make an apology; apologize

道听途说 dàotīng-túshuō　hearsay; rumour; gossip

道谢 dàoxiè　express thanks; thank: 改日登门～。I'll call to extend my appreciation some other day.

道学 dàoxué ❶ see "理学" lǐxué ❷ pedantic learning: 假～ canting hypocrite

道义 dàoyì　morality and justice: ～上的支持 moral support / 这在～上说不过去。This cannot be justified on moral grounds.

稻 dào　rice; paddy: ～草 rice straw / ～谷 paddy / ～穗 rice

ear / ～田 paddy-field; rice-field / ～种 rice seeds / ～子 rice; paddy / ～草人 scarecrow

dé

得 dé ❶ get; obtain; win: ～病 fall ill; contract a disease / ～宠 be in (sb's) good graces; find favour (with sb) / ～救 be rescued / ～空 also "得闲" be free; have leisure / ～胜 triumph; win a victory / ～知 learn; get to know / ～主 winner (of a prize, etc) / ～奖论文 prize-winning article / 三加六～九。Three plus six equals (or makes) nine. ❷ fit; proper: ～当 proper; appropriate; suitable ❸ satisfied; complacent: 面有～色 look self-satisfied; show smug complacency ❹ be finished or done; be ready: 牛排～了。The steak is done. ❺ ⟨口⟩ used to indicate agreement, prohibition or helplessness: ～，就这么办。OK! Just go ahead. / ～，我又忘带钥匙了。Oh, shoot! I forgot the key again. ❻ (usu in documents and stipulations) used before another verb to show permission: 未经许可，不～入内。No admittance without permission.

see also de; děi

得逞 déchěng ⟨贬⟩ have one's way; succeed; prevail

得寸进尺 décùn-jìnchǐ ⟨贬⟩ reach out for a yard after taking an inch; be insatiable

得到 dédào get; obtain; receive: 得不到支持 receive no support

得法 défǎ work in the proper way; get the knack: 经营不～ (of an enterprise, etc) be badly managed

得分 défēn score: 得满分 get full marks (in a test, etc) / 连得三分 win three points in a row / 一分未得 fail to score

得过且过 déguòqiěguò muddle along

or on; drift along

得了 déle ❶ used to indicate prohibition, dismissal, or agreement: (你) ～吧,谁信你的! Come off it! Who do you think will believe you? ❷ ⟨助⟩ used to indicate affirmation and emphasis: 你走～,不用惦记我。Please go and don't worry about me. ❸ (déliǎo) used to express astonishment or shock: 这怎么～啊? Oh, my God! How will all this end?

得力 délì ❶ benefit from; get help from; be assisted by: ～于勤奋 thanks or due to one's diligence ❷ competent; capable: ～助手 competent assistant; right-hand man ❸ strong; efficient: 措施～ effective measure

得人心 dérénxīn enjoy public support; be popular

得失 déshī gain and loss; success and failure; advantages and disadvantages: 得不偿失 the loss outweighs the gain; pay too dear for one's whistle

得势 déshì be in power; get the upper hand

得手 déshǒu go smoothly; succeed; come or bring off

得体 détǐ (of language or behaviour) appropriate to the occasion; befitting one's position or dignity

得天独厚 détiāndúhòu enjoy special favours of nature; be richly endowed by nature

得心应手 déxīn-yìngshǒu ❶ with proficiency or facility: 写对子～ be in one's element when writing couplets ❷ (of a tool, etc) handy; serviceable

得益 déyì benefit; profit: ～匪浅 benefit considerably (from sth)

得意 déyì pleased with oneself; complacent; conceited: ～门生 favourite pupil / ～忘形 be intoxicated by one's success; get dizzy with success / ～扬扬 also "得意洋洋" look triumphant; be immensely proud

得志 dézhì　achieve one's ambition; have a successful career; 郁郁不～ be frustrated（in one's career）and unhappy

得罪 dézuì　offend; displease; 怕～人 afraid of giving offence

德 dé　❶ morality; virtue; moral character; ～育 moral education / ～才兼备 have both ability and virtue / ～高望重（of old people）enjoy moral eminence and high esteem ❷ mind; heart; 同心同～ of one heart and one mind ❸ kindness; favour; 有～于人 bestow favor to others ❹〔Dé〕（short for 德国 or 德意志）Germany; Deutschland; ～语 German

德行 déxíng　❶ moral conduct or integrity ❷（déxing）〈口〉（of manners, etc）disgusting; revolting; 瞧他那～! Look, how repulsive the guy is!

de

地 de　〈助〉used after an adjective, etc to form an adverbial before the verb; 轻轻～落下 fall gently
see also dì

的 de　〈助〉❶ used after an attribute　a）when modifying a noun or indicating possession; 圆圆～脸 moon face / 他～父母 his parents　b）to indicate an action received, or a role played; 开新郎～玩笑 play a joke on the bridegroom / 今天是我～东。It's my treat today. ❷ used after a verb to turn it into a noun; 理发～ barber; hair-dresser / 吃～穿～ food and clothing ❸ used between identical verbs, adjectives, etc, to form contrasts; 说一说，笑一笑。Some talk while others laugh. ❹ used for emphasis between a verb（of past time）and its object, or at the end of a statement; 她是上个月结～婚。It was last month that she got married. / 这件事

我是知道～。True, I know about this matter. ❺ used with 话 at the end of a conditional clause; 明天有空～话，我就去。I'll go if I have time tomorrow. ❻ used for enumeration; 破铜烂铁～ scrap iron and stuff ❼ see "得❷❸" de
see also dí; dì

得 de　〈助〉❶ used after certain verbs to indicate possibility or feasibility; 这东西晒～晒不～? Can we dry it in the sun or not? ❷ also "的" used between a verb and its complement to indicate possibility; 买～起 can afford（sth）❸ also "的" used after a verb or an adjective to introduce a complement of result or degree; 风刮～很大。The wind is blowing hard.
see also dé; děi

děi

得 děi　❶ need; require; take; 这事～你来做。You will have to handle the matter yourself. ❷ will certainly; be sure to; 他准～来。He is sure to come.
see also dé; de

dēng

灯（燈）dēng　lamp; light; lantern; 酒精～ alcohol burner; spirit lamp / ～会 lantern show or festival / ～具 lamps and lanterns / ～谜 riddle written on a lantern; lantern riddle / ～泡 light bulb; （electric）bulb / ～丝 filament / ～塔 lighthouse; beacon / ～头 lamp holder; electric light socket / ～罩 lampshade; chimney（of a kerosene lamp, etc）/ ～管儿 fluorescent tube

灯光 dēngguāng ❶ lamplight; ～球场 floodlit or illuminated court, field, etc ❷（stage）lighting; ～师 juicer

灯红酒绿 dēnghóng-jiǔlǜ　red lanterns and green wine— scene of feasting and revelry; night scene of colour and bustle:~的生活 life of bustling luxury or debauchery

灯火 dēnghuǒ　lights:~管制 blackout / ~辉煌 brilliantly lit or illuminated; ablaze with lights

灯笼 dēnglong　lantern:~椒 also "柿子椒" bell or sweet pepper / ~裤 sweat pants; loose sports trousers

灯心 dēngxīn　also "灯芯" (lamp) wick:~绒 also "条绒" corduroy

登 dēng ❶ climb; ascend; mount:~程 start off on a journey; set off or out / ~高 ascend a height; climb up / ~基 mount the throne; be enthroned / ~月 land on the moon / ~门求教 call on sb for advice ❷ publish; record; enter:~录 register / ~载 (of newspapers, etc) publish; carry / ~广告 advertise (in a newspaper) / ~户口 (make) residence registration ❸ also "蹬" tread; pedal; wear (shoes or trousers):~缝纫机 work on a (pedal) sewing machine / ~自行车 ride a bicycle

登报 dēngbào　publish, report, or appear in a newspaper:~声明 announce in a newspaper statement or advertisement

登场 dēngchǎng　come or go on stage; enter:首次~ (make) a début on the stage

登峰造极 dēngfēng-zàojí　(of skill, learning, etc) reach the acme of perfection; reach the limit:阴险毒辣,~ sinister and ruthless in the extreme

登革热 dēnggérè　〈医〉dengue fever

登机 dēngjī　board an airplane:~口 boarding gate / ~牌 boarding-card; boarding-pass

登记 dēngjì　register; enter one's name; check in:~簿 register / ~处 registry; registration (at a conference, etc) / ~住宿 check in (at a hotel)

登陆 dēnglù　land; disembark (from a ship):~艇 landing craft

登山 dēngshān　mountain climbing; mountaineering:~队 mountaineering expedition or party / ~运动 mountaineering / ~运动员 mountaineer

登时 dēngshí　then and there; at once; immediately

登台 dēngtái　mount the platform; go on the stage:~表演 perform on the stage / ~执政 assume political power

登堂入室 dēngtáng-rùshì　see "升堂入室" shēngtángrùshì

登徒子 dēngtúzǐ　rake; lecher; debauchee

噔 dēng　〈象声〉thump; thud:~的一声摔在地上 fall thudding on the ground

蹬 dēng ❶ 〈方〉discard; jilt; throw over:~了老婆 divorce one's wife ❷ see "登❸"

蹬腿 dēngtuǐ　〈口〉〈谑〉kick the bucket; die

děng

等 děng ❶ class; grade; rank:二~功 second-class merit / ~外品 substandard product / ~而下之 from that grade down; lower down / 划分~次 classify; grade; rank ❷ 〈助〉a) 〈书〉used for plural number:这~事 things like this / 我~三人 the three of us　b) used for enumeration:钢笔、纸张~ pens, paper and what not　c) used to end an enumeration:小提琴、钢琴、单簧管~乐器 musical instruments such as the violin, piano and clarinet ❸ equal:~号 equal-sign; equality sign / ~式 〈数〉equality / ~比级数 〈数〉geometrical progression / ~差级数 〈数〉arithmetical progression / ~额选举 nominating one candidate for each post; single-candidate election /

~边三角形 equilateral triangle ❹ wait; await; ~着瞧 wait and see / ~雨停了再走。Wait till the rain stops.

等待 děngdài *also* "等候" wait (for); await; expect; ~出发 be ready for departure / ~时机 bide one's time

等到 děngdào by the time; when; (wait) till; ~饭后再谈工作。Business can wait until after dinner. or We can discuss business after dinner.

等级 děngjí ❶ grade; rank; ~工资制 graded wage scale ❷ social stratum, estate or status; ~观念 concept of (social) status / ~森严 rigidly stratified / ~制度 hierarchy

等价 děngjià equal in value; of equal value; equivalent; ~物〈经〉equivalent / ~交换 exchange of equal values

等量齐观 děngliàngqíguān equate one with the other; put on a par; mention in the same breath

等同 děngtóng be equal to; equate; be the same

等闲 děngxián 〈书〉❶ ordinary; unimportant; ~视之 treat lightly; regard as unimportant / 非~之辈 not a person to be trifled with or to be made light of ❷ lightly; casually; for nothing

等于 děngyú be equal or equivalent to; be the same as; amount to; ~零 amount to nothing

dèng

凳(櫈) dèng *also* "凳子" stool; bench

澄 dèng *see also* chéng

澄清 dèngqīng (of water, etc) become clear; settle *see also* chéngqīng

瞪 dèng open one's eyes wide; glare; stare

瞪眼 dèngyǎn ❶ open one's eyes wide; stare; 瞪了他一眼 give him a glare ❷ get angry (with sb); glare and glower (at sb); 爱跟人~ be always glaring and glowering

镫 dèng *also* "镫子" stirrup

dī

低 dī ❶ low; inferior; 〈医〉hypo-; ~层 of or on a lower level, floor, etc; low-ranking / ~产 low yield; low-yielding / ~价 low or reduced price; low cost / ~烧 (run a) low or slight fever / ~声 in a low voice; under one's breath / ~洼地 low-lying land / ~空飞行 low-altitude or low-level flying / ~人一等 inferior (to others) / 出身~贱 of humble birth ❷ hang down; droop; 夜幕~垂。Night fell.

低潮 dīcháo low tide or ebb; lowest point; nadir; 处于~ be at a low ebb; reach the nadir

低沉 dīchén ❶ (of weather) overcast; gloomy ❷ (of voice, etc) low and deep ❸ low-spirited; downcast; 情绪~ be in low spirits

低档 dīdàng low grade or end; inferior in quality; ~服装 low-end or low-grade clothing

低调 dīdiào low-key; low-pitched; ~处理 handle (sth) in a low key

低估 dīgū underestimate; underrate

低谷 dīgǔ deep valley— all-time low; bottom; 跌入~ (of prices, markets, etc) bottom out

低级 dījí ❶ elementary; rudimentary; low; ~阶段 lower stage ❷ vulgar; coarse; low; ~趣味 bad taste; vulgar interest

低廉 dīlián cheap; low-priced

低劣 dīliè inferior; sub-standard; low-grade; ~商品 shoddy goods

低落 dīluò low; depressed; downcast; 士气~。The morale is low.

低迷 dīmí (of prices, etc) low; (of economy, etc) stagnant：经济持续~。The economy remains in the doldrums.

低能 dīnéng mental deficiency; feeble mind：~儿 (mentally) retarded child

低三下四 dīsān-xiàsì abject; servile; subservient

低声下气 dīshēng-xiàqì speak humbly and submissively; be humble and meek：~地求饶 plead piteously for mercy

低头 dītóu ❶ hang or bow one's head：~不语 hang one's head in silence ❷ yield; submit：~认罪 hang one's head and admit one's guilt; plead guilty

低温 dīwēn (of) low temperature; cryogenic：~储藏 cryo-preservation / ~疗法 cryotherapy

低下 dīxià ❶ (of status or living standard) low; inferior ❷ also "低俗" (of taste, etc) lowly; vulgar; cheap

低压 dīyā ❶ 〈理〉 low pressure; depression：~泵 low-lift pump / 低气压 low pressure; depression ❷ 〈电〉 low voltage：~电源 low-voltage power supply ❸ 〈医〉 minimum pressure; 低血压 hypotension

低音 dīyīn bass：男~ bass / 女~ alto / ~提琴 double bass; contrabass

堤(隄) dī dyke; embankment：~岸 embankment / 坝 dykes and dams / ~防 dyke; embankment

提 dī see also tí

提防 dīfang be on guard; beware of; be on the alert：隔墙有耳。Be careful: walls have ears.

嘀 dī see also tí

嘀里嘟噜 dīlidūlū also "滴里嘟噜" speak quickly and indistinctly

滴 dī ❶ drip; let drop：~灌〈农〉drip or trickle irrigation / ~剂 drops / ~水成冰 freezing cold ❷

drop; bead：水~ drops of water / 两~墨水 two drops of ink

滴答 dīdā also "嘀嗒" ❶〈象声〉tick; tick-tock；滴滴答答的秋雨 pattering autumn rain ❷ (dīda) drip：汗水~ dripping sweat

滴水不漏 dīshuǐbùlòu ❶ speak in a watertight or leak-proof manner; leave nothing for people to pick on ❷ very crowded; closely or tightly surrounded

dí

迪 dí 〈书〉enlighten; guide

迪斯科 dísīkē disco：~舞厅 discotheque

的 dí 〈书〉true; really　see also de；dì

的确 díquè indeed; really

的确良 díquèliáng dacron; terylene

敌(敵) dí ❶ enemy; foe：~后 enemy's rear / ~机 enemy plane / ~寇〈贬〉enemy (bandits); aggressors / ~人 enemy; foe / ~我矛盾 contradiction between ourselves and the enemy ❷ oppose; resist; stand up to：以寡~众 fight against heavy odds ❸ equal (in strength); match; rival：无人能~ unrivaled; invincible

敌对 díduì hostile; antagonistic; belligerent：~情绪 antagonistic feelings; hostility; enmity

敌情 díqíng enemy's situation; enemy activities：侦察~ gather information about the enemy / ~观念 alertness to the enemy; vigilance against the enemy

敌视 díshì be hostile or antagonistic to; take a hostile attitude towards

敌手 díshǒu ❶ match; opponent; adversary：不是~ not one's match or rival ❷ enemy hands：落入~ fall into enemy hands

敌意 díyì hostility; enmity; animosity：心怀 ~ hold antagonism in one's heart

涤（滌） dí ❶〈书〉wash；cleanse：~ 荡 wash away；clean up ❷（short for 涤纶）polyester fibre；dacron；terylene：~ 棉 *also* "棉的确良" mixed polyester-cotton fabric；polycotton

笛 dí ❶ *also* "横笛" (horizontal bamboo) flute；~ 子 Chinese (eight-holed) bamboo flute ❷ whistle：警 ~ police whistle

嘀 dí *see also* dī

嘀咕 dígu ❶ whisper；gossip (in a low voice)：喜欢嘀嘀咕咕 be fond of gossip ❷ have misgivings；have sth on one's mind：心里犯 ~ be uneasy in one's mind；have misgivings

嫡 dí ❶ of or by the official wife；~ 出 born of the official wife ❷ of lineal descent；closely related；authentic：~ 传弟子 disciple personally taught by the master / ~ 派真传 (receive) personal instruction and guidance by the master

嫡亲 díqīn closest by blood；by the same father；by the same paternal grandfather：~ 兄弟 blood or own brother / ~ 侄子 son of one's own brother

嫡系 díxì ❶（of）direct line of descent：~ 后裔 progeny of direct line of descent (from sb) ❷ under the direct control of a faction or chief：~ 部队 troops under the direct control of a faction or chief

dǐ

邸 dǐ residence of a high official：~ 宅 mansion (house)

诋 dǐ 〈书〉speak ill of；slander；defame：~ 毁 slander；vilify；calumniate

抵 dǐ ❶ support；prop；hold up：用木柱 ~ 着 shored or propped up by poles ❷ resist；withstand：~ 挡 withstand；keep out；ward off ❸ make up or compensate for；mortgage：~ 偿 compensate (for)；make up；make good / 用存款作 ~ mortgage one's deposit ❹ balance；be equal to；match：~ 命 give a life for a life；pay with one's life (for a murder, etc)：~ 罪 be punished for a crime / 收支相 ~。Income and expenditure are balanced. ❺〈书〉arrive at；reach：~ 达 arrive；reach

抵触 dǐchù conflict or clash (with)；contravene：有 ~ 情绪 be resentful or antagonistic

抵抗 dǐkàng resist；fight against；stand up to：顽强 ~ put up a stubborn resistance

抵赖 dǐlài deny；disavow；disclaim：无可 ~ undeniable

抵消 dǐxiāo offset；counteract；countervail：互相 ~ cancel out one another

抵押 dǐyā mortgage；pledge：以家产作 ~ mortgage one's family estate / ~ 品 security；pledge / ~ 贷款 mortgage financing or loan

抵御 dǐyù resist；withstand；ward off

抵债 dǐzhài *also* "抵账" pay a debt in kind or by labour：用房子 ~ pay off a debt with one's house

抵制 dǐzhì boycott；resist；combat

底 dǐ ❶ bottom；base；end (of a year, etc)：~ 价 base or bottom price；floor / ~ 限 lowest limit；minimum；floor / ~ 薪 basic salary；base pay / ~ 座 base；pedestal；foundation / 月 ~ end of a month ❷ origin or bottom of sth；ins and outs：~ 蕴〈书〉details；inside story；implications ❸ rough draft；draft text：~ 稿 draft；manuscript / 留个 ~ 儿 keep a copy (of sth) on file ❹ background；ground：~ 白花 white flowers on a blue background

底层 dǐcéng ❶ ground or first floor ❷ lowest rung; (rock) bottom;社会的～ bottom of society

底牌 dǐpái cards in one's hand; bottom line;亮～ show one's hand / 泄露～ leak one's bottom line (on sth)

底片 dǐpiàn also "底版" negative; photographic plate

底气 dǐqì ❶ breath; (in speech or singing) resonance;～足 have good resonance / 病后～不足 be short of breath after an illness ❷ energy; drive; vigour;做工作的～更足了 be inspired with greater energy for work

底细 dǐxì also "底里" ins and outs; inside story; true state of affairs

底下 dǐxia ❶ under; below; beneath;～人 servant; subordinate; underling ❷ next; later; afterwards;～该干什么了？ What shall we do next?

底线 dǐxiàn ❶ (of tennis court, etc) baseline;〈喻〉bottom line ❷ planted agent; stooge; stool-pigeon; 安插～ plant stooges or agents

底子 dǐzi ❶ bottom;〈喻〉base; bottom line;摸清他的～。Find out about his basic position. / 我国～薄。We have a weak economic foundation. ❷ copy kept as a record; rough draft or sketch;这份文件要留～。Keep a copy of this document on file. ❸ remnant;货～ remnants of stock ❹ see 底❹

骶 dǐ 骶骨 dǐgǔ 〈生理〉sacrum

dì

地 dì ❶ the earth;～层〈地〉stratum; layer /～心引力 (terrestrial) gravity ❷ land; soil; ground;～产 landed property; real estate /～窖 cellar /～契 title deed for land /～线 (电)ground or earth wire /～广人稀 wide but sparsely populated country ❸ place; area; locality;～痞 local ruffian /

～税 local tax /～处闹市 be located in the downtown area ❹ distance;20 里～ distance of twenty li ❺ position; situation; room;立于不败之～ be in an invincible position ❻ (short for 地区) prefecture; administrative unit below the province and above the county;～级市 prefecture-level city ❼ see 底❹ dǐ see also de

地板 dìbǎn floor; floorboard;～革 plastic floor covering or flooring /～蜡 floor wax /～砖 brick or tile flooring

地表 dìbiǎo (the earth's) surface;～水 surface water

地步 dìbù ❶ (usu bad) condition or situation; extent; degree;病到了危险的～ be critically ill / 事情还没有坏到这种～。Things are not as bad as that. ❷ room for action; leeway; elbow room;留有回旋的～ leave room for manoeuvre; have some leeway; give oneself elbow room

地大物博 dìdà-wùbó vast in territory and rich in natural resources; big country abounding in natural resources

地带 dìdài region; area; zone;绿化～ green belt (of a city, etc) / 无人～ no man's land

地道 dìdao ❶ from a place well known for the product; genuine;～货 genuine product of a locality ❷ pure; typical;～的英国口音 pure British accent ❸ up to standard; of high quality; excellent;做工～ excellent or exquisite tailoring ❹ (dìdào) tunnel;～战 tunnel warfare

地点 dìdiǎn place; site; scene

地段 dìduàn sector or section of an area; location;市中心的商业～ downtown shopping area / 不够好（的）～ rather poor location

地方 dìfāng ❶ locality (as distinct from central administration);～财政 local finance /～观念 localism; localistic prejudice /～保护主义 local protectionism ❷ (of) this locality (as distinct from others); (of) local government and people (as distinct from the garrison): ~病 endemic (disease) / ~志 also "方志" local chronicles or records; annals of local history / ~特产 local speciality ❸ (dìfang) place; space; room: 她是什么~人? Where is she from? / 他的建议有些~我同意。I agree in part with his proposal.

地基 dìjī foundation; ground; subgrade: 打好~ lay a good foundation

地界 dìjiè ❶ demarcation of land; boundary ❷ space; area; jurisdiction: 进入河北省~ enter the jurisdiction of Hebei Province

地老天荒 dìlǎo-tiānhuāng for ages and ages; for all eternity: ~,此心不变。Even if heaven and earth get old, my heart shall remain faithful.

地雷 dìléi (land) mine: 埋~ plant or lay mines

地理 dìlǐ ❶ geographical features of a place: ~环境 geographical surroundings ❷ geography: 自然~ physical geography

地面 dìmiàn ❶ earth's surface; ground: ~站 ground (satellite) station / ~部队 land or ground forces ❷ ground; floor: 水磨石~ terrazzo floor ❸ see "地界❷"

地盘 dìpán territory under one's control; turf; domain: 争夺~ fight for turf; compete for spheres of influence

地皮 dìpí ❶ land for building; plot ❷ ground; surface

地平线 dìpíngxiàn horizon

地壳 dìqiào earth's crust: ~运动 crustal movement

地勤 dìqín ground service (for aviation): ~人员 ground crew or personnel

地球 dìqiú earth; globe: ~村 global community or village / ~仪 terrestrial globe

地区 dìqū ❶ area; district; region: ~冲突 regional conflict ❷ see "地❻" ❸ region (of the world as distinguished from an independent state); territory: 港澳 ~ Hong Kong-Macao region

地热 dìrè terrestrial heat: ~资源 geothermal resources

地势 dìshì physical features of a place; terrain; topography

地毯 dìtǎn carpet; rug: ~式轰炸 carpet or blanket bombing

地铁 dìtiě ❶ (short for 地下铁道) subway; tube; underground (railway): ~站 subway or Metro station ❷ underground train: 坐 ~ ride or take the subway; go by subway

地头蛇 dìtóushé local villain or bully

地图 dìtú map: ~集 atlas

地位 dìwèi ❶ position; standing; place: 国际~ international standing or prestige ❷ geographical position; location: ~重要 of geographical importance

地下 dìxià ❶ underground; subterranean: ~室 basement; cellar / ~水 groundwater ❷ secret (activity); underground: 转入~ go underground / ~党 underground Party (organization) / ~工厂 underground or unlicensed factory ❸ (dìxia) on the ground: 把~扫干净 sweep the floor clean

地形 dìxíng topography; terrain: ~图 topographic or relief map

地狱 dìyù hell; inferno: 打入~ be condemned or consigned to hell

地域 dìyù ❶ vast area or region: ~辽阔 (have a) vast territory ❷ locality: ~观念 regionalism

地缘 dìyuán geographically-related; geo-: ~优势 geographical advantages / ~政治 geopolitics

地震 dìzhèn earthquake; seism; tremor: ~波 seismic wave / ~仪 seismograph / ~地区 earthquake-stricken area / ~震级 (earthquake) magnitude

地支 dìzhī twelve Earthly Branches

see also "干支" gānzhī

地址 dìzhǐ address；～不详 unclear address

地质 dìzhì geology：～构造 geological structure／～年代 geological age

地中海 Dìzhōnghǎi the Mediterranean (Sea)；～气候 Etesian climate／～国家 Mediterranean country

地主 dìzhǔ ❶ landlord ❷ host：尽～之谊 extend the courtesies of a host; play the host

地租 dìzū (land or ground) rent；实物～ rent in kind

弟 dì ❶ younger brother：～兄 brothers ❷ younger brother-in-law or (male) cousin ❸〈谦〉(usu in letter writing) I

弟弟 dìdi ❶ younger brother ❷ younger male cousin：叔伯～(younger) first cousin

弟妹 dìmèi ❶ younger brother and sister ❷ *also* "弟妇"、"弟媳" younger brother's wife; sister-in-law

弟子 dìzǐ disciple; pupil; follower

的 dì bull's-eye; target：众矢之～ target of public criticism *see also* de；dí

帝 dì ❶ Supreme Being; the Divine；天～ supreme ruler of heaven ❷ emperor; monarch：～王 emperor; monarch／～制 monarchy ❸ (short for 帝国主义) imperialism：反～斗争 struggle against imperialism; anti-imperialist struggle

帝国 dìguó empire：大英～ the British Empire／石油～〈喻〉oil empire

帝国主义 dìguózhǔyì imperialism；～分子 imperialist

递(遞) dì ❶ hand over; pass; deliver：～送 pass on; deliver ❷ successively; in the proper order：～补 fill vacancies in the proper order／～减 decrease progressively or successively; decrease by degrees／～升 rise progressively; pro-

mote to the next grade or rank／～增 increase progressively or by degrees

递交 dìjiāo hand over；present; submit

递解 dìjiè escort (usu a prisoner) from one place to another：～出境 deport

递眼色 dìyǎnsè wink at; give a wink；她向我递了个眼色。She gave me a knowing look.

第 dì ❶ *used to indicate ordinal numbers*：～一产业 primary industry or sector／～二产业 secondary industry or sector／～三产业 tertiary industry; service sector／宪法～三条 Article 3 of the Constitution ❷ (旧) residence of a high official：～宅 mansion

第二 dì'èr second; No 2；～人称〈语言〉second person／～职业 second or sparetime job; moonlighting

第六感觉 dìliùgǎnjué sixth sense；凭～(go) by one's sixth sense；(go) by hunch

第三 dìsān third; No 3；～世界 Third World／～人称单数〈语言〉third person singular

第三者 dìsānzhě ❶ third party (to a dispute) ❷ person having an affair with either the husband or the wife; third party；～插足 involvement of a third party in one's family life

第一 dìyī first; No 1；考～ come first in an exam／～卷 first volume; volume one／～流 *also* "一流" first rate or class; top-grade; top-notch／～手 firsthand／～把手 *also* "一把手" first in command; number one man／～夫人 First Lady／～人称〈语言〉first person ❷ most important; primary; foremost：安全～. Safety first.

第一线 dìyīxiàn ❶ front (line)：把兵力集中在～ concentrate troops at the front ❷ forefront; first line：教学～ classroom lecturing／农业生产～ field work in farming

谛 dì 〈书〉❶ attentively; carefully; ~ 视 examine closely; scrutinize ❷ meaning; significance; 妙 ~ ingenious remark; wisdom

蒂 dì base of a fruit

棣 dì 〈书〉younger brother; 贤 ~ my worthy brother

缔 dì form; establish; conclude; ~ 姻 be united in wedlock
缔交 dìjiāo ❶ 〈书〉establish a friendship ❷ establish diplomatic relations
缔结 dìjié conclude; establish; ~ 贸易协定 conclude a trade agreement
缔约 dìyuē conclude or sign a treaty or an agreement; ~ 方 contracting party / ~ 国 signatory state; (high) contracting party
缔造 dìzào found; create; establish; 共和国的 ~ 者 founders of a republic

diǎ

嗲 diǎ 〈方〉act or speak like a pampered child, or in a coquettish manner; 发 ~ play the coquet; act the pampered child

diān

掂 diān weigh in the hand; appraise
掂量 diānliáng weigh in the hand or mind; think over; ~ 着办 act as one sees fit

滇 diān another name for Yunnan (云南)

颠 diān ❶ crown (of the head); top; peak; 山 ~ mountain top ❷ jolt; bump; ~ 簸 jolt; bump; toss ❸ fall; topple down; turn over; ~ 来倒去 over and over; again and again ❹ 〈方〉jump up and run; make off ❺ see “癫” diān
颠倒 diāndǎo ❶ put or turn upside down; invert; ~ 乾坤 reverse heaven and earth; create total chaos ❷ confuse; confound; ~ 黑白 confound black and white; stand the facts on their heads
颠覆 diānfù overturn; subvert; topple; ~ 活动 subversive activities
颠沛流离 diānpèi-liúlí drift from place to place; wander about homeless and penniless
颠扑不破 diānpū-bùpò indestructible; indisputable; irrefutable
颠三倒四 diānsān-dǎosì disorderly; confused; disconnected; 说话 ~ talk incoherently or disconnectedly

巅 diān mountain top; peak; summit; ~ 峰 peak; summit

癫 diān mentally deranged; insane; ~ 狂 insanity; schizophrenia; (of behaviour) frivolous and arrogant / ~ 痫 (usu known as 羊角风) 〈医〉epilepsy

diǎn

典 diǎn ❶ standard or definitive work; canon; law; ~ 籍 important literature of a country; canon / ~ 章 institutions, decrees and regulations ❷ also “典故” allusion; literary quotation ❸ ceremony; ~ 礼 ceremony; celebration ❹ pawn; lease; mortgage; ~ 当 also “典押” mortgage; pawn
典范 diǎnfàn model; example; paragon; 树立 ~ set up a model
典型 diǎnxíng typical case or example; model; ~ 的书呆子 hundred-percent or typical bookworm / 具有一定的 ~ 性 be quite representative or typical
典雅 diǎnyǎ refined; elegant; in good taste

点（點） diǎn ❶ drop (of liquid); spot; stain; 霉 ~ 儿 specks of mould ❷ dot stroke (in

Chinese characters) ❸〈数〉(decimal point):七~一 seven point one (7.1) ❹〈量〉*used in counting items or to indicate a small amount or degree*:两~意见 two proposals or comments / 觉得尾~儿了 feel somewhat better ❺ mark; point; aspect:~面结合 combine work at selected spots with that of the whole area ❻ put a dot or point (to sth); punctuate; embellish:~句 punctuate a sentence or text / ~染 touch up or polish (a painting, etc); decorate ❼ touch on (briefly); make clear; point out:~明 point out; pinpoint / ~评 comment (on); review / ~题 bring out the theme / ~到要害 hit the nail on the head; hit or drive home ❽ incline one's head or hand briefly ❾ drip; dibble:~眼药水 put drops in the eyes ❿ check or count one by one:~钱 check or count the money / ~收 check and accept ⓫ select; choose:~菜 choose dishes from a menu; order food (in a restaurant) / ~歌 select a song for singer to sing ⓬ light; kindle; ignite:~炉子 make a fire in a stove ⓭ appointed time:快到~了。It's about time. ⓮ refreshments; snack; cake:糕~ cake; pastry

点播 diǎnbō ❶ also "点种"〈农〉dibble seeding; dibbling ❷ request an item or a programme to be broadcast or televised:~服务 service on demand

点拨 diǎnbo teach; instruct; show how (to do sth)

点滴 diǎndī ❶ a bit; a little; a small amount:~经验 limited experience / ~小事 insignificant detail; humble job ❷ (short for 静脉点滴)〈医〉intravenous drip

点火 diǎnhuǒ ❶ light a fire; ignite; fire:火箭~ firing of a rocket / ~装置 ignition device; igniter; squib ❷ stir up trouble

点击 diǎnjī〈信息〉hit; click

点将 diǎnjiàng assign sb a particular job; name sb for a given task

点名 diǎnmíng ❶ call the roll:~册 roll (book) ❷ mention by name; name explicitly:~表扬 praise (sb) by name

点破 diǎnpò bring to light; lay bare; point out bluntly:~其中奥妙 reveal the secret (of sth); let the cat out of the bag

点球 diǎnqiú〈体〉penalty kick

点燃 diǎnrán light; kindle; ignite

点铁成金 diǎntiěchéngjīn also "点石成金" turn stone into gold with a touch; turn sth worthless into sth valuable

点头 diǎntóu nod (one's head):~哈腰 bow servilely or unctuously; bow and scrape / ~同意 nod assent or approval / ~之交 nodding or bowing acquaintance

点心 diǎnxin refreshments; pastry; dim sum

点缀 diǎnzhuì ❶ embellish; adorn; decorate ❷ use merely for show

点子 diǎnzi ❶ drop (of liquid); spot; dot:泥~ speck of mud ❷ beat (of percussion instruments):鼓~ drumbeat ❸ key point; crux:说到~上 speak to the point; hit the nail on the head (in one's speech) ❹ idea; pointer:出~ offer advice; make suggestions

碘 diǎn〈化〉iodine:~酒 also "碘酊" tincture of iodine / ~缺乏病 iodine deficiency

跕 diǎn stand on tiptoe:~着脚看 look at (sth) standing on one's tiptoe

diàn

电(電) diàn ❶ electricity; electric power:~表 kilowatt-hour or electric meter / ~波 electric or radio wave / ~厂 (electric) power plant / ~镀 electroplate / ~费

power rate or bill / ～缆 electric cable / ～流 electric current / ～炉 electric stove or furnace / ～路 circuit / ～闸 main or master switch / ～饭煲 *also* "电饭锅" electric cooker ❷ give or get an electric shock ❸ (send a) telegram or cable; ～告 inform by telegraph / ～贺 telegraph one's congratulations; cable a message of congratulations; (telegraphic) code / ～唁 send a telegram or message of condolence / 草拟～文 draw up a telegram

电报 diànbào　telegraph; telegram; cable; ～机 telegraph / ～挂号 cable or telegraphic address

电车 diànchē　tram; tramcar; streetcar; 有轨～ tram; tramcar; streetcar / 无轨～ trolley (bus)

电池 diànchí　cell; battery

电传 diànchuán　fax; telex; 发～ send a fax

电磁 diàncí　electromagnetism; ～波 electromagnetic wave / ～场 electromagnetic field / ～感应 electromagnetic induction

电大 diàndà　(short for 电视大学) TV University

电灯 diàndēng　electric lamp or light; ～泡 electric (light) bulb

电动 diàndòng　power-driven; electrically-operated; electric; ～机 motor / ～玩具 electric toy

电工 diàngōng　❶ electrical engineering ❷ electrician

电焊 diànhàn　electric welding; ～条 welding electrode or rod

电话 diànhuà　❶ telephone; phone; (telephone) line; ～机 telephone / ～局 telephone office; exchange / ～亭 telephone box or booth / ～用户 telephone subscriber / ～占线。Number engaged. or The line is busy. ❷ telephone or phone call; ～卡 phone or calling card / ～会议 telephone conference; audio conferencing / ～听不清。The connec-

tion is poor.

电汇 diànhuì　telegraphic money order or transfer; remittance by telegram; ～一万元 remit or send 10,000 yuan by telegram

电机 diànjī　electric machinery or engineering; ～系 electric engineering (E. E.) department

电教 diànjiào　(short for 电化教学 or 电化教育) education with electrical audio-visual aids; audio-visual education; ～设备 (electrical) audio-visual aids

电解 diànjiě　electrolysis; ～质 electrolyte

电力 diànlì　(electric) power; ～网 power network or grid / ～线 electric flux line; power line or main

电疗 diànliáo　〈医〉electrotherapy

电脑 diànnǎo　(popular word for 计算机) electronic brain; computer; ～化 computerization / ～迷 computer buff or enthusiast / ～洗印 computer-controlled developing and printing (of photos)

电钮 diànniǔ　(push) button

电瓶 diànpíng　storage battery; accumulator; ～车 electric car; electromobile

电气 diànqì　electric; ～化 electrification / ～设备 electrical equipment

电器 diànqì　electric device, appliance or equipment

电热 diànrè　electric heat; electrothermal; ～杯 electric heating mug / ～毯 electric blanket

电容 diànróng　❶ electric capacity; capacitance ❷ *also* "电容器" condenser; capacitor

电视 diànshì　television (TV); television programme; ～机 television set / ～剧 TV play / ～迷 telefan; couch potato / ～片 television film; telefilm / ～观众 televiewer; TV viewer / ～会议 TV conference; teleconference / ～实

况转播 live television coverage; live
telecast

电台 diàntái ❶ transmitter-receiver;
transceiver ❷ broadcasting or radio
station

电梯 diàntī lift; elevator

电筒 diàntǒng *also* "手电筒" (pocket) torch; flashlight

电网 diànwǎng ❶〈军〉electrified wire
netting; live wire entanglement ❷ electric network; power grid

电线 diànxiàn wire; ~杆 (wire) pole

电信 diànxìn telecommunications; ~
业务 telecommunications service

电讯 diànxùn ❶ (telephone, telegraph, or radio) dispatch ❷ telecommunications

电压 diànyā voltage; ~表 voltmeter

电影 diànyǐng film; movie; motion
picture; ~节 film festival / ~院 cinema; movie (house) / ~大片 big-budget movie; hit-movie; blockbuster / ~
剧本 scenario; screen play

电源 diànyuán power supply or
source; mains; ~开关 power switch

电子 diànzǐ electron; ~表 quartz
watch; accutron / ~管 electron tube;
valve / ~琴 electronic organ or keyboard / ~工业 electronics industry /
~邮件 E-mail; electronic mail / ~商
务 E-commerce; electronic commerce /
~游戏 video game / ~出版物 electronic publication

电阻 diànzǔ resistance; ~器 resistor

佃 diàn rent land (from a landlord); ~户 tenant (farmer) / ~
农 tenant peasant or farmer / ~租 land
rent

甸 diàn 〈书〉open country outside
a town; outskirts (esp used in
place names)

店 diàn ❶ inn; 客~ inn ❷ shop;
store; ~面 shop front / ~铺
shop; store / ~员 shop assistant;
salesclerk / ~小二〈旧〉waiter; attend-

ant

玷 diàn ❶ flaw in a piece of jade
❷ tarnish; disgrace; ~辱 bring
disgrace or shame on; be a disgrace to

玷污 diànwū ❶ stain; sully; ~名声
tarnish one's name ❷ ravage; rape;
seduce

垫（墊） diàn ❶ put (sth) under sth else to raise it;
spread (sth) over sth else; make level
by filling up; ~肩 shoulder pad (for a
carrying pole); shoulder padding (for a
jacket, etc) / ~平 level up / ~圈
washer; cushion ring; grommet / ~子
mat; mattress; cushion / ~脚石 stepping-stone ❷ fill in a gap; insert; ~戏
fill-in performance ❸ pay for sb to be
repaid later; ~付 *also* "垫支" pay for
sb and expect to be repaid later

垫背 diànbèi 〈方〉take the blame for
sb; be a scapegoat

垫底 diàndǐ ❶ put or spread on the
bottom;〈喻〉use as a last resort ❷ take
a bite to stave off hunger ❸ lay the
foundation (for sth); serve as a basis

淀（❶澱） diàn ❶ form sediment; settle; precipitate; ~粉 starch ❷ (often used in
place names) shallow lake

惦 diàn be concerned about; keep
thinking about; ~记 *also* "惦念"
be concerned about; worry about; cannot take one's mind off

奠 diàn ❶ establish; settle; ~都
北京。Beijing has been made the capital. ❷ make offerings to the spirits of
the dead; ~祭 (perform) libation;
(hold a) memorial ceremony

奠定 diàndìng establish; settle; ~基
础 lay a foundation

奠基 diànjī lay a foundation; ~礼
foundation-laying ceremony / ~人
founder

殿 diàn ❶ hall; palace; ~堂 (hall
in a) palace or temple ❷ at or in

the rear；～后 bring up or close the rear；follow in the rear

殿下 diànxià　His, Her, or Your Highness (for addressing princes or princesses)；太子～ His Royal Highness the Crown Prince

靛 diàn ❶ also "靛蓝" indigo ❷ indigo-blue；～青 indigo-blue

癜 diàn　purplish or white patches on the skin

diāo

刁 diāo　sly; cunning; tricky；～悍 cunning and ferocious / ～滑 cunning; crafty; artful / 发球～钻 (have) a tricky service

刁难 diāonàn　create difficulties (for sb)；make things difficult (for sb)；百般～ create obstacles of every description；raise all manner of difficulties

叼 diāo　hold in the mouth：嘴角～着雪茄 with a cigar dangling from a corner of one's mouth

凋 diāo　wither

凋敝 diāobì ❶ in straitened circumstances; destitute：民生～。The people lived in destitution. ❷ (of business) languishing; depressed

凋零 diāolíng ❶ withered; fallen and scattered about：万物～。All things fell into decay. ❷ decline; go downhill; be on the wane

凋谢 diāoxiè　also "凋落" ❶ wither and fall：秋风起处，树叶～。Chilly gusts of the autumn wind denuded the trees of their leaves. ❷ die of old age

貂 diāo　marten; ermine：黑～ sable / 水～ mink / ～皮 fur or pelt of any of these animals

碉 diāo　also "碉堡" pillbox; blockhouse

雕 diāo ❶ carve; engrave; sculpt：～镂 write in a laboured, ornate style / ～饰 carve and decorate; overdecorate; overdo / ～花玻璃 cut glass / ～虫小技 insignificant or trifling (literary) skill ❷ decorated with coloured drawings：～梁画栋 richly ornamented building ❸ (动物)eagle; vulture

雕刻 diāokè　carve; engrave; sculpt：～刀 carving tool; burin

雕塑 diāosù　sculpture：～家 sculptor / ～ sculpture

雕像 diāoxiàng　statue; carved figure：半身～ bust / 全身～ full-length statue

雕琢 diāozhuó ❶ cut and polish (jade, etc)；carve ❷ write in an ornate or elaborate style；过于～ too elaborate or ornate; laboured

diào

吊(弔) diào ❶ hang; suspend; lift up or let down (with a rope, etc)：～床 hammock / ～灯 pendent lamp / ～环〈体〉rings / ～桥 drawbridge; suspension bridge / ～扇 ceiling fan ❷〈体〉drop (the ball or shuttle) where one's rival finds it hard to retrieve ❸ retrieve; revoke; withdraw：～销 revoke; withdraw ❹ crane：～车 also "起重机" crane; hoist ❺ condole; mourn：～孝 call on the bereaved to offer one's condolences; pay a condolence call

吊儿郎当 diào'erlángdāng　fool around; be careless and casual

吊嗓子 diàosǎngzi　(of a singer, etc) train or exercise one's voice

吊胃口 diàowèikǒu　whet sb's appetite (without satisfying it); hold in suspense; tantalize

吊唁 diàoyàn　pay homage to the deceased and offer condolences to the bereaved; condole：～函电 messages of condolence

钓 diào　fish (with a hook and line); angle; hunt for：～饵 bait / ～竿

fishing rod or pole / ~钩 fishhook / ~具 fishing tackle / ~鱼 angle; go fishing

调 diào ❶ transfer; shift; move：~档 ask for the transfer of a file of records / ~回 recall / ~离 be transferred from one place or job (to another) / ~令 transfer order / ~运 allocate and transport ❷ accent; tune; melody：两个人一个～儿。They are harping on the same view. ❸〈乐〉key：B～ key of B / D大～ D major ❹〈语言〉tone; tune

see also tiáo

调拨 diàobō ❶ transfer and allocate (goods or funds); allot：~款项 allocate funds ❷ *see* "调遣"

调查 diàochá investigate; inquire or look into; survey；彻底～ get to the bottom of sth / ～团 fact-finding mission / ～报告 report on the findings of an investigation; investigative report

调动 diàodòng ❶ transfer; shift; move (troops)：~工作 transfer (sb) to another post ❷ bring into play; arouse; mobilize：~群众积极性 arouse the enthusiasm of the people

调度 diàodù ❶ manage; control; dispatch (trains, buses, etc)：生产～ production management / ～室 dispatcher's office; control room ❷ *also* "调度员" dispatcher; controller

调虎离山 diàohǔlíshān lure the tiger out of his mountain or lair; tempt sb into leaving vantage ground

调换 diàohuàn *see* "掉换" diàohuàn

调集 diàojí assemble; muster：~防汛器材 mobilize or muster flood prevention equipment

调门儿 diàoménr pitch (of one's voice, etc); tone (of one's words)：~定得太低 pitch a tune too low; make an argument too mild

调配 diàopèi allocate; deploy *see also* tiáopèi

调遣 diàoqiǎn dispatch; assign：听从 ～ (be ready to) accept an assignment; be at sb's disposal or command / 调兵遣将 dispatch troops; deploy forces; mobilize and organize manpower

调研 diàoyán (short for 调查研究) investigate and study：~员 researcher

调子 diàozi ❶ tune; melody; tone ❷ view; argument; tone (of one's words)

掉 diào ❶ fall; drop; shed：~眼泪 shed tears / ~脑袋 be beheaded; get killed ❷ fall or lag behind：~队 drop out or off; fall or lag behind ❸ lose; be missing：钱包~了 lose one's wallet ❹ reduce; cut down; lose：~色 lose colour; fade / 体重~了5公斤 lose 5 kg (in weight) ❺ turn (round or back)：~转 *also* "调转" turn (sth) round / ~过脸去 turn one's face away; avert one's face ❻ change; exchange; swap ❼ *used after some verbs to indicate the result of an action*：脱~鞋袜 pull off one's shoes and stockings

掉包 diàobāo *also* "调包" stealthily replace sth genuine or valuable with sth fake or worthless; change

掉换 diàohuàn *also* "调换" exchange; swap; change：~工作 change to a new job

掉价 diàojià ❶ (of prices) go down; fall or drop in price ❷〈喻〉lower one's social status; lose face

掉头 diàotóu ❶ turn (round or about)：掉过头去 turn one's head away ❷ *also* "调头" (of vehicles, vessels, etc) turn round or about; make a U-turn：车辆~处 turnaround

掉以轻心 diàoyǐqīngxīn be off one's guard (against sth); treat lightly

diē

爹 diē〈口〉father; dad; pa

跌 diē fall; tumble; drop：~倒 fall or tumble down / ~幅 volume or

amount of fall (in price) / ～价 go down in price; devalue / ～落 fall; drop / ～破 fall and break; fall below (a certain mark)

跌宕 diēdàng　*also* "跌荡"〈书〉❶ free and easy; bold and unconstrained; ～不羁 free and unrestrained ❷ undulating; varied; ～起伏的乐曲 well-modulated tune

跌跌撞撞 diēdie-zhuàngzhuàng stagger or dodder along; totter

跌跤 diējiāo　(trip or stumble and) fall; make a mistake; suffer a setback; 这一跌跤摔得很重 make a grievous mistake; suffer a serious setback

dié

迭 dié　❶ alternate; replace; change; ～为宾主 play host by turn ❷ repeatedly; time and again; ～出 *also* "迭起" crop up one after another; happen again and again

谍 dié　espionage; intelligence agent; spy

谍报 diébào　information obtained through espionage; intelligence; ～网 spy ring; intelligence network / ～员 intelligence agent; spy / ～部门 secret service

喋 dié

喋喋不休 diédiébùxiū　chatter away; rattle on; talk endlessly

喋血 diéxuè　*also* "蹀血"〈书〉extensive bloodshed; bloodbath

䐈 dié　❶ official document; certificate ❷ record; book

叠（疊） dié　❶ pile up; duplicate; repeat; ～影 *also* "重像" ghosting / ～字〈语言〉reduplication of words / ～罗汉〈体〉pyramid ❷ fold; ～衣服 fold up clothes

碟 dié　*also* "碟子" (small) dish; saucer

蝶（蜨） dié　butterfly; ～泳〈体〉butterfly stroke

dīng

丁 dīng　❶ male adult; man; ～壮 able-bodied man (subject to conscription); male adult ❷ members of a family; population ❸ person engaged in certain types of labour; 园～ gardener ❹ 4th of the Heavenly Stems; fourth　*see also* "干支" gānzhī ❺ small cube (of meat or vegetable); 萝卜～ diced turnip ❻〈书〉meet; encounter; ～忧 be in mourning for one's parent

丁当 dīngdāng　*also* "叮当"; "玎珰" 〈象声〉(of metal, jade or china) ding-dong; jingle; clatter; 穷得～响 poor as a church mouse; penniless

丁点儿 dīngdiǎnr　〈方〉〈量〉tiny bit; wee bit; jot; ～不错 entirely right / 这么～事 such a trifle / 只有一～面粉了。There is only a handful of flour left.

丁东 dīngdōng　*also* "丁冬"〈象声〉(of metal, jade or stone) tinkle; 泉水～ gurgling brook

丁零 dīnglíng　〈象声〉(of bell or small metal ware) jingle; ～当 jingle-jangle; ding-dong

丁宁 dīngníng　*also* "叮咛" urge again and again; exhort; admonish

丁是丁，卯是卯 dīngshìdīng, mǎoshì mǎo　*also* "钉是钉，铆是铆" be meticulous, precise, or unaccommodating

丁香 dīngxiāng　〈植〉❶ lilac ❷ clove

丁字 dīngzì　T-shaped; ～尺 T-square / ～街 T-shaped road junction

叮 dīng　❶ sting; bite; 蚊虫的～咬 mosquito bites ❷ urge again and again; exhort; admonish; ～嘱 urge again and again; admonish; exhort ❸ say or ask again to make sure; 再～他

一句，免得忘了。Remind him again just in case.

叮当 dīngdāng *see* "丁当" dīngdāng

叮咛 dīngníng *see* "丁宁" dīngníng

盯 dīng *also* "钉" fix one's eyes on; gaze or stare at: ～住这个坏蛋。Keep a close watch on the scoundrel.

盯梢 dīngshāo *see* "钉梢" dīngshāo

钉 dīng ❶ nail; tack: ～锤 nail or claw hammer / ～鞋〈体〉spiked shoes; spikes ❷ follow closely; shadow; tail:(人)～人防守〈体〉man-for-man or man-to-man defence ❸ urge; press; keep asking or reminding: ～着点，让他们快点修。Keep pressing them to speed up the repairs. ❹ *see* "盯" dīng

see also dìng

钉梢 dīngshāo *also* "盯梢" shadow; tail; stalk

钉子 dīngzi ❶ nail; tack; pin ❷ snag; obstacle: ～户 person or household who is a big obstacle to a relocation project; snag ❸ planted agent, stool, or saboteur

疔 dīng〈中医〉malignant boil or furuncle

酊 dīng tincture: ～剂 tincture

dǐng

顶 dǐng ❶ top; peak; crown (of the head) ～灯 top-light; dome light; overhead light (of a car) / ～点 apex; zenith / ～楼 attic / ～棚〈建筑〉ceiling ❷ hold or carry on the head; strike with head or horn; butt: ～球〈体〉head (a ball) ❸ push from below or behind; push or prop up: 把车～起 jack up a vehicle / 把门～上 prop up the door ❹ 冒: ～着暴风雨 in the teeth of a storm ❺ answer back; retort; rebuff: ～牛 (willfully) oppose;

clash; quarrel / ～撞 contradict (one's elder or superior); answer or talk back / ～嘴〈口〉reply defiantly; answer or talk back ❻ manage with difficulty; stand up to: ～住 withstand; resist; hold out (against sth or sb) ❼ equal; be equivalent to: 一个～俩 do the work of two; serve better than two ❽ take the place of; substitute; replace: ～班 take over sb's shift; serve as a temporary substitute; (of an executive, etc) work on a regular shift as a manual worker / ～替 take sb's place; replace; substitute ❾ transfer a business license or lease of real estate; sublease ❿〈量〉used of sth that has a top: 一～帽子 a cap ⓫ most; very; extremely: ～多 at (the) most; at best / ～好 best; excellent / ～刮刮 *also* "顶呱呱"〈口〉tip-top; first-rate; excellent

顶端 dǐngduān ❶ top; peak; apex ❷ end

顶风 dǐngfēng ❶ against the wind: ～作案〈喻〉commit a crime in defiance of a law-enforcement campaign ❷ head wind: 回程正好是～ face a head wind on the way back

顶峰 dǐngfēng peak; summit; pinnacle: 事业的～ pinnacle of one's career

顶尖 dǐngjiān ❶ top; tip ❷ best; first-rate: ～的象棋高手 topmost master of chess

顶礼膜拜 dǐnglǐmóbài prostrate oneself in worship; make a fetish (of sth or sb); pay homage (to sth or sb)

顶梁柱 dǐngliángzhù pillar; backbone: 社会的～ pillar of society; salt of the earth

顶事 dǐngshì *also* "顶用" be useful or effective; serve the purpose: 不～ be no good / 他在我们这里可～啦！He is a great asset to us here.

顶天立地 dǐngtiān-lìdì of titanic, noble stature; of the highest order: ～的汉子 dauntless or heroic man; he-man

~的事业 earth-shaking undertaking

顶头上司 dǐngtóushàngsi immediate superior or boss; institution of an immediately higher level

顶针 dǐngzhen thimble

顶罪 dǐngzuì ❶ also "顶缸" bear punishment for sb else's wrongdoing or crime; be a scapegoat ❷ (of punishment, etc) be equal to the crime; be appropriate: 罚不~。The punishment falls short of the crime.

鼎 dǐng ❶ ding — ancient cooking vessel with two loop handles and three (sometimes four) legs: ~立 stand like the three legs of a tripod; (of three parties) confront one another on an equal footing ❷ 〈书〉great; grand; ~~大名 well-known; renowned; celebrated

鼎沸 dǐngfèi 〈书〉like a boiling cauldron; clamorous; noisy and confused: 群情~。Public feeling runs high.

鼎力 dǐnglì 〈书〉〈敬〉your kind effort; your great help: ~相助 make unstinting efforts to help (esp in an undertaking)

鼎盛 dǐngshèng in a time of great prosperity; at the height of power and glory: 国力~ in the heyday of national power

dìng

订 dìng ❶ fix or set through consultations, etc; conclude; draw up: ~立 conclude (an agreement, etc); make (a contract, etc) / ~合同 draw up or enter into a contract / ~日子 fix or set a date ❷ subscribe to (a newspaper, etc); book (a seat, ticket, etc); order (merchandise, etc): ~单 also "定单" order (for goods); order form / ~户 also "定户" subscriber; person or household with a standing order (for milk, etc) / ~阅 also "定阅"

subscribe to (a periodical, etc) / ~房间 make a room reservation ❸ make corrections; revise: ~正 make corrections; emend ❹ staple together: ~书机 stapling machine; stapler; book-binding machine

订购 dìnggòu also "定购" order (goods); place an order (for sth)

订婚 dìnghūn also "定婚" be engaged or betrothed: ~戒指 engagement ring

订货 dìnghuò also "定货" order goods; place an order: ~单 order (list)

订金 dìngjīn also "定金" "定钱" deposit; down payment; earnest (money)

订做 dìngzuò also "定做" have sth made to order or measure: ~的套服 tailor-made or custom-made suit

钉 dìng ❶ nail; drive in (a wedge): ~鞋掌 nail on a sole; sole a shoe ❷ sew on: ~扣子 sew a button on

see also dīng

定 dìng ❶ calm; still; stable: 心~ calm (down); feel at ease ❷ fix; set; decide: ~编 fix the number of staff; set the personnel quota or complement / ~都 choose a site for the capital; make (a place) the capital / ~级 grade (a product, etc); rank (sb or sth) / ~亲 engagement (usu arranged by parents); betrothal / ~调子 set the tone or keynote; call the tune / ~计划 make a plan ❸ determined; stipulated; fixed: ~理 theorem / ~律 law ❹ *see* "订②" ❺ 〈书〉surely; certainly; definitely: ~然 certainly; definitely

定案 dìng'àn decide on or pass a verdict; reach a conclusion (on a case, etc); make the final decision

定点 dìngdiǎn chosen location; designated place; selected point: ~厂 designated factory / ~供应 supply at designated locations

定夺 dìngduó make a final decision; decide: 这事要由经理~。This is for the manager to decide.

定额 dìng'é　stipulate an amount or norm; fix or set a quota:生产～ production quota / ～补贴 set quota subsidy

定稿 dìnggǎo　finalize a manuscript, text, etc; final text or manuscript

定价 dìngjià　fix a price:明码～ marked price

定居 dìngjū　settle (down) in; reside or live in:～点 settlement

定局 dìngjú　❶ final decision ❷ foregone conclusion; inevitable outcome

定量 dìngliàng　❶ determine the amounts of the components of a substance:～分析〈化〉quantitative analysis ❷ fix the amount or quantity:～供应 fixed quantity supply; rationing

定论 dìnglùn　accepted opinion; final conclusion:不作～ leave a matter open / 尚无～ no consensus of opinion

定名 dìngmíng　name; denominate

定期 dìngqī　❶ fix a schedule; set a date ❷ at regular intervals; regular; periodical:～存款 fixed or time deposit / 付款 scheduled payment / ～交货 time delivery; delivery on term

定情 dìngqíng　(of lovers) pledge enduring affection: ～物 token of love (given when first pledging love)

定神 dìngshén　❶ concentrate one's attention:～细看 look hard; scrutinize ❷ collect or compose oneself; pull oneself together:先定神再往下讲。Calm down before you go on.

定时 dìngshí　at fixed time; at regular intervals: ～器 timer / ～炸弹 time bomb; delayed-action bomb;〈喻〉hidden danger; latent crisis

定式 dìngshì　also "定势" fixed pattern; stereotype; set:心理～ psychological set

定位 dìngwèi　❶ orientate; position:全球～ global positioning / 船舶～ determine a ship's position ❷ put in

proper perspective and evaluate:给新产品～ evaluate and price a new product (in relation to other products); rank a new product

定向 dìngxiàng　find or determine the direction of; orient; direct:～爆破 directional or directed blasting / ～培养 training for a certain region or work unit; target training

定心丸 dìngxīnwán　sth capable of setting sb's mind at ease; reassurance:吃了～ be reassured; feel at ease

定型 dìngxíng　finalize the design; fall into a pattern; take shape or form:思想～ fixed in outlook

定性 dìngxìng　❶ determine the nature (of an offence or a case) ❷〈化〉determine the chemical composition of a substance:～分析 qualitative analysis

定义 dìngyì　definition:下～ give a definition; define

定语 dìngyǔ　〈语言〉attribute:～从句 attributive clause

定员 dìngyuán　fixed or stipulated number of staff, passengers, etc:超过～ be overloaded or over-staffed / ～15 人。(Of a lift, etc) Stipulated capacity: 15 persons.

定罪 dìngzuì　declare guilty; convict:要量刑~。Penalty should be given in accordance with guilt.

碇 dìng　heavy stone used as an anchor; killick:拔锚起～ weigh anchor / ～泊 anchor; berth

锭 dìng　❶ spindle:~子 spindle (in a textile mill) ❷ ingot: (of medicine, etc) ingot-shaped tablet:～剂 lozenge; pastille; troche ❸〈量〉*used of sth like an ingot*:一～银子 a silver ingot

diū

丢 diū　❶ lose; mislay: ～弃 abandon; discard; get rid of / ～

失 lose; let slip; miss / ～三落四 be always forgetting things; be careless and sloppy ❷ throw; cast; put or lay aside：～卒保车 give up a pawn to save a castle—sacrifice minor things to save major ones

丢丑 diūchǒu　be disgraced; make a fool of oneself：太～了! What a disgrace!

丢掉 diūdiào　❶ lose：～饭碗 lose one's job ❷ throw or cast away; discard：～原则 discard or give up one's principles

丢人 diūrén　also "丢脸"; "丢面子" lose face; be disgraced; 丢人现眼 make a fool or spectacle of oneself; be disgraced

dōng

东(東) dōng　❶ east：～方 east; the East or Orient / ～经(地) east longitude / ～亚 East Asia / ～洋(旧) Japan / ～半球 Eastern Hemisphere ❷ master; owner：～家 master; boss ❸ host：今天我做。I'll stand host today. or It's on me today.

东北 dōngběi　❶ northeast：～风 northeast wind; northeaster ❷ (Dōngběi) northeast China (formerly known as Manchuria); the Northeast：～虎 Manchurian or Siberian tiger

东倒西歪 dōngdǎo-xīwāi　❶ stumble; stagger; totter：～地向前走 stumble or stagger along ❷ lying in disorder or aslant; tumbledown (house, etc); rickety (furniture, etc)

东道 dōngdào　host：做～ play host; be the host / ～国 host country / ～主 host

东风 dōngfēng　east or spring wind; (喻) propitious or favourable circumstance：万事俱备，只欠。Everything is ready except one key element.

东京 Dōngjīng　Tokyo, capital of Japan

东南 dōngnán　❶ southeast：～亚国家

联盟 (shortened as 东盟) ASEAN (Association of Southeast Asian Nations) ❷ (Dōngnán) southeast China; the Southeast

东山再起 dōngshānzàiqǐ　stage or make a comeback

东施效颦 dōngshīxiàopín　blind imitation with ludicrous effect

东西 dōngxī　❶ east and west; from east to west：～交通 east-west transportation ❷ (dōngxi) stuff; thing; creature：可爱的小～ cute little thing (a baby or pet) / 蠢～! What a fool! / 那是什么～? What is that?

东…西… dōng…xī…　here and there; this and that：东奔西跑 run here and there; bustle or rush about / 东拉西扯 drag in all sorts of irrelevant matters; ramble / 东拼西凑 scrape or knock together / 东张西望 look about in all directions; peer or glance around / 东家长，西家短 also "张家长，李家短" gossip about people; backbite / 东一榔头，西一棒子 act or speak haphazardly; act in a hit-or-miss fashion

东正教 Dōngzhèngjiào　Eastern Orthodox Church

冬(❷鼕) dōng　❶ winter：～菇 (dried) mushrooms picked in winter / ～季 also "冬天" winter / ～眠 winter sleep; hibernation / ～泳(体) winter swimming also "咚"(象声)：战鼓～～ booming of war drums / ～～地敲门 drum at or thump on the door

冬瓜 dōngguā　wax gourd; white gourd

冬至 dōngzhì　Winter Solstice, 22nd seasonal division point　see also "节气" jiéqi

dǒng

董 dǒng　director; trustee：校～ school trustee

董事 dǒngshì　director; trustee: ～会 board of directors; (of schools, etc) board of trustees / ～长 chairman of the board of directors

懂 dǒng understand; know: ～行 know the business; know the ropes or tricks / ～事 sensible; intelligent; well-behaved / ～规矩 know the rules; be well-behaved; have good manners

dòng

动(動) dòng ❶ move; stir; act: ～产 movable or personal property; movables / ～土 break ground; start construction ❷ change; alter: ～容〈书〉change countenance; be visibly moved / ～几个字 change a few words ❸ use; wield; resort to: ～兵 resort to force; appeal to arms / ～武 resort to or use force; start a fight; come to blows / ～脑筋 use one's head ❹ touch (one's heart); move; arouse: ～感情 be carried away by emotion; get worked up ❺ begin; start: ～笔 take up the pen or brush; start writing or painting / ～工 begin construction; start building; be under construction ❻ easily; often: 游客～以万计. The number of tourists easily exceeds ten thousand.

动不动 dòngbudòng　easily; frequently; at every turn: ～就发火 flare up at the slightest provocation

动词 dòngcí　〈语言〉verb: ～短语 phrasal verb; verbal phrase / 动名词 gerund

动荡 dòngdàng　❶ undulating (water, etc); rolling ❷ turbulent; in turmoil or upheaval: ～不安 turbulent; in turmoil / ～年代 age of turmoil; turbulent years

动画片 dònghuàpiàn　(animated) cartoon

动机 dòngjī　motive; intention: ～不纯 have mixed motives; have one's own axe to grind

动静 dòngjing　❶ sound of sth astir: 周围没有一点～. It was dead quiet all around. ❷ movement; activity: 打听～ try to find out how things stand

动力 dònglì　(motive) power; driving force; impetus: 前进的～ motive force of progress / ～系统 dynamic or power system

动乱 dòngluàn　turmoil; upheaval; turbulence: 制止～ curb disturbances / ～时代 times of turmoil; years of upheaval

动脉 dòngmài　〈生理〉artery: ～瘤 aneurysm; arterial tumour / ～硬化 arteriosclerosis

动怒 dòngnù　also "动气" flare up; lose one's temper; get worked up

动迁 dòngqiān　relocate; resettle; remove: ～户 family or household to be relocated

动情 dòngqíng　❶ be moved or touched; get worked up; become excited ❷ become enamoured (of sb); fall for

动人 dòngrén　moving; touching; stirring: ～心弦 strike or touch a deep chord in one's heart; touch one's heart

动身 dòngshēn　go or set out on a journey; leave (for a distant place)

动手 dòngshǒu　❶ start work; get to work; do: 人人～. Let everyone join in. ❷ touch; handle: ～动脚 paw (sb); take liberties (with a woman) ❸ raise a hand to strike or hit; hit out: 先动手 strike the first blow

动手术 dòngshǒushù　❶ perform or have an operation; operate or be operated on ❷〈喻〉effect a big change; overhaul: 对管理制度～ overhaul the management regime

动态 dòngtài　❶ developments; trends: 舆论～ trend of public opinion /

最新～ latest developments ❷ dynamic; mobile; kinetic：～分析 dynamic analysis

动弹 dòngtan　move; stir：他的嘴唇～了一下。His lips twitched.

动听 dòngtīng　interesting or pleasant to listen to：～的言辞 fine-sounding words

动物 dòngwù　animal; fauna：～园 zoological garden; zoo

动向 dòngxiàng　trend; tendency：摸清他的～ find out what he is up to

动心 dòngxīn　have one's enthusiasm or interest aroused; be attracted or lured

动摇 dòngyáo　❶ vacillate; waver：在不同意见之间～不定 vacillate between differing opinions ❷ shake; undermine：～军心 undermine the morale (of an army)

动议 dòngyì　motion：提出休会～ move for recess of a meeting

动用 dòngyòng　use; employ; draw on：～存款 draw on one's deposit / ～武力 use force

动员 dòngyuán　❶ national or general mobilization：～令 mobilization order ❷ arouse; mobilize：～大会 mobilization rally / 作～报告 give a mobilization speech; give a pep talk

动真格的 dòngzhēngéde　〈口〉do sth for real; work in earnest; take sth seriously

动辄 dòngzhé　〈书〉easily; frequently; at every turn：～得咎 be taken to task at every turn / 花费～上千元 easily spend more than one thousand yuan

动作 dòngzuò　movement; motion; action：搞小～ make petty moves; play little tricks / ～片 action movie; actioner

冻（凍） dòng　❶ freeze：～土 frozen earth / ～雨 sleet ❷ jelly：果～ fruit jelly ❸ feel

very cold; freeze; be frost-bitten：～疮 frostbite; chilblain / ～僵 frozen stiff; numb with cold / ～死 freeze to death; die of cold

冻结 dòngjié　❶ freeze; congeal：～存款 freeze an account ❷ suspend：～双方关系 suspend bilateral relations

栋（棟） dòng　❶〈书〉ridgepole：～梁 ridgepole and beam；〈喻〉pillar (of society, etc)❷〈量〉used of housing：一～楼房 a building

洞 dòng　❶ hole; cavity; opening：～窟 also "洞穴" cave; cavern / ～眼 small hole / 小～不补，大～吃苦。A stitch in time saves nine. ❷ penetratingly; thoroughly：～若观火 see (sth) as clearly as a blazing fire

洞察 dòngchá　see clearly; have an insight into：～力 insight; discernment; acumen / ～秋毫 be perceptive of the minutest detail; have discerning eyes

洞房 dòngfáng　bridal or nuptial chamber；闹～ celebrate a wedding by making noisy fun of the couple in the bridal chamber / ～花烛 wedding (festivities)

洞天 dòngtiān　dwelling of immortals; scenery of exceptional charm

洞悉 dòngxī　know clearly; understand thoroughly：～内情 know the inside story; be in the know

恫 dòng　〈书〉fear; fright; terror：～吓 threaten; intimidate

胴 dòng　trunk; body：～体 trunk (of a slaughtered animal); carcass; (human) body

dōu

都 dōu　〈副〉❶ all; both; every：～怪你！It's all your fault. ❷ used for emphasis：连他老婆～不知道。Even his wife knew nothing about it. / ～是这场暴雨把庄稼给毁了了。It was the storm that ruined the crops.

see also dū

兜 **dōu** ❶ pocket; bag: 布～子 cloth bag ❷ wrap up or hold as if in a bag: ～ also "兜肚" diamond-shaped cloth worn (usu by a child) over the chest and abdomen; bib / 用手～着几个苹果 hold some apples in a towel ❸ move round; go in a circle; make a detour: ～圈子 go round in circles; beat about the bush ❹ canvass; solicit: ～售 also "兜销" peddle; hawk / ～生意 canvass business; solicit customers ❺ take upon oneself; assume responsibility for:一切后果我～着。I'll take all the consequences. ❻ confronting; facing: ～头一棒 (deal a) head-on blow

兜底 **dōudǐ** disclose all the details; expose; show up: 兜人老底 drag up the seamy side of sb's life or past / 这回他可全兜了底。He's made a clean breast of it this time.

兜风 **dōufēng** ❶ (of a sail, etc) catch the wind ❷ go for a (joy-)ride or sail: 开车～ go for a ride or spin

兜揽 **dōulǎn** ❶ canvass; solicit: ～生意 tout for business ❷ take upon oneself (sb else's work); take up the cudgels for others: 爱～事儿 like to take everything upon oneself

dǒu

斗 **dǒu** ❶ unit of dry measure for grain (now about a decalitre) ❷ cubic wooden or bamboo measure for grain; sth shaped like such a measure: ～笠 wide-rimmed bamboo hat / ～篷 sleeveless cloak; cape ❸ whorl of a fingerprint: ～箕 fingerprint ❹ (short for 北斗星) Big Dipper: ～转星移 turning of the Dipper and rotating of the stars—change of season; passage of time

see also dòu

斗胆 **dǒudǎn** 〈谦〉make bold; venture: 恕我～进言。I venture to offer a suggestion.

斗室 **dǒushì** 〈书〉tiny room

抖 **dǒu** ❶ tremble; shiver; quiver: 浑身直～ tremble all over ❷ shake; jerk; flick: ～掉衣服上的土 shake dirt off one's clothes ❸ disclose the inside story; expose: ～老底儿 expose sb's past; rake up old scores ❹ rouse; muster or stir up: ～起精神 pluck up one's spirits; cheer up ❺ 〈讽〉throw one's weight about; preen oneself: ～起来 throw one's weight around; swagger about / ～起来了 become purse-proud or drunken with power

抖动 **dǒudòng** ❶ shake; tremble; quiver: ～的手 trembling hand ❷ shake; jerk; flick: 把单子～～ flick a sheet

抖搂 **dǒulou** 〈方〉❶ see "抖❷" ❷ shake out (a container, etc); make a clean breast; expose: ～箱子底儿 shake out a suitcase / 把事儿全～出来 make a clean breast of it all; give the whole show away ❸ squander: 一年不到,把家产～干净 squander all the family fortune before the year is out

抖擞 **dǒusǒu** rouse; pluck up; invigorate: ～精神 brace or cheer up; pull oneself together; pep oneself up

陡 **dǒu** ❶ steep; precipitous: ～壁 cliff; precipice / ～立 steeply / ～峭 precipitous; sheer ❷ suddenly; abruptly: ～然发怒 flare up all of a sudden; explode into a rage

dòu

斗(鬥) **dòu** ❶ (make) fight; struggle; denounce: ～士 fighter (for a cause); champion; proponent / ～鸡 gamecock; cockfighting ❷ compete or contend with; con test；~法 fight（each other）with magic powers；contend by artifice or trickery / 群芳~艳。All flowers vie with each other for beauty。❸ come together；fit or put together：~眼 also "斗鸡眼" cross-eye

see also dǒu

斗牛 dòuniú bullfighting；bullfight；~场 bullring / ~士 matador；bullfighter

斗殴 dòu'ōu fight with fists；have a fisticuff

斗气 dòuqì act perversely out of resentment or anger；be in a fit of pique

斗争 dòuzhēng ❶ struggle；fight；strive：思想~ ideological struggle；soul-searching / 与迷信作~ struggle against or combat superstition ❷ denounce；accuse：~会 public accusation meeting

斗志 dòuzhì will to fight；fighting will；morale：~昂扬 have high morale；be militant

斗智 dòuzhì have a duel of wits；pit one's intelligence against sb's：~斗勇 have a contest of wits and courage

斗嘴 dòuzuǐ ❶ quarrel；have an angry exchange：怄气 quarrel and sulk ❷ exchange banter；joke with each other：~取笑 poke fun at and play practical jokes on each other；pull each other's leg

豆（荳） dòu ❶ legumes；beans；peas：~豉 fermented soy beans / ~荚（bean）pod / ~浆 also "豆腐浆" soybean milk / 奶 mixed soybean and cow milk drink / ~油 soybean oil / ~汁 fermented drink made from water used in grinding green beans / ~花儿〈方〉condensed bean curd jelly / ~角儿 fresh beans in pod / ~芽儿 also "豆芽菜" bean sprouts / ~制品 bean product / ~瓣儿酱 thick broad bean sauce ❷ sth like a bean：玉米~儿 grain of corn

豆腐 dòufu tofu；bean curd：老~ also "北豆腐" firm tofu / 嫩~ also "南豆腐" tender tofu / ~干 dried bean curd / ~皮 skin of soybean milk；thin sheet of dried bean curd / ~乳 also "腐乳" "酱豆腐" fermented bean curd / ~脑儿 jellied bean curd

豆腐渣 dòufuzhā also "豆渣" bean dregs（after making soybean milk）："~"工程 "bean dregs" or jerry-built project

豆沙 dòushā sweetened bean paste：~包 steamed bun with sweetened bean paste filling

逗 dòu ❶ tease；provoke：~乐儿〈方〉be amusing or funny / ~趣儿〈方〉set people laughing（by making jokes,etc）；try to amuse / 他在~你们呢！He's pulling your leg。❷〈方〉amusing；funny：这故事真~。What a funny story！❸ stay；stop：~留 also "逗遛" stay；stop ❹ also "读" short pause in reading a Chinese sentence

逗号 dòuhào also "逗点" comma（,）

逗弄 dòunong also "逗引" ❶ play with：~小狗 play with a puppy ❷ tease；kid；make fun of：把孩子~哭了 tease a child till it cries

痘 dòu ❶ also "痘疮" smallpox ❷ vaccine（lymph）；种~ vaccinate；be vaccinated / ~苗 also "牛痘苗"（bovine）vaccine ❸ smallpox pustule

窦（竇） dòu hole；opening；aperture：狗~ dog hole

dū

都 dū ❶ also "都城" capital（city）❷ also "都会" big city；metropolis

see also dōu

都市 dūshì city；metropolis：~化 urbanization

督 dū superintend；supervise；oversee：~办 superintend and direct；oversee / ~促 supervise and press; urge / ～学 inspector of schools / ～战 urge on in battle; supervise (military) operations / ～阵 supervise and direct a battle at the front; supervise (a project, etc) on the spot

督察 dūchá ❶ superintend; supervise; inspect ❷ superintendent; supervisor; inspector

督导 dūdǎo supervise and direct; superintend; ～员 superintendent; supervisor; inspector

嘟 dū 〈象声〉(of a car, etc) toot; honk ❷ 〈方〉pout: 气得～着嘴 pout peevishly

嘟囔 dūnang also "嘟哝" mutter to oneself; mumble

dú

毒 dú ❶ poison; toxin: ～草 poisonous weed; 〈喻〉sth harmful (esp writing) / ～瘤 malignant tumour; cancer / ～素 toxin; poison; pernicious influence / ～液 also "毒汁" liquid poison; venom / ～药 poison; toxicant / ～性 poison; poisonous made itself felt. ❷ narcotic drug; ～品 drugs; narcotics / ～枭 drug baron or lord / ～贩子 drug trafficker or pusher ❸ kill with poison; poison ❹ vicious; sinister; cruel: ～打 beat up; give a vicious beating / ～计 deadly trap / ～辣 sinister; diabolic; malignant / 太阳很～。The sun is scorching.

毒害 dúhài poison (sb's mind); harm (sb's health): 吸烟对人～很大。Smoking is very harmful to health.

毒化 dúhuà poison; defile: ～社会风气 contaminate social morals; debase social morality

毒气 dúqì poisonous (or toxic) gas; ～弹 gas shell or bomb / ～室 gas chamber

毒蛇 dúshé poisonous or venomous snake; viper; vicious person (usu woman)

毒手 dúshǒu murderous scheme; wicked trap: 下～ resort to violent treachery; lay murderous hands (on sb)

毒瘾 dúyǐn drug addiction: ～发作 have a craving for the drug; be craving the drug

独(獨) dú ❶ one; single; lone: ～白 monologue; soliloquy / ～苗 only son of a family or clan / ～舞 solo dance / ～子 only son / ～幕剧 one-act play / ～来～往 keep to oneself; be a loner ❷ the old and childless ❸ only; alone: ～有她持不同意见。She alone held a different view.

独霸 dúbà dominate exclusively; monopolize: ～市场 corner the market / ～一方 lord it over a locality; dominate an area

独裁 dúcái dictatorship; autocratic rule: ～者 autocrat; dictator / ～政权 dictatorship; autocracy

独唱 dúchàng (of a vocalist) solo: ～音乐会 recital

独出心裁 dúchūxīncái show originality; be original or novel

独创 dúchuàng original creation: ～性 originality / ～一格 create a distinctive style of one's own

独当一面 dúdāngyīmiàn cope with one sector or field on one's own; assume sole responsibility for one's job

独到 dúdào original: 见解～ show originality in one's views; hold original views / ～之处 distinctive feature; unique style

独断专行 dúduàn-zhuānxíng behave arbitrarily or despotically; act wilfully on one's own

独家 dújiā exclusive: ～代理 sole agency; exclusive agent / ～新闻 exclusive (report)

独角戏 dújiǎoxì also "独脚戏" monodrama; one-man show: 唱～ put on a one-man show; go it alone

独具匠心 dújùjiàngxīn show unusual ingenuity; have originality: 情节构思～。The plot is ingenious in structure.

独揽 dúlǎn arrogate to oneself; monopolize: ～大权 arrogate all power to oneself

独立 dúlì ❶ independence: ～核算 keep separate accounts; practise independent accounting / ～思考 think for oneself / ～王国〈喻〉independent realm (brooking no supervision whatever): exclusive preserve / ～自主 maintain independence and keep the initiative in one's own hands; act independently and rely on oneself 闹～性 assert one's "independence"—disregard established discipline and refuse to obey the leadership ❷ become independent or separate

独联体 Dúliántǐ (short for 独立国家联合体) CIS (Commonwealth of Independent States)

独门 dúmén ❶ (of a family, etc) having one's own entrance or gate: ～户 single house or apartment with its own entrance ❷ (of a skill, recipe, etc) possessed by one individual or family only

独木 dúmù (made of) a single plank or log: ～桥 single-plank or single-log bridge; 〈喻〉difficult path / ～木舟 dugout canoe / ～难支 a single log cannot support a big house—one person alone cannot accomplish a major undertaking; cannot save the situation singlehanded / ～不成林 one tree does not make a woods—one person without support cannot achieve anything of significance

独辟蹊径 dúpìxījìng blaze a new trail for oneself; create a new style or method of one's own

独善其身 dúshànqíshēn seek one's

personal edification alone; be self-centred

独身 dúshēn unmarried; single; celibate: ～主义 remaining unmarried as a principle; celibacy

独生子女 dúshēngzǐnǚ only child: ～家庭 one-child family

独树一帜 dúshùyīzhì fly one's own colours; blaze one's own path; be unique

独特 dútè unique; distinctive; peculiar: ～风光 sight of no ordinary attraction; unusual tourist attraction

独一无二 dúyī-wú'èr unique; unrivalled; unmatched

独占 dúzhàn have all to oneself; monopolize: ～鳌头 come out first; be the champion

独资 dúzī single proprietorship: ～经营 exclusive ownership and management / ～企业 enterprise of exclusive ownership (by foreign investors, etc)

独自 dúzì alone; by oneself: ～谋生 earn one's own bread

独奏 dúzòu (of instrumental music) solo: ～音乐会 recital

读（讀） dú ❶ read out or aloud; pronounce: ～音 pronunciation ❷ read: ～本 reader; textbook / ～后感 impressions of or notes on a book or an essay ❸ attend (school): ～中学 attend secondary school

读书 dúshū ❶ read (a book): ～笔记 reading notes ❷ study; attend school: 在大学～ go to college / ～人 scholar; intellectual; 〈方〉student

读数 dúshù reading: 温度计～ thermometer reading

读物 dúwù reading matter or material; 儿童～ reading matter for children; children's books

读者 dúzhě reader: ～来信 letters from readers; letters to the editor

渎（瀆） dú 〈书〉show disrespect or contempt: ～职

malfeasance; dereliction of duty

犊(犢) dú calf:~子 calf

牍(牘) dú ❶ wooden tablets or slips for writing (in ancient times) ❷ documents; archives; correspondence

黩(黷) dú 〈书〉❶ sully; defile ❷ act rashly:~武 abuse one's military might; be militaristic or warlike

dǔ

肚 dǔ tripe:~子 tripe / ~丝儿 shredded tripe　*see also* dù

笃 dǔ ❶ faithful; earnest; sincere:~厚 honest and kind-hearted ❷ be seriously ill; be in a critical condition

笃定 dǔdìng 〈方〉❶ be sure or certain of:~成功 be bound to succeed ❷ be at ease; be composed:神情~ look completely at ease

笃实 dǔshí ❶ honest and loyal ❷ solid; sound:学问~ sound scholarship

笃信 dǔxìn faithfully believe; be an ardent believer:~不疑 believe firmly without a shadow of doubt

堵 dǔ ❶ stop up; block; suffocate:~击 intercept and attack / ~截 intercept / ~窟窿 plug up a leak or hole / 心里一～得慌 feel suffocated; have a load on one's mind / 用钱～人家的嘴 gag criticism with money ❷ 〈量〉一～墙 a wall

堵车 ·dǔchē traffic jam or congestion; 这街～得很严重。The street is often congested with traffic.

堵塞 dǔsè stop or block up; congest: 交通～ traffic jam or hold-up / ~工作中的漏洞 stop or plug up loopholes in work

赌 dǔ ❶ gamble:~本 gambling money or capital / ~场 gambling

house or den; casino / ~鬼 (incorrigible) gambler / ~棍 professional or hardened gambler / ~局 gambling party or den / ~具 gambling paraphernalia or device / ~钱 gamble / ~徒 gambler / ~债 gambling debt / ~资 money to gamble with; gambling money ❷ be:~东道 a treat (on sth)

赌博 dǔbó gambling:政治～ political gamble / ~成瘾 be addicted or given to gambling

赌气 dǔqì do (sth) in a pique; act wilfully:~不吃饭 refuse to eat out of pique

赌咒 dǔzhòu take an oath; swear:指天～ swear to heaven

赌注 dǔzhù stake; bet:下～ put down a stake; place or lay a bet

睹(覩) dǔ see:~物思人 think of the person at the sight of the thing; the souvenir reminds one of the person who gave it

dù

杜 dù ❶ *also* "杜梨";"棠梨"〈植〉birchleaf pear ❷ block; stop; forestall

杜鹃 dùjuān ❶ *also* "布谷";"子规"〈动物〉cuckoo ❷ *also* "映山红"〈植〉azalea

杜绝 dùjué stop; put an end to; uproot:~后患 destroy the root of future trouble / ~漏洞 plug a loophole

杜撰 dùzhuàn fabricate; make up:纯系～ (be) pure fabrication or fiction

肚 dù ❶ belly; abdomen; stomach; ~脐 *also* "肚脐眼儿" navel; belly button / 填饱～皮 fill the stomach　*see also* dǔ

肚量 dùliàng *see* "度量" dùliàng

肚子 dùzi ❶ belly; abdomen; stomach:生一～气 be overcome with anger; be filled with pent-up fury / 她~大了。She is in a family way. ❷ bulging and

round part (of sth):这瓶子是口小 ~
大。The bottle is narrow at the neck
and big in the body.

妒（妬） dù be jealous or envi-
ous of; envy:~忌 also
"妒嫉" be jealous or envious of / ~火
中烧 burn with jealousy; be green with
envy

度 dù ❶ linear measure:~量衡
length, capacity and weight;
weights and measures ❷ degree of a
given quality;灵敏 ~ sensitivity ❸ degree as a unit of measure:两 ~ 电 2
kilowatt-hours / 45 ~ 角 an angle of
45 degrees / 这种酒是 38 ~。This
liquor contains 38 per cent alcohol. ❹
standard; limit; tolerance:以能熔化为
~ to the point of melting ❺ space or
time of a given extent;季 ~ quarter (of
a year) ❻ spend (time); pass:~荒 tide
over a famine / ~命 keep oneself alive;
subsist / ~夜 spend or stay the night
❼ (of Buddhists or Taoists) convert:
普 ~ 众 生 deliver all living creatures
from suffering ❽〈量〉occasion; time:
一年两 ~ twice a year; bi-annually
see also duó

度假 dùjià spend one's holidays; go
vacationing:~村 holiday village / ~者
holiday-maker; vacationer

度量 dùliàng *also* "肚量" tolerance;
magnanimity: 有 ~ large-minded;
broad-minded; magnanimous / ~ 小
narrow-minded; petty-minded

度日 dùrì eke out a living or an existence:~如年 every hour seems an eternity; time hangs heavy

度数 dùshù ❶ number of degrees; read-
ing:用电 ~ reading on electricity consumed; consumption of power

渡 dù go or carry across; cross;
tide over:~口 *also* "渡头" ferry
(crossing) / ~ 轮 *also* "渡船"
ferryboat; ferry / ~过难关 tide over a
difficulty; pull through

镀 dù plating; coating:~层 coat-
ing / ~银 silver-plating; silver-
ing

镀金 dùjīn ❶ gold-plating; gilding:~
器皿 gilded utensils ❷ become gilded;
acquire a gilded reputation: 出 国 ~
study or work abroad for prestige

蠹 dù ❶ insect that eats into
books, clothing, etc; moth:~虫
moth; worm:〈喻〉vermin ❷ (of moths
or worms) eat:~蚀 moth-eaten

duān

端 duān ❶ tip; end; point:笔 ~
tip of a pen ❷ reason; cause; occasion:~由 cause; reason ❸ upright;
proper:~坐 sit bolt upright ❹ hold
(sth) level with both hands; carry (in
this manner):~茶 carry (cups of) tea;
serve tea / ~架子 put on airs

端倪 duānní clue; indication; inkling:
问题解决已见 ~。The solution of the
problem is in sight.

端平 duānpíng hold level; be impartial or unbiased:一碗水 ~ hold a bowl
of water level—treat (all parties) even-
handedly; be even-handed

端午 Duānwǔ *also* "端阳" Dragon
Boat Festival (5th day of the 5th lunar
month)

端详 duānxiáng ❶ details; particu-
lars:细说 ~ give a detailed account (of
sth); speak in detail ❷ (of manner,
etc) dignified and serene ❸
(duānxiang) *also* "端量" look up and
down; size up; look searchingly:仔细
~ scrutinize

端正 duānzhèng ❶ balanced and
symmetrical; regular; upright:五官 ~
have regular features / 穿得端端正正
be neatly dressed ❷ (make) proper;
upright; correct:人品 ~ be upright; be
a person of integrity / ~态度 change
one's wrong attitude; take the right at-

titude

端庄 duānzhuāng　stately; dignified and sedate: 神情 ～ look calm and sedate; look dignified

duǎn

短 duǎn ❶ short; brief: ～波〈通信〉short-wave / ～发 (for a woman) bobbed hair / ～裤 short pants; shorts / ～命 die young; be short-lived / ～评 short commentary; brief comments / ～视〈喻〉short-sighted; lacking in foresight / ～袜 socks; anklets / ～训班 short-term training course / ～篇小说 short story / ～距离赛跑 short-distance run; dash; sprint ❷ lack; owe: ～秤 give short weight / ～人 5 元 owe sb 5 yuan ❸ shortcoming; deficiency; fault: ～处 shortcoming; failing; weakness / 揭别人的～ rub sb on the raw

短兵相接 duǎnbīngxiāngjiē　fight at close quarters; engage in hand-to-hand fight: 一场～的外交斗争 a cut-and-thrust diplomatic battle

短程 duǎnchéng　short distance or range: ～导弹 short-range missile / ～运输飞机 short-haul airplane

短促 duǎncù　very short or brief: 呼吸～ short of breath; gasp / 期限～ little time allowed; short notice

短工 duǎngōng　casual or seasonal labourer: 打～ work as a casual labourer

短见 duǎnjiàn ❶ short-sighted view / suicide: 寻～ attempt or commit suicide

短路 duǎnlù〈电〉short (circuit) / ～事故 short-out accident

短跑 duǎnpǎo　dash; sprint: ～运动员 dash man; sprinter

短平快 duǎn-píng-kuài ❶〈体〉short, quick smash (as in volleyball) ❷ (enterprise or project) of little investment, short duration but quick returns

短期 duǎnqī　of short duration; short-term: ～行为 action aimed at achieving short-term results; short-sighted action / ～内完成 accomplish in a short time

短浅 duǎnqiǎn　narrow (in vision) and shallow (in understanding); superficial: 目光～ short-sighted

短缺 duǎnquē　short; deficient; scarce: 资金～ be short of funds / 商品～ commodity or item; goods in short supply

短途 duǎntú　short distance: ～运输 short-distance transport; short haul

短线 duǎnxiàn　in short supply; in great demand: ～产品 goods in short supply; under-supplied product

短小 duǎnxiǎo　short and small: ～精悍 (of a person) short and dapper; (of writing) short and forceful

短信 duǎnxìn　also "短信息"〈信息〉short message: 发～ send a short message (by mobile phone) / 文字～ text message

短语 duǎnyǔ〈语言〉phrase: ～动词 phrasal verb

短暂 duǎnzàn　of short duration; transient; brief: ～停留 brief or short stop

duàn

段 duàn ❶〈量〉used of a section or segment of sth long: 一～话 a passage of a speech / 一～木头 a section of a log ❷ (of ranks in weiqi) level; dan: 九～国手 level 9 weiqi master; ninth-dan go master ❸ (in a mine, factory, etc) section: 机务～ engineering section

段落 duànluò ❶ paragraph: ～大意 main idea of a paragraph ❷ phase; stage: 告一～ come to the end of a stage

段子 duànzi〈戏〉piece: 这相声～挺逗。This comic dialogue is very amusing.

断(斷) duàn ❶ cut; break; snap: ～裂 snap; ～流 (of a river) run dry / ～头台 guillotine / ～子绝孙〈粗〉die without issue ❷ break or cut off; stop; quit; ～顿 also "断顿" can't keep the pot boiling; go hungry / ～电 cut power; have a blackout / ～根 be completely cured (of a disease, etc); effect a permanent cure / ～交 cut ties; sever (diplomatic) relations / ～球 intercept the ball / ～粮 run out of grain or food / ～面 section / ～奶 wean / ～了联系 break off relations; be out of touch ❸ judge; decide; ～案 try or hear a case; settle a lawsuit / 我～他不敢这样做。I just don't think he has the nerve to do so. ❹〈书〉(usu in the negative) absolutely; decidedly; ～无可能 absolutely impossible; decidedly untrue

断层 duàncéng ❶〈地〉fault; ～带 fault line or zone ❷〈喻〉break (in a continuum); gap; 文化～ break or gap in cultural continuity

断肠 duàncháng be heartbroken; be overwhelmed with grief

断代 duàndài division of history into periods; periodization; ～史 dynastic or periodic history

断档 duàndàng (of goods, etc) out of stock; sold out

断定 duàndìng form a judgement; conclude; determine; 我敢～, 他会后悔的。I am sure he will be sorry for this.

断断续续 duànduàn-xùxù on and off; intermittently; ～的枪声 intermittent shooting; sporadic gunfire

断后 duànhòu ❶ have no (male) progeny or offspring; be childless ❷ cover a retreat; bring up the rear

断句 duànjù read correctly; punctuate (ancient writings)

断绝 duànjué break or cut off; sever; ～交通 cut off transport; stop all traffic / ～后患 remove causes of future trouble

断气 duànqì breathe one's last; die

断然 duànrán ❶ resolute; drastic; ～

措施 drastic measure ❷ absolutely; categorically; ～没有这个道理 absolutely unreasonable

断送 duànsòng forfeit or lose (one's life, etc); ruin (one's career, etc)

断想 duànxiǎng brief comments or notes; 新春～ random thoughts on New Year's Day

断言 duànyán say or state with certainty; assert or affirm categorically

断章取义 duànzhāngqǔyì quote out of context; garble a statement, etc

缎 duàn satin; ～子 satin

椴 duàn 〈植〉(Chinese) linden

锻 duàn also "煅" forge; ～工 forging; forger; blacksmith / ～件 forging(s) / ～压 forge and press / ～造 forging; smithing

锻炼 duànliàn ❶ forge; smelt ❷ exercise; have physical training; temper; ～坚强的意志 build up a strong will

duī

堆 duī ❶ pile; heap; stack; 沙～ sand heap / ～放 pile up; stack ❷〈量〉used of what can be gathered (as) in a heap; 一～灰烬 a heap of ashes / 一大～谎话 a pack of lies

堆积 duījī pile or heap up; ～如山 (of things) heap in a mound; (of work, etc) pile up like a mountain

堆砌 duīqì ❶ pile up neatly (to build sth); 用乱石～而成 built with cobbles and rocks ❷ pile up (fancy vocabulary); write in an ornate, redundant style

duì

队(隊) duì ❶ row or file of people; line; queue; ～形 formation ❷ team; group; band; ～友 fellow member of a group or team; fellow player / ～员 team member / ～长 team leader;〈体〉captain ❸ (standing for 少年先锋队) Chinese Young Pioneers;～礼 Young Pioneer's salute ❹〈量〉used of a line or group of people, etc:一～士兵 a column of soldiers

队旗 duìqí ❶ Young Pioneers' flag ❷〈体〉team pennant

队伍 duìwu ❶ armed force; troops ❷ contingent; force:知识分子～ contingent of intellectuals ❸ ranks; formations:游行～ procession; parade

队形 duìxíng formation:以密集～ in close order; in massed formation / 以散开～ in open order

对（對） duì ❶ reply; answer:无以为～ not know how to answer / ～答如流 respond fluently; reply readily ❷ treat; cope with:～事不～人 be concerned with facts rather than individuals ❸ be trained on; be directed at; face:～准靶子 aim at the target / 甲队～乙队 team A versus team B ❹ facing or opposite (each other):～岸 opposite bank / ～白〈戏〉dialogue / ～唱 also "对歌" antiphonal singing / ～过 opposite; across / ～骂 trade abuse; call each other names / ～讲机 intercom / ～着干 adopt a confrontational approach; set oneself against sb ❺ bring into coordination or contact; match; fit:～胃口 suit one's taste; be interesting or pleasant ❻ compare; check; identify:～暗号 exchange code words / ～台词 (of actors) practise lines together ❼ set; adjust:～表 set one's watch; synchronize watches ❽ right; correct; normal:你～了。You've got it (right). ❾ add; mix; adulterate:～了水的酒 adulterated or diluted wine ❿ divide into halves; split even:～半 half-and-half; fifty-fifty / ～折 (at) 50% discount; (fold sth) in half ⓫ (antithetical) couplet:～联 antithetical couplet ⓬〈量〉pair; couple:一～石狮子 a pair of stone lions ⓭ concerning; regarding:～问

题的看法 view on a question; how one looks at a problem

对比 duìbǐ ❶ compare; contrast:力量～ balance of forces / ～度〈通信〉contrast / ～之下 by comparison ❷ ratio

对簿公堂 duìbùgōngtáng〈书〉be cross-examined or interrogated in court; go to court (against sb over sth)

对不起 duìbuqǐ also "对不住" ❶〈套〉I am sorry; excuse or pardon me:～,叫你久等了。Sorry to have kept you waiting so long. ❷ let down; be unworthy of; be unfair to:我决不做任何～你们的事情。I shall never do any disservice to you.

对策 duìcè way to cope with a situation; countermeasure; solution:上有政策,下有～。Whatever policy the higher-ups may adopt, people down below know how to circumvent it.

对称 duìchèn symmetry; 布局～ symmetrical in layout / ～美 symmetrical beauty

对待 duìdài treat; approach:客观地～一切事物 take all things objectively

对得起 duìdeqǐ also "对得住" treat fairly; do justice to:～朋友 not let one's friends down / ～自己的良心 have a clear conscience

对等 duìděng reciprocal; equal in rank or status; ～贸易 counter-trade / ～原则 principle of reciprocity

对调 duìdiào also "对换" exchange; swap

对方 duìfāng other side or party; opposite side; rival:～付费电话 collect call

对付 duìfu ❶ deal or cope with; handle; tackle:此人不易～。The chap is a hard nut to crack. ❷ make do:～着用 make do with sth

对号 duìhào ❶ check the number:～入座 take the number before taking one's seat;〈喻〉see where one fits into sth, or how sth relates to one ❷ fit;

tally；match ❸ mark used to show that an answer is correct（usu "O" or "√"）

对话 duìhuà　dialogue；conversation：南北～ North-South dialogue

对劲 duìjìn ❶ be to one's liking；suit one：这笔写起来～。This pen writes well. ❷ see"对头❷❸"

对抗 duìkàng ❶ antagonism；hostility：～性矛盾 antagonistic contradiction ❷ resist；oppose；confront：～赛〈体〉dual meet / ～上级指示 disobey or defy instructions from above

对口 duìkǒu （of two parties, etc) correspond in nature or speciality；（of training, etc) fit in with one's job：～会谈 negotiations between counterparts / 专业～ the kind of work one is trained for

对垒 duìlěi　also"对阵"（in battle or contest) confront or meet each other；be pitted against each other

对立 duìlì ❶ contradict；oppose；be antagonistic to：～面 opposite；antithesis；〈喻〉adversary / ～情绪 antagonistic mood；antagonism / ～统一规律〈哲〉law of the unity of opposites

对路 duìlù ❶ meet the requirement；satisfy the need；be just right：～商品 marketable goods；goods that sell well ❷ be to one's liking；suit one：这工作对我的路。This job suits me fine.

对面 duìmiàn ❶ opposite；across ❷ right ahead：～走过来一群小学生。A group of school kids came towards us. ❸ face to face；vis-à-vis

对内 duìnèi　internal；domestic；home：～销售 sell in the home market

对牛弹琴 duìniútánqín　play the lute to a cow—address the wrong audience；cast pearls before swine

对偶 duì'ǒu　〈语言〉antithesis：～句 antithetical sentences

对手 duìshǒu ❶ opponent；adversary；rival ❷ match；equal：下棋你不是他的～。You are no match for him in chess.

对头 duìtóu ❶ right and proper；correct：这办法～。This is the right solution. ❷ (often in the negative) normal；right：脸色不～ not look well ❸ (often in the negative) get on well；hit it off；be on good terms：两个人的脾气不～。The two do not agree（with each other）in temperament. ❹ (duìtou) enemy；opponent；adversary：死～ sworn enemy

对外 duìwài　external；foreign：～开放 opening to the outside world；opening up / ～扩张 external expansion / ～贸易 foreign trade

对虾 duìxiā　also"明虾" prawn

对象 duìxiàng ❶ target；object：攻击～ target of attack / 本书的～是大中学生。This book is intended for college and high-school students. ❷ prospective partner in marriage；boy or girl friend：找 ～ look for a prospective spouse

对眼 duìyǎn　cross-eye

对应 duìyìng　homologous；corresponding；relevant：～词〈语言〉equivalent / ～措施 corresponding or reciprocal measure；countermeasure

对于 duìyú　concerning；with regard to；about：～他，我们要严格些。We must be strict with him.

对照 duìzhào ❶ check（a piece of writing）against another；place side by side：英汉～读物 bilingual English-Chinese reader ❷ contrast；compare：形成鲜明的～ make a striking contrast；contrast sharply

对症 duìzhèng　give a correct diagnosis；be the right cure（for sth）：～下药 give the right prescription for an illness；take proper steps；adopt effective measures

对质 duìzhì　confront（as）in court；verify by confrontation

对峙 duìzhì　face off；confront：两军～ two armies locked in a face-off / 武装～ military confrontation

对子 duìzi ❶ antithetical couplet；对～ provide the second of a pair of anti-thetical sentences ❷ pair of persons or things；结成～ pair off (to do sth)

兑 duì ❶ exchange；convert：用人民币～美元 convert RMB into US dollars ❷ honour (a bill, etc)；cash (a cheque, etc)；～付 cash (a cheque, etc) / ～奖 claim a prize；cash in a lottery ticket (that has won a prize) ❸ mix；mingle：～了水的牛奶 diluted milk ❹ see "八卦" bāguà

兑换 duìhuàn exchange；convert：～率 rate of exchange；exchange rate / 可～货币 convertible currency

兑现 duìxiàn ❶ cash (a cheque, etc)；pay a dividend, bonus or balance in cash ❷ honour (a commitment, etc)；fulfil；make good：说了话不～ fail to live up to one's word

dūn

吨(噸) dūn ❶ ton；tonnage：～公里 ton kilometre ❷ also "吨位" register ton

敦 dūn sincere；honest：～促 urge；press；request / ～厚 honest and sincere / ～请 sincerely request；cordially invite

敦实 dūnshi 〈方〉stocky；thickset；squat

墩 dūn ❶ mound ❷ block of stone or wood；foundation made of brick or cement ❸ mop (the ground, etc)：～布 mop / ～地 mop the floor ❹ 〈量〉cluster：一～稻秧 a cluster of rice seedlings

蹲 dūn ❶ squat (on the heels)：～坑〈口〉squat over a latrine pit to relieve oneself ❷ stay (in one place)：～点 (of leaders) etc) work at a chosen grass-roots unit (to get firsthand experience) / ～班房 also "蹲大牢" be in jail；be imprisoned

dǔn

盹 dǔn doze；take a nap：打个～儿 take a nap；doze off

趸(躉) dǔn ❶ buy or sell) wholesale：～货 buy goods wholesale / ～批 wholesale

趸船 dǔnchuán landing stage；pontoon

dùn

囤 dùn grain bin　see also tún

炖(燉) dùn ❶ stew：～牛肉 stewed beef ❷ warm (sth) by putting it in a container in boiling water：～酒 warm wine

钝 dùn ❶ blunt；dull：～角〈数〉obtuse angle / ～器 blunt tool ❷ stupid；dull-witted

盾 dùn ❶ shield；buckler；shield-shaped thing：～牌 shield；pretext；excuse ❷ money unit of Vietnam (dong), Indonesia (rupiah), etc

顿 dùn ❶ pause：～号 slight-pause mark (、) (in Chinese calligraphy) pause to reinforce the beginning or ending of a stroke ❸ kowtow；stamp：～首 knock one's head against the ground / ～足 stamp one's feet ❹ arrange；handle：安～ settle ❺ suddenly；immediately；～时 at once；instantly / ～悟 realize in a flash；instant or sudden enlightenment ❻ tired：困～ dog-tired；fatigued ❼ 〈量〉used to indicate frequency：一日三～ three meals a day / 痛打一～ give (sb) a sound beating

遁(遯) dùn ❶ escape；flee；run away：～入空门 withdraw from secular life and become a Buddhist monk or nun ❷ hide；lie low；disappear：～词 subterfuge；quibble / ～迹 live in seclusion；lead a

D

reclusive life / ～形 lie low; hide one's identity

duō

多 duō ❶ many; much; multi-；～云 cloudy / ～党制 multi-party system / ～媒体 multimedia / ～面手 many-sided or versatile person; all-rounder / ～劳～得 more work, more pay / ～民族国家 multinational country / 请～～指教. Please feel free to make your suggestions. ❷ be or have too many or too much：～虑 over-anxious / ～退多补 (after a round sum is paid in advance) refund for any overpayment and supplementary payment for any deficiency / ～喝了一点儿 have a drop too much ❸ (used after a numeral) more; over; odd：二百～人 over two hundred people / 5 点～钟 a little past five ❹ much or far more; much or far less；好～了 much better / 差～了 much worse; far poorer ❺ also "多么"〈副〉used in questions to indicate degree or extent：这男孩儿～大了？ How old is the boy? ❻ also "多么"〈副〉used in exclamations to indicate a high degree or a great extent：～好的年轻人啊! What a fine young man! ❼ also "多么"〈副〉used to a great extent: 不管～忙，他总挤时间读书. However busy he was, he always found time for reading.

多半 duōbàn ❶ greater part; majority; most：～个月 (for the) better part of a month ❷ probably; most likely: 台风～发生在夏季. Typhoons usually occur in summer.

多边 duōbiān multilateral：～形〈数〉polygon / ～会谈 multilateral talks / ～主义 multilateralism

多变 duōbiàn changeable; fickle; varied; 形势～ volatile situation / 性情～ mercurial temperament

多才多艺 duōcái-duōyì versatile; of many talents

多层 duōcéng of many layers; multi-layer：～板 plywood / ～建筑 multi-storeyed building (usu of less than eight storeys)

多愁善感 duōchóu-shàngǎn excessively sentimental; mawkish

多此一举 duōcǐyījǔ be superfluous; make an unnecessary move; carry coals to Newcastle

多次 duōcì many times; repeatedly; on many occasions：～提出忠告 offer repeated advice / ～入境签证 multiple entry visa

多动症 duōdòngzhèng 〈医〉attention-deficit hyperactivity disorder (ADHD); hyperactivity: 这孩子像有～. The child seems to be hyperactive.

多多益善 duōduō-yìshàn the more, the better; the more, the merrier

多发 duōfā occur frequently：～病 frequently occurring disease / 事故～地段 accident-prone area (of a road, etc)

多方 duōfāng in many ways; in every way：～阻挠 hinder in many ways; place many obstacles (in sb's way, etc)

多方面 duōfāngmiàn many-sided; multiple; in many ways: 失败的原因是～的. The defeat was due to a number of factors.

多功能 duōgōngnéng multifunction; multi-purpose：～厅 multi-purpose hall

多国 duōguó multinational：～公司 multinational corporation

多极 duōjí multi-polar：～化 multi-polarization; multi-polarity

多亏 duōkuī thanks to; luckily：～你的支持. We owe everything to your support.

多么 duōme see "多❺-❼"

多情 duōqíng tender and affectionate (to a person of the opposite sex); loving; sentimental

多如牛毛 duōrúniúmáo too numerous

to enumerate; countless; innumerable

多少 duōshǎo ❶ number; amount: ~不等 vary in amount or number ❷ more or less; somewhat; a little: ~有点凉 somewhat cold / ~知道些 hear something of it ❸ (duōshao) how many or much: 这苹果～钱一公斤? How much are those apples per kilo? ❹ (duōshao) indicating an uncertain quantity: 要～给～ give (sb) as much as he or she wants

多事 duōshì ❶ do what is unnecessary or superfluous; be officious or meddlesome: 别～。Mind your own business. ❷ troubled; eventful: ~之秋 eventful period of time; troubled times

多数 duōshù majority; most: 绝大～overwhelming majority / 微弱～ small or narrow majority / 相对～ relative majority; plurality / ~人 most people; the majority

多维 duōwéi 〈数〉multidimensional: ~空间 multidimensional space; hyperspace

多谢 duōxiè 〈套〉many thanks; thanks a lot: ~~。Thank you ever so much.

多心 duōxīn oversensitive; suspicious: 你别～。Please don't take it to heart.

多样 duōyàng diverse; varied: 形式～diversified or varied in form / ~化diversify; vary

多疑 duōyí over-suspicious; given or prone to suspicion

多余 duōyú ❶ surplus; extra; unnecessary; superfluous; redundant: 你的猜疑是～的。Your suspicion is uncalled for.

多元 duōyuán multi-factor or -element; multivariate: ~论〈哲〉pluralism / ~社会 pluralistic society

多种 duōzhǒng diversified; varied; manifold: ~多样 varied; manifold / ~经营 diversified economy; diversification

多嘴 duōzuǐ shoot off one's mouth; have a big mouth: ~多舌 gossipy and meddlesome; long-tongued / 别～! Keep your mouth shut!

咄 duō

咄咄 duōduō used to show amazement or wonder: ~逼人 overbearing; aggressive / ~怪事 height of absurdity

哆 duō

哆嗦 duōsuo tremble; shiver: 吓得直～ shiver with fright

掇 duō pick up: 拾～ tidy up

duó

夺(奪) duó ❶ take by force; seize; wrest: ~权 seize power ❷ win through competition: ~冠 win the championship; come first; take first place ❸ 魁 come first; win the first prize or championship / ~走金牌 carry off the gold medal ❸ force one's way through; rush into or out of: ~门而出 make for the door and rush out ❹ 〈书〉decide: 定～ make a final decision

夺标 duóbiāo ❶ win the trophy; win a championship: ~呼声最高 be favoured for the championship ❷ have one's tender accepted; win a bid

夺目 duómù dazzle the eyes: 光彩～的项链 shining necklace

夺取 duóqǔ ❶ capture; seize; take by force ❷ strive for: ~更大的胜利 strive for even greater victories

度 duó 〈书〉surmise; estimate: ~德量力 take a proper measure of one's own (moral) reputation and ability; correctly appraise one's own position see also dù

踱 duó stroll; pace: ~着方步 stroll with measured steps; walk in a leisurely manner

D

duǒ

朵（朶） duǒ 〈量〉 *used of flowers, clouds, etc*：一～玫瑰 a rose (blossom) / 一～白云 a whitish cloud

垛 duǒ ❶ *also* "垛子" battlement; outward buttress (of a wall) ❷ 〈量〉 *used of a window, wall, etc*：砌一～砖墙 build a brick wall

see also duò

D

躲 duǒ ❶ go into hiding; hunker down；～藏 hide or conceal oneself; go into hiding ❷ avoid; dodge：～让 dodge; make way for / ～闪 dodge; evade / ～雨 take shelter from rain / ～债 avoid a creditor

躲避 duǒbì ❶ hide (oneself) ❷ avoid; elude; dodge：～困难 shy away from difficulties

躲躲闪闪 duǒduo-shǎnshǎn not face the reality; evade；话说得～ speak evasively; hum and haw

duò

驮 duò *see also* tuó

驮子 duòzi ❶ load carried by a pack animal; pack ❷ 〈量〉 *used of caravan goods*：三～货 three loads of goods

剁 duò chop; cut：～肉馅 chop up or mince meat

垛 duò ❶ pile up neatly ❷ pile; stack：柴禾～ pile of firewood

see also duǒ

舵 duò rudder; helm：～手 (often figuratively) steersman; helmsman

堕（墮） duò fall; sink：～胎 have an (induced) abortion / ～入情网 be snared in the coils of love; fall in love

堕落 duòluò degenerate; sink low；走向～ head towards one's downfall; sink into degeneration / ～风尘 (of a woman) be driven to prostitution

惰 duò lazy; idle; indolent

惰性 duòxìng inertia; passive attitude；～气体 inert or noble gas

踩 duò stamp (one's foot)

E

ē

阿 ē pander or cater to; ~附权贵 attach oneself to bigwigs *see also* ā

阿胶 ējiāo *also* "驴皮胶"〈中药〉donkey-hide gelatin

阿弥陀佛 Emítuófó 〈宗教〉Amitabha, name of Buddha; merciful Buddha; 南无~。Blessed be *Amitabha*.

阿谀 ēyú fawn on; flatter: ~奉承 curry favour with sb; lick sb's boots

屙 ē 〈方〉discharge (excrement or urine)

婀 ē

婀娜 ēnuó （usu of a woman's bearing or figure）lithe and graceful; supple and charming: ~多姿 graceful and charming; lithe and pretty

é

讹 é ❶ erroneous; wrong; mistaken: ~脱〈书〉errors and omissions / ~误 error (in a text, etc); mistake / ~字 wrong word (in a text) ❷ blackmail; extort; bluff: ~钱 extort money by blackmail / ~人 blackmail or bluff sb

讹传 échuán false or unfounded rumour: ~老张病了。Lao Zhang was rumoured to be ill.

讹诈 ézhà extort; blackmail; bluff: 核~ nuclear blackmail / ~善良 black-

mail honest people

俄 é ❶〈书〉shortly; presently; suddenly: ~而 before long; not long after / ~顷 in a moment; presently ❷（俄）(short for 俄罗斯) Russia: 沙~ Tsarist or Czarist Russia / ~国 Russia / ~语 *also* "俄文" Russian (language)

俄罗斯 Éluósī Russia: ~人 Russian

俄延 éyán delay; stall: 此事不可~。This brooks no delay.

峨（峩） é 〈书〉high; lofty: 峨博带 high hats and wide waist-belts (worn by officials and scholars in ancient China)

娥 é pretty young woman: 宫~ palace maid; maid of honour

娥眉 éméi *also* "蛾眉" ❶ delicate eyebrows: ~月 new moon; crescent (moon) / ~皓齿 fine eyebrows and white teeth — female beauty; beautiful woman ❷ beautiful woman

鹅（鵝） é goose: ~黄 light yellow / ~蛋脸 egg-shaped or oval face / ~卵石 cobblestone; cobble

鹅毛 émáo goose feather: ~大雪 heavy snow / ~扇子 goose-feather fan

蛾 é moth: 蚕~ silk moth / ~子 moth

蛾眉 éméi *see* "娥眉" éméi

额 é ❶ *also* "额头" forehead ❷ specified number, volume, or amount: ~度 quota; specified amount

额定 édìng specified (number or amount); rated: ~值 nominal value;

〈机〉rating / ～马力 rated horsepower /～人数 stipulated number of personnel; authorized complement

额手称庆 éshǒuchēngqìng lay one's hand on one's forehead in jubilation; be overjoyed: 国人无不～。The entire nation was beside itself with joy.

额外 éwài extra; additional; added: ～负担 added burden / ～开支 extra expense

ě

恶（惡、噁）ě *see also* è; wù

恶心 ěxīn ❶ feel nauseated; be disgusted ❷ disgust; embarrass; humiliate; let sb ～: disgusting; repugnant / 找个机会～～他 find an opportunity to embarrass or humiliate him

è

厄 è disaster; adversity; hardship: ～境 miserable plight; predicament / ～运 adversity; misfortune

厄尔尼诺现象 è'ěrnínuò xiànxiàng El Nino phenomenon

扼 è ❶ grasp tightly; clutch; grip: ～死 strangle to death; throttle /～腕〈书〉wring one's hands (in sorrow or despair) ❷ guard; hold; control: ～守阵地 hold a position / ～制怒火 restrain or contain one's anger

扼杀 èshā strangle; smother; throttle: ～积极性 throttle or frustrate sb's enthusiasm / ～在摇篮里 strangle (sth) in the cradle / ～于萌芽状态中 nip (sth) in the bud

扼要 èyào concise; brief and to the point: ～介绍情况 give a briefing (on sth); give a brief account (of sth)

恶（惡）è ❶ evil; bad; wicked: ～鬼 evil spirit; demon; wicked person / ～棍 ruffian;

scoundrel; bully / ～迹 *also* "恶行" abominable behaviour; evil conduct or deed / ～疾 foul or pernicious disease / ～兆 *also* "噩兆" ill or bad omen; writing on the wall / ～势力 evil force; pernicious pressure group / ～有～报。Evil is rewarded with evil. ❷ fierce; vicious; ferocious:～狼 ferocious wolf / ～战 *also* "恶仗" fierce or gruelling battle; savage fighting / ～声～气 angry voices and rude remarks　*see also* ě; wù

恶霸 èbà local tyrant; despot or bully:～地主 despotic landlord

恶臭 èchòu foul smell; stench: 名声～ foul or stinking reputation

恶毒 èdú vicious; malicious; venomous: 用心～ (harbour) malicious intent

恶感 ègǎn (bear) ill or hard feeling; ill will; grudge

恶贯满盈 èguànmǎnyíng be guilty of too many crimes to escape punishment: ～的毒枭 drug baron whose sum of iniquity is made up for retribution

恶果 èguǒ evil consequence; bad result; bitter end: 必食～ be bound to come to a bitter end

恶狠狠 èhěnhěn venomous; fierce; ferocious

恶化 èhuà worsen; deteriorate

恶劣 èliè bad; vile; odious: 心情～ be in a bad mood / ～的天气 inclement or foul weather

恶名 èmíng bad name or reputation; infamy: 背～ suffer infamy (for sb else); be subjected to vilification / ～昭著 infamous; notorious

恶魔 èmó demon; devil; monster

恶人 èrén evil person; vile creature; villain: 做～ act the villain; play the role of bad guy / ～先告状〈俗〉the guilty party files charges first; he who offends is always the first to complain

恶习 èxí bad or pernicious habit: 染上～ get into or contract a bad habit; fal into evil ways

恶性 èxìng malignant; pernicious; vicious;～竞争 cut-throat competition /～贫血 pernicious anaemia /～循环 vicious circle /～肿瘤 malignant tumour; cancer /～通货膨胀 galloping or runaway inflation /～刑事案件 case of vicious crime

恶意 èyì evil or ill intention; ill will; malice;心怀～ bear (sb) malice or ill will

恶语 èyǔ vicious slander; foul language;～中伤 viciously slander; calumniate

恶作剧 èzuòjù mischief; prank; practical joke;闹～ be up to mischief; play a practical joke

饿 è be hungry; starve;～死 starve to death; die of hunger /～极了 be famished /～虎扑食 like a hungry tiger pouncing on its prey

鄂 È another name for Hubei(湖北);～西北 northwestern Hubei

萼 è 〈植〉calyx

遏 è check; restrain; prohibit;～抑 keep down; suppress; contain

遏止 èzhǐ hold back; check; restrain;～侵略 check aggression / 不可～的洪流 irresistible tide

遏制 èzhì restrain; curb; contain;～政策 policy of containment /～内心的恐惧 try to keep one's fear under control

愕 è astounded; stunned; dazed;～视 look in astonishment; stare wide-eyed /～然失色 be taken aback and turn pale

腭 è 〈生理〉palate;软～ soft palate / 硬～ hard palate

颚 è ❶ mandible (of an arthropod); jaw;上～ upper jaw /～骨 jawbone ❷ see "腭" è

噩 è shocking; frightening;～耗 also "恶耗" sad news (as of the

death of sb one loves, etc) /～梦 also "恶梦" nightmare; frightening or horrible dream /～运 also "恶运" bad luck

鳄(鱷) è crocodile; alligator;～梨 also "油梨" alligator pear; avocado

鳄鱼 èyú (popular term for 鳄) crocodile; alligator;～眼泪 crocodile tears

ēn

恩 ēn kindness; favour; grace;～将仇报 return evil for good; bite the hand that feeds one /～同再造 kindness tantamount to giving one a new lease of life /～威并用 combine justice and mercy; use the carrot and the stick /～重如山 kindness as heavy as a mountain; great favour

恩爱 ēn'ài conjugal love;～夫妻 affectionate or loving couple

恩赐 ēncì bestow (favours, charity, etc); patronize;大自然的～ bounty of nature /～的态度 patronizing attitude

恩德 ēndé kindness; favour; grace;～无量 infinite kindness; numerous favours

恩典 ēndiǎn favour; grace; kindness;求～ beg for a favour

恩惠 ēnhuì favour; kindness; bounty;小恩小惠 petty favours

恩情 ēnqíng loving kindness; favour;～似海 kindness as extensive as the sea

恩人 ēnrén (kind) benefactor;以～自居 assume the airs of a benefactor; play the benefactor

恩师 ēnshī esteemed teacher; honourable master

恩怨 ēnyuàn (gratitude and) resentment; grievance;～分明 also "恩仇分明" know whom one should love or hate; distinguish clearly between friend and foe / 不计较个人～ not allow oneself to be swayed by personal feelings

èn

摁 èn　press (with the hand or finger)：～钮 press or push a button /～钉儿 drawing pin；thumbtack /～扣儿 snap fastener /～门铃 ring a doorbell /～手印 register one's fingerprint

ér

儿（兒） ér ❶ child；baby：～歌 children's song；nursery rhyme /～时 childhood ❷ son：～子 son /～媳妇儿 daughter-in-law /～不嫌母丑.《俗》A mother never looks ugly to her son. ❸ male：～马（口）male horse；stallion ❹ used as a suffix (called 儿化) a) after a noun to indicate smallness：帽～ cap / 零碎～ odds and ends b) to turn a verb or an adjective into a noun：吃～ eatables；food / 亮～ light c) to render a concrete noun abstract or different：油水～ profit / 白面～ heroin

儿科 érkē　(department of) paediatrics：～医生 paediatrician

儿女 érnǚ ❶ sons and daughters；children：一对～ a son and a daughter / 中华～ children of China ❷ young man and woman (in love)：～情长 (of a man and a woman) enduring affection for each other

儿孙 érsūn　children and grandchildren；descendants；～满堂 have many children and grandchildren in the family

儿童 értóng　children：～节 Children's Day (1 June) /～文学 children's or juvenile literature /～医院 children's hospital

儿戏 érxì　child's play；trifling matter：视同～ regard as mere child's play；treat as a matter of no consequence

而 ér 〈连〉❶ used to express coordination a) by joining two parallel adjectives, etc：朴素～大方 simple but with good taste b) by joining two elements that form a sequence in meaning：战～胜之 fight and defeat sb c) by joining two elements opposite in meaning that contrast with, or complement each other：忙～不乱 busy but not disorderly / 不在数量多～在质量好. It is not quantity but quality that counts. d) by connecting cause and effect, or aim and means：由于成功～骄傲 be dizzy with success ❷ used to indicate change from one state to another：由上～下 from top to bottom / 一～再，再～三 again and again；time and again ❸ used to connect an adverbial phrase of time or manner with a verb：日出～作 start working at sunrise / 顺流～下 go downstream ❹ inserted between subject and predicate to indicate a condition：科学研究～无进取精神，是不会有所成就的. Scientific research would never get anywhere without the pioneering spirit.

而后 érhòu　(used only after another element) after that；then：学～知不足. One discovers one's ignorance only through learning.

而今 érjīn　now；at the present time：～而后 from now on

而且 érqiě 〈连〉(often used after an element introduced by 不但 or 不仅) and (also)；but also；moreover：他不但是历史学家，～还是诗人. He is not only a historian, but also a poet.

而已 éryǐ 〈助〉nothing more；nothing but；only；不过是个烟幕弹～ nothing but a smoke-screen

ěr

尔（爾） ěr 〈书〉❶ you；your：～曹 you people；you

and your kind / ～父 your father / 虞我诈 each trying to cheat or outdo the other; mutual deception ❷ so; like that; 果～ if so / ～ 尔 *also* "尔尔" nothing out of the ordinary; just so-so ❸ that; this; ～来 since then; lately

耳 ěr ❶ ear; ～背 hard of hearing; somewhat deaf / ～垂 earlobe / ～垢 *also* "耳屎" earwax / ～聋 deaf / ～鸣〈医〉ringing in the ear / ～膜 *also* "鼓膜" eardrum; tympanum / ～报神〈方〉one who reports on sb's activities; informer / 根清净 have peace for one's ears (free from nagging, quarrel, etc) ; enjoy peace and quiet / ～听八方, 眼观六路 be very alert to what is going on all around ❷ any ear-like appendage; ear of a utensil ❸ flanking; side; ～房 side room (usu in a courtyard); wing / ～门 side door

耳鼻喉科 ěr-bí-hóu kē ENT (ear-nose-throat) department; ～医生 ENT specialist

耳边风 ěrbiānfēng *also* "耳旁风" sth that goes in one ear and out the other; unheeded words; 把忠告当作～ make light of or turn a deaf ear to well-meant advice

耳聪目明 ěrcōng-mùmíng have good eyesight and hearing; be clear-headed and clear-sighted

耳朵 ěrduo ear; 尖 *also* "耳尖" (with) sharp ears; sharp of hearing / ～软 *also* "耳软" susceptible to flattery and gossip; credulous; gullible

耳光 ěrguāng *also* "耳刮子" slap on the face; box on the ear; 打～ slap sb's face; box sb's ear

耳机 ěrjī *also* "听筒" earphone; earpiece; receiver

耳目 ěrmù ears and eyes; 〈喻〉informer; information; 充人～ be sb's informer / ～闭塞 be ill-informed / ～一新 find everything fresh and new

耳濡目染 ěrrú-mùrǎn be imperceptibly influenced by what one constantly sees and hears

耳塞 ěrsāi ❶ mini-earphone ❷ earplug

耳熟 ěrshú familiar to the ear; ～能详 get to know pretty well what one often hears; (of sth) be familiar to (through repetition)

耳提面命 ěrtí-miànmìng pour advice and exhortations (into sb's ears); constantly give (sb) one's advice and instructions

耳闻 ěrwén hear of or about; ～目睹 what one sees and hears / ～不如目见。Seeing is believing.

耳语 ěryǔ whisper (in sb's ear)

迩(邇) ěr〈书〉near; ～来 recently; lately

饵 ěr bait; trap; ～雷〈军〉booby-trap / ～料 fishing bait; insect killer; insecticide / ～子 fishing bait

èr

一 èr ❶ two; second; sub-; ～老〈敬〉father and mother; parents / ～流 second-class; second-rate / ～楼 (UK) first floor; (US) second floor / ～把手 number two; second-in-command / ～次能源 secondary energy (source) (such as electricity, etc) / ～级市场 secondary market / ～氧化碳〈化〉carbon dioxide / ～者必居其一。It's one or the other. / ～者不可兼得。You can't eat your cake and have it too. / ～虎相斗, 必有一伤。〈俗〉When two tigers fight, one is bound to be the loser. ❷ different; 不～ different; 米饭～ boiled rice mixed with millet or corn / 并无～致 not different; the same

二百五 èrbǎiwǔ〈口〉one who is not all there; stupid person; smatterer

二重 èrchóng dual; ～唱 (vocal)

duet /～性 duality / ～奏 (instrumental) duet

二等 èrděng   second-class or-rate; ～舱 second-class cabin / ～奖 second prize

二噁英 èr'èyīng   also "二恶英" 〈化〉 dioxin, a cancer-causing chemical

二胡 èrhú   erhu, a two-stringed Chinese fiddle

二话 èrhuà   (usu in the negative) demur; objection; complaint: 决无～ not hesitate (to do sth) / ～没说 without more ado

二进制 èrjìnzhì   〈数〉binary system or mode: ～编码器 binary coder

二郎腿 èrlángtuǐ   (sit) with one's legs crossed

二愣子 èrlèngzi   rash fellow

二流子 èrliúzi   also "二赖子"; "二混子" loafer; idler; bum

二手 èrshǒu   second-hand: ～货 second-hand goods

二线 èrxiàn   second line of defence; 〈喻〉semi-retirement for veteran cadres: 退居～ step down or withdraw from active service

二心 èrxīn   also "二意"; "贰心" ❶ disloyalty; unfaithfulness: 决无～ be absolutely faithful or loyal ❷ half-heartedness; two minds: 做事不可有～. If you want to do something, concentrate on it.

二一添作五 èryītiānzuòwǔ   share on a fifty—fifty basis; go halves

二元 èryuán   duality; binary: ～论 〈哲〉dualism / ～方程式 〈数〉binary equation /～化学武器 binary chemical weapon

二月 èryuè   ❶ February ❷ second month of the lunar year; second moon

贰 (弍) èr   ❶ two (used for the numeral 二 to avoid mistakes or alterations) ❷ turncoat: ～臣 turncoat official

F

fā

发（發） fā ❶ issue; send; discharge / ~车 dispatch a car, etc; (of a car, etc) depart / ~炮 discharge a gun; fire a cannon / ~信 send a letter / ~奖金 distribute bonuses / ~号施令 issue orders; order people about / 把报纸~给订户 distribute newspapers to subscribers ❷ generate; produce; bring or come into existence / ~奶 (of food or medicine) promote lactation / ~疟子 have an attack of malaria; suffer from malarial fever ❸ speak; utter; express; ~话 say the word; give a verbal order / ~问 ask or put a question / ~议论 air one's views; make comments ❹ develop; expand; (of foodstuffs) rise or expand when fermented or soaked / ~海带 soak dried kelp in water / ~面 了。The dough has risen. ❺ prosper; become rich; ~家致富 build up a family fortune; get rich / 他这几年~了。He's made a pile the last few years. ❻ get into a certain (usu unpleasant) state; become; feel; ~麻 feel numb; tingle / ~黏 (of sth) feel or become sticky / ~酒疯 be in a drunken fit; get roaring drunk ❼ show; look; elicit; ~旧 (of sth) look used / ~威 show one's strength or authority; throw one's weight about ❽ start; begin; set out or off; ~端 also "发轫" make a start; begin; originate / ~难 rise in revolt;

start a rebellion; launch an attack / 发大水 be in flood / ~祥地 place of origin; birthplace ❾ 〈量〉 used for ammunition; 两~子弹 two rounds of ammunition; two cartridges or bullets

see also fà

发案 fā'àn (of a criminal case) occur; take place; ~率 incidence (of crime) / ~地点 scene of a crime

发榜 fābǎng publish a list of successful candidates or applicants

发报 fābào transmit a message (by radio); send a telegram; ~机 transmitter

发表 fābiǎo announce; issue; publish; ~公报 issue a communiqué / ~任命 announce an appointment / ~社论 publish or carry an editorial

发病 fābìng (of a person) fall ill; be taken ill; ~率 incidence of a disease / ~原因 cause of a disease

发布 fābù issue; promulgate; release; ~命令 issue an order; promulgate a decree / ~消息 give out information; release news

发财 fācái get rich; make a fortune; 发横财 get a windfall; make money illegally / 发洋财 get a windfall; strike it rich

发愁 fāchóu worry (about or over sth); be anxious; become sad

发出 fāchū ❶ produce; generate; send forth; ~热能 generate thermal energy / ~刺耳的声音 produce a piercing sound ❷ issue; send out; promulgate; ~传票 issue a summons / ~警报

send out or sound a warning

发达 fādá　develop; flourish: ～国家 developed country / 欠～ underdeveloped / 生意～ do a flourishing business / 四肢～ have a powerful physique

发呆 fādāi　also "发愣"; "发怔" look blank; be in a trance or daze; be stupefied

发电 fādiàn　❶ generate electricity or power: ～厂 power or generating plant / ～机 generator; dynamo ❷ send a telegram: ～吊唁 send a message of condolences

发动 fādòng　❶ start; launch: ～机 engine; motor / ～引擎 start an engine; set an engine going / ～战争 unleash or start a war ❷ call into action; arouse; mobilize: 放手～群众 boldly arouse or mobilize the masses

发抖 fādǒu　also "发颤"; "发战"; shiver; shake; tremble: 冻得～ shiver with cold

发放 fāfàng　provide; grant; distribute: ～贷款 grant or extend credits / ～救济品 distribute relief

发奋 fāfèn　❶ work energetically; exert oneself: ～有为 energetic and promising ❷ see "发愤"

发愤 fāfèn　also "发奋" make a firm resolution; make a determined effort: ～图强 make determined efforts to better oneself or to make the country strong

发疯 fāfēng　go mad or crazy; be out of one's mind: 爱得～ be madly in love (with sb) / ～似地工作 work like crazy or mad

发福 fāfú　(usu said of older people as a euphemism for 发胖) put on weight; grow stout

发稿 fāgǎo　send a manuscript or dispatch (to the press): 截至～时 at press time

发光 fāguāng　shine; glow; be luminous or luminescent: ～体 luminous body; luminant / 有一分热, 发一分光 give as much light as one has heat for; do one's utmost

发汗 fāhàn　(induce) perspiration; sweat; diaphoresis: ～药 sudorific; diaphoretic

发狠 fāhěn　❶ make a determined effort (to do sth hard) ❷ be furious (with sb about sth); fly into a rage

发慌 fāhuāng　feel nervous; get flustered or flurried: 饿得～ be faint with hunger

发挥 fāhuī　❶ bring into play; give play or scope to: ～优势 exploit one's advantage / ～想像力 give (free) rein to one's imagination / ～骨干作用 play a key role ❷ develop (an idea, a theme, etc); elaborate; expand: ～主题思想 develop a theme

发昏 fāhūn　feel giddy or dizzy; 〈喻〉lose one's head; be out of one's mind

发火 fāhuǒ　❶ catch fire; ignite ❷ get angry; flare up; lose temper

发货 fāhuò　dispatch or deliver goods: ～单 dispatch list; (consignment) invoice; delivery order / ～人 consignor; shipper

发迹 fājì　(of sb poor and obscure) gain fame and fortune; rise to power and position; make the grade

发酵 fājiào　ferment; leaven: ～粉 yeast or baking powder / ～饲料 fermented feed

发觉 fājué　find; discover; realize: ～情况不对 find sth amiss; smell a rat

发掘 fājué　excavate; unearth; explore: ～遗址 excavate an ancient site / ～潜力 tap potentials / ～人才 seek out talented people; hunt for talent

发狂 fākuáng　go mad or crazy; go berserk: 使人～ drive one mad or crazy

发牢骚 fāláosāo　complain; grumble; grouse: 爱～的人 grouser; grumbler

发令 fālìng　give or issue an order (to

do sth)：～枪〈体〉starting gun or pistol

发聋振聩 fālóng-zhènkuì also "**发聩振聋**" rouse the deaf and awaken the unhearing; enlighten the ignorant and the benighted

发落 fāluò deal with (an offender)

发霉 fāméi go mouldy; become mildewed：～的味道 mouldy smell

发明 fāmíng invent：～家 inventor / 专利 patent for an invention

发怒 fānù get angry; flare up; fly into a rage

发泡 fāpào foam; bubble：～剂 foaming agent / ～饮料 fizz

发脾气 fāpíqi also "**发态度**" lose one's temper; fly into a rage; throw a tantrum

发票 fāpiào bill; invoice：开～ make out a bill; write an invoice / ～存根 invoice stub

发起 fāqǐ ❶ initiate; sponsor：～人 initiator; sponsor; promoter ❷ start; launch：～进攻 launch an attack

发情 fāqíng 〈动物〉(be in) heat; oestrus; rut：～期 heat (period); oestrus

发球 fāqiú 〈体〉serve a ball：换～ change service / ～失误 miss a service / 由你～。It's your service.

发热 fārè ❶ see "发烧❶" ❷ generate heat; give out heat ❸ be hotheaded：头脑～ be hot-headed or impetuous

发人深省 fārénshēnxǐng also "**发人深醒**" make one wake up to reality or the truth; make one wide awake; stir up one's soul

发烧 fāshāo ❶ also "发热" have or run a fever or temperature：发高烧 run a high fever ❷ be infatuated or obsessed：～友 enthusiast；(esp) audiophile

发射 fāshè ❶ launch; discharge; fire：～场 launch(ing) site / ～架 launcher / ～井 launch(ing) silo ❷

〈理〉 transmit; emit：～机 transmitter / ～功率 transmitting power

发生 fāshēng happen; occur; arise：～冲突 come to a clash; have a conflict / ～兴趣 become interested; take an interest / ～关系 establish a relationship; have sexual intercourse

发誓 fāshì take an oath; vow; pledge；～戒烟 pledge not to smoke again; swear off smoking

发售 fāshòu sell; put on sale：公开～ be for general sale; have sth for general sale

发酸 fāsuān ❶ turn or taste sour ❷ (of one's nose, eyes, etc) tingle with sorrow, grief or compassion ❸ feel weak and sore; ache：浑身～ feel sore all over

发条 fātiáo spiral power spring; clockwork spring：上～ wind up (a watch, etc)

发现 fāxiàn find; discover; detect：考古～ archaeological find / ～错误 spot a mistake; detect an error / ～自己陷入困境 find oneself in a dilemma

发笑 fāxiào burst out laughing; laugh：引人～ make people laugh or funny or ridiculous

发泄 fāxiè give vent to; let off：～不满 air one's grievances; give vent to one's discontent

发行 fāxíng issue; publish; distribute：～量 amount or number issued; circulation / ～人 publisher / ～渠道 channel for distribution / ～债券 issue bonds; float bond issues

发芽 fāyá germinate; sprout：～率 germination or sprouting percentage

发言 fāyán speak; make or deliver a speech; take the floor：～稿 text of a speech / ～权 right to speak / ～人 spokesman; spokesperson; speaker

发炎 fāyán become inflamed：～处 inflammation

发扬 fāyáng　carry on or forward; promote; foster: ~光大 carry forward; build on; further develop / ~民主 promote democracy

发音 fāyīn　pronounce; articulate; enunciate: ~部位 point of articulation / ~器官 vocal or speech organ / ~准确 pronounce accurately; have an accurate pronunciation

发育 fāyù　grow; develop: 充分 ~ reach full growth; be fully grown / ~期 period of growth; (of people) adolescence / ~不全 underdevelopment; 〈医〉hypoplasia

发源 fāyuán　rise; originate: ~地 place of origin; source; birthplace

发运 fāyùn　send by freight; ship (goods): ~单 shipping order / ~人 shipper

发展 fāzhǎn　❶ develop; expand; grow: ~组织 expand an organization; recruit new members / ~壮大 go from strength to strength / ~中国家 developing world / 有~前途 have good prospects; be promising ❷ recruit; admit: ~新会员 recruit or admit new members

发作 fāzuò　❶ break out; show effect: 胃病 ~ have a stomachache / 药性 ~。The medicine began to take effect. ❷ have a fit of anger; flare up

fá

乏 fá　❶ lack; be short of: ~力 lacking in strength; worn-out; incapable (of doing sth) / ~术 lack means; have no effective measures / 不~其人。There is no lack of such people. ❷ tired; weary: 旅途 ~ 困 fatigued by a journey; travel-worn

乏味 fáwèi　tasteless; dull; insipid: 生活 ~。Life seems flat.

伐 fá　❶ fell; cut (down): ~竹编筏 cut bamboo to make rafts ❷ send an expedition against; attack: ~罪 〈书〉 launch a punitive expedition against an oppressive ruler, etc

伐木 fámù　lumbering; logging; felling: ~场 lumber-mill / ~工人 lumberman; lumberjack

罚（罸） fá　punish; fine; forfeit: ~金 fine; forfeit / ~没 fine and confiscate; forfeit / ~出场 send (a player) off the field (for foul play); foul out / ~不当罪 the punishment is not commensurate with the wrong; be unduly punished / ~酒一杯 (make sb) drink a cup of wine as a forfeit

罚款 fákuǎn　impose a fine or forfeit; fine; 免除 ~ remit a fine / ~一万元 fine (sb) ten thousand yuan (for sth)

罚球 fáqiú　〈体〉penalty kick or shot; free throw: ~得分 score a penalty shot; convert a free throw / 罚点球 take a penalty shot / 罚角球 take a corner kick / 罚任意球 take a free kick

阀 fá　❶ powerful person or family: 学 ~ scholar-tyrant / ~阅之家 distinguished family ❷ valve: 汽 ~ 〈体〉 steam valve / ~门 valve

筏 fá　also "筏子" raft: 竹 ~ bamboo raft

fǎ

法 fǎ　❶ law; statute: ~办 deal with according to law; bring to justice / ~典 (legal) code; law book / ~警 bailiff / ~盲 (person) ignorant of the law / ~统 legally constituted authority ❷ method; way: 操作 ~ method of operation / 解决问题 ~子 way to solve a problem ❸ standard; criterion; model: 不足为 ~ be not fit to serve as a standard; cannot be taken as a model or an example ❹ 〈宗教〉dharma; the Law or Way; Buddhism: ~师 (title of respect for a Buddhist or Taoist priest) master (of the Law) / ～ 轮常转。The power of dharma is constant and infinite. ❺ magic (arts)：作～ resort to or exercise magic / ～宝 sth of magic power; magic weapon or formula: talisman / ～术 magic arts; witchcraft

法案 fǎ'àn proposed law; bill：提出～ propose or introduce a bill / 通过～ pass or adopt a bill

法场 fǎchǎng 〈旧〉execution ground：劫～ raid an execution ground to rescue the condemned

法定 fǎdìng legal; statutory; official：～多数 statutory or required majority / ～汇率 official or pegged rate of exchange / ～假日 legal or official holiday / ～人数 (legal) quorum / ～继承人 legal heir; heir at law

法官 fǎguān judge; justice：大～ chief justice

法规 fǎguī laws and regulations; statutes：～汇编 statute book

法国 Fǎguó France：～菜 French cooking or cuisine / ～人 (the) French; Frenchman / ～梧桐 plane tree / ～白兰地 cognac

法纪 fǎjì law and discipline：～观念 awareness of law and discipline

法郎 fǎláng (French) franc：瑞士～ Swiss Franc

法理 fǎlǐ legal principle; theory of law：～学 jurisprudence / ～依据 legal basis

法令 fǎlìng laws and decrees; decree; order

法律 fǎlǜ law; statute：～界 legal circles / ～承认 (extend) de jure recognition / ～程序 legal procedure or process / ～地位 legal status / ～顾问 legal adviser or counsel / ～效力 legal validity or effect / ～责任 legal liability or responsibility / ～事务所 law office or firm

法人 fǎrén 〈法〉legal or juridical person; corporation：～股 corporate shares / ～代表 legal representative / ～团体 body corporate; corporate body; corporation

法庭 fǎtíng court; tribunal：仲裁～ arbitration tribunal; court of arbitration / 道德～ forum of conscience

法网 fǎwǎng net of justice; arm of the law：～难逃 cannot escape the reach of the law; will eventually be brought to justice

法西斯 fǎxīsī fascist：～分子 fascist / ～主义 fascism

法学 fǎxué science of law; jurisprudence：～家 jurist; jurisprudent / ～士 bachelor of laws (LL B)

法医 fǎyī legal medical expert：～鉴定 medico-legal expertize

法语 Fǎyǔ French (language)：～区 Francophone or French-speaking area

法院 fǎyuàn court of justice; (law) court：～判决 court sentence / ～院长 president of a court

法则 fǎzé law; rule：自然～ law of nature

法治 fǎzhì rule of law; government by law：～国家 country under the rule of law

法制 fǎzhì legal system or institutions; legality：～化 legalize; institutionalize / ～教育 education or instruction in law

砝 fǎ

砝码 fǎmǎ weight (used on a balance)：～盘 scale-pan

fà

发(髮) fà hair：～菜 〈植〉hair weeds / ～带 (hair) ribbon; hair-band / ～箍 hair slide; headband / ～髻 bun; chignon / ～胶 hair jelly; gel-mousse / ～廊 also

"发屋" barber's; hairdresser's; beauty salon / ～卡 also "发夹" hairclip; hairpin; barrette / ～乳 hair cream / ～型 also "发式" hairstyle; hairdo; hair fashion / ～油 hair oil or tonic; brilliantine　see also fā

珐(琺)　fà

珐琅 fàláng　enamel; ～质〈生理〉enamel (of teeth) / ～制品 enamelware

fān

帆

帆 fān　sail;〈书〉sailing boat:～船 sail(ing) boat or ship; junk / ～板运动〈体〉sailboarding; windsurfing

帆布 fānbù　canvas; sailcloth; ～包 canvas or kit bag / ～床 cot; campbed / ～鞋 canvas or deck shoes; plimsolls

番

番 fān ❶ barbarian; foreign:～邦〈旧〉barbarian land; alien people or nation / ～薯〈方〉sweet potato ❷〈量〉used with 一, 几, or 三 in given collocations:几～较量 repeated trials of strength / 呈现一～新气象 put on a new look ❸〈量〉used after "翻❸" fān

番号 fānhào　designation (of a military unit)

番茄 fānqié　also "西红柿" tomato:～酱 tomato sauce; ketchup / ～汁 tomato juice

幡

幡 fān　long narrow flag; streamer:～儿 (long narrow white) funeral streamer

幡然 fānrán　see "翻然" fānrán

藩

藩 fān ❶ also "藩篱"〈书〉fence; hedge; (protective) screen or barrier ❷ also "藩属" feudatory; vassal state

翻

翻 fān ❶ turn (over, upside down, etc); overturn; rummage:～地 turn up the soil / ～供 overturn or revoke a confession; retract a testimony / ～老账 bring up old scores again; rake up old grievances / ～资料 look for data / ～箱倒柜 rummage through chests and cupboards (in a thorough search); ransack boxes and chests ❷ climb or get over; cross:～墙头 climb over a wall / ～山越岭 cross over mountain after mountain; go uphill and down dale ❸ multiply; double:～一番 double; be twice as much / ～两番 quadruple ❹ reproduce (with or without alterations); remake:～盖 also "翻建" rebuild (a house, etc); renovate / ～改大衣 have an overcoat turned or remade / ～印必究. Those responsible for unauthorized reproduction will be prosecuted. ❺ translate; interpret (into another language) ❻〈口〉fall out (with sb); break up:把人惹～了 get sb's back up

翻案 fān'àn　reverse or overturn a verdict; present a radically different view (from established canon)

翻本 fānběn　win back (money lost in gambling, etc); make up or recoup one's losses

翻车 fānchē　(of a vehicle) overturn;〈喻〉suffer a setback midway through sth

翻船 fānchuán　(of a boat) capsize;〈喻〉suffer a setback or an upset:阴沟里～ capsize in a ditch; suffer an upset with all odds on one's side

翻跟头 fāngēntou　also "翻斤头"、"翻筋斗" ❶ turn a somersault; loop the loop;〈喻〉suffer a setback ❷ (of prices, etc) double

翻滚 fāngǔn　(as of waves) seethe; churn; roll:麦浪～ rolling sea of wheat

翻悔 fānhuǐ　also "反悔" go back on one's word; renege (on one's promise); back out (of a commitment, etc)

翻江倒海 fānjiāng-dǎohǎi　also "倒海翻江" overwhelming; earthshaking;

tremendous

翻来覆去 fānlái-fùqù ❶ toss and turn (in bed); toss from side to side ❷ again and again; repeatedly

翻脸 fānliǎn suddenly turn hostile; turn (against sb): ～不认人 turn against sb; cut sb dead / ～无情 be treacherous and ruthless

翻然 fānrán also "幡然" (change) quickly and completely: ～改进 make quick, marked improvements / ～悔悟 wake up to one's error; make a clear break with one's past

翻身 fānshēn ❶ turn over: ～又睡着了 turn over in bed and fall asleep again ❷ 〈喻〉stand on one's own feet; improve dramatically: ～农奴 emancipated serfs / 大打～仗 work hard to bring about a decisive change for the better

翻腾 fānteng ❶ (as of waves) seethe; churn; surge ❷ turn (sth) over and over; rummage

翻天覆地 fāntiān-fùdì ❶ earth- or world-shaking: ～的时代 world-shaking era; era of turbulence and upheaval ❷ make a violent noise or row; 吵了个～ start a violent quarrel; kick up a terrific row

翻新 fānxīn revamp; recondition; make over: 旧车～ revamp an old car / 手法～ do the same old thing in a new guise; try a new trick

翻修 fānxiū rebuild; restore to good condition; renovate

翻译 fānyì ❶ translate; interpret: 笔头～ written translation / 口头～ interpretation ❷ translator; interpreter

翻云覆雨 fānyún-fùyǔ (short for 翻手为云,覆手为雨) wield one's power capriciously; play fast and loose; be shifty and capricious

fán

凡 fán ❶ (of) this mortal world; commonplace; ordinary: ～人 mortal or ordinary man; human / ～庸 (of a person) mediocre; commonplace / ～夫俗子 mortals; common run of people; philistines / 非同～响 quite extraordinary ❷ all; every; any: ～木有本,是水有源。Every tree has its roots, and every river has its source. ❸〈书〉altogether; in all: 全书～十二章。The work has twelve chapters in all.

凡例 fánlì notes on or guide to the use of a reference book, etc

凡士林 fánshìlín vaseline; petrolatum

凡事 fánshì everything: ～小心 be prudent in whatever one does / ～开头难。It's the first step that costs.

凡是 fánshì every; any; -ever: ～违反本规定者将予以罚款。Whoever breaks this regulation is subject to a fine.

矾（礬） fán 〈化〉vitriol; alum: ～土 alumina

烦 fán ❶ upset; irritated; worried: ～忧 worried and depressed / ～躁 irritable and restless; fretful; fidgety / 无需～神 need not bother (with sth) ❷ fed up; tired: 听～了 be tired of hearing (sth) / ～人 vexing; annoying / ～心的事 trouble; worry; vexation ❸ superfluous and confusing: 事务～冗 daily chores of all sorts ❹ 〈敬〉trouble: ～请 request; ask / 此件～交王先生。Please forward this to Mr Wang.

烦劳 fánláo 〈敬〉trouble: 能～您给我买本书吗? Would you mind buying a book for me?

烦闷 fánmèn dull and unhappy; moody; depressed: ～不安 depressed and uneasy

烦恼 fánnǎo vexed; upset; worried: 自寻～ bring vexation upon oneself; go to unnecessary trouble

烦琐 fánsuǒ also "繁琐" over-elaborate; petty and tedious: 手续～ over-elaborate procedures / ～哲学 scholasticism; 〈喻〉over-elaboration; hair-

蕃 fán ❶ (as of vegetation) luxuriant; lush: ～茂 luxuriant; lush ❷ reproduce rapidly; multiply: ～衍 multiply; increase gradually in number or quantity

樊 fán 〈书〉fence: ～篱 fence; hedge; 〈喻〉restriction: ～笼 bird cage — place or condition of confinement

繁 fán ❶ numerous; complicated: ～复 numerous and complicated / ～体字 original complex form of a simplified Chinese character; full-form character / 文缛节 over-elaborate formalities; red tape ❷ propagate; procreate; multiply: ～育 breed; raise (crops or animals) / ～衍生息 live and procreate / 枝叶～茂 thickly covered with foliage

繁多 fánduō various; numerous: 花样～ (of) all shapes and colours

繁华 fánhuá flourishing; prosperous; bustling: ～的商业区 busy downtown area

繁忙 fánmáng busy; bustling: ～的海港 bustling seaport

繁荣 fánróng flourishing; thriving; prosperous: ～昌盛 thriving and prosperous / ～富强 rich, powerful and prosperous / ～市场 stimulate the market

繁杂 fánzá also "烦杂" many and diverse; various; miscellaneous: ～的家务活 miscellaneous household chores

繁殖 fánzhí breed; reproduce; procreate: ～场 breeding ground / ～率 rate of reproduction; breeding rate

繁重 fánzhòng heavy; strenuous; onerous: ～的负担 onerous burden

fǎn

反 fǎn ❶ turn over; turn or go in an opposite direction; reverse: ～身 (of a person) turn round; face about / ～弹 rebound / ～过来 conversely; the other way round / ～败为胜 turn defeat into victory; turn the tables (on sb) ❷ return; counter: ～证 counter-evidence; disproof / ～建议 counterproposal / ～求诸己 seek the cause in oneself (not in sb else) ❸ oppose; combat; be against: ～霸 anti-hegemonistic / ～义词〈语言〉antonym / ～腐倡廉 combat corruption and build a clean government / ～病毒软件〈信息〉anti-virus (software) ❹ revolt; rebel: 官逼民～. Oppressive government drove the people to revolt. ❺ on the contrary; instead

反比例 fǎnbǐlì also "反比"〈数〉inverse proportion or ratio: 成～ in inverse proportion (to sth); inversely proportional (to sth)

反驳 fǎnbó refute (sb's accusation, etc); retort; rebut

反差 fǎnchā contrast: 强烈～ (in) striking contrast (to sth)

反常 fǎncháng unusual; abnormal; perverse: 冷得～ unusually cold

反刍 fǎnchú also "倒嚼" ruminate; chew the cud: ～动物 ruminant

反动 fǎndòng reactionary; reaction: ～派 reactionaries; reaction

反对 fǎnduì oppose; be against; combat: ～党 opposition party; the opposition / ～票 dissenting or negative vote

反而 fǎn'ér also "反倒" on the contrary; instead: 失败～更坚定了我们的决心. The failure only strengthened our determination.

反复 fǎnfù ❶ repeatedly; again and again: ～较量 (have) repeated trials of strength ❷ chop and change; go back on one's word: ～无常 be changeable or capricious; play fast and loose ❸ reversal; setback; relapse: 病情～ suffer a relapse

反感 fǎngǎn be disgusted with; loathe: 对吸烟～ have an aversion to smoking

反戈一击 fǎngēyījī turn against one's own side; change sides and turn back to hit

反革命 fǎngémìng counterrevolutionary; counterrevolution: 镇 压 ～ crack down on counterrevolutionaries / ～ 政变 counterrevolutionary coup d'état

反攻 fǎngōng counteroffensive; counter-attack: ～ 倒算 strike back to settle old scores; stage a vindictive counter-attack; retaliate

反躬自问 fǎngōngzìwèn *also* "抚躬自问" examine oneself or one's conscience; search one's heart or soul

反光 fǎnguāng reflect light: ～ 镜 reflector

反话 fǎnhuà irony; 说 ～ speak ironically

反悔 fǎnhuǐ see "翻悔" fānhuǐ

反击 fǎnjī strike or hit back; counter-attack; 自卫 ～ (launch a) counter-attack in self-defence

反季节 fǎnjìjié 〈农〉 out of season: ～蔬菜 out-of-season vegetables

反间 fǎnjiàn sow distrust or discord; set (people) at odds: ～计 stratagem or trick to drive a wedge (between people)

反抗 fǎnkàng revolt or rebel (against sb); resist; 消极 ～ passive resistance / ～精神 spirit of revolt; rebellious spirit

反客为主 fǎnkèwéizhǔ turn from a guest to a host — gain the initiative (from a passive position); turn the tables (on an earlier comer, etc)

反馈 fǎnkuì feedback: ～ 机制 feedback mechanism / 读者的 ～ feedback from readers

反面 fǎnmiàn ❶ reverse or wrong side; back: 布料的 ～ wrong side of a cloth / 从 ～ 提出问题 ask questions about the other side (of a problem, etc) ❷ opposite; contrary; negative: 走 ～ change or turn into one's opposite / ～教材 negative example which may serve as a lesson / ～意见 adverse or dissenting opinion

反目 fǎnmù fall out (esp between husband and wife): ～ 成仇 quarrel with each other and become enemies

反派 fǎnpài villain (in drama, etc); negative character or role

反叛 fǎnpàn betray; revolt; defect: ～ 投敌 defect to the enemy

反倾销 fǎnqīngxiāo anti-dumping: ～ 税 anti-dumping duties

反射 fǎnshè ❶ reflect: ～光 reflected light / ～热 reverberated heat ❷ 〈生理〉reflex: 条件 ～ conditioned reflex / 膝腱 ～ knee-jerk (reflex)

反手 fǎnshǒu ❶ 〈体〉backhand: ～ 抽球 backhand drive / ～ 握拍 backhand grip ❷ turn one's hand over; have one's hand(s) behind one's back: ～把门关上 pull the door to behind one

反思 fǎnsī reflect; introspect: ～过去 reflect upon the past / 值得认真 ～ provide much food for thought

反贪 fǎntān fight graft; battle corruption: ～ 局 anti-corruption bureau / ～斗争 struggle against corruption

反胃 fǎnwèi *also* "翻胃" feeling nauseated or queasy; 〈医〉regurgitation

反问 fǎnwèn *also* "反诘" ask (a question) in reply or in retort: 反问句 〈语言〉rhetorical question

反响 fǎnxiǎng repercussion; echo; reverberation: ～ 热烈 be warmly received

反省 fǎnxǐng introspection; self-questioning or-examination: ～自己的言行 examine one's own words and deeds

反咬 fǎnyǎo *also* "反诬" 〈贬〉trump up a countercharge (against one's accuser, etc): 反咬一口 retort with a false countercharge

反应 fǎnyìng react; respond: ～ 堆 〈理〉reactor / ～ 迟钝 slow in response / ～ 良好 respond (to sth)

F

favourably; receive (sth) well

反映 fǎnyìng ❶ reflect; mirror; show;～论〈哲〉theory of reflection /～时代 mirror the times ❷ report; make known;～群众意见 report or transmit opinions at the grassroots

反正 fǎnzhèng any way; anyhow; all the same;～我不信。I don't believe it anyhow. /～都一样。It makes no difference one way or the other.

反之 fǎnzhī conversely; on the other hand; otherwise; whereas;～亦然 vice versa

反作用 fǎnzuòyòng counteraction; reaction;～力〈理〉reacting force / 起～ be counterproductive

返 fǎn return; come or go back; become (again);～潮 get damp or moist /～工 do (poorly-done work) over again; redo /～航 return to base or port; be on the homeward journey /～青〈农〉(of winter crops or transplanted seedlings) turn green /～老还童 regain one's youthful vigour; feel rejuvenated in one's old age

返程 fǎnchéng return journey; one's way back;～车票 return ticket

返回 fǎnhuí return; come or go back;～原处 go back where one was; return to the starting point /～式卫星 retrievable or recoverable satellite

返聘 fǎnpìn also "反聘" be employed or reposted after one's retirement

fàn

犯 fàn ❶ violate; go against;～禁 violate a ban or prohibition /～人 prisoner; convict ❷ attack; invade;～境 make inroads into another country ❸ criminal; offender; culprit; 初～ first offender or offence ❹ experience (sth unpleasant); have an attack of (an illness, etc); commit (a mistake, crime, etc);～戒 conduct oneself below

one's dignity; cheapen oneself /～困 feel sleepy or drowsy /～嘀咕 have misgivings or doubts about sth; have sth on one's mind /～糊涂 become confused; get mixed up /～烟瘾 crave to have a smoke /～主观主义 succumb to subjectivism

犯案 fàn'àn (of an offender) be found out and brought to justice

犯病 fànbìng have an attack of (an old illness); fall ill again; have a relapse (of a bad habit);犯胃病 have a stomach-ache

犯不着 fànbuzháo also "犯不上" (口) not worthwhile; not worth doing;～为小事生气。It's not worthwhile getting angry over trifles.

犯愁 fànchóu worry; feel uneasy; anxious

犯得着 fàndezháo also "犯得上" (often used in rhetorical questions) is it worthwhile;～麻烦他吗? Is it worthwhile bothering him?

犯法 fànfǎ violate or break the law;～行为 illegal act; offence against the law

犯规 fànguī ❶ break rules; violate regulations;犯校规 break or breach school discipline ❷〈体〉foul;发球～ foul service / 技术～ technical foul / 侵人～ personal foul /～者 offender

犯忌 fànjì also "犯忌讳" touch sb's sore spot; break or violate a taboo

犯罪 fànzuì commit a crime or an offence;～率 crime rate /～未遂 attempted crime; criminal attempt /～疑人 suspect in a crime / 犯死罪 commit a capital crime

饭 fàn ❶ cooked rice or other cereal;～菜 meal; repast; food /～锅 pot for cooking rice; rice cooker ❷ meal; food;～盒 lunch-box; mess kit; dinner pail /～局 dinner party; feast /～票 meal ticket; mess card /～厅 dining hall or room; mess hall ❸

用 to be taken after meals ❸ means of livelihood or living; job: 这口～不好吃。It is no cushy job.

饭店 fàndiàn ❶ hotel: 五星级～ five-star hotel; first-class hotel ❷〈方〉restaurant

饭馆 fànguǎn *also* "饭庄" restaurant; eatery: 风味～ restaurant specializing in a distinctive cuisine

饭来张口，衣来伸手 fànlái-zhāngkǒu, yīlái-shēnshǒu have only to open one's mouth to be fed and hold out one's arms to be dressed — lead an easy life with everything provided; live the life of a parasite

饭量 fànliàng appetite: ～不大 have a small appetite; be a light eater

饭桶 fàntǒng ❶ rice bucket; 〈喻〉big eater; gourmand ❷ fathead; good-for-nothing

饭碗 fànwǎn ❶ rice bowl ❷ job; means of livelihood: 铁～ iron rice bowl — secure lifelong job / 自己把～儿砸了 get fired through one's own fault

泛（汎、⁴氾） fàn 〈书〉 ❶ float: 月夜～舟 go boating on a moonlit night ❷ emerge; turn; send forth: 树叶～黄了。The leaves are turning yellow. ❸ extensive; general; superficial: ～称 general term / ～读 extensive reading / ～指 make a general reference (to sth); be used in a general sense ❹ flood; inundate; overflow

泛泛 fànfàn ❶ general; superficial: ～而谈 speak in superficial terms; talk in generalities / ～之交 nodding or casual acquaintance ❷ common; ordinary: ～之辈 mediocre person; mediocrity

泛滥 fànlàn be in flood; overflow; spread unchecked: ～成灾〈of flooding waters〉cause a disaster; 〈喻〉run rampant or wild

范（範） fàn ❶ model; criterion; example; model / ～文 model essay or writing ❷ limits; range: 就～ submit; give in

范畴 fànchóu ❶ category: 基本～ basic or primary category ❷ domain; scope; range: 不在我研究的～内 outside my range (of research)

范围 fànwéi scope; range; extent: 在可能的～内 within the range of possibilities

贩 fàn ❶ buy to resell; traffic: ～私 traffic in smuggled or illegal goods / ～粮食 buy grain for resale ❷ trader; pedlar; vendor: 摊～ street pedlar or vendor / ～夫走卒 small tradesmen and porters; people of lowly occupations

贩卖 fànmài peddle; sell; trade: ～牲口 deal in draught animals / ～人口 traffic in human beings (esp women); engage in white slavery

贩运 fànyùn transport goods for sale; traffic: ～服装 traffic in clothing

贩子 fànzi trader; trafficker: 毒～ drug trafficker / 战争～ warmonger

梵 fàn ❶ of ancient India: ～文 *also* "梵语" Sanskrit ❷ of Buddha; Buddhist: ～典 Buddhist sutra

fāng

方 fāng ❶ square; 〈数〉power: ～格 square; check / ～糖 sugar cube; lump sugar / X 的五次～ fifth power of X ❷〈量〉a) *used for sth square or rectangular*: 一砚台 an ink-stone b) *short for* 平方 *or* 立方: 6,000～土 6,000 cubic metres of earth ❸ direction: 北～ north ❹ side; party: 多～协作 coordinated efforts by all quarters ❺ place; region; locality: 一～水土，一～人情。Conditions and customs vary from place to place. ❻ method; means; way: ~ 略 general plan or programme; overall strategy / ~子〈中医〉prescription; recipe ❼ 〈副〉only; just (then): ~将离开 just about to depart / ~兴未艾 be just unfolding; be on the upswing

方案 fāng'àn　work plan or programme; scheme

方便 fāngbiàn ❶ convenient; handy; instant (food): 为了~ for convenience / ~面 instant noodles / ~食品 instant or convenience food / 在~的时候 at one's convenience ❷ appropriate; proper; suitable: 如果~的话 if it is proper; if it suits you ❸〈婉〉have money to spare or lend ❹〈婉〉go to the lavatory; wash one's hands

方才 fāngcái ❶ just now; just ❷ only then; not until

方程 fāngchéng　also "方程式"〈数〉equation: 解~ solve an equation

方法 fāngfǎ　method; way; approach: ~论 methodology / ~灵活 adopt a flexible approach

方块 fāngkuài ❶ square; ~字 square-shaped (Chinese) characters / ~ 钻 diamond (in cards): ~老 K diamond king

方面 fāngmiàn　respect; aspect; side: 在这~ in this respect or regard / 方方面面 all sides or parties; all concerned

方式 fāngshì　way; mode; pattern

方位 fāngwèi　point of the compass; direction and position: ~词〈语言〉noun of direction or locality / 测定~ locate one's position; take a bearing (on sth)

方向 fāngxiàng　direction; orientation: ~盘 steering wheel / 迷失~ lose one's bearings / 善于辨别~ have a good sense of direction

方言 fāngyán　(local) dialect; patois

方圆 fāngyuán ❶ neighbourhood; surrounding area ❷ circumference: ~

数百里 for hundreds of miles around

方针 fāngzhēn　policy; guiding principle: 总~ general guiding principle

坊 fāng ❶ lane; alley: ~巷 lane; alley; street ❷ memorial archway or gateway
see also fáng

芳 fāng ❶ (like) flowers and plants; fragrant; youthful: ~龄 age (of a girl) / ~草如茵 a carpet of green grass ❷ good (name or reputation); virtuous:〈书〉〈敬〉your: ~邻 good neighbour; your neighbour

芳名 fāngmíng ❶〈敬〉name (usu of a girl) ❷ good name or reputation: ~远扬 be known far and wide

芳香 fāngxiāng　(of flowers, etc) fragrant; aromatic: ~油 perfume oil / ~植物 aromatic plant

fáng

防 fáng ❶ prevent; guard or provide against: ~旱 prevent or control drought / ~波堤 breakwater / ~盗门 burglar-proof or anti-theft door / ~风林 windbreak (forest) / ~腐剂 antiseptic; preservative / ~沙林 sandbreak (forest) / ~晒剂 anti-UV lotion; sun cream / ~水衣 waterproof watch / ~雨布 waterproof cloth; tarpaulin / ~不胜~ very hard to guard against (sb); impossible to defend (oneself) effectively / ~弹背心 bulletproof vest / ~毒面具 gas mask / ~锈涂层 antirust coating ❷ defend; protect: ~区〈军〉defence or garrison area; station (of a unit) / ~身术 art or skill of self-defence

防暴 fángbào　anti-riot: ~警察 riot police or squad

防备 fángbèi　be on the alert for; guard against; take precautions against

防潮 fángcháo ❶ damp-proof; moisture-proof: ~剂 drying agent / ~密封

moisture seal ❷ protection against the tide:～闸门 tidal gate

防冻 fángdòng antifreeze; frostbite-prevention:～剂（for engines, etc）anti-freezing agent; antifreeze / ～药品 frostbite preventive

防范 fángfàn be on guard against; keep a lookout for:严加～ keep a close lookout; take every precaution

防洪 fánghóng prevent or control flood:～标准 flood control standard / ～大堤 flood dyke

防护 fánghù protect; shelter:～林 shelter-forest / ～涂层 protective coating

防患未然 fánghuànwèirán take preventive measures; provide against possible trouble:与其补救于已然,不如防患于未然。To forestall is better than to amend, or Prevention is better than cure.

防火 fánghuǒ fire-prevention; fire-proof:～墙 fire wall / ～防盗 guard against fire and theft

防空 fángkōng air or antiaircraft defence:～洞 air-raid shelter;〈喻〉cover for evil / ～部队 air defence force / ～警报 air-raid warning; air alert

防守 fángshǒu defend; guard:人盯人～〈体〉man-to-man defence

防暑 fángshǔ heatstroke or sunstroke prevention:～药 heatstroke preventive / ～降温 lower the temperature to prevent heatstroke

防微杜渐 fángwēi-dùjiàn nip (evil) in the bud; check at the outset

防伪 fángwěi fight forgery; guard against faking:～标志 anti-forgery mark or seal

防卫 fángwèi defend; guard:正当～ rightful self-defence / ～能力 defence capabilities

防务 fángwù defence (matters)

防线 fángxiàn line of defence:突破～ break through sb's defence line

防汛 fángxùn flood prevention or control:～器材 flood-relief equipment / ～人员 flood-fighters

防疫 fángyì epidemic prevention or control:～站 epidemic prevention station / ～针 (prophylactic) inoculation

防御 fángyù defend; guard:～战 defensive warfare / ～工事 defences; fortifications; defence works

防震 fángzhèn ❶ shockproof:～表 shockproof watch ❷ take precautions against earthquakes:～棚 temporary shelter for earthquake victims / ～建筑 anti-seismic building

防止 fángzhǐ prevent; guard against; avoid:～传染 keep off the infection of a disease

防治 fángzhì prevent and cure (diseases); prevent and control (pests)

坊 fáng (traditional) workshop or mill; shop:油～ oil mill *see also* fāng

妨 fáng hinder; hamper; harm:害治安 threaten public security; obstruct law and order / 不～事 no harm done; no hindrance

妨碍 fáng'ài hinder; hamper; impede:～进步 impede or hinder progress / ～视线 obstruct the view

房 fáng ❶ house; housing:～顶 roof (of a house); housetop / ～东 landlord or landlady (of a house or room) / ～客 tenant; lodger / ～屋 *also* "房子" house; building; housing / ～租 *also* "房钱" rent (for a house, room, etc) ❷ room:～间 room / 两～一厅 (apartment with) two bedrooms and a sitting room ❸ branch or member of an extended family:长～ eldest branch (ie eldest son and his family) / 正～ legal wife

房产 fángchǎn house (property); real estate:～证 housing property title deed

房地产 fángdìchǎn real estate or property:～公司 real estate agency /

～开发商 developer

fǎng

仿（倣） fǎng ❶ imitate; model on; copy:～建 copy the style or build in imitation of another building /～宋体 imitation Song-Dynasty-style typeface; handwriting in such a style ❷ resemble; be like

仿单 fǎngdān instructions on the use of a commodity sold; instruction manual

仿佛 fǎngfú *also* "彷彿" ❶ seemingly; as if:～生气了 seem angry ❷ be more or less the same; be similar:年纪相～ be about the same age

仿古 fǎnggǔ modelled after the antique; in the style of the ancients:～瓷器 imitation ancient porcelain /～建筑 pseudo-classic architecture

仿冒 fǎngmào counterfeit; forge:～名牌 counterfeit of a well-known brand

仿生 fǎngshēng bionic:～学 bionics /～装置 bionic device

仿效 fǎngxiào imitate; pattern after; model on

仿造 fǎngzào copy; model on:～的机器 machine modelled on another

仿照 fǎngzhào pattern on or after; imitate; follow:～办理 follow the example; do or act accordingly

仿真 fǎngzhēn simulate; emulate:～喉 artificial throat /～技术 simulation technology /～手枪 imitation pistol

仿制 fǎngzhì copy; imitate; model on:～品 imitation; replica; copy

访 fǎng ❶ visit; call on:互～ exchange visits /～客 visitor; caller; guest /～谈 call on and talk with; interview ❷ seek by inquiry or search:～查 go about making inquiries; investigate; inquire /～求 search or look for; seek

访问 fǎngwèn visit; call on; interview:～团 visiting mission or group /～学者 visiting scholar

纺 fǎng ❶ spin:～车 spinning wheel /～锭 spindle /～纱机 spinning machine ❷ thin silk fabric

纺织 fǎngzhī spinning and weaving; textile:～厂 textile mill /～品 textile; fabric /～工业 textile industry

舫 fǎng boat:游～ pleasure-boat

fàng

放 fàng ❶ let go; (set) free; release:～权 delegate or devolve powers to lower levels /～生 (of Buddhists) free captive or bought animals /～人质 release a hostage ❷ put out to pasture; graze; tend:～牛 put cattle out to pasture; pasture or graze cattle ❸ stop (work, etc); knock off:～工 get off work; knock off /～学 dismiss class; school is over ❹ let oneself go; give way to:～声 at the top of one's voice /～胆去干 go ahead boldly (with one's work) ❺ send out or forth; release; fire:～光 give off or shed light /～枪 fire a gun /～冷箭 injure with an arrow shot from behind; stab in the back /～长线，钓大鱼 throw a long line to catch a big fish — adopt a long-term plan to secure sth big; fly at higher game ❻ lend (money) at interest; loan:～债 *also* "放账" lend money for or at interest ❼ show; play; turn on:～电影 show a film /～录像 play a video tape ❽ light; set (off); let off:～火 set fire; commit arson /～爆竹 let or set off firecrackers ❾ expand; make larger; let out:～照片 make enlargements of a photograph; have a photograph enlarged ❿ (of flowers) blossom; bloom; open ⓫ put; place; lay:～毒 put poison (in food, water, etc); poison (minds) with evil ideas /

～置 lay up or aside; place; put / ～包袱 lay down a burden; take a load off one's mind / ～下武器 lay down one's arms / ～在首位 place above everything else; give first priority to / 这问题暂时～一～吧。Let's shelve the question for the time being. ⑫ readjust or moderate (one's attitude, behaviour, etc)：～尊重些。Behave yourself.

放大 fàngdà enlarge; blow up; amplify；～机 (photo) enlarger / ～镜 magnifying glass; magnifier / ～点声 speak a bit louder; turn up the volume (of TV, etc) a little

放荡 fàngdàng ❶ dissolute; debauched; dissipated ❷ unconventional；～不羁 unconventional and unrestrained; Bohemian

放风 fàngfēng ❶ let in fresh air; ventilate (a room, etc) ❷ let prisoners out for exercise or to relieve themselves ❸ divulge or leak information; circulate news or rumours

放过 fàngguò let off; let (an opportunity) slip by; 不～一个罪犯 not let a single criminal go unpunished

放虎归山 fànghǔguīshān see "纵虎归山" zònghǔguīshān

放假 fàngjià have a holiday or vacation; have a day off / ～三天 have three days off / 放暑假 be on summer vacation

放开 fàngkāi relax or loosen control; give a free hand to; let go；～搞活 decontrol and invigorate (an enterprise, etc); adopt a flexible policy to enliven (the economy, etc) / ～价格 decontrol prices / ～手脚干 work or act with a free hand

放空气 fàngkōngqì (usu derogatory) drop a hint; spread word; create an impression

放宽 fàngkuān relax (restrictions); liberalize (control)；～尺度 relax the requirements / ～期限 extend or pro-

long the time limit / ～政策 introduce or adopt more flexible policies

放款 fàngkuǎn also "放贷" grant or extend credit; make loans; lend

放疗 fàngliáo (short for 放射疗法) radiotherapy；接受～ undergo radiotherapy

放牧 fàngmù put out to pasture; pasture; graze；～地 grazing land/～牛羊 herd or graze sheep and cattle

放炮 fàngpào ❶ fire a gun; set off firecrackers or an explosion; blast ❷ (have a) blowout (of a tyre, etc) ❸ speak bluntly and forcefully; shoot one's mouth; 放大炮 shoot one's mouth off; talk big; boast / 放空炮 talk big; spout hot air; pay lip service / 放马后炮 fire belated shots; flog a dead horse

放屁 fàngpì ❶ break wind; fart ❷ (粗) talk nonsense; crap; rot

放弃 fàngqì abandon; give up; renounce；～国籍 renounce one's nationality / ～使用武力 renounce the use of force

放晴 fàngqíng (of weather) clear up

放任 fàngrèn let alone; indulge; laissez-faire；～政策 policy of laissez-faire / ～自流 let things drift or slide; let people do as they like; take an indulgent attitude

放哨 fàngshào stand sentry or sentinel; be on patrol

放射 fàngshè radiate; emit；～线 active rays / ～光芒 radiate light

放射性 fàngshèxìng 〈理〉 radioactivity；～污染 radioactive pollution / ～元素 radioactive element

放手 fàngshǒu ❶ let go (one's hold, etc); give up ❷ remove one's control; give a free hand; go all out; 不肯～ keep hold (of sth); keep (sth) in one's own hands / ～发动群众 mobilize the people with a free hand

放肆 fàngsì unbridled; wanton; impudent: 不许～! No impudence!

放松 fàngsōng relax; slacken; loosen; ～警惕 lower one's vigilance; let down one's guard / ～一下 relax a little

放血 fàngxiě ❶〈医〉blood-letting ❷〈口〉bleed (sb); make (sb) spend money

放心 fàngxīn set one's mind at rest; rest assured; ～不下 be kept in suspense; feel anxious

放行 fàngxíng let pass; get clearance; 免税～〈grant〉duty-free clearance

放眼 fàngyǎn take a broad view; scan widely; ～世界 have the whole world in view

放羊 fàngyáng ❶ graze or pasture sheep; look after sheep; ～娃 shepherd boy ❷〈贬〉throw (the) reins off; be uncared-for; drift along

放养 fàngyǎng breed (fish, silkworm, etc) in a suitable environment; culture

放映 fàngyìng show; project; ～队 film projection team / ～机 (film) projector

放逐 fàngzhú send into exile; exile; banish

放纵 fàngzòng let (sb) have his own way; indulge; pamper

fēi

飞(飛) fēi ❶ fly; flit; hover or flutter in the air; ～播 aerial seeding or sowing / ～虫 winged insect / ～船 spaceship; spacecraft; (旧) airship / ～弹 rocket; missile; stray bullet / ～禽走兽 birds and beasts; fauna ❷ swiftly; rapidly; speedily; ～跑 run very fast; tear along; dash / 时光～逝. Time flies. ❸ unexpected; accidental; groundless; ～来横祸 unexpected disaster; sudden accident; bolt from the blue

飞奔 fēibēn speed off; dash; tear along

飞驰 fēichí (of a horse or vehicle) gallop or speed along

飞碟 fēidié ❶ flying saucer; unidentified flying object (UFO) ❷〈体〉clay pigeon; ～射击 clay pigeon shooting

飞短流长 fēiduǎn-liúcháng also "蜚短流长" spread embroidered stories and malicious gossip

飞蛾投火 fēi'étóuhuǒ also "飞蛾扑火" (act like) a moth darting into a flame —— bring destruction upon oneself; court one's own doom

飞黄腾达 fēihuángténgdá make rapid advance in one's career; rise quickly in the world (esp in officialdom)

飞机 fēijī aircraft; aeroplane; plane; 双引擎～ twin-engine plane / ～场 airfield; airport; aerodrome

飞溅 fēijiàn splash; spatter

飞快 fēikuài ❶ very fast; at lightning speed ❷ (of a knife, etc) extremely sharp; keen-edged

飞毛腿 fēimáotuǐ ❶ swift or fleet of foot; fleet-footed (runner); 你就是长了～也来不及啊. You couldn't get there in time even with a pair of wings.

飞盘 fēipán frisbee; 玩～ play frisbee

飞速 fēisù at full speed; ～发展 develop rapidly; make great headway

飞吻 fēiwěn blow a kiss (to sb)

飞舞 fēiwǔ dance in the air; whirl; flutter

飞翔 fēixiáng fly; circle in the air; hover

飞行 fēixíng fly; ～服 flight suit / ～器 (flight) vehicle; aircraft / ～员 pilot; aviator; flyer

飞扬 fēiyáng also "飞飏" ❶ fly upward; rise; float; 尘土～. Clouds of dust rose. ❷ in high spirits; elated; 神采～ glowing with pride and happiness

飞扬跋扈 fēiyáng-báhù be unruly and haughty; act in an arrogant and domineering manner; throw one's weight around

飞跃 fēiyuè leap (swiftly upward or forward); ~发展 develop by leaps and bounds

飞涨 fēizhǎng (of prices, etc) soar; shoot up; skyrocket

妃 fēi ❶ *also* "妃嫔"; "妃子" imperial concubine ❷ wife of a prince, etc; 王~ princess consort

非 fēi ❶ not (non-, un-, in-, etc); against; counter to; ~暴力 non-violence / ~卖品 (article) not for sale / ~正式 unofficial; informal / ~处方药 OTC (over-the-counter) medicine / ~军事区 demilitarized zone / ~人生活 inhuman life / ~常设机构 ad hoc organization / ~关税壁垒 non-tariff barrier / ~婚生子女 children born out of wedlock; illegitimate children / ~政府组织 non-governmental organization (NGO) / ~言语所能表达 beyond words ❷ wrong; error; evil; 以为~ not regard (sth) as wrong or evil ❸ (often followed by 莫,不得 or 不可) *used to indicate necessity, wilfulness or determination*; ~公莫入。No admittance except on business. / 为什么他~要来? Why did he insist on coming? ❹ (short for 非洲) Africa; ~盟 (short for 非洲联盟) AU (African Union)

非常 fēicháng ❶ extraordinary; unusual; special; ~举动 unusual action; extraordinary behaviour / ~时期 time of emergency ❷ very; extremely; ~感谢 very grateful / ~健康 as fit as a fiddle

非但 fēidàn not only; ~长得俊,手还特别巧 not only beautiful but also very clever with her hands

非得 fēiděi (usu followed by 不 or 才) have (got) to; must; 凡属技艺~常练不可。All skills need constant practising.

非典 fēidiǎn (common name for 严重急性呼吸综合征) SARS (severe acute respiratory syndrome)

非法 fēifǎ illegal; unlawful; illegitimate; ~集会 unlawful assembly / ~监禁 illegal detention / ~手段 illegal means / ~出版物 illegal publication

非凡 fēifán outstanding; extraordinary; uncommon; 抱负~ cherish extraordinary aspirations

非⋯非⋯ fēi⋯fēi⋯ neither... nor...; 非敌非友 neither friend nor foe / 非驴非马 neither ass nor horse; neither fish nor fowl / 非亲非故 neither kith nor kin; not in any way related

非分 fēifèn not one's due; presumptuous; ~之财 ill-gotten money / ~之想 inordinate ambition and desire

非⋯即⋯ fēi⋯jí⋯ either... or...; 非此即彼 either this or that; one or the other / 非涝即旱 (suffer from) either flood or drought

非礼 fēilǐ ❶ rude; im-polite; improper; ~之举 indecorous conduct; improper behaviour ❷ assault (a woman) sexually; violate; rape; 欲行~ attempt to assault or rape a woman

非难 fēinàn blame; censure; reproach; 无可~ above criticism; blameless; irreproachful

非同小可 fēitóngxiǎokě no small or trivial matter

非议 fēiyì reproach; condemn; censure; 招致~ get censured or condemned

菲 fēi (of flowers and grass) luxuriant and rich with fragrance; 芳草~~。The grass gives off a sweet fragrance. *see also* fěi

绯 fēi red; ~红 *also* "飞红" bright red; crimson; scarlet / ~闻 amorous affair; sex scandal

扉 fēi door leaf

扉页 fēiyè title page (of a book, etc)

蜚 fēi 〈书〉 see "飞" fēi

蜚声 fēishēng 〈书〉 make a name; become famous: ~海内外 be renowned at home and abroad

霏 fēi 〈书〉 ❶ (of snow, rain, etc) fall thick and fast: 雨雪~ ~。The snowflakes fell thick and fast. ❷ flutter; disperse; diffuse: 烟~云敛。The smoke diffused while the clouds dispersed. or It cleared up.

féi

肥 féi ❶ (make) fat; lucrative; profitable: ~差 also "肥缺" fat or plum job / ~肉 fat meat; 〈喻〉 fat / ~育 (of animals) fattening / 以公~私 fatten oneself on public funds ❷ (make) fertile; luxuriant; rich: ~田 fertilize or enrich the soil / ~美的牧场 rich or luxuriant pasture ❸ fertilizer; manure; compost: ~料 fertilizer; manure / ~效 fertilizer or manure efficiency ❹ loose-fitting; loose: 腰身~大 large in girth / 瘦儿挺合适 (as of garment) fit (sb) very well

肥肠 féicháng pig's large intestines (used as food); chitterlings

肥大 féidà ❶ loose; large: ~的外套 loose coat ❷ fat; plump; corpulent ❸ 〈医〉 hypertrophy: 心脏~ hypertrophy of the heart

肥厚 féihòu plump; fleshy: 果肉~。The pulp is full and fleshy.

肥胖 féipàng fat; corpulent; obese: ~症 obesity / ~基因 obesity gene

肥硕 féishuò (of fruit) big and fleshy; (of limbs and body) large and firm-fleshed

肥沃 féiwò 〈of land〉 fertile; rich

肥皂 féizào soap: ~粉 soap powder / ~盒 soap box / ~剧 〈戏〉 soap opera / ~泡 soap bubble / ~水 soap-suds

肥壮 féizhuàng (of crops, animals, etc) stout and strong

腓 féi calf (of the leg): ~骨 〈生理〉 fibula

fěi

匪 fěi ❶ bandit; robber; gangster: ~帮 bandit gang / ~首 also "匪酋" bandit chieftain / ~徒 robber; gangster; bandit / ~穴 also "匪巢" bandits' lair or den ❷ 〈书〉 not; no: ~夷所思 (of ideas, events, etc) out of the ordinary; fantastic; bizarre

诽 fěi slander; calumniate

诽谤 fěibàng slander; calumniate; defame: ~罪 crime of defamation; (offence of) libel / ~名誉 character assassination or defamation

菲 fěi 〈书〉 humble; poor; unworthy: ~仪 also "菲礼" 〈谦〉 small or humble gift / ~酌 〈谦〉 simple meal or dinner / 所值不~ be worth quite a lot   see also fēi

菲薄 fěibó ❶ humble; poor: ~生活 plain living ❷ belittle; look down on; despise: 前人 belittle one's predecessors

斐 fěi 〈书〉 teeming with literary grace or talent

斐然 fěirán 〈书〉 of striking literary grace or talent; brilliant; prominent: ~成章 compose beautiful prose / ~成风 become a prominent trend / 成绩~ (make) outstanding accomplishment

翡 fěi

翡翠 fěicuì also "硬玉" jadeite: ~绿 jade green

fèi

吠 fèi bark; yap; yelp

肺 fèi lung: ~癌 carcinoma of the lung; lung cancer / ~炎 pneumonia / ~叶〈生理〉lobe of the lung / ~活量 (of lungs) vital capacity / ~结核 *also* "肺病" pulmonary tuberculosis (TB) / ~气肿〈医〉pulmonary emphysema

肺腑 fèifǔ bottom of one's heart: ~之言 words from the bottom of one's heart / ~之交 bosom friend; deep and sincere friendship

废（廢） fèi ❶ give up; abolish;〈书〉depose: ~耕 (of land) be left uncultivated; lie waste / ~置 put aside as useless; abandon / ~太子 depose a crown prince ❷ waste; useless; disused: ~钢 scrap steel / ~井 disused well / ~矿 abandoned mine / ~料 waste (material); scrap; junk / ~票 invalidated ticket or ballot; spoilt vote / ~渣 waste residue; slag; dross / ~铜烂铁 metal scrap ❸ disabled; maimed: ~人 disabled person; simpleton; good-for-nothing

废除 fèichú abolish; abrogate; repeal: ~债务 cancel a debt / ~农奴制 abolish serfdom / ~不平等条约 abrogate an unequal treaty

废黜 fèichù〈书〉dismiss from office; dethrone; depose

废话 fèihuà (talk) nonsense; rubbish: ~连篇 reams of rubbish; pages and pages of nonsense / 别~! Don't talk nonsense!

废品 fèipǐn ❶ waste product; reject: ~率 reject rate ❷ scrap; waste; junk: ~袋 litterbag / ~处理 waste treatment or disposal / ~回收 waste recovery; recycling or salvage of waste

废气 fèiqì waste gas or steam; exhaust: 汽车~ car exhaust

废弃 fèiqì discard; abandon; (of sth) fall into disuse

废寝忘食 fèiqǐn-wàngshí (so ab-

sorbed or occupied as to) forget all about food and sleep: ~地工作 devote oneself whole-heartedly to one's work

废水 fèishuǐ waste water; liquid waste: ~处理池 purification tank for liquid waste

废物 fèiwù ❶ waste material; junk; trash: ~利用 convert waste into useful material; recycle wastes ❷ (fèiwu)〈粗〉dimwit; good-for-nothing

废墟 fèixū ruins; debris

废止 fèizhǐ abolish; annul; nullify: ~协议 nullify an agreement

废纸 fèizhǐ waste paper; ~篓 wastebasket / ~篓 scrap basket

沸 fèi boil; bubble: ~点 boiling point / ~水 boiling water / ~滚的油锅 cauldron full of boiling oil

沸扬 fèiyáng seethe (with excitement); bubble over: 沸沸扬扬 (as of discussion or gossip) bubbling and gurgling; in a hubbub

沸腾 fèiténg boil (over); seethe; hubbub: ~的熔岩 bubbling lava / 人声~ hubbub of voices.

费 fèi ❶ fee; expense; fare; 水~ charge for water / ~改税 change fees into taxes; (carry out) fee-to-tax reform ❷ cost; spend; take: ~工 take a lot of work / ~钱 cost a lot; be costly / ~时 take time; be time-consuming / ~唇舌 take a lot of talking or explaining / ~眼神 strain or tax the eye / ~尽心机 rack one's brains (in scheming, etc) / 十多岁的孩子很~鞋。Teenagers wear out shoes quickly.

费解 fèijiě hard to understand; obscure; unintelligible

费力 fèilì exert or require much effort; go to or take great pains: ~不讨好 do a hard but thankless job; (of a task, etc) be arduous but fruitless

费神 fèishén *also* "费心" ❶ tax one's energy; be exhausting: 这事真~。This is quite a headache. ❷〈套〉may I trouble you (to do sth); would you mind (doing sth):请您～给照看一下。Would you be so kind as to take care of it?

费事 fèishì give or take a lot of trouble; be troublesome

费用 fèiyong cost; expenses:生活～cost of living; living expense / ～概算 cost estimate

痱 fèi

痱子 fèizi prickly heat:～粉 prickly-heat powder

fēn

分 fēn

❶ divide; separate; assign:～任务 assign tasks / ～而治之 divide and rule / ～门别类 put into different categories; classify / ～片包干 divide up the work and assign a part to each (individual or group) ❷ tell; distinguish; differentiate:不～伯仲 be equally matched ❸ branch (of an organization):～店 branch (of a shop) / ～行 branch (of a bank) / ～校 branch school or campus / 第三～册 book III; third volume ❹ fraction; one-tenth; percentage:～米 decimetre (dm) / 五～之二 two fifths ❺ *fen*, a traditional measure **a)** as a unit of length (=1/10 of a *cun* or 1/3 of a centimetre) **b)** as a unit of area (=1/10 of a *mu*, or 66.66 square metres) **c)** as a unit of weight (=1/10 of a *qian*, or 1/2 gram) ❻ (as money) *fen*, 1/100 of a yuan or 1/10 of a *jiao* ❼ minute (=1/60 of an hour):～针 minute hand (of a watch or clock) / ～钟 minute / ～秒必争 seize every minute and second; make the best use of time ❽ minute (=1/60 of a degree):北纬70度23～ 70 degrees and 23 minutes (70°23′) north latitude ❾ *of interest rate*:年利一～ 10% annual interest / 月息二～ a monthly interest of 2% ❿ point; mark:考了95～ get 95 marks (out of 100) in an exam / 领先五～ lead by five points

see also fèn

分贝 fēnbèi 〈理〉decibel (dB)

分崩离析 fēnbēng-líxī disintegrate; fall to pieces; come or fall apart

分辨 fēnbiàn ❶ distinguish; differentiate:～是非 distinguish between right and wrong; tell right from wrong ❷〈理〉resolution:～率 resolution (ratio or power)

分辩 fēnbiàn *also* "分说" defend oneself (against a charge); offer an explanation:不容～ allow or brook no explanation

分别 fēnbié ❶ part; say goodbye to each other:～多年 have been parted for years ❷ distinguish; differentiate; differ:～好坏 distinguish good from bad ❸ respectively; separately:～处理 deal with separately / ～对待 treat differently

分布 fēnbù be distributed or spread (over an area); be dispersed or scattered:人口～ population distribution

分成 fēnchéng divide into tenths; share:四六～ divide into two shares with one party getting 40% and the other 60%

分词 fēncí 〈语言〉participle:～短语 participial phrase

分寸 fēncun sense of propriety or proportion:有失～ go too far; overstep the limits

分担 fēndān share; contribute:平均～(divide sth) share and share alike

分道扬镳 fēndàoyángbiāo separate and go different ways; part company

分发 fēnfā distribute; hand out; issue

分割 fēngē divide; separate; break or

split up:不可～的领土 inalienable or inseparable territory

分工 fēngōng division of labour:～负责 divide work and responsibility

分管 fēnguǎn assume personal responsibility for; be in charge of

分毫 fēnháo fraction; iota:～不差 *also* "分毫不爽" precisely the same; without an iota of difference or error

分号 fēnhào ❶ semicolon (;) ❷ branch (of a firm, etc)

分红 fēnhóng share out bonuses; draw dividends or profits

分洪 fēnhóng flood diversion:～区 flood-diversion area

分化 fēnhuà divide; split or break up:～瓦解 divide and demoralize; disintegrate / 两极～ polarization

分机 fēnjī (telephone) extension:～号 extension number

分家 fēnjiā ❶ (of family members) divide up family property and live apart; (喻) split or break up:分工不～ divide the work but coordinate each other's efforts

分解 fēnjiě resolve; decompose; disintegrate:力的～〈理〉 resolution of force / 从内部～ disintegrate from within; fall apart

分界 fēnjiè (draw a) dividing line or demarcation line; boundary:军事～线 military demarcation line

分居 fēnjū ❶ (of a married couple) live separately; separate ❷ (of family members) live apart

分句 fēnjù 〈语言〉 clause:并列～ parallel clauses

分开 fēnkāi ❶ be away or separate from each other:～讨论 hold separate discussions; discuss (sth) separately ❷ (cause to) separate or part

分类 fēnlèi classify:～法 (method of) classification / ～广告 classified ads / ～数字 breakdown figures / ～索引 classified index

分离 fēnlí separate; sever; part:～多年的老友 long-parted friends / 从空气中～稀有气体 separate rare gases from air

分裂 fēnliè divide; split:细胞～ cell division / ～主义 splittism

分泌 fēnmì 〈生理〉 secrete; excrete:～物 secretion; secreta / ～腺 secreting gland

分娩 fēnmiǎn childbirth; delivery; labour:～室 *also* "产房" delivery room / ～顺利 (have a) smooth delivery

分明 fēnmíng clear; obvious; distinct:赏罚～ be strict and fair in meting out rewards and punishments / 从～不对 obviously wrong

分母 fēnmǔ 〈数〉 denominator:公～ common denominator

分派 fēnpài assign (a task, etc); share (expenses, etc)

分配 fēnpèi distribute; allocate; assign:～工作 assign (sb) a job / ～住房 allot housing / 收入～制度 income distribution system

分期 fēnqī by stages or instalments:～付款 payment by instalment / ～实施 implement (sth) by stages

分歧 fēnqí dispute; differ; diverge:观点～ divergence of views; conflicting opinions

分清 fēnqīng distinguish; tell (one from another):～是非 distinguish between right and wrong

分散 fēnsàn disperse; scatter; diffuse:～精力 fritter away one's energies / ～注意力 distract or divert attention; take sb's mind off sth

分身 fēnshēn spare or find time (from one's main work):～无术 attend to many things at the same time

分手 fēnshǒu part (company); say goodbye to each other

分数 fēnshù ❶ mark; grade; score:～线 bottom or floor mark (for enrolment, etc) ❷ 〈数〉 fraction; fractional

number

分水岭 fēnshuǐlǐng watershed; divide;〈喻〉line of demarcation

分摊 fēntān share; apportion; contribute

分庭抗礼 fēntíng-kànglǐ stand up to sb (as an equal); make rival claims; act independently and defiantly

分头 fēntóu ❶ separately; severally ❷ parted hair

分文 fēnwén (usu used in the negative) single cent or penny;～不取 not taking a single cent; free of charge; gratis /～不值 not worth a cent or straw; worthless

分析 fēnxī analyse;～能力 analytical ability /～国际形势 analyse the international situation

分享 fēnxiǎng share (joy, rights, etc); partake of

分晓 fēnxiǎo outcome; result; solution;未见～。The outcome is still uncertain.

分心 fēnxīn also "分神" ❶ divert or distract one's attention; be distracted;～的事太多 have too many distractions ❷〈套〉please give some attention:这件事您多～吧。Would you be kind enough to give this some attention?

分野 fēnyě dividing line; line of demarcation; domain

分忧 fēnyōu share (sb's) worries; help solve difficult problems;为国～ do one's bit for the country in times of trouble

分赃 fēnzāng divide the spoils; share ill-gotten gains or power;～不均 quarrel over the spoils

分支 fēnzhī branch (of an organization, etc); affiliate; ～学科 subdiscipline

分子 fēnzǐ ❶〈数〉numerator (in a fraction) ❷〈化〉molecule;～量 molecular weight or mass /～式 molecular formula

see also fènzǐ

分组 fēnzǔ divide into groups:按年龄～ be grouped according to age /～学习 study in groups; group study

芬 fēn sweet smell; fragrance;～芳 sweet-smelling; fragrant

吩 fēn

吩咐 fēnfù also "分付" tell; bid; order:按咐～办事 do as told / 听候～ be at sb's disposal or command

纷 fēn diverse; numerous; confused or confusing;～繁 numerous and complicated /～飞 swirl in the air; fly about in a disorderly way;～乱 numerous and disorderly; helter-skelter; chaotic /～扰 tumult; turmoil /～争 dispute; quarrel; wrangle /～至沓来 come thick and fast; keep pouring in; occur in quick succession / 诸事～纭 be caught in a confusion of matters

纷纷 fēnfēn ❶ numerous and confused; profuse:～扬扬 (of snowflakes, etc) fly or flutter in confusion ❷ one after another; in succession; all at once:～离开 leave one after another; depart all at once

氛 fēn

氛围 fēnwéi atmosphere; ethos:文化～ cultural ethos

fén

坟(墳) fén grave; tomb:看～ take care of a grave or graveyard; be a cemetery-keeper / ～地 also "坟场" graveyard; cemetery / ～头 also "坟包" grave mound / ～茔〈书〉grave; tomb; graveyard

坟墓 fénmù grave; tomb:自掘～ dig one's own grave; be one's own undoing

焚 fén burn;～毁 destroy by fire; burn down / ～烧 burn; set on fire / ～香 burn joss sticks; burn incense

焚化 fénhuà　incinerate; cremate; ～炉 incinerator; cremator

fěn

粉 fěn ❶ powder; chalk; 磨成～ grind into powder; pulverize / ～盒 powder box; compact / ～剂 powder; 〈农〉 dust / ～末 powder / ～底霜 foundation cream ❷ noodles made from rice flour, bean starch, etc; starch; 炒～ fried rice noodles / ～皮 (bean or sweet potato starch) sheet jelly / ～芡 pasty mixture of water and starch (for cooking) / ～丝 bean vermicelli / ～条 starch noodles ❸ white; white-powdered; ～墙绿瓦 white(-washed) walls and green tiles ❹ pink; ～红 pink; rosy

粉笔 fěnbǐ　chalk; 彩色～ coloured chalk; pastel / ～画 chalk drawing; crayon

粉尘 fěnchén　(industrial) dust; ～污染 dust pollution

粉刺 fěncì　also "痤疮"〈医〉acne

粉墨登场 fěnmòdēngchǎng　〈贬〉make oneself up and go on stage — embark upon a political venture

粉饰 fěnshì　gloss over; whitewash; ～门面 window dressing / ～太平 present a fake picture of peace and prosperity

粉刷 fěnshuā　whitewash; ～一新 look brand new after being whitewashed

粉碎 fěnsuì　break into pieces; smash; crush; ～机 pulverizer; grinder / ～阴谋 crush a conspiracy / ～性骨折〈医〉comminuted fracture / ～身碎骨,在所不辞 not flinch or shrink even if one is threatened with destruction

fèn

分 fèn ❶ component; element; 水～ moisture content ❷ what is

within one's right or obligation; ～内 within one's job or duty ❸ friendly feeling; affection; 看在老关系的～上 for old times' sake ❹ see "份" fèn
see also fēn

分量 fènliàng　weight; 有～ carry a lot of weight / 给足～ give full measure / ～不足 give short measure; be lacking in weight or importance

分外 fènwài ❶ particularly; especially; ～明亮 all the brighter ❷ beyond one's duty or job; more than one's due; ～之想 inordinate wish or ambition

分子 fènzǐ　member; element; 动摇～ vacillating element; waverer　*see also* fēnzǐ

份 fèn ❶ share; portion; part; ～额 share; portion / 分成三～ divide into three parts ❷ 〈量〉 set; 两～儿快餐 two sets of fast food / 三～冰淇淋 three ice-creams b) copy; 一～报纸 a copy of a newspaper / 一～电报 a telegram ❸ *used after* 年,月,省,县 *to form a unit*; 省～ province / 月～ month

份儿 fènr ❶ portion; share; ～菜 set-portion dish / ～饭 table d'hôte; set meal ❷ status; position; 没有我说话的～。I've no voice.

份子 fènzǐ　one's share of expenses for a joint undertaking; gift in the form of cash; 出～ pay one's share (of expenses, etc) / 凑～ club together to present a gift (to sb)

奋(奮) fèn ❶ brace up; exert oneself; act vigorously; ～飞 spread the wings and soar; 〈喻〉take off; develop rapidly / ～进 advance bravely; forge ahead / ～战 fight bravely; work strenuously ❷ take up; raise; lift; ～臂高呼 raise one's arms and fist

奋不顾身 fènbùgùshēn　(charge forward) regardless of personal safety; ～的战斗精神 dauntless militant spirit

奋斗 fèndòu　struggle; work hard; strive; ～ 目标 objective of a struggle; target of one's efforts

奋发 fènfā　rouse or exert oneself; brace oneself up; ～图强 go all out to achieve success / ～有为 be energetic and promising

奋力 fènlì　do all one can; spare no effort; ～抢救 spare no effort to rescue (sb) / ～挣扎 struggle with all one's might

奋起 fènqǐ　rise or lift with force and spirit; brace up; ～自卫 rise in self-defence / ～直追 do one's utmost to catch up

奋勇 fènyǒng　summon up all one's courage and energy; be dauntless; ～当先 charge at the forefront of struggle

粪(糞) fèn　excrement; faeces; dung; ～车 dung-cart; night-soil cart / ～池 manure pit; cesspool / ～堆 dunghill; manure heap / ～肥 manure; muck; dung / ～坑 manure pit; latrine

粪便 fènbiàn　excrement and urine; night soil; ～无害处理 decontamination of faeces

粪土 fèntǔ　dung and dirt; muck; 视名利如～ look upon fame and fortune as dirt

愤(忿) fèn　anger; indignation; resentment; ～懑 disgruntled; resentful / ～～不平 fume or seethe with anger; be indignant and resentful / ～然作色 flush with anger

愤恨 fènhèn　indignantly resent; detest; ～不已 remain angry

愤激 fènjī　excited and indignant; furious; 群情～。Popular feelings were running high.

愤慨 fènkǎi　(righteous) indignation; 令人～ arouse one's indignation

愤怒 fènnù　indignation; fury; anger; ～声讨 angrily denounce / ～到了极点 be overwhelmed with indignation

愤世嫉俗 fènshì-jísú　detest human injustices; loathe the ways of the world; be cynical about life; ～者 cynic/ ～之作 work that is highly critical of the world and its ways

fēng

丰(豐) fēng　❶ rich; plentiful; abundant; ～美 (of vegetation, etc) abundant and rich; lush / ～年 bumper harvest year; year of abundance; good year / ～饶 rich (and fertile) / ～衣足食 have ample food and clothing; be well-fed and well-clad / 粮草～裕 be well-stocked with grain and fodder ❷ great; ～功伟绩 also "丰功伟业" signal or monumental contributions; magnificent exploits

丰碑 fēngbēi　monument; monumental work

丰产 fēngchǎn　high yield; bumper crop or harvest; ～田 high-yield cropland

丰富 fēngfù　(make) rich or wealthy; plentiful; abundant; ～多彩 rich and varied; diverse and colourful / 读书～我们的知识。Reading enriches our knowledge.

丰厚 fēnghòu　rich (and thick); generous; 植被～ rich vegetation / 待遇～ excellent or generous pay and perks

丰满 fēngmǎn　full; full-grown; plentiful; ～的麦穗 full ears of wheat / ～的身材 well-rounded or plump figure

丰盛 fēngshèng　rich; abundant; sumptuous; ～的宴席 sumptuous banquet; lavish feast

丰收 fēngshōu　bumper or big harvest; 小麦～ (reap a) bumper wheat harvest / 教学科研双～ score great achievements in both teaching and research

丰硕 fēngshuò　plentiful and enormous; abundant; rich; 成果～ rich rewards; great successes

丰腴 fēngyú ❶ also "丰盈" (of one's figure) full; plump; well-rounded ❷ rich and fine; fertile; abundant; 水草~ abundant water and lush grass

风（風）

fēng ❶ wind; breeze; gale: 大~ strong or high wind / ～灯 storm or hurricane lamp or lantern / ～镜 goggles / ～沙 sand blown by the wind; dust storm / ～速 wind speed or velocity / ～衣 windcheater; windbreaker ❷ air-dried or -driven; winnowed; pneumatic: ～鸡 air-dried chicken / ～动工具 pneumatic tool / 晒干～净 sun-dried and well-winnowed ❸ practice; custom; atmosphere; 校～ school spirit / ～土人情 local conditions and customs ❹ scene; view ❺ bearing; character; style: view ❺ bearing; character; style / ～骨 strength of character; vigour of style / ～华正茂 in the flower of youth; in one's prime ❻ news; hearsay; rumour: ～闻 learn through hearsay; get wind of; hear / ～言～语 slanderous gossip; groundless talk / 传他已逃走。He is rumoured to have fled.

风暴 fēngbào windstorm; storm; tempest

风波 fēngbō disturbance; rumpus; trouble

风采 fēngcǎi also "丰采" graceful bearing; elegant demeanour; charisma: ～依旧 retain one's former charisma or charm

风餐露宿 fēngcān-lùsù eat in the wind and sleep in the dew — go through the rigours of arduous journey or fieldwork; endure the hardships of living in the open

风潮 fēngcháo agitation; unrest; disturbance: 闹～ agitate (for a cause); stir up unrest

风车 fēngchē ❶ windmill ❷ winnower ❸ pinwheel (a toy)

风尘 fēngchén ❶ travel fatigue: ～仆仆 travel-worn and weary; travel-stained ❷ hardships and uncertainties of an unstable society or life: ～女子 prostitute; street walker

风驰电掣 fēngchí-diànchè swift as wind and quick as lightning

风吹草动 fēngchuī-cǎodòng rustle of grass in the wind — sign of disturbance or trouble brewing: 有什么～要及时通报。Inform us immediately if there is anything untoward brewing.

风度 fēngdù demeanour; manner; bearing: ～翩翩 elegant demeanour; graceful manner or bearing

风风火火 fēngfēng-huǒhuǒ hasty and rash; hustling and bustling; hectic

风格 fēnggé character; style; integrity: 独特的～ unique style / ～高尚 of noble character / ～奖〈体〉award for sportsmanship

风光 fēngguāng scene; view; sight: ～旖旎 beautiful or wonderful view / ～片 scenic

风寒 fēnghán cold; chill: 难挡～ (of clothing, etc) too thin to keep out the cold / 偶染～ catch a chill or cold by chance

风花雪月 fēnghuā-xuěyuè ❶ effete and sentimental writings ❷ love affair; Bohemian life

风化 fēnghuà ❶ morals; decency: 有碍～ offend against decency ❷〈地〉weathering: ～石 weathered rock

风景 fēngjǐng scenery; landscape: ～画 landscape (painting) / ～区 scenic spot

风卷残云 fēngjuǎncányún a strong wind scatters wisps of clouds — make a clean sweep of sth

风口 fēngkǒu place where there is a draught: 站在～ stand in the draught

风浪 fēnglàng stormy waves; storm and stress: 风口浪尖 in the teeth of a storm; at the centre of storm and stress / 风平浪静 calm and tranquil;

F

plain sailing

风力 fēnglì force or power of wind：
～发电 wind power (generation)

风凉 fēngliáng cool：～话 irresponsible and sarcastic remarks; derisive comments / 在～处休息 rest in the cool

风流 fēngliú ❶ distinguished and accomplished; outstanding：～人物 truly great man; hero ❷ talented in letters and unconventional in life style：～倜傥 of easy and elegant bearing ❸ romantic; dissolute; loose：～韵事 romantic affair; romance

风马牛不相及 fēngmǎniúbùxiāngjí have nothing at all to do with each other; be totally irrelevant or beside the point

风貌 fēngmào ❶ characteristic style and features; ethos：时代～ style and features of the time; ethos ❷ appearance and manner; view; scene：恢复小城的古老～ restore a small town to its ancient appearance

风靡 fēngmǐ also "风行" fashionable; in vogue：～一时 become fashionable for a time; be all the rage

风起云涌 fēngqǐ-yúnyǒng surging and fast-developing; forging ahead or rolling on with full force

风气 fēngqì general mood; common practice; atmosphere：学习～很浓 good learning climate

风琴 fēngqín organ：～手 organist

风情 fēngqíng ❶ amorous sentiment; flirtatious expression：卖弄～ play the coquette; be coquettish ❷ lifestyle; local conditions and customs

风趣 fēngqù humour; wit；～话 witty remarks; wisecrack

风骚 fēngsāo ❶〈书〉literature; literary excellence ❷ coquettish; flirtatious：～女人 flirtatious woman; coquette

风尚 fēngshàng prevailing custom or practice

风声 fēngshēng ❶ sighing or soughing of the wind；～鹤唳 moaning of the wind and cry of cranes —（fleeing army's）suspicion of danger at the slightest sound ❷ news; word; rumour：听到～ get wind of sth / ～越来越紧. The situation is getting tense.

风湿 fēngshī 〈医〉rheumatism：～性关节炎 rheumatic arthritis / ～性心脏病 rheumatism of heart

风霜 fēngshuāng wind and frost—hardships experienced in life or on a journey：久经～ weather-beaten

风水 fēngshuǐ feng shui, traditional Chinese practice of determining the siting and orientation of a house, tomb, etc; geomantic omen; fortune：看～ practise feng shui or geomancy / ～宝地 place of good geomantic omen / ～轮流转〈俗〉even fortune rotates; your mileage may vary

风俗 fēngsú social custom：～画 genre (painting) / ～习惯 customs and habits

风调雨顺 fēngtiáo-yǔshùn propitious winds and rains; favourable weather (for the crops)

风头 fēngtou ❶ straw in the wind; trend of things：避～ lie low until the dust has settled or till the trouble blows over ❷ public attention; the limelight：～颇健 very much in the limelight

风味 fēngwèi distinctive flavour; local colour：～菜 typical local dish; local delicacy

风险 fēngxiǎn risk; hazard; danger：冒～ run or take a risk / ～评估 risk evaluation / ～资本 venture or risk capital

风向 fēngxiàng wind direction; trend of events; evolving circumstances：～标 weather-vane; wind vane; weathercock

风雅 fēngyǎ polite; elegant; refined：举止～ have refined manners; be elegant in manner

风雨 fēngyǔ　wind and rain; stress and storm; trials and hardships; ～飘摇 swaying in the midst of a raging storm; precarious; tottering / ～同舟 be in the same storm-tossed boat; tide over difficulties together / ～无阻 regardless of the weather; rain or shine / 风风雨雨 repeated difficulties and hardships; groundless talk; gossip / 风里来，雨里去 come in the wind and go in the rain — be busy running about despite hardship

风云 fēngyún　wind and cloud — stormy or unstable situation; ～变幻 changeable or fast-changing situation; ～人物 man of the hour or time

风韵 fēngyùn　also "丰韵" (usu of a woman) graceful bearing; charm

风疹 fēngzhěn　〈医〉nettle rash; ～块 weal

风筝 fēngzheng　kite; 放～ fly a kite

风烛残年 fēngzhúcánnián　old and ailing like a candle guttering in the wind; with one foot in the grave; last remaining years

风姿 fēngzī　also "丰姿" graceful bearing; charm; charisma; ～绰约 (of a woman) carry oneself in a graceful manner

枫 fēng　also "枫树" Chinese sweet gum; maple

封 fēng　❶ seal; close; block; ～存 seal up for safe keeping / ～港 close a port / ～火 bank a fire / 用钱～人的嘴 seal sb's lips with money ❷ envelope; wrapper; cover; ～底 (of a book) back cover / ～里 inside front or back cover (of a book) / ～面 title page of a thread-bound book; front and back cover of a book; front cover / ～套 big envelope (for holding documents, books, etc) ❸ confer (a title, territory, etc); ～官许愿〈贬〉promise high posts and other favours ❹ (short

for 封建主义) feudalism;反帝反～ struggle against imperialism and feudalism

封闭 fēngbì　seal (off or up); close (down);～机场 seal off or close an airport / ～性社会 closed society / ～非法 网吧 close down an illegal Internet bar

封顶 fēngdǐng　(of a building) be topped off or roofed;〈喻〉put a ceiling (on sth);奖金不～ put no ceiling on or set no maximum for bonuses

封冻 fēngdòng　(of a river, etc) freeze over; (of soil) be frozen over;～期 period of freezing weather; freeze

封建 fēngjiàn　feudalism;～主 feudal lord / ～社会 feudal society / ～主义 feudalism

封口 fēngkǒu　❶ seal; close; (of a wound, etc) heal;没有～的信 unsealed letter ❷ also "封门" speak with a tone of finality; close one's door (to further compromise, etc)

封皮 fēngpí　❶ front and back cover of a book ❷ envelope ❸ wrapper; paper wrapping ❹ strip of paper used for sealing

封山 fēngshān　seal or close a mountainous area;～育林 close hillsides to facilitate reafforestation

封锁 fēngsuǒ　blockade;～线 blockade (line) / ～边境 seal or close the border / ～消息 (impose a) news blackout

封条 fēngtiáo　strip of paper bearing an official seal and the date of the sealing; paper strip seal

疯 fēng　(like) mad; crazy; wild;～话 incoherent utterance; rot; nonsense / ～玩 enjoy oneself with abandon / ～子 lunatic; madman; nut / ～牛病 mad cow disease / ～人院 lunatic asylum; madhouse; mental hospital

疯癫 fēngdiān　insane; mad; demented;疯疯癫癫 be mentally deranged; act like a lunatic; be dotty or flighty

疯狂 fēngkuáng　crazy; frenzied; unbridled; (of sb's face) frenzied revenge / ~抢购 panic buying

峰 (峯)　fēng　peak; summit; anything like a peak; ~会 summit (meeting) / ~峦 ridges and peaks / ~年 peak year (of an activity, etc) / ~回路转 (of mountain paths) be full of twists and turns; be circuitous; (of writing) make an abrupt transition

烽　fēng　beacon; ~烟 beacon (fire); flames of war

烽火 fēnghuǒ　❶ beacon (fire); ~台 beacon tower ❷ flames of war; ~连天 with flames of war raging all over the land

锋　fēng　❶ sharp point or cutting edge of a knife, etc ❷ van; front; leading edge; 冷~ cold front / 前~ vanguard; forward

锋利 fēnglì　sharp; keen; piercing; ~的匕首 keen dagger / ~的爪子 sharp claws / ~的目光 piercing look

锋芒 fēngmáng　❶ cutting edge; spearhead; 斗争的~ spearhead of struggle ❷ outward show of one's talent or ability; ~毕露 show off one's ability or talent; be aggressive

蜂　fēng　❶ wasp; (esp) bee; ~巢 also "蜂房" beehive; honeycomb / ~蜡 beeswax / ~蜜 honey / ~箱 (bee-) hive / ~音 hum; buzz ❷ in swarms; flocking; ~拥而至 come swarming or flocking

蜂王 fēngwáng　queen bee or wasp; ~浆 also "蜂皇精"; "蜂乳" royal jelly

蜂窝 fēngwō　honeycomb; sth honeycomb-like; ~炉 honeycomb briquet stove / ~煤 (honeycomb) briquet / ~式电话 cellular phone

féng

逢　féng　meet; encounter; come on or upon; ~集 on market day /

年过节 on New Year's Day or other festivals / ~人便问 ask everyone one meets

逢场作戏 féngchǎngzuòxì　join in the fun on occasion; have fun when possible; play a game

逢凶化吉 féngxiōnghuàjí　turn ill luck into good; turn misfortune into fortune

逢迎 féngyíng　ingratiate oneself or curry favour with; fawn on

缝　féng　stitch; sew; ~补 (sew and) mend / ~被子 stitch a cover on a quilt / ~刀口 (in a surgery) stitch up an incision / ~扣子 sew on a button / ~连连 do sewing and mending　*see also* **fèng**

缝合 fénghé　suture; sew up; ~线 *also* "缝线" 〈医〉suture / ~伤口 sew up or suture a cut

缝纫 féngrèn　sewing; tailoring; ~机 sewing-machine / ~车间 tailoring workshop

fěng

讽　fěng　allude or admonish euphemistically; satirize; mock; ~嘲 satirize; mock; sneer / ~示 hint at; allude euphemistically to

讽刺 fěngcì　satirize; ridicule; mock; ~画 satirical cartoon; caricature / ~小品 satirical essay or skit

讽喻 fěngyù　parable; allegory; ~诗 allegorical poem / ~时政 allude to current politics in parable

fèng

凤 (鳳)　fèng　phoenix, traditional symbol for the empress or queen; ~冠 phoenix coronet (worn by an empress or as a bride's headdress)

凤凰 fènghuáng　phoenix; 凤求凰 young man seeking a girl's love

凤毛麟角 fèngmáo-línjiǎo phoenix feathers and unicorn horns — rarity of rarities

凤尾鱼 fèngwěiyú (general term for 鲚) anchovy

奉 fèng ❶ present with respect; submit; offer:～茶 serve tea (to a guest) ❷ receive (orders, etc):～召 receive a summons / 上级指示 on orders from above ❸ regard with respect; esteem; revere:～公守法 be law-abiding / ～若神明 make a fetish of; worship / ～为楷模 hold up or look upon as a model ❹ believe in; espouse (a religion):～佛 believe in Buddhism ❺ wait upon; attend to:～养父母 support and look after one's parents ❻ 〈敬〉*used to refer to sth one does for the other party*:～告 inform you; let you know / ～还 return or repay with thanks

奉承 fèngcheng flatter; fawn upon; 当面～ flatter sb to his or her face / 爱听～话 fall for or dote on flatteries

奉命 fèngmìng be ordered (to do sth):～行事 act on or under orders / ～声明 be authorized or instructed to make a statement

奉陪 fèngpéi 〈敬〉keep (sb) company:～到底 keep (sb) company till the very end; take (sb) on and fight to a finish / 恕不～ I'm afraid I'll have to beg off.

奉劝 fèngquàn 〈敬〉offer a piece of advice:～你不要鲁莽从事。You would be well advised not to act rashly.

奉送 fèngsòng give away free; offer as a gift

奉献 fèngxiàn present or offer with respect; devote (oneself):～精神 spirit of self-sacrifice; selfless devotion / 为听众～一首歌 sing a song for the audience

奉行 fèngxíng pursue; follow:～独立自主的和平外交政策 pursue an independent foreign policy of peace

俸 fèng salary; stipend; pay:～禄 〈旧〉official's salary or stipend

缝 fèng ❶ chink; crack; crevice:～隙 fissure; crack; crevice / 衣柜裂了～儿。The wardrobe has cracked. ❷ seam:焊～ welding seam or line

see also féng

fó

佛 fó ❶ Buddha; image or statue of Buddha:拜～ worship Buddha; pay respects to Buddha / ～像 image or statue of Buddha / ～爷 Buddha / ～要金装,人要衣装。〈俗〉As Buddha needs a gilt statue, so man needs fine clothes. or Fine clothes make the man. / ～争一炷香,人争一口气。〈俗〉As Buddha needs incense, so man needs self-respect. ❷ Buddhism:信～ believe in or espouse Buddhism / ～经 Buddhist scripture or sutra / ～事 (hold a) Buddhist service or ceremony / ～塔 Buddhist pagoda; dagoba / ～学 Buddhist learning or philosophy ❸ name of Buddha (*Amitabha*); Buddhist scripture or sutra:念～ pray to Buddha (by chanting *Amitabha*)

佛法 fófǎ ❶ Buddha's teachings; Buddhist doctrine:弘扬～ spread Buddha's teachings; spread the dharma ❷ power of Buddha:～无边。The power of Buddha is infinite.

佛教 Fójiào Buddhism:～徒 Buddhist

佛门 fómén Buddhism:～弟子 follower of Buddha; Buddhist

fǒu

否 fǒu ❶ negate; deny:方案被～了。The proposal was turned down. ❷ no; not:能～出发,尚待决

定。Whether or not to start off is yet to be decided.

see also pǐ

否定 fǒudìng　negate; deny; ~一切 negate everything / 持～态度 hold a negative attitude

否决 fǒujué　vote down; veto; over-rule; ~权 veto (power)

否认 fǒurèn　deny; disavow; repudiate

否则 fǒuzé　otherwise; if not; or else; 快穿上大衣，～会受凉的。Put on your overcoat or (else) you'll catch cold.

fū

夫 fū　husband; ~妇 husband and wife; married couple / ~唱妇随 (traditional concept of conjugal harmony) the husband sings and the wife follows; the wife is her husband's echo

夫妻 fūqī　husband or man and wife; ~店 mom-and-pop store / ~恩爱 conjugal affection; connubial love

夫人 fūrén〈敬〉lady; madame; 大使～ wife of an ambassador

夫子 fūzǐ　term of address for a scholar or teacher (formerly esp Confucius); pedant; ~庙 Confucian Temple / ~气 pedantic ways; pedantry

肤(膚) fū ❶ skin; ~色 colour of skin ❷ skin-deep; superficial; ~浅 superficial; shallow; skin-deep

麸 fū *also* "麸皮"; "麸子" (wheat) bran

跗 fū〈生理〉instep; ~骨 tarsal bones; tarsus / ~面 instep

孵 fū　hatch; brood; incubate; ~卵鸡 brooding hen; sitter / ～出一窝小鸭 hatch a brood of duck-lings

孵化 fūhuà　hatch; incubate; 人工～ artificial incubation / ～器 hatcher; (literal or figurative) incubator

敷 fū ❶ apply (powder, ointment, etc); ~药 apply ointment / ~粉 powder (one's face) ❷ spread; lay out; elaborate; ~设铁轨 lay a railway track / ~陈其事〈书〉relate sth in detail; elaborate sth ❸ sufficient; enough; ~用 be barely enough

敷衍 fūyǎn　be perfunctory; go through the motions; muddle through; ~几句 dismiss with a few perfunctory remarks; say sth just for the occasion / ~搪塞 go through the motions; stall (sb) off; explain (sth) away

fú

弗 fú〈书〉not; ~如 not as good as; not equal to

伏 fú ❶ lean or bend over; lie prostrate; ~卧 lie on one's stomach; lie prone / ~案写作 bend over one's desk writing ❷ fall; subside; go down; 起～ rise and fall; up and down ❸ hide; 无处～藏 have nowhere to conceal oneself ❹ any of the three nine-day periods constituting high summer; dog days; ~天 high summer; dog days / ~汛 summer flooding ❺ yield; admit; subdue; ~法 be executed / ~罪 plead guilty; admit one's guilt ❻ (short for 伏特)〈电〉volt

伏笔 fúbǐ　*also* "伏线" foreshadowing; 为后文设下～ foreshadow later developments

伏兵 fúbīng　(troops in) ambush; 设～ lay an ambush

伏击 fújī　ambush; ambuscade; 打～ ambush (the enemy); lay an ambush / 中～ fall into an ambush

伏贴 fútiē ❶ (of clothing) fit perfectly ❷ *also* "伏帖" comfortable; at ease; 心里很～ feel at ease

凫(鳬) fú ❶ wild duck ❷ swim：～水 swim

芙 fú

芙蓉 fúróng ❶ cottonrose hibiscus ❷ lotus：～出水 lotus flower appearing just above the water；〈喻〉delicate and charming woman

扶 fú ❶ place a hand on (sb or sth) for support or work；support or work with the hand：～犁 put one's hand to the plough；follow the plough / ～杖 lean on a stick / ～病人上车 help an invalid into a car ❷ hold or straighten up：～不起的阿斗 weakling whom nobody can help to succeed ❸ lend a hand；help；assist：～危济困 help those in danger and relieve those in need；rescue the endangered and succour the needy / ～助穷人 assist the poor

扶病 fúbìng (do sth) in spite of illness

扶持 fúchí give aid to；help sustain；foster：～正气 help sustain a healthy atmosphere；foster healthy trends (in a society, etc)

扶老携幼 fúlǎo-xiéyòu help the aged along and lead the young by the hand；bring along both the old and the young

扶贫 fúpín help the poor；aid a poverty-stricken area；alleviate poverty：科技～ help the poor or a poverty-stricken area through scientific and technological assistance / ～计划 aid-the-poor programme

扶手 fúshou ❶ handrail；rail；banister ❷ armrest：～椅 armchair

扶梯 fútī staircase with banisters；〈方〉ladder

扶养 fúyǎng provide for；support；bring up：～费 support payment；alimony / ～老人 provide for the elderly；support one's parents

扶摇直上 fúyáozhíshàng (of prices,

etc) soar；rise steeply；skyrocket

扶植 fúzhí foster；cultivate；promote：～新生力量 foster new emerging forces

孚 fú inspire (confidence)：以信～人 win trust with good faith / 不～众望 not command public confidence or trust

拂 fú ❶ stroke；caress；touch：～动 sway gently；flap；brush slightly against ❷ whisk；flick：～去身上的尘土 whisk or brush the dust off one's clothes ❸〈书〉run counter to or go against (sb's wishes)

拂晓 fúxiǎo dawn；daybreak

拂袖 fúxiù 〈书〉give a flick of one's sleeve in anger：～而去 leave in a huff；storm out

服 fú ❶ (wear) clothes, dress, or mourning：～饰 dress (and personal adornment)；garment (and accessories) / ～孝 wear mourning clothes or be in mourning for one's parent ❷ take (medicine, etc)：内～ to be taken orally / ～毒 take poison / ～药 take medicine ❸ serve：～刑 serve a sentence；serve time / ～兵役 serve in the army ❹ obey；be convinced；persuade：～劝 accept advice；be amenable to advice / 不～裁判 refuse to obey the referee ❺ be accustomed, used or acclimated to：这东西我吃不～。This food does not agree with me.

see also fù

服从 fúcóng obey；submit (oneself) to；be subordinated to：～法律 submit to or obey the law / ～全局利益 subordinate personal or local interests to the overall interests

服老 fúlǎo be reconciled to one's age and failing health：不～ refuse to give in to age

服气 fúqì be convinced；be won over；be reconciled to one's defeat, inferiority, etc

服侍 fúshì also "服事"; "伏侍" wait upon; attend to; nurse: ~病人 nurse the sick / ~老人 wait upon or care for the old

服输 fúshū also "伏输" admit or acknowledge defeat; take defeat hands down

服帖 fútiē ❶ also "伏帖" docile; obedient; submissive ❷ fitting; neat; well-arranged

服务 fúwù serve; give or render service to; be in the service of:为祖国~ serve one's motherland / ~费 service charge or fee / ~器 (信息) server / ~台 (as on a hotel floor) service desk or counter; (as in a hotel lounge) information and reception desk / ~员 attendant; assistant; waiter or waitress / ~行业 service trades or sector / ~态度 attitude in serving one's customers; (quality of) service

服役 fúyì be on active service; enlist; serve:超期~ be on an extended term of service / 服后备役 be on reserve duty; be in reserve service

服装 fúzhuāng clothing; dress; garment:~厂 clothing factory / ~表演 fashion show / ~款式 dress style or fashion / ~模特儿 (fashion) model; mannequin / ~设计师 apparel stylist; fashion designer

服罪 fúzuì also "伏罪" plead guilty; admit one's guilt:认罪~ admit one's guilt and be determined to atone for it

怫 fú 〈书〉indignant; angry:~然作色 flush with anger; glower

茯 fú

茯苓 fúlíng 〈中药〉 *fuling*, edible fungus often used as tonic; tuckahoe

氟 fú 〈化〉fluorine (F):~化物 fluoride / ~利昂 also "氟氯烷" freon; CFC / ~缺乏症〈医〉fluorine deficiency / 无~冰箱 CFC-free refrigerator

俘 fú ❶ capture; seize; take prisoner:生~ capture alive; take a prisoner alive / ~获 capture (captives, weapons, etc) ❷ prisoner of war; captive:遣~ repatriate prisoners of war

俘虏 fúlǔ ❶ capture; take prisoner ❷ captive; captured personnel; prisoner of war (POW):抓~ take prisoners of war / ~营 prisoner or POW camp

浮 fú ❶ float; emerge:~冰 floating ice; (ice) floe / ~萍〈植〉duckweed / ~桥 pontoon or floating bridge / ~出水面 emerge from the water; surface / ~想联翩 random thoughts thronging one's mind ❷ on the surface; superficial:~泛 superficial; too generalized / ~土 loose surface soil; surface dust ❸ temporary; provisional; movable:~财 movable or portable property ❹ flighty; shallow; superficial:工作很~ superficial or shallow work / 习性~滑 given to slick and frivolous ways ❺ hollow; empty; inflated:~名 empty name; vain glory; bubble reputation / ~文 verbiage; padding (in writing) / ~艳 showy and unsubstantial; flashy; gaudy ❻ exceed; be surplus or redundant:~员 redundant personnel / ~报开支 report more expenditure than actually defrayed

浮标 fúbiāo buoy:灯~ light buoy

浮沉 fúchén go up and down; drift along:与世~ swim with the current; follow the trend

浮雕 fúdiāo relief:浅~ low relief / 深~ high relief

浮动 fúdòng rise and fall; fluctuate; 〈经〉float:~工资 floating or fluctuating wages / ~汇率 floating (exchange) rate / 人心~ widespread feeling of insecurity

浮光掠影 fúguāng-lüèyǐng　skimming over the surface; hasty and casual; cursory

浮华 fúhuá　vain; showy; flashy

浮夸 fúkuā　be boastful; exaggerate: ~风 trend to boast and exaggerate (achievements, etc)

浮力 fúlì　〈理〉buoyancy: 海水比淡水更有~。Sea water is more buoyant than fresh water.

浮皮潦草 fúpí-liáocǎo　also "肤皮潦草" superficial and careless; cursory; perfunctory

浮现 fúxiàn　appear in one's mind; show: ~绝望的神色 show an expression of despair

浮游 fúyóu　swim: ~生物 plankton

浮躁 fúzào　impetuous; impulsive: 办事~ act on impulse

浮肿 fúzhǒng　〈医〉dropsy; oedema

符 fú　❶ symbol; mark; sign (magical or otherwise): 音~ musical note / 画一张~ draw a magic sign ❷ match; tally or accord with: 与事实不~ not tally with the facts

符号 fúhào　❶ symbol; mark; sign ❷ insignia: 胸前佩戴~ wear an insignia on one's chest

符合 fúhé　accord or tally with; be in line with; ~标准 meet a criterion; be up to standard / ~实际 conform to reality; be realistic

幅 fú　❶ width (of cloth, etc); breadth (in general); size: ~面 width of cloth / 双~ double width / 巨~画像 portrait of gigantic size ❷〈量〉used for cloth, pictures, scrolls, etc: 一~画 a drawing or painting / 一~地毯 a carpet

幅度 fúdù　range; margin; scope: 大~上升 increase by a big margin

幅员 fúyuán　(of a country, etc) area; size: ~辽阔 (of) vast territory

辐 fú　spoke (of a wheel): ~条 〈口〉spoke (of a wheel)

辐射 fúshè　radiate: ~病 radiation disease / ~波 radiation or radiated wave / ~热 radial or radiated heat / ~线 radiation ray / ~源 radiation source / ~光芒 radiate light / ~强度 radiation intensity; radiance

福 fú　❶ good fortune; blessing; happiness: ~祉〈书〉happiness; well-being / ~、禄、寿 happiness, high rank and longevity / 如东海, 寿比南山〈套〉happiness as boundless as the sea and longevity comparable to that of the hills; may you live a long and happy life / ~无双至, 祸不单行。〈谚〉Blessings do not come in pairs and calamities never come singly. or Luck comes but once but trouble comes in droves. ❷ short for Fujian (福建): ~橘 tangerine produced in Fujian

福地 fúdì　place where immortals live; place of happiness or luck

福分 fúfen　〈口〉happy lot; good fortune: ~不浅 no small fortune; good fortune

福利 fúlì　material benefit; well-being; welfare: ~院 (state-run) old folks' home / ~彩票 welfare (foundation) lottery / ~国家 welfare state / ~事业 welfare projects or services

福气 fúqi　happy lot; good fortune: 有~ have the good fortune; be fortunate (enough)

福相 fúxiàng　features or countenance of good fortune: 长得一副~ have features suggestive of good fortune; look as if born under a lucky star

福星 fúxīng　lucky star; mascot: ~高照 have one's star in the ascendant; ride the high tide of luck

福音 fúyīn　❶〈宗教〉gospel: ~书 Gospels (of the Bible) / ~音乐 gospel music ❷ happy news; glad tidings: 高血压病人的~ good news for those who suffer from hypertension

蝠 fú 〈动物〉bat

fǔ

甫 fǔ 〈书〉just; only (just); 年二八 only just turned sixteen

抚(撫) fǔ ❶ comfort; console; ～慰 comfort; console; soothe ❷ protect; nurture; foster; ～孤 bring up the orphaned ❸ press lightly; stroke; ～弄 keep stroking; caress; fondle / ～琴〈书〉play the zither ❹ also "拊"〈书〉clap; ～掌 clap one's hands

抚爱 fǔ'ài　caress; fondle; take care of

抚今追昔 fǔjīn-zhuīxī　contemplate the present and recall the past; reflect on the past in the light of the present

抚摩 fǔmó　also "抚摸" stroke; caress

抚恤 fǔxù　comfort and compensate; ～金 pension for the disabled or for the family of the deceased

抚养 fǔyǎng　raise; rear; bring up; ～费 child support payment (after divorce) / ～成人 bring up a child

抚育 fǔyù　foster; nurture; tend; ～孤儿 bring up an orphan / ～森林 tend a forest

斧 fǔ axe; hatchet; ～柄 shaft or handle of an axe / ～头 also "斧子" axe; hatchet

斧正 fǔzhèng　also "斧削"〈书〉〈敬〉(please) make corrections

府 fǔ ❶ (official) residence; mansion; 〈敬〉your home or house; ～第 also "府邸" mansion (house); residence / ～总统 presidential palace ❷〈旧〉prefecture (above the county); ～尹 prefect

府上 fǔshàng 〈敬〉❶ your home, house or family; 改日到～拜访。I'll call at your home some other day. ❷ your native place; ～在哪里? Where are you from?

俯 fǔ ❶ bow (one's head); bend forward or down; ～伏 lie prostrate / ～身 bend down; stoop ❷〈敬〉deign; condescend; ～就 condescend to take or accept (a post, etc) / ～允 condescend to grant; deign to approve

俯冲 fǔchōng　(of a plane) dive; ～扫射 (dive-) strafe

俯拾即是 fǔshíjíshì　can be found everywhere; be easily available; be extremely common

俯视 fǔshì　also "俯瞰" look down at; overlook

俯首 fǔshǒu ❶ bow one's head; stoop; ～作画 stoop to paint a picture ❷ obey submissively; ～称臣 bow one's head to acknowledge one's allegiance; admit one's inferiority or defeat / ～帖耳 be docile and obedient; be servile; take (sth) lying down

俯卧 fǔwò　lie on one's stomach; lie prostrate; ～撑〈体〉press-up; push-up

釜 fǔ 〈旧〉a kind of cauldron; ～底抽薪 take away the firewood from under a cauldron — take drastic measures to deal with a critical situation; cut the ground from under sb's feet / ～底游鱼 also "釜中之鱼" fish swimming in the bottom of a cauldron — person whose fate is sealed

辅 fǔ assist; complement; supplement; ～币 fractional currency or money / ～料 supplementary or subsidiary materials / ～路 subsidiary road (alongside a trunk highway) / ～音〈语言〉consonant / ～佐 assist (a ruler, etc); serve as adviser for

辅导 fǔdǎo　give guidance in study or training; guide; coach; 个别～ individual coaching or tutorial / ～员 counselor; instructor / ～材料 guidance material

辅助 fǔzhù ❶ assist; aid ❷ supplementary; auxiliary; subsidiary; ～读物

supplementary reading material / ～劳动 auxiliary labour / ～人员 auxiliary personnel or staff

脯 fǔ dried meat; preserved fruit　see also pú

腐 fǔ ❶ rotten; putrid; stale; ～臭 smelly; stinking; putrid / ～儒〈贬〉pedantic scholar; pedant ❷ beancurd; tofu; ～乳 fermented beancurd or tofu / ～竹 (rolls of) dried bean-milk cream

腐败 fǔbài ❶ putrid; rotten; decayed; ～变质的食品 putrid or rotten food ❷ degenerate; corrupt; ～无能的政府 corrupt and inept government

腐化 fǔhuà ❶ degenerate; corrupt; dissipated; ～堕落 become corrupt and degenerate / ～分子 corrupt elements; depraved persons; degenerates ❷ see "腐烂❶"

腐烂 fǔlàn ❶ rot; decompose; go putrid ❷ see "腐败❶"

腐蚀 fǔshí ❶ corrode; etch; ～剂〈化〉corrosive; corrodent / ～性物质 corrosive material ❷ corrupt; deprave; ～人的灵魂 corrode people's souls; corrupt people's mind

腐朽 fǔxiǔ ❶ rot; decay; degenerate; ～的生活方式 degenerate way of life / 木结构已经～。The wooden structure has rotted.

fù

父 fù ❶ father; ～辈 (people of) father's or elder generation / ～母 father and mother; parents / ～亲 father / 有其～必有其子。Like father, like son. ❷ male relative of a senior generation; 祖～ grandfather

父老 fùlǎo elders (of a country or community); ～乡亲 fellow countrymen

父系 fùxì ❶ paternal; ～亲属 paternal relatives ❷ paternal line; ～社会 patrilineal society

讣 fù (usu 讣告) ❶ announce sb's death ❷ obituary

付 fù ❶ hand or turn over; give; commit; ～印 send to the press; turn over to the printing shop (after proof-reading) / ～邮 send by mail; post; mail / ～之一笑 laugh away; dismiss with a smile / ～诸一炬 also "付之一炬" commit to the flames; set on fire; burn / ～诸东流 have all one's efforts wasted; come to naught; go down the drain ❷ pay; ～清 pay in full; pay off or up / ～账 pay or foot a bill / ～出牺牲 make sacrifice ❸ see "副❷"fù

付款 fùkuǎn pay; make payment; ～人 payer / ～凭证 payment voucher or certificate

负 fù ❶ carry on the back or shoulder; shoulder; bear; ～法律责任 bear legal responsibility ❷ suffer; sustain; ～疚〈书〉feel conscience-stricken or guilty; be apologetic / ～罪感 sense of guilt ❸ have; enjoy; boast; 久～盛名 have long been famous ❹ fail (in one's duty, obligation, etc); disappoint; betray; ～约 break a promise; go back on one's word / 有～厚望 fail to come up to expectations; let sb down ❺ lose (a battle, game, etc); be defeated; 一胜一～ win a round and lose another ❻〈数〉〈电〉negative; 〈数〉minus; ～号 negative sign (-) / ～片 (in photography) negative / ～数 negative number / ～离子 also "阴离子"〈理〉anion / ～增长〈经〉negative growth

负担 fùdān ❶ bear; carry; shoulder; ～不起 cannot afford / ～全部家务劳动 do all the housework ❷ burden; load; (mental) strain

负荷 fùhè also "负载""载荷" load; performance capacity; 超～ overload; above capacity / 低～ under-load; under capacity / 满～ full-load; (at)

full capacity

负荆请罪 fùjīngqǐngzuì　proffer a birch and ask for a flogging — make a humble and heartfelt apology

负面 fùmiàn　negative：～影响 negative impact；unfavourable influence

负伤 fùshāng　sustain an injury；be wounded：负重伤 suffer or sustain serious injuries；be severely wounded

负心 fùxīn　*also* "负情" untrue (esp in love)；ungrateful；heartless：～薄幸 be inconstant or fickle in love

负隅顽抗 fùyúwánkàng　*also* "负嵎顽抗"〈贬〉put up a desperate resistance with one's back to the wall；put up a frantic struggle and refuse to surrender

负责 fùzé　❶ be responsible for；be in charge of：～人 person in charge；leader／为事故～ bear responsibility or be held responsible for an accident／对公众～ be accountable to the public ❷ conscientious

负债 fùzhài　❶ be in debt；incur debts：～率 debt ratio／～经营 operate in debt／～累累 be heavily in debt ❷ liabilities

负重 fùzhòng　bear a (heavy) load or weight；shoulder an important task：～行军 (make a) loaded march

妇（婦） fù　❶ woman：～联 (short for 妇女联合会) Women's Federation ❷ married woman；daughter-in-law ❸ wife

妇科 fùkē　(department of) gynaecology：～病 *also* "妇女病" gynaecological or women's disease／～医生 gynaecologist

妇女 fùnǚ　woman：～能撑半边天 women hold up half the sky；women are just as essential as men

妇幼 fùyòu　women and children：～卫生 maternity and child hygiene／～保健站 health centre for women and children

附 fù　❶ add；attach；append：～笔 *also* "附言" additional note；postscript (PS)／～图 attached map or drawing；figure／～页 attached sheet／～注 note appended to a book, etc；annotation ❷ get close to；be close by；be near：～耳密谈 speak in each other's ears；talk in whispers ❸ attach oneself to；depend on；comply with：～议 second a motion；support a proposal

附带 fùdài　❶ in passing；incidentally；by the way ❷ attach；append：不～条件 with no strings attached；unqualified ❸ subsidiary；supplementary；additional：～的损失 incidental damage

附和 fùhè　chime in with (sb)；echo；parrot

附会 fùhuì　draw wrong conclusions by false analogy；make an irrelevant comparison or interpretation

附加 fùjiā　add；append；attach：～费 surcharge；additional charge／～税 surtax；additional tax or duty／～值 value added

附件 fùjiàn　❶ appendix (to sth)；annex；enclosure (in sth) ❷ accessory；attachment；peripherals

附近 fùjìn　nearby；close by；adjacent

附录 fùlù　appendix (to a book, etc)；addenda

附设 fùshè　have as an attached institution

附属 fùshǔ　auxiliary；attached；affiliated：～国 dependent state；dependency／～品 accessory；appendage／～小学 (shortened as 附小) attached or affiliated primary school

附庸 fùyōng　❶ dependency；vassal (state) ❷ appendage；hanger-on：～风雅 mingle with men of letters and pose as a lover of culture；behave like a connoisseur of art and literary works when one is not

附着 fùzhuó　adhere；cling；stick：～

力〈理〉adhesive force；adhesion ation

服 fù （of Chinese medicine）dose：三～药 three doses of Chinese medicine　*see also* fú

驸 fù

驸马 fùmǎ　emperor's or king's son-in-law

赴 fù　go to；be bound for；attend：～会 attend a meeting；meet（sb）by appointment／.～任（of an official）go to one's post／～宴 *also* "赴席" go to a banquet／～约 meet（sb）by appointment；keep an appointment／～汤蹈火 go through hell and high water；be ready to face all difficulties and dangers／共～国难 join in a united effort to save the nation

复（❶複、❷-❹復） fù　❶ repeat；double；compound：～本 extra copy／～利〈经〉compound interest／～种〈农〉multiple cropping ❷ answer；reply：～电 telegram in reply；reply by telegram／～命 report（to one's superiors）on completion of a task／～信（write a）letter in reply ❸ regain；recover；resume：～出 resume one's official post after rehabilitation；make a comeback／～工 return to work（after a strike or layoff）／～会 resume（a session or sitting）／～婚 restore or resume matrimonial relations after divorce／～课 resume classes ❹ again；repeatedly：～读 study at school again and review what one has learnt／～赛〈体〉intermediary heat；semi-finals／～试 re-examination；second round of examinations／～诊 further consultation（with a doctor）；subsequent visit（to a doctor）

复辟 fùbì　restore a dethroned monarch or an old order；make a comeback

复查 fùchá　check again；re-examine：住院～ be in hospital for re-examin-

复仇 fùchóu　revenge；avenge：为死者～ avenge the dead／～心理 vindictiveness；desire for revenge

复发 fùfā　have a relapse；recur：旧病～ suffer a relapse of an old ailment；return to one's old bad habit／～率 recurrence rate

复古 fùgǔ　restore old customs, traditions, etc；return to the ancients：～主义 doctrine of "back to the ancients"

复合 fùhé　compound；complex；composite：～词〈语言〉compound（word）／～句 *also* "复句"〈语言〉compound or complex sentence

复核 fùhé　❶ check；cross-check ❷〈法〉(of the Supreme People's Court) review（a case involving a death sentence）

复活 fùhuó　come or bring back to life；revive；resurrect：～节〈宗教〉Easter

复旧 fùjiù　restore old ways；return to the past；rehabilitate（sth old）

复审 fùshěn　❶ re-examine；re-check ❷〈法〉review（a case）；retrial

复述 fùshù　❶ repeat：～说过的话 repeat what is said ❷ retell（in language learning）：～课文 retell a text

复数 fùshù　〈语言〉plural（number）；〈数〉complex number：第三人称～ third person plural

复苏 fùsū　come back to life or consciousness；revive；〈经〉recover

复习 fùxí　review；revise：～功课 review one's lessons／～提纲 outline for review

复写 fùxiě　make carbon copies：～纸 carbon paper

复兴 fùxīng　revive；reinvigorate；rejuvenate

复印 fùyìn　duplicate；photocopy；xerox：～机 duplicator；xerox（copier）；photocopier／～件 xerox（copy）；duplicate copy

复员 fùyuán　demobilize；～军人 demobilized soldier；ex-serviceman

复原 fùyuán　❶ *also* "复元" recover from an illness；be restored to health. ❷ restore；rehabilitate；文物～ restoration of cultural relics

复杂 fùzá　complicated；intricate；complex；～劳动 complex labour／～的心情 mixed feelings／使问题～化 complicate matters

复制 fùzhì　duplicate；reconstruct；reproduce；～品 replica；reproduction

副 fù　❶ deputy；associate；assistant；队～ deputy team-leader／～手 assistant；deputy／～校长 vice-president (of a college, etc)；vice-principal (of a school) ❷ complementary；auxiliary；secondary；～品 substandard goods；seconds／～职 (person in) position of a deputy／～标题 *also* "副题" subheading；subtitle／～产品 by-product ❸〈量〉 a) set；pair；一～眼镜 a pair of glasses b) *used to indicate facial expression*：一～笑脸 a smiling face

副本 fùběn　duplicate；transcript；copy

副词 fùcí　〈语言〉 adverb：～短语 adverbial phrase

副刊 fùkān　supplement：文学～ literary supplement

副食 fùshí　non-staple food：～品 non-staple food or foodstuff／～商店 grocery

副业 fùyè　sideline；side occupation；moonlighting

副作用 fùzuòyòng　side effect；by-effect：产生～ produce a harmful by-effect；play a counter-productive role

赋 fù　❶ bestow；endow；vest；人民～予的权力 power bestowed by the people／～有学者风度 have the natural bearing of a scholar ❷ (agricultural) tax：～税 land and other taxes；taxes and levies ❸ compose；write；即

席～诗 compose a poem impromptu

赋闲 fùxián　(of an official, etc) be unemployed；be out of office

傅 fù　❶ teacher；instructor：师～ master；teacher ❷〈书〉 lay on；apply：～粉 put powder on；powder (one's face)

富 fù　❶ rich；wealthy：～豪 rich and powerful people／～矿 rich or high-grade ore；bonanza／～翁 rich man；man of wealth／～人和穷人 the rich and the poor；the "haves" and "have-nots" ❷ make rich；enrich：～国强兵 make one's country rich and build up its military might／～民政策 policy of enriching the people ❸ abundant；rich；plentiful：～足 affluent；plentiful；abundant；rich／～于心计 adept at scheming；very calculating

富贵 fùguì　riches and honour；wealth and rank：～病 rich man's disease／～人家 wealthy and influential family

富丽 fùlì　splendid；gorgeous：～堂皇 sumptuous；gorgeous；grand

富强 fùqiáng　rich and powerful；prosperous and strong：～之路 road to prosperity and strength

富饶 fùráo　fertile；abundant：～的黑土地 fertile black soil

富庶 fùshù　rich and prosperous；thriving：～的鱼米之乡 prosperous and populous rice-and-fish country

富态 fùtài　〈婉〉 plump；stout：老太太长得真～。What a full figure the old lady has!

富有 fùyǒu　❶ rich；affluent；wealthy：生于～的家庭 born with a silver spoon in one's mouth ❷ rich in；replete with；full of：～才华 talented／～个性 of strong personality

富裕 fùyù　prosperous；well-to-do；well off：共同～ common prosperity

富余 fùyu　have more than needed；have enough and to spare：～的钱 spare money／～人员 redundant staff；sur-

腹 fù ❶ belly; abdomen; stomach;~肌 abdominal muscle / ~腔〈生理〉abdominal cavity / ~泻〈医〉diarrhoea / ~胀 abdominal distension / ~膜炎〈医〉peritonitis / 下~部 underbelly ❷ heart; innermost part;打~稿 make mental notes

腹背受敌 fùbèishòudí be exposed to attacks from the front and the rear; find oneself in a dilemma

腹地 fùdì hinterland; interior

腹心 fùxīn vital organs; key parts;~要地 important place; strategic area

缚 fù tie up; bind fast; ~住双手 tie up sb's hands

覆 fù ❶〈书〉cover; envelop;~土 cover up with soil ❷〈书〉overturn; capsize; upset;~辙 track of an overturned cart; lesson drawn from another's mistakes / ~水难收 spilt water can't be gathered up; what is done can't be undone ❸ see "复❷、❸" fù

覆被 fùbèi cover; overspread; screen;森林~ forest cover

覆巢无完卵 fùcháowúwánluǎn when the nest is overturned no egg stays unbroken — in an all-embracing disaster, no one can escape safe and sound

覆盖 fùgài cover; plant cover; vegetation:~面 (forest- or rain-) covered area;(TV, etc) coverage

覆灭 fùmiè destruction; ruin; total collapse

覆没 fùmò ❶〈书〉(of ships) sink ❷ (of troops, etc) be overwhelmed or destroyed:全军~ the whole army is wiped out; suffer a total defeat

覆亡 fùwáng (of an empire, etc) fall; downfall; collapse

馥 fù〈书〉fragrance:~郁 strong fragrance; heavy perfume

F

G

gā

夹(夾) gā *see also* jiā; jiá

夹肢窝 gāzhiwō armpit

旮 gā

旮旯儿 gālár 〈方〉❶ nook; corner:
旮旮旯旯儿 every nook and cranny ❷
out-of-the-way place: 背～ inaccessible
recess

伽 gā

伽马射线 gāmǎ shèxiàn *also* "γ 射
线"〈理〉gamma ray

咖 gā *see also* kā

咖喱 gālí curry: ～鸡 curried chicken;
chicken curry

嘎 gā 〈象声〉screech: ～～ (of
ducks, etc) honk; quack; (of
boots, etc) creak

gāi

该 gāi ❶ ought to; should: 本～
如此。That's just as it should
be. / ～出发了。It's time we were
starting off. ❷ fall to sb; be sb's turn
(to do sth): ～你了。It's your turn. ❸
deserve; merit: 你～当何罪?〈书〉
What punishment do you think you deserve? ❹ probably; most likely; it is
expected: 明天他～出院了。He is due
to leave hospital tomorrow. ❺ used in
*exclamatory sentences to indicate specu-
lation and emphasis*: 他～多累呀! He
must be exhausted. ❻ owe: ～账 be in
debt ❼〈书〉this; that; said: ～国 the
said country

该死 gāisǐ 〈口〉*used to express resentment or anger*: 你这～的笨蛋! You
damn fool! / 真～, 忘了密码了! Oh
shit, I forget the PIN number.

gǎi

改 gǎi ❶ change; convert: ～行
change one's profession / ～嫁
(of a woman) remarry / ～期 change
the date; reschedule / ～选 hold a new
election; re-elect / ～乘轮船 change to
a steamboat ❷ alter; revise; polish:
～动 change; alter; modify / ～写 re-
write; adapt / 把大衣～瘦点儿 make a
coat a bit tighter ❸ correct; rectify;
remedy: ～错儿 correct a mistake

改编 gǎibiān ❶ adapt; rearrange;
revise: 把小说～成电视剧 adapt a novel for TV ❷ reorganize (an army,
etc); re-designate

改变 gǎibiàn change; alter; transform: ～落后面貌 rid (a place) of its
backwardness

改革 gǎigé reform: ～开放 reform
and open to the outside world; reform
and open up

改观 gǎiguān change in appearance;
take on a new look

改过 gǎiguò correct one's mistakes;
mend one's ways: ～自新 correct one's

errors and make a fresh start; turn over a new leaf

改换 gǎihuàn change; replace; substitute: 改朝换代 (have a) change of dynasty or regime; (make a) dynastic change / 改名换姓 change one's name; assume an alias / 改头换面 〈贬〉change the appearance but not the substance; dish up something old in a new form

改进 gǎijìn improve; make better

改口 gǎikǒu withdraw or modify one's previous remark; correct oneself; change one's tune or topic

改良 gǎiliáng ❶ improve; ameliorate ❷ reform: ～派 reformists; reformers / ～主义 reformism

改日 gǎirì also "改天" another day; some other day

改善 gǎishàn improve; ameliorate: ～投资环境 provide a better environment for investment

改弦更张 gǎixián-gēngzhāng also "改弦易辙" change one's course; strike out on a new path; make a fresh start

改邪归正 gǎixié-guīzhèng also "改恶从善" mend one's ways; turn over a new leaf

改造 gǎizào transform; reform; remould: ～思想 remould one's outlook / ～旧企业 refurbish an old plant

改正 gǎizhèng correct; amend; rectify: ～错案 redress miscarriages of justice / ～缺点 overcome one's shortcomings

改装 gǎizhuāng ❶ repackage; repack: ～费用 repacking charge; reconditioning expense ❷ re-equip; refit: ～电脑 refit a computer

改锥 gǎizhuī also "螺丝刀" screwdriver

改组 gǎizǔ reorganize; reshuffle; restructure: ～内阁 reshuffle the cabinet

gài

丐 gài 〈书〉beggar: ～帮 ring of beggars

芥 gài see also jiè

芥菜 gàicài see "盖菜" gàicài see also jiècài

芥蓝 gàilán 〈植〉cabbage mustard

钙 gài 〈化〉calcium (Ca): 缺～ calcium-deficient / ～片 calcium tablet

盖(蓋) gài ❶ lid; cover; cap: ～碗 tea-bowl with a lid ❷ shell; carapace: 乌龟～ tortoise shell ❸ cover; put (over or on); overwhelm: ～戳 also "盖图章" affix a seal (on sth); put a stamp (on sth) / 欢呼声～过了起哄声。Cheers drowned the booing and hooting. ❹ build; put up (housing) ❺ 〈书〉approximately; about: around ❻ 〈书〉for; because: 文章错误甚多，作者不学之故。The essay teems with errors, because the author is but an indifferent scholar.

盖菜 gàicài also "芥菜" 〈植〉leaf mustard

盖棺论定 gàiguānlùndìng no final verdict can be pronounced on a person until after death

盖帽儿 gàimàor ❶ (of basketball) shot blocking ❷ also "盖了" 〈方〉terrific; tops; great

盖世 gàishì unsurpassed; matchless; peerless: ～无双 unrivalled; second to none / ～英雄 peerless hero

盖子 gàizi lid; cover; cap: 揭～ lift up the lid; 〈喻〉uncover; expose ～ keep the lid on; 〈喻〉try to cover up the truth

概 gài ❶ general; approximate: ～论 introduction; survey / ～数 approximate or round number / ～算

〈经〉 budgetary estimates / ～言之 generally speaking; all told ❷ without exception; absolutely; categorically; 不负责 will not assume any responsibility / ～莫能外 admit of no exception whatsoever ❸ bearing; deportment; 气～ mettle; manner; spirit

概况 gàikuàng general situation; overall picture; brief account or survey

概括 gàikuò ❶ sum up; summarize; epitomize; 从个别～一般 generalize from particulars ❷ briefly; in broad outline; ～地说 to sum up; to put it in a nutshell / ～介绍 give a brief account (of sth)

概率 gàilǜ also "几率"〈数〉probability; ～论 probability theory; law of probability

概略 gàilüè outline; summary; brief; 计划～ outline of a programme / ～说明 brief account

概念 gàiniàn concept; notion; idea; 基本～ fundamental conception; basic concept / ～化的作品 stereotyped literary work

概述 gàishù outline; (give a) brief account (of sth)

概要 gàiyào essentials; outline

gān

干(❺-❽乾) gān ❶ shield; ～城〈书〉defence; defenders ❷〈书〉offend; affront; go against; ～犯法规 break laws and regulations ❸ have to do with; be concerned with; be implicated in; ～政 meddle in state affairs / 不～你的事。It has nothing to do with you. or It's none of your business. ❹ Heavenly Stems ❺ dry; arid; ～果 nuts; dried fruit / ～花 dehydrated flower / ～咳 dry cough / ～裂 (of parched earth, skin, etc) crack; chap / ～尸 also "木乃伊" mummy / ～瘦 skinny; bony;

emaciated / 笋～儿 dried bamboo shoots / 油漆未～. Wet paint. / 水缸～了. The water vat is empty. ❻ without substance; hollow; futile; ～等 wait idly / ～笑 give a hollow laugh / ～着急 be anxious but to no avail; be helplessly worried ❼ (relatives) of nominal kinship; not linked by blood; ～爹 nominally adoptive father; godfather ❽ cold-shouldered; slight; 别把客人～在那里. Don't leave the guests out in the cold.

see also gàn

干巴 gānba *also* "干巴巴的" ❶ dried up; (of skin) desiccated; ～老头儿 wizened old man ❷ dry and dull; insipid; ～文章 insipid or dull writing

干杯 gānbēi drink a toast; ～! Cheers! or Bottoms up! / 为你的健康～! (Here's) To your health!

干瘪 gānbiě ❶ shrivelled; wizened; ～的脸 wizened face ❷ *see* "干巴❷"

干草 gāncǎo hay; ～make hay / ～垛 haystack; hayrick

干脆 gāncuì ❶ frank and straightforward; candid; clear-cut; 办事～ act with decision ❷ simply; just; ～一言不发 simply refuse to talk

干打雷, 不下雨 gāndǎléi, bùxiàyǔ 〈俗〉all thunder but no rain — much clamour but no action

干饭 gānfàn cooked rice (as distinct from porridge); 吃～的 parasite; good-for-nothing

干戈 gāngē weapons of war; arms; war; 动～ take up arms; go to war

干股 gāngǔ〈经〉unpaid-for or gratuitous share

干旱 gānhàn (of weather or soil) arid; dry; 连年～ be afflicted by drought for years / ～地区 arid area

干涸 gānhé dry up; run dry

干净 gānjìng ❶ clean; neat and tidy; 保持～ keep (sth) clean and tidy / ～利落 efficient and smart; in a neat and tidy manner ❷ completely; entirely; totally:把责任推了个～ deny all responsibility (for sth)

干枯 gānkū dry up; wither; shrivel:～的树叶 dry leaves

干粮 gānliáng （solid) food; field rations; rations for a journey:～袋 ration bag; haversack

干扰 gānrǎo disturb; distract; interfere:不受外界～ not be distracted by the outside world / ～台〈通信〉jamming station

干涉 gānshè interfere (in sth or with sb); intervene; meddle:武力～ armed intervention / ～别人私事 meddle in other people's private affairs

干洗 gānxǐ dry-clean:～店 dry-cleaner's (shop)

干系 gānxì responsibility; implication:摆脱～ (try to) escape one's responsibility / ～重大 be deeply implicated (in a case)

干薪 gānxīn ❶ salary drawn for a sinecure:领～ hold a sinecure ❷ (basic) salary (apart from bonuses, etc)

干预 gānyù also "干与" interfere (in sth); intervene; meddle

干燥 gānzào ❶ dry; arid:～剂 drier; drying or desiccating agent ❷ dull; uninteresting:～乏味 dull as ditchwater

干支 gānzhī （short for 天干地支) ten Heavenly Stems (甲、乙、丙、丁、戊、己、庚、辛、壬、癸) and twelve Earthly Branches (子、丑、寅、卯、辰、巳、午、未、申、酉、戌、亥) — the two sets of signs are variously combined to designate years and days, whereas the latter are also used to designate the 12 two-hour periods of the day (时辰) and the 12 symbolic animals (生肖)

甘 gān ❶ sweet; honeyed; pleasant:～霖 good or timely rain / ～美 sweet and refreshing / ～甜 sweetness; joy / 时雨～露 (like) timely rain and sweet dew ❷ willingly; of one's

own accord:～当重罚 be ready to accept a heavy penalty / ～受屈辱 take an insult lying down ❸ (Gān) short for Gansu (甘肃)

甘拜下风 gānbàixiàfēng candidly admit or concede defeat; sincerely acknowledge sb's superiority

甘草 gāncǎo 〈中药〉licorice root

甘苦 gānkǔ ❶ joys and sorrows; weal and woe:～与共 share joys and sorrows; go through weal and woe together ❷ hardships and difficulties experienced:～自知。One knows best what one has gone through.

甘蓝 gānlán 〈植〉wild cabbage

甘心 gānxīn ❶ willing; ready:～情愿 willingly and gladly ❷ be content with or reconciled to:不～失败 refuse to resign oneself to defeat

甘休 gānxiū give up; take (sth) lying down:不达目的，决不～ never give up until one's purpose is achieved

甘油 gānyóu 〈化〉glycerine

甘愿 gānyuàn willingly; readily; gladly:～冒此风险 be ready to take the risk

甘蔗 gānzhè sugarcane

甘之如饴 gānzhīrúyí enjoy sth bitter as if it were malt sugar — gladly endure hardships

杆 gān also "杆子" pole; staff:斜～ slanting pole see also gǎn

肝 gān liver:～癌〈医〉cancer of the liver / ～病 liver trouble / ～脏〈生理〉liver; hepar / ～功能〈生理〉liver function / ～硬化〈医〉cirrhosis of the liver

肝肠寸断 gānchángcùnduàn afflicted with profound grief; heartbroken

肝胆 gāndǎn ❶ liver and gall; 俱裂 feel as if one's liver and gall were torn up — be overwhelmed by grief or terror ❷ true heart; sincerity:～相照 treat each other with an open heart ❸ heroic spirit; courage:～过人 be un-

肝火 gānhuǒ　irascibility; spleen：动~ vent one's spleen; get worked up / ~ 旺 hot-tempered; irascible

肝脑涂地 gānnǎotúdì　be ready to lay down one's life (for a cause); be willing to repay a favour with extreme sacrifice：~，在所不惜 would grudge nothing, not even one's life

肝炎 gānyán　〈医〉hepatitis; 丙型~ hepatitis C / 慢性~ chronic hepatitis

坩 gān

坩埚 gānguō　〈化〉crucible

泔 gān

泔水 gānshui　swill; slops; hogwash

柑 gān　mandarin orange：~橘 oranges and tangerines; citrus

竿 gān　also "竿子" (bamboo or wooden) pole; rod

尴（尷） gān

尴尬 gāngà　❶ in a predicament or dilemma; cornered：处境~ find oneself on the horns of a dilemma ❷〈方〉uneasy; embarrassed; unnatural：神情~ look uneasy or embarrassed; look not quite oneself

gǎn

杆（桿） gǎn　❶ also "杆子" shaft or arm of sth：箭~ arrow shaft / ~秤 steelyard ❷〈量〉used for implements with a shaft：一~笔 a pen
see also gān

秆（稈） gǎn　stalk; stem

赶（趕） gǎn　❶ run after or for; hurry to; go to：~集 go to a local market or country fair / ~路 hurry on with one's journey; rush / ~早 as early as possible; before

it is too late / ~任务 rush through a task; hurry to meet a deadline / ~末班车 try or hurry to catch the last bus / ~前不~后〈俗〉rather be early than late ❷ drive (a vehicle); tend (a herd); drive (an invader) out or away ❸ encounter; come across; find oneself in (a situation) ❹ by; till; until：这事~下月再说吧。Let's put this off till next month.

赶超 gǎnchāo　catch up and overtake：~世界先进水平 catch up with and surpass the world's advanced levels

赶尽杀绝 gǎnjìn-shājué　drive away and root out; spare none; be ruthless to the extreme

赶快 gǎnkuài　also "赶紧"; "赶忙"; hurry; hasten：~做 do without delay; do in a hurry

赶巧 gǎnqiǎo　happen to; it so happens; as luck would have it：我去看他时,他~不在家。He happened to be out when I went to see him.

赶上 gǎnshàng　❶ catch up with; keep pace with：~科学的新发展 keep pace with new developments in science / 学习成绩赶不上姐姐 be not as good as one's sister in academic grades; lag behind one's sister in studies ❷ encounter; come across; run into (a situation)：回家路上~一场雨 be caught in a rain on one's way back home / 赶得上吃晚饭 will be in time for supper

赶时髦 gǎnshímáo　also "赶潮流"; "赶浪头" follow the fashion; try to be in the trend; be a fashion-monger

赶趟儿 gǎntàngr　〈口〉be in time; make it

赶鸭子上架 gǎnyāzishàngjià　〈俗〉make sb do sth entirely beyond him; force a donkey to dance

敢 gǎn　❶ brave; bold; daring：~死队 dare-to-die corps; suicide squad / ~想~干 dare to think and dare to act; be bold of vision and courageous in action / ～怒而不～言 be forced to keep one's resentment to oneself; hold one's tongue with pent-up indignation / ～于承担责任 have the courage to shoulder a responsibility ❷ be sure or certain; ～保 surely; assuredly; certainly ❸〈书〉〈谦〉make bold; take the liberty; venture:～问家住何方? May I ask where you live? ❹ can it be that:～是他们走错了路? Is it possible that they have taken the wrong road?

敢情 gǎnqing 〈方〉〈副〉❶ why; so; I say; 哟! ～夜里下了大雪啊。Why! There was a heavy snow last night. ❷ of course; indeed; really:去长城? 那～好! Going to the Great Wall? That's really great.

感 gǎn ❶ feel; sense; be aware; ～怀 recollections; reflections; thoughts / ～略～不适 be slightly indisposed; be a little under the weather ❷ move; touch; affect: ～奋 be moved and inspired; be fired with enthusiasm / ～天动地 deeply moving ❸ be thankful, grateful or obliged: ～戴 show gratitude and respect (usu for a superior) / ～念 remember with gratitude; recall with deep emotion / ～愧交加 be tormented by mixed feelings of gratitude and shame ❹〈中医〉be affected (by cold); catch (cold):外～风寒 be affected by the cold; catch a cold ❺ sense; sensation; impression:荣誉～ sense of honour

感触 gǎnchù thoughts and feelings (aroused by what one sees or hears):～很深 be deeply impressed or touched

感到 gǎndào feel; sense; perceive:～骄傲 be proud (of); take pride (in)

感动 gǎndòng move; touch; affect:～得说不出话来 be too moved to utter a word

感恩 gǎn'ēn feel grateful; be thankful:～节 Thanksgiving / ～戴德 be profoundly grateful; bear a debt of deep gratitude / ～图报 owe a debt of gratitude and hope to repay it; be grateful and seek ways to return the kindness

感官 gǎnguān （short for 感觉器官）sense or sensory organ

感光 gǎnguāng （in photography）sensitization / ～纸 sensitive paper

感化 gǎnhuà reform (an erring person) through persuasion, etc; help to reform:～院 reformatory

感激 gǎnjī feel grateful or indebted; be thankful:～涕零 be moved to tears of gratitude

感觉 gǎnjué feel; perceive; become aware of:～轻松 feel relaxed / ～神经 sensory nerve

感慨 gǎnkǎi sigh with emotion:～万千 all sorts of feelings well up in one's mind

感冒 gǎnmào also "伤风"（catch）cold

感情 gǎnqíng ❶ emotion; feeling; sentiment:动～ be carried away by one's emotions; get worked up / ～用事 give way to or be swayed by one's emotions ❷ affection; love; fondness; ～深 be deeply attached (to sb); cherish a deep affection (for sb)

感染 gǎnrǎn ❶ infect; taint:轻度～ light infection ❷ arouse; inspire; affect:～力 power to inspire or influence; appeal

感人 gǎnrén moving; stirring; inspiring:～肺腑 touch one to the heart; tug or pull at one's heartstring

感伤 gǎnshāng （feel）sad; (be) sentimental or mawkish

感受 gǎnshòu ❶ be affected by; catch;～风寒 be affected by the cold; catch a chill ❷ experience; feel; be impressed

感叹 gǎntàn sigh or exclaim with feeling；～词 interjection；exclamation／～号 exclamation mark（!）／～句 exclamatory sentence

感同身受 gǎntóngshēnshòu feel as though one experienced sth personally；empathize；feel indebted as if the favour were received in person

感悟 gǎnwù come to realize；become aware（of sth）

感想 gǎnxiǎng impressions；reflections；thoughts

感谢 gǎnxiè thank；be thankful or grateful；～信 letter of thanks

感性 gǎnxìng perception；perceptiveness；～认识 perceptual knowledge

感应 gǎnyìng ❶ response；reaction；interaction；天人～ interaction between heaven and man ❷〈电〉induction；irritability；～场 induction field

感召 gǎnzhào move and inspire；impel；influence；～力 inspiration；power to influence

感知 gǎnzhī feel；sense；〈哲〉perceive

橄 gǎn

橄榄 gǎnlǎn Chinese olive；（oil）olive；～绿 olive green／～球〈体〉rugby／～油 olive oil／～枝 olive branch — symbol of peace

擀 gǎn

擀 gǎn roll（dough, etc with a rolling pin）：～面条 make noodles／～面杖吹火，一窍不通〈俗〉try to blow the fire with a rolling pin — be completely ignorant or irrelevant

gàn

干（幹）gàn

❶ trunk；stem；main part；～道 main road；trunk line／～线 main or trunk line；artery／～细胞 stem cell ❷（short for 干部）cadre；～警 police officers and constables／～训班 in-service training course／～群关系 relations between the cadres and the masses ❸ do；act；work；～掉〈口〉kill；get rid of；put out of the way／～活儿 work（on a job）／～架 also "干仗"〈方〉quarrel；squabble；come to blows／～得过 be superior to sb（in doing sth）；can get the better of sb；beat／～尽坏事 do all kinds of evil things；stop at no evil／没～头儿 not worth doing；not worthwhile ❹ competent；capable；able；～才 ability；capability；capable or able person／～将 capable or able person；go-getter；competent assistant ❺〈方〉go wrong；become a mess；这事眼看要～。This is going to be a disaster.

see also gān

干部 gànbù cadre；public functionary or servant；government or Party employee

干劲 gànjìn drive；vigour；enthusiasm；鼓～ rouse one's enthusiasm／～十足 brim over with vigour or drive；have plenty of go

干练 gànliàn capable and experienced

干吗 gànmá（口）❶ why；whatever for：～这么认真？Why take it so seriously? ❷ what to do；你想～？What do you want? or What are you up to?

干事 gànshì secretary or clerical worker in charge of sth

赣 Gàn

another name for Jiangxi（江西）：～剧 Jiangxi（local）opera

gāng

冈（岡）gāng

（low and flat）ridge（of a hill）

扛 gāng

lift with both hands see also káng

刚（剛）gāng

❶ stiff；firm；strong；～度 stiffness；rigidity／～健（of character, style, etc）vigorous；forceful；robust／～劲（of handwriting, bearing, etc）forceful and vigorous; bold; sturdy / ～性 rigidity; inflexibility / ～毅 resolute and steadfast / ～直 upright and outspoken / ～烈女子 woman of strong character and integrity / ～柔相济 combine firmness and flexibility; temper toughness with gentleness ❷〈副〉 exactly (a test); barely; just: ～～及格 barely pass (a test) / 大小～合适 just the right size ❸〈副〉 only a short while ago; just: 会议～开始。The meeting has just begun. ❹〈副〉 (used with 就 to indicate immediacy); only at this moment: 我～想给他打电话，他就来了。He came just as I was about to call him.

刚愎自用 gāngbìzìyòng bent on having one's own way; self-willed; headstrong

刚才 gāngcái just now; a moment ago

刚好 gānghǎo also "刚巧" ❶ no more, no less; just (right); exactly ❷ happen to; it so happens; as luck would have it

刚强 gāngqiáng firm; steadfast; staunch: 意志～ strong-willed; iron-willed

刚正 gāngzhèng staunch and upright; principled: ～不阿 upright and never stooping to flattery; keeping to principles and not yielding to pressure

肛 gāng (usu 肛门) anus: ～表 anal or rectal thermometer

纲（綱） gāng ❶ key link; guiding principle; outline: ～常 three cardinal guides and five constant virtues (of Confucian ethics) / ～举目张。Once you seize hold of the key link, everything falls into place. ❷ class: 亚～ subclass

纲领 gānglǐng ❶ programme: 最高～ maximum programme (of a political party) ❷ guiding principle; guidelines: ～性文件 programmatic document

纲目 gāngmù ❶ general outline and its details; major and minor items: ～不清 poorly organized ❷ (usu used in the title of a book) detailed outline (of a subject); compendium

纲要 gāngyào ❶ outline; sketch ❷ (usu used in the title of a book or document) essentials; compendium

钢（鋼） gāng steel: ～材 steel products; rolled steel / ～锭 steel ingot / ～管 steel tube or pipe / ～枪 rifle / ～水 molten steel　see also gàng

钢板 gāngbǎn ❶ (steel) plate; 薄～ steel sheet; sheet steel ❷ spring (of a motorcar, etc) ❸ stencil steel board

钢笔 gāngbǐ also "自来水笔" (fountain) pen: ～尖 pen nib / ～帽 pen cap

钢筋 gāngjīn reinforcing (steel) bar; steel reinforcement: ～铁骨 have muscles of steel and bones of iron — be extremely tough / ～混凝土 reinforced concrete

钢精 gāngjīng also "钢种" aluminium (as used for utensils): ～锅 aluminium pan

钢琴 gāngqín piano: 弹～ play the piano / ～家 pianist

钢丝 gāngsī (steel) wire: 走～ walk a tightrope; high-wire walking / ～床 spring bed / ～绳 steel cable

钢铁 gāngtiě iron and steel; steel: ～厂 steelworks; steel mill; iron and steel plant / ～意志 iron or indomitable will

钢印 gāngyìn steel or embossing seal; embossed stamp

缸 gāng ❶ vat; jar; sth shaped like a jar or vat: 搪瓷～子 enamel mug ❷ compound of sand, clay, etc, for making earthenware: ～砖 clinker (tile)

gǎng

岗（崗） gǎng ❶ hillock; mound: ～峦起伏 undulating hills ❷ ridge; welt; wale ❸ sentry; post; ~楼 watchtower / ~哨 sentry post; sentry; sentinel / ~亭 sentry box; police booth

岗位 gǎngwèi　post; station; job; ~津贴 job subsidy / ~培训 on-the-job training / ~责任制 system of responsibility for the work done by each individual at his post; system of post responsibility

港 gǎng ❶ port; airport; harbour; 出~ clear a port; leave port / ~湾 harbour / ~务局 port or harbour authority / 国际~埠 international port ❷ tributary of a river; ~汊 branching stream ❸ (Gǎng)(short for 香港) Hong Kong; HK; ~币 Hong Kong dollar / ~澳办 Hong Kong and Macao Affairs Office / ~人治~ Hong Kong people administering Hong Kong

港口 gǎngkǒu　port; harbour; ~吞吐量 traffic (of a port)

gàng

杠(槓) gàng ❶ thick stick or club; 〈体〉bar; rod-shaped spare part (of a machine) ❷ thick line drawn beside or under words as a mark ❸ cross out; delete; ~去赘词 cross or strike out the redundant words ❹ standard; criterion; 过了~儿 exceed the limit of propriety; go too far

杠杆 gànggǎn ❶ lever; pry bar; ~原理 lever principle / ~作用 leverage ❷ leverage; 经济~ economic leverage

杠杠 gànggang ❶ rule; regulation; 年龄~ age limit (for sth) ❷ criterion; standard

杠铃 gànglíng　〈体〉barbell

钢(鋼) gàng ❶ sharpen; whet; strop; ~菜刀 sharpen a kitchen knife ❷ reinforce the edge (of a knife, etc) by adding steel and re-tempering

see also gāng

戆 gàng 〈方〉foolish; silly; foolhardy; ~头~脑 silly-looking　*see also* zhuàng

gāo

高 gāo ❶ tall; high; ~地 highland; upland; 〈军〉height / ~举 hold high or aloft / ~楼 high building; high-rise / ~个儿 *also* "高个子" tall person / ~跟鞋 high-heeled shoes; high heels ❷ advanced; high; senior; ~干 senior cadre; high-ranking official / ~工 (short for 高级工程师) senior engineer / ~频 high frequency / ~徒 *also* "高足" brilliant or outstanding disciple; best pupil / ~温 high temperature / ~校 (short for 高等学校) institutions of higher learning; colleges and universities / ~中 (short for 高级中学) senior secondary school / ~蛋白 high protein / ~血压〈医〉hypertension; high blood pressure / 清晰度电视 high definition television (HDTV) ❸ loud; ~调 lofty tone; high-sounding words / ~喊 shout at the top of one's voice ❹ 〈敬〉your; his; their; ~见 *also* "高论" your opinion or view / ~就 (find a) better job

高矮 gāo'ǎi　height; ~不一 Some are tall and some short.

高昂 gāo'áng　high; elated; jubilant; 斗志~ have high morale / ~的代价 high or dear price

高傲 gāo'ào　supercilious; arrogant; haughty; ~自大 self-important

高不成，低不就 gāobùchéng, dībùjiù 〈俗〉can't have one's heart's desire but won't accept less

高不可攀 gāobùkěpān　too high to reach; far beyond one's reach; unattainable

高才生 gāocáishēng　brilliant or top student; whiz kid

高参 gāocān senior staff officer;〈喻〉able adviser or counsellor

高层 gāocéng high level;～会议 summit (meeting) / ～建筑 high-rise (building)

高产 gāochǎn high yield or production;～作物 high-yield crop

高唱 gāochàng ❶ sing loudly or with spirit;～赞歌 sing the praises (of sb or sth) ❷ prate; talk glibly about

高超 gāochāo superb; outstanding; excellent

高潮 gāocháo ❶ high tide; upsurge ❷ climax

高大 gāodà ❶ tall and big; high;身材～ be of great stature ❷ lofty; noble

高档 gāodàng top grade; superior quality;～货 high-grade or high-end goods

高等 gāoděng higher; senior; advanced;～动物 higher animal / ～法院 high court (of justice) / ～教育 higher or tertiary education / ～数学 higher mathematics

高低 gāodī ❶ height;～杠〈体〉uneven or asymmetric bars ❷ also "高下" relative superiority or inferiority; difference in degree;争～ vie with each other to see who is superior ❸ sense of propriety or discretion; appropriateness;不知～ have no sense of discretion ❹〈方〉on any account; just; simply;～不答应 just wouldn't say yes

高度 gāodù ❶ altitude; elevation; height;飞行～ flying altitude ❷ highly; to a high degree;～发达 highly developed / ～赞扬 speak highly of; pay high tribute to / ～自治 high degree of autonomy

高额 gāo'é huge (amount); great (number);～利润 huge profit

高尔夫球 gāo'ěrfūqiú golf (ball);～棒 golf club / ～场 golf course

高风亮节 gāofēng-liàngjié exemplary conduct and noble character; sterling integrity

高峰 gāofēng peak; summit; height;～期 peak period; rush hours / ～会议 summit (meeting)

高高在上 gāogāozàishàng set oneself high above the masses; be divorced from the people and reality

高歌 gāogē sing loudly or with a resounding voice;～猛进 forge ahead triumphantly

高官 gāoguān high-ranking or senior official;～厚禄 high office and fat salary / ～会谈 talks by senior officials

高贵 gāoguì ❶ noble; exalted; high; ～品质 noble quality ❷ highly privileged; elitist;出身～ be from an exalted family

高级 gāojí ❶ high-ranking; senior; advanced;～法院 higher court / ～职称 senior academic or professional rank / ～工程师 senior engineer / ～神经中枢〈生理〉high nerve centre ❷ high-grade; high-quality;～宾馆 first-class hotel / ～化妆品 de luxe cosmetics

高技术 gāojìshù high technology; high-tech;～园 high-tech park / 高新技术 high and new technology; newly-emerging high technology

高价 gāojià high or excessive price; ～油 high-priced oil / ～出售 sell at a high price

高架 gāojià elevated; overhead;～桥 viaduct / ～铁道 overhead or elevated railway

高精尖 gāo-jīng-jiān high-grade, precision and advanced (technology, etc);～设备 state-of-art equipment

高亢 gāokàng loud and sonorous (singing); elevated (mood); resounding

高考 gāokǎo college entrance examination

高科技 gāokējì high-tech; ～成果 high-tech result / ～犯罪 high-tech crime

高空 gāokōng　high altitude; upper air; ～作业 work high above the ground

高利贷 gāolìdài　usury; usurious loan; 放 ～ practise usury / ～ 者 usurer; loan shark

高粱 gāoliang　*kaoliang*; Chinese sorghum; ～ 酒 liquor made from Chinese sorghum / ～ 米 husked *kaoliang*

高龄 gāolíng　❶〈敬〉(of people over sixty) advanced or venerable age ❷ older than usual; ～ 社会 also "老龄社会" aged society / ～ 学生 student (far) above normal age

高帽子 gāomàozi　also "高帽儿" empty title or honour; flattery; 爱戴 ～ take to flattery

高明 gāomíng　❶ brilliant; smart; wise; 医术 ～ superb medical skill ❷ wise or skilful person; 另请 ～。Find someone better qualified (than myself).

高能 gāonéng　〈理〉high-energy; ～ 粒子 high-energy particle

高攀 gāopān　〈套〉claim ties of friendship or kinship with someone of a higher social position; 不敢 ～ I dare not aspire to such an honour.

高朋满座 gāopéngmǎnzuò　with many guests of exalted rank present; (have) a galaxy of distinguished guests

高跷 gāoqiāo　stilts; 踩 ～ walk on stilts

高人一等 gāorényīděng　a cut above other people; a notch higher than others

高山 gāoshān　high mountain or altitude; ～ 病 also "高山反应" altitude or mountain sickness / ～ 滑雪〈体〉alpine skiing

高尚 gāoshàng　❶ noble; lofty; 品德 ～ noble character ❷ refined; elegant; cultivated; ～ 的谈吐 refined speech

高烧 gāoshāo　high fever; 发 ～ have or run a high fever

高射炮 gāoshèpào　antiaircraft gun or artillery; ack-ack gun

高深 gāoshēn　advanced; profound; 学问 ～ erudite scholarship

高升 gāoshēng　advance from a lower to a higher position; be promoted

高视阔步 gāoshì-kuòbù　carry oneself proudly; swagger; strut

高手 gāoshǒu　past master; expert; master-hand; ～ 如 云 a galaxy of master-hands

高寿 gāoshòu　❶ longevity; long life; Wishing you a long life! ❷〈敬〉*used of age of elderly people*; 您 ～? How old are you, sir?

高耸 gāosǒng　stand tall and erect; tower; ～ 入云 reach to the clouds

高速 gāosù　high speed; ～ 发展 develop at high speed; grow by leaps and bounds / ～ 公路 expressway; superhighway

高抬贵手 gāotáiguìshǒu　〈套〉be generous or lenient; not be too hard on sb

高谈阔论 gāotán-kuòlùn　indulge in loud and empty talk; talk volubly or bombastically

高汤 gāotāng　❶ (meat or chicken) soup-stock ❷ thin soup

高堂 gāotáng　〈书〉parents; ～ 老母 aged mother

高头大马 gāotóudàmǎ　❶ big strong horse ❷ (of people) tall and big

高危 gāowēi　highly venerable (to a disease); prone; 艾滋病 ～ 人群 group highly vulnerable to AIDS; AIDS-prone group

高位 gāowèi　❶〈书〉prominent position ❷ upper part (of a limb); ～ 截瘫 upper-part paraplegia

高屋建瓴 gāowūjiànlíng　sweep down irresistibly from a commanding height; operate from a strategically advantageous position

高消费 gāoxiāofèi　high or excessive

consumption：～社会 high consumption society

高效 gāoxiào　highly effective or efficient；～政府 highly efficient government／～肥料 concentrated fertilizer

高薪 gāoxīn　high salary or pay；～阶层 high-salaried stratum／～聘请 engage（sb）at a high salary

高兴 gāoxìng　❶ glad；happy；pleased；谈得很～ enjoy a conversation ❷ be willing or happy to：～干什么就干什么 do whatever one pleases

高压 gāoyā ❶〈电〉high tension or voltage：～线 high-tension line ❷〈理〉high pressure：～泵 high-pressure pump／～锅 also "压力锅" pressure cooker／～水龙 water cannon ❸〈医〉maximum pressure ❹ high-handed：～政策 high-handed policy

高雅 gāoyǎ　elegant and in good taste；refined and graceful

高音 gāoyīn〈乐〉high pitch（voice）：男～ tenor／女～ soprano／～喇叭 tweeter

高原 gāoyuán　plateau；highland；tableland；～冰川 plateau glacier／～反应 altitude reaction

高瞻远瞩 gāozhān-yuǎnzhǔ　stand high and see far；show great foresight；be farsighted：～的政治家 statesman of vision

高涨 gāozhǎng　rise；upsurge；run high；空前～ rise to an unprecedented height

高招 gāozhāo　also "高着儿"〈口〉clever move；brilliant idea；smart trick

高枕无忧 gāozhěnwúyōu　shake up the pillow and have a good sleep；sit back and relax

高姿态 gāozītài　take a lofty stance（showing tolerance and generosity）；be generous and tolerant

羔 gāo lamb；kid；fawn；产～ lambing；fawning／～皮 lambskin；kidskin；kid／～羊 lamb；kid；

innocent and helpless person

睾 gāo

睾丸 gāowán〈生理〉testis；testicle

膏 gāo ❶ fat；grease；oil；吸干～血 bleed（sb）white／～粱子弟 children of wealthy families ❷ paste；ointment；plaster；～剂 medicinal extract／贴～药 apply a plaster ❸ fertile

膏肓 gāohuāng　vital organs（of a body）：～之疾 disease that is beyond cure

篙 gāo punt-pole

糕（餻） gāo cake；pudding；～点 cake；pastry

gǎo

搞 gǎo ❶ do；go in for；make；～掉 do away with；get rid of；put out of the way／～定〈方〉fix；settle；wangle／～法 method or way of doing things／～对象（of a man and woman）go steady；date／～研究 do research／～小动作 play an underhand trick；hit sb under the belt／有一年头 have a point（in doing sth）；be worth doing ❷ make （sb）suffer；make things difficult for（sb）；fix（sb）❸ set up；start；organize／～（get hold of）scarce；wangle；～票 get tickets ❺（followed by a complement）produce a certain effect or result；cause to become；～臭 discredit；humiliate／～垮 get（sth）wrong；mistake（sth for sth else）；be mistaken／～笑〈方〉try to be amusing or entertaining／把人～糊涂 confuse people

搞鬼 gǎoguǐ　play tricks；scheme in secret；be up to mischief

搞好 gǎohǎo　do a good job of；do well；～关系 foster or cultivate good relations

搞活 gǎohuó　invigorate；enliven；rejuvenate；～市场 invigorate the market

搞通 gǎotōng　come to understand; grasp：～思想 straighten out one's ideas / ～基本道理 grasp the fundamentals

缟 gǎo ❶ thin white silk ❷ white：～素 white mourning dress

槁 gǎo withered：～木 withered or dead tree

镐 gǎo also "镐头" pick; pickaxe：丁字～ T-shaped pick / 十字～ pick; pickaxe; mattock

稿 gǎo draft; sketch; manuscript：约～ (of editors) make an arrangement in advance with sb for his contribution / ～费 also "稿酬" payment for an article or a book written; author's remuneration / ～件 manuscript; contribution / ～纸 squared or lined paper for making drafts or copying manuscripts / ～子 draft; manuscript; contribution

gào

告 gào ❶ tell; inform; report：～白 (issue a) public notice; profess; express / ～慰 comfort (the deceased); console (the bereft) / 无人～知。Nobody informed me of it. ❷ sue; accuse：～官 lodge a complaint (against sb) with the authorities ❸ ask for; request; solicit：～便 〈婉〉 excuse oneself / ～贷 also "告借" go and borrow money ❹ declare; announce：～病 beg off on account of illness / ～老还乡 〈旧〉 retire in one's old age and return to one's native place ❺ announce a result; declare a condition：～负 be defeated; lose / ～竣 (of work or project) be completed / ～破 (of a criminal case) be solved / ～罄 run out; be used up or exhausted / ～缺 be scarce; be in short supply / ～一段落 be completed for the time being

告别 gàobié ❶ take leave of; leave; part from ❷ bid farewell to; say goodbye to：～宴会 farewell banquet / 向遗体～ pay one's last respects to the deceased

告吹 gàochuī fizzle out; fall through; fail

告辞 gàocí take leave (of one's host)；就此～。I'm afraid I must be off now.

告发 gàofā inform against (sb to the police); accuse; denounce

告急 gàojí report an emergency; ask for emergency help; be in emergency or danger

告假 gàojià ask for leave：～一周 ask for a one-week leave

告捷 gàojié ❶ win victory; be victorious；首战～ win the first battle ❷ report a victory

告诫 gàojiè also "告戒" warn; exhort; admonish

告警 gàojǐng report an emergency; give or sound an alarm

告密 gàomì 〈贬〉 inform (on or against sb)：～者 informer

告饶 gàoráo beg for mercy; ask pardon

告扰 gàorǎo 〈套〉 disturb or bother sb：不敢～。I don't think I should be bothering you.

告示 gàoshi official notice; bulletin; (esp) slogan

告诉 gàosù ❶ accuse in court; sue (sb for sth) ❷ (gàosu) let know

告退 gàotuì ❶ ask for leave to withdraw from a meeting, etc ❷ resign (a position); withdraw (from an organization)

告终 gàozhōng come to an end; end up；以失败～ end in failure; come to grief at last

告状 gàozhuàng ❶ bring an action, a case, or a lawsuit (against sb) ❷ lodge a complaint against sb (with one's superior, etc)；向老师告同学的

状 complain to the teacher about one's fellow student

告罪 gàozuì 〈谦〉beg pardon; ask forgiveness; apologize

诰 gào imperial mandate: ～ 封 confer honorary titles by imperial mandate

锆 gào zirconium (Zr)

gē

戈 gē dagger-axe, an ancient weapon

戈壁 gēbì 〈地〉Gobi (Desert)

疙 gē

疙瘩 gēda also "疙疸" ❶ swelling on the skin; pimple; wart ❷ lump; knot: ～汤 dough drop soup ❸ knot in one's heart; hang-up

疙疙瘩瘩 gēge-dādā also "疙里疙瘩" ❶ knotty; thorny; hard ❷ not smooth; lumpy: 胃里～的 feel lumpy in the stomach

咯 see also kǎ; lo

咯噔 gēdēng also "格登"〈象声〉click; clump; thump: ～～的皮鞋声 clicking of leather shoes

咯吱 gēzhī 〈象声〉creak; groan: 地板踩得～～响。The floor creaked underfoot.

格 see also gé

格格 gēgē 〈象声〉❶ also "咯咯" (as a child) chuckle; giggle ❷ (of a machine-gun) rattle ❸ (of a hen, etc) cackle

哥 gē ❶ elder brother ❷ elder male cousin ❸ friendly way of addressing a male older than oneself or of about the same age: 张～ Brother Zhang

哥哥 gēge ❶ elder brother ❷ elder

male cousin

哥们儿 gēmenr also "哥儿们"〈口〉❶ brothers ❷ buddies; cronies; pals: 讲～义气 go by cronyism

胳(肐) gē

胳膊 gēbo also "胳臂" arm: ～肘子 elbow / ～拧不过大腿〈俗〉the arm is no match for the thigh — the weak cannot contend with the strong

鸽 gē (usu 鸽子) pigeon; dove

鸽派 gēpài 〈喻〉dove: ～观点 dovish view / ～人物 dove

搁 gē ❶ put; place; lay: 把东西～好 put things where they belong ❷ add; put in: 茶里～点糖。Put some sugar in the tea. ❸ put aside; leave over; shelve: ～笔 lay down the brush or pen; stop writing or painting see also gé

搁浅 gēqiǎn run aground; 〈喻〉become stranded; be at a deadlock

搁置 gēzhì shelve or put or lay aside; pigeonhole: ～脑后 put (sth) out of mind

割 gē cut; sever; mow: ～破 cut; gash; slash / ～弃 throw away; discard; part with / ～地赔款 cede territory and pay indemnities

割爱 gē'ài give up what one treasures; part with a valued or cherished possession

割断 gēduàn sever by cutting; cut off: ～联系 sever relations; break off ties / ～历史 garble (sth) out of the historical context

割据 gējù set up a separatist regime by force of arms; carve up a country and establish one's independent regime: 军阀～ separatist warlord rule

割裂 gēliè cut apart; sever; separate: 不可～ inseparable

割舍 gēshě give up or away; part with (sth): 忍痛～ give up reluctantly

歌 gē ❶ song：~本 songbook / ~词 words of a song；libretto (of an opera) / ~喉 singer's or singing voice / ~迷 fan (of a singer, etc) / ~谱 music of a song / ~曲 song / ~手 singer / ~坛 song circles / ~厅 song and karaoke hall / ~星 star singer；singing star / ~片儿 song sheet ❷ sing；chant：缓~慢舞 sing and dance gently

歌唱 gēchàng ❶ sing (a song)：~家 singer；vocalist ❷ sing the praises of；eulogize

歌剧 gējù opera：~团 opera troupe or company / ~院 opera house

歌声 gēshēng singing (voice)；vocal part in a performance

歌颂 gēsòng sing the praises of；extol；eulogize：歌功颂德 eulogize (sb's) virtues and achievements；sing the praises of (one's superior, etc)

歌舞 gēwǔ song and dance；singing and dancing：~剧 song and dance drama；musical / ~厅 song and dance hall / ~团 song and dance ensemble / ~升平 extol the good times by singing and dancing — put on a fake or an exaggerated show of peace and prosperity

歌谣 gēyáo ballad；folk song；nursery rhyme

歌咏 gēyǒng singing：~队 choir；chorus / ~比赛 singing contest

革 gé ❶ leather；hide：~履 leather shoes ❷ change；alter；transform：~故鼎新 abolish the old and introduce the new ❸ remove from office；expel；get rid of

革除 géchú ❶ abolish；get rid of；eliminate ❷ expel；dismiss；remove from office：~公职 expel from public service

革命 gémìng revolution：~化 revolutionize / ~家 also "革命者" revolutionary；revolutionist / ~性 revolutionary character or spirit / ~导师 teacher of revolution / ~圣地 sacred place of a revolution；cradle of revolution

革新 géxīn innovation；renovation：~思想 innovative ideas / ~者 innovator

革职 gézhí remove from office；cashier；dismiss：~查办 discharge sb from office and prosecute him or her

阁 gé ❶ traditional pavilion ❷ 〈旧〉 woman's chamber；boudoir：出~ (of a girl) get married ❸ cabinet；入~ become a cabinet minister / ~员 also "阁僚" member of a cabinet

阁楼 gélóu attic；garret；loft

阁下 géxià 〈敬〉 Your, His or Her Excellency：首相~ Your Excellency Mr Prime Minister；His or Her Excellency the Prime Minister

格 gé ❶ square；check ❷ standard；pattern；character：自成一~ have a style of one's own ❸ 〈语言〉 case：宾~ objective case ❹ 〈书〉 probe；delve into；study thoroughly：致 (short for 格物致知) study the world in order to gain knowledge ❺ fight；hit：~斗 grapple；wrestle；fistfight

see also gē

格调 gédiào ❶ (literary or artistic) style；ethos；quality：~优雅 (in) elegant style ❷ 〈书〉 one's style of work and moral quality：~高尚 of integrity and lofty ideals

格格不入 gégébùrù incompatible (with)；out of tune (with)

格局 géjú pattern；layout；setup：世界多极化的~ multi-polar structure of the world

格律 gélǜ rules and forms of classical poetic composition；poetical meter；rules for versification：~诗 poem with a strict tonal pattern and rhyme scheme

格杀勿论 géshāwùlùn kill on sight (without fear of prosecution); kill on the spot without mercy

格式 géshi form; pattern; 〈信息〉format

格外 géwài ❶ especially; particularly; all the more ❷ extra; additional

格言 géyán maxim; motto; aphorism

格子 gézi check; chequer; ～布 checked fabric; check / ～窗 lattice window

葛 gé ❶ (usu 葛麻) ko-hemp; kudzu ❷ poplin

搁 gé bear; stand; endure; ～不住 (of sb) can't bear; can't keep to oneself; (of sth) spoil easily *see also* gē

蛤 gé ❶ *also* "蛤蜊" clam ❷ *also* "蛤蚧" gecko
see also há

隔 gé ❶ separate; partition; stand or lie between; ～层 interlayer; partition / ～热〈建筑〉heat insulation; heat-proof / ～着一条河 be separated by a river ❷ at a distance or an interval; ～代遗传〈生理〉reversion; atavism / ～年黄历 calendar of the past year — sth outdated; yesterday's newspaper

隔岸观火 gé'ànguānhuǒ watch a fire from the other side of the river — look on at sb's trouble with indifference; show no concern for another's trouble

隔壁 gébì next door (to)

隔断 géduàn ❶ cut off; sever; separate ❷ (géduàn) *also* "隔扇" partition (wall, etc)

隔行 géháng ❶ of different professions or trades; ～如隔山〈俗〉Difference in profession makes one feel worlds apart. ❷ interlace; interleave; ～打印 (as in typing) double space

隔阂 géhé estrangement; barrier; misunderstanding

隔绝 géjué cut off completely; isolate; 与世～ be cut off from the outside world; live in seclusion

隔离 gélí ❶ separate; keep apart; segregate; ～层 separation layer / 被审查 be taken into custody and under investigation ❷ isolate (the sick, etc); quarantine; ～病房 isolation ward

隔膜 gémó ❶ lack of mutual understanding; estrangement; 感到～ feel alienated or estranged ❷ unfamiliar; not versed ❸ diaphragm

隔墙有耳 géqiángyǒu'ěr walls have ears; beware of eavesdroppers

隔日 gérì ❶ day after the next ❷ every other day

隔三差五 gésān-chàwǔ *also* "隔三岔五" every now and then; time and again

隔山 géshān relationship between siblings of different mothers; ～兄妹 half brothers and sisters (by the same father)

隔世 géshì be separated by a whole generation; belong in the remote past; 有～之感 feel as if a whole generation had elapsed

隔靴搔痒 géxuēsāoyǎng scratch an itch from outside one's boot — fail to strike home; do sth ineffective; be irrelevant

隔夜 géyè *also* "隔宿" of the previous night; last night; ～菜 last night's leftovers / 家无～粮。There is no food left for tomorrow in the house.

隔音 géyīn sound insulating; soundproof; ～室 soundproof room / ～符号〈语言〉syllable-dividing mark (')

嗝 gé ❶ belch ❷ hiccup; hiccough

槅 gé ❶ latticed door; partition board; lattice; ～扇 partition board ❷ set of shelves

膈 gé (usu 膈膜)〈生理〉diaphragm

镉

gé cadmium (Cd)

gè

个（個）

gè ❶ 〈量〉a) *used before a noun having no particular classifier*：一～西瓜 a watermelon b) *used after a verb and before an approximate figure*：来～一两趟 come once or twice c) *used between a verb and its object*：讨～吉利 invite luck d) *used between a verb and a complement*：看～仔细 have a careful look / 问～没完 keep asking questions ❷ individual：～例 particular or isolated case / ～展 individual exhibition (of paintings), etc；one-man show ❸ *as suffix to* 些：那么些～书呀！What a lot of books!

个案 gè'àn (individual or special) case：～处理 deal with (sth) on a case-to-case basis / ～研究 case study

个把 gèbǎ *also* "个把子" one or two；a couple or so：～月 a month or so；about a month

个别 gèbié ❶ individual；specific；particular：～差异 individual difference / ～谈话 private talk ❷ very few；exceptional：～情况 isolated or exceptional case

个个 gègè each and every one；all

个儿 gèr ❶ *also* "个头儿" size；build；stature：大～ big guy ❷ taken singly；each：挨～ one by one；by turn

个人 gèrén ❶ individual；personal：～电脑 personal computer (PC) / 简历 curriculum vitae (CV) / ～迷信 *also* "个人崇拜" personality cult；cult of the individual / ～密码 (in banking, etc) personal identification number (PIN) / ～隐私 privacy / ～主义 me-first mentality；egoism；(of philosophy) individualism / ～所得税 personal income tax ❷ (used on formal occasions to refer to oneself) I：～认为 in my view

个体 gètǐ ❶ individual：～户 individual or household engaged in small-scale business；small-scale privately-owned business / ～经济 individual economy / ～商贩 small retailer；pedlar / ～劳动者 self-employed labourer / ～经营执照 licence for an individually-run enterprise ❷ individual or household engaged in small-scale business：干～ run one's own business；be self-employed

个性 gèxìng individual character；personality；individuality：～很强 of strong character / ～解放 liberation of the self / ～化装饰 personalized decoration

个中 gèzhōng 〈书〉therein：～老手 expert in a given field；old hand；past master / ～缘由 the whys and wherefores (of sth)

个子 gèzi ❶ height；stature；build：不大个 of small stature；small ❷ bundle；bunch；bale

各

gè ❶ all；every；each or either：～半 half and half；fifty-fifty / ～不相让 neither is willing to yield；each is trying to excel the other / ～抒己见 each airs his or her own views；everyone speaks up / ～显神通 each shows his or her own prowess；each tries for all he or she is worth / ～有千秋 each has sth to recommend him or her；each has his or her own merits / ～有所好 each has his or her likes and dislikes；each follows his or her own bent / ～族人民 people of all nationalities ❷ various；different：～级政府 governments at various levels / ～界人士 personages of various circles；public figures from various walks of life

各奔前程 gèbènqiánchéng each pursues his or her own course；each goes his or her own way

各别 gèbié ❶ distinct；different：～对待 treat differently；treat each on its own merits ❷〈方〉out of the ordinary; unusual; novel ❸〈贬〉odd; freakish; eccentric

各持己见 gèchíjǐjiàn　also "各执己见" each sticks to his or her own view; each sticks to his or her guns

各打五十大板 gèdǎwǔshídàbǎn　〈俗〉blame both sides without discrimination; punish the innocent and the guilty alike

各得其所 gèdéqísuǒ　each is in his or her proper place; each is properly provided for; each has a role to play

各个 gègè　❶ each; every; various ❷ one by one; separately; ～击破 crush or tackle one by one; divide and conquer

各…各… gè…gè…　❶ each… his or her own …; 各就各位〈军〉man your posts;〈体〉on your marks? ❷ all kinds of; all; 各行各业 all walks of life; all trades and professions / 各式各样 all kinds

各尽所能 gèjìnsuǒnéng　from each according to his ability; let each do his or her best; ～，按劳分配 from each according to his ability, to each according to his work

各取所需 gèqǔsuǒxū　each takes what he or she needs; 对法律断章取义、～ garble the laws and bend them to one's own use

各色 gèsè　of all kinds; of every description; assorted; ～服装 clothes of all styles

各位 gèwèi　❶ (as a term of address) everybody; ～请入坐。Be seated please, everybody. ❷ every; ～女士、～先生 ladies and gentlemen

各行其是 gèxíngqíshì　each does what he or she thinks is right; each goes his or her own way

各自 gèzì　each; respective; individual; ～为政 each administers his or her affairs (regardless of the overall interest); each does things in his or her own

way / 根据他们～的需要 according to their respective needs

圪 gē

圪蚤 gēzao　flea

硌 gè

gè　(of sth hard or bulging) press or rub against; ～牙 (of vegetables, etc) taste gritty

铬 gè

also "克罗米" 〈化〉chromium (Cr)

gěi

给 gěi

gěi　❶ give; present; grant; ～出路 give or grant (sb) a way out / ～脸不要脸 be fool enough to reject a face-saving offer / ～人颜色看 make it hot for sb; show or tell sb a thing or two ❷ *used to introduce* a) *object or target of an action*; ～人看孩子 babysit for sb b) *agent of an action*; 衣服～雨淋湿了。The clothes got wet in the rain. ❸〈助〉*used directly before the verb of a passive sentence, etc, to show emphasis*; 茶杯叫他～摔碎了。The cup was broken by him.
see also jǐ

给面子 gěi miànzi　save (sb's) face; do (sb) a favour

给以 gěiyǐ　(interchangeable with 给予 except when an indirect object is inserted between 给 and 以) give; allow; grant; ～适当照顾 show due consideration (for sb) / 给敌人以沉重的打击 deal the enemy a heavy blow

gēn

根 gēn

gēn　❶ root (of a plant); ～雕 tree-root carving / ～蔓 root and stem; cause; origin / ～系〈植〉root system / ～深叶茂 have deep roots and thick foliage — be well established and flourishing ❷ offspring; progeny; 独儿 only son of a family ❸ root; foot;

base：齿～ root of a tooth / 城墙～儿 foot of a city wall ❹ cause；origin；root：寻～ trace or seek one's (family) roots ❺ foundation；basis：无～之谈 groundless talk；sheer nonsense ❻ thoroughly；completely；entirely：～究 make a thorough investigation of；get to the bottom of ❼〈量〉*used for sth long and thin*：几～头发 several strands of hair ❽〈数〉(short for 方根) root：～号 radical sign /～式 radical (expression) ❾〈化〉radical：酸～ acid radical

根本 gēnběn ❶ source；base；foundation：从～上解决问题 tackle a problem at its roots；solve a problem once and for all ❷ basic；fundamental；essential；cardinal：～法 fundamental or basic law；constitution /～原因 basic reason；root cause ❸ (often used in the negative) at all；ever：～没说过这种话 never make such remarks ❹ thoroughly

根除 gēnchú *also* "根绝" root or stamp out；eradicate：～腐败 stamp out or eradicate corruption

根底 gēndǐ ❶ foundation；groundwork：～好 have a solid foundation；be well-grounded (in sth) ❷ what lies at the bottom or back of sth；origin；cause

根基 gēnjī ❶ foundation；groundwork；basis：打好～ build up or lay a solid foundation ❷〈喻〉property，resources，etc，as foundation for a family，enterprise，etc

根据 gēnjù ❶ on the basis of；according to；in the light of：～同样理由 for the same reason；by the same token ❷ basis；grounds；foundation：～地 base (area) / 没有科学～ be devoid of scientific basis

根苗 gēnmiáo ❶ root and shoot；〈喻〉source；root ❷ (male) offspring；posterity；progeny

根深蒂固 gēnshēn-dìgù *also* "根深柢固" deep-rooted；ingrained；firmly established

根由 gēnyóu cause；origin；问个～ ask about the whys and wherefores (of sth)

根源 gēnyuán ❶ source；cause；root ❷ originate；stem：～于传统文化 stem or come from traditional culture

根治 gēnzhì effect a radical cure；cure once and for all；bring under permanent control

根子 gēnzi〈口〉❶ root (of a plant)：～扎得很深 be deep-rooted；strike deep roots ❷ source；origin；root

跟 gēn ❶ heel ❷ follow：～风 (贬) follow the trend or vogue (blindly) /～进 follow up；follow suit /～形势 keep abreast of the current situation ❸ (of a woman) marry sb ❹ *used to introduce* a) *orientation or target of an action*：～人打听事 ask sb about sth b) *object of comparison*：～你一般高 as tall as you ❺〈连〉*used to join two or more items*：一楼～三楼 first and third floors

跟班 gēnbān ❶ join a regular shift or class；work with a group，team or class：～听课 audit a class ❷ *also* "跟班的"；"跟差"〈旧〉footman；attendant

跟脚 gēnjiǎo〈方〉❶ (of shoes) fit well ❷ close upon sb's heels：我刚进门，他～儿就来了。He came to see me the moment I got home.

跟前 gēnqián ❶ in front of；close to；near：请你到我～来。Please come over here. ❷ just before：新年～ shortly before New Year's Day ❸ (gēnqian) (of one's children) living with one：孩子们都不在她～。None of her children lives with her.

跟上 gēnshàng ❶ keep pace with；catch up with：跟不上形势 fail to keep up with the times; fall behind the times ❷ be as good as; can be compared with：他的身高都赶得上他哥哥了。He is as tall as his elder brother.

跟随 gēnsuí follow; come or go after

跟头 gēntou *also* "跟斗"；"筋斗" somersault; fall；〈喻〉setback：翻～ do a somersault / 栽了～ have a setback

跟着 gēnzhe ❶ follow；～感觉走 follow one's hunch ❷ following; right after：一到家～就做饭 start cooking as soon as one comes back home

跟踪 gēnzōng track; tail；电子～ electronic tracking / ～调查 follow-up investigation / ～追击 pursue and attack; go in hot pursuit

gěn

艮 gěn 〈方〉❶ (of character or speech) brusque; blunt; stiff ❷ (of food) not crisp; tough; hard：发～ taste tough and leathery

gèn

亘(亙) gèn extend; stretch; span：～古及今 from time immemorial down to the present day

gēng

更 gēng ❶ change; alter; replace：～迭 change; alternate / ～番 alternately; by turns / ～名改姓 change both one's given name and surname; change one's name? ❷〈书〉experience：～事不多 inexperienced ❸〈旧〉one of the five two-hour periods into which the night was divided; watch：～夫 night watchman / ～深人静 *also* "更阑人静" all is quiet in the

dead of night
see also gèng

更动 gēngdòng change; modify; alter：人事～ personnel changes

更改 gēnggǎi change; alter：～路线 change a route / 无法～的事实 unalterable fact

更换 gēnghuàn change; replace; renew；～零件 renew or replace parts

更年期 gēngniánqī 〈生理〉climacteric; menopause

更替 gēngtì interchange; alternate; replace；季节～ change of seasons

更新 gēngxīn renew; update; replace：设备～ updating of equipment / ～换代 replace the old by the new; upgrade

更衣 gēngyī ❶ change one's clothes：～室 locker room; changeroom ❷〈婉〉go to the lavatory

更正 gēngzhèng emend; make corrections

庚 gēng ❶ 7th of the Heavenly Stems *see also* "干支" gānzhī ❷ age：同～ be of the same age

耕 gēng ❶ plough; till; cultivate：～畜 farm or draught animal / ～具 tillage implement; farmtool / ～者有其田 land to the tiller ❷ work (for a living); do：笔～ make a living by writing

耕地 gēngdì ❶ *also* "耕田" plough; till ❷ cultivated land；可～ arable land / ～面积 area under cultivation; cultivated area

耕耘 gēngyún plough and weed; cultivate

耕种 gēngzhòng plough and sow; till; cultivate

耕作 gēngzuò till; cultivate; farm：～技术 farming technique / ～制度 cropping system

羹 gēng thick soup; custard：～匙 soup spoon; tablespoon / ～汤 thick soup; broth

gěng

埂 gěng ❶ low earth dike, embankment or bank；田～子 low bank of earth between fields；ridge ❷ long, narrow mound；ridge

耿 gěng honest and just；upright；～介〈书〉honest and straightforward；upright

耿耿 gěnggěng ❶ devoted；staunch；dedicated ❷ have on one's mind；be troubled：～于怀 nurse a grievance；smoulder with resentment

耿直 gěngzhí also "梗直"；"鲠直" honest and frank；candid and outspoken；upright

哽 gěng ❶ choke：吃饭～着了 choke over food ❷ choke with emotion；feel a lump in one's throat；～咽 also "哽噎"；"梗咽" choke with sobs／喉头～塞 feel a lump in one's throat

梗 gěng ❶ stalk；stem ❷ straighten；stiffen；hold stiff；～着脖子一句话也不说 stiffen one's neck without saying a word ❸ straightforward；frank ❹ hinder；obstruct；block

梗概 gěnggài broad outline；gist；synopsis；～电影 synopsis of a film

梗塞 gěngsè ❶ block；obstruct；clog：河道～ clogging of a river course ❷ also "梗死"〈医〉infarction

梗阻 gěngzǔ ❶ block；obstruct；hinder ❷〈医〉obstruction：肠～ intestinal obstruction

鲠 gěng ❶〈书〉fishbone ❷ (of a fishbone) get caught in one's throat

gèng

更 gèng〈副〉❶ (even) more；still more：～加容易 even easier／

～其如此〈书〉even more so／～高、～快、～强 swifter, higher and stronger ❷〈书〉in addition；furthermore：～胜一筹 go one better；be a cut above (sb)／～有甚者 what is more／～上一层楼 scale new heights；attain yet better results

see also gēng

gōng

工 gōng ❶ worker；labourer；working class：～潮 labour unrest；strike movement／～会 trade or labour union／～匠 craftsman；artisan／～头 foreman；overseer／～运 (short for 工人运动) workers' or labour movement／～贼 scab；blackleg／～长 section chief (in a workshop, etc)；foreman ❷ work；labour；construction：～场 (usu of handicrafts) workshop／～地 building or construction site／～棚 builders' temporary shed；work shed／～效 work efficiency／～序 working procedure；process／～种 (as in a factory) type of work；kind of job ❸ man-day ❹ industry：～矿企业 industrial and mining enterprises ❺ (delicate) skill；(exquisite) craftsmanship；(excellent) workmanship：～画 (traditional) painting made with fine, delicate strokes；meticulous traditional painting ❻ be expert or versed in；be good at：～诗善画 be well versed in painting and poetry／～于心计 be adept at scheming；be very calculating

工本 gōngběn labour and other costs；expense (of production)：～费 cost of production

工兵 gōngbīng also "工程兵" (army) engineer；engineering corps：～连 engineer company

工厂 gōngchǎng factory；plant；works

工程 gōngchéng ❶ engineering; construction；～队 construction team or brigade / ～师 engineer ❷ project; programme

工读 gōngdú ❶ study through work; work one's way through school ❷ education for juvenile delinquents：～生 juvenile delinquent enrolled in a reform school / ～学校 reformatory for juvenile delinquents; reform school

工夫 gōngfu ❶ time；费～ time-consuming / 白花～ sheer waste of time ❷ free or spare time; leisure：有～吗? Are you free? ❸ also "功夫" skill; workmanship：诗画都有～ be accomplished in both poetry and painting

工具 gōngjù tool; implement; instrument：交际的～ means of communication / ～袋 kit bag; workbag / ～房 tool storeroom; toolhouse / ～书 reference book; dictionary

工科 gōngkē engineering (course)：～大学 engineering university

工力 gōnglì ❶ expertise; skill; craftsmanship：颇见～ display much skill; show the hand of an expert / ～悉敌〈书〉be matched in expertise ❷ manpower (for a project, etc); labour

工料 gōngliào ❶ labour and materials (for sth)：～成本 flat cost ❷ materials for a construction project

工龄 gōnglíng length of service; standing; seniority：～工资 pay based on years of service; seniority pay / ～津贴 seniority allowance / 有十年～的工人 worker of ten years' standing

工农 gōngnóng ❶ workers and peasants：～大众 the broad masses of workers and peasants / ～联盟 alliance of workers and peasants; worker-peasant alliance ❷ industry and agriculture：～差别 difference between industry and agriculture / ～业总产值 gross output value of industry and agriculture

工期 gōngqī time limit, schedule or deadline for a project：延误～ be behind schedule / ～定为两年 be scheduled to be completed in two years

工钱 gōngqian ❶ money paid for an odd job; charge for a service：做条裙子要多少～? How much does it cost to have a skirt made? ❷〈口〉wages; pay

工人 gōngrén worker; working man; workman：～贵族 labour aristocracy / ～阶级 working class

工伤 gōngshāng injury suffered on the job; industrial injury：～事故 industrial accident

工商 gōngshāng industry and commerce; business：～界 industrial and commercial circles; business community / ～局 (short for 工商行政管理局) administrative bureau for industry and commerce / ～联 (short for 工商业联合会) association of industry and commerce / ～业 industry and commerce / ～管理 business administration; business (management)

工事 gōngshì fortifications; defence works

工薪 gōngxīn salary; wages; pay：～阶层 also "工薪族" salaried workers; wage-earners

工休 gōngxiū ❶ (have a) holiday：～日 day off; holiday ❷ (work) break

工业 gōngyè industry：～国 industrial or industrialized country / ～化 industrialization / ～园 also "工业园区" industrial park

工艺 gōngyì ❶ technology：～流程 technological process ❷ craft; handicraft：～品 handicraft (article); handiwork / ～美术 industrial art; arts and crafts

工余 gōngyú spare time; after-hours; leisure

工整 gōngzhěng orderly; neat：字迹～ neatly lettered

工资 gōngzī wages; salary; pay：～表 payroll; pay sheet / ～级别 (grade in the) wage scale / ～外收入 extra-wage income

工作 gōngzuò work; job; task; ～餐 working meal / ～服 work clothes; boiler suit / ～狂 workaholic / ～量 amount of work; workload / ～日 working day; workday / ～站〈信息〉workstation / ～证 employee's card; ID card / ～表现 (work) performance / ～单位 work unit / ～人员 working personnel; staff member / ～语言 working language / ～作风 style of work; work style / ～许可证 work permit

弓 gōng ❶ bow; anything bow-shaped; ～箭 bow and arrow / ～弦 bowstring / 小提琴～ bow of a violin ❷ bend; arch; bow; ～腰驼背 hunchbacked

公 gōng ❶ public; state-owned; official; ～干 (official) business / ～函 official letter or correspondence / ～休 also "公休日" official or public holiday / ～债 public or government bonds / ～章 official seal / ～而忘私 be selfless ❷ common; public; general; ～厕 public convenience; lavatory or restroom / ～敌 public enemy / ～愤 public indignation; popular anger / ～筷 serving chopsticks / ～墓 cemetery / ～演 (of a play) perform in public; give a performance / ～映 (of a film) be shown to the public / 是非自有～论。Public opinion is the best judge. ❸ international; metric; ～尺 also "米" metre (m) / ～斤 kilogram (kg); kilo / ～里 kilometre (km) / ～顷 hectare (ha) / ～制 metric system ❹ make public; ～之于世 make public; publicize / ～诸同好 share enjoyment with, or show sth to people of similar taste ❺ equitable; impartial; fair; ～断 arbitrate; make an impartial judgement ❻ public affairs; official business; 因～致残 be disabled by work-related injury ❼ duke; 大～ grand duke / ～国 duchy; dukedom; principality / ～爵 duke ❽ *respectful term of address for an elderly or senior man;* 万～ revered Mr Wan / 诸～请坐。Will you gentlemen please be seated? ❾ husband's father; father-in-law; ～婆 husband's father and mother; parents-in-law ❿ (of animals) male; ～鸡 cock; rooster

公安 gōng'ān public security; ～机关 public security organ or agency / ～人员 public security officer

公案 gōng'àn complicated legal case; controversial issue; mystery; 无头～ intricate case without a clue

公报 gōngbào communiqué; bulletin

公报私仇 gōngbàosīchóu *also* "官报私仇" avenge a personal wrong in the name of public interests; abuse one's official position to punish sb for a private grudge

公布 gōngbù make public; promulgate; issue; ～法令 promulgate laws and decrees / ～名单 publish a name list

公差 gōngchāi public errand; official business; 出～ go on official business

公道 gōngdào ❶ justice; 讨个～ demand justice / 主持～ uphold justice ❷ (gōngdao) fair; evenhanded; reasonable; ～话 impartial or just remarks

公德 gōngdé public morality; social ethics; 讲～ have a strong sense of public morality

公费 gōngfèi at public or state expense; ～旅游 go on a sightseeing tour at public expense; be off on a junket / ～留学 study abroad on a government scholarship / ～医疗 free medical care; public health service

公告 gōnggào public notice; announcement; proclamation; ～栏 bulletin board

公共 gōnggòng public; common; communal; ～课 common required course (at a college) / ～财产 public property / ～场所 public places / ～汽车 (public) bus / ～秩序 public order

公公 gōnggong ❶ husband's father; father-in-law ❷ *reverent term of address for an elderly man*

公关 gōngguān （short for 公共关系） public relations (PR)；～部门 public relations department / ～手法 public relations ploy / ～小姐 public relations girl or lady

公馆 gōngguǎn residence (of a rich or important person)；mansion

公海 gōnghǎi high seas；open sea；～自由 freedom of the high seas

公害 gōnghài public hazard, plague or scourge；无 ～ 食品 pollution-free food

公积金 gōngjījīn accumulation fund；public reserve fund

公家 gōngjia 〈口〉 the state, public, organization or enterprise：爱护～的东西 take good care of public property

公检法 gōngjiǎnfǎ public security organs, procuratorial organs and people's courts；law-enforcing departments

公交 gōngjiāo （short for 公共交通） public transport or transit；～路线 public transport route

公开 gōngkāi ❶ open；overt；public；～化 make public；come out into the open / ～赛〈体〉 open (tournament) / ～信 open letter / ～性 openness；transparency / ～发表 publish / ～露面 appear in public / ～招标 (invite) public bidding ❷ make public；make known to the public / ～内幕 divulge an inside story / ～账目 make an account known to the public

公款 gōngkuǎn public money or fund；～宴请 wine and dine at public expense

公理 gōnglǐ axiom；self-evident truth；justice

公历 gōnglì ❶ Gregorian calendar ❷ see "公元"

公了 gōngliǎo settle according to law or policy；～还是私了 settle in court or out of it

公路 gōnglù highway；road；～桥 highway bridge

公民 gōngmín citizen；～ 权 civil rights；citizenship / ～投票 (shortened as 公投) referendum；plebiscite / ～意识 awareness of the obligations of a citizen

公平 gōngpíng fair；evenhanded；equitable；～秤 fair scales (used in a market as standard scales) / ～地说 to be fair；in all fairness / ～交易 fair deal

公仆 gōngpú public servant；～意识 right attitude of a public servant

公然 gōngrán 〈贬〉openly；flagrantly；brazenly

公认 gōngrèn generally acknowledged；universally accepted；established

公社 gōngshè commune；原始 ～ primitive commune

公审 gōngshěn 〈法〉 public or open trial；～大会 public trial rally / ～战犯 try war criminals in public

公使 gōngshǐ minister；～馆 legation / ～衔参赞 minister-counsellor

公式 gōngshì formula；～化 (as in art and literature) formulistic；stereotyped

公事 gōngshì public affairs；official business or duties；～公办 discharge official duties strictly according to rules；not let personal considerations interfere with execution of public duties

公司 gōngsī company；corporation；firm；～ 法 corporation or corporate law / ～标识 corporate logo

公私 gōngsī public and private (interests)；～分明 be scrupulous in separating public from private interests / ～合营 joint state-private ownership / ～兼顾 take both public and private interests into consideration；do sth private on the side while discharging official business

公诉 gōngsù 〈法〉(public) prosecution：提起～ bring a public charge；institute prosecution / ～人 public prosecutor；the prosecution / ～书 bill of indictment or prosecution；public indictment

公堂 gōngtáng law court；tribunal；私设～ set up a clandestine tribunal or a kangaroo court

公文 gōngwén official document：～包 briefcase；portfolio / ～旅行 travel of documents；red tape

公务 gōngwù public service；official business or affairs：～护照 service passport

公务员 gōngwùyuán ❶ orderly ❷ public or civil servant；civil service：～考试 civil service examination / ～考绩制 merit system

公心 gōngxīn ❶ fair-mindedness ❷ public spirit；selflessness

公益 gōngyì public good or welfare：热心～ public-spirited / ～金 public welfare fund / ～劳动 volunteer labour / ～事业 public service；welfare undertaking

公用 gōngyòng for public use；common：～电话 public telephone；pay phone / ～事业 (public) utilities

公有 gōngyǒu publicly owned：～制 public ownership (of means of production) / ～土地 public land

公寓 gōngyù flat；apartment (house)：～大楼 apartment building / 外交～ diplomatic compound

公元 gōngyuán Common Era；Christian era；AD：～前 206 年至～220 年 206 BC to 220 AD

公园 gōngyuán park：国家～ national park

公约 gōngyuē ❶ convention；pact；covenant ❷ joint pledge：治安～ public security pledge (for a neighbourhood)

公允 gōngyǔn impartial；even-handed；

fair and equitable：持论～ be just and fair in one's argument

公正 gōngzhèng fair；just；impartial：～待遇 equitable treatment；fair play or deal

公证 gōngzhèng notarize；attest：～处 notary office / ～费 notarial fee / ～人 notary (public) (NP) / ～书 notarial certificate or document

公职 gōngzhí government office；official post；public employment：担任～ hold a public office / ～人员 government employee；public servant

公众 gōngzhòng the public：～集会 public rally or gathering / ～领袖 leader of the public or community / ～舆论 public opinion

公主 gōngzhǔ princess：长～ princess royal

公转 gōngzhuàn 〈天文〉revolution：～周期 period of revolution

公子 gōngzǐ son of a prince or high official；〈敬〉sb's son：～哥儿 pampered son of a wealthy or influential family；dandy

功 gōng ❶ meritorious service or deed；merit；achievement：～臣 person who has rendered outstanding service；hero / ～过 merits and demerits / ～勋 exploit；feat；meritorious service / ～业 exploits；feats；achievements ❷ effect；result；success：～效 efficacy；efficiency；effect / ～用 function；use ❸ effort；skill；qigong or qi-energy：～力 skill；ability；efficacy / ～到自然成.〈俗〉Constant effort yields sure success. ❹〈理〉work；机械～ mechanical work

功败垂成 gōngbàichuíchéng fail on the verge of success；suffer defeat when victory is within one's grasp

功成 gōngchéng (used in certain phrases) achieve success；be successful：～名就 win success and recognition；be successful and famous：～身

退 retire after achieving success; withdraw from public life when one's work is done

功德 gōngdé　merits and virtues; beneficence; good deeds or works: ～无量 boundless beneficence; great service / ～圆满 achieve perfect virtues and merits; come to a successful conclusion

功底 gōngdǐ　basic training; foundation: ～扎实 have a solid grounding or foundation (in sth)

功夫 gōngfu　❶ skill; workmanship; kung fu: ～茶 kung fu tea (a kind of black tea) / ～片 kung fu film; action movie / ～不负苦心人. Those who work hard will be rewarded. ❷ see "工夫" gōngfu

功绩 gōngjì　merits and achievements; meritorious deed or service; contribution

功课 gōngkè　❶ schoolwork; lesson; course: 复习～ review one's lessons / 门门～都优秀 get straight A's for all the courses ❷ homework: 做～ do one's homework

功亏一篑 gōngkuīyīkuì　fall short of success for lack of a final effort

功劳 gōngláo　contribution; meritorious service; credit: ～簿 record of merits

功利 gōnglì　❶ utility; efficacy; use: ～婚姻 marriage of convenience / ～主义 utilitarianism ❷ official position and material gain; fame and wealth

功率 gōnglǜ　〈理〉power; capacity; output: ～输出 output rating; rated output / 大～发动机 large capacity motor

功名 gōngmíng　〈旧〉scholarly honour and official rank: ～利禄 official position and wealth; rank, fame and fortune

功能 gōngnéng　function: 语法～ grammatical function / ～性疾病 functional disease / 肾～正常. The kidneys function normally.

攻 gōng　❶ attack; assault; take the offensive: ～打 attack; assault / ～破 break through; breach; capture / ～取 also "攻占" attack and seize; storm and capture / ～陷 also "攻下" capture; seize / 全～型选手 all-out attack player ❷ accuse; refute; charge: ～人之短 attack sb at his or her weakest point / ～其一点, 不及其余 seize upon one point and ignore all others; attack sb for a single fault without considering other aspects ❸ study; specialize in: 专～法学 specialize or major in jurisprudence

攻读 gōngdú　❶ study assiduously; work diligently: ～博士学位 work for a doctorate ❷ specialize or major in; read: ～地质学 major in or read geology

攻关 gōngguān　storm a strategic pass; 〈喻〉tackle a key problem or project: ～成果 result obtained in tackling a key problem / ～小组 task team

攻击 gōngjī　❶ attack; assault; launch an offensive ❷ accuse; vilify; attack: ～性广告 attack advertisement

攻坚 gōngjiān　storm fortifications; assault fortified positions; 〈喻〉tackle a thorny problem: ～战 storming of heavily fortified positions / ～部队 assault troops

攻克 gōngkè　capture; seize; take: ～难关 surmount a great obstacle; solve a thorny problem / 攻无不克 carry everything before one; be all-conquering or ever-victorious

攻势 gōngshì　offensive; offence: 发动～ launch an offensive / 宣传～ publicity campaign

攻守 gōngshǒu　offence and defence; offensive and defensive: ～同盟 offensive and defensive alliance; 〈喻〉agreement (as between partners in crime) not to give each other away; pact or pledge to shield each other

攻其不备 gōngqíbùbèi　strike where

or when the enemy is unprepared; take sb by surprise; catch sb unawares: 出其不意, ~。 Do the unexpected; attack the unprepared.

攻心 gōngxīn mount a psychological attack; try to win over: 政策 ~ try to win sb over, or persuade sb to confess by 'explaining the Party's policy' / ~ 战 psychological warfare; war of nerves

供 gōng supply; furnish; provide: ~ 稿 contribute (an article, etc) / ~ 不应求 supply falls short of demand; be in short supply / ~ 电系统 power supply system; power network / ~ 孤儿上学 provide for the education of an orphan

see also gòng

供给 gōngjǐ supply; provide; furnish: ~ 制 supply system — an equalitarian system of payment in kind

供求 gōngqiú *also* "供需" supply and demand: ~ 规律 law of supply and demand / ~ 平衡 balance between supply and demand

供销 gōngxiāo supply and marketing: ~ 合作社 *also* "供销社" supply and marketing cooperative

供养 gōngyǎng provide for (one's parents or elders); support

供应 gōngyìng supply; provide: ~ 舰 (船) depot or supply ship; tender / ~ 线 supply line / ~ 充足 be in abundant supply

宫 gōng ❶ palace; anything compared to a palace: ~ 灯 palace lantern / ~ 殿 palace / ~ 女 *also* "宫娥" maid in an imperial palace; maid-in-waiting ❷ place for cultural activities and recreation: 少年 ~ children's palace ❸ 〈生理〉 womb; uterus: ~ 颈 uterine neck / ~ 外孕 〈医〉 ectopic or extrauterine pregnancy

宫廷 gōngtíng imperial palace; royal or imperial court: ~ 侍卫 imperial

bodyguard / ~ 政变 palace revolution or coup

宫刑 gōngxíng 〈史〉 castration (as punishment)

恭 gōng respectful; courteous; reverent: ~ 候 await respectfully / ~ 谨 respectful and cautious / ~ 顺 respectful and submissive / ~ 请光临。 Your company is respectfully requested.

恭贺 gōnghè congratulate: ~ 新禧。 Happy New Year!

恭敬 gōngjìng respectfully; with great respect: ~ 不如从命。 The best way to show respect is to do as you say.

恭维 gōngwei *also* "恭惟" flatter; compliment: ~ 话 flattering remarks; compliments / 不敢 ~ 〈套〉 have no compliments (for); beg to differ (from)

恭喜 gōngxǐ 〈套〉 congratulate: ~ 发财! May you be prosperous!

躬 gōng ❶ oneself; in person; personally: ~ 逢其盛 〈书〉 be present on the grand occasion in person; live in times of prosperity ❷ bend forward; bow; stoop: ~ 身下拜 bow down and worship; bend the knee in obeisance

觥 gōng 〈史〉 wine vessel made of bronze: ~ 筹交错 wine cups and gaming chips lie about in disarray; wine and dine

gǒng

巩(鞏) gǒng

巩固 gǒnggù consolidate; strengthen; solidify: ~ 国防 consolidate national defence / ~ 安定团结的局面 further enhance stability and unity

汞 gǒng *also* "水银" 〈化〉 mercury (Hg)

拱 gǒng ❶ cup one hand in the other before the chest (as a form of salutation) ❷ encompass; encircle; surround：～卫 surround and protect; defend or guard on all sides ❸ arch; hump or raise back：猫把身子～了一。The cat arched its back. ❹ arch：～门 arched door / ～桥 arch bridge / ～券〈建筑〉arch ❺ (of people) push with one's body; (of pigs, etc) dig with the snout; (of shoots, etc) sprout up

拱手 gǒngshǒu fold one's hands in a bow; make an obeisance by cupping one hand in the other before one's chest：～称谢 join one's hands together in salute to express one's thanks / ～让人 give up submissively; hand over on a silver platter

gòng

共 gòng ❶ common; general; universal：～通 universal; applicable to all; common / ～性 general character; generality / 用天线 common antenna ❷ share; do the same thing; do together：～度 spend or pass (time) together; celebrate (a festival) together / ～勉 encourage each other (in sth); make joint efforts / ～患难 go through hardships together / ～担风险 share risks / ～赴国难 unite to meet a national crisis ❸ altogether; in all; all told：～盈利 50 万元 make a total profit of 500,000 yuan ❹ short for 共产党 or 共产主义：中～ CPC (Communist Party of China) / ～运 communist movement / ～青团 Communist Youth League

共产党 gòngchǎndǎng Communist Party：～员 member of the Communist Party; Communist

共产主义 gòngchǎnzhǔyì communism：～者 communist

共处 gòngchǔ coexist：和睦～ live in

harmony / 难以～ hard to get along with

共和 gònghé republicanism; republic：～党 (US) Republican Party / ～国 republic / ～制 republicanism

共计 gòngjì total; amount to; add up to

共鸣 gòngmíng ❶〈理〉resonance ❷ sympathetic response：引起～ arouse sympathy; strike a ready chord; get a ready response

共识 gòngshí common understanding; consensus：达成～ reach consensus

共事 gòngshì work together; be fellow workers：易于～ easy to work with

共同 gòngtóng common; shared; joint：～体 community / ～被告 joint defendant; co-defendant / ～富裕 common prosperity / ～语言 common language / ～主持会议 co-chair a meeting

共享 gòngxiǎng enjoy together; share

贡 gòng tribute：～赋 also "贡税" tribute and taxes / ～酒 tribute wine; fine quality wine / ～品 (article of) tribute

贡献 gòngxiàn contribute; dedicate; devote：重大～ important contribution (to) / ～一份力量 do one's bit (for sth)

供 gòng ❶ worship; lay (offerings)：～佛 enshrine and worship Buddha's statue ❷ offerings：～案 also "供桌" altar (table) / ～品 offerings ❸ confess; admit; own up：～称 confess; own up; admit / ～词 confession / ～状 written confession; deposition / ～出犯罪事实 admit to the details of a crime
see also gōng

供奉 gòngfèng enshrine and worship; consecrate

供认 gòngrèn confess：～不讳 confess without hiding anything; candidly confess

供职 gòngzhí hold office：在市政府～

work in the city government

gōu

勾 gōu ❶ tick off; check; cross or strike out:～出正确答案 tick off or check the correct answer ❷ delineate; sketch; draw:～脸 (in traditional opera) make up or paint the face ❸ evoke; call to mind:～动食欲 arouse or whet one's appetite / ～起伤心事 evoke memories of past miseries ❹ entice; inveigle; collude with:～魂慑魄 (of a woman) bewitch; cast a spell (on sb) ❺ mix; blend:～兑 mix or blend (different types of wine) / ～芡 thicken (soup, etc) with starch *see also* gòu

勾搭 gōuda ❶ gang up with; be in collusion or work hand in glove with ❷ seduce; carry on (an affair) with

勾画 gōuhuà *also* "勾描" draw; delineate; sketch:～蓝图 (喻) draw or paint a blueprint (for the future, etc)

勾结 gōujié collude or collaborate with; gang up with

勾勒 gōulè delineate; draw (the outline of sth); sketch (the contours of sth)

勾通 gōutōng collude; work hand in glove:～作弊 work together to cheat (in an exam, etc)

勾销 gōuxiāo cancel; write off; strike out:～债款 cancel a debt / ～宿怨 sink a feud; bury the hatchet

勾心斗角 gōuxīndòujiǎo *see* "钩心斗角" gōuxīndòujiǎo

勾引 gōuyǐn ❶ *see* "勾结" ❷ entice; seduce; lure ❸ induce; evoke; call to mind

gōu

佝 gōu

佝偻 gōulóu with arched shoulder and back:～病 rickets / ～着背 arch one's back; be hunchbacked

沟(溝) gōu ❶ ditch; drain; trench; ～渠 irrigation canals and ditches ❷ rut; furrow; gully:～壑纵横 crisscrossed by gullies and ravines / 划了一道～子 have a long, deep scratch

沟沟坎坎 gōugōu-kǎnkǎn 〈口〉setback; reverse:人生的～ vicissitudes of life

沟通 gōutōng link up; connect; join:～南北 (of a railway, etc) connect the south and the north / ～思想 exchange ideas; compare notes

钩(鈎) gōu ❶ hook; sth like a hook:打～ tick off; check / ～虫病 hookworm disease ❷ hook stroke (in Chinese characters) ❸ secure (as) with a hook; hook:～背 bend arms round each other's shoulders ❹ explore; search after:～深致远 seek profound truths or meanings ❺ crochet:～针 *also* "勾针" crochet hook ❻ sew with large stitches:～贴边 sew on an edging

钩心斗角 gōuxīndòujiǎo *also* "勾心斗角" intrigue or scheme against each other; jockey for position

篝 gōu

篝火 gōuhuǒ bonfire; campfire:～晚会 campfire party

gǒu

苟 gǒu ❶ temporary; expedient; for the time being:～安 seek momentary peace; be contented with temporary ease and comfort / ～活 drag out an ignoble existence; live on in degradation / ～全性命 preserve one's own life at the cost of principle; just manage to save one's bacon ❷ casual; careless; negligent:～得 〈书〉 obtain without effort or justification ❸ 〈书〉 provided; if

苟合 gǒuhé ❶ agree with or echo (sb) from expediency ❷ have illicit sexual relations

苟且 gǒuqiě ❶ drift along; muddle on; be resigned to circumstances: ～度日 muddle along / ～偷安 rest content with temporary ease and comfort; seek a moment's peace without any thought of the future ❷ perfunctorily; casually; carelessly; 从不～ never do anything shoddy ❸ illicit (sexual relations): ～之事 illicit affair; liaison

苟同 gǒutóng 〈书〉(often used in the negative) agree without giving serious thought; readily subscribe to (sb's views)

苟延残喘 gǒuyáncánchuǎn drag out a feeble existence; linger on in a steadily worsening condition; be on one's last legs

狗 gǒu (usu derogatory when used figuratively) dog; cur: ～屎 dog's droppings — worthless stuff / ～崽子 puppy 〈粗〉son of a bitch / ～胆包天〈口〉monstrous audacity; sheer impudence / ～咬～的争斗 dog-eat-dog fight

狗急跳墙 gǒují tiàoqiáng a dog will leap over a wall in desperation; despair gives courage even to a coward

狗拿耗子，多管闲事 gǒunáhàozi, duōguǎnxiánshì 〈俗〉poke one's nose into other people's business; be a busybody

狗皮膏药 gǒupígāoyao ❶〈中药〉dogskin plaster (for curing rheumatism, etc) ❷ quack medicine; fake stuff: 卖～ practise quackery

狗屁 gǒupì 〈粗〉baloney; bullshit; rubbish: ～不通 unreadable rubbish; mere trash / 放你的～! Cut the crap!

狗头军师 gǒutóujūnshī person who offers bad advice — inept or villainous adviser

狗腿子 gǒutuǐzi 〈口〉lackey; flun-

key; henchman

狗尾续貂 gǒuwěixùdiāo dog's tail joined to a marten — a wretched sequel to a fine (literary) work

狗窝 gǒuwō kennel; doghouse; 〈谦〉one's humble home

狗熊 gǒuxióng ❶ black bear ❷ coward; good-for-nothing

狗血喷头 gǒuxuèpēntóu pour invective upon sb's head: 骂得～ let loose a stream of abuse (against sb); heap curses (on sb)

狗仗人势 gǒuzhàngrénshì 〈贬〉be a bully with the support of a powerful patron

枸 gǒu

枸杞 gǒuqǐ 〈中药〉Chinese wolfberry

gòu

勾 gòu see also gōu

勾当 gòudang 〈贬〉business; transaction; deal

构(構) gòu ❶ construct; build; fabricate: ～件 (structural) member; component (part) / ～图 composition of a picture / ～词法〈语言〉word-building; word-formation ❷ literary composition: 妙～ fine writing

构成 gòuchéng constitute; form; compose: 土壤的～ composition of soil / ～威胁 pose a threat

构架 gòujià ❶ (structural) frame; framework; skeleton ❷ see "构建"

构建 gòujiàn (usu of sth abstract) set up; establish; construct

构思 gòusī conceive; construct; work out: ～小说 construct a novel / ～新颖 original in conception

构想 gòuxiǎng ❶ see "构思" ❷ idea; concept; plan: "一国两制"的～ concept of "one country, two systems"

构造 gòuzào　structure; construction: ～精密 precise in construction

构筑 gòuzhù　construct; build: ～工事 construct fortifications; dig in

购（購）gòu　purchase; buy: ～置 purchase (durables, etc) / ～销两旺 brisk buying and selling

购买 gòumǎi　purchase; buy: ～力 purchasing power

购物 gòuwù　shopping: 出外～ go shopping / ～袋 (UK) carrier bag; (US) shopping bag / ～中心 shopping centre

诟 gòu　〈书〉❶ shame; disgrace; humiliation ❷ rebuke; reprimand; talk abusively: ～病 censure; condemn; castigate / ～骂 revile; abuse; vilify

垢 gòu　〈书〉❶ soiled; dirty; filthy: ～污 filth; dirt ❷ see "诟 ❶" gòu

够（夠）gòu　❶ enough; sufficient: ～数 enough to make up a required number; sufficient in quantity / ～本儿 (of a deal, etc) break even; get one's money's worth (out of sth); be quits or even / 受一了 have had enough (of sth or sb) / 分量～不～? Did you give me full measure? ❷ quite; rather; really: ～受的 〈口〉 quite an ordeal; hardly endurable / ～损的 〈口〉 (of words) bitterly sarcastic; (of behaviour) tart and mean / ～味儿 just the right flavour; just the thing ❸ reach (sth by stretching); reach or be up to (a certain standard, etc): ～条件 be eligible or qualified (for sth) / ～不到天花板 can't reach the ceiling

够格 gòugé　be qualified; be up to standard: 当教练不～ not qualified to be a coach

够交情 gòujiāoqing　❶ sufficient or profound friendship: 我要他帮这个忙

还不～。He and I are not friends enough for me to ask for such a favour. ❷ see "够朋友"

够劲儿 gòujìnr　〈口〉❶ see "够瞧的" ❷ strong (in taste, strength, etc)

够朋友 gòupéngyou　be worthy of the name of a true friend; be a friend indeed

够瞧的 gòuqiáode　also "够戗" 〈口〉 awful; terrible; really too much: 累得～ tired out; dog-tired / 这天气真～。What awful weather!

够意思 gòuyìsi　〈方〉❶ (of sth) up to a high standard; really something; terrific ❷ (of sb) generous; friendly; really kind

媾 gòu　〈书〉❶ wed: 婚～ marriage ❷ reconcile; make (peace): become reconciled: ～和 make peace ❸ coition: ～合 copulate; have sexual intercourse

gū

估 gū　estimate; assess; appraise: ～产 estimate the yield (of a crop); appraise the assets / ～算 estimate; calculate; consider

估计 gūjì　estimate; calculate; reckon: 错误～ miscalculate / ～过低 underestimate / ～过高 overestimate

估价 gūjià　❶ estimated or appraised price: ～单 list of cost estimates ❷ appraise; evaluate

估量 gūliáng　appraise; estimate; assess: 无法～ inestimable

估摸 gūmo　〈口〉 reckon; suppose; guess

咕 gū　〈象声〉 (of hens, etc) cluck; (of turtledoves, etc) coo: 肚子饿得～～ be so hungry that one's stomach keeps rumbling

咕咚 gūdōng　〈象声〉 thud; splash; plop: ～掉下水 fall into the water with a splash

咕嘟 gūdū　❶ 〈象声〉 bubble; gurgle；gulp；～～地喝水 gulp water down ❷〈方〉boil；stew

咕唧 gūjī *also* "咕哜" "咕叽" ❶〈象声〉squelch：在泥地里～～地走着 squelch along in the mud ❷（gūji）whisper；murmur；mumble（to oneself）

咕隆 gūlōng *also* "咕隆隆"〈象声〉(usu of sth heavy) rumble；rattle；roll；～～的雷声 rumbling thunder

咕哝 gūnong *also* "咕噜" murmur；mumble；grumble

沽 gū〈书〉❶ purchase；buy：～酒 buy wine / ～名钓誉 fish for fame and compliments ❷ sell：待价而～ wait for a good price or the highest bid

姑 gū ❶ father's sister；(paternal) aunt：～父 *also* "姑夫" husband of father's sister；uncle /〈口〉father's sister；aunt / ～妈 *also* "姑母" father's married sister；aunt / ～表姊妹 daughters of a brother and those of his sister；female cousins ❷ husband's sister；sister-in-law：～嫂 woman and her brother's wife；sisters-in-law / 大～子 husband's elder sister ❸〈书〉husband's mother；mother-in-law ❹ nun；priestess：～子〈口〉Buddhist nun ❺〈书〉just；for the time being：～妄听之 might as well hear sb out；see no harm in hearing what sb has to say

姑老爷 gūlǎoye *also* "姑爷" respected form of address for a man used by family members of his wife

姑奶奶 gūnǎinai〈口〉❶ sister of one's paternal grand father；great-aunt ❷ form of address for a married woman used by members of her family ❸ used of or by a shrewish woman：～，饶了我吧。Spare me, auntie.

姑娘 gūniang ❶ girl ❷ daughter

姑且 gūqiě〈副〉tentatively；for the moment：～不论 leave (sth) aside for the moment

姑妄言之 gūwàngyánzhī venture an opinion or a remark；tell sth for what it's worth

姑息 gūxī appease；placate；indulge：～养奸。To tolerate evil is to abet it.

孤 gū ❶ (of a child) fatherless；orphaned；～女 orphan girl ❷ lone；solitary；isolated：～本 only existing copy / ～岛 isolated island / ～身一人 all alone；all by oneself ❸ we (used by a monarch)

孤傲 gū'ào proud and aloof；standoffish and arrogant：～不群 too haughty to get along with others

孤单 gūdān ❶ lonely；friendless；solitary ❷ weak；inadequate：工程仅靠两个人，太～了。A team of two is far from adequate for the project.

孤独 gūdú lonely；solitary：～症〈医〉autism

孤儿 gū'ér fatherless child；orphan：～院 orphanage

孤芳自赏 gūfāngzìshǎng lone soul admiring its own purity；indulging in self-admiration；narcissism

孤寡 gūguǎ ❶ widows and orphans ❷ solitary；lonely；lone

孤家寡人 gūjiā-guǎrén solitary or lonely person；person in utter isolation；odd man out：变成～ become totally isolated；find oneself without a following

孤军 gūjūn isolated force：～奋战 fight single-handed；fight a lone battle

孤苦 gūkǔ poor and helpless；friendless and wretched：～伶仃 *also* "孤苦零丁" friendless and uncared-for；forlorn and alone

孤立 gūlì isolated；on one's own；helpless：～无援 isolated and cut off from help / ～主义 isolationism / ～地看问题 look at a problem in isolation

孤零零 gūlínglíng solitary；lone；all alone

孤陋寡闻 gūlòu-guǎwén　ignorant and ill-informed

孤僻 gūpì　unsociable and eccentric

孤掌难鸣 gūzhǎngnánmíng　it's impossible to clap with one hand; it's difficult to achieve anything without support

孤注一掷 gūzhùyīzhì　stake everything on a single throw; risk everything on a single venture; put all one's eggs in one basket

轱 gū

轱辘 gūlu　also "轱轳" ❶ 〈口〉 wheel ❷ turn; roll; ~~转 turn over and over; turn round and round

骨 gū　see also gǔ

骨朵儿 gūduor　〈口〉 flower bud

骨碌碌 gūlūlū　roll round and round; move rapidly

骨碌 gūlu　roll; 钢镚儿~到桌子下面去了。The coin rolled under the table.

菇 gū　also "菰" mushroom

辜 gū ❶ guilt; crime; 死有余~ deserve more than death ❷ 〈书〉 abandon; betray; ~负 let down; be unworthy of; fail to live up to

箍 gū ❶ fasten round; bind fast; hoop ❷ hoop; band; 铁~ iron hoop; hoop iron

gǔ

古 gǔ ❶ ancient; age-old; old; ~ 奥 archaic and abstruse / ~都 ancient capital / ~籍 ancient books or texts / ~旧 antiquated; archaic; out of date / ~人 ancients; forefathers / ~ 时(候) (in) ancient times / ~训 precept from ancient times; old adage / ~ 汉语 archaic or classical Chinese / ~如此 have been so since time immemorial / 文明~国 country with an ancient civilization / 从~到今 from ancient times to the present ❷ 〈书〉 of ancient style; simple and sincere; ~拙 simple and unsophisticated; of primitive simplicity / 人心不~。People nowadays are no longer simple and honest. ❸ *short for* 古体诗；五~ classical poem with five characters to a line

古板 gǔbǎn　old-fashioned and inflexible; outmoded and rigid; prim and proper

古代 gǔdài　ancient times; antiquity; ~史 ancient history / ~社会 ancient society

古道 gǔdào ❶ ancient road; 〈喻〉 ancient ways, rules or methods ❷ kind; considerate; generous; ~热肠 considerate and warm-hearted; honest and compassionate

古典 gǔdiǎn ❶ classical allusion ❷ classical; ~文学 classical literature / ~主义 classicism / ~式摔跤〈体〉 Graeco-Roman style wrestling

古董 gǔdǒng　also "骨董" ❶ antique; ~店 antique shop / ~商 antiquary; antiquarian ❷ 〈喻〉 old fogey; outdated stuff; anachronism

古风 gǔfēng ❶ ancient customs; antiquities ❷ see "古体诗"

古怪 gǔguài　odd; strange; eccentric; 古里~的家伙 strange bird; queer fish; oddball

古迹 gǔjì　historic site; place of historic interest

古今 gǔjīn　from the ancient times to the present; past and present; for all time; ~中外 in modern or ancient times, in China or elsewhere / 古往今来 through the ages; since time immemorial

古兰经 Gǔlánjīng　also "可兰经" (of Islam) Koran; Quran

古老 gǔlǎo　ancient; age-old; old; ~ 的习俗 ancient or old custom

古朴 gǔpǔ　simple and unaffected; of

primitive simplicity

古色古香 gǔsè-gǔxiāng of antique flavour; of antique or classical beauty; antique

古生物 gǔshēngwù ancient extinct life;~学 palaeontology / ~化石 fossils of ancient extinct life

古体诗 gǔtǐshī also "古诗"; "古风" form of classical poetry originated before the Tang Dynasty and flexible in poetics; pre-Tang style poetry

古铜色 gǔtóngsè bronze-coloured; bronze; deep brown

古玩 gǔwán antique; curio; curiosity

古为今用 gǔwéijīnyòng make the past serve the present;~，洋为中用 make the past serve the present and foreign things serve China

古文 gǔwén ❶ prose written in the classical literary style; classical prose ❷ Chinese script before the Qin Dynasty; pre-Qin script

古稀 gǔxī seventy years of age; 已逾 ~ more than seventy years old

古装 gǔzhuāng ancient costume;~戏 opera in ancient costume; costume play

谷(❷-❹穀) gǔ ❶ valley;

ravine; gorge;~地 valley ❷ cereal; grain;~粒 grain (of rice, millet, etc) / ~物 grain; cereal (crop) / ~贱伤农.〈俗〉Low prices for grain hurt the farmers. ❸ also "粟" millet;~草 millet straw / ~穗儿 ears of millet ❹〈方〉unhusked rice; paddy

谷底 gǔdǐ bottom of a valley; 到达~〈喻〉touch bottom; bottom out

谷雨 gǔyǔ Grain Rain, 6th seasonal division point see also "节气" jiéqì

股 gǔ ❶ thigh;~骨 thighbone ❷

section (of an office, etc); 财务 ~ financial or accounting section ❸ strand; ply; 把线捻成 ~ 儿 twist threads into a strand ❹ share of stock (in a company); one of several equal parts: 分为三 ~ divide into three equal parts / ~本 capital (stock); equity / ~东 shareholder; stockholder / ~价 share price / ~金 money paid for shares; share capital / ~民 person who buys and sells stocks / ~市 (short for 股票市场) stock market / ~息 also "股利" dividend ❺〈量〉used for a) sth long and narrow:一~清泉 a stream of clear spring water b) gas, smell, etc:一~浓烟 a column of heavy smoke c)〈贬〉a group of people: 小~土匪 small bands of bandits

股份 gǔfèn also "股分" share; stock; ~公司 joint-stock company / ~转让 stock transfer / ~制企业 shareholding enterprise / ~有限公司 limited-liability company; limited company (Ltd.)

股票 gǔpiào share (certificate); stock;~行情 current stock prices; quotations on the stock exchange / ~交易所 stock exchange / ~经纪人 stockbroker; stockjobber / ~价格指数 (shortened as 股指) stock index

骨 gǔ ❶ bone;~癌 cancer in the

bones; osteocarcinoma / ~刺〈医〉spur / ~粉 bone meal or dust / ~胶 bone glue / ~节〈生理〉joint / ~盆〈生理〉pelvis / ~子里〈喻〉in one's bones; in reality; at heart ❷ skeleton; structure; framework; 扇子 frame or ribs of a fan ❸ character; quality; spirit;~力 (as in Chinese calligraphy) strength or force of strokes see also gū

骨董 gǔdǒng see "古董" gǔdǒng

骨干 gǔgàn backbone; core; mainstay;~分子 core or key member / 起 ~作用 serve as the mainstay; play a major role

骨骼 gǔgé〈生理〉skeleton;~系统 skeletal system

骨鲠在喉 gǔgěngzàihóu〈喻〉have a fishbone caught in one's throat; 如~，不吐不快 can't rest unless one spits it out

骨灰 gǔhuī ashes of the dead; ~盒 cinerary casket / ~堂 cinerarium / ~安放仪式 ceremony for laying sb's ashes to rest

骨架 gǔjià skeleton; framework; ~大 have big bones / 大楼的~ framework of a building

骨科 gǔkē 〈医〉(department of) orthopaedics; ~医生 orthopaedist

骨气 gǔqì ❶ strength of character; moral integrity; backbone ❷ vigour and force shown in calligraphy

骨肉 gǔròu flesh and blood; kindred; ~同胞 be flesh and blood / ~相连 linked together by flesh and blood / ~之情 ties of blood; kindred feelings

骨髓 gǔsuǐ 〈生理〉bone marrow; ~移植〈医〉marrow transplant

骨头 gǔtou ❶ bone; ~架子 skeleton; very thin person ❷ person of a certain character or behaviour; 软~ spineless creature / 硬~ person of unyielding integrity

骨血 gǔxuè flesh and blood; offspring; 亲~ one's own flesh and blood

骨折 gǔzhé fracture; 开放~ open or compound fracture / 粉碎性~ comminuted fracture

骨质 gǔzhì 〈生理〉sclerotin; ~软化 osteomalacia / ~疏松 osteoporosis / ~增生 osteoproliferation

牯

gǔ (usu 牯牛) bull

贾

gǔ ❶ merchant; 书~ book seller ❷ trade; do business; buy or sell; 多财善~。A lot of money helps in doing business.

钴

gǔ 〈化〉cobalt (Co); ~60 〈医〉cobalt-60 (60 Co)

蛊(蠱)

gǔ

蛊惑 gǔhuò also "鼓惑" poison; harm; bewitch; ~人心 confuse and

corrupt people's minds; resort to demagogy

鼓

gǔ ❶ drum; drum-shaped object; 石~ drum-shaped stone block / ~槌 drumstick / ~角 battle drum and horn / ~楼 drum-tower / ~膜 also "耳膜"〈生理〉tympanic membrane; eardrum / ~手 drumbeater; drummer / ~乐 (strains of) music accompanied by drumbeats / ~点子 drumbeats; (clapper beats which set the) tempo ❷ beat; strike; play; ~舌 wag one's tongue; talk glibly ❸ blow (as) with a bellows; fan; ~风机 blower or fan; blow engine ❹ rouse; agitate; stir up; ~起精神 pluck up or summon one's spirit ❺ bulge; swell; ~包 swelling; bump; lump / ~胀 bulge; bloat / ~~的 also "鼓鼓囊囊的" bulging; swollen

鼓吹 gǔchuī ❶ advocate; promote; espouse ❷〈贬〉preach; trumpet

鼓捣 gǔdao 〈方〉❶ tinker or fiddle with; ~钟表 tinker with clocks and watches ❷ egg (sb) on; stir up; incite; 暗中~ pull strings behind the scenes

鼓动 gǔdòng agitate; arouse; incite; 政治~ political agitation / ~学潮 stir up student unrest

鼓惑 gǔhuò see "蛊惑" gǔhuò

鼓劲 gǔjìn boost the morale; pluck up courage; stir up enthusiasm or spirit; 给球队~ cheer (on) a ball team / 鼓足干劲 go all out; exert one's utmost

鼓励 gǔlì encourage; urge; spur (on); 精神~和物质~相结合 combine moral encouragement with material rewards

鼓舞 gǔwǔ encourage; hearten; inspire; 令人~ heartening; inspiring / ~士气 boost or enhance the morale

鼓噪 gǔzào clamour; make an uproar; raise a hubbub; ~而进 move ahead uproariously

鼓掌 gǔzhǎng applaud; clap one's hands:起立 ～ give a standing ovation / ～通过 approve by acclamation

臌 gǔ bloating (of the abdomen, etc); tympanites:～胀 also "鼓胀"〈中医〉distension of the abdomen caused by accumulation of gas or fluid; tympanites

gù

固 gù ❶ (make) firm; strong; solid:～态〈理〉solid state / ～氮作用〈农〉nitrogen fixation / ～若金汤 strongly fortified; impregnable; invulnerable / ～沙林带 sand-fixing forest belt ❷ resolutely; persistently; firmly:～守 defend tenaciously; be firmly entrenched in; cling or adhere to (sth outmoded or conventional) ❸〈书〉just; originally; as a matter of course:～所愿也. It is just what I wish. ❹〈书〉admittedly; no doubt:务农 ～可，经商亦无不可. Farming is all right, but it is just as good to do business.

固步自封 gùbùzìfēng see "故步自封" gùbùzìfēng

固定 gùdìng fixed; static; regular:～汇率 fixed exchange rate / ～职业 permanent occupation / ～资本 also "固定资金" fixed capital / 用～眼光看问题 take a static view of things / 把螺丝一下 fix a screw

固然 gùrán used to acknowledge a statement before raising one's main argument or the other side of the question:步行 ～ 安全，可就是慢得多. It is true it would be safer to walk, but it would be much slower.

固体 gùtǐ solid (body):～燃料 solid fuel / ～物理 solid-state physics / ～酱油 solidified soy sauce

固有 gùyǒu intrinsic; inherent; innate:～权利 inherent right / ～的文化 indigenous culture

固执 gùzhí ❶ obstinate; stubborn; self-willed ❷ persist in; stick or cling to:～己见 cling or adhere stubbornly to one's own opinion

故 gù ❶ incident; accident ❷ reason; cause; excuse:不知何 ～ … I wonder why … ❸ intentionally; deliberately; on purpose:～ 杀〈法〉premeditated or wilful murder ❹ hence; therefore; consequently:此段重复，～删去. This paragraph was deleted as a mere repetition. ❺ of the past; former; old:～道 old road; beaten track; old river course / ～地 former home; old haunt / ～都 former capital / ～国〈书〉native land, soil or place; motherland / ～旧 old friends and acquaintances / ～居 former residence or home ❻ (usu 故去 or 故世) pass away; die

故步自封 gùbùzìfēng also "固步自封" hold fast to established ways of doing things; be complacent and conservative

故此 gùcǐ also "故而" therefore; for this reason; on this account

故技 gùjì also "故伎" stock trick; old dodge or tactic:～重演 be up to one's old tricks again; repeat the same old tactics

故弄玄虚 gùnòngxuánxū purposely turn a simple matter into a mystery; deliberately mystifying

故人 gùrén ❶ old friend ❷〈书〉the deceased or dead ❸ former wife or husband

故事 gùshi ❶ story; tale:～会 storytelling session / ～片 feature film ❷ plot:～性不强 (of a literary work) not have a vivid plot

故态 gùtài one's old ways:～复萌 slip back into one's old ways; revert to type

故土 gùtǔ native land or soil:～难离

It is hard to leave one's native land.

故乡 gùxiāng *also* "故里" native place or village; hometown; birthplace; 荣归～ return to one's native place with honours; return home in glory

故意 gùyì intentionally; wilfully; deliberately;～捣乱 make trouble on purpose /～犯规〈体〉commit a deliberate foul /～杀人〈法〉intentional homicide

故友 gùyǒu ❶ deceased friend ❷ old friend

故障 gùzhàng ❶ breakdown; failure; trouble; 排除～ trouble-clearing; trouble-shooting /〈信息〉bug

故作 gùzuò (used in certain phrases) pretend; feign;～高深 pretend to be erudite and profound /～镇静 feign composure; strive to maintain an outward calm /～姿态 strike a pose; make a deliberate gesture; put on airs

顾（顧） gù ❶ (turn round and) look at;～盼自如〈书〉look round with ease; behave in a free and easy way /～左右而言他 look left and right, and talk about other matters; evade the subject under discussion ❷ attend to; take care of; take into consideration;～家 care for or attend to one's own family /～恋 concern oneself with; be reluctant to part (from sb or with sth) /～面子 save face; keep up appearances;～前不～后 drive ahead without considering the consequences; act rashly ❸ visit; call on; patronize (a shop);～主 customer; client; patron

顾此失彼 gùcǐ-shībǐ attend to one thing and lose sight of another; have too many things to take care of at the same time; be unable to look after everything at once

顾及 gùjí attend to; look after; take into consideration; 无暇～ be too busy to attend to sth

顾忌 gùjì scruple; qualm; misgiving;

毫无～ make no scruple (of doing sth); do (sth) with no qualms; act unscrupulously

顾客 gùkè customer; client; patron;～盈门 filled with customers or shoppers /～至上 customers first

顾虑 gùlǜ misgiving; apprehension; worry;～重重 be full of apprehensions; have no end of worries

顾名思义 gùmíng-sīyì as the name implies; as the term suggests; by definition

顾全 gùquán show consideration for and take care to preserve; keep in mind;～大局 take the interests of the whole into account; bear the overall interest in mind /～名誉 take care to preserve one's reputation; act for the sake of one's name

顾问 gùwèn adviser; consultant; counsellor; 法律～ legal adviser or counsel /～班子 advisory group; team of consultants

顾惜 gùxī cherish; treasure; take good care of;～名节 treasure one's name and integrity /～身子 take care of one's health; look after oneself

顾影自怜 gùyǐngzìlián ❶ look at one's shadow and lament one's lot; feel self-pity ❷ admire oneself in the mirror; be narcissistic

雇（僱） gù hire; employ; engage;～农 farmhand; farm labourer /～员 employee /～主 employer; one who hires a vehicle or boat

雇工 gùgōng ❶ hire labour; hire hands; 雇短工 hire a day-labourer ❷ hired labourer; farmhand

雇佣 gùyōng *also* "雇用" employ; hire;～军 *also* "雇佣兵" mercenary army or troops; mercenary (soldier) /～观点 "hired-hand" mentality — the attitude of one who won't do more than he is paid for /～关系 employer-employee relationship / ～劳动 wage labour / ～文人 hack (writer)

痼 gù chronic; enduring; inveterate; ～疾 chronic disease or malady; incurable or obstinate disease / ～癖 addiction; inveterate weakness / ～习 inveterate or confirmed habit

guā

瓜 guā melon; gourd; ～农 melon grower

瓜代 guādài 〈书〉succeed (sb to an office)

瓜分 guāfēn carve or divide up; partition

瓜葛 guāgé connection; implication; association; 此事与他有些～。He is somehow implicated in this.

瓜熟蒂落 guāshú-dìluò everything comes easy at the right time; ～之时 when conditions are ripe

瓜田李下 guātián-lǐxià (be in) suspicious circumstances or surroundings

瓜子 guāzǐ melon seeds (usu cooked and flavoured); ～仁 kernel of a melon seed / ～脸 oval face

呱 guā

呱嗒 guādā also "呱哒"〈象声〉clip-clop; clack; clatter; ～板儿 bamboo clappers; 〈方〉clogs

呱呱 guāguā 〈象声〉(of ducks) quack; (of frogs) croak; (of crows) caw; ～叫 also "刮刮叫"〈口〉tiptop; top-notch; terrific

刮(❸颳) guā ❶ scrape; scratch; shave; ～宫〈医〉dilatation and curettage (D and C) / ～痧〈中医〉(as treatment for sunstroke, etc) scraping the patient's neck, chest or back / ～奖卡 scratch card ❷ plunder; fleece; extort; ～地皮〈喻〉batten on the fat of the land; bleed the people white ❸ (of wind)

blow

刮脸 guāliǎn shave (the face); ～刀 razor / ～膏 shaving cream

刮目 guāmù look at (sb) with new eyes; ～相看 also "刮目相待" regard (sb) in a totally different light; treat (sb) with increased respect; sit up and take notice

guǎ

剐(剮) guǎ ❶〈史〉(as capital punishment) cut to pieces ❷ cut; slit; 胳臂上～了个口子 have a cut on one's arm

寡 guǎ ❶ few; scarce; scant; ～不敌众 lose a battle against overwhelming odds; be hopelessly outnumbered / ～廉鲜耻 lost to shame; brazen / ～言少语 taciturn; of few words ❷ tasteless; thin; bland; ～酒 wine without any food to go with it / ～淡无味 tasteless (food, etc) ❸ widowed; 新～ newly widowed (woman) / ～妇 widow / ～母 widowed mother; widow with children

寡人 guǎrén (used by a monarch to refer to himself) I, the sovereign; we

寡头 guǎtóu oligarch; ～政治 oligarchy

guà

卦 guà one of the Eight Trigrams (八卦) as a divinatory symbol; fortune-telling

挂(掛) guà hang; put up; suspend; ～历 wall calendar / ～毯 tapestry / ～图 wall map; hanging or wall chart / ～靴 also "挂鞋" (of a footballer, etc) hang up one's sports shoes for good; retire as a pro / ～钟 wall clock / ～冠而去〈书〉resign (one's position) and leave / ～免战牌 hang up a "no battle" sign; refuse battle or debate / 把案子～起来 leave a case unsettled; shelve a case ❷ be anxious or concerned about; have sth (weighing) on one's mind: ~怀 have (sth) weighing on one's mind; show concern (for) ❸ register (at a hospital): make an appointment (with a doctor): ~急诊 register as an emergency case / ～皮肤科 register for dermatology ❹ (量) set; string: 一～珠子 a string of pearls

挂彩 guàcǎi *also* "挂花" (be) wounded in action

挂齿 guàchǐ 〈谦〉mention: 区区小事，何足～。Such a trifle is not worth mentioning.

挂电话 guàdiànhuà make a (telephone) call: 挂通电话 put through a call / 把电话挂了 hang up (on sb) / 给家里挂个电话 give one's family a ring; call back home

挂斗 guàdǒu *also* "拖车"; "拖斗" trailer

挂钩 guàgōu ❶ hook: 挂衣钩 clothes hook ❷ link up or get in touch (with): establish contact (with): 奖金与工作表现～ link up bonuses with performance / ～单位 institution one has regular links with

挂号 guàhào ❶ register (at a hospital, etc): ～处 registration office / ～费 registration fee / 挂专家号 register for an appointment with a specialist ❷ send by registered mail: ～信 registered letter / ～邮资 registration charge

挂靠 guàkào be attached, affiliated or subordinate to; be linked with: ～单位 umbrella institution (to which a smaller entity is attached)

挂零 guàlíng (used after a round number) odd: 七十～ seventy-odd

挂面 guàmiàn fine dried noodles; vermicelli

挂名 guàmíng in name only; titular; nominal: ～差事 nominal job; titular

position; sinecure / ～头头 titular or nominal head; figurehead / ～合伙人 sleeping partner

挂念 guànniàn *also* "挂记" worry about (sb absent); miss

挂牌 guàpái ❶ (usu of a professional or businessman) hang out one's shingle; put up one's brass plate; go into practice or business: ～营业 start business officially / 挂头牌 (as in traditional opera) play the leading role; be the leading star ❷ (经) list: ～公司 listed or quoted company / ～汇价 posted exchange rate ❸ (of service personnel, etc) wear a name plate

挂失 guàshī report or declare the loss of sth

挂帅 guàshuài be in command; assume command or leadership; take command or charge (of sth)

挂心 guàxīn concern oneself with; care for; worry about

挂羊头，卖狗肉 guàyángtóu, màigǒuròu 〈俗〉hang out a sheep's head and sell dog-meat; cry up wine and sell vinegar; sell horse-meat as beefsteak

挂一漏万 guàyī-lòuwàn (shortened as 挂漏) 〈谦〉be far from exhaustive; leave much to be desired: 限于水平，难免～。Due to my limited knowledge, incompleteness is hardly avoidable.

挂职 guàzhí serve in a lower level unit while retaining one's original position: ～下放 be seconded to a grass-roots unit to temper oneself

褂 guà (usu 褂子) traditional-style garment or jacket; gown: 长～儿 long gown

guāi

乖 guāi ❶ well-behaved; obedient; good: 这孩子真～! What a

good child! ❷ clever; smart; alert:学 ~ become smarter or wiser ❸〈书〉contrary (to reason); perverse; abnormal:~舛 wrong; false; not smooth or consistent / ~戾 perverse; recalcitrant; cantankerous / ~僻 eccentric; odd / ~张 eccentric and unreasonable; perverse; recalcitrant / 有~人情 run counter to human nature

乖乖 guāiguāi ❶ little dear or darling ❷ well-behaved; compliant; docile ❸ (guāiguai)〈叹〉gosh; my; boy

乖觉 guāijué alert; quick; smart

乖巧 guāiqiǎo ❶ cute; lovely; 伶俐 ~ bright and cute ❷ clever; smart:有一张~的嘴 have a honeyed tongue; be honey-mouthed

掴(摑) guāi also guó slap; smack:~一耳光 slap (sb) on the face

guǎi

拐(❹枴) guǎi ❶ change direction; turn:~角 turning; corner / ~回去 turn back ❷ limp ❸ (used verbally only, as over the telephone) seven:洞洞~ zero, zero, seven ❹ crutch:拄着双~走 walk with crutches ❺ swindle; abduct; make away with:~卖 abduct and sell (children, etc) / ~骗 swindle; abduct; kidnap / 被人~走一个金项链 be swindled out of a gold necklace

拐棍 guǎigùn ❶ (popular term for 拐杖) walking stick; crutch ❷〈喻〉indispensable aid

拐弯 guǎiwān ❶ turn (a corner); 〈喻〉turn round (in thinking or speech); reorient:~抹角 go or travel in a zigzag manner; talk in a round-about way; beat about the bush / 思想~不过弯来 find it hard to reorient one's thinking ❷ turning; corner

拐子 guǎizi ❶〈口〉〈贬〉cripple ❷ crutch ❸ abductor; swindler

guài

怪 guài ❶ strange; odd; eccentric:毫不足~ nothing to wonder at / ~病 strange disease / ~话 cynical remark; grumble; complaint / ~癖 eccentric habit or behaviour; eccentricity / ~僻 eccentric; cranky / ~人 eccentric person; crank; weirdo / ~胎 genetic freak; monster ❷〈口〉rather; quite:那地方~远的。It is quite far. ❸ monster; fiend; evil spirit ❹ blame; reproach:~罪 reproach; blame; reprove

怪不得 guàibude ❶ no wonder; so that's why:夜里下大雪了,~这么冷! It snowed heavily last night! No wonder it's so cold. ❷ not to blame:这事~别人, 他自作自受。Nobody but himself is to blame for it.

怪诞 guàidàn weird; strange; fantastic:~不经 weird and uncanny; fantastic; crazy

怪里怪气 guàiliguàiqì eccentric; queer; weird

怪模怪样 guàimú-guàiyàng queer in appearance or manners; grotesque

怪圈 guàiquān vicious circle

怪声怪气 guàishēng-guàiqì also "怪腔怪调" in a strange or affected voice; in a disagreeable falsetto

怪物 guàiwù ❶ monster; monstrosity ❷ eccentric person; crank; weirdo

怪异 guàiyì ❶ strange; bizarre; grotesque ❷ unusual or strange phenomenon

guān

关(關) guān ❶ shut or close (down); turn or switch

off; lock up;～灯 turn off a light /～张 (of a shop) close down; go out of business /～进牢房 put behind bars; jail ❷ mountain pass; checkpoint; customs (house);通～ clear the customs /～内 also "关里" inside or south of the Great Wall /～山阻隔 separated by mountains and passes ❸ barrier; critical juncture; crucial point ❹ involve; implicate; concern;事～全局 have a bearing on the situation as a whole

关爱 guān'ài concern and care; love and care

关闭 guānbì ❶ close; shut ❷ (of a factory, etc) close or shut down

关东 Guāndōng the Northeast; northeast China;闯～ go and seek a livelihood in northeast China

关怀 guānhuái show loving care, concern or solicitude for;～备至 show the greatest solicitude (for sb); be extremely considerate (of sb)

关键 guānjiàn door bolt;〈喻〉key; crux;～时刻 crucial or critical moment /～所在 crux of a matter

关节 guānjié ❶〈生理〉joint;～炎〈医〉arthritis ❷ key link; crucial point ❸ clandestine dealings through the backdoor, etc;疏通～ try to wangle sth by greasing sb's palm

关口 guānkǒu ❶ strategic pass; checkpoint ❷ see "关头"

关联 guānlián also "关连" be linked, related or connected; 相互～ inter-related /～词〈语言〉connective

关门 guānmén ❶ close or shut (the door); stop operation;～大吉 (of a business, etc) wind up or close down for good ❷ close the door; refuse discussion, consideration, etc;关上了谈判的大门 shut the door on negotiations ❸ last (before stoppage);～弟子 last disciple (of a master)

关卡 guānqiǎ outpost or checkpoint (for taxation or security);～林立

There are checkpoints everywhere.

关切 guānqiè be deeply concerned (about); show concern (over)

关税 guānshuì customs duty; tariff;～率 tariff rate /～壁垒 tariff wall; customs barrier

关头 guāntóu juncture; moment;生死～ moment of life and death

关系 guānxì ❶ relations; ties; connections;相互～ relations with each other / 发生～ have sexual relations (with sb) ❷ personal connections or network;～户 people who have preferential business dealings with each other; (person with) special connections /～网 network of friends; connections ❸ bearing; relevance; impact;大有～ have much to do (with) / 没～! Never mind. ❹ (often used after 由于, 因, etc) because of; since;由于资金短缺的～ for lack of funding ❺ membership or personal credentials; organizational connection or identity; 转党、团～ transfer one's Party or League membership credentials ❻ also "关乎" concern; affect; have a bearing on;～国计民生 have a direct bearing on the national economy and people's livelihood

关心 guānxīn be concerned with; show solicitude for; care for;共同～的问题 matter of common concern

关于 guānyú about; on; concerning

关照 guānzhào ❶ look after; take care of;多谢～. Thank you for your kindness. ❷ notify by word of mouth;离开时请～一声. Please let me know when you leave.

关注 guānzhù follow with interest; pay close attention to; show concern for;引起～ draw attention; cause concern

观(觀) guān ❶ look; see; watch;～看 look at;

watch; view / ～感 impressions (of);
observations ❷ sight; spectacle; view
❸ outlook; view; concept: 人生～ outlook on life
see also guàn

观测 guāncè observe and survey: ～站
observation station or post / ～资料
observational data; observations

观察 guānchá observe; watch; size
up: ～哨 observation post or sentry /
～员 observer / ～病情 keep a patient
under observation

观点 guāndiǎn point of view; viewpoint; standpoint

观光 guānguāng go sightseeing; see
the sights; tour: ～客 sightseer; tourist / ～团 sightseeing party; tour or
tourist group / ～市容 make a tour
round a city

观礼 guānlǐ attend a celebration or
ceremony: ～台 reviewing or visitor's
stand

观摩 guānmó view and emulate: ～演
出 demonstration performance

观念 guānniàn sense; concept; mentality

观赏 guānshǎng view and admire; enjoy the sight of; watch (with appreciation): ～植物 ornamental or decorative
plant

观世音 Guānshìyīn *also* "观音" 〈宗
教〉Guanyin, goddess of mercy

观望 guānwàng ❶ wait and see;
look on (from the sidelines): ～不前
look on and make no move ❷ look
about or around: 四下～ look around

观众 guānzhòng audience; spectator;
viewer: ～席 auditorium (of a theatre);
grandstand (of a stadium) / ～收视率
audience rating

官 guān ❶ (government) official;
(military) officer: ～兵 officers
and men / ～邸 official residence or

mansion / ～吏 government official /
～迷 obsessed office-seeker; careerist /
～员 official; officer / ～本位 official
status taken as the only criterion for
judging social worth; official rank
standard / ～复原职 be restored to
one's former rank or office; be re-
instated / ～～相护。Bureaucrats
shield one another. ❷ government-
run; government-sponsored; official:
～价 official price / ～腔 official jargon; bureaucratese; bureaucratic tone /
～衔 official title ❸ organ: 感～ sense
organ

官场 guānchǎng 〈贬〉officialdom;
official circles: ～得意 be successful in
officialdom; rise rapidly up the official
ladder

官倒 guāndǎo ❶ profiteering by governmental organizations or public servants ❷ official speculator or racketeer

官方 guānfāng of or by the government; official: ～消息 news from official or government sources

官话 guānhuà ❶ (old name for 普通
话) official dialect — Mandarin ❷ official jargon; language of officialdom

官僚 guānliáo bureaucrat; bureaucracy: ～机构 bureaucratic apparatus /
～主义 bureaucratism / ～资本
bureaucrat-capital

官能 guānnéng organic function;
sense; physical faculty: ～症 functional
disease

官气 guānqì *also* "官架子" bureaucratic airs; bureaucratism: ～十足
bursting with bureaucratic airs; very
haughty in manners

官商 guānshāng (personnel) in a
state-run business; government enterprise or commerce: 改变～作风 change
one's bureaucratic way of doing business

官司 guānsi 〈口〉lawsuit: 人命～
case of homicide

官样文章 guānyàngwénzhāng　mere formalities；officialese

官瘾 guānyǐn　craving after office；obsession for official post；～ 极 大 be an addicted office-seeker

官运 guānyùn　official or political career；fortunes of officialdom；～ 亨通 have a successful official career；advance smoothly in officialdom

冠 guān　❶ cap；hat：～盖〈书〉official hats and canopies — officials ❷ sth like a cap；corona；crest：～子 crest；comb / ～状病毒 coronavirus ～状动脉 coronary artery
see also guàn

冠冕 guānmiǎn　❶ royal crown；official hat ❷ high-sounding；pompous；highfalutin：～ 堂皇 high-sounding；high-sounding

冠心病 guānxīnbìng　〈医〉coronary heart disease：～ 患者 coronary heart patient

棺 guān　coffin：～ 材 *also*「棺木」coffin / ～椁 inner and outer coffins

鳏 guān　wifeless；widowered：～夫〈书〉old wifeless man；widower / ～寡孤独 widowers, widows, orphans and the childless

guǎn

馆（舘） guǎn　❶ accommodation for guests；mansion ❷ embassy，legation or consulate ❸ term for certain service establishments：～子 restaurant；eatery ❹ place for cultural activities，(esp) library or museum：～藏丰富 have a rich collection (of books，etc)

管 guǎn　❶ tube；pipe；valve：～材 tubing ❷ wind instrument：～风琴〈乐〉(pipe) organ / ～乐队 wind band ❸ manage；run；administer：～界 area or land under one's jurisdiction /

～区 *also*「管片」district under one's jurisdiction；jurisdiction / 她～账，我～卖货。She keeps the books while I do the business. ❹ subject (sb) to discipline；take in hand：这孩子得～一～了。The boy needs discipline. ❺ concern oneself with；bother or care about；mind：大家的事大家～。Everybody's business，everybody's care. / ～他是谁，违纪犯律就得批评。Whoever violates the regulations shall be criticized. ❻ provide；ensure；guarantee：～吃～住 provide board and lodging ❼ *used in the pattern*「管…叫…」：大家都～这孩子叫小嘎子。Everyone calls the boy Naughty Imp.

管保 guǎnbǎo　guarantee；assure：～灵验。Efficacy guaranteed. / 他～不是我的对手。He's certainly not my match.

管道 guǎndào　❶ pipeline；piping；conduit：～工 plumber / ～系统 piping system ❷〈方〉channel；way

管家 guǎnjiā　❶ steward；butler；housekeeper：～婆（female）housekeeper；housewife ❷ manage a household；run a house

管见 guǎnjiàn　〈谦〉(in) my humble opinion；(according to) my limited understanding

管教 guǎnjiào　❶ subject (sb) to discipline；discipline：严加～ impose strict discipline (upon sb) ❷ put under surveillance and re-educate through labour：～所 reformatory

管理 guǎnlǐ　❶ manage；run；administer：～费 management fee；cost of administration / ～科学 management science / ～人员 administrative personnel；managerial staff；administrator ❷ take care of；look after；tend：～员 storekeeper；janitor / ～犯人 watch over prisoners

管事 guǎnshì　❶ run affairs；be in charge；be responsible：不 ～ 的职务

nominal post ❷ see "管用" ❸ 〈旧〉
steward; butler; manager

管束 guǎnshù supervise; restrain;
control:～不严 be lax in supervision

管辖 guǎnxiá have jurisdiction over;
exercise control over; administer:～权
jurisdiction

管闲事 guǎnxiánshì meddle in what
does not concern one; poke one's nose
into others' business: 爱～ be nosy or
meddlesome / 别～! Mind your own
business!

管弦 guǎnxián wind and string instruments:～乐 orchestral music / ～乐队
(symphony) orchestra

管用 guǎnyòng also "管事" efficacious; effective; useful: 他说话不～。
His words carry no weight.

管制 guǎnzhì ❶ control: 外汇～ foreign exchange control / 灯火～ blackout ❷ put (criminals, etc) under surveillance:～劳动 labour under surveillance

管中窥豹 guǎnzhōngkuībào look at a
leopard through a tube — see only a
part; have a limited view of sth

管子 guǎnzi tube; pipe:～工 plumber; pipe fitter

guàn

观(觀) guàn Taoist temple
see also guān

贯 guàn ❶ pass through; penetrate; pierce ❷ be connected;
proceed in succession; follow in a continuous line

贯彻 guànchè carry out (a policy,
etc); implement; execute

贯穿 guànchuān ❶ run through;
penetrate ❷ also "贯串" fill; permeate:求实精神～全文。The article is
permeated with pragmatism.

贯通 guàntōng ❶ have a thorough
understanding of; master (a subject);

be well-versed in:～中西医学 master
both Chinese and Western medicine ❷
link or join up; thread together:～南北
(of a railway, etc) run north and south

贯注 guànzhù ❶ concentrate on;
give full attention to; be absorbed in ❷
(of meaning, tone, etc) connected;
consistent

冠 guàn ❶ give a name; crown
with (a title):～名权 (exclusive)
right to name a contest, etc / ～以大师
的 称号 crown (sb) with the title of
"grand master" ❷ first place; champion:～军 champion; first-prize winner; gold medallist
see also guān

冠词 guàncí 〈语言〉article: 定～ definite article

惯 guàn ❶ be used, accustomed
or inured to or be in the habit of:
～犯 habitual offender; hardened criminal; recidivist / ～技〈贬〉customary
tactic; old trick / ～例 convention;
usual practice; precedent ❷ also "惯
纵" indulge; spoil; pamper

惯常 guàncháng ❶ habitual; customary; usual ❷ often; frequently

惯性 guànxìng 〈理〉inertia:～定律
law of inertia / ～制导 inertial guidance; inertia-guided

惯用 guànyòng habitually practise;
consistently use:～法 usage / ～语 idiom / ～的 伎俩 customary tactics;
stock-in-trade

盥 guàn 〈书〉wash (the hands or
face)

盥洗 guànxǐ wash one's hands or
face; wash up:～室 washroom; toilet /
～台 washstand / ～用品 toilet articles

灌 guàn ❶ irrigate; water:～区
irrigated area / ～渠 irrigation
canal or channel ❷ fill; pour; cram:～
到瓶里 pour into a bottle / 把人～醉
get sb drunk ❸ record (on a tape or
disc):～唱片 make a gramophone re-

cord; cut a disc

灌肠 guàncháng ❶〈医〉give an enema ❷ starch sausage

灌溉 guàngài irrigate; water: ~面积 area under irrigation / 引水~ irrigated area

灌米汤 guànmǐtāng *also* "灌迷魂汤" bewitch with honeyed words; lay it on thick; soft-soap

灌木 guànmù bush; shrub: ~丛 brush(-wood); shrubbery

灌输 guànshū instill (sth) into (sb); inculcate; imbue (sb) with (sth)

灌注 guànzhù pour: ~混凝土 pour concrete / ~全部心血 devote oneself heart and soul (to sth)

鹳 guàn 〈动物〉stork

罐 guàn jar; pot; tin: ~装食品 tinned or canned food / 水~子 water pitcher / 一~茶叶 a caddy of tea

罐头 guàntou tinned or canned food: 水果~ canned fruit / ~厂 cannery

guāng

光 guāng ❶ light; ray; brightness: ~波〈理〉light wave / ~缆 fibre-optic cable / ~年〈天文〉light-year / ~速〈理〉speed or velocity of light / ~合作用〈植〉photosynthesis / ~控开关 photo-switch; light-operated switch ❷ scenery; landscape; sight ❸ honour; glory; credit ❹ smooth; glossy: ~洁度 degree of finish ❺ use up; exhaust; finish: 喝~ drink up ❻ bare; naked: ~脚 bare-footed / ~膀子 stripped to the waist / ~秃秃 bald ❼ merely; solely; only: ~打雷下不下雨 all thunder and no rain; all words and no action

光标 guāngbiāo 〈信息〉cursor

光彩 guāngcǎi ❶ lustre; splendour; brilliance: ~夺目 dazzlingly bright; brilliant / ~照人 brilliant; resplendent ❷ honour; glory: 觉得不~ feel disgraced or humiliated

光大 guāngdà carry forward(a tradition, etc); promote; enhance

光复 guāngfù recover; regain

光杆儿 guānggǎnr bare trunk or stalk; 〈喻〉one who has no family or following: ~司令 general with no troops under his command; leader without a following

光顾 guānggù (of customers) patronize (a shop, etc): 欢迎~。Your patronage is cordially invited.

光怪陆离 guāngguài-lùlí grotesque and gaudy; bizarre and motley; fantastic

光棍儿 guānggùnr unmarried man; bachelor: 打~ remain a bachelor; be unmarried

光滑 guānghuá smooth; glossy; slick

光环 guānghuán ring of light; luminous ring; (as of a deity) halo

光辉 guānghuī radiance; brilliance; glory: ~灿烂 shining with splendour; magnificent

光火 guānghuǒ get angry; fly into a rage; flare up

光景 guāngjǐng ❶ conditions; circumstances: 如今的~强多了。Things are much better now. ❷ probably; likely: 天又阴了, ~是要下雪了。It's overcast again and looks like snow. ❸ (usu used to modify time, quantity, etc) about; around: 十六七岁~ about sixteen

光亮 guāngliàng ❶ bright; luminous; shiny: ~如新 as bright as new ❷ light: 透出一线~。A beam of light peeped through.

光临 guānglín 〈敬〉presence (of a guest), etc): 敬请~指导。Your presence and comments are cordially requested.

光溜溜 guāngliūliū ❶ *also* "光溜" smooth; slippery ❷ bare; naked

光芒 guāngmáng rays of light; radiance；～万丈 shining with boundless brilliance；resplendent

光明 guāngmíng ❶ light：广场上大放～。The square was brilliantly lit. ❷ bright：通体～的水晶球 transparent crystal ball ❸ promising；bright：～前景 brilliant prospects ❹ openhearted；guileless；aboveboard：～磊落 open and aboveboard；frank and openhear-ted

光盘 guāngpán *also*"光碟"(optical) disc；compact disc（CD）

光谱 guāngpǔ 〈理〉spectrum：～分析 spectral analysis

光驱 guāngqū （short for 光盘驱动器）〈信息〉CD drive

光荣 guāngróng honour；glory；credit：～榜 honour roll / ～使命 glorious mission

光天化日 guāngtiān-huàrì in broad daylight；in the light of day

光头 guāngtóu ❶ bareheaded；hatless ❷ shaven head：剃～ have one's head shaved clean ❸ bald head

光纤 guāngxiān （short for 光导纤维）light-guide or optical fibre；fibre-optic：～电缆 fibre-optic cable

光线 guāngxiàn light；ray：～充足 well lighted

光学 guāngxué optics：～玻璃 optical glass

光耀 guāngyào ❶ brilliant；radiant；splendid ❷ glory；honour：光宗耀祖 bring honour to one's ancestors ❸ shine brilliantly：～千秋 shine through the ages

光阴 guāngyīn time：～似箭。Time flies. / 一去不复返〈谚〉Lost time is never found again. or Time and tide wait for no man.

光泽 guāngzé lustre；sheen；gloss：无～的眼睛 lacklustre eye

光照 guāngzhào shine；illuminate：～度〈理〉intensity of illumination；illuminance / ～期〈植〉light period / ～日月 shine like the sun and the moon

咣 guāng 〈象声〉bang；crash：门～当一声关上了。The door was shut with a bang.

guǎng

广（廣） guǎng ❶ wide；extensive；numerous：～度 scope；breadth；range / ～为流行 be all the rage / ～种薄收 extensive cultivation or farming；〈喻〉extensive effort with little gain ❷ expand；spread；extend：以～声势 extend one's power and prestige ❸ （Guǎng）short for 广东 or 广州：老～〈口〉Guangdong man / ～柑 a kind of orange originally produced in Guangdong / ～式月饼 Guangdong-style mooncakes

广播 guǎngbō broadcast；be on the air：～剧 radio play / ～室 broadcasting room；studio / ～员 (radio) announcer / ～电台 radio or broadcasting station / ～讲话 broadcast speech；radio talk / ～电视大学 radio and television college

广博 guǎngbó （of knowledge，etc）extensive；wide：广见博识 have rich experience and extensive knowledge

广场 guǎngchǎng （public) square

广大 guǎngdà ❶ vast；wide；extensive ❷ large-scale；widespread；broad ❸ numerous；many：～观众 numerous viewers；large audiences

广泛 guǎngfàn wide；extensive；wide-ranging：～宣传 give wide publicity (to) / ～征求意见 solicit opinions from all quarters

广告 guǎnggào advertisement；ad：～画 poster / ～栏 advertisement column / ～牌 billboard / ～公司 advertising agency

广开 guǎngkāi open wide；provide extensive possibilities：～门路 tap all possible channels (for sth)；explore every avenue or possibility / ～言路 en-

G

courage the free airing of views; provide wide opportunities for people to express their opinions

广阔 guǎngkuò　vast; wide; extensive

广袤 guǎngmào　〈书〉vast; broad; immense; ~无垠 boundless

广漠 guǎngmò　vast and bare; ~浩瀚的戈壁滩 vast and bare Gobi Desert

广义 guǎngyì　broad or general sense; ~的文化 culture in its broad sense / ~相对论〈理〉general theory of relativity

犷（獷）guǎng　〈书〉rustic; uncouth; boorish; ~悍 tough and intrepid; rough and ferocious

guàng

逛 guàng　stroll; roam; saunter; ~荡 also "逛游" loaf about; loiter; ~街〈口〉take a stroll in the streets; go window-shopping / ~窑子 visit a brothel; go whoring

guī

归（歸）guī　❶ return; give back; go or come back; ~客 returnee / ~侨 (short for 归国华侨) returned overseas Chinese / ~途 also "归程" homeward or return journey; way home or back / ~国留学生 returned student / 物~原主 return sth to its rightful owner ❷ tend; converge; come or group together; ~类 sort out; classify; categorize / ~入 be included (in sth); go under (sth) ❸ belong to; be in sb's charge; put under sb's care; 派自己 ~ 他管。He's in charge of assigning jobs. ❹ used between identical verbs to indicate irrelevance: 玩儿 ~ 玩儿，不能耽误正事。Fun may be fun but we mustn't neglect business.

归案 guī'àn　bring to justice; 逮捕 ~ apprehend and bring to justice / 尚未 ~

(of a suspect, etc) be still at large

归并 guībìng　❶ incorporate or merge into; amalgamate ❷ add up; put or lump together

归档 guīdàng　place on file; file; ~备查 file for future reference

归队 guīduì　rejoin one's unit; 〈喻〉return to the profession one was trained for

归根结底 guīgēn-jiédǐ　also "归根结蒂" in the final analysis; to put it in a nutshell

归公 guīgōng　be turned over to the state or the group; be made a public possession

归功 guīgōng　give the credit to; attribute the success to

归还 guīhuán　give back; return; revert

归结 guījié　❶ sum up; conclude; put in a nutshell; 问题可以 ~ 为三大类。The problems fall into three main categories. ❷ conclusion; end (of a story, etc)

归拢 guīlǒng　put or gather together

归纳 guīnà　induce; infer; draw; ~法 inductive method

归属 guīshǔ　belong to; come under the jurisdiction of; be affiliated to or with; ~未定。The jurisdiction is uncertain.

归顺 guīshùn　come over and pledge allegiance (to the government, etc)

归宿 guīsù　place where one belongs; home to return to; destination

归天 guītiān　also "归西"〈婉〉go to one's glory; pass away; die

归向 guīxiàng　turning (towards the righteous side); inclination; 人心 ~ swing of popular support; trend of popular feeling

归心 guīxīn　desire to return (home); homesickness; ~似箭 be anxious to return home as soon as possible; be impatient to return

归因 guīyīn　ascribe; attribute; ~于运

气 attribute or ascribe (sth) to luck

归于 guīyú ❶ belong to; be attributed to:把错误～别人 attribute errors to sb else; put the blame on others ❷ tend to; result or end in:～一致 reach consensus

归真返璞 guīzhēn-fǎnpú *also* "返璞归真" (drop all affectation and) return to original purity and simplicity; return to nature; rediscover one's true self

归置 guīzhi *also* "归整" sort out; arrange; put in order; tidy up

归总 guīzǒng in total; all together; to put in a nutshell

归罪 guīzuì *also* "归咎" put the blame on; attribute or impute a fault to; blame

圭 guī ❶ tapering jade tablet (for ceremonial occasions in ancient times) ❷ sundial:～桌〈书〉sundial;〈喻〉criterion; standard

龟(龜) guī tortoise; turtle:～甲 tortoise-shell /～龄 long life /～缩 huddle up (like a turtle); hole up　*see also* jūn

龟头 guītóu 〈生理〉glans penis

规 guī ❶ dividers; compasses; gauge ❷ rule; regulation; convention:～章 rules; regulations /～整 regular; standard; (make) neat and tidy /无～可循 have no precedents or conventions to go by ❸ admonish; counsel; advise:～劝 admonish; counsel; advise

规避 guībì evade (responsibility, etc); shun; dodge

规程 guīchéng rules; regulations; 操作～rules of operation

规定 guīdìng stipulate; specify; provide:～动作〈体〉compulsory exercise or programme /～价格 stipulate or fix a price

规范 guīfàn standard; model; norm:～化 standardization /～语法 normative grammar /～市场管理 regulate

market management

规格 guīgé specifications; standards; norms

规划 guīhuà （draw up a) plan;（map out a) programme:统一～商业网点 draw up a unified plan for a commercial network

规矩 guīju ❶ rule; established practice; custom:坏了～violate established practice / 规行矩步 stick to established practice; follow the beaten track ❷ well-behaved or well-disciplined; honest:放～点儿。Behave yourself!

规律 guīlǜ law; regular pattern:～性 regularity; pattern; law

规模 guīmó scale; scope; dimensions:～宏大 broad in scale or scope /～经济 economy of scale /～效应 scale effect

规则 guīzé ❶ rule; regulation; law ❷ regular;不～irregular

皈 guī

皈依 guīyī *also* "归依" be converted to (Buddhism or some other religion)

闺 guī boudoir:～房〈书〉inner chambers (of husband and wife); boudoir /～阁 women's quarters; boudoir /～女 girl; maiden;〈口〉daughter /～秀 daughter of a rich and powerful family

硅 guī 〈化〉(formerly called 矽) silicon (Si):～肺〈医〉silicosis /～钢 silicon steel /～胶 silica gel /～酸盐 silicate

瑰 guī 〈书〉rare; marvellous; magnificent:～宝 treasure; gem /～丽 surpassingly beautiful; splendid; magnificent

鲑 guī salmon

guǐ

轨 guǐ ❶ rut; track; rail ❷ course; orbit; order

轨道 guǐdào ❶（railway）track ❷ orbit; trajectory; path; 送人〈书〉put（a satellite）into orbit ❸〈喻〉course; track; path: 走上～get on the right track

轨迹 guǐjì ❶〈数〉locus ❷ see"轨道 ❷"❸〈喻〉track; footmark: 人生～ journey through life

诡 guǐ ❶ deceitful; sly; cunning: 一谲〈书〉strange and changeable; mysterious; treacherous / ～秘 surreptitious; secretive; furtive / ～诈 crafty; cunning; treacherous ❷〈书〉 weird; uncanny; eerie: 一诞 unfounded and absurd; incredible / ～异 queer; strange; bizarre

诡辩 guǐbiàn sophistry; sophism; quibble; ～术 sophistry

诡计 guǐjì cunning scheme; trick; ruse: ～多端 have a lot of tricks up one's sleeve; be foxy and wily

鬼 guǐ ❶ ghost; spirit; apparition: 镇～lay a ghost / ～魂 ghost; spectre; apparition / ～火 also "磷火" will-o'-the-wisp; jack-o'-lantern / ～蜮 伎俩 devilish stratagem; sinister trick ❷ derogatory term for a person with a certain vice or problem: 讨厌～bore; spoilsport ❸ stealthy; clandestine; surreptitious: ～头～脑 thievishly; in a hole-and-corner fashion; furtively ❹ sinister; wicked; ～把戏 also "鬼名堂" sinister plot; treacherous scheme; mischief / 其中有～。There's something fishy about it. ❺〈口〉clever; smart; quick: ～才 person having some peculiar talent; special talent / ～点子 also "鬼主意" wicked or smart idea; trick

鬼斧神工 guǐfǔ-shéngōng （of architecture, etc) uncanny or incredible workmanship; prodigious craftsmanship

鬼怪 guǐguài also "鬼魅" ghosts and monsters; bogeys; forces of evil

鬼画符 guǐhuàfú ❶ poor handwriting; (illegible) scrawl ❷ deceptive device; hypocritical remark

鬼话 guǐhuà fake story; falsehood; lie: ～连篇 a pack of lies

鬼混 guǐhùn lead an aimless or irregular life; fool or loaf around; hang about

鬼哭狼嚎 guǐkū-lángháo wail like ghosts and howl like wolves; give bloodcurdling cries and howls

鬼脸 guǐliǎn ❶ mask (used as a toy) ❷ funny or wry face; grimace: 做～ (make a) grimace

鬼门关 guǐménguān gate of hell; jaws of death; danger spot

鬼迷心窍 guǐmíxīnqiào （act as if） possessed; (be) obsessed (by a craze)

鬼神 guǐshén ghosts and gods; spirits; supernatural beings: 鬼使神差 as inexplicably as if manipulated by supernatural beings; as if designed by providence; by curious coincidence

鬼祟 guǐsuì ❶ furtive; secretive: 鬼鬼祟祟 in a hole-and-corner fashion; sneaky; on the sly ❷ see"鬼怪"

鬼胎 guǐtāi sinister design; ulterior motive; evil plot: 心怀～harbour sinister designs

鬼子 guǐzi （term of abuse for foreign invaders）devil: ～兵（during WWII）Japanese soldiers; Japs / 洋～foreign devil

癸 guǐ 10th of the Heavenly Stems see also"干支" gānzhī

guì

柜（櫃） guì ❶ cupboard; cabinet: ～橱（usu for bowls, glasses, etc）cupboard / ～子（usu for clothes or files）cabinet; cupboard ❷ cashier's office or desk: ～房 cashier's office or desk; shop cashier

柜台 guìtái counter; bar: 站～serve behind the counter; work as a shop assistant / ～承包 concession (in a shop)

剁（剗） guì

剁子手 guìzishǒu executioner; butcher

贵 guì ❶ expensive; costly; dear ❷ (deem) valuable or precious; highly valued / ～客 distinguished or honoured guest / ～重 valuable; precious; expensive / ～金属 noble or precious metal ❸ of high rank; exalted; noble；～妃〈史〉highest-ranking imperial concubine / ～族 noble; aristocrat; patrician ❹〈敬〉your；～姓? May I know your name? ❺（Guì）short for Guizhou（贵州）

贵宾 guìbīn honoured or distinguished guest; VIP；～卡 VIP card / ～席 seats for distinguished guests; VIP gallery / ～休息室 VIP lounge or room

贵人 guìrén person of eminence；～多忘事 (often with mild sarcasm) people of eminence have short memories; great men easily forget

桂 guì ❶ cassia; cinnamon；～皮 cassia or cinnamon bark ❷ also "桂花" sweet-scented osmanthus ❸ laurel; bay tree; 折～ win the laurel; win victory ❹（Guì）another name for Guangxi（广西）

桂冠 guìguān laurel；摘取～ win the laurel; gain distinction / ～诗人 poet laureate

桂鱼 guìyú (popular term for 鳜) mandarin fish

桂圆 guìyuán〈植〉longan；～肉 dried longan pulp

跪 guì kneel; go down on one's knees；～拜 worship on bended knees; kowtow / ～倒 throw oneself on one's knees; fall to one's knees; prostrate oneself

gǔn

辊 gǔn roller

滚 gǔn ❶ roll; trundle; tumble; 前一翻〈体〉forward roll / 一下悬崖 tumble from a cliff ❷〈贬〉get away; beat it; scram；～蛋〈粗〉get out; scram; beat it ❸ boil; seethe；～水 boiling water ❹ very; extremely；～热 also "滚烫" boiling, piping or burning hot / ～圆 round as a ball; perfectly round ❺ trim; hem; bind; 袖口～边 bind cuffs (with embroidered borders)

滚动 gǔndòng roll; trundle；〈喻〉circulate or accumulate continuously；～摩擦〈理〉rolling friction / ～播放 show or televise (a series of movies, etc) one after another / ～投放〈经〉rolling launch

滚瓜 gǔnguā used in the following phrases；～烂熟 be extremely fluent; master thoroughly; know pat / ～溜圆 (as of an animal) fat and round

滚滚 gǔngǔn roll; surge; come or occur continuously；波涛～ rolling seas; surging waves / 财源～. Money keeps rolling in.

滚筒 gǔntǒng cylinder; rotary drum；～式洗衣机 cylindrical or drum-type washing machine

滚雪球 gǔnxuěqiú roll a snowball; snowball；他的财富像～一样越滚越多. His wealth snowballed.

滚轴滑冰 gǔnzhóuhuábīng （体）(roller-) blading / ～鞋 (roller-) blades; in-line skates

滚珠 gǔnzhū ball；～轴承 ball bearing

磙 gǔn ❶ also "磙子" roller; 石～ stone roller ❷ level (ground) with a roller

gùn

棍 gùn ❶ rod; stick; cudgel；～棒 club; cudgel; stick / 竹～儿 bamboo stick; cane ❷ scoundrel; rascal; ruffian; 淫～ licentious man; libertine; wolf

guō

郭 guō　outer wall of a city

聒 guō　noisy；～噪 be clamorous or long-winded；nag；din

锅（鍋） guō　❶ pot；pan；cooker：饭～ rice pot / ～巴 crust of cooked rice；rice crust / ～盖 lid of a cooking pot / ～炉 boiler / ～台 top of a kitchen range；kitchen / ～贴儿 lightly fried dumpling；potsticker ❷ bowl (of a pipe, etc)：烟袋～儿 (bowl of a) pipe

蝈（蟈） guō

蝈蝈儿 guōguor　〈动物〉katydid；long-horned grasshopper

guó

国（國） guó　❶ country；state；nation：～别 (as an entry in a form) country；nationality / ～道 national road or highway / ～都 (national) capital / ～度 country；state；land / ～父 father of a republic / ～歌 national anthem / ～号 title of a reigning dynasty or state / ～花 national flower / ～徽 national emblem / ～界 national boundary or border / ～君 monarch / ～旗 national flag / ～土 territory or land (of a country) / ～王 king；monarch / ～威 international prestige of a state；national power and influence / ～宴 state banquet / ～葬 state funeral / ～破家亡 with one's country subjugated and family wrecked ❷ of the state；national；(esp) Chinese：～宝 national treasure / ～货 national or domestic goods；Chinese (-made) goods ❸ best in the country：～脚 〈口〉member of the national football team / ～手 top-notch person in the country (in chess, medicine, etc)；member of the national team

国宾 guóbīn　state guest：～馆 state guesthouse

国策 guócè　basic policy of a state or nation；state or national policy

国产 guóchǎn　home-made；(esp) made in China：～影片 Chinese-made movie；Chinese film

国耻 guóchǐ　national humiliation：～纪念日 day in remembrance of national humiliation

国粹 guócuì　quintessence or best of Chinese culture：保护～ preserve Chinese cultural treasures

国法 guófǎ　law of the land；(national) law：～难容 not to be tolerated by law

国防 guófáng　national defence：～部 ministry of defence；(China) Ministry of National Defence；(US) Department of Defence / ～工业 (national) defence industry

国格 guógé　nation's dignity；national prestige：有损～ harmful or damaging to the dignity of one's nation

国画 guóhuà　traditional Chinese painting：～家 traditional Chinese painter

国会 guóhuì　(UK) Parliament；(US) Congress；(Japan) Diet：～山 (US) Capitol Hill；the Hill / ～议员 congressman；member of parliament (MP)；(Japan) Dietman

国籍 guójí　❶ nationality；citizenship：无～ stateless ❷ (of a plane, ship, etc) national identity：～不明的飞机 unidentified aircraft

国计民生 guójì-mínshēng　national economy and people's livelihood

国际 guójì　international；foreign；world：～法 (short for 国际公法) international law；law of nations / ～歌 The Internationale / ～化 internationalize / ～法院 International Court of Justice；

World Court / ～关系 international relations / ～惯例 international practice / ～社会 international community; family of nations / ～私法 private international law / ～象棋 chess / ～形势 international situation / ～音标〈语言〉international phonetic symbols or alphabet / ～主义 internationalism / ～互联网 also“因特网”Internet / ～日变更线 international date line

国家 guójiā country; state; nation;～队 national team / ～大事 state or national affair / ～机关 state agency or organ;（central）government office / ～机密 state secret / ～机器 state machine or apparatus / ～行为 act of state; state act / ～元首 head of state / ～主权 state or national sovereignty / ～主席 president（head of state of PRC）/ ～指导价格 state-guided price / ～兴亡，匹夫有责。The rise and fall of the nation is the concern of every citizen.

国境 guójìng ❶ national territory:出入～leave and enter a country ❷ national border or boundary:偷越～illegally cross the border / ～线 boundary（line）of a country; frontier

国库 guókù national or state treasury; exchequer;～券 treasury bond（TB）; treasury bill（T-bill）; treasury stock / ～空虚 depletion of the national treasury

国力 guólì national power, strength or capabilities:综合～comprehensive or overall national power

国门 guómén gateway of a country; border:拒敌于～之外 keep the enemy beyond the national borders

国民 guómín people of a nation; national;～党 Kuomintang（KMT）or Nationalist Party / ～待遇（条款）national treatment（clause）/ ～经济 national economy / ～收入 national income / ～心态 national psyche / ～生产总值 gross national product（GNP）

国难 guónàn national crisis or calamity（caused by foreign aggression）:～当头 at a time of national crisis

国内 guónèi internal; domestic; home;～法 domestic or national law / ～生产总值 gross domestic product（GDP）

国情 guóqíng condition or state of a country; national conditions or circumstances:～咨文（US）state of the union message / 从中国的～出发 proceed from China's actual conditions

国庆 guóqìng National Day;～节 National Day（October 1, in China）

国人 guórén compatriots;（fellow）countrymen; people of the country

国色天香 guósè-tiānxiāng of ravishing beauty and heavenly fragrance（referring to the peony or a beautiful woman）

国事 guóshì state or national affairs;～访问 state visit

国书 guóshū letter of credence; credentials:递交～present credentials

国泰民安 guó tài-mín'ān the country enjoys prosperity and the people live in peace

国体 guótǐ ❶ state system ❷ national prestige or dignity:有失～impair national prestige

国外 guówài external; overseas; abroad;～市场 overseas or foreign market / ～资产 assets abroad

国务 guówù state affairs;～卿（US）Secretary of State / ～院 State Council;（US）State Department / ～部长 minister of state / ～委员 member of the State Council; state councillor

国营 guóyíng state-run; state-operated;～经济 also“国有经济”state sector of the economy

国有 guóyǒu state-owned;～股 state-owned stock or shares / ～化 nationalize / ～企业（shortened as 国企）state-owned enterprise (SOE); state enterprise

国语 guóyǔ national language of a country; Chinese (as taught in school); (旧) Mandarin Chinese

国债 guózhài ❶ national debt ❷ also "国库券" treasury or government bond

guǒ

果(❶菓) guǒ ❶ fruit; nut; ~冻 (fruit) jelly; jello / ~脯 preserved or candied fruit / ~酱 jam / ~木 fruit tree / ~农 fruit grower; orchardman / ~品 (fresh and dried) fruit / ~仁 meat of a nut; kernel / ~园 fruitery; orchard / ~汁 fruit juice ❷ result; consequence; outcome; ~报 〈宗教〉 karma; (esp) retribution for sin ❸ strong-willed; resolute; determined; ~断 resolute; decisive / ~敢 courageous and resolute ❹ really; as expected; ~不其然 just as expected; sure enough

果然 guǒrán also "果真" as expected; sure enough; indeed

果实 guǒshí ❶ fruit; ~累累 laden with fruit ❷〈喻〉 gains; fruits;劳动~ fruits of labour

果子 guǒzi ❶ fruit; ~酱 jam / ~酒 fruit wine / ~露 fruit syrup ❷ also "馃子" deep-fried doughnut

裹 guǒ ❶ tie up; wrap; bind; ~扎伤口 dress a wound / ~足不前 hesitate to move forward; mark time; flinch ❷ press into service; round up; make away with

裹胁 guǒxié also "裹挟" force to take part (in evildoing); coerce;被~当了土匪 become a bandit under duress

裹挟 guǒxié ❶ (of current, etc) carry away (mud and sand, etc) ❷ involve; sweep along; be caught up in;受形势~ be swept along by the force of circumstances ❸ see "裹胁"

guò

过(過) guò ❶ go from one place to another; cross; pass;~道 passageway; corridor; doorway / ~客 passing traveller; transient (guest) / ~厅 hallway; lobby / ~街天桥 overhead pedestrian crossing; overpass ❷ spend or pass (time); undergo; go through or over;~磅 (usu of sth heavy) weigh (on the scales) / ~冬 pass the winter; winter / ~年 celebrate or spend the New Year / ~手 take in and give out (money, etc); receive and distribute; handle / ~筛子 sift (out); go over or select carefully; scan / 今天~一天，算一天 muddle along with no thought of tomorrow; while away the time as best one could ❸ transfer; adopt ❹ exceed; go beyond; be over; ~谦 too modest / ~半数 more than half; majority / 经济~热 overheated economy ❺ fault; error; mistake ❻〈量〉 time;洗了三~ wash (sth) three times ❼〈助〉 used after a verb to indicate a) (plus 得 or 不) superiority or inferiority, success or failure, etc;说不~ can't out-argue (sb) / 信得~ have confidence (in sb) b) completion of an action;账付~了。The bill has been paid. c) past action or experience;他当~水手。He has been a sailor (before).

过不去 guòbuqù ❶ cannot get through or across; (of a sth) be impassable;胡同太窄,卡车~。The alley is too narrow for the truck to pass through. ❷ be hard on (sb); make things difficult for; make it hot for ❸ feel uneasy or sorry (about sth)

过程 guòchéng course; process;认识~ process of cognition

过错 guòcuò fault; error

过得去 guòdeqù ❶ be able to pass;

can get through ❷ not bad; passable; okay:日子还~can get by / 他的字还~。His handwriting is presentable. ❸ (usu used in rhetorical questions) feel at ease;光拿钱不干活,你心里~吗? Do you feel comfortable about getting money without working for it?

过度 guòdù excessive; undue; over-:劳累~ overworked

过渡 guòdù transition; interim; stop-gap:~时期(period of)transition; transitional period / ~性人物 transitional figure; flash-in-the-pan

过分 guòfèn going too far; excessive; too much

过关 guòguān cross a mountain pass;〈喻〉pass a test; reach a standard:~斩将 beat one's adversaries one by one; overcome one obstacle after another / 质量不~。The quality is not up to standard.

过河 guòhé cross the river:~拆桥 demolish the bridge as soon as the river's crossed; kick down the ladder / ~卒子(in Chinese chess)pawn that has crossed the border and cannot go back; desperate person with no retreat

过后 guòhòu afterwards; then; later on

过户 guòhù transfer ownership (of property, etc):房地产~ transfer of real estate ownership

过活 guòhuó make or eke out a living:靠储蓄~ live on one's savings

过火 guòhuǒ go beyond the proper limit; go to extremes; overdo:这玩笑开得~了。This is going beyond a joke.

过激 guòjī excessive; extremist; radical:~分子 extremist; radical

过奖 guòjiǎng also "过誉"〈谦〉over-praise; undeserved compliment:您~了。You flatter me.

过街老鼠 guòjiēlǎoshǔ rat crossing the street — person hated by everyone

过继 guòjì (of a heirless person) adopt a young relative; (of a child) be adopted by a relative

过境 guòjìng pass through a country; be in transit:~签证 transit visa

过来 guòlái ❶ come over or up; go or pull through:~人 experienced person; old hand ❷(guolai) *used after a verb to indicate* a)(plus 得 or 不)*ability or inability; success or failure*:干得~can manage or handle / 忙不~ have too much to do b)*direction (towards the speaker) or tendency (towards normalcy)*:转~turn round / 醒~wake up; come to

过量 guòliàng excessive; immoderate; over-:饮酒~ drink to excess

过路 guòlù pass by on one's way:~人 passer-by / ~财神 "god of wealth in transit" — one who handles large sums of money in transit

过虑 guòlǜ be over-anxious; worry unnecessarily

过滤 guòlǜ filter; filtrate:~器 filter / ~嘴儿 filter-tip; filter-tipped cigarette

过门 guòmén (of a girl) move into the husband's house upon marriage; marry

过门儿 guòménr〈乐〉opening bars; short prelude or interlude

过敏 guòmǐn ❶〈医〉allergy (to sth):~性鼻炎 allergic rhinitis ❷ over-sensitive; hypersensitive

过目 guòmù look over (a draft, etc); glance through or over; check:~不忘 not forget sth after reading it just once; have a photographic memory / ~成诵 memorize with one reading

过期 guòqī pass the deadline; expire; be overdue:~胶卷 expired film / ~杂志 back numbers of a magazine / ~作废 become invalid after the expiry date

过去 guòqù ❶ past; former; previous ❷(guoqu) go over; pass by:~的事就让它~吧。Let bygones be bygones. ❸ (guòqu) see "过世" ❹ (guoqu) used after a verb to indicate a)*motion away from the speaker*: 把头扭～ turn round one's head b) *loss of normalcy or of original state*: 昏迷～ lose consciousness; be in a coma c) *success or completion of action*: 挤～ push one's way through; squeeze in

过人 guòrén ❶ outstanding; excellent; 记忆力～ unusual memory ❷ (in certain ball games) get past or round; 带球 ～ dribble past (an opponent); break through

过日子 guòrìzi live; get along; 不会～not know how to lead a frugal life; be a poor housekeeper

过甚 guòshèn exaggerate; overstate; overdo; ～ 其 词 overstate a case; stretch the truth

过剩 guòshèng excess; surplus; 人口～ overpopulation / ～ 商品 surplus goods

过失 guòshī fault; error; mistake; ～杀人〈法〉involuntary homicide; manslaughter

过时 guòshí ❶ outdated; outmoded; obsolete ❷ past the appointed time; ～不候 no waiting after the set time

过世 guòshì *also* "过去" pass away; die

过头 guòtóu exceed the limit; overdo; ～话 excessive or extreme words; overstatement / 聪明～ be too clever by half

过往 guòwǎng ❶ come and go; pass; ～ 行 人 pedestrians; pedestrian traffic ❷ *also* "过从" have friendly

contact with; associate with; ～基密 be on close terms (with sb); be a close associate (of sb)

过问 guòwèn concern oneself with; take an interest in; bother about; 无人～ be left neglected

过细 guòxì meticulous; careful; painstaking

过眼云烟 guòyǎnyúnyān transient as a fleeting cloud; like a puff of smoke; ephemeral

过夜 guòyè ❶ *also* "过宿" pass the night; put up for the night; stay overnight ❷ of the previous evening or night

过意不去 guòyìbùqù *also* "不过意" feel guilty, sorry or apologetic; 给您添了不少麻烦, 真～。I'm sorry to have put you to so much inconvenience.

过瘾 guòyǐn satisfy an urge; enjoy oneself to the full; do sth to one's heart's content; 玩儿得真～ have the time of one's life

过硬 guòyìng *also* "过得硬" be able to stand all tests; have a perfect command (of sth); 苦练～本领 practise hard to master true skills

过犹不及 guòyóubùjí going too far is tantamount to falling short; too much is as bad as too little

过于 guòyú too; over-; excessively; ～啰嗦 too long-winded; over-elaborate

过招 guòzhāo (in martial arts, etc) measure one's strength (against sb's); 〈喻〉 have a contest; compete (in strategy, etc)

H

hā

哈 hā ❶ blow (one's breath); breathe out; ~气 breathe out; gasp; pant ❷ 〈象声〉 *usu repeated to describe laughter*: ~~大笑 roar with laughter; laugh heartily ❸ 〈叹〉 *usu repeated to indicate complacency or satisfaction*: ~~, 我说对了。Aha, so I was right. ❹ *see* "~腰"
see also hǎ

哈哈镜 hāhājìng distorting mirror

哈密瓜 hāmìguā *Hami* melon — muskmelon produced in Hami, Xinjiang

哈欠 hāqian yawn: 一面打~一面伸懒腰 stretch oneself with a yawn

哈腰 hāyāo ❶ bend one's back; stoop ❷ bow slightly (as a greeting)

há

蛤 há clam: ~壳 clamshell *see also* gé

蛤蟆 háma ❶ frog: ~镜 frog sun glasses ❷ toad

hǎ

哈 hǎ *see also* hā

哈巴狗 hǎbagǒu ❶ *also* "狮子狗" Pekinese (pet dog) ❷ toady; sycophant

哈达 hǎdá *hada*, silk scarf used as a greeting gift among Tibetans and Mongolians

hāi

咳 hāi 〈叹〉 *used to express sorrow, regret, surprise, etc*: ~, 他怎么病成这个样子! Good heavens! How ill he is! *see also* ké

嗨 hāi

嗨哟 hāiyō 〈叹〉 (chanted while doing collective labour) heave-ho; yo-heave-ho; yo-ho

hái

还(還) hái ❶ still; yet; nevertheless: ~来得及。There's still time. ❷ even more; in addition; also: 他弟弟比他~要高。His brother is even taller than he is. ❸ *used to concede a point*: 这公园~不小。The park is fairly big. ❹ *usu used in the first half of a rhetorical question to set off the second half*: 老师~弄不懂, 何况我们呢? Even our teacher cannot understand it, how can we? ❺ *used for emphasis or astonishment*: ~在 80 年代 back in the 80's / 这~假得了! It can't be a fake! *see also* huán

还好 háihǎo ❶ not bad; passable: "今天考得怎么样?" "~。" "How did today's exam go?" "Not so bad." ❷ fortunately; luckily: ~, 飞机安全着陆了。Fortunately, the plane landed safely.

还是 háishi ❶ still; yet; all the same:他最后~成功了。Nevertheless, he succeeded in the end. ❷ unexpectedly; beyond expectation:议案~真通过了！The proposal was adopted after all! ❸ had better; it would be best:你~亲自去一趟好。It would be best if you could go in person. ❹ 〈连〉or:不管刮风~下雨 rain or shine

孩 hái child; kid

孩子 háizi child; ~话 silly childish talk; baby talk / ~气 childishness

骸 hái ❶ bones of the body; skeleton:~骨 human bones (usu of the dead); skeleton ❷ body:病~ ailing body

hǎi

海 hǎi ❶ sea; lake; ocean:出~ put out to sea / ~草 seaweed / ~产 marine product / ~岛 island (in the sea) / ~堤 also "海塘" sea wall or embankment / ~港 seaport; harbour / ~轮 seagoing vessel or ship; ocean-liner / ~滩 (sea) beach / ~域 sea area; maritime space / ~战 sea warfare; naval battle / ~平面 sea-level ❷ vast expanse; 〈喻〉sea:林~ vast stretch or expanse of forest ❸ extra large; of great capacity; immense:~碗 extra-big or huge bowl

海岸 hǎi'àn (sea) coast; sea-shore:~线 coastline

海拔 hǎibá height above sea-level; elevation:~高度 altitude / ~3,000米 3,000 metres above sea level

海报 hǎibào playbill; notice:出~ put up a playbill or notice

海滨 hǎibīn seashore; seaside:~胜地 seaside resort / ~浴场 bathing beach

海带 hǎidài 〈植〉kelp

海盗 hǎidào pirate:~船 pirate ship; sea rover / ~行为 piracy

海底 hǎidǐ bottom of the sea; seabed; sea floor:~捞针 also "大海捞针" fish for a needle in the ocean; look for a needle in a haystack / ~电缆 submarine cable

海防 hǎifáng coast defence:~部队 coastal defence force

海关 hǎiguān customhouse; customs:~放行 customs clearance / ~检查 customs inspection or examination / ~总署 customs head office; (China) General Administration for Customs / ~申报单 customs declaration (form)

海归 hǎiguī also "海归派" returned overseas Chinese

海涵 hǎihán 〈敬〉be magnanimous enough to forgive or tolerate (one's error or shortfall)

海疆 hǎijiāng coastal areas and territorial seas

海军 hǎijūn navy; naval forces; ~基地 naval base / ~航空兵 naval aviation; naval air service or force / ~陆战队 marine corps; marines

海口 hǎikǒu ❶ estuary (of a river into the sea) ❷ seaport ❸ bragging; boasting; 夸下~ boast about what one can do; talk big

海枯石烂 hǎikū-shílàn (even if) the seas should run dry and the rocks crumble; ~不变心 remain loyal whatever happens

海阔天空 hǎikuò-tiānkōng as boundless as the sea and sky; unrestrained and far-ranging; ~地聊个没完 shoot the bull endlessly

海蛎子 hǎilìzi also "牡蛎" oyster

海量 hǎiliàng ❶ have an enormous capacity for alcoholic drinks; can hold one's liquor ❷ see "海涵"

海路 hǎilù sea route; sea-lane; sea-way:走~ travel by sea / ~运费 maritime transit charge

海洛因 hǎiluòyīn heroin

海米 hǎimǐ　dried shrimps

海绵 hǎimián　sponge; foam rubber or plastic；～垫 foam-rubber cushion or mattress

海难 hǎinàn　marine or maritime peril; shipwreck；～救助 salvage at sea

海内 hǎinèi　throughout the land；～外 at home and abroad

海鸥 hǎi'ōu　seagull

海派 hǎipài　Shanghai school of Beijing opera; Shanghai style；～文化 Shanghai subculture

海上 hǎishàng　offshore; maritime; marine；～运输 marine transport／～作业 offshore operation; operation at sea

海参 hǎishēn　sea cucumber; sea slug

海市蜃楼 hǎishìshènlóu　mirage; 〈喻〉castle in the air; illusion

海事 hǎishì　❶ maritime affairs；～法庭 maritime or admiralty court／～仲裁 maritime arbitration ❷ accident or disaster at sea

海誓山盟 hǎishì-shānméng　lover's pledge of eternal loyalty; vow of eternal love

海水 hǎishuǐ　sea water; brine; sea；～浴 sea bathing／～养殖 marine culture; sea water aquaculture／～不可斗量。〈谚〉Great minds cannot be fathomed by common measure.

海豚 hǎitún　dolphin

海外 hǎiwài　overseas; abroad；～版 overseas edition／～市场 overseas market／～奇谈 strange story from over the seas; traveller's tale; tall story

海湾 hǎiwān　❶ bay; gulf ❷ (short for 波斯湾) (Persian) Gulf

海味 hǎiwèi　(choice) seafood; 山珍～ all sorts of delicacies

海峡 hǎixiá　strait (esp the Taiwan Strait); channel；～两岸 both sides of the (Taiwan) Strait

海鲜 hǎixiān　(fresh) seafood

海啸 hǎixiào　tidal wave; tsunami

海牙 Hǎiyá　The Hague (of Holland)；～国际法庭 International Court at the Hague

海燕 hǎiyàn　(storm) petrel

海洋 hǎiyáng　seas and oceans; ocean；～生物 marine organism／～渔业 sea or marine fishery／～性气候 maritime or marine climate

海员 hǎiyuán　seaman; sailor; marine

海运 hǎiyùn　sea or marine transport; ocean shipping

海藻 hǎizǎo　marine alga; seaweed

海蜇 hǎizhé　jellyfish

hài

亥 hài　12th of the Earthly Branches *see also* "干支" gānzhī

骇 hài　frighten; shock; astonish；～然 gasp with astonishment; be struck dumb with amazement／～人听闻 shocking; appalling; horrifying

害 hài　❶ harm; injury; damage; 霜～ frost damage or injury／处～ harm; injury; damage ❷ harmful; destructive; injurious；～虫 injurious or destructive insect／吸烟有～。Smoking is harmful to health. ❸ do harm or cause trouble to; impair；～人不浅 do people great harm／～群之马 one who brings disgrace or is a danger to one's group; rotten apple (in the barrel); black sheep／～人终～己 (a trick, etc) boomerang (against the schemer); harm set, harm get ❹ kill; murder；～命 take sb's life; kill; murder ❺ contract (an illness); suffer from；～病 fall ill; be sick／～眼 have eye trouble ❻ feel (ashamed, etc)；～羞 *also* "害臊" be shy or bashful; be ashamed

害怕 hàipà　be afraid, scared or frightened；～困难 be afraid of difficulties／～得要命 be scared to death

氦 hài　(commonly called 氦气) 〈化〉helium (He)

嘻 hài 〈叹〉 *used to express sorrow or regret*：～，你怎么不早点告诉我！Oh, why didn't you tell me earlier?

hān

蚶 hān *also* "蚶子"〈动物〉blood clam

酣 hān heartily; deeply；(drink, etc) to one's heart's content：～畅 merry and lively (drinking); sound (asleep); (of writing, painting, etc) with ease and verve / ～歌 sing lustily / ～梦 sweet dream / ～睡 *also* "酣眠" be fast asleep; sleep soundly / ～战 hard-fought or pitched battle; (be locked in) fierce fighting

憨 hān ❶ foolish; silly：～头～脑 with a stupid head and a dull brain; foolish-looking ❷ naive; ingenuous; innocent：～厚 *also* "憨实" simple and honest; straightforward and good-natured / ～笑 smile artlessly, guilelessly or fatuously / ～直 honest and straightforward / ～态可掬 charmingly naive

鼾 hān snore：打～ snore / ～睡 sound, snoring sleep / ～声如雷 snore thunderously

hán

邯 hán

邯郸学步 Hándānxuébù imitate others slavishly only to lose one's own individuality; attempting to walk like a swan, the crow loses its own gait

含 hán ❶ keep or hold in the mouth：～口水 hold some water in the mouth / 此药须～服。This medicine is to be sucked. ❷ contain; bear：～水层〈地〉water-bearing stratum; aquifer / ～苞欲放 (of a bud) ready to

burst; (of a girl, etc) in early puberty / ～泪告别 say goodbye with tears in one's eyes / ～铅汽油 leaded gasoline or petrol / ～泪吞声 choke down one's tears ❸ nurse; cherish; harbour：～垢忍辱 endure contempt and insults / ～怒不语 hold one's tongue in fury

含糊 hánhu *also* "含胡" ❶ ambiguous; equivocal; vague：回答得很～ give an equivocal or a noncommittal reply ❷ careless; perfunctory：～不得 (of sth) must be handled with meticulous care ❸ (usu used in the negative) show weakness or cowardice：乒乓球打得真不～ be not half bad at table-tennis

含混 hánhùn unclear; indistinct; ambiguous：概念～ confused concept

含金量 hánjīnliàng gold content; 〈喻〉real worth or value：矿石的～ gold content of ore / 文凭的～ real worth of a diploma

含量 hánliàng content：净～ net content

含情脉脉 hánqíngmòmò exude tenderness and love：～地一笑 smile with tenderness and love

含沙射影 hánshāshèyǐng attack by innuendo; make insinuating remarks

含笑 hánxiào have a smile on one's face：～九泉 smile in the underworld — have nothing to regret in life; die happy / ～相迎 meet (sb) with a smile

含辛茹苦 hánxīn-rúkǔ endure all kinds of hardships; suffer hardships and privations

含羞 hánxiū with a shy look; bashfully：～不语 feel too shy to speak / ～自尽 commit suicide from shame

含蓄 hánxù *also* "涵蓄" ❶ contain; embody; imply：～的批评 implicit or veiled criticism ❷ reserved：态度～ reserved manner

含血喷人 hánxuèpēnrén make slanderous or vicious accusations

against sb; throw dirt at sb

含义 hányì　*also* "涵义" meaning; implication

含冤 hányuān suffer an injustice; be victim of a false charge; ～负屈 be wronged on a false charge / ～莫白 bear an injustice one cannot clear up

函 hán ❶ letter; ～大 (short for 函授大学) correspondence university / ～电 letters and telegrams; correspondence / ～调 investigate through correspondence / ～告 inform by letter / ～件 letters; mail / ～索即寄 be sent on application; be available on request

函购 hángòu purchase by mail (order); ～部 mail-order department

函授 hánshòu teach by correspondence; give a correspondence course; ～学校 correspondence school

函数 hánshù 〈数〉function; ～表 function table

涵 hán ❶ contain; embody; bear; ～容 be magnanimous enough to bear or excuse ❷ culvert; ～洞 culvert / ～管 culvert pipe; pipe-shaped culvert

涵盖 hángài contain; cover; embody; ～面 what is covered; coverage

涵蓄 hánxù *see* "含蓄" hánxù

涵养 hányǎng ❶ ability to control oneself; self-restraint ❷ conserve; ～地力 conserve soil fertility

涵义 hányì *see* "含义" hányì

韩(韓) Hán (short for 韩国) Republic of Korea; South Korea

寒 hán ❶ cold; frigid; chilly; 受～ catch cold; catch a chill / ～带〈地〉frigid zone / ～流 cold (ocean) current;〈气象〉cold wave / ～冬腊月 severe or freezing winter; the dead of winter / ～风刺骨 The cold wind chills one to the bone. or The wind cuts one to the marrow. / ～气袭人.

There is a nip in the air. ❷ be stricken with terror; tremble with fear ❸ poor; needy; humble; ～儒 needy scholar / ～窗苦读 persevere in one's studies in spite of hardships / 出身～微 be born of a poor family; be of humble origin

寒碜 hánchen　*also* "寒伧" ❶ ugly; unsightly; shabby; 长得～ bad-looking; plain ❷ disgraceful; shameful; disreputable; 你干这事也不嫌～? Aren't you ashamed of yourself for doing that? ❸ ridicule; put to shame; 拿话～人 make caustic remarks about sb; ridicule sb

寒假 hánjià winter vacation

寒冷 hánlěng cold; frigid; 天气～ cold weather

寒露 hánlù Cold Dew, 17th seasonal division point　*see also* "节气" jiéqì

寒毛 hánmáo　*also* "汗毛" fine hair on the human body; ～直竖 make one's hair stand on end; scare one stiff

寒舍 hánshè 〈谦〉my humble home

寒暑 hánshǔ ❶ cold and heat; ～表 thermometer ❷ winter and summer; whole year; 十余～ a dozen years or so

寒酸 hánsuān shabby and miserable; too meagre to be handsome; 穿得～ be shabbily dressed

寒心 hánxīn be bitterly disappointed; be disillusioned; 如此忘恩负义, 真让人～。Such ingratitude chills one to the marrow.

寒暄 hánxuān exchange conventional greetings; exchange amenities or compliments; pass the time of day

寒战 hánzhàn　*also* "寒颤" shiver with cold or fear; 他打了个～。A shiver ran over his body.

hǎn

罕 hǎn rarely; seldom; ～见 seldom seen; rare / ～有 rare; unusual; exceptional / 人迹~至 show little trace of human habitation

喊 hǎn ❶ shout; cry (out); call: ~叫 shout; cry out / ~救命 cry "Help! Help!" / ~冤叫屈 cry out about one's grievances; complain loudly about an alleged injustice / 人接电话 call to sb to answer the phone ❷ 〈方〉call; address; ~我老王就行。Just call me Lao Wang.

hàn

汉（漢） Hàn ❶ Han Dynasty (206 BC-220 AD) Han nationality: ~人 also "汉民" Han (people or person) / ~族 Han ethnic group, China's majority people ❸ Chinese (language): ~学 Sinology ❹ (hàn) man: 大~ big fellow

汉白玉 hànbáiyù white marble

汉堡 Hànbǎo Hamburg, major port in northwestern Germany: ~包 hamburger

汉奸 hànjiān traitor (to China): ~卖国贼 traitor and collaborator; quisling

汉语 Hànyǔ Chinese (language): ~拼音字母 Chinese phonetic alphabet / ~水平考试 Chinese language proficiency test (HSK)

汉字 Hànzì Chinese character: 简化~ simplified Chinese characters / 日语~ kanji / ~显示 (shortened as 汉显) Chinese character display / ~处理软件〈信息〉Chinese character processing software

汗 hàn sweat; perspiration: ~斑 also "汗碱" sweat stain / ~臭 bad smell of perspiration; stink of sweat / ~脚 feet that sweat easily; sweaty feet / ~水 sweat; perspiration / ~腺〈生理〉sweat gland / ~珠子 beads of sweat / ~流浃背 be soaked with sweat; sweat all over / ~

如雨下 drip with perspiration

汗马功劳 hànmǎgōngláo distinctions won on the battlefield; great contributions or services

汗毛 hànmáo see "寒毛" hánmáo

汗衫 hànshān undershirt; vest

旱 hàn ❶ dry spell; drought: ~季 dry season / ~象 signs of drought / ~灾 drought ❷ (used in contrast with 水) (dry) land: ~稻 land or dry rice / ~地 also "旱田" non-irrigated farmland; dry land / 走路 travel by land

旱冰 hànbīng 〈体〉roller-skating: ~场 roller-skating rink / ~鞋 roller skates

旱井 hànjǐng ❶ water-retention well ❷ dry well (used to store vegetables in winter)

旱涝保收 hànlàobǎoshōu ensure stable yields despite drought or excessive rain; ensure a safe income: ~田 land that gives stable yields irrespective of drought or excessive rain

旱情 hànqíng how bad a drought is; damage caused by a drought: ~严重 be afflicted with severe drought

旱鸭子 hànyāzi 〈谑〉person who cannot swim; non-swimmer

旱烟 hànyān pipe tobacco: ~袋 long-stemmed Chinese pipe

捍 hàn

捍卫 hànwèi defend; guard; protect

悍 hàn ❶ doughty; dauntless; bold; 强~ intrepid; valiant; dauntless ❷ fierce; ferocious; unreasonable: ~妇 shrew

悍然 hànrán outrageously; brazenly; flagrantly: ~宣布 brazenly or outrageously declare / ~不顾 (act) in gross defiance of; (fly) in the face of

焊（銲、釬） hàn weld; solder: ~工 welding; soldering; welder / ~枪 welding torch; welding gun / ～ 条 welding rod; solder-stick / ～ 接钢管 welded steel pipe

翰 hàn 〈书〉❶ writing brush; ～墨〈书〉brush and ink — writing, painting or calligraphy / 挥 ～ write (with a brush) ❷ writing; letter:华 ～〈敬〉your letter

翰林 hànlín 〈史〉member of the Imperial Academy (from the Tang Dynasty onward)

撼 hàn shake; ～ 天动地 shake heaven and earth; be earth-shaking

憾 hàn regret; ～事 matter for regret / 死而无 ～ die without regret; die contented / 引以为 ～ consider sth a matter for regret; deem sth regrettable

瀚 hàn 〈书〉vast; immense: ～海 vast desert

hāng

夯 hāng ram or tamp; rammer or tamper: 石 ～ stone rammer or tamper / ～歌 rammers' chant / ～土 rammed earth

háng

行 háng ❶ line; row: ～距 space between rows; (row) spacing / ～列 ranks ❷ seniority (among brothers and sisters, etc): ～辈 seniority in the family or clan / 我 ～二。 I'm the second child in my family. ❸ trade; profession; line of business: ～业 trade; profession; industry / ～～出状元〈谚〉every profession produces its own leading authority; one may distinguish oneself in any trade ❹ business firm; bank:车 ～ car or bicycle dealer's shop / ～长 president (of a bank); governor (of a central bank) ❺〈量〉

used of sth that forms a line:两 ～眼泪 two streams of tears
see also xíng

行当 hángdang ❶ see "行❸" ❷〈戏曲〉type of role:京剧的武生 ～ the martial role in Beijing opera

行话 hánghuà jargon

行家 hángjia expert; connoisseur; specialist: ～里手 experts and master hands

行情 hángqíng quotations (esp on the financial market); prices; market conditions: ～看跌。 The market is bearish. / ～看涨。 The market is bullish.

行市 hángshi quotations or prices (on the market): ～变化不定。 Prices fluctuate constantly.

吭 háng throat:引 ～高歌 sing at the top of one's voice; sing lustily
see also kēng

杭 háng

杭育 hángyō 〈象声〉(chanted by teams doing hard labour) heave-ho; yo-heave-ho; yo-ho

航 háng ❶ ship; vessel; plane: ～标 navigation mark; buoy / ～程 voyage; flight; distance travelled / ～船 ship (on regular or scheduled service) / ～模 (short for 航空模型) model airplane / ～速 speed of a ship or plane / ～线 air or shipping line; route; course / ～向 course (of a ship or plane) / ～运 shipping ❷ navigate; sail; fly: ～海 sailing the seas; navigation / 出 ～ set out on a voyage or flight; set sail; take off

航班 hángbān scheduled flight; flight (number): ～号 flight number

航道 hángdào channel; sea-lane; fairway:主 ～ main channel / 国际 ～ international sea-lane / 偏离 ～ be off course

航空 hángkōng aviation: ～港 air harbour; airport / ～公司 airline company; airlines; airways / ～母舰 (shortened as 航母) aircraft carrier; flattop

航天 hángtiān space flight; aerospace: ～器 also "航天飞行器" spacecraft / ～飞机 space shuttle; shuttlecraft

航行 hángxíng navigate by water or air; sail; fly: 逆风～ sail or fly against the wind; sail or fly to windward / 顺风～ sail or fly before the wind; sail or fly downwind

hàng

巷 hàng tunnel　*see also* xiàng

巷道 hàngdào tunnel: ～掘进 tunnelling

hāo

蒿 hāo 〈植〉 wormwood; artemisia: ～子秆儿 tender leaves and stem of crown daisy chrysanthemum

薅 hāo pull up (weeds, etc); weed by hand

háo

号(號) háo ❶ howl; yell; bawl: ～叫 yell; scream; howl ❷ wail: ～啕痛哭 wail inconsolably; cry one's eyes out　*see also* hào

蚝(蠔) háo oyster: ～油 oyster sauce

毫 háo ❶ fine tapering hair; writing brush (made of such hair) ❷ (used in the negative) least bit; slightest degree: ～不在乎 not care a damn; couldn't care less / ～发不爽 〈书〉 not deviate a hair's breadth; be perfectly accurate / ～厘不差 not different in the least; just right / ～无二致 without a fraction of difference; as

like as two peas; identical ❸ milli-: ～克 milligram (mg) / ～米 millimetre (mm) / ～升 millilitre (ml)

毫毛 háomáo soft hair on the body; down: ～无损 not suffer the slightest harm; remain unharmed / 你敢动他一根～! Don't you dare to touch a single hair on his head!

嗥 háo (of a wolf, etc) howl

豪 háo ❶ person of extraordinary powers or endowments: ～杰 person of exceptional ability; hero / ～气 heroic spirit; heroism ❷ bold and unconstrained; magnanimous and forthright: ～赌 gamble in huge amounts / ～举 bold move; munificent or magnificent act; extravagance / ～言壮语 heroic or brave words; bold promise ❸ rich and powerful; bullying; arrogant: ～门 rich and powerful family; wealthy and influential clan / ～宅 large, expensive house; mansion / 逞～强 give free rein to one's arrogance; have a free hand in doing what one wishes

豪放 háofàng uninhibited; bold and unconstrained; ～不 羁 unconventional and free; vigorous and unrestrained

豪华 háohuá ❶ (of living) extravagant; luxurious ❷ (of buildings, furniture, ornaments, etc) sumptuous; splendid; lavish: ～巴士 de luxe bus

豪迈 háomài bold and generous; heroic: ～地宣告 declare with pride

豪情 háoqíng lofty sentiments: ～满怀 filled with pride and enthusiasm; full of spirit

豪爽 háoshuǎng bold and unconstrained; uninhibited and straightforward; forthright

壕 háo ❶ also "濠" moat ❷ trench; dugout

嚎 háo ❶ howl; yell; bawl ❷ wail; cry loudly: ～天哭地 weep and wail

hǎo

好 hǎo ❶ good；fine；nice：～闻 pleasant to smell；sweet-smelling / ～坏参半 partly good and partly bad；ambivalent / ～离～散 (of a divorced couple, etc) part peacefully；part friends / 病～了 be all right now；have recovered / ～景不长。Good times don't last long. ❷ friendly；kind：～友 great or good friend ❸ be easy (to do)；be convenient；～办 easy to handle or do / ～商量 can be settled through consultation；be no problem ❹ *used after a verb to indicate the completion of an action*：计划订～了。The plan has been drawn up. ❺ *used to express approval, conclusion, etc*：～，就照你说的办。OK, we'll do as you say. ❻ *used for emphasis or intensity, sometimes with exclamatory force*：～多 *also* "好些" a great many；a good deal；quite a lot / ～半天 quite a while / 五十～几 well over fifty / 一个人权卫士！A human rights champion indeed!

see also hào

好比 hǎobǐ can be compared to；may be likened to；be just like

好不 hǎobù *used before bi-syllabic words for emphasis*：～高兴 very glad；so happy

好吃 hǎochī tasty；delicious；nice (to eat)

好处 hǎochu ❶ benefit；advantage：戒烟～多。There are many advantages in giving up smoking. ❷ gain；profit；mileage：～费 favour fee；kickback

好歹 hǎodǎi ❶ *also* "好赖"good and bad；what's good and what's bad ❷ mishap；disaster：万一有个～ in case of a mishap；should something happen ❸ *also* "好赖" in a makeshift manner；somehow (or other)：～吃一点 just

have a bite ❹ *also* "好赖"no matter in what way；at any rate；anyhow：～你得去一趟。You should go there anyhow.

好端端 hǎoduānduān （used to show regret or surprise）in perfectly good condition；when everything is all right：她～的怎么就晕倒了? How come she fainted all of a sudden?

好感 hǎogǎn favourable impression；good opinion：对其颇有～ have quite a good opinion of sb；be favourably impressed by sb；take to sb

好过 hǎoguò ❶ have an easy time；be in easy circumstances：日子很不～ have a hard time ❷ feel well：觉得～些了 feel a bit better

好汉 hǎohàn brave man；true man；hero：～不吃眼前亏。〈俗〉A wise man does not fight against obvious odds. / ～不提当年勇。〈俗〉A true hero is silent about his past glories. / ～做事～当。〈俗〉A true man has the courage to accept the consequences of his own action.

好好儿 hǎohāor ❶ *see* "好端端" ❷ all out；to one's heart's content：～干 do one's best / ～想一想 give (sth) careful thought；～ mull over

好话 hǎohuà ❶ good or useful words；well-meant advice ❷ words of praise；pleasant words：～说尽 do every fine word and do every foul deed；be a sinner under the guise of a saint ❸ words of persuasion；plea；apology：替人说句～ put in a good word for sb

好家伙 hǎojiāhuo 〈叹〉〈口〉good lord；good heavens；gosh：～,这机器真沉。Gosh, the machine is real heavy.

好看 hǎokàn ❶ good-looking；attractive；interesting：好吃不～ delicious though not much to look at ❷ honoured；proud：脸上～ feel honoured ❸ in an embarrassing situation；on the spot：成心要人～ be bent on embarrassing sb

好莱坞 Hǎoláiwù Hollywood，centre of US movie industry：～明星 Hollywood star

好评 hǎopíng favourable comment or reception；high opinion；acclaim：～如潮 favourable comments pour in like a tidal wave；be widely acclaimed

好儿 hǎor 〈口〉❶ favour；kindness ❷ benefit；advantage；gain：有你什么～？ How could you have anything to gain? ❸ good wishes；regards；greetings：给我带个～。 Say "Hello" for me. ❹ praise；acclamation；cheers：讨个～ fish for praise

好人 hǎorén ❶ good or fine person；decent person：～好事 good people and good deeds ❷ healthy person ❸ person who tries to get along with everyone；Mr Please-all

好日子 hǎorìzi ❶ auspicious day ❷ wedding day ❸ good days；happy or comfortable life

好容易 hǎoróngyì also "好不容易" manage with great difficulty；have a hard time (doing sth)

好声好气 hǎoshēng-hǎoqì in a gentle voice；in a kindly or friendly manner；gently

好事 hǎoshì ❶ good deed or turn；〈书〉happy event：～多磨 good things never come easy；the course of true love never runs smooth ／ ～从天降 It's a godsend. ❷ used ironically：瞧你做的～! See what a mess you've made!
see also hàoshì

好手 hǎoshǒu good hand；expert；past master：烹调～ expert in cooking；good cook

好受 hǎoshòu feel good or well；feel comfortable：一身臭汗，真不～。 It feels awful to be soaked with sweat.

好说 hǎoshuō ❶〈套〉used as a po-

lite response to expressions of gratitude or compliments：～，～，这点事算不了什么。 Don't mention it. That was nothing. ❷ used to express (possible) agreement：只要您想买，价钱～。 Price won't be a problem if you want to buy this.

好说歹说 hǎoshuō-dǎishuō use every possible means of persuasion；try every way to persuade sb

好说话儿 hǎoshuōhuàr open to persuasion；obliging；good-natured：欺负人家～ take advantage of sb's good nature

好听 hǎotīng ❶ (of sound or voice) pleasant to hear；pleasant to the ear ❷ (of language) satisfactory；palatable；fine：净拣～的说 say nothing but what is palatable；always try to please

好玩儿 hǎowánr interesting；amusing；fun：这可不是～的! This is no joking matter.

好戏 hǎoxì good play or show；(used ironically) fun：看他的～ see him make a fool of himself

好像 hǎoxiàng also "好似" seem；be like

好笑 hǎoxiào laughable；funny；ridiculous：幼稚得～ ridiculously naive

好心 hǎoxīn kind heart；good intention：～自有好报。〈俗〉Good-heartedness is sure to be rewarded.

好样儿的 hǎoyàngrde 〈口〉great fellow；regular guy

好意 hǎoyì good intention；kindness：出于～ out of good intentions；well intentioned

好意思 hǎoyìsi have the nerve or cheek (to do sth)

好在 hǎozài (used in a bad situation) fortunately；luckily：～我带着伞 Luckily I have an umbrella with me.

好转 hǎozhuǎn take a turn for the better；improve

好自为之 hǎozìwéizhī conduct one

self well; do one's best; look out for oneself

hào

号(號) hào ❶ (assumed or alternative) name; title：国～ name of a dynasty or state ❷ business house; firm；本～ this shop or firm ❸ mark; sign; signal：击掌为～ clap as a signal ❹ order; grade; ordinal number：中～ medium size / 门牌～ street or house number / 这一人〈口〉 people of this sort ❺〈量〉 used of people：三百多～人 over three hundred people ❻ put a mark on; give a number to：～房子 mark out houses (as billets, etc) ❼ feel (the pulse)：～脉〈中医〉 feel the pulse ❽ order; verbal command：～令三军 issue orders to the army ❾ any brass wind instrument; anything used as a horn：军～ bugle / ～手 trumpeter; bugler ❿ call made on a bugle; bugle call
see also háo

号称 hàochēng ❶ be known as ❷ claim to be (usu sth one is not)

号角 hàojiǎo bugle; horn; bugle call (to do sth)

号码 hàomǎ number：电话～ telephone number

号外 hàowài extra (of a newspaper)

号召 hàozhāo call; appeal：发出～ issue a call; call for (sth); call on (sb)

好 hào ❶ like; love; be fond of：～动 be active or restless / ～战 bellicose; warlike / ～出风头 like to be in the limelight; enjoy public attention / ～学不倦 never tire of learning ❷ be liable to：～晕船 easily get seasick
see also hǎo

好吃懒做 hàochī-lǎnzuò be fond of food and averse to work; be gluttonous and lazy

好大喜功 hàodà-xǐgōng have a passion for the grandiose; crave grandeur and success：～，不切实际 be over-ambitious and unrealistic

好高务远 hàogāo-wùyuǎn *also* "好高骛远" reach for what is beyond one's grasp; aim too high; bite off more than one can chew

好客 hàokè be hospitable; keep open house

好奇 hàoqí curious (about); full of curiosity：～心 curiosity

好强 hàoqiáng be eager to do well in everything; always put one's best foot forward：～的性格 unyielding nature

好色 hàosè (of a man) be lecherous; be fond of women：～之徒 lecher; womaniser

好胜 hàoshèng eager to excel in everything; keen to outdo others

好事 hàoshì meddlesome; interfering; officious：～之徒 busybody; Nosy Parker
see also hǎoshì

好为人师 hàowéirénshī be fond of teaching others; like to lecture people

好恶 hàowù likes and dislikes; taste

好逸恶劳 hàoyì-wùláo love ease and comfort but hate to work; detest work and seek after comforts

好整以暇 hàozhěngyǐxiá remain calm and composed while handling pressing business; take things easy

耗 hào ❶ consume; take; cost：～费 expend; cost; consume / ～尽 *also* "耗竭" exhaust; use up; deplete / ～时 time-consuming / ～资 consume or expend money; cost / ～电量 power consumption or input ❷〈方〉 waste time; dawdle：别～着了，快开始吧。Stop dillydallying and get started. ❸ bad news

耗子 hàozi 〈方〉 mouse; rat：～药 ratsbane

浩 hào great; vast; numerous：～大 (of scale or momentum) very

great; huge; vast / ～荡 vast and mighty; expansive; immense / ～繁 vast and numerous; (of expenditure) heavy / ～瀚 (of water) vast; numerous; immense / ～劫 disaster; calamity; catastrophe / ～森 also "浩渺"〈书〉(of water) extensive; vast / ～如烟海 (of data, etc) as vast as the open sea; tremendous amount

浩气 hàoqì　also "浩然之气" noble spirit

浩叹 hàotàn　heave a deep sigh; sigh deeply

皓 hào

❶ white; ～髯 white beard / ～首 hoary head ❷ bright; luminous; ～月 bright moon

hē

呵 hē

❶ breathe out (with the mouth open); exhale; ～手 blow on one's hands (to warm them) ❷ scold; ～责 scold severely; give (sb) a dressing-down / ～斥 also "呵叱"; "喝叱" scold loudly; berate; excoriate ❸ see "嗬" hē

呵呵 hēhē　〈象声〉laugh loudly; guffaw

呵护 hēhù　〈书〉❶ (of a deity, etc) bless ❷ cherish; take good care of

喝 hē

❶ drink; ～墨水 "drink ink" — study in a school / ～西北风 suffer from cold and hunger; starve ❷ drink alcoholic liquor; ～多了 have a drop too much; be drunk
see also 喝 hè

嗬 hē

also "呵" 〈叹〉indicating astonishment; ～, 真棒! Oh, it's terrific!

hé

禾 hé

standing grain (esp rice); ～苗 seedlings of cereal crops, esp rice / ～本科〈植〉grass family

合 hé

❶ close; shut; ～拢 come or join together; gather / ～眼 close one's eyes; sleep; pass away ❷ come together; join; combine; ～办 operate or run jointly / ～金 alloy / ～谋 conspire or plot together / ～十 (as a Buddhist greeting, etc) hold the palms together before one / ～得来 get along well; be compatible / ～订本 (of a newspaper, etc) bound volume ❸ whole; entire; ～家大小 whole family ❹ conform with; suit; agree; ～身 (of clothing) fit / ～辙 be in agreement; rhyme; be rhythmical / ～规矩 conform with the rules; follow the convention / ～胃口 suit or be to one's taste / ～情～理 fair and reasonable; fair and square ❺ be equal to; add up to

合抱 hébào　also "合围" (of a tree, etc) so big that one can just put one's arms around

合璧 hébì　(of two different things) combine harmoniously; match well; 诗画～ painting matched with poetry; painting with a poem inscribed on it

合并 hébìng　❶ merge; amalgamate ❷ (of an illness) be complicated by another illness / ～症〈医〉complication

合唱 héchàng　chorus; 混声～ mixed chorus / 无伴奏～ unaccompanied chorus / ～团 chorus; choir

合成 héchéng　❶ compose; compound; 录音～ dubbing / ～镜头 process shots ❷〈化〉synthetic; ～纤维 synthetic fibre

合法 héfǎ　legal; lawful; legitimate; ～化 legalize; legitimize / ～权益 legitimate rights and interests / ～收入 lawfully earned income / ～要求 lawful or rightful claim

合该 hégāi　〈口〉should; ought to; ～如此。That is as it should be.

合格 hégé　qualified; up to standard; ～率 acceptance rate / ～证 certificate of inspection or qualification

合股 hégǔ ❶ pool capital; form a partnership ❷ plying;～线 ply or plied yarn; twine

合乎 héhū conform with or to; correspond to; accord or tally with:～要求 meet the requirements /～逻辑 be logical

合伙 héhuǒ form a partnership (with sb); enter into partnership (with sb):～人 partner /～经营 run a business in partnership

合计 héjì ❶ amount to; add up to; total ❷ (héji) think or mull over; figure out ❸ (héji) consult:～一个办法 work out a plan together

合理 hélǐ rational; reasonable; equitable;～安排 rational or proper arrangement /～收费 reasonable charge /～化建议 rationalization proposal

合力 hélì ❶ join forces; combine efforts ❷〈理〉resultant (of forces)

合流 héliú ❶ flowing together; confluence;〈喻〉merger ❷ collaborate; work hand in glove

合龙 hélóng〈建筑〉join the two sections of a bridge or dam built from two ends

合拍 hépāi ❶ in time, step or harmony (with) ❷ collaborate (on a film, etc); shoot or produce (a film) in collaboration ❸ see "合影"

合群 héqún get on well with others; be sociable or gregarious

合适 héshì suitable; appropriate; right:工作的～人选 right person for the job

合算 hésuàn ❶ worthwhile ❷ reckon; calculate; consider:我们应该再～。We've got to reconsider it.

合同 hétong contract:～方 party to a contract; contracting party /～工 contract worker /～医院 assigned hospital (under medical insurance, etc)

合叶 héyè also "合页" hinge:～片 hinge strap

合议 héyì discuss (together); consult;〈法〉try or hear (a case) together:～庭〈法〉collegiate bench or panel

合意 héyì suit; be to one's liking or taste

合营 héyíng jointly operate; run in partnership;公私～企业 enterprise under joint public-private ownership

合影 héyǐng also "合照" have a photo taken together; take a group photo or picture

合用 héyòng ❶ share ❷ fit for use; of use

合约 héyuē contract:签～ sign a contract

合资 hézī invest or own jointly; pool capital; enter into partnership:中外～企业 jointly-owned Chinese-foreign enterprise; Chinese-foreign joint venture

合奏 hézòu instrumental ensemble:～一曲 perform a piece (of music) together

合作 hézuò cooperate; collaborate; work together:～社 cooperative; co-op /～经营 jointly run or operate; manage in cooperation; run a cooperative business

何 hé ❶ used in specific questions a) what; which; who:～去～从 which way to take; what course to follow / 有～不同? What is the difference? / ～谓大学? What is a university? b) where:～处 what place; where / 公道～在? Where can one find justice? c) why:～以 why; what for ❷ used in rhetorical questions or exclamations, usu to indicate negation or emphasis:～足挂齿 not worth mentioning /～必当真 Why take it so seriously? /～不再试一下? Why not try again? /～其相似乃尔! What a striking likeness! / 人们～尝知道。People never knew.

何等 héděng ❶ what kind:你是～

人，敢来干涉我的事？ Who are you to interfere with me? ❷ *used in exclamations*:～聪明！ How clever!

何妨 héfáng　*used in rhetorical questions to suggest sth*:说说又～？ Why not speak up?

何苦 hékǔ　why take the trouble; why bother; why:～自寻烦恼？ Why worry yourself sick?

何况 hékuàng　much less; let alone; moreover:牺牲尚且不怕，～这些困难。We fear no death, let alone these difficulties.

何首乌 héshǒuwū　*also* "首乌"〈中药〉tuber of multiflower knotweed

何以 héyǐ　❶〈书〉with what; how:此等情况～解释？ How can you explain all this? ❷ for what reason; why:～他要提前离开？ Why does he want to leave earlier?

何止 hézhǐ　*used to indicate a number or extent far greater than the one given*:方圆～百里 extend far than a hundred *li* in periphery

和 hé　❶ gentle; mild; kind:～善 kind and gentle; kindly; genial /～煦 pleasantly warm; genial /～颜悦色 have a kind or genial expression; be kindly and affable ❷ harmonious; on good terms:失～ be at odds with each other; fall out with each other /～美 harmonious and happy /～睦 harmony; concord; amity /～为贵 harmony is most precious; nothing is more precious than peace ❸ peace:～谈 *also* "和议" peace talks or negotiations /～约 peace treaty ❹〈体〉draw; tie:～棋 draw or tie in chess or other board games ❺ together with:～衣而眠 sleep in one's clothes ❻〈介〉*used to indicate relationship, comparison, etc*:他无关。have nothing to do with him ❼〈连〉and:丈夫～妻子 man and wife ❽〈数〉sum ❾ (Hé) Japan; Japanese:～服 (Japanese) kimono

see also hè; hú; huó; huò

和蔼 hé'ǎi　kindly; affable; amiable:～可亲 gentle and affable; genial; amiable

和风细雨 héfēng-xìyǔ　like a gentle breeze and light rain-in a gentle and mild way

和好 héhǎo　❶ harmony; concord; amity:关系～ live in harmony ❷ become reconciled:～如初 become reconciled; be on good terms again; restore good relations

和缓 héhuǎn　❶ gentle; mild:语气～ in a gentle voice; in a mild tone ❷ ease up; relax:～紧张气氛 relieve the tension

和解 héjiě　become reconciled:～的态度 conciliatory attitude

和盘托出 hépántuōchū　make a clean breast of everything; hold nothing back

和平 hépíng　❶ peace:～鸽 dove of peace /～演变 peaceful evolution /～共处五项原则 Five Principles of Peaceful Coexistence (mutual respect for territorial integrity and sovereignty, mutual non-aggression, non-interference in each other's internal affairs, equality and mutual benefit, and peaceful coexistence) ❷ (usu 平和) mild; gentle; tranquil:心境～ peaceful mind; ease of mind

和气 héqi　❶ gentle; amiable; courteous:说话～ speak politely or gently; be soft-spoken ❷ friendship; harmony:别为这事伤了～。Don't let this hurt our friendship.

和尚 héshang　Buddhist monk:～头〈口〉shaven head; man or boy

和事老 héshìlǎo　peacemaker; mediator

和谐 héxié　harmonious:颜色搭配～ well-blended or well-matched colours

和衷共济 hézhōng-gòngjì　work together with one accord (in time of difficulties); make concerted efforts to overcome difficulties

河 hé ❶ river：～岸 river bank / ～床 also "河槽" riverbed / ～道 (usu navigable) river course / ～防 flood-prevention work done on rivers, esp the Yellow River / ～谷 river valley / ～口 river mouth：estuary / ～滩 flood land (in a river) ❷ (usu 河汉)〈天文〉Milky Way ❸ (Hé) Yellow River：～套 Great Bend of the Yellow River

河马 hémǎ hippopotamus；hippo；river horse

河山 héshān rivers and mountains；land；territory：重整～ rebuild one's country

河豚 hétún also "鲀" globefish；balloonfish；puffer

饸 hé

饸饹 héle a kind of noodles made from buckwheat or sorghum flour (with a special press)

荷 hé lotus see also "莲" lián see also hè

荷包 hébāo ❶ small bag (for carrying money and odds and ends)；pouch；～蛋 fried or poached egg ❷ pocket (in a garment)

荷尔蒙 hé'ěrméng 〈生理〉(now called 激素) hormone

荷兰豆 hélándòu snow peas；mangetout；sugar snap

核 hé ❶ (of fruit) pip；stone：～仁 kernel ❷ nucleus：细胞～ cell nucleus ❸ atomic nucleus；nuclear energy or weapon：～弹 nuclear bomb；N-bomb / ～弹头 nuclear warhead / ～电厂 also "核电站" nuclear power plant / ～辐射 nuclear radiation / ～试验 nuclear test / ～威慑 nuclear deterrence / ～污染 nuclear or radioactive pollution / ～武器 nuclear weapon；nuke / ～战争 nuclear war or warfare / ～保护伞 nuclear umbrella ❹ examine；

check：～查 examine；check；verify / ～定 check and ratify；appraise and decide / ～发 approve and issue / ～计 assess；calculate / ～资 verify capital or assets
see also hú

核对 héduì check；verify；identify or examine：～账目 check accounts

核实 héshí verify；check：～数据 verify the data

核算 hésuàn examine and calculate；assess：成本～ cost accounting

核桃 hétao also "胡桃" hútáo walnut：～仁 walnut kernel / ～酥 walnut cake

核心 héxīn nucleus；core；kernel：～部门 key department / ～家庭 nuclear family / ～人物 key person or figure / ～问题 heart of the matter

盒 hé box；case：～饭 box lunch / ～子 box；case；casket / ～式磁带 (shortened as 盒带) cassette tape / ～式录像带 videocassette；videocartridge

涸 hé 〈书〉dry up；run dry：～辙之鲋 fish trapped in a dry rut — person in a desperate situation who needs immediate relief

颔 hé jaw：上～ upper jaw

貉 hé (usu 貉子 or 狸) raccoon dog

阖 hé 〈书〉❶ entire；whole：～家团圆 reunion of all family members；family reunion ❷ shut；close：～眼 close the eyes；sleep

hè

吓（嚇） hè ❶ threaten；intimidate ❷〈叹〉used to express disapproval or resentment：～，你也太不像话了！Humph, how impudent you are!
see also xià

和 hè ❶ join in the singing ❷ write a poem in reply (to sb's poem)
see also hé; hú; huó; huò

贺 hè congratulate; felicitate; celebrate; ~词 speech or message of congratulation / ~电 congratulatory telegram; message of congratulation / ~卡 greeting card / ~礼 *also* "贺仪" congratulatory gift / ~喜 offer congratulations or felicitations

贺年 hènián *also* "贺岁" extend New Year greetings; pay a New Year call; 贺年片儿 New Year card / 贺岁片儿 film produced for the New Year; New Year movie

荷 hè ❶ carry on one's shoulder or back; ~枪实弹 carry loaded rifles ❷〈书〉bear; take on; ~重〈建筑〉weight a building can bear; weight load ❸ burden; responsibility ❹〈书〉(usu used in letter writing) obliged; grateful; 敬请示复为~。I will appreciate it very much if you kindly reply.
see also hé

荷载 hèzài ❶ carry or bear (a load or weight) ❷ *also* "载荷"; "负荷" load; ~系数 load factor

喝 hè shout loudly; ~彩 cheer; acclaim / ~令 shout (out) a command / ~问 shout (out) a question or interrogation / ~倒彩 boo; hoot; make catcalls *see also* hē

赫 hè ❶ conspicuous; distinguished; grand; ~有名 distinguished; very famous / ~~战功 outstanding or impressive military exploit ❷ (short for 赫兹)〈电〉hertz (Hz); Hertz

赫然 hèrán ❶ unexpectedly and shockingly; ~在目 be suddenly confronted with ❷ terribly (angry); ~而怒 fly into a violent rage

褐 hè brown; ~斑 (of paper) foxing; brown stain / ~铁矿 brown

iron ore; limonite

鹤 hè crane; ~嘴镐 pickaxe; pick; mattock / ~立鸡群 (of a person) be like a crane standing among chickens; stand head and shoulders above others / ~发童颜 (of elderly people) with white hair and youthful complexion; hale and hearty

壑 hè gully; big pool

hēi

黑 hēi ❶ black; ~洞 *also* "坍缩星"〈天文〉black hole; collapsed star / ~豆 black soya bean / ~纱 black armband; mourning band / ~面包 black or brown bread; rye bread / ~黢黢 *also* "黑漆漆" pitch-black; pitch-dark ❷ dark; dusk; ~洞洞 pitch-dark; pitch-black / ~压压 *also* "黑鸦鸦" dense, dark mass / ~灯瞎火 dark and unlighted ❸ secret; unlawful; reactionary; ~车 unlicenced taxi or vehicle / ~户 household or person without residence registration; shop or firm without a business licence / ~钱 money obtained by unlawful means; ill-gotten money / ~窝 nest of illegal activities; gangsters' or criminals' lair or den / ~社会 underworld; criminal syndicate ❹ wicked; evil; vicious; ~店 (口) shop, hotel or restaurant which cheats customers; (often used in the early vernacular) inn run by outlaws / ~哨 corrupt judge, referee or umpire (in sports, esp ball games) / 心~手狠 evil-minded and ruthless ❺ (Hēi) (short for 黑龙江) Heilongjiang

黑暗 hēi'àn ❶ dark ❷ corrupt; evil; reactionary; 揭露~ expose evils; show up the seamy side; rake muck

黑白 hēibái black and white; (喻) right and wrong; good and evil; ~片 black-and-white movie / ~电视 black-

and-white television / ～分明 black-and-white；　black　contrasted　with white；（good and evil，etc）in sharp contrast

黑板 hēibǎn　blackboard；～擦（black-board）eraser / ～报 blackboard news-paper

黑道 hēidào　❶ unlighted road（at night）❷ illegal activity；～买卖 shady trade ❸ underworld；banditry；～人物 underworld figure；gangster

黑管 hēiguǎn　〈乐〉（popular term for 单簧管）clarinet

黑糊糊 hēihūhū　also "黑乎乎" ❶ black；blackish ❷ dim；dusky；darkish ❸ indistinct in the distance；blurred；～的人影 blurred figure

黑话 hēihuà　❶ （thieves'）cant；（bandits'）argot ❷ malicious；obscure words；double-talk

黑金 hēijīn　❶ "black gold" — petrol-eum ❷〈方〉money used in corrupt politics；～政治 money politics

黑客 hēikè　〈信息〉hacker；cyber-punk

黑马 hēimǎ　dark horse — little-known person who unexpectedly becomes suc-cessful or prominent

黑麦 hēimài　rye

黑名单 hēimíngdān　blacklist；上了～be on a blacklist；be blacklisted

黑幕 hēimù　（sinister）inside story；shady deal；～重重 shrouded in sinister secrecy

黑人 hēirén　❶ （Hēirén）Black；Ne-gro：美国～ Afro-American；Black American ❷ person without residence registration；unregistered immigrant；person in hiding

黑色 hēisè　black；～素〈生化〉mel-anin / ～火药 black powder / ～金属 ferrous metal / ～幽默 black humour

黑市 hēishì　black market；～交易 black market deal；under-the-counter sale

黑手 hēishǒu　wicked person manipulat-ing from backstage；evil backstage ma-nipulator；～党 Mafia；Black Hand

黑桃 hēitáo　（of cards）spade；～皇后 queen of spades；spade queen

黑体 hēitǐ　boldface；～字 boldface type

黑匣子 hēixiázi　black boxes，popular name for flight data and cockpit voice recorders

黑猩猩 hēixīngxing　chimpanzee

黑黝黝 hēiyǒuyǒu　❶ also "黑油油" shiny black；jet-black ❷ dim；dark；一片～的松林 a dark mass of pine trees

黑鱼 hēiyú　（popular term for 乌鳢）snakeheaded fish；snakehead

黑子 hēizǐ　❶ （in weiqi or go）black pieces ❷〈天文〉sunspot

嘿（嗨）hēi　❶〈叹〉used as a form of greeting or to call attention：～，准备停当了吗？Hey! Are you all set? ❷〈叹〉used to express satisfaction or self-congratu-lation：～，写得真不错呀! Hey! This is really well-written. ❸〈叹〉used to ex-press surprise：～，下雨了! Why，it's raining! ❹〈象声〉usu used in dupli-cation for sneering or silly laughter：～～地冷笑 laugh ironically；ha ha

hén

痕 hén　mark；trace：泪～ tear stain / ～迹 mark；trace；vestige

hěn

很 hěn　〈副〉very；quite；awfully

狠 hěn　❶ ruthless；relentless：～毒 vicious；wicked；venomous / ～巴巴 fierce；ferocious ❷ make a painful effort；harden（one's heart，etc）：～命 do all one can；do one's ut-most；make an all-out effort ❸ reso-lute；firm；vigorous：～～打击 take resolute measures against

狠心 hěnxīn ❶ harden one's heart; make up one's mind; set one's heart; 狠了狠心 steel one's heart ❷ heartless; merciless; cruel

hèn

恨 hèn ❶ hate; resent; ～之入骨 *also* "恨入骨髓" hate to the marrow of one's bones; hate like poison ❷ regret; remorse; ～事 matter for regret

恨不得 hènbude *also* "恨不能" be anxious to; be dying or itching to; ～立刻回到家乡 wish one could get back to one's hometown right away

恨铁不成钢 hèntiěbùchénggāng wish that iron could turn into steel at once — be anxious for sb to improve

hēng

亨 hēng

亨通 hēngtōng go smoothly or well; prosper

哼 hēng ❶ snort; groan; ～哧〈象声〉puff and blow / ～哈二将 Generals Heng and Ha, two fierce-looking divinities guarding a Buddhist temple gate; pair of (truculent) men serving a powerful master or working hand in glove with each other ❷ hum; croon; ～民歌 hum a folksong / ～儿哈儿 *also* "哼哼哈哈" hem and haw; hum and ha
see also hng

哼唷 hēngyō 〈叹〉heave ho; yo-heave-ho; yo-ho

héng

恒(恆) héng ❶ lasting; persevering; permanent; ～久 long lasting; enduring / ～齿 *also* "恒牙" permanent tooth / ～心 perseverance; constancy of purpose / ～星〈天文〉(fixed) star ❷ usual; common; constant; ～量〈理〉constant / ～温 constant temperature

桁 héng 〈建筑〉purlin; ～条 purlin; stringer / ～架 truss

横 héng ❶ horizontal; transverse; ～梁〈建筑〉crossbeam; cross girder / ～批 horizontal scroll bearing an inscription (usu hung over a door and flanked by two vertical scrolls forming a couplet) ❷ from east to west or from west to east; across; sideways; ～穿 cross; go across / ～ 扯 lie across or between; span / ～跨 stretch over or across; span / ～越太平洋 fly across the Pacific ❸ horizontal stroke (in a Chinese character) ❹ in disorder or confusion; in profusion; overflowing; 老泪～流 tears streaming down one's aged face ❺ unreasonably; wilfully; forcibly; ～加指责 make unfounded charges; hurl abuses / ～插一杠子 interfere flagrantly; butt in
see also hèng

横冲直撞 héngchōng-zhízhuàng *also* "横冲直闯" dash around like mad; jostle and elbow one's way; barge or charge about

横幅 héngfú ❶ horizontal scroll of painting or calligraphy ❷ streamer; banner

横膈膜 hénggémó 〈生理〉diaphragm

横贯 héngguàn pass through from east to west or from west to east; traverse

横眉 héngméi frown in anger; scowl; ～怒目 glare hatred (at); dart an angry look (at)

横肉 héngròu ugly, ferocious facial muscles; 满脸～ (of sb) look ugly and ferocious

横扫 héngsǎo ❶ sweep across; sweep away; make a clean sweep of ❷ glance quickly from side to side

横生 héngshēng ❶（of vegetation）grow wildly ❷ crop up; bring up wilfully: ~枝节 deliberately complicate a problem by raising side issues;（wilfully）throw obstacles in the way ❸ be overflowing with; be full of: 妙趣~ be overflowing with wit

横…竖… héng…shù… *used respectively before two identical or similar words for vividness or emphasis*: 横七竖八 in disorder; in a mess or clutter; higgledy-piggledy / 横说竖说 speak over and over again（to convince sb）; exhaust all means of persuasion / 横躺竖卧（of people）lie here and there / 横挑鼻子竖挑眼 find fault; pick holes; nitpick

横竖 héngshù 〈口〉 in any case; anyhow; anyway

横向 héngxiàng crosswise; horizontal; lateral: ~比较 cross comparison / ~经济联系 horizontal or lateral economic ties; cooperation between enterprises

横心 héngxīn resolve; be determined: 横下一条心 steel oneself（to do sth despite consequences）; make a firm resolve

横行 héngxíng run wild or amok; be on a rampage: ~霸道 ride roughshod; tyrannize; domineer

横溢 héngyì ❶（of a river）overflow; brim over ❷（of talent, feelings, etc）brimming; overflowing; abundant: 才华~ be brimming or bursting with talent; have superb talent

横征暴敛 héngzhēng-bàoliǎn extort excessive taxes and levies; levy heavy or exorbitant taxes

衡 héng ❶ weighing apparatus: ~器 weighing apparatus ❷ weigh; measure; judge: ~情度理 consider the circumstances and judge by common sense — all things considered ❸〈书〉levelled; balanced

衡量 héngliáng ❶ measure; judge: ~是非 measure right and wrong; tell right from wrong ❷ weigh; consider: ~得失 weigh（up）the gains and losses

hèng

横 hèng ❶ rude; fierce and brutal; harsh and unreasonable: ~蛮 violent and unreasonable; perverse and brutal / ~蛮 rough and unreasonable; tyrannical ❷ inauspicious; unexpected: ~财 ill-gotten wealth or gain; windfall / ~死 die a violent or unnatural death / ~祸 unexpected disaster or misfortune

see also héng

hng

哼 hng 〈叹〉 *used to express dissatisfaction or suspicion*: ~, 我就不信她不知情。Humph! I don't believe she is not in the know. *see also* hēng

hōng

轰（轟） hōng ❶〈象声〉（of thunder, etc）bang; boom; roar: ~隆 rumble; roll / ~鸣 thunder; roar / 火车~~地前进。The train rumbled on. ❷ bombard; explode: ~击 shell; bombard; blast / ~ shoo away; drive（off）: ~下台 boo（sb）off the platform

轰动 hōngdòng *also* "哄动" cause a sensation; make a stir: ~一时 create a furore; cause a great sensation; be a great hit / 产生~效应 produce a sensational effect; make quite a stir

轰轰烈烈 hōnghōng-lièliè on a grand and spectacular scale; with vim and vigour; dynamic

轰然 hōngrán with a loud crash or

bang; with loud noise: 全场～。 There was general commotion in the audience.

轰炸 hōngzhà bomb; bombard; ～机 bomber / 地毯式～ carpet bombing

哄 hōng ❶〈象声〉 *used to describe roars of laughter or uproarious talk*: ～的一声大笑起来 burst into uproarious laughter ❷ hubbub; din: ～传 (of rumours) circulate widely / ～然 boisterous; uproarious / ～抬 (of speculators, etc) drive up (prices) / ～堂大笑 whole room rocking with laughter; all the audience roaring with laughter

see also hǒng; hòng

哄动 hōngdòng *see* "轰动" hōngdòng

哄抢 hōngqiǎng (of a crowd of people) ❶ panic-buying ❷ scramble for; engage in mass looting

烘 hōng ❶ dry; warm; bake: ～焙 cure (tea or tobacco leaves) / ～干 dry over fire or heat / ～烤 toast; bake / ～箱 (baking) oven ❷ set off: ～染 set off by shading; embroider on (sth)

烘托 hōngtuō (in Chinese painting) set off by shading; make conspicuous by contrast; throw into sharp relief: ～手法 technique of contrast / 烘云托月 paint clouds off the moon; provide a foil to set off sb or sth; portray through contrast

薨 hōng (of feudal lords or high officials) die; pass away

hóng

弘 hóng (now often written as 宏) ❶ great; grand; magnificent: ～大 grand; great; vast ❷ enlarge; expand: ～扬〈书〉 promote and develop; carry forward; enhance

红 hóng ❶ red: ～榜 honour roll (on red paper) or board (in red

ink) / ～牌 red card (in soccer) / ～叶 red autumnal leaves / ～油 (red) chilli oil / ～扑扑 ruddy; rosy / ～彤彤 *also* "红通通" bright red; glowing / ～细胞 *also* "红血球" red blood cell or corpuscle / ～艳艳 bright or brilliant red / ～光满面 with one's face glowing with health; in ruddy health / ～十字会 Red Cross (Society) ❷ red bunting, etc, used on festive occasions; festivity: ～白喜事 red and white affairs — weddings and funerals ❸ symbol of success, favour or popularity: ～火 flourishing; prosperous; thriving / ～人 favourite (with sb in power); fairhaired boy / ～得发紫 (of sb) be extremely popular; be at the height of one's power and influence / ～极一时 enjoy great popularity for a time; be all the rage ❹ revolutionary; red: ～军 Red Army; Red Army soldier / ～领巾 red scarf (worn by a Young Pioneer); Young Pioneer / ～卫兵〈史〉 Red Guards ❺ bonus; dividend: ～包 red envelope (containing money as a gift, tip, or bribe) / ～利 bonus; dividend

红宝石 hóngbǎoshí ruby

红茶 hóngchá black tea

红尘 hóngchén world of mortals; vanity fair: 看破～ see through the vanity of the world; be disillusioned with human society

红灯 hóngdēng red light;〈喻〉 obstacle; ban: 闯～ jump a red (traffic) light / 设置～ place obstacles (for) / ～区 red-light district (haunted by prostitutes) / 红绿灯 traffic lights or signals

红豆 hóngdòu ❶ red pea shrub; Indian licorice *also* "相思子" seeds of this shrub used as token of love; love peas *also* "红小豆" red bean

红果 hóngguǒ〈方〉 fruit of large Chinese hawthorn; haw

红花 hónghuā ❶〈中药〉false saffron；safflower；~ 油 safflower oil ❷ red flower；~ 虽好，也要绿叶扶持。〈俗〉Beautiful as the red flower is, it takes the green leaves to set it off. or However capable one is, one has to have the support of those around one.

红脸 hóngliǎn ❶ red-painted face (in traditional opera)；〈喻〉honest, candid guy ❷ blush ❸ flush with anger；be angry；他俩口从来没红过脸。The old couple have never exchanged angry words.

红娘 hóngniáng maid in the classical play *The West Chamber* (西厢记)；〈喻〉kind-hearted go-between；well-meaning matchmaker

红旗 hóngqí red flag or banner；~ 手 red-banner pacesetter；model worker / ~ 单位 red-banner or advanced unit

红色 hóngsè red；revolutionary；~ 根据地 revolutionary base

红烧 hóngshāo braise in soy sauce

红薯 hóngshǔ （common name for 甘薯）sweet potato

红糖 hóngtáng brown sugar

红桃 hóngtáo heart (in cards)；叫四 ~ bid four hearts

红头文件 hóngtóu-wénjiàn 〈口〉document issued by a Party or government office (with the title printed in red)；official document

红外 hóngwài （short for 红外线）infrared (ray)；近 ~ near infrared / 远 ~ far infrared / ~ 扫描 infrared scanning / ~ 通信 infrared communication / ~ 制导 infrared guidance / ~ 夜视系统 infrared night vision system

红颜 hóngyán rosy cheeks；pretty face；beautiful woman；~ 薄命。Beautiful women are often ill-fated.

红眼 hóngyǎn ❶ see red；become desperate or furious；输 ~ 了眼 become desperate due to loss in gambling ❷ be jealous；be green with envy；~ 病〈医〉acute conjunctivitis；〈喻〉jealousy；green-eyed monster

红药水 hóngyàoshuǐ （popular term for liquid solution of 红汞 or 汞溴红）mercurochrome

红运 hóngyùn *also* "鸿运" good luck；走 ~ *also* "交红运" have a spate of good luck；ride on the crest of fortune

红晕 hóngyùn blush；flush

红肿 hóngzhǒng red and swollen；眼睛 ~ bloodshot, swollen eyes

宏 hóng great；grand；magnificent；~ 大 grand；great / ~ 论 learned argument；intelligent view；informed opinion / ~ 图 *also* "鸿图" great plan；lofty aspiration；grand prospect / ~ 伟 magnificent；grand / ~ 愿 great aspirations；noble ambition / ~ 旨 main theme；leading idea / ~ 程序〈信息〉macro program

宏观 hóngguān macro；macroscopic；~ 结构 macrostructure / ~ 经济 macro-economy / ~ 世界 macro-world；macrocosm / ~ 调控 macro-adjustment and control

泓 hóng 〈书〉❶ (of water) deep ❷〈量〉*used of clear water after* 一：一 ~ 清泉 a clear spring

虹 hóng *also* "彩虹" rainbow

虹吸 hóngxī 〈理〉siphonage；~ 管 siphon / ~ 现象 *also* "虹吸作用" siphonage

洪 hóng ❶ big；great；vast；~ 恩 great favour or kindness / ~ 亮 *also* "宏亮" loud and clear；sonorous / ~ 流 mighty torrent；powerful current / ~ 炉〈喻〉great furnace or crucible (for tempering people) / ~ 福齐天 limitless blessing；boundless bliss / 声如 ~ 钟 have a stentorian or sonorous voice (like a big bell) ❷ flood；~ 峰 flood crest or peak / ~ 水 flood；floodwater / ～灾 damages done by flood or inundation / ～水猛兽 fierce floods and savage beasts; great scourge

洪荒 hónghuāng　primeval chaos; primeval times; ～时代 primeval age; remote antiquity

鸿 hóng ❶ swan; Chinese goose; ～鹄 swan; 〈喻〉person of lofty aspirations / ～毛〈书〉goose feather; 〈喻〉sth very light or insignificant ❷ 〈书〉letter; 远方来～ letter from afar ❸ great; grand; ～ 沟 wide gap; chasm / ～儒〈书〉man of great learning; erudite scholar / ～篇巨制 magnum opus; monumental work

鸿门宴 Hóngményàn banquet at Hongmen — a feast or meeting set up as a trap for the invited

鸿雁 hóngyàn　see "鸿❶❷"

hǒng

哄 hǒng ❶ fool; humbug; kid; ～骗 cheat; humbug; hoodwink ❷ keep in good humour; coax; humour; ～劝 persuade by coaxing / ～孩子睡觉 lull a baby to sleep
see also hōng; hòng

hòng

讧 hòng 〈书〉quarrel; discord; 内～ internal strife

哄(鬨) hòng uproar; clamour; horseplay; ～闹 (make an) uproar; hubbub see also hōng; hǒng

hōu

齁 hōu ❶ snore; ～～熟睡 snore away in sound sleep ❷ (usu indicating distaste) awfully; too; 甜得～人 so sweet as to make one sick; too sweet; cloying / 天气～冷。It's aw-fully cold.

hóu

侯 hóu ❶ marquis; ～爵 marquis / ～爵夫人 marquise; marchioness ❷ nobleman; high official; ～门似海。The mansions of the nobility are inaccessible to the common man.

喉 hóu 〈生理〉larynx; throat; ～管 windpipe; trachea / ～结〈生理〉Adam's apple; larynx / ～舌 mouthpiece / ～痛 (have a) sore throat / ～炎 laryngitis / 清清～嗓 clear one's throat

猴 hóu ❶ monkey; ～子 monkey / ～戏 monkey show; 〈戏〉performance with the Monkey King (孙悟空) as the hero ❷ 〈方〉(usu of children) smart; clever; mischievous; ～头～脑 looking funny and mischievous

猴皮筋儿 hóupíjīnr also "猴筋儿" rubber band; 跳～ rubber-band rope skipping

瘊 hóu (usu 瘊子) wart

hǒu

吼 hǒu roar; howl; shout; ～声 roaring; loud shouts / 你～什么? What are you shouting for? / 狂风～叫。The wind was howling.

hòu

后(❷-❺後) hòu ❶ empress; queen; ～妃 empress and imperial concubines ❷ back; rear; behind; ～背 back (of the human body) / ～跟 heel (of a shoe or sock) / ～襟 back of a garment / ～排 back-row (seat) / ～腰 small of the back / ～级〈语言〉suffix; postfix; ～滚翻〈体〉backward roll ❸ after; afterwards; later; ～爹 also "后爸" 〈口〉stepfather / ～记 postscript; afterword / ～妈 also "后娘"〈口〉stepmother / ～年 year after next / ～期 later stage or period / ～人 also "后裔" later generations; descendants; offspring / ～会有期 meet again some day; see you again ❹ last; later; ～者 the latter / ～起之秀 up-and-coming or promising young person; rising star ❺ offspring; progeny

后半 hòubàn latter or second half; ～生 also "后半辈子" latter half of one's life / ～天 also "后半晌" afternoon / ～夜 after midnight; (in the) small hours

后备 hòubèi reserve; ～军 reserves; reserve force / ～物资 reserve materials / ～系统 back-up or stand-by system

后辈 hòubèi ❶ see "后代❷" ❷ juniors; younger generation

后代 hòudài also "后世" ❶ later periods or ages; ～学者 later scholars ❷ later generations; descendants; posterity; ～子孙 descendants; later generations

后盾 hòudùn backing; back-up (force); support

后发制人 hòufāzhìrén gain mastery by striking only after the adversary has struck

后方 hòufāng ❶ rear; ～医院 rear or base hospital ❷ behind; at the back; in the rear

后顾 hòugù ❶ turn back (to take care of sth); ～之忧 disturbance in the rear; trouble back at home; family worries ❷ look back

后果 hòuguǒ consequence; aftermath

后患 hòuhuàn future trouble; ～无穷 no end of trouble for the future; endless trouble in store

后悔 hòuhuǐ regret; remorse; ～莫及 too late to regret; cry over spilt milk / 吃～药 be overcome with remorse

后继 hòujì succeed; carry on; follow up; ～无人 have no successor

后进 hòujìn ❶ junior (in rank, service, etc) ❷ less advanced; underdeveloped; lagging behind; ～生 slow or problem student / ～地区 underdeveloped areas

后劲 hòujìn aftereffect; staying power; stamina; 有～ (in work, etc) have (plenty of) stamina; (of liquor) produce strong aftereffect

后来 hòulái ❶ afterwards; later; (since) then ❷ newly come or arrived; ～居上 the latecomers come out first; catch up from behind

后路 hòulù ❶ communication lines to the rear; route of retreat; 抄人 ～ outflank sb; attack sb from the rear ❷ room for manoeuvre; way of escape; 不留～ burn one's boats

后门 hòumén ❶ back door or gate ❷ back-door; backstairs; under-counter; ～交易 under-the-counter or back-door deal

后面 hòumian ❶ at the back; at or in the rear; behind ❷ later

后勤 hòuqín rear or general service; logistics; ～服务 rear service / ～人员 rear-service personnel

后生 hòushēng young man; youth; ～可畏 the young deserve to be regarded with awe; a ragged colt may make a good horse

后事 hòushì ❶ what happened afterwards ❷ funeral (affairs); 料理～ see about sb's funeral

后台 hòutái ❶ backstage ❷ backstage supporter; behind-the-scenes backer; patron; ～很硬 have very strong backing / ～老板 backstage boss; wire puller

后天 hòutiān ❶ also "后儿"; "后儿

后退 hòutuì　draw or fall back; retreat; back away

后卫 hòuwèi　❶〈军〉rear guard ❷ (in soccer) full back ❸ (in basketball) guard

后续 hòuxù　follow up:～投资 follow-up investment

后遗症 hòuyízhèng　❶〈医〉sequelae ❷ after-effect; residual effect; hangover

后援 hòuyuán　reinforcements; backup force; backing:～会 backup institution; fans' club (of a sports team)

后院 hòuyuàn　backyard; rear; home:～起火〈喻〉have trouble at home

厚 hòu　❶ thick:～度 thickness ❷ deep; profound; rich in flavour:～爱〈敬〉your kindness; your care and support /～望 great expectations; high hopes /～谊 deep feeling; profound friendship ❸ kind; magnanimous; generous:～道 honest and kind /～礼 generous present /～谢 thank (sb) with a generous gift /～意 kindness; generosity; kind thought /～葬 elaborate funeral ❹ value; favour; stress

厚薄 hòubó　❶ thickness:～正好 (be) of the right thickness ❷ *used to show contrast in degree* a) *of accumulation*:厚积薄发 be so well versed in a subject as to be able to write about any part of it with ease; be well-grounded or well-prepared b) *of favour or intimacy*:厚此薄彼 favour one and discriminate against the other; treat with partiality / 厚古薄今 stress the past, not the present; praise the past and belittle the present

厚脸皮 hòuliǎnpí　*also* "厚脸" cheeky; brazen; thick-skinned:他可真是～! The nerve of him!

厚实 hòushi　❶ thick; broad and sturdy ❷ profound and sound; deep and solid:学术基础～ have a solid academic foundation ❸ wealthy; abundant; rich:家底～ financially solid family; family with substantial resources

厚颜 hòuyán　thick-skinned; impudent; brazen:～无耻 shameless; brazen as brass

厚重 hòuzhòng　❶ thick and heavy; 〈喻〉solid and profound ❷ (of a gift, etc)generous; munificent ❸〈书〉(of a person) honest and serious

候 hòu　❶ wait; await:～审〈法〉await trial /～诊 wait to see the doctor / ～车室 waiting room (in a railway or coach station) /～机楼 air terminal (building) /～机室 airport lounge; airport waiting room ❷ inquire after:请代我向他致～. Please give him my best regards. ❸ time; season:～鸟 migratory bird; bird of passage ❹ condition; state:征～ symptom; sign

候补 hòubǔ　be an alternate; candidate or substitute:～委员 alternate member / ～演员 understudy

候选人 hòuxuǎnrén　candidate:提出～ nominate or put up a candidate / ～资格 candidacy; candidature

hū

乎 hū　❶〈书〉〈助〉*used like* 吗 *or* 呢 *in a question*:然～,否～? Yes or no? ❷〈书〉〈助〉*used to express supposition or doubt*:其是之谓～? Is this what it is about? ❸ *used after a verb like* 于:出～意料 be beyond or exceed one's expectations ❹ *used for rhythm after an adjective or adverb*:断～不可 absolutely impossible; out of the question

呼 hū　❶ breathe out; exhale:长长地～了一口气 exhale a long breath ❷ shout; cry out:～救 call or cry for help; (of a ship) send out GMDSS signals / ～口号 shout slogans ❸ call; 直～其名 address sb by name / ～来挥去 order around; have at one's beck and call ❹〈象声〉*used of the loud sound of wind or sth like it*; ～～大睡 snore loudly in one's sleep; snore away

呼哧 hūchī *also* "呼蚩"〈象声〉puff; ～～直喘粗气 puff and blow; pant heavily

呼风唤雨 hūfēng-huànyǔ summon wind and rain — exercise magic powers; exert great influence; stir up trouble

呼号 hūháo ❶ wail; cry out in distress ❷ appeal (to people); campaign (for a cause); 四处～ go around campaigning ❸〈通信〉call sign; catchword (of an organization); motto

呼唤 hūhuàn ❶ shout; call out ❷ call (on); summon

呼机 hūjī *also* "寻呼机" pager; beeper

呼叫 hūjiào ❶ *also* "呼喊" call out; shout ❷〈通信〉call; ring; ～信号 calling signal / ～装置 calling device

呼啦 hūlā *also* "呼啦啦"; "呼喇喇"〈象声〉*used of flapping sounds*; 窗纸～～地响。The window paper was flapping in the wind.

呼噜 hūlū ❶〈象声〉wheeze; 喉咙里～直响 have a wheezy voice ❷ (hūlu)〈口〉snore

呼哨 hūshào *also* "嗅哨" whistle; 打～ give a whistle

呼声 hūshēng cry; voice; 人民的～ voice of the people / ～最高 be tipped to win (in an election, etc)

呼天抢地 hūtiān-qiāngdì lament to heaven and knock one's head on earth; utter cries of anguish; ～，痛不欲生 cry one's eyes out, wishing oneself dead

呼吸 hūxī breathe; respire; ～道〈生理〉respiratory tract / ～器 respirator / ～衰竭 respiratory failure / ～系

统 respiratory system / ～相通〈喻〉be of the same mind; share feelings and sentiments

呼啸 hūxiào whistle; scream; whiz

呼应 hūyìng echo; work in concert (with sth); 前后～ be consistent

呼吁 hūyù appeal; call on; ～书 (letter of) appeal

呼之欲出 hūzhīyùchū (of sth artistic or literary) be lifelike; be vividly portrayed

忽 hū ❶ neglect; overlook; ignore ❷ suddenly; ～地刮起大风。A high wind rose all of a sudden.

忽…忽… hū…hū… now…, now…; 忽高忽低 now high, now low; fluctuate (in tune, etc) / 忽明忽暗 now bright, now dim; bright one moment and dim the next / 忽而皱眉，忽而微笑 frown one minute and smile the next

忽略 hūlüè neglect; overlook; lose sight of; ～不计 not take into account; overlook; (of sth) be negligible

忽然 hūrán suddenly; all of a sudden

忽闪 hūshǎn ❶ (of light) flash; sparkle ❷ (hūshan) (of eyes, etc) flash; glitter; sparkle

忽视 hūshì ignore; neglect; make light of; 不可～ not to be trifled with; to be reckoned with / 渐被～ fall into neglect

糊 hū plaster (a wall, hole, etc) *see also* hú; hù

hú

囫 hú

囫囵 húlún whole; ～觉 a whole night's sleep; a sound sleep without interruption / ～吞枣 gulp down without chewing; lap up information without digesting it

和 hú win a game of mahjong or cards *see also* hé; hè; huó;

huò

狐 hú　fox；～媚 bewitch by coquettish cajolery；entice by flirtatious charm / ～裘 fox-fur robe / ～朋狗友 evil associates；dissolute company / ～群狗党 pack of rogues；bad lot

狐步舞 húbùwǔ　foxtrot

狐臭 húchòu　body odour；bromhidrosis

狐假虎威 hújiǎhǔwēi　bully people by virtue of sb else's influence

狐狸 húli　fox；～精 fox spirit — seductive woman；coquette；vamp / ～尾巴 fox's tail — cloven hoof

狐疑 húyí　doubt；suspicion；misgivings；～不决 suspicious and hesitating；indecisive

弧 hú　〈数〉arc；～度 also "弳" radian（measurement）；circular measure / ～线 arc；curve；curved line．/ ～光灯 arc lamp

胡（④**鬍**）hú　❶（Hú）〈史〉Hu, general term for non-Han nationalities living in north and west China：～人（member of）such ethnic minorities ❷ introduced from such minorities or from abroad：～笳〈乐〉reed pipe used by northern tribes in ancient China / ～椒 pepper / ～麻 oil-bearing flax / ～桃 walnut ❸ recklessly；wantonly；outrageously：～吹 boast outrageously；talk through one's hat / ～话 ravings；wild talk / ～闹 act wildly；make trouble；do mischief / ～诌 fabricate（wild tales）；cook up / ～编乱造 cook up（a tale）；fabricate；concoct ❹ moustache；beard；whiskers：～须 beard and/ or moustache

胡扯 húchě　❶ talk nonsense；drivel ❷ chat；chitchat

胡搞 húgǎo　❶ mess（sth）up；meddle or tamper with ❷ carry on an affair（with）；be promiscuous

胡搅 hújiǎo　❶ pester（sb）；be mischievous；～蛮缠 harass with unreasonable demands；pester endlessly ❷ argue tediously and vexatiously；wrangle

胡来 húlái　❶ see "胡搞" ❷ run wild；make trouble；commit all kinds of outrages

胡乱 húluàn　❶ carelessly；casually；perfunctorily：～扒拉了几口饭 eat a hasty meal；grab a quick bite ❷ at will or random；arbitrarily；unreasonably：～怀疑 have wild suspicions

胡萝卜 húluóbo　carrot：～素（beta-）carotene / "～加大棒"政策 carrot and stick policy

胡说 húshuō　speak groundlessly, unreasonably or recklessly；drivel：～八道 talk nonsense；twaddle

胡思乱想 húsī-luànxiǎng　imagine things；go off into wild flights of fancy

胡同 hútòng　lane；alley

胡言乱语 húyán-luànyǔ　talk nonsense；rave；shoot one's mouth off

胡子 húzi　❶ beard；moustache；whiskers：大 ～（man with a）heavy beard / ～拉碴 stubbly beard；bristly unshaven chin / ～工程 project that drags on for years；unduly long project ❷ also "胡匪"〈方〉bandit

胡作非为 húzuò-fēiwéi　act wildly in defiance of the law or public opinion；commit all kinds of outrages

壶（**壺**）hú　kettle；pot；can：水 ～ kettle ❷ bottle；flask；暖 ～ thermos bottle or flask

核 hú　see also hé

核儿 húr　〈口〉❶ stone；pit；core；桃 ～ peach stone ❷ sth resembling a fruit stone：冰 ～ ice nucleus / 煤 ～ partly burnt coals or briquettes；cinders

葫 hú

葫芦 húlu　bottle gourd；calabash；酒 ～ wine calabash / ～瓢 gourd ladle /

他～里卖的是什么药？What has he got up his sleeve?

鹄

鹄 hú swan

鹄候 húhòu 〈书〉await respectfully; expect

鹄望 húwàng 〈书〉wait on tiptoe (for); eagerly look forward (to)

猢

猢 hú

猢狲 húsūn a variety of macaque; monkey

湖

湖 hú lake: ～泊 lake / ～泽 also "湖沼" lakes and marshes / ～光山色 landscape of lakes and mountains; natural or scenic beauty

煳

煳 hú burnt: 饼烙～了。The pancake is burnt.

蝴

蝴 hú

蝴蝶 húdié also "胡蝶" butterfly: ～结 bow; bow-tie

糊（²餬）

糊 hú ❶ stick (paper, etc) with paste; paste ❷ gruel; porridge; congee ❸ see "煳" hú

see also hū; hù

糊口 húkǒu keep body and soul together; make both ends meet; keep the pot boiling: 养家～ provide for one's family

糊涂 hútu also "胡涂" ❶ muddled; confused; bewildered: 糊里～ muddle-headed; mixed up; confused / ～虫 blunderer; bungler; blockhead ❷ confusing; confused; chaotic: ～账 chaotic account; mess

hǔ

虎

虎 hǔ ❶ tiger: ～狼 like tigers and wolves; ferocious and ruthless / ～崽 tiger cub / ～踞龙盘 like a coiling dragon or a crouching tiger — a forbidding strategic point ❷ like a tiger; brave; vigorous: ～将 brave general / ～背熊腰 broad-shouldered and thick-waisted; muscular and sturdy / ～头脑 (usu of a child) naive and robust / ～～有生气 brim (over) with vigour and vitality; be vigorous and energetic ❸ see "唬" hǔ

虎口 hǔkǒu ❶ tiger's mouth — jaws of death: ～拔牙 pull a tooth from the tiger's mouth — brave the greatest danger; beard the lion in his den / ～余生 escape from the tiger's jaws — escape by the skin of one's teeth; have a narrow escape ❷ part of the hand between the thumb and the index finger

虎视 hǔshì glare like a tiger — with malice or avarice; stare in an awe-inspiring manner: ～眈眈 glare like a tiger eyeing its prey; eye greedily or menacingly

虎头蛇尾 hǔtóu-shéwěi in like a lion, out like a lamb; (make a) fine start but poor finish

虎穴 hǔxué tiger's den: ～追踪 track a tiger to its lair; pursue the enemy to his base

虎牙 hǔyá 〈口〉protruding canine tooth

唬

唬 hǔ bluff: 别～人了。Stop bluffing.

琥

琥 hǔ

琥珀 hǔpò also "虎魄" amber

hù

互

互 hù mutual; each other; one another: ～补 mutually complementary / ～动 interaction / ～访 visit each other; exchange visits / ～换 exchange; swap / ～利 mutually beneficial; of mutual benefit; reciprocal / ～不相容 mutually repellent; incompatible / ～为条件 each is the condition of the other; be mutually conditional

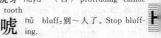

为因果 interact as both cause and effect; act on and reinforce each other / ～不侵犯条约 (mutual) non-aggression treaty or pact

互…互… hù … hù … mutual; each other; 互敬互爱 love and respect each other; show mutual respect and love / 互让互利 mutual accommodation and benefit

互惠 hùhuì mutually beneficial; mutually preferential; reciprocal; ～待遇 reciprocal preferential treatment / ～原则 principle of reciprocity

互联网 hùliánwǎng *also* "因特网" 〈信息〉internet; ～协议 Internet Protocol (IP)

互通 hùtōng communicate with each other; exchange; ～消息 exchange information / ～姓名 introduce each other / ～有无 supplies what the other needs; meet each other's needs; exchange needed goods

互相 hùxiāng mutual; each other; ～拆台 cut the ground or pull the rug from under each other's feet; hinder each other's work / ～排斥 be mutually exclusive or repellent

互助 hùzhù help each other; 团结～ unity and mutual help / ～组 mutual aid group or team / ～基金 mutual fund

户 hù ❶ door; ～内 indoor; indoors / ～外 outdoor; outdoors ❷ household; family; ～主 head of a household (as registered on the residence card) ❸ family status ❹ (bank) account; ～头 (bank) account

户籍 hùjí ❶ household register or registration; ～警 policeman in charge of household registration ❷ registered permanent residence

户口 hùkǒu ❶ number of households and population; ～稀少 sparsely populated ❷ registered residence; 报～ register one's residence; apply for residence / 查～ check residence cards; check on household residents / 销～ cancel one's residence registration / ～簿 *also* "户口本儿" (permanent) residence book / ～普查 census

户枢不蠹 hùshūbùdù a door-hinge is never worm-eaten — constant activity staves off decay

护(護) hù ❶ protect; guard; shield; ～栏 guardrail; railings; rail fence / ～送 escort; convoy / ～腿〈体〉shin-guard or -pad / ～腕〈体〉bracer / ～膝〈体〉knee-pad; kneecap / ～腰 back belt / ～佑 (bless and) protect; safeguard / ～城河 city moat / ～发素 hair conditioner / ～肤霜 face cream; body lotion / ～林员 forest ranger / ～路队 road maintenance crew ❷ be partial to; shield; shelter; ～犊子〈口〉be partial to one's child; shield one's child

护短 hùduǎn shield or hide a shortcoming or fault (of one of one's own)

护航 hùháng escort (a ship, etc); 舰队 escort flotilla; convoy

护理 hùlǐ nurse; tend; take care of; ～草坪 tend a lawn / ～人员 nursing staff

护身符 hùshēnfú *also* "护符" ❶ amulet; protective charm or talisman ❷ person or thing that protects one; shield

护士 hùshi (hospital) nurse; ～长 head nurse / ～学校 *also* "护校" nurses' school

护卫 hùwèi ❶ protect; guard; ～舰 escort vessel; frigate; corvette ❷ *also* "护兵" bodyguard

护照 hùzhào passport

沪(滬) Hù another name for 上海: 京～路 Beijing-Shanghai Railway

怙 hù 〈书〉rely or count on; ～恶不悛 persist in evil and refuse to repent; be steeped in iniquity and refuse to reform

戽 hù ❶ *also* "戽斗" bailing bucket (for irrigation) ❷ bail；～水抗旱 bail water to combat the drought

笏 hù 〈史〉ceremonial official tablet

扈 hù 〈书〉retinue；～从 retinue；entourage；retainer

糊 hù paste；面　 （flour ） paste　*see also* hū；hú

糊弄 hùnong 〈方〉❶ fool；deceive ❷ go through the motions；be slipshod in work；～事 do sth in a sloppy way；muddle through

huā

化 huā *same as* "花❾" huā *see also* huà

花 huā ❶ flower；blossom；ornamental plant；～瓣 petal / ～草 (ornamental) flowers and plants / ～店 florist's (shop)；flower shop / ～房 greenhouse (for flowers) / ～冠〈植〉corolla；(formerly for a bride) flowery coronet / ～环 garland；lei；wreath / ～匠 gardener；florist / ～蕾 *also* "花骨朵" bud / ～蜜〈植〉nectar / ～盆 flowerpot / ～圃 flower nursery or garden；parterre / ～期 *also* "花令" florescence (of plants)；flowering season / ～市 flower market or fair / ～束 bunch of flowers；bouquet / ～坛 *also* "花台" (raised) flower bed or terrace；parterre ❷ anything resembling a flower；fireworks；cotton；弹～ fluff cotton (with a bow) / 放～ shoot off fireworks / 挂～ get wounded (in battle) / ～卷 steamed twisted roll / ～炮 fireworks and firecrackers / 冰～儿 ice flower / 泪～儿 tears ❸ flowered design；decorative pattern；(multi-) color；～布 (cotton) print / ～猫 spotted cat / ～呢 fancy suiting / ～衣服

bright-coloured clothes ❹ mix；blend；～搭着吃 eat a mixed diet (of cereals, etc) ❺ blurred；dim；bleary；～镜 presbyopic glasses / ～眼 presbyopia ❻ showy；tricky；false；～头〈方〉trick；knack；novel idea / ～点子 trick / fancy but impractical idea / ～架子 showy but useless *wushu* movements；〈喻〉sth fancy but of no practical value；show-piece / ～样子〈喻〉scheme；trick；crafty person / ～拳绣腿 useless fancy boxing；mere ostentation ❼ romantic (in love)；promiscuous；of prostitution；～心 (usu of men) fickle (in love)；inconstant / ～～公子 dandy；playboy；swinger / ～～事儿 (extramarital) affair；sex scandal / ～街柳巷 red-light district；disreputable quarters ❽〈喻〉young, pretty woman；警～ young policewoman ❾ spend；expend；～钱 spend money / ～子 *also* "花子" beggar / ～功夫 take time；be time-consuming

花白 huābái （of hair, etc) grey；grizzled

花边 huābiān ❶ decorative border；fancy lace；金色的～ golden bordering ❷ fancy borders in printing；～新闻 interesting sidelights；tabloid news

花茶 huāchá *also* "香片" scented tea；茉莉～ jasmine tea

花旦 huādàn (in traditional Chinese opera) lively or spirited female role

花灯 huādēng festive or colourful lantern；闹～ display (a riot of) colourful lanterns

花朵 huāduǒ flower；blossom

花费 huāfèi ❶ spend；expend；cost；～心血 take great pains (with) ❷ (huáfei) money spent；expenditure；expense

花粉 huāfěn 〈植〉pollen；～过敏 pollen hypersensitivity or allergy；hay fever

花岗岩 huāgāngyán granite；granite-like; incorrigibly obstinate: ~ 脑袋 granite-like skull; ossified thinking

花好月圆 huāhǎo-yuèyuán （usu used as compliment for the newly wed) blooming flowers and full moon — perfect conjugal bliss

花花绿绿 huāhuālǜlǜ brightly coloured; multicoloured; colourful: 穿得 ~ dressed in bright colours

花花世界 huāhuāshìjiè （贬）dazzling world with its myriad temptations; world of sensual pleasures; vanity fair

花卉 huāhuì flowers and plants; painting of flowers and plants in traditional Chinese style: ~ 栽培 floriculture; floristry / 擅长 ~ be good at painting flowers and plants

花甲 huājiǎ sixty years of age

花季 huājì 〈喻〉blooming or tender age: ~ 少女 young girl in her mid or late teens

花椒 huājiāo 〈植〉Chinese prickly ash; seeds of such plants

花轿 huājiào bridal sedan chair

花篮 huālán flower basket; gaily decorated basket

花里胡哨 huālihúshào 〈口〉gaudy; showy; not reliable: ~ 的小伙子 superficially clever boy

花脸 huāliǎn （in traditional Chinese opera) male character with a darkish painted face

花柳病 huāliǔbìng venereal disease (VD); sexually-transmitted disease (STD)

花露水 huālùshuǐ toilet water or lotion; cologne water

花名册 huāmíngcè register （of names); membership roster; muster roll

花瓶 huāpíng ❶（flower）vase ❷ (woman, post, etc, serving as an) ornament; decoration: 只不过是个 ~ merely decorative

花旗 huāqí Stars and Stripes; Star-Spangled Banner; USA: ~ 参 American ginseng

花枪 huāqiāng trickery: 掉 ~ play tricks

花腔 huāqiāng ❶〈乐〉coloratura: ~ 女高音 coloratura (soprano) ❷ guileful talk; sweet-talk

花圈 huāquān （floral）wreath; garland: 献 ~ place or lay a wreath

花容月貌 huāróng-yuèmào （of a woman) fair as a flower and beautiful as the moon; extremely beautiful

花色 huāsè ❶ pattern and colour ❷ (of merchandise) variety of designs, sizes, colours, etc: ~ 品种 variety of colours and designs

花哨 huāshao （of decoration, ornament) garish; flowery; showy

花生 huāshēng peanut; groundnut: ~ 酱 peanut butter / ~ 米 also "花生仁" shelled peanut; peanut kernel / ~ 油 peanut oil

花天酒地 huātiān-jiǔdì live in the world of wine and women; indulge in dissipation; lead a decadent and dissolute life

花团锦簇 huātuán-jǐncù rich multicoloured decorations; splendid and beautiful: 布置得 ~ most gorgeously decorated

花纹 huāwén decorative pattern; figure

花消 huāxiāo also "花销" spend; expend (money); cost

花絮 huāxù titbits (of news); interesting sidelights: 大会 ~ (interesting) sidelights on the conference

花言巧语 huāyán-qiǎoyǔ sweet or honeyed words; slick talk; blandishments

花样 huāyàng ❶（floral）design; (embroidery) pattern; variety: ~ 繁多 have a great variety of designs and patterns ❷ of particular form, figure or skill: ~ 滑冰 〈体〉figure skating / ~ 游

泳 also "水上芭蕾"〈体〉synchronized swimming; water ballet ❸ trick;耍～ play pranks (on sb)

花园 huāyuán (flower) garden; park

花招 huāzhāo also "花着" showy movement in *wushu*（武术）; flourish; trick;耍～ play tricks; resort to chicanery

花枝招展 huāzhīzhāozhǎn (of a woman) be gorgeously dressed

哗(嘩) huā 〈象声〉*used of prolonged loud sounds*;～～流淌的小溪 babbling brook *see also* huá

huá

划(❸劃) huá ❶ paddle; row;～艇〈体〉rowboat; Canadian canoe; canoeing / ～船运动 boating ❷ be to one's profit; pay;～不来 it doesn't pay; it's not worthwhile or profitable ❸ scratch; cut the surface of;～火柴 strike or light a match *see also* huà

划拉 huála 〈方〉❶ whisk away or off; brush lightly; sweep;～几下 give a quick dust or sweep ❷ scrawl; scribble;很快就把卷子～完了 scribble through the paper quickly

划拳 huáquán also "搳拳"、"豁拳" finger-guessing game — a drinking game at feasts;～行令 play a drinking game

划算 huásuàn ❶ calculate; weigh;来回～ weigh the pros and cons ❷ *see* "划❷"

华(華) huá ❶ radiance; magnificence; splendour;～灯 colourfully decorated lantern; (coloured) light / ～丽 sumptuous; resplendent; gorgeous / ～贵 gorgeous and expensive; sumptuous / ～而不实 flashy and without substance; superficially clever; ostentatious ❷〈书〉〈敬〉your; his; her;～章 your beautiful writing; your brilliant work / 60～诞 sixtieth birthday ❸ prosperous; flourishing ❹ best part; cream;年～ one's best years; youthful years; youth ❺ time; years;年～ time; years ❻ grizzled; grey;～发〈书〉grey hair ❼ (Huá) China; Chinese;～东 east China / ～侨 overseas Chinese (nationals) / ～人 Chinese, esp foreign citizens of Chinese descent / ～裔人士 foreign personages of Chinese origin

华尔兹 huá'ěrzī waltz;跳～ dance a waltz

华夏 Huáxià ancient name for China; Cathay;～子孙 descendants of Cathay

哗(嘩、譁) huá ❶ noise; clamour;～变 mutiny / ～然 in an uproar; in commotion / ～笑 uproarious laughter / ～众取宠 seek popularity by demagogy; play to the gallery *see also* huā

铧(鏵) huá ploughshare

猾 huá *see* "滑❸" huá

滑 huá ❶ slippery; smooth; glossy;～腻 (of skin) satiny; velvety; creamy / ～润 smooth; well-lubricated ❷ slip; slide; glide;～板〈体〉skateboard / ～道 chute; slide; ski run / ～动 slide; glide; slip / ～水〈体〉water ski / ～梯 (children's) slide ❸ also "猾" cunning; crafty; sly;～吏 fraudulent or cunning official

滑冰 huábīng 〈体〉(ice-) skating;花样～ figure skating / ～场 skating rink / ～鞋 skates / 滑旱冰 roller skating

滑稽 huájī funny; amusing; comical;～戏 a kind of farce, popular in and around Shanghai

滑溜 huáliū ❶ stir-fry or sauté with starchy sauce;～里脊 sauté fillet with thick gravy ❷ (huáliu) 〈口〉smooth; slippery

滑轮 huálún　also "滑车" pulley; block

滑坡 huápō　❶〈地〉landslide; landslip ❷ decline; slump; deteriorate; 国民经济严重～. The national economy slumped.

滑石 huáshí　talcum; talc; ～粉 talcum powder

滑头 huátóu　slippery (fellow); sly (customer); slick; 耍～ act in a slick way; try to shirk work or responsibility / 小～ petty or young slicker

滑翔 huáxiáng　glide; ～机 glider; sailplane / ～着陆 (make a) glide landing

滑行 huáxíng　❶ slide; coast; ～下坡 coast down a slope ❷ (of a plane) taxi; ～道 taxiway

滑雪 huáxuě　ski; skiing; ～板 skis / ～场 ski run / ～运动 skiing

huà

化 huà　❶ change; turn; transform; ～除 clear up; dispel; remove ❷ melt; dissolve; burn up; ～冻 thaw; defrost ❸ digest; eliminate; dispel; ～食 help digestion / ～痰〈中医〉reduce phlegm; resolve sputum ❹〈宗教〉beg alms; ～缘 also "化募" beg alms / ～斋 beg a (vegetarian) meal ❺ short for 化学; ～肥 chemical fertilizer / ～疗 chemotherapy / ～纤 chemical fibre ❻ used as a suffix to a noun or an adjective to make a verb: 深～ deepen / 现代～ modernize

see also huā

化工 huàgōng　(short for 化学工业) chemical industry; ～产品 chemical products / ～原料 industrial chemicals

化合 huàhé　〈化〉chemical combination; ～物 chemical compound / ～反应 combination reaction

化解 huàjiě　resolve; eliminate; ～矛盾

resolve contradictions

化境 huàjìng　sublimity; perfection; 已入～ reach perfection; be superb

化名 huàmíng　assumed name; alias; ～刘玉 go by the alias Liu Yu

化脓 huànóng　fester; suppurate

化身 huàshēn　❶〈宗教〉incarnation ❷ embodiment; 真理的～ embodiment of truth

化石 huàshí　〈考古〉fossil

化为 huàwéi　change or turn to; transform or convert into; ～灰烬 turn over or crumble to dust; be reduced to ashes; be consumed by fire / ～泡影 vanish like soap bubbles; come to naught / ～乌有 vanish into thin air; go up in smoke / 化敌为友 convert an enemy into a friend / 化公为私 turn public property into one's own; embezzle public property / 化险为夷 get out of danger unscathed; head off a disaster / 化整为零 break up the whole into parts / 化悲痛为力量 turn sorrow into strength / 化腐朽为神奇 make rotten things miraculous; turn bad into good / 化干戈为玉帛 cease hostilities and make peace; bury the hatchet

化学 huàxué　❶ chemistry; ～变化 chemical change / ～成分 chemical composition / ～反应 chemical reaction / ～武器 chemical weapon / ～性质 chemical property / ～元素 chemical element ❷〈口〉celluloid

化验 huàyàn　chemical or physical examination; laboratory test; ～单 laboratory test report

化妆 huàzhuāng　put on make-up; make up; apply cosmetics; ～品 cosmetics

化装 huàzhuāng　❶ make up; ～舞会 costume or fancy dress ball; masquerade ❷ disguise (oneself); ～侦察 go reconnoitering in disguise

划（劃） huà　❶ delimit; differentiate; ～定 delimit;

designate / ～清 differentiate clearly (between); draw a clear line of demarcation (between); make a clean break (with) / ～范围 delimit a sphere / ～框框 set limits; place restrictions ❷ transfer; assign;～归 put under (sb's administration; etc) incorporate into / ～账 transfer accounts ❸ plan; 筹～ plan and prepare ❹ see "画❹" huà see also huá

划拨 huàbō ❶ transfer: 通过银行～ transfer through a bank ❷ allocate; allot: ～物资 allocate goods and materials

划分 huàfēn ❶ divide; partition: ～权限 redefine sb's competence / ～势力范围 carve out spheres of influence ❷ differentiate; distinguish: ～产品等级 grade the quality of products

划价 huàjià (of a hospital pharmacy) calculate medical expenses for a patient

划时代 huàshídài epoch-making (event, etc)

划一 huàyī standardized; uniform; consistent: 尺寸～ be of uniform size / ～体例 make the style (of writing) consistent / ～不二 fixed; unalterable; rigid

画(畫) huà ❶ draw; paint: ～笔 (painting) brush / ～布 canvas (for painting) / ～舫 gaily-painted pleasure boat / ～符 (of a Taoist priest) draw a magic figure to exorcise or invoke spirits and bring good or ill fortune / ～家 painter; artist / ～匠 artisan-painter; inferior painter / ～具 painter's paraphernalia / ～师 master in painting; professional painter / ～儿 draw a picture ❷ drawing; painting; picture: ～报 pictorial / ～册 album of paintings; picture album / ～刊 pictorial section of a newspaper; pictorial / ～帖 book of model paintings or drawings / ～展 art exhibition or show / ～外音 (in a

movie, etc) off-screen voice; voice-over; narration ❸ draw a line or write a character as a mark: ～到 also "画卯" register one's attendance; sign in / ～押 make one's cross or mark; sign ❹ stroke (of a Chinese character): 笔～ strokes of a Chinese character

画饼充饥 huàbǐngchōngjī draw cakes to allay hunger — feed on illusions

画地为牢 huàdìwéiláo draw a circle on the ground to serve as a prison — restrict activities to a designated area or sphere

画虎类狗 huàhǔlèigǒu also "画虎类犬":"画虎不成反类犬" set out to draw a tiger and end up with the likeness of a dog — aim high but achieve little; make a poor imitation

画卷 huàjuàn picture scroll; magnificent scenery; moving spectacle

画廊 huàláng ❶ painted corridor ❷ (picture) gallery

画龙点睛 huàlóngdiǎnjīng bring the painted dragon to life by putting in the pupils of its eyes — add the touch that brings sth to life; add the finishing touch; ～之笔 the finishing touch; what clinches the point

画眉 huàméi ❶ (动物) a kind of song bird ❷ draw or paint eyebrows

画面 huàmiàn ❶ general appearance of a picture; tableau ❷ (in film and TV) frame; ～清晰 high definition frame

画皮 huàpí disguise or mask of an evildoer

画蛇添足 huàshétiānzú draw a snake and add feet to it — ruin the effect by adding sth superfluous; gild the lily

画图 huàtú ❶ draw designs, maps, etc; ～员 draftsman; draughtsman; designer ❷ picture

画像 huàxiàng draw or paint a portrait; portray: 自～ self-potrait

话 huà ❶ word；talk：洋 ～ foreign language or expression / ～锋 thrust of discourse；topic or focus of conversation / ～题 subject of a talk；topic of conversation / ～头 thread of discourse / ～语 speech；remark；utterance / ～中有刺 hidden barbs or catch in one's words；sarcastic remark ❷ talk or speak about：～别 say a few parting words；bid goodbye / ～旧 talk over old times；reminisce about good old days / ～家常 chitchat；exchange small talk ❸（short for 电话）telephone：～费 phone bill / ～机 telephone set / ～务员（telephone）operator

话柄 huàbǐng also "话把儿" subject for ridicule；handle

话不投机 huàbùtóujī have a disagreeable conversation；can't see eye to eye（with sb）：～半句多。〈俗〉A disagreeable conversation, however short, is a waste of time

话茬儿 huàchár 〈方〉❶ thread of discourse or conversation：接着他的 ～说 continue from where he left ❷ tone of one's speech：露出 ～ suggest by one's tone of speech

话剧 huàjù modern drama；stage play：～团 modern drama troupe；theatrical company

话里有话 huàlǐyǒuhuà words mean more than they say；there's more to it than meets the ear

话梅 huàméi preserved plum

话说 huàshuō ❶（used to begin a story, etc）the story says ... ；as the story has it ❷ talk；narration；account：～中国 talk about China

话筒 huàtǒng ❶ telephone transmitter ❷ microphone ❸ also "传声筒" megaphone

话匣子 huàxiázi 〈方〉❶ radio（receiving set）：听～ listen to the radio ❷ chatterbox

话音 huàyīn ❶ one's voice（in speech）；accent ❷ tone；implication

桦（樺） huà 〈植〉birch：白～ white birch / ～木 birch wood

huái

怀（懷） huái ❶ chest；bosom：抱在 ～ 里 hold in one's bosom ❷ mind；heart；sentiment：书 ～（of poetry, etc）express one's sentiments ❸ think of；yearn for；miss：～古 meditate on the past；reflect on an ancient event / ～恋 think fondly of；look back upon nostalgically；miss ❹ conceive；cherish；harbour：～春 〈书〉（of a young girl）be lovesick / ～胎 be pregnant；conceive（a baby）/ ～才不遇 have no opportunity to use one's talents；be unrecognized for all one's talents

怀抱 huáibào ❶（hold or carry in one's）arms；embrace；bosom：睡在母亲的 ～ 里 sleep in mother's arms ❷ 〈喻〉cherish（ideals, etc）

怀表 huáibiǎo pocket watch

怀鬼胎 huái guǐtāi 〈喻〉harbour evil designs；have ulterior motives；have a bad conscience

怀恨 huáihèn cherish hatred；bear ill will；nurse grievances：对人 ～ 在心 bear a grudge against sb

怀旧 huáijiù recall past events or old friends（with kindly thoughts）；be nostalgic for old times or friends

怀念 huáiniàn also "怀想" cherish the memory of；think of longingly；miss

怀柔 huáiróu control through mollification or conciliation：～政策 policy of conciliation or placation

怀疑 huáiyí ❶ doubt；scepticism；suspicion：毫不 ～ without the slightest suspicion；without a shadow of doubt ❷ suspect：～对象 suspect

怀孕 huáiyùn be pregnant or expecting; be with child

淮 Huái Huaihe River

槐 huái 〈植〉Chinese scholartree

踝 huái 〈生理〉ankle;～骨 ankle-bone / ～关节 ankle

huài

坏(壞) huài ❶ bad; evil; defective: ～处 harm; disadvantage / ～人 bad or wicked person; evildoer; scoundrel / ～账 bad debt or loan / ～心眼儿〈口〉evil intention ❷ (of food, etc) go bad; (of a machine, etc) break down ❸ spoil; ruin:电视看多了～眼睛。Watching too much TV is bad for eyesight. ❹ badly; awfully; very:饿～了 be very hungry; be famished ❺ evil idea; dirty trick:一肚子～ full of evil ideas or dirty tricks

坏蛋 huàidàn bad egg; rascal; bastard

坏东西 huàidōngxi ❶ sth bad or rotten ❷ rogue; rascal; scoundrel

坏话 huàihuà ❶ unpleasant words ❷ malicious remarks; vicious talk:说别人的～ speak ill of others

坏事 huàishì ❶ ruin or spoil sth; make things worse ❷ bad thing; evil deed:～做绝 stop at nothing in doing evil

坏水 huàishuǐ 〈口〉〈喻〉deceit; craft and guile:一肚子～ full of craft and guile

坏死 huàisǐ 〈医〉necrosis:肌肉～ necrosis of muscle

huān

欢(歡) huān ❶ joyous; merry; happy:～喜 elated; joyous / ～快 cheerful and light-hearted; lively / ～庆 celebrate joyously / ～笑 laugh merrily; smile happily ❷ love; fancy; what one loves or fancies:偷～ seek illicit sexual pleasure; have an affair / 男～女爱 (mutual) love between man and woman ❸ 〈方〉vigorously; with a vengeance; in full swing:干得～ work vigorously

欢蹦乱跳 huānbèng-luàntiào dancing and jumping with joy; healthy-looking and vivacious; alive and kicking

欢度 huāndù spend (an occasion, etc) joyfully:～晚年 spend one's old age in happiness

欢呼 huānhū hail; cheer; acclaim:雀跃 shout and jump for joy; be elated

欢聚 huānjù happy get-together or reunion:～一堂 gather happily under the same roof; get together joyously; be together on a happy occasion

欢乐 huānlè happy; merry; joyous

欢声 huānshēng cheers; applause:～雷动 cheers resound like rolls of thunder; give a thundering ovation / ～笑语 cheers and laughter

欢送 huānsòng see or send off; bid farewell:～会 farewell or send-off party

欢腾 huānténg great rejoicing; jubilation:举国～ nationwide jubilation

欢喜 huānxǐ ❶ joyful; happy; delighted:～冤家 quarrelsome and loving couple; quarrelsome lovers / 欢天喜地 wild with joy; overjoyed ❷ like; be fond of; delight in

欢心 huānxīn favour; liking; love:博取～ win sb's heart or favour

欢欣鼓舞 huānxīn-gǔwǔ be filled with exultation; jubilant

欢迎 huānyíng ❶ welcome; greet; meet:～词 welcoming speech; address of welcome ❷ receive favourably:深受观众的～ be warmly received by the audience

獾(貛) huān also "狗獾" badger

huán

还(還) huán ❶ go or come back; return; restore; ~魂 *also* "还阳"〈迷信〉revive after death; return from the grave / ~家 go back or return home / ~俗 (of a Buddhist or Taoist priest) resume or return to secular life ❷ give back; return; repay; ~钱 repay; pay back / ~账 pay one's debt or bill; repay a loan / ~本付息 repay the principal with interest ❸ give or do sth in return; ~击 fight back; return fire; counterattack / ~席 give a return banquet or dinner / ~嘴〈口〉answer or talk back

see also hái

还价 huánjià （make a) counter-offer or counter-bid; bargain

还礼 huánlǐ ❶ return a salute ❷ give a gift in return

还原 huányuán ❶ restore to the original state or shape ❷〈化〉reduction; ~剂 reducing agent; reducer

还愿 huányuàn redeem a vow (as to the Buddha);〈喻〉fulfil one's promise

环(環) huán ❶ ring; hoop; loop; ~岛 traffic circle; roundabout; rotary / ~线 ring or circular route / ~城赛跑 round-the-city race / 二~路 second ring road ❷〈体〉ring; 射中八~ hit the 8-point ring / ~靶 round target ❸ link; ~相扣 each linked with another; closely linked with one another ❹ surround; encircle; hem in; ~抱 surround; encircle; embrace / ~顾〈书〉look about / ~绕 surround; encircle; revolve round / ~视 look around

环保 huánbǎo （short for 环境保护） environmental protection; ~部门 environmental protection departments / ~型汽车 environment-friendly car

环节 huánjié ❶〈动物〉segment; ~动物 annelid ❷ link; 主要~ key link

环境 huánjìng ❶ environment; ~污染 environmental pollution or contamination / ~意识 environmental awareness / ~质量 environmental quality ❷ surroundings; circumstances; conditions

环球 huánqiú ❶ round the world; ~旅行 round-the-world tour ❷ *see* "寰" huá ❸ 环球网 *also* "万维网"〈信息〉World Wide Web (WWW)

环卫 huánwèi （short for 环境卫生）environmental sanitation; ~部门 public sanitation department

环行 huánxíng go in a circle; make a circuit; ~公路 ring road; beltway; belt highway

环形 huánxíng annular; ring-like; loop-like; ~山〈天文〉lunar crater; ring structure / ~交叉 roundabout; traffic circle; rotary

寰 huán extensive region

寰球 huánqiú *also* "环球"; "寰宇"; "环宇" Earth, whole world

缳 huán〈书〉noose; 投~ hang oneself (with a noose) / ~首 be hanged

huǎn

缓 huǎn ❶ slow; unhurried; sluggish; ~步 walk slowly; stroll / ~坡 gentle slope / 不济急 slow action cannot save a critical situation; a slow remedy cannot meet an urgency ❷ delay; postpone; put off; ~付 delay or defer payment / ~征 postpone the imposition of a tax or levy ❸ revive; come to; recuperate; ~（口）气 get a breathing space; have a respite; take a breather / ~一劲儿 feel refreshed; recoup one's strength

缓兵之计 huǎnbīngzhījì　stratagem to

gain a respite; trick to gain time; stalling tactics;中了敌人的～ be taken in by the enemy's stalling tactics

缓冲 huǎnchōng buffer; cushion; ～地带 also "缓冲区" buffer zone or area / ～作用 buffer or cushioning effect

缓和 huǎnhé relax; ease off or up; alleviate; ～气氛 ease up the atmosphere / 口气～ speak in a mild tone

缓解 huǎnjiě alleviate; allay; ease up; 病情～ improvement of a patient's condition

缓慢 huǎnmàn slow; sluggish;进展～ make slow progress

缓期 huǎnqī postpone a deadline; suspend; delay; ～执行 suspend a court sentence; sentence with a reprieve

缓行 huǎnxíng ❶ move, drive or walk slowly ❷ put off; postpone

缓刑 huǎnxíng 〈法〉temporary suspension of a sentence; reprieve; probation;～犯 probationer

huàn

幻 huàn ❶ unreal; imaginary; illusory;～景 illusion; mirage / ～境 dreamland; fairyland / ～觉 hallucination; illusion / ～梦 dream; fantasy; illusion / ～灭 disillusion / ～象 phantom; phantasm; mirage / ～影 unreal image; phantom ❷ change or conjure magically; ～术 magic; conjuring

幻灯 huàndēng slide show; slide projector;放～ show slides / ～机 slide projector / ～片 (lantern) slide; filmstrip

幻想 huànxiǎng ❶ fancy; dream; imagine;～曲〈乐〉fantasia ❷ illusion; fantasy;不抱～ cherish no illusions

奂 huàn 〈书〉❶ numerous; plentiful ❷ bright; brilliant

宦 huàn official; ～海〈喻〉(sea of) officialdom; official

circles / ～游〈书〉office-hunting ❷ (usu 宦官) eunuch

换 huàn ❶ exchange; barter; trade;～工 exchange labour / ～购 purchase by way of barter / ～取 exchange or barter for; get in return / ～文 exchange of notes or letters ❷ change; substitute; relieve; ～车 change trains or buses; transfer / ～乘 change or transfer to / ～挡〈机〉shift gears / ～防〈军〉relieve a garrison / ～岗〈军〉relieve a sentry; change the guard / ～毛〈动物〉moult / ～牙 (of a child) grow permanent teeth / ～脑筋〈喻〉change one's way of thinking / ～气扇 also "排风扇" ventilation fan / ～言之〈书〉in other words; namely; viz ❸ convert:把人民币～成美元 convert or change Renminbi (RMB) into US dollars

换班 huànbān ❶ change shifts; relieve sb on duty ❷〈军〉changing of the guard

换代 huàndài (of a product, etc) replace; regenerate: ～产品 new model (of a product)

换汇 huànhuì earn foreign exchange;出口～ foreign exchange earnings from export (of sth)

换季 huànjì change (garments) with the season; put on different clothes for a new season

换届 huànjiè replace or re-elect when a term of office expires: ～选举 re-election (when the current term expires)

换钱 huànqián ❶ change money; break a bill or note ❷ sell;典当衣服 pawn clothing for cash

换算 huànsuàn conversion; ～公式 conversion formula

换汤不换药 huàntāngbùhuànyào old wine in a new bottle; change in name only

换血 huànxiě blood transfusion; reorganization by introducing fresh personnel; reshuffle of a team

唤 huàn　call (out); summon; ～醒 wake up; awaken; arouse

唤起 huànqǐ　❶ arouse; ～民众 arouse the masses of the people ❷ call; draw; recall; ～人们的注意 call or draw attention (to sth)

涣 huàn　dissolve; dissipate; vanish; ～然 melt away; dissipate; vanish / ～散 lax; slack; demoralized

浣 huàn　〈书〉wash; rinse; ～纱 rinse yarn / ～衣 wash clothes

患 huàn　❶ trouble; peril; disaster; 水～ flood ❷ anxiety; worry; ～得～失 worry about personal gains and losses; be swayed by considerations of gain and loss ❸ contract; suffer from (an illness); ～病 fall or be ill / ～处 affected part (of a patient's body) / ～者 patient; invalid; sufferer

患难 huànnàn　trials and tribulations; adversity; trouble; ～与共 share hardships and dangers; go through trials and tribulations together / ～之交 friend in adversity; friend in need; tested friend

焕 huàn　shining; glowing; ～然一新 take on an entirely new look; look brand new

焕发 huànfā　❶ shine; glow; irradiate; 英姿～ dashing and spirited ❷ display vigour; cheer up; ～青春 (of older people, etc) radiate the vigour of youth; have a new lease of life; be rejuvenated

豢 huàn　(usu 豢养) feed; groom; keep

鲩 huàn　(popularly known as 草鱼) grass carp

huāng

荒 huāng　❶ waste; uncultivated; ～地 wasteland / ～芜 (of land, etc) lie waste; be overgrown with weeds ❷ desolate; wild; barren; ～岛 uninhabited island / ～凉 bleak and desolate; wild / ～僻 wild and remote; desolate and out-of-the-way / ～山 barren hill / ～野 wilderness; wild country; the wilds / ～原 wild country; wilderness / ～无人烟 desolate and uninhabited / ～乱的年代 years of social upheaval or turmoil ❸ famine; shortage; scarcity; ～年 year of famine; lean year / ～歉 crop failure; famine / 粮～ grain shortage; scarcity of grain ❹ neglect; be out of practice; ～疏 out of practice; (of skill) rusty ❺ unreasonable; absurd

荒诞 huāngdàn　❶ absurd; preposterous; fantastic; ～不经 (incredibly) fantastic; preposterous; absurd ❷ the absurd; ～派 the absurd / ～哲学 philosophy of the absurd

荒废 huāngfèi　❶ leave (land) uncultivated; (of land) lie waste ❷ neglect (one's studies, etc); be out of practice ❸ (of sth) fall into disuse or disrepair; waste (time)

荒谬 huāngmiù　absurd; preposterous; ～绝伦 absolutely preposterous; absurd to the extreme; height of absurdity

荒漠 huāngmò　❶ desolate and vast ❷ desert; wilderness; ～化 desertification

荒唐 huāngtang　❶ absurd; preposterous; ridiculous ❷ dissolute; dissipated; loose

荒淫 huāngyín　dissolute; licentious; debauched; ～无耻 dissipated and shameless; openly given to debauchery

慌 huāng　❶ flurried; confused; panicky; ～乱 alarmed and confused; flurried / ～神儿 be scared out of one's wits; panic / ～不择路 flee along any path one stumbles upon;

〈喻〉seize on any solution when hard pressed / ～里～张 in a hurried and confused manner; in a flurry / ～作一团 be thrown into utter confusion; be totally at a loss ❷ (huang)〈口〉(used after 得 as a modifier) unbearably; awfully: 饿得～ be awfully hungry; be famished

慌忙 huāngmáng in a great rush; in a hurry; hurriedly: 说话不慌不忙 speak in a poised manner; speak with composure

慌张 huāngzhāng flurried; flustered; confused: 沉住气，别～! Keep calm, don't panic!

huáng

皇 huáng ❶〈书〉grand; magnificent: ～～巨著 voluminous work; masterpiece ❷ emperor; sovereign: ～储 also "皇太子" crown prince / ～帝 emperor / ～宫 imperial palace / ～冠 imperial or royal crown / ～后 empress; queen / ～陵 imperial mausoleum / ～权 imperial power or authority / ～上 (reigning) emperor; His or Your Majesty / ～位 throne / ～族 royal or imperial clan; people of imperial lineage / ～太后 empress dowager / ～亲国戚 kinsman or relative of the emperor / ～天后土 Heaven and Earth

皇历 huángli also "黄历"〈口〉(lunar) almanac

皇粮 huángliáng ❶〈旧〉public grain; grain tax to the government ❷ funds, goods, etc provided by the government: 吃～ be paid by the government; be a government employee

皇室 huángshì ❶ imperial family; royal house ❷ royal court; imperial government

黄 huáng ❶ yellow; sallow: ～酒 (yellow) rice or millet wine; Shaoxing wine / ～米 glutinous millet /

～铜 brass / ～灿灿 bright yellow; golden / ～澄澄 glistening yellow; golden / ～种人 Mongoloid or yellow person ❷ (of) pornography: 扫～ wipe out pornography and prostitution ❸ (Huáng) short for 黄河: ～泛区 area (formerly) flooded by the Yellow River ❹ (Huáng) short for 黄帝: ～老之学 the philosophy of Huangdi and Laotse ❺〈口〉(of a project, plan, etc) fizzle out; fall through; be off

黄疸 huángdǎn also "黄疸病"; "黄病"〈医〉jaundice

黄道 huángdào 〈天文〉ecliptic: ～带 zodiac / ～吉日 propitious or auspicious date; lucky day

黄帝 Huángdì Huangdi or Yellow Emperor — legendary ruler and ancestor of the Chinese nation

黄豆 huángdòu soya bean; soybean: ～芽 soya bean sprouts

黄蜂 huángfēng wasp

黄瓜 huánggua cucumber: 酸～ pickled cucumber

黄河 Huánghé Yellow River, second longest river in China: ～流域 Yellow River Valley

黄花 huánghuā ❶ chrysanthemum ❷ also "黄花菜" (popular term for 金针菜) (dried) day lily ❸ without sexual experience; virgin: ～闺女 also "黄花女儿" virgin

黄昏 huánghūn dusk; twilight; gloaming: ～恋 love between old people; twilight love

黄金 huángjīn gold: ～储备 gold reserve / ～地段 most valuable section (of a city) / ～时代 golden age; prime of one's life / ～时间 (as on TV) prime time; peak viewing time

黄鹂 huánglí also "黄莺" oriole

黄连 huánglián 〈中药〉rhizome of Chinese goldthread

黄粱梦 huángliángmèng also "黄粱美梦" Golden Millet Dream;

daydream; pipe dream

黄毛丫头 huángmáoyātou 〈谑〉〈贬〉 chit of a girl; saucy miss

黄梅天 huángméitiān *also* "黄梅季节" rainy season (usu April and May in the middle and lower reaches of the Yangtze River)

黄梅雨 huángméiyǔ *also* "梅雨"; "霉雨" prolonged intermittent drizzles (characteristic of 黄梅天)

黄牛 huángniú ❶ ox; cattle ❷〈方〉 tout; scalper:～票 scalper's ticket

黄牌 huángpái 〈体〉 yellow card:吃了一张～ get a yellow card;〈喻〉 get a serious warning

黄泉 huángquán netherworld:命归～ go to the netherworld; die

黄色 huángsè ❶ yellow:～炸药 trinitrotoluene (TNT) ❷ decadent; vulgar; pornographic:～电影 pornographic movie; sex or blue film /～书刊 obscene publication

黄鳝 huángshàn *also* "鳝鱼" rice-field eel; finless eel

黄鼠狼 huángshǔláng *also* "黄鼬" yellow weasel

黄土 huángtǔ 〈地〉 loess:～高原 loess plateau

黄油 huángyóu ❶ grease (for bearings, etc) ❷ butter

黄鱼 huángyú *also* "黄花鱼" yellow croaker

遑 huáng ❶〈书〉 leisure ❷ *see* "惶" huáng 〈书〉 in haste /～论 〈书〉 out of the question; much less

惶 huáng fear; dread; trepidation:～～ *also* "皇皇" anxious and alarmed; on tenterhooks /～惑 perplexed and alarmed; apprehensive /～恐 scared; terrified

煌 huáng bright; brilliant

潢 huáng dye or colour paper

蝗 huáng locust:～虫 locust /～灾 plague of locusts

磺 huáng sulphur:～胺〈医〉 sulphanilamide (SN)

簧 huáng ❶ reed (in a musical instrument):～乐器 reed instrument ❷ spring:锁～ lock spring

huǎng

恍 huǎng ❶ all of a sudden; suddenly:～然大悟 realize all of a sudden; suddenly see the light ❷ (used with 如 or 若) seem; as if:～如隔世 it seems as if a whole generation had passed; feel as if cut off from the outside world for ages

恍惚 huǎnghū *also* "恍忽" ❶ in a trance; absent-minded:神情～ look absent-minded ❷ dimly; faintly; seemingly:～记得 faintly remember; seem to remember

晃 huǎng ❶ dazzle:灯光～眼。The light is dazzling. ❷ flash past:一～〈眼〉暑假就过完了。The summer vacation passed in a flash. *see also* huàng

谎 huǎng lie; falsehood:～报 make a false report (about sth); give false information /～称 falsely claim /～话 *also* "谎言" lie; falsehood

幌 huǎng

幌子 huǎngzi ❶〈旧〉 shop sign; signboard ❷ pretence; cover; front:在和谈的～下 under the cover of peace talks

huàng

晃 huàng shake; sway:～动 shake; rock; sway /～悠 shake from side to side; wobble; stagger *see also* huǎng

晃荡 huàngdang ❶ rock; sway;

swing:一瓶子不响，半瓶子~〈俗〉the half-filled bottle sloshes, the full bottle remains quiet — the dabbler chatters away, the wise man stays silent ❷ saunter; loaf:成天在外面~ loaf around all day long

huī

灰 huī ❶ ash:~烬 ashes / ~飞烟灭 become ash and smoke; vanish like so much smoke ❷ dust; powder:~尘 dust / ~土 dust; dirt ❸ lime; (lime) mortar:抹~ apply mortar / ~浆 mortar / ~泥 plaster ❹ grey:~暗 murky grey; gloomy / ~白 greyish white; ashen; pale / ~熊 grizzly bear / ~沉沉 (usu of the sky) dull (grey); gloomy / ~蒙蒙 dusky; overcast / ~指甲〈医〉ringworm of the nails ❺ disheartened; discouraged:~溜溜 gloomy; dejected; crestfallen

灰色 huīsè ❶ grey; ashy:深~ dark or Oxford grey ❷ pessimistic; gloomy; dispirited ❸ obscure; ambiguous:持~的态度 be ambiguous about sth ❹〈喻〉grey — halfway between legal and illegal; of questionable origin:~收入 grey income

灰心 huīxīn lose heart; be discouraged or disheartened:~丧气 very much disheartened; dejected and crestfallen

诙 huī〈书〉banter; tease; ridicule:~谐 humourous; jocular; witty

挥 huī ❶ wave; brandish; shake:~动 brandish; wave; shake / ~毫〈书〉wield one's brush; write or paint (with a brush) / ~拳 shake one's fist (at sb) / ~手 wave (one's hand) / ~舞 wave; brandish; shake ❷ wipe off:~泪 wipe off one's tears; shed tears / ~汗如雨 (of weather) so hot that perspiration falls like rain; (of people) dripping with sweat; wet

through ❸ command (an army):~师前进 command an army to march forward ❹ scatter; disperse:~金如土 throw gold about like dirt; spend money like water / ~洒热血 shed one's blood (for a worthy cause)

挥发 huīfā volatilize:~性 volatility / ~油 volatile oil / ~作用 volatilization

挥霍 huīhuò spend freely; squander:~无度 spend without restraint; squander wantonly

咴 huī

咴儿咴儿 huīrhuīr〈象声〉(of a horse, etc) neigh; whinny

恢 huī broad; vast; extensive:~弘 also "恢宏"〈书〉extensive; vast; great

恢复 huīfù ❶ go back or return to normal; renew; resume:~原状 return to the original state; resume the original shape ❷ recover; regain; resume:~期 convalescence; recovery; recuperation period / ~名誉 rehabilitate one's reputation

晖 huī sunshine; sunlight:春~ spring sunshine

辉（輝） huī ❶ radiance; splendour; glow ❷ shine; glow:~映 also "晖映" shine; reflect

辉煌 huīhuáng brilliant; splendid; glorious:再创~ regain one's former splendour / ~灿烂 splendid; glorious

麾 huī ❶ standard of a commander:~下〈书〉(troops under) sb's command;〈敬〉commander; your or his excellency ❷〈书〉command:~军进击 command an army to attack the enemy

徽 huī ❶ emblem; badge; insignia:~记 mark; sign; logo / ~章 badge; insignia ❷ fine; glorious:~号 glorious title; title of honour

huí

回（囬、●迴） huí ❶ circle; wind; ~廊 winding corridor / ~形针 (paper) clip ❷ return; go or come back; ~程 return trip / ~荡 resound; reverberate; echo / ~放 play-back / ~国 return to one's country or native land / ~航 return to base or port / ~聘 also "返聘" re-engage (usu retirees) for work; re-employ / ~乡 return to one's home village or town / ~娘家 (of a married woman) visit one's parents; 〈喻〉 return to one's place of origin or former place of work ❸ turn round; ~身 turn round / ~马枪 (give a) back-thrust; (fire a) Parthian shot ❹ answer; reply; return; ~拜 also "回访" pay a return visit or call / ~驳 refute; rebut / ~电 wire back; (send a) return cable / ~馈 repay; requite; give in return / ~请 return hospitality; give a return banquet / ~赠 give (sb a present) in return ❺ decline; cancel; dismiss; ~掉邀请 decline an invitation ❻ 〈量〉 used to indicate frequency of occurrence; 来过两~ have been here twice ❼ 〈量〉 chapter (of a novel); section; session ❽ (Huí) Hui; ~族 Hui ethnic group / ~民 Hui (people)

回报 huíbào ❶ report back (to sb on sth); 据实~ report the facts; make a factual report ❷ repay; requite; reciprocate; ~率 〈经〉 rate of return; return rate ❸ retaliate; get one's own back; 行恶者，必遭~。Retribution is certain to overtake the evildoer.

回避 huíbì ❶ evade; dodge; avoid ❷ (as of a judge or witness) avoidance; challenge; recuse; 要求证人~ challenge or recuse a witness

回肠荡气 huícháng-dàngqì (of music, poetry, etc) soul-stirring; thrilling; inspiring

回潮 huícháo ❶ get damp or moist ❷ 〈贬〉 (of once-extinct old customs, etc) resurgence; reversion

回春 huíchūn ❶ return of spring ❷ also "回生" bring back to life; ~乏术。 There is no way to bring the patient back to life.

回答 huídá answer; reply; response

回复 huífù ❶ reply (to a letter) ❷ restore; return to; ~原状 return to the original state or status quo ante

回顾 huígù look back; review; 频频~ look back again and again / ~展 review; retrospective exhibition / ~起来 in retrospect

回光返照 huíguāngfǎnzhào last glow of the setting sun — temporary clearing up of mind or momentary recovery of consciousness before death; sudden spurt of activity prior to death or collapse

回归 huíguī return; ~年 〈天文〉 tropical year / ~线 〈地〉 Tropic of Capricorn or Cancer / ~自然 return or go back to nature

回锅 huíguō cook again; ~肉 stir-fried boiled pork in hot sauce; twice-cooked pork

回合 huíhé round; bout; 大战 80 多~ (have) eighty rounds of fierce battle

回话 huíhuà ❶ (usu used by a junior to a senior in reply to the latter's inquiry, etc) reply; 回大人话 in reverent reply to your inquiry, sir ❷ reply; answer; confirm; 带个~ take or bring a message by way of reply

回击 huíjī fight back; return fire; counterattack

回见 huíjiàn 〈套〉 see you later or soon; cheerio; goodbye

回敬 huíjìng ❶ return a compliment or gift ❷ retaliate; give tit for tat; give as good as one gets

回绝 huíjué decline; refuse; reject

回扣 huíkòu also "回佣" (of sales) commission; kickback: 拿～ accept a kickback

回来 huílái ❶ come or get back; return ❷ (huilai) used after a verb to indicate direction: 带～ bring back

回礼 huílǐ ❶ return a salute ❷ (give a) gift in return

回笼 huílóng ❶ steam again; resteam ❷ withdraw (currency) from circulation

回炉 huílú ❶ melt down: ～重造 melt down and recast ❷ bake again ❸ (of staff, etc) retrain by taking a refresher course

回落 huíluò (of water level, price, etc) fall after a rise; drop

回去 huíqù ❶ return; go or be back ❷ (huiqu) used after a verb to indicate direction: 拿～ take (sth) back

回升 huíshēng rise again (after a fall); pick up

回声 huíshēng echo: 山谷～ echoes in a valley

回收 huíshōu ❶ recycle (waste, etc); recover: ～率 rate of recovery / ～站 (waste matter) collection depot ❷ get back (a loan, etc); retrieve (a satellite, etc); recover

回首 huíshǒu ❶ see "回头❶" ❷ 〈书〉 look back; recollect: 不堪～当年 cannot bear to talk about the past

回天 huítiān reverse a hopeless situation: 无力～ also "回天乏术" be incapable of reversing a hopeless situation; know no way to save a situation

回条 huítiáo also "回执" note that acknowledges receipt of sth; receipt

回头 huítóu ❶ turn one's head; turn round ❷ come back; return: ～客 regular or repeat customer; frequenter / ～路〈喻〉road back to where one started; road of retrogression ❸ repent; mend one's way: ～是岸〈喻〉turn

from one's evil ways; repent and be saved ❹ later; some other time: ～见 see you later; cheerio

回味 huíwèi ❶ aftertaste ❷ call to mind and ponder over; ponder retrospectively; ruminate over: ～无穷 leave prolonged aftertaste; afford much food for thought

回响 huíxiǎng reverberate; echo; resound: 激起强烈的～ evoke strong repercussions

回想 huíxiǎng think back; recall

回心转意 huíxīn-zhuǎnyì change one's mind; come round; think better (of sth)

回信 huíxìn write back; reply: 至今未见～. I haven't received any reply.

回旋 huíxuán ❶ circle round; wheel ❷ (room for) manoeuvre: 留点儿～余地 allow a little latitude

回忆 huíyì call to mind; recall; recollect: ～录 reminiscences; memoirs; recollections

回音 huíyīn ❶ see "回声" ❷ reply; response

回应 huíyìng reply; answer; response: 积极～ (give) positive responses (to a proposal, etc)

茴 huí

茴香 huíxiāng fennel; aniseed

洄 huí 〈书〉(of water) flow back; whirl: ～游 also "回游" (of fish) migration

蛔 huí (usu 蛔虫) roundworm

huǐ

悔 huǐ regret; repent: ～改 repent and mend one's ways / ～棋 also "回棋" retract a false move in a chess game / ～悟 realize and regret one's error; repent / ～罪 show penitence or repentance (for a crime, etc)

悔不当初 huǐbùdāngchū　regret not having pursued a different course; regret having done sth

悔过 huǐguò　repent one's error; be repentant; ～书 written confession; statement of repentance / ～自新 repent and turn over a new leaf

悔恨 huǐhèn　deeply regret; be filled with remorse; ～交加 be stung by remorse and shame

悔之无及 huǐzhīwújí　also "悔之晚矣" it is too late to repent; it is no use regretting it

毁（③譭） huǐ ❶ destroy; ruin; demolish; ～坏 destroy; damage; ruin / ～灭 destroy; exterminate; wreck / ～容 disfigure / ～约 annul a contract or treaty; go back on one's word / ～于一旦 be destroyed in a day; be ruined overnight ❷ burn up; burn down. ～于战火 be burnt down in war ❸ defame; slander; ～谤 slander; malign; calumniate / ～誉参半 (of sb) get both praise and censure; be as much censured as praised; (of sth) have a mixed reception

huì

卉 huì　(usu decorative) grass

汇（滙、匯、②③彙） huì ❶ converge; ～合 converge; join / ～流 flow together; converge ❷ gather together; collect; ～集 also "会集" collect; converge; assemble / ～总 gather; collect; pool ❸ things collected; assemblage; collection / ～展 joint exhibition ❹ remit; ～费 remittance fee ❺ foreign exchange; ～率 exchange or conversion rate / ～市 foreign exchange market or quotations

汇报 huìbào　report; give an account of; 思想～(give an) account of one's ideological progress and problems / ～工作 report (to sb) on one's work

汇编 huìbiān ❶ compile; collect: 资料～ corpus of data / ～成册 collect in book form ❷ 〈信息〉 assembly; ～语言 assembly or assembler language

汇兑 huìduì ❶ remittance: 国内～ domestic remittance ❷ exchange: ～率 rate of exchange

汇款 huìkuǎn　remit money; ～单 money order; remittance slip / ～收款人 beneficiary of remittance

汇票 huìpiào　draft; bill of exchange; money order: 银行～ bank draft / 邮政～ postal money order

汇演 huìyǎn　see "会演" huìyǎn

会（會） huì ❶ get together; assemble; do jointly; ～餐 dine together; have a dinner party / ～合 join; meet; converge / ～聚 also "汇聚" assemble; meet; flock together / ～考 standard or uniform examination (for students from various schools) / ～商 hold a conference or consultation; negotiate / ～审 (hold a) joint hearing or trial; (make a) joint checkup / ～师 join forces; effect a junction ❷ meet; see: ～见 have a meeting with (sb) / ～面 meet ❸ meeting; party; conference; ～场 meeting place; site or venue of a conference / ～堂 meeting or assembly hall; (conference) hall ❹ association; society; union; ～标 symbol of an event or a gathering; emblem of an association; logo / ～费 membership dues or fees / ～徽 emblem of an organization or association; logo ❺ major city; capital; 大都～ big city; metropolis ❻ opportunity; occasion ❼ understand; comprehend; grasp; ～心 understanding; knowing ❽ be able to; be good at; be likely or sure to; ～水 be able to swim / 天～下雨吗? Is it going to rain? ❾ pay (a bill) ～账 also "会钞" pay or foot the bill ❿ (usu used with 一) 一 ~儿 period of time; some time; a while or moment

see also kuài

会话 huìhuà　(usu of a foreign language) conversation

会客 huìkè　receive a visitor or guest; ~室 reception room / ~时间 visiting hours

会谈 huìtán　talks; negotiation; 双边~ bilateral talks

会同 huìtóng　together with; jointly with

会晤 huìwù　meet; confer (with)

会演 huìyǎn　also "汇演" joint performance (by a number of theatrical troupes, etc)

会议 huìyì　❶ meeting; conference; convention; ~室 meeting or conference room / ~地点 venue; meeting place ❷ council; conference (as an organization); 部长~ council of ministers

会意 huìyì　❶ see "六书" liùshū ❷ understanding; knowing; ~地一笑 smile knowingly

会员 huìyuán　member; 正式~ full member / ~国 member (state or nation) / ~证 membership card / ~资格 status of a member; membership

会战 huìzhàn　❶〈军〉meet or engage in a decisive battle ❷〈喻〉join in a battle (for a project, etc); launch a mass campaign (to do sth)

会诊 huìzhěn　(of doctors) group consultation; multi-disciplinary consultation; 专家~ (hold) consultations of specialists

会址 huìzhǐ　❶ site or address of a society, etc ❷ site of a conference or meeting

讳(諱) huì　❶ avoid as taboo; ~言 dare not mention; would not speak up / ~疾忌医 hide one's illness for fear of treatment; 〈喻〉refuse to face up to one's prob-

lems; ~莫如深 carefully avoid mentioning sth; guard a secret closely ❷ taboo; sth regarded as a taboo; forbidden word; 犯~ say or do something that is taboo

荟(薈) huì　〈书〉luxuriant growth (of plants); ~萃 (of fine people or things) collect; gather together; assemble

诲 huì　teach; instruct; ~人不倦 be tireless in teaching; teach with tireless zeal / ~淫~盗 propagate sex and violence; stir up base passions

绘(繪) huì　paint; draw; ~画 drawing; painting / ~图 mapping; plotting; sketch / ~声~色 also "绘影绘声" vivid; lively; graphic

恚 huì　〈书〉hate; resent; be angry

贿 huì　bribe; ~赂 bribe / ~选 rig an election by bribery

烩(燴) huì　❶ braise in thick sauce and add starch when almost ready ❷ cook (rice, etc) with meat, vegetables and water

彗 huì　〈天文〉comet; ~星 comet / ~尾 tail of a comet / ~星 comet

晦 huì　❶ dark; dim; obscure; ~暗 dark and gloomy / ~涩 (of language, etc) obscure; hard to understand ❷ night; ~明〈书〉day and night

晦气 huìqì　❶ unlucky; 真~! What rotten luck! ❷ pale and gloomy look; 一脸~ unhealthy look that threatens ill luck

秽(穢) huì　dirty; ugly; abominable; ~土 rubbish; refuse; dirt / ~行〈书〉abominable behaviour; promiscuous conduct / ~闻〈书〉ill repute (usu in reference to promiscuity) / ~语 vulgar remarks; dirty words; obscene language

惠 huì ❶ favour; kindness; benefit; ~而不费 do a kindness that does not cost much; be of great profit without much cost ❷〈敬〉you; your; ~顾 your patronage / ~赠 your kind gift / ~存 please keep this as a souvenir; to So-and-So

喙 huì 〈书〉bill or beak (of a bird); snout (of an animal); mouth

溃(殨) huì (of a sore) run; fester; 伤口～脓。The wound festered and ran with pus. *see also* kuì

慧 huì intelligent; bright; clever; 早～ mature early (in intelligence) / ~黠〈书〉clever and sly; shrewd / ~眼 discerning eye; penetrating insight / ~中秀外 intelligent within and beautiful without; both intelligent and beautiful

蕙 huì 〈植〉orchid; ~质兰心 also "蕙心兰质" pure-hearted and charming

hūn

昏 hūn ❶ dusk; gloaming ❷ dark; dim; murky; ~暗 dim; dusky / ~黑 dusky; dark / ~黄 pale yellow; faint; dim ❸ confused; muddled; fatuous; ~君 fatuous and self-indulgent ruler / ~聩 decrepit and muddle-headed ❹ lose consciousness; faint; ~倒 fall unconscious; faint / ~厥 also "晕厥" faint; swoon / ~死 faint; swoon; (go into a) coma / ~眩 also "昏晕" dizzy; giddy; faint

昏沉 hūnchén ❶ murky; dim ❷ dazed; befuddled

昏花 hūnhuā dim-sighted; 老眼～ dim-sighted from old age

昏昏欲睡 hūnhūnyùshuì drowsy; sleepy

昏乱 hūnluàn ❶ dazed and confused;

befuddled ❷〈书〉confusion and disorder; 世道～ social disarray

昏迷 hūnmí (fall into a) stupor; coma; shock

昏睡 hūnshuì lethargic sleep; lethargy; ~病〈医〉sleeping-sickness; lethargy

昏天黑地 hūntiān-hēidì ❶ pitch-dark;〈喻〉dark; chaotic; ~的社会 dark and lawless society / 吵了个～ have a hell of a quarrel ❷ dizzy; faint; unconscious ❸ perverted; decadent; wanton

昏头昏脑 hūntóu-hūnnǎo *also* "昏头胀脑" with one's mind numb; confused and dizzy; addle-brained

昏庸 hūnyōng fatuous; muddle-headed; stupid; ~无能 fatuous and incompetent

荤 hūn ❶ meat or fish; ~菜 meat dish / ~素搭配 (have a) balanced diet of meat and vegetables ❷ filthy; indecent; ~笑话 dirty joke

阍 hūn 〈书〉❶ (palace) gate ❷ guard the door or gate; 司～ *also* "阍者" doorkeeper; gatekeeper; janitor

婚 hūn wed; marry; 未～ unmarried / ~变 divorce; extramarital affair (that disrupts a marriage) / ~礼 wedding (ceremony) / ~期 wedding day / ~纱 (lady's) wedding garment / ~事 marriage; wedding / ~约 marriage contract; engagement / ~外恋 *also* "婚外情" extramarital love or sex; affair / ~生子女〈法〉children born in wedlock; legitimate children

婚龄 hūnlíng ❶ years of marriage ❷ (legally) marriageable age

婚前 hūnqián before marriage; ~检查 premarital physical check-up / ~协议 pre-marriage or pre-nuptial agreement / ~性关系 pre-marital sex

婚姻 hūnyīn marriage; matrimony; ~法 marriage law / ~自主 marry of one's own free will / ~状况 marital status / ～介绍所 matrimonial agency

hún

浑 hún ❶ *also* "混" muddy; murky; turbid:～水摸鱼 fish in troubled waters; try to gain advantage out of other people's troubles ❷ *also* "混" addle-brained; foolish; stupid:～蛋〈粗〉wretch; bastard; son of a bitch / ～话 nonsense; fatuous talk; impudent remark / ～～噩噩 fatuous and ignorant; simple-minded; muddle-headed ❸ simple and natural:画风～朴 paint in a plain and simple style ❹ whole; full; all over:～圆 perfectly round / ～似其父 look exactly like one's father; be a chip of the old block

浑厚 húnhòu ❶ simple and honest ❷ (of writing, painting, etc) simple and vigorous ❸ (of a voice) deep and sonorous

浑然 húnrán ❶ integrated; unified; integral:～一体 integrated mass; integral whole ❷ completely; fully; entirely:～不觉 be entirely unaware

浑身 húnshēn from head to heel; all over:～是胆 be the very embodiment of valour; be every inch a hero / 使出～解数 do all one can; do one's level best

珲 hún 〈书〉a kind of jade

馄 hún

馄饨 húntún wonton; dumpling soup

混 hún see "浑❶❷" hún see also hùn

魂 hún ❶ soul:～灵 soul (of the dead) / ～魄 soul / ～不附体 feel as if one's soul had left one's body; be shaken to the depths of one's soul / ～不守舍 in a trance; absent-minded; panic-stricken / ～飞魄散 panic-stricken; go out of one's mind; be half dead with fright ❷ mood; spir-

it;军～ spirit of an army; army spirit / ～牵梦萦 miss very much; pine for

hùn

诨 hùn joke; jest:打～ make gags; crack jokes / ～名 *also* "诨号" nickname

混 hùn ❶ mix; mingle; confuse:～纺 blending (of textiles) / ～双 (short for 混合双打)〈体〉mixed doubles / ～同 confuse; mix up / ～杂 mix; mingle; confound / ～战 tangled warfare; tangled fighting / ～血儿 person of mixed blood; half-breed ❷ pass for; pass or palm off as:～进 *also* "混入" infiltrate; sneak into; worm one's way into / ～～儿 *also* "混子" quack; conniving idler; street rowdy ❸ muddle along or on; drift along:～饭吃 make a living as best one can; work just to get by / ～日子 muddle or drift along; scrape by / ～事儿 scrape a living; muddle along (in one's job) ❹ get along with;和当地人～得很熟 hit it off with the locals ❺ at random; irresponsibly:～说 speak thoughtlessly

see also hún

混沌 hùndùn ❶ chaos (as primeval state of the universe):～理论 chaology ❷ innocent; simple-minded and ignorant

混合 hùnhé mix; blend; mingle:～物 mixture

混乱 hùnluàn confusion; chaos; disorder:引起～ create confusion; throw (people, etc) into disarray / ～局面 chaotic state or situation

混凝土 hùnníngtǔ 〈建筑〉concrete

混为一谈 hùnwéiyītán lump or jumble together; confuse sth with sth else

混淆 hùnxiáo obscure; mix up; confuse:～视听 mislead the public; befuddle or confuse public opinion

混账 hùnzhàng 〈粗〉scoundrel; rascal; bastard; ～话 impudent language; vile rubbish / ～东西 bastard; son of a bitch

混浊 hùnzhuó （of water) muddy; (of air) foul; (of eyes, etc) dull

huō

粏 huō hoeing; ～子 hoe

劐 huō 〈口〉❶ slit or cut with a knife ❷ see "粏" huō

嚄 huō 〈叹〉wow; ～! 这么多水果呀! Wow! Such a lot of fruit!

豁 huō ❶ split; crack; breach; ～嘴 harelip; harelipped person / ～口 opening; breach; crack ❷ (be ready to) pay any price (for sth one must do); sacrifice; ～命 risk one's life; (do sth) at any price / ～出去 be ready to risk everything

see also huò

huó

和 huó mix with water; ～面 mix flour with water; make or knead dough　see also hé; hè; hú; huò

活 huó ❶ live; be alive or active; keep alive; ～佛 〈宗教〉Living Buddha / ～埋 bury alive / ～血 〈中医〉invigorate blood circulation / ～捉 capture alive / ～靶子 live target (for criticism, etc) / ～化石 living fossil / ～火山 active volcano / ～菩萨 Buddha incarnate; person full of compassion / ～受罪 have a terrible life or time / ～字典 walking dictionary / 没～头儿 have nothing to live for / ～到老,学到老 live and learn; one is never too old to learn ❷ vivid; lively; like real; ～现 appear vividly; come alive / ～地狱 hell on earth; living hell / ～像真的一

样 like real; lifelike ❸ movable; flexible; moving; ～话 indefinite, vague, or open-ended remark; non-committal words / ～水 flowing or running water / ～用 apply in a creative way; make flexible use of / ～字印刷 movable-type printing; letter press ❹ work; job; product; 不出～儿 not productive; not efficient / 体力～儿 physical work; manual labour or work

活宝 huóbǎo bit of a clown; funny fellow

活蹦乱跳 huóbèng-luàntiào skip and jump about; be alive and kicking; be full of life

活动 huódòng ❶ move about; exercise; ～筋骨 limber up (the joints) ❷ shaky; unsteady; loose ❸ mobile; movable; flexible; ～房屋 mobile home; Nissen hut ❹ activity; manoeuvre; event; ～家 activist; public figure / ～范围 sphere of activities; scope of operation / ～余地 room for manoeuvre; leeway; latitude / 庆祝～ celebration ❺ use personal influence or irregular means; manoeuvre; jockey (for sth)

活该 huógāi ❶ serve sb right; 他～! Serves him right! ❷ 〈方〉be decreed by fate; ～受苦 be predestined to suffer

活活 huóhuó ❶ while still alive; ～打死 be beaten to death ❷ simply; completely; literally; ～累死 literally die of overwork

活计 huójì ❶ handicraft work; manual labour; 针线～ needlework ❷ handiwork; work

活见鬼 huójiànguǐ you're imagining things; it's sheer fantasy; how preposterous

活结 huójié also "活扣" slipknot; bowknot; 打个～ make a slipknot

活口 huókǒu living witness to a crime; survivor of a murder attempt; person who can furnish information; 留

下～ leave sb behind who can tell about a case

活力 huólì vigour; vitality; energy:增强经济～ invigorate the economy

活灵活现 huólíng-huóxiàn also "活龙活现" vivid; lifelike:说得～ give a vivid account

活路 huólù ❶ thorough path ❷ workable method; feasible approach ❸ means of subsistence; way to keep alive

活命 huómìng ❶ earn a bare living; scrape along; eke out an existence ❷ 〈书〉 save sb's life; survive:～哲学 philosophy of survival; keeping oneself alive at all costs ❸ life:留人一条～ spare sb's life

活泼 huópo lively; vivacious; vivid

活期 huóqī current:～储蓄 current (savings) deposit; demand deposit

活生生 huóshēngshēng ❶ real; living; in actual life:～的现实 living reality ❷ while still alive:～被逼死 be driven to death

活页 huóyè loose-leaf; detachable leaf:～本 loose-leaf notebook

活跃 huóyuè ❶ dynamic; active; lively:思想～ dynamic thinking; active mind ❷ enliven; invigorate; stimulate

huǒ

火 huǒ ❶ fire:～把 torch / ～场 scene of a fire / ～光 flame; blaze; firelight / ～海 sea of fire / ～炉 (heating) stove / ～苗 also "火舌" tongues of fire; licking flame / ～源 source of combustion; fire starter ❷ firearms; firing; fire:～器 firearm ❸ 〈中医〉 internal heat, one of the six causes of disease ❹ red as fire; fiery; flaming:～烧云 morning or evening glow; crimson clouds at sunrise or sunset ❺ urgent; pressing:～速增援 rush up or speed reinforcements ❻ anger; temper:～冒三丈 fly into a

rage; flare up ❼ prosperous; thriving; flourishing:买卖很～。Business is brisk. ❽ see "伙" huǒ

火暴 huǒbào also "火爆" ❶ fiery; impetuous:脾气～ have a fiery temper ❷ 〈方〉 vigorous; prosperous; exciting:～的场面 a scene of bustle and excitement

火并 huǒbìng also "火拼" open fight between factions or among associates; intramural strife

火柴 huǒchái match:～盒 matchbox

火车 huǒchē train:～头 engine; locomotive / ～站 railway or train station / ～车厢 railway coach or car / ～时刻表 railway or train schedule

火电 huǒdiàn (short for 火力发电) thermal power (generation):～厂 thermal power plant

火锅 huǒguō chafing dish; hotpot; dip-boiled dish

火红 huǒhóng red as fire:〈喻〉 fiery; flaming:～的心 〈喻〉 honest and warm heart

火候 huǒhou ❶ duration and degree of cooking, smelting, etc:欠～ not properly done; half-cooked; underdone / 掌握好～ keep good control over timing and temperature ❷ level of attainment:戏艺上已有相当～ be quite accomplished in theatrical art ❸ crucial moment:来得是～ come at the right moment

火花 huǒhuā ❶ sparks ❷ matchbox picture

火化 huǒhuà also "火葬" cremate:～场 crematorium; crematory

火鸡 huǒjī turkey

火急 huǒjí urgent; pressing:十万～ most urgent; extra-urgent / ～燎 be extremely worried; be terribly anxious

火箭 huǒjiàn rocket:发射～ fire or launch a rocket / ～筒 rocket launcher; bazooka

火警 huǒjǐng fire alarm:报～ report a

fire; sound the fire alarm / ～电话 fire number

火炬 huǒjù　torch; torchlight: ～赛跑 torch race

火坑 huǒkēng　pit of hell; abyss of suffering: 救出～ get (sb) out of living hell

火辣辣 huǒlālā　❶ burning; scorching; hurtful: ～的骄阳 scorching sun / 伤口～地疼痛。The wound hurts badly. ❷ (of a person, etc) bold and resolute; (of language) acerbic; sharp

火力 huǒlì　❶ thermal power: ～发电 thermal power; thermo-power generation ❷〈军〉firepower; fire: ～网 network of fire; fire net / ～侦察 reconnaissance by firing ❸ also "火气" cold-resistant capacity of the human body: 年轻人～旺。Young people could better resist cold.

火气 huǒqì　❶ anger; temper: ～大 have a fiery temper ❷〈中医〉internal heat: 败～ reduce internal heat

火热 huǒrè　❶ burning hot:〈喻〉fervent; passionate: ～的恋情 passionate love ❷ intimate: 谈得～ be in the middle of an intimate conversation ❸ fierce; intense: ～的斗争 fierce fight

火山 huǒshān　volcano: ～灰 volcanic ash / ～口 crater / ～喷发 volcanic eruption / ～熔岩 lava

火上加油 huǒshàngjiāyóu　also "火上浇油" pour oil on the fire; add fuel to the flames

火烧 huǒshāo　❶ set or be on fire; burn ❷ (huǒshao) baked wheaten cake

火烧火燎 huǒshāo-huǒliáo　❶ feel terribly hot or very painful: 伤口～地疼。The wound hurt terribly. ❷〈喻〉be restless with anxiety: 心里～的 be on pins and needles

火烧眉毛 huǒshāoméimao　the fire is singeing the eyebrows — extremely urgent; pressing

火势 huǒshì　intensity or state of a fire: 控制～ get a fire under control

火速 huǒsù　at top speed; posthaste: ～前往 go there posthaste

火头 huǒtóu　❶ (of an oil lamp, etc) flame; fire ❷ see "火候❶" ❸ place where a fire started: ～在三楼。The fire started somewhere on the 3rd floor. ❹ (be in a) fit of anger

火腿 huǒtuǐ　ham: ～蛋 ham and egg

火险 huǒxiǎn　❶ fire insurance ❷ fire danger: ～季节 fire season

火线 huǒxiàn　❶ battle line; frontline; battlefield ❷〈电〉live wire; power line

火星 huǒxīng　❶〈天文〉Mars ❷ sparks: ～四溅 throw off sparks in all directions; there is a shower of sparks

火性 huǒxìng　also "火性子" hot or quick temper

火焰 huǒyàn　flame; 熊熊的～ blazing flames / ～喷射器〈军〉flame-thrower

火药 huǒyào　gunpowder; powder: ～桶 powder keg; danger spot / ～味 smell of gunpowder

火灾 huǒzāi　fire (as a disaster); conflagration: ～保险 fire insurance

火中取栗 huǒzhōngqǔlì　pull chestnuts out of the fire; be a cat's paw

火种 huǒzhǒng　kindling (material); tinder: 科学～ sparks of science

火烛 huǒzhú　anything that may cause a fire: 小心～! Be careful about fires!

伙(火、❷⁻⁵夥)　huǒ　❶ mess; board; food: ～房 kitchen (in a school, etc) / ～夫 also "火夫"〈旧〉mess cook ❷ partner; mate ❸ partnership; company ❹〈量〉group; band; gang: 一一伙青年人 a group of young people ❺ combine; join; club: ～耕 also "伙种" work the land together; cultivate (land) as partners

伙伴 huǒbàn　partner; companion;

pal：～关系 partnership

伙计 huǒji ❶ partner；〈口〉fellow；mate ❷〈旧〉hired hand；salesman

伙食 huǒshí mess；food；board；～费 board expenses；money spent on meals

伙同 huǒtóng act in collusion with；gang up with

huò

或 huò ❶ also "或者"；"或许"；also "或者" or；either ... or ...；或迟或早 sooner or later / 你～他，谁都可以。You or he, either will do. ❸〈书〉somebody；some；～曰 it is said that...；some say ❹〈书〉slightly；a little bit；不可～缓 cannot be postponed at all；brook no delay

或然 huòrán probably：～率 also "概率" probability / ～性 chance；probability

和 huò ❶ mix；blend；～面 mix flour with water；prepare dough / ～稀泥〈喻〉mediate differences at the sacrifice of principle；try to paper things over ❷〈量〉(number of) rinses；boilings (of medicinal herbs)：一剂药要煮两～。Each dosage should be boiled twice.

see also hé；hè；hú；huó

货 huò ❶ currency；money ❷ goods；commodity；product：～舱 (cargo) hold (of a ship)；cargo bay (of a plane) / ～车 freight or goods train；goods van or wagon / ～单 manifest；waybill；shipping list / ～柜 (goods) counter；〈方〉container / ～款 money or payment for goods / ～摊 stall；stand / ～物 goods；commodity；merchandise / ～源 source or supply of goods / ～栈 warehouse / ～架子 goods shelves；luggage-carrier (of a bicycle) / ～比三家 compare different of-

fers ❸〈粗〉used of a person：好吃懒做的～ lazybones

货币 huòbì money；currency：～贬值 currency devaluation or depreciation / ～回笼 withdrawal of currency from circulation；currency recovery / ～政策 monetary policy / ～流通量 currency in circulation；money supply

货船 huòchuán freight or cargo ship；cargo vessel：定期～ cargo liner / 不定期～ tramp (steamer)

货色 huòsè ❶ goods；kinds and quality of goods：～齐全 have goods of every description ❷〈贬〉(of sb or sth) stuff；trash；rubbish

货运 huòyùn freight transport；shipment of commodities：～单 waybill / ～码头 cargo terminal / ～业务 cargo service

货真价实 huòzhēn-jiàshí ❶ quality goods at a fair price ❷ through and through；out-and-out；dyed-in-the-wool：～的骗子 a downright crook

获（⓵⓶获、⓷穫） huò ❶ capture；catch；seize ❷ get；obtain；win：～奖 win a prize；receive an award / ～救 be saved or rescued / ～利 earn or make a profit / ～取 acquire；obtain；gain / ～准 secure approval；get permission ❸ harvest；reap

获得 huòdé get；gain；acquire：～好评 win acclaim / ～性免疫〈医〉acquired immunity

获胜 huòshèng win；be victorious；triumph：5：1～ win a match five to one / ～率 average of wins

获释 huòshì be released or freed；be set free

获悉 huòxī learn (of an event)；get to know

祸（禍） huò ❶ misfortune；disaster；calamity：～根 root or source of trouble；cause of ruin；bane / ～首 chief culprit；arch-criminal / ～水 person（esp a woman）or thing that brings trouble; bane; peril / ～不单行 misfortunes never come singly; it never rains but it pours / ～从口出 disaster results from careless talk; a loose tongue is a source of evil / ～从天降 disaster comes like a bolt from the sky / ～起萧墙 trouble starts from within the family; there is internal strife afoot ❷ bring disaster upon; ruin; damage:～心 evil intent / ～国殃民 wreck the country and ruin the people; bring calamity to the nation

祸害 huòhai ❶ disaster; ruin; bane ❷ damage; destroy; ruin:～别人 ruin others

惑 huò ❶ be puzzled or bewildered:～然不解 feel puzzled or confused ❷ delude; mislead:～乱人心 confuse people's minds

霍 huò suddenly; quickly:～地冲了出去 dash or rush out all of a sudden

霍霍 huòhuò ❶〈象声〉sound of grinding knives，etc;磨刀～ sharpen one's knife ❷ flash:他两眼～闪光。His eyes flashed.

霍乱 huòluàn 〈医〉cholera

霍然 huòrán ❶ suddenly; quickly:～云消。Quickly the clouds dispersed. ❷〈书〉(of an illness) be cured quickly:病体～ get well quickly

豁 huò ❶ open; open-minded; generous:～达 be generous and open-minded /～亮 roomy and bright; open and clear; (of one's voice) loud and clear /～然开朗 (of terrain) open out;〈喻〉see the light clearly; be fully enlightened ❷ (usu 豁免) exempt (sb from sth); remit; make immune (from sth)

see also huō

嚯 huò ❶〈叹〉oh; wow:～，真漂亮! Wow, how beautiful! ❷〈象声〉:～～大笑 guffaw

J

jī

几(幾) jī ❶ small table ❷ 〈书〉close to; nearly; almost: ~近于零 next to nothing; almost nothing
see also jǐ

几乎 jīhū ❶ close to; nearly; all but ❷ hardly; almost: ~遇难 have a narrow escape

讥(譏) jī ridicule; mock; satirize: ~讽 ridicule; mock / ~笑 scoff, sneer or jeer at

击(擊) jī ❶ beat; hit; strike: ~打 beat; lash / ~剑〈体〉fencing / ~球 (as in baseball) batting ❷ attack; assault; assail: ~败 defeat; beat; crush / ~毙 shoot or strike dead / ~毁 smash; destroy / ~溃 rout; thoroughly defeat / ~以猛掌 give sb a shove / ~中要害 strike a serious warning / ~中要害 strike or hit home; hit the bull's eye or the nail on its head ❸ come in contact with; bump into: 目~witness; see with one's own eyes

叽(嘰) jī 〈象声〉chirp: ~咕 *also* "唧咕" talk in a low voice; whisper; mutter / ~~喳喳 *also* "唧唧喳喳" chirp; twitter / ~里咕噜 (of sb) gabble; (of sth) rumble / ~里呱啦 talk noisily

饥(²饑) jī ❶ hungry; starving: ~渴 hunger and thirst / ~肠辘辘 one's stomach rumbling with hunger; rumblings of an empty stomach / ~寒交迫 suffer from hunger and cold; be poverty-stricken ❷ crop failure; famine: ~馑〈书〉famine; crop failure / ~民 famine victim or refugee

饥不择食 jībùzéshí a hungry person is not choosy about food; all food is delicious to the starving

饥饿 jī'è be hungry; starve: ~难挨 suffer from unbearable hunger / 挣扎在~线上 struggle along on the verge of starvation

饥荒 jīhuang ❶ famine: 闹~ be famine-stricken / 〈喻〉be hard up ❷ debt: 拉~ be in debt

机(機) jī ❶ machine; engine; motor: ~车 locomotive; engine / ~床 machine tool / ~井 motor-pumped well / ~油 engine oil; (esp) lubricant oil / ~帆船 motor sailboat; motorized junk ❷ aircraft; aeroplane; plane: ~场 airport; airfield / ~库 (airplane) hangar / ~票 plane or flight ticket / ~长 crew commander; captain (of an airplane) ❸ chance; occasion; opportunity: ~遇 favourable circumstance; luck; opportunity / ~不可失，时不再来. Don't slip the opportunity; it may never come again. *or* Opportunity knocks but once. ❹ flexible; quick-witted; clever: ~敏 alert and resourceful; quick-witted

机舱 jīcāng ❶ engine room (of a ship) ❷ passenger or freight compartment (of an aircraft); cabin

机电 jīdiàn　electromechanical；～产品 mechanical and electrical products

机动 jīdòng　❶ motor-driven；motorized；～车 motor vehicle；vehicle in reserve ❷ flexible；adaptable；mobile；～性 flexibility；mobility；manoeuvrability ❸ in reserve；for emergency use；～力量 reserve force／～财力 standby financial resources

机构 jīgòu　❶ mechanism；液压～ hydraulic pressure mechanism ❷ organ；organization；institution；教育～ educational institution ❸ internal structure of an organization；set-up；～改革 structural reform or streamlining；restructuring／～臃肿 inflated organization

机关 jīguān　❶ mechanism；device；gear；～失灵 breakdown or failure of a mechanism ❷ machine-operated；～枪 also "机枪" machine-gun ❸ office；agency；organ；～刊物 organ；official publication (of a party, government, etc) ❹ stratagem；scheme；trick；～算尽 do much plotting and scheming；use every stratagem

机会 jīhuì　chance；opportunity；opening；～均等 equal opportunity for all／～主义 opportunism

机警 jījǐng　alert；watchful；vigilant

机灵 jīlíng　also "机伶" clever；smart；agile；～鬼 smart fellow；clever guy

机密 jīmì　❶ secret；classified；confidential；～文件 classified papers；confidential documents ❷ secret；泄露～ leak a secret

机能 jīnéng　〈生理〉function；faculty

机器 jīqì　machine；machinery；apparatus；～人 robot／～翻译 machine translation

机体 jītǐ　〈生理〉organism

机械 jīxiè　❶ machinery；machine；mechanism；～手 mechanical arm／～工业 machine-building industry／～运动 mechanical movement ❷〈喻〉mechanical；inflexible；rigid；～唯物主义 also "机械论"〈哲〉mechanical materialism

机械化 jīxièhuà　mechanize：农业～ mechanization of agriculture／～部队 mechanized forces

机型 jīxíng　❶ type (of an aircraft) ❷ model (of a machine)

机要 jīyào　confidential；掌握～ in control of confidential matters／～员 cipher officer

机宜 jīyí　principles of action；guidelines：请示～ ask for guidelines (from one's superior)

机缘 jīyuán　good luck or fortune；lucky chance；～巧合 by happy coincidence；by sheer luck

机载 jīzài　airborne；air-launched；～导弹 air-launched missile／～雷达 airborne radar

机制 jīzhì　❶ machine-processed；machine-made；～水饺 machine-made dumplings ❷ mechanism：引入竞争～ introduce competition

机智 jīzhì　quick-witted；resourceful；～老练 resourceful and experienced

机组 jīzǔ　❶ unit；set：发电～ generating set ❷ aircrew；flight crew：～人员 (members of a) crew

肌 jī　❶ muscle ❷〈书〉skin：～肤 (human) skin／～理 skin texture

肌肉 jīròu　muscle：～发达 muscular；brawny／～注射 intramuscular injection

肌体 jītǐ　human body；〈喻〉organism

鸡(鷄) jī　chicken；fowl；～雏 chick；chicken／～肉 chicken (as food)／～舍 chicken coop；henhouse；roost／～汤 chicken broth／～飞狗跳 with hens flying and dogs running—mass confusion；great disorder

鸡蛋 jīdàn　(hen's) egg；～糕 (sponge) cake／～羹 steamed egg custard／～碰石头〈俗〉like an egg striking a rock — attack sb far stronger than oneself / ～里挑骨头〈俗〉look for a flaw where there is none; nit-pick

鸡飞蛋打 jīfēi-dàndǎ 〈俗〉the hen has flown away and the eggs in the coop are broken — all is lost; fall between two stools

鸡奸 jījiān 〈commit〉sodomy; buggery

鸡肋 jīlèi 〈书〉chicken ribs — things of small value that one hesitates to throw away; white elephant

鸡毛 jīmáo chicken feather: ～掸子 feather duster / ～蒜皮 trifles; trivialities

鸡皮疙瘩 jīpí gēda goose pimples or bumps; gooseflesh; 吓得浑身起～ be so terrified that one's flesh creeps

鸡犬不留 jīquǎnbùliú even fowls and dogs are not spared — commit ruthless mass slaughter

鸡犬不宁 jīquǎnbùníng even fowls and dogs are not left in peace — general disturbance or turmoil; 闹得班里～ throw the whole class into confusion

鸡尾酒 jīwěijiǔ cocktail; ～会 cocktail party or reception

鸡胸 jīxiōng 〈医〉pigeon or chicken breast

鸡眼 jīyǎn 〈医〉corn; clavus

奇 jī odd (number); ～偶 odd and even numbers *see also* qí

唧 jī ❶ spurt; squirt; ～筒 pump / ～了一身水 squirt water all over sb ❷ *see* "叽" jī

积（積） jī ❶ gather; store up; accumulate; ～存 store up; stockpile / ～德 accumulate merit (for one's salvation); do good deeds / ～肥 collect (farmyard) manure; store compost / ～聚 gather; amass; build up / ～攒〈口〉save bit by bit; collect piecemeal / ～久成习 form a habit or custom over the years; (of sth) become one's second nature ❷

accumulated; long-standing; long pending; ～案 long-pending case / ～弊 accumulated malpractice; long-standing abuse / ～淀 accumulation over the years or ages / ～愤 pent-up indignation or grievances / ～习 deep-rooted habit; long-standing practice / ～怨 accumulated rancour; piled-up grievances ❸ 〈数〉product; 求～ find the product by multiplication

积非成是 jīfēichéngshì repeated lies become truths; (of sth wrong) become accepted through repeated usage

积分 jīfēn ❶ 〈数〉integral; ～学 integral calculus ❷ accumulated points

积极 jījí ❶ positive; ～因素 positive factor ❷ active; energetic; vigorous; ～性 zeal; initiative; enthusiasm / ～分子 activist; active element; enthusiast / ～进取精神 enterprising spirit

积劳成疾 jīláochéngjí break down from constant overwork; fall ill through prolonged overwork

积累 jīlěi accumulate; gather; ～经验 gain or accumulate experience

积木 jīmù building blocks; toy bricks

积少成多 jīshǎochéngduō accumulate little by little; amass gradually; many a little makes a mickle

积蓄 jīxù put aside; accumulate; save; ～物资 store up resources / 有点～ have some savings

积压 jīyā keep long in stock; overstock; ～商品 overstocked goods / ～的资金 tied-up funds

积重难返 jīzhòngnánfǎn bad old practices die hard; ingrained or inveterate habits are difficult to get rid of

屐 jī clogs; 木～ clogs

基 jī ❶ base; foundation; 房～ foundations (of a house) / ～价 base price ❷ basic; fundamental; primary; ～色 *also* "原色" primary colour

基本 jīběn ❶ base; foundation; 国家

的 ~ foundation of a country ❷ basic; fundamental; main; ~法 basic law / ~ 功 basic training or skill; fundamentals/ ~国策 basic state policy ❸ basically; in the main; on the whole

基本建设 jīběn jiànshè ❶ (shortened as 基建) capital construction; ~投资 investment in capital construction ❷ undertaking of primary importance

基本上 jīběnshang ❶ principally; mainly ❷ on the whole; in the main; by and large

基层 jīcéng　basic or primary level; grass roots; ~选举 elections at the grass roots

基础 jīchǔ ❶ base; foundation; basis: 打好 ~ lay a solid foundation / ~教育 elementary education / ~科学 basic science / ~设施 infrastructure ❷ (short for 经济基础) economic base

基地 jīdì　base: 能源 ~ energy base; source of energy

基点 jīdiǎn　basis; point of departure; starting point: 以互相信任为 ~ based on mutual trust

基调 jīdiào ❶ 〈乐〉fundamental or main key ❷ keynote: 会议的 ~ keynote for a conference

基督 Jīdū 〈宗教〉Christ; ~徒 Christian / ~纪元 Christian era

基督教 Jīdūjiào ❶ Christianity; Christian religion ❷ also "耶稣教" Protestantism

基金 jījīn　fund: 教育 ~ education fund / ~会 foundation

基石 jīshí ❶ foundation stone; 奠定 ~ lay a foundation stone ❷ 〈喻〉cornerstone: 外交政策的 ~ cornerstone of a foreign policy

基数 jīshù ❶ cardinal number ❷ base: 以此为 ~ take the amount as the base

基因 jīyīn 〈生理〉gene; ~组 genome / ~变异 geno-variation / ~工程 genetic engineering / ~疗法 gene ther-

apy / ~芯片 gene chip

基于 jīyú　because of; in view of; on account of

基准 jīzhǔn ❶ (in cartography) datum; ~点 datum point ❷ standard; criterion

犄 jī

犄角 jījiǎo 〈口〉❶ corner ❷ (jījiao) horn; 牛 ~ ox horn

缉 jī

seize; arrest; apprehend; ~查 search; ransack / ~毒 crack down on drug trafficking; arrest drug traffickers / ~获 capture; catch / ~拿 also "缉捕" seize; arrest; apprehend / ~私 seize smugglers or smuggled goods; crack down on or suppress smuggling

畸 jī

❶ lopsided; unbalanced: ~轻 ~重 attaching too much weight to one to one and too little to another; now too much, now too little; unbalanced ❷ irregular; eccentric; abnormal: ~变 abnormal change

畸形 jīxíng ❶ deformity; malformation; 肢体 ~ (have a) deformed limb ❷ lopsided; uneven; unbalanced: ~发展 lopsided development

跻 (躋) jī 〈书〉ascend; climb

; mount; ~(身)于世界强国之列 rank among the great powers of the world

稽 jī

❶ check; examine; investigate; ~核 audit; check; examine ❷ 〈书〉delay; linger; procrastinate; ~留 hold up; delay; detain

see also qǐ

稽查 jīchá ❶ check (to prevent tax evasion, etc) investigate ❷ inspector; customs officer

激 jī

❶ (of water, etc) swash; splash; dash; ~起浪花 dash up or raise spindrift ❷ arouse; stimulate; stir (up); ~起众怒 arouse popular indignation; stir up public wrath / ~于

义愤 be stirred by righteous indignation ❷ 心潮～荡 feel an upsurge of emotion ❸ fierce; violent; radical：～剧 intense；fierce；rapid／～浪 turbulent waves；torrential waters／～增 increase sharply；rise steeply；shoot up／～战 fierce fighting；pitched battle／形势～变。The situation took a radical turn.

激昂 jī'áng　excited and impassioned；vehement；roused：～地发表演说 deliver an impassioned speech

激动 jīdòng　excite；stir（up）；inspire：～人心 moving；touching／～地叫嚷 shout in an agitated tone

激发 jīfā　arouse；stimulate；spur：～灵感 stimulate imagination

激奋 jīfèn　rouse to action；stir into activity：～人心的场面 stirring scene

激愤 jīfèn　also "激忿" wrathful；indignant；enraged：群情～。Popular feelings ran high.

激光 jīguāng　also "莱塞"；"镭射" laser（light amplification by stimulated emission of radiation）：～器 laser；laser device／～束 laser beam／～打印机 laser printer／～制导导弹 laser-guided missile

激化 jīhuà　sharpen；intensify；aggravate：日趋～ intensify with each passing day／～矛盾 sharpen contradictions

激活 jīhuó　stimulate；invigorate；〈理〉activate：～市场 stimulate the market

激将 jījiàng　goad or prod sb into action：～法（method of）prodding or goading sb into doing sth（as by ridicule，sarcasm，etc）

激进 jījìn　radical；militant：～分子 radical／～主义 radicalism

激励 jīlì　encourage；urge；inspire：～机制 incentive mechanism／～士气 boost the morale

激烈 jīliè　intense；fierce；sharp：冲突～ conflict sharply（with sb）／～的比赛 gruelling match

激流 jīliú　torrent；turbulent current：～险滩 turbulent currents and dangerous shoals；rapids

激怒 jīnù　enrage；infuriate；exasperate：易于～的小伙子 irascible young man

激情 jīqíng　passion；fervour；enthusiasm：～满怀 full of enthusiasm

激素 jīsù　also "荷尔蒙"〈生理〉hormone：性～ sex hormone

激扬 jīyáng　❶ excited and high-spirited；vehement：～的歌声 spirited singing ❷ encourage；urge：～士气 boost the morale

羁（羈） jī　〈书〉❶ bridle；headstall；halter ❷ control；restrain；restrict：～绊 trammels；fetters；shackles／～押候审 commit（sb）for trial ❸ stay；delay；detain：～旅异乡 stay far away from one's hometown for a long time

羁留 jīliú　❶ stay；stop over；短期～上海 short sojourn at Shanghai ❷ keep in custody；detain

jí

及 jí　❶ catch or keep up with；reach；attain：赶不～ cannot catch or keep up；cannot manage（to do sth）in time ❷ be in time for；seize（an occasion）❸〈连〉*used to join two or more nouns or noun phrases，usu with the one following* 及 *subordinate in meaning*：部长～其随行人员 the minister and his entourage

及格 jígé　pass（a test，etc）：～赛〈体〉qualifying contest／考试不～ fail（in）an exam

及时 jíshí　❶ timely；in time；seasonable：～雨 timely or auspicious rain；〈喻〉timely help／～行乐 seize every opportunity to enjoy life；eat，drink and be merry ❷ promptly；at once

及物动词 jíwù dòngcí　〈语言〉transitive verb（v. t.）

及早 jízǎo　as soon as possible; without delay; before it is too late

及至 jízhì　by (a given time); up to; until

吉 jí　lucky; auspicious; propitious; ~ 期 wedding day / ~ 言 auspicious remark; blessing / ~ 兆 good omen; propitious sign / ~ 日良辰 lucky or happy day / ~ 凶未卜 no one knows how it will turn out; one's fate is in the balance / ~ 星高照。one's star is rising.

吉卜赛人 Jíbǔsàirén　Gipsy; Gypsy

吉利 jílì　lucky; fortunate; auspicious; 图个 ~ (do sth) for good luck / 大吉大利 extremely fortunate

吉尼斯 Jínísī　(short for 吉尼斯世界纪录大全) Guinness (Book of Records)

吉普 jípǔ　also "吉普车" jeep, a kind of land-rover

吉庆 jíqìng　auspicious; propitious; happy; ~ 有余 luck and happiness in superabundance

吉人天相 jírén tiānxiàng　heaven helps a good or virtuous man; heaven helps the good or out of harm's way

吉他 jítā　〈乐〉guitar

吉祥 jíxiáng　lucky; auspicious; propitious; ~ 物 mascot / ~ 如意 be as lucky as one wishes

岌 jí

岌岌 jíjí　〈书〉precarious; ~ 可危 be in imminent danger; hang by a thread / ~ 不可终日 live in constant fear

汲 jí　draw (water); ~ 取营养 derive nourishment (from sth)

级 jí　❶ level; rank; grade; ~ 一 grade A; first-class / 各 ~ 领导 leaders at all levels / 工资 ~ 别 (grade on the) wage scale ❷ (of a school) grade; class ❸ step; 石 ~ stone step / 多 ~ 火箭 multi-stage rocket ❹ 〈语言〉degree; 比较 ~ comparative degree

极（極） jí　❶ utmost; extreme; highest; ~ 品〈书〉highest grade; best quality / ~ 小〈数〉minimum / ~ 刑 capital punishment; death penalty / ~ 右 extreme right; ultra-right / ~ 盛期 heyday; zenith / 荒谬到了 ~ 点 be absurd in the extreme; be the height of absurdity ❷ pole; ~ 地 polar region / ~ 光 polar lights; aurora ❸ do one's utmost; reach the limit; ~ 目远望 as far as the eye can see ❹〈副〉extremely; exceedingly; very; ~ 少 very few or little / ~ 为不满 extremely dissatisfied

极度 jídù　extreme; utmost; limit; ~ 疲劳 tired out; exhausted; overcome with fatigue

极端 jíduān　❶ extreme; 走 ~ go to the extreme ❷ extreme; utter; exceeding; ~ 分子 extremist / ~ 腐化 corrupt to the core / ~ 贫困 dire or abject poverty

极力 jílì　exert oneself to the utmost; do one's best (to do sth); spare no effort (in doing sth)

极其 jíqí　most; extremely; exceedingly; ~ 艰巨 most arduous; extremely difficult / ~ 仇恨 hate to the bones

极权 jíquán　totalitarian; ~ 主义 totalitarianism

极限 jíxiàn　limit; maximum; the ultimate; 达到 ~ reach the maximum or outside limit / ~ 运动 extreme sports

即 jí　❶ approach; reach; attain; ~ 位 ascend the throne ❷ just presently; about (to do sth); ~ 将来 just round the corner ❸ prompted by the occasion; on the spot; ~ 景生情 the scene brings back memories; the scene touches a chord in one's heart ❹〈书〉be; mean; that is; 非亲 ~ 友 if not relative, then a friend ❺〈书〉at once; immediately; in no time; ~ 刻 at once; immediately; instantly / ~ 食面 instant noodles

J

即日 jírì ❶ this or that very day; today：自～起生效 take effect as of today ❷ within the next few days；soon

即时 jíshí immediately；instantly：～起程 set out at once

即使 jíshǐ also "即便" even；even if；(even) though

即席 jíxí 〈书〉❶ impromptu；extemporaneous；offhand：～讲话 give an impromptu speech；speak off the cuff ❷ take one's seat (at a dinner table, etc)

即兴 jíxìng impromptu；extemporaneous：～诗 extempore verse / ～之作 improvisation

佶 jí

佶屈聱牙 jíqū'áoyá also "诘屈聱牙" (of writing, etc) not read smoothly；be sth of a tongue-twister

亟 jí

亟 jí 〈书〉urgently；promptly；anxiously：～须改变 must be speedily changed

急 jí

急 jí ❶ impatient；anxious；angry：～脾气 hot-tempered；impatient / ～不可待 be extremely anxious；can scarcely wait / ～于求成 over-anxious for quick results；impatient for success ❷ hasty；sudden；violent：～匆匆 hurriedly；in a hurry / ～就章 hurriedly-written essay；hasty work；improvisation / ～行军 (make a) rapid or forced march / ～风暴雨 violent storm；hurricane；tempest ❸ urgent；compelling；pressing：～事 urgent matter / ～待解决 call for immediate solution / ～如星火 in a frantic hurry；extremely pressing；post-haste / 留着用钱等着急用 be eager to help；～公好义 zealous for public welfare；public-spirited / ～群众之所～ keen on meeting the needs of the people

急促 jícù ❶ also "急骤" hurried；rapid ❷ (of time) short；pressing：时～ be pressed for time

急功近利 jígōng-jìnlì eager for quick success and instant benefit；anxious to get quick results and instant profits

急进 jíjìn ❶ also "激进" radical：～派 radical (party) ❷ also "疾进" move quickly or rapidly

急救 jíjiù (give) emergency treatment；first aid：～车 ambulance / ～箱 first-aid kit

急剧 jíjù rapid；sharp；sudden：～的变化 abrupt turn；drastic change

急流 jíliú strong current；rapid stream；rapids：～险滩 rapids and shoals；difficulties and obstacles / ～勇退 resolutely retire at the height of one's career；extricate oneself from a difficult situation in good time

急忙 jímáng in a hurry or rush；in haste

急迫 jípò urgent；pressing；imperative

急起直追 jíqǐzhízhuī rouse oneself to catch up；strive to overtake

急切 jíqiè ❶ eager；impatient；urgent：语气～ (in an) urgent or impatient tone ❷ hurriedly；in haste：～间拿不出什么好办法 cannot come up with any good idea on the spur of the moment

急刹车 jíshāchē ❶ slam the brakes on (a car, etc) ❷ bring to a sudden halt；stop abruptly

急速 jísù very fast；rapidly；quickly

急先锋 jíxiānfēng daring vanguard—one of those eager to take the lead；shock force

急性 jíxìng acute；〈喻〉impetuous；impatient：～病 acute disease；impetuosity / ～子 impatient or impetuous person

急需 jíxū be badly in need of；need urgently：～照料 be in need of immediate care / 满足顾客的～ meet the pressing needs of customers

急躁 jízào ❶ irritable；hot-tempered；

irascible：爱～ get worked up easily ❷
impetuous；rash；impatient

急诊 jízhěn　emergency call or treatment：挂～ register as an emergency case／～室 emergency ward

急中生智 jízhōngshēngzhì　have a sudden flash of inspiration；suddenly hit upon a way out of a predicament；show resourcefulness in an emergency

急转直下 jízhuǎnzhíxià　（of a situation，etc）take a sudden turn and then develop rapidly；（of a patient，etc）take an unexpected turn for the worse

疾 jí ❶ disease；sickness；illness：～病丛生 be infested with all kinds of diseases ❷ suffering；pain；distress：～苦 sufferings；hardships ❸ hate；loathe；abhor：～恶如仇 hate evil like an enemy；hate the wicked like enemies ❹ swift；fast；quick：～书 write swiftly／～步而行 walk quickly

疾驰 jíchí　gallop away；go by quickly；whirl off：～的火车 train running at full speed

疾风 jífēng　strong wind；gale：～暴雨 violent storm；tempest；hurricane／～（知）劲草 the force of the wind tests the strength of the grass—adversity is the measure of a man

疾首蹙额 jíshǒu-cù'é　with aching head and knitted brows—frown in disgust；express deep abhorrence

疾言厉色 jíyán-lìsè　harsh words and stern look；angry or stern look

棘 jí　sour jujube；thorn bushes；brambles

棘手 jíshǒu　thorny；sticky；troublesome：～的问题 tough problem；hard nut to crack

集 jí ❶ gather；collect；assemble：～资 raise money or funds；pool resources／～散地 collecting and distributing centre；hub of trade／～聚一堂 assemble or gather together in one hall ❷ market；fair：～市 country fair；

market／～贸 市场（open）fair；market ❸ collection；anthology：画～ album of paintings／～锦 collection of choice specimens／～子 collection；collected works；anthology ❹ volume；book；part：分五～出版 be published in five volumes／二十五～电视剧 25-part TV serial

集成电路 jíchéngdiànlù　〈信息〉integrated circuit（IC）／～卡 IC card／～块 integrated circuit block

集大成 jídàchéng　be a culmination or comprehensive expression；epitomize：～者 one who epitomizes sth；quintessential representative（of sth）

集合 jíhé　assemble；gather；call together：～！Fall in！

集会 jíhuì　assembly；gathering；meeting：～自由 freedom of assembly／群众～ mass rally

集结 jíjié　mass；concentrate；build up：～力量 muster forces；build up strength

集权 jíquán　centralization of state power：～统治 centralized rule

集思广益 jísī-guǎngyì　draw on collective wisdom and absorb all useful ideas；solicit opinions extensively and pool wisdom

集体 jítǐ　collective：～化 collectivization／～舞 group dance／～婚礼 group wedding／～宿舍 dormitory／～主义 collectivism／～所有制 collective ownership

集团 jítuán　group；clique；circle：小～ coterie；small clique／～军 army group／～公司 group corporation or company／～购买力 group or institutional purchasing power

集训 jíxùn　assemble for training：～队 team of athletes in training

集腋成裘 jíyèchéngqiú　little drops of water make a mighty river；many a little makes a mickle；every little bit helps

集邮 jíyóu　stamp collecting；philately;～册 *also* "集邮簿" stamp album / ～爱好者 stamp-collector; philatelist

集约 jíyuē intensive;～化 intensification / ～农业 intensive farming or agriculture

集中 jízhōng concentrate; centralize; focus;思想不～ absent-minded / ～营 concentration camp / ～管理 centralized management / ～优势兵力 muster superior forces

集注 jízhù ❶ focus; concentrate;把心思～到工作上 focus one's attention on work ❷ *also* "集解"; "集释" variorum;～本 variorum edition

集装箱 jízhuāngxiāng *also* "货柜" container;～船 container ship / ～运输 containerized traffic

楫 jí 〈书〉oar;舟～ vessels

辑 jí ❶ collect; compile; edit;～要 summary; abstract / ～录成册 be compiled into a book ❷ part; volume; division

嵴 jí ridge of a mountain or hill

嫉 jí ❶ jealous; envious; covetous;～恨 envy and hate; hate out of jealousy ❷ hate; detest;～视 look upon with hatred / ～恶如仇 hate evil like an enemy; hate the wicked like enemies

嫉妒 jídù be jealous of; envy;心怀～ be consumed with jealousy / 嫉贤妒能 *also* "忌贤妒能" envy the good and be jealous of the capable; be jealous of people of worth and ability

瘠 jí 〈书〉❶ lean; emaciated; thin and weak ❷ barren; poor;～薄 barren; unproductive

籍 jí ❶ book; record; register;古～ ancient books ❷ (usu 籍贯) place of origin; native place; hometown ❸ membership; nationality;会～ membership (of an association) / 美～华人 Chinese American

jǐ

几（幾） jǐ how (many); what;～时 what time; when / ～许 〈书〉how much; how many ❷ a few; several; some;～分 a little; somewhat; rather / ～次三番 time and again; repeatedly / ～经波折 experience ups and downs / ～起～落 up and down again; on and off *see also* jī

几何 jǐhé ❶ 〈书〉how much; how many;人生～! How fleeting life is! ❷ 〈数〉geometry;～体 *also* "立体" solid / ～学 geometry / ～级数 geometric progression

己 jǐ ❶ self; oneself; one's own;～方 one's own side / ～所不欲,勿施于人 do not do to others what you would not have them do to you ❷ 6th of the Heavenly Stems *see also* "干支" gānzhī

挤（擠） jǐ ❶ crowd; cram; pack;～兑 run on a bank / ～作一团 huddle together; be packed like sardines ❷ jostle; push or squeeze (out) / 〈喻〉exclude;你推我～ hustle and bustle / ～占 squeeze in and forcibly occupy; squat; commandeer / ～进去 push one's way in; squeeze in / 互相～轧 try to put each other down; do each other in ❸ squeeze; press;～奶 milk (a cow, etc) / ～压 extrude; press / ～牙膏 〈喻〉act like squeezing toothpaste out of a tube—be forced to tell the truth bit by bit / ～眉弄眼 make eyes; wink

济（濟） jǐ *see also* jì

济济 jǐjǐ (of people) many; abundant; numerous;～一堂 (of many people) gather together under the same roof

给 jǐ ❶ supply; provide; furnish;～水 supply water / ～养 provisions; victuals / ～予 also "给与"〈书〉give; render; offer ❷ ample; abundant; well provided for: 家～户足。Every household is well provided for. *see also* gěi

脊
jǐ ❶ spine; backbone; vertebra: ～背 back (of a vertebrate) / ～柱 spinal or vertebral column; backbone; spine ❷ sth like a spine; ridge: 书～ spine of a book

脊梁 jǐliang ❶ back (of a human body): 光～ stripped to the waist ❷ (usu 脊梁骨) backbone; spine: 没有～ spineless; weak

脊髓 jǐsuǐ spinal cord: ～灰质炎 (popularly called 小儿麻痹症)〈医〉poliomyelitis (polio); infantile paralysis

脊椎 jǐzhuī vertebra; spine; backbone: ～病 spinal disease / ～动物 vertebrate

掎
jǐ 〈书〉pull; pin down; draw: ～角之势 tactic or posture of dividing one's forces to pin down the enemy

戟
jǐ 〈史〉halberd

麂
jǐ 〈动物〉muntjac: ～皮 chamois (leather)

jì

计
jì ❶ count; calculate; number: 数以万～ numbering tens of thousands / ～费〈通信〉billing / ～程车 also "出租车" taxi / ～数器 counter ❷ metre; gauge ❸ idea; plan; stratagem: ～策 also "计谋" stratagem; scheme; device / ～出万全 (make a) sure-fire plan / ～穷力竭 at the end of one's tether; at one's wits' end ❹ make plans; aim; intend: ～议 deliberate; consider; consult / 不～成本 whatever the cost; not concerned about the cost

计划 jìhuà ❶ plan; project; programme: ～经济 planned or command economy / ～生育 family planning birth control / ～外产品 non-planned product / ～单列城市 city specifically designated in the state plan ❷ map out; plan: 明天～干什么？What do you intend to do tomorrow?

计件 jìjiàn reckon by the piece: ～工资 piece (rate) wage

计较 jìjiào ❶ bother or fuss about; haggle over ❷ argue; dispute; 从不与人～ never quarrel with anyone ❸ think or mull over; consider

计量 jìliàng count; calculate; measure; 无法～ immeasurable; inestimable

计日程功 jìrìchénggōng have the completion of a project well in sight; be certain of success in time

计时 jìshí reckon by time: ～器 hour meter; timer / ～赛〈体〉time trial / ～工资 payment by the hour; time-rate wage

计算 jìsuàn ❶ count; calculate; compute: ～器 calculator / ～尺 slide rule ❷ consider; plan ❸ also "算计" trick; scheme: 相互～ scheme against each other

计算机 jìsuànjī computer; calculating machine: ～程序 computer program / ～配置 computer configuration / ～辅助设计 computer-aided design (CAD) / ～情报检索 information retrieval by computer

记
jì ❶ remember; recall; bear in mind: ～仇 bear grudges; harbour resentment / ～得 remember; recall; keep in memory / ～起 recall; collect; call to mind / ～住 learn by heart; bear in mind / ～事儿 (of a child) begin to remember things ❷ write down; record; jot or take down: ～功 cite for meritorious service; record a merit / ～名 put down one's name (on a cheque, etc); sign / ～述 record and narrate; give an account

of / ～账 keep accounts or books; charge to an account / ～笔记 take notes ❸ note; record; narrative:目击～ eyewitness account ❹ mark; stamp; birthmark:暗～儿 secret mark

记分 jìfēn ❶ (in a game) keep the score; record the points:～牌 scoreboard / ～员 scorekeeper; scorer; marker ❷ register a student's marks:～册 mark-book

记号 jìhào mark; sign:做个～ make a mark (on sth); mark (sth)

记录 jìlù also "纪录" ❶ take notes; note down; record:～本 minutes book/～片 documentary (film) / ～在案 be or go on record; put (sth) on record ❷ minutes; notes; record:原始～ original records ❸ note-taker; recorder ❹ record:平～ equal or match a record / 保持～ hold a record / 打破～ break a record

记念 jìniàn ❶ remember; think of; miss ❷ see "纪念❷" jìniàn

记事 jìshì ❶ keep a record of events; make a memorandum:～本 notebook ❷ account or record of events; annals; chronicle

记性 jìxing memory:～极好 have a retentive memory / ～特差 have a memory like a sieve

记叙 jìxù narrate:～体 narration; narrative (style) / ～文 narration; (written) narrative

记忆 jìyì ❶ remember; recall ❷ memory:～力 (faculty of) memory / ～犹新 remain fresh in one's memory

记载 jìzǎi ❶ put down in writing; record ❷ record; account:历史～ historical records

记者 jìzhě reporter; correspondent; journalist:～席 press gallery / ～招待会 press or news conference

伎 jì see "技" jì

伎俩 jìliǎng trick; intrigue; manoeu-

vre:骗人的～ deceptive ploy; ruse

纪 jì ❶ discipline:～检 discipline inspection ❷ put down in writing; write down; record:～实 record of actual events; on-the-spot report / ～要 also "记要" summary (of minutes) / ～传体 history presented in a series of biographies ❸ twelve years' cycle or period:(地)～ period; epoch

纪录 jìlù see "记录" jìlù

纪律 jìlǜ discipline:给予～处分 take disciplinary action (against sb); discipline (sb)

纪年 jìnián ❶ way of numbering the years:干支～ designate the years by the Heavenly Stems and Earthly Branches ❷ chronological record of events; chronicles; annals:～体 chronological order

纪念 jìniàn ❶ pay tribute to; commemorate; mark:值得～ memorable / ～碑 monument; memorial / ～册 commemorative album; autograph book/ ～馆 memorial hall; museum in memory of sb / ～日 commemoration day / ～章 souvenir badge / ～邮票 commemorative stamp ❷ also "记念" souvenir; keepsake; memento

纪事 jìshì ❶ record facts; narrate:～文 narrative writing; narration ❷ record of facts or events; account

纪元 jìyuán ❶ beginning of an era ❷ epoch; era

技 jì skill; ability; trick:～法 technique; skill and method / ～工 skilled worker; mechanic; technician / ～能 technical ability; mastery of a technique; skill / ～穷 at one's wits' end; at the end of one's resources / ～师 (senior) technician / ～校 technical school / ～痒 crave to display one's skill; itch to have a go (at sth) / ～艺 skill; skilfulness; artistry

技巧 jìqiǎo ❶ skill; technique; craftsmanship ❷ also "技巧运动"〈体〉

acrobatic gymnastics; sports acrobatics:～运动员 gymnast

技术 jìshù　technology; technique; skill:～员 technician / ～革新 technological or technical innovation / ～骨干 mainstay in technology; backbone of a technical force / ～科学 applied sciences / ～职称 titles for technical personnel / ～转让 technology transfer / ～密集产品 technology-intensive product

系(繫) jì　tie; fasten; do or button up　*see also* xì

忌 jì ❶ be jealous of; envy ❷ fear; dread; scruple:～惮〈书〉dread; fear / ～恨 hate; bear a grudge against ❸ avoid; quit; abstain or refrain from:～酒 give up alcohol; abstain from wine / ～口 *also* "忌嘴" avoid certain food; be on a diet / ～食生冷 avoid cold and uncooked food

忌辰 jìchén　*also* "忌日" anniversary of the death (of sb held in esteem)

忌妒 jìdu　be jealous of; envy:～心 jealousy

忌讳 jìhuì ❶ taboo; 犯～ violate or break a taboo ❷ avoid as bad or harmful; abstain from:～人家揭短儿 resent any attempt to rake up one's shortcomings

际(際) jì ❶ border; boundary; edge; 脑～ in one's head / 春夏之～(time) between spring and summer ❷ between (each other); among; 校～合作 intercollegiate cooperation ❸ occasion; moment; time:危急之～ at a critical moment ❹〈书〉happen to be on an occasion; experience:～遇 (mostly good) opportunity; spell of good fortune / ～逢盛世 happen to live in a flourishing age

妓 jì　prostitute; whore:～女 prostitute; whore; streetwalker / ～院 brothel

季 jì ❶ period of time that has a distinctive characteristic; season; quarter:～度 quarter (of a year) / ～风 monsoon / ～刊 quarterly (publication) ❷ last period (of a dynasty); las month (of a season) ❸ fourth or youngest among brothers:伯仲叔～ eldest second, third and youngest of brothers

季节 jìjié　season:～性 seasonal (nature) / ～变化 seasonal variation

季军 jìjūn　third place in a contest

剂(劑) jì ❶ pharmaceutica tion;〈化〉agent:干燥～ drying agent desiccant / ～量 dosage; dose / ～型 form of a drug ❷〈量〉*used of concoctions of herbal medicine*:连服三～ take three doses in a row

荠(薺) jì

荠菜 jìcài　〈植〉shepherd's purse

迹(跡、蹟) jì ❶ mark trace:油～ oi stain ❷ remains; ruins; vestige ❸ outward sign; indication:～象 sign; indication; straw in the wind

济(濟) jì ❶ ferry; cross river; go across stream ❷ relieve; aid; help:～世 help the people and society ❸ be helpful benefit; 不～事 not help matters; be useless
see also jǐ

既 jì ❶ already:～定 set; fixed established / ～成事实 accomplished fact; fait accompli / ～得利益 vested interest ❷ as; since; now that ～来之，则安之 since one is here, one may as well stay and make the best o it; take things as they come ❸ both and …; as well as

既而 jì'ér　〈书〉afterwards; later subsequently:始则同意，～反对 agre at first but oppose later

既然 jìrán　〈连〉since; as; now that ～下雨，那就呆在家里看电视吧 Since it's raining, we may as well watch TV at home.

既往 jìwǎng ❶ past;一如～ as in the past; as always ❷ past affairs; what one has done in the past;～不咎 forgive sb's past misdeeds; let bygones be bygones

觊(覬) jì

觊觎 jìyú 〈书〉covet; cast greedy eyes on

继(繼) jì

❶ continue; succeed; adopt;～父 step-father / ～任 succeed (sb) in a post / ～位 succeed to the throne / ～往开来 carry forward (a cause) and forge ahead into the future ❷ also "继而" then; afterwards;才离去,～又返回 re-turn immediately one leaves

继承 jìchéng ❶ inherit; succeed;～法 law of succession; inheritance law / ～权 right of succession or inheritance; heirship / ～人 heir; successor; inheri-tor ❷ carry on or forward; carry on sb's unfinished work;～衣钵 take over sb's mantle; step into sb's shoes

继续 jìxù continue; remain; go on;～教育 continuing education / ～有效 re-main valid; remain in force

祭 jì

❶ offer sacrifices to;～典 ceremony to offer sacrifices / ～品 sacrificial offering; oblation / ～祀 offer sacrifices (to gods or ances-tors) / ～坛 sacrificial altar ❷ hold a memorial ceremony for (the dead);～扫 sweep a grave and pay respects to the dead / ～文 funeral oration; elegiac address / ～奠亡灵 hold a memorial ceremony for the dead

悸 jì

〈书〉(of the heart) throb with terror;～动 palpitate

寄 jì

❶ send by post; post; mail; also "寄钱" remit or send money / ～情 express or vent one's feel-ings / ～语 〈书〉send word or a mes-sage (to sb) ❷ entrust; deposit;

place;～卖 also "寄售" consign for sale (on commission); put up for sale / ～养 entrust (one's child) to the care of sb; ask sb to bring up (one's child) ❸ depend on; attach oneself to;～人篱下 live under sb's roof; depend on sb for a living or for support ❹ adopted;～父 foster father / ～女 adopted daughter

寄存 jìcún also "寄放" deposit; leave; check;行李～处 left-luggage of-fice; checkroom

寄居 jìjū also "寄寓" live away from home;～海外 live overseas

寄生 jìshēng parasitism;～虫 para-site — insect or person who leads a parasitic life / ～植物 parasitic plant

寄宿 jìsù ❶ lodge; put up;～友人家 lodge with a friend; put up at a friend's place ❷ (of students) board;～生 resi-dent student; boarder / ～学校 board-ing school; residential college

寄托 jìtuō ❶ entrust (sth) to the care of (sb); leave (sth) with (sb) ❷ place (hope, etc) in; find sustenance in; repose;精神～ spiritual sustenance

寄予 jìyǔ also "寄与" ❶ place (hope, etc) in ❷ show; give; ex-press;～关怀 show solicitude (for sb)

寂 jì

❶ still; quiet; silent; ～然 〈书〉silent; quiet / ～静无声 dead still; all quiet ❷ lonely; lonesome; solita-ry;～苦 lonely and distressed

寂寞 jìmò ❶ (of a person) lonely; lonesome ❷ (of a place) quiet; still

绩 jì

achievement; contribution; performance;～优质 (经) blue chip / ～效显著 marked achievements

霁(霽) jì

〈书〉❶ (of sky, etc) clear up after rain or snow ❷ calm down after being angry

暨 jì

〈书〉❶ and; as well as; with ❷ to; up to;从古～今 from ancient times to the present

稷 jì

❶ (broomcorn) millet ❷ god of grains

鲫 jì　（usu 鲫鱼）crucian carp

髻 jì　hair worn in a bun or coil; chignon

冀 jì　〈书〉❶ hope; long or yearn for; look forward to: 心有所~ long for sth / ~求 hope to get ❷ (Jì) another name for Hebei (河北)

骥 jì　〈书〉thoroughbred horse; 〈喻〉virtuous and competent person

jiā

加 jiā ❶〈数〉add; plus: ~法 addition / ~号 plus sign (+) ❷ increase; raise; add: ~倍 double; be twice as much; redouble (efforts, etc) / ~大 increase; augment; enlarge / ~固 reinforce; consolidate; strengthen / ~紧 step or speed up; intensify / ~剧 aggravate; intensify / ~快 quicken; speed or step up; accelerate / ~宽 broaden; widen / ~码 raise the quota or price; overcharge / ~深 deepen; enhance; aggravate / ~温 raise the temperature; heat up / ~碘盐 iodized salt / ~塞儿〈口〉butt in a line; jump a queue / ~湿器 humidifier / ~官进爵 receive official promotion; advance in rank and position ❸ same as 加以 but used after a monosyllabic adverb: 不~干涉 not interfere / 严~管制 exercise strict control

加班 jiābān　work overtime; work an extra shift: ~费 overtime pay or cost / ~加点 work extra shifts; put in extra hours

加工 jiāgōng ❶ process: ~工业 processing industry / 艺术~ artistic treatment or recreation ❷ polish (writing, etc); finish; refine

加仑 jiālún　gallon

加盟 jiāméng　ally oneself to; join (a team, etc)

加密 jiāmì　〈通信〉encrypt: ~节目 encrypted programme / ~电报 code telegram

加冕 jiāmiǎn　coronation; crowning

加强 jiāqiáng　strengthen; intensify; enhance: ~法制 strengthen the legal system / ~管理 tighten up or improve management

加入 jiārù ❶ add; mix; put in ❷ join; accede to: ~国 acceding state / ~中国国籍 acquire Chinese citizenship

加速 jiāsù　quicken; speed up; accelerate: ~度〈理〉acceleration / ~器〈理〉accelerator / ~步伐 quicken one's steps / ~资金流转 expedite cash flow

加以 jiāyǐ ❶ *used before disyllabic verbs*: 对某事~分析 make an analysis of sth ❷ in addition; moreover

加意 jiāyì　with special care; with close attention: ~提防 be particularly watchful

加油 jiāyóu ❶ lubricate; refuel: ~站 filling station; petrol or gas station / ~飞机 tanker aircraft ❷ encourage sb to make an extra effort; cheer: ~干 work with added vigour / "~! ~!" "Go! Go! Go!"

加油添醋 jiāyóu-tiāncù　*also* "加枝添叶" add inflammatory or highly-coloured details; embellish; exaggerate

加重 jiāzhòng ❶ increase the weight; make or get heavier: ~自行车 heavy-weight-bearing bike ❷ make or become more serious; aggravate: 危机日益~ deepening crisis

夹（夾） jiā ❶ press from both sides; place or stay in between; clip: ~攻 *also* "夹击" attack from both sides; (make a) converging or pincer attack / ~在中间 be sandwiched in between / ~起尾巴做人 be modest and prudent (as if with one's tail between one's legs); pull in one's horn / 受~板气 be caught in crossfire;

get blamed by both sides ❷ carry under one's arm ❸ mix; mingle; intersperse; ～杂 be mixed up with; be cluttered or mingled with / ～七～八 incoherent; confused; cluttered (with irrelevant remarks) ❹ *also* "夹子" clip; clamp; folder; 报～ newspaper holder / 点心～ cake tongs / 活页～ loose-leaf bind

see also gā; jiá

夹带 jiādài ❶ carry secretly; smuggle ❷ notes smuggled into an examination hall

夹道 jiādào ❶ narrow lane; passageway ❷ line both sides of the street; ～欢迎 line the street to welcome

夹缝 jiāfèng narrow space between two adjacent things; crack; crevice; 在～中求生存 seek to survive in the opposing forces

夹克 jiākè *also* "茄克" jacket

夹生 jiāshēng half-cooked; half-baked; ～饭 half-cooked rice; half-done task

夹竹桃 jiāzhútáo 〈植〉 sweet-scented oleander

佳

佳 jiā good; excellent; beautiful; ～话 story on everybody's lips; much-told tale / ～句 beautiful line; well-turned phrase / ～丽 good; beautiful (woman); beauty / ～酿 vintage wine / ～偶〈书〉happy married couple; ideal spouse / ～期 wedding day; lover's time for dating / ～人〈书〉beautiful woman / ～肴 delicious food; delicacy / ～音 welcome news; glad tidings; favourable reply / ～作 fine piece of writing; excellent literary work / 新春～节 happy Spring Festival / 十～民歌手 top ten folksong singers

枷

枷 jiā wooden yoke for a prisoner

枷锁 jiāsuǒ yoke; chains; shackles; 摆脱殖民主义的～ shake off the yoke of colonialism

浃（浹）

浃（浹） jiā 〈书〉 soak through; spread all over; 汗流～背 soaked with sweat

痂

痂 jiā scab; crust; 结～ form a scab; crust

家

家 jiā ❶ family; household; home; ～传 (sth) handed down in the family; sth that runs in the family/ ～当〈口〉family belongings; property/ ～电 (short for 家用电器) household (electric) appliance / ～境 "家景" family financial situation; family circumstances / ～具 *also* "像具" furniture / ～信 *also* "家书" letter to or from one's family / ～训 *also* "家诫"〈书〉family or parental instruction / ～业 (family) property; assets (of an enterprise, etc) / ～园 home; homeland / ～学渊源 (benefit from) a line of scholars in the family / ～贼难防 a thief in the family is hard to detect; it's most difficult to guard against a thief within the house / ～和万事兴.〈俗〉Harmony in the family leads to prosperity in all undertakings. ❷ person or family engaged in a certain trade; 店～ shopkeeper ❸ specialist in a certain field; expert; 法学～ jurist ❹ school of thought; 诸子百～ various schools of thought ❺ one of the opposite parties (in a game, etc); 两～下成和棋。The chess game ended in a draw. ❻〈谦〉my; ～父 *also* "家严" my father / ～母 *also* "家慈" my mother ❼ domestic; tame; cultivated; ～畜 domestic animal; livestock / ～禽 domestic fowl; poultry ❽〈量〉*used of families or enterprises* ❾ (jia) *used after certain nouns, indicating their category*; 姑娘～ girl(s)

家财 jiācái family property; ～万贯 (have) a huge family fortune; (be from a) wealthy family

家产 jiāchǎn *also* "家私" family property or fortune

家常 jiācháng　daily life of a family; domestic trivia: 拉 ～ engage in small talk / ～菜 home cooking; home-style dish / ～便饭 also "家常饭" homely or plain food: 〈喻〉common occurrence; routine

家丑 jiāchǒu　family scandal; skeleton in the closet: ～不可外扬.〈俗〉Don't wash dirty linen in public.

家道 jiādào　family financial situation: ～中落 decline in family fortunes

家底 jiādǐ　(family) property accumulated over a long time; resources (of an enterprise, etc): ～薄 without substantial resources; financially shaky

家伙 jiāhuo　also "傢伙"〈口〉❶ tool; utensil; weapon: 锣鼓 ～ gongs and drums ❷ fellow; chap; guy; 坏～ scoundrel; villain / 小 ～ little chap; kid ❸ (often as a term of endearment) domestic animal; livestock

家家 jiājiā　every or each family or household: ～户户 each and every family or household / ～有本难念的经.〈俗〉Each family has its own problems.

家教 jiājiào　❶ family education; upbringing: 缺 ～ not properly brought up; ill-bred ❷ (short for 家庭教师) private tutor; private tutoring

家眷 jiājuàn　also "家口"; "家室"; "家小" family dependents; wife (and children)

家门 jiāmén　❶ house gate; home ❷〈书〉family: 有辱～ bring disgrace to one's family ❸ family background: 自报 ～ give one's family background; tell about one's family

家破人亡 jiāpò-rénwáng　with one's family broken up, some gone away, some dead

家谱 jiāpǔ　family tree; genealogy; pedigree: 查 ～ trace one's family tree / 修～ compile one's genealogy

家世 jiāshì　〈书〉family background:

family social status: ～寒微 be of plebeian origin

家什 jiāshi　also "傢什"〈口〉utensils, tools, furniture, etc

家属 jiāshǔ　family member; family dependent: 随军 ～ family members that live in the barracks; families that follow the army

家庭 jiātíng　family; household: 大 ～ extended family / 小 ～ also "核心家庭" nuclear family / ～出身 family origin; class status of one's family / ～妇女 housewife / ～观念 attachment to one's family; strong sense of family / ～影院 family cinema; home theatre / ～作业 homework / ～联产承包责任制〈经〉household contract responsibility system with remuneration linked to output

家徒四壁 jiātúsìbì　have nothing but the bare walls in one's house — live in miserable penury

家务 jiāwù　household duties: ～劳动 housework; household chores

家乡 jiāxiāng　hometown; native place: ～菜 food from one's hometown; food cooked in hometown style / ～话 native dialect

家用 jiāyòng　❶ family expenses; housekeeping money: 贴补 ～ supplement housekeeping money; help pay family expenses ❷ for household use; domestic

家喻户晓 jiāyù-hùxiǎo　known to every household; on everybody's lips; known to all

家长 jiāzhǎng　❶ head of a family; patriarch: ～作风 patriarchal behaviour; high-handed way of dealing with people / ～式统治 arbitrary rule as by a patriarch; paternalism ❷ parent or guardian of a child: ～会 teacher-parent meeting

家政 jiāzhèng　household management; home economics: ～学 home economics

家族 jiāzú　clan；family；～公司 family firm

袈 jiā

袈裟 jiāshā　*kasaya*, a patchwork outer vestment worn by a Buddhist monk

傢 jiā

same as "家" in such combinations as "傢伙"，"傢具"，and "傢什"

嘉 jiā

❶ good；nice；fine：～宾 also "佳宾" honoured or welcome guest ❷ praise；laud；commend：～勉〈书〉praise and encourage / ～许〈书〉praise；approve

嘉奖 jiājiǎng　commend；cite：～令 citation

jiá

夹(夾) jiá

double-layered；lined；～袄 lined jacket / ～被 double-layered quilt see also gā；jiā

荚(莢) jiá

pod：结～ bear pods；pod / ～果 pod；legume

戛(戞) jiá

戛然 jiárán〈书〉❶〈象声〉loud cry of a bird；～长鸣 cry loud for a long time ❷ stop abruptly or suddenly：～而止 stop all of a sudden

铗(鋏) jiá

〈书〉❶ pincers；pliers；tongs；火～ fire tongs / 剪票～ conductor's punch ❷ sword；sabre ❸ handle of a sword；hilt

颊(頰) jiá

cheek：～骨〈生理〉cheekbone

jiǎ

甲 jiǎ

❶ 1st of the Heavenly Stems see also "干支" gānzhī ❷ first；A：～等 first-rate；first-class / ～肝 (short for 甲型肝炎) hepatitis A ❸ 富～天下 richest in the country ❸ shell；carapace：～虫 beetle / ～壳 crust；shell / ～鱼 soft-shelled turtle ❹ nail；指～ fingernail ❺ armour：披～ wear a suit of armour

甲板 jiǎbǎn　deck (of a ship)：后～ afterdeck or quarterdeck / 前～ foredeck

甲骨文 jiǎgǔwén　oracle bone inscriptions (of the Shang Dynasty, 16th-11th centuries BC)；language used in such inscriptions

甲醛 jiǎquán　〈化〉formaldehyde

甲状腺 jiǎzhuàngxiàn　thyroid (gland)：～肿大〈医〉goitre / ～功能亢进 (shortened as 甲亢)〈医〉hyperthyroidism

岬 jiǎ

❶ cape；promontory；headland ❷ space or narrow passage between mountains

胛 jiǎ

shoulder：～骨 shoulder blade

钾 jiǎ

〈化〉potassium (K)：～肥 potash fertilizer

假 jiǎ

❶ false；fake；psuedo-：～币 counterfeit or fake money / ～发 wig；hairpiece / ～话 falsehood / ～山 rockery / ～死〈医〉suspended animation；asphyxia / ～象 also "假相" false appearance / ～慈悲 crocodile tears / ～小子 tomboy / ～正经 hypocrisy；prudery / ～模～式 also "假模假样" put on an act；pretend to be serious；feign sincerity / ～仁～义 pretended benevolence and righteousness；hypocrisy / ～性近视〈医〉pseudomyopia / ～意应承 pretend to promise ❷ suppose；presume；assume ❸ borrow；avail oneself of；make use of；～道 via；by way of / ～公济私 use public office for private gain；exploit public office for private ends

see also jià

假定 jiǎdìng　❶ suppose；assume；

presume；～成本 assumed or hypothetical cost ❷ *see* "假设❷"

假借 jiǎjiè　make use of（sb else's name, etc）；use false pretences；～别人名义到处招摇 go about cheating people in the name of sb else

假冒 jiǎmào　disguise oneself as；pose as；palm off（a fake as genuine）：～签名 forge a signature／谨防～。Beware of fakes.

假面 jiǎmiàn　*also* "假面具" mask；false front；pretence：揭穿～ tear the mask off sb；expose sb's hypocrisy；unmask sb

假名 jiǎmíng　❶ pseudonym；alias；false name ❷ *kana*, a Japanese syllabary

假如 jiǎrú　*also* "假若""假使" if；supposing；in case：～出了问题，我们该怎么办？Supposing something should go wrong, what shall we do?

假设 jiǎshè　❶ suppose；assume；presume：～情节 fictitious plot ❷ *also* "假说""假定" hypothesis

假释 jiǎshì　〈法〉release on parole or probation：～犯 parolee

假手 jiǎshǒu　❶ do sth through sb else；make a cat's-paw of sb：～于人（achieve one's end）through sb else；make sb else do the work ❷ artificial hand

假托 jiǎtuō　❶ on the pretext or pretence of ❷ under sb else's name；pass oneself off as：～之作 work written under sb else's name；fake ❸ by means of；through the medium of

假想 jiǎxiǎng　imagination；hypothesis；supposition：～敌〈军〉imaginary enemy；hypothetical foe

假惺惺 jiǎxīngxīng　hypocritically；unctuously；insincerely

假造 jiǎzào　❶ forge；counterfeit：～的文件 forged document ❷ invent；fabricate；cook up：～理由 work out or invent an excuse

假装 jiǎzhuāng　pretend；feign；make

a show of：～不知 affect ignorance

jià

价（價） jià　❶ price：～目 *also* "价码" price（marked）price／～钱 price／～位 price（level）／～廉物美 cheap but good；inexpensive but of fine quality ❷ value ❸〈化〉valence：一～元素 one-valence element

价格 jiàgé　price：～杠杆 lever of prices；pricing leverage／～结构〈经〉price mechanism or structure

价值 jiàzhí　value；worth；cost：～观 values／～规律 law of value／～连城 worth several cities — invaluable；priceless

驾 jià　❶ harness（a horse to a cart, etc）❷ drive；pilot；sail：～校（short for 驾驶学校）driving school／～照（short for 驾驶执照）driver's license／～飞机 pilot a plane ❸ vehicle；carriage：劳～ you；候～ await you／～临寒舍 your arrival at my humble abode；your esteemed presence at my home ❹ emperor's carriage；emperor：～崩（of an emperor）pass away；die

驾轻就熟 jiàqīng-jiùshú　drive a light carriage on a familiar road；do a familiar job with ease

驾驶 jiàshǐ　drive（a vehicle）；pilot（a ship or plane）：～舱 pilot house；control cabin；（of a plane）cockpit／～盘 steering wheel／～室 driver's or engineer's cab／～员 driver；pilot

驾驭 jiàyù　*also* "驾御" ❶ drive（a horse, cart, etc）：～烈马 control a mettlesome horse ❷ control；tame；master：～局势 control a situation；have a situation in hand

架 jià　❶ frame；shelf；stand：工具～ tool rack／葡萄～ grape trellis ❷ prop up；put up；support：～桥 put up or build a bridge／～设 erect；

put or set up / ～不住 cannot sustain (the weight)；cannot stand or withstand；be no match for ❸ fight；quarrel；骂～ quarrel；wrangle ❹〈量〉 *used of sth with a stand or mechanism*：～次 (of planes) sortie / 两～钢琴 two pianos

架豆 jiàdòu kidney bean

架空 jiàkōng ❶ built on stilts；overhead；aerial：～管道 overhead pipe ❷ impracticable；impractical；unpractical ❸ make sb a mere figurehead；kick upstairs

架势 jiàshì also "架式" ❶ posture；air；manner：摆出高人一等的～ assume a posture of superiority ❷〈方〉 appearances of things；trend：看～ judging by the appearances of things

架子 jiàzi ❶ frame；stand；shelf：床～ bedstead ❷ framework；outline：搭～ set up a framework (for sth) ❸ airs；arrogance；haughty manner：没有～ be easy of approach；be modest and unassuming / ～十足 overbearing；on one's high horse ❹ *see* "架势❶"

假 jià ❶ holiday；vacation；leave of absence：续～ extend one's leave of absence / ～期 vacation；holiday；period of leave / ～条 application for leave；leave permit；absence slip / ～日 holiday；day off　*see also* jiǎ

嫁 jià ❶ (of a woman) marry：～婆 marriages / ～人〈口〉 get married；marry / ～妆 ＝"嫁装" dowry；trousseau / ～鸡随鸡，嫁狗随狗〈旧〉 throw in one's lot with one's husband，whatever he is ❷ shift (blame，loss，etc)；transfer：～接〈植〉 graft / ～祸于人 shift misfortune onto sb else；put blame on sb else；lay one's own fault at sb else's door

稼 jià ❶ sow；～穑〈书〉 sowing and reaping；farming；farm work ❷ cereals；crops

jiān

尖 jiān ❶ point；tip；sharp or tapering end；削～ sharpen / ～兵〈军〉 point；vanguard；pioneer / ～嘴猴腮 thin angular face；ugly looks ❷ shrill；sharp；piercing：～叫 shriek；scream；yell ❸ acute；sharp；keen：眼睛～ have a sharp eye；be sharp-sighted ❹ best of the kind；pick of the bunch；cream of the crop：～子运动员 top-notch athlete ❺ sharp-tongued；caustic：～嘴薄舌 have a caustic and flippant tongue

尖端 jiānduān ❶ pointed end；tip；peak ❷ sophisticated；most advanced：～科学 most advanced branch of science；frontier science / ～武器 state-of-the-art weaponry

尖刻 jiānkè caustic；cutting；biting：～的讽刺 biting or poignant satire

尖利 jiānlì ❶ sharp；biting；keen：～的匕首 sharp dagger / 笔锋～ poignant writing ❷ shrill；piercing

尖锐 jiānruì ❶ sharp；sharp-pointed ❷ keen；penetrating；sharp：眼光～ have a keen eye ❸ shrill；sharp：～的汽笛声 shrill whistle ❹ intense；sharp；acute：～化 intensify；aggravate

尖酸 jiānsuān acrid；harsh；acrimonious：～刻薄 tart and mean；bitterly sarcastic

奸(❸姦) jiān ❶ false；crafty；treacherous：～计 evil scheme；treacherous plot / ～商 unscrupulous merchant；profiteer / ～笑 sinister smile / ～雄 arch-careerist；unscrupulous schemer ❷ disloyal to one's country or monarch；traitorous：～党 clique or people disloyal to the country / ～贼 traitor；conspirator ❸ illicit sexual relations；adultery：～夫 adulterer / ～妇 adulteress / ～情 adulterous affair

奸猾 jiānhuá　*also* "奸滑" treacher-ous; deceitful; cunning

奸污 jiānwū　rape; violate; seduce; ~处女 deflower a virgin

奸细 jiānxi　spy; enemy agent

奸险 jiānxiǎn　wicked and crafty; treacherous; malicious

奸淫 jiānyín　❶ illicit sexual relations; adultery ❷ rape; seduce; ~烧杀 com-mit rape, murder and arson

奸诈 jiānzhà　fraudulent; crafty; de-ceitful; 心怀~ harbour treacherous mo-tives

歼(殲) jiān　annihilate; wipe out; exterminate

歼击 jiānjī　attack and destroy; ~机 fighter plane

歼灭 jiānmiè　annihilate; exterminate; wipe out; ~战 war or battle of annihi-lation

坚(堅) jiān　❶ solid; hard; strong; ~固 strong; firm; solid / ~果 nut / ~毅 firm and persistent; staunch and determined; ~硬 hard; rigid; solid　~不可摧 in-destructible; impregnable　~如磐石 solid as a rock; rock-firm ❷ armour; heavily fortified point; fortification ❸ firmly; flatly; determinedly; ~守阵地 hold fast to one's position; hold one's ground; dig in / ~执不允 firmly re-fuse to permit; be adamant

坚壁 jiānbì　hide (supplies to prevent the enemy from seizing them); place in a cache; cache; ~清野 strengthen the defences and clear the fields (of provi-sions and livestock)

坚持 jiānchí　persist or persevere in; insist on; stick or adhere to; ~不懈 (be) unremitting; unswerving; persis-tent / ~到底 stick it out; carry through to the end / ~己见 hold on to one's own view; be opinionated

坚定 jiāndìng　❶ firm; resolute; staunch; ~不移 firm and unshakable;

unswerving; adamant ❷ strengthen; fortify; ~决心 harden one's resolve

坚决 jiānjué　firm; resolute; deter-mined; 口气~ (speak) in a firm tone / ~完成任务 fulfil one's task without fail

坚苦 jiānkǔ　persevering despite diffi-culty; arduous; hard; ~卓绝 showing or requiring the utmost fortitude; tire-less and indomitable

坚强 jiānqiáng　❶ strong; firm; in-domitable; ~不屈 firm and unyielding; staunch and unbending ❷ strengthen (one's ranks, etc)

坚忍 jiānrěn　steadfast and persever-ing; firm and unbending; ~不拔 firm and indomitable; stubborn and unyield-ing; tenacious

坚韧 jiānrèn　tough and tensile; tena-cious

坚实 jiānshí　solid; strong; sturdy; 打下~的基础 lay a solid foundation

坚挺 jiāntǐng　❶ strong and powerful; stiff and straight ❷ 〈经〉 strong; ro-bust; 美元~ strong dollar

坚信 jiānxìn　firmly believe; be deeply convinced; be fully confident; ~不疑 have not a shadow of doubt; have pro-found faith

坚贞 jiānzhēn　faithful; staunch; con-stant; ~不渝 be always faithful; re-main loyal forever

间(間) jiān　❶ between; among; ~距 distance between (two trees, etc) / ~不容发 there is not a hair's breadth in be-tween—the situation is extremely ur-gent or critical ❷ within (a definite time or space); 乡~ in the countryside ❸ room; 里~ inner room / 两~卧室 two bedrooms
see also jiàn

间架 jiānjià　❶ framework or struc-ture of a house ❷ form of a Chinese character; structure of an essay

肩 jiān ❶ shoulder:～膀 shoulder / ～章 epaulette / ～胛骨 shoulder blade / 并～而行 walk side by side ❷ undertake; shoulder; bear:～负重大的责任 shoulder heavy responsibilities

艰(艱) jiān difficult; arduous; hard:～巨 onerous; arduous; formidable / ～涩 involved and abstruse; intricate and obscure / ～深 difficult to comprehend; abstruse / ～险 hardships and dangers; perils / ～辛 distress; hardship

艰苦 jiānkǔ difficult; hard; tough:～朴素 hard work and plain living / ～卓绝 extreme hardship and difficulty

艰难 jiānnán difficult; arduous; hard:处境～ find oneself in straitened circumstances; be in a predicament / ～险阻 difficulties and obstacles; trials and tribulations

监(監) jiān ❶ supervise; inspect; watch:～管 keep watch on; supervise and control / ～票 examine ballots; be a scrutineer / ～听 monitoring / ～制 supervise the manufacture or production (of sth) / ～守自盗 steal what is entrusted to one's care; defalcate ❷ prison; jail:～禁 take into custody; imprison; put in jail or behind bars / ～牢 prison; jail / ～外就医〈法〉receive medical treatment outside the prison under surveillance

see also jiàn

监测 jiāncè monitor; observe and measure:～器 monitor

监察 jiānchá supervise; inspect; examine:～部 Ministry of Supervision / ～制度 supervisory system

监督 jiāndū ❶ supervise; superintend; control:～权 authority to supervise / 在严格的～下 under strict supervision ❷ supervisor

监工 jiāngōng ❶ supervise (work); oversee ❷ overseer; superintendent

监护 jiānhù〈法〉guardianship; tutelage:～权 guardianship / ～人 guardian / 被～人 ward

监考 jiānkǎo ❶ monitor (an exam); invigilate ❷ monitor; invigilator

监控 jiānkòng ❶ monitor and control:～器 monitor / ～程序 monitor routine ❷ supervise and control (suspects, prices, etc)

监理 jiānlǐ ❶ inspect and handle; supervise:工程～公司 construction supervision company ❷ inspector; supervisor

监视 jiānshì keep watch on; keep lookout over:电子～ electronic surveillance / ～器 monitor

监狱 jiānyù prison; jail:关进～ put in prison; imprison / ～长 warden

兼 jiān ❶ double; twice:～人之勇 unusual courage; extraordinary bravery ❷ simultaneously; concurrently:～课 do teaching in addition to one's main occupation; hold two or more teaching jobs concurrently / ～而有之 have both at the same time / ～施并用 employ various methods at the same time / ～听则明，偏信则暗 listen to both sides and you will be enlightened, and heed only one side and you will be benighted; a clear head comes from an open mind

兼备 jiānbèi have both ... and ...; as well as:文武～ be well versed in civilian as well as military affairs

兼并 jiānbìng annex (territory, property, etc); acquire:企业～ amalgamation or merger of enterprises

兼程 jiānchéng travel at double speed:日夜～ travel day and night

兼顾 jiāngù give consideration to or take account of two or more things:需要与可能～ match needs with possibilities

兼容 jiānróng embrace all; be compatible (with); be tolerant:～性（理）compatibility; compatibleness / ～并包

tolerant; all-embracing; all-inclusive / ～软件 compatible software

兼收并蓄 jiānshōu-bìngxù　incorporate things of diverse nature; take in everything

兼职 jiānzhí　also "兼任" ❶ hold two or more posts concurrently ❷ concurrent post; part-time job; ～教师 part-time teacher

笺（箋、❶❷❸牋）jiān　❶ annotation; commentary ❷ writing paper ❸ letter; ～札〈书〉letter; correspondence

犍 jiān　castrated bull; bullock; ～牛 bullock

缄 jiān　〈书〉seal; close; ～封 seal a letter / ～默 keep silent; be reticent / ～口结舌 be tongue-tied and silent — not dare to say anything

搛 jiān　pick up (with chopsticks)

煎 jiān　❶ fry in shallow oil; ～饼 thin pancake made of millet flour, etc ❷ simmer in water; decoct; ～药 decoct medicinal herbs / ～熬〈喻〉suffering; distress; torture ❸〈量〉decoction; 头～药 first decoction (of herb medicine)

jiǎn

拣（揀）jiǎn　❶ choose; select; pick; ～选 select; choose; pick / ～便宜 buy on the cheap; get the better of a bargain ❷ see "捡" jiǎn

茧（繭）jiǎn　❶ cocoon; ～绸 pongee; tussah silk ❷ also "趼" callus; ～子 also "老趼" callus

柬 jiǎn　card; note; letter; ～帖 note; short letter

俭（儉）jiǎn　thrifty; frugal; 朴～ thrifty and simple; economical / ～省 economical; thrifty

捡（撿）jiǎn　pick up; collect; gather; ～漏 find and take advantage of a loophole / ～破烂儿 pick odds and ends from refuse heaps; 〈喻〉take over what is left over or discarded by another / ～了芝麻丢了西瓜〈俗〉be mindful of minor matters to the neglect of major ones; penny wise and pound foolish

检（檢）jiǎn　❶ check up; inspect; examine; ～测 test and determine / ～票 check tickets or ballots / ～修 overhaul; maintenance / ～疫 quarantine ❷ restrain oneself; be careful in one's conduct; 言语失～ be careless about one's words; speak indiscreetly

检查 jiǎnchá　❶ check up; inspect; examine; 全身～ general check-up / ～站 checkpoint; checkpost; inspection station / ～证件 examine sb's papers ❷ make self-criticism; review; ～错误 review one's mistakes (and their causes)

检察 jiǎnchá　prosecute; ～官 public procurator or prosecutor; prosecuting attorney / ～院 procuratorate / ～长 chief procurator; (US) attorney-general

检点 jiǎndiǎn　❶ examine; check; ～行李 check the luggage ❷ be discreet or cautious; 行为不～ be indiscreet in one's conduct

检举 jiǎnjǔ　report (an offence) to the authorities; inform against (an offender); ～人 informant; accuser / ～信 letter of accusation; written accusation

检索 jiǎnsuǒ　look up sth; retrieve; search; 目录～ catalogue-search / ～系统 searching system

检讨 jiǎntǎo　❶ make self-criticism; examine critically ❷〈书〉review; inspect; study

检验 jiǎnyàn　test; examine; inspect; ～员 inspector / ～真理的标准 criterion of truth

检阅 jiǎnyuè ❶ review (troops, etc); inspect ❷ browse (data, etc); look or glance over; leaf through

减(減) jiǎn subtract; minus; reduce; ~产 reduction of output; fall or decline in production / ~低 reduce; lower; diminish / ~法〈数〉subtraction / ~号〈数〉minus sign (一) / ~价 reduce the price; mark down / ~速 slow down; decelerate / ~员 depletion of numbers (in an army, etc); staff or personnel reduction / ~灾 reduce damages by natural disasters / 八～二等于六。Eight minus two is equal to six.

减肥 jiǎnféi reduce fat; lose weight; slim; ~操 slimming exercises / ~疗法 weight-reducing therapy

减缓 jiǎnhuǎn retard; slow down; reduce; ~衰老 decelerate ageing

减免 jiǎnmiǎn mitigate or annul (punishment, etc); reduce or remit (taxation, etc); ~学费 reduce or remit tuition; grant a partial or total tuition waiver

减轻 jiǎnqīng lighten; lessen; alleviate; ~负担 ease sb's burden; lighten sb's load / ~压力 relieve pressure

减弱 jiǎnruò weaken; relax; abate; 体质～ be debilitated / 风势～。The wind abated or subsided.

减色 jiǎnsè lose lustre; impair excellence; 情节拖沓使小说～不少。The loose plot spoils the novel.

减少 jiǎnshǎo reduce; decrease; lessen; ~错误 commit fewer errors

减退 jiǎntuì subside; abate; decline; 记忆力～ failing memory

剪 jiǎn ❶ scissors; clippers; scissor-shaped tool; 火～ fire-tongs; tongs ❷ cut (with scissors); clip; trim; ~报 newspaper cutting or clipping / ~彩 cut the ribbon / ~断 cut off; nip; snip / ~发 also "剪头" have

one's hair cut / ~票 punch a ticket / ~贴 clip and paste (in a scrapbook, etc); cut-out / ~影 paper-cut silhouette; outline; vignette / ~纸 paper-cut / ~羊毛 shear a sheep ❸ wipe out; exterminate; ~除 wipe or weed out; annihilate

剪裁 jiǎncái ❶ cut out (a garment); tailor ❷ cut out unwanted material (from a piece of writing, etc); prune

剪刀 jiǎndāo scissors; shears; ~差〈经〉scissors movement of prices; scissors differential or difference

剪辑 jiǎnjí ❶ also "剪接" montage; film editing ❷ re-cut; re-edit; 录音～ edited recording

睑(瞼) jiǎn eyelid

简 jiǎn ❶ simple; terse; brief; ~编 short course; concise edition; abridged version / ~短 terse; succinct; brief / ~介 (give a) brief introduction; synopsis / ~括 brief but comprehensive; compendious / ~历 biographical note; curriculum vitae (CV); résumé / ~图 sketch; diagram; simplified scheme / ~讯 news in brief / ~章 general regulations / ~装 plainly-packed or plainly-packaged / ~写本 simplified edition (of a book) / ~而言之 in short; in brief; in a nutshell / ~政放权 streamline administration and devolve powers to lower levels ❷ bamboo slip (used for writing in ancient times) ❸ note; letter; ~札〈书〉letters; correspondence ❹〈书〉select; choose

简报 jiǎnbào bulletin; brief report; 新闻～ news bulletin

简便 jiǎnbiàn simple and convenient; handy

简称 jiǎnchēng ❶ acronym; abbreviation ❷ be called (sth) for short

简单 jiǎndān ❶ simple; brief; uncomplicated; ~劳动〈经〉simple labour ❷ (often used in the negative) commonplace; ordinary ❸ oversimplified; cursory; offhand: ～化 oversimplification

简化 jiǎnhuà simplify: ～字 *also* "简体字" simplified Chinese character / ～程序 simplify procedures

简洁 jiǎnjié succinct; terse; pithy: ～有力 pithy and vigorous

简捷 jiǎnjié simple and direct; simple and quick; forthright

简练 jiǎnliàn terse; concise; pithy: 文字～,寓意深刻 be succinct in language and pregnant with meaning

简陋 jiǎnlòu simple and crude: 陈设～ be sparely furnished

简略 jiǎnlüè simple (in content); compact; brief

简明 jiǎnmíng simple and clear; succinct; concise: ～扼要 terse and clear; brief and to the point; concise

简朴 jiǎnpǔ simple and unadorned; plain: 生活～ lead a simple and frugal life

简谱 jiǎnpǔ 〈乐〉numbered musical notation

简省 jiǎnshěng simplify; use sparingly; economize: ～费用 economize on expenses / ～手续 simplify procedures

简要 jiǎnyào brief and to the point; concise; laconic

简易 jiǎnyì ❶ simple and easy: ～读物 easy reader ❷ simply constructed or equipped; unsophisticated: ～楼 economically constructed building / ～机场 airstrip

简直 jiǎnzhí simply; just; at all: ～难以想像 virtually unimaginable

碱 jiǎn ❶ alkali base: ～地 alkaline land / ～性 alkalinity; basicity ❷ soda ❸ alkalinize; basify

jiàn

见(見) jiàn ❶ see; witness; catch sight of: ～世面 see the world; enrich one's experience / ～机行事 do as one sees fit; use one's discretion / ～死不救 see sb in mortal danger without lifting a finger to save him; watch people die and not lend a helping hand / ～树不见林 fail to see the wood for the trees / ～不得人 不得人的事 unseemly deed; scandal / ～人说人话、鬼说鬼话〈俗〉be all things to all men; doublespeak; speak with a forked tongue ❷ meet with; be exposed to: ～风流泪 One's eyes water when exposed to wind. ❸ show evidence of; appear or seem to be: ～报 appear or be published in the newspapers / ～老 look old for one's age; age visibly / ～效 become effective; produce the desired result / ～之于行动 be translated into action ❹ refer to; see: ～后 see below / ～前 see above ❺ meet; receive; see: ～客 receive guests / ～上帝〈婉〉go to see God—go the way of all flesh; die ❻ view; opinion: ～解 view; idea; understanding / 依我之～ in my opinion; to my mind ❼ 〈助〉 *used before a verb to indicate* a) *the passive idea*: ～弃 be rejected or discarded b) *sth done for one*: 希～告。Please let me know.

见长 jiàncháng ❶ be good at; be expert in: 以音乐～ be good at music ❷ (jiànzhǎng) (of a child) grow well

见得 jiàndé (used in the negative or interrogative) seem; appear: 不～ may not be right / 何以～? How so?

见地 jiàndì insight; judgement: 很有～ show remarkable insight

见多识广 jiànduō-shíguǎng experienced and knowledgeable

见风使舵 jiànfēngshǐduò *see* "看风使舵" kànfēngshǐduò

见缝插针 jiànfèngchāzhēn stick in a pin wherever there's room — make use of every bit of time, space or opportunity

见怪 jiànguài mind; take offence: 请

勿～! No offence.

见怪不怪 jiànguàibùguài not be surprised by anything unusual; be used to uncommon things:～,其怪自败〈俗〉ignore a monster and it will defeat itself; fear not the fearful, and its fearfulness disappears

见鬼 jiànguǐ ❶ ridiculous; absurd; funny:真是见了鬼了,剪子怎么转眼就不见了? That's funny! How come the scissors disappeared in the twinkling of an eye? ❷〈粗〉go to hell; to hell with it

见好 jiànhǎo ❶ (of a patient's condition) get better; pick up ❷ see or show improvement:～就收 leave well enough alone; stop before going too far

见教 jiànjiào 〈套〉favour me with your advice; instruct me:有何～? Is there something you want to enlighten me about? or What can I do for you?

见利忘义 jiànlìwàngyì sacrifice principle for profit; sell one's honour for money

见谅 jiànliàng 〈书〉〈套〉excuse me; forgive me

见面 jiànmiàn meet; see:～熟〈口〉hail-fellow-well-met / 这部电影从明日起和观众～。The film will be released tomorrow.

见仁见智 jiànrén-jiànzhì different people have different views; opinions differ

见识 jiànshi knowledge; experience:～短浅 lacking in knowledge and experience; shallow; superficial

见外 jiànwài regard sb as an outsider:请不要～。Don't bother please. or Make yourself at home.

见微知著 jiànwēizhīzhù from one small clue one can see what is coming; a little straw shows which way the wind blows

见闻 jiànwén what one sees and hears; knowledge; information:以广～(so as to) enrich one's experience or knowledge; widen one's horizon

见习 jiànxí learn on the job; be on probation:～生 intern; probationer /～医生 intern

见笑 jiànxiào be laughed at; incur ridicule:诗写得不好,真是～了。〈谦〉The poem is not well-written; hope you won't mind.

见义勇为 jiànyìyǒngwéi be ready to take up the cudgels for a just cause; have the courage to do what is right

见异思迁 jiànyìsīqiān change one's mind the moment one sees something new; be inconstant or irresolute:～,终无所获。A rolling stone gathers no moss.

见证 jiànzhèng ❶ be a witness to; bear witness to:～人 eyewitness; witness ❷ evidence; witness

件 jiàn ❶ letter; paper; document:要～ important document ❷ *used of sth that can be counted*:工～ workpiece / 配～ fittings of a machine ❸〈量〉piece:三～家具 three items of furniture

间 jiàn ❶ space or time in between; opening; discord:团结无～ united as one / 当～儿 in the middle ❷ separate; intersperse:～杂 be intermingled or mixed (with) / 多云～晴 cloudy with occasional sun ❸ sow discord ❹ thin out (seedlings); remove *see also* jiān

间谍 jiàndié spy:～活动 espionage

间断 jiànduàn be disconnected or interrupted:从未～ without interruption

间隔 jiàngé ❶ interval; intermission; spacing:～均匀 evenly spaced /～15米 fifteen metres apart ❷ separate:～号〈语言〉separation dot (·)

间或 jiànhuò occasionally; once in a while

间接 jiànjiē indirect; second-hand:～经验 indirect experience /～证据 circumstantial evidence

间隙 jiànxì　interval; gap; space: 比赛 ~ time-out; break

间歇 jiànxiē　intermittence; intermission; interval: ~泉〈地〉geyser; intermittent spring

饯(餞) jiàn ❶ give a farewell dinner: ~行 give a farewell dinner (for sb) ❷ candy (fruit)

建 jiàn ❶ build; construct; erect: ~材 (short for 建筑材料) building materials / ~造 build; construct; make ❷ establish; set up; found: ~都 establish a capital; make (a place) the capital / ~国 found or establish a state; build up a country / ~功立业 render meritorious service and make a distinguished career ❸ propose; put forward; advocate: ~言〈书〉state one's views and proposals; offer advice or suggestions

建构 jiàngòu　establish; construct (usu sth abstract): ~新的理论体系 set up a new theoretical system

建交 jiànjiāo　establish diplomatic relations: ~国 country having diplomatic relations (with China)

建军 jiànjūn ❶ found an army: ~节 Army Day (1 August) ❷ build up an army: ~原则 principles of army building

建立 jiànlì ❶ found; start; set up: ~一支教学队伍 organize a teaching staff ❷ build up; establish: ~威信 establish one's prestige

建设 jiànshè　build; construct: 城市 ~ urban development / 富有~性的会谈 very constructive talks

建树 jiànshù　make a contribution; contribute: 有所~ make one's contribution (to); do one's bit (for)

建议 jiànyì　propose; suggest: ~权 right to make suggestions or recommendations / ~价格 recommended price

建制 jiànzhì　organizational or

set-up (of an army, etc)

建筑 jiànzhù　build; construct; erect: ~群 architectural complex / ~学 (art of) architecture / ~面积 (built) floor space

荐(薦) jiàn　recommend; introduce

贱(賤) jiàn ❶ low-priced; inexpensive; cheap: ~卖 hold a sale; sell cheap ❷ lowly; common; humble: ~民〈旧〉person of a low social status; pariah ❸ lowdown; mean; base: ~骨头〈粗〉miserable or contemptible wretch; 〈谑〉self-imposed sufferer; trouble seeker ❹ 〈谦〉my: ~内 my wife

剑(劍) jiàn　sword; sabre: ~柄 hilt / ~客〈旧〉swordsman / ~鞘 scabbard; sheath / ~拔弩张 with swords drawn and bows bent; at daggers drawn; rattling one's sabres

涧 jiàn　(stream in a) ravine or gully: 山~ mountain stream

监(監) jiàn　imperial office: 国子~ Imperial College, highest educational administration in dynastic China　*see also* jiān

健 jiàn ❶ healthy; robust: ~美 strong; ~儿 strong agile men (usu referring to soldiers or athletes) / ~朗 healthy and strong; hale and hearty / ~旺 healthy and vigorous / ~壮 healthy and strong; robust ❷ strengthen; fortify; invigorate: ~胃药 stomach tonic ❸ be strong in; be good at: ~谈 be a good talker or conversationalist

健步 jiànbù　(walk with) vigorous strides: ~如飞 walk as if on wings; walk quickly and vigorously

健将 jiànjiàng ❶ master; expert: 文坛~ master in the world of letters ❷ master of a sport; ace player: 游泳~ top-notch swimmer

健康 jiànkāng ❶ health; physique;提高～水平 improve one's health / 祝您～长寿！To your health! ❷ healthy; fit; sound; ～的思想 sound idea; wholesome thought

健美 jiànměi ❶ strong and handsome; vigorous and graceful ❷ body-building; ～操 body-building exercises; calisthenics

健全 jiànquán ❶ sound; healthy; perfect;神经不～ out of one's mind ❷ strengthen; improve; perfect; ～法制 perfect the legal system

健身 jiànshēn keeping fit; body-building; ～操 physical exercises / ～房 gymnasium; gym; fitness centre

健忘 jiànwàng be forgetful; have a bad memory; ～症〈医〉amnesia

健在 jiànzài (of a person of advanced age) alive and well; hale and hearty

舰（艦） jiàn warship; naval vessel; man-of-war;～队 fleet; naval force / ～艇 naval vessels / ～载 ship-based; carrier-borne or carrier-based / ～长 captain

渐 jiàn gradually; little by little; ～变 gradual change / ～～ gradually; by degrees / ～进 advance gradually; progress step by step / ～入佳境 (of a situation, etc) be improving; become better and better / 夜色～浓。It's getting dark.

谏 jiàn 〈书〉expostulate with (one's superior or friend); admonish; ～阻 dissuade sb from (doing sth); advise sb not to (do sth)

践（踐） jiàn ❶ trample; tread;～踏 tread on;〈喻〉trample underfoot; violate ❷ act on; carry out; execute; ～约 keep an appointment

毽 jiàn shuttlecock; 踢～子 kick the shuttlecock (as a game)

腱 jiàn 〈生理〉tendon; ～鞘 tendon sheath / ～子 (beef or mut-ton) shank

溅（濺） jiàn splash; spatter; splatter; ～落 fall into water (from a height); splash down (esp of a satellite)

鉴（鑒、鑑） jiàn ❶ ancient bronze mirror; 〈喻〉warning; object lesson; ～戒 warning; object lesson ❷ reflect; mirror;光可～人 (of sth) so shining and bright that it can serve as a looking glass ❸ inspect; survey; scrutinize;～证 distinguish and confirm

鉴别 jiànbié discern; distinguish; differentiate;～能力 discernment / ～真伪 distinguish the false from the genuine

鉴定 jiàndìng appraisal; evaluation; ～人 identifier; appraiser / ～书 testimonial; written appraisal

鉴谅 jiànliàng 〈书〉〈套〉used to ask for understanding and forgiveness;招待不周,务乞～。Please forgive us for any negligence in our service.

鉴赏 jiànshǎng appreciate;～家 connoisseur / ～水平 connoisseurship / 很有～力 have a keen eye (for sth)

鉴于 jiànyú in view of; seeing that; considering

键 jiàn key; ～盘 keyboard; fingerboard

槛（檻） jiàn ❶ banister; balustrade ❷ cage

see also kǎn

僭 jiàn 〈书〉exceed one's responsibility of office; usurp; ～位 usurp the throne / ～越 overstep one's authority; go beyond proper bounds

踺 jiàn

踺子 jiànzi 〈体〉somersault

箭 jiàn arrow;～筒 quiver / ～镞 metal arrowhead / ～靶子 target for archery / ～在弦上,不得不发。When the arrow is on the string, it must go.

箭步 jiànbù   sudden big stride forward；一个～蹿上去 dash forward with a sudden big stride

箭楼 jiànlóu   embrasured watchtower over a city gate

jiāng

江 jiāng ❶ river；～岸 river bank ❷ (Jiāng) Yangtze River；～汉 Yangtze-Hanshui (Valley) / ～南 (areas) south of the lower reaches of the Yangtze; south of the Yangtze / ～东父老 elders of one's native region or place; old country folks

江河日下 jiānghérìxià   go from bad to worse; be on the decline

江湖 jiānghú ❶ rivers and lakes ❷ all corners of the country；走～ go from place to place to earn a living / 流落～ lead a vagrant life / ～好汉 valorous man of the wide world; Robin Hood ❸ itinerant, quack, etc；～郎中 quack; mountebank / ～骗子 swindler; charlatan

江郎才尽 Jiānglángcáijìn   Jianglang written out — a writer whose creative powers are exhausted

江米 jiāngmǐ   polished glutinous rice

江山 jiāngshān ❶ rivers and mountains; land; landscape；～如画 picturesque landscape; beautiful scenery / ～易改，秉性难移〈谚〉it's easy to change rivers and mountains but hard to change a person's nature; a leopard cannot change his spots ❷ country; state power；打～ fight for state power

将(將) jiāng ❶〈书〉support; take; bring ❷ take care of (one's health, etc)；～养 also "将息" rest and recuperate; convalesce ❸ (in chess) check; ～死 checkmate ❹ incite; challenge; put

(sb) on the spot；你再～我也没用。It is useless trying to egg me on. ❺ also "将将" just; barely；～够 barely enough ❻ used to introduce the object before the verb；～门关上 shut the door ❼ and; by；～功赎罪 also "将功折罪" atone for a crime by meritorious acts; expiate one's crime by good deeds / ～心比心 put oneself in another's shoes; empathize ❽ be going to; be about to; will ❾ and; also；～信～疑 half believing, half doubting; hover between doubt and belief

see also jiàng

将近 jiāngjìn   close to; nearly; approximately

将就 jiāngjiu   make do with; make the best of; put up with；～着吃 put up with the food / 事事～ pamper or accommodate (sb) in everything

将…就… jiāng … jiù …   used before two identical words to indicate following an existing trend or accepting an accomplished fact；将错就错 leave a mistake uncorrected and make the best of it; leave an error alone / 将计就计 turn sb's trick against him or her; beat sb at his or her own game

将军 jiāngjūn ❶ (in chess) check; 〈喻〉put on the spot; challenge ❷ general; high-ranking military officer；～肚 〈谑〉pot-belly; beer belly or gut

将来 jiānglái   future

将要 jiāngyào   be going to; will; shall

姜(薑) jiāng   ginger；～汤 ginger tea / ～是老的辣 〈俗〉old ginger is hotter than new — old hands are better than greenhorns

豇 jiāng

豇豆 jiāngdòu   cowpea

浆(漿) jiāng ❶ thick liquid, esp bean milk ❷ soak in rice or starch soup；～洗 wash and starch

僵（❶**殭**）jiāng ❶ stiff; rigid; numb：～死 dead；rigid／～直 stiff and rigid; unbending／政治～尸 political mummy ❷ deadlock; impasse; stagnation：～局 deadlock; impasse; stalemate／搞～ strain (relations, etc)

僵持 jiāngchí neither (party) is willing to give in or yield; refuse to budge; be at a deadlock

僵化 jiānghuà become rigid; ossify：头脑～ ossified way of thinking; stereotyped thinking

僵硬 jiāngyìng ❶ stiff：手指～ feel stiff in the fingers ❷ rigid; hidebound; inflexible

缰（**韁**）jiāng also "缰绳" reins; halter

疆 jiāng ❶ boundary; border; frontier：～土 also "疆域" territory／划分～界 delimit the boundary ❷ (Jiāng) (short for 新疆) Xinjiang

疆场 jiāngchǎng battlefield：久历～ battle-hardened

jiǎng

讲（**講**）jiǎng ❶ speak; talk; say：～述 tell about; give an account of; recount／～演 lecture; speech; talk／～笑话 crack a joke／～心里话 bare or open one's heart／～几点意见 make a few remarks ❷ explain; make clear; interpret：～道 (of a priest) preach; sermonize／～课 teach; lecture／～评 comment on; appraise／～授 lecture; instruct; teach／～学 give or deliver lectures (usu as a guest scholar)／～义 lecture sheets; teaching materials ❸ discuss; negotiate：～价钱 also "讲价" bargain; haggle over prices; negotiate terms／不～条件 unconditionally ❹ pay attention to; consider; be particular about：～交情 (do sth) for the sake

of friendship／～面子 be face-loving; care about sb's sensibilities／～排场 put up a show; go in for pomp／～义气 set store by personal loyalty

讲和 jiǎnghé make peace; settle a dispute; become reconciled or conciliated

讲话 jiǎnghuà ❶ speak; talk; address；敢～ dare to air one's views; be outspoken／会～ be a good talker; have a ready tongue ❷ (often used in book titles) talk; guide; introduction

讲解 jiǎngjiě explain; expound; explicate：～员 guide; commentator; announcer

讲究 jiǎngjiu ❶ be particular or fastidious about; pay attention to; stress：～吃穿 be fastidious about one's food and clothing／～ sth worth of study or observation；教学法大有～。Teaching is quite an art. ❸ exquisite; superb; tasteful

讲理 jiǎnglǐ ❶ reason (with sb); argue ❷ listen to reason; be reasonable or sensible

讲情 jiǎngqíng intercede (on sb's behalf); plead (for sb); put in a good word

讲求 jiǎngqiú be particular about; pay attention to; strive for：～效率 lay emphasis on efficiency; stress or underline performance

讲师 jiǎngshī lecturer：～团 lecture team; teaching group

讲坛 jiǎngtán ❶ also "讲台" platform; rostrum ❷ forum

讲座 jiǎngzuò lecture; course of lectures：举办～ sponsor or hold lectures

奖（**獎**）jiǎng ❶ praise; commend; reward：～杯 cup (as a prize)／～金 money award; bonus; premium／～牌 medal (as an award)／～品 prize; award; trophy／～赏 award; reward; premium／～章 medal; decoration／～状 certificate of merit; citation／～学金 scholarship；

(student) grant / ～被后进 encourage and promote one's juniors ❷ award; prize; reward;颁～ hand out prizes

奖惩 jiǎngchéng　rewards and punishments;～严明 strictly abide by regulations on rewards and disciplinary sanctions

奖励 jiǎnglì　(encourage and) reward; award;～工资 premium wages; incentive pay

奖券 jiǎngquàn　lottery ticket; gift coupon;对～ check a lottery ticket against the prize numbers

奖项 jiǎngxiàng　prize in a particular item or field;共设九个～ give prizes in nine fields

桨（槳） jiǎng　oar;荡起双～ pull on the oars; go boating

jiàng

匠 jiàng　❶ craftsman; artisan ❷〈书〉person of remarkable achievements in a particular field; master;文学巨～ literary giant

匠心 jiàngxīn　〈书〉ingenuity; craftsmanship;颇具～ be quite ingenious or imaginative mind / ～独运 exercise one's inventive mind; give play to one's ingenuity or creativity

降 jiàng　❶ go down; fall; drop; ～水 precipitation / ～雪 snowfall / ～旨 issue an imperial edict ❷ lower; reduce;～价 reduce or cut the price / ～职 demote / ～半旗 hoist a flag to half-mast　*see also* xiáng

降低 jiàngdī　reduce; drop; lower;～要求 lower one's standards; moderate one's demands / ～成本10% cut costs by 10 per cent

降格 jiànggé　〈书〉lower one's standard or status;～以求 settle for the second best

降级 jiàngjí　❶ reduce in rank; demote ❷ send (a student) to a lower grade

降解 jiàngjiě　〈化〉degradation;可～塑料 degradable plastic

降临 jiànglín　〈书〉befall (sb); arrive; come

降落 jiàngluò　descend; land; alight; ～伞 parachute

降生 jiàngshēng　*also*"降世"〈书〉(as of the founder of a religion, etc) be born

降温 jiàngwēn　❶ lower the temperature; drop in temperature ❷〈喻〉cool down; decrease; wane

降压 jiàngyā　❶〈电〉reducing voltage; step-down;～变电站 step-down sub-station ❷ bring down the blood pressure;～药 hypotensive (medicine)

将（將） jiàng　❶ general; commander; military officer;～才 ability to command troops; man with military talent; born general / ～领 high-ranking officer; general / ～士〈书〉officers and men; commanders and fighters / ～遇良材 meet one's equal; find one's match; diamond cuts diamond ❷〈书〉command; lead;善于～兵 be good at commanding troops; be a good general　*see also* jiāng

绛 jiàng　deep red; crimson;～紫 *also*"酱紫" dark reddish purple

强 jiàng　stubborn; obdurate; unyielding;～嘴 *also*"犟嘴" reply defiantly; answer or talk back　*see also* qiáng; qiǎng

酱（醬） jiàng　❶ thick sauce or paste made from soya beans, flour, etc;～油 soy (sauce) / ～园 sauce and pickle shop ❷ food cooked or pickled in soy sauce;～菜 vegetables pickled in soy sauce; pickles / ～肉 pork cooked in soy sauce; braised pork seasoned with soy sauce ❸ sauce; paste; jam: 草莓 ～ strawberry jam

酱豆腐 jiàngdòufu *also* "豆腐乳" fermented bean curd

犟 jiàng obstinate; stubborn; self-willed: 脾气 ～ headstrong / ～劲 tenacious will

糨 jiàng thick

糨糊 jiànghu *also* "糨子" paste

jiāo

交 jiāo ❶ hand in; hand or turn over; deliver: ～班 hand over to the next shift; change shift / ～公 hand over to the collective or the state / ～心 lay one's heart bare; open one's heart / ～学费 pay a tuition fee; 〈喻〉pay for a lesson ❷ meet; converge; intersect: ～界 have a common boundary / ～运 have good luck ❸ associate with; befriend; ～道 dealings; contact / ～好 be on friendly terms; have friendly relations / ～朋友 make friends; date / ～游广阔 have a wide range of friends ❹ friend; friendship; relationship: 多年之 ～ friendship of many years ❺ copulate; mate; breed: ～媾（have）sexual intercourse; copulation; coitus / ～尾 (of insects and animals) mate; pair; couple ❻ mutual; reciprocal: ～杯酒 mutual toasting by bride and bridegroom drinking from each other's cup / ～相辉映 add radiance and beauty to each other; enhance each other's beauty ❼ together; simultaneous: ～集 (of different feelings) occur simultaneously; be mixed in ❽ *see* "跤" jiāo

交保 jiāobǎo bail: ～释放 allow or take bail; be released on bail

交兵 jiāobīng 〈书〉*see* "交战"

交叉 jiāochā ❶ cross; intersect; criss-cross: ～点 intersection / ～火力

crossfire ❷ overlap: ～学科 interdisciplinary branch of learning ❸ alternate; stagger: ～进行 do alternately

交差 jiāochāi report (to the leadership) after accomplishing a task; report on the fulfilment of one's duty: 无法 ～ no way to account for one's mission

交错 jiāocuò 〈书〉interlock; interlace; criss-cross: 枝杈 ～ interlaced branches

交代 jiāodài ❶ hand or turn over; transfer ❷ tell; leave word; order: ～清楚 give clear-cut instructions; give a clear account ❸ *also* "交待" explain or clarify to people concerned; account for; confess: 彻底 ～ make a clean breast (of sth) / ～任务 brief sb on his or her assignment

交待 jiāodài ❶ *see* "交代❸" ❷〈谑〉end (one's life, etc); kill

交底 jiāodǐ tell (sb) what one's real intentions are; give the bottom line; put all one's cards on the table

交锋 jiāofēng cross swords; engage in a battle or contest; have a trial of strength: 思想 ～ confrontation of ideas; clash of views

交付 jiāofù ❶ pay: ～定金 make a down payment ❷ hand or turn over; deliver; consign: ～审判 commit (sb) for or submit (sb) to trial / ～使用 put (sth) into commission or operation; make available

交割 jiāogē ❶ complete a business transaction ❷ transfer; deliver; hand or turn over: ～日期 date of delivery; due date

交互 jiāohù ❶ each other; mutual: ～式电视 interactive television (ITV) ❷ alternately; in turn

交换 jiāohuàn exchange; interchange; swap: ～看法 exchange opinions; compare notes / ～条件 give-and-take condition; quid pro quo

交火 jiāohuǒ open or exchange fire;

fight

交货 jiāohuò　deliver goods；~单 delivery order / ~付款 cash on delivery (COD)

交际 jiāojì　social intercourse；communication：善于~ be a good mixer / ~花〈贬〉social butterfly or beauty / ~舞 *also* "交谊舞" ballroom or social dancing / ~应酬 business entertainment；social obligations

交加 jiāojiā　(of two things) accompany each other；occur simultaneously：拳足~ punch and kick (sb) / 风雨~ raging rainstorm

交接 jiāojiē　❶ join；connect：冬春~ transition from winter to spring ❷ hand over and take over：~班 relieve a shift ❸ associate with；make friends with

交警 jiāojǐng　(short for 交通警察) traffic police or policeman

交卷 jiāojuàn　hand in an examination paper；complete one's task；carry out an assignment：交白卷 hand in a blank examination paper；fail completely；lay an egg

交口 jiāokǒu　speak in unison；~称誉 praise (sb) unanimously；be praised by one and all；receive unanimous acclaim

交流 jiāoliú　❶ flow simultaneously：涕泪~ shed tears and have a runny nose ❷ exchange；interflow；interchange：思想~ exchange of views or ideas / ~学者 exchange scholar；visiting scholar

交流电 jiāoliúdiàn　alternating current (AC)

交纳 jiāonà　pay (to the state or an organization)；hand in

交配 jiāopèi　mating；copulation：~期 mating season

交情 jiāoqíng　friendship；friendly relations：有~ be on friendly terms (with sb)

交融 jiāoróng　blend；mix；mingle：不

同文化的~ blending or mutual assimilation of cultures

交涉 jiāoshè　negotiate；take up (sth with sb)；make representations (to sb about sth)：继续~ pursue a matter further

交手 jiāoshǒu　fight hand to hand；fight in a game or contest：交起手来 come to blows

交替 jiāotì　❶ give place to；replace；supersede ❷ alternately；one after another；in turn：昼夜~。Day alternates with night.

交通 jiāotōng　❶ communicate：阡陌~ criss-crossing paths on farmland ❷ traffic；communications：~不便 have poor transport facilities；be inconveniently located / ~工具 means of transport / ~阻塞 traffic jam；congested traffic ❸〈书〉associate or collude with

交头接耳 jiāotóu-jiē'ěr　speak in each other's ears；whisper to each other

交往 jiāowǎng　associate；contact：少有~ have little contact (with sb)

交响乐 jiāoxiǎngyuè　symphony；symphonic music；~团 symphony or philharmonic orchestra

交椅 jiāoyǐ　ancient folding chair；〈喻〉leading position：坐头把~ occupy the highest post；be first in command

交易 jiāoyì　trade；bargain；deal：~会 trade fair / ~所 exchange / ~成本 transaction cost

交战 jiāozhàn　be at war；fight a war：~方 belligerent party / ~状态〈法〉belligerency；state of war

交账 jiāozhàng　❶ hand over accounts ❷ account for：这事儿怎么~? How are we going to account for this?

交织 jiāozhī　(of fabrics, etc) interweave；(of plants, etc) intertwine；〈喻〉mingle

郊 jiāo　suburbs or outskirts (of a city)：~外 country around a city；outskirts / ~游 outing；excursion / ~

区居民 suburban；suburbanite

茭 jiāo
茭白 jiāobái 〈植〉wild rice stem

浇（澆） jiāo ❶ pour (liquid on sth)；sprinkle (water on sth)：～水 sprinkle water / ～冷水〈喻〉pour or throw cold water (on) ❷ irrigate；water：～菜 water vegetable plots ❸ cast：～注 also "浇筑"（建筑）pour (concrete, etc)；casting；pouring

浇灌 jiāoguàn ❶ pour；mould：～混凝土 pour concrete ❷ water；irrigate

娇（嬌） jiāo ❶ tender；delicate；charming：～嫩 delicate；tender and lovely / ～娆〈书〉enchantingly beautiful / ～柔 gentle and charming；delicate and lovely ❷ squeamish；fragile；frail ❸ pamper；spoil：～宠 indulge；spoil；dote on / ～惯 coddle；pamper；spoil / ～纵 indulge (a child)；pamper；spoil

娇滴滴 jiāodīdī ❶ delicately pretty；affectedly sweet ❷ too delicate；frail

娇贵 jiāoguì ❶ enervated (by good living)；pampered ❷ fragile；delicate；easy to break：～的玻璃器皿 fragile glassware

娇媚 jiāomèi ❶ coquettish；flirtatious ❷ sweet and charming

娇气 jiāoqì ❶ delicate；squeamish；coquettish：娇声～（speak in a) seductive tone ❷ (of things) easily broken or damaged；fragile；delicate

娇生惯养 jiāoshēng-guànyǎng pampered and spoiled：他绝不是～的孩子。He is no mama's boy.

娇小 jiāoxiǎo small and delicate；petite：～玲珑 delicate and exquisite；petite and charming

娇艳 jiāoyàn delicate and charming；tender and beautiful

姣 jiāo 〈书〉beautiful；handsome：～妍 beautiful；pretty

骄（驕） jiāo ❶ proud；arrogant；conceited：胜不～ not be dizzy with success / ～矜〈书〉self-important；arrogant；haughty / ～躁 arrogant and impetuous / ～气十足 be swell-headed；be full of arrogance / ～奢淫逸 arrogant，luxury-loving，loose-living and idle；given to dissipation and debauchery / ～兵必败。An arrogant army is doomed to defeat. ❷〈书〉intense；fierce；violent：～阳似火 scorching sun

骄傲 jiāo'ào ❶ arrogant；haughty；conceited；～自满 conceited and self-satisfied；arrogant and complacent ❷ be proud (of)；take pride (in)

骄横 jiāohèng arrogant and tyrannous；overbearing：～跋扈 be arrogant and overweening；throw one's weight about

骄子 jiāozǐ 〈喻〉favoured or favourite son；favourite：天之～ God's favoured one；golden boy or girl

骄纵 jiāozòng arrogant and headstrong：～放恣 overbearing and debauched

胶（膠） jiāo ❶ glue；gum：～水 mucilage；glue / ～囊 capsule / ～质 gel ❷ stick with glue；glue：～粘剂 adhesive ❸ rubber：～布 also "胶带"（rubberized）adhesive tape / ～鞋 rubber overshoes；galoshes；sneakers

胶版 jiāobǎn offset plate：～印刷 also "胶印" offset (printing)；offset lithography

胶卷 jiāojuǎn also "胶片"（roll of）film；冲～ have one's film developed；develop film

胶着 jiāozhuó deadlocked；stalemated：～状态 stalemate

教 jiāo teach；instruct：～学 teach / ～书育人 impart knowledge and educate people；pass on knowledge and

enlighten people　*see also* jiāo

椒 jiāo　any of several hot spice plants；～盐 roasted prickly ash and salt；spiced salt

蛟 jiāo

蛟龙 jiāolóng　flood dragon；～得水 like the flood dragon going into water — be in one's element；get a good opportunity to display one's talent

焦 jiāo　❶ burnt；scorched；charred；～黄 sallow；brown / ～土 scorched earth — ravages of war ❷ coke；～炭 coke ❸ worried；anxious；～灼〈书〉deeply worried；extremely anxious / ～思苦虑 cudgel one's brains ❹（short for 焦耳）〈理〉joule，a measure of energy

焦点 jiāodiǎn　❶〈数〉〈理〉focal point；focus ❷〈喻〉central issue；focus；point at issue

焦急 jiāojí　anxious；agitated；worried；～万分 be all anxiety

焦虑 jiāolù　feel anxious；be troubled；have worries and misgivings

焦头烂额 jiāotóu-làn'é　badly battered；in a terrible fix；in a sorry plight；忙得～ be up to one's neck with work

焦躁 jiāozào　restless with anxiety；impatient；～不安 fidgety；on pins and needles；like a cat on hot bricks

跤 jiāo　tumble；fall

鲛 jiāo　（usu known as 鲨）shark

蕉 jiāo　any of several broadleaf plants；香～ banana

礁 jiāo　reef；rock；触～ strike a reef；run up on a rock / 环～ atoll

jiáo

嚼 jiáo　masticate；chew；munch

嚼舌 jiáoshé　also "嚼舌头"；"嚼舌根" ❶ wag one's tongue；chatter；gossip ❷ argue meaninglessly；squabble

jiǎo

角 jiǎo　❶ horn；horn-shaped thing：牛～ ox horn / 豆～ fresh kidney beans ❷ bugle；horn ❸ cape；promontory；headland；好望～ Cape of Good Hope ❹ corner：～楼 watchtower at a corner of a city wall；corner tower；turret / ～落 corner；nook；remote place / ～球 corner kick ❺〈数〉angle；～尺 angle square ❻ jiǎo，fractional unit of money in China（=⅒ of a yuan or 10 *fen*）
see also jué

角度 jiǎodù　❶（degree of）angle ❷ point of view；angle：从不同的～来看 view（sth）from a different angle

角膜 jiǎomó　〈生理〉cornea

侥（僥） jiǎo

侥幸 jiǎoxìng　lucky；by luck；by a fluke；～脱险 have a close shave / ～心理 idea of leaving things to chance；trusting to luck

佼 jiǎo　〈书〉beautiful；handsome；pretty

佼佼 jiǎojiǎo　〈书〉above average；outstanding

狡 jiǎo　crafty；cunning；sly：～辩 argue without reason；quibble；resort to sophistry / ～猾 also "狡滑" sly；wily；crafty / ～计 tricky plot；crafty trick；wily trap / ～诈 crafty；cunning / ～诈 deceitful；crafty；cunning / ～兔三窟 a wily hare has three burrows—a crafty person has more than one hideout or option

饺 jiǎo　a kind of dumpling；蒸～ steamed dumplings

饺子 jiǎozi dumpling；包～ make dumplings／～皮 dumpling wrapper／～馅 filling or stuffing for dumplings

绞 jiǎo ❶ twist (two or more strands) into one；wind；wind：～车 winch；windlass／把床单～干 wring out a wet bed sheet ❷ hang by the neck：～架 gallows (tree)／～索 (hangman's) noose／～刑 execution by hanging ❸ cut or bore by a revolving cutter；ream：～肉机 meat grinder；mincing machine ❹〈量〉skein；hank：一～ a hank of yarn

绞尽脑汁 jiǎojìnnǎozhī rack one's brains；task one's mind；cudgel one's brains

绞杀 jiǎoshā ❶ hang (sb) ❷ strangle；throttle：～于摇篮中 strangle in the cradle；nip in the bud

绞痛 jiǎotòng〈医〉angina：肚子～ abdominal angina；colic

铰 jiǎo ❶〈口〉cut with scissors：～条裤子 cut out a pair of trousers ❷ see "绞❸" jiǎo ❸ hinge：～接 join with a hinge；articulate／～链 hinge

矫(矯) jiǎo ❶ rectify；remedy；correct：～治 correct and cure (stammer, etc) ❷ strong；powerful；brave：～捷 vigorous and nimble；agile；brisk／～若游龙 as dynamic as a flying dragon；as strong and brave as a lion ❸ pretend；feign；counterfeit：～饰 feign in order to conceal sth；dissemble；dissimulate

矫健 jiǎojiàn strong and vigorous；brisk and dynamic；sturdy：～的步伐 (at a) brisk pace

矫揉造作 jiǎoróuzàozuò affected；artificial：～的姿态 affectations

矫枉过正 jiǎowǎngguòzhèng exceed the proper limits in righting a wrong；overcorrect

矫形 jiǎoxíng〈医〉orthopaedic：～外科 orthopaedic or plastic surgery／

医师 orthopaedist

矫正 jiǎozhèng correct；remedy；rectify

皎 jiǎo〈书〉clear and bright；white and luminous：～洁 bright and clear

脚(腳) jiǎo foot；base：墙～ foot of a wall／～板 also "脚底板儿" sole (of the foot)／～背 also "脚面" instep／～法〈体〉footwork／～尖 tip of a toe；tiptoe／～力 strength of one's legs／～镣 fetters；shackles／～印 footmark；track／～趾 also "脚指头" toe／～注 footnote

see also jué

脚本 jiǎoběn script；scenario

脚步 jiǎobù footstep；step；stride：～声 footfalls／～跟跄 walk unsteadily；stagger

脚跟 jiǎogēn also "脚根" heel：站稳～ gain a firm foothold；stand firm

脚气 jiǎoqì〈医〉❶ beriberi ❷ also "脚癣" ringworm of the foot；athlete's foot

脚踏 jiǎotà ❶ foot-operated：～板 pedal (of a bike, etc)；treadle (of a sewing machine)／～车〈方〉bicycle ❷ put one's feet (on sth)：～实地 have one's feet planted on solid ground—be earnest and down-to-earth／两只船 also "脚踩两只船" have a foot in either camp；hedge one's bet

脚丫子 jiǎoyāzi also "脚鸭子"〈方〉foot；光着～ barefooted／忙得～朝天 be up to one's neck in work

搅(攪) jiǎo ❶ stir；mix；mingle：～混〈口〉mix；blend；mingle ❷ disturb；upset；annoy：～局 upset the apple cart；make a mess of sth／～扰 disturb；annoy；upset

搅拌 jiǎobàn stir；mix：～机 mixer

搅动 jiǎodòng ❶ stir；mix ❷ disturb；mess up

搅浑 jiǎohún　stir into a muddy state; stir into a mess: 把水～ throw (things) into turmoil or confusion; create a disturbance

搅和 jiǎohuo　〈口〉❶ mix; mingle; involve: 这是我的事, 你别往里头～。This is my business; don't you butt in. ❷ also "搅乱" throw into confusion; mess up; spoil: 把会～了 disrupt a meeting

剿 (勦) jiǎo　send armed forces to suppress; put down; quell: ～灭 wipe out; exterminate; annihilate

缴 jiǎo　❶ pay; hand over or in: ～纳 pay / ～销 hand in for cancellation / ～枪不杀! Lay down your arms and you'll be spared! ❷ capture (arms): ～获 capture; seize

缴械 jiǎoxiè　❶ disarm (sb) ❷ surrender one's weapons; lay down one's arms

jiào

叫 (呌) jiào　❶ cry; shout; yell: ～春 (of cats) make mating calls / ～号 call a number / ～骂 shout curses / ～卖 cry one's wares; peddle; hawk / ～屈 complain of being wronged; protest against an injustice / ～嚷 shout; howl; clamour / ～醒 wake (sb) up; awaken / ～阵 also "叫板" challenge (an opponent) to a fight; throw down the gauntlet ❷ greet; call; summon: ～门 call or knock at the door ❸ hire; order; get: ～菜 order dishes / ～出租车 hail or call a taxi ❹ name; call; designate: ～做 be called; be known as / 他～什么名字? What's his name? ❺ make; cause; allow: ～人为难 put sb in a dilemma; make sb feel embarrassed ❻ used to introduce the doer of an action: ～雨淋了 be caught in a rain

叫好 jiàohǎo　shout "Bravo!" or "Well done!"; applaud; cheer: 博得全场～ bring the house down

叫花子 jiàohuāzi　also "叫化子"〈口〉beggar

叫唤 jiàohuan　❶ cry or call out: 疼得直～ cry out in pain ❷ (of animals or birds) cry; shout

叫劲 jiàojìn　see "较劲" jiàojìn

叫绝 jiàojué　applaud as the very best (one has seen, etc); shout "Bravo!"

叫苦 jiàokǔ　complain (of hardship): ～不迭 complain incessantly; pour out endless grievances / ～连天 complain to high heaven; ventilate one's bitter grievances

叫嚣 jiàoxiāo　clamour; raise a hue and cry: 疯狂～ clamour frantically (for or about sth); raise a terrible hullabaloo

叫座 jiàozuò　draw a large audience; appeal to the audience; be a box-office success: 叫好不～ win favourable critical comments but no box office success

觉 (覺) jiào　sleep: 睡了一大觉 have a sound sleep　see also jué

校 jiào　❶ check; proof-read; collate: 二～ second proof / ～勘 collate / ～样 proof-sheet; proof / ～注 check (against the authoritative text) and annotate ❷ (usu 校量) compare; contest　see also xiào

校对 jiàoduì　❶ proof-read; proof ❷ proof-reader

校阅 jiàoyuè　❶ read and revise ❷〈书〉review

校正 jiàozhèng　(proof-read and) correct; rectify

轿 (轎) jiào　sedan (chair); litter: 坐～ be carried in a sedan; go by sedan chair / ～夫 sedan carrier

轿车 jiàochē　bus or car: 大～ bus

较 jiào ❶ compare；～为 comparatively；fairly；quite ❷〈书〉clear；obvious；evident

较劲 jiàojìn　also "叫劲" ❶ match one's strength with；have a contest with ❷ set oneself against；be at odds with：这天儿真～儿，冻死人！ What disagreeable weather! It's freezing cold. ❸ require special effort；play a crucial role：眼下正是～的时候。Now is the time we must put our shoulders to the wheel.

较量 jiàoliàng　have a contest；have a trial or test of strength；compete：综合国力的～ contest of comprehensive national power

较真 jiàozhēn　also "叫真"〈方〉serious；earnest：干活～儿 be very serious with work；be meticulous

coach / 小～ car；limousine；sedan

教 jiào ❶ teach；instruct：～案 teaching or lesson plan / ～材 teaching material；textbook / ～程 course of study；(published) lectures / ～官 (army) drillmaster；instructor / ～具 teaching aid / ～益〈书〉enlightenment；benefit from advice or instruction / ～科书 textbook / ～研室 teaching and research section or division ❷ religion：～父 godfather / 皇～ pope；pontiff / ～派 religious sect；denomination / ～士 priest；clergyman；missionary / ～廷 the Vatican；the Holy See / ～徒 believer or follower of a religion / ～义 religious doctrine；creed；tenet / ～主 founder of a religion；patriarch ❸ see also "叫"❺❻ jiào

教导 jiàodǎo　instruct；teach；give guidance：～员 political instructor / ～有方 teach in the right way

教化 jiàohuà〈书〉educate；cultivate；edify：～作用 educational role

教会 jiàohuì　(Christian) church；～法

规 canon law / ～学校 missionary school

教诲 jiàohuì〈书〉teaching；instruction

教练 jiàoliàn ❶ train；drill；coach：～机 trainer (aircraft) ❷ coach；instructor：～兼队员 playing coach

教师 jiàoshī　teacher；schoolteacher；～节 Teachers' Day (10 Sept. in China)

教室 jiàoshì　classroom；schoolroom：大～ lecture room or hall

教授 jiàoshòu ❶ professor；副～ associate professor / 客座～ visiting or guest professor ❷ instruct；teach

教唆 jiàosuō　instigate；abet；put (sb) up to (sth)：～犯 abettor；instigator / ～罪 instigation to a crime；solicitation

教堂 jiàotáng　(Christian) church：cathedral；大～ abbey；cathedral

教条 jiàotiáo ❶〈宗教〉creed；canon；tenet ❷ dogma；doctrine；tenet：～主义 dogmatism；doctrinism

教头 jiàotóu ❶ drill master；instructor ❷〈口〉(sports) coach

教务 jiàowù　educational administration：～处 dean's office / ～长 dean of studies；academic dean

教学 jiàoxué ❶ teaching；education：～法 pedagogy；teaching method / ～大纲 teaching programme；syllabus / ～方针 principle of teaching ❷ teachers and students；teaching and learning：相长。Teaching benefits teacher and student alike.

教训 jiàoxun ❶ chide；teach (sb) a lesson；give (sb) a talking-to or dressing-down ❷ lesson；moral：吸取～ draw a lesson (from sth)；take warning (from sth) / 血的～ lesson paid for with blood；lesson written in blood

教养 jiàoyǎng ❶ bring up and teach；educate ❷ breeding；upbringing；education：有～ be well-bred / 缺乏～ lack breeding；be uncouth ❸〈法〉correction; reeducation: ～院 house of correction; reformatory; workhouse

教育 jiàoyù ❶ education; schooling: ～家 educationist; educator / ～学 pedagogy; education / ～学院 college of education; teacher's college ❷ teach; educate; inculcate

教员 jiàoyuán teacher; instructor: ～休息室 common room

教正 jiàozhèng 〈书〉〈套〉instruct and correct: 敬希～. With the compliments of the author.

窖 jiào ❶ cellar or pit (for storing things) ❷ store (sth) in a cellar or pit

酵 jiào ferment; leaven: ～母 also "酵母菌" yeast

醮 jiào ❶〈旧〉libation at a wedding ceremony: 再～ (of a woman) remarry ❷ Taoist sacrificial ceremony: 打～ perform a Taoist ritual

jiē

节（節） jiē see also jié

节骨眼 jiēguyǎn 〈方〉critical juncture; vital link

阶（階） jiē ❶ steps; stairs ❷ rank

阶层 jiēcéng (social) stratum; class: 高薪～ high-salary class

阶段 jiēduàn stage; phase; period: ～性成果 result of one phase of a project; initial product

阶级 jiējí ❶〈书〉steps ❷ (social) class: ～斗争 class struggle / ～社会 class society

阶梯 jiētī flight of stairs; ladder: ～教室 lecture theatre; terrace classroom / 向上爬的～ stepping stone; ladder of promotion

阶下囚 jiēxiàqiú prisoner; captive

疖（癤） jiē

疖子 jiēzi 〈医〉furuncle; boil

皆 jiē all; each and every: 大欢喜 everybody is happy; all are satisfied; (sth is done) to the satisfaction of all

结 jiē bear (fruit); form (seed); produce: 只开花不～果 blossom without bearing fruit; 〈喻〉produce no substantive result despite outward show　see also jié

结巴 jiēba ❶ stammer; stutter: 结结巴巴的英语 faltering English ❷ stammerer; stutterer

结实 jiēshi ❶ (of sth) solid; sturdy; durable ❷ (of sb) strong; sturdy; tough: 身体～ sturdily built

接 jiē ❶ come into contact with; get close to; be in touch with: ～壤 border (on); be contiguous (to); be bounded (by) ❷ connect; join; put together: ～口（信息）interface / ～上页 continued from the preceding page / ～通电话 put a call through; switch through to ❸ catch or take hold of: ～力 relay / ～球 receive a service ❹ receive; take; accept: ～客 receive guests (esp of a prostitute) entertain a client / ～茬儿〈方〉pick up the thread of a conversation; chime in / ～电话 answer the phone; receive or take a phone call ❺ meet; welcome: ～机 go to the airport to meet sb / ～驾〈谑〉greet or welcome sb as an emperor / ～见 receive; give an interview to / ～站 meet (sb) at a (train, etc) station ❻ take over; succeed: ～管 take over (control) / ～任 take over a job or post; succeed / ～手 take over (duties, etc)

接班 jiēbān take one's turn on duty; take over from; carry on: ～人 successor

接触 jiēchù ❶ come into contact with; get or keep in touch with: ～不良 〈电〉loose or poor contact / ～传染

〈医〉contagion / ～政策 policy of engagement ❷ engage：脱离～ (of two armies, etc) disengage

接待 jiēdài　receive; host; admit：～日 reception day / ～人员 reception personnel; receptionist

接二连三 jiē'èr-liánsān one after another; in quick succession; repeatedly

接风 jiēfēng　also "接风洗尘" give a welcome dinner (for a visitor from afar)

接轨 jiēguǐ ❶ connect the rails ❷ get onto the track; switch over to; integrate：与国际惯例 ～ follow international practice / 与世界经济 ～ get integrated into the world economy

接火 jiēhuǒ ❶ start to exchange fire ❷ (of an installation, etc) be joined to the power main

接济 jiējì　give material assistance or financial aid to; supply (materials, etc)：受人 ～ get pecuniary help from people ❷ keep up the supply

接近 jiējìn ❶ be close to; be near; approach；难以～ difficult to approach; stand-offish ❷ (of views, etc) similar; close

接连 jiēlián　on end; in a row; in succession：～ 不 断 continuously; incessantly; in rapid succession / 几年 for years running

接纳 jiēnà ❶ admit (into an organization); accept (as a member) ❷ accept (advice, etc); adopt (a view, etc)

接洽 jiēqià　take up (a matter); arrange or talk (business, etc); consult

接生 jiēshēng　deliver a child; practise midwifery：～婆 (traditional) midwife

接收 jiēshōu ❶ receive; pick up; accept：～ 机 receiving set ❷ take over (property, etc); expropriate ❸ see "接纳❶"

接受 jiēshòu　accept; take; learn：～国 recipient or accepting country / ～教训 learn a lesson / ～考验 face up to a test

接替 jiētì　take over; succeed; replace：～某人当大使 succeed sb as ambassador

接头 jiētóu ❶ connect; join; contact：～地点 contact point; rendezvous / 四通～儿〈电〉four-way connection ❷ know about; be familiar with; be in the know

接吻 jiēwěn　kiss

接续 jiēxù　continue; follow

接应 jiēyìng ❶ come to sb's aid; back up; reinforce：派人 ～ send sb to meet (a visitor) ❷ give material assistance; supply

接踵 jiēzhǒng　〈书〉follow behind sb's heels or in the wake of sth

接种 jiēzhòng　〈医〉have an inoculation; inoculate：～卡介苗 have a BCG vaccine

秸（稭）jiē　grain stalk after threshing; straw：麦 ～ wheat straw

揭 jiē ❶ tear or take off; remove; uncover：～牌 unveil a signboard, etc; officially launch; inaugurate / ～疮疤 pull the scar right off sb's sore; rub salt in sb's old wound; touch sb on the raw / ～不开锅 have nothing in the pot; run out of food ❷ expose; show up; bring to light：～丑 expose the ugly side (of sth) / ～秘 break a secret; unveil a mystery ❸ 〈书〉raise; hoist：竿而起 rise in rebellion; start an uprising

揭榜 jiēbǎng ❶ announce the results of an examination ❷ 〈旧〉take off a notice (as a sign of accepting what is offered)

揭穿 jiēchuān　expose; lay bare; show up：～阴谋 uncover a plot / ～ 西洋景 give away the show

揭底 jiēdǐ　reveal the inside story; lay bare; expose：揭老底 expose sb's unsavoury past; drag the skeleton out of sb's closet

揭短 jiēduǎn　rake up sb's faults; disclose sb's shortcomings; 爱揭别人的短儿 be always ready to rub people on the raw

揭发 jiēfā　expose; unmask; lay bare; ～丑闻 blow the lid off a scandal

揭开 jiēkāi　uncover; reveal; make public; ～谜底 solve a riddle / ～序幕 raise the curtain (on an event, etc)

揭露 jiēlù　expose; unmask; lay bare; ～真面目 expose sb in his or her true colours; show sb up for what he or she is

揭幕 jiēmù　❶ unveil (a monument, etc); inaugurate; ～式 unveiling ceremony ❷ the curtain rises (on an event, etc); begin; start

揭示 jiēshì　❶ announce; make public; promulgate; ～牌 notice board ❷ reveal; disclose; bring to light; ～客观规律 shed light on an objective law

揭晓 jiēxiǎo　announce (results, etc); make known; publish

嗟 jiē　〈书〉sigh; lament; ～叹 (heave a) sigh / ～来之食 food handed out in contempt; handout

街 jiē　street; ～区 block; neighbourhood / ～市 downtown street / ～谈巷议 street gossip; talk of the town / ～心广场 square at an intersection

街道 jiēdào　❶ street ❷ residential district; neighbourhood; ～办事处 subdistrict (government) office

街坊 jiēfang　〈口〉neighbour

街头 jiētóu　street; ～叫卖 hawk one's wares in the street / ～巷尾 (in) streets and lanes

jié

孑 jié　〈书〉lonely; all alone

孑孓 jiéjué　〈动物〉wiggler; wriggler

孑然 jiérán　〈书〉solitary; lonely;

alone; ～一身 all alone in the wide world

节(節) jié　❶ joint; node; knot; 藕～ node of lotus root / 竹～ bamboo joint ❷ division; section; part; 第二～ Section Two / 一～钢管 a length of steel tube ❸ festival; red-letter day; holiday; 过～ celebrate a festival ❹ save; check; reduce; ～能 save energy / ～食 eat moderately; go on a diet / ～育 (practise) birth control / ～欲 restrain one's carnal desires; check one's selfish desire / ～支 cut down expenses; ～衣缩食 economize on food and clothing; tighten one's belt ❺ abridge; ～选 excerpts; extracts / ～译 abridged translation ❻ moral integrity; chastity; ～操 high moral principle; moral integrity ❼ knot (nautical mile per hour)

see also jiē

节哀 jié'āi　restrain one's grief

节俭 jiéjiǎn　thrifty; frugal; economical

节节 jiéjié　successively; continuously; steadily; ～后退 make one retreat after another; keep on retreating

节令 jiélìng　climate and other natural phenomena of a season; ～不等人。Don't miss the right season (for farming, etc).

节略 jiélüè　❶ capsule; excerpt; extract ❷ memorandum; aide-memoire ❸ reduce and save; omit; leave out

节目 jiémù　programme; item (on a programme); number; ～主持人 host; anchorperson

节拍 jiépāi　〈乐〉metre; tempo; 合着 ～ keep time

节气 jiéqì　❶ one of the twenty-four seasonal division points by which the solar year is divided under the traditional Chinese calendar according to the sun's apparent movement on the ecliptic (黄经), with 春分 (Vernal Equinox) marking 0° on this imaginary line and each of the twenty-four points spaced by 15° from the next. The traditional Chinese calendar, however, starts the solar year with (1) 立春 (Beginning of Spring) marking the sun's position at 315° falling between 3-5 Feb., followed successively by (2) 雨水 (Rain Water, 18-20 Feb.), (3) 惊蛰 (Waking of Insects, 5-7 Mar.), (4) 春分 (Vernal Equinox, 20-21 Mar.), (5) 清明 (Pure Brightness, 4-6 Apr.), (6) 谷雨 (Grain Rain, 19-21 Apr.), (7) 立夏 (Beginning of Summer, 5-7 May), (8) 小满 (Grain Budding, 20-22 May), (9) 芒种 (Grain in Ear, 5-7 Jun.), (10) 夏至 (Summer Solstice, 21-22 Jun.), (11) 小暑 (Slight Heat, 6-8 Jul.), (12) 大暑 (Great Heat, 22-24 Jul.), (13) 立秋 (Beginning of Autumn, 7-9 Aug.), (14) 处暑 (Limit of Heat, 22-24 Aug.), (15) 白露 (White Dew, 7-9 Sept.), (16) 秋分 (Autumnal Equinox, 22-24 Sept.), (17) 寒露 (Cold Dew, 8-9 Oct.), (18) 霜降 (Frost's Descent, 23-24 Oct.), (19) 立冬 (Beginning of Winter, 7-8 Nov.), (20) 小雪 (Slight Snow, 22-23 Nov.), (21) 大雪 (Great Snow, 6-8 Dec.), (22) 冬至 (Winter Solstice, 21-23 Dec.), (23) 小寒 (Slight Cold, 5-7 Jan.), (24) 大寒 (Great Cold, 20-22 Jan.) ❷ day marking such a seasonal division point ❸ period lasting from such a seasonal division point till the next one; solar term

节日 jiérì　festival; red-letter day; holiday

节省 jiéshěng　economize; save; cut down on:过日子很～ live a frugal life

节外生枝 jiéwàishēngzhī　❶ side issues or new problems crop up unexpectedly ❷ raise obstacles; deliberately complicate an issue

节余 jiéyú　❶ save; have in surplus ❷ surplus; money or material saved; saving

节约 jiéyuē　practise thrift; economize; save

节制 jiézhì　❶ command and manage (troops, etc) ❷ control; check; be moderate:有～ practise temperance or abstinence

节奏 jiézòu　rhythm; tempo

劫 jié

❶ rob; plunder; attack by surprise:～匪 highwayman; robber / ～掠 plunder; loot; maraud / ～狱 break into a jail and rescue a prisoner / ～富济贫 rob the rich to give to the poor ❷ coerce; compel; hijack:～持 kidnap; hijack; abduct / ～机 hijack an aircraft; commit air piracy ❸〈宗教〉predestined disaster or trial; (natural or man-made) calamity:～难 disaster; calamity / ～数 inexorable doom; predestined fate / ～后余生 survive a disaster

杰 (傑) jié

❶ outstanding person; hero ❷ outstanding; prominent; distinguished:～出 outstanding; remarkable / ～作 masterpiece

诘 jié

〈书〉closely question; interrogate:～难 censure; blame; condemn / ～问 closely question; interrogate; cross-examine

拮 jié

拮据 jiéjū　in straitened circumstances; short of money; hard up

洁 (潔) jié

clean; pure; clear:～净 clean; spotless; neat and tidy / ～具 sanitary equipment / ～癖 fastidiousness about cleanliness; mysophobia

洁白 jiébái　spotlessly or pure white; ～无瑕 spotless and flawless; pure and innocent

洁身自好 jiéshēnzìhào　❶ refuse to

be contaminated by evil influence; preserve one's purity ❷ mind one's own business; stand aloof (out of self-interest)

结 jié ❶ tie; knit; knot;打个～ tie a knot / ～网 weave a net ❷ form; forge; associate;～伴 go together; do sth together; work in company / ～伙 form a gang; gang up / ～交 make friends with; associate or mix with / ～社自由 freedom of association / ～为夫妻 be tied in wedlock ❸ settle; finish; conclude;～案 settle a lawsuit; wind up or close a case / ～欠 balance due / ～清 settle; square up; liquidate / ～余(cash) surplus; balance / ～语 concluding remarks / ～账 settle or square accounts; balance the books ❹ 〈生理〉node

see also jiē

结疤 jiébā *also* "结痂" scab; become scarred

结拜 jiébài *also* "结义" become sworn brothers or sisters; ～兄弟 sworn brothers

结冰 jiébīng freeze; ice up or over

结存 jiécún cash or goods on hand; balance; inventory; ～商品 goods in stock

结党营私 jiédǎng-yíngsī form a clique to pursue selfish interests; gang up for selfish purposes;一群～的政客 a gang of self-seeking politicians

结发夫妻 jiéfà fūqī husband and wife by the first marriage

结构 jiégòu structure; composition; construction;组织～ framework of an organization / ～严密 well-organized (essay); tightly-knit (unit)

结果 jiéguǒ ❶ result; outcome; fruit ❷ kill; finish off

结合 jiéhé ❶ combine; integrate; link;中西医～ combine or integrate traditional Chinese medicine and Western medicine / ～具体情况 in the light

of specific conditions ❷ be united in wedlock

结核 jiéhé 〈医〉tubercule; tuberculosis; consumption;～病 tuberculosis; TB

结婚 jiéhūn marry; get married; ～年龄 age for marriage; matrimonial or marriageable age / ～证书 marriage certificate or lines

结集 jiéjí ❶ collect articles, etc. into a volume ❷ assemble; concentrate (troops)

结晶 jiéjīng ❶ crystallize;～体 *also* "晶体" crystal ❷ crystallization;知识的～ quintessence of knowledge

结局 jiéjú final result; outcome; ending

结论 jiélùn deduction; conclusion; verdict;匆匆下～ jump to conclusions

结盟 jiéméng form an alliance; ally; align;不～政策 non-aligned policy

结亲 jiéqīn ❶ get married ❷ (of two families) become related by marriage

结石 jiéshí 〈医〉stone; calculus;排出～ discharge stones

结识 jiéshí get acquainted (with sb); get to know (sb); make friends with

结束 jiéshù end; conclude; close; ～语 concluding remarks / ～混乱状态 put an end to a chaotic situation

结算 jiésuàn settle accounts; close or wind up an account;非现金～ settle through accounts / ～单据 document of settlement

结尾 jiéwěi ending;～阶段 final or winding-up stage

结业 jiéyè complete a course; finish one's studies;～证书 certificate for completing a course

结缘 jiéyuán form ties (of affection, etc); take a liking; become attached; 与绘画～ take a fancy to painting

结怨 jiéyuàn *also* "结仇" bear grudges; contract enmity; incur hatred

桔 jié *see also* jú

桔槔 jiégāo　well sweep (for drawing water)

榤 jié

榤骜 jié'ào　〈书〉wild and stubborn：～不驯 stubborn and intractable；obstinate and unruly

捷 jié

jié ❶ prompt；agile；quick ❷ victory；triumph；success

捷报 jiébào　news of a victory；report of a success：～频传 news of victory keep pouring in；reports of success keep flooding in

捷径 jiéjìng　short cut；royal road：走～ take a short cut；cut corners

捷足先登 jiézúxiāndēng　the swift-footed arrive first；the race is to the swiftest；it's the early bird that catches the worm：我申请那个工作时,发现已有人～了。I found that someone had beaten me to it when I applied for the job.

睫 jié

jié　eyelash；lash：～毛 eyelash；lash

截 jié

jié ❶ cut；separate；sever：～面 also "剖面" section / ～取 cut out / ～肢〈医〉amputation / ～长补短 take from the long to add to the short；even up scarcity and plenty / ～头去尾 cut off both ends ❷ also "截子" section；chunk；length：话说了半～儿 break off halfway；finish only half of what one has to say ❸ stop；check；intercept：～流 dam a river / ～球 intercept a pass ❹ (usu 截至) by (a specified time)；up to：～稿日期 closing date (for contribution of articles)

截断 jiéduàn　cut off；block：～联系 cut off communications / ～退路 block the retreat

截获 jiéhuò　intercept and capture：～逃犯 capture a criminal at large

截留 jiéliú　hold back；withhold；retain：～税款 keep back tax payment

截然 jiérán　sharply；distinctly；completely：～不同 poles apart；completely different

截止 jiézhǐ　end；close：报名～日期 closing date for signing up

碣 jié

jié　(round-topped) stone tablet

竭 jié

jié　exhaust；use up：～力 do one's utmost；go all out；try by every possible means / ～泽而渔 drain the pond to get all the fish；kill the goose that lays the golden eggs

竭诚 jiéchéng　wholeheartedly；with all one's heart：～帮助 go all out to help；help in all sincerity

竭尽 jiéjìn　use up；exhaust：～所能 work to the best of one's ability；do the best one can

jiě

姐 jiě

jiě ❶ (elder) sister：～夫 elder sister's husband；brother-in-law ❷ elder female relative (of one's own generation) ❸ general term for young women

姐姐 jiějie　❶ elder sister ❷ elder female cousin

姐妹 jiěmèi　❶ sisters：～城市 sister or twin cities ❷ brothers and sisters

解(觧) jiě

jiě ❶ separate；divide；split ❷ untie；undo；solve：～谜 solve a riddle or mystery / ～衣 take off one's clothes；undress / ～扣儿 undo a button；〈喻〉get rid of a hang-up；remove ill will / ～甲归田 take off one's armour and return to one's native place；be demobilized ❸ relieve；remove；dispel：～馋 satisfy a craving for good food / ～愁 free from worries；relieve depression / ～饿 satisfy or appease one's hunger；stay one's stomach / ～乏 recover from fa-

tigue; refresh oneself / ～恨 vent one's hatred; have one's hatred slaked / ～禁 lift a ban / ～酒 relieve or neutralize the effect of alcohol / ～渴 quench or satisfy one's thirst / ～忧 assuage sorrow; dispel worry ❹ explain; construe; clear up; ～疑 dispel doubts and misgivings; clear up a doubt ❺ understand; comprehend; be clear; ～悟 come to understand; realize / 不～其意 not know what sb means ❻ relieve oneself; ～手 relieve oneself; go to the toilet or restroom ❼〈数〉solution
see also jiè; xiè

解嘲 jiěcháo　try to explain things away when ridiculed; console oneself

解除 jiěchú　free; relieve; remove; ～合同 terminate or dissolve a contract / ～警报 (sound the) all-clear / ～宵禁 lift a curfew / ～职务 remove sb from his or her post; relieve sb of his or her office

解答 jiědá　answer; explain; solve

解冻 jiědòng　(as of ice) thaw; unfreeze; ～资产 unfreeze assets / 两国关系～。There was a thaw in the relations between the two countries.

解毒 jiědú　〈医〉detoxify; detoxicate; ～药 *also* "解药" antidote

解读 jiědú　❶ read and explain; explicate; ～古籍 explicate ancient texts ❷ analyse; interpret; understand; 对政策的不同～ different interpretations or constructions of a policy

解放 jiěfàng　liberate; emancipate; free; ～思想 emancipate the mind; free oneself from outmoded ideas / ～战争 War of Liberation (1946-1949) / ～生产力 liberate or unfetter the productive forces

解放军 jiěfàngjūn　❶ (short for 中国人民解放军) the Chinese People's Liberation Army; the PLA ❷ PLA man

解雇 jiěgù　*also* "解聘" dismiss from employment; discharge; fire

解救 jiějiù　save; rescue; deliver

解决 jiějué　❶ solve; resolve; overcome; ～争端 settle a dispute / ～问题的能手 troubleshooter ❷ dispose of; finish off; eliminate

解困 jiěkùn　❶ relieve sleepy feeling ❷ overcome a difficulty; tide over hardships

解铃系铃 jiělíng-xìlíng　(short for 解铃还须系铃人) let him who tied the bell on the tiger take it off—whoever started the trouble should end it

解闷 jiěmèn　divert (oneself from boredom); amuse; 读闲书～ do light reading for amusement

解密 jiěmì　declassify; decipher; ～高手 cypherpunk / ～文件 declassified document

解难 jiěnán　❶ relieve sb of difficulties; explain difficult points; solve problems ❷ (jiènàn) rescue sb from danger or disaster

解囊 jiěnáng〈书〉open one's purse; 慷慨～ make generous contributions of money / ～相助 dig in one's pocket to help sb

解剖 jiěpōu　❶ dissect; anatomize; autopsy; ～刀 scalpel; dissecting knife / ～学 anatomy ❷〈喻〉analyse; examine; critique; 自我～ self-examination / ～麻雀 (method of) analysing a typical case

解气 jiěqì　vent one's spleen; work off one's anger

解散 jiěsàn　❶ dismiss (as a command) ❷ break up; dissolve; disband

解释 jiěshì　explanation; interpretation; exposition; 作出错误的～ put a false construction (on sth) / ～权 right of interpretation

解说 jiěshuō　explain orally; comment; ～词 commentary; captions (for a movie, etc) / ～员 commentator; narrator; guide (to an exhibition), etc)

解体 jiětǐ　decompose; disintegrate

collapse:封建社会的～ disintegration or breakup of the feudal system

解脱 jiětuō free (oneself); extricate (oneself); absolve

解围 jiěwéi ❶ raise or lift a siege; rescue sb (as) from a siege ❷ help sb out of a predicament; save sb from embarrassment

解析 jiěxī 〈数〉analyse:～几何 analytic geometry

解职 jiězhí dismiss from office; relieve sb of his or her post:～金 severance pay

jiè

介 jiè ❶ be (situated) between; interpose:～乎两者之间 be between the two ❷ introduce ❸ have in mind; take to heart ❹ armour; shell ❺〈量〉used of persons (often to indicate humility):一～书生 a (mere) scholar

介词 jiècí 〈语言〉preposition:～短语 prepositional phrase

介入 jièrù intervene; interpose; get involved:～他人私事 intervene in others' private affairs

介绍 jièshào ❶ introduce; recommend; sponsor:～人 one who introduces or recommends sb; sponsor; go-between / ～信 letter of introduction; recommendation; reference ❷ let know; brief; give an account of:向人～情况 brief sb on the situation; put sb in the picture; fill sb in

介意 jièyì (often used in the negative) take offence; mind:毫不～ not mind at all; not take the least offence

戒 jiè ❶ guard against; be on the alert against; be prepared against:～骄～躁 guard against arrogance and rashness; be on guard against conceit and impetuosity ❷ give up; drop; stop:～除 also "戒绝" give up; stop; get rid of ❸ religious precept or commandment; abstinence; taboo:～律 also "戒条"〈宗教〉religious discipline; commandment / 开杀～ break an abstinence from killing ❹ (usu 戒指) (finger) ring:钻～ diamond ring

戒备 jièbèi guard; take precautions; be on the alert:～森严 enforce tight security; guard heavily

戒心 jièxīn vigilance; wariness:对拍马的人要存～。Be wary of sycophants.

戒严 jièyán enforce martial law; impose a curfew; cordon off (an area):撤销～ call off or lift a curfew / ～地区 district under martial law

芥 jiè ❶ mustard:～菜 leaf mustard / ～末 mustard (powder) ❷ sth tiny and trivial:草～ trifle; mere nothing

see also gài

芥蒂 jièdì 〈书〉ill feeling; unpleasantness; grudge:不存～ harbour no grudge; nurse no ill feelings

届 jiè ❶ fall due:～时 when the time comes; at the appointed time; on the occasion ❷〈量〉session; class:本～毕业生 this year's graduates

届满 jièmǎn (of a term of office, etc) expire

界 jiè ❶ boundary; border:～碑 boundary marker / ～内〈体〉in bounds ❷ scope; range; extent:动物～ animal kingdom / 学术～ academic circles

界定 jièdìng specify the limits; delimit; define

界面 jièmiàn 〈信息〉interface

界说 jièshuō also "定义" definition

界限 jièxiàn ❶ demarcation or dividing line; limits:打破学科～ break the bounds among academic disciplines ❷ limit; end:贪欲是没有～的。Greed knows no limit.

界线 jièxiàn ❶ boundary line; dividing or demarcation line; bounds:是非

J

~ dividing line between right and wrong ❷ edge; verge

疥 jiè scabies; ~ 癣之疾 minor trouble; immaterial illness

诚 jiè warning; admonish; advise

借(❸❹ **藉**) jiè ❶ borrow; ~ 词〈语言〉 borrowed word; loan (word) / ~ 据 also "借条" receipt for a loan; IOU / ~ 喻〈语言〉 metonymy / ~ 风使船 also "借水行舟" sail before the wind—attain one's own end through the agency of sb else / ~ 尸还魂 (of sth evil) revive in a new guise ❷ lend; loan; ~ 书处 loan or circulation desk ❸ use as a pretext; ~ 古讽今 use the past to disparage the present; borrow a current lesson to criticize a current practice ❹ make use of; take advantage of; rely on; ~ 酒浇愁 drown one's worries in the wine cup; drink sorrow down

借贷 jièdài ❶ borrow or lend money ❷ debit and credit sides

借刀杀人 jièdāoshārén murder with a borrowed knife — make use of sb else to get rid of an adversary; kill by another's hand

借调 jièdiào temporarily transfer (staff); loan; second

借读 jièdú study at a school away from one's registered permanent residence; study at a school on a temporary basis; ~ 生 (usu unenrolled) temporary student

借故 jiègù use as a pretext; make an excuse; find an excuse; ~ 寻衅 pick a quarrel on some pretext or other

借光 jièguāng ❶ benefit from association with sb or sth ❷〈套〉〈口〉excuse me

借花献佛 jièhuāxiànfó present Buddha with borrowed flowers — borrow sth to make a gift of it

借鉴 jièjiàn use for reference; draw on (the experience of)

借口 jièkǒu use as an excuse or a pretext; 找 ~ find an excuse (to do sth)

借款 jièkuǎn ❶ borrow or lend money; ask for or offer a loan ❷ loan; 收回 ~ recall a loan

借题发挥 jiètífāhuī make use of the subject under discussion to put over one's own ideas; seize on an incident to expatiate on sth else; take an opportunity to grind one's own axe

借以 jièyǐ so as to; with a view to; by way of

借用 jièyòng ❶ borrow ❷ use sth for another purpose

借重 jièzhòng rely on (for support); enlist (sb's help)

借助 jièzhù have the aid of; draw support from; with the support of; ~ 双拐行走 walk with crutches

借住 jièzhù stay at sb else's place temporarily; put up for the time being

解 jiè carry or take under guard; escort; ~ 送 escort; take (to a place, etc) under guard see also jiě; xiè

裰 jiè

裰子 jièzi 〈方〉diaper

jīn

巾 jīn piece of cloth (used as a towel, scarf, etc)

巾帼 jīnguó 〈书〉woman; ~ 英雄 heroine

斤(**觔**) jīn jin, unit of weight (= ½ kilogram); ~ 两 weight; importance / ~~计较 haggle over every ounce; be calculating

今 jīn ❶ modern; present-day; now; 古诗 ~ 译 modern translation of ancient poetry; ancient poems rendered into modern Chinese ❷ this; today; ~ 年 this year / ~ 朝有酒 ~ 朝醉 today's wine I drink today; enjoy while you can

今后 jīnhòu from now on; in the days to come; in the future: ~ 的道路 the road ahead

今日 jīnrì ❶ today ❷ present; now

今世 jīnshì ❶ this contemporary age; ~ 贤人 wise man of the present world ❷ *also* "今生" this life

今天 jīntiān ❶ today: ~ 运气不好。 Today just isn't my day. ❷ present; current; now

今昔 jīnxī present and past; today and yesterday: 今非昔比 things today are different from what they were; be no longer the person one used to be

金 jīn ❶ metal: ~ 城汤池 ramparts of metal and a moat of boiling water — impregnable fortress / ~ 戈铁马 shining spears and armoured horses; gallant, formidable warriors ❷ gold: ~ 婚 golden wedding, 50th wedding anniversary / ~ 块 gold bullion / ~ 元 gold or US dollar / ~ 本位 〈经〉 gold standard ❸ money: ~ 额 amount of money / ~ 库 treasury ❹ precious as gold; sterling: ~ 贵 〈口〉 precious, valuable / ~ 曲 〈口〉 extremely popular song; great hit / ~ 嗓子 beautiful or sweet voice / ~ 钥匙 golden key—very effective way ❺ golden; gilt: ~ 发 golden or blonde hair / ~ 黄 golden (yellow) / ~ 鱼 goldfish / ~ 灿灿 glittering like gold; golden bright and dazzling / ~ 銮殿 Hall of Golden Chimes; throne room; imperial palace ❻ (Jīn) Jin Dynasty (1115-1234)

金榜题名 jīnbǎngtímíng find one's name on the list of successful candidates (in the final imperial examination); succeed in official examinations

金碧辉煌 jīnbìhuīhuáng (as of a building) looking splendid in green and gold; resplendent and magnificent

金蝉脱壳 jīnchántuōqiào slip out of a predicament like a cicada sloughing its skin; escape by cunning manoeuvres; get away by putting pursuers off the scent

金刚 jīngāng ❶ Buddha's warrior attendant: 四大 ~ Buddha's four guardian warriors / ~ 怒目 glare like a temple door god — be fierce of visage ❷ 〈喻〉 capable assistant or underling; lieutenant

金刚石 jīngāngshí *also* "金刚钻" "钻石" diamond: ~ 婚 60th or 75th anniversary of a marriage

金科玉律 jīnkē-yùlǜ golden rule and precious precept: 奉为 ~ take sth as infallible canon

金口玉言 jīnkǒu-yùyán emperor's words; unalterable oracular saying

金兰 jīnlán sworn brothers

金牌 jīnpái 〈体〉 gold medal: ~ 得主 gold medallist

金钱 jīnqián money: ~ 万能 money is almighty; money talks

金融 jīnróng finance; banking: ~ 家 financier / ~ 危机 financial crisis

金石 jīnshí ❶ 〈书〉 metal and stone — a symbol of firmness and strength ❷ inscriptions on ancient bronzes and stone tablets ❸ musical instruments made of copper and stone: ~ 丝竹 musical instruments or music of all kinds

金属 jīnshǔ metal: ~ 加工 metal processing; metalworking

金丝猴 jīnsīhóu golden monkey; snub-nosed monkey

金童玉女 jīntóng-yùnǚ 〈宗教〉 Golden Boy and Jade Maiden—boy and girl attendants of a god or goddess; 〈喻〉 lovely boy and girl

金文 jīnwén *also* "钟鼎文" 〈考古〉 inscriptions on ancient bronze objects; ancient language used in such inscriptions

金星 jīnxīng ❶ (Jīnxīng) 〈天文〉 Venus ❷ golden star ❸ spark; star: 两眼冒 ~ see stars

金玉 jīnyù 〈书〉gold and jade; treasures: ~良言 golden saying; pearls of wisdom; invaluable advice / ~其外，败絮其中 rubbish coated in gold and jade; fair without, foul within

金字塔 jīnzìtǎ pyramid

金字招牌 jīnzìzhāopái gold-lettered signboard of a shop; prestigious or vainglorious title

津 jīn ❶ saliva: ~液《中医》body fluid; saliva ❷ sweat: 遍体生~ perspire all over ❸ moist; humid; damp ❹ ferry crossing; ford: ~梁〈书〉ferry crossing and bridge; 〈喻〉guide (to learning) ❺ (Jīn) (short for 天津) Tianjin

津津 jīnjīn ❶ tasty; interesting; with relish: ~乐道 take delight in talking about (sth); dwell upon (sth) with great relish / ~有味 with relish or gusto; with great enjoyment; with keen pleasure ❷ (of liquid) flow; come out: 汗~ moist with sweat; sweaty

津贴 jīntiē ❶ allowance; subsidy: 生活~ living allowance ❷ grant an allowance; subsidize

矜 jīn ❶ pity; sympathize with; have compassion for ❷ be self-conceited or self-important; sing one's own praises: ~夸 conceited and boastful ❸ prudent; reserved; prim; ~持 prim and affected; restrained; reserved

筋 jīn ❶〈旧〉muscle ❷ tendon; sinew: ~疲力尽 also "精疲力竭" exhausted; worn or tired out; played out ❸〈口〉veins that stand out under the skin ❹ anything resembling a tendon or vein: 钢~ steel bar / 叶~ ribs of a leaf

筋道 jīndao 〈方〉❶ (of food) tough and chewy ❷ sturdy, hale and hearty

筋斗 jīndǒu somersault; tumble

筋骨 jīngǔ muscles and bones—physique: 活动~ limber up

禁 jīn ❶ bear; stand; endure; ~得住 also "禁得起" be able to bear or endure; can stand or withstand ❷ hold back; contain oneself; restrain oneself: ~不住大笑起来 can't help laughing out loud

see also jìn

襟 jīn ❶ front of a garment ❷ (breadth of) mind: ~怀坦白 have a broad mind; be honest and above board

jǐn

仅(僅) jǐn *also* "仅仅"〈副〉only; just; barely: ~供参考 for (your) reference only

尽(儘) jǐn ❶ to the greatest extent or degree possible: ~早 as early or as soon as possible; at your earliest convenience / ~可能 try one's best ❷ within the limits, bounds, or time: ~着一周完成 get it finished within a week ❸ give priority or precedence to; put first: ~先考虑住房问题 give first priority to the housing problem; put housing first ❹ (used before phrases indicating direction or location) furthest; most: ~后头 rearmost; furthest back

see also jìn

尽管 jǐnguǎn ❶ feel free to; not hesitate to: 有劲~使 do as much as you can ❷ (even) though; despite; in spite of

尽量 jǐnliàng to the best of one's ability; as far as possible　*see also* jìnliàng

紧(緊) jǐn ❶ tight; taut: 把弦绷得太~ stretch the strings too tight; press too hard on sb; overwork oneself ❷ fast; firm; close: ~~盯住他 keep a close watch on him; fix one's eyes on him ❸ close; too tight: 这双鞋子太~。These shoes pinch. ❹ urgent; pressing; following (each other) closely；～跟形势 keep pace with the times ❺ hard up; hard-pressed; short of money

紧巴巴 jǐnbābā also "紧梆梆" ❶ tight; taut；这件上衣我穿～的。The jacket is a tight fit for me. ❷ hard up；日子过得～的 live in straitened circumstances; be hard up

紧绷绷 jǐnbēngbēng ❶ tight; taut；～的绳子 tight or taut rope ❷ strained; stiffened; sullen；脸上～的 look strained

紧逼 jǐnbī press hard; close in on；半场～ half-court press (in basketball)

紧凑 jǐncòu compact; terse; succinct；结构～ well-organized; well-knit

紧促 jǐncù hurried; short and pressing；呼吸～ be short of breath; gasp for breath

紧急 jǐnjí urgent; emergent; pressing；～关头 critical moment / ～信号 urgent or distress signal

紧锣密鼓 jǐnluó-mìgǔ beat gongs and drums wildly—make intense publicity (before the appearance of sb or beginning of some undertaking)：准备工作正在～地进行着。Preparations are going on intensely.

紧密 jǐnmì ❶ close together; inseparable；～相连 closely linked ❷ rapid and intense

紧迫 jǐnpò pressing; critical; urgent；时间～ pressed for time / ～感 sense of urgency

紧俏 jǐnqiào (of goods, etc) have a ready market; sell like hot cakes; be salable

紧缺 jǐnquē lack; be short of; be in short supply；～商品 commodities that are in short supply; scarce items

紧缩 jǐnsuō reduce; retrench; tighten；～银根 tighten money supply / ～政策〈经〉deflation policy; policy of retrenchment

紧要 jǐnyào critical; crucial; vital；事

关～ be of vital importance

紧张 jǐnzhāng ❶ nervous; edgy; keyed up ❷ tense; intense; strained；缓和～局势 ease tension ❸ in short supply; tight；人手～ be short of hands

锦

锦 jǐn ❶ brocade；～缎 brocade / ～旗 silk banner (as an award or a gift) / ～上添花 add flowers to the brocade — make what is good still better ❷ bright and gorgeous

锦标 jǐnbiāo prize; trophy; title；～赛 championship (contest)

锦囊妙计 jǐnnángmiàojì stratagem to deal with an emergency; wise counsel

锦绣 jǐnxiù as beautiful as brocade; splendid; magnificent；～河山 land of charm and beauty; beautiful land / ～前程 glorious or splendid future

谨

谨 jǐn ❶ careful; cautious; prudent；～防有误 beware of or guard against possible error ❷ solemnly; sincerely; respectfully；～启 also "谨上"〈套〉yours respectfully; sincerely yours / ～致谢意 Please accept our sincere thanks.

谨慎 jǐnshèn prudent; cautious; circumspect；谨小慎微 overcautious in small matters; timid and wary; punctilious / 谨言慎行 speak and act cautiously; be discreet in word and deed

谨严 jǐnyán careful and precise; meticulous；学风～ meticulous scholarship

jìn

尽（盡）

尽（盡） jìn ❶ exhaust; use up；(do or go) to the utmost or limit；～头 end (of sth) / ～其所有 give everything one has; give one's all / ～善～美 acme of perfection; flawless / 用～办法 exhaust every means; be at the end of one's tether / 发挥～致 bring into full play ❷ do all one can; try one's best; put to the best use；～责 do one's best to fulfil one's responsibility; do one's duty / ～义务 do one's duty; work without asking for reward; do (sth) free of charge ❸ all; entire: ～干坏事 do nothing but evil / ～人皆知 be known to all; be common knowledge / ～如人意 just as one wishes; entirely satisfactory / ～释前嫌 *also* "尽捐前嫌" forget all former grudges; let bygones be bygones / ～收眼底 have a panoramic view (of a place, etc)

see also jìn

尽力 jìnlì do all one can; try one's best: ～而为 do one's best; do everything in one's power; exert every effort

尽量 jìnliàng (drink or eat) to the full

see also jǐnliàng

尽情 jìnqíng to one's heart's content; as much as one likes: ～欢笑 laugh to one's heart's content; make merry as best one can

尽心 jìnxīn with all one's heart: ～竭力 (do sth) with all one's heart and might; exert one's utmost

尽兴 jìnxìng to one's heart's content; (enjoy oneself) to the full

尽忠 jìnzhōng ❶ be loyal to: ～尽孝 be loyal to one's country and filial to one's parents ❷ sacrifice or lay down one's life (for one's country)

进（進） jìn ❶ advance; move forward; march or press onward: ～逼 advance on; close in on; press on towards / ～兵 *also* "进军" (of troops) drive on; forge ahead; march towards / ～发 set out or off; start ❷ enter; come or go into; get or put into: ～出 enter and exit; pass in and out; (business) turnover / ～球〈体〉 score a goal / ～站 draw up at a station; pull in / ～驻 enter and be stationed in; enter and garrison / ～入角色 enter into the spirit of a character; live one's part ❸ receive; take; buy: ～货 lay in a new stock of mer-

chandise; replenish one's stock ❹ submit; present: ～谏〈书〉 remonstrate with the monarch / ～香 go on a pilgrimage to a temple; offer incense / ～言 offer an opinion; voice or air one's view / ～献礼物 present a gift ❺ eat; drink; take: ～补 take tonic; take extra nourishment / ～餐 eat; take a meal

进步 jìnbù ❶ advance; improve; move forward; 取得～ make progress ❷ (politically) progressive

进程 jìnchéng course; process; progress

进度 jìndù (rate of) progress or advance: ～表 progress chart / 加速技术革新的～ step up technical innovations

进而 jìn'ér next; (and) then

进犯 jìnfàn intrude into; invade: 抗击～之敌 resist the aggressor troops

进攻 jìngōng attack; assail; assault: 发起～ launch an offensive

进贡 jìngòng ❶ pay tribute (to a suzerain or emperor) ❷ grease or oil sb's palm

进化 jìnhuà evolution: ～论 theory of evolution; evolutionism

进见 jìnjiàn *also* "晋见" call on (sb holding high office); have an audience with

进口 jìnkǒu ❶ enter port; sail into a port: ～港 port of entry ❷ import: ～商 importer / ～替代〈经〉 import substitution / 进出口贸易 import and export trade; foreign trade ❸ entrance

进来 jìnlái ❶ come in; get in; enter: ～坐坐 drop in ❷ (jinlái) (used after a verb) in; into: 走～ walk in

进门 jìnmén ❶ enter (the gate) ❷ learn the rudiments (of sth); be initiated ❸ (of a woman) get married and move into the bridegroom's family: 刚～的媳妇 new bride

进取 jìnqǔ keep forging ahead; be eager to make progress; be dynamic or enterprising: ～心 enterprising spirit;

initiative; drive

进去 jìnqù ❶ go in or into; enter ❷ (jinqu) (used after a verb) in; into; 把手伸～ stretch one's hand in

进深 jìnshēn (of a house or a room) distance from the entrance to the rear; depth; 三米～ three metres in depth

进士 jìnshì 〈史〉 successful candidate in the palace (civil service) examination; palace graduate

进退 jìntuì ❶ advance and retreat; ～维谷 be on the horns of a dilemma; find oneself between the devil and the deep blue sea / ～自如 be free to advance or retreat; have plenty of room for manoeuvre ❷ sense of propriety; 不知～ have no sense of propriety

进项 jìnxiang also "进账" income; receipts

进行 jìnxíng ❶ (of a meeting, etc) be in progress; be under way; go on ❷ carry on; conduct; ～讨论 hold a discussion ❸ march; advance; be on the march; ～曲 march

进修 jìnxiū engage in advanced studies; take a refresher course; ～生 student engaged in further studies

进一步 jìnyībù further; ～改进 further improve

进展 jìnzhǎn progress; headway; 毫无～ (make) no progress whatever

近 jìn ❶ near; close; immediate; ～东 Near East / ～景 close-by scenery; (in photography) close shot; close-up (shot) / ～况 recent developments; current situation; how things stand / ～邻 near or immediate neighbour / ～年 in recent years / ～因 immediate cause / ～照 recent photo / 在咫尺 close at hand; well within reach; just around the corner ❷ approaching; nearly; close to; 年～不惑 approaching forty; getting on for forty ❸ intimate; closely related; ～友 close or bosom friend ❹ 〈书〉 easy to understand; simple and obvious; 言～旨远 simple words with deep meaning; plain remarks of profound significance

近代 jìndài ❶ modern times (from the 1840's to 1919 in Chinese history) ❷ capitalist era (in world history); modern times

近道 jìndào also "近路" short cut; 走～ follow or take a short cut; 〈喻〉 cut corners

近古 jìngǔ recent antiquity (in Chinese history, roughly from the Song Dynasty to the Opium Wars); from the 10th century to the 1840s

近海 jìnhǎi also "近洋" coastal waters; inshore; offshore; ～渔业 inshore fishing

近乎 jìnhu ❶ nearly; close to; almost; ～神话的宣传 propaganda little short of a fairy tale ❷ 〈方〉 intimate; friendly; clubby

近来 jìnlái recently; of late; lately

近期 jìnqī in the near future; over the short or near term; ～展望 near-term prospect

近亲 jìnqīn close relative; near relation; ～繁殖 close breeding; inbreeding / ～婚姻 consanguineous marriage

近视 jìnshì ❶ myopia; near-sightedness; ～眼 short-sightedness; myopic or near-sighted person ❷ 〈喻〉 short-sightedness

近水楼台 jìnshuǐlóutái waterside pavilion—advantageous position; ～先得月 a waterfront pavilion gets the moonlight first—enjoy the advantage of being in a favoured position

近似 jìnsì approximate; near; similar; ～值 〈数〉 approximate value / 相貌～ look alike

近朱者赤，近墨者黑 jìnzhūzhěchì, jìnmòzhěhēi one who stays near vermilion gets stained red, and one who stays near ink gets stained black—one takes on the colour of one's company;

he who lies with dogs will rise with fleas

妗 jìn

妗子 jìnzi 〈口〉 wife of one's mother's brother; aunt

劲（勁） jìn

❶ physical strength; power; energy:手～ (muscular) strength of the hand ❷ spirit; mood; drive ❸ air; manner; look:瞧他那骄傲～儿! How arrogant he looks! ❹ interest; relish; savour:没～儿 not interesting; boring
see also jìng

劲头 jìntóu 〈口〉 ❶ strength; power; energy ❷ vigour; drive; zeal:～十足 be full of drive or enthusiasm; be keen on

晋（晉） jìn

❶ enter; advance:～京 go to the capital / ～见 *see* "进见" jìnjiàn / ～谒 *also* "进谒"〈书〉call on (sb holding high office); have an audience with ❷ promote:～升 *also* "晋级" promote to a higher office ❸ (Jìn) Jin Dynasty (265-420) ❹ (another name for 山西) Shanxi

烬（燼） jìn

cinder; ashes

浸 jìn

soak; steep; immerse:～没 submerge; flood; immerse / ～泡 soak; immerse / ～渍 soak; ret; macerate

浸礼 jìnlǐ 〈宗教〉(of Christianity) baptism; immersion:为孩子施～ baptize a child / ～会 Baptist Church

浸染 jìnrǎn be contaminated or gradually influenced:～不良习气 contract bad habits

浸透 jìntòu ❶ soak; steep; infuse:汗水～ soaked with sweat / 雨水～了表土。The rain infiltrated the topsoil. ❷〈喻〉immerse; engross:～了旧伦理道德 immersed in old ethics

禁 jìn

❶ prohibit; forbid; ban:～毒 prohibit drugs or narcotics /

～果〈宗教〉〈喻〉forbidden fruit / ～绝 totally prohibit; completely forbid / ～赛 forbid sb to participate in a match (due to violation of rules); suspend from competition (as punishment) / ～书 banned book / ～伐林 forest preserve / ～飞区 no-fly zone ❷ put behind bars; imprison; detain:～押 take into custody ❸ what is forbidden by law or custom; taboo ❹ forbidden area:～城 imperial palace wall / ～地 forbidden or restricted area; out-of-bounds area
see also jīn

禁闭 jìnbì confinement (as a punishment):～室 guardroom

禁锢 jìngù ❶ keep in custody; imprison; jail ❷ confine; enthral; shackle

禁忌 jìnjì ❶ taboo ❷ avoid; abstain from;〈医〉contraindicate:～生冷 avoid eating anything raw or cold

禁军 jìnjūn *also* "禁卫军"〈史〉armed escort of a monarch; imperial guard

禁令 jìnlìng prohibition; ban:解除～ lift or remove a ban

禁脔 jìnluán chunk of meat for one's exclusive consumption; one's exclusive domain or preserve

禁区 jìnqū ❶ forbidden or restricted zone; out-of-bounds area ❷ (of wildlife or vegetation) preserve; reserve; natural park ❸〈体〉(of football) penalty area; (of basketball) restricted area

禁食 jìnshí fast:～疗法 fasting treatment; starvation cure

禁欲 jìnyù suppress sensual enjoyment; be ascetic:～主义 asceticism

禁运 jìnyùn embargo:～品 contraband

禁止 jìnzhǐ prohibit; ban; forbid:～超车区 no-passing zone / ～人入内。No admittance. / ～通行。No thoroughfare. or Closed to traffic. / ～招贴 Post no bills.

觐 jìn

❶ (usu 觐见) present oneself before (a monarch) ❷ go on

a pilgrimage

噤 jìn ❶〈书〉keep silent；～若寒蝉 as silent as a cicada in cold weather—keep silent out of fear ❷ shiver with cold

jīng

茎（莖） jīng （of a plant）stem；stalk；anything like a stem or stalk

京 jīng ❶ capital of a country；～都 also "京城"；"京华" capital of a country／～畿〈书〉capital city and its environs ❷（Jīng）（short for 北京）Beijing：～白〈戏〉parts in Beijing opera spoken in Beijing dialect／～剧 also "京戏" Beijing opera／～腔 also "京片子" Beijing accent／～味之特别 special Beijing flavour；characteristic of Beijing

泾（涇） Jīng （short for 泾河）Jing River：～渭分明 as different as the waters of the Jing and Wei rivers—wholly different

经（經） jīng ❶（usu 经纱）warp ❷〈中医〉channels in the human body；～络 main and collateral channels ❸（usu 经度）〈地〉longitude ❹ manage；rule；deal or engage in：～商 engage in trade；be in business ❺ constant；regular；normal ❻ scripture；canon；classic：～卷 scrolls of Buddhist sutras／～书 Confucian classics ❼〈生理〉menses；menstruation ❽（pass）through；via；by way of：～年累月 year in and year out；for years（on end）／～一事，长一智 live and learn；a fall in the pit，a gain in the wit ❾ stand；bear；endure：～风雨，见世面 see the world and brave the storms；see life and stand its tests

经办 jīngbàn　handle；manage；deal with：一手～ handle sth by oneself

经常 jīngcháng ❶ day-to-day；every-day；regular：～化 become a regular practice ❷ often；frequently；regularly

经典 jīngdiǎn ❶ classics ❷ scriptures ❸ classical：～著作 classical works

经费 jīngfèi　fund；outlay

经管 jīngguǎn　be in charge of；steward

经过 jīngguò ❶ process；course：事情的～ course of an incident ❷ pass（by）；go through；undergo：～认真考虑 after careful consideration ❸ last；continue

经纪 jīngjì ❶ manage（a business）：老于～ experienced in business ❷ also "经纪人" broker；middleman；agent

经济 jīngjì ❶ economy：～师 economist；（as a professional rank）economic administrator／～学 economics／～基础 economic base or basis／～衰退 recession／～特区 special economic zone／～体制 economic structure／～效益 economic efficiency；economic results or effects／～总量 total supply and demand／～一体化 economic integration／～技术开发区 also "经济开发区" economic（technological）development zone ❷ of industrial or economic value；economic：～作物 industrial or cash crop ❸（of）financial condition：～宽裕 well-off；well-to-do；comfortably off ❹ economical；frugal；thrifty：～舱 economy class or cabin

经久 jīngjiǔ ❶ prolonged：～不息 prolonged；enduring ❷ durable；fast：色泽～ fast colour／～耐用 durable；lasting

经理 jīnglǐ ❶ handle；manage ❷ manager；director

经历 jīnglì　experience；undergo；go through：工作～ work experience／长期的磨炼 undergo a long process of tempering

经贸 jīngmào　economy and trade：～公司 trading company

经手 jīngshǒu　handle；manage；deal

with：～人 person handling a particular transaction, job, etc

经受 jīngshòu experience；sustain；stand：～许多苦难 undergo much suffering

经售 jīngshòu ❶ sell on commission；distribute ❷ also "经销" sell；deal in

经心 jīngxīn also "经意" careful；mindful；conscientious：不～地打碎了花瓶 inadvertently break a vase

经验 jīngyàn ❶ experience：～论〈哲〉empiricism / ～之谈 wise counsel of an experienced person / 从～中学习 learn by experience ❷ go through；experience

经营 jīngyíng ❶ manage；operate；run：～权 power of management；managerial authority / ～成本 operating or operation cost；handling cost / ～家电 deal in household electrical appliances ❷ plan and organize：经过十年了，这些树都成林了。The trees have grown into woods after ten years' painstaking care.

经传 jīngzhuàn ❶ Confucian classics and their commentaries；Confucian canon ❷ classical works；classics：名不见～ be not well known；be a mere nobody

荆 jīng chaste tree；bushes：～条 twigs of the chaste tree (used for weaving baskets, etc)

荆棘 jīngjí thistles and thorns；brambles；thorny undergrowth：～丛生 overgrown with brambles—beset with difficulties

菁 jīng

菁华 jīnghuá essence；cream；quintessence

旌 jīng

旌旗 jīngqí banners and flags：～招展 with banners and pennants fluttering in the wind

惊（驚） jīng ❶ start；get alarmed；be frightened；～呆 be stunned or stupefied / ～骇〈书〉be frightened, scared or panic-stricken / ～叫 cry in fear；scream with terror；give a cry of alarm / ～悉〈书〉be shocked or distressed to learn ❷ surprise；shock；amaze：～世骇俗 astounding the world (with an extraordinary idea, etc)；amazing ❸ shy；stampede：～马 startled or runaway horse

惊诧 jīngchà 〈书〉surprised；amazed；astonished

惊动 jīngdòng alarm；alert；disturb：消息～了全校。The whole school was startled by the news.

惊愕 jīng'è 〈书〉shocked；stunned；stupefied：～不已 unable to recover from one's shock；totally stupefied

惊弓之鸟 jīnggōngzhīniǎo (like a) bird that shies at the sight of a bow；badly frightened person

惊慌 jīnghuāng alarmed；scared；frightened：～失措 frightened out of one's wits；seized with panic；paralysed with fear

惊惶 jīnghuáng alarmed；terrified；panic-stricken

惊魂 jīnghún state of terror；frightened expression；panic-stricken look：～未定 have not yet recovered from fright；be still badly shaken

惊恐 jīngkǒng terrified；panic-stricken；seized with terror：～万状 in great panic；convulsed with fear

惊奇 jīngqí wonder；marvel；be surprised or amazed：令人～ surprising；amazing

惊扰 jīngrǎo alarm；agitate；disturb：自相～ raise a false alarm

惊人 jīngrén astounding；astonishing；amazing：～之举 masterstroke；*coup de maitre*

惊师动众 jīngshī-dòngzhòng mobilize many people (for a task); make a tremendous fuss (over sth); 别为这点小事一啦。Don't try to arouse so many people for such a petty cause.

惊叹 jīngtàn exclaim with admiration; wonder; marvel; ～号 exclamation mark (!)

惊涛骇浪 jīngtāo-hàilàng terrifying waves; stormy sea; hazards in life

惊天动地 jīngtiān-dòngdì (of sound) extremely loud; earth-shaking; world-shaking

惊喜 jīngxǐ pleasantly surprised; ～交集 be filled with elation and amazement; have mixed feelings of surprise and joy

惊吓 jīngxià frighten; terrify; scare

惊险 jīngxiǎn alarmingly dangerous; breathtaking; thrilling; ～片 thriller; adventure film

惊心动魄 jīngxīn-dòngpò soul-stirring; profoundly moving

惊醒 jīngxǐng ❶ wake up with a start ❷ rouse suddenly from sleep

惊讶 jīngyà surprised; amazed; astonished

惊异 jīngyì astonished; amazed; taken aback;～得说不出话来 be struck dumb

惊蛰 jīngzhé Waking of Insects, 3rd seasonal division point　*see also* "节气" jiéqì

晶 jīng ❶ bright; shiny; glittering;～莹 sparkling and crystal-clear; glittering and translucent ❷ quartz; (rock) crystal ❸ any crystal-line substance;冰～ ice crystal

晶体 jīngtǐ crystal;～管 transistor /～结构 crystal structure

睛 jīng eyeball;定～细看 give (sth or sb) a good look

粳(粳) jīng (usu 粳稻) round-grained non-glutinous rice;～米 polished round-grained rice

兢 jīng

兢兢业业 jīngjīngyèyè cautious and conscientious

精 jīng ❶ refined; polished; choice; ～盐 refined or table salt /～白米 polished white rice /～饲料 concentrated feed; concentrate; rich nourishing feed ❷ essence; concentrate; extract;～华 cream; essence; quintessence / 樟脑～ spirit of camphor ❸ excellent; exquisite; intensive; ～度 precision; accuracy /～妙 exquisite and ingenious /～耕细作 intensive and meticulous farming; intensive cultivation ❹ smart; astute; shrewd;～明 astute; shrewd; smart ❺ skilled; versed; proficient;～于算术 be skilled in numbers ❻ energy; vigour; spirit; 无～打采 listless; lackadaisical ❼〈生理〉sperm; semen; seed;～子 sperm; spermatozoon ❽ goblin; spirit; demon ❾〈方〉extremely; very; awfully;～光 with nothing left; completely (finished) /～瘦 as thin as a lath

精兵 jīngbīng picked troops; crack troops;～强将 picked troops and good generals; crack forces

精兵简政 jīngbīng-jiǎnzhèng better troops and simpler administration; better staff and streamlined administration

精彩 jīngcǎi brilliant; marvelous; wonderful

精诚 jīngchéng〈书〉absolute sincerity; good faith;～团结 unite as one /～所至,金石为开。Absolute sincerity can conquer all.

精粹 jīngcuì pure and exquisite; pithy; succinct;品质～(of) pure and excellent quality

精打细算 jīngdǎ-xìsuàn careful calculation and strict budgeting

精当 jīngdàng precise and appropriate;评论～ make pertinent comments

精到 jīngdào precise and penetrating;

careful and thorough

精雕细刻 jīngdiāo-xìkè　*also* "精雕细镂" work (at sth) with the care and precision of a sculptor; work (at sth) with meticulous care

精读 jīngdú　❶ read carefully and thoroughly ❷ intensive reading (as a course)

精干 jīnggàn　❶ (of a body of troops, etc) small in number but highly trained; crack ❷ keen-witted and capable; smart and efficient

精悍 jīnghàn　❶ smart and efficient; capable and energetic ❷ pithy and poignant; terse: 文笔~ terse writing

精简 jīngjiǎn　simplify; streamline; cut (down): ~机构 simplify or streamline administrative structure; downsize management

精力 jīnglì　energy; vitality; vigour: ~充沛 vigorous; energetic; full of vim and vigour

精练 jīngliàn　*also* "精炼" concise; terse; succinct

精良 jīngliáng　(of weapons, etc) excellent; superior; of the best quality

精灵 jīnglíng　❶ spirit; demon ❷ 〈方〉 clever guy; smart fellow: 小~ smart kid

精美 jīngměi　superb; delicate; elegant: ~的工艺品 exquisite handicraft

精密 jīngmì　precise; exact; accurate: ~仪器 precision instrument / ~的分工 clear-cut division of labour

精明 jīngmíng　astute; shrewd; smart: ~强干 intelligent and capable; able and efficient

精疲力竭 jīngpí-lìjié　*also* "筋疲力尽" exhausted; worn or tired out; played out

精辟 jīngpì　penetrating; incisive; insightful

精品 jīngpǐn　work created with painstaking effort; work of a high order;

top-quality product

精巧 jīngqiǎo　fine; exquisite; ingenious

精确 jīngquè　accurate; exact; precise: ~度 measure of precision

精锐 jīngruì　crack; picked: ~的王牌军 elite army

精深 jīngshēn　deep; profound: 学术造诣~ profound scholarship

精神 jīngshén　❶ spirit; mind; consciousness: ~病〔医〕mental disease or disorder; psychosis / ~境界 mental outlook; spiritual ethos / ~疗法 mental therapeutics; psychotherapy; mind cure / ~世界 inner or mental world / ~文明 cultural and ideological progress; (advanced) culture and ideology or ethics; spiritual civilization / ~支柱 mental or ideological prop ❷ essence; gist; spirit: 宪法的~与文字 spirit and letter of the constitution ❸ (jīngshen) vigour; energy; drive: 振作~ bestir oneself; summon up one's energy; get up steam / ~焕发 be in high spirits; one's spirits rise / ~头儿〔口〕vim and vigour

精髓 jīngsuǐ　marrow; pith; quintessence

精通 jīngtōng　be proficient in; be well versed in; have a good command of: ~法律 have an intimate knowledge of law

精细 jīngxì　❶ meticulous; fine; careful: 做工~ fine workmanship ❷ sharp and careful; shrewd; smart: 为人~ be a shrewd guy

精心 jīngxīn　take great pains; work painstakingly; be meticulous or elaborate: ~治疗 give meticulous (medical) treatment

精选 jīngxuǎn　carefully select or choose: ~本 select version / ~的良种 choice seeds of improved strains

精益求精 jīngyìqiújīng　constantly improve; keep improving: 业务上~ constantly improve and perfect one's professional skill

精英 jīngyīng ❶ cream; essence; quintessence ❷ the best and the brightest; elite:学术～ outstanding scholars

精湛 jīngzhàn consummate; superb; exquisite

精制 jīngzhì make with extra care; refine:～品 highly finished products; superfines / ～糖 refined sugar

精致 jīngzhì fine; exquisite; delicate

精装 jīngzhuāng ❶ (of books) clothbound; hardback; hardcover:～本 de luxe edition ❷ (commodities) elegantly or elaborately packed

精壮 jīngzhuàng able-bodied; strong; robust

鲸 jīng (usu 鲸鱼) whale:～吞 swallow like a whale; gobble up; annex (a large tract of territory, etc)

jǐng

井 jǐng ❶ well; sth in the shape of a well:～底之蛙 frog at the bottom of a well—person with a very limited outlook or vision ❷ in good order:～～有条 in perfect order; shipshape; methodical

井然 jǐngrán 〈书〉orderly; neat and tidy; systematic:～有序 in apple-pie order; orderly; methodical

井水不犯河水 jǐngshuǐbùfànhéshuǐ I'll mind my own business, you mind yours; not interfere with each other

刭(剄) jǐng 〈书〉cut the throat:自～ cut one's own throat; commit suicide

颈(頸) jǐng neck; anything shaped like the neck:～椎〈生理〉cervical vertebra

景 jǐng ❶ view; sight; scene:～点 scenic spot / ～区 scenic spot or area / ～物 scene; sight; view / ～致 also "景观" landscape; scenery; sight worth seeing ❷ situation; condition;

circumstances ❸ scenery (of a play or film); setting ❹ scene (of a play):第一幕第二～ Act I, Scene II ❺ admire; esteem; respect:～仰其人格 admire sb for his or her integrity

景况 jǐngkuàng situation; condition; circumstances:～不佳 be in straitened circumstances; not get on very well

景气 jǐngqì prosperity; boom; state of the economy:～周期 business cycle / 市场不～. The market is sluggish.

景色 jǐngsè scenery; landscape; view:～如画 picturesque

景泰蓝 jǐngtàilán cloisonné (enamel)

景象 jǐngxiàng scene; sight; picture:一派忙碌的～ a scene of hustle and bustle

儆 jǐng warn; admonish:～戒 warn (sb) against making mistakes again; warn (sb) to correct mistakes

憬 jǐng (usu 憬悟)〈书〉wake up to reality; come to see the truth, one's error, etc

警 jǐng ❶ alert; vigilant; keen ❷ (give a) warning; alarm; emergency:～示 serve as or give a warning / ～世良言 wise counsel that admonishes the world ❸ (short for 警察) police; policeman:～方 the police (authorities) / ～衔 police rank / ～匪片 cop-and-robber movie

警报 jǐngbào alarm; warning; alert:～器 siren; alarm / 发布台风～ issue a typhoon warning

警备 jǐngbèi guard; garrison:～区〈军〉garrison command / ～森严 tightly garrisoned; heavily guarded

警察 jǐngchá police; policeman:女～ policewoman / ～局 police station

警告 jǐnggào ❶ remind; alert; put on one's guard ❷ warn; caution; admonish:受到严重～处分 be given a serious warning (as a disciplinary measure)

J

警戒 jǐngjiè ❶ *also* "警诫" warn; admonish ❷ be on the alert; guard; keep a close watch: ~哨 outguard; picket guard / ~线 cordon; security line; warning line (for water level, etc)

警句 jǐngjù aphorism; epigram; witty remark

警觉 jǐngjué ❶ vigilance; alertness; awareness: 提高~ be more vigilant ❷ sound an alarm; warn against; awaken (to a danger, etc)

警惕 jǐngtì be vigilant or on guard; watch out; be on the alert: ~性 vigilance; alertness

警卫 jǐngwèi ❶ guardsman; guard: ~员 bodyguard ❷ guard (a place, etc)

警醒 jǐngxǐng ❶ be a light sleeper ❷ *also* "警省" warn; caution; alert

警钟 jǐngzhōng alarm bell; tocsin: 敲~ sound the alarm

jìng

劲（勁） jìng strong; vigorous; powerful: ~敌 formidable adversary; strong opponent or foe / ~旅 crack troops; strong contingent or team / ~射 (in football, etc) make a forceful or powerful shot / ~拔的苍松 tall sturdy pine　*see also* jìn

径（徑） jìng ❶ footpath; trail; track: ~赛〈体〉track event ❷ way; road; means ❸〈副〉directly; straight; straightaway: ~直 straightly; straightaway / ~自 without leave; without consulting anyone / ~行处理 dispose of sth directly; handle sth straightaway ❹ (short for 直径) diameter

净（淨） jìng ❶ clean: ~水 clean water / ~土 clean, unpolluted place ❷ wipe (sth) clean; wash: ~菜 ready-to-cook vegetable / ~场 *also* "静场" have spectators leave the cinema or theatre after the show ends / ~化 purify; cleanse; clean / ~手 wash one's hands;〈婉〉relieve oneself ❸ with nothing left; completely: 用~ use up ❹ net; pure: ~高 clear height (of a structure, etc) / ~余 remainder; surplus / ~值 net worth or value / ~重 net weight ❺ nothing but; only; merely: ~尽 completely; utterly / 遍地~是树叶。The ground was covered with leaves. ❻ *also* "花脸" (in traditional Chinese opera) male character with a darkish painted face

胫（脛） jìng shin; ~骨〈生理〉shin bone; tibia

痉（痙） jìng

痉挛 jìngluán convulsion; spasm; fit: 胃~ spasm of the stomach

竞（競） jìng compete; contend; vie: ~标 compete for a bid or tender / ~拍 auction; compete by bidding; bid / ~走〈体〉(heel-and-toe) walking race

竞技 jìngjì sports; athletics: ~场 arena; sports ground / ~运动 athletic sports / ~状态好 be in good form

竞赛 jìngsài contest; competition; race

竞相 jìngxiāng compete or vie with each other: ~购买 vie in buying; fall over each other to buy (sth); scramble to buy

竞选 jìngxuǎn enter into an election contest; campaign for (office); stand or run for: ~纲领 election programme / ~总统 run for the presidency

竞争 jìngzhēng compete; vie; contend: ~性 competitiveness / ~机制 competitive mechanism / ~意识 competition-awareness / ~优势 competitive edge

竟 jìng ❶ end; finish; complete: 未~事业 unfinished task or work ❷ from beginning to end; throughout;

whole；～日 throughout the day；all day long ❸〈书〉in the end；finally；eventually ❹〈副〉 *used to indicate unexpectedness or surprise*：～至（于）go so far as to；go to the length of；have the impudence or effrontery to

竟然 jìngrán〈副〉*same as* 竟❹：～如此简单？As simple as that？

敬

jìng ❶ respect；honour；esteem：～辞 term of respect；polite expression／～意 respect；tribute／～重 deeply respect；esteem；honour／～老院 home of respect for the aged；old folk's home ❷ respectfully；reverently：～告 beg to inform or notify／～献 present politely；offer respectfully／谢不敏〈套〉beg to be excused；regret being unable to comply with the request／～祝身体健康。Wish you good health. ❸ offer politely：～茶 serve tea

敬爱 jìng'ài respect and love：～的老师（respected and）beloved teacher

敬而远之 jìng'éryuǎnzhī stay at a respectful distance from（sb）；hold at arm's length；give（sb or sth）a wide berth

敬贺 jìnghè〈敬〉congratulate（sb on sth）；offer congratulations：～新年快乐！Wishing you a Happy New Year！

敬酒 jìngjiǔ propose a toast；toast：～不吃吃罚酒〈俗〉refuse a toast only to drink a forfeit—be forced to do what one at first declined

敬礼 jìnglǐ ❶ give a salute；send greetings；salute ❷ *used at the end of a letter*：此致～ with high respect；with best wishes

敬佩 jìngpèi look up to；admire

敬畏 jìngwèi hold in awe and veneration；revere：心存～ stand in awe（of sb）

敬仰 jìngyǎng *also*"敬慕"respect and admire（sb for sth）；hold in high esteem；revere：受人～的学者 scholar who commands reverence

敬业 jìngyè dedicate oneself to work or study：～精神 professional dedication or ethics

靖

jìng ❶ peace；tranquillity ❷ pacify；suppress：～乱 put down a rebellion

静

jìng ❶ still；calm；motionless：～寂的山谷 still mountain valley ❷ silent；noiseless：～谧〈书〉quiet；calm；tranquil／～穆 solemn and quiet／～养 rest quietly to recuperate；convalesce／～候佳音 quietly awaiting the good news／请大家～一～。Please be quiet.

静电 jìngdiàn〈理〉static（electricity）：～感应 electrostatic induction

静脉 jìngmài〈生理〉vein：～炎〈医〉phlebitis／～曲张〈医〉varicosity／～注射 intravenous injection

静默 jìngmò ❶ become silent ❷ mourn in silence；observe silence：～三分钟 observe three minutes' silence

静悄悄 jìngqiāoqiāo very quiet：四处～。It was quiet all round.

静态 jìngtài static（state）：～分析 static analysis

静物 jìngwù still life：～画 still life（drawing）

静心 jìngxīn ease or peace of mind：～读书 be engrossed in study or reading

静止 jìngzhǐ static；motionless；at a standstill：～地看待事物 view things as static／风～下来了。The wind subsided.

静坐 jìngzuò ❶ sit quietly and still ❷ sit down；sit in：～示威 sit-in demonstration；sit-down protest

境

jìng ❶ border；boundary：～外 abroad；overseas ❷ place；area；territory：～域〈书〉area；domain；realm／进入山东～内 enter Shandong Province ❸ condition；situation；circumstances：～况 condition；circumstances

境地 jìngdì condition；circumstances；

plight: 陷入尴尬 ～ find oneself in an embarrassing situation

境界 jìngjiè ❶ boundary ❷ extent reached; plane attained; state; 崇高的精神～ lofty realm of spirit

境遇 jìngyù (usu undesirable) circumstances; one's lot: ～不佳 be in wretched circumstances

镜 jìng ❶ looking glass; mirror: ～框 picture frame / ～花水月 flowers in a mirror or the moon in the water—illusion ❷ lens; eyeglass: ～片 lens

镜头 jìngtóu ❶ camera lens ❷ shot; scene: 电影～ cinema scene / 特技～ special effects or trick shot

jiǒng

迥 jiǒng 〈书〉 ❶ remote; far away ❷ widely different: ～异 widely different; diametrically opposed / 性情～然不同 poles apart in temperament

炯 jiǒng 〈书〉 bright; shining: ～～有神 (of eyes) gleaming and penetrating

窘 jiǒng ❶ hard up; short of money; in straitened circumstances ❷ awkward; embarrassed; ill at ease; ～况 also "窘境" awkward situation; predicament; plight / ～态 embarrassed look ❸ embarrass; upset; disconcert

窘迫 jiǒngpò ❶ poverty-stricken; very poor ❷ hard-pressed; embarrassed; in a predicament

jiū

纠 jiū ❶ entangle; involve: ～葛 entanglement; dispute / ～结一团 an entangled mass ❷ band together; assemble: ～集 also "鸠集" 〈贬〉 get together; collect; muster ❸ correct; rectify; right: ～风 rectify professional malpractices or unhealthy trends / ～偏 correct or rectify a deviation

纠察 jiūchá maintain order at a public gathering; picket: ～队 pickets / ～线 picket line

纠缠 jiūchán ❶ get entangled or involved; be in a tangle ❷ trouble (sb); bother; pester

纠纷 jiūfēn dispute; quarrel; issue

纠合 jiūhé also "鸠合" 〈贬〉 band or gather together; collect: ～多数 line up or muster a majority

纠正 jiūzhèng correct; rectify; redress: ～冤案 redress or right a wrong verdict

鸠 jiū ❶ turtledove ❷ see "纠❷"

究 jiū ❶ study carefully; probe into; investigate: ～其根源 get to the bottom (of sth); trace (sth) to its very source; find out the whys and wherefores ❷ 〈书〉 actually; really; after all

究竟 jiūjìng ❶ outcome; truth; whole story ❷ used in questions for emphasis: ～是谁说了算? Who exactly has the final say? ❸ after all; in the final analysis

赳 jiū

赳赳 jiūjiū valiant; gallant

阄(鬮) jiū lot: 抓～儿 draw lots

揪 jiū ❶ hold tight; grab; seize: ～辫子 also "抓辫子" seize upon sb's faults or errors; capitalize on sb's weak point ❷ pull; tug; drag: ～出 ferret out; uncover; catch

揪心 jiūxīn 〈方〉 anxious; troubled; worried: 叫人～ worrisome

啾 jiū

啾啾 jiūjiū 〈象声〉 ❶ used of small birds and insects: 小鸟～ chirping or twittering birds ❷ used of *horses*，*bells*，*etc*战马声～。The war-horses were neighing.

鬏 jiū （of hair）bun；knot；chignon：把头发梳个～ wear one's hair in a bun

jiǔ

九 jiǔ ❶ nine：～层 ninth floor／～折 ten per cent discount／～族〈旧〉nine forms of kinship—all one's relatives／～成新 ninety per cent new／～～表 multiplication table／～头鸟 legendary evil bird with nine heads；cunning and deceitful man ❷ each of the nine nine-day periods following the Winter Solstice ❸ numerous；many

九九归一 jiǔjiǔguīyī *also* "九九归原" when all is said and done；all in all；in the last analysis

九牛二虎之力 jiǔniú'èrhǔzhīlì herculean effort；utmost exertion：费尽～ exert oneself to the utmost；use every ounce of one's strength；do all one can

九牛一毛 jiǔniúyìmáo a single hair out of numerous ox hides—a drop in the ocean；just peanuts

九曲 jiǔqū （with）numerous bends；twists and turns：～桥 zigzag bridge／～回肠 knot in one's stomach；pent-up feelings of sadness

九泉 jiǔquán 〈书〉grave；nether world：～之下 in the nether world；after death

九死一生 jiǔsǐ-yìshēng escape by the skin of one's teeth；miss death by a hair's breadth

九天 jiǔtiān ninth heaven；highest of heavens

九霄 jiǔxiāo highest heavens；sky of the skies：～云外 beyond the highest heavens；immeasurably far away

九月 jiǔyuè ❶ September ❷ ninth month of the lunar year；ninth

moon

九州 jiǔzhōu （nine administrative divisions of ancient）China

久 jiǔ ❶ for a long time；long：～别重逢 meet again after a long separation／～～不能成眠。It was quite a while before he fell asleep. ❷ of a specified duration：他去了多～了？How long has he been away？

久病 jiǔbìng be ill for a long time：～初愈 have just recovered from a long illness／～成医。〈俗〉Prolonged illness makes a doctor of a patient.

久而久之 jiǔ'érjiǔzhī after a long time；in the course of time；over time

久旱逢甘雨 jiǔhànfénggānyǔ have a welcome rain after a prolonged spell of drought—have a long-felt desire satisfied

久经 jiǔjīng experience for a long time；go through repeatedly：～风霜 weather-beaten；seasoned／～考验 long-tested

久违 jiǔwéi 〈套〉It's a long time since we last met；I haven't seen you for ages.

久仰 jiǔyǎng *also* "久慕"〈套〉（usu said at first meeting）long admire；long look forward to：～大名。I've long been looking forward to meeting you.

久远 jiǔyuǎn far back；ages ago；time-honoured

玖 jiǔ nine（used for the numeral 九 on cheques，etc，to avoid mistakes or alterations）

灸 jiǔ 〈中医〉moxibustion

韭（韭） jiǔ （usu 韭菜）Chinese chives：青～ young chives／黄～ hotbed chives

酒 jiǔ alcoholic drink；wine；liquor：～吧 bar（room）／～鬼 drunkard；sot；tippler／～会 cocktail party／～量 capacity for liquor；drinking capacity／～令 drinkers' wager game／～水 drinks；beverages and alcohol / ～席 also "酒宴" banquet; feast / ～囊饭袋 wine pot and rice bag — good-for-nothing / 撒～疯 throw a drunken fit; be crazy drunk / 不胜～力 cannot hold (that) much liquor

酒店 jiǔdiàn ❶ also "酒馆" wine shop; public house; pub ❷ hotel

酒后 jiǔhòu after drinking alcohol; when drunk; ～开车 drunk driving; driving when under the influence of alcohol / ～失言 make indiscreet remarks under the influence of alcohol; when wine is in, wit is out

酒精 jiǔjīng (ethyl) alcohol; ～灯 spirit lamp; alcohol burner / ～中毒 alcoholism

酒酿 jiǔniàng fermented glutinous rice; ～圆子 dumplings cooked in fermented glutinous rice soup

酒肉朋友 jiǔròupéngyǒu wine-and-meat friend; fair-weather friend

酒色 jiǔsè wine and women; ～财气 wine, women, avarice, and pride—the four cardinal vices / ～之徒 one who lusts after wine and women; libertine; debauchee

酒意 jiǔyì signs of getting tipsy; tipsy feeling; 有几分～ somewhat drunk; squiffy

酒窝 jiǔwō also "酒涡" dimple

酒糟鼻 jiǔzāobí also "酒渣鼻" acne rosacea; brandy nose

jiù

旧（舊） jiù ❶ past; outdated; old; ～时 also "旧日" old times or days / ～俗 old custom / ～病复发 have a relapse; slip back into old ways / ～事重提 rake up sth of the past; bring up an old score / ～瓶装新酒 new wine in an old bottle; new content in old form / ～石器时代（考古）Old Stone Age; Palaeolithic era / 不念～恶 forgive an old wrong; let bygones

be bygones ❷ used; worn; second-hand; ～车 used or second-hand car ❸ former; one-time; ～居 former residence; old home / ～址 former site / ～地重游 revisit a once-familiar place / 不忘～情 remember an old-time friendship / 恢复～观 restore (sth) to its former look ❹ old friendship; old friend or acquaintance; ～交 old acquaintance / ～雨新知 acquaintances, old and new

旧调重弹 jiùdiàochóngtán also "老调重弹" play the same old tune; rehash old ideas

旧货 jiùhuò old or used goods; second-hand goods; junk; ～店 second-hand shop; junk shop

旧历 jiùlì old Chinese calendar; lunar calendar; ～年（now 春节）Chinese New Year; Spring Festival

旧式 jiùshì old type or fashion; ～房子 old-style building / ～婚姻 traditional marriage

旧体诗 jiùtǐshī also "旧诗" classical poetry (as distinct from vernacular poetry)

旧物 jiùwù ❶ old books, records and institutions; old relics ❷ former territory; 光复～ recover lost territories

臼 jiù ❶ mortar; 石～ stone mortar ❷ any mortar-shaped thing; ～齿 molar

咎 jiù ❶ fault; blame; ～由自取 have only oneself to blame; be one's own worst enemy ❷ censure; punish; blame; 自～ blame or reproach oneself ❸ ill luck; bad fortune

疚 jiù 〈书〉remorse; guilt; compunction; 愧～ guilty conscience; compunction

柩 jiù coffin with a corpse in it; ～车 hearse

厩（廐） jiù stable; cattle-shed; pen; ～肥 〈农〉barnyard manure

救 jiù rescue; save; salvage;～驾 save the emperor from danger;〈谑〉save one from an awkward situation, etc /～星 saviour; liberator; emancipator /～灾 provide disaster relief; fight a disaster /～死扶伤 heal the wounded and rescue the dying

救兵 jiùbīng relief troops; reinforcements;搬～ call in or ask for reinforcements

救护 jiùhù relieve (a sick or injured person); give first-aid; rescue:～车 ambulance /～站 ambulance corps /～站 first-aid station

救荒 jiùhuāng send relief to a famine area; help to tide over a crop failure:生产～ relieve famine by promoting production

救火 jiùhuǒ fire-fighting;～车 fire engine or truck /～队 fire brigade or company /～队员 fireman; fire fighter

救急 jiùjí help cope with an emergency; help meet a pressing need:～不救贫.〈俗〉You can help someone cope with an emergency but you can't save him from poverty.

救济 jiùjì relieve; succour /～金 relief money or fund

救苦救难 jiùkǔ-jiùnàn help the needy and relieve the distressed; relieve people of their sufferings:～的观世音 benevolent Goddess of Mercy

救命 jiùmìng save sb's life:～稻草 straw to clutch at /～恩人 saviour /～! Help!

救生 jiùshēng life-saving:～圈 lifebuoy or life ring /～艇 lifeboat /～衣 life jacket /～员 lifeguard; life-saver

救世主 Jiùshìzhǔ the Saviour; the Redeemer

救亡 jiùwáng save the nation from subjugation; strive for national salvation

救援 jiùyuán come to sb's rescue or relief; rescue; relieve;～物资 relief supplies

救助 jiùzhù help (sb) in danger or difficulty; succour

就 jiù ❶ come near; move towards:～着烛光看书 read by candlelight ❷ get into or onto; engage in; embark on:～餐 have one's meal /～读 also "就学" attend school; study /～医 also "就诊" seek medical advice; get medical treatment; see a doctor ❸ used to introduce a passive action:～聘 accept an invitation or appointment /～擒 be arrested or caught /～刑 be punished or executed ❹ accomplish; attain; make:草草写～ finish writing hastily ❺ take advantage of; accommodate oneself to; suit ❻ (of food, etc) go with (wine, rice, etc):～菜吃饭 eat rice with the dishes; act according to circumstances ❼〈副〉at once; right away; immediately:我这～来. I'm coming. or I'll be right there. ❽〈副〉used to indicate concession or supposition:你～跪下求他,他也不答应. He would not relent, even if you begged him on bended knees. ❾〈副〉used for emphasis or affirmation:办公室～在这里. The office is right here. ❿〈副〉used between two identical words or expressions to express tolerance or resignation:去～去! I'll go if I must. ⓫〈副〉only; merely; just:怎么～你去? Why are you the only one going? ⓬ with regard to; as far as; concerning:～目前况来看 as matters now stand

就伴 jiùbàn keep (sb) company; be in (sb's) company

就便 jiùbiàn also "就手" at one's convenience; while one is at it:～把信发了 post a letter on one's way

就此 jiùcǐ at this point; here and now; thus:～告一段落 thus come to a close

就地 jiùdì on the spot; on site:～取材

make use of indigenous materials; draw on local resources or talents / ～正法 execute (a criminal) on the spot; execute summarily

就范 jiùfàn　submit; give in; conform

就教 jiùjiào　〈敬〉ask for advice; consult: 有个问题向大家～。I have a question to discuss with you.

就近 jiùjìn　(do or get sth) nearby; in the neighbourhood: ～上学 (of children, etc) go to a nearby school

就里 jiùlǐ　inside information: 不知～ have no inside information; be at sea

就寝 jiùqǐn　retire for the night; turn in; go to bed

就任 jiùrèn　take up one's post; take or assume office: ～要职 take up an important post

就势 jiùshì　❶ make use of the momentum of sth or sb ❷ (do sth) while one is at sth else; at one's convenience

就事论事 jiùshìlùnshì　consider or judge sth as it stands; deal with a matter on its merits

就是 jiùshì　❶ usu used with 了 at the end of a sentence to express affirmation: 我一定照办, 你放心～了。Please rest assured that I'll do as you wish. ❷ that is so; exactly; precisely: ～, ～, 你的意见很好嘛。Exactly, your suggestion is quite good. ❸ used for emphasis: 随你怎么说, 我～不愿意。You may say what you like, but I just won't do it. ❹ only; simply; just: 他～喜欢钓鱼。He likes nothing but fishing. ❺ see "就算"

就是说 jiùshìshuō　that is to say; in other words; namely

就算 jiùsuàn　(used together with 也) even if; granted that: ～有困难也得干。We must do it even if there are difficulties.

就位 jiùwèi　take one's place or seat; be seated at the table

就绪 jiùxù　be in order; be all set; be

ready

就要 jiùyào　(usu used with 了) near; about to; on the point of: 春节～到了。The Spring Festival is drawing near.

就业 jiùyè　find employment; take up an occupation; get a job: ～率 employment rate / ～机会 job opportunity / ～人口 working population / ～指导 vocational or placement guidance

就义 jiùyì　die a martyr: 英勇～ die a hero's death

就正 jiùzhèng　〈敬〉solicit comments (on one's writing, etc)

就职 jiùzhí　assume office: ～典礼 inaugural ceremony; inauguration / ～演说 inaugural speech

就座 jiùzuò　also "就坐" take one's seat; be seated

舅 jiù　❶ mother's brother; maternal uncle: ～～ also "舅父"〈口〉mother's brother; uncle / ～妈 also "舅母"〈口〉wife of mother's brother; aunt ❷ wife's brother; brother-in-law: 大～子〈口〉wife's elder brother

鹫 jiù　also "雕"〈动物〉vulture

jū

车(車) jū　❶ (of Chinese chess) chariot ❷ (of chess) castle; rook
see also chē

拘 jū　❶ arrest; detain; take into custody: ～捕 also "拘拿" arrest / ～禁 also "拘押" detain; take into custody / ～役 short term of forced labour under detention ❷ adhere to rigidly; be inflexible ❸ restrain; confine; restrict: ～礼 be punctilious (about etiquette); stand on ceremony

拘谨 jūjǐn　overcautious; reserved; punctilious

拘留 jūliú　detain; hold in custody; intern：～所 house of detention；lock-up／～审讯 detain for interrogation

拘泥 jūnì　be a stickler for（form）；cling to（formalities，etc）；be confined to

拘束 jūshù　❶ restrain；restrict；行动受到～ be restricted in one's activities ❷ constrained；embarrassed；ill at ease

狙 jū

狙击 jūjī　ambush；snipe at：～手 sniper／～战（军）sniping action

居 jū　❶ reside；dwell；live：～家 stay at home；keep house／～丧 *also*「居哀」〈书〉observe mourning for one's deceased parent／～孀〈书〉live as a widow；be widowed／～所 residence；dwelling（place）❷ residence；house；home ❸ be（in a certain position）；occupy（a place）：厂里女工～多。Women workers make up the majority in the plant. ❹ claim；assert：以老资格自～ flaunt one's seniority ❺〈书〉stay put；be at a standstill ❻ *used in the names of some restaurants*：同和～ Tonghe Restaurant

居安思危 jū'ānsīwēi　think of danger in times of peace；be vigilant in peace time

居高临下 jūgāo-línxià　occupy a commanding position；〈喻〉take on a condescending air

居功 jūgōng　claim credit for oneself；parade one's merits：～自傲 be arrogant because of one's achievements

居留 jūliú　reside：～权 right of residence or abode／～证 residence permit

居民 jūmín　resident；inhabitant；dweller：～点 residential area；settlement／～委员会（shortened as 居委会）neighbourhood or residents' committee

居然 jūrán　unexpectedly；to one's surprise；(go) so far as：他～会干出这样的事来！He went so far as to do

such a thing！or Fancy his doing it！

居士 jūshì　❶ lay Buddhist ❷ retired scholar

居室 jūshì　❶ housing：～狭小 cramped housing ❷（bed-）room：三～ three-bedroom flat or apartment

居心 jūxīn　harbour（evil）intentions：你是何～？ What are you up to？

居中 jūzhōng　❶ *also*「居间」（work）between two parties：～调停 mediate between two parties；act as a mediator ❷（be）in the middle

居住 jūzhù　live；reside；dwell：～面积 living space／多民族～地区 region inhabited by a number of ethnic groups

驹 jū　❶ fine young horse；colt：千里～ winged steed ❷ foal：怀～ be in foal

掬 jū　hold with both hands：～诚相待 treat sb with all sincerity

锔 jū　mend（crockery，etc）with clamps

裾 jū〈书〉full front（and back）of a Chinese gown

鞠 jū　❶ rear；bring up ❷〈书〉bend

鞠躬 jūgōng　❶ bow：鞠了个 90 度的躬 bow to a 90° angle；make a deep bow ❷〈书〉in a discreet and scrupulous manner：～尽瘁 bend oneself to a task and exert oneself to the utmost；spare no effort in the performance of one's duty

jú

局（⑤偏）jú　❶ chessboard；chess game ❷ game；set；(of baseball，etc) innings ❸ situation；position；state of affairs：～内人 *also*「局中人」one of the inner circle；insider ❹ gathering；party：饭～ dinner party ❺ restrain；constrain；confine：～于一隅 be confined to a locality or part ❻ part；portion：～麻（short for

局部麻醉〈医〉local anaesthesia / ~域网〈信息〉intranet ❼ bureau; department；税务 ~ tax bureau ❽（functional）office; shop; 书 ~ publishing house; bookshop

局部 júbù　part; locality; ~地区 parts of an area; some areas / ~现象 local phenomenon / ~优势 partial superiority

局促 júcù　❶（of a place, etc）narrow; constricted; cramped ❷〈方〉（of time）short ❸ feel or show constraint; be ill at ease; ~不安 be ill at ease; feel embarrassed

局面 júmiàn　phase; prospect; situation; ~一新 enter a new phase; take on a new aspect / 打开 ~ open up a new prospect; make a breakthrough

局势 júshì　situation; 紧张 ~ tense situation; tension

局外 júwài　have nothing to do with (sth); 置身 ~ stand aloof from sth; refuse to be drawn into sth / ~人 outsider

局限 júxiàn　limit; confine; ~性 limitations

桔 jú　see "橘" jú　see also jié

菊 jú　（usu 菊花）chrysanthemum

焗 jú　❶〈方〉steam cooking：盐 ~ 鸡 salted and steamed chicken ❷（usu 焗油）treat hair with cream and steam it to make it soft and shiny

橘 jú　（usu 橘子）tangerine; mandarin orange; ~红 tangerine (colour); reddish orange / ~黄 orange (colour) / ~汁 orange juice

jǔ

咀 jǔ　chew; ~嚼 masticate; chew (the cud); mull over

沮 jǔ

沮丧 jǔsàng　dejected; depressed; dispirited

矩 jǔ　❶ carpenter's square; square; ~尺 also "曲尺" carpenter's square / ~形 also "长方形" rectangle ❷ rules; regulations

举（舉） jǔ　❶ lift; raise; hold up; ~杯 raise one's glass (to propose a toast) / ~重若轻 lift a heavy load easily;〈喻〉handle task difficult with ease ❷ act; work; move; ~步维艰 (find it) difficult to take a step; hard to start ❸ start; begin; initiate; ~义 also "举事"〈书〉stage an uprising; rise in rebellion ❹ elect; choose; recommend; ~代表 elect a representative ❺（short for 举人）〈史〉successful candidate in the imperial examinations at the provincial level ❻ cite; enumerate; give; ~例 give an example; cite an instance / ~要 (give) essentials / ~证 provide evidence / ~不胜 ~ too numerous to mention ❼〈书〉all; whole; entire; ~家 whole family / ~坐 also "举座" all those present

举哀 jǔ'āi　hold a funeral; go into mourning

举办 jǔbàn　conduct; hold; run; ~酒会 give a cocktail party

举报 jǔbào　report (an offence); inform (against an offender); ~信 letter reporting an offence or offender / ~电话 informants' hotline telephone

举措 jǔcuò　move; act; measure; ~失当 make an ill-advised move; take an unwise measure

举动 jǔdòng　movement; move; act; 一举一动 every act and move

举国 jǔguó　whole nation; ~上下 from the leaders of the nation to the common people; the entire nation

举火 jǔhuǒ　〈书〉❶ light a fire; ~为号 light a beacon ❷ light a kitchen fire; do cooking

举荐 jǔjiàn　recommend (a person); 举

贤荐能 recommend the virtuous and the able; promote gifted people

举借 jǔjiè borrow (a large amount of money); raise (a loan)

举目 jǔmù 〈书〉raise the eyes; look: ~远望 look into the distance / ~无亲 have no one to turn to (for help); be a stranger in an alien land

举棋不定 jǔqíbùdìng hesitate about what move to make; be unable to make up one's mind; be irresolute

举世 jǔshì throughout the world; universally: ~闻名 of world renown; world-famous / ~无双 unrivalled; matchless

举手 jǔshǒu raise or put up one's hand(s): ~礼 hand salute / ~表决 vote by a show of hands / ~之劳 (by) lifting a finger / 举双手赞成 be totally in favour; fully support

举行 jǔxíng hold (a meeting, etc); stage; conduct: ~罢工 go on strike

举一反三 jǔyī-fǎnsān draw inferences about other cases from one instance; learn by analogy and judge the whole from the part

举债 jǔzhài 〈书〉borrow money: ~度日 live on borrowed money

举止 jǔzhǐ bearing; manner: ~失措 lose one's presence of mind and show it / ~像军人 bear oneself like a soldier

举重 jǔzhòng weightlifting: ~运动员 weightlifter; lifter

举足轻重 jǔzúqīngzhòng hold the balance; be of crucial importance; prove decisive: ~的影响 decisive influence

龃 jǔ

龃龉 jǔyǔ 〈书〉disagreement; incongruity; discord

踽 jǔ

踽踽 jǔjǔ 〈书〉(walk) alone: ~独行 walk all by oneself

jù

巨（钜） jù huge; great; tremendous: ~变 great or radical change; sea change / ~额 huge sum or amount; enormous; immense / ~富 (person of) immense wealth; billionaire; magnate / ~匠 〈书〉great master (in science, art, etc) / ~头 giant; magnate; tycoon / ~著 monumental work; magnum opus / ~奸大猾 past master of machination and manoeuvre; wily old fox; arrant swindler

巨大 jùdà tremendous; gigantic; enormous: 影响~ exert an enormous influence

巨人 jùrén giant; colossus: 文化~ literary giant / ~症〈医〉gigantism

巨万 jùwàn 〈书〉millions; tens of thousands: 耗资~ spend or cost an immense fortune

巨子 jùzǐ also "巨擘"〈书〉authority; leading figure; tycoon

句 jù ❶ sentence: ~法 sentence structure; syntax / ~号 also "句点" full stop; period (。) (.) / ~型 sentence pattern ❷〈量〉used of language: 几~诗 a few lines of verse / 一~口号 a slogan

拒 jù ❶ resist; repel; ward off: ~捕 resist arrest / ~守 defend (a strategic pass, etc) ❷ refuse; reject: ~付〈经〉refuse payment; dishonour (a cheque) / ~载 (of a taxi driver) refuse to take a passenger

拒绝 jùjué refuse; reject; turn down

具 jù ❶ utensil; tool; implement ❷〈量〉一尸体 a corpse / 一座钟 a desk clock ❸ be endowed or furnished with; possess; have: ~体而微 small but complete; miniature / 各~特色 Each has its own style. ❹〈书〉state; write out; sign: ~名 one's name (to a document, etc); affix

one's signature

具备 jùbèi　possess; have; be provided with: ~信心 have confidence; be confident / ~条件 be qualified (for sth or to do sth)

具体 jùtǐ　❶ concrete; specific; detailed: ~化 specify / ~劳动〈经〉concrete labour　❷ particular; specific; given: ~人选 specific candidate

具有 jùyǒu　possess; have; be provided with: ~约束力 be binding (on sb)

炬 jù　torch; flame

俱 jù　〈书〉all; complete: ~全 complete in all varieties; comprehensive / ~乐部 club

倨 jù　〈书〉haughty; overbearing; arrogant: ~傲无礼 rude and supercilious

剧(劇) jù　❶ drama; play; opera: ~本 play; drama; script / ~场 theatre / ~情 story or plot of a play, etc / ~团 theatrical company; troupe / ~院 theatre; theatrical company; troupe / ~中人 character in a play; cast of characters; dramatis personae / ~作家 playwright; dramatist　❷ acute; sharp; intense: ~毒 deadly poison; highly toxic (matter) / ~烈 violent; severe; fierce / ~增 increase drastically or sharply

据(據) jù　❶ occupy; hold; seize: ~点 strongpoint; stronghold; base / ~守 defend; guard; be entrenched in / ~为己有 take (forcible) possession of; seize (by force); appropriate / ~有一方 occupy an area　❷ rely on or depend on: be based on (rumour, etc): ~传 it is rumoured; people are saying / ~说 also "据称" it is said; they say; reportedly / ~悉 it is reported / ~理力争 argue strongly on just grounds / ~险顽抗 stubbornly resist by taking advantage of strategically difficult terrain　❸ evidence;

proof; certificate: 言必有～ always speak on good grounds; never speak without evidence

距 jù　distance: 株～ distance or space between two plants / ~开幕只有一星期了. It is only one week before the opening day.

距离 jùlí　distance; range: ~远 be at a long distance; be far off / 与期望有很大～ fall far short of one's expectations

惧(懼) jù　fear; dread; frighten: ~内〈书〉henpecked / ~怕 be afraid; fear; dread / 毫无～色 look undaunted

飓 jù

飓风 jùfēng　hurricane

锯 jù　❶ saw: ~末 also "锯屑" sawdust / ~条 saw blade / ~齿形 zigzag　❷ cut with a saw; saw: ~木厂 sawmill; lumber-mill

聚 jù　assemble; gather; get together: ~餐 dine together (usu on festive occasions); have a dinner party / ~赌 gambling party / ~歼 round up and wipe out; annihilate en masse / ~焦 focus (on sth) / ~齐 assemble (at an appointed place) / ~首〈书〉spotlight / ~光灯 spotlight / ~散无常 meet and part by chance / ~众闹事 incite a mob disturbance or riot / 下星期天~一~好吗? Shall we have a get-together next Sunday?

聚宝盆 jùbǎopén　treasure bowl—place rich in natural resources; cornucopia

聚变 jùbiàn　〈理〉fusion: 受控～ controlled fusion

聚会 jùhuì　gather; assemble; get together

聚积 jùjī　accumulate (capital, etc); amass; collect

聚集 jùjí　gather; assemble; crowd: ~力量 gather forces; build up strength

聚精会神 jùjīng-huìshén　concentrate one's attention; be all attention; be all eyes and ears: ~地听课 listen attentively in class

聚居 jùjū　inhabit a region (as a group); live in a compact community: ~点 settlement / ~地区 inhabited region

聚拢 jùlǒng　(of people, etc) gather round or together; gather (things, etc) together

踞 jù　❶ crouch; squat; sit ❷ be entrenched; occupy

遽 jù　hurriedly; speedily; hastily: ~然〈书〉suddenly; abruptly

juān

捐 juān　❶ relinquish; abandon; give up: ~躯 also "捐生" sacrifice one's life; lay down one's life / ~弃前嫌 give up or cast away past grievances; let bygones be bygones ❷ contribute; donate: ~款 (make a) donation or contribution / ~献 donate (clothing, money, etc for a good cause); contribute; present / ~赠 contribute (as a gift); donate; present / ~助 offer (financial or material) assistance; contribute; donate ❸ tax; levy: ~税 taxes and levies

涓 juān　〈书〉tiny stream; trickle: ~滴 tiny drop; dribble; driblet / ~~清泉 trickling clear spring

娟 juān　〈书〉beautiful; graceful: ~秀 (of a girl) beautiful; graceful; (of handwriting, etc) elegant / ~明月 lovely bright moon

圈 juān　shut (pigs, etc) in a pen; (of an animal) confine (to a small space, etc); detain　see also juàn; quān

镌(鐫) juān　(usu 镌刻) 〈书〉engrave; carve; inscribe

juǎn

卷(捲) juǎn　❶ roll (up); curl; fold; ~发 curly or wavy hair; crimp or curl one's hair / ~帘 folding curtain / ~缩 curl up; huddle oneself up / ~烟 cigarette; cigar / ~铺盖〈喻〉pack up and quit; get the sack ❷ sweep along, up, or off; carry along: ~逃 abscond with valuables ❸ sth cylindrical; roll; 纸儿 roll of paper ❹ 〈量〉roll; spool; reel: ~一线 a spool of thread　see also juàn

卷入 juǎnrù　be drawn into; be involved in; get mixed up with; 军事 military involvement

卷土重来 juǎntǔchónglái　stage or make a comeback

juàn

卷 juàn　❶ book, painting, etc, that can be rolled up: ~轴 scroll (of a mounted painting, etc) ❷ volume; fascicle ❸ (usu 卷子) examination paper: 阅~ grade papers ❹ file; dossier: ~宗 file; dossier; folder　see also juǎn

隽(雋) juàn　〈书〉meaningful: ~永 pregnant with implication; significant; enchanting / ~语 pithy remark

倦 juàn　❶ tired; worn out; weary: ~容 tired look / 毫无~意 not feel in the least tired ❷ be weary, tired or bored: ~游归来〈书〉return when weary of vacationing and sightseeing

绢 juàn　thin tough silk: ~花 silk flower

圈 juàn　(of livestock) pen; fold; sty: ~肥 barnyard manure; muck / ~养 rear (livestock) in pens or sties　*see also* juān；quān

眷 juàn ❶ family dependant；～属 family dependants；family；married couple ❷〈书〉have tender feelings for；～恋 be sentimentally attached to；have tender thoughts or deep affection for /～念 think fondly of；feel nostalgic about；have tender thoughts for

juē

撅 juē ❶ stick up；pout（one's lips）；～嘴 pout one's lips；sulk ❷ embarrass openly；contradict ❸〈口〉break（sth long and narrow）；snap；一～两段 break（sth）in two

jué

决（決） jué ❶ make a decision；decide；determine；～议 resolution /～意 set one's mind（on sth）；be determined（to do sth）❷（used before negatives）definitely；absolutely；under any circumstances；～不可能 absolutely impossible；no way /～非偶然 by no means accidental ❸ decide the final result；win or lose；～一胜负 *also* "决一雌雄" fight it out ❹ execute（a person）❺（of flood，etc）breach；burst；堤 breach or burst a dyke

决策 juécè make policy；make a strategic decision；～人 decision or policy maker /～过程 policy-making process

决定 juédìng decide；determine；resolve；～因素 decisive factor；determinant /这事由你～。It's for you to decide. or It's up to you.

决斗 juédòu duel；（喻）life-and-death or decisive struggle；进行～ fight a duel；engage in a life-and-death struggle

决断 juéduàn ❶ make a decision ❷ resolve；determination；resolution；为人颇有～ be a person of resolve

决计 juéjì ❶ decide；make up one's mind（to do sth）❷ definitely；certainly；surely；坚持下去，～成功。Perseverance will surely lead to success.

决绝 juéjué ❶ break off；cut off；sever；与世～ have nothing to do with the world any more ❷ firm；resolute；态度～ be adamant（on a question，etc）

决口 juékǒu （of a dike，etc）be breached；burst；堵住～ stop up or close a breach

决裂 juéliè break with；part company with；rupture；和旧我～ turn over a new leaf

决然 juérán 〈书〉❶ firmly；resolutely；determinedly ❷ definitely；inevitably；undoubtedly

决赛 juésài finals；半～ semi-finals / 四分之一～ quarter-finals

决胜 juéshèng decide the outcome of a battle；determine the victory；～局〈体〉deciding game or set /～阶段 decisive phase

决算 juésuàn final accounting of revenue and expenditure；final accounts；～表 final statement

决心 juéxīn determination；resolution；下～ resolve；make up one's mind / 有～ be resolved（to do sth）

决战 juézhàn decisive battle or engagement；～决胜 fight a decisive battle for the final victory / 决一死战 fight a life-and-death battle；fight to the bitter end

诀 jué ❶ rhymed formula ❷（usu 诀窍）knack；key to success；tricks of the trade ❸（usu 诀别）bid farewell；part（usu for good）

抉 jué

抉择 juézé 〈书〉choose；生死～ choose between life and death

角 jué ❶〈戏〉(type of) role；par ❷（famous）actor or actress ❸ contend; struggle; fight; ~斗 wrestle; fight / ~力 have a trial of strength; wrestle / ~逐 contend (for sth); contest; compete

see also jiāo

角色 juésè role; part: 进入 ~ enter into the spirit of a character; live one's part

觉(覺) jué ❶ sense; feel: 视 ~ sight / ~察 sense; become aware of; perceive ❷ wake (up); awake; become aware or conscious: ~醒 awaken; rouse up from sleep

see also jiào

觉得 juéde ❶ feel: ~恶心 feel sick; be disgusted ❷ think; feel: ~不妥 当 feel sth to be unwise

觉悟 juéwù ❶ consciousness; awareness; understanding: 提高 ~ heighten one's awareness ❷ begin to understand; come to realize; become politically awakened

绝 jué ❶ cut or break off; sever: ~交 break off relations (with sb) / ~经 menopause / 人生路 ~ cut off sb's livelihood ❷ exhaust; use up; finish: ~版 (of a publication) out of print / ~户 childless person or family / ~迹 disappear; be extinct; be stamped out *also* "绝产" crop failure / ~种 *also* "绝灭" become extinct / ~子~孙〈粗〉without offspring ❸ desperate; beyond help; hopeless: ~症 incurable disease; fatal illness / ~处逢生 be unexpectedly rescued from a desperate situation; find one's way out of an impasse ❹ stop breathing; die: ~笔 last words written before one's death; last work of an author or a painter / ~命书 suicide note; note written on the eve of one's execution ❺ unique; superb; matchless: ~ 代佳人 woman of unsurpassed beauty; beauty of beauties / ~世珍品 peerless

treasure / 这真叫 ~ 了。That is superb! or Can you beat that! ❻ extremely; most: ~密 most confidential; top secret; for your eyes only / ~早 extremely early / ~大部分 most part ❼ (used before negatives) absolutely; in the least; on any account: ~无此意 have absolutely no such intentions ❽ *short for* "绝句"

绝壁 juébì precipice

绝唱 juéchàng ❶ acme of perfection: 古今 ~ best for all time ❷ swansong

绝顶 juédǐng ❶ extremely; utterly: 聪明 ~ exceptionally intelligent ❷ 〈书〉highest peak

绝对 juéduì absolute; unconditional: ~多数 absolute majority / ~零度 absolute zero (−273.15℃) / ~正确 perfectly right / ~真理〈哲〉absolute truth / 不要把话说得太 ~ 了。Don't be so sweeping in what you say.

绝技 juéjì *also* "绝活"; "绝艺" unique or consummate skill: 献 ~ show one's superb skill

绝句 juéjù *jueju*, a classical poem of four lines, of five or seven characters each, with a strict tonal pattern and rhyme scheme

绝口 juékǒu (used only in the negative) ❶ cease talking: 赞不 ~ give unstinted praise; praise profusely ❷ keep one's mouth shut: ~不提 never say or breathe a single word (about sth)

绝路 juélù road to ruin; blind alley; impasse: 走上 ~ take the road to ruin; head for one's doom

绝伦 juélún 〈书〉unsurpassed; unrivalled; peerless: 美妙 ~ absolutely wonderful; superb

绝妙 juémiào extremely clever; superb; excellent

绝情 juéqíng be heartless; be heartless: ~的话 harsh, inconsiderate words; words meant to break off relations

J

绝食 juéshí　fast; go on a hunger strike

绝望 juéwàng　hopelessness; despair; 陷入～的心境 sink into despair

绝无仅有 juéwú-jǐnyǒu　only one of its kind; unique

绝育 juéyù　〈医〉sterilization; ～手术 sterilization operation

绝域 juéyù　〈书〉out-of-the-way or inaccessible place; remote foreign land; ～殊方 remote foreign lands and remote regions

绝缘 juéyuán　❶ be cut off or isolated from; 与烟酒～ never smoke or drink ❷〈电〉insulation; ～体 insulator / ～材料 insulating material

绝招 juézhāo　also "绝着" ❶ unique skill ❷ unexpected tricky move; 想出一个～ think up a most unusual trick; conceive an uncommon idea

倔 jué　see also juè

倔强 juéjiàng　also "倔犟" stubborn; unyielding; unbending

掘 jué　dig; excavate; ～墓人 gravedigger / ～土机 excavator / ～地三尺 dig to a depth of three feet; dig deep

崛 jué

崛起 juéqǐ　〈书〉❶ (of a mountain, etc) stand abruptly; rise suddenly ❷ (of a political force, etc) rise; spring into being

脚(腳) jué　see also "角❶❷" jué see also jiǎo

厥 jué　faint; swoon; fall into a coma

谲 jué　〈书〉❶ cheat; swindle; ～诈 cunning; crafty ❷ strange; odd

蕨 jué　〈植〉brake (fern); ～菜 edible tender leaves of brakes

橛 jué　short wooden stake; peg

爵 jué　❶ rank of nobility; peerage; ～位 rank or title of nobility ❷ ancient wine vessel with three legs and a loop handle

爵士 juéshì　❶ knight ❷ (a British title) sir

爵士乐 juéshìyuè　jazz

蹶 jué　fall; setback; ～败 fail

夌

攫 jué

夌铄 juéshuò　〈书〉hale and hearty

攫 jué　(usu 攫取) seize; snatch; grab

镢 jué　(usu 镢头)〈方〉pick; pickaxe

juè

倔 juè　gruff; blunt; irascible; ～脾气 irascible temper / ～头～脑 blunt of manner and gruff of speech　see also jué

jūn

军 jūn　❶ armed forces; army; troops; ～车 military vehicle / ～方 the military / ～费 military expenditure or spending / ～号 bugle / ～舰 also "兵舰" warship; naval vessel / ～龄 length of military service / ～旗 army flag; military banner; colours / ～权 military power or leadership / ～人 soldier; serviceman; armyman / ～士 non-commissioned officer (NCO) / ～衔 military rank / ～训 military training / ～医 medical officer; military surgeon / ～营 military camp; barracks / ～装 also "军服" (military or army) uniform / ～兵种 arms and services of the armed forces / ～烈属 family members of servicemen and martyrs / ～转民 convert military enterprises to civilian production ❷ army; corps; ～部

army headquarters / ～长 army or corps commander

军备 jūnbèi armament; arms;～竞赛 armament or arms race / ～控制 (shortened as 军控) arms control

军队 jūnduì armed forces; army; troops;～番号 designation of a military unit

军阀 jūnfá warlord; military strongman;～割据 separatist warlord regime or rule

军法 jūnfǎ military criminal code; military law;～从事 punish by military law / ～审判 court-martial

军工 jūngōng ❶ (short for 军事工业) war industry;～生产 war production ❷ (short for 军事工程) military project

军功 jūngōng military exploit;～章 medal for military merit

军官 jūnguān officer;～学校 (shortened as 军校) military school; military college or academy

军管 jūnguǎn (short for 军事管制) military control;实行～ put under military control; place on a war footing

军国主义 jūnguózhǔyì militarism;～化 militarization / ～者 militarist

军火 jūnhuǒ munitions; arms and ammunition;～库 arsenal / ～商 munitions merchant; arms dealer

军机 jūnjī ❶ military plan ❷ military secret;泄露～ leak a military secret

军籍 jūnjí military status; one's name on the army roll; 开除～ strike sb's name off the army roll; dismiss (sb) from the army

军垦 jūnkěn reclamation of wasteland by the army;～农场 army (reclamation) farm

军令 jūnlìng military order;～状 written pledge to fulfil a mission or task (making oneself liable to punishment by military law in case of failure) / ～如山。A military order must be obeyed on all accounts.

军旅 jūnlǚ 〈书〉army; armed forces; troops;～生涯 military career

军民 jūnmín army and people; soldiers and civilians; military and civilian;～联防 army-civilian joint defence / ～两用技术 technology for both military and civilian service

军区 jūnqū military region; (military) area command; 大～ greater military area; major military region / 省～ provincial military command / 军分区 military sub-area or sub-region

军师 jūnshī 〈史〉imperial official with power to supervise military affairs; (military) counsellor; 〈喻〉adviser

军事 jūnshì military affairs;～化 militarize / ～法庭 military tribunal or court; court-martial / ～素质 military qualities; fighting capability / ～演习 military exercise; war manoeuvre

军威 jūnwēi military prestige;～大振 greatly boost (one's) military prestige; raise (one's) military morale immensely

军委 Jūnwěi (short for 军事委员会) Military Commission (of the Central Committee of the CPC, etc);中央～ Central Military Commission

军械 jūnxiè ordnance; armament;～处 ordnance department / ～库 ordnance or arms depot; armoury

军心 jūnxīn soldiers' morale;动摇～ sap the army's morale

军需 jūnxū military supplies;～品 military supplies; military stores

军用 jūnyòng for military use; military;～物资 military supplies; matériel

军乐 jūnyuè martial or military music;～队 military band

均 jūn ❶ equal; even; average;～等 equal; impartial; fair / ～势 balance (of power); equilibrium (of forces); parity / ～沾 share (benefits, etc) equally; have equal access to (advantages, etc) / 损失~摊 share a loss equally ❷ without exception; every one; all

均衡 jūnhéng balanced; proportionate; even; ~发展 balanced or harmonious development

均匀 jūnyún even; well-distributed; 呼吸~ even breathing / 把饲料拌~ get the fodder well mixed up

龟(龜) jūn *see also* guī

龟裂 jūnliè ❶ *see* "鞁裂" jūnliè ❷ (of parched earth) be full of cracks

君 jūn ❶ monarch; sovereign; supreme ruler; ~权 monarchical power / ~王 monarch; sovereign / ~临天下 rule a country as the monarch ❷ 〈书〉 gentleman; Mr: 杨~ Mr Yang

君主 jūnzhǔ monarch; sovereign: ~国 monarchical state; monarchy / ~制 monarchy / ~立宪 constitutional monarchy / ~专制 autocratic or absolute monarchy

君子 jūnzǐ man of noble character; superior man; gentleman: ~协定 gentlemen's agreement / ~一言，驷马难追。〈俗〉A gentleman is as good as his word. or A word spoken is past recalling.

君子兰 jūnzǐlán 〈植〉kaffir lily

钧 jūn ❶ ancient unit of weight (equal to 15 kilos) ❷ potter's wheel ❸ 〈书〉〈敬〉you; your: ~安 wishing you good health

菌 jūn ❶ fungus ❷ bacterium: 杀~ disinfect; sterilize / ~落 colony (of microbes) / ~苗〈医〉vaccine
see also jùn

鞁 jūn

鞁裂 jūnliè *also* "龟裂"〈书〉(of skin) chap

jùn

俊 jùn ❶ handsome; pretty; beautiful: ~美 pretty; good-looking / ~俏〈口〉pretty and charming; handsome / ~秀 pretty; of delicate beauty ❷ person of outstanding talent: ~杰 person of outstanding talent; hero

郡 jùn ❶ 〈史〉prefecture ❷ (in the UK, etc) county; shire

峻 jùn ❶ (of mountains, etc) high and steep: ~峭 high and steep / ~险 precipitous; dangerously steep ❷ harsh; severe; stern: ~刻〈书〉severe and harsh

浚(濬) jùn dredge (a river, etc)

骏 jùn (usu 骏马) fine horse; steed

菌 jùn mushroom *see also* jūn

竣 jùn complete; finish: ~工 (of a project) be completed

K

kā

咔 kā 〈象声〉(sound of breaking or impact) click; clack *see also* kǎ

kā

咖 kā *see also* gā

加啡 kāfēi coffee; ~馆 also "咖啡厅" coffee bar; café / ~因 also "咖啡碱" caffeine

喀 kā 〈象声〉*of noise made in coughing or breaking*

喀嚓 kāchā *also* "咔嚓" 〈象声〉crack; snap: 树枝 ~ 一声断了。The twig snapped.

喀斯特 kāsìtè *also* "岩溶" 〈地〉karst: ~溶洞 karst cave

kǎ

卡 kǎ ❶ (short for 卡路里) calorie ❷ *also* "卡片" card: 索引 ~ index card ❸ cassette: 双 ~ 录音机 double-cassette recorder *see also* qiǎ

卡车 kǎchē truck; lorry: 轻型 ~ pick-up (truck)

卡介苗 kǎjièmiáo BCG or TB vaccine

卡拉OK kǎlā'ōukèi karaoke

卡通 kǎtōng ❶ animated cartoon: ~片 animated cartoon (film) ❷ comic strip; (strip) cartoon

咔 kǎ *see also* kā

咔叽 kǎjī *also* "卡其" khaki (a fabric)

kǎ

咯 kǎ cough up (phlegm, blood, etc) *see also* gē; lo

kāi

开(開) kāi ❶ open; turn or be on: ~ 灯 turn or switch on a light / ~奖 draw and announce the winning ticket ❷ make an opening; open up; reclaim: ~ 荒 open up or reclaim wasteland / ~矿 open up or exploit a mine / ~ 膛 gut; disembowel (poultry, etc) / 在墙上 ~ 个洞 make an opening in the wall ❸ open out; come loose or undone: ~胶 come unglued / 你的鞋带 ~ 了。Your shoe-laces have come undone. ❹ thaw; melt; open: 河 ~ 了。The river thawed. ❺ lift (a ban, etc): ~禁 lift a ban; rescind a prohibition ❻ operate; start; run: ~船 (set) sail; weigh anchor / ~ 溜 slip (away); sneak or slink off / ~球 (in soccer) kick off; (in tennis, etc) serve ❼ set up; establish; run: ~饭馆 set up or run a restaurant ❽ begin; start: ~播 (of a station or programme) begin broadcasting; (in farming) start sowing / ~端 beginning; start / ~价 charge or ask a price; make a quotation / ~(先)例 set a precedent / ~拍 start shooting (a film, etc) / ~学典礼 school's opening ceremony ❾ hold (a meeting, etc); convene: ~小会 talk to each other in a low voice at a meeting ❿ write or make out: ~列 draw up (a list); list / ~收条 make out a receipt

⓫ pay（wages，fares，etc）⓬〈方〉kick out；fire；sack；把总经理 ~ 了give the general manager the sack ⓭boil；锅 ~ 了 The pot is boiling. ⓮serve（a meal，banquet，etc）；~ 席serve dinner *used after a verb to indicate a result or extent*：谣言传 ~ 了The rumour spread all over. ⓰ *used after an adjective to indicate the beginning of a state*：头场雪后，天就冷 ~ 了. It got cold after the first snow. ⓱percentage；proportion（in round numbers）：利润按四六 ~ 分成divide the profit in the proportion of four to six ⓲division of standard size printing paper；（corresponding）book size：32 ~ 32mo ⓳（of gold）carat：18 ~ 金18carat gold

开拔 kāibá （of troops，etc）move；set or start out

开办 kāibàn open；set up；start：~ 费opening or initial expenses；preliminary cost / ~ 学校 run a new school

开采 kāicǎi mine；exploit；recover：~ 天然气 tap or extract natural gas

开场 kāichǎng begin；open；start：~ 白prologue（of a play）；opening speech；introductory remarks

开车 kāichē drive or start a car，train，etc：开快车 drive at a high speed；〈喻〉hurry through work / 开倒车 back a car；〈喻〉go against the trends of the times or the will of the people / 开夜车 work late into the night；burn the midnight oil

开诚 kāichéng open one's heart；be sincere and frank；~ 布公be open-hearted；lay all the cards on the table / 相见 be frank and open（with sb）

开除 kāichú expel；discharge；dismiss：~ 学籍 expel（sb）from school / ~ 公职 discharge（sb）from public employment；take sb's name off the books

开创 kāichuàng open；initiate；pio-

neer：~ 精神 initiative；pioneering spirit / ~ 新纪元 open or usher in a new epoch

开刀 kāidāo ❶ make（sb or sth）the first target of attack；拿小张 ~ make an example of Xiao Zhang ❷ perform or have an operation；operate or be operated on

开导 kāidǎo show（sb）what is right or sensible；give guidance to；enlighten

开道 kāidào clear the way：~ 车 lead vehicle（a car or motorcycle going in advance of a motorcade）

开动 kāidòng start；set in motion：~ 马达 start a motor / ~ 脑筋 use one's brains；think things over

开恩 kāi'ēn （sometimes said humorously）show or have mercy；bestow or grant a favour：~ 放行 be kind enough to let sb go

开发 kāifā ❶ develop；open up；exploit：~ 区 open economic zone（OEZ）；（investment and）development zone ❷bring into play；tap；develop：~ 智力 tap intellectual resources

开方 kāifāng ❶ also "开方子" write（out）a prescription ❷〈数〉extraction；evolution：开立方 extraction of the cube root

开放 kāifàng ❶（of flowers）come into bloom；blossom ❷ open（to traffic or public use）；be open（to the public）；deregulate：~ 城市 open city（ie open to foreigners）/ ~ 政策 opening-up or open policy / ~ 式基金 open-end fund ❸ outgoing；uninhibited；open-minded

开赴 kāifù march to（the front，etc）；be bound for

开工 kāigōng （of a factory，etc）go or be put into operation；（of a project，etc）start（work）：~ 率 utilization of capacity；operating rate / ~ 不足 operate under capacity / 破土 ~ break the ground for the construction（of a project）

开关 kāiguān ❶ *also* "电门" switch; switchgear; ~盒 switch box; switchgear cabinet ❷ button; knob; 油门~ button for oil; oil button

开国 kāiguó found a state;〈旧〉establish a dynasty; ~元勋 founding father(s) of a country

开航 kāiháng ❶ become open for navigation; begin flight service ❷ (of a ship) set sail

开后门 kāihòumén 〈喻〉open the back door — offer or obtain advantages by underhand means; resort to backstair or under-the-counter deals; 利用职务~ abuse one's position to secure benefits (for one's friends, etc)

开户 kāihù open or establish an account; ~银行 bank of deposit

开花 kāihuā ❶ (also used figuratively) blossom; bloom; ~结果 blossom and bear fruit — yield (positive) results ❷ explode; break up; open; ~馒头 split-top steamed bun ❸ burst with joy; beam with smiles

开化 kāihuà become civilized; 未~ uncivilized

开怀 kāihuái to one's heart's content; heartily; ~畅饮 drink to one's heart's content; go on a drinking spree

开荤 kāihūn ❶ begin or resume a meat diet; end a meatless diet ❷ have a novel experience; 开洋荤 taste, see or experience sth exotic; have sth as a special treat

开火 kāihuǒ *also* "开战" ❶ open fire; fire ❷ attack (in speech or writing); assail (with words)

开伙 kāihuǒ (of an institution) run a mess or cafeteria; (of a canteen) provide food

开架 kāijià *also* "开架式" open-stack; open-shelf; ~借阅 (of a library) open-stack circulation; open access

开局 kāijú (of a chess or ball game) start; begin; ~不利 make an unfavour-able beginning; set off to a bad start

开卷 kāijuàn ❶〈书〉open a scroll or book; read; ~有益 Reading is always profitable. ❷ *also* "开卷考试" open-book examination

开垦 kāikěn open up or reclaim (wasteland); bring under cultivation

开口 kāikǒu ❶ open one's mouth; start to talk; ~闭口 whenever one speaks; say again and again / 不便~ find it difficult to bring sth up or to broach sth ❷ put the first edge on (a knife); sharpen (for the first time)

开阔 kāikuò ❶ open; wide; vast; ~地 open terrain ❷ tolerant; liberal; 心胸~ broad-minded; unprejudiced ❸ widen; ~眼界 broaden one's outlook

开朗 kāilǎng ❶ open and clear; 天空渐渐~了。The sky was clearing up. ❷ sanguine; cheerful; optimistic; ~活泼 lively and cheerful

开路 kāilù ❶ open a road; blaze a trail ❷ take the lead; lead the way; ~先锋 path breaker; trailblazer; pioneer

开绿灯 kāilǜdēng give the green light; give the go-ahead

开门 kāimén ❶ open the door; make a beginning; do sth in public; ~红 make a good beginning; get off to a flying start / ~揖盗 open the door to robbers — invite disaster by letting in evildoers; court trouble / ~见山 come straight to the point; speak bluntly ❷ (of a bank, etc) open; begin business for the day

开明 kāimíng *also* "开通" enlightened; liberal

开幕 kāimù ❶ the curtain rises; begin a performance ❷ open; inaugurate; ~式 inauguration; opening or inaugural ceremony

开炮 kāipào open fire with artillery;〈喻〉fire or level criticism at; fiercely criticize; 开头炮 be the first to fire; be the first to make a speech (often critical in nature)

开辟 kāipì ❶ open; start; establish: ~新路子 blaze new trails ❷ develop; promote; explore: ~工作 promote work (in a given area, etc); push work forward

开票 kāipiào ❶ open the ballot box and count the ballots ❷ make out an invoice or bill

开启 kāiqǐ ❶ open: ~闸门 lift a floodgate ❷ start; begin: ~一代新文风 set a new style of writing

开腔 kāiqiāng open one's mouth or lips; begin to speak: 一生气就不～ keep mum when angry

开窍 kāiqiào ❶ have one's ideas straightened out; be enlightened; begin to realize ❷ (of a child) start to understand things ❸ 〈方〉see (the ways of) the world; experience life

开山 kāishān ❶ cut into a mountain (for quarrying); open a (closed) mountain for grazing or lumbering ❷ establish or found a new sect, etc: ～祖师 founder; founding father

开设 kāishè ❶ open (a shop, etc) ❷ offer (a course in college, etc)

开审 kāishěn start a trial; sit at session: ～日期 hearing time

开始 kāishǐ ❶ start; begin: ～生效 take on or come into effect ❷ initial stage; beginning; outset

开释 kāishì release; acquit; set free: 无罪～ be released as innocent

开水 kāishuǐ boiling or boiled water: 白～ plain boiled water

开司米 kāisīmǐ also "开士米"; "羊绒" cashmere

开天辟地 kāitiān-pìdì creation of the world; genesis or dawn of history: ～第一回 for the first time in history

开庭 kāitíng 〈法〉open or hold a court session; call the court to order

开通 kāitōng ❶ (of communication lines or routes) be put into use; be

open to traffic ❷ (kāitong) see "开明"

开头 kāitóu start; begin; set on foot: 好的～ good beginning

开脱 kāituō absolve; exonerate; vindicate: ～责任 absolve or free (sb) of responsibility

开拓 kāituò open up; pioneer; create: ～进取 forge ahead and open new paths / ～型人才 pioneering talent; trailblazer

开外 kāiwài over; above; beyond: 60 ～ over sixty years old

开玩笑 kāiwánxiào crack, make or play a joke; make fun of; pull sb's leg: 经不起～ can't take a joke / 不是～的事 no joking matter

开往 kāiwǎng (of a train, ship, etc) leave for; be bound for: ～上海的特快列车 the Shanghai express

开胃 kāiwèi ❶ whet or stimulate the appetite: ～菜 appetizer; antipasto ❷ amuse oneself; make fun of; pull sb's leg: 拿人～ amuse oneself at sb's expense

开销 kāixiāo ❶ pay or cover expenses ❷ expense: 日常～ daily or running expenses

开小差 kāixiǎochāi ❶ (of a soldier) desert; go AWOL; sneak off ❷ be absent-minded; be in a brown study

开小灶 kāixiǎozào prepare special food for sb (as a privilege); give special favour or treatment

开心 kāixīn ❶ feel happy; rejoice; be delighted ❷ amuse oneself (at sb's expense); make fun (of sb)

开心果 kāixīnguǒ pistachio

开眼 kāiyǎn open sb's eyes; widen sb's view or horizon; broaden sb's vision: 去了趟深圳, 真～。 The trip to Shenzhen was really an eye-opener.

开业 kāiyè (of a shop, etc) start business; (of a lawyer, doctor, etc) open a private practice: ～行医 practise medicine

开源节流 kāiyuán-jiéliú　open up the source and regulate the flow; increase income and reduce expenditure

开凿 kāizáo　cut (a canal, tunnel, etc); dig

开展 kāizhǎn　❶ develop; launch; carry out ❷ (of an exhibition) open ❸ open-minded; enlightened; politically progressive

开张 kāizhāng　❶ start or open a business; begin doing business; ～大吉 (as of a business) have an auspicious beginning; open to a flying start ❷ make the first transaction for the day

开支 kāizhī　❶ pay; disburse; spend ❷ expenses; expenditure; spending ❸ 〈方〉 pay wages or salaries; 今天～。Today is payday.

开宗明义 kāizōng-míngyì　make clear the purpose and main theme from the very beginning; state the purpose at the very beginning

开罪 kāizuì　offend; displease

揩 kāi　wipe; rub; ～汗 wipe the sweat away / ～油 get petty advantages (at sb else's expense); scrounge

kǎi

凯(凱) kǎi　triumphant (strains); ～歌 song of victory or triumph; paean / ～旋 (make a) triumphant or victorious return

铠(鎧) kǎi　(usu 铠甲) armour

慨 kǎi　❶ indignant ❷ deeply touched; ～叹 lament with a sigh; sigh with regret ❸ generous; ～诺 consent readily; kindly promise

慨然 kǎirán　❶ with deep feeling; emotionally; ～长叹 let out a sigh of regret ❷ generously; without stint; ～相

助 help without stint; help readily

楷 kǎi　❶ model; pattern; ～模 (role) model; example; paragon ❷ (of Chinese calligraphy) regular script; ～书 also "正楷" regular script

kài

忾(愾) kài　〈书〉 hatred; 同仇敌～ common hatred for the enemy

kān

刊 kān　❶ print; publish; ～载 also "刊登" publish (in a newspaper or magazine); carry ❷ periodical; publication; ～物 publication ❸ delete; correct; rectify; ～误 correct errors in printing

看 kān　❶ look after; take care of; tend; ～小孩 take care of a baby; babysit ❷ keep under surveillance; keep watch over; detain; ～押 take into custody; detain

see also **kàn**

看管 kānguǎn　❶ guard (sb); watch ❷ look after (sth); attend to

看护 kānhù　❶ nurse; look after ❷ 〈旧〉 hospital nurse

看家 kānjiā　❶ look after or mind the house; house-sit; ～狗 watchdog; snitch ❷ outstanding (ability); special (skill); ～本领 one's outstanding skill, stock-in-trade or forte

看守 kānshǒu　❶ look after; take care of; ～内阁 caretaker cabinet ❷ watch; guard; keep under surveillance; ～所 lock-up; detention house ❸ jailer; turnkey; warder; 女～ wardress

勘 kān　❶ read and correct; collate; ～正 proofread and correct ❷ investigate; survey; ～测 survey / ～定界 survey and determine a border

勘察 kānchá　also "勘查" ❶ reconnoitre; ~ 敌情 reconnoitre an enemy position; gather intelligence about the enemy ❷ prospect; survey; ~ 煤层 prospect a coal bed

勘探 kāntàn explore; prospect; ~ 队 prospecting team

勘误 kānwù correct errors in printing; ~ 表 errata; corrigenda

龛（龕） kān niche; shrine

堪 kān ❶ may; can; ~ 当重任 can fill a position of great responsibility; be capable of performing important tasks ❷ bear; endure; 不~重负 can hardly bear the heavy burden

戡 kān suppress; put down; ~ 乱 suppress or put down a rebellion

kǎn

坎 kǎn bank; ridge; 土~儿 earthen bank

坎肩儿 kǎnjiānr （usu padded or lined) sleeveless jacket; vest; waistcoat

坎坷 kǎnkě ❶ bumpy; rough; rugged ❷ 〈书〉 full of frustrations; 生活 ~ lead a frustrated life

坎儿 kǎnr ❶ critical moment; point of great importance; crux; 说到～上 speak to the point; drive a point home ❷ streak of bad luck; predicament

侃 kǎn also "砍" 〈方〉 chat idly; tattle; ~ 儿爷 big talker; gossip; tattler / ~ 大山 chat idly; gossip; shoot the breeze

侃侃而谈 kǎnkǎn'értán speak with ease and assurance; speak freely and frankly

砍 kǎn ❶ cut; chop; hack; ~ 柴 cut firewood / ~ 伐 fell (a tree) ❷ reduce; cut; ~ 价 also "侃价" cut down on price; bargain for discount ❸ see "侃" kǎn

槛（檻） kǎn threshold see also jiàn

kàn

看 kàn ❶ look at; see; read; ~ 台 stands; bleachers; grandstand / ~ 戏 see a play, etc; go to the theatre / ~ 热闹 watch the fun; gloat over sb's trouble / ~ 眼色 take a hint; take one's cue ❷ think; consider; judge; ~ 风色 also "看风头" see or find out which way the wind blows / ~ 着办 do as one pleases; do as one sees fit ❸ call on; visit; go to see ❹ look upon; regard; treat; ~ 扁 underestimate; belittle / ~ 开 accept (sth unpleasant) with equanimity; not take to heart ❺ treat (a patient or an illness); ~ 急诊 treat an emergency patient / ~ 中医 see a doctor of traditional Chinese medicine ❻ (of market, etc) tend to; be expected to; ~ 跌 be expected to fall; be on the decline ❼ depend or rely on; ~ 情况而定 depend on the circumstances / ~ 菜吃饭，量体裁衣 〈俗〉 act according to actual circumstances ❽ *used to show sth is going to happen, or as a warning*; ~ 车! Watch out for the traffic! ❾ *used after a verb to indicate a tentative action*; 等等 ~ wait and see

see also kān

看不起 kànbuqǐ look down upon; despise; belittle

看出 kànchū perceive; detect; 看不出真假 cannot tell whether sth is genuine or fake

看待 kàndài look upon; consider; treat; 当人 ~ consider (sb) a human being; treat decently

看得起 kàndeqǐ have a good opinion of; think highly or much of

看法 kànfǎ ❶ (point of) view; opinion; ~ 一致 hold identical views; see eye to eye ❷ 〈口〉 unfavourable opinion or judgement

看风使舵 kànfēngshǐduò also "见风

使舵" trim one's sails to the wind; serve the time; ～ 的人 time-server; weathercock

看惯 kànguàn　become accustomed to the sight of (sth or sb); 看惯 "看不过"〈口〉can't bear (to see) any more of (sth or sb); cannot stand by and watch

看好 kànhǎo　❶ look up; get better: 外贸形势～. Foreign trade is picking up. ❷ expect sb or sth to win: 人们～北京队. The Beijing team is the favourite (for a contest, etc).

看见 kànjiàn　catch sight of; see

看来 kànlái　also "看起来"; "看样子"〈口〉it seems or appears; it looks as if or as though: ～我只能靠自己了. Apparently, I have to rely on myself.

看破 kànpò　❶ also "看穿" see through: ～骗局 see through a swindle ❷ become disillusioned: ～红尘 be disillusioned with the ways of the world

看齐 kànqí　❶ dress: 向右～! Dress right, dress! ❷ keep up with; emulate

看轻 kànqīng　underestimate; look down upon; take lightly

看上 kànshàng　also "看中" take a fancy to; settle on; fall in love with

看望 kànwàng　call on; visit; see

看相 kànxiàng　〈迷信〉tell sb's fortune by reading his or her face, etc

看笑话 kànxiàohua　watch sb make a fool of himself or herself; have a good laugh at sb's expense: 不要给人家～. Don't make a laughing-stock of yourself.

看重 kànzhòng　regard as important; value; set store by

看做 kànzuò　also "看作" look upon as; take as or for

瞰 kàn　look down from a height; overlook

kāng

康 kāng　❶ healthy: ～健 (in) robust health ❷〈书〉well-being; abundance; affluence

康复 kāngfù　recover; recuperate; rehabilitate: 病体～ recover from an illness; recuperate / ～中心 rehabilitation centre

康乐 kānglè　peace and happiness; recreation: ～球 also "克郎球" caroms

康乃馨 kāngnǎixīn　〈植〉carnation

康庄大道 kāngzhuāng-dàdào　〈喻〉broad or main road

慷 kāng

慷慨 kāngkǎi　❶ fervent; ardent: ～陈词 speak with fervour; present one's views ardently / ～激昂 impassioned; vehement; passionate / ～就义 go to one's death like a hero; die a martyr's death ❷ generous; liberal; magnanimous: ～解囊 help generously with money; give money freely and generously / 慷他人之慨 be liberal with other people's money; be generous at the expense of others

糠(粇) kāng　❶ chaff; bran; husk: ～秕 chaff; bran; worthless stuff ❷ (usu of a radish) spongy: ～心儿 be spongy at heart

káng

扛 káng　carry on the shoulder; work by hand; shoulder: ～活 work as a farm labourer　see also gāng

kàng

亢 kàng　❶ high; haughty; arrogant: 不～不卑 neither haughty nor humble; neither arrogant nor servile ❷ excessive; extreme: ～奋 stimulated; excessively excited / ～进〈医〉hyperfunction

伉 kàng　〈书〉(of spouse) matching or fit: ～俪 married couple

抗 kàng　❶ resist; fight; defy: ～击 resist; fight back / ～命 defy orders; disobey; defy one's destiny / ～体〈医〉antibody / ～灾 fight natural disasters / ～震 earthquake-resistant; anti-seismic; ～药性〈医〉resistance to drugs ❷ contend with; be a match for.

抗辩 kàngbiàn ❶ contradict; refute; speak in self-defence ❷〈法〉counterplea; demurrer

抗旱 kànghàn fight or resist drought; ～作物 drought-resistant crop

抗衡 kànghéng rival; contend; match; 无法～ be no match (for)

抗拒 kàngjù resist; defy; ～心理 negativism

抗生素 kàngshēngsù (formerly called 抗菌素) antibiotic; microbiotic

抗议 kàngyì protest; remonstrate; object; 提出～ lodge a protest (with sb against sth)

抗争 kàngzhēng make a stand against; resist; 奋起～ rise to resist; rise in resistance

炕 kàng ❶ *kang*, a heatable brick or earthen bed; ～头 warmer end of a *kang* ❷〈方〉bake or dry by the heat of a fire

kǎo

考（攷）kǎo ❶ ask sb to answer (a difficult question); quiz; question; 你把我～住了。You've got me there. ❷ give or take an examination; test; ～场 examination hall or room / ～点 examination place, site or venue / ～取 pass an entrance examination for (a school or college); be admitted to (after an examination) / ～生 candidate for an entrance examination; examinee / ～题 examination question or paper / ～研 sit for postgraduate enrolment examinations ❸ check; inspect; assess; ～查 check;

examine / ～绩 assess or appraise staff performance ❹ study; investigate; verify; ～订 examine and correct; do textual research / ～量 consider; ponder; mull over ❺〈书〉one's deceased father; ～妣 deceased parents

考察 kǎochá ❶ inspect; investigate on the spot; 出国～ go abroad on a study tour ❷ observe and study; ～问题的实质 go into the crux of a matter

考古 kǎogǔ (engage in) archaeological studies; ～学 archaeology / ～学家 archaeologist

考核 kǎohé check; assess; appraise; 定期～制度 routine check-up system

考究 kǎojiu ❶ observe and study; investigate ❷ fastidious; particular; choosy; 衣着～ particular about one's dress ❸ exquisite; fine; 用料～ made of high-quality material

考虑 kǎolǜ consider; think over; deliberate; 出自人道主义的～ out of humanitarian considerations

考评 kǎopíng assess and evaluate; 学术～ academic assessment and evaluation

考勤 kǎoqín check on work attendance; 记～ register or record the attendance

考试 kǎoshì examination; test; 参加～ sit for or take an examination / ～及格 pass an examination; get a pass

考验 kǎoyàn test; trial; ordeal; 经不住时间的～ cannot stand the test of time

考证 kǎozhèng (engage in) textual research and criticism; ～古书的作者 ascertain or find out the author of an ancient book through research

拷 kǎo flog; beat; torture; ～打 beat; torture / ～问 torture during interrogation; interrogate with torture

拷贝 kǎobèi copy; 电影～ copies of a film

烤 kǎo ❶ bake; roast; toast; ～肉 barbecue; roast (meat) / ～箱 oven; toaster / ～烟 flue-cured tobacco

～面包 toasted bread; toast / ～羊肉串 mutton shish kebab ❷ (usu 烤火) warm oneself (by a fire, etc)

kào

铐 kào (put) handcuffs (on sb)

犒 kào reward with food and drink; ～劳 reward (troops, etc) with food and drink / ～赏 reward a victorious army, etc, with bounties

靠 kào ❶ lean on or against; come up to; near; ～岸 (of a ship) pull in to shore; draw alongside / ～背 back (of a chair) / ～垫 cushion / ～近 (draw) near; (come) close to; by / ～拢 draw close; close up / ～山临水 with hills at the back and water in the front; between a mountain and a river ❷ depend or rely on:～山 patron; backing; support / ～天吃饭 depend on Heaven for food; live at the mercy of the elements ❸ trust; ～不住 unreliable; untrustworthy

靠边 kàobiān keep to the side; ～儿站 stand aside; get out of the way; 〈喻〉be out of power

靠山吃山，靠水吃水 kàoshānchīshān, kàoshuǐchīshuǐ those living on a mountain live off the mountain, those living near the water live off the water — make use of local resources

kē

苛 kē ❶ severe; rigorous; exacting; ～刻 harsh; relentless; mean and exacting / ～求 make excessive demands; be exacting or overcritical / ～责 criticize severely; excoriate / ～政猛于虎 oppressive government is fiercer than a tiger; tyranny is worse than a tiger ❷ over-elaborate; tedious:～捐杂税 exorbitant taxes and levies; multifarious and onerous taxes

科 kē ❶ branch or division of activity; subject of instruction or study; (esp) science:工～ engineering; technology / ～盲 person ignorant of science; science-illiterate / ～普 popularization of science; popular science / ～室 administrative or technical offices (of a factory), etc) / ～协 (short for 科技协会) association of science and technology / ～教兴国 make the country prosperous and strong through science and education ❷ imperial civil examinations; subject in such examinations:～举制度 〈史〉 imperial civil examination system ❸ 〈书〉 law; rule:犯有前～ have a criminal record ❹ impose (a punishment, etc); pass (a sentence)

科班 kēbān old-type traditional opera school;〈喻〉regular professional training:～出身 have received regular professional training; be a professional by training

科幻 kēhuàn (short for 科学幻想) science fiction:～小说 science fiction (novel)

科技 kējì (short for 科学技术) science and technology; sci-tech:～园 sci-tech park / ～兴农 invigorate agriculture by applying science and technology

科目 kēmù ❶ subject (in a curriculum); course:必修 ～ obligatory or compulsory course / 选修～ elective or optional course ❷ headings in an account book

科学 kēxué ❶ science:～家 scientist / ～院 academy of sciences ❷ scientific:～社会主义 scientific socialism

科研 kēyán (short for 科学研究) scientific or academic research; R&D research / ～开发能力 R & D capacity

棵 kē 〈量〉usu used of plants:一～草 a cluster of grass

棵儿 kēr size (of plants):这白菜～大。This Chinese cabbage is big.

K

颏 kē (generally known as 下巴 or 下巴颏儿) chin

嗑 kē 〈方〉words; talk; chat; 唠～ have a chat or talk　*see also* kè

稞 kē

稞麦 kēmài　*also* "青稞" highland barley

窠 kē nest; burrow; ～臼〈书〉set pattern (of writing, etc); convention

颗 kē 〈量〉*used of grains and grain-like things*; ～～汗珠 drops or beads of sweat

颗粒 kēlì ❶ anything small and roundish; ～物质 particle; particulate matter ❷ (of cereals) each grain; ～无收 total crop failure

磕 kē ❶ knock (against sth hard); bump; ～～撞撞 stagger along; stumble; reel / 膝盖～破了皮 graze or scrape one's knee ❷ (sth out of a container, etc); ～掉鞋上的泥巴 knock the mud off one's shoes

磕巴 kēba 〈方〉❶ stutter; stammer ❷ stammerer

磕磕绊绊 kēke-bànbàn ❶ stumble; limp; walk with difficulty ❷ bumpy; rough ❸ obstacle; difficulty; setback

磕碰 kēpèng ❶ knock or bump against; collide with; 瓷器经不起～。 Chinaware will not stand bumping. ❷ clash; squabble; 两人一起生活,有些～是难免的。 For two people living together, friction over petty matters is hardly avoidable. ❸ (kēpeng)〈方〉chip in a utensil;〈喻〉setback; frustration

磕头 kētóu kowtow; ～如捣蒜 kowtow again and again (to beg for sb's mercy or express one's gratitude)

磕头碰脑 kētóu-pèngnǎo ❶ (push and) bump against each other (in a crowd, etc) ❷ rub elbows (with each other); frequently contact ❸ clash; squabble; conflict

瞌 kē

瞌睡 kēshuì sleepy; drowsy; 打～ be sleepy; doze or nod off / ～虫 drowsiness; sleepyhead

蝌 kē

蝌蚪 kēdǒu　*also* "科斗" tadpole

ké

壳(殻) ké shell; 脑～ skull / 子弹～ (bullet) shell　*see also* qiào

咳 ké cough; ～得很厉害 have a bad cough / ～嗽药 cough drops or medicine　*see also* hāi

kě

可 kě ❶ approve; agree; 不置～否 say neither yes nor no; decline to comment ❷ can; may; -able; ～鄙 contemptible; despicable; mean / ～耕地 arable or cultivable land / ～燃物 combustible (matter); inflammable (matter) / ～塑性 plasticity; adaptability / ～进～退 be free to press forward or back out; can either attack or retreat / ～视电话 picture-phone; videophone / ～有～无 not essential or indispensable / ～持续发展 sustainable development / ～支配收入 disposable income / ～意会而不～言传 can be appreciated but not clearly defined; be beyond words ❸ (often used with a monosyllabic verb to form an adjectival phrase) need (doing); be worth (doing); ～读 readable / ～歌～泣 moving (one to song and tears); stirring ❹ 〈书〉about; some; 年～20 about twenty years of age ❺ 〈方〉go as far as is possible; make the best or most of; ～着嗓子喊 shout at the top of one's voice ❻ 〈副〉but;

K

yet：～事情没那么容易。Well, things are not that easy. ❼〈副〉*used for emphasis* a）*in a statement*：他～真是个大好人。He is really kind-hearted. b）*in a rhetorical question*：这么大的北京城，到哪儿去找他呀? Beijing is such a big city. Where on earth should we find him? c）*in a question to indicate doubt*：这件事他～同意? Has he really approved of this? ❽ fit；suit：脚～〈方〉(of shoes) etc) fit well / ～心 *also* "可意" after one's heart；satisfying

可爱 kě'ài lovable; lovely; likeable；绿得～ beautifully green

可悲 kěbēi sad; lamentable; deplorable：愚蠢得～! What deplorable stupidity!

可比 kěbǐ comparable：～价格〈经〉comparable or constant price

可变 kěbiàn variable; changeable：～性 variability

可不 kěbù *also* "可不是"(used to express emphatic agreement) right; exactly："这东西太贵了!" "～，有多少人能买得起!" "This is too expensive." "You said it! I wonder how many people can afford it?"

可乘之机 kěchéngzhījī opportunity that can be exploited to sb's advantage; opening：给人～ play into sb's hands

可耻 kěchǐ shameful; disgraceful; ignominious

可观 kěguān ❶ be worth seeing ❷ considerable; sizable; impressive

可贵 kěguì valuable; commendable; praiseworthy

可恨 kěhèn hateful; detestable; abominable：～之至 most hateful

可见 kějiàn ❶ it is thus clear or evident that ❷ visible; visual：～度 *also* "能见度" visibility

可卡因 kěkǎyīn *also* "古柯碱" cocaine：～瘾 cocaine addiction; cocainism

可靠 kěkào reliable; dependable; trustworthy：～性 reliability / ～性试验 fail-test

可可 kěkě *also* "蔻蔻" cocoa

可口 kěkǒu (of food) palatable; tasty; nice：～菜肴 delicious food

可兰经 Kělánjīng *also* "古兰经"〈宗教〉Koran

可乐 kělè ❶ funny; amusing; laughable ❷（short for 可口可乐）Coca-Cola; coke; soft drink similar to Coca-Cola

可怜 kělián ❶ pity; arouse pity：～虫 pitiful creature; miserable wretch ❷ meagre; miserable; wretched：穷得～ as poor as a church mouse

可能 kěnéng ❶ possible; probable; likely：～性 possibility; probability; feasibility / ～范围内 in so far as it is possible; as much as one can ❷ probably; perhaps; maybe：她～回家了。She's probably gone home.

可怕 kěpà fearful; dreadful; horrible

可欺 kěqī ❶ easily cowed or bullied ❷ gullible; easily duped

可巧 kěqiǎo *also* "可好" just at that moment; just then; by happy coincidence

可取 kěqǔ desirable; advisable：各有～之处。Each has its own advantages.

可是 kěshì ❶ but; yet; however ❷〈副〉*used for emphasis*：这人～不简单。He is no sucker.

可望而不可即 kěwàng'érbùkějí within sight but beyond reach; unattainable; inaccessible

可谓 kěwèi 〈书〉it may be said; one may well say：他对国事～鞠躬尽瘁。One may well say that he exerted himself to the utmost for his country.

可恶 kěwù hateful; detestable; abominable：～之极 utterly detestable; extremely loathsome

可惜 kěxī unfortunately; it's a pity; it's too bad

可喜 kěxǐ　gratifying；heartening：～的进步 encouraging improvement

可想而知 kěxiǎng'érzhī　one can imagine；one may well imagine：他对自己的父母都是这么粗鲁，对别人就可想而知了。He is rude to his own parents，let alone other people.

可笑 kěxiào ❶ ridiculous；ludicrous；～之至 extremely foolish；height of absurdity ❷ funny；amusing；laughable

可行 kěxíng　feasible；workable：～性研究 feasibility study

可疑 kěyí　suspicious；dubious：～分子 dubious character；suspect

可以 kěyǐ ❶ can；may：～为鉴 may be taken as an example or warning ❷ pretty good；not bad；passable ❸ terrible；awful；dreadful：她那张嘴真够～的。She's got such a sharp tongue.

可遇而不可求 kěyù'érbùkěqiú　sth that comes by chance，not through seeking；sth so rare that one can only stumble upon it by luck

可憎 kězēng　hateful；repulsive；detestable

渴

渴 kě ❶ thirsty；dry：～死了 dying for a drink；die of thirst ❷ yearningly；eagerly：～慕 admire greatly／～盼 look forward to；expect eagerly／～求 hope earnestly for；hunger or strive for／～望 long，thirst or yearn for

kè

克（剋、尅） kè ❶〈书〉can；be able to：～勤～俭 be industrious and frugal；practise diligence and thrift ❷ overcome；restrain：～星 jinx；natural enemy ❸ capture；conquer；subdue：～敌制胜 defeat an enemy and win a victory／～复失地 recover lost territory ❹ also "刻" set a time limit：～日完工 be completed within the deadline ❺ gram

(g)：500～ 500 grams；half a kilogram

克服 kèfú ❶ overcome；surmount；conquer：～缺点 rectify one's shortcoming／～私心杂念 do away with selfish considerations ❷ put up with (hardships，etc)；make do；endure

克己 kèjǐ ❶ be strict with oneself；exercise self-denial；be unselfish：～奉公 deny oneself and work wholeheartedly for the public interest ❷ (used by shopkeepers) reasonable：价钱～ reasonable price ❸ frugal：生活～ live a frugal life

克扣 kèkòu　pocket part of employees' pay，etc；dock

克拉 kèlā　carat (about 0.2 gram)

克里姆林宫 Kèlǐmǔlíngōng　the Kremlin

克隆 kèlóng　clone：～技术 cloning technology

克制 kèzhì　restrain；control：采取～态度 exercise or show restraint

刻

刻 kè ❶ carve；engrave；cut：～本 block-printed edition／～度 graduation (on an instrument，etc)；scale division／～记在心 bear (sth) in mind ❷ quarter (of an hour)：两点一～ quarter past two ❸ moment；time ❹ cutting；biting；harsh：～薄 mean；sarcastic；cynical／～毒 venomous；spiteful；malignant ❺ see "克❹" kè

刻板 kèbǎn ❶ also "刻版" cut wood or metal blocks (for printing) ❷ stiff；inflexible；mechanical

刻不容缓 kèbùrónghuǎn　be extremely urgent；demand immediate attention；brook no delay

刻骨 kègǔ　engraved on one's bones；deeply ingrained；deep-seated or -rooted：～铭心 also "镂骨铭心" be engraved on one's mind or in one's heart；be remembered with gratitude

刻画 kèhuà ❶ engrave or draw ❷ depict；portray：人物～ characterization／～入微 depict or portray to the last detail

刻苦 kèkǔ ❶ hardworking; assiduous: ~好学 be studious and diligent ❷ simple and frugal; thrifty

刻意 kèyì strive or seek sedulously: ~讨好 go out of one's way to please sb

刻舟求剑 kèzhōuqiújiàn cut a mark on the gunwale of a moving boat to indicate where one's sword dropped into the river — take measures without regard to changing circumstances

恪 kè 〈书〉 scrupulously and respectfully; meticulously: ~守 scrupulously abide by or adhere faithfully to (a promise, principle, etc) / ~尽职守 be whole-heartedly devoted to one's duty

客 kè ❶ guest; visitor: ~队〈体〉 visiting team / ~随主便 the guest must suit the convenience or comply with the wishes of the host ❷ live or settle in a strange place: ~居 live abroad or away from home ❸ passenger; travelling merchant: ~舱 passenger cabin (on a ship, plane, etc) / ~店 inn / ~流 volume of passenger traffic; passenger flow / ~商 itinerant or travelling trader; visiting businessman / ~运 passenger transport ❹ customer; patron; client: ~户 customer; client / ~满 (of theatre, hotel, etc) be filled to capacity; have a full house / ~源 source of tourists; potential customers or tourists ❺ 〈方〉〈量〉 used for food or drinks sold in portions: 两~冰激凌 two ice-creams

客场 kèchǎng 〈体〉 other team's home court or ground: ~比赛 away game — game played on the other team's court

客串 kèchuàn (usu of an amateur) participate in a show as a guest performer: ~演员 guest actor or actress

客观 kèguān objective: ~性 objectivity; objectiveness

客家 Kèjiā Hakka: ~话 Hakka (dialect) / ~人 Hakka (people)

客气 kèqi ❶ polite; courteous: 你太~了。You're very kind. ❷ modest ❸ speak or behave politely; stand on ceremony: ~了一番 exchange or say a few words of courtesy

客人 kèrén ❶ guest; visitor ❷ guest (at a hotel, etc); patron; customer ❸ passenger; traveller

客套 kètào ❶ also "客套话" polite formulas; civilities ❷ make polite remarks; exchange courtesies

客厅 kètīng parlour; drawing or sitting room; lounge

客座 kèzuò ❶ seat or place for a guest or client ❷ professional person invited to work temporarily in an institution: ~教授 guest or visiting professor

课 kè ❶ class; lesson; period: ~本 textbook / ~表 school or class schedule / ~间 break (between classes) / ~时 class hour; period / ~文 text / ~余 after school or class ❷ subject; course: 必修~ required or mandatory course ❸ (now 科) subdivision of an administrative unit; section: 会计~ accounting section ❹ levy; impose: ~税 levy taxes; charge duties / ~以罚金 impose a fine

课程 kèchéng course; curriculum: ~计划 syllabus / ~设置 curriculum; courses offered

课堂 kètáng classroom: ~教学 classroom instruction or teaching

课题 kètí ❶ topic for class discussion ❷ question or topic for study; problem; task

课外 kèwài outside class; after school; extra-curricular: ~辅导 (as of a teacher) help (a student) outside class; give tutorials

氪 kè 〈化〉 krypton (Kr)

骒 kè female (mule or horse): ~马 mare

嗑 kè crack sth between the teeth；～牙〈方〉indulge in idle talk；gossip　*see also* kē

溘 kè〈书〉suddenly：～然长逝 suddenly pass away；die a sudden death

kēi

剋（尅） kēi ❶ beat；fight：～架〈方〉have a fist fight ❷ scold；curse：挨～ get a scolding

kěn

肯 kěn agree；consent；be willing or ready (to do sth)
肯定 kěndìng ❶ affirm；confirm；regard as positive ❷ doubtless；certain；sure：口气～ speak with certainty

垦（墾） kěn turn up (soil)；cultivate (land)；reclaim (wasteland)：～荒 reclaim wasteland；open up virgin soil；bring wild country under cultivation／～区 reclaimed area／～殖场 reclamation farm

恳（懇） kěn ❶ sincerely；earnestly：～请 earnestly request；cordially invite／～求 beg sincerely；implore；entreat／～谈会 get-together where participants are engaged in free and cordial conversation／语调～切 speak in a sincere or an earnest tone ❷ request；entreat；beg；敬～ respectfully request

啃 kěn gnaw；nibble：～骨头 gnaw at a bone；crack a hard nut；work painstakingly at a difficult task／～大部头 delve into big volumes (of books)

kēng

坑（阬） kēng ❶ pit；depression；hollow：～～洼洼 full of bumps and hollows；bumpy；〈喻〉full of setbacks and frustrations ❷ tunnel；hole；pit：～道 pit；gallery；〈军〉tunnel ❸ bury alive：～杀 bury alive (usu in a pit) ❹ harm by cunning or deceit；cheat；hoodwink：～害 entrap；ensnare；do harm to (by scheming, etc)／～蒙拐骗 swindle, cheat and abduct

吭 kēng utter a sound or word；speak：～哧 puff (and blow)；work hard；hem and haw／～声 *also* "吭气" utter a sound；breathe a word　*see also* háng

铿（鏗） kēng
铿锵 kēngqiāng (of gongs, cymbals, etc) rhythmic and sonorous；sonorous and forceful：～有力的讲话 ringing and powerful speech

kōng

空 kōng ❶ empty；void；unoccupied：～喊 clamour without taking action；loud and empty talk／～炮 empty talk or promise；idle boasting／～身 carry no luggage；carry nothing／～驶 travel empty；deadhead／～载 (of machinery, etc) operate without load／～荡荡 empty；deserted／～架子 mere skeleton；bare outline；framework without substance ❷ air；sky：～防〈军〉air defence／～难 air disaster；air or plane crash／～域 airspace／～降兵 airborne force；paratroops；parachutists／～勤人员 aircrew；flight crew／～对地导弹 air-to-ground missile ❸ in vain；for nothing；to no avail：～欢喜 rejoice too soon；rejoice only to be let down／一纸～文 a mere scrap of paper　*see also* kòng
空城计 kōngchéngjì empty-city stratagem — presenting a bold front to con-

K

ceal a weak defence：我们总得留个人在后面照料，不能唱～啊！It won't do for us all to pack up and go. We'll have to leave somebody behind to keep an eye on things.

空挡 kōngdǎng neutral gear；挂～ put (a car, etc) in neutral gear

空洞 kōngdòng ❶ empty；hollow；devoid of substance；～无物 empty；windy；devoid of content ❷ cavity；肺～ pulmonary cavity

空泛 kōngfàn vague and general；not specific；内容～ devoid of specifics

空腹 kōngfù on an empty stomach；～服用 to be taken on an empty stomach

空话 kōnghuà hollow words；empty or idle talk；lip-service；～连篇 long-winded empty talk；reels of empty verbiage

空幻 kōnghuàn visionary；illusory

空寂 kōngjì open and silent；deserted and quiet

空间 kōngjiān space；～站 also "航天站" space station

空军 kōngjūn air force；～基地 air base；air force base (AFB)

空空如也 kōngkōngrúyě completely or all empty；肚子里～ have an empty stomach；be hungry；〈喻〉have an empty head

空口 kōngkǒu ❶ eat dishes without rice or wine；eat rice or drink wine with nothing to go with it ❷ merely give a verbal statement；pay lip service；～无凭 also "口说无凭" a verbal statement or promise is no guarantee；words alone are no proof

空旷 kōngkuàng (of land, etc) open and spacious；wild

空灵 kōnglíng (of art, writing, etc) indescribably free；free and natural

空门 kōngmén ❶ 〈宗教〉Buddhism；遁入～ become a Buddhist monk or nun；take a monastic vow ❷ (of football) unguarded or open goal

空濛 kōngméng 〈书〉hazy；misty

空气 kōngqì ❶ air：～浴 air-bath／～传染〈医〉airborne infection／～加湿器 humidifier ❷ atmosphere：这里学术～浓厚。One feels great enthusiasm in academic studies here.

空前 kōngqián unprecedented；unparalleled：～高涨 be at an all time high／～绝后 unprecedented and unrepeatable；unique

空手 kōngshǒu ❶ empty-handed；with bare hands：～道〈体〉karate ❷ (usu used in painting or embroidery) without a model or sample

空谈 kōngtán (indulge in) empty or idle talk；prattle；(go in for) windy abstractions

空调 kōngtiáo air-conditioning；air-conditioner

空头 kōngtóu ❶ 〈经〉(of the stock exchange) bear；shortseller：做～ bear；shortsell／～市场 bear market ❷ nominal；empty；phony：～人情 empty gesture of friendship or sympathy；lip-service／～政治家 armchair politician

空头支票 kōngtóuzhīpiào ❶ bounced or bad cheque ❷ empty promise；lip service

空投 kōngtóu air-drop；paradrop：～场 dropping ground／～救援物资 air-drop relief supplies

空袭 kōngxí air raid or attack；躲～ run for shelter during an air raid

空想 kōngxiǎng (indulge in) day-dreaming or fantasy：～家 dreamer；visionary／～社会主义 utopian socialism

空心 kōngxīn ❶ (of a plant, etc) become hollow or spongy inside ❷ hollow (core)；air core：～菜 also "蕹菜"〈植〉water spinach／～砖 air or hollow brick／～萝卜 hollow turnip — person without genuine ability or knowledge see also kòngxīn

空虚 kōngxū hollow；empty；void：填

补精神上的～ fill the vacuum in one's heart

空穴来风 kōngxuéláifēng　an empty hole invites wind — weakness lends wings to rumours

空运 kōngyùn　air transport; airlift:～费 air freight

空中 kōngzhōng　in the air or sky; overhead:～加油 air or in-flight refueling /～劫机 (aerial) hijacking /～楼阁 castle in the air /～小姐 (shortened as 空姐) air hostess; stewardess /～走廊 air corridor

kǒng

孔 kǒng ❶ hole; opening; aperture:～道 narrow passage; pass /～穴 hole; cavity /三～桥 three-arched bridge ❷〈方〉〈量〉used for caves:两～砖窑 two brick-lined cave-dwellings

孔夫子 Kǒngfūzǐ　also "孔子" (respectful term of address for 孔丘, 551 BC-479 BC) Confucius, Chinese philosopher, educator and founder of Confucianism

孔雀 kǒngquè　peacock:～开屏 peacock fanning out its tail in a splash of colours

恐 kǒng ❶ be afraid; fear; dread:～高症〈医〉acrophobia /～水病 hydrophobia; rabies ❷〈书〉perhaps; probably:～非原意。This may not be what was meant

恐怖 kǒngbù　terror; horror:～分子 terrorist /～主义 terrorism

恐吓 kǒnghè　intimidate; threaten; blackmail:～信 blackmailing or threatening letter

恐慌 kǒnghuāng　panic:陷入～ fall into a panic; be seized with panic

恐惧 kǒngjù　fear; dread; terror:突然感到～ be seized with fear

恐龙 kǒnglóng　〈考古〉dinosaur

恐怕 kǒngpà　〈副〉❶ indicating doubt or anxiety about consequences:她踮着脚尖进了屋,～吵醒了妹妹。She tiptoed into the room for fear of waking up her sister. ❷ indicating an estimation:～你得亲自去一趟。I think you'd better go in person.

kòng

空 kòng ❶ leave empty, blank or unoccupied; vacate:每段开头要～两格。Indent the first line of each paragraph by two spaces. ❷ vacant; unoccupied; blank:～额 vacancy /～格 blank; blank space (as on a form) ❸ unoccupied or empty space; room ❹ free, spare or leisure time:没～儿 have no time; be occupied ❺ see "控❸❹" kòng
see also kōng

空白 kòngbái　blank space:填补～ fill a gap

空当 kòngdāng　also "空当子" ❶ gap; empty space ❷ break; interval (in a schedule, etc)

空地 kòngdì ❶ unused land; open space; vacant lot ❷ extra room; space available

空缺 kòngquē ❶ vacant position; vacancy:出～ vacate a position ❷ gap; vacancy:填补～ fill a gap or vacancy

空隙 kòngxì ❶ space; gap; interval ❷ opening or opportunity (usu for evildoing)

空闲 kòngxián ❶ also "空余" free; leisurely:～时间 free or spare time ❷ also "空眼" leisure; free or spare time ❸ also "空余" unused; idle:～房间 vacant room

空心 kòngxīn　on an empty stomach
see also kōngxīn

空子 kòngzi ❶ unoccupied space; free time; gap ❷ opening; chance; opportunity (usu for wrongdoing):钻

exploit an opportunity; avail oneself of a loophole

控 kòng ❶ accuse (sb.of sth); charge (sb with sth); denounce: ~方〈法〉prosecuting party ❷ control; dominate:~速行驶 drive within a speed limit ❸ also "空" keep (one's body or part of one's body) hanging in the air; keep unsupported ❹ also "空" turn (usu a container) upside down to let the liquid trickle out

控告 kònggào charge; accuse; arraign:提出~ file a charge (in court) / ~人 accuser; accusing party

控股 kònggǔ 〈经〉holding:~方 party holding a controlling interest / ~公司 holding company

控诉 kòngsù denounce; accuse; condemn:~书 written accusation or complaint

控制 kòngzhì control; curb; dominate;~论〈数〉cybernetics / ~因素 governing factor / ~自己的感情 control or restrain one's feelings

kōu

抠(摳) kōu ❶ dig (out) with a finger or sth pointed; scratch:~鼻子 pick one's nose / 雕~ cut; carve:~花纹 cut a pattern ❸ study punctiliously; delve into:~书本 儿 bury oneself in books / ~字眼儿 be a stickler for words ❹〈方〉stingy; closefisted; penny-pinching:~门儿 stingy; closefisted; miserly / ~搜搜 penny-pinching

眍(瞘) kōu also "眍䁖" (of eyes) become or be sunken

kǒu

口 kǒu ❶ (of a human or an animal) mouth:~疮 mouth ulcer;

canker / ~红 lipstick / ~技 vocal mimicry or imitation / ~紧 close-mouthed; tight-lipped / ~粮 grain for one's own consumption; provisions / ~琴 mouth organ; harmonica / ~试 oral examination / ~述 oral account / ~误 (make) a slip of the tongue / ~ 罩 gauze or surgical mask / ~蹄疫 foot-and-mouth disease / ~香糖 chewing gum / ~出狂言 talk boastfully or wildly; brag; boast / ~惠而实不至 make an empty promise; pay lip-service ❷ taste in food:~咸 also "口重" like salty food ❸ (of a vessel, etc) sth resembling or functioning as a mouth:碗 ~ rim of a bowl ❹ opening; (esp) gateway of the Great Wall; pass:~北 also "口外" (area) north of the Great Wall (esp of Zhangjiakou 张家口) ❺ cut; crack; chip:花瓶缺了个个~儿。 The vase has a chip in the rim. ❻ general category grouping institutions or enterprises of similar nature loosely together; departments of such a category:工交~ departments of industry and transport ❼ sharp edge; blade ❽ age of a draught animal;两岁~的母马 two-year-old mare ❾〈量〉:四一之家 a family of four / 讲一~流利的英语 speak fluent English

口岸 kǒu'àn port; port of call

口碑 kǒubēi public praise or evaluation; reputation:~不佳 have a poor reputation

口才 kǒucái talent for speaking; eloquence

口吃 kǒuchī also "结巴" stutter; stammer

口齿 kǒuchǐ ❶ enunciation:~不清 speak with a mumble / ~伶俐 have a glib or ready tongue ❷ teeth or age of draught animals

口袋 kǒudai ❶ bag; sack ❷ pocket

口风 kǒufēng one's intention or opinion as revealed in what one says; 探探

~ sound (sb) out

口服 **kǒufú** ❶ profess to be convinced：~心不服 say one is convinced but be not so at heart ❷ take orally (medicine)：~液 oral liquid

口福 **kǒufú** luck to enjoy delicious food; gourmet's luck：一饱 ~ satisfy one's appetite for delicious food; enjoy a gourmet's luck

口感 **kǒugǎn** texture of food；~ 好 have a nice chewy texture; feel wonderful in the mouth

口供 **kǒugòng** confession; testimony

口号 **kǒuhào** slogan; watchword

口径 **kǒujìng** ❶ bore; calibre; diameter：小 ~ 步枪 small-bore rifle ❷ requirements; specifications ❸ line of action; approach; version：对 ~ compare notes so as to give the same story / 对外 ~ unified statement for the public

口诀 **kǒujué** pithy formula or table (often in rhyme); mnemonic rhyme：乘法 ~ (rhyming) multiplication table

口角 **kǒujué** quarrel; bicker; wrangle

口口声声 **kǒukou-shēngshēng** say or claim repeatedly; keep on saying

口令 **kǒulìng** ❶ word of command ❷ password; watchword; countersign：对 ~ exchange passwords

口蜜腹剑 **kǒumì-fùjiàn** honey-mouthed but dagger-hearted; hypocritical and sinister

口气 **kǒuqì** ❶ manner of speaking; way of speaking：~ 挺 大 speak in a grand manner; talk big ❷ what is actually meant; implication：听听他的 ~ find out his intention ❸ tone; note：~ 婉转的声明 mildly worded statement

口腔 **kǒuqiāng** 〈生理〉oral cavity：~ 溃疡 canker; mouth ulcer / 一 医院 stomatological hospital

口若悬河 **kǒuruòxuánhé** let loose a torrent of words; speak eloquently and volubly

口哨儿 **kǒushàor** whistle (with one's lips)

口舌 **kǒushé** ❶ quarrel, dispute or misunderstanding caused by what one says：搬弄 ~ sow dissension; tell tales ❷ talking (round)：白费 ~ waste one's breath; talk in vain

口实 **kǒushí**〈书〉❶ cause for gossip; handle ❷ excuse; pretext：制造 ~ create a pretext or an excuse (for doing sth)

口是心非 **kǒushì-xīnfēi** say yes and mean no; say one thing and mean another; play a double game

口授 **kǒushòu** ❶ teach by oral instruction; pass on by word of mouth ❷ dictate：~笔录 (verbatim record of a) dictation

口水 **kǒushuǐ** saliva：流 ~ slobber / 仗〈方〉battle of words

口头 **kǒutóu** ❶ words (as distinct from thoughts or actions)：~ 禅 platitude; pet phrase / ~语 pet phrase; habitual turn of phrase ❷ oral; verbal：~ 表决 (put to) voice vote

口味 **kǒuwèi** ❶ (of food) flavour; taste ❷ one's taste or liking：合 ~ suit one's taste; be to one's liking

口吻 **kǒuwěn** ❶〈动物〉muzzle; snout ❷ tone; note：讥笑的 ~ sneering tone

口信 **kǒuxìn** oral message：捎 ~ take a message

口音 **kǒuyīn** ❶ voice：听出 ~ recognize sb's voice ❷ accent：家乡 ~ native accent

口语 **kǒuyǔ** spoken language：~ 体 colloquialism; colloquial style

口诛笔伐 **kǒuzhū-bǐfá** condemn both in speech and in writing; denounce by tongue and pen; castigate in all forms

口子 **kǒuzi** ❶〈量〉*used of people*：百八十 ~ 人 a hundred people or so ❷〈口〉husband or wife：我那 ~ my wife or husband ❸ opening; breach：山谷的 ~ mouth of a valley / 这个 ~ 开不得！ We can never set such a precedent！❹

cut; crack; hole

kòu

叩 kòu ❶ knock; tap; rap: ～门 knock at the door ❷ (usu 叩头) kowtow: ～拜 show one's respect by kowtowing / ～谢 express earnest thanks (by kowtowing) ❸ also "叩问" 〈书〉inquire; ask

扣(⁶鈕) kòu ❶ button up; buckle; bolt: ～上门 bolt the door ❷ 扳机 pull the trigger ❷ place upside down; cover; 〈喻〉put a label on:～帽子 put a (usu political) label on (sb); brand (sb) / ～屎盆子 clamp a dirty name (on sb); level dirty charges (against sb) ❸ take into custody; detain; apprehend ❹ deduct; discount:八～ 20% discount / ～发 withhold (what should be issued); hold / ～压 withhold (what should be dealt with); shelve; pigeonhole ❺ knot; loop ❻ button; buckle:～眼 buttonhole ❼〈体〉smash; spike:～篮 (make a) dunk shot / ～球 also "扣杀" smash or spike (the ball)

扣除 kòuchú deduct:～税款 deduct the tax (from income, etc)

扣留 kòuliú detain; arrest; hold in custody

扣人心弦 kòurénxīnxián exciting; thrilling; soul-stirring: ～ 的悬念 breathtaking suspense

扣题 kòutí keep to the point; be relevant to the subject

扣押 kòuyā ❶ detain; hold in custody ❷〈法〉distrain; seize

扣子 kòuzi ❶ knot ❷ button ❸ abrupt break in a story to create suspense

寇 kòu bandit; invader; enemy:～仇 mortal enemy; foe

kū

枯 kū ❶ (of a plant, etc) withered; (of a well, river, etc) dried

up; (of a person) thin and haggard;～干 dried-up; withered; shriveled / ～槁 withered; shriveled; haggard / ～竭 dry up; exhaust; deplete / ～荣 (of grasses, etc) luxuriate and wither; 〈喻〉prosper and decline; rise and fall / ～萎 wither; shrivel (up) / ～木逢春 〈喻〉get a new lease of life; enjoy good fortune after a long spell of bad luck / ～木朽株〈喻〉senile or sick persons; decadent and weak force / 心如～井 with one's heart like a dry well; devoid of any desire or dream ❷ dull; uninteresting:～涩 dry and puckery; dull and heavy / ～坐 sit idly / ～燥无味 dry as dust; dull as ditchwater

哭 kū cry; weep:～泣 sob; weep / ～穷 go about saying how hard up one is; pretend to be hard up / ～诉 complain tearfully; sob out; accuse while weeping / ～鼻子〈口〉cry; weep; snivel / ～啼啼 keep crying or sobbing; whimper endlessly / ～丧着脸 wear a long face; sulk / ～天抹泪〈贬〉wail and whine; cry piteously / ～笑不得 not know whether to laugh or to cry / ～得死去活来 cry one's heart out / ～着～着就睡着了 cry oneself to sleep

窟 kū ❶ hole; cave; grotto / ～den; lair:蛇～ den of snakes

窟窿 kūlong ❶ hole; cavity; hollow:～眼儿 small hole ❷ deficit; debt:拉～ run into debt ❸ loophole:堵住税收中的～ stop up loopholes in taxation

骷 kū

骷髅 kūlóu ❶ human skeleton ❷ human skull; death's head

kǔ

苦 kǔ ❶ bitter:～胆 gall (bladder) / ～寒 bitterly cold; frigid / ～命 bitter or sad fate; ill-fated life / ～尽甜来 *also* "苦尽甘来" when bitterness ends, sweetness begins; after suffering comes happiness; sweet after sweat ❷ hardship; suffering; misery:～熬 endure; go through (years of suffering, etc) / ～楚 suffering; misery; distress / ～笑 (give a) forced, wry or strained smile / 不堪言 (of a person) suffer untold misery and hardship; the misery or hardship is beyond words / 大仇深 have suffered bitterly and nurse deep hatred (for sth) / ～中作乐 enjoy life in adversity; seek joy in hardship ❸ cause sb to suffer; give sb a hard time ❹ suffer from; be troubled by:～夏 *also* "疰夏" (suffer from) loss of appetite and weight in summer / ～于 be troubled (over a problem); suffer (from a disadvantage) ❺ painstakingly; assiduously:～干 work hard; make painstaking effort / ～功 painstaking effort; hard work / ～～恋 persistent unrequited love / ～～思索 ponder hard; rack one's brains / ～思冥想 ponder long and hard; cudgel or rack one's brains

苦差 kǔchāi *also* "苦活儿" hard and unprofitable job; thankless job

苦处 kǔchu suffering; hardship; difficulty:做父母的 ～ what one has to endure as a parent

苦工 kǔgōng ❶ forced (hard) labour ❷ person who does hard labour; coolie

苦瓜 kǔguā balsam pear; (喻) bitter gourd:一副～脸 a miserable look / 一根藤上的 ～ be bitter gourds on the same vine; suffer the same lot

苦果 kǔguǒ bitter fruit — evil consequence; bitter pill:自食 ～ swallow one's own bitter pill; reap what one has sown

苦海 kǔhǎi sea of bitterness; abyss of misery:～无边, 回头是岸 (formerly a Buddhist admonition) the sea of bitterness is boundless, repent and the shore is at hand — it is never too late to mend one's ways

苦口 kǔkǒu ❶ (admonish) in earnest:～婆心 (admonish) in earnest words and with the best of intentions; with patience and sincerity ❷ bitter to the taste:良药～, 忠言逆耳. Candid advice always sounds unpleasant, just as good medicine tastes bitter.

苦力 kǔlì ❶ coolie ❷ hard (manual) work; great effort:卖～ do heavy manual work; work hard (for sb) / 下～ work hard (at sth)

苦闷 kǔmèn depressed; dejected; feeling low

苦难 kǔnàn suffering; misery; distress:～的深渊 abyss of misery

苦恼 kǔnǎo distressed; frustrated; vexed:令人～ distressing; frustrating

苦肉计 kǔròujì trick of inflicting an injury on oneself to win the trust of one's enemy or critic; ruse of self-injury

苦涩 kǔsè ❶ bitter and astringent; acrid ❷ pained; agonized; anguished:～地一笑 force a smile

苦水 kǔshuǐ ❶ bitter water ❷ gastric secretion rising to the throat; reflux suffering; misery:吐～ pour out one's grievances

苦头 kǔtóu suffering:尝够了 ～ endure untold sufferings; have had enough (of sth)

苦心 kǔxīn trouble or pains taken:～经营 nurse (an enterprise, etc) with every care; painstakingly build up

苦行 kǔxíng (宗教) ascetic practice; asceticism:～僧 ascetic (monk) / ～主义 asceticism

苦役 kǔyì hard labour; penal servitude:服～ serve one's time in hard labour; do hard labour

苦战 kǔzhàn ❶ bitter fighting; pitched battle ❷ wage an arduous struggle; work hard

苦衷 kǔzhōng　private suffering; trouble or difficulty: 体谅别人的～ make allowance for others' difficulties

kù

库 kù　warehouse; storehouse; bank or treasury: ～藏 (have in) storage / ～（boast a）collection / ～房 storeroom; stacks (of archives, etc) / ～券（short for 国库券）treasury bond / ～容 storage capacity (of a reservoir, warehouse, etc)

库存 kùcún　stock; reserve; inventory: 盘点～ take stock / ～现金 cash on hand; cash holdings

裤（袴） kù　trousers; pants: ～衩 underpants; undershorts / ～兜 trouser pocket / ～袜 pantyhose / ～线 creases (of trousers)

酷 kù ❶ cruel; oppressive: ～吏 cruel, ruthless official / ～刑 cruel or savage torture ❷ very; extremely: ～爱 love ardently; be very fond of; adore / ～寒 bitter cold / ～好 be extremely fond of; be very keen on / ～暑 intense heat of summer / ～似 be the very image of; be exactly like ❸ cool: 扮相～ look cool in costume and make-up / ～哥 cool or smart guy

kuā

夸（誇） kuā ❶ exaggerate; boast; brag; ～饰 give an exaggerated account; embellish (writing, etc, with exaggerations) / ～耀 brag about; show off; flaunt / ～（口）boast; brag ❷ praise (sb for sth); compliment (sb on sth) / ～奖 praise; commend; compliment

夸大 kuādà　exaggerate; overstate; magnify: ～其词 make an overstatement; exaggerate / ～事实 stretch the facts / ～的数字 inflated figures

夸口 kuākǒu　boast; brag; talk big: 夸海口 talk big

夸夸其谈 kuākuāqítán　indulge in empty talk; shoot one's mouth off; be full of hot air

夸张 kuāzhāng ❶ exaggerate; overstate ❷ (in rhetoric) hyperbole

kuǎ

侉 kuǎ ❶ speak with an accent (esp a provincial one): 说话～里～气的 speak with a heavy provincial accent ❷ big and clumsy; unwieldy: ～大个儿 clumsy fellow; lout

垮 kuǎ　collapse; fall in; break down: ～台 collapse; fall from power / 累～ break down; collapse / 身体～了 suffer a physical breakdown; ruin one's health

kuà

挎 kuà ❶ carry on the arm: ～臂而行 walk arm in arm ❷ carry over one's shoulder, or round one's neck, or at one's side: ～包 satchel / ～斗 sidecar (for a motorcycle)

胯 kuà　〈生理〉hip: ～裆 crotch (of trousers) / ～骨 hipbone / ～下之辱 humiliation of being forced to crawl between sb's legs; cup of humiliation

跨 kuà ❶ step; stride: ～入新世纪 stride or enter into a new century ❷ sit or stand astride; straddle: ～上自行车 mount a bicycle ❸ cut across; go beyond: ～地区 transregional; inter-regional / ～世纪 cross-century; trans-century / ～学科 interdisciplinary / ～国公司 also "多国公司" transnational corporation; multinational（corporation）❹ attach to the side of sth: ～间 small side room

跨度 kuàdù ❶ also "跨径"〈建筑〉

span ❷ distance; span; 时间～大 tremendous time span

跨栏 kuàlán　*also* "跨栏赛跑"〈体〉 hurdle race; the hurdles

跨行业 kuàhángyè　(of an enterprise) concurrently engage in different trades or industries; ～公司 conglomerate company / ～组织 multi-trade organization

跨越 kuàyuè　stride or cut across; step over; span; ～界限 surpass the bounds / ～栏杆 clear a fence

kuǎi

抠（擓）kuǎi　〈方〉❶ scratch; ～破了皮 have one's skin scraped ❷ carry on the arm ❸ ladle out; scoop up

kuài

会（會）kuài　(grand) total *see also* huì

会计 kuàijì　❶ accounting; ～报表 accounting statement / ～年度 accounting or fiscal year / ～事务所 accounting firm ❷ bookkeeper; accountant; ～师 accountant; (UK) chartered accountant; (US) certified public accountant

块（塊）kuài　❶ lump; piece; chunk; ～根 root tuber / ～茎 (stem) tuber / ～儿糖 lump or loaf sugar / 大～头 big burly fellow / 大一儿的煤 big lumps of coal ❷ block; 功能～ function(al) block ❸〈量〉a) *used of sth cubical or flat in shape*: 一～菜地 a vegetable plot / 一～肥皂 a cake of soap b) *used as a unit of money (such as yuan or dollar)*: ～儿八毛 one yuan or less; about one yuan

快 kuài　❶ quick; fast; rapid; ～班 advanced class / ～攻〈体〉quick attack (in volleyball, etc); fast break (in basketball) / ～件 express delivery

luggage, goods or mail / ～进 (with a tape, etc) fast-forward / ～镜头 snapshot / ～慢适中 neither quick nor slow — the right speed ❷ hurry (up); make haste; ～马加鞭 (ride) whip and spur; at top speed; posthaste ❸ *also* "快要" soon; before long; 寒假～到了。The winter vacation is drawing near. ❹ sharp; keen; ～刀斩乱麻 cut a tangled skein of jute with a sharp knife — cut the Gordian knot ❺ straightforward; forthright; plainspoken; ～人一语 straightforward talk from a straightforward person ❻ pleased; happy; gratified; ～感 pleasant sensation; delight; pleasure / ～事 delightful event; delight / ～慰 (feel) gratified and comforted; (be) pleased / ～意 pleased; delightful; comfortable

快板儿 kuàibǎnr　rhythmic comic talk to the accompaniment of bamboo clappers; clapper talk; 说～ perform a clapper talk

快步 kuàibù　❶〈军〉half step; trot ❷ quick pace; ～舞 quickstep

快餐 kuàicān　quick meal; snack; fast food; ～店 fast food restaurant

快车 kuàichē　❶ express train or bus ❷ fast traffic; 开～ drive fast; speed / ～道 fast (traffic) lane

快递 kuàidì　express delivery; ～服务 express delivery service; fast mail service

快活 kuàihuo　happy; jolly; merry

快捷 kuàijié　(of speed) quick; fast; nimble

快乐 kuàilè　happy; joyful; delightful; 生日～! Happy birthday (to you)!

快门 kuàimén　(camera) shutter; ～开关 shutter release

快手 kuàishǒu　quick worker; deft hand; ～快脚 be deft of hand and nimble of foot; do things very fast

快速 kuàisù　fast; quick; rapid; ～部队 mobile force or troops / ～倒带 fast-rewind / ～反击〈体〉fast counter-attack;/～反应〈军〉rapid response; quick or fast reaction

快讯 kuàixùn （news）flash;向各地发～ flash the news to various places

快嘴 kuàizuǐ loose tongue; big mouth; gossip

脍（膾） kuài

脍炙人口 kuàizhìrénkǒu win universal praise; be on everybody's lips; be a household word

筷 kuài also "筷子" chopsticks

kuān

宽（寬） kuān ❶ wide; broad;～度 width; breadth /～银幕电影 wide-screen film / 管得太～ take too much into one's own hands; poke into other people's business ❷ relax; relieve; extend;～解 ease (sb's anxiety); relieve (sb of his or her trouble) / 心情～畅 be carefree; feel free and happy ❸ generous; lenient;～待 treat with leniency; be lenient in dealing with /～让 tolerant; lenient /～打窄用 budget liberally and spend sparingly / 从～处理 treat with leniency ❹ comfortably off; well-off;手头～ be well-off; be liberal with one's money

宽敞 kuānchang spacious; roomy; commodious

宽绰 kuānchuo ❶ see "宽敞" ❷ broad-minded; at ease; relaxed;把心放～些。Take things easy. ❸ comfortably off; well-off

宽大 kuāndà ❶ spacious; roomy;～的睡袍 loose nightgown ❷ lenient; magnanimous;～为怀 treat leniently; be willing to let bygones be bygones

宽带 kuāndài also "宽频带"〈通信〉broadband; wide-band (WB);～网 broadband network

宽广 kuānguǎng broad; extensive;

vast;眼界～ farsighted

宽宏 kuānhóng also "宽洪" large-minded; magnanimous;气度～ be of magnanimous bearing /～大量 also "宽宏大度" large-minded; magnanimous

宽厚 kuānhòu ❶ thick and broad ❷ generous and kind ❸ (of voice) deep and rich

宽阔 kuānkuò ❶ broad; wide ❷ broad-minded

宽容 kuānróng tolerant; lenient;～大度 tolerant and generous

宽舒 kuānshū ❶ free of worry; relaxed and happy ❷ spacious; broad

宽恕 kuānshù forgive; pardon;请求～ ask for forgiveness

宽松 kuānsōng ❶ spacious; commodious; not crowded ❷ relaxed; free; happy:政策～ relaxed or liberal policy ❸ ample; well off:时间～ have ample time ❹ (of clothes) loose and comfortable

宽慰 kuānwèi comfort; console;～某人几句 say sth to comfort sb

宽限 kuānxiàn extend a time limit;～期 grace period /～两周 give two weeks' grace

宽心 kuānxīn feel relieved;～话 reassuring words /～丸儿 comforting words; sth reassuring

宽衣 kuānyī ❶〈敬〉take off your coat ❷ undress

宽余 kuānyú ❶ spacious and comfortable ❷ ease of mind ❸ see "宽裕"

宽裕 kuānyù well-to-do; comfortably off; ample:时间～ have plenty of time / 手头不～ have little money to spare; be in financial straits

髋（髖） kuān hip;～骨 also "胯骨"〈生理〉hipbone

kuǎn

款（欵） kuǎn ❶ sincere;～留 cordially urge (a guest)

to stay ❷ receive with hospitality; entertain: ～待 treat cordially; entertain / ～客 entertain a guest ❸ section (of an article in a legal document); paragraph ❹ sum of money for a specific purpose; fund;～项 sum of money (for a specific purpose); fund / ～爷〈方〉moneybags; nouveau riche ❺ name of author or recipient (inscribed on a painting, etc);题 inscribe one's name and comments (on a painting, etc) / ～识 signature (of author on a painting, etc); inscription (on bronzes, etc) ❻ style; kind; type:～式 pattern; style; design / 三～点心 three kinds of pastry ❼〈书〉leisurely; slow:～～而行 walk slowly

kuāng

匡 kuāng ❶〈书〉rectify; correct:～谬正俗 rectify the erroneous and help to form good customs ❷〈书〉assist; save; rescue ❸ calculate roughly; estimate:～算 roughly calculate; estimate

诓 kuāng deceive; cheat; hoax:～哄 deceive; dupe / ～骗 also "诓诈" cheat; swindle

哐 kuāng （usu 哐当）〈象声〉crash; bang

筐 kuāng basket:柳条～ wicker basket

kuáng

狂 kuáng ❶ mad; crazy; insane:～乱的人群 frantic, confused crowds ❷ violent; fierce:～暴 violent; wild; furious / ～奔 run swiftly and violently; run like mad ❸ unrestrained; wild:～吠 bark furiously;〈喻〉slander viciously / ～喜 wild with joy / ～放不羁 totally unconventional and untrammelled ❹ arrogant; overbearing; presumptuous

狂飙 kuángbiāo hurricane;〈喻〉storm and stress

狂风 kuángfēng fierce wind:～暴雨 violent storm / ～大作. A high wind sprang up.

狂欢 kuánghuān revelry; carnival:～节 carnival; festival

狂犬病 kuángquǎnbìng also "恐水病" hydrophobia; rabies

狂热 kuángrè fanaticism; fever:宗教～ religious fever; zealotry

狂人 kuángrén ❶ madman; maniac; lunatic ❷ person of extreme arrogance and conceit; supercilious person

狂妄 kuángwàng wildly arrogant; presumptuous:～自大 arrogant and conceited

狂想 kuángxiǎng ❶ fancy; fantasy:突发～ be struck with a fancy / ～曲〈乐〉rhapsody; fantasia ❷ vain hope; wishful thinking; illusion

狂言 kuángyán ravings; wild language; delirious utterances:口出～ talk wildly; rave

诳 kuáng deceive; dupe; fool:～语 also "诳话" lie; falsehood

kuàng

旷（曠） kuàng ❶ open and empty; vast; spacious:～野荒郊 uninhabited open country; wilderness ❷ free from worries and petty ideas; relaxed; expansive:～达〈书〉broad-minded; big-hearted ❸ neglect (duty, etc); waste (time, etc):～废 neglect; waste / ～工 be absent or stay away from work without leave / ～课 cut school; play truant / ～费时日 neglect the passage of time; squander one's time ❹ loose (-fitting):这双鞋我穿着太～了. This pair of shoes is too large for me.

旷古 kuànggǔ ❶ from time immemorial; ~ 奇闻 unheard-of story ❷ remote antiquity; ancient times

旷日持久 kuàngrìchíjiǔ long-drawn-out; protracted; time-consuming: ~ 的战争 prolonged or protracted war

旷世 kuàngshì 〈书〉❶ also "旷代" unrivalled by one's contemporaries; matchless in one's age; unique: ~ 无双 unmatched in one's time ❷ last a long, long time: ~ 难成 can hardly be completed even for ages

况（況） kuàng ❶ condition; situation ❷ compare: 以物~人 compare things to people ❸ 〈书〉moreover; besides; let alone; 且 moreover; besides; in addition / 困兽犹斗，~人乎？Even beasts at bay will fight back, let alone men.

矿（礦、鑛） kuàng ❶ mineral or ore deposit; ore: ~产 mineral deposits; minerals / ~床 also "矿体" (mineral or ore) deposit / ~层 ore bed; seam ❷ mine: ~ 工 miner; pitman / ~ 山 mine / ~业 mining industry

矿藏 kuàngcáng mineral resources: ~量 (ore) reserves

矿井 kuàngjǐng mine (shaft); pit: ~通风 mine ventilation / ~瓦斯 damp; fire-damp

矿泉 kuàngquán mineral spring; spa: ~水 mineral water / ~疗养地 spa

矿山 kuàngshān mine: ~机械 mining machinery / ~运输 mine haulage

矿石 kuàngshí mineral; ore: 富~ high-grade ore

矿物 kuàngwù mineral: ~质 mineral substance / ~燃料 fossil or mineral fuel

框 kuàng ❶ frame; case: 眼镜~儿 rims (of spectacles) ❷ (formerly pronounced kuāng) restrict; restrain; confine: ~得太死 impose or make too rigid restrictions

框架 kuàngjià ❶〈建筑〉frame; 钢筋混凝土~ reinforced concrete frame ❷ framework; 小说的~ plot of a novel /

~协议 framework agreement

框框 kuàngkuang ❶ frame; circle; restriction; convention; set pattern: 打破旧~ break the set patterns; break free of the old rut

眶 kuàng socket of the eye

kuī

亏（虧） kuī ❶ lose (money, etc); have a deficit; fall short: ~秤 give short measure; lose weight / ~耗 (sustain) loss by a natural process / ~空 (be in) debt; (have a) deficit / ~折 lose (one's capital, etc) / 月满则~。The moon begins to wane upon reaching the full. ❷ treat unfairly or shabbily: ~待 treat unfairly or shabbily / ~良心 have a guilty conscience ❸ also "亏得" fortunately; luckily; thanks to: ~我早有准备。Fortunately, I had taken precautions beforehand. ❹ also "亏得" used to indicate irony: ~你还有脸来见我！And you have the cheek to come and see me!

亏本 kuīběn lose money (in business); lose one's capital: ~出售 sell at a loss / ~生意 losing business or proposition

亏欠 kuīqiàn have a deficit; be in arrears; owe: 谁也不~谁 be quits / ~妻子很多 owe a great deal to one's wife

亏损 kuīsǔn ❶ loss; deficit: ~企业 losing enterprise ❷ general debility; 身体~ be debilitated (by illness), etc)

亏心 kuīxīn have a guilty conscience; ~事 matter that troubles one's conscience; cause for remorse

岿（巋） kuī

岿然 kuīrán 〈书〉towering; lofty: ~不动 steadfastly stand one's ground

盔 kuī helmet; any helmet-shaped hat: ~甲 suit of armour / 头~

(cyclist's, etc) helmet

窥 kuī　peep; pry; spy: ～见 get or catch a glimpse of; detect / ～豹一斑 see one spot on a leopard — have a limited view; see a typical segment of a whole

窥测 kuīcè　watch; spy out: ～方向 spy out the land; see which way the wind blows

窥视 kuīshì　peep at; spy on; pry about: ～镜 also "猫眼儿" peephole; spyhole

窥伺 kuīsì　lie in wait for; be on watch for: ～良机 lie in wait for a good chance; bide one's time

窥探 kuītàn　spy upon; pry about: ～别人的隐私 nose into sb's privacy

kuí

奎 kuí

奎宁 kuíníng　also "金鸡纳霜" quinine

葵 kuí　common name for certain herbaceous plants with big flowers: ～花 sunflower

揆 kuí　〈书〉❶ conjecture; surmise; speculate: ～度 estimate; surmise ❷ manage; control: 阁～ premier; chief minister

魁 kuí　❶ chief; head: ～首 also "魁元" best (of all); one who is head and shoulders above others ❷ tall and burly; of stalwart build: ～伟 strongly-built / ～梧 big and tall; powerfully-built

睽 kuí

睽睽 kuíkuí　stare; gaze: ～相视 stare at each other

kuǐ

傀 kuǐ

傀儡 kuǐlěi　puppet; marionette; stooge

跬 kuǐ　(usu 跬步) 〈书〉small step: ～步千里 one can cover a thousand *li* by small steps — continued efforts may lead to great successes

kuì

匮 kuì　〈书〉deficient; lacking: ～乏 short (of supplies, etc); deficient

喟 kuì　〈书〉heave a sigh; sigh: ～叹 sigh with deep feeling

馈(餽) kuì　make a present of; present (a gift): ～赠 present (a gift); make a present of (sth)

溃 kuì　❶ (of floodwater, etc) burst a dyke or dam; break: ～决 (of a dyke or dam) burst ❷ be routed; fall to pieces: ～败 be crushed or routed / ～散 be routed and dispersed / ～退 retreat in confusion; beat a disorderly retreat / ～不成军 (of an army, etc) be utterly routed ❸ (of muscles, etc) fester: ～烂 (of a wound, etc) fester; ulcerate / ～疡 〈医〉ulcer; canker

see also huì

愧(媿) kuì　ashamed; abashed; conscience-stricken: ～恨 (ashamed and) remorseful / ～悔 ashamed and regretful / ～疚 〈书〉feel ashamed and remorseful; be conscience-stricken / ～领 〈谦〉accept humbly / ～色 look of shame / ～不敢当。〈谦〉I do not deserve such an honour. or I am flattered.

kūn

坤(堃) kūn　female; feminine: ～包 lady's handbag or

昆 kūn 〈书〉❶ elder brother：～仲 brothers ❷ offspring；progeny：后～ descendents；children ❸ (short for 昆曲；昆剧) *Kunqu* opera，oldest traditional Chinese opera extant

昆虫 kūnchóng insect：～学 entomology；insectology

鲲 kūn

鲲鹏 kūnpéng enormous legendary fish and bird；roc：～展翅 like the roc flapping its wings — taking off with tremendous power and momentum

kǔn

捆（綑） kǔn ❶ tie；bind；bundle up：～住手脚 bind sb hand and foot — restrict sb's freedom of action ❷〈量〉*used of sth bundled up*：一～菠菜 a bundle of spinach

捆绑 kǔnbǎng truss up (people)；bind；tie up：～销售 bundling / ～式火箭 rocket with strap-on boosters

kùn

困（³睏） kùn ❶ be stranded，stricken or trapped；hold in check：～境 difficult position；predicament；straits / ～守孤城 defend a lone city against a siege / ～兽犹斗 a cornered beast will turn and fight；a person at bay will put up a desperate fight ❷ difficulty；hardship：～苦 hardship and privation ❸ tired；sleepy；drowsy：～倦 tired and sleepy

困顿 kùndùn ❶ worn out；exhausted ❷ in financial straits or difficulties：～潦倒 be frustrated in life and poverty-stricken

困乏 kùnfá ❶ tired；fatigued ❷〈书〉(financial) difficulties；shortage (of supplies)：生计～ lack means of livelihood

困惑 kùnhuò perplexed；puzzled；confused

困窘 kùnjiǒng ❶ embarrassed；awkward ❷ in straitened circumstances；poverty-stricken

困难 kùnnan ❶ difficulty：克服～ overcome or surmount difficulties ❷ financial hardship；poverty：～补助 subsidy to those who are hard up

困扰 kùnrǎo ❶ besiege and harass ❷ haunt；trouble；perplex

kuò

扩（擴） kuò extend；expand；enlarge：～版 (of a newspaper，etc) enlarge the format；increase the number of pages / ～编 (of an army) enlarge the establishment；increase the size of one's forces / ～建 extend (an existing factory，etc) / ～容 enlarge：〈信息〉expand the capacity / ～展 expand；spread；develop / ～招 increase enrolment (of students) or recruitment (of workers) / ～音器 loudspeaker；microphone；audio amplifier / ～军备战 arms expansion and war preparations

扩充 kuòchōng expand and strengthen；augment；enlarge：～内容 add to or expand the contents (of a book，etc)

扩大 kuòdà enlarge；expand；extend：～会议 enlarged meeting or session / ～就业 create more jobs；enlarge employment / ～内需 expand domestic demand

扩大化 kuòdàhuà magnify or extend wrongly，unrealistically or unnecessarily：矛盾～ aggravation of a contradiction / 不要使事态～ not let the trouble get out of hand；keep an incident under control

扩散 kuòsàn spread；diffuse；proliferate；癌 ～ proliferation or spread of cancer / ～谣言 spread a rumour

扩张 kuòzhāng ❶ expand；extend；spread；～主义 expansionism ❷〈医〉dilate：血管～ blood vessel dilatation

括 kuò ❶ tie (up)；tighten up；contract (muscles, etc) ❷ include；comprise：～号 brackets / ～弧 parentheses / 兼 ～ 各家之长 incorporate advantages of all schools

阔(濶) kuò ❶ wide；broad；vast：～步 take big strides；stride / ～边草帽 broad-brimmed straw hat ❷ wealthy；rich；～绰 extravagant；lavish；liberal with money / ～佬 also "阔老" rich or wealthy

guy；moneybags / ～少 wealthy man's son；young man from a rich family

阔别 kuòbié have been long separated；have not seen (each other) for quite some time：～故乡 have long been away from one's hometown

阔气 kuòqi extravagant；luxurious；lavish：摆 ～ show off one's wealth；flaunt an ostentatious life-style

廓 kuò ❶ wide；extensive；vast ❷ expand；extend：～地千里 extend the territory by a thousand *li* ❸ outer features；outline

廓清 kuòqīng clean up；clarify；clear away：～障碍 clear away obstacles / ～异端邪说 dispel evil ideas and heresy

L

lā

垃 lā

垃圾 lājī garbage; trash; junk;~箱 dustbin; garbage can / ~处理 garbage disposal; refuse treatment / ~食品 junk food

拉 lā ❶ pull; draw; drag;~面 also "押面" hand-pulled noodles / ~网 draw in a net; tighten a ring of encirclement / ~下马 pull off the horse;〈喻〉cause to fall from power / ~下水 drag into the mire;〈喻〉corrupt; make an accomplice of / ~开序幕 raise the curtains on (a performance, etc) / ~伤肌肉 injure one's muscle by straining; pull a muscle / ~长调子说话 speak in a drawn-out voice; drawl ❷ transport by vehicle; haul: 这车能~50人。This van can carry 50 passengers. ❸ organize; set up; put together: ~帮结伙 form a clique; band together; engage in factional activities ❹ play (certain instruments, etc); sound:~二胡 play the erhu / ~鼻儿〈口〉sound a siren; blow a whistle ❺ give or lend a hand; help:~他一把 give him a helping hand; help him out ❻ drag in; implicate; involve:~人当垫背的 make sb a scapegoat / ~账 owe (a debt); run (a deficit);~亏空 run a deficit; get into

debt ❽ draw or drag in; canvass; solicit:~客 (of restaurants, etc) solicit customers or clients; (of taxis, etc) carry passengers; (of prostitutes) solicit patrons / ~广告 solicit advertisements (from companies, etc) / ~皮条 〈贬〉act as a pimp; pander; procure ❾ chat; engage in chit-chat:~家常 chat about homely things; chit-chat ❿ have a bowel movement; empty the bowels; ~肚子〈口〉have loose bowels; have diarrhoea / ~屎~尿〈口〉piss and shit;〈喻〉do whatever one pleases in a despotic manner; treat (people) like shit

see also lá

拉扯 lāche ❶ drag; pull; tug:拉拉扯扯,打打闹闹 pull at each other and kick up a din ❷ bring up (a child) ❸ help and support; promote ❹ gang up with; rope in:吃吃喝喝, 拉拉扯扯 wine and dine, and exchange flatteries and favours ❺ drag in; implicate:放心吧, 我不会~你们的。Don't worry. I won't get any of you involved. ❻ chat; chit-chat

拉倒 lādǎo forget about it; leave it at that; drop it

拉丁 Lādīng Latin:~文 Latin (language) / ~美洲 (shortened as 拉美 or 拉) Latin America / ~字母 Latin or Roman letters

拉动 lādòng stimulate; boost; jumpstart

拉关系 lā guānxi 〈贬〉try to establish a relationship (with sb useful);

cultivate：拉同学关系 make use of old school ties

拉后腿 lāhòutuǐ　*also* "扯后腿" hold (sb) back; be a drag on (sb)

拉家带口 lājiā-dàikǒu have a family to provide for; be burdened with a family

拉架 lājià try to stop a brawl by separating the brawlers; try to stop people from fighting each other

拉近乎 lājìnhu *also* "套近乎"〈贬〉 cultivate (unfamiliar people); try to get in with (sb)

拉锯 lājù ❶ work a two-handed saw ❷ be locked in back-and-forth warfare; fight a seesaw battle：～战 seesaw battle

拉拉队 lālāduì *also* "啦啦队" cheering squad; rooters：～长 cheer leader

拉力赛 lālìsài 〈体〉(cross-country) rally

拉链 lāliàn *also* "拉锁" zip fastener; zipper：把～拉上 fasten a zipper; zip up

拉拢 lālǒng draw over to one's side; win over; rope in：～感情 win (people) over by appealing to their sentiments; curry favour (with sb)

拉纤 lāqiàn ❶ tow a boat ❷ act as go-between or middleman：为人～ serve as sb's broker or middleman; lobby or plead on sb's behalf; canvass for sb

拉手 lāshǒu ❶ shake hands ❷ (lāshou) handle：门～ doorknob; door handle

拉下脸 lāxiàliǎn 〈口〉❶ not spare sb's sensibilities：拉不下脸 be afraid of hurting others' feelings ❷ pull a long face; put on a stern expression

拉杂 lāzá rambling; jumbled; ill-organized

邋 lā

邋遢 lātā slovenly; sloppy; unkempt

lá

拉 lá cut; slit; slash：～双眼皮 have plastic surgery on one's eyelids (to make them double-fold) *see also* lā

lǎ

喇 lǎ

喇叭 lǎba ❶ trumpet or similar wind instrument; sth with a flared end：吹～ blow a trumpet; play the *suona* /～花〈口〉(white-edged) morning glory /～裤 flared trousers; bell-bottoms ❷ loudspeaker; horn (of a vehicle)：高音～ tweeter

喇嘛 lǎma lama：～教 Lamaism /～庙 lamasery

là

落 là ❶ leave out or behind; forget to bring; be missing：老～东西 have a habit of leaving things behind; lag or fall behind：～了三天的作业 be three days behind with one's homework *see also* lào; luò

腊(臘) là ❶ (usu 腊月) twelfth lunar month ❷ (of fish, etc) cured in winter (esp in the twelfth lunar month)：～肉 cured meat; bacon /～味 cured meat, fish, etc /～肠 sausage

腊八 làbā *laba* day, eighth day of the twelfth lunar month：～粥 *laba* porridge (porridge made with cereals, beans, nuts and dried fruit, eaten on *laba* day)

腊梅 làméi *also* "蜡梅"〈植〉wintersweet

蜡(蠟) là ❶ wax：～黄 yellow; waxen; sallow / ～人 also "蜡像" wax statue or figure / 给地板打～ wax or polish the floor ❷ candle

蜡版 làbǎn mimeograph stencil;刻～ cut a stencil

蜡笔 làbǐ wax or colour crayon;～画 crayon drawing

蜡染 làrǎn wax printing;～布 wax print;batik

蜡纸 làzhǐ ❶ waxed paper ❷ stencil paper;stencil

蜡烛 làzhú candle;～台 candlestick;candleholder / ～芯儿 candlewick

癞 là

癞痢 làlì 〈方〉favus of the scalp

辣 là

辣 là ❶ peppery;hot;pungent;～酱 thick chilli sauce;chilli paste ❷ (of smell or taste) burn;bite;sting ❸ vicious;ruthless:嘴甜心～ sweet-mouthed but wicked-hearted;hypocritical and malignant

辣椒 làjiāo capsicum;chilli;hot pepper

辣手 làshǒu ❶ ruthless method;vicious device ❷ 〈方〉vicious;ruthless / ❸ thorny;knotty

辣子 làzi ❶ hot pepper;chilli ❷ impetuous, hot-tempered girl or woman;termagant

镴 là also "焊锡";"锡镴" solder

la

啦

啦 la 〈助〉a combination of 了 (le) and 啊 (a) expressing exclamation, interrogation, etc:上课～!Hey! Time for class.

lái

来(來)

来(來) lái ❶ come; arrive:～宾 guest; visitor / ～访 come to visit or call / ～稿 manu-

script received; contribution / ～函〈书〉incoming letter; letter received;your letter / ～～往往 come and go; go to and fro / ～者不拒 all comers are welcome; nobody's request or offer is refused / ～无影去无踪 come without a shadow and leave without a trace; never betray one's whereabouts / ～而不往非礼也。One should take as good as one gets. ❷ crop up; take place ❸ used as a substitute for a more specific verb:会一事儿〈方〉know how to cope with people; have a way with people / 我自己～吧! I'll help myself (to food). or Let me do it myself. ❹ used with 得 or 不 to indicate possibility,capability, or the lack of it:合得～get along well;对不上 / 划不～ it doesn't pay (to do sth) ❺ used before a verb to indicate an intended or suggested action:大家都～出主意。Let's put our heads together. ❻ used after a verb, or between two verbs, to indicate intention or purpose:他回国探亲～了。He returned from abroad to visit his family. / 这件事应写篇报道～宣传。This calls for a special feature to give it enough publicity. ❼ used after a verb to indicate having done sth:你说什么～着? What did you say? or I beg your pardon? ❽ future; coming; next:～年 coming year; next year / ～生 also "来世" next life; sweet by-and-by ❾ used after a time phrase to indicate a duration that lasts from the past up to the present:一周～ for the last week ❿ used after round numbers like 十,百,千 to indicate approximation:十～个 about or around a dozen ⓫ used after numerals 一,二,三 to enumerate reasons or points of argument:练书法,一～有用,二～陶冶性情。Practising calligraphy is useful for one thing; for another, it helps to refine one's sentiment. ⓬ used as filler-word for

L

rhythm and euphony：不愁吃～不愁穿。We are neither worried about food nor clothing. ⑬（lai）*used after a verb to indicate motion towards the speaker*：进～ come in ⑭（lai）*used after a verb to indicate a result or an estimation*：信手写～ write down one's ideas as they come to one's mind

来不得 láibude　won't do; be impermissible：科学～半点虚假。Science permits of no dishonesty.

来得 láide ❶ be able or competent：家务活样样～ be good at every chore in the house ❷ emerge（from a comparison）; come out as：打针比吃药效力～快。Injections produce quicker effects than oral medicine.

来得及 láidejí　there's still time (to do sth); be able to do (sth) in time：来不及 there's not enough time (to do sth); it's too late (to do sth)

来电 láidiàn ❶ incoming telegram or phone call; your telegram or message：～显示 caller ID service ❷ send a telegram; make a telephone call：～祝贺 cable congratulations; send congratulations over the phone

来回 láihuí ❶ go to a place and come back; make a round trip：～票 round-trip ticket; (UK) return ticket ❷ to and fro; back and forth：～走 walk to and fro; pace up and down / ～变 chop and change / ～来去（口）back and forth; over and over again

来劲 láijìn ❶ in high spirits; full of enthusiasm：越干越～ become more enthusiastic as one works on ❷ exciting; exhilarating; thrilling：玩得真～ have a terrific time ❸ gloat (at one's own perceived success, etc); be contrary, unreasonable or perverse (in face of reproach, etc)

来历 láilì　origin; source; background：～不明 (of things) of unknown origin; (of people) of dubious background

来临 láilín　come; arrive; approach

来龙去脉 láilóng-qùmài　origin and evolution; beginning and end; ins and outs

来路 láilù ❶ incoming way; approach ❷ source; origin：断了生活～ cut off the source of sb's support ❸ see "来历"

…来…去 …lái…qù　*used after two identical or synonymous words to indicate the repetition of an action*：想来想去 turn (sth) over and over in one's mind

来日 láirì　the future; days to come：～方长。There will be ample time (for that).

来势 láishì　oncoming force; gathering momentum：～汹汹 come to look for trouble; break in (upon sb) in full fury

来头 láitou ❶ background; backing; connections：大有～ have rather powerful backing ❷ motive; reason; cause：他这话有～。There's something more to what he said. ❸ see "来势" ❹ fun; interest：跟你下棋没～。It's no fun playing chess with you.

来往 láiwǎng ❶ come and go：～账目 current account ❷ (láiwang) contact; intercourse; dealings：和一些不三不四的人～ hang around with some dubious characters

来由 láiyóu ❶ reason; cause：毫无～ without rhyme or reason ❷ see "来历"

来源 láiyuán ❶ source; origin ❷ originate; stem from

来之不易 láizhībùyì　not easily come by; hard-earned

莱（萊）lái

莱菔 láifú　〈植〉radish

莱塞 láisè　*also* "激光"〈理〉laser

lài

睐(睞) lài 〈书〉❶ squint ❷ look at; glance

赖 lài ❶ depend; rely: 以~以生存 rely on sth for existence ❷ impudent; cheeky; rascally: 这人真~。 What a brazen guy! ❸ drag out (beyond what is necessary or welcome); hang on where one does not belong: ~床 linger in bed after waking up ❹ deny (what was previously said or done); renege; shirk: ~账 repudiate a debt; default; go back on one's word ❺ put the blame on (sb else); shift the blame onto (sb else); blame: 这事不~你。 You are not to blame for this. ❻ no good; poor

赖皮 làipí ❶ rascally; brazen; unreasonable ❷ also "要赖皮" act shamelessly or brazenly

癞 lài also "麻风" 〈医〉leprosy ❷ 〈方〉favus of the scalp: ~皮狗 mangy dog; 〈喻〉loathsome creature

癞蛤蟆 làiháma also "癞虾蟆" toad: ~想吃天鹅肉 〈俗〉act like a toad lusting after a swan's flesh; crave for sth one is not worthy of

籁 lài sound; noise: 天~ sounds of nature

lán

兰(蘭) lán ❶ orchid: ~花 also "兰草"; "春兰" orchid; (sword-leaved) cymbidium ❷ also "兰草" fragrant thoroughwort

岚 lán 〈书〉mountain haze or mist

拦(攔) lán ❶ block; bar; hold back: ~击 intercept and attack / ~截 stop and rob; waylay; mug / ~网 〈体〉block (in volleyball) / ~阻 block; stop; obstruct / ~洪坝 flood-control dam / ~路虎 stumbling block; obstacle / ~一辆出租车 stop or get a taxi ❷ direct (a blow, etc) right at: ~头一棍 give (sb) a head-on blow with one's club / ~腰截断 cut in the middle; block (a river) with a dam; dam (a river)

栏(欄) lán ❶ fence; railing; hurdle: ~杆 also "阑干" railing; banister; balustrade ❷ pen; shed; barn: 羊~ sheep pen ❸ (usu 栏目) column (in a newspaper, or form): 征聘 "~" "wants" column ❹ board (for putting up notices or newspapers)

阑 lán ❶ see "栏❶" lán ❷ see "拦❶" lán ❸ (usu 阑珊) 〈书〉draw to an end; wane; be late

阑尾 lánwěi 〈生理〉(vermiform) appendix: ~炎 〈医〉appendicitis

蓝(藍) lán ❶ blue: ~靛 indigo (blue); dark blue / ~领 also "蓝领工人" blue-collar worker / ~宝石 sapphire / ~筹股 blue chip (stock) / ~晶晶 (of water, gems, etc) blue and glittering; bright blue / ~盔部队 Blue Berets — UN peace-keeping force / ~莹莹的天 azure sky ❷ indigo plant

蓝本 lánběn source material; original version on which later work is based

蓝图 lántú blueprint; 〈喻〉plan; scheme

谰 lán 〈书〉❶ calumniate; slander; malign: ~言 calumny; slander ❷ deny; disavow

澜 lán billows; waves: 微~ ripples

褴(襤) lán

褴褛 lánlǚ also "蓝缕" ragged; tattered: 衣衫~ in rags or tatters; out at elbows

lán

篮（籃） lán ❶ basket ❷〈体〉 goal; basket; 补～ tip-in or follow-up shot / 塞～ dunk shot / 上～ lay up / 投～ shoot (a basket) / ～板 backboard; bank / 框 basket; ring hoop / ～圈 ring; hoop / ～板球 rebound ❸ basketball (team); ～坛 basketball circles

篮球 lánqiú 〈体〉 basketball; ～场 basketball court

lǎn

览（覽） lǎn ❶〈书〉look at; see; view; ～胜 see sights; tour scenic spots ❷ read

揽（攬） lǎn ❶ pull or take in to one's arms; hold; fasten with a rope, etc; 把孩子～在怀里 clasp a child to one's bosom ❷ take on; take upon oneself; canvass; ～承 undertake (to do sth); take on (a job, etc) / ～活 undertake jobs; solicit work / ～事 take on what is not one's business; mind others' business ❸ grasp; exercise control over; monopolize; ～权 arrogate power to oneself; seize or monopolize power / ～总 take overall charge; assume overall responsibility; take on everything

缆（纜） lǎn ❶ hawser; mooring rope or cable ❷ thick rope; cable; ～车 cable car / ～道 cableway ❸ moor (a ship)

罱 lǎn ❶ rectangular net used for fishing or dredging ❷ dredge up (silt, mud, etc)

溂 lǎn ❶ season (vegetables, etc) in salt or other dressings ❷ remove puckery taste (of persimmons, etc)

懒（嬾） lǎn ❶ lazy; indolent; ～虫 also "懒鬼"; "懒骨头"〈口〉lazybones / ～惰 lazy; indolent / ～汉 lazybones; sluggard;

idler ❷ sluggish; languid; listless; ～ 散 sluggish and careless; indolent and slack / ～洋洋 (of one's manner) sluggish; languid; spiritless

懒怠 lǎndai ❶ lazy; indolent ❷ see "懒得"

懒得 lǎnde have no inclination (to do sth); not feel like (doing sth); ～开会 be tired of meetings

làn

烂（爛） làn ❶ sodden; pappy; mushy; ～烂 (of food) mushy; pulpy / ～泥 mud; slush; mire / 一煮就～ (of food) cook quickly ❷ rot; fester; decay; ～肠子 also "烂肚肠"〈口〉have rotten bowels —be wicked or evil / ～嘴角儿 canker of the mouth ❸ broken; tattered; worn-out; ～货〈口〉shoddy stuff;〈贬〉lazy woman of easy virtue; slatternly hussy / 破衣～衫 worn-out clothes; rags ❹ messy; confused; ～账 messy account; bad debt or loan / ～摊子 awful mess; shambles ❺ thoroughly; very; ～熟 be thoroughly cooked; know thoroughly; learn off pat / ～醉如泥 be dead drunk; drink oneself into a stupor

烂漫 lànmàn also "烂缦"; "烂缦" ❶ bright-coloured; brilliant; 春光～。Spring is very much in the air. ❷ unaffected; unpretentious; 一颗～的童心 a heart as innocent as that of a child

滥（濫） làn ❶ overflow; flood; inundate ❷ excessive; indiscriminate; unrestrained; ～调 hackneyed tune; worn-out theme; platitude / ～杀无辜 wantonly or indiscriminately slaughter innocent people / ～用职权 abuse one's power

滥觞 lànshāng 〈书〉❶ origin; beginning ❷ (usu used with 于) originate; begin

滥竽充数 lànyúchōngshù （of incompetent people or inferior goods）be there just to make up the number; pass off as an expert or a brand name

lāng

啷

啷 lāng

啷当 lāngdāng （of age）about; around;20～岁 just about twenty years old

láng

郎

郎 láng ❶ young man:～才女貌 (a perfect match between)a talented man and a beautiful woman ❷ *usu used by a woman to address her husband or lover*:～君 husband ❸ 〈旧〉son of another person:令～ your son

郎中 lángzhōng 〈俗〉physician of herbal medicine; doctor of Chinese medicine:江湖～ quack doctor

狼

狼 láng wolf:～狗 wolfhound; wolf dog /～嗥 wolf's howl /～奔豕突 (of a crowd, etc) tear about like mad (like wolves or boars); go on the rampage /～吞咽 wolf (down); gobble up; devour ravenously /～子野心 wolf cub with a savage heart — vicious nature with wild ambitions

狼狈 lángbèi in a difficult position; in a tight corner:～为奸 act in cahoots; work hand in glove; band together /一副～相 cut a sorry figure

狼藉 lángjí also "狼籍"〈书〉in disorder; in a mess:声名～ ruin one's reputation; be notorious

狼心狗肺 lángxīn-gǒufèi ❶ cruel and unscrupulous; brutal and cold-blooded ❷ ungrateful

狼烟 lángyān smoke or flames of war:～四起 smoke of war rising from

all sides; war alarms raised everywhere

琅（瑯）

琅 láng

琅琅 lángláng 〈象声〉tinkle; jingle:～上口 easy to read out loud /～书声 ringing sound of reading aloud

廊

廊 láng porch; corridor; veranda

榔

榔 láng

榔头 lángtou hammer

锒

锒 láng

锒铛 lángdāng also "郎当"❶〈书〉iron chains; ～入狱 be chained and thrown into prison ❷ clank; clang:～作响 go clanging or clanking

lǎng

朗

朗 lǎng ❶ light; bright;天～气清 clear sky and fresh air ❷ loud and clear:～读 read aloud; read loudly and clearly /～声大笑 burst into loud laughter

朗朗 lǎnglǎng ❶〈象声〉loud and clear sound, as of reading aloud ❷ bright; light

朗诵 lǎngsòng read aloud with expression; recite; declaim:～会 recitation

làng

浪

浪 làng ❶ wave; billow; breaker:～花 spray or foam of breaking waves; spindrift /～涛滚滚 rolling waves ❷ sth undulating like waves:热～ heat wave /～船 swingboat ❸ unrestrained; dissolute:～语 lewd or obscene remarks; bawdy speech /～游四方 wander from place to place

浪潮 làngcháo tide; wave:抗议的～ waves of protest

浪荡 làngdàng ❶ loiter, loaf or idle about ❷ dissolute; debauched; dissipated：～鬼 roué；rake

浪费 làngfèi　waste；squander；be extravagant：～时间 idle or fritter away one's time；waste time

浪迹 làngjì　drift about with no fixed lodging；lead a vagrant life：～江湖 lead a wandering and vagabond life

浪漫 làngmàn ❶ romantic；poetic；imaginative：～史 romance / ～主义 romanticism ❷ abandoned；lax；loose

浪头 làngtou ❶ wave；billow ❷ trend：赶～ follow the trend

浪子 làngzǐ　prodigal；loafer；wastrel：～回头金不换〈俗〉a prodigal who turns over a new leaf is more precious than gold；broken bones well set become stronger

lāo

捞（撈）

lāo ❶ drag or fish for；dredge up；scoop up（from the water）：～面 noodles cooled in cold water after being boiled / 捕鱼～虾 net fish and shrimps ❷ get（usu by improper means）；wangle：～本 win back lost wagers；recover one's losses；recoup oneself / ～钱 make money（by questionable means）/ ～外快 earn extra income；moonlight / ～一把 also "捞一票" rake in（usu illegal）profits；profiteer；gain advantages（in politics, etc）/ 他中了个大奖，算是～着了。He was lucky enough to draw the grand prize.

捞稻草 lāodàocǎo ❶ clutch at a straw ❷（try to）take advantage of sth；capitalize on sth：利用别人的失误～ cash in on others' mistakes

捞取 lāoqǔ ❶ drag for；dredge up；scoop up（from the water）❷ fish for；gain：～名利 grab fame and fortune

láo

劳（勞）

láo ❶ work；labour：～作 labour；work / 逸结合 strike a proper balance between work and rest ❷〈敬〉used in asking sb to do sth or for a favour：这事有～您啦。I'll depend on you for that. ❸ labourer；labour：～方 labour ❹ fatigue；toil：～乏 physically exhausted；tired；run-down / ～民伤财 tire the people and drain the treasury；waste money and manpower / 请勿～步.〈敬〉Please don't bother to come（and visit）. ❺ meritorious deed；service：～绩卓著 outstanding merits and accomplishments ❻ express one's appreciation or thanks；reward：～军 greet and bring gifts to the army；comfort the soldiers（with entertainment, etc）

劳保 láobǎo ❶（short for 劳动保险）labour insurance ❷（short for 劳动保护）labour protection

劳动 láodòng ❶ work；labour；（esp）physical or manual labour：～布 denim / ～节（short for 五一国际劳动节）Labour Day（1 May）/ ～模范（shortened as 劳模）model worker / ～人民 working or labouring people / ～合同制 contract labour system / ～密集型 labour-intensive / ～生产率（labour）productivity ❷（láodong）〈敬〉bother；trouble：不敢～大驾. I would not dream of bothering you（with sth）.

劳动力 láodònglì ❶ labour or work force；labour：～不足 short of manpower；short-handed ❷ capacity for physical labour：丧失～ lose one's ability to work；be disabled ❸ able-bodied person；labourer

劳顿 láodùn（�）fatigued；wearied：旅途～ fatigued by a journey；travel-worn

劳改 láogǎi（short for 劳动改造）re-

form (of criminals) through labour：~
犯 criminal serving a sentence of reform
through labour / ~产品 prison labour
product

劳工 láogōng ❶ labourer；worker；
labour；~ 运动 labour movement ❷
〈旧〉coolie

劳驾 láojià 〈套〉excuse me；may I
trouble you (to do sth)

劳教 láojiào (short for 劳动教养) reeducation (of juvenile delinquents, etc)
through labour

劳苦 láokǔ toil；hard work；不辞~
spare no pains / ~大众 toiling masses

劳累 láolèi ❶ tired；run-down；ex-
hausted；~ 过度 overworked ❷ 〈敬〉
trouble (sb)；~您去一趟。I'm afraid
you'll have to make this trip.

劳力 láolì ❶ labour；work ❷ labour
force；able-bodied person ❸ use one's
physical strength；do manual work；
费心 exert one's strength and rack
one's brains

劳碌 láolù work hard；toil；~ 命
(person) destined to toil all one's life；
born for hard work

劳神 láoshén ❶ be trying；be a tax
on (one's mind) ❷ 〈套〉may I trouble
you；will you please

劳师动众 láoshī-dòngzhòng mobilize
too many troops；drag in lots of
people

劳损 láosǔn 〈医〉strain；腰肌 ~
strain of lumbar muscles；psoatic strain

劳务 láowù (labour) services；~ 费
service charge / ~ 输出 export of labour services

劳燕分飞 láoyànfēnfēi (usu of man
and wife or lovers) part；separate

劳役 láoyì ❶ 〈法〉penal servitude；
forced labour ❷ corvée ❸ use (as a
draught animal)

劳资 láozī labour and capital；~ 关系
relations between labour and capital；
labour-management relations / ~ 纠纷

dispute between labour and manage-
ment；industrial dispute

牢 láo ❶ 〈书〉animal enclosure；
pen；fold ❷ prison；jail；~ 房
cell；ward (of a prison) / ~ 狱 prison；
gaol；jail ❸ firm；fast；~ 固 firm；
fast；solid / ~ 记 keep firmly in
mind；remember well；bear in mind /
~不可破 unbreakable；indestructible

牢靠 láokào ❶ firm；strong；sturdy
❷ dependable；reliable

牢笼 láolóng ❶ cage；bonds；冲出~
shake off bonds ❷ trap；snare；误入~
be caught in a trap；fall into a trap；
be entrapped ❸ 〈书〉win or draw over ❹
〈书〉tie；bind up；fetter

牢骚 láosāo ❶ discontent；grievance；
complaint；~ 满腹 be full of grievances；
be querulous ❷ complain；grumble

唠(嘮) láo see also lào

唠叨 láodao be garrulous；chatter；
nag

痨(癆) láo consumption；
tuberculosis (TB)

醪 láo

醪糟 láozāo fermented glutinous rice；
~汤圆 dumplings cooked in fermented
rice soup

lǎo

老 lǎo ❶ old；aged；elderly；程~
〈敬〉venerable Mr Cheng / ~ 辈
(one's) elder；old folk；ancestor / ~
伯〈敬〉(used to address people of
father's generation) uncle / ~ 汉 old
man / ~ 路 old road；same route；
beaten path / ~ 区 old liberated area /
~大娘〈敬〉(usu of an elderly woman
one doesn't know) aunty；granny / ~
掉牙 hoary；corny；ancient / ~ 东西
〈粗〉useless old thing；silly old fool /
~干部 veteran cadre；retired cadre /

～古董 antique; museum piece; old fogey / ～皇历 yesterday's newspaper; obsolete practice or rule / ～顽固 old stick-in-the-mud; diehard; fogey / ～一套 *also* "老套" same old stuff or story / ～字号 store of long standing / ～有所养. Elderly people will be properly provided for. ❷ seasoned; experienced; veteran: ～辣 seasoned and vicious; (of handwriting, etc) smooth and vigorous / ～手 old hand; veteran / ～于此道 experienced in this line (of tricks, etc) ❸ old-fashioned; outdated; obsolete: ～式 old-fashioned; outdated / ～把戏 same old stuff; old trick; outmoded method / ～套子 outdated custom; outmoded method ❹ original; former; same: ～坟 ancestral grave / ～汤 sauce specially reserved from previous cooking to be used as a condiment / ～地方 same place ❺ (usu of vegetables or food) overgrown; tough; overcooked: 鸡蛋炒嫩点儿还是～点儿? Do you like the eggs underdone or well-done? ❻ for a long time; long: 最近～没见他。I haven't seen him for a long time. ❼ always; constantly; frequently: ～是自作主张 always like to act on one's own ❽ very; extremely; terribly: ～大不小〈口〉fully grown; no longer little / 天气～热 terribly hot weather ❾〈口〉youngest: ～叔 youngest paternal uncle / ～儿子 youngest son ❿ *used as a prefix before a person or certain animals or things*: ～爸〈口〉(usu used by a younger person to refer to his or her father) the old man; guv, guvnor / ～鸨 woman running a brothel; procuress; madam / ～粗 *also* "大老粗" uneducated person; rough and ready chap / ～公〈口〉husband; hubby / ～婆〈口〉wife; missus / ～鹰 black-eared kite; hawk; eagle / ～玉米〈方〉maize; (Indian) corn; boiled

tender corn / ～丈人 wife's father; father-in-law

老百姓 lǎobǎixìng　common or ordinary people; civilians; men in the street

老板 lǎobǎn　shopkeeper; proprietor; boss; ～娘 proprietress; boss's wife

老伴儿 lǎobànr　〈口〉old spouse: 我～ my old man or woman; my hubby or missus

老本 lǎoběn　principal; capital: 吃～(喻) live off one's past gains; rest on one's laurels / 输光～ lose one's last stakes

老巢 lǎocháo　nest; den; lair: 端了土匪的～ completely destroy the bandits' den

老成 lǎochéng　experienced; steady; prudent: ～持重 experienced and prudent; prudent and cool-headed; mature

老大 lǎodà　❶〈书〉old: 少小离家～回 leave home when young and return home an old man ❷ eldest child (in a family); eldest among siblings; first among equals: ～哥〈敬〉oldest (of a group, etc) / 本行业的～ No 1 or flagship of the industry ❸〈方〉boatman of a sailing vessel; captain; skipper ❹ boss (of a gang) ❺ greatly; very: 心中～不忍 feel extremely reluctant

老大难 lǎodànán　long-standing, big and difficult (problem): ～问题 problem that has long defied solution; difficult problem of long standing; hard nut to crack

老当益壮 lǎodāngyìzhuàng　be aspiring despite old age; be old but vigorous

老到 lǎodao　(in doing things) experienced and thoughtful; mature and prudent

老底 lǎodǐ　❶ inside or true story; unsavory background; past: 揭～ reveal the inside story about sth or embarrassing facts about sb's past; drag the skeleton out of sb's closet ❷ family fortune; savings; nest-egg: ～儿厚 have a considerable family fortune; have much (savings, etc) to fall back upon

老弟 lǎodì (familiar form of address to a man younger than oneself) young fellow; buddy; my boy

老调 lǎodiào hackneyed theme; platitude: ～重弹 harp on the same string; sing the same old tune

老豆腐 lǎodòufu ❶ processed bean curd ❷ also "北豆腐" bean curd made in the northern style; firm tofu

老夫 lǎofū〈书〉(used by an old man to refer to himself) I; me

老夫子 lǎofūzǐ ❶〈旧〉a term of respect for a teacher in a private school or a scholar-staffer ❷ pedant

老姑娘 lǎogūniang ❶ also "老处女" spinster; old maid ❷ also "老闺女" youngest daughter

老好人 lǎohǎorén one who tries to please everybody (without regard to principles); Mr Please-All

老虎 lǎohǔ tiger: 母～ tigress; shrew / ～机 slot machine (for gambling) / ～钳 vice; pincer pliers / ～屁股摸不得〈俗〉won't allow any different opinions; be not to be crossed / ～头上拍苍蝇〈俗〉invite trouble; court disaster

老花 lǎohuā presbyopic: ～镜 presbyopic glasses / ～眼 presbyopia

老化 lǎohuà ageing: 人口～ ageing population / 知识～ obsolete or outdated knowledge

老黄牛 lǎohuángniú willing ox — person who serves wholeheartedly

老骥伏枥，志在千里 lǎojìfúlì, zhìzàiqiānlǐ an old steed in the stable still aspires to gallop a thousand *li* — old people may still cherish high aspirations

老几 lǎojǐ ❶ order of seniority among siblings; birth order: 你排行～? Where

do you come in the family? ❷ *usu used in rhetorical questions to indicate a negligible status*: 你算～? Who do you think you are?

老家 lǎojiā ❶ old home; native place ❷ family living in one's native place; ancestral home

老奸巨滑 lǎojiān-jùhuá old hand at trickery; crafty old scoundrel

老茧 lǎojiǎn also "老趼" callosity; callus: 长满～的手 callused hand

老练 lǎoliàn seasoned; experienced; knowing one's way around: ～通达 seasoned and sensible; experienced and reasonable

老马识途 lǎomǎshítú〈谚〉an old horse knows the way; an old man is a good guide; an old hand knows the ropes

老迈 lǎomài aged; senile: ～昏庸 senile and fatuous; old and muddle-headed

老谋深算 lǎomóu-shēnsuàn circumspect and far-sighted; experienced and astute; calculating and crafty

老年 lǎonián old age: ～斑 also "老人斑" senile plaque; old-age speckle / ～人 senior citizen; old people; the aged / ～学 gerontology / ～人口 elderly population / ～性痴呆〈医〉senile dementia

老牛 lǎoniú old ox or cow: ～破车 also "老牛拉破车"〈俗〉creep slowly along; drag along at a snail's pace / ～舐犊 old cow licking her calf — parental love

老牌 lǎopái ❶ old brand ❷ old-timer; veteran: ～儿特务 seasoned spy

老气 lǎoqì ❶ mature; old-mannish: ～横秋 arrogant on account of one's seniority; decrepit; lacking in youthful vigour ❷ (of clothes, etc) dark and old-fashioned

老人 lǎorén ❶ old man or woman; the aged: ～政治 also "老人统治"

L

gerontocracy ❷ one's aged parents or grandparents

老人家 lǎorénjia ❶〈敬〉venerable old person ❷ parent

老生常谈 lǎoshēngchángtán commonplace remark; mere platitude; truism

老师 lǎoshī ❶ teacher: 中小学～ school teacher; schoolmaster; schoolmistress ❷ used as a polite term of address: 李～ Mr or Ms Li

老实 lǎoshi ❶ honest; frank: ～交待 come clean; own up; make a clean breast (of sth) ❷ well-behaved; lawabiding; good: ～巴交〈方〉wellbehaved and law-abiding; circumspect and timid ❸〈婉〉simple-minded; naive; easily taken in

老鼠 lǎoshǔ mouse; rat: ～药 rat-poison; ratsbane / ～过街，人人喊打〈俗〉be chased after like a rat; be extremely unpopular

老太太 lǎotàitai〈敬〉old lady; your or my mother or mother-in-law

老太爷 lǎotàiyé〈敬〉old or elderly gentleman; your or my father or father-in-law

老态龙钟 lǎotàilóngzhōng senile and doddering; old and clumsy; weighed down with age

老天 lǎotiān〈口〉God; Heaven: ～有眼 heaven has eyes — there is divine justice after all

老头子 lǎotóuzi ❶ old man; old fogey or codger ❷ (used for one's aged husband) my old man ❸ (often used by those under him) chief of a secret society; boss

老外 lǎowài〈口〉❶ layman; raw hand; nonprofessional ❷ foreigner

老王卖瓜，自卖自夸 Lǎowángmàiguā, zìmàizìkuā〈俗〉a melon pedlar always says his melons are sweet; every cook praises his own broth

老乡 lǎoxiāng fellow-townsman;

fellow-villager ❷ (form of address to a rural person whose name one doesn't know) buddy; chap

老相 lǎoxiàng look older than one's age

老小 lǎoxiǎo grown-ups and children; one's family: 一家～ one's whole family

老兄 lǎoxiōng (usu used among men) brother; mate; buddy: 此事就拜托了。Old chap, I would leave it to you, OK?

老羞成怒 lǎoxiūchéngnù also "恼羞成怒" be shamed into anger; fly into a rage out of shame; lose one's temper from embarrassment

老朽 lǎoxiǔ ❶ decrepit and behind the times; old and useless ❷〈谦〉(used by old people) I; me

老爷 lǎoye ❶〈贬〉bureaucrat: ～兵 pampered soldiers / ～作风 bureaucratic attitude ❷〈旧〉(used by domestic servants) master; lord ❸ see "姥爷" lǎoye ❹ old-fashioned; old (and dilapidated): ～车 vintage car

老油子 lǎoyóuzi also "老油条" wily old bird; old slicker

老于世故 lǎoyúshìgù versed in the ways of the world; sophisticated; worldly-wise

老账 lǎozhàng ❶ old or long-standing debt ❷ old scores: 翻～ bring up old scores

老子 lǎozi〈口〉❶ father; dad ❷ (used to show contempt for others, or said in anger, pride, etc) I; me: ～天下第一 regard oneself as number one under heaven

老总 lǎozǒng〈口〉❶ marshal ❷ term of address for 总经理, 总工程师, etc: 刘～ General Manager Liu ❸〈旧〉(used to address a soldier) sir

佬 lǎo〈贬〉man; guy; fellow: 美国～ Yankee / 乡巴～儿 country bumpkin

姥 lǎo

姥姥 lǎolao　*also "老老"* (maternal) grandmother or grandma

姥爷 lǎoye　*also "老爷"* (maternal) grandfather or grandpa

lào

唠（嘮） lào

〈方〉talk; speak; chat; ~嗑 chat; chit-chat　*see also* láo

烙 lào

❶ brand; sear; iron ❷ bake in a pan; ~饼 pancake　*see also* luò

烙铁 làotie　❶ flatiron; iron ❷ soldering or searing iron; solder-iron

烙印 làoyìn　brand; stamp: 时代的~ brand of the times / 在心灵上留下深深的~ be deeply engraved upon one's mind

涝（澇） lào

waterlogging; floodwater (on low-lying land): ~灾 extensive damage caused by waterlogging / 排~ drain off floodwater; drain a waterlogged area

落 lào

usu used in the following entries　*see also* là; luò

落不是 làobùshi　get blamed for an alleged fault; be blamed;落了一身不是 earn nothing but blame

落汗 làohàn　have sweat (on a human body) evaporate; stop sweating

落价 làojià　drop or fall in price; lower or reduce the price; mark down

落枕 làozhěn　❶ stiff neck (caused by cold or awkward sleeping posture) ❷ (of one's head) touch the pillow; 着 fall asleep as soon as one's head hits the pillow

酪 lào

❶ junket: 奶~ cheese ❷ fruit jelly; sweet paste (made from crushed nuts): 杏仁~ apricot kernel cream

lē

肋 lē *see also* lèi

肋脦 lēde　*also* lēte〈方〉(of clothes) slovenly; sloppy; dirty and untidy

lè

乐（樂） lè

❶ happy; cheerful; joyful: ~呵呵 cheerful and merry; happy and gay; buoyant / ~滋滋 contented; pleased / ~极生悲 extreme joy begets sorrow; when the cup of happiness overflows, disaster follows ❷ be glad to; find pleasure in; enjoy: ~善好施 be happy to do good and give alms; be glad to give to charities / ~于助人 be happy to help others / ~在其中 find pleasure in sth / ~得玩玩儿 readily take an opportunity to enjoy oneself ❸ laugh; be amused
see also yuè

乐不可支 lèbùkězhī　be overwhelmed with joy; one's joy knows no bounds

乐不思蜀 lèbùsīshǔ　indulge in pleasure and forget home and duty; abandon oneself to pleasures

乐此不疲 lècǐbùpí　*also "乐此不倦"* always enjoy sth; never tire of sth

乐观 lèguān　optimistic; hopeful; sanguine; 前景~ have a bright future; be optimistic about the future / ~主义 optimism

乐趣 lèqù　delight; pleasure; joy

乐天 lètiān　carefree; optimistic; happy-go-lucky: ~派 carefree and happy-go-lucky person; optimist / ~知命 submit to the will of heaven and be content with one's lot; be easily contented

乐意 lèyì　❶ be willing or ready to ❷ pleased; happy

乐园 lèyuán　❶ *also "乐土"* land of happiness; promised land; paradise: 人

间～ paradise on earth; land of milk and honey ❷ amusement park:儿童～ children's playground

勒 lè ❶〈书〉headstall; halter ❷ rein in (a horse) ❸ force; compel; coerce:～索 extort (money); blackmail (sb) ❹〈书〉carve; engrave; inscribe:～碑 inscribe on a stone tablet
see also lēi

勒令 lèlìng compel (by legal authority); order:～停工 order (sb) to stop work; order (a plant, etc) shut down /～退学 rusticate (a student)

le

了 le〈助〉❶ used after a verb or an adjective to indicate the completion of an action or a change:我买～房。I've bought a house. ❷ used at the end or in the middle of a sentence to indicate **a)** new circumstances that have occurred or are about to occur:天快亮～。It will soon be dawn. **b)** result of a condition:天一下雨，我们就不出门～。If it rains, we will stay indoors. **c)** change in understanding, opinion, action, etc:她明白～是自己的错。She realized that she had been wrong. **d)** urging or dissuasion:别哭～! Stop crying!
see also liǎo

lēi

勒 lēi ❶ tie or strap tight:～紧裤腰带 tighten one's belt — practise austerity ❷〈方〉force; compel; coerce
see also lè

累(纍) léi see also lěi; lèi

累累 léiléi ❶〈书〉haggard and dejected; gaunt and listless:～若丧家之狗 wretched as a homeless cur ❷ clusters of; heaps of:果实～ fruit hanging in clusters
see also lěilěi

累赘 léizhui also "累坠" ❶ (of things) superfluous; burdensome; (of writing) wordy ❷ (be a) burden; encumbrance; nuisance

雷 léi ❶ thunder:～雨 thunderstorm /～电交作 lightning accompanied by thunder /掌声～动 thunderous applause /〈军〉mine; detonator:～管 detonator; primer

雷池 léichí〈喻〉limit; confinement:不可越～一步 must not go beyond the limits

雷达 léidá radar (radio detection and ranging):～干扰 radar jamming /～跟踪 radar tracking

雷打不动 léidǎbùdòng unshakable; unyielding; (of a schedule, etc) not to be altered under any circumstances

雷厉风行 léilì-fēngxíng (carry out orders, etc) resolutely and swiftly; (perform a task) with drive and sweep

雷鸣 léimíng ❶ roaring or rumbling thunder ❷ thunderous

雷声 léishēng thunderclap; thunder:隆隆～ rumble of thunder /～大，雨点小〈俗〉loud thunder but small raindrops; much said but little done; much promise but little performance

雷霆 léitíng thunderclap; thunderbolt; thunder-like power or rage:～万钧 (like a) powerful thunderbolt; devastating punch; crushing blow

雷同 léitóng duplicate; identical:如有～，纯属巧合。Any resemblance is accidental.

擂 léi ❶ grind; pestle; pound:～钵 mortar ❷ hit; beat; punch
see also lèi

léi

镭 léi 〈化〉radium (Ra) / ～疗 〈医〉radium therapy

镭射 léishè see "激光" jīguāng

lěi

垒(壘) lěi ❶ build by piling up bricks, stones, earth, etc ❷〈军〉rampart; fort; fortification ❸〈体〉base / ～球 softball / 全～打 home run

累(❶·❷ 纍) lěi ❶ pile up; gather; accumulate:累进税 progressive tax / 势如～卵 be like a stack of eggs — be in an extremely dangerous or precarious situation ❷ repeated; continuous; running:～次 time and again; repeatedly / ～犯 recidivist; recidivism ❸ implicate; involve:～及无辜 involve innocent people see also léi; lèi

累积 lěijī accumulate; collect; gather:～数 accumulated number / ～量 cumulative quantity

累计 lěijì ❶ add up (to); total ❷ accumulative, grand or sum total

累累 lěilěi ❶ again and again; many times ❷ innumerable; countless:血债～ owe many blood debts
see also léilěi

磊 lěi

磊磊 lěilěi 〈书〉heaps (of stones)

磊落 lěiluò ❶ open and upright:胸怀～ open-hearted and upright ❷〈书〉many and jumbled

蕾 lěi (flower) bud

lèi

肋 lèi rib; costal region:～骨 also "肋条" rib; costa / ～膜炎 pleurisy / 两～ both sides of the chest see also lē

泪(淚) lèi tear; teardrop:～痕 tear stains / ～花 tears in one's eyes / ～腺 tear or lachrymal gland / ～珠 teardrop; tear / ～汪汪 tearful; (eyes) brimming with tears / 如雨下 tears fall like rain; tears stream down one's cheeks; shed a flood of tears / 流下感激的～ shed tears of gratitude

类(類) lèi ❶ kind; type; category:～别 classification / ～型 type; category; genre / ～型 type; category; kind ❷ resemble; be similar to:～似 similar; analogous / ～人猿 anthropoid (ape) / ～平神话 sound like a fairy tale

类比 lèibǐ analogy:把心脏和水泵相～ draw an analogy between the heart and a pump

类推 lèituī analogize; reason by analogy:照此～ by this analogy; by analogy to this

累 lèi ❶ tire; fatigue; weary:～坏了 dead tired; worn out; exhausted ❷ work hard; toil:～死～活 work one's fingers to the bone; work like a dog:
see also léi; lěi

擂 lèi ring (for martial contests); arena:～主 one who gives an open challenge see also léi

擂台 lèitái ring or stage (for martial art contests); arena:摆～ give an open challenge / ～赛 open contest or challenge

lei

嘞 lei 〈助〉similar to 嘞 but with a lighter tone:好～,我听您的! Okay, I'll do as you say.

léng

棱(稜) léng ❶ edge:有～有角 angular ❷ corrugation; ridge

棱角 léngjiǎo ❶ edges and corners 〈喻〉edge; pointedness:不露～ draw in one's horns / ～毕露 make a full display of one's talent

棱镜 léngjìng （glass）prism; optical prism; edge glass:三～ triangular prism

lěng

冷 lěng ❶ cold; chilly; frigid; ～盘 also "冷菜" cold dish; hors d'oeuvre / ～色 cold colour / ～飕飕 (of wind, etc) chilly; chilling / ～血动物 cold-blooded animal; 〈喻〉unfeeling or cold-hearted person / 出～汗 be in a cold sweat ❷ cold in manner; frosty; icy: ～峻 cold and sharp; sober and grave; stern / ～嘲热讽 taunt and jeer; scathing sarcasm / ～若冰霜 (usu of women) as cold as ice; frosty ～言～语 sarcastic comments; ironical remarks ❸ unfrequented; deserted; out-of-the-way:～凄凄 cold and dreary; lonely; deserted ❹ strange; rare; unpopular:～货 unpopular or unattractive goods; unsalable goods / ～字 rarely-used word ❺ covert; underhanded; sudden:～炮 sporadic and unexpected shelling ❻ dishearten; discourage; dampen:我的心一下子～了。I was struck cold at heart.

冷冰冰 lěngbīngbīng （of an object, one's manner, etc）ice-cold; icy; frigid

冷不防 lěngbùfáng also "冷不丁" unawares; off one's guard; by surprise

冷藏 lěngcáng refrigeration; cold storage: ～室 refrigerating chamber; cold closet

冷场 lěngchǎng awkward silence on the stage or at a meeting, etc:说个笑话打破～ crack a joke to break the ice

冷淡 lěngdàn ❶ slack; sluggish ❷ cold; indifferent; apathetic ❸ treat coldly; cold-shoulder; slight

冷冻 lěngdòng freezing:～食品 frozen food / ～手术 cryosurgery

冷风 lěngfēng ❶ cold wind or draught; cold air: ～机 air cooler ❷ negative or unfavourable remarks:吹～ make negative remarks; spread malignant gossip

冷宫 lěnggōng cold palace — part of the palace to which disfavoured queens or concubines were banished; 〈喻〉limbo:打入～ consign to limbo; shelve

冷箭 lěngjiàn arrow shot from hiding; sniper's shot:放～ make a sneak attack

冷静 lěngjìng ❶ deserted and quiet; still; hushed ❷ calm; sober; composed:遇事要～。Play it cool when in trouble.

冷酷 lěngkù cold-hearted; cold-blooded; callous

冷落 lěngluò ❶ unfrequented; desolate:门庭～ have few visitors, guests or customers ❷ treat coldly; cold-shoulder; slight

冷门 lěngmén ❶ little-known profession, trade or branch of learning ❷ unexpected winner; dark horse; upset

冷面 lěngmiàn ❶ cold noodles ❷ stern-looking face; cold eye; poker face:～滑稽 telling a joke with a poker face; dry humour

冷漠 lěngmò cold and detached; indifferent; nonchalant

冷暖 lěngnuǎn changes in temperature;〈喻〉shifting ways of the world; everyday life: ～自知 know what's what by one's own experience / 关心群众的～ be concerned with the well-being of the people

冷僻 lěngpì ❶ deserted; desolate; out-of-the-way:性格～ be given to solitude ❷ unfamiliar; rare

冷气 lěngqì ❶ cold or cool air ❷ air conditioning

冷枪 lěngqiāng sniper's shot:打～

fire a sniper's shot; snipe (at sb)

冷清 lěngqīng　cold and cheerless; deserted; lonely: 日子～（lead a）lonely life / 生意～（have）sluggish business

冷却 lěngquè　make cool; cool: ～剂 coolant

冷笑 lěngxiào　laugh grimly; sneer

冷眼 lěngyǎn　❶ cold eye; (cold) detachment: ～旁观 look on coldly; stand aloof; watch with a critical eye ❷ cold-shoulder; slight

冷遇 lěngyù　cold reception or treatment: 屡遭～ be cold-shouldered time and again

冷战 lěngzhàn　❶ cold war: ～心态 cold-war mentality ❷（lěngzhan）shiver: 吓得浑身打～ shiver all over with fear

lèng

愣 lèng　❶ distracted; stupefied; blank: ～神儿〈方〉stare blankly; be in a daze; be lost in thought ❷ blunt; rash; reckless: ～干〈口〉act recklessly; persist in going one's own way whatever the cost / ～头～脑 reckless; rash; impetuous / ～头青儿〈方〉rash fellow; hothead ❸〈方〉stubbornly; wilfully: ～是不听 just wouldn't listen

lī

哩 lī　see also lǐ

哩哩啦啦 līli-lālā　scattered; on and off; here and there

哩哩啰啰 līli-luōluō　wordy and unclear in speech; rambling and indistinct

lí

厘（釐） lí　❶（of certain measurements）one hundredth; ～米 also "公分" centimetre (cm) ❷ li, as a measurement a) of length (= ⅓ millimetre) b) of weight (= 0.05 grams) c) of area (= 0.666 square metres) ❸〈旧〉li, a unit of Chinese currency, equal to 0.1 fen（分）or 0.001 yuan ❹ li, a unit of monthly (= 0.1%) or annual interest rate (= 1%) ❺ very small amount; fraction; the least ❻〈书〉put in order; regulate: ～定 collate and stipulate (rules and regulations, etc)

狸 lí

狸猫 límāo　also "豹猫"; "狸子" leopard cat

离（離） lí

❶ leave; part or depart from; be away from: ～愁 sorrow at parting / ～乱 be separated or rendered homeless by war / ～谱〈口〉go beyond what is proper; be out of place; go too far / ～任 leave one's post; terminate one's tour of duty / ～经叛道 deviate from the dominant values of a society; be heretical / ～退人员 retirees ❷ off; away; from: ～这儿不远 not far away from here ❸ without; independent of: 孩子～不开母亲。Children cannot leave their mothers.

离别 líbié　part; leave; bid farewell

离婚 líhūn　divorce: 跟丈夫～ divorce one's husband

离间 líjiàn　sow discord; play (people) off (against each other); drive a wedge (between people)

离境 líjìng　leave a country or place; exit: ～签证 exit visa

离奇 líqí　fantastic; bizarre; eccentric

离群索居 líqúnsuǒjū　live in solitude; live the life of a hermit; plough a lonely furrow

离散 lísàn　(of family members) disperse; scatter about; separate from one another

离题 lítí stray from the point or subject; branch out; digress:~万里 be a thousand *li* from the topic; stray far afield

离乡背井 líxiāng-bèijǐng *see* "背井离乡"

离心 líxīn ❶ be at odds with the community or the leadership; ~离德 disunity; dissonance; dissension and discord; divided loyalty ❷〈理〉centrifugal:~力 centrifugal force / ~倾向 centrifugal or divisive tendency

离休 líxiū (of those who joined the revolutionary ranks before October 1949) retire:~干部 retired veteran cadre

离异 líyì divorce:父母~ with one's parents divorced

离职 lízhí ❶ leave one's job temporarily:~学习 be on an off-the-job study programme ❷ resign:打~报告 present one's resignation request

离子 lízǐ〈理〉ion

梨(棃) lí pear:~园 Pear Garden (name of a Tang Dynasty opera academy) — theatre; theatrical world

犁(犂) lí ❶ plough ❷ work with a plough; plough:~耕 ploughing / ~沟 furrow

黎 lí ❶ *also* "黎族" Li nationality, living in Guangdong and Hainan ❷〈书〉multitude; host:~民 common people; the multitude; the masses ❸〈书〉yellowish black:~黑 *also* "黧黑" (of complexion) dark

黎明 límíng dawn; daybreak

罹 lí〈书〉suffer (from):~难 die in a disaster or an accident; be murdered

篱(籬) lí fence; hedge:~笆 bamboo or twig fence

lǐ

礼(禮) lǐ ❶ ceremony; rite; ritual:~教 Confucian or feudal ethical code / ~堂 assembly hall; auditorium ❷ courtesy; etiquette; manners:~数 courtesy; etiquette / ~遇 courteous reception / 多人不怪〈俗〉you will offend no one by being polite; no one will blame you for being too polite ❸ present:~物 present; gift / ~轻情意重 the gift is trifling but the sentiment is profound; the thoughtfulness is far weightier than the gift itself ❹〈书〉treat with courtesy; be courteous to:~赞 sing the praise of; commend

礼拜 lǐbài ❶ religious service:做~ go to church ❷ (colloquial for 星期) week ❸ (colloquial for 星期) day of the week ❹ *also* "礼拜日"; "礼拜天"〈口〉Sunday

礼宾 lǐbīn protocol:~司 protocol department

礼法 lǐfǎ rules of etiquette; decorum:不合~ be at variance with the accepted rites

礼服 lǐfú ceremonial robe; full dress; formal attire:晚~ (for women) evening dress or gown; (for men) evening or dinner suit

礼花 lǐhuā fireworks (for ceremonies or festivals):放~ let off fireworks

礼节 lǐjié etiquette; protocol; courtesy:社交~ social etiquette / ~性拜会 courtesy call

礼貌 lǐmào courtesy; politeness; manners:讲~ mind one's manners; be polite

礼炮 lǐpào salvo; (gun) salute:鸣放~21 响 fire a 21-gun salute or a salvo of 21 guns

礼品 lǐpǐn gift; present:~券 *also* "礼券"coupon for free goods; gift coupon

礼让 lǐràng give precedence (to sb) out of courtesy or thoughtfulness; comity:行车~ yield right of way when driving

礼尚往来 lǐshàngwǎnglái ❶ courtesy demands reciprocity ❷ deal with a man as he deals with you; give as good as one gets

礼贤下士 lǐxián-xiàshì be courteous to the wise and respectful to the learned; go out of one's way to enlist the services of the talented and learned

礼仪 lǐyí ceremony and propriety; etiquette; rite; ~小姐 young lady serving at a ceremony

李 lǐ plum; ~子 plum / ~代桃僵 substitute this for that; take the blame for sb else

里(❶-❸ 裏、❶-❸ 裡) lǐ ❶ lining; inside; 被~儿 inside of a quilt ❷ inner; inside; 圈~人 insider / ~勾外联 also "里勾外连" collusion between forces within and without; (of insiders) hand in glove with outsiders / ~通外国 have illicit relations with a foreign country; turn traitor to one's country ❸ used after 这,那,哪 to indicate a location; 哪~ where ❹ neighbourhood ❺ hometown; native place; 返~ return to one's hometown ❻ also "市里" li, Chinese unit of length (= ½ kilometre)

里边 lǐbian also "里头";"里面" inside; in; within; 这~有文章。 There is something fishy about it.

里程 lǐchéng ❶ mileage; ~碑 milestone; marker; landmark / ~表 also "里程计" mileage meter; odometer ❷ course (of development)

里脊 lǐji tenderloin

里手 lǐshǒu ❶ left-hand side (of a running vehicle or machine) ❷ expert; old hand

里外 lǐwài ❶ inside and outside; ~受气 be blamed both at home and outside ❷ (used after round numbers) approximately; about; or so; 40 岁~ about forty

里巷 lǐxiàng also "里弄" side street; alley; lane

里应外合 lǐyìng-wàihé act from inside in coordination with forces attacking from outside; collaborate from within with forces from without

俚 lǐ popular; vulgar; ~俗 vulgar; unrefined / ~语 slang

哩 lǐ also "英里" mile see also li

浬 lǐ also "海里" nautical or sea mile

理 lǐ ❶ texture; grain (of wood, stone, skin, etc) ❷ reason; logic; truth; 懂~ 数〈口〉be reasonable or sensible ❸ natural science,esp physics; ~工科 science and engineering ❹ put in order; manage; tidy up; ~财 manage money matters; conduct financial transactions / ~家 keep house; manage family affairs / ~赔 settle claims / ~顺 straighten or sort out; rationalize ❺ (usu used in the negative) pay attention to; acknowledge

理睬 lǐcǎi (often used in the negative) pay attention to; heed; show interest in; 不加~ ignore; take no notice of; pay no heed to

理发 lǐfà get a haircut; have one's hair done; ~馆 barbershop; barber's; hairdresser's

理会 lǐhuì ❶ understand; comprehend; grasp ❷ (usu used in the negative) take notice of; pay attention to; heed

理解 lǐjiě understand; comprehend; ~力 (faculty of) understanding; comprehension

理亏 lǐkuī be in the wrong; ~心虚 feel apprehensive for not being on solid ground; have a bad conscience

理疗 lǐliáo 〈医〉physiotherapy; 进行~ undergo or have physiotherapy

理论 lǐlùn ❶ theory; doctrine; principle; ~家 theoretician; theorist / ~联

系实际 link theory with practice ❷ argue; reason

理念 lǐniàn　principle; 〈哲〉idea:经营～ managerial principle

理屈 lǐqū　have a weak case; be in the wrong:～词穷 fall silent on finding oneself bested in argument; be unable to advance any further arguments to justify oneself

理事 lǐshì　❶ handle matters; administer affairs; 当家～ rule the roost ❷ member of a council; director:～会 executive council; board of directors

理所当然 lǐsuǒdāngrán　(as a matter) of course; naturally

理想 lǐxiǎng　❶ ideal; aspiration:～化 idealize /～主义 idealism ❷ ideal; perfect:～结果 optimum result

理性 lǐxìng　❶ rational;感性和～ the perceptual and the rational ❷ rational faculty; reason:恢复～ come to one's senses

理学 lǐxué　also "道学"〈哲〉Confucian school of idealist philosophy of the Song and Ming dynasties; neo-Confucianism

理应 lǐyīng　also "理当" ought to; should; deserve:～如此 just as it should be; only right and proper

理由 lǐyóu　reason; ground; cause:毫无～ be without rhyme or reason; be utterly groundless

理喻 lǐyù　(usu used negatively) persuade or convince with reason; 难以～ (of sb) is impervious to reason; there's no reasoning with (sb)

理直气壮 lǐzhí-qìzhuàng　feel confident with justice on one's side; be bold and assured because of the righteousness of one's cause:～地提出批评 criticize firmly and forcefully

理智 lǐzhì　reason; intellect:保持～ keep one's senses

锂 lǐ　〈化〉lithium (Li):～电池 lithium battery

鲤 lǐ　carp

鲤鱼 lǐyú　carp:～跳龙门〈俗〉(as of an obscure person) gain immediate fame and advancement; make a success of oneself

lì

力 lì　❶ force; (physical) strength; capacity:～臂〈理〉arm of force /～作 tour de force; masterpiece /～不能支 unable to stand the strain any longer; too weak to stay on one's feet ❷ do all one can; make every effort; exert oneself:～战 fight with might and main; fight gallantly /～戒自满 be vigilant against conceit

力不从心 lìbùcóngxīn　one's ability falls short of one's wishes; one's talent is not equal to one's ambition

力度 lìdù　❶ strength; force;加强改革的～ strengthen or beef up the reforms ❷ intensity; depth; power:有～的作品 powerful work

力量 lìliang　❶ see "力气"❷ power; force; strength;动员一切～ mobilize all the forces available ❸ potency; efficacy; effect:这种农药～很大。This pesticide is very potent.

力排众议 lìpáizhòngyì　prevail over or override all dissenting views

力气 lìqi　physical strength; effort:～活儿 manual labour; strenuous or heavy work

力所能及 lìsuǒnéngjí　in one's power; within one's ability:予以～的帮助 help (sb) to the best of one's ability

力透纸背 lìtòuzhǐbèi　❶ (of calligraphy, etc) vigorous; forceful; powerful ❷ (of literary works) deep and powerful; penetrating

力挽狂澜 lìwǎnkuánglán　make vigorous efforts to turn the tide; strive to save a desperate situation

力学 lìxué　❶ mechanics; dynamics ❷ 〈书〉study hard:～不倦 be tireless in one's pursuit of knowledge

力争 lìzhēng　❶ work hard for; do all

one can to：～上游 aim high；strive for the best；strive to get the upper hand ❷ argue strongly；contend vigorously

历（歷、⁴曆）lì ❶ go through；undergo；experience：～时十年 last or take ten years；be decade-long / ～久不衰（long-）lasting；abiding ❷ all previous（years，occasions，etc）：～次 all previous（meetings，etc）/ ～届政府 all previous governments ❸ all；one after another：～陈利弊 explain all the advantages and disadvantages item by item / ～数其犯罪事实 enumerate sb's crimes ❹ calendric system；calendar：～法〈天文〉calendric system；calendar / ～书 almanac

历程 lìchéng course；experience：人生～ life's journey

历代 lìdài ❶ successive or past dynasties；all ages ❷ all previous generations；successive generations：～务农 engage in farming from generation to generation

历经 lìjīng experience repeatedly；suffer again and again：～沧桑 experience the vicissitudes of life

历来 lìlái always；all along；throughout the ages：～如此 has always been the case

历历 lìlì distinctly；clearly：～在目 leap up vividly before one's eyes；come clearly into view

历练 lìliàn ❶ experience；see the world ❷ experienced；seasoned

历任 lìrèn ❶ have successively held（posts）；have served successively as ❷ successive；all previous（holders of an office，etc）

历史 lìshǐ ❶ history；historical record：～性胜利 historic victory / ～唯物主义 also "历史唯物论"；"唯物史观" historical materialism ❷ past experiences or events：～包袱 burdens from the past / ～清白 have a clean

record ❸ history（as an academic discipline）；historiography：～学家 historian；historiographer

厉（厲）lì ❶ strict；rigorous；rigid：～禁毒品（impose a）strict ban on drugs ❷ stern；severe；fierce：～声斥责 rebuke in a stern voice

厉兵秣马 lìbīng-mòmǎ see "秣马厉兵" in "秣"

厉害 lìhai also "利害" terrible；formidable；serious：她那张嘴可真～. She's got a sharp tongue.

厉行 lìxíng strictly enforce；make rigorous efforts to carry out：～节约 practise strict economy

立 lì ❶ stand；stand or set（sth）up；erect：～标牌 put up a signboard / ～于不败之地 be invincible；remain impregnable ❷ upright；erect；vertical：～灯 also "落地灯" floor lamp / ～柜 clothes closet；wardrobe ❸ set up；found；establish：～功 render meritorious service；win honour；make contributions / ～誓 take an oath；vow；make a pledge / ～项 put（a project）under an authorized plan；register（a project）with the competent authorities / ～业 build a career；buy an estate / 另～门户 break away from the old establishment and set up one's own ❹ sign；conclude：～字据 write and sign a pledge，contract，etc ❺ exist；live；grow ❻ immediately；at once；right away：～等 wait for sth to be done at once / ～见功效 produce an immediate effect

立案 lì'àn ❶ register；put on record：申请～ apply for registration（with the competent authorities，etc）❷〈法〉accept a case for investigation and prosecution：～调查 start an investigation into a case

立场 lìchǎng position；stand；standpoint：～坚定 be steadfast in one's stand; take a firm stand

立春 lìchūn Beginning of Spring, 1st seasonal division point *see also* "节气" jiéqì

立定 lìdìng ❶ halt; ~! Halt! ❷ stand firm; ~脚跟 gain a foothold; become established ❸ resolutely determine; ~志向 set one's resolve

立冬 lìdōng Beginning of Winter, 19th seasonal division point *see also* "节气" jiéqì

立法 lìfǎ legislate; make or enact law; ~权 legislative power / ~机构 legislative body; legislature

立方 lìfāng ❶ 〈数〉cube; 5 的~ cube of 5 *also* "正方体" (short for 立方体) cube ❸ *also* "立米" (short for 立方米) cubic metre

立竿见影 lìgānjiànyǐng do sth to get instant results; produce an immediate effect

立户 lìhù ❶ register for a household residence card; set up housekeeping ❷ open or establish an account with a bank

立即 lìjí immediately; without delay; promptly

立交桥 lìjiāoqiáo (short for 立体交叉桥)(US) overpass;(UK) flyover; cloverleaf intersection

立刻 lìkè *also* "立时" immediately; at once; right away

立论 lìlùn set forth one's view; present one's argument; ~新颖(present a)novel view or argument

立马 lìmǎ 〈方〉 straight or right away; ~给个回话 give an immediate reply

立秋 lìqiū Beginning of Autumn, 13th seasonal division point *see also* "节气" jiéqì

立身处世 lìshēn-chǔshì *also* "立身行世" the way one conducts oneself in society; ~，诚信为本。Trustworthiness is essential in human relationship.

立体 lìtǐ ❶ three-dimensional; stereoscopic; ~感(produce a)three-dimensional effect / ~声 stereophony; stereophonics; stereo / ~电影 stereoscopic or 3-D film; stereo-screen ❷ 〈数〉 solid; ~几何 solid geometry; stereogeometry ❸ multi-level; all-round; 交叉 grade separation

立夏 lìxià Beginning of Summer, 7th seasonal division point *see also* "节气" jiéqì

立宪 lìxiàn constitutionalism; ~政体 constitutional government; constitutionalism

立意 lìyì ❶ be determined; make up one's mind ❷ conception; approach; ~深刻(of writing, etc)have a profound meaning

立约 lìyuē conclude an agreement or a treaty; sign or draw up a contract; ~人 contractor / ~双方 contracting parties

立正 lìzhèng stand at attention; ~! Attention!

立志 lìzhì be resolved or determined

立锥之地 lìzhuīzhīdì tiny bit of land; 贫无~ not possess a speck of land; be penniless

立足 lìzú ❶ *also* "立脚" gain a foothold; establish oneself; ~点 foothold; standpoint; stand / ~之地 footing; foothold ❷ base oneself on; 立足中国，放眼世界 have one's feet firmly planted in China while keeping the whole world in view

吏 lì ❶〈旧〉petty official; government clerk ❷ official; mandarin

丽(麗) lì pretty; beautiful; ~人 beautiful woman; beauty / 天生~质 born beautiful

励(勵) lì encourage; urge; ~精图治 exert oneself to make the country prosperous; make vigorous efforts to build a strong country

利 lì ❶ sharp; keen; ～器 sharp weapon; good tool; efficient instrument / ～嘴 glib or sharp tongue ❷ favourable; smooth; convenient; ～于团结 be conducive to unity / 不计～钝 regardless of consequences; at all costs ❸ advantage; benefit; gain; ～禄〈书〉(of an official) money and status; wealth and position / ～令智昏 be blinded by lust for gain; be befuddled by greed ❹ profit; interest; ～钱 interest / ～税〈经〉profit and tax / ～滚～ compound interest; usurious loan ❺ do good to; benefit; ～国～民 benefit both the country and the people

利弊 lìbì advantages and disadvantages; pros and cons; ～各半 The advantages and disadvantages cancel each other out. / 利多弊少。The advantages outweigh the disadvantages.

利害 lìhài ❶ advantages and disadvantages; gains and losses; pros and cons; ～攸关 have a stake in (sth); (of sth) concern one's vital interests / 有～关系的人 interested party ❷ (lìhai) see "厉害" lìhai

利己主义 lìjǐzhǔyì egoism; 民族～ national egoism / ～者 egoist

利率 lìlǜ 〈经〉interest rate; 年～ annual interest rate

利落 lìluo also "利索" ❶ agile; nimble; dexterous; 说话～ 干脆 straightforward and articulate ❷ neat; orderly; 穿戴不～ sloppily dressed ❸ finished; settled; completed; 屋子里收拾～了吗? Is the room tidied up?

利润 lìrùn profit; ～率 profitability; profit rate / ～留成 profit retention

利息 lìxī interest; 应计～ interest accrued / ～税 interest tax

利益 lìyì interest; profit; benefit; 个人～ individual or personal interest

利用 lìyòng ❶ make use of; use; utilize; ～率 utilization ratio ❷ take advantage of; exploit

利诱 lìyòu lure by promise of gain; 不受～ not succumb to the temptation of personal gain

利欲熏心 lìyùxūnxīn one's mind is clouded with avarice; be blinded by greed; be overcome by covetousness

沥(瀝) lì ❶ drip; trickle; ～干 (of clothing) drip-dry / ～胆披肝 open up one's heart; be all sincerity ❷ drop; 余～ last drops; dregs

沥青 lìqīng pitch; asphalt

例 lì ❶ example; instance; ～句 sentence serving as an example; illustrative sentence / ～题 illustrative question or problem (in a textbook, etc) / ～言 introductory remarks; notes on the use of a book / ～子 also "例证" example; instance; case / 援～ quote or follow a precedent / ～行公事 routine (business); mere formality ❸ case; instance ❹ rule; regulation; 定～ usual practice; set pattern ❺ regular; routine; ～会 regular meeting

例假 lìjià ❶ official or legal holiday ❷〈婉〉menstruation; period

例如 lìrú for instance; for example (eg); such as

例外 lìwài exception; 不得～ make no exception / ～情况 exceptional case

戾 lì〈书〉❶ crime; sin ❷ perverse; unreasonable

隶(隸) lì ❶ be subordinate or affiliated ❷ person in servitude ❸〈旧〉yamen runner ❹ also "隶书" official script, simplified from xiaozhuan (小篆) and current in the Han Dynasty

隶属 lìshǔ be subordinate to; be under the jurisdiction or command of; ～关系 relationship of administrative subordination

荔 lì

荔枝 lìzhī〈植〉litchi; lichee

栎（櫟） lì also "柞树"; "麻栎"〈植〉oak

俪（儷） lì ❶ paired; parallel; ～辞 antithetic prose ❷ husband and wife; married couple; ～影 photograph of a married couple; wedding picture

苈（藶） lì 〈书〉arrive; be present; ～会 be present at a meeting / ～临 arrive; be present

栗（❷慄） lì ❶〈植〉chestnut; 板～ Chinese chestnut / ～色 chestnut colour; maroon / 糖炒～子 sugar-roasted chestnuts ❷〈书〉tremble; shudder

砺（礪） lì ❶〈书〉whetstone; grindstone; ～石 whetstone ❷ whet; sharpen; 磨～ steel oneself

砾（礫） lì gravel; grit

蛎（蠣） lì oyster

唳 lì cry (of a crane, wild goose, etc)

笠 lì large bamboo or straw hat with a conical crown and broad brim

粒 lì ❶ grain; granule; pellet; 米～儿 grains of rice ❷〈量〉used with granular objects; 五～药丸 five pills

粒子 lìzǐ ❶〈理〉particle; ～加速器 particle accelerator ❷ (lìzi) grain; 盐～ grain of salt

痢 lì (usu 痢疾) dysentery

liǎ

俩（倆） liǎ 〈口〉❶（两 and 个 combined）two; 你们～ you two / 爷儿～ grandpa and

grandson; father and son; uncle and nephew ❷ a few; a little; some; 给他～钱儿。Give him some money.

lián

连 lián ❶ link; join; connect; ～词〈语言〉conjunction / ～坐〈旧〉be punished for being related to or friendly with sb who has committed an offence / ～裤袜 panty hose / ～衣裤 catsuit; jumpsuit / ～衣裙（women's）one-piece dress ❷ in succession; repeatedly; continuously; ～亘〈书〉continuous / ～年 in successive years; for years running or on end / ～任 be reappointed or reelected consecutively; renew one's term of office / ～轴 work round the clock / ～～摇头 shake one's head again and again ❸ including; ～根拔 tear up by the roots; eliminate; eradicate / ～锅端 remove or destroy lock, stock and barrel; get rid of the whole lot ❹〈军〉company; ～长 company commander ❺ even; ～我都不认识了？Couldn't you even recognize me?

连带 liándài ❶ related; connected;〈法〉joint; ～责任 joint liability / ～在一起的事件 related incidents ❷ involve; implicate ❸ incidentally; in passing

连…带… lián…dài… ❶ indicating the inclusion of two items; 连本带利 both principal and interest; capital and profit ❷ indicating that one action follows another or that two actions occur almost simultaneously; 连说带笑 talking and laughing

连裆裤 liándāngkù ❶ child's pants with no slit in the seat ❷（usu 穿连裆裤）collude; gang up

连贯 liánguàn also "联贯" ❶ link up; join or piece together ❷ coherent; consistent; ～性 coherence; continuity

连环 liánhuán　chain of rings；～画 picture-story book / ～计 series of stratagems / ～漫画 comic strip；comics；strip cartoon

连接 liánjiē　also "联接" join；link；～号〈语言〉hyphen

连襟 liánjīn　husbands of sisters；我的～ my wife's sister's husband；my brother-in-law

连累 liánlěi　implicate；involve；get (sb) into trouble

连理 liánlǐ〈书〉❶ also "连理枝" trees or plants whose branches interlock or join together ❷ marital love；loving couple；结为～ get married

连忙 liánmáng　hasten (to do)；(do sth) promptly；at once

连绵 liánmián　also "联绵" continuous；unbroken；uninterrupted；阴雨～ succession of rainy days

连篇累牍 liánpiān-lěidú　lengthy and tedious；at great length；～的空话 endless empty talk

连锁 liánsuǒ　chain；linkage；～店 chain store / ～反应 chain reaction；sequence of events

连同 liántóng　together or along with

连续 liánxù　continuous；successive；in a row；～性 continuity；continuance / ～电视～剧 TV serial

连夜 liányè　❶ the same night；that very night ❷ for several nights running

连载 liánzǎi　publish in instalments；serialize

连轴转 liánzhóuzhuàn　work day and night；work round the clock；work 24/7；忙得～ be terribly busy

连珠炮 liánzhūpào　continuous firing；drumfire；continuous sequence (of things)；说话像～似的 speak at machine-gun pace；chatter away like a machine-gun

怜（憐） lián ❶ sympathize with；pity；～悯 pity；take pity on；have compassion for / ～惜 show compassion and concern for；take pity on / ～恤 take pity on；have pity for ❷ love tenderly；have tender affection for：～香惜玉 be tender towards women；have a tender heart for the fair sex

帘（❷簾） lián ❶ flag or banner used as shop sign；酒～ wine shop sign ❷ curtain；(hanging) screen

莲 lián （also known as 荷 or 芙蓉）〈植〉lotus；lotus seed；～藕 lotus and its root；lotus root / ～子 lotus seed / ～蓬头〈方〉shower nozzle

涟 lián〈书〉❶ ripples；～漪 ❷ 不兴 (of a lake, etc) without ripples；perfectly calm ❷ continual flow (of tears)：泣下～～ stream with tears

联（聯） lián ❶ ally oneself with；unite；combine；～翩 also "连翩" in close succession；together / ～姻〈书〉be related by marriage / ～营 joint management / ～席会议 joint conference or meeting / ～产承包责任制 system of contracted responsibility linking remuneration to output；contract system with remuneration linked to output ❷ antithetical couplet：春～ Spring Festival couplets

联邦 liánbāng　federation；confederation；commonwealth；英～ British Commonwealth of Nations / 俄罗斯～ Russian Confederation / ～国家 federal state / ～调查局 (US) Federal Bureau of Investigation (FBI)

联播 liánbō　broadcast over a radio or TV network；radio or TV hookup；新闻～ network news

联防 liánfáng ❶ joint defence；joint command of defence forces；治安～ joint effort to maintain public security ❷〈体〉joint defence

联合 liánhé　unite；ally；有条件的～ conditional alliance / ～王国 United Kingdom (of Great Britain and Northern

Ireland) — official name for Britain; UK ❷ joint; combined; ～会 federation; union / ～经营 coordinated management; joint venture / ～声明 joint statement / ～政府 coalition government / ～收割机 also "康拜因" combine (harvester)

联合国 Liánhéguó　United Nations (UN); ～大会 UN General Assembly / ～宪章 United Nations Charter / ～秘书处 UN Secretariat / ～安全理事会 UN Security Council

联欢 liánhuān　(have a) get-together; ～会 get-together; party

联结 liánjié　also "连结" bind; tie; join

联络 liánluò　get in touch with; come into contact with; 失去～ lose contact or be out of touch (with sb) / ～处 liaison office / ～感情 make friendly contacts; promote friendship

联袂 liánmèi　also "连袂"〈书〉come or go hand in hand; ～登台献艺 give a joint performance

联盟 liánméng　(form an) alliance; coalition; union

联名 liánmíng　jointly (signed); ～倡议 jointly initiate or sponsor

联赛 liánsài　〈体〉(basketball, etc) league matches

联手 liánshǒu　join hands (with a person); ～调查 (make a) joint investigation

联网 liánwǎng　network (access); 计算机～ computer networking / ～用户 on-liner

联系 liánxì　❶ relate; connect; be in touch with; 保持～ keep touch with (sb); be in touch with (sb) / 密切～群众 maintain close ties or links with the people ❷ arrange; negotiate; ～工作 talk business

联想 liánxiǎng　associate; connect in the mind; ～力 ability or capacity for

association / ～记忆 associative memory

联谊 liányì　friendship ties; fellowship; ～会 fraternity; sorority; friendship association

联运 liányùn　through transport or traffic; 水陆～ land-and-water coordinated transport; through transport by land and water / ～票 through ticket; connection ticket

廉 lián　❶ honest and clean; ～正 also "廉直" honest and upright / ～政 honest and clean government ❷ low in price; inexpensive; cheap; ～价 cheap; low-priced; at a bargain price

廉耻 liánchǐ　sense of honour or shame; integrity; 不顾～ shameless

廉洁 liánjié　honest and clean; ～奉公 be honest in performing one's official duties; honest and incorruptible

鲢 lián　silver carp

镰(鐮) lián　sickle; 开～ start harvesting (with sickles)

liǎn

敛(斂) liǎn　❶〈书〉hold or keep back; restrain; ～迹 restrain oneself; go into hiding; lie low / ～容 assume a serious expression / ～声屏气 lower one's voice and hold one's breath; be awed into silence ❷ collect; ～财 accumulate wealth by unfair or illegal means

脸(臉) liǎn　❶ face; front; facial expression; ～颊 also "脸蛋儿" cheeks; face / ～上贴金 cover the face with gold foil — gild; touch up; prettify / 鞋～儿 front of a shoe; instep / 笑～相迎 greet with a smiling face ❷ sensibilities; credit; 没皮没～ shameless; brazen / ～薄 also "脸嫩" thin-skinned;

shy; bashful / ～上无光 (make sb) lose face; bring discredit on sb

脸红 liǎnhóng ❶ blush (with shame):～耳赤 flush up to one's ears (with shame or anger); become red in the face and ears ❷ flush with anger; get excited or worked up:～脖子粗 get red in the face from anger or excitement; flush with agitation

脸面 liǎnmiàn ❶ face self-respect; sensibilities; feelings

脸盘儿 liǎnpánr *also* "脸庞" cast of one's face; 圆～ round-faced

脸盆 liǎnpén washbasin; washbowl

脸皮 liǎnpí ❶ skin of the face ❷ feelings; sensibilities; 撕不破～ cannot bear to hurt others' sensibilities; spare others' sensibilities ❸ face; cheek; sense of shame; ～厚 thick-skinned; shameless

脸谱 liǎnpǔ (in traditional opera) type of facial make-up. 〔喻〕mask; stereotype:～化 stereotyping of people or things)

脸色 liǎnsè ❶ complexion; look:～不好 be off colour ❷ facial expression; countenance:看别人～行事 take cues from others

liàn

练(練) liàn ❶ white silk; 〈书〉boil and scour raw silk ❷ practise; train; drill; ～笔 practise writing or calligraphy / ～兵 (troop) training; drill / ～功 do exercises in gymnastics, *wushu*, etc; practise one's skill / ～手 practise one's skill; keep one's hand in / ～武 practise *wushu* or military skills / ～好功夫 perfect one's skill (in martial arts, etc) ❸ experienced; skilled; seasoned; ～达 〈书〉experienced and worldly-wise

练习 liànxí ❶ practise; learn ❷ exercise:做～ do exercises / ～簿 exercise book

炼(煉、鍊) liàn ❶ smelt; refine; temper:～钢 steel-making; steel-smelting / ～乳 condensed milk / ～油厂 (oil) refinery ❷ polish; improve; refine:～句 work hard at improving one's diction; polish and repolish a sentence

炼金术 liànjīnshù alchemy; ～士 alchemist

炼狱 liànyù ❶ 〈宗教〉purgatory ❷ abyss of sufferings or misery

恋(戀) liàn ❶ 情 love (affair); attachment; love / ～人 lover; sweetheart ❷ long for; feel attached to:～家 reluctant to leave one's home; be much of a homebody / ～旧 be homesick or nostalgic / ～战 be over-zealous in fighting / ～～不舍 be reluctant to part; hate to see sb go

恋爱 liàn'ài love; be in love; have a courtship or love affair; 谈～ be in love; have a love affair; date

殓(殮) liàn put a body into a coffin; encoffin; ～衣 clothes put on the dead body; grave clothes; cerements

链(鍊) liàn chain:～球〈体〉hammer (event) / ～条 (transmission) chain / 〈方〉roller chain (of a bicycle) / ～式反应 *also* "连锁反应"〈化〉chain reaction

链接 liànjiē 〈信息〉link:新闻～〔喻〕news link

链霉素 liànméisù streptomycin

潋(瀲) liàn

潋滟 liànyàn 〈书〉rippling, wavy:湖光～ sparkling lake

liáng

良 liáng ❶ good; fine; ～策 good plan or idea; sound strategy /

～机 good or golden opportunity / ～宵〈书〉happy evening; pleasant night / ～种〈农〉improved variety or strain; fine breed / ～家妇女 woman of good family / ～师益友 good teacher and helpful friend / ～莠不齐 The good and the bad are intermingled. ❸〈书〉very (much)：～久 (for a) good while; long time / 获益～多 benefit a great deal

良辰 liángchén ❶ auspicious day; propitious time：～吉日 bright and propitious day; auspicious occasion ❷ fine day; pleasant time：～美景 beautiful scene on a fine day; good weather and beautiful scenery

良好 liánghǎo　good; fine：健康状况～ in the pink (of health) / ～的开端意味着成功的一半。A good beginning means half the success — well begun is half done.

良心 liángxīn　conscience：～发现 be stung by conscience / 凭～说 to be fair; in all conscience

良性 liángxìng ❶ good; favourable; healthy：～循环 virtuous or beneficial cycle ❷ not malignant; benign：～肿瘤〈医〉benign tumour

良药 liángyào　good or effective medicine：～苦口利于病，忠言逆耳利于行。〈谚〉Just as bitter medicine cures sickness, so unpalatable advice benefits conduct.

良缘 liángyuán　happy fate which brings lovers together：喜结～ be happily married

良知 liángzhī ❶ (in Confucian philosophy) innate or intuitive ability to tell good from bad; reason ❷ see "良心"

凉(涼) liáng ❶ (to keep) cool; cold：～拌 (of food) cold and dressed with sauce / ～菜 cold dish / ～粉 bean jelly / ～台 balcony; veranda / ～亭 wayside pavilion; summer house; kiosk / ～席 summer sleeping mat (of woven split bamboo, etc) / ～鞋 sandals / ～白开〈口〉boiled water that has been chilled / 倒抽一口～气 gasp with surprise, fear, etc ❷ discouraged; disappointed：心里～了半截 be chilled with disappointment; be disheartened
see also liàng

凉快 liángkuai ❶ nice and cool; pleasantly cool ❷ cool oneself; cool off

凉棚 liángpéng ❶ mat-awning; mat shelter ❷ (usu 手搭凉棚) hand or hands spread out above one's eyes (to shelter them from strong light)

凉爽 liángshuǎng　nice and cool; pleasantly cool

凉丝丝 liángsīsī　coolish; a bit cool

凉飕飕 liángsōusōu　(of wind) chilly; chill

凉意 liángyì　chill or nip in the air; 初春时节，仍有～。The chill lingers in the early spring.

梁(樑) liáng ❶ roof beam; purlin：正～ ridge purlin / ～上君子 gentleman on the beam — burglar; thief ❷ bridge：桥～ bridge ❸ ridge：山～ mountain ridge

量 liáng ❶ measure; weigh：～杯 measuring glass; graduate / ～尺寸 take (sb's) measurements / ～度单位 unit of measurement / ～具 刃具 measuring and cutting tools ❷ appraise; estimate; assess：思～ consider; turn over in one's mind
see also liàng

粮(糧) liáng ❶ grain; food; provisions：～仓 granary; barn; breadbasket / ～草 food and forage; army provisions / ～秣 food and forage; army provisions / ～库 grain depot / ～食 grain; cereals; food / ～饷〈旧〉provisions and pay for troops ❷ grain tax paid in kind

粱 liáng〈书〉❶ fine strain of millet ❷ fine grain; choice (staple) food：～肉 fine grain and meat; good

food

liǎng

两(兩) liǎng ❶ (used before a classifier or 半, 千, 万, 亿, etc) two: ～倍 twice; twofold / ～半儿 in half; in two / ～党制 two-party or bipartisan system / ～回事 also "两码事" entirely different things / ～口子 husband and wife; couple / ～路人 totally different people / ～小无猜 (of a young boy and a young girl) be innocent childhood playmates ❷ both (sides); either (side): ～相情愿 also "两厢情愿" both parties are willing; (do sth) by mutual consent / ～条腿走路 walking on two legs — do two interrelated things simultaneously ❸ a couple; a few; some: 再等～天 wait for a few more days ❹ liǎng, a unit of weight (＝50 grams) ❺〈旧〉tael, a unit of weight for silver or gold (about 31 grams)

两岸 liǎng'àn ❶ both banks or sides; either bank or side ❷ both sides of the Taiwan Strait: ～关系 relations between the mainland and Taiwan

两败俱伤 liǎngbàijùshāng both sides suffer or lose; neither side wins or gains — a no-win game

两边 liǎngbiān ❶ both or two sides ❷ both directions or places ❸ both parties or sides: ～倒 lean now to one side, now to the other; waver; sit on the fence / ～下注 hedge one's bet

两便 liǎngbiàn ❶ be convenient to both; make things easy for both ❷ be advantageous or beneficial to both

两极 liǎngjí ❶ poles of the earth ❷〈理〉poles of a magnet or an electric battery ❸ division into two opposing extremes: ～分化 polarization

两可 liǎngkě ❶ both or either will do: 这种事干不干～。It does not matter one way or the other. ❷ also "两可之间" could go either way; maybe, maybe not; hang in the balance

两面 liǎngmiàn ❶ two or both sides ❷ both directions or places: ～夹攻 close in from both sides; make a pincer attack ❸ opposite sides; dual or double character; Janus face: ～光 (try to) please both parties / ～派 double-dealer; double-dealing; Janus-faced / ～三刀 double-dealing; duplicity

两难 liǎngnán be in a dilemma; face a difficult choice: ～处境 predicament; dilemma

两栖 liǎngqī ❶ amphibious: ～动物 amphibious animal; amphibian / ～作战〈军〉amphibious warfare ❷ working or engaged in two fields or spheres: 影视～明星 star in both films and TV programmes; movie-cum-TV star

两全 liǎngquán be satisfactory to both parties; have regard for both sides; do both: ～其美 gratify both sides; satisfy rival claims

两手 liǎngshǒu ❶ also "两下子" skill; ability; trick: 露～儿 show a trick or two ❷ both hands or aspects; dual tactics: 做好～准备 prepare oneself for both eventualities

两头 liǎngtóu ❶ both ends; either end ❷ both parties or sides: ～落空 fall between two stools / ～为难 find it hard to satisfy either side; find oneself on the horns of a dilemma ❸ two or both places

两性 liǎngxìng (of) both sexes: ～人 bisexual person; hermaphrodite / ～关系 relations between the sexes; sexual relations or intercourse

两袖清风 liǎngxiùqīngfēng (of an official) have clean hands; be free from corruption

两样 liǎngyàng not the same; different: ～对待 regard as different; treat differently

两用 liǎngyòng　dual purpose or use：～衫 *also* "春秋衫" jacket for spring and autumn wear / ～沙发 sofa-bed；convertible sofa

liàng

亮 liàng　❶ bright；light：～敞 (of a house, etc) light and spacious；roomy / ～点 bright spot (in an otherwise gloomy affair, etc)；silver lining / ～度 brightness；brilliance；luminance　❷ shine；flash：天快～了。It's getting light.　❸ loud and clear；clarion：嗓音又高又～ in a loud and clear voice；in a resounding voice　❹ enlightened；clear：～话 blunt words；naked truth　❺ show；lay open；make public：～底 disclose one's real plan，stand，view，etc；put one's cards on the table / ～分 (of a judge or an umpire) show or display the marks one has given / ～牌 lay one's cards on the table；have a showdown / ～明观点 make public one's view；declare one's position；air one's opinion

亮光 liàngguāng　❶ light：一道～ a shaft of light　❷ shine；reflection：洁白而有～ white and shiny

亮晶晶 liàngjīngjīng　glittering；glistening；sparkling：～的星星 twinkling stars

亮丽 liànglì　bright and beautiful：～的色彩 bright colours / 外观～的跑车 splendid-looking sports car

亮儿 liàngr　〈口〉lamp；light：照个～。Please give me a light.　❷ light；glow

亮堂堂 liàngtāngtāng　brightly or well lit；brilliant：心里～ feel as clear as clear can be

亮堂 liàngtáng　❶ light；bright　❷ clear；enlightened：心里～ feel enlightened；be clear-headed　❸ loud and clear；resonant：嗓门～ rich voice

亮相 liàngxiàng　❶ (of Beijing opera, dancing, etc) strike a pose on the stage　❷ make one's debut　❸ declare one's position；state one's views

凉（涼） liàng　make or become cool；把粥～一～ let the porridge cool a bit　*see also* liáng

谅 liàng　❶ forgive；excuse；understand　❷ I think or expect；presumably：～必不假。I believe it is true.

谅解 liàngjiě　understand；appreciate；make allowance for：达成～ reach an understanding / ～备忘录 memorandum of understanding

辆（輛） liàng　〈量〉used with vehicles：两～大卡车 two trucks

靓 liàng　〈方〉beautiful；handsome；good-looking：～女 beautiful girl

量 liàng　❶ bulk measure　❷ capacity；capability：～小力微 small in capacity and weak in strength　❸ quantity；number；volume：～变 quantitative change / ～化 quantify；quantize / ～降雪 snowfall　❹ estimate；appraise；measure：～刑 〈法〉measurement of penalty / ～才录用 give sb work suited to his or her talents；employ sb on the basis of his or her merits / ～入为出 keep expenditure within the limits of income；live within one's means / ～体裁衣 cut the garment according to the figure；act according to actual circumstances　*see also* liáng

量词 liàngcí　〈语言〉classifier (as 个，次，件)；measure word

量力 liànglì　estimate one's own strength or ability (and act accordingly)：～而行 do what one's strength allows；act according to one's capability

量子 liàngzǐ　〈理〉quantum：～论 quantum or Planck's theory

晾 liàng ❶ dry in the air or sun; air-dry; sun; ~晒 sun; air / ~台 terrace or veranda for sunning clothes / ~衣绳 clothesline ❷ ignore; slight; give the cold shoulder to; 把客人~在一边 let one's guests cool their heels ❸ see "凉" liàng

踉 liàng

踉跄 liàngqiàng stagger; totter

liāo

撩 liāo ❶ hold or lift up (a curtain, etc from the bottom); ~一下头发 brush back one's hair ❷ sprinkle (with one's hand)
see also liáo

liáo

辽(遼) liáo ❶ distant; far-away; ~阔 vast; extensive / ~远 distant; faraway; remote ❷ (Liáo) short for Liaoning (辽宁)

疗(療) liáo treat; cure; 泥~ mud-bath treatment / ~程〈医〉course of treatment / ~法 therapy; treatment / ~效 curative effect

疗养 liáoyǎng recuperate; convalesce; rest up; ~院 sanatorium; rest home / ~胜地 health resort

聊 liáo ❶ barely; merely; just; ~以自慰 just to console oneself; merely to seek relief ❷ a little; somewhat; slightly; ~表寸心 as a small token of one's feelings / ~胜于无 (it's) better than nothing ❸〈书〉rely; depend; ~赖 (usu used in the negative) sth to rely on (for a living); sth to occupy one's mind; chat; chew the fat; 边喝茶,边~天儿 chat over a cup of tea

僚 liáo ❶ official ❷ associate in office; ~机〈军〉wing plane; wingman / ~属〈旧〉subordinates; staff

寥 liáo ❶ few; scanty; ~~无几 very few; hardly any / ~若晨星 as sparse as the morning stars; few and far between ❷ silent; deserted; ~寂〈书〉solitary; lonesome ❸ broad and empty; vast; ~廓 boundless; infinite; vast / ~无人烟 no trace of human habitation in sight

寥落 liáoluò ❶ few and far between; sparse; deserted ❷ desolate; lonesome; lonely

撩 liáo tease; provoke; stir up (emotions, etc); ~拨 tease; incite; provoke / ~逗 provoke; tease; annoy see also liāo

嘹 liáo

嘹亮 liáoliàng resonant; loud and clear; clarion

獠 liáo

獠牙 liáoyá long, sharp, protruding tooth; fang; bucktooth

潦 liáo

潦草 liáocǎo ❶ (of handwriting) hasty and careless; illegible; ~的字迹 scribble; scrawl ❷ sloppy; slipshod; slovenly

潦倒 liáodǎo frustrated; dispirited

寮 liáo small house; hut

缭 liáo ❶ curled up; entangled; confused ❷ sew with slanting stitches; ~缝儿 stitch up a seam

缭乱 liáoluàn also "撩乱" in a tangle or turmoil; confused; 心绪~ with one's mind in a tangle / 山花~ (of a mountain) overgrown with wild flowers

缭绕 liáorào curl up; wind around; 白云~ veiled in clouds

燎 liáo （of fire）spread；burn；～泡 blister raised by a burn or scald / ～原 set a prairie ablaze　*see also* liǎo

liǎo

了（❹ 瞭） liǎo ❶ end；finish；settle；～事 dispose of a matter；get through with sth / 安排～当 properly arranged ❷ （used with 得 or 不 after a verb）can；去得～ be able to go / 跑不～ cannot escape ❸ 〈书〉（usu used in the negative）entirely；～无痕迹 without the least trace；traceless ❹ know clearly；understand；～如指掌 know like the palm of one's hand；be thoroughly familiar （with sth）；have at one's fingertips　*see also* le

了不得 liǎobudé ❶ terrific；extreme；extraordinary；多得～ innumerable / 没什么～ nothing remarkable terrible；dreadful；awful

了不起 liǎobuqǐ amazing；remarkable；extraordinary；他有什么～ What's so remarkable about him any way?

了得 liǎode ❶ *used at the end of a sentence，mostly following* 还，*to indicate seriousness*：随便打人，这还～？How outrageous to beat people at will! ❷ （often used in the early vernacular）extraordinary；outstanding；本事～ extremely capable

了结 liǎojié *also* "了断" end；finish；settle；自作～ settle （the business） by oneself；commit suicide （as a solution）

了解 liǎojiě ❶ know；understand；comprehend；相互的～ mutual understanding ❷ find out；acquaint oneself with；～情况 size up the situation

了了 liǎoliǎo 〈书〉❶ know clearly；不甚～ know little （about sth）❷ clever；smart；intelligent；小时～，大未必佳。A smart boy may not grow up

a wise man.

了却 liǎoquè finish；settle；solve；～心愿 fulfil a wish

了然 liǎorán understand；be clear；了然于怀 know well；have a pretty good idea

燎 liǎo singe　*see also* liáo

liào

尥 liào

尥蹶子 liàojuězi ❶ （of horses，etc）give a backward kick ❷ lose one's temper；get angry；爱～ have an irascible disposition

料 liào ❶ expect；anticipate；～事如神 predict like a prophet；foretell with miraculous accuracy ❷ material；stuff；备～ prepare materials （for a project，etc） / ～酒 cooking wine / 当演员的～ have the makings of an actor ❸ （grain） feed；forage；fodder ❹ synthetic jade；opaque coloured glass；～器 glassware ❺ 〈量〉〈中药〉：配两～药 make up a prescription twice

料定 liàodìng know for sure；我～他会来。I'm sure he will come.

料理 liàolǐ ❶ arrange；attend to；take care of；～后事 make arrangements for a funeral ❷ cooking；cuisine；日本～ Japanese cuisine

料峭 liàoqiào 〈书〉chilly；北风～ chilly north wind

料想 liàoxiǎng expect；think；anticipate

料子 liàozi ❶ material for making clothes；dress length ❷ 〈方〉wooller fabric ❸ makings；stuff；搞科研的好～ have got what it takes to do scientific research

 撂 liào ❶ put down；leave behind；shelve；这事先～一～，

Let's shelve it for the time being. ❷ throw, knock or shoot down ❸ abandon; discard; cast aside:～挑子 throw up one's job

瞭 liào　watch from a height or a distance

瞭望 liàowàng ❶ look far into the distance (usu from a height):～全城 have a bird's-eye view of the city ❷ watch from a height or a distance; keep a lookout:～台 observation or lookout tower

镣 liào　fetters; shackles:～铐 fetters and handcuffs; shackles; chains

liě

咧 liě　grin:～着嘴笑 grin from ear to ear

liè

列 liè ❶ arrange; line up; list:～出名单 make a name list / 队欢迎 line or queue up to welcome sb / ～入计划 be listed in a plan / 名～第一 stand or rank first on a list ❷ row; file; sort; rank:排成一～ form a line or file ❸ kind; sort; category:不在此～ not fall into this category ❹ various; each and every:～强 big powers / ～位 all of you; ladies and gentlemen / ～祖～宗 successive generations of ancestors ❺〈量〉used of a series or row of things:一～火车 a train

列兵 lièbīng 〈军〉private

列车 lièchē　train:旅客～ passenger train

列岛 lièdǎo　chain of islands; archipelago

列举 lièjǔ　enumerate; list:～事实 cite facts

列席 lièxí　attend (a meeting) without voting rights:～代表 non-voting delegate

劣 liè　bad; inferior; of low quality:～等 of inferior quality; low-grade; poor / ～种 inferior strain; inferior breed / ～根性 deep-rooted or ingrained bad habit

劣迹 lièjì　misdeed; evildoing:～昭彰 flagrant evildoing

劣势 lièshì　inferior strength or position; unfavourable or disadvantageous situation:扭转～ turn the tables (on one's opponent)

劣质 lièzhì　of poor or low quality; inferior:～产品 substandard product

冽 liè〈书〉cold; chilly

冽 liè〈书〉(of water or wine) clear; limpid

烈 liè ❶ strong; fierce; intense:～暑 scorching summer days; dog days / ～火 fierce fire; raging flames / ～日 burning or scorching sun ❷ staunch; upright; stern ❸ dying for a just cause:～属 members of a revolutionary martyr's family

烈度 lièdù　intensity:地震～ earthquake intensity

烈士 lièshì ❶ martyr ❷〈书〉person of high endeavour; man of heroic ambitions

烈性 lièxìng ❶ upright and unyielding; spirited; fiery:～子 fierce temper; person with a violent temper; spitfire ❷ strong; intense:～酒 strong drink; hard liquor

猎（獵） liè ❶ hunt:～物 prey; quarry; game / ～艳〈书〉seek ornate phrases; hunt for beauties; philander with women ❷ hunting:～狗 also "猎犬" hunting dog; hound / ～枪 shotgun; fowling piece; hunting rifle / ～人 hunter; huntsman

猎奇 lièqí〈贬〉hunt for or seek novelty:～心理 partiality for novelty

猎取 lièqǔ ❶ hunt ❷ pursue; seek; hunt for

猎头 liètóu headhunting: ～公司 headhunting or talent-search company

裂 liè split; crack; rend: ～变〈理〉fission / ～缝 (long and narrow) crack; crevice; fissure / ～口 crack; breach; split

裂痕 lièhén rift; breach; estrangement: 弥合～ span a breach; heal a rift

裂纹 lièwén ❶ also "裂墨" crack ❷ crackle (on pottery or other vessels as decoration)

趔　liè

趔趄 lièqie stagger; reel

鬣　liè mane

līn

拎 līn carry; hold; lift: ～包〈方〉handbag; (shopping) bag

lín

邻(鄰) lín ❶ neighbour: ～居 neighbour ❷ neighbouring; near; adjacent: ～国 also "邻邦" neighbouring country

邻接 línjiē border on; be next or contiguous to; adjoin

邻近 línjìn ❶ near; close or adjacent to ❷ in the neighbourhood; nearby

邻里 línlǐ ❶ neighbourhood: ～之情 neighbourliness ❷ people of the neighbourhood; neighbours

林 lín ❶ forest; woods; grove: ～带 forest belt / ～立 stand in great numbers (like trees in a forest) / ～区 forest zone or region / ～阴道 boulevard; avenue ❷ cluster of similar things; circles: 艺～ art circles ❸ forestry: ～场 forestry centre; tree farm / ～业 forestry (as an industry)

林林总总 línlín-zǒngzǒng in great abundance; numerous; manifold

临(臨) lín ❶ arrive; be present: 大祸将～。A grave danger is imminent. ❷ face; overlook; be close to: ～河 be close to or overlook a river ❸ about to; on the point of; just before: ～盆 be giving birth to a child; be confined; be in labour / ～别赠言 words of advice at parting / ～产阵痛 labour pains; birth pangs ❹ se "临摹"

临场 línchǎng ❶ take an examination; enter a competition: ～发挥好 do well in a match, an examination etc; be in good form ❷ be personally present (at a place): ～指导 (render) on-the-spot guidance

临床 línchuáng〈医〉clinical: ～学 clinical medicine / ～医生 clinician

临到 líndào ❶ just before; about to; on the point of ❷ befall; happen to (sb)

临机 línjī as the occasion requires; on the spur of the moment; in an emergency: ～应变 suit one's actions to changing conditions; cope with any contingency

临界 línjiè〈理〉critical: ～点 critical or breakthrough point; point of transition

临近 línjìn close to or on: ～春节 the approach of the Spring Festival

临渴掘井 línkějuéjǐng make no preparation until the last moment; start acting too late

临摹 línmó copy (a model of calligraphy or painting)

临时 línshí ❶ at the time when st happens: ～抱佛脚 seek help at the eleventh hour; make a frantic last minute effort ❷ temporary; interim; provisional: ～工 casual labourer / ～代办 chargé d'affaires ad interim

临头 líntóu ❶ befall; happen; 大难～ when disaster strikes ❷ imminent; pending; 死到～ at death's door

临危 línwēi ❶ be dying (from illness) ❷ facing death or deadly peril; in the hour of danger; ～不惧 face danger fearlessly; betray no fear in an hour of danger

临战 línzhàn just before going into battle or a contest; ～状态 readiness for battle / ～训练 training just before a game

临阵 línzhèn on the eve of a battle; at the eleventh hour; at a critical moment; ～磨枪 start to prepare only at the last moment; take belated action / ～脱逃 sneak away at a critical juncture

临终 línzhōng approach one's end; be on the point of death; be on one's deathbed; ～关怀 solicitude for the dying / ～遗言 deathbed testament; last words

淋 lín pour; drench; sprinkle; 风吹雨～ wind-beaten and rain-drenched; exposed to the elements / ～浴 shower (bath) see also lìn

淋巴 línbā 〈生理〉lymph; ～结 also "淋巴腺" lymph node or gland

淋漓 línlí ❶ dripping; streaming; pouring; 大汗～ dripping with sweat; sweating all over ❷ free from inhibition; unrestrained; ～尽致 incisively and vividly; thoroughly

淋淋 línlín dripping; drizzling; pouring; 全身湿～的 be drenched all over; be soaked to the skin

琳 lín

琳琅 línláng beautiful jade; gem; ～满目 superb collection of beautiful things; feast for the eyes

粼 lín

粼粼 línlín 〈书〉(of water, etc)

clear; limpid; crystalline

嶙 lín

嶙峋 línxún 〈书〉❶ (of rocks, cliffs, etc) jagged; rugged; craggy ❷ (of a person) bony; thin; 瘦骨～ bag of bones; bony ❸ upright; unyielding

潾 lín

潾潾 línlín (of water) clear; limpid

霖 lín

霖霖 línlín continuous heavy rain

辚 lín

辚辚 línlín 〈象声〉rattle; 车～，马萧萧 chariots rattling and horses neighing

磷(燐) lín 〈化〉phosphorus (P); ～肥 〈农〉phosphate fertilizer / ～火 also "鬼火" will-o'-the-wisp; phosphorescent light

鳞 lín ❶ scale (of fish, etc) ❷ like the scales of a fish; ～伤 be covered with wounds / ～爪 〈书〉small bits; fragments / ～次栉比 row upon row (of houses, etc)

麟(麐) lín 〈书〉(short for 麒麟) kylin; (Chinese) unicorn; ～凤龟龙 (Chinese) unicorn, phoenix, turtle, and dragon; talented people

lǐn

凛 lǐn ❶ cold; frigid; ～冽 piercingly or bitingly cold ❷ strict; rigorous; stern; ～然 stern; awe-inspiring / ～若冰霜 (of manner) as cold as ice; icy; forbidding ❸ 〈书〉afraid; fearful; ～于夜行 be afraid to walk at night

凛凛 lǐnlǐn ❶ cold; frigid; 朔风～ piercing north wind ❷ stern; awe-inspiring; ～正气 awe-inspiring integrity

檩 lǐn 〈建筑〉purlin; ～条 purlin

lìn

吝 lìn　stingy; miserly; closefisted; ~色 reluctance to give; unwillingness to spare / 不~赐教 not stint on comments; not be grudging in giving advice

吝啬 lìnsè　stingy; niggardly; mean; ~鬼 miser; niggard; skinflint

吝惜 lìnxī　grudge; stint; 毫不~金钱 spend money without stint; be liberal with money

赁 lìn　rent; hire; lease; ~费 rent; rental

淋 lìn　strain; filter　*see also* lín

淋病 lìnbìng　〈医〉gonorrhoea

líng

〇 líng　(usu used in numbers) zero sign; nought

伶 líng　*also* "伶人"〈旧〉actor or actress

伶仃 língdīng　*also* "零丁" ❶ left all alone; solitary; lonely ❷ thin and weak; 瘦骨~ mere skeleton; all skin and bones

伶俐 línglì　clever; bright; smart; 伶牙俐齿 have the gift of the gab; have a glib tongue

灵（靈） líng ❶ quick; clever; flexible; 脑子~ have a sharp mind; 周转不~ have difficulty in liquidity or cash flow ❷ mind; soul; intelligence; ~气 intelligence; power of understanding ❸ deity; fairy; skil; ~怪 legendary deity; goblin ❹ efficacious; effective; ~丹妙药 miraculous cure; panacea; cure-all ❺ coffin containing a corpse; remains of the deceased; bier; ~车 hearse / 枢 coffin containing a corpse; bier / ~堂 mourning hall

灵便 língbiàn ❶ nimble; agile; quick ❷ (of sth) easy to handle; handy

灵感 línggǎn　inspiration

灵魂 línghún ❶ soul; spirit; ~不死〈迷信〉immortal soul ❷ conscience; soul; 触及~ touch one to the soul / 丧失~的人 person devoid of conscience; conscienceless person ❸ decisive factor; soul; 球队的~ soul or playmaker of a team

灵活 línghuó ❶ nimble; agile; quick; 脑筋~ be quick-witted; have a supple mind ❷ flexible; elastic; ~性 flexibility; elasticity; adaptability / ~上班制 flexible working hours

灵机 língjī　sudden inspiration; brainwave; ~一动 have a brainwave; strike on a bright idea

灵敏 língmǐn　sensitive; keen; agile; ~度〈信息〉sensitivity; accuracy; precision

灵巧 língqiǎo　dexterous; smart; ingenious; 心思~ have a dexterous mind / ~炸弹〈军〉smart bomb

灵通 língtōng　having quick access to information; well-informed

灵性 língxìng ❶ intelligence; aptitude; wisdom ❷ (of animals) sagacity; intelligence

灵验 língyàn ❶ efficacious; effective ❷ (of a forecast, etc) accurate; true; right

灵长目 língzhǎngmù　〈动物〉Primates; ~动物 primate

灵芝 língzhī　〈植〉glossy ganoderma

囹 líng

囹圄 língyǔ　*also* "囹圉"〈书〉gaol; jail; prison; 身陷~ be behind (prison) bars

泠 líng

泠泠 línglíng　〈书〉❶ cool; chilly ❷ clear and melodious

玲 líng

玲玲 línglíng 〈书〉〈象声〉tinkling of jade pieces

玲珑 línglóng ❶ (of things) ingeniously and delicately made; exquisite; cute ❷ (of people) nimble and smart

玲珑剔透 línglóngtītòu ❶ (of things) exquisitely made; delicately shaped ❷ (of people) bright and quick; very smart

铃 líng bell; sth in the shape of a bell; ～铛 small bell

凌 líng ❶ insult; bully; ～辱 insult; humiliate; treat insolently ❷ approach; draw close; ～晨 in the small hours; before daybreak ❸ rise high; tower aloft; ～云 志 high aspirations ❹ ice; ～汛 ice run

凌迟 língchí also "陵迟" 〈史〉put to death by dismembering the body

凌驾 língjià place oneself above; override; 把自己的利益～于他人之上 place one's own interests above those of others

凌空 língkōng be high up in the air; soar high into the air; ～射门 make a volley shot

凌厉 línglì quick and powerful; swift and fierce

凌乱 língluàn also "零乱" in disorder or confusion; in a mess

陵 líng ❶ hill; mound ❷ imperial tomb; mausoleum; ～墓 also "陵寝" mausoleum; tomb / ～园 tombs surrounded by a park; cemetery ❸〈书〉bully; violate; 以强～弱 bully the weak by dint of one's strength

聆 líng 〈书〉listen; hear; ～听 listen (respectfully) / ～取教诲 follow instructions

菱 líng (usu 菱角) 〈植〉water caltrop; ～形 rhombus; lozenge; diamond

棂(櫺) líng (window) lattice; latticework

翎 líng ❶ plume; tail or wing feather; quill; ～毛 未羊 unfledged ❷ (usu 翎子) peacock feather worn at the back of a Qing Dynasty official's hat

羚 líng ❶ (usu 羚羊) antelope; gazelle ❷ also "羚角" 〈中药〉antelope's horn

绫 líng silk fabric resembling satin but thinner; damask silk; ～罗绸缎 silks and satins

零 líng ❶ fractional; fragmentary; part; ～食 also "零嘴" between-meal nibbles; snacks / ～工 odd jobs / 存整取 instalment savings account ❷ fraction; odd lot; extra; ～数 remainder (beyond a round number); fractional amount / 三百挂～儿 three hundred odd ❸ placed between two numbers to indicate a smaller quantity following a larger one; 一年～五天 a year and five days ❹ zero sign (0); nought; ～点 五 0.05 (point nought five) ❺ nought; zero; nil; 3：0 three-nil; three-nothing / ～点 also "零时" zero hour; twelve o'clock at night; midnight / ～和游戏 zero-sum or zero game ❻ wither and fall

零蛋 língdàn zero (0); nothing; 考试得了个～ get a zero mark in an exam; lay an egg in an exam

零的突破 língdetūpò sth achieved for the first time in history; breakthrough; 实现～ make a breakthrough

零工 línggōng ❶ odd job; short-term hired labour; 打～ do odd jobs; odd-job ❷ odd-job man; casual labourer

零花 línghuā also "零用" ❶ spend on minor items; pay or defray incidental expenses; ～钱 pocket money ❷ pocket money; 挣～儿 earn a little extra money

零件 língjiàn spare parts; spares

零落 língluò ❶ wither and fall ❷ decline; decay：家境 ～ live in declining family circumstances ❸ scattered; sporadic

零七八碎 língqībāsuì ❶ scattered and disorderly：～地乱放东西 leave things about ❷ miscellaneous and trifling things; odds and ends

零钱 língqián ❶ small change ❷ pocket money ❸ extra money; tip

零敲碎打 língqiāo-suìdǎ do sth bit by bit, off and on; adopt a piecemeal approach

零散 língsǎn scattered; dispersed

零售 língshòu （sell) retail：～商 retail trader; retailer

零碎 língsuì ❶ scrappy; fragmentary; trivial：～事儿 odd jobs ❷ odds and ends; oddments; bits and pieces

零头 língtóu ❶ fractional amount; odd-lot piece：只剩几毛钱 ～ have only several jiao left ❷ remnant; oddments; bits and pieces：～布 remnant (of cloth)

零星 língxīng ❶ fragmentary; odd; piecemeal：零零星星 in dribs and drabs ❷ scattered; sporadic：～小雨 occasional drizzles; scattered showers

龄 líng ❶ age; years：90 高 ～ advanced age of ninety ❷ length of time or service; duration ❸ instar; stadium

鲮 líng （usu 鲮鱼）〈动物〉dace

鲮鲤 línglǐ also "穿山甲" pangolin

lǐng

令 lǐng 〈量〉ream (of paper) see also lìng

岭（嶺） lǐng ❶ (ridge of a) mountain ❷ mountain range ❸ (short for 五岭) Five Ridges that separate Guangdong and Guangxi from the hinterland：～南 (area) south of the Five Ridges; Guangdong and

Guangxi

领 lǐng ❶ neck：～巾 scarf; neckerchief ❷ collar (band); neckband; 鸡心 ～ V-shaped collar; V neck / ～结 (bow) tie / ～口 collar band; neckband; place where the two ends of a collar meet / ～章 badge or insignia ❸ 〈量〉used on gowns, mats, etc：一～ 新长袍 a new robe ❹ lead; usher; take：～唱 lead a chorus; leading singer (of a chorus) / ～港 pilot a ship into or out of a harbour; (harbour) pilot / ～路 lead the way ❺ have jurisdiction over; be in possession of：～有 possess; own ❻ receive; get; accept：～ 款 draw money / ～受 accept (kindness, etc) / receive / ～罪 plead guilty; admit or confess a crime ❼ understand; comprehend; grasp：～略 have a taste of; experience; appreciate

领班 lǐngbān ❶ lead or head (a work team or group) ❷ foreman; supervisor

领带 lǐngdài necktie; tie：打 ～ knot a necktie / ～卡 also "领带夹" tie clip

领导 lǐngdǎo ❶ lead; ～ 权 leadership; authority / ～ 核心 leading nucleus or core ❷ leader; leadership

领地 lǐngdì ❶ 〈史〉manor (of a feudal lord); fief ❷ territory

领队 lǐngduì ❶ lead a group ❷ leader of a group, team, etc；〈体〉manager

领海 lǐnghǎi territorial waters or sea：～ 权 sovereign right over territorial waters

领航 lǐngháng ❶ navigate; pilot：～ 权 pilotage ❷ also "领航员" navigator; pilot

领会 lǐnghuì understand; comprehend; grasp：～精神 grasp the essence (of sth)

领教 lǐngjiào ❶ 〈套〉used to express one's appreciation for advice, instruction, or performance：今日大开眼界，～，～。Thank you very much for opening our eyes today. ❷ ask advice; consult：～几个问题 seek sb's advice on some questions ❸ witness; experience；你的手段，早已～。We are no strangers to your tricks.

领空 lǐngkōng territorial sky or air; territorial air space

领情 lǐngqíng feel grateful to sb; appreciate the kindness

领取 lǐngqǔ draw; receive：～护照 get one's passport

领事 lǐngshì consul：总～ consul general / ～馆 consulate

领水 lǐngshuǐ ❶ inland waters ❷ territorial waters ❸ also "领水员"（harbour）pilot

领头 lǐngtóu take the lead (in doing sth)；be the first (to do sth)：～羊 bellwether

领土 lǐngtǔ territory：割让～ cede territory / ～完整 territorial integrity

领悟 lǐngwù comprehend; realize; grasp：～个中奥妙 come to see what is behind it all

领先 lǐngxiān be in the lead; lead；遥遥～ hold a safe lead; be way ahead (of sb) / 3：1～ lead by 3：1 / ～水平 leading or cutting edge

领衔 lǐngxián head the list of signers (of a document)；be the first on a name list；～主演 star in a film, etc; be a featured actor or actress

领袖 lǐngxiù leader：～欲 strong desire to be a leader

领养 lǐngyǎng adopt (a child)；～人 adopter

领域 lǐngyù ❶ territory; domain ❷ field; sphere; realm；艺术～ world of art

lìng

另 lìng other; another; separate：～案处理 handle as a separate case / 谋生另路 find another way of earning a living / ～请高明 find someone better qualified / ～行通知 be notified later；(wait) till further notice / ～有所图 have other fish to fry; have ulterior motives / 打入～册 be registered as undesirable or disreputable

另当别论 lìngdāngbiélùn be viewed differently; be considered from another perspective

另类 lìnglèi alternative; different; maverick：～音乐 alternative music / ～作家 maverick writer / 视为～ regard as alien or heretical

另起炉灶 lìngqǐlúzào ❶ make a fresh start; start all over again ❷ set up for oneself; go one's own way

另外 lìngwài in addition (to)；moreover; besides：～一个问题 a different question; another problem

另眼相看 lìngyǎnxiāngkàn ❶ regard or look up to sb with special respect ❷ view sb in a new, more favourable light; see sb in a new light

令 lìng ❶ command; order; decree：～箭〈史〉arrow-shaped token of military authority；〈喻〉token of authority / ～行禁止 strict enforcement of orders and prohibitions ❷ make; cause：～人费解 elude understanding / ～时～ season ❸〈书〉good; excellent：～名 also "令誉" good name or reputation ❺〈敬〉your：～爱 also "令媛" your daughter / ～堂 your mother / ～尊 your father
see also líng

liū

溜 liū ❶ slide; glide ❷ also "蹓" sneak off; slip away：～号〈方〉sneak away; slink off / ～之乎也〈书〉steal away; slink off; make oneself scarce ❸ smooth：～圆 smooth and round; very round / ～光〈方〉very smooth; glossy; with nothing left ❹ along：～边 keep to the edge (of a road, etc)；〈喻〉dodge；avoid ❺ see "熘" liū

see also liù

溜冰 liūbīng　　skate：～场 skating rink／溜旱冰 roller-skate

溜达 liūda　*also* "蹓跶" stroll；saunter；go for a walk

溜门 liūmén　break into (a house) to steal；burglarize；housebreak；～撬锁 burglary and lock-picking

溜须拍马 liūxūpāimǎ　〈口〉fawn；suck up to sb；shamelessly flatter

溜之大吉 liūzhīdàjí　seek safety in flight；make oneself scarce；sneak away

熘 liū　*sauté* (with thick gravy)；quick-fry；～腰花 kidney *sauté*

蹓 liū　see "溜❷" liū

liú

刘(劉) liú

刘海儿 liúhǎir　bang；fringe；垂着～ wear one's hair in bangs

浏(瀏) liú　〈书〉❶ (of water) clear；limpid ❷ (of wind) swift

浏览 liúlǎn　glance over；skim through；browse：～器〈信息〉browser

留 liú ❶ remain；stay：～鸟〈动物〉resident (bird)／～校 be employed at the school or university one graduates from ❷ study abroad：～美 study in the United States ❸ ask sb to stay；keep sb where he is；detain：～人吃饭 ask sb to stay for dinner ❹ reserve；retain；keep：～成 retain a portion or percentage (of sth)；take a cut／～任 retain a post；remain or continue in office／～后路 *also* "留后手" keep a way open for retreat；leave room for manoeuvre；keep other op-

tions／～胡子 grow a beard or moustache／～面子 let (sb) keep some self-respect；not completely disgrace (sb) ❺ accept；take；keep ❻ leave (behind)：～尾巴 leave sth unfinished；leave loose ends／～下深刻印象 make a deep impression (on sb)

留步 liúbù　〈套〉don't bother to see me out；don't come any further

留传 liúchuán　leave sth to posterity；pass on to later generations；hand down：～至今 come down to this day

留级 liújí　*also* "留班" (of pupils, etc) repeat the year's work；stay down：～生 repeater

留兰香 liúlánxiāng　〈植〉spearmint

留恋 liúliàn　be reluctant to leave (a place)；can't bear to part (from sb or with sth)；recall with nostalgia

留念 liúniàn　as a souvenir or keepsake：合影～ have a group picture taken as a souvenir

留情 liúqíng　show mercy or forgiveness；be lenient；relent

留神 liúshén　see "留心❷"

留声机 liúshēngjī　gramophone；phonograph

留守 liúshǒu　stay behind for garrison or liaison duty or to take care of the family：～人员 rear personnel

留宿 liúsù　❶ put up (a guest) for the night ❷ stay overnight；put up for the night

留心 liúxīn　❶ *also* "留意" concern oneself with；pay attention to：～时事 be concerned with current affairs ❷ *also* "留神" be careful；take care；稍不～，就可能出差错。Errors will crop up at the slightest carelessness.／～别让牛奶煮溏了。Watch the milk doesn't boil over.

留学 liúxué　study abroad：～生 student studying abroad；returned student；foreign student studying in China

留言 liúyán　leave one's comments or a message; ~簿 visitors' book / ~牌 notice board

留意 liúyì　see "留心❶"

留影 liúyǐng　❶ take a photo as a memento; have a photo taken as a souvenir ❷ photo or picture taken as a souvenir

留用 liúyòng　continue to employ; keep on; ~察看 be kept in office on probation

留职 liúzhí　retain one's post; remain on the roster; ~停薪 remain on the roster without pay; be on leave without pay

流 liú　❶ flow; ~量 (rate of) flow; discharge; flow of traffic / ~食 liquid diet / ~速 velocity of flow; current velocity / ~淌 (of liquids) flow (out); run (down) / ~体 〈理〉fluid / ~向 (of water) flow direction; (of people, gas, etc) moving direction / ~鼻涕 have a running nose / ~口水 slobber; slaver ❷ moving from place to place; drifting; wandering: ~弹 stray bullet / ~寇 roving bandits / ~民 refugee; displaced person / ~沙 drifting or shifting sand; quicksand; river silt ❸ spread; circulate; propagate ❹ change for the worse; degenerate: ~于形式 be reduced to a mere formality ❺ banish; send into exile ❻ stream (as) of water; current; torrent: 人~ stream of people ❼ class; rate; grade: 一~大学 first class university

流弊 liúbì　(long-standing) malpractice; abuse

流产 liúchǎn　❶〈医〉(have an) abortion; miscarriage ❷〈喻〉miscarry; abort; fall through

流畅 liúchàng　easy and smooth; fluent: 文笔~ write with ease

流程 liúchéng　❶ flow path; distance of the flow of water: 生命的~ life span ❷ (short for 工艺流程) technological process; work flow: ~图 flow chart

流传 liúchuán　also "流布" spread; circulate; hand down: 广为~ spread far and wide

流窜 liúcuàn　flee hither and thither; scurry; be on the run: ~犯 criminal on the run; fugitive criminal

流动 liúdòng　❶ flow; move; circulate ❷ going from place to place; on the move; mobile: ~性 mobility; fluidity / ~人口 floating population / ~资金 circulating fund; operating fund

流毒 liúdú　(spread) pernicious or baneful influence

流芳 liúfāng　〈书〉leave a good name or reputation: ~百世 leave a lasting reputation; gain immortal fame

流放 liúfàng　❶ banish; send into exile ❷ float (logs) downstream

流感 liúgǎn　(short for 流行性感冒) flu: 得~ catch the flu

流浪 liúlàng　roam about; wander; lead a vagrant life: ~儿 waif; street urchin / ~汉 tramp; vagrant; vagabond

流离 liúlí　〈书〉wander about homeless; live the life of a vagrant: ~失所 become destitute and homeless; be forced to leave home and wander about

流里流气 liúlǐliúqì　〈口〉(of behaviour, etc) flippant; not serious or proper; rascally

流利 liúlì　❶ fluent; glib; 文笔~ write in an easy and fluent style ❷ smooth; sleek; 书写~ (of a pen) write smoothly

流连 liúlián　also "留连" linger on; be reluctant to leave; can't tear oneself away: ~忘返 enjoy oneself so much as to forget to go home; stay on with no thought of leaving

流露 liúlù　reveal; betray; show unintentionally

L

流落 liúluò　wander poor and homeless：～他乡 live a wretched life far from home；be stranded in a remote land

流氓 liúmáng　❶ rogue；hoodlum；hooligan ❷ immoral or indecent behaviour；hooliganism：要～ behave like a hoodlum；(esp) take liberties with women；act indecently

流年 liúnián　❶〈书〉fleeting time：似水～ time passing swiftly like flowing water ❷〈迷信〉prediction of a person's luck in a given year：～不利 also "流年不顺" unlucky year

流派 liúpài　school；sect：哲学～ school of philosophy

流失 liúshī　❶ run off；be washed away；be eroded ❷ loss (of resources, etc)；drain；leaching：资产～ loss of assets／人才～ brain drain ❸ (of students) drop out

流逝 liúshì　(of time) pass；elapse

流水 liúshuǐ　❶ running water：～线 assembly line／～作业 flow process；assembly line method；conveyer system／～不腐，户枢不蠹 running water is never stale and a door-hinge never gets worm-eaten；a thing in use rots not ❷ turnover (in business)：～账 day-to-day or current account

流苏 liúsū　tassels；fringe

流俗 liúsú　〈贬〉prevalent custom；current fashion：不囿～ not confined by current customs

流通 liútōng　(of air, money, etc) flow；circulate：～货币 currency

流亡 liúwáng　be forced to leave one's native land；go into exile：～政府 government-in-exile

流线型 liúxiànxíng　streamline：～汽车 streamlined car

流星 liúxīng　also "贼星"〈天文〉meteor：shooting star；～雨 meteor or meteoric shower

流行 liúxíng　prevalent；popular；in vogue：～病 epidemic disease；widespread social evil／～色 popular colour／～歌曲 popular or pop song；pop

流血 liúxuè　bleed；shed blood：～牺牲 shed blood or lay down one's life (for a just cause)／不～的政变 bloodless coup d'état

流言 liúyán　rumour；gossip：～蜚语 also "流言飞语" rumours and slanders

流域 liúyù　river basin or valley；drainage area

琉 liú

琉璃 liúlí　coloured glaze：～瓦 glazed tile

硫 liú〈化〉sulphur (S)：～磺 also "硫黄" sulphur／～酸 sulphuric acid

馏 liú　distil：～分〈化〉fraction cut　see also liù

榴 liú　pomegranate

榴弹炮 liúdànpào　〈军〉howitzer

榴莲 liúlián　〈植〉durian

榴霰弹 liúxiàndàn　also "子母弹"〈军〉shrapnel；canister (shot)

镏 liú　see also liù

镏金 liújīn　gold-plating；gild：～戒指 gold-plated ring

瘤 liú　tumour

liǔ

柳 liǔ　willow：～编 wickerwork／～眉 (of a woman) willow-leaf shaped or arched eyebrows／～絮 (willow) catkins／～腰 (of a woman) slender waist (like a willow branch)；narrow；soft waistline

柳暗花明 liǔ'àn-huāmíng　dense willow trees and bright flowers；enchanting sight in spring time；bright new vista：～又一村。Every cloud has a silver lining.

柳条 liǔtiáo　willow twig；osier；wicker；～筐 wicker basket

绺 liǔ　〈量〉tuft；lock；skein：一～长须 a wisp of long beard

liù

六 liù　six：～月 June；sixth month or moon of the lunar year / ～边形 hexagon

六部 liùbù　〈史〉six ministries of the central government, ie 吏部（Ministry of Civil Offices），户部（Ministry of Revenue），礼部（Ministry of Rites）兵部（Ministry of War），刑部（Ministry of Punishments），and 工部（Ministry of Works）

六朝 Liùcháo　❶ Six Dynasties all with their capital located in present Nanjing（from 222 to 589, with an interval of Western Jin 西晋 281-316），namely, Wu（吴，222-280），Eastern Jin（东晋，317-420），and the four Southern Dynasties（南朝，420-589）❷ general term for the Northern and Southern dynasties（420-589）

六畜 liùchù　six domestic animals （pig, ox, goat, horse, chicken, and dog）；domestic livestock and fowl in general：～兴旺。The domestic animals and fowls are all thriving.

六合 liùhé　〈书〉six directions：east, west, north, south, heaven（up），and earth（down）；the country；universe

六亲 liùqīn　six relations（father, mother, elder brothers, younger brothers, wife, children）；one's kin；relations：～不认 disown one's kith and kin；not consider anybody's self-interest；not spare one's sensibilities

六神 liùshén　six vital organs（lung, liver, kidney, spleen；bile and heart）：～不安（with all six vital organs）rest-less；disturbed / ～无主 in a state of utter stupefaction；out of one's wits

六书 liùshū　〈语言〉six traditional categories of Chinese characters, namely, "self-explanatory" characters（指事），"pictographic" characters（象形），"pictophonetic" characters（形声），"associative" characters（会意），"mutually explanatory" characters（转注），and "phonetic-loan" characters（假借）

陆（陸） liù　six（used for the numeral six to avoid mistakes or alterations）*see also* lù

遛 liù　❶ *also* "蹓" saunter；stroll：～弯儿〈方〉take a walk；go for a stroll ❷ walk（an animal）

馏 liù　heat up（cold food in a steamer）；warm　*see also* liú

溜 liù　❶ swift current ❷ row：～新房子 a row of new houses ❸ surroundings；neighbourhood ❹〈方〉train；exercise：～嗓子 train one's voice ❺〈方〉fill（a crevice, fissure, etc）*see also* liú

镏 liù　*see also* liú

镏子 liùzi　〈方〉（finger）ring：金～ gold ring

lo

咯 lo　〈助〉*same as* 了 but more *emphatic*：那就好～！That would be much better!　*see also* gē；kǎ

lóng

龙（龍） lóng　❶ dragon：～宫 Dragon King's palace / ～王 Dragon King, god who rules the rivers and seas and is in charge of rain / ～的传人 descendants of the dragon — the Chinese nation / ～蛇混杂 good and bad mixed up；high and low mixed together ❷ dragon as the symbol of the emperor; imperial; ~袍 imperial robe ❸ anything shaped like a dragon or with the pattern of a dragon on it; ~船 *also* "龙舟" dragon boat / ~灯 dragon lantern

龙飞凤舞 lóngfēi-fèngwǔ ❶ (of mountains) undulating and winding ❷ (of calligraphy) lively and vigorous flourishes; (of handwriting) illegible scrawl

龙凤 lóngfèng　dragon and phoenix — the best; 人中~ best of talents; the best and brightest / ~呈祥 (have) extremely good fortune

龙卷风 lóngjuǎnfēng　tornado

龙盘虎踞 lóngpán-hǔjù　*see* "虎踞龙盘" in "虎"

龙潭虎穴 lóngtán-hǔxué　*also* "虎穴龙潭" dragon's pool and tiger's den; danger spot

龙套 lóngtào　actor playing a walk-on part in traditional opera; utility man; 跑~ work as a utility man; serve as a pawn

龙腾虎跃 lóngténg-hǔyuè　*also* "虎跃龙腾" (full of) vigorous, magnificent action; scene of bustling activity

龙头 lóngtóu ❶ *also* "水龙头" tap; faucet ❷〈方〉handlebar (of a bicycle) ❸〈喻〉leader; flagship; ~产品 leader product / ~企业 leading or flagship enterprise

龙虾 lóngxiā　lobster

龙眼 lóngyǎn　*also* "桂圆"〈植〉longan

龙争虎斗 lóngzhēng-hǔdòu　fierce struggle between evenly-matched opponents; contest between giants

龙钟 lóngzhōng　〈书〉decrepit; senile; ~老者 decrepit old man

茏(蘢) lóng

茏葱 lóngcōng　verdant; luxuriantly green

珑(瓏) lóng

珑玲 lónglíng　〈书〉❶ *also* "玲珑" tinkling sound of jade or metal ❷ bright; brilliant

栊(櫳) lóng

〈书〉❶ window; 帘~ curtained window ❷ (usu 栊槛) cage (for keeping animals); pen

砻(礱) lóng

❶ rice huller ❷ hull (rice); ~糠 rice chaff / ~谷舂米 hull grain and pound rice

聋(聾) lóng

deaf; hard of hearing; ~子 the deaf

聋哑 lóngyǎ　deaf and dumb; deaf-mute; ~人 deaf-mute

笼(籠) lóng

❶ cage; coop; basket; 鸡~ chicken coop / ~头 headstall; halter (for a horse, etc) / ~中鸟 caged bird; person deprived of freedom ❷ (food) steamer; ~屉 (tiers of) bamboo or wooden utensil for steaming food; food steamer ❸〈方〉put (each hand) in the opposite sleeve

see also lǒng

隆 lóng

❶ grand; solemn ❷ prosperous; thriving ❸ intense; deep; ~冬 depths of winter; midwinter / ~情厚谊 profound sentiments of friendship; great kindness and favour ❹ swell; bulge; protrude; ~胸 breast enhancement or enlargement / ~起的鼻梁 high-bridged nose

隆隆 lónglóng　〈象声〉(of thunder, cannon, etc) rumble; boom

隆重 lóngzhòng　grand; solemn; ceremonious; ~欢迎 give a ceremonious welcome; accord a grand reception

lǒng

陇(隴) Lǒng

another name for Gansu (甘肃); ~西

Western Gansu

垄(壟) lǒng ❶ ridge (in a field); ridge-like thing; ~沟〈农〉field ditch; furrow ❷ raised path between fields

垄断 lǒngduàn monopolize; ~集团 monopoly group / ~市场 corner or monopolize the market

拢(攏) lǒng ❶ close; 笑得~不上嘴 grin from ear to ear ❷ draw near; approach; reach ❸ add or sum up; ~共 also "拢总" altogether; all told; in all ❹ hold or gather together; keep close together; ~不住人 cannot keep people together; fail to keep people working for one ❺ comb (hair); ~子 fine-toothed comb

笼(籠) lǒng ❶ envelop; cover; enclose ❷ large box; chest; trunk
see also lóng

笼络 lǒngluò 〈贬〉win or draw over; rope in; ~人心 cultivate people's good will (by dispensing favours, etc); court popularity

笼统 lǒngtǒng general; sweeping; vague; ~地说 generally (speaking); in general terms

笼罩 lǒngzhào envelop; encompass; shroud; 黑暗~着大地。The earth is shrouded in darkness.

lòng

弄 lòng (usu 弄堂)〈方〉lane; alley; alleyway　*see also* nòng

lōu

搂(摟) lōu ❶ gather up; rake together; ~干草 rake up hay ❷ hold, tuck or roll up; ~起袖子 roll up one's sleeves ❸ grab or squeeze (money); extort; ~钱 grab money ❹ pull; draw; ~火 also "搂扳

机"〈口〉pull a trigger; fire
see also lóu

lóu

娄(婁) lóu 〈方〉❶ bad; poor; 身体~ (be in) poor health / 字写得~ write a poor hand ❷ (used of melons) become over-ripe and decay; go bad

娄子 lóuzi trouble; blunder; mishap; 捅~ make a blunder; get into trouble

喽(嘍) lóu　*see also* lou

喽啰 lóuluó also "喽罗" ❶ rank and file of a band of outlaws or bandits ❷ underling; flunkey; pawn

楼(樓) lóu ❶ storeyed building; multi-storey house; ~道 corridor (in a storeyed building); passageway / ~阁 pavilion; tower / ~花 futures or unfinished housing / ~盘 finished or ready-to-use housing / ~市 real estate market ❷ storey; floor; 一~ (UK) ground floor; (US) first floor / ~上 up-stairs / ~下 downstairs ❸ superstructure; tower; 望~ watchtower ❹ (used of certain kinds of shops) house; mansion; 茶~ tea house

楼梯 lóutī stairs; staircase; ~扶手 banisters; balustrade

耧(耬) lóu animal-drawn seed plough; drill (barrow); ~播〈农〉sow with a drill; drill

蝼(螻) lóu also "蝼蛄" mole cricket

蝼蚁 lóuyǐ mole crickets and ants; nobodies; nonentities

lǒu

搂(摟) lǒu ❶ hold in one's arms; hug; ~抱 hug; embrace; cuddle ❷ 〈量〉arm-span;

L

两～粗的大松树 large pine tree two arm-spans round

see also lōu

篓（簍） lǒu basket

lòu

陋 lòu ❶ plain; ugly; coarse ❷ (of a dwelling) rude; humble; mean；～室 humble room; plain house ❸ vulgar; corrupt; undesirable；～习 corrupt customs; bad habits ❹ (of knowledge) scanty; limited; shallow；～见 superficial view; narrow vision

镂（鏤） lòu engrave; carve；～刻 engrave; carve / ～空 hollow out or pierce (by carving) / ～骨铭心 *also* "刻骨铭心" bear in mind or remember forever with gratitude

瘘（瘻） lòu〈医〉fistula；肛～ anal fistula

漏 lòu ❶ trickle; ooze; leak；～电 leakage (of electricity) / ～勺 strainer; colander ❷ (usu 漏壶 or 漏刻) water clock; hourglass; sandglass；～夜 in the dead of night; midnight ❸ divulge; let out; leak；～底 let the cat out of the bag; reveal the bottom line / 说～了嘴 divulge inadvertently; make a slip of the tongue ❹ miss; omit; leave out；～检 fail to check or detect / ～税 omit to pay a tax; evade payment of a tax

漏洞 lòudòng ❶ leak ❷ flaw; hole; loophole；堵塞财务～ plug all financial loopholes

漏斗 lòudǒu funnel; hopper

漏风 lòufēng ❶ leaking air; not airtight ❷ (of information, secrets) leak out

漏网 lòuwǎng slip through or escape from the net (of law, etc); escape unpunished; get away scotfree；～之鱼 escapee; fugitive

漏子 lòuzi ❶ funnel；酒～ wine funnel ❷ flaw; mistake; loophole

露 lòu *used only in the following combinations　see also* lù

露底 lòudǐ let out a secret; reveal an inside story; disclose the ins and outs of sth

露富 lòufù show one's riches；有钱不～ never show one's wealth in public

露脸 lòuliǎn win honour or credit; cut a figure; be successful

露马脚 lòumǎjiǎo give oneself away; betray oneself; let the cat out of the bag

露面 lòumiàn show one's face; make or put in an appearance; appear on public occasions

露怯 lòuqiè *also* "露丑"〈方〉display one's ignorance or weakness; make a fool of oneself

露头 lòutóu ❶ show or raise one's head ❷ appear; emerge

露馅儿 lòuxiànr give the game away; let the cat out of the bag; spill the beans

露一手 lòuyīshǒu display one's abilities or skills; show off

lou

喽（嘍） lou〈助〉❶ *used after a verb to refer to an envisaged action*：他知道～又怎么样? What can he do about it even if he knows? ❷ *used at the end or in the middle of a sentence to attract attention*：走～，走～，戏快开演了! Let's go. The play is about to start.

see also lóu

lū

撸 lū〈方〉❶ close one's hand around (sth long) and push;

strip with the hand; ～袖子 roll up one's sleeves ❷ remove; dismiss; ～到底 be stripped of all one's posts ❸ scold; take to task; dress down

lú

卢(盧) lú
卢布 lúbù　ruble (currency used in Russia and some other countries)

芦(蘆) lú
reed; ～苇 also "苇子" reed
芦笋 lúsǔn　(popularly known as 龙须菜)〈植〉asparagus

庐(廬) lú
hut; hovel

炉(爐) lú
❶ stove; oven; furnace; ～灶 kitchen range; cooking range / ～渣 slag; cinder; clinker ❷〈量〉used of what is made in a furnace, stove or oven; 一～钢 a heat of steel
炉火纯青 lúhuǒchúnqīng　height of technical or professional proficiency; perfection

鸬(鸕) lú
鸬鹚 lúcí　also "鱼鹰"〈动物〉cormorant

颅(顱) lú
〈生理〉cranium; skull

鲈(鱸) lú
(usu 鲈鱼) perch

lǔ

卤(鹵、滷) lǔ
❶ bittern; 点～水 dribble bittern ❷ also "卤素"〈化〉halogen ❸ stew in salty water with spices or in soy sauce; ～菜 pot-stewed (meat) dish / ～虾 salted shrimp ❹ thick gravy used as sauce for noodles, etc; thick infusion; 打～面 noodles served with

thick gravy / 茶～儿 strong tea (to be diluted before drinking)

虏(虜) lǔ
❶ take prisoner; ～获 capture; men and arms captured ❷ captive; prisoner of war

掳(擄) lǔ
carry off; capture; ～掠 pillage; loot

鲁 lǔ
❶ stupid; dull; slow-witted; ～钝 stupid; obtuse; dull-witted ❷ rash; rough; rude; ～莽 also "卤莽" (crude and) rash; reckless ❸ (Lǔ) another name for Shandong (山东)

橹 lǔ
scull (at boat's stern)

lù

陆(陸) lù
land; ～地 (dry) land / ～战队〈军〉marine corps; marines / ～基导弹〈军〉land-based missile / ～海空三军〈军〉army, navy and air force; the three armed services　see also liù
陆路 lùlù　land route; 走～ take a land route; travel over land / ～交通 overland communication
陆续 lùxù　one after another; in succession

录(録) lù
❶ record; note or write down; copy; ～供〈法〉take down a confession or testimony during an interrogation ❷ tape-record; ～一盘磁带 copy a tape ❸ record; register; collection ❹ use; employ; hire
录取 lùqǔ　enrol; recruit; admit; ～通知书 admission notice; notice of acceptance
录像 lùxiàng　videotape; video-record; 放～ play a video / ～机 video (recorder); videotape player
录音 lùyīn　sound recording; ～带 (magnetic) tape / ～机 (tape) record-

er / ～电话 answer machine; telegraphone

录用 lùyòng　employ; recruit; take on the staff;择优～ employ on the basis of competitive selection; recruit selectively

录制 lùzhì　record; ～唱片 make a gramophone record; cut a disc

赂 lù ❶ give money or goods as gifts; bribe ❷ (gift of) goods or money

鹿 lù〈动物〉deer; ～角 deer horn; antler / ～茸〈中药〉pilose antler (of a young stag) / ～肉 venison / ～死谁手 who will win the prize or gain the upper hand

绿 lù　see also lǜ

绿林 lùlín　the greenwood — world of brigands and outlaws; ～好汉 hero of the greenwood; forest outlaw; bandit

禄 lù　official's salary or stipend in dynastic China; emoluments

碌 lù ❶ commonplace; mediocre ❷ busy

碌碌 lùlù ❶ mediocre; commonplace; ～无为 attempt nothing and accomplish nothing; lead a plain, humdrum life ❷ busy with miscellaneous work

路 lù ❶ road; way; route; ～边 wayside; roadside / ～标 road sign;〈军〉route marking / ～灯 street lamp / ～费 travelling expenses; fare / ～轨 (steel) rail; track / ～基 roadbed; bed / ～面 road surface; pavement / ～人 passer-by; stranger / ～障 road barrier; barricade; roadblock / 五～电车 No 5 trolley bus ❷ way (to do sth); path; means:致富之～ ways to get rich ❸ region; area; district;各～英雄 people from various places ❹ sort; grade; class:一～货色 same sort of things; people of the same ilk; birds of a feather

路不拾遗 lùbùshíyí　*also*"道不拾遗"(as descriptive of a high moral standard in society) no one picks up and pockets anything lost on the road

路程 lùchéng　distance travelled; journey

路过 lùguò　pass by or through (a place)

路径 lùjìng ❶ route; way;迷失～ lose one's way ❷ method; ways and means;寻找成功的～ seek the way to success

路口 lùkǒu ❶ crossing; junction; intersection;丁字～ T-shaped road junction ❷ end or beginning of a road or path;～的收费关卡 fee park at the beginning or end of a road

路数 lùshù ❶ way; approach;摸到了一点儿～ get some inkling of how to do it ❷ movement in martial arts ❸ ins and outs; inside story

路途 lùtú ❶ road; path ❷ distance travelled; way; journey

路线 lùxiàn ❶ route; itinerary;参观～图 visitors' itinerary ❷ line:思想～ ideological line

路遥知马力 lùyáozhīmǎlì　distance tests a horse's stamina;～,日久见人心。As distance tests a horse's strength, so time reveals a person's heart.

路子 lùzi ❶ connections; pull;～硬 have very influential backers ❷ way; approach:～对 adopt the right approach

辘 lù

辘轳 lùlú　windlass; well-pulley; hoisting tackle

辘辘 lùlù　〈象声〉*used to represent sound of wheels turning, etc*:牛车～而过。The cattle cart rumbled past.

戮 lù ❶ kill; slay ❷〈书〉unite; join;～力同心 unite in a concerted effort; make concerted efforts

鹭 lù 〈动物〉egret; heron; ~ 鸶 also "白鹭" egret

麓 lù 〈书〉foot of a hill or mountain

露 lù ❶ dew; ~ 珠 dewdrop ❷ beverage distilled from flowers, fruit or leaves; drink mixed with fruit juice; syrup; ~ 酒 alcoholic drink mixed with fruit juice ❸ in the open; outdoors; ~ 宿街头 sleep in the street ❹ show; reveal; betray; ~ 锋芒 make a showy display of one's abilities; demonstrate one's talent / ~ 头角 (of a young person) beginning to show ability or talent; budding / ~ 原形 show one's true colours; give oneself away see also lòu

露骨 lùgǔ thinly-veiled; undisguised; barefaced: 说话太 ~ be too assertive in one's words

露水 lùshui ❶ 〈口〉dew ❷ of short duration; transient; brief: ~ 夫妻 illicit lovers; one-night stand

露天 lùtiān in the open (air); outdoors: ~ 电影 open-air cinema / ~ 开采 opencast mining / ~ 看台 bleachers

露营 lùyíng ❶ 〈军〉camp (out); encamp; bivouac ❷ go camping

lú

驴(驢) lǘ donkey; ass: ~ 骡 hinny; jennet / 好心当成~肝肺 take sb's goodwill for ill intent

驴唇不对马嘴 lǘchúnbùduìmǎzuǐ also "牛头不对马嘴" beside the point; far-fetched; irrelevant

闾 lǘ 〈书〉❶ gate or entrance to an alley or lane: ~ 左 poor neighbourhood or people ❷ alley; lane; neighbourhood: ~ 里 native village; hometown / ~ 巷 alley; lane; alleyway; common people

lǚ

侣 lǚ companion; associate: ~ 伴 companion; partner; associate

捋 lǚ smooth out with the fingers; stroke: ~ 胡子 stroke beard see also luō

旅 lǚ ❶ travel; journey; live away from home: ~ 伴 travelling companion; fellow traveler / ~ 费 travelling expenses; fare / ~ 馆 also "旅店" hotel; inn / ~ 美侨胞 Chinese nationals living in the US ❷ 〈军〉brigade: ~ 长 brigade commander ❸ troops; armed forces ❹ 〈书〉jointly; ~ 进 ~ 退 go along with the majority; have no independent views of one's own

旅程 lǚchéng distance travelled; route; itinerary

旅居 lǚjū reside or live away from home; sojourn: ~ 海外 reside abroad

旅客 lǚkè hotel guest; traveller; passenger: ~ 登记簿 hotel register

旅途 lǚtú journey; trip: ~ 风光 scenes on a trip

旅行 lǚxíng travel; journey; tour: ~ 社 travel service or agency / ~ 结婚 (have a) honeymoon trip / ~ 支票 traveller's cheque / ~ 指南 guidebook

旅游 lǚyóu tour; tourism: ~ 热 travel fever or boom / ~ 鞋 sneakers; walking shoes / ~ 景点 scenic spot; sight of interest / ~ 旺季 peak tourist season / ~ 资源 tourism resources

铝 lǚ 〈化〉aluminium (Al): ~ 合金 aluminium alloy

屡(屢) lǚ repeatedly; frequently; time and again: ~ 次三番 again and again; over and over again; many times / ~ 见不鲜 nothing new; common occurrence / ~ 教不改 also "累教不改" refuse to mend one's ways despite repeated admonition / ～试不爽 put to repeated tests and proved right; time-tested / ～战～败 fight and lose repeatedly; suffer repeated defeats / ～～ 违反纪律 frequently violate discipline

缕（縷） lǚ ❶ thread ❷ detailed; in detail / ～述 state in detail; go into particulars ❸ 〈量〉 wisp; strand; lock; 几～头发 several locks of hair / ～～炊烟 wisps of smoke

膂 lǚ

膂力 lǚlì muscular or physical strength; brawn; ～过人 possessing extraordinary physical strength

履 lǚ ❶ shoe ❷ tread or walk on; ～险如夷 cross a dangerous pass as easily as walking on level ground; handle a crisis without difficulty ❸ footstep ❹ carry out; implement; fulfil; ～约 〈书〉 fulfil one's promises; keep an appointment, etc / ～职 do one's duty

履带 lǚdài caterpillar tread; track; crawler belt

履历 lǚlì ❶ personal record; antecedents ❷ also "履历表" curriculum vitae (CV); résumé

履行 lǚxíng perform; fulfil; carry out; ～诺言 keep one's word; fulfil one's promise / ～手续 go through the procedures

lǜ

律 lǜ ❶ law; rule; regulation; ～条 legal articles, clauses or provisions; law; norm ❷ also "律诗" classical Chinese poem of eight lines with a strict tonal pattern and rhyme scheme ❸ 〈书〉 restrain; keep under control; ～己 discipline oneself; exercise self-discipline; be strict with oneself

律师 lǜshī lawyer; counsel; (US) attorney; 请～ retain counsel; engage a lawyer / ～事务所 lawyer's office; law firm

虑（慮） lǜ ❶ consider; ponder; mull (over) ❷ concern; anxiety; worry

率 lǜ rate; ratio; proportion see also shuài

绿 lǜ green; ～茶 green tea / ～党 Green Party / ～地 afforested land (in urban areas) / ～肥 green manure / ～洲 oasis / ～宝石 emerald / ～茸茸 lush, bluish green / ～莹莹 glittering and green / ～油油 green and sleek; green and lush see also lù

绿菜花 lǜcàihuā (popular term for 西蓝花) broccoli

绿灯 lǜdēng green light; permission to go ahead; 开～ give the green light

绿豆 lǜdòu mung bean; green gram; ～芽 mung bean sprouts

绿化 lǜhuà make (a place) green by planting trees, flowers, etc; afforest; ～地带 green belt / ～工程 landscape engineering

绿卡 lǜkǎ green card — permanent residence permit; (US) permanent resident identification card

绿色 lǜsè ❶ green ❷ related or favourable to environmental protection; green; ～食品 green food

绿茵 lǜyīn green meadow; ～场 (green meadow) soccer field

氯 lǜ 〈化〉 chlorine (Cl); ～化物 chloride

滤 lǜ strain; filter

luán

峦（巒） luán 〈书〉 hills or mountains in a range; ～叠嶂 peaks rising one upon the other

孪(孿) luán 〈书〉twin;~生子 twin children

孪(攣) luán contract;~缩成一团 huddle (oneself) up

鸾(鸞) luán legendary bird like the phoenix,~凤 also "鸾凤"〈书〉husband and wife

銮(鑾) luán small tinkling bell (on the emperor's carriage); imperial carriage

lüǎn

卵 luǎn ❶ ovum; egg; spawn;产~ lay eggs; spawn / ~翼 cover with wings as in brooding; shield ❷ also "卵子" zygote;~巢〈生理〉ovary

luàn

乱(亂) luàn ❶ in confusion or chaos; in a turmoil; unsettled (state of mind);~码〈信息〉error or garbage code / ~作一团 in great confusion / ~蓬蓬的头发 dishevelled hair ❷ upheaval; turmoil; rebellion;~世 troubled or turbulent times; period of turmoil / ~臣贼子 traitors and usurpers ❸ confuse; mix up; jumble;~套 mess up things; turn things upside down ❹ indiscriminate; random; arbitrary;~说 speak carelessly; make irresponsible remarks / ~砍滥伐 indiscriminate felling of trees; cutting trees at random ❺ promiscuous sexual behaviour; promiscuity;~伦 (commit) incest

乱哄哄 luànhōnghōng in noisy disorder; in a hubbub; in an uproar

乱七八糟 luànqībāzāo at sixes and sevens; in a mess or muddle;脑子里~的 with one's mind in a whirl

乱弹琴 luàntánqín act or talk like a fool; talk nonsense

乱糟糟 luànzāozāo chaotic; in a mess or pickle; confused;心里~的 greatly distressed

乱子 luànzi disturbance; trouble; disorder:出~ get into trouble

lüè

掠 lüè ❶ rob; plunder; pillage;~取 seize; grab; plunder ❷ sweep or brush past; skim over;~影 bird's-eye view; panorama

掠夺 lüèduó plunder; loot; pillage;~成性 be predatory by nature / ~式开采 indiscriminate mining

掠美 lüèměi (short for 掠人之美) claim credit due to sb else; grab undue credit

略(畧) lüè ❶ brief; sketchy; rough:~~ a little; slightly; briefly / ~图 sketch (map) / ~见一斑 catch a glimpse of; get a rough idea of / ~胜一筹 a notch above; slightly better / ~知一二 know just a little; have a rough idea ❷ brief account; summary; sketch ❸ omit; delete; leave out ❹ plan; strategy; scheme ❺ capture (city or land); seize

略微 lüèwēi slightly; a little; somewhat:~有点不快 feel somewhat unhappy

略语 lüèyǔ also "略称" short form; abbreviation; acronym

lūn

抡(掄) lūn ❶ swing; brandish ❷ fling; throw; scatter

lún

伦(倫) lún ❶ human relations, esp in terms of

ethics；~常 fixed order of precedence in human relationships ② logic；order：~次 coherence；logical sequence ③ peer；match：史无~比 unequalled in history

伦巴 lúnbā rumba (a dance)

伦敦 Lúndūn London, capital of Britain：~金融区 the City

伦理 lúnlǐ ethics；moral principles：~学 ethics

沦(淪) lún sink；subside；fall：~亡 (of a country) be annexed or subjugated；perish ② 为奴隶 be reduced to slavery

沦落 lúnluò ① become a vagabond；be homeless：~街头 become a tramp or beggar ② decline；degenerate：~风尘 be driven to prostitution；become a prostitute

沦丧 lúnsàng wither away；be forfeited, lost or ruined：主权~ forfeiture of sovereignty

沦陷 lúnxiàn ① (of territory, etc) be occupied by the enemy；fall into enemy hands：~区 enemy-occupied area ② 〈书〉submerge；flood；inundate

纶(綸) lún ① 〈书〉black silk ribbon ② 〈书〉fishing line ③ synthetic fibre：锦~ polyamide fibre

轮(輪) lún ① wheel；sth resembling a wheel；ring：~胎 also "轮带" tyre / ~椅 wheelchair ② steamboat；steamer：~船 steamer；steamship；steamboat / ~渡 ferry (boat) ③ take turns；do by turns：~班 in shifts；in rotation；by turns / ~奸 gang rape / ~作〈农〉crop rotation ④ 〈量〉**a)** used of the sun, moon, etc：一~红日 a red sun **b)** used of things or actions that rotate：第二~会谈 second round of talks

轮番 lúnfān by turns；one after another：~干活 take turns at a job

轮换 lúnhuàn rotate；take turns：~警

卫人员 change of guard

轮回 lúnhuí 〈宗教〉samsara；transmigration

轮空 lúnkōng 〈体〉bye：第一轮比赛抽签~ draw a first-round bye

轮廓 lúnkuò ① outline；profile；contour ② general or rough idea

轮流 lúnliú take turns；do sth in turn

lùn

论(論) lùn ① discuss；comment；argue：~敌 opponent in a debate / ~据 grounds of argument；argument / ~坛 forum；tribune；symposium / ~战 also "论争" polemic；debate；controversy / ~著 treatise；work ② view；statement；essay：~题 proposition ③ theory；doctrine：方法~ methodology ④ measure；assess；determine：~功行赏 award people according to their contributions / ~资排辈 go by seniority；stress seniority in promotion ⑤ by；in terms of：~天计酬 pay by day

论辩 lùnbiàn argue；debate：~有力 (make a) cogent argument

论处 lùnchǔ decide on sb's punishment；punish：依法~ punish according to law；bring to justice

论点 lùndiǎn argument；thesis；point of view

论调 lùndiào 〈贬〉view；argument：蛊惑人心的~ demagogic view

论断 lùnduàn inference；judgment；thesis

论理 lùnlǐ ① reason with sb；argue：与人~ argue it out with sb ② normally；as things should be：~他今天应该来。Normally he should come today. ③ logic；reason：合乎~ be reasonable；stand to reason

论述 lùnshù discuss；explicate；expound：精辟的~ brilliant exposition or explication

论说 lùnshuō ❶ exposition and argumentation：～体 argumentation（as a category of writing）❷〈口〉see "论理❷"

论文 lùnwén thesis；dissertation；treatise；paper：毕业～ graduation thesis / ～答辩 thesis defence

论证 lùnzhèng ❶ demonstration；proof；（grounds of）argument ❷ expound and prove；appraise；evaluate：～会 meeting to appraise a project，work，etc

论罪 lùnzuì punish as guilty of a crime；decide on the nature of the guilt：按故意杀人～ find（sb）guilty of intentional homicide

luō

捋 luō rub one's palm along（sth long）；strip sth by pushing one's hand along it：～起袖子 roll up one's sleeve　see also lǚ

啰（囉） luō see also luo

啰唆（嗦） luōsuō also "啰嗦" ❶（of sb）long-winded；verbose；wordy ❷（of sth）over-elaborate；fussy；troublesome

luó

罗（羅） luó ❶ net for catching birds；catch（birds）with a net ❷ collect；recruit ❸ display；set or spread out ❹ sieve；sifter；screen：～面 sift flour ❺ silk gauze：～衣 garment of thin silk ❻〈量〉gross；twelve dozen

罗锅 luóguō ❶ hunchbacked；humpbacked ❷ hunchback；humpback ❸ arched：～桥 arch bridge

罗汉 luóhàn〈宗教〉arhat

罗口 luókǒu rib cuff or collar；rib top：～短袜 socks with rib tops / ～灯

泡 screw bulb

罗列 luóliè ❶ spread or set out ❷ enumerate；list

罗马 Luómǎ Rome：～法〈法〉Roman law / ～数字 Roman numerals / ～式建筑 Romanesque architecture / ～天主教 Roman Catholicism；Church of Rome

罗盘 luópán also "罗经" compass

罗网 luówǎng net；trap：布下～ lay or set a trap

罗织 luózhī〈书〉frame：～诬陷 frame（sb）/ ～罪名 cook up charges；frame a case（against sb）

罗致 luózhì enlist the services of；secure in one's employment；recruit

萝（蘿） luó〈植〉trailing plant；vine

萝卜 luóbo also "莱菔" radish；turnip

逻（邏） luó patrol

逻辑 luóji logic；reason；sense：不合～ contrary to reason；illogical / ～思维 logical thinking / ～炸弹〈信息〉logic bomb

锣（鑼） luó〈乐〉gong：～鼓 gong and drum；traditional percussion instruments / 破～嗓子 broken voice

箩（籮） luó square-bottomed bamboo basket：～筐 large bamboo or wicker basket

骡 luó（usu 骡子）mule

螺 luó ❶（usu 螺蛳）〈动物〉spiral shell；snail：～号 conch；shell trumpet ❷ sth with a spiral pattern；whorl；screw：～母 also "螺帽"（screw）nut；jam nut

螺钉 luódīng also "螺丝钉"；"螺丝" screw：十字槽～ Philips screw

螺纹 luówén ❶ whorl（in fingerprint）❷ also "螺丝扣" thread（of a screw）

螺旋 luóxuán spiral；helix；screw：～

桨（screw）propeller / ～式上升 spiral escalation; spiralling

luǒ

裸 luǒ　bare; naked; nude: ～机 basic machine (esp computer) / ～线〈电〉bare wire / ～眼 naked eye / ～泳 skinny-dipping

裸露 luǒlù　bare; uncovered; exposed

裸视 luǒshì　❶ see with one's naked eyes: ～视力 naked eyesight ❷ naked or unaided eyesight

裸体 luǒtǐ　nakedness; nude; nudity: ～画 painting of a nude; nude (painting)

luò

洛 Luò

洛阳纸贵 Luòyángzhǐguì　paper has become expensive (because of one's work); (of one's work) become a best seller

骆 luò

骆驼 luòtuo　〈动物〉camel: ～队 camel train; caravan

络 luò　❶ sth resembling a net ❷ hold sth in place with a net ❸ twine; coil; wind

络腮胡子 luòsāi húzi　whiskers; full beard

络绎不绝 luòyìbùjué　(come and go) in an endless stream

落 luò　❶ (let) fall or drop; let or go down; lower: ～泪 shed tears; weep / ～幕 the curtain falls; lower the curtain; close / ～日 setting sun ❷ decline; come down; deteriorate: ～寞 lonely; desolate ❸ lag or fall behind; fail; lose: ～标 fail to win a bid; fail in an election or competition ❹ stay behind; remain; settle: ～座

take one's seat; be seated / ～俗 be vulgar; act like a philistine ❺ settlement: 千村万～ myriads of villages ❻ fall onto; belong to; rest with: 任务～到我们肩上。The task fell onto us. ❼ get; gain; receive: ～个身败名裂 end up bringing shame and ruin upon oneself ❽ write; put down: ～笔 start to write or draw; put pen to paper / ～账 enter (sth) in an account; keep accounts

see also là; lào

落榜 luòbǎng　also "落第" flunk an examination for a job or school admission; fail an examination

落泊 luòbó　also "落魄"; "落拓"〈书〉❶ be in dire straits; be down and out: 一一生 go downhill all one's life ❷ bold and generous; unconstrained: 落拓不羁 unconventional and uninhibited; not fettered by formalities or conventions

落差 luòchā　❶ drop (in elevation); fall: 利用河水～发电 utilize the fall of a river for power generation ❷ gap

落成 luòchéng　completion (of a building, etc): ～典礼 inauguration ceremony

落地 luòdì　❶ fall to the ground; reach the floor: ～窗 French window / ～灯 floor lamp / ～生根 take root / 他心里一块石头落了地。A heavy burden is off his mind. ❷ (of babies) be born

落后 luòhòu　❶ fall or lag behind; fall or be behind schedule ❷ backward; underdeveloped: ～分子 laggard; backward element

落户 luòhù　❶ settle ❷ register for residence

落花流水 luòhuā-liúshuǐ　❶ (like) fallen flowers carried away by the flowing water; scene of late spring ❷ crushing defeat: 打得～ soundly defeat; utterly rout

落脚 luòjiǎo stay (for a time); stop over; put up; ~点 foothold; standpoint; stand

落井下石 luòjǐngxiàshí *also* "投井下石" hit a person when he's down

落空 luòkōng come to nothing; fail; fall through

落款 luòkuǎn ❶ names of the sender and the recipient written on a painting, letter or gift; inscription (on a gift, etc) ❷ signature of the sender (of a letter, etc)

落落 luòluò ❶ (of demeanour) natural and unrestrained; ~大方 natural and graceful; unrestrained and at ease ❷ unsociable; ~寡合 unsociable; stand-offish

落马 luòmǎ fall off a horse; 〈喻〉be defeated (in a contest, etc)

落难 luònàn meet with misfortune; be in straits or distress

落实 luòshí ❶ practicable; workable ❷ fix or determine; ascertain; carry out; ~政策 implement a policy / ~资金 make sure of funding ❸ 〈方〉feel at ease

落水狗 luòshuǐgǒu bad guy in difficulty; 打~ flog the cur that's fallen into the water; be merciless with bad people even if they're down

落汤鸡 luòtāngjī wet like a drenched chicken; soaked through; drenched and bedraggled

落网 luòwǎng (of a criminal) fall into the net — be caught or captured

落伍 luòwǔ ❶ drop out; fall behind ❷ lag behind; become outdated or old-fashioned; 思想~ behind the times in thinking

落选 luòxuǎn fail to be chosen or elected; lose an election

落叶 luòyè ❶ (of leaves) fall down; ~归根 *see* "叶落归根" in "叶❶" ❷ fallen leaves ❸ 〈植〉deciduous leaf; ~松 larch

摞 luò ❶ pile, heap or stack up ❷ 〈量〉pile; stack

luo

啰(囉) luo 〈助〉*used at the end of a sentence to indicate affirmation*: 这件事不成问题~。Sure, that's no problem. *see also* luō

M

mā

妈 mā ❶〈口〉ma; mom; mother: ～～ mom; mum; ma / ～咪 mummy; mommy ❷ *used of an elderly married woman or a married woman of the elder generation*: 姑～ (paternal) aunt ❸ *used of a housemaid*: 老～子 maidservant

妈祖 Māzǔ Mazu, legendary goddess of the sea

抹 mā ❶ wipe; mop: ～布 rag (to wipe things with) / ～眼泪 wipe away one's tears ❷ put down; slip or take off: ～下脸来〈口〉throw sentiment or shame to the winds; have the cheek or courage (to do sth) ❸〈口〉remove from office: 一～到底 remove (sb) from all his or her posts
see also mǒ; mò

摩 mā *see also* mó

摩挲 māsā smooth out with one's hand or palm; stroke gently; caress
see also mósuō

má

吗 má〈方〉what; 干～? What for?
see also mǎ; ma

麻(❶❷蔴) má ❶ general term for fibrous crops; bast-fibre (plant): ～布 gunny (cloth); sackcloth / ～袋 *also* "麻包" gunny-bag; (gunny) sack / ～绳 bast-

fibre rope / ～线 flaxen or linen thread ❷ sesame: ～酱 sesame butter / ～油 sesame oil ❸ rough; rugged; coarse: ～玻璃 frosted or ground glass ❹ speckled; dotted; spotted: ～子 pockmarks; person with a pock-marked face ❺ numb; dead: 冻～了 numb with cold ❻ anaesthesia

麻痹 mábì ❶〈医〉paralysis; palsy; paralyze ❷ benumb; lull; blunt ❸ slacken one's vigilance; be off guard

麻烦 máfan ❶ troublesome; inconvenient; ～事 nuisance; headache ❷ trouble; inconvenience: ～你把盐递给我。May I trouble you for the salt? or Could you pass me the salt?

麻花 máhuā fried dough twist

麻将 májiàng *also* "麻雀" mah-jong: 打～ *also* "搓麻将" play mah-jong / ～牌 mah-jong pieces or tiles

麻利 máli nimble; deft; neat: 办事～ work deftly; be efficient (in work)

麻木 mámù ❶ numb; dead ❷ apathetic; lethargic; insensitive: ～不仁 apathetic; indifferent; unfeeling

麻雀 máquè ❶ (house) sparrow: ～虽小，五脏俱全。〈俗〉Small as a sparrow is, it has all the vital organs — small but complete. ❷ *see* "麻将"

麻疹 mázhěn〈医〉measles

麻醉 mázuì ❶〈医〉anaesthesia; narcosis; ～剂 *also* "麻药" anaesthetic; narcotic / ～品 narcotic; drug / ～师 anaesthetist ❷ poison; contaminate; enervate

mǎ

马(馬) mǎ　horse: ～鞍 saddle
／ ～帮 horse caravan;
pack train ／ ～鞭 horsewhip ／ ～车
carriage; wagon ／ ～厩 stable ／ ～匹
(general term for 马) horses ／ ～球
(体)(horse) polo ／ ～术 horsemanship; equestrian skill ／ ～靴 riding
boots ／ ～驹子(口)colt; pony

马不停蹄 mǎbùtíngtí　continue one's
journey non-stop; go on without a stop
or halt

马达 mǎdá　motor

马大哈 mǎdàhā　❶ careless; absent-
minded; forgetful ❷ careless person;
scatterbrain

马到成功 mǎdàochénggōng　win instant or speedy success; achieve immediate victory

马蜂 mǎfēng　hornet; wasp; 捅～窝
stir up a hornet's nest

马后炮 mǎhòupào　belated action; effort or advice; 放～ do sth or give advice
after the event; make a belated effort

马虎 mǎhu　careless; slipshod; negligent

马甲 mǎjiǎ　vest; waistcoat

马脚 mǎjiǎo　sth that gives the game
away; clue; trace; 露出～ betray oneself; give away the show

马克 mǎkè　(German) mark; (Finn-
ish) markka

马克思主义 Mǎkèsīzhǔyì　Marxism:
～者 Marxist ／ 马克思列宁主义
(shortened as 马列主义) Marxism-
Leninism

马拉松 mǎlāsōng　marathon; 〈喻〉
long and tedious; lengthy; ～谈判
marathon talks; long-drawn-out negotiations

马力 mǎlì　〈理〉horsepower (hp);开足
～ at full or top speed; full steam ahead

马铃薯 mǎlíngshǔ　(commonly known

as 土豆, 洋芋, etc)(white) potato

马路 mǎlù　road; street; avenue;～新
闻 grapevine telegraph; hearsay; rumour

马马虎虎 mǎmǎhūhū　❶ see "马虎"
❷ fair to middling; just passable or so-
so; not too bad

马屁 mǎpì　〈喻〉sycophancy; flattery;
toadyism; ～精(贬) ass-kisser; lick-
spittle ／ ～拍得不是地方 rub up or
soft-soap sb the wrong way

马前卒 mǎqiánzú　〈贬〉pawn; cat's-
paw

马赛克 mǎsàikè　〈建筑〉mosaic

马上 mǎshàng　at once; immediately;
right away

马失前蹄 mǎshīqiántí　make a mistake by accident; have an accidental
setback

马蹄 mǎtí　horse's hoof;～铁 also "马
掌" horseshoe; U-shaped magnet

马桶 mǎtǒng　❶ night stool; chamber
pot ❷ toilet bowl

马戏 mǎxì　circus; ～ 团 circus
(troupe)

马扎 mǎzhá　campstool; folding stool

吗

吗 mǎ　see also má; ma

吗啡 mǎfēi　morphine

玛

玛 mǎ

玛瑙 mǎnǎo　agate

码

码 mǎ　❶ sign or instrument indicating number: ～子 counter;
chip ❷ same thing; thing of the same
category; 两～事 two entirely different
matters; another cup of tea ❸ 〈口〉pile
up; stack; ～放整齐 pile up or place in
good order ❹ yard (yd)

码头 mǎtou　wharf; dock; quay;～工
人 docker

蚂

蚂 mǎ　see also mà

蚂蟥 mǎhuáng　〈动物〉leech

蚂蚁 mǎyǐ　ant;～啃骨头 plod away at

a big job bit by bit

mà

蚂 mà *see also* mǎ

蚂蚱 màzha 〈方〉locust

骂(罵) mà ❶ abuse; curse; swear: ～街 *also* "骂大街" shout abuse in the street; swear in public / ～名 bad name or reputation; infamy / ～～啊啊 be foul-mouthed / ～得狗血喷头 bite sb's head off; blow sb up ❷ chide; reproach; scold

ma

吗 ma 〈助〉❶ *used at the end of a (rhetorical) question*:这样做公平～? Is this fair? ❷ *used after the subject to indicate a pause in a sentence*:这件事情～,其实也不能怪他。As for this, actually he is not to blame. *see also* má; mǎ

嘛 ma 〈助〉❶ *indicating that the reason is obvious*:有意见就提～。Air your complaints if you have any. ❷ *indicating an expectation or an attempt at dissuasion*:不让你去,就别去～! Since they don't want you to go, why don't you do as they say? ❸ *used for a pause in a sentence to draw attention to what is coming*:其实～,这也并不神秘。As a matter of fact, this is nothing mysterious.

mái

埋 mái ❶ cover up; bury; embed: ～地雷 lay a landmine ❷ conceal; hide: ～名 conceal one's name; live incognito *see also* mán

埋藏 máicáng lie hidden (in the earth or in one's heart); bury; hide

埋伏 máifú ❶ ambush: 中～ fall into an ambush; be ambushed / ～重兵 have a large contingent of troops lying in ambush (for sb) ❷ hide; lie low

埋没 máimò ❶ bury or cover up (with earth, etc) ❷ neglect; hide; suppress:～人才 stifle real talents

埋头 máitóu concentrate on; be engrossed or absorbed in

埋葬 máizàng bury; destroy; wipe out

霾 mái thick haze

mǎi

买(買) mǎi buy; purchase: ～主 buyer; purchaser; customer / ～得起 can afford (sth) / ～一送一 buy one and get another free / 5 元钱～不下来。You can't get it for 5 yuan.

买办 mǎibàn comprador

买单 mǎidān *also* "埋单" bill; check; 小姐,～。Bill please, waitress.

买方 mǎifāng buying party (of a contract, etc); buyer: ～市场〈经〉buyer's market

买好 mǎihǎo *also* "卖好" go out of one's way to please; curry favour (with sb)

买空卖空 mǎikōng-màikōng buy long and sell short; speculate (in stocks, etc); engage in profiteering

买卖 mǎimài ❶ buying and selling:～公平 buy and sell at reasonable prices; be fair in business transactions / ～婚姻 mercenary marriage; wife-buying ❷ (mǎimai) business; transaction; shop: 做～ be in business / ～人 private businessman; merchant

买面子 mǎimiànzi adopt an accommodating attitude or stretch rules out of respect for sb's feelings:不买他的面子 won't make an exception in his case

买通 mǎitōng　bribe; buy off; grease sb's palm；～关节 buy off sb in a key position

买账 mǎizhàng　(usu used in the negative) show admiration or respect for：不～ won't buy it

mài

迈（邁） mài　❶ walk; step; stride：～进 forge ahead; make rapid headway; advance with big strides／～过水沟 step over a ditch／～出决定性的一步 make a decisive move ❷ advanced in age; old：年～ old; aged

麦（麥） mài　general term for wheat, barley, oats, etc; (esp) wheat：～苗 wheat seedling／～片 oatmeal／～收 wheat harvest／～穗 ear of wheat／～子 wheat／～乳精 extract of malt and milk／～芽糖 malt sugar; maltose

麦当劳 Màidāngláo　❶ (US) McDonald's ❷ hamburger

麦克风 màikèfēng　microphone; mike

卖（賣） mài　❶ sell：～点 selling point; attraction; appeal／～价 selling price／～艺 be an acrobatic performer／～不了 sb, I seller I～不动 not sell well; be unsalable／～得快 sell like hot cakes／～光了 be sold out／～狗皮膏药 sell quack remedies; fob sth off on sb ❷ betray; sell down the river：～友 betray one's friend ❸ do one's utmost; spare or stint no effort：～力 do all one can; do one's best ❹ show off; vaunt：～乖 gloat over one's petty cleverness; pretend to behave graciously／～俏 play the coquette; flirt

卖方 màifāng　selling party (of a contract, etc)；seller：～市场 seller's market

卖关子 màiguānzi　keep people in suspense; keep people guessing; be deliberately mystifying

卖国 màiguó　betray one's country; become traitor to one's country; commit treason：～贼 traitor to one's country

卖力气 màilìqi　① also "卖劲儿" exert one's utmost; spare no effort; do one's very best ❷ live by the sweat of one's brow; make a living by doing manual labour

卖命 màimìng　❶ exert one's utmost; strain oneself ❷ risk one's life; slave

卖弄 màinong　make a show of; show off; parade：～才华 parade one's talent

卖人情 màirénqíng　do sb a favour (because he is a good friend, etc); practise favouritism

卖身 màishēn　❶ sell oneself or a member of one's family; sell one's soul：～求荣 sell one's soul for material gains／～投靠 seek patronage (of the influential) through abject service ❷ 〈口〉sell one's body; be a prostitute

卖淫 màiyín　prostitution：～女 prostitute; street girl

卖座 màizuò　(of a theatre, etc) draw large audiences; (of a movie, etc) be a box-office success; (of a restaurant, etc) attract many customers

脉（脈） mài　〈生理〉arteries and veins：～管炎〈医〉vasculitis ❷ (short for 脉搏) pulse：按～ take sb's pulse ❸ vein; range; line：叶～ vein (in a leaf)

see also mò

脉搏 màibó　pulse：量～ count one's pulse／～每分钟 65 次。Pulse is 65 per minute.

脉冲 màichōng　〈理〉pulse; impulse：～功率 impulse power

脉络 màiluò　❶〈中医〉general term for arteries and veins ❷ thread of thought; sequence of ideas：～清楚

clear line of thought; clear, logical reasoning

mán

埋

埋 mán　*see also* mái

埋怨 mányuàn　complain; blame; grumble: 有～情绪 be resentful

蛮(蠻)

蛮 mán　❶ savage; fierce; unreasonable: ～横 rude and unreasonable; arbitrary; peremptory / ～荒 barbarous and remote (country) / ～不讲理 not amenable to reason; unreasonable; perverse ❷ reckless; rash; brute: ～干 act rashly or recklessly; be headstrong; be foolhardy / ～劲 sheer animal strength; mere brute force ❸〈方〉jolly; pretty: ～好 jolly good

蔓

蔓 mán　*see also* màn; wàn

蔓菁 mánjing　*also* "芜菁"〈植〉turnip

馒

馒 mán

馒头 mántou　steamed bun or bread

瞒(瞞)

瞒 mán　hide the truth from; cover up; conceal: ～天过海 practise colossal deception under a façade / 不～你说 to tell you the truth; to be quite frank

鳗

鳗 mán　eel: ～鲡 *also* "白鳝" eel

mǎn

满(滿)

满 mǎn　❶ full; filled; packed: ～分 full marks or credit / ～天飞〈喻〉go or be found everywhere / ～脑子偏见 steeped in prejudice ❷ fill; replenish: ～上一杯 fill one's glass ❸ expire; complete; reach a deadline, quota, or limit: ～假 at the end of one's vacation or leave / 定额未～ unfulfilled quota ❹ fully;

entirely; very: ～身是汗 be soaked with sweat / ～不是那么回事。That's not at all true. ❺ (of) Man or Manchu nationality

满不在乎 mǎnbùzàihu　not worry at all; not care a damn; be completely indifferent

满城风雨 mǎnchéngfēngyǔ　send rumours flying; be the talk of the town; cause a great sensation

满打满算 mǎndǎ-mǎnsuàn　counting in every item; taking everything into account; at most

满腹 mǎnfù　have one's mind filled with; be full of: ～经纶 full of learning and wisdom / ～心事 eaten up with anxiety; extremely worried

满贯 mǎnguàn　(in a game, etc) perfect score; slam: 大～ grand slam

满怀 mǎnhuái　❶ filled or imbued with: ～信心 full of confidence; fully confident ❷ bosom: 撞了个～ bump into sb

满口 mǎnkǒu　❶ whole of one's mouth: ～假牙 (have a) whole set of artificial teeth ❷ (of accent) pure; completely; unreservedly: ～答应 readily agree / ～谎言 be full of lies; tell barefaced lies / ～北京话 speak with standard Beijing dialect

满面 mǎnmiàn　one's whole face: 泪流～ (with) tears streaming down one's cheeks / 羞得～通红 flush with embarrassment

满腔 mǎnqiāng　filled with; full of: ～热忱 be filled with ardour and zest; be full of enthusiasm

满堂 mǎntáng　❶ whole house; entire audience; all those present: ～彩 (of performance) bring the house down / ～灌 (practise) saturation lecturing — cram or force-feed the students / ～红 success in every field; all-round victory ❷ (of a house, room, etc) filled; packed

满心 mǎnxīn　feel from the bottom of one's heart; genuinely feel;～欢喜 genuinely overjoyed or elated; be filled with real joy

满眼 mǎnyǎn　❶ fill one's eyes;～泪花 (with) one's eyes brimming with tears ❷ come into view; be seen everywhere;～繁华 (present a) picture of prosperity

满意 mǎnyì　satisfied; gratified; pleased;令人～ satisfactory; gratifying

满员 mǎnyuán　fully-staffed; at full strength; fully booked up

满月 mǎnyuè　❶ full moon ❷ (of a baby) one full month after birth

满载 mǎnzài　loaded to capacity; fully loaded; full load;～运行 operate under full load;～而归 return fully loaded (with shopping, gifts, etc);(喻)have a rewarding experience

满招损，谦受益 mǎnzhāosǔn, qiānshòuyì　one loses by complacency and gains by modesty; pride goes before a fall

满足 mǎnzú　❶ satisfied; gratified; contented;～现状 be content with things as they are ❷ meet; satisfy; gratify;～市场需要 meet the market demand

满座 mǎnzuò　(of a house, etc) be packed; (of a performance, etc) be attended by a capacity audience

螨(蟎) mǎn　〈动物〉mite; acarid

màn

曼 màn　❶ gracefully; gently; exquisitely;～舞 graceful dancing ❷ prolonged; long-drawn-out;～延 stretch; draw out /～声低语 speak in a low continuous voice; speak softly and unhurriedly

谩 màn

谩骂 mànmà　hurl abuses; vilify

蔓 màn　tendrilled vine　see also mán; wàn

蔓延 mànyán　(of fast-growing plant or sth like it) spread; stretch; extend

幔 màn　curtain; screen;～帐 curtain; screen

漫 màn　❶ overflow; run or brim over; flood;～过膝盖 (of water) be knee-deep ❷ all over; everywhere;～山遍野 all over the mountains and plains; over hill and dale ❸ broad; extensive; long;～长 very long; prolonged; protracted /～延 stretch; extend /长夜～～ very long night ❹ without restraint or purpose; casual; random;～笔 random thoughts or notes; sketch /～步 stroll; saunter; roam

漫不经心 mànbùjīngxīn　careless; totally unconcerned; absent-minded

漫画 mànhuà　caricature; cartoon;～家 cartoonist

漫骂 mànmà　fling abuses; hurl invectives; rail (at sb)

漫谈 màntán　informal discussion; random talk;～体会 have an informal exchange of views

漫天 màntiān　❶ all over the sky; the whole sky;～风雪 There is strong wind and drifting snow across the sky. ❷ sky-high; boundless; limitless;～大谎 outrageous lie /～要价 ask a sky-high price

漫无边际 mànwúbiānjì　❶ (of land, etc) boundless; without limit ❷ (of talk, etc) disconnected; rambling; random

漫游 mànyóu　❶ go on a pleasure trip; ramble; roam ❷〈通信〉roaming; 全球～ global roaming /网上～ surf the Internet

慢 màn　❶ slow; sluggish; tardy;～班 slow class /～火 slow or low fire /～件 regular delivery; ordinary service / ～跑 run slowly; jog; (of a horse) canter / ～动作 slow motion / ～悠悠 unhurriedly; without haste / ～～忘掉 forget by and by / ～工出细活〈俗〉a slow artisan produces skilled work; slow work brings forth fine skill / 我的表每天～3 秒。My watch loses three seconds a day. ❷ cold and indifferent; supercilious; rude

慢车 mànchē　slow or local train; slow traffic:～道 slow (traffic) lane; inside lane

慢待 màndài　❶ treat (sb) coldly; cold-shoulder:～朋友 give short shrift to one's friends ❷〈套〉treat (a guest) inadequately:太～了，请多包涵。Forgive us for our inadequate hospitality.

慢说 mànshuō　also "漫说"; "漫道" let alone; to say nothing of:～是你，谁来也不能进去。Nobody is allowed to enter, let alone you.

慢腾腾 màntēngtēng　also "慢慢腾腾"; "慢吞吞" unhurriedly; sluggishly; slowly

慢条斯理 màntiáo-sīlǐ　leisurely; slowly; unhurriedly

慢性 mànxìng　❶ chronic; slow (in taking effect):～病 chronic disease / ～中毒 slow poisoning ❷ also "慢性子" phlegmatic in character; slowcoach; slowpoke

慢走 mànzǒu　❶ wait a minute; just a minute ❷ (at parting) good-bye; take care:请～，有空再来坐坐。Goodbye. Drop in again when you are free.

máng

芒 máng　awn; beard:麦～ awn of wheat

芒刺在背 mángcìzàibèi　feel prickles down one's back; be ill at ease; feel nervous and uneasy

芒果 mángguǒ　also "杧果" mango

芒种 mángzhòng　Grain in Ear, 9th seasonal division point　see also "节气" jiéqi

忙 máng　❶ busy; fully occupied:～活 be hard at work; be busy; bustle about / ～音〈通信〉busy tone / ～不过来 have more work than one can cope with ❷ hurry; rush; hasten:～送 hastily; hurriedly; in a hurry / ～中出错 haste engenders error; haste makes waste / ～于下结论 jump to conclusions

忙里偷闲 mánglǐtōuxián　snatch a little leisure from a busy schedule; have a bit of time off on the quiet; take a breather

忙碌 mánglù　be busy; bustle about:忙忙碌碌，一事无成 be as busy as a bee but accomplish nothing

忙乱 mángluàn　confused bustle; muddled rush or haste

盲 máng　❶ blind:～从 obey or follow blindly / ～道 blind track — grooved track for the blind / ～点〈生理〉〈喻〉blind spot / ～动 blindly or rashly / ～区〈通信〉〈喻〉blind zone ❷ one who lacks knowledge; illiterate:音～ one who has no ear for music

盲肠 mángcháng　❶ blind gut ❷ (popularly for 阑尾) appendix:～炎 also "阑尾炎" appendicitis

盲流 mángliú　person or people who have blindly migrated from rural to urban areas; aimless migrant

盲目 mángmù　blind; unseeing; ignorant:～乐观 be unrealistically optimistic / ～上项目 launch new projects rashly

盲人 mángrén　blind person; the blind:～瞎马 (like a) blind man on a blind horse — galloping headlong into disaster

盲文 mángwén　braille

茫 máng　❶ (of water, etc) vast; boundless; hazy:～无边际

boundless; limitless; vast ❷ unaware; ignorant; in the dark; ~ 无头无绪 not know what to do; have no clue whatever

茫茫 mángmáng ❶ vague; unclear; 前途 ~ have an uncertain future; face a bleak prospect ❷ boundless; vast

茫然 mángrán ❶ ignorant; in the dark; at a loss; ~无措 be helpless; be at a loss ❷ frustrated; thwarted; 神情 ~ have a blank look; have a vacant expression on one's face

mǎng

莽 mǎng ❶ rank grass; thick undergrowth; ~ 原 wilderness overgrown with grass ❷ rude; crude; rash; ~ 汉 rude fellow; boor / ~ 撞 rash; impetuous; reckless

蟒 mǎng also "蟒蛇" boa; python

māo

猫（貓） māo cat; feline; ~ 叫 mewing; purring / ~ 科动物 feline / ~ 哭老鼠 shed crocodile tears; put on a hypocritical show of sorrow or sympathy

猫儿腻 māornì 〈口〉cunning plot; underhand act; trick; 玩 ~ play a trick

猫头鹰 māotóuyīng owl

猫眼 māoyǎn peephole (fixed in a door); spy-hole

máo

毛 máo ❶ hair; feather; wool; ~ 笔 writing brush / ~ 料 woollen fabrics; woollens / ~ 线 knitting wool / ~ 衣 (woollen) sweater; woolly (coat) / ~ 茸茸 downy; furry / ~ 发直立 with one's hair standing on end ❷ mildew; mould; 长 ~ become

mildewed; be covered with mildew ❸ coarse; semi-finished; ~ 糙 coarse; rough; careless / ~ 坯 semi-finished product ❹ gross; rough; ~ 估 make a rough estimate / ~ 利 gross profit or earnings; markup / ~ 重 gross weight / ~ 收入 gross income; turnover ❺ very young or little; ~ 孩子〈口〉little child; ignorant kid / ~ ~ 雨 drizzle ❻ careless; crude; rash; ~ 手 ~ 脚 careless; slipshod; brash and clumsy ❼ flurried; nervous; scared; 吓得发 ~ be frightened out of one's wits ❽ (of currency) devalue; depreciate ❾〈口〉mao, fractional money unit in China (= jiao 角，¹⁄₁₀ yuan); ~ 票 banknotes of one, two or five jiao denominations

毛病 máobìng ❶ trouble; mistake; breakdown; 出 ~ (of a car, etc) have a breakdown; break down / 心脏有 ~ have heart trouble ❷ fault; defect; 他有个偷懒的 ~。His fault is his laziness.

毛虫 máochóng also "毛毛虫" caterpillar

毛骨悚然 máogǔsǒngrán be absolutely horrified; shudder with fear; 令人 ~ make one's blood freeze; be blood-curdling

毛巾 máojīn towel; ~ 被 towelling coverlet

毛孔 máokǒng also "汗孔"〈生理〉pore

毛驴 máolǘ donkey

毛遂自荐 máosuìzìjiàn recommend oneself for a position; volunteer for a task or job; offer one's services

毛腰 máoyāo also "猫腰"〈方〉arch one's back; stoop

毛躁 máozao ❶ short-tempered; irritable; 脾气 ~ have a quick temper ❷ rash and careless; 办事 ~ act rashly

矛 máo spear; lance; pike

矛盾 máodùn ❶〈哲〉contradiction；~的对立面 opposites in a contradiction ❷ contradictory；conflicting；opposing；相互~ mutually contradictory / ~上交 pass on the buck to the higher-ups

矛头 máotóu spearhead；~所向 target of attack / 把~指向贪污腐败 spearhead one's attack on corruption

茅 máo also "茅草"〈植〉cogongrass；~屋 thatched hut

茅房 máofáng also "茅厕"〈口〉latrine；water closet

茅塞顿开 máosèdùnkāi suddenly see the light；become enlightened all of a sudden

牦(氂) máo

牦牛 máoniú yak

锚 máo anchor；~泊 lie at anchor / ~地 anchorage；anchor station

mǎo

卯 mǎo ❶ 4th of the Earthly Branches see also "干支" gānzhī ❷ also "卯眼" mortise

铆 mǎo fasten with a rivet；rivet；~钉 rivet / ~接 rivet；rivet-joint

铆劲儿 mǎojìnr ❶ (work) with a spurt of energy；再闷把劲儿 make a redoubled effort ❷〈方〉match strength；vie；compete；跟人铆上劲了 try to outdo sb

mào

茂 mào ❶ luxuriant；lush；flourishing；~密 (of grass or trees) dense；thick；lush ❷ rich and exquisite；splendid；excellent

茂盛 màoshèng ❶ luxuriant；exuberant；vigorous；草木~ luxuriant vegetation ❷ (of economy, etc) prosperous；thriving；财源~ rich in financial resources

冒 mào ❶ emit；send out, up or forth；~富 become rich quickly；get rich quick / ~火 emit fire；〈喻〉fly into a temper / ~烟 (of smoke) rise；(of a chimney, etc) belch smoke / ~金星 see stars ❷ risk；brave；~雨 in the teeth of a rainstorm / ~风险 run risks；brave danger / ~死相救 rescue (sb) at the risk of one's life / ~天下之大不韪 defy world opinion；fly in the face of universal condemnation ❸ imprudently；recklessly；rashly；~进 premature advance；rash development ❹ falsely；dishonestly；~称 falsely claim / ~名顶替 go under sb else's name；pretend to be sb else

冒充 màochōng pretend to be；pass oneself off as；~名牌货 pass goods off as brand-name products

冒犯 màofàn offend；affront

冒号 màohào colon (：)

冒尖 màojiān ❶ piled high above the brim；brimful ❷ a little over；a little more than；20 岁刚~ just over twenty years old ❸ outstanding；conspicuous；学习~ be a top-notch student / 干什么都想~儿 try to excel in whatever one does ❹ see "冒头"

冒昧 màomèi venture；make bold；be presumptuous；~行事 act presumptuously / ~提个问题 (used in a self-deprecating manner) venture to ask a question

冒牌 màopái counterfeit；imitation；fake；~货 imitation or counterfeit goods

冒失 màoshi rash；imprudent；reckless；行动~ be rash in what one does；act rashly / ~鬼 harum-scarum；madcap

冒头 màotóu (of a problem, etc) begin to crop up；emerge；appear

冒险 màoxiǎn venture；take a risk or chance；拿性命~ risk one's life / ~家

adventurer

贸 mào trade; commerce; exchange of goods: ～促会 committee for promoting trade; trade promotion council

贸然 màorán rashly; hastily; without careful thought: ～决定 make a hasty decision

贸易 màoyì trade; commerce; exchange of goods: ～战 trade war / ～壁垒 trade barrier / ～逆差 unfavourable balance of trade / ～保护主义（trade）protectionism / 自由～区 free trade zone

耄 mào advanced in years; aged: ～耋之年 advanced in age

帽 mào ❶ headgear; cap; hat: ～徽 badge on a cap; cap insignia ❷ cap-like cover: 螺～（screw）nut

帽子 màozi ❶ headgear; hat; cap: ～戏法 (in soccer, etc)（play a）hat-trick; (score a) third goal ❷ label; tag; brand; 扣～ stick political labels (on people); engage in name-calling

貌 mào looks; look; appearance: ～似 seem or appear to be / ～不惊人 quite ordinary in appearance; plain / ～合神离 (of two people or parties) look united but differ at heart; be apparently in harmony but actually at variance

me

么（麽） me used as a suffix: 怎～ how; why

méi

没 méi ❶ not have; be without; there is not: ～戏 beyond hope; hopeless / ～羞 unabashed; without shame; shameless / ～意思 uninteresting; dull / ～准儿 maybe; probably; there is no telling ❷ used for negative

assessment or comparison: ～那么严重 not that serious / 谁都～他跑得快 Nobody runs as fast as he does.

see also mò

没边儿 méibiānr ❶ groundless; baseless; unfounded: ～的话 groundless remarks ❷ without limit; excessively: 吹牛吹得～了 brag most unashamedly and wildly

没词儿 méicír 〈口〉be at a loss for words; get stuck; be tongue-tied

没错儿 méicuòr ❶ to be sure; surely; certainly: ～，就是这么回事。Sure, this is what happened. ❷ can't go wrong; be a sure success: 照我说的去做,准保～。Do as I say and you won't go wrong.

没法儿 méifǎr also "没法子" can't help it; can do nothing about it; have no alternative or choice but (to do sth): 拿他～ can do nothing with him

没关系 méiguānxi it doesn't matter; That's all right; never mind: "对不起。""～。""I'm sorry.""Never mind."

没劲 méijìn ❶ weak: 浑身～ feel very weak ❷ uninteresting; dull: 这电影真～。This film is dull as ditchwater.

没精打采 méijīng-dǎcǎi also "无精打采" listless; in low spirits; languid

没⋯没⋯ méi⋯méi⋯ ❶ used before two synonyms to emphasize negation: 没皮没脸 have no sense of shame; be shameless / 没完没了 without end; interminable; ceaseless / 没心没肺 unthinking; without thinking / 没边儿没沿儿 groundless; unfounded; excessive ❷ used before two antonyms to indicate failure to distinguish things: 没大没小 be impolite to one's superiors or elders; have no manners / 没深没浅 also "没轻没重" with no sense of propriety; tactless; improper

没门儿 méiménr 〈方〉❶ no means of

doing sth; no way; nothing doing:发奖金的事还～呢。There's nothing doing about the bonus yet. ❷ impossible:他想得头等奖，～。He hasn't got the ghost of a chance of getting the first prize.

没命 méimìng ❶ die ❷ desperately; like mad; for all one is worth:～地逃跑 flee for dear life ❸ not born under a lucky star; having no luck:没有这个命 be not predestined to enjoy such good luck

没谱儿 méipǔr 〈方〉uncertain; unsure; unimaginable:说话～ be unreliable in what one says; shoot off one's mouth at random

没趣 méiqù feel neglected or unwanted; get snubbed:自讨～ court a rebuff; ask for a snub

没商量 méishāngliáng ❶ not be open to discussion or negotiation; leave no room for mediation or compromise:你一点儿不让步，这事儿～了。There's nothing more to discuss since you wouldn't make any concession. ❷〈口〉beyond the shadow of a doubt; a hundred per cent:好吃～ extremely delicious

没什么 méishénme ❶ see "没关系" ❷ (used in reply to expressions of thanks) don't mention it; it's a pleasure; you're welcome

没事 méishì ❶ have nothing to do; be free;～找事 ask for trouble; kick up a fuss ❷ see "没关系" ❸ have no responsibility; not get involved;像个人儿似的 look as if one had nothing to do with it

没说的 méishuōde also "没的说" ❶ faultless; perfect; impeccable:这活儿～。The job is perfect. ❷ naturally; of course:这点小事我能帮忙，～。Of course, I can do something to help in this.

没完 méiwán not over or through; 雨

下个～。It rained interminably。/ 他要是欺负你，我跟他～。I won't let him off if he bullies you.

没有 méiyǒu ❶ see "没" ❷ used before 谁 or 哪个 to mean "nobody":～谁会这样做。Nobody would care to act like that.

没辙 méizhé can find no way out; be at one's wit's end; be helpless

没治 méizhì 〈方〉❶ beyond cure; incurable; hopeless ❷ not know how to deal (with sb or sth); be helpless:都拿他～ can do nothing with him ❸ first-class; perfect; superb

玫 méi

玫瑰 méigui 〈植〉rose:～红 rose-coloured; rosy

枚 méi 〈量〉used of small objects:三～印章 three seals

眉 méi ❶ eyebrow; brow; sth like a brow:～笔 eyebrow pencil /～梢 tip of the brow/～字〈书〉forehead; features /～飞色舞(of one's face) brighten up; beam with joy ❷ top margin of a page:～批 notes and comments at the top of a page

眉睫 méijié as close to the eye as the eyebrow and eyelash:祸在～。Disaster is impending.

眉毛 méimao eyebrow; brow:～胡子一把抓〈俗〉grasp the eyebrows and the beard all at the same time — try to attend to everything at once irrespective of priority

眉目 méimù ❶ one's eyebrows and eyes — one's features; looks:～传情 make sheep's eyes; cast amorous glances / 眉清目秀 fine brows and clear eyes; delicate features ❷ essentials; logic; sequence of ideas:～不清 (of writing) not well organized ❸ (méimu) sign of a possible solution; clue of an outcome:把事情弄出点～ put things into shape; get somewhere

（with sth）

眉头 méitóu　brows；~紧锁 with knitted eyebrows / 一一皱，计上心来〈俗〉knit the brows and a stratagem comes to mind

眉眼 méiyǎn　eyebrows and eyes；features：眉开眼笑 be all smiles；be wreathed in smiles / 眉来眼去 make eyes at or flirt with each other

梅 méi　Chinese *mei* flower or its tree；Chinese plum：~花 Chinese *mei* blossom / ~子 Chinese plum tree or its fruit

梅毒 méidú　〈医〉syphilis

梅花鹿 méihuālù　spotted deer

梅雨 méiyǔ　also "霉雨"；"黄梅雨" intermittent drizzles（in the rainy season in the middle and lower reaches of the Yangtze River）

媒 méi　❶ also "媒人" matchmaker；go-between ❷ intermediary；vehicle；medium

媒介 méijiè　medium；vehicle；vector：起~作用 play an intermediary role

媒体 méitǐ　medium；（mass）media：~渲染 media hype

煤 méi　coal：~层 coal seam or bed / ~球（egg-shaped）briquet / ~田 coalfield / ~烟 smoke from burning coal；(coal) soot / ~窑 coal pit / ~渣 coal cinder / ~炭基地 coal base

煤矿 méikuàng　coal mine or pit；colliery：~工人 coal miner；collier

煤气 méiqì　(coal) gas：~表 gas meter / ~罐 gas tank / ~灶 gas burner / ~中毒 carbon monoxide poisoning

煤油 méiyóu　kerosene

酶 méi　enzyme；ferment

霉 méi　mould；mildew：~变 go mouldy；become mildewed / ~菌 mould / ~烂 mildewed and rotten

糜 méi　*see also* mí

糜子 méizi　〈植〉broom corn millet

měi

每 měi　❶ every；each：~时~刻 at all time；all the time / ~人一册 a copy each ❷ every time；whenever；often：~当 whenever；every time / ~隔5米 at intervals of five metres

每况愈下 měikuàngyùxià　steadily deteriorate；get even worse than before；go from bad to worse

每每 měiměi　often；frequently；usually：~如此. That's usually the case.

美 měi　❶ beautiful；pretty；handsome：~感 sense of beauty；aesthetic perception / ~貌 good looks；beauty / ~眉 pretty eyebrows；〈喻〉pretty woman / ~学 aesthetics / ~育 aesthetic or art education ❷ beautify：~其名曰 be described euphemistically as sth ❸ satisfactory；good；gratifying：~差 enviable mission；cushy job / ~名 good name or reputation / ~缺 fat job ❹〈方〉be pleased with oneself；feel smug：~滋滋 extremely pleased with oneself ❺（Měi）*short for* 美洲：拉~ Latin America ❻（Měi）*short for* 美国：~钞 American dollar；US banknote

美不胜收 měibùshèngshōu　there are more beautiful things than the eye can take in；be of dazzling splendour or beauty

美餐 měicān　❶ delicious food ❷ eat one's fill；have a nice meal

美称 měichēng　laudatory title；good name：有"小上海"的~ enjoy the reputation of being a little Shanghai

美德 měidé　virtue；moral excellence

美发 měifà　(of men) get a haircut；(of women) go to the hairdresser's；~厅 hairdresser's；barber's

美工 měigōng　❶ art designing ❷ art designer

美观 měiguān　beautiful；artistic；

pleasing to the eye；~大方 simple and artistic；elegant and in good taste

美国 Měiguó　United States of America（USA）；America；~化 Americanization / ~佬〈贬〉Yankee / ~人 American / ~英语 American English

美好 měihǎo　happy；bright；pleasant；前途~ have a bright prospect / ~的祝愿 best wishes

美化 měihuà　beautify；prettify；embellish；~自己 make oneself look good；embellish oneself

美丽 měilì　beautiful；pretty；fair

美满 měimǎn　happy；very satisfactory；~的结局 happy ending

美美 měiměi　to one's heart's content；to one's great satisfaction；~地吃一顿 eat one's fill；enjoy a nice square meal

美梦 měimèng　fond or pipe dream

美妙 měimiào　exquisite；splendid；beautiful；生动~的文笔 graphic and graceful style of writing

美人 měirén　beautiful woman；beauty；~计 use of a woman to ensnare a man；sex-trap / ~鱼 mermaid / ~痣 beauty spot

美容 měiróng　beauty treatment；~师 beauty specialist；beautician / ~院 beauty parlour or saloon / ~手术 plastic surgery

美声唱法 měishēng chàngfǎ　bel canto

美食 měishí　delicious or choice food；delicacy；~城 food town / ~家 gourmet

美术 měishù　fine arts；（esp）painting；~馆 art gallery / ~家 artist；painter / ~品 work of art；art product / ~字 artistic calligraphy；art lettering / ~学院 school of fine arts

美谈 měitán　salutary tale；anecdote；传为~ be circulated as an anecdote worthy of emulation

美味 měiwèi　❶ delicious food；delicacy；dainty；~佳肴 slap-up meal ❷ delicious；tasty；savoury

美言 měiyán　put in a good word（for sb）

美元 měiyuán　also "美金" US or American dollar；buck；~区 dollar area / ~储备 dollar reserve

美中不足 měizhōngbùzú　flaw in something which might otherwise be perfect；感到有点~ feel not quite satisfied

美洲 Měizhōu　America；~豹 jaguar / ~狮 cougar；puma / ~国家组织 Organization of American States（OAS）

镁 měi　〈化〉magnesium（Mg）；~光灯 magnesium lamp

mèi

妹 mèi　❶ younger sister；~夫 younger sister's husband；brother-in-law ❷ junior female relative of the same generation；弟~ younger brother's wife；sister-in-law ❸ young girl；农家~ country girl / 外来~ non-local girl

昧 mèi　❶ ignorant；bewildered；confused ❷ hide；conceal；~良心（do evil）against one's conscience / ~心钱 filthy or ill-gotten money

袂 mèi　〈书〉sleeve

寐 mèi　〈书〉sleep；夜不能~ cannot go to sleep at night

媚 mèi　❶ fawn on；curry favour with；be servile to；~骨 mentality of a sycophant；servility / ~外政策 policy of toadying to foreigners ❷ charming；attractive；lovely；~眼 charming or bewitching eyes

媚俗 mèisú　cater to the vulgar tastes of society；fish for cheap popularity；play to the crowd

媚态 mèitài　❶ fawning expression；obsequiousness ❷ attractive appearance

or gestures (of a woman)

魅 mèi evil spirit; demons; monster: ～力 glamour; charm; charisma

mēn

闷 mēn ❶ stuffy; stifling: ～气 stuffy; close / ～热 hot and stuffy; sultry ❷ cover tightly: 茶还要 ～一～。 Let the tea brew a bit longer. ❸ silent; speechless: ～声不响 be silent; not say a word / ～头儿干活 plod away quietly; work with dogged perseverance ❹〈方〉(of a sound) muffled; subdued: ～声～气 (of voice, sound, etc) low; muffled ❺ shut oneself indoors: 整天在家里 shut oneself up at home all day long
see also mèn

mén

门（門） mén ❶ (of a building, etc) entrance; door; gate: ～板 door plank; shutter / ～镜 *also* "猫眼" peephole (in a door) / ～口 entrance; doorway / ～廊 porch; portico / ～铃 doorbell / ～牌 plate or house number / ～票 entrance or admission ticket / ～厅 (entrance) hall / ～卫 entrance guard / ～洞儿 gateway; doorway ❷ sth shaped or functioning like a door; opening: 炉～ opening of a stove / ～牙 front tooth ❸ way to do sth; knack: ～外汉 layman; greenhorn; outsider ❹ branch of a family or clan; family: ～第 (旧) family status ❺ sect; school of thought; (of the) same master or teacher: ～生 pupil; disciple / ～徒 disciple; follower ❻ class; category; branch ❼ 〈量〉一～大炮 a piece of artillery; a cannon / 一～亲戚 a group of relatives / 一～学科 a branch of learning; a discipline

门当户对 méndāng-hùduì (usu of a couple) be well-matched in family social status

门房 ménfáng ❶ gate house; porter's lodge ❷ gatekeeper; doorman; janitor

门户 ménhù ❶ door; gate; gateway: ～开放政策 "Open Door" policy ❷ family; home; housekeeping: 各立～ set up one's own home ❸ faction; sect: ～之见 sectarian bias; parochial prejudice ❹ family status: ～相当 be on a par in family status

门槛 ménkǎn *also* "门坎" ❶ threshold; doorsill: 迈过～ step over a threshold ❷ 〈方〉knack; trick; know-how: ～精 be shrewd (in business dealings); be calculating

门可罗雀 ménkěluóquè attract few visitors; be practically deserted

门类 ménlèi class; department; category: ～齐全 complete with all necessary departments or categories

门路 ménlu ❶ *also* "门道" knack; way; channel: 解决问题的～ key to a problem ❷ *also* "门子" social connections; pull: 找～ solicit social connections / 有～ have the backing of powerful connections

门面 ménmiàn ❶ *also* "门脸儿" façade of a shop; shop front: 三间～的铺子 shop with a three-bay front ❷ appearance; façade: 装～ keep up appearances / ～话 banal remarks; lip service

门市 ménshì retail sales: ～部 retail department; outlet

门庭若市 méntíngruòshì the courtyard is as crowded as a marketplace; have guests or customers at all times; have a constant stream of visitors

门诊 ménzhěn outpatient service (in a hospital): ～部 outpatient department (OPD); clinic / ～病人 outpatient; clinic patient / ～时间 consulting hours

mén

扪 mén 〈书〉touch; feel; stroke: ～心无愧 have a good conscience / ～心自问 examine one's own science; search one's heart

mèn

闷 mèn ❶ bored; dejected; depressed: ～得慌 be bored stiff; be bored to death / 郁郁～不乐 depressed; dejected; in low spirits / 喝～酒 drink by oneself in moments of loneliness / 生～气 have a fit of the sulks ❷ tightly closed; sealed; muffled: ～雷 muffled thunder; heavy blow for unknown reason / 感到胸～ feel oppressed in the chest
see also mēn

闷棍 mèngùn staggering blow (with a cudgel); unexpected blow

闷葫芦 mènhúlu ❶ enigma; puzzle: 被装在～里 be kept in the dark ❷ man of few words; taciturn person

焖 mèn boil in a covered pot over a slow fire; braise: ～饭 cook rice over a slow fire / ～肉 stew pork

men

们 men *suffix used to form a plural number when added to a personal pronoun or a noun referring to a person, an animal or a thing*: 女士～、先生～ ladies and gentlemen

mēng

蒙(❶❷矇) mēng ❶ cheat; deceive; fool: ～骗 deceive; hoodwink; cheat / 被～住了 be fooled / 别～人! Stop kidding! ❷ make a random or wild guess: ～对了 make a lucky guess ❸ 〈口〉unconscious; senseless: 吓～了 be scared stiff
see also méng; Měng

蒙蒙亮 mēngmēngliàng first glimmers of dawn; daybreak: 天刚～ at daybreak

蒙头转向 mēngtóuzhuànxiàng *see* "晕头转向" yūntóuzhuànxiàng

méng

虻(蝱) méng horsefly; gadfly

萌 méng sprout; bud; germinate

萌动 méngdòng ❶ *also* "萌发" bud; sprout; germinate: 草木～。The plants are coming into leaf. ❷ *also* "萌发"; "萌生" spring or start up; begin to emerge: ～邪念 conceive an evil idea

萌芽 méngyá ❶ sprout; germinate; originate ❷ rudiment; seed; germ: 消灭在～状态 nip (sth) in the bud

蒙 méng ❶ cover: ～面人 masked man / ～在鼓里 be kept in the dark; be all at sea ❷ suffer; incur; encounter: ～难 (of a celebrity, etc) encounter danger; fall into the hands of the enemy / ～冤 suffer a wrong; be wronged / ～你夸奖 〈套〉Thank you for your compliment. ❸ ignorance
see also mēng; Měng

蒙蔽 méngbì deceive; hoodwink; fool; mislead

蒙混 ménghùn fool or mislead people: ～过关 muddle through; get by under false pretenses

蒙眬 ménglóng *also* "矇眬" drowsy; half asleep; hazy: 睡眼～ drowsy eyes; eyes heavy with sleep

蒙昧 méngmèi ❶ uncivilized; uncultured; illiterate: ～状态 uncivilized state ❷ ignorant; unenlightened: ～无知 unenlightened; stupid and ignorant

蒙蒙 méngméng *see* "濛濛" méngméng

蒙受 méngshòu suffer; sustain; incur: ～耻辱 be subjected to humiliation; be humiliated / 使双方都～重大

损失 inflict heavy losses on both parties

盟 méng ❶ alliance; coalition; ～国 allied country; ally / ～军 allied forces / ～友 ally; sworn friend / ～约 oath or treaty of alliance / ～主 leader of an alliance ❷ sworn; ～兄弟 sworn brothers ❸ league (administrative division of the Inner Mongolian Autonomous Region) ❹ take (an oath); swear; ～誓 swear; vow

濛 méng

濛濛 méngméng　also "蒙蒙" drizzly; misty; hazy; ～细雨 misty drizzle

朦 méng

朦胧 ménglóng ❶ also "矇眬" dim; hazy; ～的月色 dim moonlight ❷ obscure; misty; hazy; ～的念头 vague idea / ～诗 "misty poetry" — obscure avant-garde poetry

měng

猛 měng ❶ fierce; violent; vigorous; ～火 quick fire / ～兽 beast of prey / ～药 potent medicine / 酒力很～。The liquor is very strong. ❷ suddenly; abruptly; sharply; ～跌 drop sharply; plummet / ～醒 suddenly realize / ～不防 by surprise; unexpectedly; unawares / ～然想起 remember (sth) in a flash; (of sth) occur to one all of a sudden

猛劲儿 měngjìnr 〈口〉great, concentrated force; spurt of force; dash; 用～ make a very strenuous effort / ～putting on a spurt; with a jerk

猛烈 měngliè powerful; fierce; violent; 发动～的进攻 launch a powerful offensive

蒙 Měng Mongol; Mongolian; ～族 (short for 蒙古族) Mongolian nationality　see also méng; mēng

蒙古 Měnggǔ Mongolia; ～包 (Mongolian) yurt / ～人 Mongolian; Mongol / ～语 Mongol or Mongolian language / ～人种 Mongoloid race

锰 měng 〈化〉manganese (Mn)

懵(懜) měng muddled; ignorant; ～懂 muddled; ignorant

mèng

梦(夢) mèng ❶ dream; ～见 dream about; see (sb) in one's dream / ～境 dreamland; dreamlike world / ～魇〈医〉nightmare / ～游 sleep-walk / ～之队〈体〉dream team / 进入～乡 fall asleep

梦话 mènghuà ❶ talking in one's sleep; 说～ talk in one's sleep ❷ nonsense; raving; rigmarole

梦幻 mènghuàn dream; chimera; illusion; ～般的经历 dreamlike experience

梦寐以求 mèngmèiyǐqiú long for (sth) day and night

梦想 mèngxiǎng (fond) dream; (earnest) wish; (cherished or vain) hope

mī

咪 mī

咪咪 mīmī 〈象声〉mew; miaow

眯(瞇) mī also "眯缝" narrow (one's eyes); ～着眼笑 smile with half-closed eyes ❷ 〈方〉take a short sleep; nap; doze off; ～一会儿 take a nap; have forty winks　see also mí

mí

弥(彌、❶瀰) mí ❶ full of; overflowing; all over; ～漫 permeate; diffuse;

spread all over the place / ～天大谎 monstrous or outrageous lie ❷ fill; cover; make up / ～补 make up; remedy; make good / ～合裂痕 close a rift ❸ even or still more: ～足珍贵 all the more precious

弥勒 Mílè 〈宗教〉Maitreya: ～佛 (popular name for 弥勒) Laughing Buddha

弥撒 mísa 〈宗教〉mass: 做～ say or read mass

迷 mí ❶ be confused or lost: ～航 (of a ship, etc) drift off course; get lost / ～路 lose one's way; get lost ❷ fascinated by; engrossed in; crazy about: ～恋 indulge in; be addicted to ❸ fan; buff; enthusiast ❹ bewitch; fascinate; enchant: ～宫 maze; labyrinth; mysterious and enchanting area / 令人～醉 intoxicating; enchanting

迷彩服 mícǎifú 〈军〉camouflage clothes; battle fatigues

迷糊 míhu ❶ (of vision) dim: 眼睛～ blurred eyes ❷ dazed; muddled; perplexed: 气～了 foam with rage

迷魂汤 míhúntāng 〈喻〉bewitching words or action: 灌～ flatter (sb) profusely

迷魂阵 míhúnzhèn scheme laid out to confuse the enemy; maze; trap: 摆～ set a trap (for sb) / 落入～ fall into or be caught in a trap

迷惑 míhuò confuse; puzzle; baffle: ～不解 feel baffled or perplexed / ～人心 delude the public; throw dust in the eyes of the people

迷离 mílí indistinct; blurred: 泪眼～ blurry-eyed with tears / ～恍惚 bewildered as if in a trance

迷漫 mímàn fill the air; spread all over; permeate

迷茫 mímáng ❶ vast and hazy: 一片～ a vast hazy expanse ❷ confused; baffled; dazed: 神情～ look confused

迷你 mínǐ mini-: ～裙 also "超短裙"

miniskirt

迷人 mírén ❶ enchanting; fascinating; bewitching ❷ confuse; puzzle; mislead: ～眼目 mislead or misguide people

迷失 míshī lose (one's way, etc): ～方向 lose one's bearings; get lost

迷途 mítú ❶ lose one's way ❷ wrong path: 误入～ go astray / ～知返 turn back from the wrong path; realize one's errors and mend one's ways

迷惘 míwǎng perplexed; at a loss

迷雾 míwù dense fog; miasma; unhealthy or evil influence

迷信 míxìn ❶ superstition; superstitious belief: ～鬼神 have a superstitious belief in ghosts and spirits ❷ blind faith or worship; fetish: ～权威 have blind faith in authority

眯（瞇） mí (of dust, etc) get into one's eye　*see also* mī

狝（獼） mí

狝猴 míhóu macaque; (rhesus) monkey

狝猴桃 míhóutáo 〈植〉Chinese gooseberry; kiwi fruit

谜 mí ❶ riddle; conundrum: ～底 answer to a riddle; truth / ～语 riddle; conundrum ❷ enigma; mystery; puzzle: ～团 mystery; bundle of doubts and suspicions

醚 mí 〈化〉ether

糜 mí ❶ gruel: ～粥 congee; porridge ❷ rot: ～烂 rotten; dissipated; debauched ❸ wasteful; extravagant: ～费 waste; squander; dissipate　*see also* méi

mǐ

米 mǐ ❶ rice: ～醋 rice vinegar / ～饭 cooked rice / ～粉 ground rice; rice flour; rice-flour noodles / ～

酒 rice wine; (Japanese) sake / ～色 also "米黄色" cream-coloured / ～粮 川 rich rice-producing area; granary / ～珠薪桂 every grain of rice is worth a pearl and firewood is as precious as cassia — exorbitant prices of commodities ❷ shelled or husked seed (usu edible): 高粱 ～ husked sorghum ❸ anything like a grain of rice: 海 ～ dried shelled shrimps / ～ metre; 制 metric system

弭 mǐ 〈书〉put down; quell; remove: ～谤 stop a slander / ～兵 put an end to war; cease hostilities

靡 mǐ

靡靡之音 mǐmǐzhīyīn decadent music; music or song which appeals to depraved tastes

mì

觅(覓) mì look for; seek: ～食 (of beasts, etc) hunt or search for food

泌 mì secrete

泌尿 mìniào secretion of urine; urinary secretion: ～科〈医〉urological department / ～系统〈生理〉urinary system

秘(祕) mì ❶ secret; confidential: ～传 hand down as a close secret / ～方 esoteric recipe / ～诀 recipe; secret / ～史 secret history; inside story / ～闻 unknown information: (esp) secrets of sb's private life ❷ make a secret of; keep (sth) secret: ～而不宣 keep sth secret or confidential

秘密 mìmì ❶ secret; confidential; clandestine: ～投票 secret ballot ❷ sth secret; secret; 保守～ keep a secret

秘书 mìshū secretary: ～处 secretariat / ～长 secretary-general

密 mì ❶ dense; close; thick: ～布 be densely distributed or spread;

be densely covered / ～度 density; thickness / ～林 dense forest / ～麻麻(□)thickly dotted; close and numerous ❷ intimate; familiar; close: ～友 close or bosom friend; alter ego ❸ fine; precise; meticulous / ～合 compact ❹ secret; confidential: ～件 confidential paper; classified matter / ～使 secret emissary or envoy / ～室 secret room / ～谈 secret or confidential talks; talk behind closed doors / ～探 secret agent; spy / ～信 confidential or secret letter

密闭 mìbì ❶ tightly closed: ～门窗 shut doors and windows tightly ❷ airtight; hermetic: ～容器 airtight container

密电 mìdiàn ❶ coded or cipher telegram: ～码 cipher; code ❷ send a coded telegram; secretly telegraph or wire: ～前军回师 secretly wire the advance guard to return

密封 mìfēng seal up; seal airtight or hermetically: ～ 舱 capsule; sealed cabin; airtight cabin or compartment / ～条 sealing strip or tape

密集 mìjí dense; concentrated; crowded together: 人口 ～ densely populated / ～轰炸 heavy or mass bombing

密码 mìmǎ (cipher) code: 破译～ break a code; decrypt (a text) / ～锁 trick lock / ～箱 cipher suitcase / ～电报 cipher telegram

密谋 mìmóu conspire; intrigue; plot

密切 mìqiè ❶ close; intimate: 关系～ be on intimate terms (with sb) / ～注意 pay close attention to ❷ make close; become intimate: ～干群关系 forge strong ties between cadres and the masses

蜜 mì ❶ honey; honey-like thing: 酿～ make honey / ～蜂 honeybee; bee ❷ sweet; honeyed; luscious: ～饯 candied (fruit); preserved (fruit)

蜜月 mìyuè honeymoon: 度～ spend

one's honeymoon; honeymoon / ～旅行 (make a) honeymoon trip

mián

眠 mián ❶ sleep:不～之夜 sleepless night ❷ dormancy (of an insect, etc)

绵 mián ❶ silk floss:～绸 fabric made from waste silk ❷ continuous; consecutive:～长 last a long time / ～亘 (of mountain ranges, etc) extend continuously; stretch in an unbroken chain / ～延不断 stretch endlessly ❸ thin; weak; gentle:～软 soft; weak / ～薄之力〈谦〉meagre strength; humble effort / ～里藏针 (of a person's temper) gentle but firm character; iron hand in a velvet glove

绵白糖 miánbáitáng powdered sugar; fine white sugar

绵羊 miányáng sheep

棉 mián ❶ general term for cotton and kapok:～铃 also "棉桃" cotton boll / ～农 cotton grower ❷ cotton; cotton-like material:～布 cotton (cloth) / ～签 cotton swab / ～线 cotton (thread) / ～絮 cotton wadding (for a quilt); cotton fibre / ～纺业 cotton textile industry / ～毛裤 (interlock) long cotton underwear ❸ cotton-padded:～袄 cotton-padded jacket

棉花 miánhua cotton:～胎 also "棉花套子" cotton wadding (for a quilt) / ～糖 cotton candy

棉子 miánzǐ also "棉籽" cottonseed:～饼 also "棉饼" cottonseed cake / ～油 also "棉油" cottonseed oil

miǎn

免 miǎn ❶ excuse, exempt or free (sb from sth); dispense with:～检 exempt from inspection or examination / ～烫 easy-care; permanent-press / ～于起诉 (of a suspect, etc) be exempted from prosecution / ～提式电话 hand-free telephone set ❷ remove from office; dismiss; sack:～官 dismiss from office ❸ avoid; avert; be free from:未能～俗 be unable to break away from convention; follow common practice ❹ do not (do sth):～开尊口。Keep your mouth shut.

免除 miǎnchú ❶ avoid; avert; prevent:～误会 avoid misunderstanding ❷ exempt; excuse; relieve:～债务 remit a debt

免得 miǎnde so as to avoid; so as not to:经常来信,～大家挂念。Please write regularly so we won't worry about you.

免费 miǎnfèi free (of charge); gratis:～参观 free visit

免冠 miǎnguān ❶ take off one's hat ❷ without a hat on; bareheaded:半身～正面照片 half-length, bareheaded, full-faced photo

免票 miǎnpiào ❶ free pass or ticket ❷ without having to buy a ticket; free of charge:～乘车 take a free ride (on the train, etc)

免试 miǎnshì be exempted from an examination or a test:～入学 be enrolled without taking the entrance examination

免税 miǎnshuì exempt from taxation or tariff:～商店 duty-free shop

免疫 miǎnyì immunity:～力 immunity (against a disease or sth bad) / ～接种 immunization

免职 miǎnzhí remove from office; dismiss:受到～处分 get disciplinary dismissal

勉 miǎn ❶ try to do what is almost beyond one's power; exert oneself; strive:～力支撑 exert or strain one's utmost (to keep sth going) / ～为其难 try to do what is beyond one's power; be obliged to under-take a difficult task ❷ encourage; spur; urge; ~励 encourage; urge

勉强 miǎnqiǎng ❶ manage with an ef-fort; do with difficulty ❷ reluctantly; grudgingly; unwillingly; ~答应 agree grudgingly / 笑很~ force a smile; give a strained smile ❸ force sb to do sth ❹ un-convincing; far-fetched; strained; 很~的理由 lame or poor excuse; far-fetched ar-gument ❺ barely (enough); ~够用 be just about enough / 他的英语勉勉强强强。His English is just so-so.

冕 miǎn traditional Chinese crown or coronet

缅 miǎn ❶ remote; far back; ~怀 cherish the memory of; reminisce about; recall ❷〈方〉roll up; ~袖子 roll up the sleeves

腼 miǎn

腼腆 miǎntiǎn shy; bashful; diffident

miàn

面（❼-❿**麵**）miàn ❶ face; visage; ~颊 cheek / ~孔 face / ~膜 face pack / ~庞 (contours of the) face / ~容 facial features or expression; look; face / ~色 complexion / ~巾纸 face tissue / ~不改色 remain calm; show no sign of fear or surprise / ~黄肌瘦 sallow and emaciated; lean and haggard ❷ face (a certain direction, etc) ❸ ~市 (of a prod-uct, etc) go into the market; be put on sale / ~世 (of art work, etc) be pub-lished; come out ❹ surface; side; right side / ~板 face plate; front board or panel / 江~ surface of a river / 点线 ~〈数〉point, line and surface ❺ side; aspect;

scope:上~ upper side; above / 问题的一~ one aspect of the question ❻〈量〉a) *used for flat and smooth objects*：一~锣 a gong　b) *used to indicate the times people meet one another*：见过一次~ have met once ❼ (wheat) flour; meal; ~点 pastry / ~筋 gluten / ~食 pasta; wheaten food ❽ powder; 辣椒~ chilli powder ❾ noodles ❿〈方〉(of food) soft and mealy; (of a person, etc) soft and weak-willed: 这人真~! What a softie!

面包 miànbāo bread; ~车 mini-bus; van / ~房 bakery / ~圈 doughnut / ~渣儿 (bread) crumbs

面对 miànduì face; encounter; con-front; ~现实 face reality; be realistic

面对面 miànduìmiàn face-to-face; vis-à-vis / ~站着 stand face-to-face / 地提意见 make comments and criti-cisms to sb's face

面额 miàn'é (of banknotes, etc) de-nomination; 大~的纸币 notes of large denomination

面红耳赤 miànhóng-ěrchì be red in the face; be flushed (with sth); 争得~ argue until red in the face

面积 miànjī area; space; 建筑~ floor space / 使用~ usable floor space / 占地~为 500 平方米 occupy a ground space of 160 square metres

面具 miànjù mask; 〈喻〉(false) façade; 剥去假~ unmask; expose

面料 miànliào ❶ surface cloth or ma-terial ❷ veneer (of furniture, etc); facing

面临 miànlín face; confront; be faced or confronted with

面貌 miànmào ❶ face; features; ~姣好 good-looking ❷ appearance; look; aspect; 精神~ mental outlook; moral attitude

面面 miànmiàn (used in phrases) each and every; to each other's face; ~观 comprehensive observation and analysis; multi-dimensional view /

~俱到 attend to each and every aspect of a matter; be well considered in every aspect / ~相覷 gaze at each other in blank dismay; exchange uneasy glances

面目 miànmù ❶ face; features; appearance; ~全非 be changed or distorted beyond recognition / ~一新 take on an entirely new look; have a face-lift ❷ self-respect; sense of shame; 有何~去见父母 feel too ashamed to face one's parents

面前 miànqián in front of; ahead of; before; 一大堆问题摆在我们~。We are confronted with a lot of problems.

面纱 miànshā veil; 戴~的女人 veiled woman

面试 miànshì interview (for a job, etc); audition (for a singer, etc); 通过~ pass an interview or audition

面条儿 miàntiáor noodles; 擀~ make noodles / 下~ put noodles into a boiling pan; cook noodles

面向 miànxiàng ❶ turn towards; face ❷ be geared to the needs of; be oriented towards; cater to; ~市场 market-oriented / ~世界 keep the whole world in view

面值 miànzhí ❶ par, face or nominal value; 低于~ below par ❷ denomination; 大~债券 large-denomination bond

面子 miànzi ❶ surface or face (of sth) ❷ prestige; face; 有~ enjoy due respect ❸ feelings; sensibilities; 撕破~ cast aside all considerations of face; not spare sb's feelings

miāo

喵 miāo 〈象声〉mew; miaow

miáo

M
苗 miáo ❶ sprout; shoot; seedling; ~木 nursery stock / ~圃

nursery (of young plants) ❷ offspring; male child; son; 李家的一根~儿 the only son of the Lis ❸ young of some animals; ~猪 piglet ❹ sth resembling a young plant; 扫帚~儿 broom spikes or straws ❺ vaccine ❻ Miao nationality

苗条 miáotiao (of a woman) slender; slim; 身材~ look slim; have a slender figure

苗头 miáotou symptom of a trend; straw in the wind; 事故的~ indications of an accident / ~不对。Things are not going the right way.

苗子 miáozi ❶ seedling; young plant; 〈喻〉young successor ❷ symptom of a trend; 火灾的~ possible causes of fires

描 miáo ❶ trace; copy; ~画 draw; depict; describe / ~图 tracing ❷ touch up; retouch; ~眉 pencil one's eyebrows

描绘 miáohuì depict; describe; portray; ~风土人情 depict the scenery and customs(of a place)

描摹 miáomó ❶ trace; ~花样 trace a flower pattern ❷ depict; portray; delineate

描述 miáoshù describe; 难以~ beggar description

描写 miáoxiě describe; depict; portray; 人物~ characterization

瞄 miáo (take) aim; 给他~上了 become his target

瞄准 miáozhǔn ❶ (take) aim; train (one's gun, etc) on ❷ 〈喻〉aim at; cater to; be oriented towards; ~消费者的需求 cater to consumers' needs

miǎo

秒 miǎo second (=¹⁄₆₀ of a minute); ~表 stopwatch / ~针 second hand (of a clock or watch)

渺(❶淼) miǎo ❶ (of an expanse of water)

vast; distant; nebulous: ～无人烟 bleak and desolate; uninhabited / ～无音信 not hear a word (from sb); have no news (about sb) ❷ tiny; insignificant; trivial: ～小 tiny; insignificant; paltry

渺茫 miǎománg ❶ remote and vague; distant and indistinct ❷ uncertain; indefinite: 前途～ be uncertain of one's future; have uncertain prospects

藐 miǎo ❶ small; petty ❷ despise; slight; belittle: ～视 despise; scorn; belittle

miào

妙 miào ❶ wonderful; excellent; marvelous: ～龄 (of girls) lovely age; early youth ❷ ingenious; clever; brilliant: ～处 merit; advantage; fine point / ～计 clever ruse; brilliant idea / ～诀 clever way (of doing sth); secret formula; knack / ～笔生花 ingenious writing with exquisite description

妙不可言 miàobùkěyán too wonderful for words; ingenious beyond description; most intriguing

妙趣横生 miàoqùhéngshēng be full of wit and humour; brim with interest

妙手回春 miàoshǒuhuíchūn (of a doctor) effect a miraculous cure and bring the dying back to life; restore (a patient) to health

妙语 miàoyǔ witty remark; witticism: ～如珠 full of witty remarks; sparkling discourse

庙(廟) miào ❶ temple; shrine: ～宇 temple (building) ❷ (usu 庙堂)〈书〉imperial court ❸ (usu 庙会) temple fair

miē

咩(哶) miē 〈象声〉(of sheep) baa; bleat

miè

灭(滅) miè ❶ (of a fire, etc) go out; put out or extinguish (a fire, etc); turn off: ～烟 put out a cigarette ❷ perish; exterminate; annihilate: ～迹 destroy the evidence (of one's evildoing) / ～菌〈医〉sterilize / ～口 (of a criminal) do away with a witness or accomplice to prevent leakage of information ❸ submerge; drown: ～顶之灾 getting drowned; becoming bankrupt

灭火 mièhuǒ ❶ put out or extinguish a fire: ～器 fire extinguisher ❷ (of an engine) be cut; cut or turn off (the engine)

灭绝 mièjué ❶ become extinct: 早已～的物种 long extinct species ❷ lose completely: ～人性 inhuman; savage

灭亡 mièwáng be destroyed; become extinct; perish: 濒于～ on the verge of extinction / 王朝的～ downfall of a dynasty

蔑 miè 〈书〉❶ (regard as) slight; petty; paltry: ～称 call in contempt; contemptuous name ❷ slander; malign; calumniate

蔑视 mièshì despise; scorn; look down on: 公然～人道 (act in) flagrant disregard of humanity

篾 miè thin bamboo strip

mín

民 mín ❶ (of) the people: ～风 customs and morals of the people; social customs and morals; folkways / ～歌 folk song / ～谣 folk rhyme or song / ～选政府 democratically elected government / ～以食为天 People regard food as their prime want. ❷ member of a group or nationality：汉～ a Han ❸ person of a certain occupation：盐～ salter ❹ civilian；civil：～法 civil law or code / ～防 civil defence / ～居 civilian residential housing / ～宅 private residence

民办 mínbàn　run by a community；privately-run：～大学 college or university run by the local people；privately-run college / ～教师 teacher in a community (-run) school

民兵 mínbīng　militia；militiaman

民不聊生 mínbùliáoshēng　the people have no means of livelihood；the people live in dire poverty

民愤 mínfèn　popular indignation；public grievances；people's wrath：～极大 have aroused the greatest public indignation；have earned the bitter hatred of the people

民工 míngōng　❶ labourer working on a public project ❷ farmer who does manual work in the country；casual worker from the country：～潮 tide of casual labourers flowing from the countryside to the cities

民航 mínháng　(short for 民用航空) civil aviation：～班机 civil airliner

民间 mínjiān　❶ among or of the people；popular；folk：～传说 folk legend；folklore / ～文学 folk literature / ～艺人 folk artist ❷ unofficial；non-governmental；people-to-people：～贸易 non-governmental trade / ～外交 people-to-people diplomacy / ～组织 non-governmental organization (NGO)

民警 mínjǐng　(people's) police：交通～ traffic police

民情 mínqíng　❶ condition of the people：熟悉～ be familiar with the condition of the people ❷ feelings of the people；public feelings：体恤～ care for the feelings of the people

民权 mínquán　civil rights or liberties；democratic rights：～运动 civil rights movement

民生 mínshēng　the people's livelihood：～凋敝。The people live in destitution.

民事 mínshì　〈法〉relating to civil law；civil：～案件 civil case / ～法庭 also "民庭" civil court / ～责任 civil liability / ～行为能力 capacity for civil conduct

民俗 mínsú　folk custom；folkways：～村 folk customs park

民心 mínxīn　popular feelings；common aspirations or will of the people：～向背 whether the people are for or against (sb or sth)；will of the people

民意 mínyì　opinion or will of the people；public opinion：～测验 (public opinion) poll

民营 mínyíng　run by private citizens (individually or collectively)；private management：～经济 non-state economic sector / ～企业 private enterprise

民用 mínyòng　for civilian use；civil：～产品 product for civilian use

民乐 mínyuè　music，esp folk music，for traditional instruments：～队 traditional instruments orchestra

民政 mínzhèng　civil administration：～局 Bureau of Civil Affairs

民脂民膏 mínzhī-míngāo　flesh and blood of the people：搜刮～ amass great wealth by fleecing the people

民众 mínzhòng　masses；the common people；the populace：～呼声 voice of the people

民主 mínzhǔ　democracy：～党 (US) Democratic Party / ～党派 democratic parties (working with the Chinese Communist Party) / ～人士 democratic personage / ～意识 sense of democracy；respect for democracy / ～作风 democratic work-style / ～集中制 democratic centralism

民族 mínzú　people；nation；nationality：～败类 scum of a nation / ～独立 national independence / ～风格 national or ethnic style / ～感情 national sentiments / ～英雄 national hero / ～政策 policy towards nationalities / ～主义 (principle of) nationalism / ～自治 national autonomy / ～解放运动 national liberation movement / ～区域自治 regional national autonomy / ～杂居地区 multinational area

mǐn

抿 mǐn ❶ smooth (hair, etc) with a wet brush：～了一头发 give one's hair a brush ❷ (of mouth, etc) close lightly; tuck; furl：～着嘴笑 smile with closed lips ❸ sip：～了一口酒 take a sip of wine

泯 mǐn (usu 泯灭) lose; vanish; die out

闽 Mǐn another name for Fujian (福建)：～南话 southern Fujian dialect

悯 mǐn pity; commiserate; sympathize：～惜 have compassion for; take pity on; pity

敏 mǐn quick; nimble; quick-witted

敏感 mǐngǎn sensitive; responsive; delicate：对新鲜事物～ be responsive to new things / ～的问题 sensitive issue; delicate subject

敏捷 mǐnjié quick; nimble; agile：动作～ be quick or agile in movement / 办事～ be efficient; get things done quickly

敏锐 mǐnruì sharp; acute; discerning：思想～ have a penetrating mind / ～的眼光 have a discerning eye; be sharp-eyed

míng

名 míng ❶ (given) name; appellation：～单 (name) list / ～片 visiting or calling card / ～字 (given)

name / ～存实亡 cease to exist but in name ❷ name; excuse; pretext：以…为～ in the name of; under the pretext of ❸ fame; reputation; renown：～产 famous product / ～ 贵 famous; precious; rare / ～门 eminent or illustrious family / ～望 prestige; renown / ～言 well-known saying; famous dictum / ～著 famous work; masterpiece / ～扬四海 become famous all over the world; be world-renowned / ～优产品 famous quality product ❹ 〈书〉express; describe：难以～状 defy description ❺ 〈量〉used of a number of given categories：30～学生 30 students

名不副实 míngbùfùshí also "名不符实" be in name but not in fact; be unworthy of the name

名不虚传 míngbùxūchuán be true to one's name; enjoy a well-deserved reputation; live up to one's reputation

名册 míngcè register; roll：职工～ staff register or roll

名称 míngchēng name (of a thing or an organization); appellation

名词 míngcí ❶ 〈语言〉noun; substantive ❷ term; word; phrase：化学～ chemical term or terminology

名次 míngcì position or precedence in a name list; place or grade in a competition：不计～ (of participants in a test, etc) not be graded

名额 míng'é number enrolled; quota (of people)：招聘～ vacancies for recruitment

名分 míngfèn person's social status

名副其实 míngfùqíshí also "名符其实" the name matches the reality; worthy of the name; true to one's name

名利 mínglì fame and wealth：～场 vanity fair / ～双收 gain both fame and fortune

名列前茅 mínglièqiánmáo be among the best of the successful candidates, etc; come out on top

名流 míngliú distinguished personage; eminent person; celebrity; 社会 ~ celebrities from all walks of life

名落孙山 míngluòsūnshān fail in an examination or a competition

名模 míngmó famous or first-class model; 超级 ~ super-model

名目 míngmù name (of a thing); item; ~繁多 multitude of items; names or items of every description

名牌 míngpái ❶ famous brand; brand name; ~货 goods of a famous brand; brand name commodity / ~标志 designer label (of a brand name) / ~大学 prestigious university / ~服装 designer clothes ❷ nameplate; name tag

名气 míngqi 〈口〉fame; reputation; name

名人 míngrén famous or eminent person; celebrity; ~录 who's who; list of celebrities; social register / ~效应 celebrity effect

名声 míngshēng repute; reputation; renown; ~大振 win great renown; make a big name

名胜 míngshèng well-known scenic spot; point of tourist interest; ~古迹 scenic spots and historical sites

名堂 míngtang ❶ variety; item; trick; ~多 be full of tricks ❷ achievement; result; 搞出 ~ achieve sth; produce results ❸ reason; what lies behind sth; 这部小说有点 ~。There is something in the novel.

名下 míngxià under sb's name; belonging or related to sb; 把成绩都记在个人 ~ claim all the credit for oneself

名义 míngyì ❶ name; 以…的 ~ in the name of ❷ nominal; titular; in name; ~工资 nominal wages / ~上的头头 titular head; figurehead

名誉 míngyù ❶ fame; reputation; name; ~权〈法〉right of reputation ❷ honorary; ~校长 honorary president / ~教授 professor emeritus

名正言顺 míngzhèng-yánshùn fit and proper; within one's jurisdiction; be perfectly justifiable

明 míng ❶ bright; light; brilliant; ~净 bright and clean / ~丽 bright and beautiful / ~晃晃 gleaming; shining ❷ obvious; clear; distinct; ~摆着 as clear as daylight / ~辨是非 make a clear distinction between right and wrong ❸ open; overt; explicit; ~说 speak frankly; say openly / ~面上 on the surface; apparently / ~令禁止 ban by decree; prohibit by explicit order / ~目张胆 brazenly; flagrantly ❹ sight; vision; 失 ~ go blind ❺ sharp-eyed; clear-sighted; discerning; ~眼人 person with a discerning eye; person of good sense ❻ understand; realize; know; ~达 be sensible; understand ❼〈书〉make known; make clear; ~志 state one's view, attitude, ambition, etc ❽ immediately following in time; next; ~年 next year / ~早 tomorrow morning ❾ Ming Dynasty (1368-1644)

明…暗… míng…àn… used in a parallel construction to show contrast; 明察暗访 observe publicly and investigate privately — conduct a comprehensive investigation / 明枪暗箭 open spear thrusts plus arrows shot in the back — both open and secret attacks / 明升暗降 promote in appearance but demote in reality; kick upstairs / 明争暗斗 (engage in) both open strife and veiled rivalry / 明修栈道,暗渡陈仓 make a feint in one direction while attacking in another; do one thing under cover of another

明白 míngbai ❶ clear; explicit; plain; 说得 ~ explain clearly ❷ frank; direct; unequivocal; ~地提出来意见 state one's view unequivocally ❸ sensible; reasonable; ~人 person with common sense; sensible person ❹ know; comprehend;

understand;～事理 know what's what; show good sense

明察秋毫 míngcháqiūháo be sharp-eyed enough to perceive the minutest detail; have an extremely discerning eye

明处 míngchù ❶ where there is light ❷ openly; in public:把事情摆在～ bring sth into the open

明矾 míngfán also "白矾" alum

明火 mínghuǒ ❶ burning fire ❷ carry torches (as in a robbery);～执仗 operate openly; do evil things in broad daylight

明快 míngkuài ❶ lucid and lively; vivacious; sprightly:节奏～ lively rhythm ❷ frank; straightforward; forthright

明朗 mínglǎng ❶ bright and clear ❷ clear; obvious; unambiguous:局势～。The situation is clear. ❸ forthright; straightforward; bright and cheerful

明亮 míngliàng ❶ bright; well-lit ❷ bright; dazzling; shining:～的眼睛 bright eyes ❸ become clear; be enlightened

明了 míngliǎo ❶ understand; be aware; be clear:～实际情况 know the facts ❷ clear; obvious; plain.

明码 míngmǎ ❶ plain code:～发报 send a telegram in plain code ❷ with the prices clearly marked:～标价 mark the prices clearly

明媒正娶 míngméi-zhèngqǔ 〈旧〉be legitimately and properly married; be legally married

明媚 míngmèi (of scenery) bright and beautiful; (of eyes) bright and lovely

明明 míngmíng evidently; obviously; undoubtedly:～不懂，为什么装懂 Why pretend to know what you plainly don't?

明确 míngquè (make) clear and definite; explicit; clear-cut:分工～ have a clear-cut division of work / ～任务 clarify the tasks

明儿 míngr also "明儿个"〈口〉❶ to-

morrow ❷ one of these days; some day

明人不做暗事 míngrénbùzuò'ànshì 〈俗〉an honest man will never do anything underhand

明日黄花 míngrìhuánghuā sth that is stale and no longer of interest; yesterday's newspaper

明示 míngshì ❶ state or say clearly ❷〈法〉clear and definite; express:～条款 express terms

明天 míngtiān ❶ also "明日" tomorrow ❷ near future:展望美好的～ look forward to the bright future

明文 míngwén (proclaim) in writing; (print) in black and white:～公布 announce in written form / ～规定 stipulate in explicit terms

明晰 míngxī clear; distinct:思想～ think clearly

明细 míngxì clear and detailed;～表 itemized list / ～账 minute account book; itemized bill

明显 míngxiǎn clear; obvious; evident;～的进步 marked progress

明信片 míngxìnpiàn postcard

明星 míngxīng (bright) star:电影～ film star / ～企业 star enterprise

明哲保身 míngzhébǎoshēn use one's wits to ensure one's own survival; self-preservation

明知 míngzhī know very well; be fully aware:～故犯 knowingly break (a rule, etc); deliberately violate (discipline, etc) / ～故问 ask while knowing the answer / ～不可为而为之 attempt what one knows is impossible; try the impossible

明智 míngzhì sensible; wise; judicious

明珠 míngzhū bright pearl; jewel:～暗投 cast pearls before swine; find one's ability unrecognized

鸣 míng ❶ (of birds) cry; (of insects, etc) chirp:～叫 chirp; twitter ❷ ring; sound:～笛 blow a

M

whistle / ～锣开道 beat gongs to clear the way; pave the way for ❸ express; air; voice; ～不平 complain about wrongdoing; cry out against an injustice / ～谢启事 public notice of thanks / ～冤叫屈 voice grievances and call for redress

茗 míng 〈书〉tea

冥 míng ❶ dark; dim; obscure; ～～之中 in the unseen world ❷ deep; abstruse; profound; ～想 deep thought; reverie; daydreaming ❸ dull; stupid; foolish; ～顽不灵 impenetrably thickheaded ❹ underworld; nether world; ～府 underworld; nether world

冥思苦想 míngsī-kǔxiǎng think long and hard; rack one's brains

冥王星 míngwángxīng 〈天文〉Pluto

铭 míng inscription; engraving; ～记 engrave on one's mind; remember for ever / ～文 inscription; epigraph / ～心 be engraved on one's heart; remember for ever

铭刻 míngkè ❶ inscription ❷ inscribe in one's memory; engrave on one's mind; ～在心 be engraved in the memory

瞑 míng ❶ shut one's eyes; ～目 die with one's eyes closed — die contented ❷ be dim-sighted; have blurred vision

螟 míng also "螟虫" snout moth's larva

mǐng

酩 mǐng

酩酊大醉 mǐngdǐngdàzuì be dead drunk; drink oneself blotto

mìng

命 mìng ❶ life (span); ～案 homicide or murder case / ～根子 one's very life; lifeblood; lifeline ❷ fate; destiny; lot; ～大 of extremely good fortune; very lucky / ～苦 doomed to a life of misfortunes; born under an unlucky star / ～里注定 it is one's lot; be predestined ❸ order; command; instruct; 奉～出发 receive orders to set out ❹ grant or assign (a name, title, etc); name

命令 mìnglìng command; order; instruct; ～句(语言) imperative sentence / ～发起总攻 order (sb) to launch a general attack

命脉 mìngmài lifeline; lifeblood; 交通～ lifelines of transportation

命名 mìngmíng give a name to; name; ～典礼 naming ceremony / 以孙中山先生～ be named after Dr Sun Yat-sen

命题 mìngtí ❶ set a question; assign a topic; ～作文 give a topic for composition; composition with an assigned topic ❷ proposition; statement

命运 mìngyùn fate; destiny; predestination; ～不济 have a bad fate

命中 mìngzhòng score a hit; hit (a target)

miù

谬 miù ❶ false; wrong; erroneous; ～论 absurd theory; falsehood; fallacy / ～误 error; falsehood; mistake / ～种 error; fallacy ❷ 〈谦〉 *used in reference to sb else's praise of oneself*; ～奖 misplaced or undeserved compliment

mō

摸 mō ❶ feel; stroke; caress; ～着很软 (of sth) feel soft / ～老虎屁股(喻) touch the backside of a tiger; beard the lion in his den ❷ grope; fumble; ～黑儿(口) grope in the dark / ～出钢笔 fish or take out a pen (from sth) ❸ try to find out; feel or sound out：～透 get to know well；have at one's fingertips / ～情况 find out how things stand / ～不着头脑 also "摸不着门儿" be unable to make head or tail (of sth)；be totally at a loss / ～着石头过河〈俗〉try to gain experience while actually doing the job

摸底 mōdǐ　(get to) know the actual situation；have a clear picture (of sb or sth)；摸清对方的底 sound out the other side's bottom line

摸索 mōsuǒ ❶ grope；fumble；～前进 grope one's way forward ❷ try to find out (direction，etc)；～经验 gather experience bit by bit

mó

馍（饃） mó 〈方〉steamed bun

摹 mó copy；trace：～本 book of reproductions / ～写 copy；imitate；portray

摹仿 mófǎng　see "模仿" mófǎng

摹拟 mónǐ　see "模拟" mónǐ

模 mó ❶ pattern；standard：～式 pattern；model ❷ imitate ❸ model：～范 model；example

see also mú

模仿 mófǎng　also "摹仿" imitate；mimic；copy

模糊 móhu ❶ blurred；hazy；fuzzy：图像～ blurred picture / ～理论〈数〉fuzzy theory ❷ blur；film：～是非界限 obscure or blur the distinction between right and wrong

模棱两可 móléngliǎngkě equivocal；ambivalent；ambiguous

模拟 mónǐ　also "摹拟" imitation；simulation；analogue：～考试 simulated or mock examination / ～软件 simulation software

模特儿 mótèr model；dummy：超级～ supermodel

模型 móxíng ❶ model：飞机～ model

aircraft ❷ mould；matrix

膜 mó ❶ membrane ❷ film；thin coating

膜拜 móbài prostrate oneself in worship；worship

摩 mó ❶ rub；scrape：～肩接踵 rub shoulders or elbows；jostle in a crowd / ～拳擦掌 be eager for a fight / ～天大楼 skyscraper；high-rise (building) ❷ caress；stroke；touch：～掌 stroke；caress ❸ mull over；study；fathom

see also mā

摩擦 mócā　also "磨擦" ❶ rub ❷ friction；clash：～力〈理〉friction / 与人发生～ have a brush with sb

摩登 módēng modern；modish；fashionable

摩丝 mósī (styling) mousse

摩托 mótuō motor：～车 motorcycle；motorbike / ～艇 motor dory；motorboat

磨 mó ❶ rub；wear；grind：～床 grinding machine；grinder / ～砺 sharpen (a knife，etc)；〈喻〉harden or steel oneself / ～出老茧的手 callused hands ❷ torment；plague；pester：～难 hardship；suffering / 跟人～了半天 plague sb for hours ❸ take or waste (time)；dawdle：～工夫 take time；be time-consuming / ～洋工 loaf on the job；dawdle along / ～嘴皮子 talk or argue endlessly or unnecessarily；jabber ❹ sink into oblivion；erase：～灭 wear away；rub out

see also mò

磨擦 mócā　see "摩擦" mócā

磨蹭 móceng ❶ rub slightly；scrape：双脚在地上～ with one's feet rubbing gently against the ground ❷ dawdle；loiter：快点，别～啦。Hurry up，don't loiter. ❸ nag；pester；plague：～个没完 nag (at sb) without end

磨刀 módāo grind a knife，etc：～石 grindstone；whetstone / ～不误砍柴工。〈俗〉Making preparations is not wasting time.

磨合 móhé ❶ run (a new car, etc) in; break (sth) in；～期 running-in or break-in period ❷ adapt to sth gradually：他们之间尚需～。They have yet to adjust to each other.

磨炼 móliàn　*also* "磨练" put oneself through the mill; steel or temper oneself：～才干 steel one's ability

磨损 mósǔn　wear (and tear)；abrasion：～零件 worn-out parts

磨牙 móyá ❶ grind one's teeth (in sleep) ❷〈生理〉molar

蘑 mó mushroom

蘑菇 mógu ❶ mushroom：～云 mushroom cloud／～中毒 mushroom poisoning ❷ pester; badger：别跟我～！Stop pestering me！❸ dawdle; loiter; dillydally：时间很紧，别～了。Time is pressing; don't loiter any more.

魔 mó ❶ demon; fiend; devil：～鬼 devil; demon; monster／～王 Devil; tyrant ❷ magic; occult; mystic：～法 black magic; witchcraft; sorcery／～方 Rubic's or magic cube

魔力 mólì magic (power); charm；艺术～ artistic charm

魔术 móshù　*also* "戏法" magic; sleight of hand：表演～ perform magic／～师 magician

魔掌 mózhǎng　*also* "魔爪" devil's clutches; evil hands：落入～ fall into the devil's clutches

mǒ

抹 mǒ ❶ smear; apply; put on：～粉 apply face powder; prettify；〈喻〉whitewash／～子 trowel ❷ wipe; clean off：～汗 wipe off sweat ❸ cross out; delete; erase：～去 cross (sth) out ❹〈量〉*used of cloud, etc*：一～浮云 a floating cloud

see also mā; mò

抹脖子 mǒbózi　〈口〉cut one's own throat; commit suicide

抹黑 mǒhēi　throw mud at; bring disgrace on; discredit

抹杀 mǒshā　*also* "抹煞" blot out; obliterate; cancel：一笔～ write off at one stroke

mò

末 mò ❶ point; tip; end：～端 end; bottom／～梢神经〈生理〉nerve end ❷ nonessentials; trifles; minor details：～节 minor details; trifles ❸ end; last; bottom：～代 last reign (of a dynasty); last generation／～〈口〉last; finally／～流 of the lowest quality; inferior／～路 end of one's life, career or undertaking; doom／～日〈宗教〉Doomsday; end; doom／～尾 end／～叶 last years (of a century or dynasty)／～班车 last bus or train；〈口〉last chance or turn ❹ powder; dust：胡椒～ pepper powder ❺〈戏〉role of middle-aged man

没 mò ❶ sink; submerge; disappear：～顶 be drowned／～落 decline; decay; wane／～入海中 submerge into the sea ❷ overflow; rise higher than：～堤 overflow a dyke／～膝 knee-deep ❸ confiscate; impound; seize：～收 seize; confiscate; expropriate ❹ till the end; to the last：～齿不忘 never forget to the end of one's days; remember for the rest of one's life ❺ *see* "殁" mò

see also méi

没奈何 mònàihé have no (other) way out; could do nothing (but …); be helpless

茉 mò

茉莉 mòlì　〈植〉jasmine：～花茶 jasmine tea

抹 mò ❶ daub; plaster：把地～平 make the ground level with plas-

ter / 一鼻子灰〈喻〉suffer a snub；meet with a rebuff ❷ skirt；bypass
see also mā；mǒ

抹不开 mòbùkāi　*see*"磨不开"mòbukāi

抹得开 mòdekāi　*see*"磨得开"mòdekāi

殁 mò　*also*"没"〈书〉die

沫 mò foam；froth；saliva：肥皂儿 (soap) suds；lather

陌 mò footpath between fields (running east and west)；road：～上 on a path / ～路 *also*"陌路人"〈书〉stranger

陌生 mòshēng strange；foreign；unfamiliar：～人 stranger

脉(脈) mò　*see also* mài

脉脉 mòmò affectionately；lovingly；tenderly：～含情 full of tenderness and love；amorous

莫 mò ❶〈书〉no one；none；not：～衷一是 cannot agree or decide which is right；not know whom to follow ❷ don't：～哭。Don't cry.

莫不 mòbù there is no one who doesn't or isn't；everybody does or is：～拍手称快. Everybody was clapping and cheering.

莫测高深 mòcègāoshēn unable to fathom；unfathomable

莫大 mòdà greatest；extreme；utmost：～的损失 colossal loss

莫非 mòfēi　*also*"莫不是"is it possible that…；can it be possible that…：～他生我的气了？Is it possible that he is angry with me?

莫名 mòmíng indescribable；inexpressible：～其妙 *also*"莫明其妙"unable to make head or tail (of sth)；puzzled：(of sth) inexplicable

莫逆之交 mònìzhījiāo bosom or sworn friends

莫如 mòrú　*also*"莫若"would be bet-

ter；might as well：与其替他做，～教他做. It would be better to teach him how to do it than to do it for him.

莫斯科 Mòsīkē Moscow，capital of the Russian Federation

莫须有 mòxūyǒu groundless；trumped-up；fabricated：～的罪名 trumped-up charge

秣 mò fodder；forage；feed (animals)：～马厉兵 prepare for battle

蓦 mò suddenly：～地 *also*"蓦然"all of a sudden；unexpectedly；abruptly

漠 mò ❶ desert：大～ the Gobi Desert ❷ indifferent；unconcerned：～不关心 indifferent；unconcerned / ～然 indifferent；apathetic / ～视 treat with indifference；overlook；ignore

寞 mò lonely；solitary；deserted

墨 mò ❶ Chinese ink；ink stick；pigment (for painting)：～客〈书〉man of letters；literary person / ～汁 prepared Chinese ink ❷ calligraphy or painting：～宝 treasured calligraphy or painting ❸ black；dark：～黑 inky (black)；pitch-dark / ～镜 dark glasses；sunglasses / ～绿 dark green ❹ (Mò) Mohism：～家 Mohist School

墨斗鱼 mòdǒuyú　*also*"墨鱼"inkfish；cuttlefish

墨迹 mòjì ❶ ink marks or stains：～未干 before the ink is dry ❷ sb's handwriting or painting：名人～ calligraphy and paintings of a celebrity

墨守成规 mòshǒuchéngguī stick to convention；stay in a rut；be a stick in the mud

墨水 mòshuǐ ❶ (prepared Chinese) ink：～瓶 ink bottle ❷ book learning：喝洋～ study abroad / 肚子里～不多 be fairly learned

默 mò ❶ silent；quiet；tacit：～哀 pay silent tribute；observe

silence / ～片 silent film / ～然 silent; speechless / ～认 give tacit consent or approval to; acquiesce in / ～许 tacitly consent to; acquiesce in / ～～无闻 unknown to the public; obscure ❸ write from memory; ～写 write from memory

默契 mòqì ❶ be mutually and tacitly understood or agreed; be well coordinated; 配合～ be well coordinated ❷ (reach) secret agreement; tacit understanding; 达成～ reach tacit understanding

磨 mò ❶ mill; millstones; ～坊 also "磨房" mill / ～盘 millstones, particularly the nether one ❷ grind; mill; ～豆腐 grind soya beans to make bean curd ❸ turn round; 把车～过来 turn a car round
see also mó

磨不开 mòbukāi also "抹不开" feel embarrassed; hesitate (for fear of harming personal relations, etc); ～脸 feel embarrassed or ashamed to do sth

磨得开 mòdekāi also "抹得开" be at ease; not feel embarrassed or ashamed; have the nerve (to do sth)

貘 mò 〈动物〉tapir

mōu

哞 mōu 〈象声〉(of a cow) moo; low; bellow

móu

牟 móu seek; try to gain: ～利 seek profit / ～取 try to gain
seek

眸 móu also "眸子" pupil (of the eye); eye

谋 móu ❶ design; plan; stratagem; ～划 plan; contrive / ～士 adviser; counsellor ❷ work or strive for; seek; ～反 scheme for a rebellion; conspire (against the state, etc) / ～求 seek; strive for; pursue / ～取 try to gain; seek; be after / ～财害命 murder sb for his or her money ❸ consult; discuss; deliberate

谋害 móuhài ❶ (plot to) murder ❷ plot a frame-up against: 有意～ frame (sb) deliberately

谋略 móulüè astuteness and ingenuity; resourcefulness; strategy: 有～ resourceful

谋杀 móushā (premeditated) murder; ～案〈法〉murder case

谋生 móushēng seek a livelihood; make or earn a living: ～手段 means of subsistence; livelihood

谋事 móushì ❶ plan matters; scheme: ～在人，成事在天。Man proposes, God disposes. ❷ also "谋职" seek employment; look for a job

mǒu

某 mǒu ❶ certain; some: 刘～ a certain person called Liu / ～地 somewhere / ～～ so-and-so; a certain / ～些 certain; some; a few / 从～种意义上说 in a sense ❷ used with one's surname to refer to oneself: 我张～从不说谎。Yours truly never tells a lie. ❸ used instead of sb's given name in an impolite way: 他李～实在太吝啬了。That fellow Li is a real skinflint.

某人 mǒurén ❶ somebody; a certain person ❷ see "某❷❸"

mú

模 mú mould; die; pattern: ～具 mould; matrix / 一个～子里铸出来的 cast from the same mould; as like as two peas　*see also mó*

模样 múyàng ❶ appearance; countenance; look: ～俊 good-looking ❷ (of time and age only) about；approximately ❸ trend；inclination：看～，甲队要输。It seems Team A is going to lose.

mǔ

母 mǔ ❶ mother：～爱 mother love／～乳 mother's milk／～体 mother's body；(female) parent；〈军〉matrix／～性 maternal instinct／～权制 matriarchy ❷ one's female elder：祖～ (paternal) grandmother ❸ female (animal)：～畜 female animal；dam／～狗 bitch／～夜叉 female devil；fierce and ugly woman ❹ origin；parent；mother：～本 also "母株"〈植〉female parent／～带 master tape／～校 one's old school；alma mater／～语 mother tongue；parent language／～公司 parent company

母亲 mǔqīn mother：～节 Mother's Day

母系 mǔxì ❶ maternal (side)；matrilineal：～亲属 maternal relatives ❷ matrilineal；matriarchal：～氏族 matrilineal clan

牡 mǔ male：～鹿 buck；stag

牡丹 mǔdan〈植〉(tree) peony

牡蛎 mǔlì also "蚝"；"海蛎子"〈动物〉oyster

亩(畝) mǔ mu, a Chinese unit of area (equal to ⅟₁₅ of a hectare or ⅙ of an acre)：～产 per mu yield

拇 mǔ

拇指 mǔzhǐ ❶ thumb：竖起大～ hold up one's thumb in approval；(give the) thumbs up ❷ big toe

mù

木 mù ❶ tree：～本植物 woody plant ❷ timber；lumber；wood：

～板 plank；board／～材 wood；timber／～柴 firewood／～刻 also "木版画" woodcut；wood engraving／～料 timber；lumber／～排 also "木筏" raft／～版印刷 block printing ❸ coffin ❹ simple；unsophisticated；dense；讷〈书〉simple and slow of speech／～然 stupefied／～头～脑 block-headed；slow-witted ❺ numb；wooden：冻～了 be numb from the cold

木雕 mùdiāo wood carving or sculpture：～泥塑 as wooden as a dummy

木耳 mù'ěr edible black fungus

木瓜 mùguā ❶〈植〉papaya ❷〈口〉blockhead

木匠 mùjiang carpenter：～活 carpentry

木棉 mùmián silk cotton；kapok

木乃伊 mùnǎiyī ❶ mummy ❷ sth rigid or ossified

木偶 mù'ǒu ❶ wooden figure；carved image ❷ puppet；marionette：～戏 puppet show

木薯 mùshǔ〈植〉cassava

木炭 mùtàn charcoal：～画 charcoal drawing

木头 mùtou〈口〉wood；log；timber：～人儿 wooden figure；blockhead

木星 mùxīng〈天文〉Jupiter

木已成舟 mùyǐchéngzhōu what is done cannot be undone；water under the bridge

木鱼 mùyú hollow fish-shaped wooden block used as a percussion instrument

目 mù ❶ eye；sth like an eye：～测 visual range estimation／～不识丁 not know ABC；be totally illiterate／～不转睛 fix one's eyes (upon sth or sb)；gaze intently／～无法纪 defy law and discipline／～不暇接。The eye cannot take it all in. ❷〈书〉look；see：～送 follow (sb) with one's eyes；watch (sb) go ❸ item；number；(in biology) order：～次 table of contents ❹ list；catalogue：书～ catalogue；book-

list ❺ (in *weiqi* or go) eye：负 两～半
lose (a game) by two and half eyes

目标 mùbiāo ❶ target；objective：～
管理 management by objectives (MBO) /
～市场 target market ❷ goal；aim；
objective：～一致 have a common goal

目瞪口呆 mùdèng-kǒudāi be flabber-
gasted；be stunned：吓得～ be struck
dumb with fear

目的 mùdì purpose；goal；objective：
～地 destination

目睹 mùdǔ *also*"目击" see with
one's own eyes；witness：目击者 eyewitness

目光 mùguāng ❶ look；gaze；expres-
sion in one's eyes：避开某人的～ avoid
sb's eyes ❷ sight；vision：～短浅
shortsighted / ～敏锐 keen-eyed；
sharp-sighted

目空一切 mùkōngyīqiè look·down
upon everyone else；be extremely arrogant

目录 mùlù ❶ list；catalogue；inven-
tory ❷ (table of) contents

目前 mùqián （at）present；current：
到～为止 up to the present moment；
up till now

目中无人 mùzhōngwúrén consider
nobody worth one's notice；look down
upon everyone else

沐 mù ❶ wash (one's hair, etc)；
bathe：如～春风 feel comforted
and gratified ❷〈书〉receive；be given：
～恩 receive a favour；bask in sb's
kindness (as of the emperor)

沐浴 mùyù ❶ take or have a bath：～
露 bath lotion ❷〈喻〉be bathed or im-
mersed；bask (in sth)

首 mù

首蓿 mùxu 〈植〉lucerne；alfalfa

牧 mù ❶ herd；graze；pasture：～
草 forage grass；herbage / ～场
grazing land；pasture；livestock farm
or ranch / ～歌 pastoral (song)；mad-
rigal / ～民 herdsman / ～童 shepherd

boy / ～羊人 shepherd ❷ (short for 牧
业) animal husbandry；livestock-rais-
ing：～区 pastureland；pastoral area

牧师 mùshī （Protestant）pastor；min-
ister；clergyman

募 mù raise；collect；recruit：～股
raise capital by floating shares /
～化 (of monks or nuns) collect alms /
～集 raise；collect / ～捐 take up a col-
lection；solicit donations / ～兵制 mercenary system for recruiting soldiers

墓 mù grave；tomb：～碑 tomb-
stone；gravestone / ～地 grave-
yard；burial ground / ～葬〈考古〉
grave / ～志铭 epitaph

幕 mù ❶ canopy；tent：夜～ veil
of night ❷ curtain；screen：～布
(theatre) curtain；(cinema) screen ❸
act：～间休息 interval；intermission：
四～八场 four acts with eight scenes

幕后 mùhòu backstage；behind the
scenes：～操纵 pull strings from behind
the scenes / ～交易 behind-the-scenes
or backstage deal / ～人物 wirepuller

幕僚 mùliáo 〈旧〉aide to a ranking
official or general

睦 mù peaceful；harmonious

睦邻 mùlín keep friendly relations
with one's neighbours：～政策 good-
neighbour policy

慕 mù ❶ admire：～名而来 be attracted to a place by its reputa-
tion；come to see sb on account of his
or her fame ❷ long or yearn for

暮 mù ❶ dusk；sunset；evening：
～霭 evening mist / ～色 dusk；
twilight ❷ (of time) towards the end；
late：～春 late spring；third lunar
month / ～年 old age；declining years

暮气 mùqì lethargy；apathy；languor：
～沉沉 lethargic；lifeless

穆 mù reverent；solemn

穆斯林 mùsīlín Moslem；Muslim

N

nā

南 nā *see also* nán

南无阿弥陀佛 nāmó Ēmítuófó 〈宗教〉Homage to Amita Buddha

ná

拿 ná ❶ hold; take; get：～冠军 win the championship / ～不出手 *also* "拿不出去" not presentable; not good enough / ～得起，放得下〈俗〉 never be disturbed by vicissitudes of life; be adaptable ❷ seize; capture; catch；～办 arrest and deal with (according to law); bring to justice / ～获 apprehend (a criminal); nab; catch ❸ have a firm grasp of; control; manage：～不稳 be uncertain (about sth) / ～主意 make up one's mind; make a decision ❹ put (sb) in a difficult position; make things difficult for (sb); bluff：～ 捏 make it hot for (sb); manipulate (sb) by blackmail ❺ pretend; affect; put on：～腔～调 assume a peculiar voice or tone; speak in an affected tone ❻ (used in the same sense as 用) with; by means of; by：～事实来证明 prove with facts; cite facts to prove ❼ *introducing the object of a following verbal phrase*：～别人出气 vent one's anger on sb; take it out on sb

拿人 nárén ❶ arrest or apprehend sb ❷ make things difficult; bully; black-

mail：～一把 deliberately create difficulties for sb / 拿不住人 cannot bluff sb ❸ attract; fascinate：讲起故事来很能 ～ can tell a story in a fascinating manner

拿手 náshǒu skilled; adept; expert：～好戏 part (in an opera) one plays best; forte

nǎ

哪 nǎ ❶ which; what：～个 which / ～天 what day / ～些 which; who; what ❷ any：这话对～个人都不许说。Don't breathe a word to anyone. ❸ *used in rhetorical questions*：～有你这样说话的? How could you talk like this?

see also na; něi

哪会儿 nǎhuìr ❶ when：你是～来的? When did you come? ❷ any time：不定 ～ God knows when…

哪里 nǎli *also* "哪儿" ❶ where：这是 ～? Where are we? ❷ somewhere; anywhere; no matter where：～困难就到～去。Go and work where the challenge is greatest. ❸ *used to form a rhetorical question of negation*：我～知道? How do I know? ❹〈谦〉(in response to praise, thanks, etc) not at all：～～，你过奖了。You are flattering me.

哪怕 nǎpà 〈连〉even if; even though; no matter how：～豁上性命，我也要救他。I'll rescue him even at the cost of my life.

哪样 nǎyàng ❶ (used in a question)

what kind ❷（used in the negative）any kind

nà

那 nà ❶ used to indicate sb or sth away from the speaker：～些 those / ～是谁？Who is that？❷ then；in that case：～下一步怎么办？Well，what shall we do next？
see also nèi

那个 nàge ❶ that；that thing or matter ❷ used before a verb or an adjective for emphasis：大伙儿～高兴啊！Everybody was so happy！❸〈婉〉〈谑〉used in place of a word or statement：这样是不是有点～？Isn't it a bit too much?

那会儿 nàhuìr indicating a time in the past or in the future：～我还小。I was then young.

那么 nàme ❶ like that；in that way；to that extent：～些 so much；so many / ～着（do sth）that way；like that / 墙头～高 as tall as a wall ❷（used before a number）about；some；or so：有一、两、三个人就行了。Two or three people will do. ❸ then；in that case

那儿 nàr ❶ also "那里" that place；there ❷（used after 打、从、由）that time；then：打～起 after that

那样 nàyàng like that；such；so：～坚决 so resolute / ～的机会 such chances

呐 nà

呐喊 nàhǎn cry out；shout loudly；cheer：～助威 shout encouragement；cheer

纳 nà ❶ receive；accept；take：～贿 take or accept bribes / ～凉 enjoy the cool / ～新 take in the fresh ❷ pay（tax，etc）；give：～粮〈旧〉pay grain tax ❸ sew close stitches：～鞋底儿 stitch soles（of cloth shoes）

纳粹 Nàcuì Nazi：～主义 Nazism

纳罕 nàhǎn be surprised；wonder

纳闷 nàmèn〈口〉feel puzzled（at sth）；be bewildered；wonder

纳米 nàmǐ also "毫微（米）" nanometre：～材料 nanomaterial / ～技术 nanotechnology

纳入 nàrù bring，channel or incorporate into：～计划 bring（sth）into a plan / ～正轨 put or set on the right track

纳税 nàshuì pay tax：～人 taxpayer / ～意识 sense of one's duty to pay taxes

衲 nà ❶ patch up（esp with close stitches）❷ vestment worn by a Buddhist monk — a term used by a monk to refer to himself：老～ I（the monk）

钠 nà〈化〉sodium（Na）

捺 nà ❶ press；hold back；restrain：～手印 put one's fingerprint（to a document）❷ right-falling stroke（in Chinese characters）

na

哪 na〈助〉used after a word ending in "n" to tone up what is being said：多谢您～。Thank you very much，sir.
see also nǎ；něi

nǎi

乃 nǎi〈书〉❶ be：～是 be ❷ so；therefore ❸ only then；only thus：惟努力～能成功。Only when you work hard can you expect to succeed. ❹ you；your：～兄 your elder brother

乃至 nǎizhì and even：10 年～15 年 10 or even 15 years

奶 nǎi ❶ breast：～头〈口〉nipple；tit / ～罩 also "乳罩" bra ❷

milk：吃～ suckle / ～茶 tea with milk；milk tea / ～粉 milk powder / ～酪 cheese / ～牛 (milk) cow / ～品 dairy product ❸ breastfeed；nurse；suckle：～妈 wet nurse / ～瓶 feeding bottle

奶名 nǎimíng　child's pet name；infant name

奶奶 nǎinai ❶ (paternal) grandmother；grandma ❷ respectful form of address for an elderly woman：张～ Grandma Zhang

奶声奶气 nǎishēng-nǎiqì　speak in a baby or child-like voice；lisp

奶油 nǎiyóu　cream：～色 creamy colour；cream / ～蛋糕 cake with cream on top；birthday cake / ～小生〈喻〉handsome but effeminate young man or actor

氖 nǎi　〈化〉neon (Ne)：～灯 neon lamp

nài

奈 nài

奈何 nàihé　*used to express helplessness or futility*：～不得 can do nothing about (sth or sb) / 他又怎奈我何！There is nothing he could do to me!

耐 nài　be able to bear or endure：～穿 (of clothing) stand wear and tear；be durable / ～寒 cold-resistant / ～久 long-lasting；durable / ～看 (of a work of art, etc) stand scrutiny；be of lasting interest or charm / ～力 endurance；stamina；staying power / ～磨 abrasion-resistant；wear-resisting / ～酸 acid-proof；acid-resisting / ～高温 be heat-resistant；can stand very high temperature / ～火砖 refractory brick；firebrick / ～着性子听 listen patiently

耐烦 nàifán　can endure；be patient；等得不～ wait impatiently

耐人寻味 nàirénxúnwèi　provide plenty of food for thought；thought-provoking or intriguing

耐心 nàixīn　patience：～说服 persuade with patience；use patient persuasion

耐性 nàixìng　patience；endurance：～到了限度 reach the limit of one's endurance or patience

耐用 nàiyòng　durable：～品 durable goods；durables

nān

囡（囝）nān　〈方〉child；son；daughter：～～ (used of a baby) little darling

nán

男 nán ❶ man；male：～方 (usu of a marriage) bridegroom's or husband's side / ～科 andrology；andrologic department (of a hospital) / ～篮 men's basketball (team) / ～士 man；gentleman / ～性 male sex or gender / ～傧相 best man / ～厕所 men's lavatory；(used as a sign) Men；Gents / ～朋友 boyfriend；gentleman friend / ～尊女卑 concept that men are superior to women；male superiority ❷ son；boy；长～ eldest son ❸〈史〉lowest of the five ranks of nobility；baron：～爵 baron

男盗女娼 nándào-nǚchāng　behave like thieves and whores — be full of greed and lust

男儿 nán'ér　(real) man：～志在四方。A real man goes wherever his ambition takes him.

男女 nán-nǚ ❶ man and woman：～平等 equality between men and women；gender equality ❷ sex：～关系 sexual relations；affair

男人 nánrén ❶ man；menfolk ❷ (nánren)〈口〉husband；hubby

男生 nánshēng ❶ boy or man student：～宿舍 men's dorm ❷ （方）man；boy

男装 nánzhuāng　men's clothing：扮～ dressed like a man

男子 nánzǐ　man：～气概 manly qualities；masculinity

男子汉 nánzǐhàn　（real）man；man of honour：大丈夫 true man；he-man

南 nán ❶ south：～下 go down south ／ ～美洲 South America ／ ～～合作 South-South cooperation ／ 房子～边 south of the house ❷ southern region — Yangtze River valley and areas south of the river：～宋 Southern Song Dynasty (1127-1279) ／ ～水北调 divert water from the south (ie the Yangtze) to the north

see also nā

南北 nánběi ❶ north and south：～朝 Northern and Southern dynasties (420-589) ／ ～对话 North-South dialogue ／ 南来北往 go north and south；come and go in all directions ／ 南征北战 fight north and south；fight battles all over the country ❷ from north to south：～有 8 公里 8 kilometres long from north to south

南方 nánfāng ❶ south ❷ areas south of the Yangtze River；southern China：～人 southerner

南瓜 nánguā　pumpkin；Chinese squash

南极 nánjí ❶ South Pole；the Antarctic：～洲 Antarctic Continent；Antarctica ❷ *also* "南磁极" south magnetic pole

南柯一梦 nánkēyīmèng　pipe dream；illusory joy

南腔北调 nánqiāng-běidiào　medley of north and south accents；mixed accent：说话～ speak with a mixed accent

南沙群岛 Nánshā Qúndǎo　Nansha Islands（known in the West as the Spratlys），China's southernmost territory

南洋 Nányáng　（旧）areas beyond the South China Sea

南辕北辙 nányuán-běizhé　act in a way that defeats one's purpose；be self-defeating

难（難） nán ❶ hard；uncertain；unlikely：～熬 find it difficult to endure（pain，etc）；（pain，etc）hard to bear ／ ～缠 unreasonable；hard to deal with ／ ～点 difficulty ／ ～忘 unforgettable；memorable ／ ～舍～分 cannot bear to part；loathe to part ／ ～于登天 well-nigh impossible ／ 法纪～容 not be tolerated by law or discipline ／ 毫无～色 show no signs of reluctance at all；not hesitate (to do sth) ❷ put (sb) in a difficult position；make things difficult for (sb)：～住了他 put him on the spot ／ 难不倒 cannot beat or daunt (sb) ❸ bad；unpleasant；not good：～吃 taste nasty ／ ～闻 stink；smell bad

see also nàn

难产 nánchǎn ❶ 〈医〉difficult labour or delivery ❷ (of a plan，etc) be difficult of fulfilment；be slow in coming

难处 nánchǔ ❶ difficult to deal with；not easy to get along with ❷ (nánchu) trouble；difficulty；problem：有～ have problems

难道 nándào　*used in a rhetorical question for emphasis*：这～还不明白吗？Isn't this perfectly clear?

难得 nándé ❶ hard to come by；rare：～糊涂 Where ignorance is bliss, it's folly to be wise. ❷ hardly；rarely；seldom

难怪 nánguài ❶ no wonder ❷ understandable；pardonable：这也～，她还年轻嘛。You can hardly blame her for it, as she is so young.

难关 nánguān　barrier；difficulty；crisis

难过 nánguò ❶ have a hard time ❷

feel sorry or bad; be distressed; 为人感到～ feel sorry for sb

难解难分 nánjiě-nánfēn　*also* "难分难解" ❶ be inextricably linked; be locked together; 杀得～ be locked in a stalemate (in battle or game) ❷ be sentimentally attached; not bear to part

难堪 nánkān ❶ unbearable; intolerable; unendurable; 闷热～ unbearably sultry ❷ embarrassed; embarrassing; awkward

难看 nánkàn ❶ ugly; homely ❷ shameful; disgraceful; unpleasant; 输得真～啊! What an embarrassing defeat! ❸ (of look or expression) unpleasant; not quite normal; 他的脸色变得很～. His face darkened.

难免 nánmiǎn be hard to avoid; cannot help; 人～不犯错误. Nobody is free from error.

难能可贵 nánnéngkěguì deserve credit for doing sth difficult to attain; be commendable or praiseworthy

难受 nánshòu ❶ feel unwell or uncomfortable; suffer pain; 热得～ unbearably hot ❷ feel bad or unhappy (about sth); feel sorry; 做错了事很～ feel sorry about one's mistake

难说 nánshuō it's hard to say; you never can tell; 比赛胜负很～. It's hard to tell the result of the game.

难题 nántí thorny problem; hard nut to crack; poser; 出～ pose a difficult question; put (sb) in an awkward situation

难听 nántīng ❶ unpleasant to the ear ❷ vulgar; coarse; offensive; 他的话～极了! His language was simply shocking! ❸ scandalous; disreputable; 这事说出去多～. If the story gets out, it is bound to be a scandal.

难为情 nánwéiqíng shy; embarrassed; ashamed

难为 nánwei ❶ make it hard or difficult for (sb); embarrass ❷ be a tough

job for (sb); 这事真～他了. That was not easy for him to do. ❸ 〈套〉(used to express gratitude) it is generous or kind (of sb); ～你为我准备了丰盛的晚餐. It's really very kind of you to prepare such a wonderful dinner for me.

难言之隐 nányánzhīyǐn sth difficult to express or awkward to disclose; unmentionable secret

难以 nányǐ difficult to; hard to; ～启齿 embarrassing to mention (sth) / ～为继 difficult to follow up (an example, etc); hard to keep up / ～形容 indescribable; beyond description

喃 nán

喃喃 nánnán 〈象声〉mutter; murmur

楠 nán

楠木 nánmù 〈植〉*nanmu*, an evergreen hardwood

nǎn

赧 nǎn 〈书〉blushing; ～然汗下 sweat with shame

蝻 nǎn 〈动物〉nymph of a locust

nàn

难(難) nàn ❶ trouble; disaster; calamity; ～友 fellow sufferer / ～兄～弟 fellow sufferers; people in the same boat ❷ blame; censure; take to task

see also 难

难民 nànmín refugee; ～营 refugee camp

nāng

囔 nāng

曩曩 nāngnang　murmur; mutter

náng

囊 náng ❶ bag; sack; pocket; ～中物 sth certain of attainment / ～空如洗 with empty pockets; penniless / ～中羞涩 be cash-strapped ❷ anything shaped like a bag; bladder; ～肿〈医〉cyst ❸〈书〉put into a bag; bag; ～括 embrace (all); make a clean sweep of

nǎng

攮 nǎng　stab; ～子 dagger / 让人～了一刀 be stabbed

馕 nǎng　〈口〉cram（food）into one's mouth

nàng

齉 nàng　snuffling; ～鼻儿 snuffle; speak with a twang

nāo

孬 nāo　chicken-hearted; cowardly; ～种〈口〉coward; incompetent

náo

呶 náo　〈书〉clamour; talk noisily; ～～不休 gab tediously; patter endlessly; babble on

挠（撓） náo ❶ scratch; ～痒痒 scratch an itch ❷ obstruct; hinder; block ❸ bend; twist; yield

挠头 náotóu ❶ scratch one's head; 急得直～ scratch one's head anxiously ❷ hard to tackle; thorny; ～的事 thorny issue; headache

铙（鐃） náo　a kind of cymbal; ～钹 big cymbals

蛲（蟯） náo
蛲虫 náochóng　pinworm

nǎo

恼（惱） nǎo ❶ angry; irritated; annoyed; ～恨 be angry（with）; resent; hate / ～火 annoyed; irritated / ～怒 angry; irritated / ～羞成怒 be shamed into anger; be piqued ❷ unhappy; vexed; worried; ～人 irritating; annoying

脑（腦） nǎo ❶ brain; encephalon; cerebral; ～浆 brains / ～炎 also "大脑炎"〈医〉cerebritis / ～膜炎〈医〉meningitis / ～死亡〈医〉brain death / ～血栓 also "脑栓塞"〈医〉cerebral thrombus / ～溢血〈医〉cerebral hemorrhage / ～震荡〈医〉cerebral or brain concussion ❷ head; brain; mind; ～壳〈方〉head; cranium; 动～ work with one's head ❸ see "脑儿❷"

脑袋 nǎodai ❶〈口〉head; ～搬家 get killed ❷ also "脑瓜儿" brains; ～不开窍 be dumb or stupid

脑海 nǎohǎi　also "脑际" mind; mind's eye; 浮上～ flash across one's mind

脑筋 nǎojīn ❶ brains; mind; 开动～ use one's head / ～急转弯（have an）abrupt turn in one's train of thought; (hit upon an) unexpected idea ❷ (person with a certain) way of thinking; ideas; 老～ person who moves in a rut; old fogey / 死～ inflexible person

脑力 nǎolì　brain; mind; mental power; ～劳动 mental work / ～劳动者 mental worker

脑满肠肥 nǎomǎn-chángféi　fat and idle; ～的贪官污吏 fat corrupt officials

脑儿 nǎor ❶ brains of certain animals (as food); 猪～ pig brains ❷ anything edible that looks like brains; 豆腐～ jelly bean curd

脑子 nǎozi 〈口〉❶ brain ❷ brain; mind; head; ~不清醒 be not in one's right mind

nào

闹(鬧) nào ❶ noisy; ~市 busy street; downtown area / ~哄哄 noisy; uproarious ❷ clamour; make a scene; stir up trouble; 翻 fall out (with sb) / ~哄 make a row; wrangle / ~事 make trouble; create disturbances; stir up trouble ❸ give vent to (one's anger, etc); vent; ~脾气 lose one's temper; get into a huff / ~情绪 be in a fit of pique; be disgruntled ❹ suffer from; be troubled by; ~病 fall ill; be unwell / ~鬼〈迷信〉be haunted (by ghosts) / ~别扭 be at odds with one another; clash with one another / ~肚子〈口〉have loose bowels; suffer from diarrhoea ❺ do; make; engage in: ~革命 carry out revolution ❻ joke; tease; ~剧 farce / ~洞房 have rough house in the bridal chamber

闹腾 nàoteng 〈口〉❶ wrangle; create a disturbance ❷ have fun; amuse oneself; ~得欢 have noisy fun

闹着玩儿 nàozhewánr ❶ play; have fun; amuse oneself ❷ joke (with sb); tease (sb) ❸ treat a serious matter lightly: 不是~的事儿 no joke

闹钟 nàozhōng　alarm clock

ne

呢 ne 〈助〉❶ used at the end of an interrogative sentence: 我不去, 你~? I'm not going. What about you? ❷ used at the end of a statement a) for emphasis: 他还会写诗~。He writes good poems too! b) to indicate continuation of action: 这些天我忙着~。I'm pretty busy these days. ❸ used to make a pause within a sentence (usu to show a contrast): 小孩子~, 就别去了。As for the children, well, they'd better not go.
see also ní

něi

哪 něi　colloquial pronunciation for 哪　see also nǎ; na

馁 něi　lose heart; be disheartened or discouraged: 败不~ not be discouraged by failure

nèi

内 nèi ❶ inner; inside; interior; ~宾 domestic guest or visitor / ~存 (short for 内存储器)〈信息〉inner memory; built-in storage / ~海 inland sea; continental sea / ~讧 also "内哄" internal conflict or strife / ~奸 hidden spy; mole / ~乱 internal disorder or turmoil; civil strife / ~销 (goods) for domestic market / ~秀 intelligent though seemingly unrefined; with inward grace / ~需〈经〉domestic demand / ~因 internal cause or factor / ~脏 internal organs; viscera / ~债 internal debt / ~战 civil war / ~政 internal affairs; domestic or home affairs / ~分泌 internal secretion; endocrine / ~联网〈信息〉intranet / ~燃机 internal combustion engine / ~衣~裤 underclothes ❷ one's wife or her relatives; ~弟 wife's younger brother; brother-in-law / ~亲 relative on wife's side; in-law / ~人 also "内子" my wife / ~助〈书〉wife

内部 nèibù　inside; interior; internal; ~发行 (published) for restricted circulation / ～消息 confidential news

内地 nèidì ❶ inland；interior；hinterland ❷ (as used by residents in Hong Kong or Macao) mainland

内定 nèidìng (usu of appointment) decided (at the higher level，etc) prior to official announcement：～人选 prior-determined candidate

内服 nèifú (of medicine) to be taken orally：～药 oral medicine

内阁 nèigé cabinet：～部长 cabinet minister / ～改组 cabinet reshuffle

内涵 nèihán ❶ intension (in logic)；connotation；implication：～意义 connotative meaning ❷ ability of exercising self-control；self-restraint

内行 nèiháng expert；professional：～话 comment or advice from a professional / 对金融很～ be well versed in finance

内疚 nèijiù guilty conscience；qualms (of conscience)；compunction：深感～ have deep compunction；feel very guilty

内科 nèikē 〈医〉(department of) internal medicine：～医生 physician

内陆 nèilù inland；continental；landlocked：～国 landlocked country / ～河 continental river / ～水域 inland waters

内幕 nèimù also “内情” what goes on behind the scenes；inside information or story：熟悉～ be in the know；be an insider

内勤 nèiqín (in contrast to 外勤) office work；office staff；clerk：～人员 office staff

内容 nèiróng content；substance：主要～ main points；gist / ～单薄 thin in terms of content

内伤 nèishāng internal injury；〈中医〉disorder of internal organs；〈喻〉spiritual damage

内外 nèiwài ❶ inside and outside；domestic and foreign：～交困 beset with difficulties both at home and abroad /

～有别 distinguish between what is for internal information and what is for external publicity；distinguish between one's own people and outsiders ❷ around；about：一年～ (in) a year or so

内务 nèiwù ❶ internal or interior affairs；domestic or family affairs；家庭～ family affair ❷ routine tasks to maintain cleanliness and orderliness in dormitories or barracks：整理～ tidy up the barracks

内线 nèixiàn ❶ planted agent；informer；mole：安插～ plant agents ❷ 〈军〉interior lines：～作战 fight on interior lines ❸ inside telephone connections：～电话 extension number ❹ (of politics) inside：走～ (wangle sth) through personal channels / ～人物 insider

内向 nèixiàng ❶ domestically-oriented (economy，etc) ❷ introversion：性格～ be an introvert；be introverted

内心 nèixīn innermost being；heart：～深处 at the bottom of one's heart；in one's heart of hearts / ～受到谴责 be conscience-stricken

内应 nèiyìng ❶ act in coordination with forces from outside ❷ planted agent；plant

内忧外患 nèiyōu-wàihuàn domestic trouble and foreign invasion；disturbance within and attack from without

内在 nèizài inherent；internal；inner：～美 inner beauty；beauty of the spirit

那 nèi colloquial pronunciation for 那 nà

nèn

嫩 nèn ❶ tender；delicate；sensitive：～芽 bud ❷ (of food) under-done；soft；tender：牛排要～ want one's steak rare ❸ (of colour)

light；～红 pale-red；pink ❹ inexperienced (for a post, etc)；immature；unskilled

néng

能 néng ❶ ability；capability；competence：～干 able；capable；competent／～人 able person；talent／～见度 visibility／～歌善舞 good at (both) singing and dancing／～工巧匠 skilful craftsmen；master artisans ❷〈理〉energy：～耗 energy consumption ❸ can；may：什么事都～干出来 be capable of anything／我～去吗? Can I go?

能动 néngdòng active；dynamic：～性 initiative；activity

能够 nénggòu ❶ can；be able to；be capable of：～自立 be able to stand on one's own ❷ indicating possibility, permission, etc：非会员也～参加。Non-members are also welcome.

能…会… néng…huì… introducing two phrases similar in meaning：能说会道 have the gift of the gab；have a glib tongue／能写会算 be literate

能力 nénglì ability；capability；capacity：～不够 lacking in ability

能量 néngliàng ❶〈理〉energy ❷ capabilities；capacity：这人的～不可轻视。Don't underestimate his capacity.

能耐 néngnai〈口〉ability；capability：长～ become more capable／没～的人 incompetent

能…能… néng…néng… introducing two phrases opposite in meaning：能屈能伸 submit or assert oneself as the occasion requires；be adaptable to circumstances／能上能下 be ready to accept a higher or lower post；take promotion or demotion with equal composure／能文能武 be equally capable in civilian and military affairs；be able to do both mental and manual labour

能手 néngshǒu good hand；expert；crackerjack：生产～ good hand (at one's work)；good worker

能言善辩 néngyán-shànbiàn be eloquent；have the gift of the gab；have a ready tongue

能源 néngyuán sources of energy；energy (resource)：～资源 energy resources／～密集型 energy-intensive

能者多劳 néngzhěduōláo able people should do more work；the abler one is, the more one should do

ńg

嗯 ńg also ń〈叹〉used in questioning：～，这是什么? Eh? What is this?

ňg

嗯 ňg also ň〈叹〉used to indicate surprise：～，怎么有煤气味儿? Hey, I can smell gas!

ǹg

嗯 ǹg also ǹ〈叹〉used to indicate positive response：～，你就这么办! Ok, it's settled.

nī

妮 nī

妮子 nīzi〈方〉girl；lass

ní

尼 ní nun：～庵 Buddhist nunnery；convent／～姑 Buddhist nun

尼古丁 nígǔdīng nicotine

尼龙 nílóng nylon：～绳 nylon cord

呢 ní (heavy) woollen cloth：～料 woollen (material)／～子 (heavy)

woollen cloth; wool coating　*see also* ne

呢喃 nínán　(of swallows) twitter; 〈喻〉speak in a low voice; murmur; ~ 细语 whisper tender words

泥 ní ❶ mud; silt; clay; ~巴〈方〉mud / ~浆 slurry; mud / ~泞 muddy; miry / ~鳅〈动物〉loach / ~ 人 clay figurine / ~潭 *also* "泥沼" (often figurative) mire; bog / ~石流〈地〉mud-rock flow / ~水匠 *also* "泥瓦匠" plasterer; bricklayer / ~牛入海 not to be heard of again; gone for good / 陷入~坑 get stuck in the mud; be bogged down in a morass ❷ anything shaped like mud; mashed food, esp vegetables and fruit: 土豆~ mashed potato
see also nì

泥沙 níshā　mud and sand; silt; ~含量 silt content (of water) / ~俱下,鱼龙混杂。When mud and sand are carried along and the bad mix with the good, you can't easily tell them apart.

泥塑 nísù　clay sculpture; clay figure modelling; ~木雕 motionless and lifeless; as dead as a doornail

泥土 nítǔ ❶ earth; soil; dirt ❷ clay

霓 ní　*also* "副虹" secondary rainbow

霓虹灯 níhóngdēng　neon (light)

鲵 ní　〈动物〉salamander; 大~ *also* "娃娃鱼" giant salamander

nǐ

拟(擬) nǐ ❶ draw up; draft; ~订 draw up; draft / ~定 work out; devise / ~稿 write a draft; draft (a document, etc) / ~议 draw up; draft; what is drawn up or drafted ❷ plan; intend ❸ imitate; mimic; simulate; ~人 personification / ~态 simulation; mimicry / ~音 (produce a) sound effect / ~作 work mod-

elled after a certain author; imitation

你 nǐ ❶ you; ~厂 your factory / ~好 hi; hello; how do you do / ~们 you (plural); your ❷ you; one; anyone; ~追我赶 strive to catch up and overtake one another; try to outstrip each other

你死我活 nǐsǐ-wǒhuó　life-and-death; mortal; 争得~ fight tooth and nail (oversth)

nì

泥 nì ❶ cover with plaster, etc; plaster; ~子 *also* "腻子" putty; daub ❷ stubborn; obstinate; rigid; ~ 古不化 worship the ancients and reject the moderns
see also ní

昵(暱) nì　close; intimate; confidential; ~称 intimate address; pet name

逆 nì ❶ counter; contrary; adverse; ~差 unfavourable balance of trade; trade deficit / ~光 (in photography) counterlight; backlighting / ~境 unfavourable or adverse circumstances / ~行 (of vehicles, etc) go in a direction not allowed by traffic regulations / ~耳之言 words jarring on the ear / ~时针方向 counterclockwise; anticlockwise/~水行舟,不进则退 You either forge ahead or fall behind just like sailing against the current. ❷ go against; disobey; defy; ~子 unfilial son / ~潮流而动 go against the current ❸ traitor; ~贼 traitor; rebel

逆反 nìfǎn　rebellious; adverse; ~心理 psychology of aversion; aversion (to sth)

逆来顺受 nìlái-shùnshòu　accept humiliation and adversity meekly; be submissive and patient in adversity

逆料 nìliào　foresee; anticipate; predict; 难以~ unpredictable

逆流 nìliú　adverse current；〈喻〉reactionary trend：~而上 go or sail against the current

逆向 nìxiàng　opposite or contrary direction；~思维 reverse thinking / ~行驶 drive in a direction not allowed by traffic regulations

逆转 nìzhuǎn　develop in a reverse direction；deteriorate；不可~ irreversible

匿 nì　hide；conceal；隐~ hide / ~迹 go into hiding / ~名信 anonymous letter / ~影藏形 conceal one's identity；lie low

膩 nì　❶（of food, etc）greasy；oily；cloying ❷ be fed up or bored with；be tired of ❸ dirt；filth；grime

膩烦 nìfan　〈口〉❶ be tired of；be fed up or bored with ❷ loathe；be disgusted with：从心里~这班人 find these people disgusting

膩味 nìwei　also "膩歪"〈方〉❶ see "膩烦" ❷ pester；plague：别~人了！Stop pestering me！

膩友 nìyǒu　〈书〉intimate or close friend

睨 nì　〈书〉look askance；cast an oblique look

溺 nì　❶ submerge；drown：~死 be drowned；drown / ~水 sink in water；drown / ~婴（commit）infanticide by drowning ❷ be addicted to：~爱 spoil；pamper；dote on / ~于名利 be addicted to fame and gain；lust for fame and fortune

niān

拈 niān　pick up（with the thumb and one or two other fingers）；pick；pinch：~阄儿 draw lots / ~花惹草 dally with women / ~轻怕重 pick easy jobs and shirk hard ones；be choosy about what to do

蔫 niān　❶（of flowers, etc）wither；droop；shrivel up：晒~了 droop

in the heat of the sun ❷ listless；spiritless；lethargic；~头耷脑〈口〉droopy；listless ❸〈方〉（of temperament）slow；quiet；secretive：~儿坏 apt to do harm or work mischief in secret / ~儿淘（of a child）naughty in a quiet manner

nián

年 nián　❶ year：~表 chronological table / ~底 also "年根"；"年末" end of the year；year-end / ~鉴 yearbook；almanac / ~历 calendar with the whole year printed on one sheet；single page calendar / ~谱 chronicle（of sb's life）/ ~月 days；years；times / ~复一~ year after year；year in, year out ❷ annual；yearly：~检 annual inspection（of vehicles, etc）/ ~利 also "年息" annual interest / ~轮〈植〉annual ring ❸ age；period in one's life：~迈 old；aged / ~富力强 in the prime of life；in one's prime / ~高德劭 venerable age and eminent virtue；venerable / ~事已高〈书〉advanced in age / ~幼无知 young and inexperienced ❹ period（in history）；time：~号 title of an emperor's reign ❺ harvest：~成 also "年景" year's harvest ❻（related to）Chinese New Year：~糕 New Year cake / ~画 New Year picture / ~夜饭 dinner on Chinese New Year's Eve to celebrate family reunion / ~三十儿〈口〉last day of the lunar year；Chinese New Year's Eve

年代 niándài　❶ age；years；time：~久远 of the remote past；age-old ❷ decade of a century：20 世纪 90~ the 1990's

年度 niándù　year；财政~ financial year

年份 niánfèn　❶ particular year（of an event, etc）❷ age；time：~久 old

年华 niánhuá time; years:虚度～ idle away one's time; waste one's life

年货 niánhuò special purchases for the Spring Festival:置办～ do Spring Festival shopping

年级 niánjí (at school) grade; year:高～学生 upper division students

年纪 niánjì age:上了～ advanced in age; aged / ～相仿 be of similar age; be about the same age

年龄 niánlíng age:上学～ school age / 具有～优势 enjoy an advantage on account of one's relative youth

年轻 niánqīng young:～人 young people; youth /～力壮 young and vigorous / ～～一代 younger generation / 领导班子要 ～ 化。The leading body should be younger.

年岁 niánsuì ❶ age:～不饶人。Time tells on everybody. ❷ years; time:这件事～久了。It happened many years ago.

年头儿 niántóur ❶ year:熬 ～ 过 through years of suffering; accumulate seniority as the years go by ❷ days; times

年限 niánxiàn number of years required or stipulated:使 用 ～ service life / 学习～ required years of study

粘 nián see "黏 nián" see also zhān

鲇 nián also "鲇鱼" catfish

黏 nián also "粘"sticky; glutinous:～米 glutinous rice /～土 clay / ～性 viscosity / ～着 stick together; adhere / ～合剂 binder; adhesive

黏糊 niánhu ❶ sticky; glutinous ❷ languid; slow-moving; sluggish:～性子 be the slow-moving type

niǎn

捻(撚) niǎn ❶ twist with the fingers:～麻绳 make a cord by twisting hemp fibres ❷ sth made by twisting:灯～子 lampwick

碾 niǎn ❶ roller:～ 子 (stone) roller; millstone ❷ grind with a roller; crush:～压 roll over

撵 niǎn ❶ drive out; oust; expel:～他出去! Get him out of here! ❷〈方〉try to catch up; run after; pursue:～上 catch up (with sb)

niàn

廿 niàn twenty

念(❸❹唸) niàn ❶ think of; long for; miss:～旧 remember old friends; treasure old friendships / ～～不忘 constantly bear in mind; always remember ❷ thought; idea:一～之差 wrong decision made in a moment of weakness (with serious consequences); moment's slip ❸ read aloud; recite; chant:～～有词 mutter; mumble ❹ study; attend school:～大学 study in college

念叨 niàndao also "念道" ❶ talk about again and again; harp on ❷ talk over; tell about; discuss:你把情况～～吧。Tell us about it.

念书 niànshū ❶ read; study:不好好 ～ put too little stock in study ❷ attend school

念头 niàntou thought; idea; motive:起了一个 ～ have an idea; an idea occurs to one

niáng

娘 niáng ❶ ma; mom; mother:亲 mother ❷ *term of address for an elderly married woman*:大～ aunt / 婶～ wife of father's younger brother; aunt ❸ young woman:～子军 (army) detachment of women; women soldiers; women

娘家 niángjia home or family of a married woman's parents; 回～（of a woman）return to one's parents' home（for a visit after marriage）

娘娘 niángniang ❶ empress or imperial concubine of the first rank ❷ goddess

娘儿 niángr 〈口〉woman along with her juniors（eg mother and her children）;～俩 mother and her child

娘胎 niángtāi mother's womb; 这些本领不是打～里带来的。No one is born with these skills.

niàng

酿（釀） niàng ❶ brew（beer）; make（wine or honey）; ferment;～造 make（wine, vinegar, etc）; brew（beer, etc）; distil（alcoholic drink）/ ～蜜 make honey / ～酒厂 winery; distillery; brewery ❷ lead to; result in;～成水灾 cause floods ❸ wine; 佳～ vintage wine

niǎo

鸟（鳥） niǎo bird;～粪 bird's droppings / ～笼 bird cage; aviary / ～枪 fowling piece; air gun / ～尽弓藏 put aside the bow once the birds are killed — kick out sb when his or her service is no longer needed / 作～兽散 scatter like frightened birds and beasts; flee helter-skelter / ～语花香。Birds are singing and flowers are giving forth their fragrance — a fine spring day.

鸟瞰 niǎokàn （get a）bird's-eye view; general survey;～图 bird's-eye view

袅（嫋） niǎo slender and delicate;～娜〈书〉（of a tree, etc）lithe and slender; （of a woman）lithe and graceful

袅袅 niǎoniǎo ❶（of smoke, etc）

curl upwards; coil up ❷（of slender and delicate objects）wave or sway in the wind;～婷婷〈书〉（of a woman's manner of walking）lithe and graceful ❸（of sound）linger

niào

尿 niào ❶ urine;～布 also "裤子" diaper; napkin; nappy / ～盆 chamber pot; urinal / ～素〈化〉urea / ～不湿〈口〉paper nappy; disposable diaper / ～毒症〈医〉uraemia ❷ urinate; make or pass water;～床 wet the bed; bed-wetting
see also suī

niē

捏（揑） niē ❶ hold between the thumb and other fingers; pinch / ～闸 apply the handbrake / ～一把汗 be breathless with anxiety or nervous tension; hold one's breath in suspense / ～着鼻子 pinch one's nose（to avoid a bad smell）;〈喻〉（do sth）reluctantly ❷ knead with the fingers; mould;～饺子 make dumplings by kneading the wrappers ❸ bind or put together; link;～合 bind or put together ❹ *see* "捏造"

捏造 niēzào fabricate; concoct; make or trump up;～数字 conjure up figures / ～罪名 trump up charges / 纯属～ sheer fabrication

niè

涅 niè

涅槃 nièpán 〈宗教〉nirvana — extinction of all desire and pain; absolute blessedness; death

啮（齧、嚙） niè 〈书〉gnaw;～合 clench the

teeth; (of gears) mesh; engage

嗫（囁） niè

嗫嚅 nièrú 〈书〉speak haltingly; hesitate in speech; hem and haw

镊（鑷） niè ❶ (usu 镊子) tweezers:一把～ a pair of tweezers ❷ pick up or out with tweezers

镍 niè 〈化〉nickel (Ni):镀～ nickel-plating / ～币 nickel (coin)

蹑（躡） niè ❶ lighten (one's step); walk on tiptoe:～手～脚 walk gingerly; walk on tiptoe ❷ follow; dog; track:～踪 follow along (behind sb); track

孽（孼） niè ❶ evil creature; monster ❷ evil; crime; sin:作～ do evil; commit a sin / ～种 root of trouble; unworthy offspring; worthless creature ❸〈书〉unfaithful; unfilial:～子 unfilial son

蘖 niè 〈植〉tiller

nín

您 nín 〈敬〉you:～好! How are you?

níng

宁（寧、甯） níng ❶ peaceful; serene; tranquil;～靖〈书〉(of local or frontier public order) stable; quiet; settled ❷ (Níng) another name for Nanjing (南京):沪～线 Shanghai-Nanjing Railway

see also nìng

宁静 níngjìng （of surroundings or feelings) peaceful; tranquil; calm:心里很不～ feel very uneasy

宁馨儿 níngxīn'ér 〈书〉lovely child

拧（擰） níng ❶ twist; wring:～毛巾 wring out a

towel / ～成一股绳 pull together make joint efforts ❷ pinch; tweak

see also nǐng; nìng

狞（獰） níng ferocious; hideous;～笑 grin hideously; give a grim laugh

柠（檸） níng

柠檬 níngméng lemon:～水 lemonade ～汁 lemon-juice

凝 níng ❶ congeal; curdle; coagulate:～成冰 freeze ❷ with fixed attention; attentively:～眸〈书〉(look with fixed eyes; (watch) with the utmost concentration / ～视 gaze or stare at / ～思 think deeply; be lost in thought / ～望 look far with fixed eyes; gaze into the distance

凝固 nínggù ❶ solidify; congeal; coagulate:～点〈理〉solidifying or condensation point ❷ inflexible; rigid:思想～ stereotyped in thinking

凝结 níngjié coagulate; congeal; condense:～了一层薄冰 form a thin layer of ice

凝聚 níngjù ❶ (of vapour) condense; cohere ❷ gather; accumulate:～力 cohesive force; cohesion / 这项工程～着许多人的辛勤劳动。The project is crystallization of many people's hard work.

凝练 níngliàn concise; condensed; compact:语言～ terse and succinct language

凝神 níngshén with fixed attention:～思索 deep in thought

凝滞 níngzhì stagnate; move sluggishly:神色～ look dull

凝重 níngzhòng dignified; grave; imposing:举止～ dignified manner

nǐng

拧（擰） nǐng ❶ twist; screw; turn:把灯泡～上 screw

a bulb in (a socket) ❷ wrong; at cross purposes; at odds; 把话听~了 get it the wrong way / 两个人~着劲儿。The two of them are at odds.

see also níng; nìng

nìng

宁（寧、甯） nìng would rather; better; 缺毋滥 rather go without than have something shoddy — place quality above quantity / ~死不屈 rather die than submit; prefer death to surrender / ~为玉碎，不为瓦全 rather die like a hero than live in dishonour; prefer death to dishonour　*see also* níng

宁可 nìngkě *also* "宁肯"; "宁愿" would rather; better; ~少些，但要好些。Fewer, but better.

佞 nìng given to flattery; sycophantic; ~笑 ingratiating or sinister smile

拧（擰） nìng 〈方〉pig-headed; stubborn; obstinate
see also níng; nǐng

泞（濘） nìng 〈书〉mud; slush

niū

妞 niū 〈口〉girl; ~~ little girl

niú

牛 niú ❶ ox; cattle; 公~ bull / 母~ cow / ~犊 calf / ~柳〈方〉beef sirloin / ~马 oxen and horses — beasts of burden / ~排（beef）steak / ~肉 beef ❷ 〈方〉capable; competent; 咱们厂最~的钳工 most skilful fitter in our factory ❸ 〈方〉stubborn; proud; arrogant; ~气 self-important; conceited / 发~脾气 fly into a mulish temper /

有点儿钱就~起来了 become purse-proud with a little money

牛刀小试 niúdāoxiǎoshì display just a bit of one's talent; reveal the tip of an iceberg

牛痘 niúdòu ❶ cowpox ❷ smallpox pustule; vaccine; 种~ be vaccinated

牛劲 niújìn ❶ great strength; tremendous efforts; 费了~ take tremendous efforts ❷ stubbornness; obstinacy; tenacity; 犯~了 get stubborn

牛郎织女 niúláng-zhīnǚ ❶〈天文〉Altair and Vega ❷ "the Cowherd and the Girl Weaver", mythical couple in heaven who meet just once a year; husband and wife who live far apart

牛奶 niúnǎi milk; ~场 dairy (farm)

牛皮 niúpí ❶ cattle hide ❷ pliable and tough; ~癣〈医〉psoriasis / ~纸 kraft or brown paper ❸ brag; boast; ~大王 person given to gross exaggerations; braggart

牛市 niúshì 〈经〉bull or bullish market (with generally rising stock prices)

牛头不对马嘴 niútóubùduìmǎzuǐ *see* "驴唇不对马嘴" lúchúnbùduìmǎzuǐ

牛头马面 niútóu-mǎmiàn two armed runners under the king of the underworld, one with an ox head and the other a horse face — hideous lackeys; wicked people of all descriptions

牛仔 niúzǎi cowboy; ~服 cowboy clothing / ~裤 jeans

niǔ

扭 niǔ ❶ turn; ~过脸去 turn aside / ~亏增盈 make up losses and increase profits ❷ twist; contort; wrench; 把铁丝~在一起 twist wires together ❸ sprain; wrench; strain; ~了脚 sprain one's ankle ❹ (usu of manner of walking) swing; sway; ~秧歌 do a *yangge* dance ❺ seize; grapple; ~打 be locked in a fistfight;

wrestle / ～送 (of citizens) seize (sb) and hand over (to the public security authorities) / ～住不放 seize hold of; grapple

扭捏 niǔnie be affectedly bashful; be coy; hum and haw; displayed 显出一副一副 put on a show of coy reluctance / 说话别扭捏捏的。Stop humming and hawing.

扭曲 niǔqū ❶ twist; contort ❷ warp; distort:～的心态 warped mentality

扭转 niǔzhuǎn ❶ turn round:～身子 turn round ❷〈喻〉turn back or round; reverse; change radically:～局势 reverse a trend; turn the tide

怓 niǔ

怓怩 niǔní bashful; coy:～作态 behave coyly; be affectedly shy

纽 niǔ

niǔ ❶ handle; knob; 秤～ lifting cord of a steelyard ❷ (usu 纽扣) button ❸ pivot; hub

纽带 niǔdài pivot; link; bond:精神～ spiritual bond

钮 niǔ

niǔ ❶ see "纽❷"niǔ ❷ also "电钮" (push) button

niù

拗 niù

niù stubborn; obstinate; stiff-necked:脾气很～ stubborn by nature; bull-headed / 谁也～不过他。No one is able to bring him round
see also ào

nóng

农（農） nóng

nóng ❶ agriculture; farming:～活 farm work / ～机 agricultural or farm machinery / ～具 farm tool / ～闲 slack (farming) season / ～副产品 agricultural and sideline products / ～贸市场 (urban) market for farm produce; free market (primarily for agricultural prod-

ucts) ❷ farmer; peasant:～户 peasant or farm household

农场 nóngchǎng farm:～主 farm owner; farmer

农村 nóngcūn rural or agricultural area; countryside; village:～经济 rural economy

农历 nónglì ❶ Chinese lunar calendar ❷ farmer's almanac

农民 nóngmín peasant; farmer:～意识 peasant mentality / ～企业家 farmer-entrepreneur

农奴 nóngnú serf:～主 serf-owner / ～制度 serfdom

农时 nóngshí farming season:不误～ farm in the right season

农田 nóngtián farmland; cropland:～水利 irrigation and water conservancy

农药 nóngyào agricultural or farm chemical; pesticide:～残留 pesticide residue

农业 nóngyè agriculture; farming:～人口 agricultural population; people engaged in farm work

农艺 nóngyì agronomy:～师 agronomist

农作物 nóngzuòwù crops:～病虫害 plant diseases and insect pests

侬（儂） nóng 〈方〉you

哝（噥） nóng

哝哝 nóngnong murmur; mutter

浓（濃） nóng

nóng ❶ thick; dense; heavy:～茶 strong tea / ～淡 degree of density / ～度 concentration; density / ～眉 heavy or bushy eyebrows / ～烟 dense smoke ❷ (of degree or extent) strong; great; deep:睡意正～ very sleepy / 汤味不够～。The soup is rather bland.

浓厚 nónghòu ❶ (of atmosphere, etc) strong; rich:宗教色彩～ rich religious colouring / ～的生活气息 full of life ❷ (of interest) great; deep

浓烈 nónglie　rich; strong: 酒香 ～
strong scent of liquor

浓密 nóngmì　dense; thick: ～的黑发
rich black hair

浓缩 nóngsuō　❶ concentrate; condense: ～果汁 fruit juice concentrate;
condensed fruit juice ❷ enrich: ～铀
enriched uranium

浓艳 nóngyàn　rich and gaudy: 服饰～
gaudily dressed

浓郁 nóngyù　(of smell, flavour, etc)
strong; rich; deep: 兴致～ great or
deep interest

浓重 nóngzhòng　thick; heavy; strong:
～的口音 strong or thick accent / 浓墨
重彩（paint in) thick ink and rich colours; 〈喻〉(describe in a) rich and
colourful manner

浓妆 nóngzhuāng　heavy make-up: ～
艳抹 (of a woman) richly attired and
heavily made-up

脓（膿）nóng　pus

脓包 nóngbāo　❶〈医〉pustule ❷
good-for-nothing; worthless fellow

nòng

弄 nòng　❶ play or fiddle with;
fumble with; wield: ～权 manipulate or
wield power; abuse power / ～潮儿
〈喻〉one who rides the tide in times of
political or economic changes / 你在那
儿～什么? What are you fumbling
with there? ❷ do; make; get: ～不明
白 can't get it straight / ～僵关系
strain relations / 把事情～坏 mess up
things / 把人～得很苦 make sb quite
miserable ❸ play (tricks): ～鬼〈方〉
play tricks

see also lòng

弄假成真 nòngjiǎchéngzhēn　what
was make-believe has become reality;
what began in fun ends in dead earnest

弄巧成拙 nòngqiǎochéngzhuō　try to

be clever only to end up with a blunder;
outsmart oneself

弄虚作假 nòngxū-zuòjiǎ　practise
fraud; resort to deception; falsify (accounts, etc): ～，骗取信任 gain trust
(of sb) through deception

nú

奴 nú　slave; bondservant: ～婢 servant; slave / ～化 turn into a slave;
enslave / ～仆 servant; lackey / ～性十
足 abject slavishness; utter servility

奴才 núcái　lackey; flunkey; (used as
a curse or self-derogatory word) bondservant: ～相 very picture of servility;
shameless fawning

奴隶 núlì　slave: ～主 slave-owner;
slave-holder / ～社会 slave society

奴颜婢膝 núyán-bìxī　servile; subservient: 对外～ bow and scrape to foreigners

奴役 núyì　use or treat as a slave; enslave

驽 nú　〈书〉inferior horse; 〈喻〉in-
competent; dull: ～钝 dull; slow-
witted; stupid

nǔ

努 nǔ　❶ exert; strive: ～劲儿 exert oneself ❷ pout; bulge: ～嘴
pout one's lips (as a signal) ❸〈方〉in-
jure oneself through overexertion;
strain oneself

努力 nǔlì　make efforts; strive; exert
oneself: ～不懈 make unremitting efforts / ～工作 work hard

弩 nǔ　crossbow

nù

怒 nù　❶ anger; rage; fury: ～斥
rebuke angrily; denounce indig-

nantly / ～吼 roar with anger; thunder / ～目 angry or fierce stare; glaring eyes / ～容 *also* "怒色" angry look; scowl / ～不可遏 cannot restrain one's fury; boil with anger / ～发冲冠 bristle with anger; swell with rage / ～形于色 be ablaze with anger ❷ vigorous; flourishing:～放 (of flowers, etc) be in full bloom or blossom / ～号 howl; roar

怒潮 nùcháo surging tide; tidal bore: 反战的～ anti-war tide or upsurge

怒火 nùhuǒ flames of fury; fury;～中烧 be burning with anger

怒气 nùqì anger; rage; fury:～冲冲 fume with rage; be mad with fury / ～冲天 boil with rage; be in a towering rage

nǚ

女 nǚ ❶ woman; female: ～方 woman's or wife's side; bride; girlfriend / ～郎 young woman; girl ～生 girl or woman student;〈方〉girl or woman / ～声〈乐〉female voice / ～王 queen (as a monarch in her own right) / ～巫 *also* "巫婆" witch; sorceress / ～厕所 women's lavatory; (used on signs) Ladies; Women / ～孩儿 *also* "女孩子"girl; daughter / ～朋友 girlfriend; lady friend / ～强人 capable career woman; woman of strong character / ～主角 feminine lead (in a film, etc); heroine (of a story, etc) / ～主人 hostess; mistress / ～里～气 (of a man) look or act like a woman; (be a) sissy / ～流之辈〈贬〉weaker sex; women ❷ daughter:生儿育～ bear and raise children

女儿 nǚ'ér ❶ daughter; girl ❷ unmarried girl

女权 nǚquán woman's right; ～运动 feminist movement; women's lib / ～主义 feminism

女人 nǚrén ❶ woman; womenfolk ❷ (nǚren)〈口〉wife; missus

女色 nǚsè woman's beauty or sexual attraction; woman: 好～ be a womanizer; be lascivious

女士 nǚshì (polite form of address for a woman) lady; madam: ～们，先生们 ladies and gentlemen

女式 nǚshì of women's style; style that suits women: ～大衣 women's coat

女娲 Nǚwā Nüwa, Chinese goddess who created human beings and patched up the sky

女性 nǚxìng ❶ female sex; feminine gender;～化 feminization ❷ woman:职业～ career woman

女婿 nǚxu ❶ son-in-law ❷〈口〉husband; hubby

女子 nǚzǐ woman; female:～中学 female high school

nuǎn

暖（煖） nuǎn ❶ warm; genial:～冬 (abnormally) warm winter / ～色 warm colour / ～烘烘 nice and warm; warm and cosy ❷ warm up; heat: ～～手脚 warm up one's hands and feet

暖房 nuǎnfáng greenhouse; hothouse

暖和 nuǎnhuo ❶ (nice and) warm ❷ warm up;烤烤火，～～。Warm yourself up by the fire.

暖流 nuǎnliú ❶ warm current ❷ sudden surge of warmth;觉得一股～涌上心头 feel a sudden surge of warmth

暖气 nuǎnqì ❶〈口〉(central) heating; ～片 (heating) radiator ❷ central heating equipment

暖水瓶 nuǎnshuǐpíng *also* "暖瓶"; "暖壶" thermos flask or bottle

暖洋洋 nuǎnyángyáng nice and warm;～的太阳 genial warmth of the sun / 心里～的 feel gratified and happy

nüè

疟(瘧) nüè malaria；～疾 malaria；ague

虐 nüè cruel；ferocious；tyrannical：～待 ill-treat；maltreat / ～政 tyrannical government；tyranny / ～杀无辜 maltreat and kill the innocent

nuó

挪 nuó move；shift；change：～动 move；shift / ～借 get a short-term loan；borrow money (from sb) / ～地方 also "挪窝儿" move (away)；go elsewhere

挪用 nuóyòng ❶ divert (funds)：～福利经费 divert welfare funds to other purposes ❷ embezzle；misappropriate：～公款 misappropriate public money

傩(儺) nuó exorcise：～戏 local opera derived from exorcising performance

nuò

诺 nuò ❶ promise；assent：慨～ promise generously ❷ yes；yeah：～～连声 keep on saying "yes"；eagerly agree

诺贝尔奖 Nuòbèi'ěrjiǎng Nobel Prize：～得主 winner of the Nobel Prize；Nobel laureate / 诺贝尔文学奖 Nobel Prize for literature

诺言 nuòyán promise；word：违背～ go back on one's word；break one's promise

懦 nuò cowardly；faint-hearted：～夫 coward；weakling / ～弱 cowardly；weak-kneed

糯(稬) nuò glutinous (cereal)

糯米 nuòmǐ also "江米" (threshed and polished) glutinous rice：～酒 glutinous rice wine

N

O

ō

噢 ō〈叹〉indicating understanding：～，原来是你干的。So you did it.

ó

哦 ó〈叹〉indicating scepticism：～，这事我怎么没听说？Really？But I haven't heard anything about it.
see also ò

ò

哦 ò〈叹〉indicating realization or understanding：～，护照忘在家里了。Ah, I left my passport at home.
see also ó

ōu

讴（謳）ōu sing：～歌〈书〉sing the praises of；eulogize

欧（歐）ōu ❶ (Ōu)（short for 欧洲）Europe：～化 Europeanize；Westernize / ～盟 EU (European Union) / ～亚大陆 Eurasia；Eurasian land mass ❷ (short for 欧姆)〈电〉ohm：～姆 ohm

欧佩克 Ōupèikè OPEC (Organization of Petroleum Exporting Countries)

欧元 ōuyuán euro：～区 euro area

欧洲 Ōuzhōu（short for 欧罗巴洲）Europe：～中央银行 European Central Bank (Eurobank)

殴（毆）ōu beat up；hit；strike：～打 beat up；assault / ～斗 come to blows；have a fist fight

噢（嘔）ōu ❶〈叹〉indicating realization or surprise：～，我想起来了。Oh, yes, I've got it. ❷〈象声〉sound of crying：他急得～～地哭。He was so worried that he started blubbering.

ǒu

呕（嘔）ǒu vomit；throw up；retch：～吐 vomit；throw up / ～心沥血 take infinite pains；work one's heart out

偶 ǒu ❶ figure；image；idol：～人 clay or wooden figure ❷ even (number)；in pairs：～数 even number ❸ mate；spouse：佳～ good spouse ❹ by chance or accident；occasionally：～遇 meet by chance；bump into (sb) / ～发事件 chance occurrence；accident / 见解～合 coincidental agreement

偶尔 ǒu'ěr ❶ once in a while；occasionally：～为之 do (sth) occasionally ❷ accidental；chance；coincidental

偶然 ǒurán ❶ accidental；fortuitous；chance：～性〈哲〉contingency；fortuity / ～相遇 chance meeting / 事出～。It happened by chance. ❷ sometimes；occasionally

偶像 ǒuxiàng idol；icon；image：～化 idolization / ～崇拜 worship of idols；idolatry

耦 ǒu

耦合 ǒuhé 〈理〉coupling：～器〈机〉coupler

藕 ǒu

lotus root：～粉 lotus root starch / ～荷色 *also* "藕合色" pale pinkish purple；lavender *see also* "莲" lián

藕断丝连 ǒuduàn-sīlián （usu of separated lovers who cherish lingering affection for each other）be still in each other's thoughts though apparently separated

òu

沤（漚） òu

soak；steep；macerate：～肥 make compost

怄（慪） òu

〈方〉annoy；upset；provoke：～气 be sulky and difficult；be in a fit of the sulks

P

pā

趴 pā ❶ lie on one's stomach; lie prone：～下 lie down ❷ lean on; bend over：～在桌子上写字 bend over a desk writing

啪 pā 〈象声〉 *indicating the sound of clapping, striking, or shooting*：～嚓摔碎了 break with a crash / ～～两声枪响 two cracks of rifle fire

葩 pā 〈书〉flower

pá

扒 pá ❶ gather up or spread out (with a rake, etc) ❷ steal; pinch：～窃 pick (people's) pockets / ～手 pickpocket ❸ stew; braise：～鸡 braised chicken
see also bā

爬 pá ❶ crawl; creep：～虫 reptile。❷ climb; clamber：～得高，跌得重。〈喻〉The higher the climb, the harder the fall. ❸ sit, stand, or get up：在哪里跌倒，就在哪里～起来。Get up from where you slip and fall.
爬格子 págézi 〈口〉write (on ruled paper); make a living by one's pen
爬行 páxíng ❶ crawl; creep：～动物 reptile ❷ slavishly follow the convention or imitate others：跟在别人后面～ trail behind others at a snail's pace

耙 (钯) pá ❶ *also* "耙子" rake ❷ make smooth with a rake; rake
see also bà

pà

帕 pà *also* "帕子" kerchief; handkerchief
帕金森氏病 pàjīnsēnshìbìng Parkinson's disease; shaking palsy

怕 pà ❶ be afraid or worried; fear; dread：～生 (of a child) be afraid of or shy with strangers / ～事 shy away from responsibility; be fearful of trouble; be overcautious ～羞 coy; shy; bashful / ～老婆 under the thumb of one's wife; henpecked ❷ I suppose; maybe; probably：这箱子～有百来斤吧。The trunk may be over fifty kilos.
怕人 pàrén ❶ be afraid or shy of people ❷ frightening; terrible; dreadful：山峰险得～。The cliff is terribly precipitous.

pāi

拍 pāi ❶ pat; clap; beat：～球 bounce a ball / ～胸脯儿〈口〉slap one's chest as a gesture of promise or guarantee ❷ bat; racket ❸ 〈乐〉beat; time：打～子 beat time / 二分之一～ one-half time ❹ take (a photo); shoot (a film)：～照 take a picture; have a picture taken / ～电影 shoot or make a film ❺ *also* "拍发" send (a telegram, etc) ❻ 〈口〉flatter; fawn on

拍案 pāi'àn　strike the table (in anger, wonder, etc); ~叫绝 thump the table and cry out with admiration

拍板 pāibǎn ❶ rap the gavel (to clinch a business deal); ~成交 conclude or clinch a deal ❷〈喻〉call the shots; make a final decision; have the final say; ~定案 give the final verdict; make a final decision

拍打 pāidǎ　pat; beat; flap; ~尘土 pat or beat off the dust

拍马屁 pāimǎpì　also "拍马"〈口〉lick (sb's) boots; soft-soap; toady to

拍卖 pāimài ❶ auction; ~会 auction / ~师 auctioneer / ~古玩 auction antiques ❷ sale (at reduced prices); 大~ bargain sale

拍摄 pāishè　take (a photo); shoot (a film); ~外景 go on location

拍手 pāishǒu　clap one's hands; applaud; ~称快 clap and cheer (with great satisfaction)

pái

排 pái ❶ arrange in order; line up; ~班 arrange the order of shifts; take turns / ~版 set type; compose / ~名第三 rank third ❷ line; row; ~尾 last person in a row; (person at the) end of a procession or line / ~头兵 file leader;〈喻〉pace-setter ❸〈军〉platoon; ~长 platoon leader ❹〈量〉row; line; 一~树 a row of trees ❺ also "排练", "排演" rehearse; ~节目 rehearse a performance ❻ raft; salvo; sth like a raft or salvo; ~筏 timber or bamboo raft ❼ push; exclude; dispel; ~放 discharge; release; emit / ~涝 drain waterlogged land / ~雷〈军〉remove mines; clear (a place of) mines / ~气量 engine capacity / ~气扇 also "排风扇" ventilating fan; ventilator / ~忧解难 relieve anxieties and resolve difficulties; solve problems and alleviate sufferings / ~他性集团 exclusive bloc ❽ large meat slice; 大~ (pork) chop

排比 páibǐ　parallelism; ~句 parallel sentences

排场 páichǎng　(grand) style; ostentation; extravagance; 大~ (do things in a) grand style / 集体婚礼既~,又省钱。A group wedding is both dignified and economical.

排斥 páichì　repel; exclude; discriminate against; ~异己 discriminate against those outside one's coterie; exclude people of different views; tolerate no dissenting voices

排除 páichú ❶ get rid of; remove; exclude; ~故障 fix a breakdown / ~一种可能性 rule out a possibility ❷ excrete; discharge; clean out; ~体内毒素 discharge toxins from the body; purge the body of toxins

排队 páiduì　form a line; line or queue up; ~购票 line up for tickets / 把问题排排队 sort out problems

排骨 páigǔ　spare-ribs

排行 páiháng　seniority among siblings; ranking; ~榜 ranking; (bestseller) list / ~老二 be the second child of the family

排挤 páijǐ　push out; exclude; discriminate against

排解 páijiě ❶ mediate; reconcile; ~纠纷 mediate a dispute; reconcile a quarrel ❷ also "排遣" dispel; assuage; relieve (sorrow, boredom, etc); 难以~的惆怅 melancholy that is hard to get rid of; unassuaged melancholy

排列 páiliè　put in order; rank; 按姓氏笔画~ be listed according to the number of strokes in one's surname

排球 páiqiú　volleyball; 沙滩~ beach volleyball

排山倒海 páishān-dǎohǎi　great in momentum and irresistible

排水 páishuǐ　drain off water; ~沟

drainage ditch; gutter / ～量 displacement (of a ship, etc); discharge capacity (of a canal, etc)

排外 páiwài　anti-foreign; xenophobic;～心理 *also* "排外情绪" xenophobia; anti-foreign sentiments

排泄 páixiè　❶ drain (water, etc) ❷ excrete; void;～物〈生理〉excrement; excretion

徘 pái

徘徊 páihuái　❶ pace up and down; walk to and fro;～不前 mark time; stand still; remain stagnant ❷ hesitate; waver; oscillate;在两种意见之间～ waver between two views ❸ move up and down; fluctuate;销量在百万台上下～。The sales volume fluctuate around one million sets.

牌 pái

❶ board; plate; sign;～匾 board with characters carved or written on it; plaque / ～位 memorial tablet (for worshipping the deceased, a deity, etc) ❷ brand; make; trademark;杂～ unknown brand / ～号 trademark; brand (-name) ❸ cards; dominoes; tiles;打～ play cards / ～局 gambling at dominoes, cards or mah-jong; bridge or mah-jong party ❹ title (of a *ci* or *qu* tune)

牌坊 páifāng　memorial arch

牌价 páijià　❶ list or posted price ❷ market quotation;外汇～ foreign exchange quotations

牌楼 páilou　❶ *pailou*, or decorated archway ❷ temporary ceremonial gateway

牌照 páizhào　licence (plate, tag or certificate):汽车～ automobile licence or number plate / 营业～ business (operation) licence

牌子 páizi　❶ board; plate; tablet;存车～ parking check (for a bicycle, etc) ❷ brand; make; trademark;创～(of

enterprises) produce and establish a brand name

pǎi

迫 pǎi *see also* pò

迫击炮 pǎijīpào　(trench) mortar

pài

派 pài

❶ sect; school; faction;～别 group; school; clique / ～系 faction (within a political party, etc); clique / 各～学者 scholars of various schools ❷ style; bearing; manner and air;有～ have an impressive bearing ❸〈书〉branch of a river ❹ send; assign; appoint;～活 assign jobs / ～用场 put to use; turn to account ❺〈量〉*preceded by* 一 *and used with words indicating scenery, atmosphere, language, etc*;一～欣欣向荣的气象 a thriving atmosphere ❻ pie;苹果～ apple pie

派出所 pàichūsuǒ　precinct or local police station; police substation

派遣 pàiqiǎn　send; dispatch;～大使 accredit an ambassador (to a foreign country)

派生 pàishēng　derive;～词〈语言〉derivative

派头 pàitóu　bearing; manner;讲～ have a penchant for grandeur / 摆首长～ put on airs of a leader; pose as a leader

派驻 pàizhù　post; station; accredit;～国外 be accredited to a foreign country

pān

攀 pān

❶ climb; clamber;～岩〈体〉rock-climbing ❷ cling or hold to; attach oneself to (sb powerful, etc) ❸ involve; implicate;～扯 involve or implicate (sb in a crime, etc)

攀比 pānbǐ compete (regardless of actual circumstances); vie:互相～ keep up with the Joneses; beggar thy neighbour

攀登 pāndēng climb; clamber; scale:～科学高峰〈喻〉scale the heights of science

攀附 pānfù ❶ (of a plant) climb; cling to ❷ attach oneself to (sb powerful); seek connection with:攀龙附凤 play up to people of power and influence

攀高 pāngāo ❶ see "攀升❷" ❷ also "攀高枝儿" make friends or claim ties of kinship with someone of a higher social position

攀亲 pānqīn ❶ claim kinship (with sb useful):～道故 claim ties of blood or friendship ❷ arrange a match or a betrothal (for one's son), etc)

攀升 pānshēng ❶ climb by holding onto sth; negotiate one's way up (a peak, etc) ❷ also "攀高" (of prices, etc) rise; soar

攀谈 pāntán engage in chit-chat; chat up

攀援 pānyuán also "攀缘" ❶ climb; clamber:抓住绳子向上～ climb up by holding on to a rope ❷ seek the patronage of influential people or the powers that be

攀折 pānzhé pull down and break off (twigs, flowers etc)

pán

盘(盤) pán ❶ tray; plate; dish:～儿菜 ready-to-cook dish of meat, vegetables, etc ❷ sth shaped like or used as a tray, etc:～秤 steelyard with a pan ❸ market quotation; current price: 开～ open quotations ❹ coil; wind; twist:～跌 (of stock prices, etc) be on the downturn; spiral down / ～绕 twine; coil; wind / ～腿 (sit) cross-legged / ～陀路 also "盘陀路"〈书〉winding path / ～山公路 winding mountain highway ❺ build (a cooking range, etc) with bricks ❻ check; examine; investigate:～查 interrogate and check; question and examine / ～根究底 try to get to the root of sth ❼ transfer; sell:～店 sell a shop along with its stock, furniture and equipment ❽〈量〉一～菜 a dish (of food); a course / 两～单打 two singles matches

盘剥 pánbō exploit by practising usury, etc:～渔利 reap unfair gains through exploitation

盘缠 pánchan also "盘川" travel money; travelling expenses

盘点 pándiǎn check; make an inventory of:～存货 (shortened as 盘存 or 盘货) take inventory

盘根错节 pángēn-cuòjié with twisted roots and gnarled branches; intricate (case, etc); deep-rooted (influence, etc)

盘桓 pánhuán ❶〈书〉linger; stay:～数日 stay a few days / ～脑际 linger in one's mind ❷ see "盘旋"

盘活 pánhuó (经)take stock of and activate; revitalize:～国有资产 make optimal use of or revitalize state-owned assets

盘踞 pánjù also "盘据" illegally or forcibly occupy; be entrenched in

盘算 pánsuàn consider; calculate; plan:～下一步怎么办 ponder over what to do next

盘问 pánwèn also "盘诘" question; interrogate; cross-examine

盘旋 pánxuán spiral; circle; wheel:在上空～ (of a plane, etc) circle above / ～而上 wind one's way up

磬 pán

磐石 pánshí　*also* "盘石" huge rock; monolith

蹒 pán

蹒跚 pánshān　*also* "盘跚" stagger; falter; limp;～而行 stagger along

蟠 pán coil; curl;～伏 lie curled up

蟠桃 pántáo ❶ flat peach ❷ legendary peach of longevity

pàn

判 pàn ❶ distinguish; differentiate; separate;～明情况 find out the facts ❷ obviously (different);～然不同 markedly different ❸ judge; decide; grade;～定 judge; decide; determine /～罚 (as of a referee) decide to penalize; penalize /～分 give a mark; mark; score ❹ sentence; condemn;～案〈case〉make a judgement /～例 legal or judicial precedent /～刑 pass or impose a sentence; sentence /～罪 declare guilty; convict /～处劳役 sentence (sb) to penal servitude /～为无罪 declare (sb) not guilty

判别 pànbié　distinguish; differentiate; tell apart;～是非 distinguish between right and wrong /～真伪 tell the true or genuine from the false or fake

判断 pànduàn ❶ judge; decide; determine;～力 (ability to make correct) judgement ❷ (in logic) judgement

判决 pànjué ❶ court decision; judgement /～书 written judgement ❷ decision; judgement; 服从裁判～ respect the decision of the umpire

判若 pànruò　as different as;～鸿沟 as different as if separated by a yawning gulf; completely different /～两人 be no longer one's old self; become a totally different person /～云泥 *also* "判若天渊" as far removed as heaven is from earth; poles apart

盼 pàn ❶ hope, yearn, or long for; expect;～头 sth to hope for or look forward to; good prospect /～望 eagerly await; hope for; look forward to /～复〈套〉await your reply eagerly. ❷ look;～顾 look left and right

叛 pàn betray; revolt; rebel;～变 betray (one's country, etc); turn traitor; defect /～卖 betray; be treacherous; sell out /～逃 defect; desert /～徒 traitor; rebel

叛国 pànguó betray one's country; commit treason;～罪 (high) treason

叛乱 pànluàn rebellion; insurrection; revolt;～分子 rebel; insurgent

叛逆 pànnì ❶ rebel; revolt;～行为 act of rebellion ❷ rebel; 封建礼教的～ a rebel against feudal ethics

畔 pàn ❶ side; bank; 桥～ beside a bridge ❷ border (of a field); edge

襻 pàn ❶ loop for fastening a button; 纽～儿 button loop ❷ sth shaped like a button loop or used for a similar purpose; 鞋～儿 shoe strap

pāng

乒 pāng 〈象声〉bang;～地一声摔碎了 smash with a bang

滂 pāng 〈书〉(of water) overflowing; rushing;～湃的浪涛 roaring waves

滂沱 pāngtuó　torrential;～大雨 torrential rain /涕泣～。Tears streamed down one's cheeks.

膀 pāng swell; 腿～了 have got swollen legs　*see also* bǎng; páng

páng

彷(徬) páng

彷徨 pánghuáng hesitate; waver;～观

望 hesitate and choose to wait and see

庞（龐） páng ❶ tall and large; huge：～然大物 huge monster; colossus ❷ numerous and disordered：～杂 numerous and jumbled ❸ face; 脸～ face

庞大 pángdà huge; immense; enormous：规模～ immense or extensive scale / 机构～ unwieldy organization

旁 páng ❶ side：～白 (in a play) aside / ～门侧道 side door / ～证 circumstantial or collateral evidence / 马路～边 (by the) road side ❷ else; other：～落 (of power) slip into other people's hands / ～人 other people; sb else ❸ lateral radical of a Chinese character (eg 亻, 氵, etc)

旁观 pángguān look on; be an onlooker：～者清 the spectator is often a better judge of the game (than the player); the onlooker sees the game best

旁敲侧击 pángqiāo-cèjī beat about the bush; make oblique references; speak or write in a roundabout way

旁若无人 pángruòwúrén act as if there were no one else present — be self-assured or arrogant

旁听 pángtīng attend as a visitor or auditor; audit：～生 auditor / ～席 visitors' seats; public gallery

旁系 pángxì collateral line：～血亲 collateral relative by blood

旁征博引 pángzhēng-bóyǐn quote copiously from a great variety of sources; be well documented (with copious quotations, etc)

膀 páng see also bǎng; pāng

膀胱 pángguāng (urinary) bladder

磅 páng see also bàng

磅礴 pángbó ❶ boundless; majestic：气势～ of great momentum; powerful and majestic ❷ fill; permeate：热情～ be full of enthusiasm

螃 páng

螃蟹 pángxiè crab

pàng

胖 pàng fat; stout; plump：～子 fat person; fatty / ～墩儿〈口〉chubby child / ～乎乎 plump; fleshy /～头鱼 (popular term for 鳙) variegated carp; bighead

pāo

抛 pāo ❶ throw; hurl; toss：～撒 throw about; scatter / ～掷〈书〉throw; cast; abandon ❷ leave behind; cast aside; abandon ❸ expose; show：～光（机）burnish; polish; buff / ～头露面〈贬〉appear in public; seek the limelight ❹ also "抛售" sell (goods, shares, etc) in big quantities; dump; unload

抛锚 pāomáo ❶ (of a ship) drop or cast anchor; (of a vehicle) break down ❷〈方〉(of a project, etc) discontinue; be suspended

抛弃 pāoqì abandon; desert; discard

抛物线 pāowùxiàn 〈数〉parabola

抛砖引玉 pāozhuānyǐnyù 〈谦〉offer sth (an ideas, a work, etc) commonplace to elicit sth valuable: (of idea, work, etc) serve as a modest spur to induce sth better：我先说几句算作～。Let me say a few words to set the ball rolling.

泡 pāo ❶ sth puffy and soft：眼～ upper eyelid ❷ spongy; puffy and soft ❸〈口〉〈量〉used of excrement and urine：拉一～屎 take a shit
see also pào

páo

刨 páo ❶ dig; excavate：～根儿问底儿〈口〉get to the root of a mat-

ter ❷〈口〉exclude；not count；minus；
～除 deduct；minus / ～分儿（in exam）
subtract marks

see also bào

咆 páo〈书〉(of a beast) howl；
roar：～哮 (of a beast) roar；(of
a human being) roar with fury；(of torrents) thunder away

狍（麅） páo (usu 狍子)〈动物〉roe (deer)

庖 páo〈书〉❶ kitchen ❷
chef；cook

庖代 páodài *also* "代庖"〈书〉act in
sb's place；do what is sb else's job

庖丁解牛 páodīngjiěniú　work methodically and expertly（like a butcher
cutting up an ox carcass）

炮 páo〈书〉bake；roast　*see also*
bāo；pào

炮制 páozhì ❶〈中医〉prepare（herbal
medicine）by roasting，baking，etc；de-
coct ❷〈贬〉concoct；invent；cook up

袍 páo *also* "袍子" robe；gown；
皮～ fur coat

pǎo

跑 pǎo ❶ run；race；gallop：～表
also "马表"〈体〉stopwatch / ～
步 run；jog；march at the double / ～
车 racing bike or car / ～道（for a
plane）runway；tarmac；〈体〉track / ～
鞋 running or track shoes ❷ run away；
leak；(of a liquid) evaporate：～调 (of
singing) go out of tune / ～气 (of a
tyre，etc) leaky；flat / ～题 stray from
the subject；digress from the point ❸
run or go about (doing sth)；busy oneself (with sth)：～外 travel around handling business for a shop，etc；work as
a travelling agent / ～账 go round collecting money owed / ～江湖 wander
about making a living (as an acrobat,
fortune-teller，etc) / ～买卖 go from
place to place buying or selling goods；

work as a commercial traveller / ～～
颠颠 bustle about；be always on the
go / ～冤枉路 do legwork for nothing

跑龙套 pǎolóngtào　〈戏〉〈喻〉play a
walk-on role；be a utility man

跑腿儿 pǎotuǐr　〈口〉run errands；
fetch and carry；do legwork；～的 er-
rand-boy

pào

泡 pào ❶ bubble：气～ air bubbles /
～～糖 bubblegum；chewing gum
❷ sth shaped like a bubble：脚上起～
get blisters on one's feet ❸ steep；
soak：～菜 pickled vegetables；pickles /
～茶 make or steep tea / ～澡 soak
one's body in bath water；take a soaking bath ❹ dawdle；loiter：～妞 dally
with women (esp prostitutes)；woman-
ize / ～病号 sham illness；malinger /
整天～在电子游戏里 play video games
all day

see also pāo

泡蘑菇 pàomógu ❶ use delaying tac-
tics；go slow；dawdle：干活～ dawdle
at work ❷ plague；pester

泡沫 pàomò　foam；froth；bubble：～
塑料 foam plastic / ～经济 bubble
economy

泡汤 pàotāng　〈方〉come to nothing；
fall through

泡影 pàoyǐng　〈喻〉bubble；illusion：化
为～ burst like a bubble；fizzle out
completely

炮（砲） pào ❶（big）gun；
cannon；artillery（piece）：
～兵 artillery；artilleryman / ～弹
shell / ～轰 bombard；shell / ～火 artillery fire；gunfire / 当～灰 serve as
cannon fodder ❷ firecrackers：～仗
also "鞭炮" firecrackers ❸ load of ex-
plosive：点～ set off an explosion or
blast

see also bāo；páo

疱（皰） pào blister；bleb；~疹〈医〉bleb；herpes

pēi

呸 pēi 〈叹〉(indicating contempt or censure) bah；pooh；pah

胚 pēi 〈生物〉embryo；~芽〈植〉bud；sprout

胚胎 pēitāi 〈生物〉〈喻〉embryo；~移植 embryo transfer／处于~状态 be in embryo；be embryonic

péi

陪 péi ❶ accompany；keep (sb) company；~伴 accompany；keep (sb) company／~读 be a companion (to sb) in study／~嫁 dowry／~葬〈旧〉〈喻〉be buried with the dead；(of a dead person) be buried close to the grave of one's husband or overlord ❷ assist；help；~床 stay in a ward to look after a bedridden patient

陪衬 péichèn serve as a contrast or foil；set off

陪审 péishěn act or serve as an assessor (in China)；serve on a jury；~团 jury／~员 assessor；juror／~制 jury system

陪同 péitóng ❶ accompany (in an activity)；主要~人员 main members of sb's party ❷ tourist guide；地方~ (shortened as 地陪) local guide／全程~ (shortened as 全陪) guide for the entire tour

培 péi ❶ (usu 培土) bank up (with earth)；earth up ❷ cultivate；foster；train

培训 péixùn cultivate；train；~班 training class

培养 péiyǎng ❶〈生物〉culture；~基 culture medium ❷ foster；train；develop；边工作边~ train on the job

培育 péiyù cultivate；foster；breed；~新品种 breed new strains／~一代新人 rear a new generation

培植 péizhí ❶ plant；grow；cultivate；人工~ artificial cultivation ❷ foster；build up；~亲信 foster one's trusted followers；build up one's coterie

赔 péi ❶ compensate；pay for；refund；~付 pay in compensation／~款 (make) compensatory payment ❷ apologize；~笑 also 赔笑脸" smile placatingly or apologetically／~不是 apologize；offer one's apologies／~小心 try hard to placate；apologize in a humble way／~礼道歉 make a humble apology；offer formal apologies ❸ stand or incur a loss；lose；生意~了 lose money in business／~了夫人又折兵〈俗〉suffer a double loss instead of making a gain

赔本 péiběn sustain losses in business；~出售 sell at a loss／~买卖 bad deal；unprofitable business

赔偿 péicháng compensate；indemnify；pay for；战争~ war reparations or indemnity／~名誉损失 (pay an) indemnity for defamation

赔钱 péiqián ❶ sustain losses in business；~货 loss-making commodity；unprofitable product ❷ compensate for the loss or damage of property

赔罪 péizuì apologize (usu for having offended sb)；是我不对,我向你~。It is all my fault. Please accept my apology.

pèi

沛 pèi 〈书〉copious；abundant；~然雨降。It rained heavily.

佩（❷珮） pèi ❶ wear (at the waist, etc)；~剑〈体〉sabre ❷ pendant worn at the waist；玉~ jade pendant ❸ admire；~服 admire (sb for sth)

佩带 pèidài ❶ carry at the waist；~手枪 carry a pistol at one's waist ❷ wear:~式话筒 body mike

配 pèi ❶ (of people) join or match in marriage; (of animals) mate: ~偶 spouse / ~种 breeding ❷ blend; mix; prepare by blending, etc.: ~餐 prepare food according to given standards or needs; assorted food / ~料 prepare various materials (for making sth); trimmings (in cooking) / ~色 mix colours in the right proportion / ~药 make up a prescription ❸ distribute; apportion; assign: ~送 distribute; allocate / ~电〈电〉power distribution / ~助手 assign an assistant (to sb) ❹ fit; make up; replace: ~曲 set (words of a song) to music; compose music (for words of a song) / ~眼镜 have a pair of glasses made (for one's eyes) / ~钥匙 have a key made (to fit a lock) ❺ foil; set off; be ancillary to: ~殿 side hall (in a palace or temple) / ~戏 support a leading actor; play a supporting role / ~乐 provide background music; write a score (for a film, etc) ❻ match; deserve; be worthy of: ~不上 be unworthy of; not deserve / 裤子与上衣不~。The trousers and the jacket don't match.

配备 pèibèi ❶ provide; equip; fit out: ~技术力量 provide technical personnel (for) ❷ dispose (troops, etc); deploy: ~火力 dispose firepower

配对 pèiduì ❶ pair; match:这两只鞋不~儿。The two shoes aren't a pair. ❷ (of animals) mate

配额 pèi'é quota:移民~ immigration quota

配方 pèifāng ❶ make up or fill a prescription ❷ (dispensation or production) formula; recipe

配合 pèihé ❶ coordinate; cooperate; concert:整顿市容要各方面~行动。It takes concerted action from all sides to keep the city clean and tidy. ❷ (pèihe) match; go well together:这小

两口~得太理想了。The young couple are perfectly matched.

配件 pèijiàn fitting (of a machine, etc); replacement; spare part:汽车~ car parts

配角 pèijué supporting or minor role;唱~(喻)play a supporting role / 最佳女~奖 award for best supporting actress

配套 pèitào form a complete set:~产品 complete set of products; accessory product / ~措施 supporting or supplementary measure

配音 pèiyīn dub (a film, etc):~演员 dubbing actor or actress

配制 pèizhì ❶ compound; make up:~药丸 compound (medicinal) pills ❷ supplement; accompany:书内~了多幅精美插图。There are quite a few beautiful plates in the book.

配置 pèizhì dispose (troops, etc); deploy; allocate:资源~ allocation of resources / 电脑的~ PC package; PC accessories

pēn

喷 pēn gush; spray; sprinkle;~灌〈农〉sprinkling irrigation / ~泉 fountain / ~洒 spray; sprinkle / ~射 spray; spurt / ~头 also "莲蓬头" shower nozzle; sprinkler head / ~涌 (of liquid) gush; spout / ~雾器 sprayer; atomizer / 令人~饭 be tremely funny; make one split one's sides with laughter see also pèn

喷发 pēnfā (as of a volcano) erupt; explode:怒火~ explode in anger

喷气 pēnqì jet:~式飞机 jet (plane)

喷嚏 pēntì also "嚏喷" sneeze:打~ sneeze

pén

盆 pén ❶ basin; tub; pot: ~景 potted landscape; bonsai / ~栽

plant or grow in a flowerpot；〈农〉pot culture / ~~ 罐罐 pots and pans；all the household utensils ❷ sth like a basin：~ 腔〈生理〉pelvic cavity / ~ 地〈地〉basin

pèn

喷
喷　pèn　*see also* pēn

喷香　pènxiāng　richly fragrant；very delicious

pēng

抨
抨　pēng

抨击　pēngjī　attack；lash out at；criticize：~ 时弊 denounce current evil practices

怦
怦　pēng　〈象声〉(of the heart) pound；thump：~ 然心动 miss a beat (from excitement, etc)

砰
砰　pēng　〈象声〉thump；bang：~ 的一声关上门 bang the door shut

烹
烹　pēng　❶ cook；boil：~ 茶 make tea / ~ 调 *also* "烹饪" cooking；cuisine ❷ quick-fry in hot oil and stir in sauce

嘭
嘭　pēng　〈象声〉bang；thud：~ ~ 的敲门声 repeated banging at the door

péng

朋
朋　péng　❶ friend ❷〈书〉form a clique；gang up：~ 党 clique；faction / ~ 比为奸 gang up to do evil；collude with each other ❸ match；equal

朋克　péngkè　*also* "鹏克" punk

朋友　péngyou　❶ friend：交 ~ make friends (with sb) ❷ boyfriend or girlfriend：他俩正在交 ~。They are dating.

棚
棚　péng　❶ awning propped up with poles to keep off wind and

rain ❷ shed；shack：~ 户 slum or shanty dwellers

蓬
蓬　péng　❶ fluffy；dishevelled：~ 乱 (of hair or weeds) growing in disorder；untidy / ~ 松 fluffy；puffy / ~ 头垢面 with dishevelled hair and a grimy face；dirty and untidy ❷〈量〉(of flowers or grass) clump；tangle

蓬荜增辉　péngbìzēnghuī　*also* "蓬荜生辉"〈谦〉your gift lends lustre to my humble abode；my humble house is honoured by your presence

蓬勃　péngbó　prosperous；vigorous；flourishing：~ 兴起 flourish；forge ahead vigorously

硼
硼　péng　〈化〉boron (B)：~ 砂 borax / ~ 酸 boric acid

鹏
鹏　péng　roc, a huge legendary bird：~ 程万里 have a brilliant career

澎
澎　Péng　(short for 澎湖列岛) (called Pescadores in the West) Penghu Islands

澎湃　péngpài　surging (waves, etc)；〈喻〉vast and mighty：心潮 ~ feel an upsurge of emotion

篷
篷　péng　❶ covering or awning on a car, boat, etc ❷ sail (of a boat)：扯 ~ hoist the sails

膨
膨　péng　expand；swell：~ 化食品 dilated or inflated food

膨胀　péngzhàng　❶ expand；swell；dilate ❷ inflate：机构 ~、人浮于事 (of an institution) inflated and overstaffed

pěng

捧
捧　pěng　❶ hold or carry in both hands：~ 杯 (in a sports competition) win the cup；become a champion ❷〈量〉*used of what can be held in both hands*：一 ~ 花生 a double handful of groundnuts ❸ flatter；promote；boost：~ 杀 destroy (sb) by excessive flattery

捧场 pěngchǎng　support (an activity) by being present; boost (an actor, etc)

捧腹 pěngfù　split or burst one's sides with laughter: 令人~ set people roaring with laughter / ~大笑 be convulsed with laughter

pèng

碰(**挷**、**踫**)　pèng ❶ touch; knock; bump: ~杯 clink glasses; exchange toasts / ~撞 collide (with); strike (against); 〈喻〉provoke: ~一鼻子灰 get the cold shoulder; be snubbed ❷ meet; come across; run into: ~见 also "碰到" meet unexpectedly; run or bump into; chance upon / ~面 meet ❸ take (a chance); try: ~运气 try one's luck; take a chance

碰壁 pèngbì　run into a stone wall; be rebuffed; suffer a setback

碰钉子 pèngdīngzi　meet with a rebuff; be up against a brick wall: 碰了个软钉子 be politely but firmly turned down; receive an implicit rebuff

碰巧 pèngqiǎo　by chance or coincidence; accidentally

碰头 pèngtóu　meet (and discuss); put ones' heads together: ~会 brief meeting / 碰个头研究一下 meet for a discussion

pī

批 pī ❶ write instructions or comments; officially approve: ~复 reply to a request, etc (submitted by a subordinate) / ~条子 write out a note with instructions on it / ~阅文件 read over and comment on documents ❷ criticize; refute; rebuke: 挨~ be criticized ❸ wholesale ❹〈量〉batch; lot; group: 刚到的一~货 a new lot of goods

批驳 pībó ❶ reject (an opinion or a request from a subordinate) ❷ refute; criticize

批发 pīfā ❶ wholesale: ~商 wholesale dealer; wholesaler / ~价格 wholesale price ❷ authorize or approve the issue of (a document, etc)

批改 pīgǎi　correct; revise; go over: ~作业 correct students' papers

批量 pīliàng　(produce) in batches; 生产 batch-produce; serial-produce

批判 pīpàn　criticize; critique: ~地吸收 critically assimilate / ~的眼光 critical insight / ~现实主义 critical realism

批评 pīpíng ❶ criticism (involving both positive and negative aspects); critique: 文艺~ literary and art criticism ❷ criticize; censure

批示 pīshì　(write) comments or instructions (as on a memo submitted by a subordinate): 请领导~ ask for instructions from above

批语 pīyǔ ❶ comments on a piece of writing ❷ see "批示"

批注 pīzhù ❶ annotate and comment on; put notes and commentary to (a book, etc) ❷ notes and comments; marginalia

批准 pīzhǔn　ratify (a treaty, etc); approve (a plan, etc); sanction: ~书 instrument of ratification

纰 pī　(of cloth, thread, etc) ravel; come undone

纰漏 pīlòu　careless mistake; slip

坯 pī ❶ unfired earthen brick; adobe: 脱~ mould adobe blocks ❷ semi-finished product; base: 钢~ steel billet

坯子 pīzi ❶ semi-finished product; base; blank: 搪瓷的金属~ metal base for enamel ❷ makings; material: 踢足球的~ (have) the makings of a good soccer player

披 pī　drape or wear over one's shoulders; wrap around: ~风 cape; cloak / ~挂上阵 buckle on one's armour and go into battle; be armed to the teeth / ~红戴花 have red silk draped over one's shoulders and flowers pinned on one's breast (as a token of honour) ❷ open; unfold; break open:~览 also "披阅"〈书〉open and read (a book); peruse / ~荆斩棘 break through brambles and thorns; hew one's way through difficulties / ~头散发 with dishevelled hair; with hair hanging loose ❸ split open; crack:指甲~了 have one's nail broken

披肝沥胆 pīgān-lìdǎn　bare one's heart; unbosom oneself; be sincere and faithful

披肩 pījiān　❶ cape ❷ shawl ❸ wear one's hair over one's shoulders:~发 (w   r) shoulder-length hair

披露 pīlù　❶ publish; announce:~内幕 make public inside information ❷ reveal; show; disclose:~无遗 thoroughly disclose; lay bare

披靡 pīmǐ　❶ (of trees and grass, etc) cannot stand the force of wind ❷ collapse before a formidable enemy

披星戴月 pīxīng-dàiyuè　(travel) under the moon and stars; (work) from before dawn till after dark

砒 pī　❶ (old name for 砷) arsenic (As) ❷ also "砒霜" (white) arsenic

劈 pī　❶ split; cop; crack:~波斩浪 (of a ship) cleave through the waves / 〈喻〉surmount difficulties and forge ahead / ~成两半 split (sth) in two ❷ right against (one's face, etc):~头盖脸 also "劈头盖脸" right in the face; suddenly and fiercely ❸ 〈书〉(of lightning) strike ❹ also "尖" wedge see also pǐ

劈里啪啦 pīlipālā　also "噼啪啪啦"〈象声〉used of the sound of clapping, cracking, etc:~的鞭炮声 splutter of firecrackers / 竹子烧得 ~ 响。The bamboo cracked in the fire.

霹 pī

霹雳 pīlì　thunderbolt; thunderclap:~舞 break-dance; break-dancing

pí

皮 pí　❶ skin; cutis; peel:擦破~ scrape skin off / 西瓜~ watermelon rind / ~科〈医〉dermatological department; dermatology / ~试〈医〉skin test / ~包骨 skin and bones; bag of bones / ~下注射〈医〉subcutaneous or hypodermic injection ❷ leather; fur:~袄 fur coat or jacket / ~尺 tape (measure) / ~带 leather belt / ~革 leather; tanned hide / ~夹子 wallet; pocketbook; purse ❸ cover; wrapper; package:~重 tare (weight) ❹ surface:地~ ground ❺ thin, flat piece; sheet ❻ not crisp; tough; case-hardened:饼干~了。The biscuits are no longer crisp. / 他让你说~了。He's apathetic to your repetitive scolding. ❼ (of a child) naughty; mischievous ❽ rubber:~筋儿〈口〉rubber band

皮包 píbāo　leather handbag; briefcase; portfolio:~商 wildcat merchant; fly-by-nighter / ~公司 bubble company; fly-by-night company

皮蛋 pídàn　also "松花蛋" preserved duck egg

皮肤 pífū　skin; dermis:~白 fair or pale skin / ~病 skin disease

皮开肉绽 píkāi-ròuzhàn　with the skin torn and the flesh gaping open (after a beating or flogging)

皮毛 pímáo　❶ fur ❷ smattering; inkling:仅知 ~ have only a superficial knowledge (of sth)

皮肉 píròu　skin and flesh:~之苦 physical suffering or pain / ~生涯 make a living by selling one's body; be a prostitute

皮实 píshi　❶ (of people) sturdy;

tough ❷ (of things) durable; stout

皮笑肉不笑 píxiàoròubùxiào　〈俗〉
put on a false smile

皮鞋 píxié　leather shoes;擦～ polish
shoes / ～油 shoe polish

枇 pí

枇杷 pípá　〈植〉loquat

毗 pí

毗连 pílián　also "毗邻"〈书〉adjoin;
border on

疲 pí
❶ tired; weary; exhausted;
～急 tired out / 疲于
奔命 be kept constantly on the run; be
always on the go ❷ weaken; slump;畅
销不～ sell well on the market

疲乏 pífá　weary; tired;累得睁不开眼
too tired to keep one's eyes open

疲倦 píjuàn　tired; weary;不知～ be
tireless or indefatigable

疲劳 píláo　❶ tired; fatigued; weary;
～战术 gruelling tactic / 不顾～ despite the fatigue ❷〈生理〉〈理〉fatigue;
金属～ metal fatigue

疲软 píruǎn　❶ fatigued and weak;
weak and frail;浑身～ feel weak all
over ❷ weak; slumping; sluggish;
股市～ sluggish or bearish stock market

疲塌 píta　also "疲沓" slack; negligent;工作拖拉～ dilatory and lackadaisical in one's work

啤 pí

啤酒 píjiǔ　beer;生～ draught beer /
～厂 brewery / ～肚 beer belly

琵 pí

琵琶 pípá　pipa, plucked string instrument with a fretted fingerboard

脾 pí
also "脾脏" spleen

脾气 píqi　❶ temperament; disposition; temper;～好 be good-tempered;

have a good disposition ❷ bad temper;
～大 be hot-tempered

脾胃 píwèi　temperament; taste;不合
～ not fit one's temperament / ～相投
be kindred spirits

裨 pí
〈书〉assistant; secondary;～
将 adjutant general　see also bì

罴(羆) pí
〈动物〉brown bear

pǐ

匹(❸❹疋) pǐ
❶ be equal to;
be a match for; ri-
val;～配〈书〉match; mate; marry ❷
alone; single;～马单枪 single-handed;
all by oneself ❸〈量〉used of horses,
mules, etc.;一～马 a horse ❹〈量〉used
of bolts of silk or cloth;一～布 a bolt
of cloth

匹敌 pǐdí　be equal (to); match;
rival;无可～ matchless; peerless

匹夫 pǐfū　❶ ordinary or common
man;～有责. Everyone has the duty.
❷ (usu used in the early vernacular)
ignorant person;～之勇 reckless physical courage; fool-hardiness

仳 pǐ

仳离 pǐlí　〈书〉❶ (of husband and
wife) be separated ❷ divorce one's
spouse (esp wife)

否 pǐ
❶ bad; evil;～极泰来. Ex-
treme adversity marks the beginning of fortune. ❷ censure; condemn
see also fǒu

痞 pǐ
❶ also "痞块"〈中医〉lump
in the abdomen ❷ (usu 痞子)
ruffian; hooligan; riff-raff

劈 pǐ
❶ cut; split; divide;～账 divide a sum of money / ～成 deduct a percentage (from a sum) / ～柴
kindle; firewood ❷ see "擗" pǐ ❸
open one's legs or fingers (too) wide;
～〈体〉do the splits

see also pī

擗 pǐ break off (from the stem, etc); ~棒子 pick corn

癖 pǐ addiction; ~好 (favourite) hobby; fondness / ~性 natural inclination; propensity / 爱洁成 ~ make a fetish of cleanliness

pì

屁 pì ❶ wind (from bowels); fart; ~滚尿流 piss in one's pants (in terror); be frightened out of one's wits ❷ 〈粗〉damned rubbish; worthless stuff; ~话 shit; nonsense; rubbish / 你懂个~! A fat lot you know!

屁股 pìgu ❶ buttocks; bottom; ass; ~沉〈口〉simply love to sit and chat; (of a caller, etc) be apt to stay longer than one should ❷ (of animals) rump; haunch; hindquarters ❸ back of an object; end of a slender object; butt; 烟~ cigarette butt; fag end

睥 pì

睥睨 pìnì 〈书〉look sideways in an arrogant manner; consider every one and everything beneath one's notice

辟(闢) pì ❶ open up (territory, land, etc); reclaim; ~为旅游区 be opened up as a tourist attraction ❷ penetrating; incisive; refute; repudiate; ~谣 refute a rumour

see also bì

媲 pì be equal to; match; ~美 compare well with; rival

僻 pì ❶ out-of-the-way; secluded; ~静 secluded ❷ eccentric; odd ❸ rare; uncommon; ~典 unfamiliar allusion

譬 pì example; analogy; ~如 for example or instance; such as / ~喻 metaphor; simile; analogy

piān

片 piān (used of photo, record, etc) flat, thin piece; 画~儿 picture

see also piàn

片子 piānzi ❶ (roll of) film; movie; 拍部~ shoot or make a film ❷ (negative of a) radiograph; X-ray; 给胸部拍个~ have one's chest X-rayed ❸ gramophone record; disc

偏 piān ❶ inclined to one side; slanting; deviating; ~题 catch question; tricky question (in an exam) / ~远 remote and out-of-the-way / ~安一隅 (of a regime) be content to exercise control over part of the country ❷ partial; prejudiced; ~好 have a particular liking (for sth) / ~颇〈书〉unfair; biased / ~食 have a partiality for a particular kind of food / ~心 also "偏心眼儿" partiality or bias (for) / ~听~信 heed and trust only one side; be partial / ~重数量，忽略质量 stress quantity at the expense of quality ❸ supplementary; auxiliary; ~殿 side hall in a palace or temple ❹ also "偏偏"〈副〉showing perversity, stubbornness or ill luck; 我~不去。I just won't go. / ~不凑巧，他出门了。Unfortunately, he was out.

偏爱 piān'ài have partiality for; show favour to; ~小儿子 dote on the youngest son

偏差 piānchā deviation; error

偏方 piānfāng folk prescription (for a disease)

偏废 piānfèi do one thing to the neglect of another; emphasize one thing at the expense of another

偏激 piānjī go to extremes; be extreme; ~分子 extremist / ~情绪 extreme emotions

偏见 piānjiàn prejudice; bias; one-sided attitude

偏离 piānlí　deviate (from the right course); veer

偏旁 piānpáng　〈语言〉radical (of a character)

偏僻 piānpì　secluded; out-of-the-way

偏偏 piānpiān　〈副〉*see* "偏❹" ❷ *showing dissatisfaction or perplexity at limit of range or scope*: 为什么～是他? Why him, of all the people?

偏巧 piānqiǎo　❶ it so happens; as luck would have it ❷ fortunately ❷ against one's expectation; unluckily; unfortunately

偏袒 piāntǎn　be partial (to one side)

偏向 piānxiàng　❶ erroneous tendency; deviation ❷ tend towards (sth); favour (sb)

偏执 piānzhí　extreme; stubborn: ～狂 〈医〉paranoia

篇 piān　❶ (main section of a) piece of writing: 通～ throughout the piece (of writing, etc) / ～目 table of contents (of a book) / ～章 sections and chapters; writing ❷ 〈usu 篇子〉 printed sheet (of paper, etc) ❸〈量〉 *used of writing, paper, or publication*: 两～纸 two sheets of paper

篇幅 piānfu　❶ length (of a piece of writing): ～不长 not long ❷ space (of printed matter): ～有限 (owing to) limited space

翩 piān　〈书〉fly swiftly

翩翩 piānpiān　❶ *also* "翩跹" lightly (and gracefully): ～起舞 dance gracefully ❷〈书〉graceful; elegant: ～少年 elegant young man

pián

便 pián　*see also* biàn

便宜 piányi　❶ cheap: ～没好货。Cheap goods are not good. ❷ undeserved gain; undue advantage; windfall: 捡了个～ get a windfall / 占人家～ take advantage of sb ❸ let (sb) off lightly
see also biànyí

骈 pián

骈文 piánwén　ornate rhythmical prose characterized by parallelism; parallel prose

胼 pián

胼胝 piánzhī　callosity; callus; 胼手胝足的拓荒者 hard-working pioneer

蹁 pián

蹁跹 piánxiān　〈书〉whirl about (in dancing)

piàn

片 piàn　❶ flat, thin piece; slice; flake: 面包～ slices of bread / 剂〈药〉tablet ❷ motion picture; TV film: ～酬 payment for acting in a film or TV play / ～头 title and credits ❸ section of a place; sub-area; neighbourhood: ～儿警 neighbourhood police ❹ cut into slices; slice: ～羊肉片儿 slice mutton ❺ incomplete; partial; brief: ～言只语 a few isolated words / 杀得～甲不留 destroy (an army, etc) thoroughly; completely wipe out ❻〈量〉: a) *of things in the form of flat, thin pieces*: 两～药 two tablets b) *of land, water, etc*: 一～树林 a stretch of woods c) (used after 一) *of scenery, sound, feeling, etc*: 一～真心 be all sincerity
see also piān

片断 piànduàn　❶ *also* "片段" fragment; passage; extract ❷ scrappy; fragmentary; incomplete

片刻 piànkè　short while; instant; moment: ～之间 in an instant

片面 piànmiàn　unilateral; one-sided;

～性 one-sidedness / ～之词 one party's version (of sth)

骗 piàn ❶ deceive; cheat; fool; ～局 fraud; hoax / ～术 deceitful trick; ruse / ～子 impostor; swindler; fraud / 不～你。No kidding. ❷ gain by swindle; ～钱 get money by swindle; cheat or swindle sb of his money / ～税 (practise) tax fraud ❸ jump onto (a horse, etc); lift one leg over the saddle (of a bicycle, etc)

骗取 piànqǔ obtain by cheating; trick sb out of sth; wangle; ～选票 wangle votes / ～信任 worm one's way into sb's confidence; gain sb's confidence by sham loyalty

piāo

剽 piāo ❶ rob; loot; plunder; ～窃 also "剽袭" plagiarize; lift; copy ❷ nimble; swift; ～悍 quick and fierce; intrepid

漂 piāo float; stay afloat; drift; ～移 drift (about) / ～洋过海 cross the seas; go abroad to a faraway country　*see also* piǎo; piào

漂泊 piāobó also "飘泊" lead a wandering life; drift aimlessly; ～海外 wander overseas

漂浮 piāofú ❶ float; 朝雾在群山间～。Morning mists floated about the hills. ❷ float or hover before the eyes; hover in one's mind ❸ (of style of work) superficial; shallow

漂流 piāoliú ❶ be driven by the current; drift about; 随波～ drift along with the waves ❷ *see* "漂泊" ❸ 〈体〉rafting

缥 piāo

缥缈 piāomiǎo dimly discernible; misty; elusive

飘(飄) piāo flutter; float (in the air); waft; ～带 streamer; ribbon / ～舞 flutter or dance in the air / ～扬 flutter; fly / ～～欲仙 feel as if one were in paradise; be intoxicated with happiness

飘荡 piāodàng ❶ (in the air or on water) wave; flutter; flutter ❷〈喻〉drift about; wander

飘忽 piāohū ❶ (of wind, clouds, etc) float in the air; move quickly ❷ float about; ～不定 (of sth) float about; (of one's whereabouts) uncertain

飘零 piāolíng ❶ (of flowers, leaves, etc) wither and fall; whirl about and scatter ❷〈喻〉wander alone; drift about homeless

飘飘然 piāopiāorán ❶ feel as if treading on air or as if one were drunk ❷ drunk with self-satisfaction; smug; complacent; ～忘乎所以 be swollen-headed

飘洒 piāosǎ ❶ (of fine snow, rain, etc) fall gently; swirl down ❷ (piāosa) (of a person) elegant; (of calligraphy) graceful; free and easy

飘摇 piāoyáo (of smoke, etc) sway or toss about in the wind;〈喻〉totter

飘逸 piāoyì ❶ graceful; elegant; 才气～ overflow with talent ❷ also "飘散" float and scatter; drift apart; disperse

piáo

嫖 piáo frequent brothels; go whoring; ～妓 visit prostitutes; go whoring / ～客 brothel frequenter; (prostitute's) client

瓢 piáo gourd ladle; wooden dipper; ～泼大雨 pouring or torrential rain; downpour

piǎo

漂 piǎo ❶ bleach; ～白粉 bleaching powder ❷ (usu 漂洗) rinse　*see also* piāo; piào

瞟 piǎo　look sidelong at；glance sideways at

piào

票 piào ❶ printed slip as certificate；ticket：～价 price of a ticket；admission (fee) fee / ～贩子 tout；scalper ❷ (usu 票子) banknote；bill；零～儿 notes of small denominations；small change ❸ person held for ransom；hostage ❹ amateur performance (of Beijing opera，etc)：～友 amateur performer

票房 piàofáng　booking office；box office (of a theatre，etc)：～价值 box-office value / 很有～号召力 be a box-office success

票据 piàojù ❶ bill；note：流通～ negotiable instruments or papers ❷ voucher；receipt：凭～提货 delivery of cargo against voucher

票面 piàomiàn　face，par，or nominal value；denomination：～数额 nominal amount / 大～伪钞 fake banknotes of large denomination / 低于～价值 below par

漂 piào　see also piāo；piǎo

漂亮 piàoliang ❶ handsome；beautiful；good-looking：打扮得漂漂亮亮 be beautifully or smartly dressed ❷ remarkable；brilliant；wonderful：说一口～的英语 speak flawless English ❸ fine (-sounding)；high-sounding：～的大道理 high-flown rhetoric

piē

撇 piē ❶ put aside；discard；leave behind：～弃 discard；throw up ❷ skim：～沫子 skim off the scum
see also piě

瞥 piē　shoot a glance at；catch a glimpse of：～见 catch sight of

piě

苤 piě

苤蓝 piělan〈植〉kohlrabi

撇 piě ❶ throw；fling；cast：～在脑后 cast (sth) out of one's mind ❷ left-falling stroke (in a character) ❸〈量〉两～胡子 two strokes of moustache
see also piē

pīn

拼(拚) pīn ❶ put or piece together：～接 join；piece together / ～盘 assorted cold dish / ～板玩具 jigsaw puzzle ❷ risk all (in doing sth)；fight tooth and nail；exert one's utmost：～抢 fight or wrest (for a ball) / ～杀 fight fiercely or desperately (in battle) / ～体力 spend one's strength recklessly / 有一劲儿 have resolution and perseverance；be full of drive

拼搏 pīnbó　take (a challenge) head-on；go all out in one's struggle；stand up to hardship：～精神 spirit of going all out to win success

拼凑 pīncòu　piece，knock or throw together

拼命 pīnmìng ❶ risk one's life；fight tooth and nail ❷ exert one's utmost；strain every nerve；desperately：～奔跑 run like crazy

拼死 pīnsǐ　risk one's life；fight desperately：～抵抗 put up a stubborn resistance

拼写 pīnxiě　spell：～练习 spelling exercise

拼音 pīnyīn ❶ spell；phoneticize：～文字 alphabetic or phonetic language ❷ pinyin，phonetic system for transcribing Chinese characters

姘 pīn have illicit relations with：~
夫 (illicit) lover (of a woman) /
~妇 mistress；paramour / ~居 cohabit (usu between a married person and
someone who is not his or her spouse) /
~头 mistress；lover

pín

贫 pín ❶ poor；needy；impover-
ished：~富悬殊 extremes of poverty and wealth；wide gap between the
rich and the poor ❷ inadequate；defi-
cient；poor：~油 poor in oil deposits；
oil-poor ❸〈方〉garrulous；loquacious；
~嘴 be loquacious or flippant

贫乏 pínfá ❶ poor；destitute ❷ defi-
cient；scanty；poor：知识~ deficient in
knowledge

贫寒 pínhán poor；poverty-stricken：
出身~ from an impoverished family

贫瘠 pínjí (of land, etc) poor；bar-
ren；infertile

贫贱 pínjiàn poor and lowly；in straitened and humble circumstances：~之交
those who befriend one when one is
poor and unknown / ~不能移 remain
firm in one's principle despite poverty；
poverty cannot alter one's resolve

贫苦 pínkǔ poor；destitute：生活~
live in poverty and misery

贫困 pínkùn poor；impoverished；in
straitened circumstances：~线 poverty
line；subsistence level / ~地区 poverty-stricken area

贫民 pínmín poor people；pauper：城
市~ urban poor；city pauper / ~窟
slum；ghetto

贫穷 pínqióng poor；needy；impover-
ished：过着~的生活 live in poverty

贫血 pínxuè〈医〉anaemia：这孩子~。
The child is anaemic.

频 pín ❶ frequently；repeatedly：~
~ time and again；repeatedly /
~仍〈书〉frequent；repeated ❷〈理〉

frequency：~道 (frequency) channel

频繁 pínfán frequent；incessant：交往
~ have frequent contacts / 车辆往来
~。Traffic is heavy.

频率 pínlǜ ❶〈理〉frequency：高~
high frequency ❷ frequency (of words,
etc)；incidence (of accidents, etc)

嫔（嬪） pín〈书〉concubine of
an emperor：~妃 imper-
ial concubines

pǐn

品 pǐn ❶ article；product；goods：
~名 name of an article ❷ grade；
class；kind：~级 grade (of a product,
etc) ❸ character；quality：~貌 character and looks / ~学兼优 excellent both
in character and in scholarship ❹ sam-
ple；savour：~茶 sip tea and taste its
flavour / ~尝 taste (food, etc)；sa-
vour；sample

品德 pǐndé moral character：~高尚 of
(high) moral integrity

品格 pǐngé ❶ one's character and
morals ❷ quality and style (of artistic
or literary works)：~低下 of low taste

品牌 pǐnpái brand (name)；make：~
形象 brand image / ~意识 brand-name
awareness

品评 pǐnpíng judge；appraise；com-
ment on：~优劣 assess the quality (of
sth)

品头论足 pǐntóu-lùnzú　*see*"评头论
足"píngtóu-lùnzú

品位 pǐnwèi ❶ grade；quality：低~矿石
low-grade ore / ~不高 (of literary
work, etc) lowly；vulgar

品味 pǐnwèi ❶ taste；savour；sam-
ple：细细~诗中的含义 ponder on the
meaning of a poem ❷ quality；flavour；
taste

品行 pǐnxíng conduct；behaviour：~
不端 of loose morals

品性 pǐnxìng moral character：~恶劣

morally corrupt

品质 pǐnzhì ❶（moral）character; quality ❷ quality（of commodities, etc）:～与样品不符的情况 quality variation from sample

品种 pǐnzhǒng ❶（of crops or domestic animals）breed; strain; variety ❷ variety; assortment:～单调 lacking in variety

pìn

牝 pìn （of some birds and animals）female:～鸡司晨。〈旧〉The hen cackles in the morning — it is the wife who wears the trousers in the family.

聘 pìn ❶ engage; employ; appoint:～期 term of engagement or appointment /～任 engage; appoint to a position /～书 letter of appointment /～约 contract of employment ❷ betroth:～金 betrothal money（from the bridegroom's to the bride's family）/～礼 betrothal gift

聘请 pìnqǐng engage; employ; hire:～律师 engage a lawyer

聘用 pìnyòng engage; employ; recruit:～制 also "聘任制" system of appointment /～条件 conditions for employment

pīng

乒 pīng ❶〈象声〉used for short high-ringing sound:～的一声暖水瓶爆炸了。The thermos bottle burst with a bang. ❷（short for 乒乓球）table tennis; ping-pong:～坛新星 rising star in table tennis

乒乓 pīngpāng ❶〈象声〉used for rattling or clattering sound:乒乒乓乓 with a great rattle or clatter ❷ also "乒乓球" table tennis; ping-pong:～拍 table tennis bat

píng

平 píng ❶ flat; level; smooth:～滑（level and）smooth /～坦（of land, etc）level; even; smooth /～胸〈生理〉flat chest /～板车 flat-bed tricycle /～顶房 flat-roofed house /～底鞋 low-heeled shoes /～铺直叙 tell in a simple, straightforward way; speak or write in a flat style ❷ be on the same level; equal;〈体〉draw:～辈（people of the）same generation /～列 place side by side; place on a par /～起～坐 sit as equals at the same table; be of equal status ❸ just; fair; impartial:～议 judge or assess fairly ❹（make）calm; peaceful; stable:～民愤 assuage popular indignation /～抑物价 stabilize the prices ❺ put down; quell; suppress:～叛 quell a revolt; suppress a rebellion ❻ common; ordinary; usual:～民 commoner; common people /～年〈天文〉non-leap or common year;〈农〉average year（in crop yield, etc）/～信 ordinary or surface mail /～装本 paperback（book）; paperbound edition ❼ also "平声"〈语言〉level tone　see also "四声" sìshēng

平安 píng'ān safe and sound; without mishap; well:～抵达 arrive safe and sound /～无事. All is well.

平白 píngbái also "平白无故" for no reason whatever; for no apparent reason; gratuitously

平步青云 píngbùqīngyún suddenly rise to fame; have a meteoric rise

平常 píngcháng ❶ ordinary; usual; common; 手艺～（of）average craftsmanship /～人 ordinary people; man in the street ❷ also "平日" generally; ordinarily; as a rule:和～一样 as usual

平川 píngchuān level land; flat, open country; plain:一马～ a large stretch of flatland

平淡 píngdàn dull; insipid; prosaic；~无奇 commonplace; trite; prosaic / ~无味 dull as ditchwater

平等 píngděng equal；~协商 consultation on an equal basis

平地 píngdì ❶ level the land or ground；〈农〉rake the soil smooth ❷ level or flat ground；~风波 sudden storm on a calm sea; unexpected turn of events; unforeseen trouble

平定 píngdìng ❶ calm; settled；~情绪 calm down ❷ also "平靖" suppress; quell; put down (a riot, etc)

平凡 píngfán ordinary; common：不~的业绩 extraordinary or outstanding achievements

平反 píngfǎn redress (a mishandled case); reverse an unjust verdict; rehabilitate (sb)

平方 píngfāng ❶〈数〉square；~公里 square kilometre ❷ also "平米"; "平方米" square metre

平房 píngfáng single-storey house; one-storey building

平分 píngfēn divide equally; divide share and share alike; go halves；~秋色 (of two parties) share (power, glory, etc) equally; share on a fifty-fifty basis

平复 píngfù ❶ calm down; subside; be pacified；~如初 regain one's calm ❷ (of a wound, etc) be cured or healed; recover

平和 pínghé ❶ gentle; mild; moderate：药性~ mild medicine ❷ serene; tranquil：心境渐渐~下来 gradually recover one's composure; calm down little by little

平衡 pínghéng balance; equilibrium；~膳食 balanced diet / 心态~ mental equilibrium / 发展不~ uneven development

平缓 pínghuǎn ❶ (of terrain) level; (of slopes) gentle; (of currents) slow and steady ❷ (of feeling, voice, etc)

mild; placid; gentle：语气~ speak unhurriedly

平价 píngjià ❶ stabilized price；~米 rice sold at government-controlled price; low-price rice ❷ reasonable price；~商店 low-price or bargain shop

平静 píngjìng calm; quiet; peaceful：生活~ lead a quiet life / 打乱内心的~ upset one's mental composure

平局 píngjú also "平手" draw; tie：打成~ equalize the score / 打成~ end in a draw or tie; tie (with sb)

平均 píngjūn ❶ average; mean：~数〈数〉average; mean value / 按人口~ per capita ❷ equally; share and share alike：~发展 equal or even development / ~分配 share out equally / ~主义 equalitarianism; egalitarianism

平面 píngmiàn plane；~图 plan; plane figure / 几何〈数〉plane geometry

平平 píngpíng average; middling; mediocre；技术~ (of) middling skill / 她这次表现~。Her performance this time was just so-so.

平生 píngshēng all one's life; one's whole life; ever；~的志愿 lifelong aspiration / ~从不抽烟 never smoke in one's life

平时 píngshí ❶ also "平素" ordinarily; usually；~很少来往 seldom call on each other ❷ (in) peacetime; uneventful period

平台 píngtái platform：计算机~ computer platform

平添 píngtiān increase naturally; add to：孩子给家庭~了许多乐趣。Children add greatly to the joys of families.

平头 píngtóu ❶ closely cropped hair; crew-cut：理个~ have a crew-cut ❷ common; ordinary (people)；~百姓 common people

平稳 píngwěn steady; normal; stable；~过渡 (make a) smooth transition

平息 píngxī ❶ calm, quiet, or die

down; subside; ~怒火 calm down; appease (sb's) anger ❷ put down (a rebellion, etc); quell; suppress; ~争端 settle a dispute

平心而论 píngxīn'érlùn　in all fairness; to be fair; to do (sb) justice

平心静气 píngxīn-jìngqì　calmly; dispassionately

平行 píngxíng　❶〈数〉parallel; ~线 parallel lines ❷ of equal rank; on an equal footing; parallel ❸ simultaneous; parallel; ~不悖的利益 parallel interests

平易 píngyì　❶ unassuming; amiable; ~近人 modest and easy of access; modest and unassuming ❷ (of a piece of writing) easy; plain; 语言~ (in) simple or plain language

平庸 píngyōng　mediocre; commonplace; ~之辈 mediocre people; mediocrities

平原 píngyuán　plain; flatland

平整 píngzhěng　❶ level; ~土地 level the land ❷ neat; smooth; level; 这块地很~。 The field is level and smooth.

评 píng　❶ comment on; criticize; ~介 review (a new book, etc) / ~述 appraise through comments; review / ~语 comments; remarks / ~注 annotate (often with textual commentary); notes and commentary / ~传 critical biography ❷ judge; assess; appraise; ~级 grade (staff, etc) through assessment; grade (products, etc) according to quality / ~奖 give awards after panel discussion / ~卷 (short for 评阅试卷) mark exam or test papers / ~审 comment on and examine; evaluate / ~委 (member of a) review committee / ~功摆好 evaluate and praise (sb's) merits; enumerate (sb's) merits in flattering terms / 群众~议 popular appraisal

评比 píngbǐ　appraise through comparison; compare and evaluate

评点 píngdiǎn　❶ edit (classical works, etc) with comments; annotate ❷ comment on and advise

评定 píngdìng　pass judgement on; evaluate and determine; decide through assessment; ~名次 decide on the relative places (of contestants, products, etc)

评分 píngfēn　give a mark; mark or grade (homework, performance, etc)

评估 pínggū　evaluate and estimate (assets, etc)

评价 píngjià　pass judgement on; appraise; evaluate; 高度~ have a very high opinion of sth

评理 pínglǐ　give a verdict on a dispute; pass judgement on a matter; 这个理很难评。 It's difficult to pass judgement on this matter.

评论 pínglùn　❶ discuss; comment; ~家 critic; reviewer / ~员 commentator / ~好坏 comment on (sb's) merits and demerits ❷ review (a book, etc); commentary (on current affairs, etc)

评判 píngpàn　pass judgement on; judge; decide; ~得失 judge the advantages and disadvantages

评书 píngshū　(traditional) storytelling; ~艺人 professional storyteller

评头论足 píngtóu-lùnzú　also "品头论足" ❶ make frivolous remarks about a woman's looks ❷ carp at; nitpick

评选 píngxuǎn　choose through public appraisal (by ballot); 观众~的最佳影片 best movie chosen by audience

坪 píng　level ground; flat land; 停机~ aircraft park; tarmac

苹(蘋) píng

苹果 píngguǒ　apple; ~酱 apple jam / ~园 apple orchard

凭(憑) píng　❶ lean on or against; ~栏沉思 lean on a railing lost in thought ❷ rely or depend on：～手艺吃饭 make a living by one's craftsmanship ❸ evidence；proof；guarantee：～据 evidence；proof ❹ by；based on；according to：～良心说 in all conscience；to be fair／～单据报销 refund by invoices／你～什么不让我进？What is your ground for not admitting me？ ❺〈连〉no matter（what，how，etc）：～他是谁，也得遵守交通规则。Everybody has to abide by the traffic rules，no matter who he is.

凭吊 píngdiào visit（a historical site，etc）and meditate on the past

凭借 píngjiè take advantage of；rely or depend on：～权势胡作非为 commit outrages by abusing one's power and influence

凭空 píngkōng out of thin air；without foundation；groundless：～捏造 make something out of nothing；concoct；fabricate

凭眺 píngtiào gaze（from a high place）into the distance；enjoy a distant view：～大海 gaze into the distant sea

凭信 píngxìn trust；believe：不足～ not trustworthy；unreliable

凭证 píngzhèng certificate；voucher：纳税～ tax payment receipt

枰 píng〈书〉chessboard；checkerboard：推～认输 concede defeat in a chess game

屏 píng ❶ screen：～风 screen（for blocking draught or view）／电视～幕 TV screen；telescreen ❷（usu 屏condensed）〈set of〉hanging scrolls of painting or calligraphy ❸ shield（sb or sth）；screen：天然～障 natural protective screen

see also bǐng

瓶 píng bottle；jar；flask：～装啤酒 bottled beer／三～汽水 three bottles of soda-water

瓶颈 píngjǐng ❶ neck of a bottle；bottleneck ❷〈喻〉bottleneck：制约经济发展的～ bottleneck in economic de-

velopment

萍 píng duckweed：～踪〈书〉whereabouts（of a wanderer）

萍水相逢 píngshuǐxiāngféng （of strangers）meet by chance like patches of drifting duckweed

pō

坡 pō slope：上～ go up a slope；go uphill／一度～ slope；degree of incline／～跟鞋 wedge heels

泊 pō lake（often used in place names）*see also* bó

泼（潑） pō ❶ sprinkle；splash；spill：～冷水 pour or throw cold water on；discourage／～脏水 sling mud at；slander ❷ rude and unreasonable；shrewish：～皮 hooligan；hoodlum／～妇骂街 like a shrew shouting abuse in the street

泼辣 pōlà ❶ rude and unreasonable；shrewish：～女人 shrew；termagant ❷ pungent and forceful；bold and vigorous：工作～ bold and decisive in one's work

颇 pō〈书〉❶ inclined to one side；oblique；partial ❷ quite；rather；considerably：～为感动 be quite moved

pó

婆 pó ❶ old woman ❷ woman in a certain occupation：巫～ witch；sorceress ❸ husband's mother；mother-in-law

婆家 pójia husband's family：找～ find a husband（for one's daughter，etc）

婆婆 pópo ❶ husband's mother；mother-in-law；〈喻〉leader or leading body：～太多，难办事。It's hard to get anything done when you have too many bosses. ❷〈方〉grandmother

婆婆妈妈 pópo-māmā ❶ act slowly

like an old woman:你快一点吧,别这么~的了。Hurry up! Don't dawdle any more. ❷ sentimental; mawkish; maudlin

婆娑 pósuō　whirling; dancing:~起舞 start dancing

pǒ

叵 pǒ

叵测 pǒcè　〈贬〉unfathomable; unpredictable

筶 pǒ

筶箩 pǒluo　shallow (usu round) basket made of wicker or bamboo strips

pò

迫(廹) pò
❶ compel; force; press:~使 force; compel / ~不得已 be compelled (to do sth); have no choice (but to do sth); (do sth) against one's will / ~于形势 be compelled by the exigencies of the situation ❷ urgent; critical; pressing:~不及待 be too impatient to wait; be unable to hold oneself back; itch (to do sth) ❸ approach; go toward or near:~近 approach; get close; draw near / ~在眉睫 extremely urgent; imminent

see also pǎi

迫害 pòhài　persecute:受~者 victim of persecution / 被~致死 be harassed to death

迫降 pòjiàng　(make a) forced or crash landing

迫切 pòqiè　urgent; pressing; imperative:~愿望 fervent wish / ~的需要 crying need

破 pò
❶ broken; torn; worn-out;:~旧 old and shabby; dilapidated / ~罐~摔 act recklessly and irresponsibly when in adversity or

despair; write oneself off as hopeless and behave wantonly / 手上~了个口儿 have a cut on one's hand ❷ break; damage; split:~晓 daybreak; dawn / ~冰船 icebreaker / ~浪前进 cleave or ride the waves ❸ break (a banknote) into small change ❹ break; surpass:~世界记录 break a world record ❺ defeat; capture (a city, etc); break through:大~敌军 rout the enemy thoroughly ❻ spend; expend:~财 suffer unexpected loss of money / ~工夫 take pains; require plenty of efforts ❼ reveal the truth; lay bare; show up:~案 solve or crack a (criminal) case / ~解 break (a code); decode; solve ❽ 〈贬〉lousy; wretched; damned:~地方 lousy or damned place / ~嗓子 wretched voice

破败 pòbài　❶ ruined; dilapidated; decrepit ❷ deteriorate; decline:家道~ (with) declining family fortune

破产 pòchǎn　❶ bankruptcy; insolvency:宣告~ (of a company, etc) declare bankruptcy; go into bankruptcy ❷ (plan) come to naught; fall through

破除 pòchú　do away with; get rid of; eradicate:~迷信,解放思想 do away with blind faith and emancipate the mind

破费 pòfèi　spend (money or time):不好意思让您~。It wouldn't be right to put you to expense.

破釜沉舟 pòfǔ-chénzhōu　cut off all means of retreat to show one's determination to press ahead; burn one's boats or bridges

破格 pògé　break a rule or convention; make an exception:~提拔 break a rule to promote sb

破坏 pòhuài　❶ destroy; undermine; sabotage:~性 destructiveness / ~分子 saboteur ❷ violate (an agreement, etc); break; go against:~纪律 break or violate discipline

破获 pòhuò uncover (a criminal gang, etc); crack (a case)

破镜重圆 pòjìngchóngyuán (usu of a couple) put together the wreckage of a married life; retie a marriage knot after a separation; achieve reunion and reconciliation after a rupture

破口大骂 pòkǒudàmà let loose a torrent of filthy abuse

破烂 pòlàn ❶ tattered; ragged; worn-out;～货 worthless stuff; rubbish;〈粗〉whore ❷〈口〉junk; scrap; waste;收～儿 collect waste

破例 pòlì break a rule; make an exception;～喝了一杯 drink a glass of wine as an exception

破裂 pòliè burst; split; break;感情～ become estranged / 水管～。A water pipe burst. / 谈判～。The negotiation broke down.

破落 pòluò decline (in wealth and position);家景～ live in straitened circumstances

破门 pòmén ❶ burst or force the door open;～而入 break into a house ❷〈体〉(of soccer, etc) score a goal

破灭 pòmiè be shattered; melt into thin air; evaporate;～的希望 dashed hope

破伤风 pòshāngfēng 〈医〉tetanus

破碎 pòsuì ❶ broken; in pieces or tatters;～的心 broken heart ❷ smash to pieces; shatter; crush;～机 crusher; breaker

破损 pòsǔn damaged; broken; 如有～,包退包换。The goods can be returned or exchanged if damaged.

破涕为笑 pòtìwéixiào smile through tears; smile away one's tears

破天荒 pòtiānhuāng occur for the first time; be unheard-of or unprecedented

破土 pòtǔ ❶ break ground;～动工 break ground on a construction project /～仪式 ground-breaking ceremony ❷

start spring ploughing ❸ (of a seedling) break through the soil

破相 pòxiàng (of facial features) be marred by a scar, etc; be disfigured

破译 pòyì decode (an intercepted message); decipher;～敌军密码 break an enemy code

破绽 pòzhàn flaw; loophole; weak point;看出～ discover sb's Achilles' heel; see through the game / 露出～ give away the show; let the cat out of the bag /～百出 full of flaws or loopholes

破折号 pòzhéhào 〈语言〉dash (—)

魄

魄 pò ❶ soul ❷ vigour; energy; spirit:～力 daring and resolution; boldness; drive

pōu

剖

剖 pōu ❶ cut or rip open ❷ analyse; examine:～白 explain or vindicate oneself /～明 analyse clearly /～视 dissect and observe; analyse

剖腹 pōufù cut open one's belly:～产〈医〉Caesarean (birth) /～自杀 (Japanese) (commit) hara-kiri

剖面 pōumiàn also "断面" section; profile:横～ cross section

剖析 pōuxī analyse; dissect:～细密 make a minute and in-depth analysis

póu

抔

抔 póu 〈书〉hold with cupped hands:一～土 a handful of earth

pū

扑(撲)

扑 pū ❶ throw oneself on; pounce on; attack:～鼻 (of a strong smell, etc) assail the nostrils /～向匪巢 (of police, etc) pounce on a bandits' den /～出好几个球 pull off quite a few saves /～一心～在工作上 throw oneself heart and soul into one's work; devote oneself to one's job ❷ pat; flap; plop: ~去衣服上的尘土 pat the dirt from one's clothes; dust dirt off one's clothes ❸ 〈方〉bend over: ~在机器上查看毛病 bend over a machine looking for defects

扑哧 pūchī　*also* "噗嗤" 〈象声〉*sound of laughter, gushing water or air*: ~一笑 give a snigger / ~一声撒了气了(of a ball, etc) go soft with a hiss

扑打 pūdǎ　❶ swat (flies, etc) ❷ (pūda) beat; pat: ~身上的雪花 beat the snow off one's clothes

扑救 pūjiù　put out; fight (a fire, etc)

扑克 pūkè　playing cards: 打~ play cards

扑空 pūkōng　❶ pounce but miss ❷ fail to find what one looks for; come away empty-handed: 我上次去他家扑了个空。He was out the last time I went to see him.

扑灭 pūmiè　stamp or put out; eradicate: ~蝗虫 exterminate or wipe out locusts / ~森林大火 put out a forest fire

扑朔迷离 pūshuòmílí　bewildering; confusing; complicated

扑簌 pūsù　(of tears) trickle or course down

扑腾 pūteng　❶ (pūtēng) 〈象声〉thump; thud: ~掉下 drop or fall with a thud ❷ beat the water with one's feet when swimming ❸ move up and down; flop; throb: 吓得心里直~。One's heart thumps with fear. ❹ 〈方〉wangle; wheel and deal: 挺能~ be adept at wangling; be quite a wheeler-dealer ❺ spend lavishly; squander

扑通 pūtōng　〈象声〉flop; splash: ~跳下水 jump into the water with a splash

铺 pū　spread; lay; pave: ~轨 lay a railway track / ~床 make the bed / ~设电缆 lay a cable / 工程已全面~开。The project is in full swing.
see also pù

铺陈 pūchén　*also* "铺叙" narrate in detail; describe at length; elaborate

铺垫 pūdiàn　❶ bedding ❷ foil; set off: 为戏的高潮作~ set off the climax of a play

铺盖 pūgai　bedding; bedclothes: ~卷儿 bedroll; bedding or luggage roll / 打~走人 pack and go

铺路 pūlù　pave a road; 〈喻〉pave the way (for sth): ~石 people who sacrifice themselves for the benefit of others

铺天盖地 pūtiān-gàidì　blanket the earth and eclipse the sky: 暴雨~而来。The storm came and seemed to block out the sky.

铺张 pūzhāng　extravagant; ostentatious: ~浪费 extravagance and waste

噗 pū　〈象声〉puff: ~的一声吹灭了蜡烛 blow out the candle with one puff

潽 pū　(as of a liquid) boil over

pú

仆(僕) pú　servant: ~从 footman; flunkey / ~人 (domestic) servant

匍 pú

匍匐 púfú　❶ crawl; creep: ~而行 crawl on all fours; inch one's way forward ❷ lie prostrate; (of a plant) trail; creep: ~在地 lie prostrate on the ground / ~植物 creeper

菩 pú

菩萨 púsà　〈宗教〉Bodhisattva; Buddha; 〈喻〉Buddha-like person: ~心肠 with the heart of a Buddha; kind-hearted

葡 pú

葡萄 pútáo　grape: ~干 raisin / ~酒 (grape) wine; port / ~糖 grape sugar; glucose / ~藤 grapevine / ~柚

脯 grapefruit / ～园 vineyard；grapery

脯 pú chest；breast：鸡～儿 chicken breast　*see also* fǔ

蒲 pú 〈植〉❶ cattail；reed mace；club grass：～扇 cattail leaf fan ❷ calamus；sweet flag

蒲公英 púgōngyīng 〈植〉dandelion

璞 pú uncut jade：～玉浑金 uncut jade and unrefined gold — unadorned beauty；unsophisticated nobility

pǔ

朴(樸) pǔ simple；plain；honest：～质 simple and unaffected；natural；unsophisticated

朴实 pǔshí ❶ simple and plain：陈设～ simply furnished ❷ sincere；honest：为人～ sincere and honest ❸ solid and unpretentious；matter-of-fact：～无华 simple and unaffected

朴素 pǔsù ❶ simple；plain；frugal：～大方 simple and in good taste ❷ spontaneous；undeveloped：～的感情 spontaneous sentiment

圃 pǔ plot of land for growing plants；garden

浦 pǔ (used in place names) water's edge；river mouth

普 pǔ general；common；universal：～查 general investigation or survey / ～降喜雨 (there is) widespread timely rain /．～天同庆 nationwide or worldwide jubilation；universal rejoicing

普遍 pǔbiàn universal；general；common：～应用 universal application / ～感兴趣的问题 matter of common interest

普及 pǔjí ❶ extend far and wide；spread；popularize：～教育 make education universal / ～法律常识 (shortened as 普法) spread or disseminate general knowledge of law among the people / 这书已～全国。This book is used throughout the country. ❷ popular；common；universal：～本 popular edition / ～读物 popular books

普通 pǔtōng ordinary；common；average：～话 (formerly known as mandarin) *putonghua* — common speech of the Chinese language；standard Chinese pronunciation / ～人 ordinary person；man in the street / ～邮票 postage stamp

普选 pǔxuǎn general election：～权 universal suffrage

谱 pǔ ❶ chronology；record；register：～系 pedigree；family tree ❷ music (score)；(chess) manual：打～ study chess manuals / 识～ read music scores ❸ set to music；compose：～写 compose (music) / 给一首诗～曲 set a poem to music ❹ sth to count on；assurance；confidence：心里有～儿 know what is what；be assured

蹼 pǔ web (of the feet of ducks, frogs, etc)：～趾 webbed toe

pù

铺(舖) pù ❶ (usu 铺子) shop；store：肉～ butcher's (shop)；butchery / ～面 shop front ❷ plank bed；板～ plank board / ～位 bunk or berth (on a ship, etc)；bed (in a hospital or hotel)　*see also* pū

瀑 pù (usu 瀑布) waterfall；cataract；cascade

曝 pù 〈书〉expose to the sun：～露 expose to the open air / ～晒 (of the sun) shine upon；scorch　*see also* bào

P

Q

qī

七 qī ❶ seven; ~巧板 seven-piece puzzle; tangram / ~言诗 (classical) poem with seven characters to a line / ~品芝麻官 grade-seven lowly official ❷ *also* "七七"; "断七" "seven sevens" — an old custom requiring a memorial ceremony to be held for the deceased every seven days after his or her death until the seventh ceremony is over on the 49th day

七…八… qī…bā… *used in conjunction with verbs or nouns to indicate multiplicity or disorder*: 七零八落 scattered here and there; in great confusion; in disarray / 七拼八凑 knock together / 七上八下 be on tenterhooks; be on pins and needles / 七手八脚 with many people taking part or pitching in; with everybody lending a hand / 七嘴八舌 with many people speaking all at once; with everybody talking at the same time

七窍 qīqiào seven apertures in the human head, i.e. the eyes, ears, nostrils and mouth; ~流血 bleeding from every orifice / ~生烟 infuriated; mad with rage

七情六欲 qīqíng-liùyù various human emotions and desires

七十二行 qīshí'èrháng all sorts of trades; in every conceivable line of work; ~，行行出状元。One can chalk up outstanding achievements in every profession or trade.

七夕 qīxī seventh evening of the seventh moon of the lunar calendar (when the Cowherd 牛郎 and the Weaver Maid 织女 meet every year in Heaven)

七月 qīyuè ❶ July ❷ seventh month of the lunar year; seventh moon

沏 qī infuse; ~茶 make tea

妻 qī wife; ~室〈书〉wife / ~小 wife and children / ~子 wife (and children) / ~管严〈谑〉(as a near homophone of 气管炎) with wife in tight control; hen-pecked / ~儿老小 one's parents, wife and children / ~离子散 breaking up of a family, with the wife and children drifting apart

柒 qī seven, used for the numeral 七 on cheques, etc to avoid mistakes or alterations

栖(棲) qī ❶ *also* "栖息"; "栖宿" (of birds) perch; rest ❷ dwell; live; stay; ~居 (of animals) dwell; inhabit / ~身 stay; sojourn; reside

凄(❸ 悽) qī ❶ chilly; freezing; cold; ~寒 *also* "凄冷" chilly; desolate and cold ❷ bleak and desolate; dreary; ~寂 desolate and still; dreary and lonely ❸ sad; wretched; melancholy; ~惨 wretched; horrible; dreadful / ~楚〈书〉grieved; sad; sorrowful / ~厉 (of sound) mournful and shrill / ~切 sad and plaintive; melancholy / ~然〈书〉sorrowful; sad; mournful

凄风苦雨 qīfēng-kǔyǔ　chilly wind and unrelenting rain — foul weather; wretched circumstances; sad plight

凄凉 qīliáng ❶ bleak; desolate:晚景～ spend the evening of one's life in great misery ❷ lonely; dismal; miserable:琴声～ melancholy notes from the zither

凄清 qīqīng ❶ chill; chilly:月色～。 There was a chilly touch about the moonlight. ❷ see "凄凉❷"

凄婉 qīwǎn ❶ sad; mournful; doleful:神情～ (with) a doleful expression on the face ❷ (of sound) sad and moving; plaintive

萋 qī

萋萋 qīqī　(of grass) lush and luxuriant

戚 qī ❶ relative; kin ❷ sorrow; grief:神态～然 wear a woeful expression

期 qī ❶ schedule; appoint (a time):～满 expire; end / 不～而遇 meet by chance; run into (sb) ❷ period of time; term; stage:～刊 periodical / ～考 (end-of-) term examination / 春节～间 during the Spring Festival / 两～培训班 two terms of a training course ❸ await (sb by appointment); expect; hope:～冀〈书〉 expect; hope / ～盼 look forward to; expect; await

期待 qīdài　expect; await; anticipate:不辜负父母的～ live up to the expectations of one's parents

期货 qīhuò　〈经〉futures:～大豆 soybean futures / ～市场 (shortened as 期市) futures market / ～交易所 futures exchange

期求 qīqiú　hope to get; want; desire:无所～ have nothing to desire

期望 qīwàng　hope; expect; look forward to:～值 expectations; aspirations

期限 qīxiàn　allotted or set time; deadline

欺 qī ❶ cheat; dupe; deceive:～哄 deceive by lying; hoodwink / ～瞒 dupe; hoodwink; pull the wool over sb's eyes / ～诈 deceive; cheat; swindle / ～人之谈 deceitful words; deceptive talk ❷ bully; intimidate; take advantage of:～凌 bully; insult; humiliate / ～侮 behave rudely towards; bully; insult / ～软怕硬 bully the weak and fear the strong

欺负 qīfu ❶ act like a bully towards weaker people; bully:你这不是～人吗？What a bully you are! ❷ take advantage of (sb's ignorance, weaknesses, etc); cheat

欺行霸市 qīháng-bàshì　bully others in the same trade and monopolize the market; bully others for control of the market

欺骗 qīpiàn　deceive; cheat; dupe:～性 duplicity

欺生 qīshēng　bully or cheat strangers; be inhospitable to strangers; (of horses, etc) be refractory to strangers

欺世盗名 qīshì-dàomíng　gain fame by dishonest means; win popularity by deception

欺压 qīyā　bully and oppress; ride roughshod over; tyrannize

喊 qī

喊哩喀喳 qīlikāchā　(of speech) directly and succinctly; (of action) decisively and effectively

喊喊喳喳 qīqī-chāchā　〈象声〉chatter or jabber away; rattle or babble on

漆 qī　lacquer; paint; varnish:～布 varnished cloth / ～雕 carved lacquer / ～黑 pitch-dark; pitch-black

蹊 qī　see also xī

蹊跷 qīqiāo　odd; mysterious; suspicious:内中定有～。There must be something wrong with it.

qí

齐(齊)

qí ❶ neat; even; in order:~整 neat; well-arranged / ~步走 (军) quick march; (as a command) Quick-time, march! / ~刷刷 neat; uniform ❷ be of or reach the same level:~名 enjoy equal renown; be equally famous / 河水~腰深。The river is waist-deep. ❸ same; together; in unison:心不~ not of the same mind / ~唱 (乐) sing in unison / ~奏 (乐) play in unison; unison / ~声叫好 applaud in chorus ❹ all (ready); completely:~备 all ready

齐全 qíquán complete; ready:商品~ have a whole array of commodities in stock / 设备~ have all necessary equipment

齐头并进 qítóubìngjìn advance in parallel; undertake tasks at the same time

齐心 qíxīn be of one mind; have a common goal; act in concert:~协力 work as one; act in concert

其

qí ❶ he; she; it; they:听~自然 let matters take their own course; let sb go his or her own way ❷ that; those; such:~后 after that; later on; afterwards / ~间 during; in the course of; in the interval / ~乐无穷 infinite delight or joy ❸ used as a functional word:大上~当 walk straight into a trap; play right into sb's hands ❹ 〈书〉〈助〉indicating conjecture or retort:欲加之罪,~无辞乎? He who is bent on condemning sb can always trump up a charge. ❺ 〈书〉〈助〉indicating an order or instruction:尔~无忘乃父之志! Always bear your father's wish in mind! ❻ used as a suffix for an adverbial:极~困难 extremely difficult

其次 qícì ❶ next; then ❷ second; secondary

其貌不扬 qímàobùyáng unprepossessing to look at; of undistinguished appearance

其实 qíshí in reality; actually; as a matter of fact:说是花园,~是果园。A garden in name, it is actually an orchard.

其他 qítā also "其它" other (than); else:~人 other people; others

其余 qíyú the rest or remainder; the others

其中 qízhōng among (which, them, etc); in (which, it, etc):~蹊跷,一言难尽。It's hard to explain the tricks involved in a word.

奇

qí ❶ strange; unusual; extraordinary:~才 outstanding talent; (person of) genius / ~功 outstanding service; extraordinary exploit / ~巧 (of workmanship, etc) of unusual ingenuity / ~谈 bizarre tale; absurd argument / ~效 (of medicine) extraordinary efficacy / ~闻逸事 strange stories and anecdotes ❷ unexpected; surprising:~兵 troops moving swiftly and making a surprise attack / ~袭 (make a) surprise attack or raid ❸ wonder; be surprised or astonished:~观 marvellous spectacle; marvel / ~妙 wonderful; marvelous / ~想 fantastic idea; extraordinary thought
see also jī

奇耻大辱 qíchǐ-dàrǔ great shame and humiliation; deep disgrace

奇怪 qíguài ❶ strange; odd; eccentric:奇形怪状 of grotesque shapes and appearances; fantastic in form ❷ unexpected and hard to understand; incomprehensible:这没有什么好~的。There is nothing to be surprised at.

奇货可居 qíhuòkějū rare commodity worth hoarding (for a better price); anything regarded as an unusual advantage or possession

奇迹 qíjì　miracle; wonder; marvel;创造～ work wonders / 一般地康复 recover miraculously

奇葩 qípā　exotic, enchanting flower;文坛～ outstanding work in the literary world

奇缺 qíquē　be extremely short (of sth); be scarce

奇特 qítè　unusual; singular;构思～ingenious conception

奇异 qíyì　❶ queer; strange; bizarre;奇花异草 exotic flowers and rare herbs / 奇装异服 exotic costume; bizarre dress; outlandish attire or outfit ❷ curious; astounded:显露出～的神色 look curious

奇遇 qíyù　happy or lucky encounter; fortuitous meeting; adventure

歧 qí　also "岐" ❶ fork; branch;～路 branch; forked road / ～途 wrong path ❷ divergent; varied; different:～义 different meanings; polysemy; ambiguity / ～视 discriminate against

祈 qí　❶ pray:～祷 pray; say one's prayers / ～雨 pray for rain ❷ request; entreat:～盼 earnestly hope; expect / ～求 plead for; earnestly hope / ～望 hope; wish / ～使句 〈语言〉imperative sentence

耆 qí　over sixty years of age:～老〈书〉man of advanced age; respected old man / ～宿 esteemed old people (of a community)

颀 qí　〈书〉tall:～长 tall; of high stature

脐(臍) qí　❶〈生理〉navel; umbilicus:～带 umbilical cord ❷ abdomen of a crab

畦 qí　rectangular pieces of land in a field surrounded by ridges:～灌〈农〉plot-by-plot irrigation

崎 qí

崎岖 qíqū　rugged; rough:～不平 rough and uneven; 〈喻〉full of twists and turns

骐 qí　〈书〉black horse:～骥 thoroughbred horse

骑 qí　❶ ride; sit (on a horse, etc):～车 ride a bicycle; cycle / ～射 horsemanship and archery / ～手 also "骑师" (professional) rider; jockey / ～术 horsemanship; equestrian skill ❷ straddle:～缝印 (put a) seal across (two sheets of) a document or voucher ❸ horse or other animal one rides ❹〈usu 骑兵〉cavalry; cavalryman; horseman

骑虎难下 qíhǔnánxià　ride a tiger and find it hard to dismount; find oneself on the horns of a dilemma; have no way to back down

骑墙 qíqiáng　sit on the fence:～派 fence-sitter; weathercock

骑士 qíshì　knight; cavalier:～称号 knighthood

琪 qí　〈书〉fine jade

琦 qí　〈书〉❶ fine jade ❷ out of the ordinary run; uncommon:～行 fine virtues; noble character

棋 qí　❶ chess or any board game:～局 situation confronting the players in a chess game; chessboard / ～盘 chessboard; chequerboard; draughtboard / ～谱 chess manual / ～圣 (honorary title) grand master of chess or weiqi / ～手 (skilful) chess or weiqi player / ～艺 technique of playing chess or weiqi; skill in chess or weiqi / ～子 chessman; piece / ～逢对手 also "棋逢敌手" meet one's match in a game of chess; diamond cut diamond ❷ piece; chessman:落～无悔。No retracting any move (in chess) once you've made it.

祺 qí　〈书〉good luck; blessing:敬颂近～。(used at the end of a letter) Wishing you the best of luck.

旗(❶ 旂) qí ❶ flag; banner; pennant；～杆 flag-pole; flag post / ～舰 flagship / ～手 standard-bearer; pioneer / ～语 flag signal; semaphore / 旗开得胜 triumph in the first battle; be off to a flying start ❷ "Eight Banners" (八旗), military-administrative setup of the Manchu before and during the Qing Dynasty：～人 bannerman; Manchu ❸ banner, an administrative division of county level in Inner Mongolia：敖汉～ Aohan Banner

旗鼓相当 qígǔxiāngdāng　be equal in strength; be well matched

旗号 qíhào　〈贬〉banner; pretext; disguise：打着别人的～ under sb else's banner

旗袍 qípáo　*qipao* — close-fitting woman's dress as worn by the Manchu nationality; *cheongsam*

旗帜 qízhì ❶ banner; flag; colours：～鲜明 fly unambiguous colours — be clear-cut in one's stand ❷ example; model

鳍 qí　〈动物〉fin：背～ dorsal fin / 尾～ caudal fin

麒 qí

麒麟 qílín　(shortened as 麟) kylin, an auspicious legendary animal with a horn and scales all over; (Chinese) unicorn

qǐ

乞 qǐ　beg (for alms, etc); seek (charity); supplicate：～丐 beggar / ～怜 beg for pity or mercy / ～求 beg for; entreat; implore / ～讨 beg; go begging

岂(豈) qǐ　〈书〉*used to introduce a rhetorical question*：～止 not just; not merely / ～有此理 outrageous; shameless / ～能无

动于衷？How could one remain aloof and indifferent?

岂但 qǐdàn　not only：～你我不知道，恐怕连他自己也不清楚。Not only are you and I in the dark; he himself may not be at all clear about it.

岂敢 qǐgǎn ❶ how dare：我～单独行动！How dare I go it alone? ❷ (often duplicated) 〈套〉you flatter me; I don't deserve such praise

企 qǐ　stand on tiptoe; look forward to; expect：～待 look forward to; expect / ～盼 expect; hope for / ～求 seek; yearn; hanker after (sth) / ～望 look forward to; hope for; aspire / 难以～及 can hardly expect to attain (sth); (of sth) be beyond (one's) reach

企鹅 qǐ'é　〈动物〉penguin

企划 qǐhuà　plan; scheme; contrive；～人员 planning staff

企图 qǐtú　〈贬〉attempt; try; strive

企业 qǐyè　enterprise; business；～家 entrepreneur; enterpriser / ～管理 (shortened as 企管) business management / ～文化 corporate culture

杞 qǐ

杞人忧天 Qǐrényōutiān　*also* "杞忧" like the man of Qi who feared that the sky might fall — haunted by imaginary fears

启(啟、啓) qǐ ❶ open：～齿 open one's mouth; mention / ～封 break or remove the seal; open an envelope ❷ enlighten; inspire; awaken：～迪 〈书〉enlighten; inspire; shed light on ❸ start; begin; initiate：～程 set out or off; start on a journey / ～航 set sail; weigh anchor / ～用 start using; employ ❹ 〈书〉state; declare; inform：～奏 (of officials) present one's views or clarify issues to the emperor ❺ 〈书〉letter; note：小～ brief note

启动 qǐdòng　start (a machine, etc); turn or switch on;〈经〉start up;~资金 start-up fund; seed money / ~消费需求 stimulate consumer demand

启发 qǐfā　arouse; inspire; enlighten;~式 elicitation or heuristic method (of teaching) / ~诱导 enlighten and persuade

启蒙 qǐméng　❶ impart elementary knowledge to beginners; initiate;~教师 teacher who initiates a student into a specific field of study; initiator / ~书籍 children's primers ❷ enlighten;~运动 Enlightenment

启示 qǐshì　enlightenment; inspiration; revelation;~人思索问题 provide much food for thought; set people thinking

启事 qǐshì　notice; announcement

起 qǐ　❶ get or stand up; rise; move;~床 get up; get out of bed / ~立 stand up; rise to one's feet / ~夜 get up in the night to urinate / ~早贪黑 start work early and knock off late; work from dawn to dusk ❷ rise; go up;~降 (of airplanes) take off and land / ~落 go up and come down; rise and fall / 面~了。The dough has risen. ❸ grow; get; appear;~泡 blister; bubble; foam / ~痱子 get prickly heat ❹ remove; draw; extract;~获 recover (stolen goods or contraband) from a hoarding place /~锚 also "起碇"weigh anchor; set sail ❺ begin; launch; occur;~兵 also "起师"launch an expedition; start an armed revolt / ~程 start a journey; set out / ~航 begin a voyage or flight; take off; set sail / ~疑 begin to suspect; become suspicious / ~运 start shipment / ~跑线 starting line (for a race); scratch line (for a relay race) / ~风了。The wind rose. ❻ draft; make; work out;~稿 also "起草稿" make or work out a draft; draft

❼ set or put up; build;~道墙 build a wall ❽ obtain; secure; buy;~护照 obtain a passport ❾ start or begin from; 从头做~ start from the very beginning; start all over again ❿〈量〉a) case; instance; 两~恶性刑事案 two cases of vicious crime b) batch; group; party; 分三~上车 board the train in three batches ⓫ (qǐ) *used after a verb to indicate* a) an upward movement; 举~孩子 lift up the baby / 引~注意 attract or draw attention b) (often preceded by 不 or 得) *whether it is within or beyond one's power to do sth*; 惹不~ cannot afford to offend (sb) / 经得~考验 be able to stand a test

起步 qǐbù　leave; start to move; start doing sth;~较晚 start later than one should

起草 qǐcǎo　draft; draw up;~人 draftsman / ~委员会 drafting committee

起初 qǐchū　*also* "起先";"起头" at the outset or beginning; at first; originally

起点 qǐdiǎn　❶ starting point;~站 starting station ❷〈体〉starting line or mark of a race

起动 qǐdòng　❶ start (a machine, etc); set in motion ❷ start the implementation or execution (of a plan, project, etc)

起飞 qǐfēi　❶ (of aircraft) take off ❷ (of an enterprise or economy) be off to a flying start; take off; 经济~ economic takeoff

起伏 qǐfú　❶ rise and fall; undulate;~的群山 mountains upon mountains ❷ (of emotions, etc) rise and fall; surge and subside; fluctuate

起哄 qǐhòng　❶ gather together to create a disturbance; 大伙儿别跟着~。You people should stay away from the row. ❷ (of a crowd of people) make fun of; play a joke on

起家 qǐjiā　build up; grow and prosper; make one's fortune, name, etc

起见 qǐjiàn　(used together with 为) for the purpose of; in order to: 为慎重 ~，你还是去做一次检查吧。To make doubly sure, you'd better go and have a checkup.

起劲 qǐjìn　vigorously; energetically; zealously: 谈得 ~ talk enthusiastically

起居 qǐjū　daily life: ~室 living-room; sitting-room / ~有恒 observe a regular schedule in daily life; keep regular hours

起来 qǐlái　❶ stand or sit up; rise ❷ get out of bed; get up ❸ rise; arise; be aroused: ~造反 rise in rebellion ❹ (qǐlái) *used after a verb to indicate* **a)** *upward movement*: 把头抬 ~ raise one's head **b)** *commencement and continuation of an action or a state*: 欢呼 ~ start to cheer **c)** *completion of an action or achievement of a goal*: 把意见集中 ~ pool ideas **d)** *an impression, estimate or idea*: 说 ~ 容易, 做 ~ 难。It's easier said than done.

起码 qǐmǎ　❶ minimum; basic; elementary: ~ 的条件 basic or minimum requirements ❷ at least

起色 qǐsè　signs of improvement: 未见 ~ show no (signs of) improvement

起身 qǐshēn　❶ set out; depart; leave ❷ get up; get out of bed ❸ stand up; rise

起誓 qǐshì　take an oath; swear; vow: 对天 ~ swear by God

起死回生 qǐsǐ-huíshēng　(of a doctor) bring life to the dying; raise from the dead; 〈喻〉turn a desperate situation round

起诉 qǐsù　〈法〉bring a suit or an action (against sb); sue; prosecute: ~ 人 suitor; prosecutor / ~ 书 indictment; bill of complaint

起眼儿 qǐyǎnr　(usu used in the nega-

tive) attractive; eye-catching: 不 ~ 的徒弟 run-of-the-mill apprentice

起义 qǐyì　❶ revolt; insurrection; uprising: ~ 军 insurrectionary army ❷ defect to the righteous side: ~ 投诚 revolt and cross over

起因 qǐyīn　cause; source; origin

起用 qǐyòng　❶ reinstate (an official who had been relieved of his duties) ❷ employ or promote: ~ 新人 promote new people to leading posts

起源 qǐyuán　originate; begin: 生命的 ~ origin of life / 知识 ~ 于实践。Knowledge stems from practice.

起重机 qǐzhòngjī　hoist; crane; derrick: 塔式 ~ tower crane

起子 qǐzi　❶ bottle opener ❷ 〈方〉screwdriver ❸ 〈方〉baking powder

绮 qǐ　❶ figured woven silk material; damask: ~ 罗 gorgeous silk fabrics ❷ beautiful; exquisite: ~ 丽 exquisite; beautiful; gorgeous

稽 qǐ　*see also* jī

稽首 qǐshǒu　kowtow

qì

气（氣） qì　❶ gas: ~ 体 gas / ~ 田 gas field ❷ air: ~ 泵 air pump / ~ 浪 blast (of an explosion) / ~ 流 air current or stream; airflow / ~ 泡 (air) bubble / ~ 枪 air gun / ~ 筒 *also* "打气筒" inflator; bicycle pump / ~ 温 air or atmospheric temperature ❸ breath: ~ 急 panting and exasperated; incoherent with rage / ~ 绝 stop breathing; die / ~ 喘吁吁 *also* "气咻咻" pant; gasp for breath ❹ weather; season ❺ smell; odour; scent ❻ mental state; spirit; drive: ~ 昂 spirited; dashing / ~ 贯长虹 lofty as the rainbow spanning the sky; full of noble aspirations ❼ airs; manners; bearing: 书呆子 ~ bookishness; pedantry ❽ anger; rage; infuriate: ～话 unguarded remark made in a fit of fury; angry words / ～恼 offended; angry; ～盛 apt to flare up; quick-tempered / ～冲人 be furious; fume with rage / ～死人 infuriating; exasperating ❾ insult; ridicule; bully ❿〈中医〉qi — vital energy; life force: ～虚 deficiency of vital energy ⓫〈中医〉certain symptoms of disease: 痰～ phlegm as symptom of disease

气喘 qìchuǎn ❶ also "哮喘"〈医〉asthma; be out of breath; breathe hard; pant: ～吁吁 huff and puff

气窗 qìchuāng transom (window); fanlight

气度 qìdù ❶ see "气量" ❷ appearance; bearing; demeanor: ～不凡 impressive-looking

气短 qìduǎn ❶ also "气促" breathe hard; be short of breath ❷ depressed; in low spirits: 屡受挫折而不～ be undaunted despite repeated setbacks

气氛 qìfēn atmosphere; air: 政治～ political climate

气愤 qìfèn indignant; enraged; furious

气概 qìgài noble quality or spirit; mettle; drive: 大无畏的～ dauntless mettle

气功 qìgōng qigong, a system of deep breathing exercises: ～疗法 qigong therapy; breathing technique therapy

气管炎 qìguǎnyán ❶〈医〉tracheitis ❷〈谑〉(as a near homophone of 妻管严) (as a near homophone of 妻管严) with one's wife in tight control; hen-pecked

气候 qìhòu ❶ climate ❷ progress; achievement: 成不了～ won't achieve anything; will get nowhere

气急败坏 qìjíbàihuài flustered and exasperated; flurried and furious; ～地跳起来 jump up in uncontrollable anger

气节 qìjié moral integrity or courage

气力 qìlì strength; energy; effort: 用尽～ exert oneself to the utmost; with all one's strength / ～不如从前 be less strong than one used to be

气量 qìliàng also "气度"; "器量" magnanimity; forbearance; tolerance: ～大 large-minded; generous / ～小 narrow-minded; petty

气闷 qìmèn ❶ upset; vexed ❷ stuffy; close: 屋里真～. It's so stuffy in the room.

气馁 qìněi be disheartened; lose heart: 失败了不～ keep one's chin up despite failure; refuse to take one's defeat lying down

气派 qìpài ❶ manner; style: 学者的～ manner of a scholar ❷ impressive; imposing; spirited: ～的大厦 imposing building

气魄 qìpò ❶ (of people) courage; daring; boldness of vision: 显示了领导者的～ demonstrate the sweep and determination of a leader ❷ see "气势"

气球 qìqiú balloon

气色 qìsè colour; complexion: ～很好 the very picture of health; in the pink / ～不大好 a bit off colour

气势 qìshì momentum; impetus; imposing manner or appearance: ～磅礴 full of power and grandeur / ～汹汹 truculent; overbearing; aggressive

气味 qìwèi ❶ smell; scent; flavour ❷〈贬〉odour; reek; taste: ～相投 two of a kind; like-minded; birds of a feather / 宣传～太浓 savour or smack too much of propaganda

气息 qìxī ❶ breath: ～均匀 breathe evenly / ～奄奄 be at one's last gasp; be breathing one's last ❷ scent; smell; tang: 时代～ ethos of the times

气象 qìxiàng ❶ meteorological condition or phenomenon; meteorology: ～台 meteorological observatory / ～预报 meteorological report; weather forecast ❷ atmosphere; scene: ～万千 with a myriad scenes; spectacular; majestic

气压 qìyā　atmospheric or barometric pressure: 低～ low pressure

气焰 qìyàn　〈贬〉arrogance; bluster: ～嚣张 swollen with arrogance; puffed with pride

气宇 qìyǔ　*also* "器字"〈书〉bearing; carriage; deportment: ～不凡 extraordinary carriage / ～ 轩昂 impressive bearing; dignified appearance

气质 qìzhì　❶ temperament; disposition; character: 生就了的直爽～ inborn frank temperament ❷ qualities; attributes; makings

气壮山河 qìzhuàngshānhé　majestic as high mountains and mighty rivers; full of power and grandeur; imbued with sublime heroism

讫 qì　❶ settled; accomplished; completed: 付～ paid ❷ end: 起～共三年 three years from beginning to end

迄 qì　❶ up to; till; until: ～今 up to now; to this day; so far ❷ (used before 未 or 无) so far; yet: 冲突～未停止。Hostilities have not ceased yet.

弃(棄) qì　throw away; abandon; forsake: ～ 儿 abandoned child; foundling; waifs and strays / ～世 depart this world; die; pass away / ～学 drop out of school / ～置 throw aside; cast away / ～暗投明 break away from the wrong side and come over to the right side; give up the unjust cause for the cause of progress

弃权 qìquán　❶ abstain from voting: ～票 abstention ❷〈体〉default; forfeit

汽 qì　❶ gas; vapour: ～灯 gas lamp ❷ (water) steam: ～船 steamboat; steamer / ～锤 steam hammer / ～笛 steam whistle; siren; hooter / ～艇 motorboat

汽车 qìchē　automobile; motor vehicle; (motor) car: ～库 garage / ～工业 auto industry / ～旅馆 motel / ～拉力赛 car rally

汽水 qìshuǐ　aerated or soda water: 橘子～ orangeade / 柠檬～ lemonade

汽油 qìyóu　petrol; gasoline; gas

泣 qì　❶〈书〉weep; sob: ～不成声 choke with sobs; cry silently ❷ tears: ～下如雨 shed tears like rain; tears stream down one's cheeks

契 qì　❶〈书〉carve; engrave; chisel: ～刻 carve; engrave / ～文 oracle bone writing ❷ agreement; contract; deed: ～据 *also* "契券" contract; (title) deed; receipt / ～约 contract; deed; charter ❸ agree or match in temperament, etc; be congenial

契合 qìhé　❶ agree; accord; correspond ❷ get along well; share the same interest; etc

契机 qìjī　(decisive) moment; turning point; pivot: 把握～ grasp a decisive moment or opportunity

砌 qì　❶ lay (bricks or stones) ❷ step: 石～ stone steps

葺 qì　〈书〉repair; fix; mend

碛 qì　❶ moraine: ～砾 gravel ❷ desert

器 qì　❶ instrument; implement; utensil: ～材 equipment; gear; material / ～件 part (of an apparatus or appliance); component / ～具 utensil; tool; appliance / ～皿 container (esp for use in the house); household utensil or ware / ～乐〈乐〉instrumental music ❷ organ: 消化～ digestive organ ❸ magnanimity; talent; ability: ～度 ability and broad-mindedness ❹ value; think highly of: ～重 think highly of (subordinates, etc); set great store by

器官 qìguān　organ; apparatus: ～捐赠 organ donation / ～移植 organ transplant

器量 qìliàng　*see* "气量" qìliàng

器械 qìxiè ❶ apparatus; appliance; instrument;体育～ sports apparatus ❷ weapon

器宇 qìyǔ　see "气宇" qìyǔ

憩（憩） qì　〈书〉rest:小～ take a short rest /～息 rest; relax

qiā

掐 qiā ❶（with finger and nail） pinch or nip; cut:～断 nip or cut off; sever /～算 count on one's fingers /～头去尾 break off both ends; cut what is unnecessary or unimportant; quote out of context ❷ clutch; grip:～死在摇篮里 stifle in the cradle; nip in the bud

qiá

扴 qiá clutch or grip with both hands

qiǎ

卡 qiǎ ❶〈口〉wedge; stick; get stuck;鱼刺～在喉咙里 have a fishbone stuck in one's throat ❷ clutch; grip;～脖子 seize by the throat /～得很紧 keep tight control (over sth) ❸ clip; clasp; fastener ❹ checkpost; post
see also kǎ

卡壳 qiǎké ❶〈军〉jamming of cartridge ❷ (of speech or action) get stuck; be held up; be unable to proceed

卡口 qiǎkǒu 〈电〉bayonet:～插座 bayonet plug or socket /～灯泡 bayonet-socket bulb

qià

洽 qià ❶ in harmony or agreement:～妥 reach an agreement ❷

consult; discuss; arrange:～购 arrange or negotiate a purchase /～谈 hold talks; negotiate

恰 qià ❶ suitable; fitting; appropriate:～当 suitable; appropriate; proper /～到好处 just right (for the occasion, etc) /～如其分 just right; proper; appropriate ❷ precisely; exactly:～好 exactly; just right /～～ just; precisely; exactly /～巧 by chance; as chance would have it /～似
also "恰如" be just like

qiān

千 qiān ❶ thousand; kilo-:～卡 *also* "大卡" kilocalorie (kcal; Cal) /～克 kilogramme (kg) /～米 metre (km) /～瓦（电）kilowatt (kw) /～儿八百〈口〉about a thousand; a thousand or so ❷ innumerable; enormous:～斤重担 load of tremendous weight /～虑一失（short for 智者千虑，必有一失）even the wise are not always free from error /～载难逢 *also* "千载一时" not likely to occur once in a thousand years; once in a blue moon

千…百… qiān…bǎi… a thousand and one; every possible; extremely:千疮百孔 riddled with gaping wounds; afflicted with all kinds of ills / 千锤百炼 (of people) steeled and tempered; (of writing, etc) highly finished / 千方百计 (try) in a thousand and one ways; by every possible means / 千姿百态 of all shapes and postures

千古 qiāngǔ ❶ through the ages; eternal:～奇冤 stupendous wrong that is unheard of throughout the ages /～罪人 man of eternal guilt; villain of all time ❷ *used in elegiac inscription for the deceased*:某某先生～。Eternal glory to Mr So-and-so!

千金 qiānjīn ❶ thousand pieces of gold; large amount of money:一诺 a promise is worth a thousand pieces of gold — a man's promise can always be counted on ❷〈敬〉daughter (other than one's own)

千钧一发 qiānjūnyīfà　hang by a hair; be in an extremely precarious situation

千里 qiānlǐ　thousand *li* — long distance: ～马 winged steed; person of great talent / ～眼 clairvoyant (person):〈口〉telescope / ～迢迢 thousands of *li* away; from afar / ～之行，始于足下〈谚〉a thousand-*li* journey begins with the first step; the highest eminence is to be gained step by step

千篇一律 qiānpiānyīlù　harp on the same old subject; follow the same pattern; be stereotyped or monotonous

千万 qiānwàn　❶ ten million; millions; countless ❷ (used in earnest exhortation) must; be sure to:～注意防火。Do take the greatest care to prevent fire.

千…万… qiān…wàn…　❶ many; countless; numerous：千变万化 constantly changing; be subject to a myriad changes / 千军万马 thousands upon thousands of horses and soldiers / 千丝万缕 innumerable links; countless ties / 千辛万苦 all kinds of hardships; untold hardships / 千言万语 innumerable words (of solicitude); a multitude of tender words ❷ *used for emphasis*：千呼万唤 be called again and again; be called and called / 千真万确 absolutely true / 千叮咛万嘱咐 exhort sb repeatedly

仟 qiān　(capital form for the numeral 千) thousand

阡 qiān　〈书〉footpath between fields, running north and south:～陌 crisscross footpaths between fields

扦 qiān　poker; pick:～子 slender pointed stick made of metal, bamboo, etc; sharp-pointed metal prod used to extract samples from sacks of grain, etc

迁(遷) qiān　❶ move; remove:～都 move the capital (to another place) / ～居 change one's dwelling place; take up residence elsewhere; move (house) / ～徙 move; migrate / ～移 move; migrate / ～户口 change one's residence registration ❷ change:～变 changes; vicissitudes

迁就 qiānjiù　accommodate (oneself to); humour

迁怒 qiānnù　vent one's anger (on an innocent person); take it out (on sb)

迁延 qiānyán　delay; postpone; defer

钎 qiān　drill rod or steel; borer:～子 rock or hammer drill

牵(牽) qiān　❶ lead (along); pull:～着鼻子走 lead by the nose / 一发而动全身 pull one hair and you move the whole body — a slight move in one part may affect the whole situation; a minor step may lead to major consequences ❷ involve; entangle:～涉 involve; concern; drag in / ～肠挂肚 be full of anxiety and worry; worry one's head off

牵扯 qiānchě　involve; embroil; implicate

牵动 qiāndòng　❶ influence; affect; set astir:～全局 affect the situation as a whole ❷ move; touch:～了许多人的心 strike a sympathetic chord in many people

牵挂 qiānguà　worry; care; think about:无牵无挂 have nothing to worry about; be without burden; be carefree

牵累 qiānlěi　❶ tie down; burden:受家务～ be tied down with housework ❷ implicate and bring trouble to

牵连 qiānlián　❶ involve (in trouble); incriminate; implicate ❷ tie up with; be related to

牵强 qiānqiǎng　forced (interpretation, etc); strained; farfetched:～附会 stretch the meaning (of sth); draw a far-fetched conclusion; give a strained interpretation

牵头 qiāntóu take the lead (in doing sth); take the responsibility (of doing sth)

牵线 qiānxiàn ❶ pull strings or wires; manipulate from behind the scenes ❷ act as go-between; serve as intermediary: ～搭桥 act as go-between; bring one person or institution into contact with another

牵引 qiānyǐn ❶ drag; draw; tow: ～车 tractor (truck) ❷〈医〉traction: 作～ be in traction

牵制 qiānzhì also "牵掣" contain; check; pin down

铅 qiān ❶ lead (Pb): ～印 letterpress, relief or typographic printing; stereotype / ～字 type; letter ❷ lead (in a pencil); black lead

铅笔 qiānbǐ pencil: 自动～ propelling pencil / ～刀 pen-knife; pencil sharpener / ～盒 pencil case or box

铅华 qiānhuá face-powder; white lead: 洗尽～〈喻〉recover one's simplicity and purity

铅球 qiānqiú〈体〉shot: 推～ putting the shot; shot put

悭 qiān miserly; parsimonious; stingy: ～吝 鬼 skinflint; penny pincher

谦 qiān modest; unassuming: ～卑 humble; modest; meek / ～称 self-deprecatory term (in referring to oneself) / ～恭 modest and polite / ～逊 modest and unassuming; unpretentious

谦辞 qiāncí ❶ self-deprecatory expression ❷ modestly decline: ～不就 decline (an office, etc)

谦谦君子 qiānqiānjūnzǐ ❶ modest and self-disciplined gentleman ❷ (usu) hypocrite who pretends to be modest

谦让 qiānràng modestly yield (an honour, etc) or give precedence (to others); decline an offer out of modesty; decline politely

谦虚 qiānxū ❶ modest; open-minded: ～谨慎 modest and circumspect ❷ speak modestly or politely

签(籤、³⁻⁶籤) qiān ❶ sign; autograph: ～发 sign and issue (a document, etc) / ～收 sign upon receiving (sth) / ～约 sign a contract or agreement ❷ make brief comments: ～个意 见 write a brief comment (on a document) ❸ bamboo slip used for divination, gambling, etc ❹ label; sticker; tag: 行李～ luggage tag ❺ slender pointed chip of bamboo or wood: 竹～ bamboo chip or stick ❻ tack: ～被里 tack a lining on a quilt

签到 qiāndào register one's attendance (at a meeting or at an office); sign in: ～处 sign-in desk

签订 qiāndìng conclude and sign (a treaty, etc)

签名 qiānmíng put one's signature (to sth); sign one's name; autograph: ～簿 visitors' book / 为读者～ autograph for readers

签署 qiānshǔ sign: ～人 undersigned

签证 qiānzhèng (grant a) visa: 出境 ～ exit visa / 互免～ mutual exemption of visas / ～处 visa office or section

签字 qiānzì sign; affix one's signature: ～国 signatory (state or power)

愆 qiān〈书〉❶ transgression; mistake: ～尤 error; fault; sin ❷ miss the deadline; pass the time limit: ～期 exceed the time limit; delay (payment, etc)

鸽 qiān (of birds with sharp beaks) peck

qián

鄩(鄩) qián see also xún

荨麻 qiánmá 〈植〉nettle

铃 qián seal;～印 affix a seal to (a document, etc) / ～章 official stamp

前 qián ❶ front; fore; in front;～臂〈生理〉forearm / ～额 forehead / ～门 front door / ～排 front row / ～厅 antechamber; vestibule ❷ forward; ahead;～滚翻〈体〉forward roll / ～空翻〈体〉forward somersault in the air ❸ ago; past;～例 precedent / ～年 year before last / ～期 early stage or days / ～嫌 past grievances or animosity / ～半生 first half of one's life / ～几天 a few days ago ❹ former; formerly;～夫 former husband; ex-husband / ～者 the former ❺ earlier than; prior to; pre-;～资本主义 pre-capitalism ❻ prospect; future;～景 prospect; future; perspective / ～瞻性 forward-looking ❼ (short for 前线) battlefront; front;～敌 front line / ～支一物资 materials for the battlefront

前辈 qiánbèi senior (person); elder; older generation

前车之鉴 qiánchēzhījiàn warning taken from the overturned cart ahead; lesson drawn from others' mistakes

前程 qiánchéng ❶ prospect; future;～似锦 have bright prospects ❷〈旧〉career; official position; 丢了～ lose one's official position

前方 qiánfāng ❶ ahead; in front ❷ the front;～将士 officers and men at the front;～医院 field hospital

前锋 qiánfēng ❶ vanguard ❷〈体〉forward ❸ front; 冷空气的～ cold front

前赴后继 qiánfù-hòujì advance wave upon wave

前功尽弃 qiángōngjìnqì forfeit all that one has achieved; all one's previous efforts are wasted;一步走错,～。 One wrong move, and our effort will go down the drain.

前后 qiánhòu ❶ around or about (a certain time);五一～ around May first ❷ also "前前后后" from beginning to end; altogether ❸ in front and behind;～夹攻 make a frontal and rear attack at the same time / ～左右 on all sides; all around ❹ following one after another; successive;～脚儿 (of two or more people) leave or arrive nearly at the same time or in close sequence

前…后… qián…hòu… used to indicate ❶ sequence in space or in time; 前呼后拥 have attendants both in front and behind; be accompanied by numerous retainers / 前倨后恭 be first haughty and then excessively polite; change from arrogance to humility / 前松后紧 be slack at the start and have to work extra hard towards the end / 前因后果 cause and effect; entire process / 前怕狼,后怕虎 fear wolves ahead and tigers behind — be plagued by all sorts of fears; be overcautious ❷ forward or backward movements of a body;前仰后合 sway to and fro; rock backwards and forwards

前脚 qiánjiǎo ❶ forward foot in a step ❷ (used in conjunction with 后脚) no sooner … than; as soon as; the moment (when);我一～进门, 他后脚就到了。 He arrived the moment I entered.

前进 qiánjìn march on; advance; go forward

前科 qiánkē (previous) criminal record;～犯〈法〉criminal with a previous conviction; ex-convict

前列 qiánliè front row or rank; forefront; van

前列腺 qiánlièxiàn 〈生理〉prostate (gland);～炎 prostatitis / ～肥大〈医〉hypertrophy of the prostate

前面 qiánmian also "前边"; "前头" ❶ in front; forward; ahead; 走在～ walk in front ❷ above; aforementioned; preceding;～一段 preceding paragraph /～讲过 as stated above

前仆后继 qiánpū-hòujì as one falls, others step into the breach; advance fearlessly

前前后后 qiánqián-hòuhòu ❶ whole story; ins and outs;事情的～ story from beginning to end ❷ see "前后❷"

前驱 qiánqū forerunner; pioneer; precursor

前人 qiánrén forefathers; forebears; predecessors;～栽树, 后人乘凉〈俗〉 while earlier generations plant trees, posterity will enjoy the cool under the shade — profit by the labour of one's forefathers; toil for the benefit of one's descendants

前任 qiánrèn predecessor;～部长 former or previous minister

前身 qiánshēn ❶ predecessor (of an institution, etc) ❷ also "前襟" front part of a Chinese robe, etc

前世 qiánshì previous existence;～姻缘 predestined matrimonial bond

前事不忘，后事之师 qiánshìbùwàng, hòushìzhīshī 〈谚〉past experience, if not forgotten, is a guide for the future; lessons from the past can guide the future

前所未有 qiánsuǒwèiyǒu hitherto unknown; unprecedented;感到一种～的喜悦 experience a joy never felt before

前台 qiántái ❶ proscenium; stage; downstage;从幕后跳到～〈喻〉〈贬〉 jump on to the stage from behind the scenes ❷ front desk (in a hotel, etc)

前提 qiántí ❶ premise;大～ major premise /小～ minor premise ❷ prerequisite; presupposition; predicate

前天 qiántiān also "前日" day before yesterday

前途 qiántú future; prospect;～渺茫 (have a) bleak future; gloomy prospects

前往 qiánwǎng make for; go or proceed to

前卫 qiánwèi ❶〈军〉advance guard; vanguard ❷〈体〉halfback ❸ avant-garde;～作家 avant-garde author

前无古人 qiánwúgǔrén have no parallel or precedent in history;～的改革 unprecedented reform

前夕 qiánxī also "前夜" eve;建国～ on the eve of the founding of the People's Republic

前线 qiánxiàn front; battlefront; frontline;国家 frontier country

前言 qiányán ❶ preface; foreword; introduction ❷ words said earlier; previous statements;～不搭后语 talk disjointedly

前沿 qiányán 〈军〉forward position;～科学〈喻〉frontier science /～指挥所 forward command post

前兆 qiánzhào omen; augury; premonition

前奏 qiánzòu ❶〈乐〉prelude ❷〈喻〉prelude (to sth); preliminary preparations (for sth)

虔 qián pious; devout; sincere;～诚 devout; reverent; pious; sincere /～敬 highly respectful; reverent

钱(錢) qián ❶ coin; cash; money;～币 coin /～包 wallet; purse /～票〈口〉paper money or currency; banknotes /～庄 old-style banking house ❷ fund; sum; money;饭～ money for a restaurant bill; money for food ❸ wealth; fortune; money;～财 money; wealth; riches /～可通神〈俗〉money can bedevil the devil himself; money talks /～权交易 money-power exchange; trading of money for power ❹ anything that resembles a coin in shape;榆～儿 elm tree seeds ❺ qian, a unit of weight (=5 grams)

钳(箝) qián ❶ pincers; pliers; tongs;～工 fitter /

~子 pliers; pincers; forceps ❷ hold with pincers; 把铁丝～住 grip an iron wire with pincers ❸ clamp; restrain; 制 pin down; clamp down on; suppress / ～口结舌 keep one's mouth shut; keep mum

乾 qián ❶ see "八卦" bāguà ❷ 〈旧〉male

乾坤 qiánkūn heaven and earth; universe; ～再造 remake the world; rearrange the mountains and rivers

捐 qián 〈方〉carry on the shoulder; ～客 broker

潜(潛) qián ❶ hide under water; dive; submerge; ～泳 underwater swimming / ～望镜 periscope ❷ lurking; secretly; stealthily; ～藏 be latent or hidden; hide / ～逃 flee; abscond / ～行 move under water; move stealthily; slink / ～入敌后 sneak in behind the enemy lines ❸ latent; potential; ～能〈理〉latent energy / ～质 latent qualities; potentials / ～意识 the subconscious; subconsciousness

潜伏 qiánfú hide; lie low; be latent; ～期〈医〉incubation period / ～的疾病 latent disease

潜力 qiánlì potential; potentiality; latent capacity; 发挥～ tap potentials

潜流 qiánliú 〈地〉〈喻〉undercurrent; underflow; hidden opinion or feeling

潜水 qiánshuǐ go under water; dive; ～艇 also "潜艇" submarine; U-boat / ～员 diver; frogman

潜台词 qiántáicí ❶ 〈戏〉unspoken words in a play left to the understanding of the audience; subtext ❷ 〈喻〉implied meaning; implication

潜心 qiánxīn devote oneself (to doing sth); work with great concentration

潜移默化 qiányí-mòhuà exert a subtle influence (on sb's character, thinking, etc); act on subtly; influence imperceptibly

潜在 qiánzài hidden; latent; potential; ～力量 latent force; potential power / ～市场 potential market

黔 qián ❶ 〈书〉black; ～首 common people ❷ (Qián) another name for Guizhou (贵州); ～驴技穷 be at the end of one's resources

qiǎn

浅(淺) qiǎn ❶ of little depth; shallow; ～滩 shoal; shallow / ～笑 faint smile ❷ simple; easy; not difficult; ～近 simple; plain; easy to understand / ～谈 (used in book titles, etc) elementary introduction; brief talk / ～显 plain; obvious; easy to read and understand ❸ superficial; shallow; not deep or profound; ～薄 (of knowledge, etc) shallow; superficial; meager / ～见 superficial view / ～陋 meagre; mean; narrow-minded / ～尝辄止 make a superficial study only; be satisfied with a smattering of knowledge ❹ (of colour) light; ～红 light red ❺ not long in time; for a short while

遣 qiǎn ❶ send; transmit; dispatch; ～派 dispatch; send / ～送 send back; repatriate / ～词造句 choice of words and construction of sentences; wording; diction ❷ drive away; dispel; expel; ～怀 also "遣兴" 〈书〉give expression to one's feelings

遣返 qiǎnfǎn repatriate; ～原籍 send sb back to his or her native place

遣散 qiǎnsàn ❶ disband; dismiss; send away ❷ ～费 severance pay (disband and repatriate (troops), etc)

谴 qiǎn ❶ censure; reprimand; reproach; ～责 denounce; condemn; reproach; censure ❷ (usu 谪)〈书〉(of officials) be demoted on account of wrongdoing

缱 qiǎn

缱绻 qiǎnquǎn 〈书〉(of man and woman) deeply attached to each other

qiàn

欠 qiàn ❶ owe; be in debt; be in arrears: ~情 owe a favour; owe a debt of gratitude / ~条 *also* "欠单"; "欠据" receipt for a loan; IOU / ~债 be in debt ❷ be short (of sth) or deficient (in sth); lack; want: ~安〈婉〉(referring to others) not feel well; be slightly indisposed / ~佳 not good or well enough; poor; poorly / ~妥 not proper, correct or appropriate / ~揍〈口〉need a spanking ❸ raise or stretch slightly (part of one's body): ~身 (of sb sitting) rise slightly; half rise from one's seat (to be polite) ❹ yawn: ~伸 stretch oneself and yawn

欠款 qiànkuǎn ❶ owe a debt ❷ *also* "欠账" outstanding debt; arrears; balance due: 收回~ recover arrears; claim the balance due

欠缺 qiànquē ❶ be deficient or inadequate (in sth); be short (of sth) ❷ shortcoming; inadequacy; deficiency

纤(縴) qiàn rope for towing a boat; tow-rope: ~夫 boat tracker　*see also* xiān

茜 qiàn *also* "茜粉" starch used in cooking: 汤里勾点~ thicken the soup with some starch

茜(蒨) qiàn alizarin crimson: ~纱 red gauze

倩 qiàn 〈书〉beautiful; attractive: ~影 photo of a beautiful woman

堑 qiàn moat; chasm; ditch: ~壕〈军〉trench; entrenchment

嵌 qiàn inlay; embed; set: ~银 be set or inlaid with silver

歉 qiàn ❶ crop failure: ~收 crop failure; bad harvest / ~年 lean year; year of poor harvest ❷ apology; regret: ~疚 feel guilty; be remorseful / ~意 regret; apology

qiāng

呛(嗆) qiāng choke (with food or water)　*see also* qiàng

羌 Qiāng Qiang, an ancient ethnic group in western China

枪(槍、❶-❸鎗) qiāng ❶ spear ❷ rifle; gun; firearm: ~法 marksmanship / ~口 muzzle / ~炮 arms; guns / ~伤 bullet or gunshot wound / ~声 report of a gun; shot; crack / ~战 gun battle / ~子儿〈口〉cartridge; bullet; shot / ~林弹雨 hail of bullets / ~支 弹药 arms and ammunition ❸ any appliance functioning or looking like a gun: 焊~ welding torch ❹ (usu 枪替) serve as a substitute for sb at an examination

枪毙 qiāngbì ❶ *also* "枪决" execute by shooting ❷ turn down; overrule; reject: 他的意见被~了。His proposal was dismissed.

枪杆 qiānggǎn (stock of a) gun: 掌握 ~子 control the armed forces

枪手 qiāngshǒu ❶ marksman; gunner; gunman ❷ substitute for another at examinations

戗(戧) qiāng ❶ be in the opposite direction; against: ~风 against the wind ❷ verbal clash; quarrel: 他们俩说~了。Their conversation ended in a row.　*see also* qiàng

戕 qiāng 〈书〉kill: ~害 injure; damage; ruin

腔 qiāng ❶ cavity (in an organism, etc): ~骨 spine of pork ❷

speech；talk：答～ respond (to a question)；answer ❸ tune：tune；singing tunes ❹ tone；accent：一口京～ a pure Beijing accent

腔调 qiāngdiào ❶ tune ❷ tone；accent；intonation：讥讽的～ sarcastic tone

蜣 qiāng

蜣螂 qiāngláng　*also* "屎壳郎"〈动物〉dung beetle

锵(鏘) qiāng 〈象声〉clang；
锣声～～ continuous clanging of gongs

镪 qiāng

镪水 qiāngshuǐ　(popular term for 强酸) strong acid

qiáng

强 qiáng ❶ strong；mighty；powerful：～敌 formidable foe；strong opponent / ～手 person of ability and talent；strong rival / ～将手下无弱兵。〈俗〉There are no weak troops under an able general. ❷ high or strong (in degree)；demanding；resolute：责任心～ have a strong sense of responsibility / 好奇心很～ be intensely curious ❸ by force：～渡 force or fight one's way across (a river)；force (a river) / ～攻 attack violently；storm / ～占 forcibly take；seize；occupy by force of arms ❹ strengthen；enhance：～身 strengthen one's physique；keep fit / ～心剂〈医〉cardiac stimulant ❺ better；stronger：～似 *also* "强如" be better than or superior to ❻ a little over；plus：五分之二～ a little over two fifths
see also jiàng；qiǎng

强暴 qiángbào ❶ violent；ferocious；brutal：～行径 act of violence ❷ brute force；despotic strength or people：铲除

～ root out tyrannies ❸ violate (a girl)；ravish；rape

强大 qiángdà powerful；mighty；formidable：～的生命力 great vitality

强盗 qiángdào robber；bandit：～逻辑 gangster logic

强调 qiángdiào stress；emphasize；underline

强度 qiángdù ❶ intensity：劳动～ labour intensity ❷ strength：抗震～ anti-seismic strength

强国 qiángguó ❶ strong country；powerful nation；power ❷ make a nation powerful：～富民 build up the strength of a nation and enrich its people

强悍 qiánghàn valiant；intrepid；doughty：～善战 valiant and good at fighting

强横 qiánghèng brutal and unreasonable；despotic：～无理 overbearing and unreasonable；unruly

强化 qiánghuà strengthen；enhance；intensify：～课程 intensive course / ～食品 condensed food

强加 qiángjiā impose；force (people) to accept：～于人 impose (one's will, etc) on others

强奸 qiángjiān rape；defile；violate：～犯〈法〉rapist / ～民意 outrage public opinion

强健 qiángjiàn strong and healthy；sturdy

强劲 qiángjìn powerful；vigorous；forceful：势头～ forceful momentum

强力 qiánglì ❶ force：～夺取 take (sth) by force / ～机构 departments of force (the armed forces, etc) ❷ (of a material) power of resistance；strength

强烈 qiángliè ❶ strong；powerful；violent ❷ keen；sharp；striking：～的对比 sharp or striking contrast

强弩之末 qiángnǔzhīmò (like an) arrow at the end of its flight — a spent

force；at a low ebb

强权 qiángquán　power；might：～政治 power politics

强人 qiángrén ❶ strong man；女～ strong woman ❷ *also* "强徒" bandit；robber

强盛 qiángshèng　（of a country）powerful and prosperous

强项 qiángxiàng　〈体〉game or event in which one is strong；〈喻〉strength；forte

强行 qiángxíng　force：～摊派 force people to make a donation, etc／～阻止 stop (sth) by force

强硬 qiángyìng　tough；strong；hard-line：～派 hard-liner；hawk／语气～ (speak in a) forceful tone

强制 qiángzhì　force；compel；coerce：～机关 institutions of coercion／～劳动〈法〉forced labour

强壮 qiángzhuàng ❶ strong；robust；sturdy ❷ strengthen；build up：～剂〈医〉tonic

墙（牆） qiáng wall：～报 wall newspaper／～壁 wall／～角 corner formed by two walls；wall corner／～脚 *also* "墙根" foot of a wall／～纸 *also* "壁纸" wallpaper／～倒众人推〈俗〉when a wall starts tottering, everybody gives it a shove — everybody kicks somebody who is down／～里开花～外香〈俗〉the fragrance of the flowers growing in the garden smells sweeter to people outside the wall than to those inside — one's achievements are often unrecognized in one's own community／～头草，随风倒〈俗〉grass atop a wall bends with the wind — a fence-sitter goes with the crowd

蔷（薔） qiáng

蔷薇 qiángwēi　〈植〉rose

樯（檣） qiáng　〈书〉mast

qiǎng

抢（搶） qiǎng ❶ rob；loot；seize；～掠 loot；grab；sack／～球 *also* "抢断" (try to) intercept or snatch the ball／～亲 *also* "抢婚" marriage by capture ❷ hurry；rush：～渡 cross (a river) in a rush；cross speedily／～攻 grab or seize a chance to attack；race to attack／～收 rush in the harvest；get in the crops quickly／～修 rush to repair；do rush repairs；rush-repair／～时间 race against time；lose no time ❸ scrape；scratch；sharpen：～菜刀 sharpen kitchen knives

抢白 qiǎngbái　satirize；ridicule；tell off

抢夺 qiǎngduó　snatch；grab；seize：～地盘 turf grabbing

抢购 qiǎnggòu　rush to purchase；make a run on the shops：～风 panic buying

抢劫 qiǎngjié　rob；loot；plunder：～犯 robber；mugger

抢救 qiǎngjiù　rescue；save；salvage：～病人 give emergency treatment to a patient

抢手 qiǎngshǒu　(of goods, etc) sell like hot cakes；be in short supply

抢滩 qiǎngtān　〈军〉seize a beachhead；〈喻〉rush to occupy the market before others

抢先 qiǎngxiān　try to be the first (to do sth)；act before others；forestall

抢险 qiǎngxiǎn　rush to meet an emergency

抢眼 qiǎngyǎn　eye-catching；conspicuous

抢占 qiǎngzhàn ❶ race to seize or occupy ❷ take illegal possession (of sth)；occupy illegally；squat

强 qiǎng　make an effort；try hard；force：～辩 try to make out a case by false arguments; resort to sophistry / ～ 求 insist on; impose; force / ～ 词夺理 use lame arguments; resort to sophistry; be unreasonable / ～人所难 make sb do what is beyond his or her power; try to make sb do sth against his or her will　*see also* jiàng; qiáng

强迫 qiǎngpò　force; compel; coerce; ～命令 (resort to) coercion and commands / ～手段 coercive measures

襁 qiǎng

襁褓 qiǎngbǎo　swaddling clothes

qiàng

呛（嗆） qiàng　irritate (respiratory organs): 辣椒味儿太～人。The smell of pepper is too irritating.　*see also* qiāng

戗（戧） qiàng　❶ prop; wooden support ❷ buttress; shore up: ～ 面 leavened dough mixed with flour　*see also* qiāng

炝（熗） qiàng　❶ boil sth in water for a while, and then dress it with soy sauce, vinegar, etc ❷ fry sth quickly in hot oil before cooking it with dressing: 用葱花～～锅 fry chopped spring onions in hot oil (to flavour a dish)

跄（蹌） qiàng

跄踉 qiàngliàng　stagger; walk improperly

qiāo

悄 qiāo　*see also* qiǎo

悄悄 qiāoqiāo　quietly; secretly; on the quiet; ～话 whisper in private; confidential talk / ～溜出 sneak out

硗（磽） qiāo

硗薄 qiāobó　(of soil) hard and infertile; barren

跷（蹺） qiāo　❶ lift up (a leg); hold up (a finger): ～～板 seesaw ❷ on tiptoe: ～足以待 stand on tiptoe waiting; await eagerly ❸ stilts: 踩高～ walk on stilts

锹 qiāo　spade; shovel

劁 qiāo　geld; castrate

敲 qiāo　❶ knock; rap; beat: ～门 knock at the door / ～边鼓 try to assist from the sidelines; speak or act to back sb up / ～警钟 sound the alarm (bell); serve as a warning (to sb) / ～门砖 stepping stone / ～锣打鼓 beat drums and gongs ❷〈口〉force (sb) to pay through the nose; fleece: ～竹杠 make sb pay through the nose; put the lug on; fleece

敲打 qiāodǎ　❶ beat; knock; strike ❷〈方〉make sb wake up (to his faults) or keep sb in his place with criticisms, etc

敲定 qiāodìng　decide finally: ～合同 reach or make a final decision on a contract

敲诈 qiāozhà　extort; blackmail; shake down: ～勒索 swindle and squeeze

橇 qiāo　sledge; sled; sleigh

缲 qiāo　hem with invisible stitches: ～边儿 hem the edges

qiáo

乔（喬） qiáo　❶ tall: ～木〈植〉arbor; tree ❷ pretend to be; disguise: ～装 disguise; simulate

乔迁 qiáoqiān　move to a better place; be transferred to a higher post

侨（僑） qiáo resident in a foreign country; (esp) overseas Chinese：～胞 compatriots living abroad / ～汇 overseas remittance / ～居 reside or live abroad / ～属 also "侨眷" relatives of overseas Chinese / ～务 overseas Chinese affairs / ～乡 area inhabited by returned overseas Chinese and relatives of overseas Chinese / ～资 investment by overseas Chinese / 外国～民 foreign resident; alien; expatriate

荞（蕎） qiáo

荞麦 qiáomài buckwheat

桥（橋） qiáo bridge：～洞 also "桥孔" bridge opening or arch / ～墩（bridge）pier / ～拱 bridge arch / ～牌 bridge / ～头堡 bridge tower；〈军〉bridgehead

桥梁 qiáoliáng bridge：～建筑 bridge construction / 起～作用 play the role of a bridge; serve as a link

翘（翹） qiáo ❶ raise（one's head）; lift up：～足引领〈书〉stand on tiptoe and crane one's neck — eagerly await ❷ become warped or bent（with moisture, etc）

see also qiào

翘楚 qiáochǔ 〈书〉outstanding or prominent figure

翘首 qiáoshǒu 〈书〉lift up or raise one's head（to look）; crane one's neck：～企足（shortened as 翘企）crane one's neck and stand on tiptoe — eagerly await

翘望 qiáowàng ❶ raise one's head to look at sth ❷ look forward to; expect：～已久 have long been anticipating（sth）eagerly

憔 qiáo

憔悴 qiáocuì ill and emaciated; haggard; (of plants) withered

樵 qiáo 〈书〉gather firewood：～夫 woodcutter; woodman

瞧 qiáo 〈口〉look; watch; see：～病（of a patient）see or consult a doctor; (of a doctor) see or visit a patient / ～见 see; notice; catch sight of / ～不起 look down upon; despise / ～热闹 watch the fun; look on with folded arms / ～着办 do as one sees fit

qiǎo

巧 qiǎo ❶ skilful; ingenious; clever：～干 do cleverly; work ingeniously / ～计 clever device; artful scheme; smart trick / ～匠 fine craftsman / ～夺天工 so wonderful in workmanship as to excel nature; superb / ～妇难为无米之炊 even a clever housewife can't cook without rice — one can't make bricks without straw ❷ (of hand or tongue) deft; glib; clever：手～ be clever with one's hands / 嘴～ have a glib tongue ❸ opportunely; luckily; accidentally：～合 coincidence; pure chance / ～遇 encounter by chance; run into ❹ fine-sounding (words); sly; artful：巧取豪夺 get by cheating or by force; grab and keep

巧克力 qiǎokèlì chocolate

巧立名目 qiǎolìmíngmù 〈贬〉invent all sorts of names; concoct various excuses

巧妙 qiǎomiào ingenious; smart; clever

巧舌如簧 qiǎoshérúhuáng also "巧言如簧" talk glibly; sweet-talk

巧言令色 qiǎoyán-lìngsè have a glib tongue and ingratiating manner; be hypocritical

悄 qiǎo ❶ quiet; silent：～声 quietly; softly ❷ 〈书〉sad; worried; grieved

see also qiāo

悄然 qiǎorán ❶ sadly; sorrowfully：～落泪 shed tears sadly ❷ quietly; softly

雀
愀

雀 qiǎo sparrow　*see also* què

愀 qiǎo

愀然 qiǎorán 〈书〉 ❶ look grave or stern：～作色 turn stern ❷ look unhappy or displeased：～不悦 look displeased

qiào

壳（殻）

壳（殻） qiào hard outer covering；shell；crust：～菜 (as food) mussel　*see also* ké

俏

俏 qiào ❶ stylish；handsome；good-looking：～丽 *also* "俏美" charming；attractive；handsome ❷ sell well；be salable：～货 goods that sell well；highly salable goods ／ ～销 sell well；be in great demand；be highly salable ❸ 〈方〉 season (food)：～点儿 韭菜 season (food) with leeks

俏皮 qiàopi ❶ handsome；stylish；smart ❷ lively；witty：～话 sarcastic or witty remarks；witticisms

诮

诮 qiào 〈书〉 ❶ blame；censure；reproach ❷ sneer at；deride

峭（陗）

峭（陗） qiào ❶ high and steep；precipitous：～壁 cliff；precipice；steep ／ ～立 rise steeply ❷ stern；harsh：～直 stern and straightforward

峭拔 qiàobá ❶ high and steep；perilous：山峰 ～ towering peaks ❷ vigorous；robust：文笔 ～ write a vigorous style

窍（竅）

窍（竅） qiào ❶ aperture；orifice ❷ key to sth；knack：～门 key (to a problem)；trick；knack

翘（翹）

翘（翹） qiào stick or hold up；turn upwards：～尾巴 stick one's tail up；be cocky；be haughty and snooty ／ ～辫子 kick the bucket；die　*see also* qiáo

撬

撬 qiào prize；pry；jimmy：～门 pry a door open ／ ～锁 pick a lock

鞘

鞘 qiào sheath；scabbard　*see also* shāo

qiē

切

切 qiē ❶ cut；chop；slice：～除 remove；〈医〉excise ／ ～断 cut off ／ ～割 cut；carve up ❷ 〈数〉touch without crossing：～线 tangent (line)　*see also* qiè

切磋 qiēcuō learn from each other by exchanging views；compare notes

切面 qiēmiàn ❶ cut or machine-made noodles ❷ section：横 ～ cross section

切片 qiēpiàn ❶ cut into slices；slice ❷ 〈医〉section：～检查 cut sections (of organic tissues) for microscopic examination

切入 qiērù penetrate：～点 point at which to penetrate (into sth)

qié

茄

茄 qié (usu 茄子) eggplant；aubergine

qiě

且

且 qiě ❶ just；for the time being；for a while：～慢 wait a minute；hold it ❷ 〈方〉(used with 呢) for (quite) a long time：这笔～使呢。The pen will last quite some time yet. ❸ 〈书〉even：君～如此，况他人乎？If it is so with you, how could others be expected to be different？ ❹ 〈书〉also；and：水深～急。The water is both deep and rapid.

且…且… qiě…qiě… while；as：且听且记 take notes while listening ／ 且歌且舞 sing and dance at the same time

qiè

切 qiè ❶ correspond to; accord with; be close to: ～合 correspond to; accord with; fit in with / ～题 keep to the point; be relevant to the subject / ～肤之痛 keenly felt pain / 不～实际 unrealistic / 恨之～骨 hate sb to the marrow ❷ eager; keen; anxious: ～盼 eagerly look forward to; sincerely hope ❸ by all means; in all circumstances: ～记 keep firmly in mind; must always remember / ～～勿忘 be sure not to forget; must always remember

see also qiē

切齿 qièchǐ　gnash or grind one's teeth (in hatred, regret, etc): ～咒骂 curse with clenched teeth

切当 qièdàng　proper; appropriate; to the point: 用词～ be properly worded; use the right word in the right place

切忌 qièjì　must not do in any circumstances; avoid by all means: ～生冷 refrain from cold and raw food

切口 qièkǒu　password; cant

切脉 qièmài　〈中医〉feel the pulse

切身 qièshēn　❶ of immediate concern or interest to one: ～利害 immediate or vital interest ❷ personal: ～体会 intimate knowledge; keenly-felt lesson

切实 qièshí　practical; feasible; earnest: ～可行 practical and effective

切要 qièyào　❶ precise and succinct ❷ vital; essential; indispensable: ～之举 step of vital importance

切中 qièzhòng　hit (the mark): ～要害 hit the nail on the head; strike home

妾 qiè　❶ concubine ❷ 〈旧〉(used by a woman in humble reference to herself) I; me

怯 qiè　❶ timid; cowardly; nervous: ～懦 timid and afraid; weak and cowardly / ～弱 timid and weak-willed; chicken-hearted / ～生生 shy and timid; nervous ❷ 〈方〉(of accent) boorish; (of dress, etc) vulgar; outmoded: 穿得～ inelegantly dressed / 口音有点～ have a somewhat boorish accent

怯场 qièchǎng　(have) stage fright

怯阵 qièzhèn　❶ be battle-shy ❷ *see* "怯场"

窃(竊) qiè　❶ steal; pilfer; pinch: ～密 steal secret information / ～取 usurp; steal / ～贼 thief; burglar; pilferer / ～玉偷香 (of a man) have illicit sexual relations with a woman ❷ secretly; furtively; stealthily: ～笑 laugh up one's sleeve ❸ 〈旧〉〈谦〉*used to refer to oneself*: ～以为不可。In my humble opinion, this will not do.

窃据 qièjù　usurp; illegally occupy: ～要津 occupy an important post unjustly

窃窃 qièqiè　❶ *also* "切切" in a low voice; whispering: ～私语 talk privately or secretly; whisper under one's breath ❷ in secret; on the sly; stealthily: ～自喜 be secretly pleased with oneself; congratulate oneself

窃听 qiètīng　eavesdrop; wiretap; bug: ～器 tapping or listening-in device; bug; tap

挈 qiè　❶ lift; take up; raise ❷ take along: ～带家眷 take one's family along

惬(愜) qiè　〈书〉gratify; satisfy: ～意 satisfied; pleased; comfortable

惬当 qièdàng　〈书〉proper; appropriate

趄 qiè　slanting; inclined

锲 qiè　〈书〉chisel; carve; engrave: ～而不舍 work with perseverance; make unflagging efforts

箧(篋) qiè　〈书〉small suitcase or box

qīn

钦 qīn ❶ admire; adore; respect; ～佩 admire; esteem / ～仰〈书〉revere; respect; esteem ❷ of or by the emperor: ～定 (of writings, etc) authorized by the emperor

钦差大臣 qīnchāi dàchén ❶ also "钦差" imperial envoy or commissioner ❷〈喻〉person sent by the higher authorities with full powers: ～满天飞。There are imperial envoys all over the place.

侵 qīn ❶ invade; intrude into; encroach or infringe upon: ～染 be infected (with disease) / ～扰 invade and harass / ～入 intrude into; make inroads on; invade / ～袭 make incursions into; assault / ～占 invade and occupy; occupy by force; take illegal possession of ❷ approaching: ～晨 also "侵晓" approaching or towards daybreak; at the approach or crack of dawn

侵犯 qīnfàn ❶ encroach upon; infringe on; violate: ～人权 infringe on human rights ❷ invade; intrude into; make an inroad: ～别国主权 infringe or encroach upon another country's sovereignty

侵害 qīnhài invade and damage; damage or harm by force or by unlawful means: ～农作物 (of pests) harm or damage crops / ～消费者利益 harm consumers' interests

侵略 qīnlüè aggression; invasion: ～者 aggressor; invader

侵权 qīnquán〈法〉infringe on or violate others' lawful rights; commit (an act of) tort: ～行为 act of tort or infringement

侵蚀 qīnshí ❶ corrode; erode; eat into: 受旧思想～ be corroded by the influence of old ideas ❷ misappropriate or embezzle (public funds, etc) bit by bit

侵吞 qīntūn ❶ misappropriate; embezzle; defalcate: ～巨款 embezzle a large sum of money ❷ swallow up; forcibly seize; annex: ～别国领土 annex another country's territory

亲(親) qīn ❶ one's own flesh and blood; blood relation (esp) parent: ～缘 blood relationship; consanguinity / ～骨肉 one's own flesh and blood / ～姊妹 blood sister ❷ kin; relative: ～属 kinsfolk; relatives / ～友 also "亲朋" relatives and friends; kith and kin / ～痛仇快 sadden one's own people and gladden the enemy ❸ marriage; match: ～事 marriage ❹ bride: 送～ escort a bride to her groom ❺ close; intimate; near and dear: ～昵 intimate; attached; affectionate / ～疏 close and distant / ～英 pro-British; Anglophile / ～如一家 dear to each other like members of the same family ❻ in person; personally: ～睹 see with one's own eyes; personally witness / ～口 say or speak personally / ～启 (written on a letter, etc) personal; private / ～手 with one's own hands; in person; oneself / ～历其事 have had personal experience about sth ❼ kiss: ～吻 also "亲嘴" kiss *see also* qíng

亲爱 qīn'ài dear; beloved; cherished

亲笔 qīnbǐ write in one's own hand; autograph: ～信 personal letter / ～签名的照片 autographed photograph

亲和力 qīnhélì ❶〈化〉affinity ❷ appeal; popularity

亲近 qīnjìn be close to; be friendly with; be on intimate terms with: 不知不觉地～起来 feel gradually drawn towards each other

亲眷 qīnjuàn ❶ relative ❷ one's family, especially wife and children

亲密 qīnmì close; intimate; near and dear: ～无间 be on the best of terms (with each other)

亲戚 qīnqi relative; relation; kin: ~ 关系 kinship

亲切 qīnqiè ❶ warm; close; affectionate ❷ kind; hearty; cordial: ~的关怀 kind attention

亲情 qīnqíng emotional attachment among family members: 父子~ affection between father and son

亲热 qīnrè affectionate; loving; intimate

亲人 qīnrén family; kin; beloved ones

亲善 qīnshàn (esp between countries) friendship; goodwill: ~大使 goodwill ambassador

亲身 qīnshēn done or made by oneself; personal; firsthand: ~经历 personal or firsthand experiences

亲生 qīnshēng one's own: ~子女 one's own children

亲王 qīnwáng prince

亲信 qīnxìn ❶ close and trusted ❷〈贬〉trusted follower; confidant

亲眼 qīnyǎn (see) with one's own eyes; personally (witness): ~所见 see with one's own eyes

亲子 qīnzǐ parents and children: ~鉴定〈医〉DNA parental test

亲自 qīnzì in person; personally; oneself: ~处理 attend to sth oneself

衾 qīn〈书〉❶ quilt ❷ pall

骎 qīn

骎骎 qīnqīn〈书〉(of horses) gallop;〈喻〉advance rapidly: ~日上 advance with each passing day

qín

芹 qín also "芹菜" celery

秦 Qín ❶ Qin State (897 BC—221 BC) or Dynasty (221 BC—206 BC): ~兵马俑 terra-cotta warriors of Qin ❷ another name for Shaanxi

（陕西）and Gansu（甘肃）（esp Shaanxi）: ~腔 Shaanxi opera

秦晋 Qín-Jìn matrimonial ties as between the royal families of Qin and Jin: 结为~（of two families, etc）be allied through marriage / ~之好 marriage alliance

琴 qín ❶ qin, a seven-stringed plucked instrument, similar to the zither: ~棋书画（talent for）music, chess, calligraphy, and painting — artistic accomplishments of a traditional scholar ❷ general name for certain musical instruments: ~键 key（as of a piano）/ ~弦 string（as of a fiddle）

琴瑟 qínsè qin and se —（harmony between）husband and wife: ~不调 conjugal disharmony; marital discord

禽 qín ❶ bird; fowl: ~流感 bird flu ❷〈书〉fowls and animals

禽兽 qínshòu (birds and) beasts: ~不如 more beastly than beasts

勤 qín ❶ diligent; industrious; hardworking: ~恳 diligent and earnest / ~快〈口〉diligent; industrious; hardworking / ~勉 hardworking; assiduous; diligent / ~政 diligent government / ~学苦练 study diligently and train hard ❷ frequently; often: ~洗澡 take baths regularly ❸ work; duty: 内~ office work / 外~ field work ❹（at an office, a school, etc）attendance: 考~ check on attendance

勤奋 qínfèn diligent; assiduous; industrious

勤工俭学 qíngōngjiǎnxué part-work and part-study; work-study programme: ~上大学 work one's way through college

勤俭 qínjiǎn hardworking and frugal; industrious and thrifty: ~节约 work hard and practise economy

勤劳 qínláo diligent; industrious; hardworking: ~致富 get rich through honest labour

勤王 qínwáng 〈史〉(of subjects) send troops to support the emperor when he is in trouble

勤务 qínwù ❶ duty; service ❷〈军〉odd-job man；~ 兵 orderly / ～ 员 orderly；odd-job man；〈喻〉servant

勤杂 qínzá odd job; odd-job man; handyman

擒 qín capture; catch; seize：~ 获 catch；arrest；capture / ～ 贼先 ~ 王。〈谚〉To catch a gang of bandits, first catch their chieftain.

擒拿 qínná ❶ also "擒拿术" martial skills for overpowering an opponent ❷ capture; arrest：～ 归案 capture and bring to justice；track down to face criminal charges

噙 qín hold in the mouth or the eyes；be filled with；~ 化 〈中医〉dissolve (a pill) in the mouth

qǐn

寝(寢) qǐn ❶ sleep：~ 具 bed-clothes；bedding / ~ 食不安 feel worried waking or sleeping；be unable to sleep or eat peacefully ❷ bedroom：~ 室 bedroom；dormitory ❸ coffin chamber；tomb ❹〈书〉stop；cease；end：其事遂～。The matter was then dropped.

qìn

沁 qìn (of fragrance, etc) ooze; seep；exude：~ 人心脾 also "沁人肺腑" seep into the heart；be refreshing or invigorating

揿 qìn 〈方〉press；push：~ 电钮 press a button

qīng

青 qīng ❶ used of colours a) green：~ 翠 fresh or luxuriant green；verdant / ～豆 green soya bean／~ 椒 green pepper / ～ 苔 moss / ～ 纱 帐 green curtain of tall crops b) blue：~ 筋 blue veins / ～ 花瓷 blue and white porcelain / ～ 出于蓝 (short for 青出于蓝，而胜于蓝) indigo blue is extracted from the indigo plant but is bluer — the disciple surpasses the master / ～ 面獠牙 blue face with protruding fangs —(with) horrifying features c) black：~ 丝 〈书〉black hair (esp of a woman) / ～ 鱼 black carp ❷ green grass；young crop：看 ~ keep watch over young crops / ～ 苗 (of grains) young crop；green shoots ❸ young (people)：~ 工 young worker ❹ (Qīng) short for Qinghai (青海)：~ 藏高原 Qinghai-Tibet Plateau

青菜 qīngcài ❶ also "小白菜" a variety of Chinese cabbage ❷ green vegetables；greens

青春 qīngchūn ❶ youth；youthful ness；~ 痘 (common name for 痤疮 acne / ~ 期 puberty；adolescence / ～ 偶像 idol of youth ❷ (often used in the early vernacular) age of young people

青光眼 qīngguāngyǎn 〈医〉glaucoma

青红皂白 qīnghóng-zàobái black and white；right and wrong；good and bad 不问～ be undiscriminating；act rashly without first asking what the matter is about

青黄不接 qīnghuángbùjiē food short age between two harvests；temporary shortage or gap between two supplies generations，etc

青稞 qīngkē highland or qingke barley

青睐 qīnglài 〈书〉favour；good graces；受人～ win sb's favour；be in sb's good graces

青楼 qīnglóu 〈书〉brothel：~ 女子 courtesan；prostitute

青梅竹马 qīngméi-zhúmǎ childhood (playmate)：~ 的恋人 lovers who have grown up together

青霉素 qīngméisù *also* "盘尼西林" penicillin

青年 qīngnián ❶ youthful; young ❷ youth; young people:~节 Youth Day (May 4) / 青壮年 men in their twenties to forties / 青少年犯罪 juvenile delinquency; teenage crime

青史 qīngshǐ (annals of) history:~留名 leave a name in history; go down in history

青天 qīngtiān ❶ blue sky:~白日 (in) broad daylight ❷〈旧〉upright magistrate

青铜 qīngtóng bronze:~器 bronze ware / ~时代 Bronze Age

青蛙 qīngwā frog

青眼 qīngyǎn favour; good graces:~相待 treat (sb) with favour

青衣 qīngyī ❶〈戏〉female role in Beijing opera ❷ black clothes:~小帽〈旧〉plain informal clothes

青云 qīngyún high (official) position:~独步 be unrivalled in one's exalted position (in learning or career) / ~直上 make a meteoric rise in one's (political) career; rise rapidly from obscurity to fame

轻(輕) qīng ❶ of little weight or effort; light; easy:~活 light work; easy job / ~取 win or defeat without difficulty; win hands down / ~水〈理〉light water / ~装 with light packs;〈喻〉without mental burdens / ~工业 light industry / 而易举 be easy to do; come easy (to sb) / ~于鸿毛 (usu of death) lighter than a goose feather ❷ small in number or lesser in degree; slight; light:~伤 slight injury; minor wound / ~罪〈法〉misdemeanour; minor offence ❸ relaxed; light:~音乐 light music / ~歌曼舞 light music and graceful dance ❹ gently; softly:~手~脚 (walk, etc) gently; quietly; softly ❺ make light of; belittle:~敌 underestimate the en-

emy; take one's rival lightly / ~慢 treat rudely; slight ❻ rash; impetuous:~举妄动 act impetuously; make a rash move; take reckless action / ~信口供 give ready credence to confessions ❼ flighty; frivolous:~狂 excessively frivolous

轻便 qīngbiàn ❶ light; portable:~铁路 *also* "轻轨铁路" light railway / 行装~ travel light ❷ convenient; handy

轻薄 qīngbó ❶ frivolous; flirtatious ❷ behave improperly with (a woman); harass sexually

轻车熟路 qīngchē-shúlù (drive in) a light carriage on a familiar road — (do) sth one knows well enough to manage with ease

轻浮 qīngfú frivolous; flighty; lightheaded

轻贱 qīngjiàn ❶ inferior; lowly; worthless ❷ belittle; despise

轻捷 qīngjié light; brisk; agile

轻快 qīngkuài ❶ (of people, etc) brisk; light; spry ❷ (of music, etc) light; relaxed; lively

轻描淡写 qīngmiáo-dànxiě mention casually; slur over; play down

轻蔑 qīngmiè scornful; disdainful; contemptuous

轻飘飘 qīngpiāopiāo ❶ light ❷ (of movement) nimble; agile; (of a mood) buoyant:~地走了进来 sail or float in ❸ general and superficial; of little substance and use

轻巧 qīngqiǎo ❶ light and ingenious ❷ (of people) agile; nimble ❸ simple and easy:说得~ talk as if it were just a walkover; talking is easy

轻柔 qīngróu soft; gentle; pliable

轻生 qīngshēng take one's own life; commit suicide

轻声 qīngshēng ❶ in a soft voice; softly:~交谈 talk in whispers ❷〈语言〉light tone

轻视 qīngshì despise; belittle; look

down on

轻率 qīngshuài　thoughtless; rash; hasty; ～地下结论 jump to conclusions

轻松 qīngsōng　carefree; light-hearted; relaxed

轻佻 qīngtiāo　frivolous; skittish; flirtatious

轻微 qīngwēi　light; slight; negligible; ～感冒 a touch of flu

轻型 qīngxíng　light-duty; light; ～机械 light-duty machinery / ～卡车 pick-up

轻易 qīngyì　❶ easy; simple ❷ rashly; off-handed ❸ often; frequently

轻盈 qīngyíng　❶ (as of a woman) slender and graceful; nimble; lithe ❷ lighthearted; light and melodious

轻重 qīngzhòng　❶ weight ❷ (degree of) intensity; relative importance, priorities:分清～缓急 get one's priorities right ❸ proper limits; propriety:说话没个～ not know the right way to talk; speak bluntly without regard to occasion

氢（氫）qīng　〈化〉hydrogen (H); ～弹 hydrogen bomb; H-bomb

倾 qīng　❶ slant; incline; bend ❷ tendency; trend; deviation:右～ right deviation ❸ collapse; topple: ～覆 collapse; topple; overthrow ❹ overturn and pour out; dump; empty: ～谈 have a good, heart-to-heart talk; talk heartily / ～泻 rush down in torrents; pour down / ～巢出动 (as of a horde of bandits) turn out in full strength; sally forth in full force / ～囊相助 empty one's purse to help (sb); give generously to help (sb) / ～盆大雨 downpour; torrential rain ❺ 〈书〉overwhelm; overbear: ～城～国 (of a woman) ravishingly beautiful; of unmatched beauty

倾倒 qīngdǎo　❶ topple or fall over ❷ greatly admire; adore; prostrate oneself before ❸ (qīngdào) dump; empty; pour out; ～满腹的委屈 pour out all one's grievances

倾家荡产 qīngjiā-dàngchǎn　lose all one's property; be reduced to poverty and ruin; become bankrupt and homeless

倾慕 qīngmù　hold in high esteem; greatly admire; adore

倾诉 qīngsù　pour out (one's worries, grievances, etc); ～衷情 unbosom oneself; open one's heart (to sb)

倾听 qīngtīng　listen attentively or carefully to

倾吐 qīngtǔ　say freely what is on one's mind; vent (pent-up grievances, etc)

倾向 qīngxiàng　❶ be inclined to; be in favour of; prefer; ～性 tendency; preference; prejudice ❷ tendency; trend; inclination

倾销 qīngxiāo　dump:～价格 dumping price / 反～税 anti-dumping tax

倾斜 qīngxié　❶ tilt; slant; incline: ～面 inclined plane ❷ 〈喻〉lean to one side; give preferential treatment; ～政策 preferential or affirmative policy

倾心 qīngxīn　❶ greatly admire; adore; fall in love with; 一见～ fall in love at first sight ❷ wholehearted; cordial; sincere; ～长谈 have a long, heart-to-heart talk

倾轧 qīngyà　engage in factional strife (in a political party, etc)

倾注 qīngzhù　❶ pour into or down ❷ concentrate (one's energy, etc) on; ～全力 dedicate oneself to; be devoted heart and soul to

卿 qīng　〈史〉❶ minister; senior official ❷ (form of address used by the emperor for a court official, or between husband and wife) you; ～～我我 (as between man and woman) bill and coo

清 qīng　❶ (of liquid, etc) pure; clear; lucid; ～茶 green tea; tea served without refreshments / ～风 cool or refreshing breeze / ～泉 limpid spring (water) / ～样 final proof (in printing) / ～音〈语言〉voiceless sound / ～心寡欲 have a pure heart and few worldly desires ❷ quiet; silent; still; ～平 peaceful and tranquil / ～幽 quiet and secluded ❸ honest and upright; ❹ 廉 honest and upright; incorruptible ❹ plain; without any extras (esp soy sauce in cooking): ～唱 sing (Beijing opera arias) without make-up / ～ 炖 boil or stew in clear soup / ～汤 clear soup; consommé ❺ completely; entirely; thoroughly; 把债还～ pay up what one owes ❻ clear or clean up; purify; ～场 clear a public place of visitors, etc / ～剿 mop up; suppress; eliminate / ～热〈中医〉relieve inflammation or internal heat / ～扫 sweep; clean up ❼ settle (accounts); count; check; ～帐 close or wind up an account; settle accounts ❽ (Qīng) Qing Dynasty (1616-1911)

清白 qīngbái pure; clean; immaculate: ～人家 family of stainless reputation

清查 qīngchá ❶ check (accounts, etc); examine ❷ ferret or winkle out

清仓 qīngcāng make a check-up of a warehouse; ～大拍卖 clearance sale

清偿 qīngcháng pay back or off; clear off: ～旧欠 pay off old debts

清澈 qīngchè *also* "清彻" crystal-clear; limpid; transparent

清晨 qīngchén *also* "清早" early morning

清除 qīngchú clear away or up; remove; get rid of: ～路障 remove road blocks / ～出党 expel from a political party

清楚 qīngchǔ ❶ clear; explicit; distinct; 口齿不～ be inarticulate / 认识～ be clear (about sth) ❷ be aware of; know

清纯 qīngchún ❶ pretty and pure: ～少女 ingénue ❷ fresh and pure; fresh and clear

清脆 qīngcuì ❶ clear and pleasant to the ear; 嘹亮 loud and clear ❷ (of food) crisp and delicious

清单 qīngdān complete list; catalogue; inventory

清淡 qīngdàn ❶ (of smell, etc) light; plain; delicate ❷ (of food) not greasy or rich; light ❸ (of business) dull; slack

清点 qīngdiǎn sort and count; make an inventory (of sth); check

清福 qīngfú life of ease and comfort; 享～ enjoy a comfortable leisured life

清高 qīnggāo ❶ above petty politics and material pursuits; pure and lofty ❷ aloof from the common run of people; stand-offish

清官 qīngguān honest and upright official; ～难断家务事〈俗〉even an upright magistrate finds it difficult to settle a family quarrel; there is no way to straighten out family quarrels

清规戒律 qīngguī-jièlǜ (for Buddhists) regulations, taboos and commandments; (rigid) rules and conventions

清寒 qīnghán ❶ poor; impoverished ❷ *also* "清冷" clear and cold

清洁 qīngjié clean; ～工 (street) cleaner; garbage collector; housemaid / ～能源 clean energy

清净 qīngjìng ❶ peace and quiet; 耳根～ attain peace of mind by keeping away from unpleasant noise of any kind ❷ clear; limpid

清静 qīngjìng quiet; tranquil; serene

清苦 qīngkǔ simple and devoid of the ordinary comforts of life; spartan

清朗 qīnglǎng ❶ (of weather) cool and clear; 爽朗 crisp and bright ❷ (of voice, etc) clear and resounding

清理 qīnglǐ sort out; clear or tidy up;

〈经〉wind up：～欠税 clear up cases of tax arrears / ～思想 straighten out one's thinking

清凉 qīngliáng　pleasantly cool；cool and pleasant；～油 cooling ointment；Tiger balm

清明 qīngmíng　❶（of politics）characterized by good government and prevalence of justice ❷（of a person）sober and calm ❸（of weather）clear and bright ❹ 5th seasonal division point　see also "节气" jiéqì

清贫 qīngpín　poor；impoverished；～自守 maintain one's integrity despite straitened circumstances

清漆 qīngqī　varnish

清瘦 qīngshòu　〈婉〉thin；lean；spare

清爽 qīngshuǎng　❶ clean and fresh ❷ relieved；relaxed；at ease ❸〈方〉neat；tidy ❹〈方〉light and tasty

清水衙门 qīngshuǐ yámen　government office or organization with inadequate funds and scanty benefits

清算 qīngsuàn　❶ carefully calculate and check；settle；clear；～银行 clearing or settlement bank ❷ expose and condemn；liquidate

清晰 qīngxī　clear；distinct；well-defined；条理～ methodical；well-arranged / ～度（of TV）definition；（of telecommunications）articulation；（of images）resolution

清洗 qīngxǐ　❶ rinse；wash；clean ❷ purge；eliminate；get rid of

清闲 qīngxián　quiet；at leisure；～自在 be leisurely and carefree；feel very much at ease

清香 qīngxiāng　delicate fragrance；faint scent；～可口的饭菜 delicate，appetizing food

清新 qīngxīn　❶ fresh；refreshing ❷ original；tasteful

清醒 qīngxǐng　❶ fresh；clear-headed；sober-minded ❷ regain consciousness；come to

清秀 qīngxiù　pretty and graceful；fine and delicate

清雅 qīngyǎ　❶ elegant；refined；graceful ❷ delicate；cultured

清一色 qīngyīsè　❶（of mahjong）all of one suit ❷ uniform；homogeneous；all in the same way；搞～ be bent on uniformity；love to have everybody and everything in the same way

清真 qīngzhēn　Islamic；Muslim；～教 Islam；Islamism / ～寺 also "礼拜寺" mosque / ～食品 Muslim food

清正 qīngzhèng　honest and upright；～廉明 clean, honest and just

蜻 qīng

蜻蜓 qīngtíng　〈动物〉dragonfly

鲭 qīng 〈动物〉mackerel

qíng

情 qíng

情 qíng　❶ feeling；emotion；sentiment；～怀 thoughts and feelings / ～商 EQ（emotion quotient）/ ～同手足 be as intimate as brothers；regard each other as brothers / ～投合 be well suited to each other temperamentally；hit it off ❷ sensibilities；kindness；favour；～不可却 cannot refuse for the sake of friendship ❸ love；passion；lust；～敌 rival in a love triangle / ～妇 mistress / ～歌 love song / ～郎（girl's）lover；boy-friend / ～侣 lovers；sweethearts / ～书 love letter；billet-doux / ～欲 sexual urge；carnal desire；lust / ～缘 destiny of being in love；(predestined) sentimental bond / ～种 person of the sentimental type, especially one who easily falls in love / ～场失意 be disappointed in love / ～窦初开（esp of a young girl）（experience）first awakenings or stirrings of love / 坠入～网 fall in love ❹ situation；circumstance；condition；～境

circumstances; situation; occasion

情报 qíngbào information; intelligence; ～检索 information retrieval / ～人员 intelligence personnel or agents

情不自禁 qíngbùzìjīn cannot contain one's feelings; cannot refrain from; let oneself go: ～地哭出声来 cannot help sobbing

情操 qíngcāo sentiment; character; integrity

情调 qíngdiào taste; atmosphere; mood: 东方～ oriental taste

情分 qíngfèn mutual affection or love; friendship: 手足～ brotherly love; fraternity

情感 qínggǎn ❶ emotion; feeling: 复杂的～ mixed feelings ❷ affection; attachment: ～很深 be strongly attached (to)

情急 qíngjí moment of desperation: ～生智 hit on a good idea in a moment of desperation; have a brainwave on the spur of the moment

情节 qíngjié ❶ plot: ～离奇 fantastic plot ❷ (circumstances of a) case

情结 qíngjié complex: 恋母～ Oedipus complex

情景 qíngjǐng ❶ scene; sight; circumstances: ～喜剧 situation comedy; sitcom ❷ feelings and circumstances: ～交融 feeling and setting happily blended

情况 qíngkuàng ❶ situation; condition; state of affairs: ～并非如此。 That is by no means the case. ❷ military developments: 有～。 There are new developments.

情理 qínglǐ reason; sense: ～之中 within the bounds of reason

情面 qíngmiàn feelings; sensibilities; face: 讲～ spare sb's sensibilities

情趣 qíngqù ❶ temperament and taste: ～相投 have similar temperaments and tastes ❷ emotional appeal; interest: ～高雅 refined or elegant taste

情人 qíngrén sweetheart; lover: ～节 Valentine's Day (Feb 14) / ～眼里出西施。 Beauty is in the eye of the beholder.

情形 qíngxing situation; condition; state (of affairs): 看～ as it appears

情绪 qíngxù ❶ morale; feeling; mood: 稳定一下～ steady one's jangled nerves ❷ moodiness; dejection; depression: 闹～ be in a fit of depression; be in the sulks / 有～ be moody or unhappy (over sth)

情义 qíngyì mutual affection between friends, relatives and comrades; emotional attachment; ties of friendship: 最重～ value friendship above anything else

情谊 qíngyì friendly feelings or sentiments

情意 qíngyì friendly regard; affection; 有着深厚的～ cherish a profound attachment for sb)

情由 qíngyóu hows and whys; ins and outs; circumstances

情有可原 qíngyǒukěyuán excusable; forgivable; pardonable

情愿 qíngyuàn ❶ willingly; of one's own accord or free will ❷ would rather; prefer: ～死, 也不屈服 would rather die than submit

晴 qíng sunny; fine; clear: ～好 fine and beautiful / ～朗 fine; sunny / ～空万里 clear and boundless sky / 多云转～。 It will clear up after a cloudy spell. or (as a weather forecast) Cloudy to clear.

晴天 qíngtiān fine or sunny day: ～霹雳 also "青天霹雳" thunderbolt from a clear sky; bolt from the blue

晴雨表 qíngyǔbiǎo weatherglass; barometer; 〈喻〉 sth that shows (signs of) change

氰 qíng 〈化〉 cyanogen: ～化物 cyanide

擎 qíng raise; hold or lift up: ～天柱 〈喻〉 pillar of state, society, etc

黥 qíng 〈书〉❶〈史〉(as punishment) brand (in black) ❷ tattoo (usu in green or blue)

qǐng

顷 qǐng ❶ *qing*, unit of area equal to one hundred *mu* (6.66 hectares or 16.47 acres) ❷〈书〉short while; moment; instant: ~刻 in an instant; instantly ❸〈书〉just (now): ~闻噩耗 have just heard the sad news

请 qǐng ❶ request; ask; entreat: ~功 recommend that somebody be awarded (for meritorious deeds) / ~假 ask for leave (of absence) ❷ invite; engage; send for: ~帖 also "请束" invitation card; written invitation / ~不动 be unable to get sb to accept an invitation or comply with a request / ~不起 cannot afford (to hire sb, etc) / ~医生 send for a doctor ❸〈敬〉please: ~便 please or suit yourself; do as you wish / ~留步。(to a host) Please don't bother to see me out. ❹〈旧〉buy (incense, etc) or set out (statue, etc) for worship

请安 qǐng'ān ❶ pay respects (usu to elders); wish good health ❷ also "打千"〈旧〉salute by bending one's left knee and drooping one's right hand

请教 qǐngjiào consult; seek advice

请客 qǐngkè play the host; stand treat; entertain guests: 今天我~。It's on me.

请命 qǐngmìng ❶ plead on sb's behalf: 为民~ plead or speak for the people ❷〈书〉ask (higher authorities) for instructions

请求 qǐngqiú ask; entreat; request: 批准~ approve a request

请示 qǐngshì ask for or request instructions: ~工作 ask for instructions on one's work or assignment

请愿 qǐngyuàn (present a) petition

请战 qǐngzhàn ask for permission to go into battle; ask for an assignment (in a project, etc)

请罪 qǐngzuì ask for punishment because one has committed an unpardonable error; apologize: 当面~ offer an apology in person

qìng

庆(慶) qìng ❶ celebrate: ~典 celebration; ceremony / ~贺 celebrate; congratulate / ~幸 congratulate oneself; rejoice / ~祝 celebrate; mark ❷ occasion for celebration

亲(親) qìng *see also* qīn

亲家 qìngjia ❶ relatives by marriage ❷ parent-in-law of one's child: ~母〈口〉mother-in-law of one's daughter or son

磬 qìng ❶ percussion instrument made of jade or stone ❷ Buddhist percussion instrument made of bronze

罄 qìng 〈书〉use up; consume; exhaust: 售~ be sold out / ~竹难书 (of crimes, etc) be too numerous to enumerate

qióng

穷(窮) qióng ❶ poor; poverty-stricken: ~人 poor people; the destitute / ~光蛋〈口〉〈贬〉pauper; poor wretch / ~则思变。Poverty gives rise to a desire for change. ❷ wretched; bleak; desperate: ~对付〈口〉shift for oneself as best one can (in wretched circumstances) / ~讲究〈口〉be fastidious or fussy despite difficult (financial) conditions; be overly choosy or picky / ~开心 try to enjoy oneself amid misery / ~

山恶水 rugged hills and turbulent waters / ～乡僻壤 area shut off from the outside world; remote; out-of-the-way place ❸ exhaust; use up:～年累月 year after year; for many years / ～途末路 at an impasse; at a dead end; on one's last legs ❹ thoroughly (investigate); through to the end:～追 go in hot pursuit; pursue rigorously; search thoroughly:～究其理 probe deeply into a matter to find the cause ❺ utterly; extremely; wantonly:～兵黩武 wantonly engage in military ventures; indulge in wars of aggression / ～极无聊 absolutely idle and bored; totally silly or absurd / ～奢极侈 also "穷奢极欲" live in extreme extravagance; wallow in luxury / ～凶极恶 extremely brutal and vicious; incredibly ferocious and wicked; most barbarous

穷尽 qióngjìn limit; finish; end: 没有～ inexhaustible

穷苦 qióngkǔ poor and miserable; impoverished

穷困 qióngkùn poverty-stricken; impoverished; destitute:～潦倒 be hard pressed and down on one's luck

穷酸 qióngsuān (of a scholar) impoverished and pedantic

茕(煢) qióng

茕茕 qióngqióng 〈书〉❶ solitary; all alone:～孑立 stand all by oneself, quiet and solitary ❷ worried; sad: 忧心～ full of worry; eaten up by anxiety

穹 qióng

〈书〉❶ vault; dome:～顶〈建筑〉dome; crown / ～庐 tent with a vaulted roof inhabited by nomadic tribes ❷ sky:～苍 vault of heaven; the firmament

琼(瓊) qióng

❶ 〈书〉fine jade; sth exquisite:～浆 excellent wine; nectar / ～楼玉宇 beautiful palaces (as in a fairyland or the moon) ❷ (Qióng) another name

for Hainan (海南)

蛩 qióng

〈书〉❶ locust ❷ cricket

qiū

丘 qiū

❶ mound; hillock:～陵 hills / ～墓〈书〉grave; tomb / ～疹〈medical〉papule; pimple ❷ cover (a coffin) with bricks and stones prior to burial ❸ 〈量〉plot of irrigated paddy field

秋 qiū

❶ autumn; fall:～季 also "秋天" autumn (season) / ～色 autumn scenery / ～收 autumn harvest; autumn crop or produce / ～老虎 spell of hot weather in early autumn / ～高气爽 clear sky and crisp air in autumn; fine autumn weather ❷ harvest time ❸ year ❹ (troubled) period of time; juncture

秋波 qiūbō bright eyes (of a beautiful woman):～传情 give the glad eye (to sb); cast coquettish glances (at sb)

秋分 qiūfēn Autumnal Equinox, 16th seasonal division point　see also "节气" jiéqì

秋毫 qiūháo (of an animal or bird) fine autumn hair; minute detail:～无犯 (of troops) not encroach on people's interests in the least

秋后算账 qiūhòusuànzhàng wait until the dust settles to reckon with sb; bide one's time to clear the scores with sb

秋千 qiūqiān swing:打～ play on the swing

蚯 qiū

蚯蚓 qiūyǐn earthworm

qiú

囚 qiú

❶ imprison; jail:～禁 imprison; put in jail; hold in captivity ❷ prisoner; convict; ～犯 *also* "囚徒"prisoner; convict / ～牢 prison; jail / ～衣 prison clothes

犰 qiú

犰狳 qiúyú 〈动物〉armadillo

求 qiú

qiú ❶ ask; beg; entreat; ～爱 pay suit to; woo; court / ～签〈迷信〉draw a lot for an oracle / ～亲 (of a family or parent) seek a marriage alliance (with another family); make an offer of marriage (on behalf of the son, etc) / ～医 *also* "求治" seek medical treatment; see a doctor / ～雨 pray for rainfall / ～援 ask (sb) for help or assistance; request reinforcements / ～爷爷告奶奶〈口〉piteously beg everybody everywhere; go begging on all fours ❷ try; seek; strive for; ～证 seek proof or confirmation / ～贤若渴 seek talent eagerly ❸ demand; ～大于供。Demand exceeds supply.

求和 qiúhé ❶ sue for peace ❷ (in ball games or chess) try to draw a match; strive for a draw

求婚 qiúhūn ask for a lady's hand; make an offer of marriage; propose; ～者 suitor

求见 qiújiàn ask to see; request an interview; seek an audience

求教 qiújiào ask for advice; seek counsel

求救 qiújiù send (signals, etc) for help; ask sb to come to the rescue; ～信号 GMDSS (formerly SOS) signal; distress call or signal

求偶 qiú'ǒu seek a spouse; court; ～行为 courtship behaviour

求情 qiúqíng plead or beg for leniency; intercede (in sb's behalf); put in a good word (for sb)

求全 qiúquán ❶〈贬〉ask for perfection; ～思想 perfectionist ideas / ～责备 criticize a person for failing to be perfect; nitpick ❷ try to round sth off;

try to achieve sth through compromise; 忍辱～ make humiliating compromises or concessions to achieve one's purpose; stoop to compromise

求生 qiúshēng seek survival; keep oneself alive

求实 qiúshí be realistic or practical-minded; ～精神 down-to-earth approach; realism

求同存异 qiútóng-cúnyì seek common ground while reserving differences

求学 qiúxué ❶ go to or attend school; pursue one's studies ❷ seek knowledge

求之不得 qiúzhībùdé more than one could wish for; ～的机会 golden or most welcome opportunity

求知 qiúzhī seek knowledge; ～欲 thirst for knowledge

求职 qiúzhí seek a position; apply for a job; ～书 application for employment

求助 qiúzhù call for assistance; turn to sb for help; 多方～ seek help from various quarters

虬（虯） qiú 〈书〉coiled; curled; ～髯大汉 hefty fellow with curly sideburns

泅 qiú float on water; swim; ～渡 swim across (a river, etc) / ～水 float on water; swim

酋 qiú ❶ chief (of a tribe); ～长 tribal chief; emir; sheik(h) ❷ chieftain (of bandits, etc)

逑 qiú 〈书〉spouse; consort; life mate

球（❷毬） qiú ❶ sphere; globe; sth shaped like a sphere or ball; ～体 sphere; spheroid / ～形 spherical; globular / ～茎〈植〉corm ❷ ball; ball game; ～场 ground, court, or field for ball games / ～队 (ball game) team / ～杆 (golf) club / ～门 goal / ～迷 (ball game) fan; buff / ～拍 (tennis, badminton, etc) racket; (ping-pong) bat or paddle / ～

賽 ball game; match / ～鞋 gym or tennis shoes; sneakers / ～星 ball-game star; star or ace player / ～员 (short for 球类运动员) ball player ❸ globe; world

遒 qiú 〈书〉powerful; vigorous; forceful; ～劲 powerful; vigorous; sturdy

裘 qiú 〈书〉fur coat

qiǔ

糗 qiǔ 〈方〉(of rice or noodles) be clotted or caked

qū

区（區） qū ❶ distinguish; classify; subdivide; ～分 differentiate; distinguish; delineate ❷ area; zone; region; ～域 region; area; district ❸ (as an administrative division) district; region; ～划 administrative division (into districts, etc) / ～长 head of a district (as in a city)

区别 qūbié ❶ distinguish; differentiate; discriminate ❷ difference; distinction; ～极大 a world of difference

区区 qūqū ❶ petty; trivial; trifling; ～小事 mere trifle ❷ 〈旧〉〈谦〉my humble self

曲（❹麯） qū ❶ bent; curved; crooked; ～笔 euphemistic writing / ～面 curved surface; camber / ～别针 paper clip / ～径通幽 winding path leading to a secluded spot / ～～弯弯 also "曲里拐弯" full of twists and turns; winding; tortuous / ～意逢迎 go out of one's way to ingratiate oneself (with sb) ❷ bend (of sth); 河～ bend of a river ❸ wrong; false; unjustifiable; ～直 crooked and straight — right and wrong ❹ leaven; yeast

see also qǔ

曲棍球 qūgùnqiú 〈体〉field hockey; hockey ball

曲解 qūjiě （deliberately）misinterpret; distort; twist

曲线 qūxiàn ❶ curve; ～图 diagram of curves ❷ sth, esp a female body, having the shape of a curve; ～美 graceful curve

曲折 qūzhé ❶ tortuous; circuitous; winding ❷ complications; intricacies; twists and turns

驱（驅） qū ❶ drive (a horse, etc); spur; ～车前往 go in a car or carriage; drive to a place ❷ run quickly; drive ❸ expel; drive away; exorcise; ～赶 drive away; expel / ～寒 dispel cold / ～邪 ward off evils; exorcise evil spirits; drive away demons

驱除 qūchú drive out; eliminate; get rid of

驱动 qūdòng ❶ drive; ～器 〈信息〉disc drive / 风力～ wind-driven / 四轮～ four-wheel drive ❷ urge; impel; drive; 在暴利的～下 driven by lust for excessive profits

驱遣 qūqiǎn ❶ force (sb to do sth); compel; drive ❷ 〈书〉expel; banish; deport ❸ *see* "驱散❷"

驱散 qūsàn ❶ break up; scatter; disperse ❷ dispel; drive away; get rid of; ～寂寞和忧郁 relieve one's loneliness and melancholy

驱使 qūshǐ ❶ order about; push around; 任人～ be at sb's beck and call ❷ impel; prompt; spur on; 良心的～ promptings of conscience

驱逐 qūzhú throw out; expel; oust; ～舰 〈军〉destroyer / ～出境 deport

屈 qū ❶ bend; bow; crouch; ～膝 go down on one's knees; submit / ～指可数 count on one's fingers ❷ subdue; submit; 〈套〉condescend; ～从 submit to; knuckle under to / ～驾 con-

Q

descend to make the journey; be kind enough to honour us with your presence / ～就 condescend to take a post offered / ～尊 condescend; stoop / ～己待人 accommodate others by denying or inconveniencing oneself ❸ wrong; injustice; wrongful treatment; ～辱 humiliation; dishonour; mortification

屈才 qūcái　put sb on a job unworthy of his or her talents; waste sb's talents

屈打成招 qūdǎchéngzhāo　confess to false charges under torture; make a spurious confession under coercion

屈服 qūfú　succumb; yield; knuckle under

屈节 qūjié　〈书〉❶ forfeit one's honour; humble oneself; ～辱命 lose one's honour and fail in one's mission ❷ stoop; act servilely

屈居 qūjū　be reconciled to a lower position than one deserves; ～亚军 have to settle for the second place

祛 qū　dispel; prevent; remove; ～除 dispel; get rid of; drive away / ～暑 drive away or ward off summer heat / ～痰 promote or facilitate expectoration

蛆 qū　maggot

躯（軀） qū　human body;～干 trunk; torso / ～壳 body (as opposed to soul); outer form / ～体 body; soma

焌 qū　❶ put out (sth burning) ❷ burn over a slow fire ❸ stir-fry vegetables as soon as the condiments are mixed with the boiling oil

趋（趨） qū　❶ hasten; rush; hurry along; ～迎 hasten forward to meet sb / ～走 hurry; walk quickly ❷ tend towards; head for; seek;～同 tend to converge; tend to be the same / ～利避害 seek advantages or gains and avoid disadvantages or losses / ～炎附势 curry favour with

the powerful; play up to those in power / ～之若鹜 fall over each other to get sth; scramble for sth

趋附 qūfù　ingratiate oneself with; curry favour with; pander or toady to

趋时 qūshí　〈书〉follow the fashion; be trendy:穿戴～ be fashionably dressed

趋势 qūshì　trend; tendency; inclination: 多极化～ trend towards multipolarity

趋向 qūxiàng　❶ lean towards; tend or incline to ❷ see "趋势"

蛐 qū

蛐蛐儿 qūqur　〈方〉〈动物〉cricket

觑 qū　〈口〉screw up one's eyes; squint *see also* qù

黢 qū　black; dark; ～黑 pitch-black; pitch-dark

qú

劬 qú

劬劳 qúláo　〈书〉overworked; exhausted

渠 qú　canal; ditch; channel;～道 canal; channel; medium or means of communication / ～灌 canal irrigation

癯 qú　〈书〉thin; emaciated:面容清～ look quite thin

衢 qú　〈书〉thoroughfare; main road

qǔ

曲 qǔ　❶ *qu*, a type of verse for singing:～牌 names of the tunes to which *qu* is composed ❷ song; tune; melody; ～调 tune (of a song); melody / ～目 names of songs, arias, etc; repertoire / ～艺 *quyi* — folk art forms such as ballad singing, comic dialogue, etc / ～子 song; tune; melody / ～高和寡 highbrow songs find few singers; be too highbrow for common people ❸ music (of a song); 作～ compose music

see also qū

取 qǔ ❶ get; draw; fetch: ～材 draw material (from) / ～乐 enjoy or amuse oneself; make merry / ～暖 warm oneself; keep warm ❷ 证 gather or collect evidence / ～而代之 replace; supersede; take over / ～样检查 take a sample to check / ～之不尽, 用之不竭 inexhaustible; unlimited ❷ aim at; seek: ～火 drill a piece of wood to make fire ❸ adopt; assume; choose: ～道 by way of; through; via / ～景 find a view or scene (to paint, photograph, etc) / ～名 give a name; name

取保 qǔbǎo 〈法〉 get sb to go bail for one; ask sb to bail one out: ～候审 be out on bail pending trial

取长补短 qǔchángbǔduǎn overcome one's own shortcomings by learning from others' strong points; draw on the strong points of others to make up for one's own weak points

取代 qǔdài replace; substitute; supersede

取得 qǔdé get; gain; achieve: ～成绩 achieve (good) results / ～联系 get in touch (with)

取缔 qǔdì outlaw; prohibit; ban

取法 qǔfǎ follow the example of; take as one's model; draw on: ～乎上, 仅得其中。〈谚〉 Even if you take the best as your model, you may only achieve the average.

取经 qǔjīng ❶ go on a pilgrimage to India for Buddhist scriptures ❷ learn from the experience of an advanced person, enterprise or locality

取决 qǔjué be determined (by); depend or hinge (on)

取巧 qǔqiǎo resort to wiles or trickery

取舍 qǔshě decide which to accept and which not; make one's choice: 材料的～ choice of material

取胜 qǔshèng win victory; achieve success; triumph: 以多～ triumph by sheer numbers

取向 qǔxiàng sense of direction; orientation: 价值观～ orientation of values

取消 qǔxiāo *also* "取销" cancel; call off; rescind: ～比赛资格 disqualify (sb) from a contest

取笑 qǔxiào laugh at; poke fun at; ridicule

取信 qǔxìn win confidence or trust: ～于民 gain the confidence of the people; win public trust

取悦 qǔyuè try to please; curry favour with; play up to

娶 qǔ marry (a woman); take to wife: ～妻 take a wife / ～亲 (of a man) get married

龋 qǔ

龋齿 qǔchǐ tooth decay; dental caries; decayed tooth

qù

去 qù ❶ go (away); depart; leave: ～留 quit or stay (put); leave or remain / ～职 no longer hold a post; quit a job / 大势已～。The game is as good as lost. ❷ remove; get rid of; do away with: ～火〈中医〉 reduce internal heat; relieve inflammation or fever / ～壳 hull; shell / ～污粉 (household) cleanser / ～粗取精 *also* "去芜存菁" discard the dross and keep the essence; get rid of the coarse to obtain the refined / ～伪存真 eliminate the false and retain the true; sift the true from the false ❸ be away or apart from: ～此不远 not far from here ❹ past; of last year: ～年 last year ❺

Q

used after a verb-object structure to indicate **a)** *intention*:打篮球~。Let's go and play basketball. **b)** *purpose*:拿着鱼竿~钓鱼 take along one's fishing rod for angling **❻** *also* "去声"〈语言〉falling tone, *see also* "四声" sìshēng **❼** play the part or role of; act (the part of):~反派人物 play the villain **❽** (qu) *used after a verb to indicate* **a)** *movement away from the speaker*:拍~身上的尘土 flick the dust off one's clothes **b)** *continuation*:一眼看~ look far ahead

去处 qùchù **❶** *see* "去向" **❷** place; spot; site

去路 qùlù way of progress; passage; outlet;挡住~ block the way

去皮 qùpí **❶** remove the peel or skin **❷** net weight:~50 公斤 fifty kilos in net weight

去世 qùshì （of grown-ups) die; expire; pass away

去向 qùxiàng whereabouts

阒 qù 〈书〉quiet; still; silent;~无一人. It was dead still, and not a soul was around.

趣 qù **❶** interest; amuse; delight;~谈 funny remarks; amusing talk / ~闻 interesting gossip or hearsay; amusing anecdote / 童年～事 amusing childhood episodes **❷** bent; purport; inclination:~旨〈书〉purport; aim; principle

趣味 qùwèi interest; delight; taste:~性 interest; popular appeal / 低级~ in bad taste; boorish; vulgar

觑 qù 〈书〉look; stare; gaze *see also* qū

quān

圈 quān **❶** circle; ring; hoop:~椅 round-backed armchair **❷** circle; set; coterie:~里人 insider **❸** enclose; surround; encircle:~养 raise

animals in enclosures **❹** mark with a circle:~定 approve or select (an item) by drawing a circle round it / ~阅 tick off one's name listed on a circular, notice, etc after reading it
see also juàn; juàn

圈点 quāndiǎn **❶** punctuate (an ancient text, etc) while reading **❷** mark words and phrases for special attention (with dots or small circles on the side)

圈套 quāntào snare; trap; ploy:落入~ fall into a trap; play into sb's hands

圈子 quānzi *also* "圈圈" **❶** ring; circle **❷** circle; clique; set:小~ (exclusive) clique; coterie / 生活～ circle in which one moves

quán

权（權） quán **❶** 〈书〉weigh; consider **❷** power; authority:~柄 power; authority / ~贵 influential officials; powers that be / ~位 power and position / ~欲 lust for power **❸** right:~益 rights and interests **❹** advantageous or favourable position:制空～〈军〉control of the air; air supremacy **❺** expedient; tentative:~谋 expediency; adaptability; resourcefulness / ~且 for the time being; as a stopgap measure / ~作不知 pretend to be ignorant

权变 quánbiàn adaptability or flexibility in tactics; tact:长于～ be good at varying one's tactics according to circumstances

权衡 quánhéng weigh; balance:~得失 weigh the gains and losses; weigh the pros and cons; weigh the odds

权力 quánlì **❶** power; authority:~机构 organ of power / ~下放 decentralization of power **❷** jurisdiction

权利 quánlì right:~与义务 rights

and obligations

权势 quánshì power and influence；~集团 the establishment

权术 quánshù art of political manoeuvring；political trickery；Machiavellian politics

权威 quánwēi authority；authoritativeness；~人士 authoritative person or source；authority

权限 quánxiàn jurisdiction；competence；extent of authority：超越～exceed one's authority；go beyond one's brief

权宜 quányí expedient：~之计 expedient；makeshift device；stopgap measure

全 quán ❶ all ready；complete：~套 complete set ❷ keep from harm or damage；keep intact：难以两全 it is hard to satisfy both sides；can't eat the cake and keep it ❸ whole；entire；full：~称 full name；unabbreviated form /～额 full amount；in full /～景 whole scene；panorama /～貌 complete picture；full view /～年 for the whole year；annual；yearly /～胜 all-round victory /～速 full speed；top gear /～新 entirely new；brand-new /～日制 full-time /～天候 all-weather ❹ wholly；entirely；completely：~都 all；without exception /～然 (used in the negative) wholly；completely；entirely

全部 quánbù whole；entire；full

全才 quáncái multi-talented person；versatile mind；all-rounder

全场 quánchǎng ❶ whole audience；all those present ❷ 〈体〉full-court；all-court：~紧逼 all-court or full-court press

全方位 quánfāngwèi omni-directional；all-dimensional；all-round：~外交 all-round diplomacy /～开放 open in all domains；open to all countries

全副 quánfù complete；full；all：~武装 fully armed；in full battle array；armed to the teeth

全国 quánguó all over the country；nation-wide；national：~性 nationwide；countrywide；on a national scale /～人大 (short for 全国人民代表大会) National People's Congress (NPC) /～政协 (short for 中国人民政治协商会议全国委员会) National Committee of the Chinese People's Political Consultative Conference (CPPCC)

全会 quánhuì plenary meeting or session；plenum

全集 quánjí complete or collected works：《莎士比亚～》*Complete Works of Shakespeare*

全家福 quánjiāfú ❶ photograph of the whole family ❷ hotchpotch

全局 quánjú general or overall situation；situation as a whole：~观念 concept of the overall picture；keeping the general situation in mind /～利益 overall interests

全军覆没 quánjūnfùmò ❶ (as of an army) be totally destroyed；be completely annihilated ❷ be thoroughly trounced

全力 quánlì exert all one's strength；go all out；spare no effort：~推销 go all out to boost (a new product)

全面 quánmiàn overall；all-round；general：~安排 overall arrangement /～发展 all-round development

全民 quánmín whole or entire people；all the people：~动员 mobilization of the whole nation；general mobilization /～所有制 ownership by the whole people

全能 quánnéng all-round；universal：~冠军 all-round champion

全盘 quánpán overall；comprehensive；wholesale：~否认 categorical denial /～西化 wholesale or all-out Westernization

全票 quánpiào ❶ full-price ticket ❷

all the votes in an election；以～当选 be unanimously elected

全勤 quánqín　full attendance during a certain period：出～ register a full attendance

全球 quánqiú　whole world；entire globe：～化 globalization / ～战略 global strategy

全权 quánquán　full or plenary powers；full authority：～代表 plenipotentiary

全身 quánshēn　of the whole body；all over the body：～像 full-length picture / ～麻醉〈医〉general anaesthesia

全神贯注 quánshénguànzhù　absorbed or engrossed in；wrapped up in；preoccupied with：～地听 listen with rapt attention

全盛 quánshèng　in full bloom；in the prime；at the zenith：～期 zenith；heyday

全体 quántǐ　all；entire；total：～代表 all the delegates / ～会议 plenary session

全息 quánxī　holographic：～照相 holograph；hologram

全线 quánxiàn　❶ on all fronts；all along the line ❷ whole line；entire length

全心全意 quánxīn-quányì　wholeheartedly；with all one's heart；heart and soul

诠 quán　〈书〉❶ expound；annotate；interpret：～释 annotation；explanatory notes；glossary ❷ reason；logic；truth：真～ truth

泉 quán　spring；mouth or source of a spring：～水 spring water / ～眼（mouth of a）spring

泉下 quánxià　in the nether world

泉源 quányuán　fountainhead；wellspring；〈喻〉source：力量的～ source of strength

拳 quán　❶ fist：握～ clench one's fist / ～打脚踢 cuff and kick；strike and kick；beat up ❷ boxing；

pugilism：～手 boxer / ～术 Chinese boxing / ～王 boxing champion ❸ curl；warp；bend：～曲 curl；coil；twist / ～起腿来 bend one's leg

拳击 quánjī　boxing；pugilism：～台 boxing ring / ～运动 boxing / ～运动员 boxer；pugilist

拳脚 quánjiǎo　❶ fists and feet；beat and kick：～相加 rain blows (on sb) ❷ Chinese boxing

拳拳 quánquán　also〈惓惓〉〈书〉earnest；sincere：～服膺 always bear in mind；have sincere belief in；place implicit faith in

拳头 quántou　fist：～产品 highly competitive product；knockout product

铨 quán　〈书〉❶ choose or select (officials) ❷ weigh；balance

痊 quán　fully recover from an illness：～愈 be well again

蜷 quán　coil；curl or huddle up：～伏 lie coiled up；curl or huddle up / ～曲 curl；wind；twist / ～缩 huddle，curl or roll up

鬈 quán　❶ curly；wavy：满头～发 be curly-headed ❷ (of hair) lovely

颧 quán

颧骨 quángǔ　cheekbone

quǎn

犬 quǎn　dog：～齿 canine tooth / ～子〈谦〉my worthless son / ～牙交错 jigsaw-like；jagged；interlocking / ～效～马之劳 serve faithfully like a dog or horse；render one's humble service

quàn

劝(勸) quàn　❶ talk (sb) round by reasoning；try to persuade；advise：～架 try to stop a fight or quarrel; mediate / ～酒 urge sb (usu a guest) to drink more / ～慰 comfort; console; solace / ～降 try to induce (sb) to capitulate ❷ encourage; exhort; foster: ～勉 admonish and encourage / ～学 exhort people to study; encourage learning

劝告 quàngào advise; urge; exhort; 不听～ refuse to take advice

劝解 quànjiě ❶ mollify; allay (worry, anxiety, etc) ❷ mediate (as in a fight or quarrel); bring people together

劝诫 quànjiè also "劝戒" admonish; exhort; expostulate (with sb)

劝说 quànshuō exhort; admonish; advise

劝阻 quànzǔ advise sb to refrain from (doing sth); dissuade

券 quàn certificate; ticket; voucher: ～商 (short for 证券商) trader in securities *see also* xuàn

quē

炔 quē 〈化〉alkyne: 乙～ acetylene

缺 quē ❶ be short of; be deficient in; lack: ～货 be in short supply; be out of stock / ～失 defect; drawback; shortcoming / ～氧〈医〉oxygen deficiency / ～斤短两 give short measure ❷ with parts missing; incomplete; imperfect: ～漏 gaps and omissions / ～门 gap or lacuna (in a branch of learning, etc) ❸ not present; absent: ～课 be absent from class; miss a class / ～勤 absence from duty or work ❹ unfilled position; vacancy; opening: ～额 vacancy

缺德 quēdé wicked; mean; vicious: ～鬼 rascal; mean bird / ～少才 have neither ability nor virtue

缺点 quēdiǎn shortcoming; defect; failing

缺乏 quēfá be deficient or wanting in; be short of; lack

缺憾 quēhàn imperfection; disappointment; regret

缺口 quēkǒu ❶ breach; gap; crack ❷ (of funds, materials, etc) gap; shortfall

缺少 quēshǎo lack; be short of: ～雨水 have low rainfall / 不可～的支持 indispensable support

缺损 quēsǔn ❶ damaged; torn ❷ 〈医〉physiological defect: 先天性～ congenital defect

缺席 quēxí absent; not present: ～审判〈法〉trial by default / ～投票 absentee vote

缺陷 quēxiàn defect; shortcoming; fault

缺心眼儿 quēxīnyǎnr 〈口〉❶ also "缺心少肺" unwise to the ways of the world; simple-minded; scatterbrained ❷ retarded; mentally deficient

阙 quē 〈书〉❶ fault; error; mistake: ～失 mistake; fault ❷ also "缺" be short of; be deficient in; lack: ～如 deficient; yet to be provided / ～疑 leave a question open; reserve judgement for the time being

qué

瘸 qué 〈口〉lame (walk) with a limp: ～腿 lame / ～子 lame person; cripple

què

却(卻) què ❶ fall back; retreat; repulse: ～步 step back (in fear or disgust); hang back; shrink / ～敌 repulse the enemy ❷ refuse; decline; reject: ～之不恭 it would be impolite to decline ❸ lose; get rid of: ～病〈书〉ward off or cure a disease ❹ 〈副〉used to indicate a tran-

Q

sition：今天下雪，～不冷。It's snowy, but not cold.

雀 què　sparrow：～斑 freckle / ～跃 jump for joy　*see also* qiǎo

确（確） què ❶ true; reliable; authentic：～凿 conclusive; irrefutable ❷ rock-solid; firm：～保 see to it; ensure; guarantee / ～守原则 strictly abide by or firmly uphold a principle

确定 quèdìng ❶ definite; certain; for sure ❷ determine; decide; fix：～任务 set tasks

确立 quèlì　set up; establish：～协作关系 establish cooperation

确切 quèqiè ❶ definite; exact; precise：～地说 to be exact ❷ true; reliable; dependable：～的消息 reliable information

确认 quèrèn　confirm; authenticate; affirm：～航班 confirm one's flight / ～为鲁迅手迹 authenticate sth as Lu Xun's writing

确实 quèshí ❶ reliable; exact; true：证据～ ironclad evidence ❷ truly; really; indeed

确信 quèxìn ❶ be certain or sure; be convinced ❷ reliable information

确诊 quèzhěn　diagnose：～为肝炎 (one's illness) be diagnosed as hepatitis

阕 què　〈量〉❶ used in a song or ci poem：一～新词 a new ci poem ❷ one of two stanzas of a poem：上～ upper stanza / 下～ lower stanza of a ci poem

鹊 què　magpie：～桥 "Magpie Bridge" (for Cowherd and Weaver Maid to meet)；bridge or link between lovers / ～巢鸠占 seize for oneself what belongs rightfully to another / 声誉～起 gain resounding fame

権 què ❶〈书〉monopoly ❷ discuss

qūn

逡 qūn　〈书〉yield; give in; shrink from：～巡 hang back; flinch

qún

裙 qún　skirt; sth like a skirt：～裤 pantskirt; culottes / 围～ apron

裙带 qúndài　connection through one's female relatives; nepotism：～风 nepotism; petticoat influence / ～关系 networking through petticoat influence

群（羣） qún ❶ crowd; group：～岛 group of islands; archipelago / ～芳 all kinds of flowers; beautiful women / ～峰 chain of mountain peaks / ～婚 group or communal marriage (in primitive society) / ～集 crowd or assemble together / ～氓〈书〉〈贬〉common herd / ～山 continuous mountain range / ～英会 gathering or meeting of heroes ❷ large numbers of people：～殴 gang fight / ～雄 separatist warlords; numerous heroes / ～魔乱舞 demons and monsters dancing in riotous revelry — rogues of all kinds running amok / 起而攻之 rally together to attack sb; all rise against sb ❸〈量〉group; herd; flock：一～鹿 a herd of deer

群策群力 qúncè-qúnlì　pool the wisdom and efforts of the masses; make joint efforts; join hands to take concerted action

群龙无首 qúnlóngwúshǒu　a group without a leader; an army without a general

群落 qúnluò ❶ community; colony ❷ group; collection：古建筑～ group of ancient buildings

群情 qúnqíng　public sentiment; popular feelings：～激奋。Everyone was roused to action.

群体 qúntǐ ❶ colony ❷ collective; group

群众 qúnzhòng ❶ the masses or people; rank and file: ～关系 relationship with the popular masses; ties with the general run of people / ～路线 mass line / ～演员 walk-ons (in a play, etc) / 倾听～意见 listen to what people at the grass roots have to say ❷ people who are not members of the Chinese Communist Party or Youth League

麇 qún 〈书〉 in groups or large numbers: ～集 swarm; assemble; flock together

R

rán

蚺 rán *also* "蚺蛇" python; serpent

然 rán ❶ right; correct; accurate: ～也 yes; true ❷ so; like that: 不～ not so; no ❸〈连〉but; yet; however: ～而 yet; but; however / ～后 then; after that; afterwards

髯 rán whiskers; beard

燃 rán ❶ burn: ～料 fuel / ～眉之急 matter of great urgency; pressing need ❷ ignite; light; set fire to: ～放 set off; let off (fireworks, etc)

燃点 rándiǎn ❶ ignite; kindle ❷〈化〉ignition or burning point

燃烧 ránshāo ❶ burn; kindle ❷ (of strong feelings) burn; rage: 怒火～ burn with anger ❸〈化〉combustion; ignition: ～弹 fire or incendiary bomb

rǎn

冉 rǎn

冉冉 rǎnrǎn 〈书〉 ❶ (of tree branches, etc) hanging down loosely ❷ slowly; gradually: 月亮～上升。The moon rose slowly.

染 rǎn ❶ dye: ～发 dye one's hair / ～缸 dye vat; 〈喻〉place where people will degenerate / ～料 dye; dyestuff / ～指甲 paint one's fingernails ❷ catch (a disease); acquire or contract (a bad habit, etc)

染色 rǎnsè ❶ dyeing; colouring: ～剂 colouring agent ❷ colour (bacteria, etc for easy observation): ～体 chromosome

染指 rǎnzhǐ reap undeserved profit from; encroach upon: 不容他人～ allow nobody to meddle; brook no intervention

rāng

嚷 rāng *see also* rǎng

嚷嚷 rāngrang ❶ shout; yell; make an uproar ❷ make known or public; blurt

ráng

禳 ráng (usu 禳解)〈书〉keep off (evil, etc); exorcise (spirits)

瓤 ráng ❶ pulp; flesh; pith: ～子 pulp; filling ❷ interior part of certain things: 信～儿 letter inside an envelop

rǎng

壤 rǎng ❶ soil; earth ❷ earth; ground ❸ area; land; territory

攘 rǎng 〈书〉❶ reject; resist; expel: ～敌 resist the enemy ❷ seize; snatch; grab: ～夺国柄 seize state power ❸ roll or turn up (one's sleeves）：～臂高呼 roll up one's sleeves, raise one's arms and shout loudly ❹ confused; troubled：天下～～。There is great upheaval across the land.

嚷 rǎng ❶ shout; yell ❷ argue heatedly or noisily（with）; make a row
see also rāng

ràng

让（讓） ràng ❶ give or make way; give up; yield：～利 cut profit（for the benefit of customers,etc）/ ～路 make way（for）; yield the right of way; give way / ～贤 yield sb's position to a person of virtue and talent; step down in favour of a better qualified person ❷ offer; invite; treat：～茶 offer（sb）tea ❸ sell; transfer：平价一房 sell a house at a reasonable price ❹ allow; let; leave alone：谁～你这么干了? Who told you to do so? ❺ *used in a passive construction to introduce the agent*：杯子～我给打碎了。I broke the cup.
让步 ràngbù give in; give way; make a concession
让位 ràngwèi ❶ abdicate; resign ❷ *see* "让座❶" ❸ yield to; give way to
让座 ràngzuò ❶ give up or offer one's seat（to sb）❷ ask guests to be seated

ráo

饶（饒） ráo ❶ rich; abundant; plentiful：～舌 be loquacious or garrulous; shoot off one's mouth / ～有风趣 rich in wit and humour ❷ throw in; give or get sth extra for free：～头〈口〉sth thrown in as extra ❸ have mercy on; let off; forgive：～命 spare sb's life / ～恕 forgive; pardon / 得～人处且

人。Forgive where you may. ❹〈口〉although; despite

rǎo

扰（擾） rǎo harass; trouble; disturb：～乱 disturb; confuse; disrupt / ～民 harass or disturb the people / ～攘〈书〉hustle and bustle; confusion; hurly-burly / 多～了。〈套〉Thank you very much for all the trouble you've taken（to entertain us, etc）.

rào

绕（繞、❷❸遶） rào ❶ wind; coil ❷ move or go round; circle; revolve：～场一周（of athletes）go round the arena ❸ make a detour; bypass; circumvent：～道 *also* "绕路" make a detour; go by a roundabout route / ～行 go round（sth）; make a detour ❹ confuse; baffle; confound：～嘴（of a sentence, etc）tongue-twisting / ～口令 *also* "拗口令" tongue twister
绕圈子 ràoquānzi ❶ circle; go round and round ❷ *also* "绕弯儿"; "绕弯子" speak in a roundabout way; beat about the bush
绕弯儿 ràowānr ❶〈方〉go for a walk; take a stroll ❷ *see* "绕圈子❷"
绕远儿 ràoyuǎnr ❶（of a route）be longer：那条路～。That is a longer route. ❷ go the long way round

rě

惹 rě ❶ bring upon oneself（sth unpleasant）; incur：～祸 invite disaster; ask for trouble / ～事 cause trouble; commit a misdemeanour ❷ offend; provoke; tease：～恼 make angry; offend; annoy / ～是生非 provoke a dispute; kick up a fuss or row ❸ draw; cause: ～眼 eye-catching; conspicuous; showy / ～人爱 cute; charming / ～人讨厌 make a nuisance of oneself / ～人注意 attract or draw attention

rè

热（熱）

rè ❶ heat; thermal: ～量〈理〉quantity of heat / ～电厂 thermal-power plant / ～核反应〈理〉thermonuclear reaction ❷ hot: ～敷〈医〉hot compress / ～烘烘 very warm / ～气球 hot-air balloon / ～水袋 hot water bottle / ～水瓶〈口〉thermos (bottle or flask) / ～腾腾 (of food or water) steaming or piping hot ❸ make hot; heat or warm up: ～水器 water heater ❹ fever; temperature: ～退了。The temperature came down. ❺ ardent; warm; chummy: ～诚 sincere and warm-hearted; cordial / ～切 ardent; earnest; fervent / ～望 earnestly hope; ardently wish ❻ envious; eager: 眼～ feel envious ❼ in great demand; popular: ～货 also "热门货" goods in great demand; goods that sell well ❽ craze; fever; fad: 中国～ China fever / ～潮 mass enthusiasm; upsurge

热爱 rè'ài　deep affection; ardent love; devotion

热忱 rèchén　zeal; warm-heartedness; enthusiasm: 爱国～ patriotic sentiment / 待人～ treat people warmheartedly

热带 rèdài　tropical or torrid zone; the tropics: ～鱼 tropical fish

热点 rèdiǎn ❶ hot spot; flash point ❷ attraction; centre of attention: 旅游～（hot）tourist attraction / ～问题 hot issue

热度 rèdù ❶（degree of）heat ❷〈口〉fever; temperature ❸ zeal; fer-

vour: 对出国留学～很高（show）great zeal for studying abroad

热狗 règǒu　hotdog

热乎 rèhu　also "热火"; "热和" ❶ (nice and) warm ❷ (of people) warm and friendly; chummy; thick: 一见面就～上了 chum up with one another the moment they meet

热火朝天 rèhuǒcháotiān　reach the peak of enthusiasm; be in full swing; be bustling with activity

热辣辣 rèlālā　burning hot; scorching: 脸上～的 feel one's cheeks burning

热浪 rèlàng ❶ strong current of warm air; heat wave ❷〈喻〉fervour; enthusiasm; craze: 学电脑的～ craze to study computers

热泪 rèlèi　(hot) tears: ～盈眶 one's eyes brimming with tears; tears coming to one's eyes

热恋 rèliàn　be infatuated; be head over heels in love

热烈 rèliè　warm; enthusiastic; ardent: ～响应 respond enthusiastically

热门 rèmén　in great demand; popular: ～话题 topic on every one's lips; hot issue / 信息技术是个大～。Information technology is very popular.

热闹 rènao ❶ busy; bustling ❷ have a jolly good time; enjoy oneself ❸ scene of bustling activity; fun

热情 rèqíng　enthusiasm; zeal; warmth: ～奔放 overflow with enthusiasm or warmth

热身 rèshēn　warm or limber up: ～赛 warm-up match or exercise; warming-up competition

热土 rètǔ　land or place one has lived in and loves; native land or place: ～难离。It is hard to take leave of a place one loves.

热线 rèxiàn ❶ also "红外线" infra-red ray ❷〈通信〉hot-line ❸ busy route: 旅游～ busy tourist route

热销 rèxiāo　also "热卖" (of goods) in

great demand: ～商品 goods in great demand; goods that sell like hot pies

热心 rèxīn　enthusiastic; earnest; warm-hearted: ～肠〈口〉warm heart / ～公益 be devoted to public good

热血 rèxuè　warm blood; indignation: ～沸腾 one's blood boils; seethe with righteous indignation / ～男儿 red-blooded youth

热衷 rèzhōng　also "热中" ❶ hanker after or for; crave: ～名利 crave fame and gain ❷ be deeply interested in; be mad about

rén

人 rén ❶ human being; person; people: ～潮 stream or flow of people; huge crowd / ～寰〈书〉(human) world; the earth / ～伦 code of human relations, esp based on hierarchy / ～群 crowd; throng; multitude / ～像 portrait; figure; bust / ～证〈法〉(testimony of an) eyewitness / ～治 rule by man (as distinct from rule by law) / ～贩子 trafficker in human beings / ～定胜天 man is bound to conquer nature; man's will, not heaven, decides / ～多势众 enjoy numerical superiority and great strength; overwhelm or dominate by sheer numbers / ～迹罕至 (of a place) rarely visited by human beings; seldom trodden by people / ～满为患 overcrowded; over-staffed / ～面兽心 with a human face but a wolfish heart; a beast in human shape / ～声鼎沸 babel of voices; terrible din / ～微言轻 the words of a person in humble position carry little weight / ～之常情 human nature; normal practice (in human relations); ways of society / ～非圣贤，孰能无过。To err is human. ❷ everybody; each; all: ～～皆知 as is known to all; it is public knowledge that … / ～各有

志。Everyone has his own will or aspiration ❸ adult; grown-up: 长大成～ grow to manhood; come of age ❹ person engaged in or trained for a particular activity; hand; manpower: 培养～train people (for a particular purpose, etc) ❺ (other) people: ～云亦云 echo the views of others without thinking; parrot / ～言可畏 gossip is a fearful thing; one has to be wary of gossip ❻ personality; character: 他～怎么样？What do you think of him as a person? ❼ one's state of health or mind: ～在心不在 be with sb physically but have one's heart elsewhere

人才 réncái　also "人材" ❶ qualified person; person of ability; talent: ～辈出 people of talent emerge in succession; outstanding people come forward wave upon wave / ～济济 abundance of talented people; galaxy of talent / ～市场 employment market; job centre / ～外流 brain drain ❷〈口〉handsome appearance; 颇有几分～ rather pretty or handsome

人称 rénchēng　〈语言〉person: ～代词 personal pronoun

人次 réncì　person-time; man-time: 参观画展的超过一万～。Over ten thousand people visited the art exhibition.

人大 Réndà　(short for 人民代表大会) People's Congress: ～代表 deputy to the People's Congress

人道 réndào ❶ humanity; human sympathy: ～主义 humanitarianism ❷〈书〉moral standards or principles

人丁 réndīng　population; number of family members: ～兴旺 have a large or growing family; have a flourishing population

人浮于事 rénfúyúshì　have more staff than needed; be overstaffed; 改变～的状况 reduce redundancy

人格 réngé ❶ human dignity or character; moral quality:~魅力 charisma of one's personality / 以 ~ 担保 (promise) upon one's honour ❷〈法〉personality; person:~不可侵犯 inviolability of person

人工 réngōng ❶ artificial; man-made:~呼吸 artificial respiration / ~ 流产 (shortened as 人流) induced abortion or ~ 授精 artificial insemination or fertilization / ~智能 artificial intelligence ❷ manual labour or work; work done by hand; man-day:~打井 dig or drill a well by hand

人海 rénhǎi ❶ sea of faces; huge crowd (of people):人山 ~ multitude or sea of people ❷〈书〉human world:~沉浮 ups and downs of human life

人际 rénjì between persons; interpersonal:~关系 interpersonal or human relationship

人家 rénjiā ❶ household; family ❷ (of a girl) fiancé's family:她还没有 ~. She hasn't been betrothed yet. ❸ (rénjia) other people; others; certain person or persons:欠~的情 owe sb a favour ❹ (rénjia) I; me:~想要这件衣服嘛! But I really want that dress.

人间 rénjiān (human) world; the earth:~天堂 paradise on earth / ~ 奇迹 man-made miracle

人均 rénjūn per capita; per person or head:~消费 consumption per person; per capita consumption / ~国民生产总值 per capita GNP (gross national product)

人口 rénkǒu ❶ population:~爆炸 population explosion / ~普查 (population) census / ~老龄化 aging or greying of population ❷ family size; persons (esp women and children):拐卖~ abduct and sell women and children

人类 rénlèi mankind; humanity; human race or species; ~学 anthro-

pology / ~文明 human civilization

人力 rénlì manpower; labour power; ~ 资源 human or manpower resources / 非~所及 beyond human control

人马 rénmǎ ❶ troops; forces ❷ staff; set-up:原班~ original team; old set-up or cast

人们 rénmen people; the public

人民 rénmín the people:~币 renminbi; RMB / ~群众 the masses; the people / ~政府 people's government

人命 rénmìng human life:~案子 case of homicide or manslaughter / ~关天. A case involving human life is a matter of great consequence.

人品 rénpǐn ❶ moral quality or strength; character ❷〈口〉looks; bearing

人气 rénqì popular or public feeling; popularity:~急升 enjoy soaring popularity / ~最旺 most popular

人情 rénqíng ❶ human nature or feelings; sympathy:~味 human kindness; human interest / ~世故 worldly wisdom; ways of the world ❷ sensibilities; feelings:不讲~ spare no sensibilities ❸ favour:做~ do (sb) a favour / ~债 debt of gratitude ❹ etiquette; custom; convention:~往来 social exchanges ❺ gift; present:送~ give presents

人权 rénquán human rights; rights of man:~保障 guarantee of human rights

人身 rénshēn person:~安全 personal safety / ~攻击 personal attack / ~自由 personal freedom; freedom of person

人参 rénshēn ginseng

人生 rénshēng human experience; life:~观 outlook on life / ~哲学 philosophy of life

人士 rénshì personage; person; personality

人世 rénshì （human）world；this world：～沧桑 vicissitudes of man's world；tremendous changes in this world

人事 rénshì ❶ human affairs；vicissitudes in life ❷ personnel matters；human resources：～管理 human resources management；（esp in an enterprise）human engineering ❸ interpersonal relationship：～关系 interpersonal relations；organizational affiliation ❹ ways of the world ❺ what is humanly possible：尽～ do what is humanly possible；do what is regarded as one's last duty ❻ consciousness of the outside world：不醒～ be unconscious；be in a shock

人手 rénshǒu manpower；hand；staff：～不足 short of hands；shorthanded；understaffed

人梯 réntī ❶ human pyramid or ladder：搭～ stand one upon the other's shoulders ❷〈喻〉（serve as a）human ladder to success；people who willingly make sacrifices for others' progress or success

人体 réntǐ human body

人头 réntóu ❶ human head ❷ number of people：～税 poll tax ❸ relations with people：～熟 know many people（of a given place）❹〈方〉moral quality or character：～很次 be a mean guy

人为 rénwéi ❶ human effort：事在～。Where there is a will, there is a way. ❷ man-made；artificial：～失误 human error

人文 rénwén cultural activities in human society：～精神 humanistic spirit / ～景观 place of cultural interest / ～科学 humanities；humane studies / ～主义 humanism

人物 rénwù ❶ personage；figure ❷ character（in a literary work，etc）：～塑造 characterization ❸ figure painting （as a branch of traditional Chinese painting）

人心 rénxīn ❶ human or public feeling；public will or support；popularity：～大快 most gratifying to the public / ～向背 whether the people are for or against；trend of public feeling / ～隔肚皮。It is hard to tell what is going on in the minds of other people. ❷（good）sense；reason：～不古。Public morality is no longer what it used to be.

人行道 rénxíngdào pavement；sidewalk；人行横道 pedestrian or zebra crossing；crosswalk

人性 rénxìng ❶ human nature；humanity ❷ human characteristics or qualities：不通～ have no human conscience；be unfeeling and unreasonable

人选 rénxuǎn candidate：最佳～ best candidate or choice

人烟 rényān signs of human presence or habitation：～稠密 densely populated；populous

人员 rényuán personnel；staff；employee

人缘儿 rényuánr relationship with people；popularity：～不好 not get along with people；be unpopular

人造 rénzào artificial；man-made；imitation：～革 imitation leather；leatherette / ～宝石 imitation jewel or gem / ～黄油 margarine / ～卫星 man-made satellite

人质 rénzhì hostage：劫持～ take（sb）a hostage

人种 rénzhǒng ethnic group；race

壬 rén 9th of the Heavenly Stems
see also 干支 gānzhī

仁 rén ❶ benevolence；kindheartedness；humanity：～厚 kind and generous / ～政 policy of benevolence；benevolent government / ～人志士 people with lofty ideals；public-spirited people / ～者见～，智者见智。Opinions differ (from person to person). or Everyone has his own views. ❷〈敬〉 you; your: ～兄〈书〉elder brother; my dear friend ❸ kernel; stone (of a peach, etc): 杏～儿 apricot stone

仁爱 rén'ài benevolence; kindheartedness: ～之心 kind heart; benevolence

仁慈 réncí benevolence; mercy; kindness: ～的老人 kind old man

仁义 rényì humanity and justice; benevolence and virtue: ～道德 benevolence, righteousness, virtue and morality

仁至义尽 rénzhì-yìjìn treat (sb) with the utmost decency and kindness; do everything possible to help; do what is humanly possible (for sb)

rěn

忍 rěn ❶ bear; endure; tolerate: ～不住 cannot help (doing sth); be unable to bear / ～气吞声 swallow rude remarks; submit to humiliation; eat dirt / ～无可～ be pushed beyond the limit of endurance; be provoked beyond endurance ❷ have the heart to: 不～拒绝 can't find it in one's heart to refuse

忍俊不禁 rěnjùnbùjìn cannot help laughing; be unable to keep a straight face

忍耐 rěnnài exercise patience or restraint; restrain oneself: 我有点～不住了。My patience was wearing thin.

忍让 rěnràng show or exercise forbearance; be conciliatory: 互相～ bear with each other

忍辱负重 rěnrǔ-fùzhòng endure humiliation in order to discharge important duties

忍受 rěnshòu stand; bear; put up with

忍痛 rěntòng bear or suffer pain; do sth against one's own heart: ～割爱

reluctantly part with sth one loves

忍心 rěnxīn have the heart to; be hardhearted enough to

荏 rěn 〈书〉weak; cowardly: ～弱 weak

荏苒 rěnrǎn 〈书〉(of time) elapse imperceptibly; slip by: 光阴～,转瞬十年。Time flies and ten years have elapsed in the twinkling of an eye.

稔 rěn ❶〈书〉(of grain) ripe: 丰～ bumper harvest ❷ year: 一～三熟 three crops a year ❸ familiar; acquainted (usu with people): ～熟 familiar

rèn

刃 rèn ❶ edge of a knife, etc; blade ❷ sword; knife: ～具 cutting tool ❸〈书〉kill with a sword or knife

认(認) rèn ❶ recognize; identify; distinguish: ～出 recognize; make out / ～得 know; recognize; tell / ～知 cognition / ～字 be able to read; be literate / ～清形势 understand the situation clearly; see things as they are ❷ acknowledge (a certain relationship); adopt: ～干儿子 adopt sb as one's godson ❸ admit; accept; recognize: ～错 also "认不是" admit a fault; acknowledge a mistake; make an apology / ～罚 submit to punishment or a fine / ～命〈迷信〉resign oneself to fate / ～输 admit defeat; give in or up; throw in the sponge / ～罪 admit one's guilt; plead guilty / ～死理 be stubborn or inflexible; have a one-track mind / ～贼作父 regard one's foe as kith and kin; go over to the enemy and serve him abjectly ❹ offer (to pay, etc); promise; pledge: ～购 subscribe to buy ❺ (followed by 了) resign oneself to a loss, etc; accept as unavoidable: 就是吃亏, 我也～

了。Even if I suffer a loss, I will swallow it.

认定 rèndìng ❶ firmly believe; hold; maintain ❷ confirm; affirm; decide on:~目标 decide on one's aim

认可 rènkě accept; approve; confirm:点头~ nod (in) approval

认领 rènlǐng ❶ claim:~失物 claim one's lost property ❷ adopt:~孤儿 adopt an orphan

认生 rènshēng (of a child) be shy with strangers

认识 rènshi recognize; understand; know:~论 theory of knowledge; epistemology / ~水平 level of understanding

认同 rèntóng ❶ identify:民族~感 sense of national identity ❷ approve; acknowledge

认为 rènwéi consider; think; believe

认养 rènyǎng ❶ adopt and raise (an orphan, etc) ❷ undertake to pay for the care of (greenery, animals, etc)

认账 rènzhàng acknowledge a debt; admit what one has said or done; shoulder one's responsibility

认证 rènzhèng 〈法〉attestation; authentication:~费 certification fee / ~文件 authenticated document

认真 rènzhēn ❶ serious; earnest; conscientious ❷ take seriously; take to heart

仞 rèn ancient measure of length equal to seven or eight *chi* (尺):万~高山 immeasurably high mountain

任 rèn ❶ appoint; engage:~用 appoint; assign (sb) to a post / ~免名单 list of appointments and removals ❷ assume; undertake; take up:~教 teach; be a teacher; take a teaching job / ~课 give lessons; teach at a school / ~职 hold a post; be in office ❸ bear; face:~劳~怨 work hard and never feel upset by criticism;

stand the strain of labour and injustice ❹ office; official post:~期 term or tenure of office ❺ let; allow; permit:~其自然 let things run their own course; let nature take its course ❻ no matter (how, what, etc):~你怎么说,他也不听。No matter what you say, he won't listen.

任何 rènhé any; whatever; whoever

任命 rènmìng appoint:~状 commission; credential; letter of appointment

任凭 rènpíng ❶ be at one's convenience, disposal, or discretion:~处理 be dealt with as one sees fit; be at one's discretion ❷ no matter (how, who, etc):~谁都要遵守法律。No matter who you are, you must abide by the law.

任人 rènrén ❶ appoint or use people:~唯亲 appoint people by favouritism; practise cronyism ❷ let people (do what they please):~宰割 submit meekly to oppression; allow oneself to be trampled upon

任务 rènwu assignment; mission; task

任性 rènxìng wilful; self-willed; headstrong

任意 rènyì ❶ wilfully; arbitrarily; wantonly:~挥霍 spend freely ❷ unconditional; unqualified:~球 (of football) free kick; (of handball) free throw

任重道远 rènzhòng-dàoyuǎn the task is arduous and the road ahead is long — shoulder heavy responsibilities in years to come

纫 rèn ❶ thread (a needle):~针 thread a needle ❷ sew; stitch

韧(靭) rèn pliable but strong; tough:~带〈生理〉ligament / ~劲 tenacity; steadfastness; perseverance / ~性 toughness; malleability; tenacity

饪(飪)

rèn　cook：烹～ cooking；culinary art

妊(姙)

rèn　pregnancy：～娠 pregnancy；gestation

rēng

扔

rēng ❶ throw；cast；toss ❷ throw away；cast aside：～掉 throw away；shake off / ～下 leave behind；abandon；cast aside

réng

仍

réng ❶ remain：一～其旧 remain the same as before；continue as before；follow the beaten track ❷〈书〉frequently；often ❸〈书〉still；yet：～然 still；yet

仍旧 réngjiù ❶ remain the same ❷ still；yet；as ever

rì

日

rì ❶ sun：～出 sunrise / ～晷 also "日规" sundial；gnomon / ～落 sunset；sundown / ～照 sunshine / ～晒雨淋 be exposed to the sun and rain；be weather-beaten ❷ daytime：～班 day shift / ～场 day show；matinée / ～托 day care / ～～夜夜 day and night；night and day ❸ day；specified day：～复一～ day after day；day in and day out ❹ every day；daily；with each passing day：～报 daily (paper) / ～见好转 improve day by day / ～趋没落 be on the decline ❺ time；period：～后 in the days to come；in the future；some day / ～前 a few days ago；the other day ❻（Rì）(short for 日本) Japan：～语 Japanese (language) / ～圆 also "日元"(Japanese) yen

日本 Rìběn　Japan；Nippon：～人 Japanese

日薄西山 rìbóxīshān　be on the decline or wane；be drawing near one's end or doom

日不暇给 rìbùxiájǐ　be fully occupied；have no time to spare

日常 rìcháng　day-to-day；everyday；daily：～事务 day-to-day business

日程 rìchéng　schedule；programme：～表 schedule

日光 rìguāng　sunlight；sunbeam；daylight：～灯 fluorescent or daylight lamp / ～浴 sunbath；sunbathing

日积月累 rìjī-yuèlěi　by piecemeal accumulation；gradually

日记 rìjì　diary；journal：记～ keep a diary

日久 rìjiǔ　with the passage of time；over time：～天长 as the years go by；in (the) course of time / ～见人心 time reveals a person's character；it takes time to know a person

日理万机 rìlǐwànjī　(of a statesman, etc) have numerous problems to attend to every day；be busy or occupied with a myriad of (state) affairs

日历 rìlì　calendar：～手表 calendar watch

日暮途穷 rìmù-túqióng　approach the end of one's days；be on one's last legs；be doomed

日期 rìqī　date：～变更线 (international) date line

日食 rìshí　（天文）solar eclipse：～环食 annular solar eclipse / 日偏食 partial solar eclipse / 日全食 total solar eclipse

日新月异 rìxīn-yuèyì　change with each passing day；undergo daily changes

日益 rìyì　day by day；more and more；increasingly：～改善 get better and better

日用 rìyòng ❶ of everyday use：～品 articles of everyday use；house wares ❷ daily expenses

日月 rìyuè ❶ sun and moon ❷ time; days; life:苦度～ spend one's days in misery; drag out a miserable existence

日志 rìzhì　journal; daily record;航海～ logbook; log

日子 rìzi ❶ date; day ❷ days; time ❸ life; livelihood

róng

戎 róng 〈书〉❶ arms; weaponry ❷ army; military affairs; war:～马 war-horse; 〈喻〉military life / ～装 army uniform; battle dress

茸 róng ❶ (of grass, etc) newly-grown, soft and fine; downy:～毛 fine hair / ～～ soft, smooth and thick ❷ young pilose antler

荣(榮) róng ❶ grow exuberantly or luxuriantly; 〈喻〉flourish; prosper:～枯 (of vegetation) flourishing and withering; 〈喻〉rise and fall; ups and downs ❷ honour; glory:～光 honour; glory / ～获 have the honour to win (the championship, etc); be awarded / ～任 have the honour of being appointed (to a public office) / ～辱与共 share weal and woe

荣华 rónghuá　glory and splendour:～富贵 glory, wealth and rank; high position and great wealth

荣幸 róngxìng　be honoured or privileged; have the honour or privilege:很～见到您。It's my honour to meet you.

荣耀 róngyào　honour; glory

荣誉 róngyù ❶ honour; glory; credit:～感 sense of honour ❷ honorary; honourable:～奖 honourable mention / ～称号 honorary title / ～军人 (shortened as 荣军) disabled soldier

绒(絨、羢) róng ❶ fine soft hair; down:

～毛 fine hair; down ❷ nap or pile of cloth:平～ velveteen / ～布 lint; cotton flannel / ～衣 sweat shirt / ～面革 suede (leather) ❸ (usu 绒线) fine floss for embroidery

容 róng ❶ hold; contain:～积 volume / ～量 capacity / ～器 container; receptacle; vessel / ～身之地 place to stay; shelter ❷ tolerate; excuse; forgive:～情 (used usu in the negative) show mercy; put up with / ～人 tolerant towards others; broad-minded; magnanimous ❸ permit; allow; let:～留 allow to stay; take in; shelter / ～我考虑一下。Let me think it over. ❹ also "容或"〈书〉perhaps; maybe; probably ❺ facial expression; look; 〈喻〉appearance:～貌 features; looks; appearance

容光 róngguāng　glow of the face:～焕发 glowing or radiant with health; in a buoyant mood

容纳 róngnà ❶ hold; accommodate; have a capacity of ❷ accept; tolerate

容忍 róngrěn　put up with; tolerate; condone

容许 róngxǔ ❶ permit; allow; let:误差 admissible error ❷ perhaps; possibly

容颜 róngyán　looks; appearance:～憔悴 look haggard

容易 róngyì ❶ easy:说比做～。It's easier said than done. ❷ easily; likely; apt

蓉 róng ❶ mashed fruit or seeds:豆～ fine bean mash (as stuffing) ❷ (Róng) another name for Chengdu (成都)

溶 róng　dissolve; thaw; melt:～洞 (limestone) cave; cavern / ～化 also "溶解" dissolve; melt; thaw / ～剂〈化〉solvent; dissolvent / ～液〈化〉solution

榕 róng ❶ (usu 榕树) banyan ❷ (Róng) another name for Fuzhou

〈福州〉

熔 róng melt; fuse; smelt; ～点 〈理〉 melting or fusion point / ～化 also "熔解" fuse; melt / ～炉 smelting furnace; crucible / ～岩 lava

蝾(蠑) róng

蝾螈 róngyuán 〈动物〉 salamander; newt

镕 róng ❶ mould (for casting metal) ❷ see "熔"róng

融 róng ❶ melt; thaw; ～化 also "溶化"; "融解" melt; thaw; dissolve ❷ fuse; blend; be in harmony; ～会贯通 achieve thorough understanding of a subject through mastery of all relevant material ❸ circulation

融合 rónghé also "融和" fuse; merge; mix together

融和 rónghé ❶ warm and genial ❷ harmonious; friendly; genial; 气氛～ genial or harmonious atmosphere ❸ see "融合"

融洽 róngqià harmonious; on friendly terms

融融 róngróng ❶ happy and chummy; 其乐～ be happy and content ❷ warm; ～的春天 warm and cosy

融资 róngzī 〈经〉 ❶ financing; ～项目 financing project ❷ money raised through financing

rǒng

冗(宂) rǒng 〈书〉 ❶ redundant; superfluous; ～笔 redundancy or superfluity in writing or painting / ～长 lengthy; long-winded; verbose / ～员 redundant personnel ❷ loaded with trivial details; ～杂 miscellaneous; numerous and complicated ❸ busy; ～务 busy routine; daily chores

róu

柔 róu ❶ soft; supple; pliant; ～嫩 tender; delicate / ～韧 pliable; supple / ～软 soft; supple; lithe ❷ gentle; tender; mild; ～美 gentle and lovely; graceful / ～肠寸断 lovelorn; heartbroken / ～情似水 boundless tender feelings; deep affection / 中有刚 gentle but firm; iron fist in a velvet glove

柔道 róudào 〈体〉 judo; ～手 judoka

柔和 róuhé mild; gentle; soft

柔媚 róumèi ❶ gentle and lovely; tender and charming ❷ docile; complaisant; ～谦恭 complaisant and courteous

柔弱 róuruò weak; delicate; tender; ～的嫩芽 tender sprouts

柔顺 róushùn (of disposition, etc) gentle and meek

揉 róu ❶ rub; ～搓 rub ❷ knead; crumple; ～面 knead dough ❸ 〈书〉 bend; reform

糅 róu (usu 糅合) mingle; mix

蹂 róu 〈书〉 stamp; trample; ～躏 trample underfoot; ravage; ravish

鞣 róu tan; ～制 tan (hide, etc)

ròu

肉 ròu ❶ flesh; meat; ～饼 meat pie / ～店 butcher's (shop) / ～丁 diced meat / ～鸡 also "肉用鸡" roasting chicken; broiler / ～类 meats / ～末 minced or ground meat / ～丝 shredded meat / ～松 dried minced meat; dried meat floss / ～馅 meat stuffing / ～汁 gravy; meat extract / ～制品 meat product ❷ pulp; flesh (of fruit) ❸ not crisp; mushy; ～

瓤西瓜 watermelon of mushy flesh ❹
〈方〉phlegmatic：～性子 phlegmatic
temperament

肉搏 ròubó fight hand-to-hand; fight
at close quarters

肉麻 ròumá （of words, behaviour,
etc）sickening; nauseating; fulsome

肉色 ròusè flesh-coloured; yellowish
pink

肉体 ròutǐ flesh; human body：～和精
神都受到摧残 be made to suffer both
physically and mentally

肉眼 ròuyǎn ❶ naked eye ❷
layman's eyes; common or vulgar
views：～凡胎 common mortal; mediocrity; ordinary man

肉欲 ròuyù carnal or sensual desire

rú

如 rú ❶ according to; in conformity with：～实 strictly according
to the facts / ～约 keep one's appointment ❷ like; as; as if：～常 as usual /
～初 as before; as always / ～上 as
above / ～下 as follows / ～虎添翼
with added strength; further strengthened / ～获至宝 as if one had found a
treasure / ～临大敌 as if faced with a
formidable foe; extremely nervous / ～
丧考妣〈贬〉as if one had lost one's
parents; very sad or sorrowful / ～入
无人之境 encounter no resistance at
all; carry all before one ❸ used in the
negative）be as good as; can compare
with：技不～人 not so skilful ❹ for
example; such as; as ❺〈书〉go to;
arrive at; ～厕 go to the bathroom or
toilet ❻ if：～若 if; in case ❼〈书〉
used as a suffix of certain adjectives
or adverbs：空空～也 empty; penniless

如出一辙 rúchūyīzhé run in the same
groove; follow the same pattern; be
identical

如此 rúcǐ such; so; like that：～这般
and so on and so forth; in this way;
thus / 理应～. That's as it should
be.

如法炮制 rúfǎpáozhì follow sb's example; follow suit

如故 rúgù ❶ as before：依然～ remain unaltered ❷ like old friends：一见
～ feel like old friends at the first
meeting; become friends at first sight

如果 rúguǒ if; in case; in the event of

如何 rúhé how; what：你意下～?
What do you think (of it)?

如今 rújīn nowadays; now; today

如来 Rúlái also "如来佛" Tathagata;
Buddha

如雷贯耳 rúléiguàn'ěr resound like
thunder：久闻大名,～.〈套〉I have
long heard of your great name.

如期 rúqī as scheduled; on schedule;
in time

如日中天 rúrìzhōngtiān like the sun
at high noon; at the height of one's
power, career, etc

如⋯如⋯ rú⋯rú⋯ used to join two
similar words for vivid description：
如火如荼 like a raging fire; fiery; vigorous / 如醉如痴 as if intoxicated and
enthralled; be infatuated (with sth)

如释重负 rúshìzhòngfù as if relieved
of a heavy burden; greatly relieved

如数家珍 rúshǔjiāzhēn as if enumerating one's family treasures; with sth
at one's fingertips

如数 rúshù exactly the number or
amount; in full

如⋯似⋯ rú⋯sì⋯ used to join two
similar words for vivid description：如
花似玉 (of a woman) like a flower or
jade — ravishingly beautiful / 如饥似
渴 as if thirsting or hungering for sth;
eagerly; avidly / 如胶似漆 cling (to
each other) like glue or lacquer; be
deeply attached (to each other) / 如狼
似虎 as savage as wolves or tigers;

R

brutal

如同 rútóng　like; as:灯火通明,～白昼. It was brilliantly lit as if it were daytime.

如意 rúyì　❶ comply with one's wishes:～算盘 wishful thinking ❷ *ruyi*, an S-shaped wand symbolizing good fortune

如影随形 rúyǐngsuíxíng　like the shadow following the body; always in each other's company

如鱼得水 rúyúdéshuǐ　feel just like fish in water; be in congenial company or circumstances (for displaying one's talents)

如愿 rúyuàn　do as one wishes:～以偿 have one's wish fulfilled

如坐针毡 rúzuòzhēnzhān　be on pins and needles; be on tenterhooks

茹 rú　〈书〉❶ eat:～毛饮血 (of primitive man) eat the raw flesh of birds and animals ❷ suffer; endure:～苦含辛 endure hardships

R

儒 rú　❶ (Rú) Confucianism; Confucianist:～家 Confucian school; Confucianists /～生 also "儒士"〈旧〉Confucian scholar /～术 Confucian teachings ❷ scholar; learned man:～将 scholar-general /～商 scholar-merchant

儒雅 rúyǎ　〈书〉courteous and well-educated; refined:风流～ refined and elegant

嚅 rú

嚅动 rúdòng　(of lips) open and close (as if to speak)

濡 rú　〈书〉❶ immerse; dip in; moisten:～染 be immersed in; be influenced by ❷ stay; linger

孺 rú　child

孺子 rúzǐ　〈书〉child:～牛 willing horse (for a child);〈喻〉person willingly serving the interests of the peo-

ple /～可教 the kid is teachable; the young man is worth teaching

蠕 rú

蠕动 rúdòng　wriggle; squirm;〈生理〉peristalsis

rǔ

汝 rǔ　〈书〉you:～辈 you people; you

乳 rǔ　❶ breast:～房 breast; mamma; (of an animal) udder /～头 nipple; teat /～罩 brassiere; bra ❷ milk:～白 milky white; creamy /～母 wet nurse /～牛 dairy cattle; milch cow /～牙 also "乳齿" milk or primary tooth /～汁 milk /～制品 dairy product ❸ milk-like liquid:～胶〈化〉emulsion; latex ❹ new-born (animal); suckling:～名 infant name; child's pet name /～猪 suckling pig

乳臭 rǔxiù　smelling of milk; childish; green:～未干 wet behind the ears; un-fledged

辱 rǔ　❶ disgrace; dishonour ❷ humiliate; insult:～骂 abuse; curse; hurl insults (upon sb) ❸ bring disgrace or humiliation; be unworthy of:～没 bring discredit to; sully; tarnish ❹〈书〉〈谦〉:～承指教 be hon-oured by your advice; thank you for giv-ing me the benefit of your wise counsel

rù

入 rù　❶ enter; go or come in:～伏 beginning of the hottest part of summer /～库 put in storage; lay up /～托 be sent to a nursery /～狱 be put behind bars; be thrown into jail /～院 be hospitalized; be put into a hospital /～住 move in (new hous-ing, etc); put up (at a hotel, etc) /～

座 *also* "入坐" take one's seat; be seated ❷ join; become a member of; ~党 join the Party; become a Party member / ~股 buy a share; become a shareholder ❸ income; ~不敷出 income falling short of expenditure; living beyond one's means ❹ agree with; conform to; ~情~理 fair and just; logical and reasonable ❺〈语言〉(short for 人声) entering tone, now extinct in *putonghua*

入场 rùchǎng enter; be admitted; ~券 (admission) ticket

入超 rùchāo unfavourable balance of trade; trade deficit

入耳 rù'ěr pleasant to the ear; palatable

入伙 rùhuǒ ❶ join a gang; go into partnership ❷ join a mess; eat regularly at the school or factory canteen

入境 rùjìng enter a country; ~口岸 port of entry / ~签证 entry visa / ~问俗 inquire about the habits and customs on entering a foreign country

入口 rùkǒu ❶ enter the mouth ❷ entrance

入殓 rùliàn encoffin (the deceased)

入门 rùmén ❶ learn the rudiments of a subject ❷ (often used in titles of books) elementary course; introduction; ABC

入迷 rùmí be fascinated (with); be enthralled (by)

入木三分 rùmùsānfēn written in vigorous strokes; penetrating; incisive

入侵 rùqīn invade; make an incursion or inroad; intrude

入神 rùshén ❶ be entranced or spellbound; 听得~ listen spellbound ❷ superb; wonderful

入时 rùshí fashionable; a la mode

入手 rùshǒu start with; take as the point of departure

入睡 rùshuì *also* "入眠" go to sleep; fall asleep

入土 rùtǔ be buried or interred; ~为安 rest in peace after being buried

入围 rùwéi be selected, recruited or nominated (out of many); ~作品 nominated work (for a contest, etc)

入伍 rùwǔ enlist; join the services

入乡随俗 rùxiāngsuísú follow local customs wherever you are; when in Rome, do as the Romans do

入学 rùxué ❶ go to school; ~考试 entrance examination / ~教育 (freshmen's) orientation programme ❷ start school; ~年龄 school age

入赘 rùzhuì marry into the bride's family; ~女婿 man who is adopted by the family of his parents-in-law

蓐 rù 〈书〉straw mat or mattress

缛 rù elaborate; intricate; cumbersome; ~礼 elaborate rules of etiquette

褥 rù padded mattress; ~疮〈医〉bedsore; pressure sore / ~子 (cotton, etc) padded mattress

R

ruǎn

软(輭) ruǎn ❶ soft; supple; pliable; ~膏 ointment; paste / ~骨〈生理〉cartilage / ~席 (as on a train) soft or cushioned berth; soft or cushioned seat / ~科学 soft science / ~饮料 soft drinks / ~组织〈生理〉soft tissue / ~着陆 (make a) soft landing / ~体动物 mollusk; mollusc ❷ gentle; mild; soft; ~话 conciliatory words / ~钉子〈喻〉polite refusal or snub / ~磨硬泡 use soft and tough tactics alternately ❸ weak; shaky; cowardly; 两腿发~ feel weak in the legs / ~骨头 spineless person; coward ❹ poor in quality, ability, etc; 业务上~了点儿 not so competent professionally ❺ easily moved; apt to be influenced; 耳根子~ credulous;

gullible

软化 ruǎnhuà　soften (up); weaken；
～血管 soften blood vessels / ～对手
soften up an adversary

软和 ruǎnhuo　〈口〉❶ soft ❷ gentle；
kind；～话儿 kind words; conciliatory
remarks

软件 ruǎnjiàn　❶〈信息〉software；～
包 software package / ～兼容性 software compatibility ❷〈喻〉quality of
personnel, management, services, etc

软禁 ruǎnjìn　(put under) house arrest

软绵绵 ruǎnmiánmián　❶ soft；～的
音乐 sentimental music ❷ weak; limp;
浑身～的 feel weak all over

软木 ruǎnmù　❶ cork；～塞 cork (as a
stopper) ❷ softwood

软盘 ruǎnpán　〈信息〉diskette; flop-
py disk (FD); floppy；～驱动器
(shortened as 软驱) disk drive

软弱 ruǎnruò　weak; feeble; flabby；～
可欺 weak and easily bullied / ～无能
weak and incompetent; namby-pamby

软硬兼施 ruǎnyìngjiānshī　employ
both soft and hard tactics; use a combination of the carrot and the stick

ruǐ

蕊 ruǐ　stamen; pistil

ruì

蚋 ruì　buffalo gnat; blackfly

锐 ruì　❶ sharp; keen; acute；～角
〈数〉acute angle / ～不可当 irresistible ❷
vim; vigour；～气 dash; drive; élan ❸
rapid; sharp; drastic；～减 cut or drop
sharply; reduce drastically

锐利 ruìlì　❶ (of a knife, etc) sharp
❷ incisive; keen；～的笔锋 incisive

writing

锐意 ruìyì　strong determination；～改
革 be determined to carry out a reform

瑞 ruì　auspicious; lucky; good；～
雪 timely or auspicious snow / ～
兆 good omen; auspicious sign

睿 ruì　〈书〉farsighted；～智 wise
and farsighted

rùn

闰 rùn　〈天文〉intercalary；～年
leap or intercalary year

润 rùn　❶ smooth and glossy;
sleek; moist；～泽 moist; shiny
❷ moisten; lubricate；～肺〈中医〉
moisten the lungs — facilitate expectoration / ～肤露 skin lotion / ～滑油
lubricating oil ❸ embellish; touch up；
～色 also "润饰" polish; touch up ❹
profit; remuneration；～笔 also "润资"
remuneration for a writer, painter or
calligrapher

ruò

若 ruò　❶ like; seem; as if；～无其
事 as if nothing had happened;
calmly; casually / ～有所思 seem as if
deep in thought; look pensive; be lost
in thought ❷ if；～是 if / ～要人不知,
除非己莫为。If you don't want people to know sth, don't do it. ❸〈书〉
you

若非 ruòfēi　if not; were it not for;
but for；～你的帮助, 我是无法完成任
务的。I could not have accomplished
the task but for your help.

若干 ruògān　❶ some; certain；～问题
certain problems ❷ how many; how
much；存款尚余～? How much of our
savings is left?

若…若… ruò…ruò…　(used to join
two words opposite in meaning) neither
… nor …; partly … partly …；若即若离

be neither close nor distant; keep (sb) at arm's length; be ambivalent / 若明若暗 have a hazy notion (about sth); (of an attitude) non-committal; (of a situation) hard to fathom / 若隐若现 partly hidden and partly visible; discernible at one moment and gone the next

偌 ruò such; so; ～大年纪 (of) such old age; so old

弱 ruò ❶ weak; frail; delicate; ～化 become weak; weaken / ～视 〈医〉 amblyopia; weak sight / ～小 small and weak ❷ young; little; ～孙 little grandson ❸ inferior; not as good as; 手艺不比别人～ inferior to nobody in craftsmanship ❹ 〈书〉 lose; be lost; 故友又～一人。Another of one's old friends is gone. ❺ (used after a fractional number) a little less than; 八分之一～ a little less than one eighth

弱不禁风 ruòbùjīnfēng too weak to stand a gust of wind; extremely delicate or fragile; frail

弱点 ruòdiǎn weak point; weakness; failing

弱肉强食 ruòròu-qiángshí the weak are the prey of the strong — law of the jungle

弱势 ruòshì ❶ trend or tendency to weaken ❷ weak; ～群体 disadvantaged community

弱项 ruòxiàng weak event (in a contest, etc); weak area; weakness

弱智 ruòzhì weak-minded; mentally deficient; retarded; ～儿童 (mentally) retarded children

R

S

sā

仁
撒 sā (condensed from 三个) 〈口〉 three: 咱哥儿～ we three pals

撒 sā ❶ cast; loosen; let go: ～网 cast one's net / ～尿〈口〉 piss; pee; pass water / ～腿狂奔 start running wildly; scamper off ❷〈贬〉 throw off all restraint; let oneself go; run wild: ～赖 act shamelessly; make a scene / ～酒疯 be roaring drunk; be drunk and disorderly
see also sǎ

撒旦 sādàn 〈宗教〉 Satan; the Devil
撒谎 sāhuǎng 〈口〉 lie; tell a lie: ～的人 liar
撒娇 sājiāo behave like a spoiled child; play the pampered child: ～使性 throw a tantrum like a spoiled child
撒泼 sāpō make a scene and refuse to listen to reason: ～打滚 make a terrible scene by rolling in the dust
撒气 sāqì ❶ (of a ball, tyre, etc) leak; deflate; go flat ❷ vent one's anger or temper: 拿老婆孩子～ take it out on one's wife and children
撒手 sāshǒu let go one's hold; let go of sth: ～不管 shy away from (sth) / ～人世 depart this life; pass away / 使出～锏〈喻〉 play one's trump card
撒野 sāyě act rowdily (without heeding reason or decorum); behave rudely

sǎ

洒（灑） sǎ ❶ sprinkle; spray: ～落 scatter; strew; trickle down / ～水车 watering or spraying car ❷ spill; shed: ～泪告别 part in tears; take a tearful leave

洒脱 sǎtuo free and easy; unrestrained; unaffected

撒 sǎ ❶ scatter; spread; broadcast: ～种 sow seeds ❷ spill; drop: 把酒～了 spill one's wine / ～落在地 scatter all over the ground
see also sā

sà

卅 sà thirty

飒 sà sough; rustle: 房上雨声～～。The rain was pattering against the roof.
飒爽 sàshuǎng 〈书〉 of martial bearing; valiant: ～英姿 be of impressive martial bearing; look bright and brave

sāi

腮 sāi cheek: ～帮子〈口〉 cheek / ～腺炎〈医〉 mumps

塞 sāi ❶ stop; fill or squeeze in; stuff up: ～车 traffic jam / ～牙 (of food) get stuck between the teeth ❷ stopper: ～子 stopper; cork; spigot
see also sài; sè

鳃 sāi gill

sài

塞 sài stronghold of strategic importance at the border: ～外 *also* "塞北" beyond the Great Wall *see also* sāi; sè

塞翁失马，安知非福 sàiwēngshīmǎ，ānzhīfēifú〈谚〉misfortune may be a blessing in disguise

赛 sài ❶ match; game; contest；～车〈体〉cycle, motorcycle or car race；race car；racing bicycle / ～程〈体〉agenda or schedule for a tournament；(of a race) distance / ～季 season (for competitions in a particular sport) / ～马 horse race or racing / ～跑 race；dash / ～事 (sports) contest；match；game / ～艇〈体〉rowing；yachting；racing boat ❷ compete；～水平、～风格 give full display of one's skills and sportsmanship ❸ be comparable to；surpass：一个～一个（with）one surpassing the other ❹ (usu 赛神)〈旧〉offering a sacrifice to gods

sān

三 sān ❶ three：～军 three armed services；the army / ～围 chest, waist and hip measurements / ～部曲 trilogy / ～合板 three-ply board；plywood / ～脚架 tripod（mounting）；trivet；A-frame / ～联单 triplicate form / ～轮车 tricycle；pedicab / ～级跳远〈体〉hop, step and jump；triple jump / ～六九等 (of) all grades and ranks / ～权分立 separation of powers (the legislative, executive and judicial) / ～维空间 three-dimensional space / ～位一体〈宗教〉Trinity / ～喻〉three in one / ～足鼎立 tripartite confrontation；triangular balance of power / ～句话不离本行 be always talking shop ❷ more than two；several；many；～缄其口 with a closely guarded tongue；overcautious in speech / ～亲六故 (all) kinsmen and friends / ～生有幸〈套〉consider oneself most fortunate (to make sb's acquaintance, etc) / ～个臭皮匠，顶个诸葛亮〈俗〉two heads are better than one；there is wisdom in a crowd

三百六十行 sānbǎiliùshíháng all trades and professions；all walks of life：～，行行出状元. Every profession produces its top expert.

三北 Sān Běi also "三北地区" three northern areas, ie northeast, central-north and northwest (China)

三长两短 sānchǎng-liǎngduǎn mishap；unexpected misfortune or calamity：若有个～ if anything untoward should happen

三从四德 sāncóng-sìdé 〈旧〉women's three obediences (to father before marriage, to husband after marriage and to son after death of husband) and four virtues (morality, proper speech, modest manner and diligent work)

三寸不烂之舌 sāncùnbùlànzhīshé glib or silver tongue；eloquence

三点式 sāndiǎnshì also "三点式泳装" bikini (bathing suit)

三分 sānfēn ❶ 30%；a little；somewhat：让她～ yield a little to her；let her have her way / 只说～话 speak with reserve；never tell everything on one's mind ❷〈体〉three points：～球 (of basketball) three pointer ❸ (in grading) C；Fair

三伏 sānfú ❶ three ten-day periods of the hot season：～天 dog days ❷ last of the three periods of the hot season

三纲五常 sāngāng-wǔcháng also "纲常"〈旧〉three cardinal guides (ruler guides subject, father guides son, and husband guides wife) and five constant virtues (benevolence, righteousness, propriety, wisdom and fidelity)

三个代表 sānge dàibiǎo "Three Represents" (the CPC represents the development trend of advanced productive forces, the orientation of advanced cultural, and the fundamental interests of the overwhelming majority of the people in China

三顾茅庐 sāngùmáolú make three personal calls at the thatched cottage (as Liu Bei 刘备 did for Zhuge Liang 诸葛亮) — extend repeated and sincere invitations

三国 Sānguó Three Kingdoms (220-280), namely, Wei (魏, 220-265), Shu Han (蜀汉, 221-263) and Wu (吴, 222-280)

三好 sānhǎo (honorific title for students) good in study, work and physical training; ～学生 "three-good" student

三皇五帝 Sānhuáng-Wǔdì Three sage "kings" (Fuxi 伏羲, Suiren 燧人 and Shennong 神农) and five virtuous "emperors" (Huangdi 黄帝, Zhuanxu 颛顼, Di Ku 帝喾, Tang Yao 唐尧 and Yu Shun 虞舜) — legendary rulers of remote antiquity

三角 sānjiǎo ❶ triangle: ～尺 set square / ～裤 panties; briefs / ～形 triangle / ～债 (inter-corporate) triangular debt; debt chain / ～洲 delta / ～恋爱 love triangle ❷〈数〉trigonometry

三教九流 sānjiào-jiǔliú ❶ various religious sects and schools of thought ❷ (usu deprecatory) people in various trades; people of all sorts or descriptions

三九 sānjiǔ also "三九天" third nine-day period after the winter solstice — depth of winter; coldest days in the year

三昧 sānmèi〈喻〉secret; knack: 未解书法～ not grasp the essence of calligraphy

三明治 sānmíngzhì sandwich

三七 sānqī ❶〈中药〉pseudo-ginseng ❷ 30; 70 ratio: ～开 (give sb a) seventy-thirty evaluation (in which merits outweigh defects by 7 to 3); also "三七分成" split up (dividends, etc) on a

thirty to seventy ratio / 三分像人，七分像鬼 look more like a ghost than a human

三秋 sānqiū ❶〈农〉three autumn activities (harvesting, ploughing and sowing) ❷〈书〉three years:一日不见，如隔～。One day away seems as long as three years.

三三两两 sānsān-liǎngliǎng in or by twos and threes; in small groups; few and far between

三十六计，走为上计 sānshíliùjì, zǒuwéishàngjì of all the stratagems, the best is to quit; of all the alternatives, running away is the best

三思 sānsī think carefully; ponder over: ～而(后)行 think twice; look before you leap; second thoughts are the best

三天打鱼，两天晒网 sāntiāndǎyú, liǎngtiānshàiwǎng go fishing for three days and then dry the nets for two — work off and on; work by fits and starts

三天两头 sāntiān-liǎngtóu 〈口〉from time to time; almost every day

三通 sāntōng ❶〈电〉three-way connector or plug ❷ three (direct) links (in mail, transport and trade) across the Taiwan Strait

三头六臂 sāntóu-liùbì (with) three heads and six arms; (having) superhuman power

三…五… sān … wǔ … ❶ many times: 三番五次 again and again; time and again / 三令五申 repeated injunctions; repeated orders and instructions ❷ not very large in quantity, number, etc: 三年五载 in a few years

三下五除二 sānxiàwǔchú'èr neat and quick: ～地把事情办完了 finish it in a jiffy

三鲜 sānxiān three delicacies — dish or filling made of three delicious ingredients such as sea cucumber, shrimp and chicken

三弦 sānxián 〈乐〉 *sanxian*, a three-stringed plucked instrument

三心二意 sānxīn-èryì waver and hesitate; be of two minds; be half-hearted

三言两语 sānyán-liǎngyǔ in a few words; in a word or two; casually

三月 sānyuè ❶ March ❷ third month of the lunar year; third moon

三只手 sānzhīshǒu 〈方〉 pickpocket: 他遇上了～。His pocket was picked.

三资企业 sānzīqǐyè three kinds of foreign-invested enterprises: Sino-foreign joint ventures, cooperative businesses and exclusively foreign-owned enterprises

叁 sān (used for the numeral 三 on cheques, etc, to avoid mistakes or alterations) three

sǎn

伞（傘） sǎn umbrella; sth shaped or functioning like an umbrella: 阳～ parasol; sunshade / ～兵 parachute troop; paratrooper

散 sǎn ❶ come loose; break up; fall apart: ～架 collapse; fall to pieces; disintegrate ❷ loose; scattered; unorganized: ～工 odd or part-time job; casual or seasonal labourer / ～货 bulk cargo / ～记 (usu used in a title) random notes; sidelights / ～居 live scattered / ～客 individual tourist or client / ～乱 scattered and disorderly; disorganized; dishevelled (hair) / ～兵游勇 stragglers and disbanded soldiers; people not belonging to any organization ❸ medicinal powder: ～剂 〈中药〉 powder

see also sàn

散打 sǎndǎ *also* "散手" *sanda* — a form of free-style grappling in *wushu* (武术); confrontational Chinese boxing

散光 sǎnguāng astigmatism: ～眼镜 astigmatic glasses

散漫 sǎnmàn ❶ undisciplined; happy-go-lucky ❷ unorganized; loose; scattered: ～芜杂 (of writing) poorly organized and full of irrelevancies

散文 sǎnwén prose: ～家 prose-writer; essayist / ～诗 prose poem

散装 sǎnzhuāng in bulk: 白酒～ spirits in bulk / ～饼干 loose cookies

sàn

散 sàn ❶ separate; break up; disperse: ～场 (of a cinema, etc) empty after the show; (of a play, etc) be over / ～工 knock off; stop work for the day / ～会 (of a meeting) be over; break up / ～伙 (of a group) dissolve; disband; (of lovers, etc) part company / ～开 disperse / ～席 (of a dinner party) end; be over; come to a close / ～摊子 〈口〉 break up; dissolve ❷ distribute; disseminate; scatter: ～热 dissipate heat / 花香～溢 exuding fragrance of flowers ❸ (of worry) drive away; let out: 一酌～千愁 have a drink to drown one's sorrow

see also sǎn

散播 sànbō ❶ 〈农〉 broadcast (sowing) ❷ *see* "散布"

散布 sànbù spread; disseminate; scatter: ～各地 be scattered all over the country / ～谣言 spread rumours; go rumour-mongering

散步 sànbù take a walk; go for a stroll

散发 sànfā send forth; emit; distribute: ～传单 distribute leaflets / ～霉烂的气味 send forth a musty smell

散落 sànluò ❶ fall apart or down; fall scattered; disperse ❷ be scattered (over a place); straggle ❸ (of family, etc) not be heard of after being separated; be scattered

散失 sànshī ❶ scatter and disappear; vanish; be lost or missing ❷ (of moisture, etc) vapourize; dissipate

散心 sànxīn keep from worrying; relieve one's boredom; relax

sāng

丧(喪) sāng funeral; mourning; ～葬 burial; funeral / ～钟 funeral bell; (death) knell　*see also* sàng

桑 sāng (white) mulberry; ～葚 mulberry (fruit) / ～梓〈书〉〈喻〉one's native place

桑那浴 sāngnàyù *also* "桑拿浴" sauna (bath)

桑榆晚景 sāngyúwǎnjǐng *also* "桑榆暮景"〈书〉evening of one's life; old age

sǎng

搡 sǎng 〈方〉push roughly; shove

嗓 sǎng ❶ throat; larynx ❷ voice; ～音 voice / 大～门儿 loud voice

嗓子 sǎngzi ❶ throat; larynx; 清清～ clear one's throat ❷ voice; 金～ golden voice

sàng

丧(喪) sàng lose; forfeit; ～命 *also* "丧生" lose one's life; get killed / ～魂落魄 be shaken to the marrow; be overwhelmed by fear / ～家之犬 stray cur; lost pup / ～尽天良 with no conscience at all; conscienceless / ～权辱国 (of sb) surrender sovereign rights under humiliating terms; (of sth) be humiliating to a country / ～心病狂 frenzied; unscrupulous; perverse　*see also* sāng

丧气 sàngqì ❶ feel disheartened or depressed; lose heart; ～话 demoralizing remarks; gloomy talk ❷ (sàngqi)〈口〉ill-starred; out of luck

丧失 sàngshī lose; forsake; forfeit; ～警惕 lose one's vigilance; be off one's guard

sāo

搔 sāo scratch; ～首弄姿 (of a woman) preen oneself in a coquettish manner; be coquettish / ～着痒处 scratch where it itches; hit the nail on the head

骚 sāo ❶ disturb; disrupt; upset; ～乱 disturbance; turmoil; riot ❷〈书〉literary writings, esp poetry; ～人墨客 men of letters; literati ❸ coquettish; obscene; ～货〈粗〉tart; sexpot

骚动 sāodòng disturbance; turmoil; tumult; 引起～ stir up a disturbance

骚扰 sāorǎo harass; pester; molest

缫 sāo reel (silk from cocoons); filature

臊 sāo (usu 臊气) smell of urine or of a fox; foul smell; stench　*see also* sào

sǎo

扫(掃) sǎo ❶ sweep; clear away; ～墓 sweep a grave — pay respects at sb's tomb ❷ wipe out; eliminate; get rid of; ～盲 wipe out or eliminate illiteracy / ～黄打非 (launch) a campaign against pornography and illegal publications ❸ move along quickly; sweep; ～射 (of a machine-gun, etc) strafe / ～视 take a sweeping glance ❹ all together; completely; ～数入库 deliver the whole amount to the state coffers　*see also* sào

扫除 sǎochú ❶ clean (up); 大～ general cleaning ❷ clear away; eliminate; wipe out

扫荡 sǎodàng ❶ mop up (bandits, etc) ❷ wipe out; clear up; eliminate

扫地 sǎodì ❶ sweep the floor: ～出门〈喻〉be swept out (of door) like rubbish; be deprived of all one's belongings and evicted ❷ (of honour, etc) be dragged in the dust; be utterly discredited; ～以尽 be completely destroyed or discredited

扫描 sǎomiáo 〈信息〉scanning: ～器 also "扫描仪" scanner

扫尾 sǎowěi bring to an end; wind or round off: ～工程 final phase of a project

扫兴 sǎoxìng dampen one's spirits; spoil one's happiness; feel disappointed

嫂 sǎo ❶ also "嫂嫂"; "嫂子" elder brother's wife; sister-in-law ❷ form of address for a married woman about one's own age: ～夫人 (respectful form of address for a friend's wife) your wife

sào

扫(掃) sào

扫帚 sàozhou broom: ～星 comet; 〈贬〉woman who brings bad luck; jinx　see also sǎo

瘙 sào

瘙痒 sàoyáng 〈医〉pruritus

臊 sào shy; bashful; diffident: ～得脸红 blush to the ears; blush scarlet　see also sāo

sè

色 sè ❶ colour: ～调 tone; hue / ～盲 colour blindness / ～素 pigment; colouring ❷ look; countenance; expression: ～厉内荏 fierce of mien but faint of heart; ferocious in appearance but weak within ❸ kind; sort; description ❹ view; scene; scenery ❺ (of gold, etc) quality; purity ❻ woman's beautiful looks ❼ lust; eroticism: ～狼 lecher; wolf; sex maniac / ～迷迷 look erotic or lustful

see also shǎi

色彩 sècǎi ❶ colour; hue; tint: ～缤纷 colourful; riot of colour ❷ appeal; flavour; colour: 地方～ local colour or flavour

色拉 sèlā　also "沙拉" salad

色情 sèqíng pornography; sex: ～狂 sex mania or maniac / ～电影 pornographic film; porn movie

色相 sèxiàng ❶ (Buddhism) outward appearance of things ❷ feminine charm; woman's sexual appeal

色泽 sèzé colour and lustre: ～暗淡 dim and faint

涩(澀) sè ❶ puckery; astringent ❷ rough; hard-going: 这笔太～。The pen does not write smoothly. ❸ (of writing) not smooth; obscure; difficult to read or understand

啬(嗇) sè miserly; stingy; mean; close-fisted

瑟 sè 〈乐〉se, a sixteen-string or twenty-five-string plucked instrument like the zither

瑟瑟 sèsè ❶ 〈象声〉(of wind, etc) rustle ❷ shake; tremble: ～发抖 shaking all over

瑟缩 sèsuō curl up with cold; cower

塞 sè (used in certain terms and idioms) stop; block: ～责 muddle through one's job; perform one's duty perfunctorily　see also sāi; sài

sēn

森 sēn ❶ (of trees, etc) growing thickly or densely: ～林 forest ❷〈书〉in profusion ❸ dark; gloomy: ～冷的目光 dark and chilly eyes

森然 sēnrán ❶ towering in profusion; dense ❷ awesome; awe-inspiring

森森 sēnsēn ❶ dense; thick; luxuriant ❷ gloomy; gruesome; ghastly

森严 sēnyán solemn; (of guard) strict; 警戒 ~ heavily guarded; under close guard

sēng

僧 sēng (Buddhist) monk; ~侣 monks and priests; clergy / ~多粥少 many monks and little gruel — not enough to go round; inadequate

shā

杀(殺) shā ❶ kill; slay; slaughter; ~毒〈信息〉 kill a virus; anti-virus / ~机 intent to kill; murderous intention / ~生〈宗教〉killing of living things / ~手 head; decapitate; kill / ~虫剂 insecticide; pesticide / ~身成仁 sacrifice one's life for a good cause / ~一儆百 execute one as a warning to a hundred; punish one as an example to others / 大开~戒 kill or massacre a great many people ❷ fight; battle; ~出重围 fight one's way out of a heavy encirclement ❸ weaken; reduce; abate; ~价 force down the price; haggle over the price ❹ see "煞❶❷" shā ❺ in the extreme; intensely; 气~人了。It drives me mad. ❻〈方〉hurt; smart; 伤口~得慌。The cut hurts much.

杀风景 shāfēngjǐng also "煞风景" spoil the fun or show

杀鸡 shājī used in the certain idioms; ~取卵 kill the hen to get the eggs; kill the goose that lays golden eggs / ~给猴看 make an example of sb to warn others / ~用牛刀 break a butterfly on the wheel; swat a fly with a sledge hammer

杀气 shāqì ❶ murderous look; ~腾腾 bellicose; sabre-rattling ❷ vent one's ill feeling; 你别拿我~。Don't take it out on me.

杀青 shāqīng 〈喻〉finalize or finish (a book, etc)

杀人 shārén homicide; murder; ~犯 murderer; homicide / ~如麻 kill people like flies; commit innumerable murders / ~越货 murder a person and seize his goods / ~不见血 kill without spilling a drop of blood; harm by underhand means / ~不眨眼 commit murder without blinking an eye; be bloodthirsty

杀伤 shāshāng kill and wound; inflict casualties on; ~力 power of destruction

杉 shā shā used in the following; ~篙〈建筑〉fir pole / ~木 China fir see also shān

沙 shā ❶ sand; ~袋 sandbag / ~锅 earthenware pot; casserole / ~砾 grit / ~洲 shoal; sandbar; sandbank / ~子 sand; grit; small grains ❷ granulated; powdered; 豆~ bean paste ❸ (of voice) hoarse; husky; ~哑 hoarse; husky; raucous

沙场 shāchǎng battlefield; battleground; ~老将 seasoned warrior; veteran

沙尘 shāchén dust; sand; ~暴 sandstorm; dust storm

沙丁鱼 shādīngyú sardine

沙发 shāfā sofa; settee

沙里淘金 shālǐtáojīn extract the essence from an abundance of material; the result obtained is not worth the effort

沙龙 shālóng salon; 艺术~ artists' salon

沙漠 shāmò desert; ~化 also "沙化" desertification

沙沙 shāshā 〈象声〉rustle; 风吹树木~响。The wind rustled in the trees.

沙滩 shātān sandy or sand beach; sands; ~排球〈体〉beach volleyball

沙文主义 shāwénzhǔyì　chauvinism: 大国～ big-power chauvinism

沙眼 shāyǎn 〈医〉trachoma

纱 shā ❶ (cotton) yarn；～厂 cotton mill / ～锭 (cotton) spindle ❷ gauze；sth like gauze：～布 gauze / ～窗 (window) screen / ～巾 gauze kerchief；transparent scarf

纱帽 shāmào also "乌纱帽" ❶ gauze hat (worn by an official in dynastic days) ❷〈喻〉public office：丢了～ be dismissed from office

刹 shā put on the brakes；stop：～住歪风 check an unhealthy tendency　see also chà

刹车 shāchē also "煞车" ❶ (put or step on the) brake：紧急～ (apply the) emergency brakes ❷ turn off a machine；〈喻〉stop doing sth instantly

砂 shā sand；grit：～糖 granulated sugar / ～纸 abrasive paper；sandpaper　see also "沙 ❶❷" shā

铩 (鎩) shā

铩羽 shāyǔ with clipped wings：～而归 return with one's wings clipped；come back crestfallen

痧 shā〈中医〉cholera，sunstroke and such acute diseases

煞 shā ❶ stop；check；brake：～笔 stop writing (a letter, etc) / ～车 see "刹车" shāchē / ～尾 bring to an end；round off；ending ❷ tighten：～紧鞋带 tighten the shoestrings ❸ see "杀 ❸❺" shā
see also shà

鲨 shā also "鲛" shark：～鱼 also "沙鱼" shark

shá

啥 shá〈方〉what：有～说～ say what one has to say；speak one's mind

shǎ

傻 (傻) shǎ ❶ dull；stupid；muddle-headed：～笑 laugh like an idiot；giggle / ～子 fool；nitwit；simpleton / ～呵呵 also "傻乎乎" naive；unsophisticated / ～帽儿〈方〉fool；blockhead；simpleton ❷ mechanically；mindlessly；mulishly：～干 work without brain

傻瓜 shǎguā fool；blockhead；idiot：～相机 foolproof camera；point-and-shoot (camera)

傻劲儿 shǎjìnr ❶ stupid air or manner ❷ sheer animal strength

傻气 shǎqì simple(-minded)；naive：一脸～ naive-looking

傻眼 shǎyǎn be flabbergasted, dumbfounded or stunned

shà

厦 (廈) shà tall building；mansion

歃 shà〈书〉suck：～血为盟 swear loyalty by smearing blood on the mouth

煞 shà ❶ evil spirit；devil；goblin ❷ very；extremely：～白 deathly pale；ashen；pallid / ～费苦心 rack one's brains；make a painstaking effort / ～有介事 make a show of being earnest or important；be pretentious
see also shā

霎 shà very short time；moment；instant：～时 in an instant；in a flash or jiffy

shāi

筛 (篩) shāi ❶ (usu 筛子) sieve；screen；sifter ❷ sift；eliminate through selection

筛糠 shāikāng 〈口〉〈喻〉shiver; quiver; shudder

筛选 shāixuǎn screen; sift; select through extensive screening and elimination

shǎi

色 shǎi 〈口〉colour:不变～儿 not change colour; be colourfast
see also sè

色子 shǎizi dice:掷～ throw or cast dice

shài

晒(曬) shài ❶ (of the sun) shine upon ❷ dry in the sun; sun; bask:～黑 tan / ～台 flat roof (for drying clothes, etc); terrace; balcony / ～图 make a blueprint / ～太阳 bask in the sunshine; sun oneself ❸ 〈方〉ignore; give the cold shoulder to:别把客人～在一边。Be sure to slight any guest.

shān

山 shān ❶ hill; mountain:～川 *also* "山河" mountains and rivers — land; landscape / ～峰 mountain peak / ～歌 folk song (as sung in the mountains) / ～谷 mountain valley / ～脊 *also* "山梁" ridge (of a mountain or hill) / ～涧 mountain stream / ～脚 *also* "山麓" foot of a hill or mountain / ～林 wooded hills; mountain forest / ～峦 mountain chain / ～脉 mountain range or chain / ～坡 hillside; mountain slope / ～崖 cliff; crag / ～腰 halfway up a mountain / ～岳 lofty mountain / ～寨 fortified mountain village; mountain fastness / ～庄 mountain village or villa / ～地车 mountain bike ❷ anything resembling a mountain:冰～ iceberg ❸ gable (of a house)

山崩 shānbēng landslide: ～地裂 mountains collapsing and earth cracking — cataclysm

山高 shāngāo used in certain idioms: ～水长 (like the high mountain and the long river) far-reaching influence of a noble character; depth of sb's kindness or friendship / ～水远 long way off; far away; distant

山沟 shāngōu ❶ gully; ravine ❷ (mountain) valley ❸ remote mountainous area:穷～ poverty-stricken mountainous area

山洪 shānhóng mountain torrents:～暴发。Torrents of rainwater rushed down the mountains.

山货 shānhuò ❶ mountain produce (such as haws, walnuts, etc) ❷ household utensils made of wood, bamboo, clay, etc

山陵 shānlíng ❶ 〈书〉mountain ❷ royal mausoleum; imperial tomb

山明水秀 shānmíng-shuǐxiù *also* "山清水秀" green hills and clear waters; beautiful scenery

山南海北 shānnán-hǎiběi remote places or corners of the earth:～地神聊 chat about everything under the sun; shoot the breeze

山穷水尽 shānqióng-shuǐjìn be at the end of one's rope; be in a predicament

山水 shānshuǐ ❶ water from a mountain ❷ mountains and waters; scenery with hills and streams ❸ traditional Chinese painting of mountains and waters; landscape:～画 landscape (painting)

山头 shāntóu ❶ top of a mountain; hilltop ❷ mountain stronghold; 〈喻〉faction:拉～ form a faction

山羊 shānyáng goat:母～ she-goat / ～胡子 small pointed beard; goatee

山药 shānyao ❶ 〈植〉Chinese yam ❷ *also* "山药蛋" 〈方〉potato

山野 shānyě ❶ mountains and plains ❷ countryside；~村夫 country bumpkin；rustic

山雨欲来风满楼 shānyǔyùláifēngmǎnlóu a rising wind forebodes a coming storm；everything indicates imminent turmoil

山楂 shānzhā 〈植〉(Chinese) hawthorn；haw；~糕 haw jelly

山珍海味 shānzhēn-hǎiwèi mountain delicacies and seafood delights；delicacies of every kind

芟 shān mow（grass）；weed（out）；eliminate；~除 weed out；cut down；delete

杉 shān 〈植〉China fir see also shā

删 shān delete；strike or leave out；~除 also "删削" delete；remove；cut or cross out / ~改 prune away；revise / ~繁就简 simplify by weeding out superfluities

删节 shānjié abridge；abbreviate；~本 abridged edition；abbreviated version / ~号 ellipsis（dots）(······)（...）

苫 shān also "草苫子" straw mat see also shàn

衫 shān unlined upper garment；jacket；clothes

姗 shān

姗姗 shānshān slowly；leisurely；~来迟 be slow in coming；arrive late

珊 shān

珊瑚 shānhú coral；~礁 coral reef

舢 shān

舢板 shānbǎn also "舢版" sampan

扇(❶❷搧) shān ❶ fan；~炉子 fan a stove / ❷ 动翅膀 flap the wings ❷ hit with hands；box；~耳光 box sb's ears；slap sb in the face ❸ see "煽❷" shān

see also shàn

煽 shān ❶ fan（a fire）❷ incite；stir or whip up；~情 stir up feelings or passions；be stirring or rousing / ~风点火 fan the flames — stir up or instigate trouble

煽动 shāndòng instigate；incite；stir or whip up；这番话很有~性。These remarks are really inflammatory.

煽惑 shānhuò inflame；incite；agitate；~人心的演说 demagogic speech

潸 shān 〈书〉in tears；tearfully；~~（of tears or rain）fall continuously / ~然泪下 shed tears

膻(羶) shān smell（as）of mutton；~味 strong taste of mutton

shǎn

闪 shǎn ❶ move quickly to one side；dodge；~躲 avoid；dodge；evade / ~开 step aside quickly；get out of the way；dodge ❷ twist；sprain（wrist，ankle，etc）❸ lightning；打~ there's a flash of lightning；lightning strikes ❹ crop up；flash；~过一个念头 an idea flashes（across one's mind）❺ flash；sparkle；shine；~点〈化〉flash point

闪电 shǎndiàn lightning；~战 lightning warfare；blitz

闪动 shǎndòng（of light，etc）shine off and on；flash；scintillate

闪光 shǎnguāng ❶ glisten；glitter；flash；~灯 flash（light）(of a camera)；beacon light ❷ shine；be inspiring；~的语言 glittering or inspiring words

闪击 shǎnjī（carry out a）blitz（on sb）；(spring a) surprise attack

闪念 shǎnniàn sudden idea flashing across one's mind；flash of inspiration

闪烁 shǎnshuò sparkle；twinkle；glisten；电光~ flashes of lightning

闪身 shǎnshēn dodge；step sideways；

S

~进门 step sideways through the door

闪失 shǎnshī mishap; accident

闪烁 shǎnshuò ❶ twinkle; glimmer; glisten: 星光～ twinkling stars ❷ evasive; equivocal; noncommittal: ～其词 speak equivocally; hem and haw

闪现 shǎnxiàn flash; appear in a flash; come into view

闪耀 shǎnyào shine; glitter; radiate: 阳光～. The sun is shining brightly.

陕(陝) Shǎn (short for Shaanxi 陕西): ～北民歌 northern Shaanxi folk songs

shàn

讪 shàn ❶ mock; scorn; ridicule: 不怕～笑 be not afraid of mockery ❷ embarrassed; discomfited; shamefaced: ～～地走开了 leave in embarrassment

苫 shàn cover (with a tarpaulin, etc): ～布 tarpaulin / ～席 straw or reed mat　see also shān

疝 shàn also "疝气" hernia

扇 shàn ❶ fan; sth like a fan: ～子 fan / ～贝〈动物〉scallop; fan shell ❷ leaf: 门～ door leaf ❸〈量〉used of windows, doors, etc: 一～窗户 a window
see also shān

善 shàn ❶ good; virtuous; benign: ～本 (usu of an ancient book) reliable text; good edition / ～人 charitable person; philanthropist / ～心 mercy; kindness / ～男信女 devout men and women; religious believers / ～有～报，恶有恶报〈俗〉good will be rewarded with good, and evil with evil; every good or bad deed has its just reward ❷ wise; satisfactory; good: ～策 wise move; best policy ❸ friendly; kind: 相～ be friendly with each other ❹ be good at; be expert in; be apt to:

liable to: ～变 apt to change; fickle; unpredictable / ～感 oversensitive; sentimental / ～于辞令 have a ready tongue ❺ properly; well: ～待 treat well; take good care of; cherish / ～终 die a natural death; die of old age

善罢甘休 shànbà-gānxiū (often used in the negative) let the matter rest; let it go at that

善后 shànhòu properly handle the remaining problems (of an accident, etc): ～事宜 problems that are likely to arise in the aftermath

善举 shànjǔ〈书〉charitable act: 共襄～ make a concerted effort to ensure the success of a charitable activity

善良 shànliáng good and honest; kind-hearted; kind: 本性～ good and kind by nature

善始善终 shànshǐ-shànzhōng begin well and end well; stick it out; see sth through

善意 shànyì good will or intentions; bona fides: ～的忠告 well-meaning advice

禅(禪) shàn (usu 禅让 or 禅位) abdicate (from) the throne in favour of another　see also chán

骗 shàn castrate; geld; spay (a female animal): ～马 geld a horse; gelded horse; gelding

缮 shàn ❶ repair; fix; mend ❷ copy; write out: ～发 copy and dispatch

擅 shàn ❶ do sth without the approval or prior knowledge of one's superior; act or do on one's own authority; usurp: ～权 monopolize power; hold absolute power / ～离职守 be absent from one's post without leave; leave one's post without permission ❷ be good at; be versed or expert in: 不～辞令 not have the gift of gab; not be good at speech

擅长 shàncháng　be good at; be (well) versed; expert or skilled in

擅自 shànzì　act without authorization;～行动 act presumptuously

膳 shàn　meals; board; 用～ have one's meal / ～食 meals; food / ～宿 board and lodging

嬗 shàn　〈书〉❶ (usu 嬗变 or 嬗替) change; alternation; evolution ❷ see 〈禅〉shàn

赡 shàn　❶ support; keep; provide for ❷〈书〉adequate; sufficient; abundant

赡养 shànyǎng　support; maintain; provide for;～费 alimony; support payment / 赡家养口 support a family

鳝 shàn　(finless) eel;～鱼 (rice paddy) eel

shāng

伤(傷) shāng　❶ wound; injury;～亡 injuries and deaths; casualties / ～员 also "伤号" the wounded ❷ hurt; wound; impair;～感情 hurt one's feelings; wound one's pride / ～身体 impair health / ～风败俗 corrupt public morals; cause the decay of moral standards ❸ be sad or distressed; grieve;～逝 grieve over the deceased; mourn sb's death ❹ get sick from; be surfeited with;～风 catch cold; get a cold ❺ be harmful to; offend; 无～大体 not a matter of principle

伤疤 shāngbā　❶ scar ❷ past mistake or humiliation;不要揭他的～。Don't rake up all that muck about his past.

伤残 shāngcán　❶ (of finished products) damaged; defective ❷ handicap; physical disability; 因工～ be disabled on the job / ～人 the handicapped .

伤感 shānggǎn　sick at heart; sentimental; mawkish;～万分 feel a heart-breaking melancholy

伤害 shānghài　injure; harm; hurt;～感情 hurt one's feelings / ～积极性 dampen one's enthusiasm

伤寒 shānghán　❶〈医〉typhoid (fever) ❷〈中医〉disease caused by harmful cold factors; febrile disease

伤痕 shānghén　scar; bruise; gash;～累累 be covered with cuts and bruises / ～文学 "trauma" literature

伤口 shāngkǒu　wound; cut; gash;包扎～ bind up or suture a wound

伤脑筋 shāngnǎojīn　brain-racking; troublesome; vexing;让人～的事 (big) headache; hard nut to crack / 伤了一番脑筋 rack one's brains (over sth)

伤神 shāngshén　overtax one's nerves; cause great mental strain;为生计～ strain every nerve to make ends meet

伤天害理 shāngtiān-hàilǐ　in defiance of heaven and human reason; outrageous;～的勾当 inhuman act; act of gross injustice

伤痛 shāngtòng　❶ grieved; sad; broken-hearted ❷ ache; be painful

伤心 shāngxīn　sad; sorrowful; broken-hearted;～事 painful memory; heart-breaking event

殇(殤) shāng　〈书〉die young;夭～ die a premature death

商 shāng　❶ talk over; discuss; consult;～筹对策 discuss a countermeasure ❷ trade; commerce; business;～船 merchant ship; merchantman / ～店 shop; store / ～贩 small retailer; pedlar / ～海 commerce; commercial field / ～会 chamber of commerce / ～机 business opportunity / ～界 business world; commercial circles / ～情 market conditions / ～战 trade war;〈喻〉business competition ❸ merchant; businessman; dealer; 皮货～ fur trader ❹〈数〉quotient

商标 shāngbiāo　trademark;～侵权 trademark infringement / ～注册

trademark registration

商场 shāngchǎng ❶ market; bazaar; mall ❷ large department store ❸ business world

商定 shāngdìng decide through consultation; arrive at an agreement; agree

商量 shāngliáng consult; discuss; exchange views; talk over

商品 shāngpǐn commodity; goods; merchandise:~房 commercial housing / ~化 commercialization / ~粮 commodity grain / ~检验 (shortened as 商检) commodity inspection

商洽 shāngqià take up (a matter) with sb; discuss

商榷 shāngquè discuss; consider; deliberate:没有~的余地 leave no room for further consideration

商谈 shāngtán exchange views; talk about; negotiate:多方~ consultations among all parties

商讨 shāngtǎo discuss; consult; deliberate:~协作问题 hold consultations on cooperation

商务 shāngwù commercial matters; business affairs; ~代理 business or commercial agent / ~英语 business English

商业 shāngyè commerce; trade; business:~街 business or shopping street / ~片 commercial film / ~道德 business ethics /~网点 network of trading establishments; commercial network

商议 shāngyì consult; confer; discuss:~解决办法 discuss solutions

塝 shāng 〈农〉 moisture in the soil:保~ preserve soil moisture / ~情 soil moisture content

熵 shāng 〈理〉 entropy; thermal charge

shǎng

晌 shǎng 〈方〉❶ part of the day:后半~儿 afternoon ❷ (usu 晌

午) noon; midday

赏 shǎng ❶ reward; award; bestow:~金 money reward / ~罚分明 be fair and strict in meting out rewards and punishments ❷ enjoy; admire:~月 admire the bright (full) moon / ~心乐事 pleasant and enjoyable experience; happy event ❸ praise; appreciate; admire:~析 make appreciative comments (on literary works, etc) ❹ 〈套〉 used in making a request or an invitation:~脸〈套〉grant or do one the honour (of accepting)

赏赐 shǎngcì grant or bestow (a reward); award (a prize, etc):大自然的~ bounties of nature

赏光 shǎngguāng 〈套〉accept an invitation; 敬请~. The pleasure of your company is requested.

赏识 shǎngshí recognize the worth of; appreciate:备受老板~ be in the boss's good graces

赏玩 shǎngwán admire the beauty of; enjoy; delight in

赏心悦目 shǎngxīn-yuèmù pleasing to both the eye and the mind; be a feast for the eye

shàng

上 shàng ❶ upper; up; upward:~访 seek an audience with the higher authorities to appeal for intervention (in a case, etc) / ~浮 (of price, wages, etc) increase / ~交 turn over to the higher authorities; hand in / ~扬 go up; increase / ~限 upper limit; ceiling / ~肢 upper limbs / ~下 下 high and low; everyone ❷ higher; superior; better; ~宾 distinguished guest; guest of honour / ~苍 Heaven (above); God / ~策 best policy; best way out; best thing to do / ~好 ~好 "上佳" best quality; tip-top; top-notch ❸ first (part); preceding; previous;

辈 (of a family) ancestors; elder generation; elders / 一次 last time / 一古 ancient times; antiquity / 一旬 first ten days of a month / 一述 preceding; above-mentioned / 半场 also "上半时" first half (of a game, etc) / 一半夜 before midnight / 见一文 see above ❹ 〈旧〉(of the) emperor: 一谕 imperial decree ❺ go up; board; get on: 一岸 go ashore; go on shore; land / 一楼梯 ascend the stairs ❻ go to; leave for; press on: 一坟 visit a grave (to honour the memory of the dead) / 一街 go shopping; go downtown; take to the street ❼ submit; send in; present: 一书 submit a written statement to a higher authority / 一税 pay taxes ❽ add; apply; supply: 一光 glaze; polish / 一货 replenish supplies for sale; display goods on shelves / 一色 paint; colour ❾ put on record; lay on the table; carry or publish (in a paper, etc): 一菜 serve the dishes / 一晚报 be carried in the evening paper ❿ wind; tighten: 一发条 wind (a watch, toy, etc) ⓫ begin work or study at a fixed time: 一班 go to work; be on duty / 一学 go to or attend school; be at school; begin school ⓬ up to; as many as: 一档次 reach a high grade / 一千人 no fewer than a thousand people ⓭ (also shǎng) 〈语言〉falling-rising tone see also "四声" sìshēng ⓮ (shang) used after a verb to indicate a) upward movement: 飞一天 soar into the sky b) completion: 安一电话 have a telephone installed c) beginning of an action or state: 迷一了电视剧 be addicted to TV plays d) amount or extent reached: 跑一几公里 run several kilometres ⓯ (shang) used after a noun to indicate a) surface of sth: 脸一 on the face b) scope: 世一 in the world; on earth c) aspect: 技术一 technologically d) process: 路一 on the way or road

上报 shàngbào ❶ appear in the newspapers ❷ report to a higher body or the higher-ups

上层 shàngcéng upper strata; higher levels: 一社会 upper strata of society; upper-class society / 一建筑 superstructure: 走一路线 build up higher connections and get things done through their influence

上场 shàngchǎng ❶ 〈体〉enter the court or field; participate in a contest ❷ 〈戏〉appear on the stage; enter

上乘 shàngchéng ❶ (of Buddhism) Mahayana; Great Vehicle ❷ (of works) (of) superior quality; (of a) high order

上蹿下跳 shàngcuān-xiàtiào 〈喻〉〈贬〉run around on sinister errands

上当 shàngdàng be taken in; be deceived, cheated or duped

上等 shàngděng first-class or first-rate; superior; top-notch: 一货 first-class goods / 一兵 (army) private, first class

上帝 Shàngdì ❶ Lord on High that governs everything ❷ 〈宗教〉God

上吊 shàngdiào hang oneself: 急得我简直要一。I was worried to death.

上方宝剑 shàngfāngbǎojiàn also "尚方宝剑" imperial sword (as symbol of supreme authority); carte blanche

上风 shàngfēng ❶ windward: 在一头 be on the windward side; be upwind ❷ advantage; superior position; upper hand: 占一 get the upper hand

上岗 shànggǎng go to a duty post; take up a job; 择优一 take on workers on their merits / 一证 job qualification certificate

上告 shànggào complain to higher authorities; appeal to a higher court; report to a higher body

上供 shànggòng also "上贡" ❶ lay offerings on the altar ❷ grease or oil sb's palm

上钩 shànggōu swallow the bait;〈喻〉be enticed; get hooked

上火 shànghuǒ ❶（中医）suffer from excessive internal heat ❷〈方〉flare up; be upset

上级 shàngjí high level or authorities; 讨好～ curry favour with one's superiors

上将 shàngjiàng （army & air force) general; (navy) admiral

上缴 shàngjiǎo turn over (revenues, etc) to the higher authorities

上进 shàngjìn go forward; make progress;～心 desire for improvement

上镜 shàngjìng ❶ appear on TV or in movies ❷ look good on TV or in movies; be telegenic

上课 shàngkè go to or attend class; conduct a class; give a lesson or lecture

上空 shàngkōng in the sky; high above; overhead

上口 shàngkǒu ❶ be able to read aloud fluently;琅琅～ can recite fluently ❷ be easy to read; read smoothly

上来 shànglái ❶ at the beginning;一～ from the beginning or outset ❷ come up;上楼来 come upstairs ❸ used after a verb to indicate a) a movement either upward or from afar；漫～come up b) overflow with success;答～ give a correct answer (to a question) ❹ used after an adjective to indicate increasing degree：天色黑～了。Dusk is gathering.

上流 shàngliú ❶ also "上游" upper reaches (of a river) ❷ upper class; high society;～人物 people from high society

上路 shànglù ❶ hit the road; begin a journey; start out ❷ also "上轨道" on the right track；她的工作还没有～。She hasn't got the knack of her job yet.

上马 shàngmǎ ❶ mount a horse ❷

(of a project, etc) start; kick off

上门 shàngmén ❶ visit; call; drop in;送货～ deliver goods to the door ❷ shut or bolt the door; lock up for the night ❸ shut up business ❹ live with bride's family after marriage;～女婿 living-in son-in-law

上面 shàngmian also "上边";"上头" ❶ upper; above; over ❷ above(-mentioned); preceding; foregoing;～提到 as mentioned above ❸ see "上⓯a；上⓯b" ❹ higher level or authorities; higher-ups ❺ elder generation of one's family; one's elders

上年纪 shàngniánji also "上岁数"〈口〉be getting on in age

上品 shàngpǐn highest quality; top grade;茶中～ best of teas

上气不接下气 shàngqìbùjiēxiàqì gasp or pant for breath; be short or out of breath;～地说 speak in gasps

上去 shàngqù ❶ go or come up; move from a lower level to a higher level ❷ (shàngqu) used after a verb to indicate a) upward movement：跳～ jump up b) outward or forward direction；大家连忙向他迎～。Everybody hurried forward to meet him. c) rise in level；把外贸搞～ increase foreign trade ❸ addition or intensification；把劲儿使～ exert oneself

上任 shàngrèn ❶ assume an official post; take office ❷ predecessor;～校长 former principal

上身 shàngshēn ❶ （of clothes) be worn for the first time ❷ upper part of the body; above the waist；光着～ stripped to the waist; topless ❸ also "上衣" upper outer garment; blouse; jacket

上升 shàngshēng ❶ rise; go up; ascend ❷ (in grade, degree or amount) go up; grow; increase；经济～期 period of economic growth

上市 shàngshì ❶ go or appear on the market ❷ go shopping ❸〈经〉list; go public:在香港 ～ be listed in Hong Kong / ～ 公司 listed or public company

上手 shàngshǒu ❶ *also* "上首" left-hand seat; seat of honour ❷ *also* "上家" person who precedes one (in playing cards or mah-jong) ❸ set out; get started

上司 shàngsi boss; superior; chief

上诉 shàngsù 〈法〉appeal (to a higher court):提出 ～ lodge an appeal / ～ 人 appellant; petitioner / ～法院 court of appeal; appellate court

上溯 shàngsù ❶ sail or navigate upstream ❷ trace or date back to; date from

上算 shàngsuàn profitable; worthwhile

上台 shàngtái ❶ ascend the platform; appear on the stage ❷〈贬〉assume power; hold sway

上天 shàngtiān ❶ go up in the sky; go into space; fly skywards ❷〈婉〉go to heaven; pass away ❸ *also* "上苍" Heaven; Providence; God

上调 shàngtiáo (of prices, etc) be adjusted upwards; raise

上网 shàngwǎng use the Internet; go on-line:～冲浪 surf the Internet

上尉 shàngwèi (army & air force) captain; (navy) lieutenant

上下 shàngxià ❶ high and low; old and young:～推波 pass the buck either up or down / ～其手 act in an underhand way; resort to deception; play tricks in collusion ❷ from top to bottom; up and down:～文 context / 浑身～都淋湿了 be wet through ❸ relative superiority or strength:难分～ hard to tell who is better ❹ (used after a numerical-classifier compound) about; nearly; or so:50 岁～ about fifty years old ❺ go up and down:～车 get on and

off the bus

上…下… shàng…xià… *used in parallel structures*: *for contrast*:上不上,下不下 be stranded halfway; be in an awkward position / 上有政策,下有对策. Those below will always find a way to get around the policies of their superiors. ❷ *for emphasis*:上行下效. If a leader sets a bad example, his subordinates will follow suit. / 上梁不正下梁歪.〈俗〉When those above behave unworthily, those below will follow suit.

上相 shàngxiàng come out well in a photograph; be photogenic

上校 shàngxiào (army & air force) colonel; (navy) captain

上心 shàngxīn bear or keep in mind; be in earnest; be conscientious

上演 shàngyǎn (put on the) stage; perform

上瘾 shàngyǐn be addicted (to sth); get into the habit (of doing sth); get hooked (on sth)

上映 shàngyìng show (a film); screen

上游 shàngyóu ❶ *see* "上流❶" ❷ advanced position:力争～ aim high

上涨 shàngzhǎng (of water, price, etc) rise; go up

上阵 shàngzhèn go into battle; pitch into work; play in a game

上座 shàngzuò ❶ seat of honour ❷ (of a cinema, restaurant, etc) sell (well, etc):～率 box-office rate

尚 shàng ❶ esteem; value; treasure:～武精神 martial spirit / 不～空谈 set no store by empty talk ❷ prevailing custom, habits, etc ❸〈书〉(副) still; yet:年龄～小 still young ❹ *also* "尚且"〈书〉〈副〉even:他～不能,何况我! Even he failed; how could it be possible for me!

尚方宝剑 shàngfāngbǎojiàn *see* "上方宝剑" shàngfāngbǎojiàn

shāo

捎 shāo　take sth to or for sb; bring sth to sb; do (sth) on the side: ～带 incidentally; by the way; in passing / ～话 take a message to sb; have a message conveyed to sb / ～脚 pick up passengers or goods on the way / ～个好儿 give one's regards to sb　*see also* shào

烧（燒） shāo　❶ set fire to; burn: ～化 cremate (a dead body); burn (paper, etc, as offering to the dead) / ～毁 burn up; burn down / ～烤 barbecue / ～灼 burn; scorch; singe　❷ cook; bake; heat: ～饼 sesame seed cake / ～暖气 (of a building, etc) have central heating; (of workers) work at the furnace to provide central heating　❸ (of cooking) stew after frying; roast; braise　❹ run a fever; have a temperature　❺ damage or hurt (due to excessive use of chemicals, etc)　❻ have one's head turned by newly acquired riches, etc; ～包（方）be drunk with wealth or success

烧酒 shāojiǔ　spirits (usu distilled from sorghum or maize)

烧卖 shāomài　*also* "烧麦" steamed dumpling with the dough frilled at the top

烧伤 shāoshāng　〈医〉burn: 二度～ second-degree burns

烧香 shāoxiāng　❶ burn joss sticks (before an idol): 烧高香 be blessed; be thankful　❷ grease sb's palm; bribe

烧心 shāoxīn　❶ upset the stomach; have heartburn　❷（方）(of cabbages) turn yellow at the heart

梢 shāo　tip; thin end of a twig, etc: 眉～ tip of the brow

稍 shāo　〈副〉a little; a trifle; slightly: ～候 wait a little / ～微 *also* "稍为"; "稍许"〈副〉a little; somewhat; slightly: ～加润色 touch up / ～胜一筹 a notch above; slightly

better / ～事休息 take a breather / ～纵即逝 it's gone the moment the grip is slightly relaxed — transient; fleeting / ～～占上风 gain an edge (on one's opponent)　*see also* shào

艄 shāo　❶ *also* "船艄" stern　❷ rudder; helm: ～公 helmsman; boatman

鞘 shāo　（usu 鞭鞘）whiplash　*see also* qiào

sháo

勺（杓） sháo　spoon; scoop; ladle

芍 sháo

芍药 sháoyao　〈植〉Chinese herbaceous peony

韶 sháo　〈书〉beautiful; splendid: ～光 time; beautiful springtime; glorious youth / ～华 springtime; youth

shǎo

少 shǎo　❶ few; little; scanty: ～有 rare; exceptional / ～而精 fewer but better　❷ be short of; lack; not have enough: ～找钱 (give) short-change / ～不了 cannot do without; be bound to; be unavoidable　❸ lose; be missing　❹ owe　❺ a little while; a minute: ～时 after a little while; a moment later; presently / ～安毋躁 be calm and wait a while; don't get impatient　❻ stop; cut out: ～管闲事 Mind your own business.　*see also* shào

少见 shǎojiàn　❶〈套〉it's a rare pleasure to meet you　❷ seldom seen; rare: ～多怪 to one who has seen little of the world, everything is remarkable; scanty experience gives rise to many surprises

少陪 shǎopéi 〈套〉I must be leaving

少数 shǎoshù　small number; few; minority;～党 minority party /～民族 ethnic minority

少许 shǎoxǔ　also "少量" a little; some; a modicum

shào

少 shào ❶ young; youthful;～妇 young married woman /～女 young girl /～相 look younger than one's age; have a youthful appearance /～白头 be prematurely grey; young person with greying hair /～管所 reformatory for juvenile delinquents ❷ son of a wealthy family; young master;阔～ profligate son of the rich　*see also* shǎo

少不更事 shàobùgēngshì　young and inexperienced; green

少将 shàojiàng　(army & air force) major general; (navy) rear admiral

少年 shàonián ❶ early youth (from ten to sixteen) ❷ boy or girl of that age; juvenile; teenager;～犯 juvenile delinquent /～老成 old head on young shoulders; listless young person ❸ 〈书〉young man;～得志 succeed in one's early years

少尉 shàowèi　(army & air force) second lieutenant; (navy) ensign

少先队 shàoxiānduì　(short for 少年先锋队) Young Pioneers

少校 shàoxiào　(army & air force) major; (navy) lieutenant commander

少爷 shàoye　〈旧〉❶ young master (of the house); young son;要～脾气 behave like a pampered boy ❷ 〈敬〉(your, his, etc) son

少壮 shàozhuàng　young and vigorous;～派 powerful rising stars; Young Turks

劭 shào　〈书〉❶ encourage ❷ fine; noble

绍 shào ❶ carry or keep on; continue ❷ (Shào) short for Shaoxing (绍兴) in Zhejiang;～酒 also "绍兴酒" Shaoxing rice wine

绍介 shàojiè　〈书〉introduce;请为～。 Please introduce me.

捎 shào　(of draught animal) draw back a step or two; shy;～色 (of cloth) fade　*see also* shāo

哨 shào ❶ reconnaissance; patrol ❷ (sentry) post;～兵 sentry; guard /～卡 check post ❸ (of birds) warble; chirp ❹ also "哨子" whistle

稍 shào

稍息 shàoxī　〈军〉stand at ease;～! At ease!　*see also* shāo

潲 shào ❶ (of rain) slant in;西边～雨。The rain is driving in from the west. ❷ 〈方〉sprinkle (water); spray

shē

奢 shē ❶ luxurious; extravagant; profligate;～华 luxurious; sumptuous; extravagant ❷ excessive; inordinate; undue;～求 (make an) excessive or unreasonable demand /～谈 talk in a boastful manner; prate /～望 extravagant hope; wild expectation

奢侈 shēchǐ　luxurious; lavish; wasteful;～品 luxury goods; luxuries

赊 shē　buy or sell on credit;～购 buy on credit /～账 buy or sell on credit; give or get credit

shé

舌 shé　tongue; sth shaped like a tongue;火～ tongues of flame /帽～ peak of a cap /～敝唇焦 talk till one's tongue and lips are parched; talk oneself hoarse

舌苔 shétāi　〈中医〉tongue coating or

fur：～厚 have a furred tongue

舌头 shétou　tongue；大～ thick-tongued；lisper / 长～ (be a) gossip

舌战 shézhàn　engage in a battle of words；argue heatedly；cross verbal swords

折 shé ❶ break；split；snap：宁～不弯 would rather break than bend ❷ (usu 折本) suffer losses；lose money in business：不～不赚 break even

see also zhē；zhé

蛇 shé　snake；serpent：玩～ charm a snake / ～毒 snake venom；venin / ～蜕 snake slough / ～足 feet added to a snake — a superfluity / ～蝎心肠 venomous as snakes and scorpions

蛇头 shétóu　snake's head；〈喻〉ring-leader of organized illegal immigration

蛇行 shéxíng ❶ move sinuously on the ground；snake (one's way) ❷ meander；wind

shě

舍（捨） shě ❶ give up；discard；abandon；～弃 give up；forgo；abandon / ～不得 be loath to part with or give up；grudge / ～本逐末 attend to trifles to the neglect of essentials / ～己为人 place the interests of others before one's own；be altruistic / ～近求远 seek far and wide for what lies close at hand / ～车保帅 (in chess) give up a rook to save the king — sacrifice minor interests to major ones / ～身取义 sacrifice one's life for a just cause / ～生忘死 risk one's life / ～舍 give alms；dispense charity

see also shè

舍命 shěmìng　risk one's life；be ready to sacrifice oneself：～相救 come to sb's rescue at the risk of one's own life / ～陪君子〈谑〉keep sb company at all

costs

shè

设 shè ❶ set up；work out；establish：～宴 give a banquet or feast / ～计陷害 plot a frame-up；frame (sb) ❷ suppose；assume ❸〈书〉if；in case：～如 *also*"设若"supposing；provided

设备 shèbèi　equipment；installation；facilities：～精良 well-equipped

设法 shèfǎ　think of a way；try；endeavour

设防 shèfáng　set up defences；garrison and fortify：重兵～ heavily garrisoned / 处处～ guard against (sb) in every way

设计 shèjì　design；devise；plan：～师 designer；architect / ～能力 designed capacity

设立 shèlì　establish；form；set up

设身处地 shèshēn-chǔdì　put oneself in sb's place or shoes；be considerate

设施 shèshī　installation；facilities

设想 shèxiǎng ❶ imagine；assume；anticipate：从最坏处～ prepare for the worst ❷ have consideration for；give thought to

设置 shèzhì ❶ set or put up：～骗局 lay a trap ❷ install (machinery, etc)；fix

社 shè ❶ organization；society；establishment：诗～ poets' society / 茶～ teahouse / ～god of the land；sacrifices to him；altar for such sacrifices；～稷〈旧〉gods of land and grain — state；country

社会 shèhuì ❶ society：～学 sociology / ～保障 social security / ～关系 social connections；relatives and friends / ～舆论 public opinion ❷ community：～ community or social work / ～名流 noted public figure；celebrity / ～贤达 community leader

社会主义 shèhuìzhǔyì socialism：～初级阶段 primary or initial stage of socialism

社交 shèjiāo social life or contact：擅长～ be a good mixer

社论 shèlùn editorial；leading article

社区 shèqū community：～服务 community service

社团 shètuán mass organization；societies：文艺～ societies of art and literature ／ ～法人 aggregate corporation

舍 shè ❶ house：～间 also "舍下"〈谦〉my humble house ❷ shed；pen：牛～ cowshed ❸〈谦〉(of younger or junior relatives) my：～妹 my younger sister

see also shě

舍利 shèlì also "舍利子" sarira，remains from cremation of Buddha's body，often in the shape of beads：～塔 pagoda for Buddhist relics

射 shè ❶ shoot；fire；eject：～程 range (of fire) ／ ～箭〈体〉archery ／ ～猎 hunt with bow and arrow or with firearms ／ ～门〈体〉shoot (at the goal) ／ ～杀 shoot to death；shoot dead ／ ～手 shooter；marksman；〈体〉scorer ❷ discharge in a jet；spout：～精〈生理〉ejaculation ❸ emit (light，heat，etc)：光芒四～ radiate brilliant light ／ ～线〈理〉ray ❹ allude to；insinuate；intimate

射击 shèjī (open) fire；shoot：～场 shooting range ／ ～技术 marksmanship

涉 shè ❶ wade；ford：～渡 wade across a river；ford a stream ❷ go through；undergo；experience：～险 go through perils ❸ involve；implicate：～案 implicated in a case ／ ～讼 involved in a lawsuit ／ ～外事务 matters relating to foreign nationals，firms，etc

涉及 shèjí involve；relate to；deal with：作品～的生活面 aspects of life touched upon in a work

涉猎 shèliè do desultory reading；read

at random；browse：广泛～ read extensively

涉世 shèshì have experience of life；make one's way in the world：～未深 inexperienced in the affairs of the world

涉嫌 shèxián be suspected of；be a suspect：～受贿 be suspected of taking bribes

涉足 shèzú〈书〉set foot in；enter：～仕途 embark on an official career；enter politics

赦 shè remit (a punishment)；pardon；absolve：～令 decree for pardon；order of amnesty

赦免 shèmiǎn remit (a punishment)；pardon；absolve：～权 power of absolution

摄(攝) shè ❶ take in；absorb；assimilate：～食 (of animals) feed ❷ (take a) photo；shoot ❸〈书〉conserve (one's health)；keep fit：～生之道 road to longevity ❹ act for：～理 hold a position in an acting capacity

摄取 shèqǔ ❶ absorb；assimilate：～食物 take in food ❷ (take a) photo；shoot：～街景 shoot street scenes

摄氏 shèshì Celsius；centigrade：～度 ℃ (degree Celsius or centigrade)

摄像 shèxiàng make a video recording：～机 video camera

摄影 shèyǐng ❶ take a photo：～机 camera ／ ～迷 shutterbug ／ ～师 photographer；cameraman ❷ (shoot a) film or TV：～外景 exterior shooting ／ ～棚 film studio

摄政 shèzhèng act as regent：～王 prince regent

摄制 shèzhì produce (a film or TV)：～组 production unit

慑(懾) shè〈书〉fear；dread；coerce；frighten：～服 submit because of fear；be cowed into submission；be awed ／ ～于压力 submit to pressure

麝

麝 shè musk (deer)：~香 musk

shéi

谁 shéi *also* shuí ❶ who; whom; whose：他们在等~? Who are they waiting for? ❷ *used to refer indefinitely to anybody* a) *in a rhetorical question*：难道~都不懂? Is it possible that nobody understands? b) *in supposition or conjecture*：如果有~出来管管，这该有多好! It would be much better if someone came forward to take up the matter! c) *before* 都 *or* 也, *or after* 不管 *or* 无论：(不管)~来都欢迎。Whoever comes will be welcome. ❸ *used twice in the same sentence* a) *to denote different people*：我们~也不欠~。Neither of us owes anything to the other. or We're quits. b) *to refer to the same person*：~笑到最后，~笑得最好。He who laughs last laughs best.

谁谁 shéishéi *used to refer to people whose names need not be mentioned*：她向我介绍朋友中~发了财，~出了国。She told me who among our friends had made a fortune and who had gone abroad.

shēn

申 shēn ❶ state; explain; apply：~述 explain in detail; expound; state (a view, etc) / ~讨 openly condemn; censure; denounce / ~言 state; declare ❷ 9th of the Earthly Branches *see also* "干支" gānzhī ❸ (Shēn) another name for Shanghai (上海)

申办 shēnbàn apply; bid：~公证 apply for notarization / ~世博会 bid for the next world exposition

申报 shēnbào ❶ report (to higher authorities) ❷ declare (to the customs)

申辩 shēnbiàn defend oneself; argue or plead one's case

申斥 shēnchì rebuke; reprimand; reprove；~一番 give (sb) a dressing down

申明 shēnmíng make (one's stand, etc) public; declare; state

申请 shēnqǐng apply for：~人 applicant / ~书 (written) application; petition

申诉 shēnsù ❶ appeal for justice or complain about an injustice (to authorities concerned) ❷ 〈法〉present one's case in a law court; appeal：~权 right of appeal

申雪 shēnxuě *also* "伸雪" ❶ appeal for vindication ❷ vindicate (a wrong case); redress (an injustice); right (a wrong)

申冤 shēnyuān ❶ *also* "伸冤" redress an injustice; right a wrong ❷ appeal for redressing a wrong

伸 shēn put out; stretch; extend：~展 extend; reach; stretch / ~懒腰 stretch (one's limbs)

伸手 shēnshǒu stretch or hold out one's hand；〈喻〉ask or beg for sth; try to get sth that is not one's due：~不见五指 so dark that you can't see your own hand in front of you; pitch-dark / 手伸得太长 be overly ambitious or greedy; overextend oneself

伸缩 shēnsuō ❶ lengthen and shorten; stretch out and draw back：~自如 be highly elastic ❷ flexibility; latitude：没有~余地 allow no latitude

伸张 shēnzhāng uphold (justice); promote; stand up for

身 shēn ❶ body：~边 at or by one's side / ~长 height (of a person); length (of a garment, from shoulder to hemline) / ~上 on one's body; on one; with one / ~强力壮 (of a person) strong; tough; sturdy ❷ life：～后 after one's death ❸ oneself；personally：～经百战 battle-hardened / ～教言传 teach by personal example and verbal instruction / ～先士卒（of an officer）lead one's men（in a charge）；（of a leader）be at the forefront of a struggle ❹ position；moral character and accomplishment：～败名裂 bring disgrace and ruin upon oneself；fall into utter disrepute ❺ frame of a structure；body；车～ body of a car / 机～ fuselage ❻〈量〉（of clothes）suit：一～西装 a Western-style suit

身不由己 shēnbùyóujǐ involuntarily；in spite of oneself；not of one's own accord

身材 shēncái stature；figure；build

身段 shēnduàn ❶（woman's）figure ❷（dancer's）posture

身份 shēnfen also "身分" ❶ status；capacity；identity：～证 identity card；ID（card）❷ dignity：有失～ beneath one's dignity

身价 shēnjià ❶〈旧〉selling price of a person ❷ personal value（to society）；social status：～百倍（of price）skyrocket；〈喻〉have a meteoric rise in social status

身临其境 shēnlínqíjìng be present on the scene；go through the experience personally

身躯 shēnqū body；stature：～矮小 short in build；of short stature

身世 shēnshì（often unfortunate）lot；life experience

身手 shēnshǒu skill；talent；ability：～不凡 of uncommon talent or skill

身体 shēntǐ ❶ body：保持～平衡 keep one's balance ❷ health：～素质 physique

身体力行 shēntǐ-lìxíng earnestly practise what one advocates or preaches

身外之物 shēnwàizhīwù external thing；worldly possession；matter of little consequence

身心 shēnxīn body and mind：～交瘁 be worn out both physically and mentally

身孕 shēnyùn pregnancy：怀有～ be expecting；be in the family way

呻 shēn

呻吟 shēnyín groan；moan；whine

参（參）shēn general term for ginseng and similar herbs, esp ginseng　see also cān；cēn

绅 shēn gentry：乡～ country gentleman；squire

绅士 shēnshì gentleman；gentry：～风度 gentlemanly manners or airs

莘 shēn

莘莘 shēnshēn〈书〉numerous；multitudinous：～学子 large numbers of students

砷 shēn〈化〉arsenic（As）

深 shēn ❶ far downward or well inward from the outside；deep：～渊 deep pool；bottomless pit；abyss / ～山老林 remote mountains and virgin forests / ～水～齐胸 breast-deep water ❷ profound；difficult；abstruse：～奥 profound；abstruse；recondite / ～不可测 of immeasurable depth or profundity ❸ in-depth；incisive；penetrating：～究 go or probe into（a matter）seriously；thoroughly investigate / ～谈 have an in-depth conversation；go deeply into sth / ～省 come to fully realize / ～仇大恨 bitter and deep-seated hatred / ～得人心 be very popular ❹ close；intimate：～交 intimate friendship；close friends ❺ dark；rich：～蓝 dark or deep blue ❻ late：～秋 late autumn / ～更半夜 in the dead of night；in the small hours

深长 shēncháng profound：用意～ have profound meanings

深沉 shēnchén ❶ dark；deep：爱得

love (sb) deeply ❷ (of sound or voice) deep; heavy ❸ (of a person) reserved

深度 shēndù ❶ (degree of) depth; profundity;缺乏～ lacking in depth ❷ extremely; deeply; greatly;～近视 extremely myopic

深厚 shēnhòu ❶ deep; profound ❷ solid; thick; deep-seated;群众基础～ have a solid foundation among the masses

深化 shēnhuà go deeper; deepen;～改革 further or deepen the reforms

深加工 shēnjiāgōng intensive or downstream processing;～产品 downstream products; high value-added products

深居简出 shēnjū-jiǎnchū live a secluded life; live in isolation from the outside world

深刻 shēnkè profound; deep-going; incisive;印象～ be deeply impressed; have a deep impression

深明大义 shēnmíngdàyì be clear as to principles; know clearly what is right and proper

深谋远虑 shēnmóu-yuǎnlǜ think deeply and plan carefully; be thoughtful and far-sighted

深浅 shēnqiǎn ❶ depth ❷ shade (of colour); hue;～不一 .of different shades ❸ proper limits; propriety;不知～ have no sense of propriety

深切 shēnqiè ❶ profound; cordial; deep;～怀念 dearly cherish the memory of (sb) ❷ penetrating and relevant; thorough; deep

深情 shēnqíng profound feeling; deep affection;～厚谊 profound friendship

深入 shēnrù ❶ go deep into; probe or penetrate into;～浅出 explain profound ideas in plain terms;～人心 take root in the hearts of the people ❷ thorough; intensive;～思考 mull over (sth)

深思 shēnsī think deeply about; be deep in thought; ponder;～熟虑 careful consideration; mature deliberation /令人～ thought-provoking

深邃 shēnsuì ❶ going far down from the top; going far in from the outside; deep;～的目光 penetrating eyes ❷ profound; abstruse

深恶痛绝 shēnwùtòngjué cherish intense hatred for; abhor; detest

深信 shēnxìn believe strongly; be (deeply) convinced; have deep faith in;～不疑 believe without a shadow of doubt

深远 shēnyuǎn profound (significance, etc); far-reaching (repercussions, etc)

深造 shēnzào take an advanced course of study; pursue advanced studies;出国～ go abroad for advanced studies

深挚 shēnzhì profound and sincere (friendship, etc)

深重 shēnzhòng very grave; extremely serious; critical;苦难～ serious suffering; great tribulations

shén

什(甚) shén　see also shí

什么 shénme ❶ used in a question;～人? Who is it? ❷ used to refer to sth indefinite;～都不怕 fear nothing / 有～就说。 Feel free to say what's on your mind. ❸ used to express surprise, censure, or disagreement;嚷～? Why all this shouting? / 装～糊涂! Stop playing the fool. ❹ used before a string of coordinate phrases for enumeration;～绘画呀，跳舞呀，他全都会。 He can draw, dance, and what not.

什么的 shénmede 〈口〉 and so on; and what not;种点西红柿、茄子～ grow tomatoes, eggplants, and so forth

神 shén ❶ god; deity; divinity;～化 deify / ～龛 shrine (for idol or ancestral tablet) / ～明 also "神灵" gods; deities; divinities / ～职人员 clergy ❷ supernatural; miraculous; superb:～汉 sorcerer; wizard / ～童 child prodigy / ～医 miracle-working doctor / ～勇 (of) superhuman bravery / ～枪手 crack shot; dead shot; sharpshooter / ～机妙算 wonderful foresight (in military operations, etc); superb stratagem ❸ spirit; mind; energy:～似 be alike or like in spirit / ～游〈书〉 feel as if one had personally visited (a place); take an imaginary trip (to a place) / ～不守舍 look as if one's mind were unhinged; look obsessed / ～魂颠倒 be infatuated; be in a confused state of mind / ～思恍惚 in a trance; beside oneself; distracted ❹ expression; appearance; look

神采 shéncǎi expression; look:～飞扬 in fine fettle / ～奕奕 brim with energy and vitality

神出鬼没 shénchū-guǐmò move about like a supernatural being; come and go like a shadow; appear and disappear mysteriously

神道 shéndào ❶ way or path leading to a grave; tomb passage ❷ (Shéndào) Shinto, native religion of Japan; Shintoism

神父 shénfu also "神甫" (Roman Catholic or Anglican) father; priest

神乎其神 shénhūqíshén causing wonder; wonderful; miraculous:说得 ～ paint a fantastic picture (of sth)

神话 shénhuà ❶ mythology; myth ❷ 〈喻〉 tall story; fairy tale; myth

神交 shénjiāo ❶ friends with mutual understanding and trust ❷ mutual admiration without prior acquaintance:～已久 have long cherished admiration for each other without having met

神经 shénjīng nerve:～病 mental disorder / ～质 neurotic; nervous / ～错乱 mentally deranged / ～毒气 nerve

gas / ～过敏 oversensitive; hypersensitive / ～紧张 on edge; edgy / ～衰弱 〈医〉 neurasthenia

神秘 shénmì mysterious; mystical; secretive; ～莫测 unpredictable; unfathomable; inscrutable

神农 Shénnóng also "神农氏" legendary ruler supposed to have introduced agriculture and herbal medicine, also called Yandi or Red Emperor (炎帝)

神奇 shénqí magical; wonderful; miraculous

神气 shénqì ❶ expression; look; manner:说话的 ～ the way one speaks ❷ spirited; impressive; vigorous ❸ putting on airs; arrogant:～活现 very cocky; self-important; high and mighty

神情 shénqíng also "神色" air; expression; look:～自若 be calm and collected; keep one's wits about one

神圣 shénshèng sacred; holy; consecrated:～不可侵犯 sacred and inviolable

神速 shénsù marvellously swift; with lightning speed:进展 ～ make speedy progress

神态 shéntài countenance; manner; bearing:～安详 appear calm and composed

神通 shéntōng magic powers; immense capabilities:～广大 be infinitely resourceful; be a past master (at sth)

神往 shénwǎng be carried away; be rapt or fascinated:令人 ～ enchanting; fascinating

神仙 shénxiān celestial being; immortal; 〈喻〉 person with power of clairvoyance or free from worldly cares:～般的日子 (lead a) carefree life of blissful happiness

神学 shénxué 〈宗教〉 theology:～院 theological seminary; school of divinity

神韵 shényùn romantic charm (in art and literature)

S

神志 shénzhì　consciousness; senses; mind; ～清醒 be in one's right mind; be perfectly sober

神州 Shénzhōu　Sacred Land — China; ～大地 vast land of China

shěn

沈（瀋） Shěn　(short for 沈阳) Shenyang, capital of Liaoning Province

审（審） shěn ❶ careful; circumspect; ～视 look at attentively; observe carefully ❷ examine; check up; go over; ～订 examine and revise / ～定 examine and approve (a plan, etc) / ～读 read and evaluate / ～核 examine and verify (accounts, etc) / ～批 examine and approve ❸ interrogate; try; ～理〈法〉 try or hear (a case) / ～讯〈法〉 interrogate (sb); try

审查 shěnchá　examine; check; investigate～干部 (shortened as 审干) examination of cadres' personal histories including family background, work experience and social connections

审察 shěnchá ❶ observe or watch carefully ❷ examine; analyse; review

审处 shěnchǔ ❶ try (a case) ❷ examine and decide; 报上级～ submit (sth) to the higher authorities for decision

审计 shěnjì　audit; ～署 audit bureau / ～员 auditor / ～报告 audit report

审美 shěnměi　appreciation of beauty; ～观 aesthetic perspective or taste

审判 shěnpàn　bring to or put on trial; try; ～权 judicial authority; jurisdiction / ～员 judicial officer; judge / ～长 presiding judge

审慎 shěnshèn　cautious; prudent; circumspect

审时度势 shěnshí-duóshì　read the signs of the times; size up the situation

审问 shěnwèn　interrogate (sb); question; ～案情 find out about a case through interrogation

审议 shěnyì　consider; deliberate; discuss; ～中的提案 motion under deliberation

审阅 shěnyuè　check and approve; read and evaluate; ～稿件 go over a manuscript

哂 shěn 〈书〉smile; 聊博一～ just for your entertainment / ～纳〈套〉kindly accept (this humble gift)

谂 shěn 〈书〉know; be acquainted with; ～悉 know; be familiar with / ～知 be aware of

婶（嬸） shěn ❶ also "婶母" "婶子" wife of father's younger brother; aunt ❷ form of address for a woman about one's mother's age; aunt

shèn

肾（腎） shèn also "肾脏"〈生理〉kidney; ～炎〈医〉nephritis / ～功能 nephritic function / ～结石〈医〉kidney stone / ～上腺〈生理〉adrenal (gland) / ～衰竭〈医〉kidney failure

甚 shèn ❶ very; most; extremely; ～为关切 be most concerned / ～嚣尘上〈贬〉raise a riotous clamour; be all the rage ❷ more than; increasingly; 日一～日 worsen with each passing day

甚至 shènzhì　also "甚而" even; (go) so far as to; so much so that; 事隔多年，我～连他的名字都记不清了。After a lapse of so many years, I cannot even recall his name.

渗（滲） shèn　ooze; seep; leak; ～漏 seep; leak / ～入 seep into; 〈贬〉penetrate; infiltrate

渗透 shèntòu ❶〈理〉osmosis ❷ permeate; seep; soak; ～了鲜血 soaked in blood ❸ (usu used with sth abstract)

infiltrate:文化～ cultural infiltration

瘆(瘮) shèn terrify; horrify; ～人 horrifying; nauseating

慎 shèn careful; cautious; prudent:～独 guard against temptations when all alone / ～密 careful and cautious / ～重 cautious; careful; discreet / ～之又～ exercise maximum caution

shēng

升(❶❷昇、❷陞) shēng ❶ rise; go up; climb:～调〈语言〉rising tune or tone / ～幅 margin of increase; rise / ～旗 hoist or raise a flag / ～腾 (of flames, gas, etc) leap or creep up; rise / ～值〈经〉revalue (upward); appreciate ❷ promote; elevate; raise:～官 be promoted; move up (the official ladder) / ～迁 be transferred to a higher position in a new department / ～任 be promoted to the post of ❸ litre (l.) / sheng, a unit of dry measure for grain (=1 litre)

升格 shēnggé promote; upgrade:由处级单位～为局级单位 (of a unit, etc) be upgraded or raised from a division to a bureau

升华 shēnghuá 〈理〉sublimate;〈喻〉raise to a higher level; distil:生活的艺术～ artistic distillation of life

升级 shēngjí ❶ go up (one grade, etc); promote:～换代 (of products, etc) updating and upgrading ❷ (of war, etc) escalate

升堂入室 shēngtáng-rùshì also "登堂入室" reach a level of high scholarly attainments; acquire high proficiency; be initiated

升天 shēngtiān ❶ ascend heaven;〈婉〉die ❷ also "升空" (of rockets, etc) go up into the sky; lift off

升温 shēngwēn rise in temperature;〈喻〉become warm:计算机需求～。The computer market boomed.

升学 shēngxué go to a school of a higher grade:～率 proportion of students entering schools of a higher grade

生 shēng ❶ give birth to; bear; deliver:～就 be born, gifted or endowed with (a certain quality, etc) / ～来 ever since one's birth; from childhood / ～日 also "生辰" birthday / ～养〈口〉give birth to; bear / ～杀予夺 hold the power of life and death (over sb) ❷ grow:～根 take or strike root; put down roots / ～～不息 multiply endlessly ❸ live; exist; ～还 return alive; survive / ～前 (of sb who is dead) during sb's lifetime / ～擒 capture (alive); take prisoner / ～趣 joy of life / ～猪 (live) pig; hog / ～猛海鲜〈方〉fresh seafood ❹ living; livelihood:务农为～ make a living through farming ❺ cause; make; incur:～病 fall ill; be taken ill / ～事 create trouble; foment disturbance / ～锈 get rusty; rust / ～闷气 sulk; be pettish / ～财有道 have a knack of making money; be good at amassing wealth ❻ light;～火 make or light a fire / ～炉子 light a stove ❼ unripe; uncooked; unprocessed; raw;～瓜 unripe melon / ～漆 raw lacquer / ～水 unboiled water / ～铁 pig-iron ❽ unfamiliar; new; strange:面～ look unfamiliar / ～僻 (of a word, etc) uncommon; rare; obscure / ～手 sb new to a job; green hand / ～字 new word ❾ stiff; unnatural:～涩 (of language) difficult and lacking in fluency; stiff; crude ❿ (used before certain words expressing feelings) very:～疼 very painful ⓫ pupil; student; scholar:～源 source of students; source of school enrolment ⓬ also "生角" male role (as of a scholar or official) in traditional Chinese opera ⑬ *suffix of certain nouns referring to people*：后～ young man; lad ⑭ *suffix of certain adverbs*：好～为难 to be in an extremely embarrassing or difficult situation

生菜 shēngcài ❶〈植〉romaine (lettuce); cos lettuce ❷ raw vegetables

生产 shēngchǎn ❶ produce; make; manufacture：～力 productive forces / ～率 productivity / ～线 production line / ～方式 mode of production / ～资料 means of production; capital goods ❷ give birth to a baby

生存 shēngcún subsist; survive; live：～权 right of existence; right to life or subsistence / ～环境 living environment / ～竞争 struggle for survival

生动 shēngdòng graphic; vivid; lively：～活泼 vivid and vigorous; vivacious

生花妙笔 shēnghuāmiàobǐ *also*"生花之笔"gifted pen; brilliant style of writing

生活 shēnghuó ❶ live; exist; subsist：～方式 way of life; life style / ～条件 living conditions / ～作风 conduct; behaviour ❷ livelihood; living：～费 living expenses; allowance / ～资料 means of livelihood; consumer goods ❸〈方〉(usu manual) work：做～ do manual labour; work

生机 shēngjī ❶ hope of life, success, etc：一线～ an off chance of survival; a ray of hope ❷ life; vigour; vitality：盎然 vibrant with life; overflowing with vigour

生计 shēngjì (means of) livelihood; living：维持～ eke out a living; make (both) ends meet

生离死别 shēnglí-sǐbié part never to meet again; part for ever

生理 shēnglǐ physiology：～学 physiology / ～缺陷 physiological defect or deficiency

生力军 shēnglìjūn ❶ fresh troops or

reinforcements ❷〈喻〉vital contingent; new force or blood

生灵 shēnglíng ❶〈书〉common people：～涂炭。The common people were plunged into an abyss of untold suffering. ❷ life; living thing：可爱的小～ lovely little creature

生龙活虎 shēnglóng-huóhǔ full of animal spirits; full of vim and vigour; bursting with energy

生路 shēnglù ❶ means of livelihood ❷ way out (of a desperate situation)

生米煮成熟饭 shēngmǐzhǔchéngshúfàn the rice is cooked — what is done cannot be undone; a fait accompli that can't be helped

生命 shēngmìng life：～力 vitality; life-force / ～线 lifeline; lifeblood / ～科学 life science

生怕 shēngpà for fear that; so as not to; lest：～打扰别人 so as not to disturb others

生平 shēngpíng ❶ all one's life：～简介 brief introduction to sb's life ❷ ever since one's birth：～第一次 for the first time in one's life

生气 shēngqì ❶ get angry; be furious ❷ life; vitality：～勃勃 dynamic; vigorous; full of vim and vigour

生人 shēngrén ❶ be born：他是 1966 年～。He was born in 1966. ❷ stranger

生色 shēngsè add colour (to); give or lend lustre (to)

生疏 shēngshū ❶ unfamiliar：人地～ be unfamiliar with the place and have few friends there ❷ (of skill, etc) out of practice; rusty ❸ *also*"生分"(of people) not as close as before; getting more distant; estranged

生死 shēngsǐ ❶ life and death; ～存亡 life or death; survival or destruction; (matter of) vital importance / ～关头 moment when one's life or fate hangs in the balance / ～攸关 be of life and death / ～与共 go through thick and thin together ❷ share weal and woe:～之交 sworn friends

生态 shēngtài organism's biological and life habits; ecology:～圈 biosphere / ～型 eco-friendly; ecotype / ～学 ecology / ～农业 eco-agriculture / ～平衡 ecological balance; balance of nature / ～系统 ecosystem

生吞活剥 shēngtūn-huóbō swallow raw and whole; copy mechanically; accept uncritically

生物 shēngwù living thing; organism:～圈 biosphere / ～学 biology / ～钟 biological clock / ～技术 biotechnology / ～多样性 biodiversity

生息 shēngxī ❶ bear or earn interest ❷〈书〉live; exist ❸〈书〉grow; propagate; procreate

生肖 shēngxiào also "属相" any of the twelve animals representing the Earthly Branches, used to symbolize the year in which a person is born see also "干支" gānzhī

生效 shēngxiào come or go into force; take effect; become effective

生性 shēngxìng one's nature or natural disposition:～刚直 upright and outspoken by nature

生涯 shēngyá career; life:教学～ teaching career; life as a teacher

生意 shēngyì ❶ see "生机" ❷ (shēngyi) business; trade; deal:～经 knack of doing business; business expertize

生硬 shēngyìng ❶ unnatural; not smooth or polished:用词～ unnatural (in) wording ❷ blunt; rigid; stiff:作风～ inflexible in one's style

生…硬… shēng…yìng… (used before two similar verbs for vividness) by force; mechanically; unnaturally:生搬硬套 (in disregard of specific conditions) copy or apply mechanically; follow blindly / 生拉硬拽 drag (sb) along

kicking and screaming; get sb to do sth against his own will

生育 shēngyù give birth to; bear; beget:～高峰 baby boom / ～年龄 child-bearing age / 生儿育女 give birth to and rear children

生长 shēngzhǎng ❶ grow:～期 growth or growing period ❷ (of people) grow up; be brought up

生殖 shēngzhí reproduce:～器〈生理〉reproductive organs; genitals

声(聲) shēng
❶ sound; voice; noise:～波〈理〉sound wave / ～带 vocal chord; (of a film) sound track / ～卡〈信息〉sound card / ～控 audio-controlled; sound-activated / ～响 noise; noise / ～学 acoustics / ～情并茂 sing in a good voice and with much expression ❷ make a sound; state:～言 assert; claim ❸ fame; reputation:～价 fame; reputation / ～威大震 gain great fame and influence; acquire resounding prestige ❹ (usu 声母) initial consonant (of a Chinese syllable) ❺ tone:一～ 1st tone

声辩 shēngbiàn argue; justify; explain away:为自己～ (try to) justify oneself

声称 shēngchēng profess; claim; assert:～毫无所知 profess ignorance; claim to know nothing

声调 shēngdiào ❶ tone; voice note ❷〈语言〉tone of a Chinese character see also "四声" sìshēng

声东击西 shēngdōng-jīxī make a feint to the east and attack in the west; take (sb) unawares

声泪俱下 shēnglèijùxià speaking through streaming tears; in a tearful voice

声名 shēngmíng fame; reputation:～狼藉 have a bad name; fall into disrepute; be totally discredited

声明 shēngmíng state; declare;发表

~ issue or make a statement

声呐 shēngnà　sonar（sound navigation and ranging）

声色 shēngsè ❶ voice and countenance；～俱厉 look stern and sound severe；be stern in voice and countenance ❷〈书〉〈贬〉music and women；迷恋～ be fond of woman and song／～犬马（indulge in）sensual pleasures

声势 shēngshì　power；influence；momentum；～浩大 great in strength and momentum；gigantic in scale

声嘶力竭 shēngsī-lìjié　shout oneself hoarse；shout oneself blue in the face；be exhausted from shouting

声讨 shēngtǎo　denounce；condemn；decry

声望 shēngwàng　popularity；prestige；repute；～日隆 have a rising reputation

声息 shēngxī ❶（often used in the negative）sound；noise；毫无～ all quiet and still ❷ also "声气" information；message；互通～ keep each other informed of what is going on

声音 shēngyīn　sound；voice；～洪亮 deep，sonorous voice

声誉 shēngyù　reputation；fame；honour；～卓著 enjoy an excellent reputation

声援 shēngyuán　show support for；support；各方纷纷～。Support came from all quarters.

声乐 shēngyuè〈乐〉vocal music；～家 singer；vocalist

声张 shēngzhāng　also "声扬"（often used in the negative）make public；reveal；disclose；此事不可～。We must hush it up.

牲 shēng　domestic animal；～畜 livestock；domestic animal／～口 draught animal；beast of burden

笙 shēng〈乐〉sheng，a reed-pipe wind instrument；～歌 music and song

甥 shēng（usu 外甥）sister's son；nephew；～女 sister's daughter；niece

shéng

绳（繩） shéng ❶ rope；cord；string；～索 rope；cord／～梯 rope ladder ❷〈书〉restrain；punish；～之以法 punish in accordance with the law；bring to justice

shěng

省 shěng ❶ economize；save；frugal；～力 save effort or labour；be easy to do／～吃俭用 live frugally；be thrifty ❷ omit；delete；leave out；～却 save；avert；rid sb of ❸ province；～会 also "省城" provincial capital／～委 provincial Party committee／～长 governor of a province *see also* xǐng

省得 shěngde　so as to avoid；多穿点衣服～冷。Put on more clothes so you won't be cold.

省略 shěnglüè　leave out；delete；omit；～号 ellipsis（dots）；suspension points（……or …）／～句 elliptical sentence

省事 shěngshì ❶ save trouble；make things easy；simplify matters；怎么就怎么办。Do it in the simplest way possible. ❷ convenient；handy

省心 shěngxīn　save worry or anxiety；图个～ seek to save worry

shèng

圣（聖） shèng ❶ holy；sacred；sage；～洁 holy and pure／～经（Holy）Bible；（Holy）Scriptures／～人 sage；wise man／～徒〈宗教〉saint／～贤 sages and men of virtue / ～战 holy war; crusade; (of Islam) jihad ❷ superb; masterly; most accomplished; ～手 great master (in chess, etc) ❸ 〈旧〉 (of the) emperor; ～明 (as a flattering epithet for the emperor) (of) great insight and wisdom / ～上 His or Your Majesty / ～旨 imperial edict

圣诞 shèngdàn ❶ 〈旧〉 birthday of Confucius ❷ Christmas, birthday of Jesus Christ; ～节 Christmas (Day) / ～卡 Christmas card / ～树 Christmas tree / ～老人 Santa Claus; Father Christmas

圣地 shèngdì ❶ 〈宗教〉 Holy Land or City ❷ sacred place; shrine

圣母 shèngmǔ ❶ female deity; goddess ❷ (Blessed) Virgin Mary; Madonna; ～马利亚 St Maria

胜(勝) shèng ❶ win victory; succeed;～出 win victory (in a contest, etc); outplay one's rival / ～诉 win a lawsuit / ～仗 victorious battle; victory / ～不骄，败不馁 neither be dizzy with success nor lose heart because of failure ❷ defeat;以少～多 defeat the many with the few; defeat sb superior in number ❸ surpass; be superior to; get the better of;～过 excel; surpass; be better than ❹ superb; wonderful; beautiful; ～地 famous scenic spot / ～迹 renowned historical site ❺ be equal or up to; can bear;～不其烦 be pestered beyond endurance

胜负 shèngfù　also "胜败" victory or defeat; success or failure; outcome (of a war, etc);～乃兵家常事 〈俗〉 for a military commander, winning or losing a battle is a common occurrence; a commander would not fuss over a battle won or lost

胜局 shèngjú　victory; success;～已定。The battle is as good as won.

胜利 shènglì　victory; triumph; success;～者 winner; victor / ～结束 end

in success; come to a triumphant close

胜券 shèngquàn　confidence in victory;～在握。Success is within one's grasp.

胜任 shèngrèn　competent; equal to;～愉快 be fully competent; be well qualified

盛 shèng ❶ flourishing; thriving; prosperous;～开 be in full bloom / ～世 time of prosperity; flourishing age; heyday ❷ vigorous; energetic; aggressive;～年 prime of life; youth / ～怒 rage; fury ❸ magnificent; grand; sumptuous;～大 grand; majestic; magnificent / ～典 grand ceremony; great occasion / ～会 distinguished gathering; grand assembly / ～举 great or worthy undertaking / ～事 grand occasion; great event / ～宴 grand banquet; sumptuous dinner / ～装 splendid dress; Sunday or holiday best ❹ profuse; profound; great;～夏 peak of summer; high summer / ～誉 great renown; high reputation / ～赞 speak of in glowing terms; highly praise; extol ❺ popular; prevalent; extensive;～传 spread far and wide; be widely known　*see also* chéng

盛产 shèngchǎn　be rich in; teem or abound with

盛况 shèngkuàng　grand occasion; spectacular affair;～空前 exceptionally or unusually grand occasion

盛名 shèngmíng　high fame or reputation;～之下，其实难副。A high reputation is hard to live up to.

盛气凌人 shèngqìlíngrén　with overweening airs; domineering; arrogant

盛情 shèngqíng　great kindness; kind hospitality; boundless generosity;～难却。It would be ungracious not to accept a kind offer.

盛行 shèngxíng　be very popular; current or rife; be in vogue;～一时 in vogue for a time; prevalent for a time

剩（賸）

剩（賸） shèng surplus; leftover; remnant：～菜 leftover dishes / 还～下什么？What is left?

剩余 shèngyú surplus; remainder：～价值〈经〉surplus value

shī

尸（屍）

尸（屍） shī corpse; dead body; carcass：～首 also "尸身" corpse; dead body

尸骨 shīgǔ ❶ also "尸骸" skeleton; bones of the dead ❷ remains; dead body：～未寒 (while) the deceased's remains are scarcely cold yet

尸体 shītǐ corpse; dead body：～检验 (shortened as 尸检) post-mortem (examination) / ～解剖 autopsy

尸位素餐 shīwèi-sùcān hold on to one's post while doing nothing; hold down a job without doing a stroke of work

失

失 shī ❶ lose; get lost：～宠 lose favour (with sb) ; be in disfavour; be disgraced / ～聪 lose one's hearing; become deaf / ～地 lost territory / ～衡 lose balance / ～恋 be disappointed in love; be jilted / ～明 lose one's sight; go blind / ～身 (of a woman) lose one's virginity or chastity / ～主 owner of lost property ❷ lose hold of; let slip; miss：～言 (make an) indiscreet remark; (make a) slip of the tongue ❸ fail to achieve (one's end)：～察 neglect one's supervisory duties; commit an oversight / ～修 be in bad repair; fall into disrepair ❹ deviate from the normal：～态 forget oneself; be ill-mannered in one's behaviour ❺ go against; break (a promise); go back on (one's word)：～信 break one's promise; go back on one's word; lose credibility / ～约 fail to keep an appointment / ～道寡助 an unjust cause

finds scant support; one who is unjust enjoys little support ❻ mishap; defect; error：～误 faulty move; fault; mistake

失败 shībài ❶ be defeated; lose (a war, game, etc) ❷ fail：～是成功之母。Failure is the mother of success.

失策 shīcè miscalculate; be unwise or ill-advised：工作上的～ wrong decision in work

失常 shīcháng not normal; abnormal：态度～ not be one's usual self; behave strangely / 发挥～ be out of form

失传 shīchuán no longer exist; not extant：～的民间艺术 lost folk art

失措 shīcuò lose one's presence of mind; be at a loss as to what to do：茫然～ be at a total loss

失当 shīdàng improper; inappropriate; indiscreet：用人～ not choose the right person

失掉 shīdiào also "失去" ❶ lose; forfeit：～理智 be out of one's mind ❷ miss; let slip：～时机 let slip an opportunity

失和 shīhé fail to get along well (with); become estranged (from)

失魂落魄 shīhún-luòpò be panic-stricken; be scared out of one's wits

失火 shīhuǒ catch fire; be on fire：～的原因 cause of a fire

失节 shījié ❶ lose one's integrity; be disloyal ❷〈旧〉(of a woman) lose one's chastity

失禁 shījìn〈医〉incontinence：大小便～ incontinence of faeces and urine

失敬 shījìng〈套〉show inadequacy; be sorry：没有认出您来，～，～。I am awfully sorry for not having recognized you.

失控 shīkòng out of control; runaway (prices, etc)：防止局势～ prevent the situation from getting out of hand

失礼 shīlǐ ❶ breach of etiquette; discourtesy ❷〈套〉excuse me for any impropriety, lack of manners, etc, on my part

失利 shīlì suffer a setback; be defeated; 初战 ～ lose the first battle or game

失灵 shīlíng not work (properly); be out of order; be ineffective: 指挥 ～ 。The command became ineffective.

失落 shīluò ❶ lose ❷ feel lost: ～感 sense of loss; feeling of being left out

失眠 shīmián (suffer from) insomnia; sleeplessness: 彻夜 ～ lie awake all night

失陪 shīpéi 〈套〉 leave ahead of others: 我得先走一步, ～ 了。Excuse me, but I must be leaving now.

失窃 shīqiè *also* "失盗" be burgled or burglarized; have things stolen: ～案 (case of) burglary

失散 shīsàn be scattered: ～多年的兄弟 brother with whom one has lost touch for years

失色 shīsè ❶ (of things) lose colour; be discoloured ❷ (of people) lose countenance; turn pale

失神 shīshén ❶ negligent; inattentive; absent-minded ❷ out of sorts; in low spirits; dejected ❸ (of eyes, etc) lacklustre; dull

失声 shīshēng ❶ (cry out, laugh, etc) involuntarily ❷ lose one's voice: 痛哭 ～ cry oneself hoarse

失实 shīshí without foundation; inaccurate; untrue

失事 shīshì (have an) accident: 飞机 ～ plane crash

失手 shīshǒu ❶ make a slip of the hand; do sth accidentally: ～杀人 kill sb unintentionally ❷ (unexpected) loss or defeat

失守 shīshǒu (of a fortress, etc) fall; be taken

失算 shīsuàn miscalculate; misjudge; misread: 这一步～了。That was a miscalculated move.

失调 shītiáo ❶ imbalance: 营养～ unbalanced nutrition ❷ lack of proper care and rest

失望 shīwàng lose hope or confidence; be discouraged or disappointed; despair: 大失所望 be greatly disappointed

失陷 shīxiàn (of territory, etc) fall (into enemy hands); be lost to the enemy

失效 shīxiào lose efficacy; (of an agreement, etc) be no longer in force; cease to be effective: ～药品 ineffective medicine / ～日期 date of expiry; expiration date; use-by date

失学 shīxué be obliged to discontinue one's studies; drop out of school

失业 shīyè lose one's job; be out of work; be unemployed: ～率 rate of unemployment / ～保险 employment insurance / ～救济金 unemployment benefit

失意 shīyì frustrated; disappointed: 官场～ be frustrated in one's official career

失迎 shīyíng 〈套〉 fail to meet a guest personally: 原来是你, ～了。So it's you. Excuse me for not greeting you at the gate.

失真 shīzhēn ❶ (of voice, image, etc) lack fidelity or exactitude; not be true to the original ❷ 〈信息〉 distortion: 图像～ image fault

失之毫厘, 谬以千里 shīzhīháolí, miùyǐqiānlǐ an error the breadth of a single hair can lead you a thousand *li* astray — a small discrepancy may lead to a great error

失之交臂 shīzhījiāobì *also* "交臂失之" miss by a split second; 与机会～ let an opportunity slip through one's fingers

失职 shīzhí negligence or dereliction of duty

失重 shīzhòng 〈理〉 weightlessness; zero gravity

失踪 shīzōng be missing; disappear

战争～人员 personnel missing in action (MIA)

失足 shīzú ❶ also "失脚" lose one's footing; miss one's step; slip ❷ (often of a moral nature) commit a serious error in life; go astray:～青年 young offender; juvenile delinquent

师(師) shī ❶ teacher; master:～资 (used collectively) teaching staff; faculty; teachers /～道尊严 dignity or honour of the teaching profession ❷ model; example; guide:～表 model of virtue and learning ❸ person skilled in a certain profession or trade:技～ technician ❹ of one's master or teacher:～母 also "师娘" wife of one's teacher or master /～兄弟 fellow apprentices; male pupils of the same teacher ❺〈书〉learn; follow:～承 receive training in a specific school; take (sth) as one's master or teacher /～从 also "师事" study under; be taught by /～法前贤 model oneself upon sages of the past /～其所长 learn from sb's strong points ❻ troops; army:～出无名 dispatch troops without a just cause; do sth without a proper reason ❼〈军〉division (of an army):～部 division headquarters

师范 shīfàn teacher-training or normal school;～专科学校 (shortened as 师专) teacher-training or normal school

师父 shīfu ❶ see "师傅" ❷ polite form of address for a Buddhist or Taoist monk, etc

师傅 shīfu ❶ master who gives instruction in a trade, business or art ❷ polite title for one with accomplished skill (usu in a trade or handicraft) or for anyone (usu used by young blue collar workers):木工～ (master) carpenter

师长 shīzhǎng ❶〈敬〉teachers:尊敬～ respect one's teachers ❷〈军〉div-

ision commander

诗 shī ❶ poetry; verse:～歌 poems and songs; poetry /～话 notes and comments on poets and poetry /～篇 poem;〈喻〉inspiring or stirring story /～人 poet /～作 poem; verse /～情画意 poetic or idyllic beauty /～兴大发 feel greatly inspired to write poetry /～意盎然 brimming with poetic sentiment ❷ (short for 诗经) *Book of Songs*; *Classic of Poetry*

虱(蝨) shī (usu 虱子) louse

狮(獅) shī lion:母～ lioness

狮子 shīzi lion:～狗 pug-dog /～舞 lion dance /～大开口 make an excessive demand; demand an exorbitant price

施 shī ❶ execute; carry out; put into practice:～教 teach; educate; instruct /～手术 perform a surgical operation ❷ exert; bestow; impose:～礼 bow; salute /～压 exert pressure (on sb) ❸ hand out; give:～与 grant; bestow /～赈 give relief or alms /～主 (used by monks) patron; benefactor ❹ use; apply:～肥 spread manure; apply fertilizer

施暴 shībào ❶ use violence; attack ❷ rape

施放 shīfàng let off (fireworks, etc); discharge (gas, etc); fire

施工 shīgōng construction:～单位 unit in charge of construction

施加 shījiā exert; inflict:～影响 exercise one's influence (on sb)

施舍 shīshě give or dole out alms; give in charity

施行 shīxíng ❶ put in force; carry out; implement:～细则 rules for implementation ❷ perform; effect:～人工降雨 induce artificial rainfall

施展 shīzhǎn put to good use; give full play to; display

施政 shīzhèng governing; governance：～报告 report on work (by a government) / ～方针 principles for running a government; administrative policies

湿（濕、溼） shī wet; moist; damp：～地 wetland / ～度 humidity (of air, etc); moisture (of soil, etc) / ～冷 damp and chilly; dank; clammy / ～透 wet through; soaked; drenched / ～淋淋 dripping or soaking wet; drenched / ～漉漉 wet; damp

湿气 shīqì ❶ moisture; dampness ❷ eczema or fungus infection of hand or foot

湿润 shīrùn moist; damp：～的泥土 damp soil

湿疹 shīzhěn 〈医〉eczema

嘘 shī 〈叹〉(used to stop sb from doing sth or to drive sb or sth away) hush; shoo *see also* xū

shí

十 shí ❶ ten：～进制〈数〉decimal system / ～恶不赦 too wicked to be pardoned; guilty beyond forgiveness / ～年寒窗 ten years' study at a cold window — prolonged perseverance in one's studies in spite of hardships / ～室九空 nine houses out of ten are deserted — a scene of desolation / ～之八九 *also* "十有八九" in nine cases out of ten; very likely / ～八般武艺 skill in wielding the 18 kinds of traditional weapons;〈喻〉skill in various fields of work / ～项全能运动〈体〉decathlon ❷ topmost; highest：～万火急 post-haste; most urgent

十八层地狱 shíbācéng dìyù bottom or depths of hell：打入～ cast into utter darkness and misery

十二分 shí'èrfēn also "十二万分" exceedingly; extremely：～满意 be more than satisfied

十二月 shí'èryuè ❶ December ❷ twelfth month of the lunar year; twelfth moon

十分 shífēn 〈副〉fully; very; extremely：～仇ɡ恨 hate intensely / ～感谢 thank (sb) from the bottom of one's heart

十拿九稳 shínájiǔwěn *also* "十拿九准" ninety per cent sure; practically certain; as good as settled

十全十美 shíquán-shíměi perfect in every way; acme of perfection; paragon of excellence

十万八千里 shíwànbāqiānlǐ one hundred and eight thousand *li* — an extremely long distance：相差～ poles apart

十一月 shíyīyuè ❶ November ❷ eleventh month of the lunar year; eleventh moon

十月 shíyuè ❶ October：～一日 *also* "十一" October 1, National Day of PRC ❷ tenth month of the lunar year; tenth moon

十字 shízì (shaped like the) character 十; cross：～架 cross; crucifix / ～路口 crossroad

十足 shízú ❶ hundred percent; pure; sheer：～赤金 pure or 24-karat gold / ～的笨蛋 unmitigated fool ❷ full；傲气～ be puffed up with haughty airs / 派头～ put on quite a show

什 shí 〈书〉ten：～九 nine tenths ❷ assorted; varied; sundry：～物 articles for everyday use; odds and ends; sundries *see also* shén

什锦 shíjǐn assorted; mixed：～糖 assorted candy / ～果酱 mixed fruit jam

石 shí ❶ stone; rock; pebble：～板 slab stone; flagstone; slate (for writing) / ～碑 stone tablet; stele / ～壁 rock cliff / ～匠 stonemason; mason / ～窟 rock cave; grotto / ～块

(piece of) stone / ～头 stone; rock / ～子 cobblestone; cobble; pebble ❷ stone inscription: ～经 inscriptions of classics or scriptures on stone

石沉大海 shíchéndàhǎi （disappear like a) stone dropped into the sea

石膏 shígāo gypsum; plaster: ～像 plaster statue or figure / ～夹板 plaster splint

石灰 shíhuī lime: 生～ calcium or caustic lime / 熟～ white or slaked lime / ～石 also "石灰岩" limestone

石刻 shíkè also "石雕" carved stone; stone-engraving; stone inscription

石榴 shíliú 〈植〉pomegranate

石棉 shímián asbestos: ～瓦〈建筑〉asbestos shingle or tile

石墨 shímò graphite

石破天惊 shípòtiānjīng rock-shattering and heaven-shaking — (of music, writing, etc) remarkably original and forceful; staggering

石器时代 shíqìshídài 〈考古〉Stone Age: 旧～ Palaeolithic or Old Stone Age / 新～ Neolithic or New Stone Age

石英 shíyīng quartz: ～表 quartz watch

石油 shíyóu petroleum; oil: ～储藏量 oil reserve or deposit / ～化工产品 petrochemical products; petroleum chemicals

时(時)

shí ❶ time; times; days: ～空 time and space / ～区 time zone / ～限 time limit; deadline / ～钟 clock / ～来运转 time has moved in one's favour; fortune is smiling at one / ～不我待。 Time and tide wait for no man. ❷ fixed time; schedule: 按～上班 go to work on time ❸ season: ～货 goods of the season / ～鲜果蔬 fruits and vegetables just in season ❹ current; present: ～价 current price / ～局 current political situation / ～事 current affairs or events / 抨击～弊 lash out at social

evils of the day ❺ fashion: ～尚 fashion; vogue; fad / ～新 (of clothing) stylish; fashionable; trendy ❻ 7th of the twelve Earthly Branches　see also "干支" gānzhī ❼ hour: ～速 speed per hour / ～针 hands of a clock or watch; hour hand / 上午 10～ 10 a.m. ❽ opportune moment; opportunity; chance: ～不再来。 Once lost, the opportune moment will not come again. ❾ occasionally; now and then; from time to time: ～不～〈方〉from time to time; every now and then ❿ (used in pairs) now ... now ...; sometimes ... sometimes ... 断～续 on and off ⓫ also "时态"〈语言〉tense

时差 shíchā ❶〈天文〉equation of time ❷ time difference; jet lag: 倒～ get over the jet lag

时常 shícháng also "时时" often; frequently; again and again

时辰 shíchen ❶ (traditional) two-hour period of the day　see also "干支" gānzhī ❷ (right) time: ～不到。 It is not yet time.

时代 shídài ❶ age; era; epoch: ～感 sense or awareness of the times / ～潮流 trend of the times; tendency of the day / ～精神 spirit of the times; *Zeitgeist* ❷ period in one's life; years: 大学～ college years

时而 shí'ér ❶ from time to time; now and then ❷ (used in pairs) now ... now ...; sometimes ... sometimes ...: 初秋时节,～热,～冷。 In early autumn, one moment it's quite warm, the next it becomes chilly.

时分 shífēn time: 黎明～ at dawn; at daybreak

时光 shíguāng ❶ time: 消磨～ while away one's time ❷ period: 那～ in those days ❸ times; years

时过境迁 shíguò-jìngqiān times have passed and circumstances have altered; circumstances change with the passage of time

时候 shíhou ❶ (the duration of) time：他去了多少～? How long has he been away? ❷ (a point in) time; moment：来得正是～ come in the nick of time

时机 shíjī opportunity; opportune moment：掌握～很重要。Timing is important.

时间 shíjiān ❶ (the concept of) time：～表 timetable; schedule / ～差 time difference / ～性 timeliness ❷ (the duration of) time：办公～ office hours ❸ (a point in) time：出发～ departure time

时节 shíjié ❶ season：金秋～ golden autumn (season) ❷ time

时刻 shíkè ❶ moment; hour：～表 timetable; schedule ❷ constantly; always; at all times：～保持清醒的头脑 always keep a cool head

时令 shílìng season：不合～ out of season / ～病 seasonal disease

时髦 shímáo fashionable; stylish; latest；衣着～ be fashionably dressed / ～话题 topic of the day

时期 shíqī period; stage：鼎盛～ zenith of prosperity; height of power

时势 shíshì current situation; prevailing circumstances; trend of the times：～造英雄 the times produce their heroes; the hero is a product of his time

时务 shíwù prevalent circumstances; trend of the times：识～ show understanding of the times; know what's best for one; submit to the circumstances

时下 shíxià currently; at present; right now

时效 shíxiào ❶ (of medicine, etc) effectiveness for a given period of time：标明～ marked with expiry date ❷ 〈法〉prescription; limitation：诉讼～ limitation of an action

时兴 shíxīng fashionable; popular；

voguish：不～了 be no longer popular; be out of date

时宜 shíyí what suits the occasion：切合～ be compatible with the times; appropriate

时运 shíyùn luck; fortune：～不济 be down on one's luck

时装 shízhuāng ❶ fashionable dress; latest fashions：～表演 fashion show / ～模特儿 fashion model; mannequin ❷ modern clothing：～戏 (traditional) opera in modern costume

识(識) shí ❶ know：～字 know how to read and write; be literate / ～时务 know what's what; adapt to circumstances; bow to objective necessity / ～破阴谋 see through a plot / ～大体 顾大局 have the fundamental principles and overall situation in mind ❷ knowledge; learning：有～见《书》be knowledgeable and experienced

识别 shíbié distinguish; discern; identify；～力 discernment / ～真伪 distinguish between truth and falsehood; tell the false from the genuine

识货 shíhuò be able to tell good from bad; know what's what; be knowledgeable

识趣 shíqù behave or respond sensibly in a delicate situation; be tactful or judicious

识相 shíxiàng 〈方〉see which way the wind is blowing; understand the circumstances; be sensible or tactful

实(實) shí ❶ solid; full：用土填～ fill up with earth ❷ real; true; actual：～词〈语言〉notional word / ～绩 actual deeds; concrete results; real achievements / ～例 (living or concrete) example / ～情 actual state of affairs; real situation; truth / ～体 entity / ～战 actual combat or fighting / ～打～ truthful；

genuine / ～报～销 be reimbursed for one's actual expenses; (of expenses incurred) be refunded / ～弹演习 practice with live ammunition / ～话～说 speak the plain truth; call a spade a spade / 落到～处 do sth where it really matters; put sth into practice / 讲求～效 stress actual results ❸ fruit; seed

实诚 shícheng 〈口〉honest; frank; candid

实地 shídì ❶ on-the-spot; field;～调查 carry out on-the-spot investigations ❷ steadfast; practical and steady;～去做 do sth in a practical manner

实干 shígàn do solid work;～家 man of action

实惠 shíhuì ❶ real benefit; material gain ❷ substantial; solid; practical;经济～的家具 utility furniture

实际 shíjì ❶ real; true; actual;理论联系～ integrate theory with practice /～需求 effective demand /～增长 growth in real terms ❷ practical; realistic;～应用 practical application

实践 shíjiàn ❶ put into practice; carry out; implement ❷ practice;～出真知 genuine knowledge comes from practice; practice gives birth to true knowledge

实况 shíkuàng what is actually happening;～转播 live broadcast or telecast; field pick-up

实力 shílì strength; power;～地位 position of strength

实施 shíshī put into effect; implement; enforce;～政治主张 put political ideas into practice

实时 shíshí 〈信息〉real time;～监控 real-time monitoring

实事 shíshì ❶ actual thing; fact;～求是 seek truth from facts; be realistic and truthful ❷ deeds; solid or practical work;为老百姓办～ do sth practical for the people

实物 shíwù ❶ material or real object;

～教学 object lesson ❷ in kind;～工资 wages in kind /～交易 trade in kind; barter (trade)

实习 shíxí practice; fieldwork; field trip;～期 period of probation; internship /～生 trainee; intern

实现 shíxiàn realize; achieve; bring about;～利润 realize or make profits

实心 shíxīn ❶ sincere; earnest;～实意 honest and sincere; true and earnest ❷ solid;～砖 solid brick

实行 shíxíng put into practice; carry out; implement;～计划生育 practise family planning

实验 shíyàn experiment; test;～室 laboratory /～员 laboratory technician /～学校 experimental school

实业 shíyè industry and commerce; business; enterprise;～家 industrialist; businessman

实用 shíyòng ❶ practical use or application;切合～ be practical ❷ practical; applied; functional;～技术 appropriate technology /～主义〈哲〉pragmatism; expediency

实在 shízài ❶ true; honest; practical;内容～。The content is substantial. ❷ really; in all conscience;那家伙～讨厌。That fellow is a perfect nuisance. ❸ in fact; in reality; 表面上同意，心里～并不同意 pretend to agree, but actually do not ❹ (shízai) (of work) done in real earnest; well done

实至名归 shízhìmíngguī the name follows the reality — fame is a reflection of real achievements

实质 shízhì substance; essence; gist; 问题的～ crux or heart of a matter; essence of a question /～性进展 substantive progress

实足 shízú ❶ full; exact; solid;～年龄 exact age /～走了 10 公里 walk a full ten kilometres ❷ a hundred per cent; out-and-out;～的无赖 downright scoundrel

拾 shí ❶ pick up（from the ground）; gather; glean；~ 柴 collect firewood and scraps / ~ 取 pick up; gather; collect / ~ 金不昧 not pocket the money one picks up; return money found / ~ 人牙慧 pick up remarks from others and pass them off as one's own / ~ 遗补阙 make good omissions and shortcomings ❷ ten（used for the numeral 十, to avoid mistakes or alterations）

拾掇 shíduo ❶ tidy or clean up（a room, etc）; put in order ❷ repair; mend; fix ❸ settle with; take to task; punish：我非~~他不可。I must teach him a lesson.

食 shí ❶ eat; have one's meal：~ 道〈生理〉oesophagus; gullet / ~ 堂 mess hall; canteen / ~ 不甘味 eat without relish; have no appetite for food / ~ 不果腹 have not enough to eat; be ill-fed / ~ 草动物 herbivorous animal; herbivore / ~ 肉动物 carnivorous animal; carnivore ❷ food; meal; feed（for animals）：~ 疗 food therapy / ~ 盐（table）salt / ~ 油 edible or cooking oil / 鸡 ~ 儿 chicken feed ❸ also "蚀"〈天文〉eclipse

食古不化 shígǔbùhuà swallow ancient learning without digesting it; follow the ancients blindly

食客 shíkè ❶ hanger-on（of an aristocrat）❷ patron or customer of a restaurant

食粮 shíliáng food（grain）：精神 ~ nourishment for the mind

食品 shípǐn foodstuff; food; provisions：~ 加工 food processing / ~ 添加剂 food additive

食谱 shípǔ ❶ recipe; cookery book; cookbook ❷ menu：病号 ~ menu for invalids

食宿 shísù board and lodging：~ 自理 make one's own arrangements for room and board

食物 shíwù food; victuals；~ 链 food chain or cycle / ~ 中毒〈医〉food poisoning

食言 shíyán break one's promise

食用 shíyòng ❶ eat; consume：不宜 ~（of sth）not fit for human consumption ❷ edible：~ 碱 baking soda / ~ 菌 edible fungus / ~ 色素 food colouring

食欲 shíyù appetite：~ 不振 have a poor or jaded appetite

食指 shízhǐ index finger; forefinger

蚀 shí ❶ lose; erode; corrode：~ 本 lose one's capital; lose money in business / ~ 刻 etching ❷ see "食 ❸" shí

鲥（鰣） shí also "鲥鱼" hilsa herring; reeves shad

shǐ

史 shǐ history：~ 官〈史〉official historian / ~ 籍 historical records; history / ~ 料 historical materials or data / ~ 前 prehistoric / ~ 诗 epic / ~ 实 historical fact / ~ 书 historical records; history / ~ 学 science of history; historiography / ~ 无前例 without precedent in history; unprecedented; unparalleled / 载入 ~ 册 go down in history

矢 shǐ ❶ arrow ❷ take an oath; vow; swear：~ 口否认 flatly disavow / ~ 志不渝 vow to adhere unswervingly to one's chosen course; pledge steadfast devotion to a cause ❸ excrement; faeces

豕 shǐ〈书〉pig; hog; swine

使 shǐ ❶ send; have（sb do sth）：~ 人去请医生 send for a doctor ❷ use; exert; apply：~ 坏 be up to mischief; play a dirty trick; create trouble / ~ 不惯 be unfamiliar with; be unaccustomed to / ~ 绝招 play one's best or trump card / ~ 性子〈口〉

S

throw a tantrum; fly off the handle / ～眼色 wink (at sb) / ～出浑身解数 use all one's skill; do all one can ❸ make; cause; enable; ～然 (of a circumstance) make sth or sb so; (of sth or sb) is due to / ～人改变主意 make sb change his or her mind / 这场雨～空气变得新鲜. The rain cleaned up the air. ❹〈书〉if; supposing ❺ envoy; emissary; messenger; ～团 diplomatic mission or corps / ～者 emissary; envoy; messenger / ～领馆 diplomatic and consular missions; embassies and consulates

使得 shǐde ❶ can be used; will work ❷ will do; be feasible: 这可使不得. This won't do. or You mustn't do this. ❷ make; cause; bring about: 他的一席话～我深受感动. I was deeply moved by his words.

使唤 shǐhuan ❶ order about; 听人～ be at sb's beck and call / ～丫头 also "使女"〈旧〉maid; maidservant ❷ use (a horse, etc); manage; handle

使节 shǐjié (diplomatic) envoy: 各国驻华～ diplomatic envoys (accredited) to China

使劲 shǐjìn exert oneself; make efforts; ～哭 cry one's eyes out

使命 shǐmìng mission; ～感 sense of mission

使用 shǐyòng use; utilize; employ; ～权〈法〉right of use; right to use sth / ～面积〈建筑〉usable floor area / ～寿命 service life (of a machine, etc) / ～说明书 operation instructions; user's manual

始 shǐ ❶ begin; commence; start; ～发站 starting station; terminal / ～料不及 come as a surprise; be unexpected ❷〈书〉only then; not...until: 会议至晚10时～半. The meeting was not over until 10 p.m.

始末 shǐmò start to finish; beginning and end; whole story: 事故的～ ins and

outs of an accident

始终 shǐzhōng from beginning to end; from start to finish; throughout; ～不渝 unswerving; steadfast; constant / ～如一 constant; unchanging; consistent

始祖 shǐzǔ ❶ first or earliest ancestor ❷ originator or founder (of a school of thought, etc) ❸ primitive or prototypical animal

始作俑者 shǐzuòyǒngzhě creator of a bad precedent; 核军备竞赛的～ starter of the nuclear arms race

驶 shǐ ❶ (as of a vehicle) go or pass quickly; speed ❷ sail; drive; ride: ～出河湾 sail out of the estuary / ～进车站 pull into a station

屎 shǐ ❶ excrement; dung; stool; ～尿 stool and urine ❷ secretion (of the eye, ear, etc): 耳～ earwax

shì

士 shì ❶ scholar; intellectual; ～绅 (scholar-) gentry / ～大夫〈史〉scholar-officials; literati ❷ soldier; serviceman; non-commissioned officer; ～兵 rank-and-file soldier; private / ～官 non-commissioned officer (non-com) / ～气 morale; spirit ❸ person skilled in a specified field; 谋～ adviser ❹ bodyguard, one of the pieces in Chinese chess

氏 shì ❶ (now usu 姓) family name; surname; ～族 clan / 王～兄弟 Wang brothers ❷ (formerly used of a married woman) née: 李张～ Mrs Li, née Zhang ❸ used as a complimentary abbreviation, esp for famous persons: 华～表 Fahrenheit thermometer

示 shì show; produce; indicate; ～弱 show signs of weakness; wave the white feather; take (sth) lying down / ～众 publicly expose; punish before the public

示范 shìfàn　set an example; demonstrate; show;～项目 demonstration project; pioneer scheme / 起～作用 play an exemplary role

示警 shìjǐng　alert to danger; give a warning; warn;鸣枪～ a warning shot; warn by firing a shot

示威 shìwēi ❶ demonstrate; hold a demonstration;～游行 (hold a) demonstration ❷ put on a show of force; display one's prowess

示意 shìyì　show or indicate by signal, gesture, etc;～图 sketch map / 以目～ wink (at sb); tip the wink

世 shì ❶ lifetime; life;一生一～ all one's life ❷ generation;四～同堂 (have) four generations under one roof ❸ from generation to generation, esp among families;～伯 older friend of one's father / ～仇 family feud; vendetta; sworn enemy (in a family feud) / ～族 influential family of generations' standing ❹ age; era; time ❺ world; society;～道 manners and morals of the time; ways of the world / ～人 people at large; common people / ～态炎凉 snobbish ways of the world / ～风日下。 Public morals are deteriorating day by day.

世代 shìdài　generation after generation; for generations;～相传 pass on from generation to generation

世故 shìgù ❶ ways of the world;不懂人情～ new to the ways of the world; inexperienced in life ❷ (shìgu) worldly-wise; shrewd; crafty

世纪 shìjì　century;～之交 at the turn of the century

世交 shìjiāo ❶ also "世谊" friendship spanning two or more generations; long-standing friendship between two families ❷ old family friend

世界 shìjiè ❶ world;～观 world outlook / ～语 Esperanto / ～格局 world power structure ❷〈宗教〉universe;大千～ boundless universe ❸ scope; realm; world;精神～ mental world

世面 shìmiàn　various aspects of society, world or life;没见过～ have not seen much of the world; be inexperienced in life

世俗 shìsú ❶〈贬〉social conventions; the vulgar or commonplace;～之见 view of the philistines ❷ secular; worldly;～生活 secular life

世外桃源 shìwàitáoyuán　Land of Peach Blossoms — imaginary haven of peace and happiness; Shangri-La

世袭 shìxí　hereditary (title, etc)

仕 shì　hold an official post; be an official;出～ become an official; take an official post / ～途〈书〉official career

仕女 shìnǚ ❶ maid in an imperial palace ❷ also "士女" traditional Chinese painting of beautiful women

市 shì ❶ market (place);～集 fair; small (market) town / ～镇 (small) towns ❷ buying and selling; business transaction; marketing;开～ (of a shop) reopen after a cessation of business; have first transaction of a day's business / ～价 market price / ～值 current market value ❸ city; municipality (esp as administrative unit);～府 municipal government / ～话 (short for 市内电话) local telephone service; local (phone) call / ～郊 suburb; outskirts / ～区 city proper / ～委 municipal Party committee / ～长 mayor / ～中心 city centre; downtown area ❹ of traditional Chinese weights and measures;～尺 chi, a unit of length (= 0.333 metre) / ～斤 jin, a unit of weight (= 0.5 kilogram)

市场 shìchǎng　market (place); bazaar;～份额 market share / ～机制 market mechanism / ～经济 market economy / ～调节 regulation by market forces

市侩 shìkuài　vulgar and detestable person; philistine; 〜习气 philistinism

市面 shìmiàn　market conditions; business situation; 〜繁荣. Business is flourishing. or The market is brisk.

市民 shìmín　urban residents; townspeople; 〈史〉burghers

市容 shìróng　appearance of a city; 整顿〜 improve the appearance of a city

市政 shìzhèng　municipal administration; 〜建设 municipal or urban construction

式 shì　❶ type; style; fashion; 〜样 style; design; pattern ❷ (specific) pattern; form; model ❸ ceremony; celebration; ritual; 开幕〜 opening ceremony ❹ formula; 方程〜 equation ❺ 〈语言〉mood; mode; 条件〜 conditional mood

式 shì　see also sì

似的 shìde　〈助〉used after a noun, a pronoun, or a verb to indicate similarity; 像血〜红 red as blood

事 shì　❶ matter; affair; thing; 〜假 leave of absence 〈to attend to private business〉/ 〜件 incident; event / 〜例 case; example; instance / 〜出有因 be by no means accidental; there is no smoke without fire / 〜后诸葛亮 wise after the event; belated wisdom ❷ trouble; difficulty; accident; 〜主 victim of a crime; injured party / 挑起〜端 create trouble; provoke an incident ❸ job; task; work; 找个〜做 look for a job ❹ responsibility; involvement; 没他的〜。 He is not involved. ❺ 〈书〉attend or wait upon; serve ❻ go in for; be engaged in; 不〜正业 lead an idle life

事半功倍 shìbàn-gōngbèi　(do) half the work with twice the result; 收到〜的效果 achieve more with less effort

事必躬亲 shìbìgōngqīn　give personal attention to everything, big or small;

attend to every detail oneself

事变 shìbiàn　❶ incident; emergency; eventuality ❷ course of events; vicissitudes; 达于〜 take things philosophically

事故 shìgù　accident; mishap; 〜责任者 person responsible for an accident; delinquent

事过境迁 shìguò-jìngqiān　events have passed and the situation has changed; things change with the passage of time

事迹 shìjì　deed; merit; achievement; 生平〜 one's life story

事理 shìlǐ　reason; sense; logic; 晓以〜 bring sb to his or her senses through reasoning

事情 shìqíng　❶ affair; matter; business; 〜的始末 the whole story ❷ accident; 怕出〜 fear that anything untoward should happen ❸ see "事❸"

事实 shìshí　fact; 〜上 in fact; as a matter of fact / 〜胜于雄辩 facts speak louder than words; reality is stronger than rhetoric

事态 shìtài　state of affairs; developments; situation; 扩大〜 aggravate the situation

事务 shìwù　❶ work; affair; routine; 行政〜 administrative work / 〜所 office; (law) firm ❷ general affairs; 〜科 general affairs section

事物 shìwù　thing; object; reality

事先 shìxiān　also "事前" in advance; prior to; beforehand; 〜警告 forewarn

事项 shìxiàng　item; point; matter; 注意〜 items for attention

事业 shìyè　❶ cause; undertaking; career; 〜心 dedication or devotion to one's work / 搞〜的人 career-minded person; career man or woman ❷ institution; 〜费 operating expenses / 〜单位 (public) institution

事宜 shìyí　(used in documents, etc) matters concerned; relevant matters; 干部任免〜 matters concerning appointment and removal of officials

事由 shìyóu ❶ origin of an incident; specifics of a matter ❷ (used in documents) main content; gist

事与愿违 shìyǔyuànwéi things run counter or go contrary to one's wishes

事在人为 shìzàirénwéi all success hinges or depends on human effort; human effort is the decisive factor

势(勢) shì ❶ power; strength; influence:～单力薄 small in number and meagre in strength; up against great odds / ～均力敌 be evenly matched in strength ❷ momentum:～头 impetus; momentum; tendency ❸ outward appearance of a natural object or phenomenon:地～平坦 level terrain ❹ situation; circumstances; tendency:～态 position; situation / ～在必行 be imperative (under the circumstances); become inevitable ❺ sign; gesture; airs ❻ male genitals

势必 shìbì certainly; inevitably:结果～如此。It certainly will end up like this.

势不可当 shìbùkědāng irresistible; overwhelming

势不两立 shìbùliǎnglì mutually exclusive; diametrically opposed (to); irreconcilable

势力 shìlì force; power; influence:～范围 sphere of influence

势利 shìlì snobbish:～眼 snobbish attitude; snobbery; snob

势如破竹 shìrúpòzhú work like splitting bamboo; carry all before one

侍 shì wait upon; attend on; serve:～从 attendants; retinue / ～奉 look after; attend upon (parents, etc) / ～候 wait upon; look after; attend / ～女〈旧〉maidservant; maid / ～卫 (imperial) bodyguard

饰 shì ❶ adorn; polish; hide:～词 excuse; pretext ❷ decoration; ornament:～物 ornaments; jewellery;

decorations ❸ play; act the part of (a dramatic character):～演主角 play the leading role

试 shì ❶ try; attempt; test:～办 run on a trial basis; run a pilot scheme / ～表〈口〉take sb's temperature / ～播 (make a) trial broadcast or telecast / ～剂 *also* "**试药**"〈化〉reagent / ～镜(头)(have a) screen test / ～制 trial-produce; trial-manufacture / ～管婴儿 test-tube baby / ～销商品 goods for trial marketing or sale ❷ examination; test:～卷 examination or test paper / ～题 examination or test question

试点 shìdiǎn conduct an experiment at selected points; (launch a) pilot project:～班 experimental class

试飞 shìfēi ❶ (make a) test or trial flight:～驾驶员 test pilot ❷ (make an) exploratory flight (to a place)

试航 shìháng ❶ (make a) trial voyage or flight; shakedown cruise or flight ❷ shakedown (a ship or an airplane)

试金石 shìjīnshí touchstone (of truth, etc)

试探 shìtàn ❶ probe; explore ❷ (shìtan) sound or feel out:～对方的态度 sound out the other side

试图 shìtú attempt (to do sth); strive; try

试问 shìwèn (used for reproach or negation in a rhetorical question) it may well be asked:～你有什么资格这样做？May we ask what right you have to do so?

试想 shìxiǎng (used in a rhetorical question to imply mild reproach) just think or imagine:～,这样的处理会有何种后果？Just imagine what will result from the settlement of the case.

试行 shìxíng try out; experiment:～生产 (shortened as **试产**) trial-produce; produce on a trial basis / ～条例 experimental rules

试验 shìyàn　experiment；trial；test：～田 experimental plot or field；〈喻〉experimental unit；experiment

试用 shìyòng　try out；put (a new recruit, etc) on probation：～品 trial product／～期 probationary period

视 shì ❶ look；view：差 visual error／～觉 (sense of) sight；vision／～盘 visual disc (VCD)／～频〈理〉video frequency／～神经〈生理〉optic nerve ❷ regard；look upon；treat：～若无睹 shut one's eyes to；disregard／～同儿戏 treat or take (sth serious) lightly；trifle with ❸ inspect；examine；watch

视察 shìchá ❶ (of a superior) inspect (sb's work, etc) ❷ examine；look carefully at：～灾区 investigate afflicted areas

视窗 shìchuāng　(信息) Windows

视而不见 shì'érbùjiàn　look but see not；turn a blind eye to

视角 shìjiǎo ❶ visual angle；angle of view ❷ also "视点" angle；approach；perspective：以一种新的～来观察问题 look at a matter from a new angle

视力 shìlì　power of vision；eyesight：～好 have good eyesight／～表 visual chart

视死如归 shìsǐrúguī　meet one's death like a hero；face death unflinchingly

视听 shìtīng ❶ what one sees and hears；public opinion：混淆～ confuse public opinion；mislead the people ❷ audio-visual：～教学 audio-visual instruction

视线 shìxiàn ❶ line of vision or sight：挡住～ obstruct the view ❷ attention：转移～ divert one's attention (to sth else)

视野 shìyě　field of vision：～开阔 have a wide or broad vision

柿 shì　(usu 柿子) persimmon：～饼 dried persimmon／～子椒 sweet bell-pepper

拭 shì　wipe (away)；remove：～目以待 wait and see；look forward to

是 shì ❶ correct；right；true：～的 yes；right／你说的～。You're right. ❷〈书〉this；that：～可忍，孰不可忍？ If this can be tolerated, what else cannot? ❸ be：我～工人。I'm a worker. ❹ used with 的 to indicate classification：这套家具～新买的。The set of furniture was bought recently. ❺ used to indicate existence, or the state of the subject：满身～汗 sweat all over／他～一片诚心。He is all sincerity. ❻ used between two identical nouns or verbs in parallel patterns to indicate distinction：他～他，我～我，我们谁也管不着谁。We have our own wills, he and I, and neither is the other's master. ❼ used to indicate concession：书～好书，可惜贵了点儿。It's a good book all right, but a bit expensive. ❽ used for emphasis：今天天气～冷。It is cold today. ❾ used before a noun to indicate each and every one of the kind：～孩子他都喜欢。He loves all children. ❿ used before a noun to indicate suitability：你来的正～时候。You've come in the nick of time. ⓫ used in questions：你～看电视还～听音乐？ Would you like to watch TV or listen to music?

是非 shìfēi ❶ right and wrong；truth and falsehood：～曲直 right and wrong；truth and falsehood；merits and demerits ❷ quarrel；dispute；trouble：挑拨～ foment discord；stir up trouble／～之地 place where one can easily get into trouble

是否 shìfǒu　used in a general or an indirect question：你们明天～来? Are you coming tomorrow? ／他～同意，还不清楚。It's not yet clear whether he agrees or not.

适(適) shì ❶ fit；suitable；proper：～量 just the

right amount / ～口 agreeable to the taste; palatable / ～销 have a ready market; be salable / ～者生存 survival of the fittest ❷ right; opportune;～逢其会 happen to be present on the occasion; turn up at the opportune moment ❸ comfortable; well; at ease; 稍觉不～ feel somewhat unwell ❹ (usu 适才) just now ❺〈书〉go; follow;(of a woman) get married; marry;所～非人 marry the wrong man

适当 shìdàng　suitable; proper; right

适得其反 shìdéqífǎn　turn out to be just the opposite of what one wishes; run counter to one's desire; be counter-productive

适度 shìdù　just right; proper; to a moderate degree;规模～ of appropriate size; on an optimum scale

适合 shìhé　suit; fit; befit;～国情 be suited to the conditions of a country

适可而止 shìkě'érzhǐ　refrain from going too far; know when and where to stop; not exceed proper limits

适龄 shìlíng　of the right age;(入学)～儿童 children of school age

适时 shìshí　in good time; timely; seasonable;～播种 timely sowing

适宜 shìyí　suitable; proper; appropriate;～当教师 have the makings of a teacher

适意 shìyì　agreeable; pleasant; comfortable

适应 shìyìng　suit; adapt; fit;～(性)训练 adaptability training

适用 shìyòng　suit; be applicable;～范围 scope or sphere of application / ～技术 appropriate technology

适中 shìzhōng　❶ proper; appropriate;长 短～ of moderate length ❷ (of place) well located; conveniently situated

恃 shì　rely, count or depend on;～才傲物 think too much of oneself and look down upon others; be conceit-

ed and overweening / ～强凌弱 use one's strength to bully the weak; play the bully

室 shì　❶ room;～外活动 outdoor activities ❷ administrative subdivision (of an institution, etc); office;编辑～ editorial office ❸ family;(esp) wife;皇～ royal family / 继～ second wife (after the first one dies)

室内 shìnèi　indoor; interior;～乐 chamber music / ～装修 interior decorating

逝 shì　❶ (of time or flowing water) pass ❷ (usu 逝世) die; pass away

舐 shì　〈书〉lick;～犊情深 deep affection for one's children; parental love

弑 shì　〈书〉murder (one's sovereign or parent)

释(釋) shì　❶ explain; expound; elucidate;～义 explain the meaning (of a word, etc) ❷ clear up; dispel; remove;～怀 (used of sentiments in the negative) disappear; vanish / ～疑 dispel doubt (on a question, etc) ❸ let go; be relieved of;不忍～手 can't bear to put (sth) down / 心中～然〈书〉feel relieved ❹ release; set free; put down ❺ (short for 释迦牟尼) Sakyamuni; Buddhism;～教 also "释门" Buddhism

释放 shìfàng　❶ release; acquit; set free ❷ (理) release;～原子能 release atomic energy

谥(諡) shì　title given to an emperor, minister, etc, after his death;～号 posthumous title

嗜 shì　have a liking for; take to; be addicted to;～好 hobby; addiction; habit / ～血 (of insects, etc) bloodsucking;〈喻〉bloodthirsty

誓 shì　❶ take an oath; swear; vow;～死 pledge one's life; vow to die (for sth) / ～不罢休 vow not to stop; swear not to rest / ～不两立 be implacably hostile; be irreconcilable ❷ solemn promise; oath; vow: ～ 词 (words of an) oath; vow; pledge / ～ 言 oath; pledge / ～约 vow; oath; solemn promise

誓师 shìshī pledge resolution before going to war; take a solemn pledge at a mass rally: ～大会 rally to pledge mass effort (to accomplish sth important)

噬 shì bite: ～食 swallow; devour

螫 shì 〈书〉 sting

shōu

收 shōu ❶ bring in; gather together; put in proper place: ～集 bring together; collect; gather / ～殓 lay a body in a coffin; bury / ～心 get into the frame of mind for work or study ❷ recover; retrieve: ～归国有 nationalize ❸ collect (revenues); charge (fees): ～取 get (payment) / ～房租 collect rent / ～支平衡 balance of revenue and expenditure ❹ (usu 收割) reap; harvest; gather in ❺ receive; accept: ～编 incorporate into one's own forces / ～活 take orders (from customers) / ～讫 of (expenses, etc) paid; received / ～条 receipt / ～件人 addressee; consignee / ～款人 payee ❻ restrain; control: ～服 also "收伏" subdue and bring under control; win over ❼ arrest; take into custody; put in jail or prison: ～监 put behind bars; imprison / ～审 detain for interrogation / ～押 take into custody; detain ❽ end; stop: ～工 stop work (for the day); knock off / ～盘价 〈经〉 closing price or quotation / ～摊儿 wind up a day's business or the work on hand

收兵 shōubīng ❶ withdraw troops; call off a battle ❷ 〈喻〉 wind up (an

operation, etc); bring to an end

收藏 shōucáng collect; store up: ～家 collector

收场 shōuchǎng wind up; end; stop: 这事如何～? How should we end it all?

收成 shōucheng harvest; crop: 苹果～不好 have a poor crop of apples

收发 shōufā receive and dispatch: ～室 office for incoming and outgoing mail; mail office

收费 shōufèi collect toll or fees; charge: ～站 toll booth or station / ～厕所 pay toilet / ～高速公路 toll expressway

收复 shōufù recover (lost territory, etc); regain; recapture

收购 shōugòu buy; purchase; procure: ～价格 purchasing or procurement price

收回 shōuhuí ❶ regain (sovereignty, etc); recover; recall (a loan, etc) ❷ withdraw; rescind: ～成命 rescind or countermand an order; revoke a command

收获 shōuhuò ❶ gather (a crop); reap; harvest ❷ gains; rewards; results

收缴 shōujiǎo ❶ take over (arms, etc); confiscate; capture ❷ levy; collect (taxes, etc)

收据 shōujù receipt: 开～ make or write out a receipt

收看 shōukàn also "收视" view or watch (TV); tune in to (a station, etc): ～率 audience ratings

收敛 shōuliǎn ❶ (of radiance, smile, etc) weaken; diminish; disappear ❷ show restraint: 有所～ be somewhat restrained

收留 shōuliú undertake the care of (orphans, etc); take in (refugees, etc)

收拢 shōulǒng ❶ draw in (a net, etc); gather together (things) ❷ see "收买"

收录 shōulù ❶ employ; recruit; enlist **②** collect (in an anthology, etc); include **③** receive and record：～机 radio-recorder

收罗 shōuluó　collect；recruit：～人才 scout for competent personnel

收买 shōumǎi　**①** purchase；buy **②** bribe；buy (over or off)：～人心 buy popular support；court popularity

收容 shōuróng　take in and provide for：～所 collecting post (for stray soldiers, etc)；refugee camp

收入 shōurù　**①** take in；include；incorporate：～现金 take in cash / ～档案 place on file **②** income；revenue；earnings

收拾 shōushi　**①** put in order；tidy up；clear away or up：～残局 pick up the pieces / ～行装 pack one's luggage (for travel) **②** repair；mend；fix **③** settle with；punish **④** eliminate；get rid of

收受 shōushòu　receive；accept：～贿赂 take bribes

收缩 shōusuō　**①** contract；shrink **②** draw back；reduce；tighten up：～开支 cut spending

收听 shōutīng　listen (in)；tune in to (a radio station, etc)

收尾 shōuwěi　**①** wind up；bring to an end **②** final phase (of a project, etc)；concluding paragraph (of an article, etc)；ending

收效 shōuxiào　yield or produce an effect：投资少，～快 (make) small investments with quick returns

收养 shōuyǎng　adopt (an orphan, etc)：～人 adopter / ～关系 adoptive relationship

收益 shōuyì　profit；proceeds；returns

收音机 shōuyīnjī　radio (set)；wireless (set)

shóu

熟 shóu　〈口〉see "熟" shú

shǒu

手 shǒu　**①** hand：～臂 arm / ～表 wrist watch / ～袋 handbag；purse / ～鼓 hand drum；tabor / ～绢 *also* "手帕" handkerchief / ～铐 handcuffs / ～心 (centre of one's) palm；〈喻〉range of one's control / ～印 hand-print；thumbprint；fingerprint / ～语 sign language / ～掌 palm / ～杖 (walking) stick；cane / ～镯 *also* "手链" bracelet / ～抄本 handwritten copy / ～提箱 suitcase / ～把～ instruct or pass on (knowledge or skill) in person / ～拉～ hand in hand **②** hold in one's hand；possess：人～一份 a copy (of sth) for everyone **③** handy；easy to carry：～机 mobile or cellular phone **④** personally；in person：～谕 handwritten directive (as from one's superior) / ～札 *also* "手书" 〈书〉personal letter in longhand **⑤** ability；skill；stratagem：露两～ display one's abilities or skills / ～巧 handy (with needlework, etc)；deft；dexterous **⑥** person in some occupations；expert of a certain job：射～ shooter；marksman；archer

手笔 shǒubǐ　**①** sb's writing, calligraphy or painting；hand；literary or artistic skill：出自大家～ come from the hand of a master **②** style or manner (of doing sth or spending money)：～阔 liberal with money；do things in a grand style / 大～ masterly stroke or style

手不释卷 shǒubùshìjuàn　be never seen without a book in one's hand；be an avid reader

手册 shǒucè　**①** handbook；manual **②** record book；workbook：工作～ workbook

手电筒 shǒudiàntǒng　*also* "手电" electric torch；flashlight；torchlight

手段 shǒuduàn　**①** means；method；

way：法律～ legal means ❷ trick；
wiles；artifice；耍～ play tricks ❸
skill；ability：～高强 highly skilled

手法 shǒufǎ ❶ skill；technique：夸张
～ hyperbole ❷ trick；gimmick；arti-
fice

手风琴 shǒufēngqín accordion

手感 shǒugǎn （of a fabric）feel；
handle：～好 have a nice feel；feel nice

手稿 shǒugǎo original or holograph
manuscript

手工 shǒugōng ❶ handwork ❷ by
hand；manual：～业 handicraft indus-
try；handicrafts／～艺 handicraft art
or skill ❸〈口〉charge for handwork
done

手疾眼快 shǒují-yǎnkuài also "眼疾
手快" quick of eye and deft of hand；
sharp-sighted and neat-handed；agile
and swift

手迹 shǒujì original calligraphic work
or painting

手脚 shǒujiǎo ❶ movement of limbs；
motion：～勤快 quick and industrious／
～不干净 be sticky-fingered；be questionable in money matters ❷ trick：暗
中弄～ play dirty tricks on the sly

手紧 shǒujǐn ❶ close or tight with
money；tight-fisted；stingy ❷ also "手
头儿紧" short of money

手榴弹 shǒuliúdàn （hand）grenade

手忙脚乱 shǒumáng-jiǎoluàn be
thrown into confusion；be in a frantic
rush or bustle

手气 shǒuqì luck at gambling，etc：～
背 be down on one's luck／～好 be
struck with luck

手枪 shǒuqiāng pistol：气～ air pistol／
～套 holster

手球 shǒuqiú ❶〈体〉handball ❷
handball（a foul in soccer，etc）

手软 shǒuruǎn be soft-hearted；lack
firmness

手势 shǒushì gesture；sign；signal：打
～ also "做手势" make a gesture；ges-

ticulate；sign

手术 shǒushù surgical operation：动～
perform an operation；（of a patient）
have an operation／～刀 scalpel／～室
operating room or theatre／～台 operating table

手套 shǒutào gloves：无指～ mittens

手头 shǒutóu ❶ also "手边" on or at
hand：～工作 work at hand ❷ one's
present financial situation：～拮据 be
hard-pressed for money；be hard up ❸
writing or other abilities：～快 be quick
in writing；be a fast pen

手腕 shǒuwàn ❶ also "手腕子" wrist
❷ artifice；finesse；stratagem：耍～
play tricks；resort to stratagems；use
an artifice

手无寸铁 shǒuwúcùntiě without any
weapon in one's hand；bare-handed；
unarmed

手舞足蹈 shǒuwǔ-zúdǎo dance or
jump for joy

手下 shǒuxià ❶ under the leadership
or direction of：～人 subordinate；un-
derling；servant ❷ at the hands of sb：
～败将 opponent one has beaten；one's
defeated adversary／～留情 show
mercy；be lenient ❸ see "手头❶❷"

手续 shǒuxù procedure；formalities：
～费 service charge；commission

手艺 shǒuyì craftsmanship；work-
manship；skill：～人 craftsman

手淫 shǒuyín〈医〉masturbation；
self-abuse

手纸 shǒuzhǐ toilet paper；tissue

手指 shǒuzhǐ finger：～甲 fingernail／
～尖 fingertip

手足 shǒuzú ❶ hand and foot；limbs：
～无措 at a loss（as to what to do）；in
helpless confusion ❷ brothers：～之情
brotherly or fraternal affection；frater-
nity

守 shǒu ❶ guard；defend；garri-
son：～军 defending troops；de-
fenders／～门员 goalkeeper／处于～

势 be on the defensive ❷ keep watch; watch over; look after; ～灵 stand guard at the bier; keep vigil beside the coffin / ～夜 *also* "守更" keep watch or vigil at night / ～财奴 miser; tightwad; skinflint ❸ observe; abide by; adhere; ～法 obey or observe the law; be law-abiding / ～时 be punctual / ～岁 stay up all night on New Year's Eve / ～孝 observe mourning (for one's deceased parent) / ～信 keep one's word; be trustworthy ❹ by the side of; next to; near; ～着炉子取暖 sit round a stove to keep warm

守备 shǒubèi garrison; defence; ～部队 garrison (force)

守成 shǒuchéng *also* "守业"〈书〉 maintain what has been achieved by one's forefathers or predecessors; carry on an undertaking started by one's predecessors

守寡 shǒuguǎ remain a widow; live in widowhood; 守活寡 be a grass widow

守候 shǒuhòu ❶ wait; await ❷ watch over (the sick, etc); look after

守护 shǒuhù guard; protect; defend; ～神〈宗教〉guardian angel; patron saint

守旧 shǒujiù stick to old ways; be a stickler for old practices; ～思想 conservative ideology

守口如瓶 shǒukǒurúpíng keep one's mouth shut; have one's lips sealed; be tight-mouthed or -lipped

守卫 shǒuwèi keep safe; guard; defend (borders, etc)

守则 shǒuzé rules; regulations (for staff, etc)

守株待兔 shǒuzhūdàitù wait for a windfall; trust foolishly to chance and luck

首 shǒu ❶ head; 搔～ scratch one's head / ～级 chopped-off head ❷ head; leader; chief; 匪～ bandit chieftain; rebel leader / ～领 chieftain;

leader ❸ first (in importance); foremost; supreme; ～都 capital (of a country) / ～恶 arch-criminal; principal culprit / ～府 capital of a province, prefecture or dependency / ～富 richest family or person (of a place) / ～辅 prime minister (usu in a monarchy) / ～善之区〈书〉best of all places — national capital ❹ first (in time, etc) of all; first (to do sth); ～倡 initiate; begin; start / ～车 first bus or train / ～次 for the first time; first / ～航 (make a) maiden flight or voyage / ～届 first (session) / ～选 first chosen; (of) first choice / ～映 first show (of a film); première ❺〈量〉*used for poems and songs*: 三～民歌 three folk songs

首创 shǒuchuàng initiate; originate; invent; ～精神 initiative; pioneering or creative spirit

首当其冲 shǒudāngqíchōng be the first to suffer the impact (of a disaster, etc); bear the brunt

首发 shǒufā ❶ first publication or launching (of a book, etc); ～式 ceremony celebrating the first publication of a book; inaugural ceremony for launching a publication ❷〈体〉starting line-up or formation (of a soccer team, etc); 担任～ be fielded in the starting line-up; be a starter

首肯 shǒukěn nod approval or assent; approve; consent to

首脑 shǒunǎo head; leader; ～机关 leading body / ～人物 leading figure or personage

首屈一指 shǒuqūyìzhǐ come (out) or rank first; be second to none

首饰 shǒushì jewellery; ～店 jeweller's shop; jewellery store

首尾 shǒuwěi ❶ head and tail; first and last; beginning and end; ～相连 continuous without interruption; in an unbroken line ❷ from beginning to end; from start to finish

首席 shǒuxí ❶ seat of honour ❷ chief; senior; ~代表 chief representative; senior delegate / ~小提琴 first violin / ~执行官 chief executive officer (CEO)

首先 shǒuxiān ❶ first: ~报名 be the first to enroll ❷ in the first place; first (of all)

首要 shǒuyào ❶ of the first importance; primary; first: ~条件 primary condition ❷ leader; chief

首长 shǒuzhǎng senior officer or official; leading cadre: ~席 VIP seats

shòu

寿(壽) shòu ❶ long life; longevity ❷ life; age: ~命 lifespan; life; lifetime / ~数 one's destined lifespan / ~终正寝 die of old age; die a natural death; 〈喻〉 cease to exist ❸ (usu of a middle-aged or elderly person) birthday: ~辰 birthday / ~礼 birthday present / ~面 birthday or longevity noodles / ~星 god of longevity; person whose birthday is being celebrated ❹〈婉〉 for burial: ~衣 grave clothes; cerements; shroud

受 shòu ❶ receive; accept: ~粉(植) be pollinated / ~贿 take a bribe / ~奖 receive a reward; be rewarded / ~训 receive or undergo training; be trained / ~援国 recipient country / ~降仪式 ceremony to accept surrender / ~之有愧 be embarrassed to accept sth; not deserve sth ❷ suffer; be subjected to: ~潮 get moist; become damp / ~挫 be foiled; suffer a setback / ~过 bear or take the blame (for sb else) / ~窘 be embarrassed; be caught in an awkward situation / ~凉 catch cold / ~骗 be deceived, cheated or taken in / ~刑 be put to torture; be tortured / ~委屈 also "受屈" suffer

a wrong or an injustice; be wronged / ~灾地区 disaster area; stricken or afflicted area ❸ endure; stand; bear: 不了 cannot stand or bear / ~够了 have had enough (of) ❹〈方〉 pleasant; agreeable: ~听 good to hear; pleasant to the ear

受宠 shòuchǒng receive a favour; be doted on: ~若惊 be overwhelmed by an unexpected favour; feel extremely flattered

受害 shòuhài fall victim; be affected or afflicted: ~人 sufferer; victim

受惊 shòujīng frightened; scared; startled

受精 shòujīng be fertilized or inseminated: ~卵 fertilized egg; zygote

受苦 shòukǔ suffer; have a tough time: ~受难 lead a life of hardships and sufferings

受累 shòulěi ❶ be implicated or incriminated (on account of sb else) ❷ (shòulèi) be put to trouble; cause inconvenience to: 您老~了。〈套〉 Thank you for your effort, sir.

受理 shòulǐ ❶ accept and handle (business) ❷〈法〉 accept and hear (a case)

受命 shòumìng receive instructions or an assignment: ~于危难之际 receive an assignment (to save the situation, etc) in times of dire peril

受聘 shòupìn ❶ accept invitation to take a job ❷ (of a girl's family) accept a proposal to marriage with betrothal gifts

受气 shòuqì be bullied; be made to suffer: ~包 one who always takes the rap; whipping boy

受权 shòuquán be authorized or empowered: ~声明如下 be authorized to make the following statement

受伤 shòushāng be injured or wounded: 背部~ get injured in the back

受益 shòuyì benefit from; profit by:

～人 beneficiary

受用 shòuyòng ❶ enjoy; benefit from; profit by:～不尽 profit (by sth) for ever ❷ (shòuyong) (often used in the negative) feel comfortable:很不～ very uncomfortable; (of sth) quite disagreeable

受制 shòuzhì ❶ be controlled; be under control:～ 于人 be under sb's thumb ❷ suffer hardships; endure rough conditions

受众 shòuzhòng　target audience

受罪 shòuzuì　suffer hardships; endure rough conditions; have a hard time (doing sth)

狩 shòu (usu 狩猎) 〈书〉hunting (esp in winter)

授 shòu ❶ give; present; confer:～粉〖植〗pollinate / ～奖 award or confer a prize / ～人以柄 give sb a handle (against oneself) ❷ teach; instruct; tell:～计 confide a stratagem (to sb); tell (sb) what to do / ～课 give lessons or lectures

授命 shòumìng ❶ 〈书〉give or lay down one's life; sacrifice oneself ❷ (of head of state, etc) give orders; authorize:～组阁 authorize sb to organize the cabinet

授权 shòuquán　empower; authorize; delegate power to:～书 letter of authorization; power of attorney / ～范围 scope of authority

授受 shòushòu　give and receive; offer and accept:私相～ give and accept in private; illegally pass things between each other

授意 shòuyì　incite or inspire (sb to do sth); suggest an idea (to sb):这些都是谁～的？Who's behind all this?

售 shòu ❶ be on sale; sell:～价 selling price / ～货机 vending machine / ～货员 shop assistant; salesclerk / ～后服务 after-sale or post-sale service; customer service ❷ 〈书〉carry out (intrigues, tricks, etc):其计不～。The plan fell through.

售票 shòupiào　sell ticket:～处 ticket office; booking office (at a railway station, etc); box office (at a theatre, etc) / ～员 ticket seller; booking-office clerk; (of a bus) conductor or conductress

兽（獸） shòu ❶ beast; brute; animal:～医 veterinary surgeon; veterinarian; vet ❷ beastly; bestial:～行 brutal act; brutality; bestial behaviour / ～性 brutish nature; beast in a man / ～欲 animal desire; bestial lust

绶 shòu　coloured silk ribbon (usu attached to an official seal or a medal):～带 coloured silk ribbon; cordon (worn as a sash of honour or an ornament)

瘦 shòu ❶ thin; slim; lean:～长 tall and thin; lanky / ～肉 lean meat / ～弱 thin and weak; frail / ～削 very thin; emaciated; gaunt / ～骨嶙峋 thin and bony; bag of bones ❷ too close; tight:裤子太～。This pair of trousers is too tight. ❸ also "瘦瘠" infertile; poor; barren

shū

书（書） shū ❶ write; record:～写 write ❷ (style of) calligraphy; script:～ 画 painting and calligraphy / ～行 running hand ❸ book:～包 satchel; schoolbag / ～店 bookshop; bookstore; bookseller's / ～房 also "书斋" study / ～柜 also "书橱" book cabinet; bookcase / ～号 (officially registered) book number / ～籍 books; works; literature / ～架 bookshelf; book rack / ～库 stack room; stacks (of a library, etc) / ～目 booklist; title catalogue / ～皮 book cover; jacket; (dust) cover / ～评 book re-

view；～签 bookmark；bookmarker /
～市 book market or fair；～桌 (writing) desk ❹ letter；epistle；～信 *also*
"书简"；"书札" letter；correspon-
dence；written message ❺ official
paper；document

书本 shūběn ❶ books；～知识 book-
learning；book-knowledge ❷ textbooks
and exercise-books

书呆子 shūdāizi pedant；bookworm；
～气 pedantic；bookish

书法 shūfǎ calligraphy；penmanship；
～家 calligrapher

书记 shūjì ❶ secretary；总～ general
secretary / ～处 secretariat ❷ clerk；
〈法〉recorder；～员 clerk (of a court)

书卷气 shūjuànqì (of an intellectual)
air of cultured refinement；cultured；
polished

书面 shūmiàn written；in written
form；in writing；～语 written or literary language / ～通知 notify in writ-
ing；written notice

书生 shūshēng intellectual；scholar；
～气 bookishness / ～之见 pedantic
view

书屋 shūwū ❶〈旧〉study；house for
a traditional private school ❷ book-
store；bookshop

书香 shūxiāng (family) with a tradition of study；～门第 family having
noted scholars in previous generations；
scholar-gentry family

抒 shū ❶ give voice to；express；
convey / ～发 express；voice；
convey / ～怀 express one's feelings or
sentiments / ～写 describe；express ❷
see "纾" shū

抒情 shūqíng express or convey one's
emotion；～诗 lyric poetry；lyrics /
歌曲 lyric song

纾 shū 〈书〉relieve；alleviate
(hardship, etc)；free (sb) from
(danger, etc)；～忧 relieve sb from
anxiety

枢（樞） shū ❶ hinge；pivot ❷
hub；centre of activity
or importance；～纽 hub；axis；key

叔 shū ❶ father's younger broth-
er；uncle；～父 father's younger
brother；uncle / ～母 wife of father's
younger brother；aunt ❷ polite form of
address for a man about one's father's
age；uncle；李(大)～ Uncle Li ❸ husband's younger brother ❹ third son in
the family

叔伯 shūbai relationship between
cousins of the same grandfather or
great-grandfather；～姐妹 first or second female cousins on the paternal
side；cousins

叔叔 shūshu ❶〈口〉father's younger
brother；uncle ❷ (child's form of address for any man about father's age)
uncle；解放军～ uncle PLA

姝 shū 〈书〉❶ pretty；beautiful
❷ beautiful woman；beauty

殊 shū ❶ different；divergent；～
途同归 reach the same goal by
different routes；all roads lead to Rome
❷ outstanding；special；unusual；～荣
special or unusual honour ❸〈书〉very
much；exceedingly；really；～感悲痛
feel deeply grieved

殊不知 shūbùzhī *used of sth that runs
contrary to what one thought , or what
is believed or said by sb else*；原以为这
场球很容易取胜，～对手这么难对付。
I thought the game would be a walkover, and little imagined the adversary
would prove such a hard nut to crack. /
都说这趟火车准时，～今天就误点了。
They say this train is punctual, but it
was behind schedule today.

殊死 shūsǐ desperate；life-and-death；
～抵抗 put up a desperate resistance

倏 shū 〈书〉swiftly；～忽 sudden-
ly；in an instant

菽 shū beans；～粟 grain

梳 shū ❶（usu 梳子）comb ❷ comb（hair, etc）; comb（hair）; sort out（problems, etc）/ ～洗 wash and dress / ～妆 dress and make up

淑 shū〈书〉kind and gentle; fair; graceful；～女 fair maiden; virtuous woman

舒 shū ❶ stretch; relax；～筋活络〈中医〉stimulate blood circulation and relax muscles and joints ❷〈书〉easy; leisurely; slow；～畅 free from worry; relaxed; happy / ～缓 slow; leisurely; slow；～坦 comfortable; carefree

舒服 shūfu ❶ comfortable; pleasant；天气～ pleasant weather ❷ be well；你哪儿不～? What's wrong with you?

舒适 shūshì easy; comfortable; cosy；～度 comfort level

舒心 shūxīn carefree; happy; contented；～的日子 carefree life

舒展 shūzhǎn ❶ unfold; smooth out; stretch；～眉头 unknit one's eyebrows / ～筋骨 stretch one's limbs ❷ unrestrained; free；～大方 free and graceful ❸（of one's mind, etc）comfortable; at ease

疏（❶-❼ 疎） shū ❶ clear away（obstacles）; dredge（a river, etc）；～浚 dredge ❷ thin; sparse; scattered；～落 sparse; scattered / ～密有致 be well-spaced ❸（of relations）not close; distant ❹ not familiar with；人生地～ be unfamiliar with the place and the people; be a stranger in the land ❺ negligent; careless；～懒 careless and lazy; lackadaisical / ～失 careless mistake; thoughtless error ❻（of ability, learning, etc）scanty; inadequate; meagre ❼ thin out; disperse; scatter；～苗 thin out seedlings ❽〈史〉memorial to the emperor ❾ detailed annotation; 注～ notes and commentaries

疏导 shūdǎo ❶ dredge ❷ direct; regulate; guide；交通 direct the flow of traffic

疏忽 shūhu carelessness; negligence; oversight；不可～ must not overlook or neglect

疏漏 shūlòu careless omission; slip; oversight

疏散 shūsàn ❶ sparse; scattered; dispersed ❷ evacuate; vacate; disperse；～人口 evacuate residents

疏松 shūsōng ❶ loose; puffy；骨质～〈医〉osteoporosis; rarefaction of bone ❷ loosen（soil, etc）

疏通 shūtōng ❶ dredge（a ditch, etc）; remove obstacles from（a pipe, etc）❷ mediate between two parties; remove misunderstanding；～关系 mediate between two parties

疏远 shūyuǎn alienate; drift apart; estrange

输 shū ❶ transport; transmit; convey；～氧〈医〉oxygen therapy / ～油管 petroleum pipeline; oil line / ～电线路 transmission line ❷〈书〉make a gift of; contribute money; donate；～捐 pay; contribute ❸ lose; suffer defeat；～家 loser in a game or gamble / ～理 not have right on one's side; be in the wrong / ～钱 lose money at gambling

输出 shūchū ❶ send or go out; emit；（of electricity）output；～功率 output power ❷ export；～品 export / ～口岸 loading port

输入 shūrù ❶ bring in；〈电〉〈信息〉input；～数据 input data ❷ import; introduce；～港 port of import or entry

输送 shūsòng transport; send; convey；～带 conveyer belt / ～新鲜血液 infuse new blood

输血 shūxuè ❶〈医〉blood transfusion ❷〈喻〉give aid and support; shore up; give（sb）a shot in the arm

S

输液 shūyè 〈医〉infusion；给患者～ put an invalid on the drip

蔬 shū （usu 蔬菜）vegetables； greens

shú

秫 shú *kaoliang*；（Chinese）sorghum；～秸 sorghum stalks

孰 shú 〈书〉❶ who；～能当之? Who is capable of such a job? ❷ (used in comparison or choice) which； who；～是～非? Which is right and which is wrong? ❸ what；是可忍，～不可忍? If this can be tolerated, what cannot?

赎（贖） shú ❶ redeem；ransom；～金 ransom （money）/ ～买 redeem；buy (sth) back；buy (sb) out / ～身 (of a slave, etc) redeem or ransom oneself；buy back one's freedom❷ atone for or redeem (a crime)；罪不可～ (of a crime) beyond redemption

塾 shú 〈旧〉private or family school

熟 shú *also* shóu ❶ ripe；过～ overripe / ～年 good or bumper year ❷ cooked；done；～食 cooked food ❸ processed；wrought；cultivated；～皮大 processed or tanned hide；leather ❹ frequently seen or heard；well-known；familiar / ～记 learn by rote；commit to memory；memorize / ～路 familiar route；beaten track / ～人 acquaintance / ～识 be well acquainted (with)；be conversant (with) / ～语 〈语言〉idiom；idiomatic expression ❺ skilled；experienced；versed in；～手 practised or old hand / ～能生巧 skill comes from practice；practice makes perfect ❻ deeply；profoundly；～睡 sleep soundly；be fast or sound asleep / ～思 ponder deeply；consider carefully

熟练 shúliàn skilled；expert；profi-

cient；～工 skilled worker；journeyman

熟视无睹 shúshìwúdǔ pay no heed to；turn a blind eye to；ignore

熟悉 shúxī know well；be well acquainted with；～情况 know the ropes

熟习 shúxí be skilful at；be familiar with；be practised in；～计算机技术 be well versed in computer technology

shǔ

暑 shǔ summer heat；hot weather；～假 summer vacation / ～热 hot summer weather；sweltering summer heat / ～期班 summer course or school

黍 shǔ *also* "黍子" broomcorn millet

属（屬） shǔ ❶ category；genus；亚～ subgenus ❷ come within one's jurisdiction；be subordinate to；～地 possession；dependency；colony / 附～ vassal or dependent state / ～下 subordinates ❸ belong to；be part of；～性 attribute；property / ～于 belong to；be part of；be attributed to ❹ family members；dependants ❺ be；～实 (prove to) be true / 纯～虚构 be sheer fabrication ❻ be born in the year of (one of the 12 symbolic animals)；～相 *see* "生肖" shēngxiào *see also* zhǔ

署 shǔ ❶ (government) office ❷ make arrangements for；arrange；prepare ❸ *also* "署理" act as；stand proxy for；handle as proxy ❹ affix one's name to；sign；～名文章 signed article

蜀 Shǔ another name for Sichuan （四川）

鼠 shǔ mouse；rat；～辈〈粗〉rat；rascal；scoundrel / ～标〈信息〉mouse / ～窜 scamper off like a rat；scurry away / ～夹 mousetrap / ～疫 *also* "黑死病" plague / ～目寸光 see only what is under one's nose；lack foresight

数（數） shǔ ❶ count；～秒 countdown／～不清 also "数不胜数" too numerous to count；countless ❷ stand by comparison：～不着 also "数不上" not count as outstanding，important，etc／～一～二 be among the very best ❸ enumerate；list

see also shù；shuò

数典忘祖 shǔdiǎnwàngzǔ forget one's ancestral origin；disown one's forefathers

数九 shǔjiǔ （start of）the nine periods （of nine days each）following the Winter Solstice：～寒天 coldest days of the year

数落 shǔluo also "数说"〔口〕❶ scold by enumerating sb's wrongdoings；reproach；reprove ❷ cite one after another；enumerate

薯 shǔ〈植〉potato；yam：白～ sweet potato

曙 shǔ〈书〉daybreak；dawn：～光 first light of morning；daylight

shù

术（術） shù ❶ art；skill；craft：～语 technical terms；terminology ❷ method；tactics；trick

戍 shù defend；guard；garrison：～边 garrison the frontiers

束 shù ❶ bind；tie；bundle up：～腰 girdle the waist；girdle／～之高阁 shelve；pigeon-hole ❷〈量〉bundle；bunch；sheaf：一～文稿 a sheaf of manuscripts／一～玫瑰 a bouquet of roses ❸ beam：电子～ electron beam ❹ control；contain；restrain

束缚 shùfù tie；bind up；fetter：打破旧框框的～ smash the shackles of old convention

束手 shùshǒu be at one's wits' end；

be helpless；～待毙 resign oneself to death；sit idle waiting for destruction／～束脚 timid and hesitant；overcautious／～无策 feel simply helpless；be at a loss what to do

述 shù state；relate；narrate：～怀 pour out one's feelings；unburden one's heart／～评 review；commentary

述说 shùshuō state；relate；narrate：～经过 give an account of what happened；recount an incident

述职 shùzhí report （on one's work）：～报告 work report／回国～ （of an ambassador，etc）return for consultations

树（樹） shù ❶ tree：～干 （tree）trunk／～林 woods；grove／～苗 sapling／～木 trees in general／～皮 bark／～枝 branch；twig／～种 varieties or seeds of trees／～倒猢狲散〈俗〉when the tree falls，the monkeys scatter — when an influential person falls from power，the hangers-on disperse；a sinking ship is deserted by rats ❷ plant；cultivate：～人〈书〉nurture or bring up people of ability；educate the young ❸ hold or set up；establish：～敌 make enemies；arouse hostility／～典型 hold up as model

树碑立传 shùbēi-lìzhuàn〈贬〉glorify （sb）by erecting monuments and writing biographies — build up sb's prestige by an overdose of praise

树大招风 shùdàzhāofēng〈俗〉a tall tree catches the wind — a person of great reputation or power often comes under attack

树立 shùlì set or build up；establish：～全局观念 adopt an overall point of view

竖（豎） shù ❶ vertical；upright；perpendicular：～琴〈乐〉harp ❷ set upright；put up；

erect；～立 erect；raise；stand／～起耳
朵 prick up one's ears ❸ vertical
stroke (in Chinese characters) ❹〈书〉
young (servant)：～子〈贬〉boy；
(mean) fellow；bloke

恕 shù ❶ forbearance；consider-
ation for others ❷ forgive；par-
don；excuse：～罪 pardon an offence；
forgive a sin／～〈套〉excuse me；beg
your pardon；～不奉陪。Excuse me for
not keeping you company.

庶 shù ❶ multitudinous；myriad
❷〈书〉common people；the
populace：～民 commoner；man in the
street ❸〈旧〉of or by the concubine：
～出 be born of a concubine

数（數） shù ❶ number；fig-
ure：两位～ double digit
number／～额 number；amount／～以
万计 number in the tens of thousands
❷ (short for 数学) mathematics；math
❸ fate；destiny：在～难逃。There's no
escape from one's fate. ❹ several；a
few：～罪并罚〈法〉concurrent punishment for several crimes；cumulative
punishment
see also shǔ；shuò

数词 shùcí〈语言〉numeral：基～ cardinal number／序～ ordinal number
数据 shùjù data：～库 database；data
bank／～存取 data access
数控 shùkòng〈信息〉numerical control (NC)；digital control：～电话
digital control telephone
数量 shùliàng quantity；amount；vol-
ume：～词〈语言〉numeral-classifier
compound
数码 shùmǎ ❶ numeral；digital：中国
～ Chinese numerals／～相机 digital
camera ❷ number；amount
数目 shùmù sum；number；amount：
不小的～ enormous sum／～字 figure；
numeral；digit
数字 shùzì ❶ numeral；figure；digit：
～化 digitization／～编码 digital or nu-

meric coding／～激光视盘 digital video
disc (DVD) ❷ quantity；amount；fig-
ure：天文～ astronomical figure

墅 shù villa；别～ villa

漱 shù gargle；rinse：～口 rinse
the mouth；gargle

shuā

刷 shuā ❶ brush；scrub；paint
with a brush：～卡 swipe one's
card (for registration, etc)／～洗
scrub；scour；clean／～新〈喻〉reno-
vate；refurbish；break (a record)／～
子 brush；scrub／～油漆 varnish
(sth)；paint (sth)／～〈喻〉expel；dis-
charge；eliminate：第一轮就给～下来
了 be eliminated in the first round ❷
see "唰❶" shuā
see also shuà

唰 shuā ❶〈象声〉swish；rustle：
树叶被风吹得～～地响。The
leaves rustled in the wind. ❷ very
quickly；like a flash：她的脸～地就红
了。She flushed crimson.

shuǎ

耍 shuǎ ❶〈方〉play：～钱 gamble
❷ play or juggle with；manipu-
late：～把戏 perform jugglery，magic，
etc ❸ give play to (sth undesirable)；
behave (in an unsavoury manner)：～笔
杆 wield a facile pen；be skilled in literary tricks／～花腔 use honeyed words；
sweet-talk／～花招 show off one's
cleverness or skill；play tricks；resort
to deception／～威风 flaunt one's
authority or power；throw one's weight
about ❹ play with；tease：让人～了 be
had
耍滑 shuǎhuá *also* "耍滑头" try to
shirk work or responsibility；pass the
buck；dodge

耍赖 shuǎlài　also "耍无赖" act in a brazen manner; behave capriciously and unreasonably

耍弄 shuǎnòng　❶ play (tricks, etc); make use of: ～心眼儿 make use of one's petty cleverness; be calculating ❷ make a fool of; make fun of; pull sb's leg

耍笑 shuǎxiào　❶ laugh and joke; have fun ❷ make fun of; pull sb's leg

耍嘴皮子 shuǎzuǐpízi　❶ talk glibly or slickly; show off one's eloquence ❷ engage in empty talk; pay lip service

shuà

刷 shuà　see also shuā

刷白 shuàbái　〈方〉white; ashen; pale: 吓得脸色～ turn pale with fear

shuāi

衰 shuāi　decline; wane: ～败 decline; wane; fall into disrepair / ～减 weaken; diminish / ～老 old and feeble; decrepit / ～颓 weak and dejected; degenerate / 国势～微 decline of a nation

衰竭 shuāijié　〈医〉exhaustion; prostration: 心力～ heart failure

衰落 shuāiluò　decline; deteriorate; go downhill: 家境～ reduced family circumstances

衰弱 shuāiruò　❶ weak; frail; feeble ❷ flag; abate; decline in vigour

衰退 shuāituì　decline; fail; physically deteriorate: 记忆力～ failing memory

衰亡 shuāiwáng　decline and fall; wither away; become extinct

摔 shuāi　❶ fall; tumble; hurtle down: ～下楼梯 tumble down the stairs ❷ (cause to) fall and break; crash: ～了一架飞机。There was an air crash. ❸ throw; hurl; fling

摔打 shuāidǎ　❶ strike; beat; knock: 把鞋子上的泥～～。Knock the dirt off your shoes. ❷ temper oneself by roughing it

摔跤 shuāijiāo　❶ also "摔跟头" tumble; slip and fall: 当心别～! Watch your step and don't trip up. ❷ also "摔跟头" come a cropper; make a blunder ❸〈体〉wrestling: ～运动员 wrestler

shuǎi

甩 shuǎi　❶ swing; sway; wave: ～开膀子大干 go full steam ahead with one's work ❷ throw; fling; hurl ❸ throw off; leave behind: ～包袱 cast off a burden; get a load off one's back / 把女朋友～了 jilt one's girlfriend

甩干 shuǎigān　spin-dry; tumble-dry: ～机 tumbler-dryer

甩卖 shuǎimài　sell at a reduced price; have a markdown sale; dump: 清仓大～ clearance or rummage sale

甩手 shuǎishǒu　❶ swing one's arms ❷ throw up (one's job, etc); wash one's hands (of sth): ～掌柜〈口〉"hands-off" boss; "do-nothing" guy

shuài

帅(帥) shuài　❶ commander-in-chief: ～才 (person of) remarkable abilities for overall command ❷ handsome; graceful; smart: ～哥 handsome guy / ～气 handsome; elegant; graceful

率 shuài　❶ lead; command: ～领 lead; head; command / ～先 take the lead (in doing sth); be the first (to do sth) ❷〈书〉follow; comply; conform: ～由旧章 follow precedents; act in conformity with established rules ❸ hasty; rash; impetuous;

～尔成章〈谦〉written in haste ❹ frank; straightforward; forthright; 真 honest and sincere / ～直 frank and straightforward ❺〈书〉in general; generally; usually; ～皆如此. This is generally the case. ❻ see "帅❷" shuài see also lǜ

shuān

闩 shuān bolt; latch; 门～ door bolt

拴 shuān tie; bind; fasten; 把马 ～在树上 tie or hitch a horse to a tree / 被琐事～住了 be bogged down by chores

栓 shuān ❶ (rifle) bolt; plug ❷ stopper; cork; anything similar to a cork or stopper; ～剂〈医〉suppository

shuàn

涮 shuàn ❶ rinse; ～瓶子 rinse out a bottle ❷ scald (thin slices of meat, etc) in boiling water; dip-boil; ～羊肉 dip-boiled mutton slices; instant-boiled mutton ❸〈方〉trick; fool; deceive

shuāng

双(雙) shuāng ❶ two; both; double; ～倍 twofold; double / ～边 bilateral / ～打〈体〉doubles / ～杠〈体〉parallel bars / ～～ in pairs; both / ～语 bilingual / ～胞胎 twins / ～轨制〈喻〉double-track system (as in education or pricing) / ～人床 double bed / ～人舞 duet; pas de deux / ～休日 two-day weekend / ～学位 double (bachelor's etc) degree / ～眼皮 double-fold eyelid / ～喜临门 be blessed by double happiness; have two happy events occur at the same time / ～赢方案 win-win proposal ❷ even; 数 even number ❸〈量〉pair; 一～手 a pair of hands

双层 shuāngcéng double-deck; double-layered; ～床 double-decker / ～玻璃窗 double (-glazed) window / ～公共汽车 double-deck bus; double-decker

双重 shuāngchóng double; dual; twofold; ～性 dual nature; duality / ～标准 double standard

双方 shuāngfāng both or two parties or sides; 交战～ both belligerents

双关 shuāngguān having a double meaning; ～语 pun; word play

双管齐下 shuāngguǎnqíxià work along two lines; do both things simultaneously

双簧 shuānghuáng 〈戏〉two-man comic show in which the front man does the acting while the one hiding behind him does the speaking; 演～ give a two-man comic show; collaborate closely; work hand in glove

双料 shuāngliào of reinforced material; extra quality; ～瓷盆 enamel basin made of reinforced material / ～冠军 double champion (with two first prizes)

双面 shuāngmiàn two-sided; double-edged; reversible; ～绣 double-faced embroidery

双亲 shuāngqīn both parents; ～家庭 two-parent family

双全 shuāngquán enjoy a double blessing; possess both of two complementary qualities; 福寿～ enjoy happiness as well as longevity / 父母～ with both parents alive

双向 shuāngxiàng two-way; bidirectional; bilateral; ～选择 two-way selection (by employer and employee in a job market)

霜 shuāng ❶ frost; ～冻 frost / ～害 frostbite; frost damage / ～降 Frost's Descent, 18th seasonal division point see also "节气" jiéqi ❷ frostlike powder：糖～ frosting；icing ❸ white；silver；hoar：两鬓飞～ grey or hoary temples

媚 shuāng 〈书〉widow：～居 be a widow；live in widowhood

shuǎng

爽 shuǎng ❶ bright；clear；fresh：神清气～ feel fresh and clear-headed ／ ～口 tasty and refreshing ❷ frank；straightforward；forthright：～直 frank；straightforward；open ／ ～利 quick and efficient；brisk and neat ❸ feel well：身体不～ feel unwell；be under the weather ❹ 〈书〉make a mistake；deviate：～约 fail to keep an appointment

爽快 shuǎngkuai ❶ refreshed；happy ❷ also “爽气” frank；straightforward；forthright：办事～ be forthright in doing sth；do sth without fuss

爽朗 shuǎnglǎng ❶ (of weather, etc) bright and clear ❷ frank and cheerful；hearty

爽然 shuǎngrán 〈书〉feel lost；be at a loss：～若失 feel perplexed, not knowing what to do

爽心 shuǎngxīn pleased；cheerful；gratified：～悦目 refreshing；pleasing

爽性 shuǎngxìng might just as well：既已晚了，～不去了。Since it is already late, we might just as well not go.

shuǐ

水 shuǐ ❶ water；hydro-：～表 water metre ／ ～池 pool；cistern ／ ～壶 kettle；canteen；watering can ／ ～荒 shortage or scarcity of water ／ ～库 reservoir ／ ～龙 (fire) hose ／ ～牛 (water) buffalo ／ ～球 〈体〉water polo ／ ～田 also “水地” irrigated (paddy) field ／ ～文 hydrology ／ ～运 water transport ／ ～淋淋 dripping with water ／ ～龙头 (water) tap；faucet；spigot ／ ～墨画 ink and wash；wash painting ／ ～滴石穿 also “滴水穿石” dripping water wears through rock；persistent effort brings success ❷ river；general term for rivers, lakes, seas, etc：～坝 dam ／ ～系 river system ／ ～乡 region of rivers and lakes ／ ～榭 waterside pavilion ／ ～闸 sluice；watergate ❸ liquid：药～ liquid medicine；lotion ❹ times of washing：洗过两～ be washed twice

水兵 shuǐbīng seaman；sailor；blue-jacket

水彩 shuǐcǎi watercolour：～画 watercolour (painting)

水草 shuǐcǎo ❶ pasture and water：逐～而居 live where there is water and pasture；rove about for water and pasture ❷ waterweeds；water plants

水产 shuǐchǎn aquatic product：～养殖 aquaculture

水到渠成 shuǐdàoqúchéng where water flows, a channel is formed — when conditions are ripe, success is assured

水电 shuǐdiàn ❶ water and electricity ❷ see “水力”

水痘 shuǐdòu 〈医〉chickenpox

水分 shuǐfèn ❶ moisture content ❷ exaggeration；overstatement：～很大 very much exaggerated or overblown

水果 shuǐguǒ fruit：～糖 fruit drops

水火 shuǐhuǒ ❶ fire and water：～不相容 be absolutely irreconcilable as fire and water ／ ～无情。Floods and fires are inexorable. ❷ extreme misery：水深火热 abyss of suffering or misery；dire distress

水货 shuǐhuò ❶ smuggled goods ❷ fake or shoddy stuff

水晶 shuǐjīng (rock) crystal；quartz

水雷 shuǐléi 〈军〉(submarine) mine

水力 shuǐlì waterpower；hydraulic power：～发电 also “水电” hydroelectric generation / ～发电站 *also* "水电站" hydroelectric or hydropower station

水利 shuǐlì ❶ water conservancy：～枢纽 key water control project ❷ *also* "水利工程" irrigation works；water conservancy project

水灵 shuǐling ❶ (of fruit, greens, etc) fresh and juicy ❷ (of looks, eyes, etc) bright and beautiful；spirited and pretty

水流 shuǐliú ❶ rivers；streams；waters ❷ current；course；flow：～量 water flow / ～湍急 swift flow；torrent

水陆 shuǐlù land and water：～两用车 amphibian (vehicle)

水路 shuǐlù waterway；water route：走～ travel by water

水落石出 shuǐluòshíchū the truth comes to light；murder is out：把案子查个～ get to the bottom of the case

水面 shuǐmiàn ❶ water surface：～舰艇 surface vessels ❷ water area；area of waters

水母 shuǐmǔ 〈动物〉 jellyfish

水泥 shuǐní cement：～标号 cement mark or grade；strength of cement

水暖 shuǐnuǎn ❶ heating by hot-water radiator ❷ water and heating facilities；plumbing：～工 plumber

水疱 shuǐpào blister：打～ get a blister

水平 shuǐpíng ❶ horizontal；level：～面 water level；horizontal plane；level surface ❷ standard；level：不够～ be not up to standard / 管理～ art of management / ～高 (of) high calibre / ～测试 proficiency test

水乳交融 shuǐrǔjiāoróng well blended as milk and water — completely compatible；in perfect harmony

水上 shuǐshàng on or over the water：～飞机 seaplane；hydroplane / ～乐园 water amusement or sports park / ～运动 aquatic or water sports

水生 shuǐshēng living in water；aquatic：～根 water root / ～生物 aquatic life

水势 shuǐshì flow of water；rise and fall of floodwater：～汹涌 turbulent flow of water

水手 shuǐshǒu seaman；sailor：～长 boatswain

水土 shuǐtǔ ❶ water and soil：～保持 water and soil conservation / ～流失 soil erosion ❷ natural environment and climate：～不服 not accustomed to the environment and climate；not acclimatized or acclimated

水汪汪 shuǐwāngwāng ❶ (of land, etc) covered with water；wet through ❷ (of children's or young women's eyes) clear and intelligent

水位 shuǐwèi ❶ water level：警戒～ flood-warning level ❷ *also* "地下水位" water table；groundwater level

水仙 shuǐxiān 〈植〉 narcissus

水泄不通 shuǐxièbùtōng not even a drop of water could trickle through — be very crowded or tightly guarded

水星 shuǐxīng 〈天文〉 Mercury

水性 shuǐxìng ❶ skill in swimming：～好 be a good swimmer；be good at swimming ❷ condition of a river, lake, etc (such as depth, current, etc)：～杨花 (of women) fickle and lascivious (like flowing water and flying willow catkins)；of easy virtue；of loose morals

水锈 shuǐxiù ❶ *also* "水垢"；"水碱" (in a boiler, etc) scale；incrustation ❷ (in a mug, etc) water stain

水银 shuǐyín (popular term for 汞) mercury；quicksilver

水印 shuǐyìn ❶ watercolour block printing ❷ watermark (as of a banknote) ❸ water stain (on furniture, etc)

水域 shuǐyù waters；water area；body or mass of water：国际～ international waters

水源 shuǐyuán ❶ source of a river; headwaters ❷ water source

水灾 shuǐzāi *also* "水患" flood; inundation; ～面积 flood-stricken or flooded area

水藻 shuǐzǎo algae

水涨船高 shuǐzhǎngchuángāo 〈俗〉 when the river rises the boat goes up; a rising tide lifts all boats

水质 shuǐzhì water quality; ～污染 water pollution

水中捞月 shuǐzhōnglāoyuè fish for the moon in the water — make impractical or vain efforts; cry for the moon

水肿 shuǐzhǒng 〈医〉oedema; dropsy

水准 shuǐzhǔn ❶ horizontal plane; level (surface) ❷ *see* "水平❷"

水族 shuǐzú aquatic animals; ～馆 aquarium

shuì

说 shuì try to persuade or bring round; ～客 canvasser; lobbyist *see also* shuō

税 shuì tax; duty; tariff; ～单 tax return or receipt / ～额 amount of tax to be paid / ～负 tax burden / ～率 tax or tariff rate / ～后收入 income after tax; after-tax income / ～收杠杆 taxation lever; tax incentive

税务 shuìwù taxation; ～局 tax bureau / ～员 tax collector; revenue agent

睡 shuì sleep; ～袋 sleeping bag / ～梦 sleep; slumber; dream / ～袍 nightgown / ～衣 night clothes; pyjamas / ～意 sleepiness; drowsiness / ～过了 oversleep / ～眼惺忪 sleepy-eyed; eyes heavy or fogged with sleep

睡觉 shuìjiào sleep; go to bed; 睡懒觉 get up late; sleep in

睡莲 shuìlián 〈植〉water lily

睡眠 shuìmián sleep; ～不足 insuffi-

cient sleep / ～疗法 〈医〉physiological sleep therapy

shǔn

吮 shǔn suck

吮吸 shǔnxī *also* "吸吮" suck; ～乳汁 suck milk / ～老百姓的血汗 bleed the people white

shùn

顺 shùn ❶ in the same direction as; along (with); ～沟流 flow along a ditch / ～竿儿爬 chime in with sb (in order to please); readily fall in with sb's wishes / ～时针方向 clockwise ❷ arrange; sort out; 把头发梳一～ smooth the hair ❸ act at one's convenience; take the opportunity; ～访 visit on the way (to another place); stop over / ～嘴说出 say offhandedly; blurt out ❹ suitable; agreeable; favourable; ～差 (in foreign trade, etc) favourable balance; surplus / ～产 〈医〉natural labour / ～耳 pleasing to the ear / ～境 favourable circumstances / ～眼 pleasing to the eye; pleasant to look at ❺ in good luck; smoothly; successfully; ～当 smoothly; harmoniously; without a hitch / ～遂 go satisfactorily or smoothly ❻ in sequence; ～次 in order; in proper sequence; successively / ～延 postpone accordingly ❼ obey; yield or submit to; ～服 obey; submit; yield / ～民 〈贬〉docile subject; yes-man / ～我者昌, 逆我者亡. (of one's attitude towards dissidence) Those who submit will prosper; those who resist shall perish.

顺便 shùnbiàn *also* "顺带" incidentally; in passing; ～去一趟 go at one's convenience; drop in when one is free

顺畅 shùnchàng smooth; unhindered;

S

呼吸～ breathe easily / 文笔～（wield a) facile style

顺从 shùncóng ❶ obey; comply with; yield to:～民心 fall in with popular will ❷ *also*“顺服”docile; submissive; obedient

顺风 shùnfēng　go before the wind; have a favourable or tail wind:～耳 one who can hear distant voices (be well in the wind) / 〈喻〉well-informed person /～转舵 trim one's sails to the wind; chop around with the wind / 祝你一路～。Have a pleasant journey.

顺口 shùnkǒu ❶ (of writing, etc) read smoothly:～溜 doggerel; jingle ❷ speak casually; say offhandedly:～搭音儿 chime in with others; echo what others say; readily agree ❸〈方〉(of food) suit one's taste; be palatable

顺理成章 shùnlǐchéngzhāng　logical; coherent; well reasoned:这样做～。It is a matter of course.

顺利 shùnlì　smoothly; favourably; successfully:～抵达 arrive without a hitch

顺溜 shùnliu 〈方〉❶ in good order; tidy ❷ smoothly; without a hitch:日子过得～ lead a serene life

顺路 shùnlù　*also*“顺道”❶ on the way:～采购 do New Year shopping on one's way (to do sth else) ❷ direct route:这么走～。This is the most direct route (to a place).

顺势 shùnshì　take advantage of an opening, situation or momentum:一～推 push with the momentum /～溜走 seize an opportunity to sneak away

顺手 shùnshǒu ❶ (of a tool, etc) handy; convenient ❷ smooth; without difficulty or trouble:工作不～ find one's work hard-going ❸ do sth as a natural sequence or in passing:～关门 close the door after one /～牵羊 lead a goat away in passing; pick sth up by stealth; walk off with sth

顺水 shùnshuǐ　downstream; with the current:～推舟 push the boat along with the current — swim with the tide; go with the flow /～人情 favour done at little or no cost to oneself

顺藤摸瓜 shùnténgmōguā　follow the vine to get the melon — track down by following a clue; hunt for by following the traces

顺心 shùnxīn　(of sb) happy and content; (of sth) gratifying; (do sth) as one wishes:事事～ find everything to one's liking

顺序 shùnxù ❶ sequence; order:按年代～ in chronological order ❷ in proper order; in turn

顺应 shùnyìng　follow; comply with; conform to:～时代潮流 conform to the trend of the times; keep up with the march of events

瞬 shùn　wink; twinkling:(一)～间 in the twinkling of an eye / 时速度 instantaneous velocity /～息万变 undergo a myriad of changes in an instant; change rapidly

shuō

说 shuō ❶ speak; say; explain:～书（professional) storytelling /～戏 explain or explicate a play (to the cast) /～不得 unspeakable; unmentionable /～到底 in the last analysis; at bottom /～得来 see eye to eye; hit it off (with sb) /～到做到 do what one says; practise what one preaches; live up to one's word /～来话长。It's a long story. /～曹操,曹操就到。Speak of the devil and there he is. ❷ act as go-between or matchmaker; introduce:～合 bring two or more parties together; help bring about /～媒 “说亲” act as a matchmaker /～个朋友 find a girlfriend for sb ❸ theory; views; doctrine ❹ scold; criticize:把人

～哭了 scold sb into tears
see also shuì

说不定 shuōbùdìng perhaps；maybe；possibly

说不过去 shuōbuguòqù cannot be justified or explained away；be unreasonable or untenable：说得过去 justifiable；passable；so-so

说不上 shuōbushàng ❶ *also* "说不清" cannot explain clearly or predict；cannot say or tell for sure ❷ not worth mentioning；no … to speak of：这种顺口溜 ～ 是 诗。Such doggerel is no poetry (to speak of).

说辞 shuōcí alibi；excuse；pretext：编 ～ make up excuses；find a pretext

说…道… shuō…dào… *used before two parallel adjectives or numerals to indicate the range of the remark*：说长道短 comment on other people's merits and demerits；gossip / 说东道西 chatter or rattle away under anything under the sun / 说三道四 make irresponsible remarks；gossip

说法 shuōfa ❶ way of saying a thing；wording；formulation ❷ view；argument：新 ～ new theory ❸ (equitable) judgement or solution；(justifiable) explanation：讨 个 ～ demand an explanation；ask for an equitable judgement

说服 shuōfú persuade；convince；talk (sb) over：有 ～ 力 convincing；persuasive

说和 shuōhe *also* "说合" mediate a settlement；make peace between；compose a quarrel

说话 shuōhuà ❶ speak；talk；say；爱 ～ talkative；loquacious / ～算话 keep one's word / 说大话 boast；talk big；blow one's own trumpet / 说闲话 gossip；prattle；chat / 说风凉话 make irresponsible and sarcastic remarks ❷ chit-chat；chat；talk ❸ gossip；censure ❹ in a minute；right away：我～就来。I shan't be a minute.

说谎 shuōhuǎng tell untruths or lies；

lie：～的人 liar

说教 shuōjiào ❶ 〈宗教〉deliver a sermon；preach ❷ 〈喻〉preachify；preach：～式文章 didactic writing

说客 shuōkè ❶ person good at persuasion ❷ 〈贬〉person sent to win sb over through persuasion；lobbyist

说理 shuōlǐ ❶ reason (things out)；argue：没法跟他 ～. There is no reasoning with him. ❷ be reasonable or sensible：你们～不～? Don't you listen to reason?

说明 shuōmíng ❶ explain；illustrate；show：～ 书 guidebook；(technical) manual；synopsis (of a play, etc) / 文 expository writing；exposition ❷ explanation；directions；caption ❸ prove；show；uphold

说破 shuōpò *also* "说穿" expose；reveal；disclose：一 语 ～ lay bare the truth with one penetrating remark；hit the nail on the head

说情 shuōqíng *also* "说项" plead for mercy (for sb)；put in a good word；intercede

说头儿 shuōtour ❶ sth to talk about；sth worthy of discussion ❷ excuse；pretext

说笑 shuōxiào ❶ talk and laugh ❷ laugh at；ridicule：惹人 ～ invite ridicule；be a laughing stock

说一不二 shuōyī-bù'èr mean what one says；stand by one's word；never change one's view；在家里 ～ never allow anyone to contradict one at home；one's word goes in the family / 他是个 ～的人。He is a man of his word.

shuò

烁(爍) shuò bright；brilliant；shining

铄(鑠) shuò 〈书〉❶ melt (metal, etc)：～石流金 (hot enough to) melt stone and metal — intense heat; sweltering ❷ waste away; weaken

朔 shuò ❶ also "朔月" new moon ❷ also "朔日" first day of the lunar month ❸ (usu 朔方) north

硕 shuò dà huge; large. ~ 学〈书〉scholarly (person); learned (scholar)

硕大 shuòdà huge; enormous. ~ 无朋 of unparalleled size; colossal; huge

硕果 shuòguǒ rich fruit; tremendous achievement. ~ 仅存 rare survival

硕士 shuòshì master. 理学 ~ Master of Science (MS) / 文学 ~ Master of Arts (MA) / ~ (研究)生 postgraduate studying for a master's degree; MA or MS candidate / ~ 学位 master's degree

数(數) shuò〈书〉often; frequently; repeatedly. ~ 见不鲜 also "屡见不鲜" what is often seen; common occurrence; nothing new *see also* shǔ; shù

sī

司 sī ❶ take charge of; attend to; manage. ~ 机 driver; chauffeur / ~ 药 pharmacist; druggist; chemist / ~ 仪 master of ceremonies (MC) / 各 ~ 其职. Each attends to his or her own work. ❷ department (under a ministry)

司法 sīfǎ administration of justice; judicature. ~ 界 judicial circles; the bar / ~ 权 judicial powers; jurisdiction / ~ 鉴定 expert testimony or evidence

司空见惯 sīkōngjiànguàn commonly seen; common; commonplace

司令 sīlìng commander. ~ 部 command; headquarters

丝(絲) sī ❶ silk. ~ 绵 silk floss / ~ 绒 velvet; velour / ~ 织品 silk fabric or knitwear ❷ anything threadlike. 钢 ~ steel wire / ~ 竹 (music played with) traditional

stringed and woodwind instruments ❸ tiny or least bit. 一 ~ 亮光 a thread of light / 一 ~ 笑容 a trace of smile

丝绸 sīchóu silk (cloth). ~ 之路〈史〉Silk Road

丝瓜 sīguā loofah; sponge gourd. ~ 络 also "丝瓜精" loofah; vegetable sponge

丝毫 sīháo (usu in the negative) least bit; at all. ~ 不爽 tally in every detail; be perfectly right

丝丝入扣 sīsīrùkòu (of writing or performance) with flawless skill; done to perfection

私 sī ❶ personal; private. ~ 产 private property; personal possession / ~ 活 moonlighting / ~ 事 private affair; personal matter / ~ 塾 old-style tutorial school / ~ 生活 one's private life / ~ 淑弟子〈书〉self-styled disciple (of a master never studied under) / ~ 发泄 — 愤 vent personal grudges ❷ selfish. ~ 党 (member of) clique or faction privately formed to further selfish interests / ~ 利 selfish interests; personal gain / ~ 欲 selfish desire ❸ secret; stealthy; private. ~ 奔 elope / ~ 了 settle in private; settle out of court; compound ❹ illicit; illegal; unlawful. ~ 盐 contraband salt / ~ 生子 child born out of wedlock; illegitimate child / ~ 设公堂 set up an illegal court; form a kangaroo court / ~ 吞公款 embezzle or misappropriate public funds / ~ 运军火 (engage in) gun-running

私房 sīfang ❶ private savings. ~ 钱 private savings of a family member ❷ secret; confidential. 说 ~ 话 talk in confidence; exchange confidences

私访 sīfǎng visit secretly; inspect in disguise

私交 sījiāo personal friendship. ~ 甚厚 be on good terms (with sb) personally

私立 sīlì　privately run; private;～学校 private school; (UK) public school

私情 sīqíng　❶ personal friendship or sentiments ❷ illicit or secret love;儿女～ young people's secret love

私人 sīrén　❶ private;～秘书 private secretary ❷ personal; individual;～恩怨 personal gratitudes and resentments; personal friendships and enmities ❸ personal friend, relative or protégé;任用～ fill posts with one's own people; practise nepotism

私通 sītōng　❶ have secret ties with; collude secretly with ❷ have illicit intercourse or liaison; commit adultery

私下 sīxià　also "私下里" in private or secret;～了结 settle out of court

私心 sīxīn　❶ heart; innermost being;～佩服之至 admire wholeheartedly ❷ selfish motives; selfishness;～杂念 selfish ideas and personal considerations

私刑 sīxíng　extralegal punishment or torture;～处死 lynch

私营 sīyíng　privately operated or run; private;～经济 private (sector of the) economy

私有 sīyǒu　privately owned; private;～化 privatize; denationalize /～制 private ownership

私语 sīyǔ　❶ whisper; speak in a low voice ❷ talk in confidence; speak in private

私自 sīzì　without permission; on the sly

嗯（嘶） sī　〈象声〉(as of bullets) whistle

思 sī　❶ think; consider; ponder;〈书〉ponder; consider; mull over /～前想后 think over again and again; mull or ponder over ❷ think of; long or wish for; miss;～春 (of a young girl) have thoughts of love /～凡 (as of fairies or nuns) long for the secular life /～恋 remember or think of fondly /～乡 miss one's native place; be homesick /～贤若渴 thirst for the assistance of talented people; be eager to enlist able people ❸ idea; train of thought;～如泉涌 ideas gushing out like spring water; ideas teeming in one's head

思辨 sībiàn　❶〈哲〉reason; speculate;～哲学 speculative philosophy ❷ also "思辩" think and analyse;～能力 analytical ability

思潮 sīcháo　❶ trend or current of thought ❷ (surging) thoughts;～汹涌 thoughts surging in one's mind

思考 sīkǎo　think deeply; ponder; consider;经过周密～ well considered

思量 sīliang　❶ consider; turn over in one's mind;～利弊 weigh the pros and cons ❷〈方〉think of; long for; miss

思路 sīlù　train of thought; line of thinking;打断～ interrupt sb's train of thought; lose one's thread of thought /～开阔 have broad vision; be broadminded

思虑 sīlǜ　consider; reflect on; deliberate;～不周 ill-considered; ill-advised /～重重 be lost in contemplation

思慕 sīmù　think of with esteem or longing; admire

思念 sīniàn　think of; miss

思索 sīsuǒ　think deeply; reflect; ponder; 苦苦～ think long and hard; do some hard thinking

思维 sīwéi　also "思惟" thought; thinking;～方式 mode or way of thinking /～敏捷 quick-witted

思想 sīxiǎng　❶ thought; thinking; ideology;～家 thinker /～性 ideological content or level /～斗争 ideological struggle; mental conflict; soul searching /～顾虑 sth weighing on one's mind; misgivings /～境界 ideological level; moral stature /～意识 ideology /～有～准备 be mentally prepared ❷ idea;产生出国学习的～ conceive an idea of studying abroad ❸ see

"思量❶"

思绪 sīxù ❶ train of thought; line of thinking: ~万千 be lost in a myriad of thoughts ❷ feeling; mood: ~不宁 feel anxious or worried

斯 sī 〈书〉this; here: 生于~，长于~ be born and bred here

斯文 sīwén ❶ 〈书〉learning; culture; learned person: ~扫地 learning and refinement are swept into the dust; (one's) scholarly dignity is thoroughly degraded ❷ (sīwen) refined; gentle

厮(廝) sī ❶ 〈旧〉male servant ❷ each other; together: ~打 come to or exchange blows; tussle / ~混 〈贬〉live or be together; mix (in company) / ~杀 fight at close quarters; engage in hand-to-hand combat / ~守一辈子 be lifelong companions

锶 sī 〈化〉strontium (Sr)

撕 sī tear; rip; scrap: ~毁 tear up; scrap / ~票 (of kidnappers) kill a hostage / ~破脸 quarrel openly

嘶 sī ❶ 〈书〉(of horses) neigh ❷ (usu 嘶哑) hoarse ❸ 〈象声〉whistle

sǐ

死 sǐ ❶ die; cease to live; be dead: ~机(信息) (of a computer) go dead / ~难 die in an accident, etc / ~人 corpse; 〈谑〉devil; lazybones / ~者 the dead; the deceased / ~罪 capital offence or crime / ~火山 extinct or dead volcano / ~得其生 escape by the skin of one's teeth; have a narrow escape / ~无对证 the dead cannot bear witness; dead men tell no tales / ~于非命 die an unnatural or a violent death ❷ to the death; determinedly; adamantly; unyieldingly: ~党 diehard follower; sworn supporter / ~不改悔 die impenitent; be absolutely unrepentant or incorrigible / ~不要脸 be dead to all sense of shame; be utterly shameless; have no sense of shame whatever ❸ very; extremely: ~寂 〈书〉deathly stillness or silence / ~要面子 be extremely anxious to keep up appearances / 忙~了 be extremely busy; as busy as a bee ❹ implacable; deadly; irreconcilable: ~敌 deadly or mortal enemy; sworn enemy; implacable foe ❺ fixed; rigid; inflexible: ~理 rigid and inflexible rules; dogma / ~读书 study mechanically; read without thinking; be a bookworm / ~脑筋 one-track mind; old fogey / ~记硬背 learn by rote; memorize mechanically ❻ impassable; closed: ~胡同 blind alley; impasse; dead end

死板 sǐbǎn rigid (rules, etc); stiff (language, etc); inflexible (approach, etc)

死不瞑目 sǐbùmíngmù would not close one's eyes when one dies; would not rest easy in one's grave; die with regret

死地 sǐdì fatal position; death trap: 置人于~ put sb in a death trap; drive sb into a corner

死灰复燃 sǐhuīfùrán dying embers flaring up again; 〈贬〉resurgence or revival of sth that has been regarded as dead or dying

死活 sǐhuó ❶ life or death; lot; fate: 不顾别人的~ not care a damn about others ❷ 〈口〉anyway; simply: ~不同意 simply wouldn't agree / 死说活说 try to persuade by all means; importune incessantly

死角 sǐjiǎo ❶ 〈军〉dead or blind angle; dead space ❷ spot as yet unaffected by a movement, etc; backwater

死结 sǐjié also "死扣儿" fast knot: 打个~ tie a fast knot / 心头上的一个~

a fast knot on one's mind

死路 sǐlù blind alley; dead end; road to ruin or destruction: ~一条 be faced with nothing but destruction; be certain to meet one's doom

死命 sǐmìng ❶ doom; death: 制敌于 ~ deal the enemy a death blow; send the enemy to his doom ❷ also "死力" desperately; recklessly: 拼 ~ strain every effort; exert one's utmost / 逃跑 run as fast as one's legs can carry one; run for dear life

死皮赖脸 sǐpí-làiliǎn also "死气白赖" thick-skinned; utterly shameless; brazen-faced

死气沉沉 sǐqìchénchén lifeless; listless; stagnant

死囚 sǐqiú condemned prisoner: ~牢房 condemned cell; death cell

死去活来 sǐqù-huólái half dead, half alive; more dead than alive: 被折磨得 ~ be tortured within an inch of one's life

死伤 sǐshāng the dead and the wounded; casualties; toll of lives: ~惨重 (of people) suffer heavy casualties; (of a battle, etc) take a terrible toll of lives

死神 sǐshén god in charge of deaths — death: 从~手里夺回来 save (sb) from the jaws of death

死守 sǐshǒu ❶ defend (a position, etc) to the death; put up a last-ditch resistance ❷ obstinately cling to (sth outmoded, etc); stick fast to

死水 sǐshuǐ stagnant or standing water: 一潭 ~ a pool of stagnant water; a stagnant and lifeless situation

死亡 sǐwáng death; mortality; extinction: ~率 death rate; mortality / 在~线上挣扎 struggle on the verge of death; struggle for survival

死心 sǐxīn abandon an idea altogether; cherish no more illusions: 仍不 ~ would not give up (one's idea, etc)

死心塌地 sǐxīntādì (do sth) with all

one's heart; be dead set (on doing sth); completely

死心眼儿 sǐxīnyǎnr ❶ stubborn; mulish ❷ person with a one-track mind

死刑 sǐxíng 〈法〉 capital punishment; death penalty or sentence: ~缓期执行 (shortened as 死缓) death sentence with a (two-year) reprieve; stay of execution

死硬 sǐyìng stiff and inflexible; intransigent; diehard: ~派 also "死硬分子" diehard

死有余辜 sǐyǒuyúgū even death would not be sufficient punishment; the crime calls for more than death; even death is too good for sb

死战 sǐzhàn (fight a) life-and-death battle: 决一 ~ wage a life-and-death struggle; fight to the death

sì

巳 sì 6th of the Earthly Branches see also "干支" gānzhī

四 sì four; fourth; on four sides: ~化 (short for 四个现代化) four modernizations (of agriculture, industry, national defence, and science and technology) / ~季 four seasons; all the year round / ~邻 close neighbours / ~野 vast expanses of open country / ~周 all around / ~大皆空 (of Buddhism) everything in this world is void; all is vanity / ~分之一 one fourth; a quarter / ~舍五入 〈数〉 rounding (off); to the nearest whole number / ~座哗然。 The audience burst into an uproar. / ~谣言一起。 Rumours came thick and fast.

四边 sìbiān (on) four sides: ~形 quadrangle; tetragon / ~围着不少人 with many people around

四不像 sìbùxiàng ❶ (popular name for 麋鹿 〈动物〉 milu; David's deer

❷ nondescript; neither fish, flesh, nor fowl

四处 sìchù　all around; far and near; everywhere; ~寻找 search high and low; look into every nook and cranny

四方 sìfāng　❶ four directions; all sides or quarters; ~游客 tourists from everywhere ❷ square or cubic; 迈~步 walk with a leisurely and measured stride

四分五裂 sìfēn-wǔliè　fall apart; be rent asunder; disintegrate

四海 sìhǎi　four seas — the whole country or world; ~为家 make one's home wherever one is; lead a wandering life

四合院 sìhéyuàn　traditional, residential compound with houses around a courtyard; courtyard house; quadrangle

四面 sìmiàn　(on) four sides; (on) all sides; ~八方 (from) all directions or quarters; all around; everywhere / ~楚歌 be exposed to attack on all sides; be utterly isolated

四平八稳 sìpíng-bāwěn　methodical and well-balanced; stable and dependable; overcautious and lacking in initiative

四声 sìshēng　❶ the four tones of standard modern Chinese pronunciation: high and level tone (阴平, or 1st tone 一声, marked "‑"), rising tone (阳平, or 2nd tone 二声, marked "ˊ"), falling-rising tone (上声, or 3rd tone 三声, marked "ˇ"), and falling tone (去声, or 4th tone 四声, marked "ˋ") ❷ specific tone of a Chinese character

四书五经 Sìshū-Wǔjīng　Four Books and Five Classics, major works constituting the Confucian canon, with the former comprising *The Analects of Confucius* (论语), *Mencius* (孟子), *The Great Learning* (大学), and *The*

Doctrine of the Mean (中庸), and the latter made up of *The Book of Changes* (易), *Collection of Ancient Texts* (书), *The Book Of Songs* (诗), *The Rites* (礼), and *The Spring and Autumn Annals* (春秋)

四体 sìtǐ　〈书〉four limbs; arms and legs; ~不勤, 五谷不分 (贬) can neither do physical work nor tell the five grains apart

四通八达 sìtōng-bādá　extend in all directions; be accessible from all directions

四月 sìyuè　❶ April ❷ fourth month of the lunar year; fourth moon

四肢 sìzhī　four limbs; arms and legs; ~健全 be sound in body; be physically sound

寺 sì　temple; mosque; monastery; ~庙 temple (for gods or well-known historical figures) / ~院 temple; monastery; cloister

似 sì　❶ similar; like; as; ~箭离弦 run away or fly like an arrow / ~水年华 *also* "似水流年" time passes as swiftly as flowing water; youth will not endure ❷ look; seem; appear; ~曾相识 seem familiar (to one) / ~是而非 apparently true but actually false; specious; plausible ❸ *used for comparison, usu indicating superiority*; 一天好~一天 get better day by day
see also shì

似…非… sì…fēi…　*used before the same word to indicate both similarity and dissimilarity*; 似懂非懂 have half knowledge / 似醉非醉 be half-drunken

似乎 sìhū　it seems that; as if; seemingly; 他~很苦恼。He seems to be very vexed.

伺 sì　keep watch; await; observe; ~机 watch for one's chance
see also cì

祀 sì　〈书〉offer sacrifices to gods or ancestors

饲 sì ❶ raise; breed; rear ❷ (usu 饲料) forage; feed; fodder

饲养 sìyǎng raise; rear; ～场 feed lot; animal farm / ～业 livestock or poultry farming / ～员 stockman; poultry raiser; animal keeper (in a zoo)

俟(竢) sì 〈书〉wait: ～机出击 wait for the right moment to attack

肆 sì ❶ wantonly; wilfully: ～虐 indulge in wanton destruction; wreak havoc; run rampant / ～意 brazenly; recklessly; wilfully / ～无忌惮 reckless and unbridled; unscrupulous ❷ four (used for the numeral 四 to avoid mistakes or alterations) ❸ 〈书〉shop

嗣 sì ❶ succeed; inherit: ～位 succeed to the throne ❷ heir; inheritor; descendant: 子～ son; male offspring

sōng

松(❷-❺ 鬆) sōng ❶ pine: ～仁 pine nut kernel / ～涛 soughing of the wind in the pines / ～香 rosin ❷ loose; slack and flaky; fluffy: ～脆 light and crisp ❸ loosen; relax; relieve: ～手 loosen one's grip; let go / ～心 relaxed; carefree / ～紧带 elastic (cord) / ～口气 heave a sigh of relief; gain breathing space ❹ not hard up; well off: 手头～多了 be much better off ❺ dried meat or fish floss

松绑 sōngbǎng untie (sb); 〈喻〉free (an enterprise, etc) from unwarranted restrictions or control

松弛 sōngchí ❶ limp; flabby; slack ❷ lax (discipline, etc)

松动 sōngdòng ❶ become less crowded: 人群开始～. The crowd began to fall away. ❷ become loose: 牙齿～ loose tooth ❸ become flexible: 立场

～ soften in one's stance

松节油 sōngjiéyóu 〈化〉turpentine (oil)

松口 sōngkǒu ❶ relax one's bite and release what is held; let go the bite ❷ be less intransigent; moderate; relent

松快 sōngkuai ❶ at ease; relieved ❷ not crowded; spacious

松气 sōngqì ❶ relax one's breathing; breathe freely ❷ also "松劲" feel relieved; slacken (off) relax one's efforts

松软 sōngruǎn ❶ soft; spongy; loose ❷ feeble; weak: 浑身～ feel weak all over

松散 sōngsǎn ❶ loose; not firm or compact: 结构～ loosely structured / ～的土质 porous soil ❷ lax; inattentive; wandering: 注意力～ unable to concentrate; inattentive

松鼠 sōngshǔ 〈动物〉squirrel

松松垮垮 sōngsong-kuǎkuǎ ❶ (of structure) not solid or compact; rickety ❷ lax and undisciplined; slack and perfunctory

松懈 sōngxiè ❶ slacken; slack: ～斗志 slacken one's will to fight ❷ undisciplined; weak-willed ❸ see "松散❷"

嵩(崧) sōng 〈书〉high (mountain); lofty

sǒng

怂(慫) sǒng

怂恿 sǒngyǒng instigate; incite; egg on: ～闹事 foment trouble; incite a riot

耸(聳) sǒng ❶ towering; high; lofty: ～立 tower aloft; rise high / ～入云霄 tower to the skies ❷ alarm; attract (attention): ～人听闻 try to create a sensation; sensational; alarmist ❸ shrug (shoulders); prick up (ears, etc)

耸动 sǒngdòng ❶ see "耸❸" ❷ create a sensation；～视听 intend to cause a sensation

悚 sǒng 〈书〉fear；dread；毛骨～然 with one's hair standing on end

竦 sǒng ❶〈书〉respectful；deferential；～然起敬 hold（sb）in high esteem ❷ see "悚" sǒng

sòng

讼 sòng ❶ bring a case to court；～案 case in court / ～棍 legal pettifogger；shyster ❷ argue

宋 Sòng Song Dynasty（960–1279）；～体（字）Song typeface

送 sòng ❶ send；deliver；carry；～审 submit（report, etc）for approval or revision / ～信儿〈口〉convey a message；send word / ～货上门 deliver goods to the doorsteps（of a customer）；provide home delivery service ❷ give as a present；offer；give；～人情 do sb a good turn（to curry favour）；〈方〉give gifts ❸ see off；go along with；accompany；～葬 also "送丧"；"送殡" attend a funeral；take part in a funeral procession / ～终 look after a dying parent or elder relative；arrange for the burial of a deceased parent or elder relative / ～往迎来 speed the parting guests and welcome the new arrivals；engage in the work of reception

送命 sòngmìng lose one's life；get killed；die；险些～ have a narrow escape

送死 sòngsǐ 〈口〉court death；白白～ die in vain

送行 sòngxíng ❶ also "送别" see（sb）off；bid（sb）farewell；wish（sb）bon voyage ❷ also "饯行" give a send-off party ❸〈婉〉attend sb's funeral

诵 sòng ❶ read aloud；declaim；chant；～读 read aloud；chant ❷

recite；repeat from memory ❸ state；relate；narrate

颂 sòng ❶ praise；extol；laud；～扬 eulogize；laud；extol / ～古非今 eulogize the past at the expense of the present；extol the past and condemn the present ❷（usu used in letters）wish；敬～夏安。Wish you a pleasant summer. ❸ ode；paean；eulogy；～词 complimentary address or message；eulogy / ～歌 song；paean

sōu

搜（❶蒐） sōu ❶ look for；collect；gather；～集 collect；gather；solicit ❷ search；～捕 search and arrest；track down；round up / ～缴 search and confiscate / ～身 make a body search；frisk（sb）/ ～寻 search or hunt for；seek

搜查 sōuchá search；ransack；rummage；～证 search warrant

搜刮 sōuguā forcibly seize；extort；fleece；～民脂民膏 rob the people of their wealth；fleece the people

搜罗 sōuluó collect；gather；recruit；～人才 recruit qualified personnel；scout for talent

搜索 sōusuǒ search；comb；hunt for；～救援 search and rescue / ～枯肠 also "搜肠刮肚" cudgel or rack one's brains（for ideas or expressions）/ ～引擎〈信息〉search engine

嗖 sōu 〈象声〉whiz；rustle；风声～～ rustling wind / 子弹～～地飞过。Bullets whizzed past.

馊 sōu sour；spoiled（food）；～主意 also "馊点子" rotten or lousy idea

溲 sōu 〈书〉urinate

艘 sōu 〈量〉of ships：五～货轮 five freighters

sǒu

叟 sǒu old man

嗾 sǒu 〈书〉incite (a dog)；〈喻〉instigate；abet；受人～使 act at sb's instigation

薮(藪) sǒu 〈书〉(usu 渊薮) den；haunt

sū

苏(❶❷蘇、甦) sū ❶ revive；come to；～醒 revive；come to；regain consciousness ❷ (Sū) (short for 江苏 or 苏州) Jiangsu；Suzhou；～绣 Suzhou embroidery ❸ (Sū) (short for 苏维埃 or 苏联) soviet；Soviet Union；～俄 Soviet Russia / ～区 Soviet Area (established in China 1927-1937)

苏打 sūdá soda；～水 soda water / ～饼干 soda biscuit

酥 sū ❶ cheese；butter；～油茶 buttered tea ❷ crisp；fluffy；～脆 crisp；(of soil, etc) loose；porous；(of pastry, etc) flaky / ～糖 crunchy candy / ～皮点心 crisp-skinned pastry ❸ shortbread；short-cake；芝麻～ sesame shortbread ❹ limp；weak；frail；～软 limp；soft

sú

俗 sú ❶ custom；practice；convention ❷ popular；common；ordinary；～称 be generally or popularly called or termed；popular name / ～语 also "俗话" popular saying；folk adage / ～文学 popular literature ❸ vulgar；boorish；～气 inelegant；vulgar / ～物 vulgar person or thing；philistine / 不可耐 unbearably vulgar；hopelessly boorish ❹ secular；lay

俗名 súmíng ❶ popular or local name ❷ original name (of a monk or nun)

俗人 súrén ❶ layman (as distinguished from a clergyman) ❷ vulgarian；philistine

俗套 sútào conventional etiquette；convention；stereotype；落了～ conform to convention；follow the beaten track

sù

夙 sù 〈书〉❶ early in the morning；～兴夜寐 rise early and retire late — be hard at work day and night ❷ long-standing；of yore；old；～敌 also "宿敌" enemy of long standing；old enemy / ～怨 also "宿怨" long-running enmity or feud / ～愿 also "宿愿" long-cherished wish

诉 sù ❶ tell；speak out；complain；～苦 vent one's grievances；pour out one's woes / ～说 give an account of；tell；recount ❷ accuse；sue；～状 〈法〉plaint；indictment；petition / ～诸法律 go to law；have recourse to law；take (legal) proceedings / ～诸武力 resort to force；appeal to arms

诉讼 sùsòng 〈法〉lawsuit；litigation；accusation；提出～ bring a lawsuit (against sb) / ～费用 court costs；expenses of a lawsuit / ～代理人 legal representative；process attorney / ～当事人 litigant

肃(肅) sù ❶ respect；esteem；～立 stand respectfully；rise as a mark of respect / ～然起敬 hold (sb) in profound respect or in high esteem ❷ solemn；sombre；～静 solemn and silent / ～穆 solemn and quiet；solemn and respectful；grave / ～杀 〈书〉cold and lifeless ❸ eliminate；eradicate；～反 eliminate counterrevolutionaries / ～ 清 eliminate; clean up; root out / ～贪 root out corruption

素 sù ❶ white ❷ plain; simple; quiet;～净 plain and neat; quiet (colour) / ～雅 simple but elegant; quiet but tasteful / ～妆 simple make-up ❸ (as opposed to meats) vegetables, fruits, etc;～菜 vegetable dish / ～油 vegetable oil ❹ native; indigenous; prime;～材 (source) material / ～数〈数〉prime number / ～性端方 upright by nature ❺ habitually; of long standing;～来 always; regularly / ～日 also "素常" as a rule; usually; ordinarily / ～昧平生 have never met (each other); do not know at all

素描 sùmiáo ❶ sketch ❷ literary sketch

素朴 sùpǔ ❶ simple and unadorned ❷ rudimentary; undeveloped;～唯物主义 naive materialism

素食 sùshí ❶ vegetarian diet ❷ take vegetarian food;～者 vegetarian / ～主义 vegetarianism

素养 sùyǎng level of attainment; qualities;颇有文学～ be well versed in literature

素质 sùzhì quality;道德～ ethical standards / ～教育 quality-oriented education; education aimed at all-round development

速 sù fast; swift; quick; 车～ speed of a vehicle / ～递 express mail service (EMS) / ～溶 quick to dissolve; instant (coffee, etc) / ～算 short-cut counting; rapid calculation / ～战～决 (fight a) battle of quick decision

速成 sùchéng achieve by quick methods; speed up;～班 crash course

速冻 sùdòng quick-freeze;～ 食品 frozen food

速度 sùdù speed;〈理〉velocity; tempo;加～ acceleration / ～计 speedome-

ter / ～滑冰 (shortened as 速滑)〈体〉speed skating

速记 sùjì shorthand; stenography;～员 stenographer

速效 sùxiào quick acting;～药 quick-acting medicine / 有～ produce quick results

速写 sùxiě ❶ rough, quickly-made drawing; sketch ❷ (written) sketch

宿 sù ❶ put up for the night; overnight;～娼 go whoring; visit prostitutes ❷〈书〉long-standing; old;～仇 feud; old grievance / ～疾 long-standing disease; old trouble / ～志 long-cherished aspirations ❸〈书〉old; veteran;～将 battle-tested veteran general

see also xiǔ; xiù

宿命论 sùmìnglùn〈哲〉fatalism;～者 fatalist

宿舍 sùshè living quarters; dormitory; hostel;家属～ living quarters for staff with families; family dorm

宿营 sùyíng (of troops) take up quarters; pitch a tent; camp;野外～ go camping; bivouac

粟 sù millet

嗉 sù *also* "嗉子" crop (of a bird)

塑 sù ❶ model; sculpture; mould;～造 model; portray; create ❷ plastic; synthetic;～ 钢 vinyl-coated steel / ～ 胶 synthetic resin; plastic cement

塑料 sùliào plastic;可降解～ degradable plastics / ～薄膜 plastic film or sheeting / ～大棚 plastic greenhouse (for vegetables and flowers) / ～贴面 plastic-face overlay

塑像 sùxiàng statue;半身～ bust

溯 sù ❶ go up (a stream, etc);～流而上 go up a river; go upstream ❷ trace back; recall; recollect;～源 trace to the source

簌 ^{sù}

簌簌 sùsù ❶〈象声〉rustle ❷〈of tears〉streaming down ❸ shiver

suān

酸(⑤瘊) ^{suān} ❶〈化〉acid；
~性 acid；acidity／ ~雨 acid rain／~碱度 pH value ❷ sour；vinegary；tart；~菜 sauerkraut；pickles／~辣汤 hot and sour soup／ ~牛奶 yogurt；sour milk／~甜苦辣 sour，sweet，bitter，hot — joys and (esp) sorrows of life ❸ sick at heart；sad；grieved；~楚 grieved；painful；distressed／~辛 sad；grieved ❹ of impoverished pedantic scholars；~腐 dull and dogmatic ❺ prickling sensation；ache；~软 aching and limp

酸溜溜 suānliūliū ❶ sour (taste or smell) ❷ aching ❸ sadly envious；somewhat jealous ❹ pedantic

suàn

蒜 ^{suàn} also "大蒜" garlic；~苗
also "蒜薹" garlic pedicel or shoot／~泥 mashed garlic／~头 head or bulb of garlic／~瓣儿 garlic clove

算 ^{suàn} ❶ calculate；count；reckon；~式 equation／~上我。Count me in.／~起来，他今天该到家了。I suppose he'll arrive home today. ❷ plan；figure；calculate；~卦 practise divination (by the use of the trigrams)／ ~命 practise fortune-telling ❸ regard or count as；consider；take for：~得上是个专家 can be counted as an expert ❹ acknowledge；count；be effective：说话~话 mean what one says；be as good as one's word ❺ (followed by了) come；come；let it be；~了，~了，不理他就是了。Come，come，don't you mind him. ❻ also "算是" in the

end；presumably；after all：矛盾~解决了。The problem has been solved after all.

算计 suànji ❶ calculate；reckon；figure ❷ think；consider；plan ❸ expect；figure；estimate ❹ plot；scheme；intrigue：遭人~ fall into sb's trap

算盘 suànpan ❶ abacus；~子儿 beads of an abacus ❷ scheme；design；个人的小~ selfish designs or calculations

算术 suànshù arithmetic；做~ do arithmetic problems；do sums

算数 suànshù ❶ count；hold；be effective ❷ until；学会了才~。You must keep on learning until you master it.

算账 suànzhàng ❶ do accounts；balance the books；make out bills ❷〈喻〉square accounts (with sb)；settle scores；get even：我以后再跟你~！I'll make you pay for this!

suī

尿 ^{suī} urine；~脬 bladder see
also niào

虽(雖) ^{suī} (even) though；
even if：~死犹生 live in the hearts of the people (even) though dead

虽然 suīrán also "虽说" although；(even) though：这孩子~小，但却很懂事。Young as he is，the child is very sensible.

suí

绥 ^{suí}〈书〉❶ peaceful ❷ bring
peace to；pacify；~靖政策〈贬〉appeasement policy

隋 ^{Suí} Sui Dynasty (581-618)

随(隨) ^{suí} ❶ follow；~后
afterwards／~即 immediately；presently；right away／~同 accompany；

go with / ～行 accompany (sb) on a trip / ～葬品 funerary objects; burial articles ❷ comply with; adapt to; go along with; ～和 amiable; obliging; easygoing / 大溜 also "随大流"〈口〉drift with the stream; follow the herd / ～风倒 bend with the wind — be easily swayed; be a weathercock / ～波逐流 drift with the current; follow the trend ❸ (let) do at one's convenience or act at one's discretion; ～笔 informal or familiar essay; sketch; short notes / ～感 random thoughts / ～意 freely; at will; as one pleases ❹ along with (some other action) ❺〈方〉look like; be similar; resemble

随便 suíbiàn ❶ act at one's convenience, discretion, or pleasure; 随你的便. Suit yourself. ❷ as much or as little as one wishes; free; informal; ～吃 help oneself / ～谈谈看法 make some random remarks ❸ at will; at random; casually; 工作随随便便 be slipshod in one's work ❹ any; anyhow; no matter (what, when, how, etc)

随处 suíchù　in all places; everywhere; anywhere; ～可见 can be seen everywhere

随从 suícóng ❶ accompany or follow (one's superior, etc); go along with ❷ retinue; suite; entourage

随地 suídì　all over the place; everywhere; anywhere; 禁止～吐痰! No spitting!

随行就市 suíháng-jiùshì　fix prices according to market changes; (of prices) fluctuate on the basis of market conditions

随机 suíjī　random; ～抽样 random sampling / ～采访 interview at random

随机应变 suíjīyìngbiàn　act according to circumstances; be resourceful

随口 suíkǒu　speak thoughtlessly; blurt out; ～乱说 shoot off one's mouth / ～之言 words that escape one's lips;

offhand remarks

随身 suíshēn　(carry) on one's person; (take) with one; personal; ～听 walkman / ～行李 personal or carry-on luggage

随声附和 suíshēngfùhè　echo what others say; chime in with others' opinion

随时 suíshí ❶ at any time; at all times; ～随地 at any time and in any place; at all times and in all places ❷ whenever necessary or possible; as the occasion demands

随手 suíshǒu　conveniently; immediately; without extra trouble; ～拈来 pick (sth) up at random / ～关门 shut the door behind one

随…随… suí…suí…　*used before two verbs to indicate that one action is immediately followed by the other*; 随叫随到 be on call at any hour; be available at any time / 随修随取. Repairs will be done while you wait.

随心 suíxīn ❶ also "随心所欲" follow one's inclinations; have one's own way ❷ find (sth) satisfactory; be pleased or satisfied; (of sth) to one's liking or taste

随遇而安 suíyù'ér'ān　feel at home wherever one is; take the world as one finds it; be able to adapt to different circumstances

随员 suíyuán ❶ staff of a delegation; retinue; entourage ❷ attaché

suǐ

髓 suǐ ❶ also "骨髓" marrow ❷ something like marrow; 脑～ brains ❸ essence;〈植〉pith

suì

岁（歲、嵗） suì ❶ year; ～人 also "岁

收" state revenue in a fiscal year ❷ year (of age); age; 三～ three years old / 同～ of the same age ❸ 〈书〉 year's harvest

岁暮 suìmù 〈书〉 ❶ year's end ❷ ageing; old

岁数 suìshu 〈口〉 age; year; 上了～ be advanced in years

岁月 suìyuè years; time; 艰苦的～ hard times / ～易逝。How time flies.

祟 suì ❶〈迷信〉evil spirit; ghost ❷ act like an evil spirit; haunt; plague

遂 suì ❶ gratify; satisfy; fulfil; ～愿 have one's wish fulfilled; achieve what one wishes ❷ succeed; 劫机未～事件 abortive hijack ❸〈书〉then; thereupon; hence

碎 suì ❶ break or cut up (into pieces) ❷ broken; fragmentary; scattered; ～纸 scraps of paper / ～步儿 (in) quick short steps ❸ (usu 嘴碎) garrulous; long-winded; talkative

隧 suì (usu 隧道) tunnel

燧 suì flint; ～石 flint / ～木取火 get fire from wood by friction

穗 suì ❶ ear of grain; spike ❷ tassel; fringe ❸ (Suì) *another name for Guangzhou* (广州)

邃 suì 〈书〉❶ (of time or space) remote; distant ❷ profound; deep; ～密 deep; profound; recondite

sūn

孙(孫) sūn ❶ grandchild; ～女 granddaughter / ～子 *also* "孙儿" grandson ❷ generations below that of the grandchild; 孔子的 20 世～ 20th-generation descendant of Confucius ❸ relative belonging to grandchild's generation; 侄～ grandnephew ❹ second growth of a plant

sǔn

损 sǔn ❶ decrease; diminish; lose; ～兵折将 sustain heavy casualties or losses ❷ harm; injure; damage; ～耗 loss; wear and tear; wastage / ～坏 damage; break / ～人利己 harm others to benefit oneself; profit at the expenses of others / ～公肥私 line one's pocket or feather one's nest at public expense ❸〈方〉be sarcastic about; deride; ～人 make caustic remarks about sb; deride sb ❹〈方〉mean; shabby; vicious; 这可够～的! This is really mean!

损害 sǔnhài harm; impair; damage; ～名誉 damage or ruin sb's reputation; blacken sb's name

损伤 sǔnshāng ❶ harm; damage; hurt; ～肌肉 pull a muscle / ～积极性 dampen sb's enthusiasm ❷ (suffer a) loss; ～殆尽 be almost wiped out

损失 sǔnshī lose; ～额 amount of loss

损益 sǔnyì ❶ increase and decrease; 不可～一字 (of writing) admit of no addition or omission; be perfect ❷ profit and loss; gains and losses

笋(筍) sǔn bamboo shoot; ～干 dried bamboo shoots / ～鸡 young or spring chicken; broiler

隼 sǔn *also* "鹘"〈动物〉falcon

榫 sǔn tenon; ～接 joggle / ～眼 mortise

suō

唆 suō instigate; abet; incite; ～弄是非 foment discord

唆使 suōshǐ instigate; foment; abet; 受人～ at sb's instigation

梭 suō shuttle; 无～织机 shuttleless loom

梭镖 suōbiāo spear

梭子 suōzi ❶ shuttle ❷ cartridge clip ❸〈量〉(of ammunition) clip

睃 suō look askance at；偷偷地～了一眼 steal a glance (at)

蓑(簑) suō also "蓑衣" straw or palm-bark rain cape；～笠 large straw or palm-bark rain hat

嗍 suō suck：～手指头 suck fingers

缩 suō ❶ become smaller；contract；shrink：～语 abbreviation / ～印本 reduced-format edition / 微胶卷 microfilm ❷ draw or fall back；withdraw；shrink：～脖子 pull in one's horn；shrink back；flinch / ～成一团 huddle (oneself) up / ～手～脚 shrink (as with cold)；be overcautious or timid / ～头～脑 be timid or fainthearted；shrink or shy away from responsibility

缩编 suōbiān ❶ reduce the size (of the staff, etc)；trim；downsize ❷ see "缩写❷"

缩短 suōduǎn shorten；curtail：～差距 reduce the differences；narrow the gap

缩减 suōjiǎn reduce；economize；cut：～开支 cut back on spending

缩水 suōshuǐ (of cloth, etc) shrink：～率 shrinkage / 股票～。The stocks have shrunk in market value.

缩小 suōxiǎo reduce；lessen；diminish：～包围圈 tighten up a ring of encirclement

缩写 suōxiě ❶ abbreviation：～签字 sign one's initials；initial (sth) ❷ abridge (literary works, esp novels)：～本 abridged edition or version

缩影 suōyǐng miniature；epitome

suǒ

所 suǒ ❶，place；藏身之～ hiding place ❷ used as name of an institution, etc：诊疗～ clinic ❸〈量〉of houses, schools, etc：一～医院 a hospital ❹〈助〉a) used together with 为 or 被, to indicate a passive construction：为人～不齿 be held in contempt b) used before a verb followed by its object：我～敬佩的老师 the teacher I admire c) used in the "是…的" structure for emphasis：这是广大群众～喜闻乐见的。This is very popular among the people. d)〈书〉used before a verb to form a noun phrase：～部 troops under one's command / ～见～闻 what one sees and hears / ～作～为 what one has done；one's behaviour e) used with 有 or 无 to indicate some or none：无～用心 not give serious thought to anything；remain idle

所得税 suǒdéshuì income tax

所属 suǒshǔ ❶ what is under one's command or jurisdiction ❷ what one belongs to or is affiliated with：～单位 one's unit

所谓 suǒwèi ❶ what is called：～自由，就是对必然的认识。What is known as freedom consists in the cognition of necessity. ❷ (implying disagreement or disapproval) so-called：～性解放 the so-called sexual liberation

所向披靡 suǒxiàngpīmǐ also "所向无敌" carry all before one；be irresistible or invincible

所以 suǒyǐ ❶〈连〉a) used in the latter half of a sentence to indicate effect or result：临行匆忙，～未能辞行。I left in a hurry, so I didn't come to say goodbye. b) used between the subject and the predicate to stress the explanation introduced by 是因为 later on：我们之所～弃权，是因为别无选择。We abstained because we had no other choice. ❷〈口〉used with 呀 嘛 to introduce the cause or reason in a separate sentence：～呀！要不我怎么会同意呢？Well, that's just the point, otherwise I wouldn't have agreed.

used in set phrases as an object:不知～ not know what is the matter

所以然 suǒyǐrán the whys and wherefores:说不出个～ cannot explain why it is so

所有 suǒyǒu ❶ own; possess; belong to:～格〈语言〉possessive case / ～权〈法〉proprietary right; ownership; title / ～制（system of）ownership ❷ all

所在 suǒzài ❶ place; site; location ❷ where; 原因～ the reason why; exact cause

索 suǒ ❶ large rope or chain; cable:～道 cableway; ropeway ❷ search, look for:～解 search for an explanation or a solution ❸ demand; ask:～贿 extort bribes / ～价 ask a price; charge / ～取 *also* "索要" ask for; demand; exact ❹〈书〉solitary; all by oneself:～居独处 be all alone; live in seclusion ❺〈书〉dull; insipid:～然寡味 flat and insipid; dull and dry

索赔 suǒpéi claim damages or indemnity:～人 claimer; claimant

索性 suǒxìng may or might as well （do sth）

索引 suǒyǐn index:目录～ catalogue index / 地名～ gazetteer

唢 suǒ

唢呐 suǒnà *suona* horn, a woodwind instrument

琐 suǒ trivial; insignificant; petty:～事 trifles; trivial matters; trivialities / ～碎 *also* "琐细" petty; trifling; trivial

锁 suǒ ❶ lock:～匠 locksmith ❷ lock （up）:～国 close a country to the outside world ❸ chains; ～链 chain; shackles; fetters ❹ lockstitch:～扣眼儿 do a lock stitch on a buttonhole

锁定 suǒdìng ❶ locking:～开关 locking switch ❷ lock on to; zero in on:〈喻〉fix one's attention on:～目标 lock on to or zero in on a target

锁钥 suǒyuè ❶ key:搞好关系的～ key to improving a relationship ❷ strategic gateway （to）

S

T

tā

他 tā ❶ (sometimes of indefinite gender) he; him; his: ~们 (of male or indefinite gender) they; them; their / 系主任~们在开会。The dean and others are at a meeting. ❷ used between a verb and a numeral as a form word: 唱～几句 sing a few lines ❸ (some) other; another: ~人 another person; sb else; others / ～杀〈法〉 homicide / ～乡 place far away from home; alien or distant land

他妈的 tāmāde 〈粗〉hell; shit; fuck: 去～! To hell with it! or Fuck it!

它(牠) tā it; its: ～们 (non-human) they; them; their

她 tā (of female gender or of sth esteemed or treasured) she; her; ～们 (of female gender) they; them; their

趿 tā

趿拉 tāla wear shoes as slippers or with the backs trodden down; shuffle about (in slippers)

塌 tā ❶ collapse; crumble; fall down; ~方 also "坍方" (of the roof of a tunnel, etc) cave in; (of a roadbed, etc) collapse; landslide / 台collapse; fall from power / ～陷 subside; sink; cave in ❷ hang down; droop: ～秧 (of vegetables, etc) droop / ～鼻子 snub or flat nose ❸

calm or settle down: ~下心来念书 settle down to study

踏 tā see also tà

踏实 tāshi also "塌实" ❶ steady and sure; steadfast; stable: 学习认真，～ be earnest and persevering in one's study; be a conscientious student ❷ free from anxiety; at peace: 心里不～ not feel at ease

tǎ

塔 tǎ ❶ (Buddhist) pagoda ❷ tower: ~吊 tower crane / ～楼 tower building; turret

獭 tǎ 〈动物〉otter

tà

拓(搨) tà make rubbings from (inscriptions, etc): ~本 book of rubbings see also tuò

沓 tà 〈书〉crowded; repeated: ~至 come in a continuous stream; keep pouring in see also dá

挞(撻) tà 〈书〉flog; whip: ～伐 send armed forces to suppress; send a punitive expedition against

嗒 tà dejected; unhappy; at a loss: ~然若失 dispirited and at a loss; deeply despondent see also dá

榻 tà long, narrow and low bed; couch

踏 tà ❶ step; tread; walk；～步 mark time; remain where one is / ～青 go for an outing in the country in spring (to enjoy the new greenery) be on the spot；～看 make an on-the-spot investigation

see also 踏

踏勘 tàkān ❶ make an on-the-spot survey (for the design of a railway, reservoir, etc) ❷ make a personal investigation on the scene of a crime, accident, etc

tāi

胎 tāi ❶ foetus; embryo；～儿 (human) foetus; embryo / ～记 *also* "胎痣" birthmark / ～毛 foetal hair / ～生动物 viviparous animal ❷ birth; farrow ❸ padding; stuffing; wadding ❹ roughcast (in the making of china, etc) ❺ tyre；内～ inner tube (of a tyre) / 外～ cover (of a tyre)

tái

台(❶❸❹❻臺、❷檯、颱) tái ❶ terrace; platform; stage; anything so shaped：～秤 platform balance; counter scale / ～词 actor's lines / 柱子 pillar; leading light; mainstay ❷ table; desk，～布 tablecloth / ～扇 desk fan / ～式计算机 desktop (computer) ❸ 〈量〉a) *used of performance on the stage, etc*：一～音乐节目 a musical performance b) *used of a machine, etc*：一 ～收录机 a tape-recorder ❹ station; service：长途电话～ trunk call or long distance service; toll board ❺ 〈敬〉you; your；～鉴 〈套〉(used right after the salutation in a letter) I beg to inform ❻ (short for 台湾) Taiwan：～办 (short for 台湾事务办公室) Taiwan Affairs Office / ～胞 compatriots of Taiwan / ～

独分子 separatist seeking Taiwan independence ❼ (usu 台风) typhoon

台阶 táijiē ❶ (flight of) steps；再上新～〈喻〉scale a new height (in progress, etc) ❷ way or chance to extricate oneself from a predicament：找个～儿下 find a face-saving device or an out for oneself

台球 táiqiú ❶ billiards; billiard ball ❷ 〈方〉table tennis; ping-pong

苔 tái 〈植〉liverwort; moss; lichen：～藓植物 bryophyte

抬(擡) tái ❶ lift; raise：～价 jack, force or hike up prices ❷ (of two or more persons) carry; move：～轿子 carry a sedan chair；〈喻〉lick sb's boots ❸ (usu 抬扛) argue for the sake of arguing; pick a quarrel

抬高 táigāo raise; heighten; promote：打击别人，～自己 build oneself up by belittling others

抬举 táiju praise or promote (sb) to show favour; favour；不识～ not know how to appreciate favours

抬头 táitóu ❶ raise one's head；～挺胸 chin up and chest out / ～不见低头见 be bound to see much of each other ❷ gain ground; rise; look up：终有～之日 be sure to rise in life some day ❸ name of the buyer, payer or receiver (on receipts, bills, etc); space for filling in such a name

跆 tái

跆拳道 táiquándào 〈体〉tae kwon do — Korean boxing

薹 tái bolt of garlic, etc

tài

太 tài ❶ highest; greatest; imperial：～庙 Imperial Ancestral Temple / ～子 crown prince / ～上皇

"super-emperor", title of an emperor who abdicated in favour of his son; 〈喻〉overlord; backstage ruler ❷ extreme(ly); quite; very; ～古 remote antiquity / ～激动 extremely excited / 不～热情 not too enthusiastic; lukewarm ❸ (usu indicating seniority by two generations) great; ～后 emperor's mother; empress dowager; queen mother / ～爷爷 great-grandfather ❹ over; too; excessively; ～过分 going too far; excessive

太白 tàibái　*also* "太白星"〈古〉Venus; Vesper

太极 tàijí　*taiji* — quintessence of the universe; Supreme Ultimate; ～拳 *taijiquan* or t'ai chi ch'uan, a kind of traditional Chinese shadow boxing

太监 tàijiàn　(court) eunuch

太空 tàikōng　firmament; (outer) space; ～服 spacesuit / ～站 space station / ～探测器 space probe

太平 tàipíng　peace and tranquillity; ～间 mortuary; morgue / ～门 emergency exit / ～洋 the Pacific (Ocean) / ～盛世 times of peace and prosperity

太岁 tàisuì　❶ (Tàisuì) *Taisui*, legendary god living underground; ～头上动土 break ground where *Taisui* presides — provoke sb far superior in power or strength ❷ local tyrant or bully; 花花～ lecherous bully; notorious womanizer

太太 tàitai　❶ respectful title for the mistress of the house ❷ Mrs; madame; 住在隔壁的张～ Mrs Zhang next door ❸ (used with my, your, his, etc) wife

太阳 tàiyáng　❶ sun; ～镜 sunglasses / ～能 solar energy / ～系 solar system / ～黑子 sunspot ❷ sunlight; sunshine; sun; 炎热的～ scorching sun ❸ (usu 太阳穴) temples (of head)

汰 tài　discard; eliminate; 优胜劣～ survival of the fittest

态(態) tài　❶ form; state; appearance ❷〈语言〉voice

态度 tàidu　❶ manner; bearing ❷ attitude; approach; ～鲜明 clear-cut stand

态势 tàishì　posture; condition; situation

钛 tài　〈化〉titanium (Ti)

泰 tài　❶ safe; secure; peaceful ❷ extreme; most; ～古 remote antiquity

泰斗 tàidǒu　(short for 泰山北斗) Mount Tai and the Big Dipper — leading scholar of the time; 画坛～ leading painter

泰然 tàirán　calm; composed; self-possessed; ～处之 take calmly; bear with equanimity / ～自若 behave with perfect composure; be self-composed

泰山 tàishān　❶ (Tàishān) Mount Tai (a symbol of great weight or import); 有眼不识～ be so ignorant as not to recognize a celebrity, etc; entertain an angel unawares / 重如～, 轻如鸿毛 be as weighty as Mount Tai or as light as a feather — be poles apart in significance ❷ respectful term for father-in-law (used by a man)

tān

坍 tān　(usu 坍塌 or 坍陷) collapse; crumble; cave in

贪 tān　❶ (be) greedy (for sth); insatiable; corrupt; ～杯 be too fond of drinking / ～财 money-grubbing; avaricious / ～玩 be crazy about play / ～欲 greed; avarice / ～嘴 *also* "贪吃" greedy (for food); gluttonous; ～得无厌 insatiably avaricious; extremely greedy / ～官污吏 corrupt officials ❷ covet; seek; hanker after; ～小便宜 covet small gains; be keen on getting things on the cheap / ～多嚼不烂 bite off more than one can chew

贪婪 tānlán ❶ avaricious; greedy; rapacious ❷ insatiable; greedy; avid; ～地闻着花香 smell a flower greedily

贪恋 tānliàn be greedy for; be reluctant to part with

贪生怕死 tānshēng-pàsǐ cravenly cling to life instead of braving death; be mortally afraid of death; ～之徒 dastardly coward

贪天之功 tāntiānzhīgōng lay claim to what others have achieved; claim credit for what one has done nothing to deserve

贪图 tāntú seek; hanker after; covet

贪污 tānwū corruption; graft; embezzlement; ～公款 embezzle public funds

贪心 tānxīn greed; avarice; rapacity; 变得越来越～ become increasingly greedy

贪赃枉法 tānzāngwǎngfǎ take bribes and bend the law; pervert justice for bribes

摊(攤) tān ❶ spread out; unfold; ～牌 lay one's cards on the table; 〈喻〉 show one's hand; have a showdown ❷ vendor's stand; booth; stall; ～贩 street pedlar or vendor ❸ 〈量〉 used of sth that is spread out; 一～水 a pool of water / 一～工作 a whole lot of work ❹ fry batter in a thin layer; ～鸡蛋 make an omelette ❺ take a share in; share; ～钱买礼物 make a collection to buy a gift ❻ (usu of sth unpleasant) befall; happen to; 倒霉的事全叫我～着了。Bad luck always befalls me.

摊派 tānpài apportion (expenses, work, etc); portion or share out; 财政 ～ financial levies

摊子 tānzi ❶ vendor's stand; booth; stall ❷ the way sth is set out; structure of an institution; set-up; 收拾烂～ clear up a mess

滩(灘) tān ❶ beach; sands; ～地 beach or flood land / ～涂 low beach ❷ shoal; 暗～ hidden shoal

瘫(癱) tān paralysis; ～软 (of legs, etc) weak and limp / ～子 paralytic (person)

瘫痪 tānhuàn ❶ also "风瘫" paralysis; palsy ❷ be paralysed; break down; be at a standstill; 领导班子～。The leadership does not function any more.

tán

坛(❶❸壇、❹罈) tán ❶ altar; platform ❷ raised land for planting flowers, etc; terrace; 花～ (raised) flower bed ❸ (sports, etc) circles; world ❹ earthen jar; jug; ～～罐罐 pots and pans; household goods; 〈喻〉 petty belongings

昙(曇) tán

昙花 tánhuā 〈植〉 broad-leaved epiphyllum; ～一现 〈喻〉 last only briefly; be a flash in the pan

谈 tán ❶ talk; speak; chat; ～论 talk about; discuss / ～心 have a heart-to-heart talk / ～兴 mood to talk; talking mood / ～资 matter for gossip; subject of conversation / ～得来 get along well; hit it off (with sb) / ～恋爱 court (sb); be in love (with each other) / ～笑风生 talk cheerfully and humorously ❷ also "谭" tale; story

谈到 tándào speak of; refer to; mention; 谈不到 also "谈不上" not to speak of; out of the question

谈何容易 tánhéróngyì easier said than done; no easy job; by no means easy

谈虎色变 tánhǔsèbiàn turn pale at the mention of a tiger; get jittery at the mere mention of sth terrifying

谈话 tánhuà ❶ talk; chat; ~人 talk it over with sb; thrash it out with sb ❷ statement

谈判 tánpàn negotiations; talks; ~桌 negotiating table; negotiations

谈天 tántiān chat; make conversation; ~说地 chat or talk about everything under the sun

谈吐 tántǔ style of conversation; ~不俗 have a refined style of conversation; be an elegant speaker

弹（彈） tán ❶ catapult; spring; bounce; ~射 launch (as with a catapult); catapult; eject / ~跳力 jumping capacity ❷ flick; flip; ~冠相庆〈贬〉congratulate each other / ~指之间 in a flash; in the twinkling of an eye ❸ pluck; fluff; tease; ~(棉)花 fluff cotton (with a bow, etc) / ~奏 play or pluck (a stringed musical instrument) ❹ assail or attack (with words); lash out at; impeach; ~劾总统 impeach the President *see also* dàn

弹簧 tánhuáng spring; ~秤 spring balance / ~门 swing door

弹力 tánlì elasticity; resilience; stretch; ~袜 stretch socks

弹性 tánxìng elasticity; resilience; 〈喻〉flexibility; ~外交 flexible or elastic diplomacy / ~工作制 flexible hours of work; flexitime

痰 tán phlegm; sputum; ~盂 spittoon; cuspidor

潭 tán ❶ deep pool; pond ❷ pit; depression

檀 tán *also*"青檀"〈植〉wingceltis

檀香 tánxiāng 〈植〉(white) sandalwood

tǎn

忐 tǎn

忐忑 tǎntè perturbed; mentally disturbed; ~不安 uneasy; fidgety

坦 tǎn ❶ level; even; smooth; ~途 level road; 〈喻〉plain sailing ❷ open; frank; candid; ~陈 state frankly; own up / ~言 say or speak candidly ❸ calm; collected; composed; ~然 calm; unperturbed

坦白 tǎnbái ❶ honest; frank; candid ❷ confess; make a confession; own up; ~从宽, 抗拒从严 be lenient to those who confess their crimes and severe to those who do not

坦诚 tǎnchéng frank and honest; sincere and candid; ~相见 be straightforward and honest towards each other; bare one's heart to sb

坦荡 tǎndàng ❶ (of a road, etc) broad and level ❷ magnanimous; bighearted

坦克 tǎnkè tank; ~兵 *also*"装甲兵" tank or panzer forces; tank man

坦率 tǎnshuài candid; frank; straightforward; ~直言 speak without reservation; state outright

祖 tǎn ❶ leave (the upper part of the body) uncovered; have one's shirt unbuttoned; ~露 uncover; reveal; expose ❷ be biased towards; shield; shelter; ~护 be partial to; protect; shield

毯 tǎn blanket; rug; carpet

tàn

叹（嘆、歎） tàn ❶ sigh; ~气 *also*"叹息" heave a sigh; sigh ❷ recite (poetry) with a cadence; chant ❸ exclaim in admiration; acclaim; praise; ~词〈语言〉interjection; exclamation / ~号〈语言〉exclamation mark (!) / ~赏 admire; praise / ~为观止 hail or acclaim as the acme of perfection /

令人～服 compel or command admiration

炭 tàn ❶ charcoal; carbon; charcoal-like thing：～画 charcoal drawing / ～火 charcoal fire / ～精 any carbon product ❷〈方〉coal

炭疽 tànjū anthrax：～病 anthrax

探 tàn ❶ try to find out; explore; investigate：～秘 probe a secret; explore a mystery / ～风 sound (sb) out; fish for information / ～路 find out the way (to a place) / ～寻 seek; search after; look for / ～照灯 searchlight / ～本穷源 trace to the source; get to the root of a matter ❷ (usu 探子) scout; spy; detective ❸ visit; call on：～监 visit a prisoner / ～视病人 visit a patient ❹ stretch forward; crane：～身 lean forward; bend over / ～头～脑 pop one's head in and look about; pry about furtively

探测 tàncè survey; sound; probe：～器 probe; detector

探戈 tàngē tango

探囊取物 tànnángqǔwù as easy as taking sth out of one's pocket; like duck soup; walkover

探亲 tànqīn go home to visit one's family：～假 home leave

探索 tànsuǒ explore (for hidden treasures, etc); probe (space, etc); seek (truth, etc)

探讨 tàntǎo examine; inquire; probe：～改革的路子 probe new approaches in reform

探听 tàntīng try to find out; inquire about; sound out：～虚实 try to ascertain the strength (of the enemy); try to find out about (sb)

探望 tànwàng ❶ look; glance：四处～ look all around ❷ also "探问" visit; call on

探险 tànxiǎn explore; venture into the unknown：～队 exploring party; expedition / ～家 explorer

碳 tàn 〈化〉carbon (C)：～化 carbonize / ～酸 carbonic acid / ～水化合物 carbohydrate

tāng

汤（湯） tāng ❶ hot or boiling water：～壶 also "汤婆子" metal or earthen hot-water bottle ❷ soup; broth; decoction：～匙 tablespoon; soup spoon / ～料 soup stock / ～药〈中医〉medicinal decoction; herb soup / ～圆 also "汤团" (usu stuffed) dumplings

嘡 tāng 〈象声〉loud ringing sound (of gongs, shots, etc)：嘡 clang

趟 tāng also "蹚" ❶ wade; ford：～过去 wade across (a stream, etc) / ～浑水〈方〉get involved in (sth undesirable) ❷ (usu 趟地)〈农〉turn the soil and dig up weeds (with a hoe, etc)

see also táng

táng

唐 Táng Tang Dynasty (618-907), also used to stand for China：～装 (traditional) Chinese costume / ～人街 Chinatown (overseas) / ～三彩〈考古〉Tang tricolour (pottery)

唐突 tángtū〈书〉❶ brusque; rude; abrupt；行事～ be blunt in behaviour ❷ slight; tamper with; treat irreverently

堂 táng ❶ main room of a house; hall：～屋 central room of the main wing; main wing of a courtyard house ❷ hall or room for a specific purpose：大～〈旧〉principal hall in a yamen; court of law / 音乐～ concert hall ❸ used to indicate kinship with the same paternal grandfather or great-grandfather：～兄妹 first or second cousins (on the paternal side) ❹

〈量〉*used of things or activities related to a room*：两～课 two periods (of class)

堂奥 táng'ào 〈书〉❶ innermost recess of a house；〈喻〉interior of a country ❷〈喻〉depth of thought or knowledge；profundities：未登～ have not acquired profound knowledge；be uninitiated

堂而皇之 táng'érhuángzhī ❶ open；overt；public ❷ in a grand style；impressive

堂皇 tánghuáng ❶ grand；stately；magnificent ❷ high-sounding；highfalutin

堂堂 tángtáng ❶ dignified；impressive：相貌～ (with) dignified looks ❷ having noble aspirations and boldness of vision：～男子汉 man worthy of the name；real man ❸ imposing；awe-inspiring；formidable：～军威 formidable prestige of an army；awe-inspiring military strength

堂堂正正 tángtáng-zhèngzhèng ❶ open and above board：为人～ be an upright and honourable person ❷ impressive or dignified in personal appearance

棠 táng *also* "棠梨"〈植〉birchleaf pear：～棣 〈喻〉brother；brotherly love

塘 táng ❶ dyke；embankment：海～ sea wall ❷ pool；pond ❸ hot-water bathing pool

搪 táng ❶ ward or fend off；keep out (the cold, etc) ❷ evade；shirk；do perfunctorily：～塞 stall off；do perfunctorily ❸ spread (clay, paint, etc) over；daub：～瓷 enamel ❹ *see* "镗" táng

膛 táng ❶ thorax；chest ❷ enclosed space inside sth；chamber (of a furnace, etc)

镗 táng *also* "搪" boring；～床 boring machine；borer

糖 táng ❶〈化〉carbohydrate：～精 saccharin ❷ sugar：～分 sugar (-content) / ～浆 (medicinal) syrup / ～葫芦 sugar-coated haws or other fruit on a stick / ～炒栗子 sugar-roasted chestnuts ❸ *also* "糖果" sweets；candy

糖尿病 tángniàobìng diabetes：～患者 diabetic

糖衣 tángyī sugar-coating：～炮弹 〈喻〉sugar-coated bullet

螳 táng (usu 螳螂) mantis：～臂挡车 overrate oneself and try to hold back an overwhelmingly superior force / ～螂捕蝉，黄雀在后 the mantis stalks the cicada, unaware of the oriole behind — covet gains ahead without being aware of danger behind

tǎng

倘(儻) tǎng (usu 倘若 or 倘使) if；supposing；in case

淌 tǎng drip；trickle；shed：～眼泪 shed tears；weep

躺 tǎng lie；recline；rest：～椅 deck or sling chair / ～倒不干 〈喻〉refuse to work any longer

tàng

烫(燙) tàng ❶ scald；burn：～手 scalding hot；〈喻〉thorny；troublesome ❷ iron；heat up in hot water；warm：～衣服 iron or press clothes ❸ (usu 烫发 or 烫头) perm；have one's hair permed

趟 tàng ❶〈量〉*used of a round trip, etc, or a vehicle that makes such a trip*：去一～西安 make a trip to Xi'an ❷ (marching) ranks：跟不上～ lag behind
see also tāng

tāo

叨 tāo 〈书〉〈套〉 used to thank sb for a favour：～光 much obliged (to you) / ～扰 thank you for your hospitality　see also dāo；dáo

涛（濤） tāo great waves；billows

绦（縧） tāo silk ribbon or braid：～虫 tapeworm

掏 tāo ❶ take，draw or pull out；fish out；～心 open one's heart (to sb) confide one's secrets (in another) / ～耳朵 pick ears / ～腰包 pay out of one's own pocket；foot a bill；pick sb's pocket ❷ dig (a hole，etc)；hollow or scoop out

滔 tāo inundate；flood

滔滔 tāotāo ❶ (of flood，etc) torrential；surging ❷ keep up a flow of words；～不绝 (of words) tumble out in a flood；pour out (words) in a steady flow

滔天 tāotiān ❶ (of billows，etc) dash to the skies；run high ❷ towering；heinous；monstrous (crime)

韬（韜） tāo 〈书〉 ❶ sheath (for a sword，etc)；(bow) case ❷ hide；conceal；～光养晦 also "韬晦" hide one's capacities and bide one's time；lie low ❸ art of war：～略 military strategy

饕 tāo 〈书〉 greedy；gluttonous：老～ glutton；gourmand

饕餮 tāotiè ❶ taotie，a mythical ferocious animal：～纹 〈考古〉 taotie design ❷ ferocious，greedy person；glutton；gourmand

táo

逃 táo ❶ run away；escape；flee：～兵 (army) deserter；〈喻〉 sb who runs away from responsibility or hardship / ～窜 run away in panic；flee in disorder；scurry / ～犯 escaped convict；fugitive criminal / ～跑 run away；take flight；flee / ～生 flee for one's life；escape with one's life / ～脱 make good one's escape；escape scot-free；shake or cast off / ～亡 become a fugitive；flee from home；go into exile / ～之夭夭 take to one's heels；show a clean pair of heels ❷ evade；dodge；shirk：～避 evade；shun；shirk (responsibility，etc) / ～荒 flee from famine / ～课 also "逃学" play truant；cut classes / ～难 flee from a calamity；be a refugee / ～债 evade debts；dodge a creditor

桃 táo ❶ peach；peach-shaped thing：～红 pink / ～花运 〈喻〉 (used of men) luck in love；romance / ～棉 cotton boll ❷ walnut：～酥 walnut shortbread

桃李 táolǐ peaches and plums — pupils or disciples：～满天下 have pupils everywhere

桃色 táosè ❶ peach colour ❷ pertaining to an illicit affair：～新闻 illicit love story；sex scandal

陶 táo ❶ pottery；earthenware：～瓷 pottery and porcelain；ceramics / ～片 〈考古〉 potherds / ～器 pottery；earthenware / ～艺 ceramic art or craft ❷ cultivate；mould；nurture：～冶 exert a favourable influence (on a person's character，etc)；mould；refine ❸ contented；happy：乐～～ happy and gay / ～醉 be intoxicated (with success，etc)；revel in / ～然自乐 be happy and content with one's lot

淘 táo ❶ wash in a pan or basket：～金 wash for gold ❷ clean out；dredge (a well，etc) ❸ 〈方〉 naughty；mischievous

淘气 táoqì naughty；mischievous

淘汰 táotài eliminate through selection or competition: ～赛 elimination series or match

tǎo

讨 tǎo ❶ (usu 讨伐) send armed forces to suppress; send a punitive expedition against; fight ❷ denounce; decry; condemn ❸ demand; ask or beg for; seek: ～还 demand the return of sth; get sth back / ～价还价 bargain; haggle ❹ marry (a woman): ～老婆 take a wife; get married ❺ incur; court; invite: ～嫌 be a nuisance; be disagreeable or annoying / 自～没趣儿 court a rebuff for oneself ❻ explore; study; discuss

讨好 tǎohǎo ❶ try to please; ingratiate oneself with; curry favour with ❷ (often used in the negative) be rewarded with a fruitful result; have one's labour rewarded: 吃力不～的事 thankless, laborious job

讨教 tǎojiào ask for advice; consult: 向专家～ turn to an expert for advice

讨论 tǎolùn discuss; talk over: ～会 discussion; symposium; seminar

讨厌 tǎoyàn ❶ disagreeable; disgusting; repugnant ❷ hard to handle; troublesome; nasty: 眼镜又找不到了，真～! I can't find my glasses again. What a nuisance! ❸ dislike; loathe; hate

tào

套 tào ❶ sheath; case; cover: 袖～ oversleeve / ～上一件上衣 slip on a coat ❷ overlap; interlock; interlink: ～种 also "套作"〈农〉interplanting ❸ cotton padding or wadding; batting ❹ knot; noose; trap: 设～ lay a trap / 双～结 double knot ❺ hitch up; harness: ～马 harness a horse to a cart; lasso a horse ❻ coax a secret out

of; pump (sb about sth); sound out ❼ model on or after; copy; imitate: ～用 apply mechanically; use indiscriminately; copy / ～话 also "套语" polite formula; conventional remark; platitude / 俗～子 conventional pattern; convention ❽ try to win (sb's friendship); rope in; draw over to one's side: ～近乎 "拉近乎" try to form ties with; cotton up to ❾ set; series; suite: ～table d'hote; set meal / ～房 room opening off another; suite; apartment / ～服 also "套装" suit / ～路 established series of movement in *wushu*; established way of thinking, etc ❿〈量〉*used of series or sets of things*: 一～餐具 a dinner set

套汇 tàohuì 〈经〉❶ procure foreign exchange illegally ❷ engage in arbitrage (of foreign exchange)

tè

特 tè ❶ special; unusual; extraordinary: ～产 special local product; speciality / ～等 also "特级" special grade or class; top grade; ace / ～刊 (of a journal, etc) special issue or number; special / ～例 special case; exception / ～区 special (economic) zone (SEZ) / ～性 specific property or characteristic / ～大号 extra large (XL) / ～困生 (short for 特别困难学生) financially-handicapped student / ～效药 specific (drug); effective cure / ～种兵 special troops / ～立独行 be independently minded; not drift with the tide / ～型演员 typecast actor ❷ for a special purpose; specially: ～地邀请 also "特意邀请" specially invite / ～此函告。〈套〉You are hereby informed by letter.

特别 tèbié ❶ special; unusual; peculiar: ～行政区 special administrative region (SAR) ❷ going out of one's way (to do sth); especially ❸ (usu used with 是) especially; particularly; in particular

特长 tècháng　what one is skilled in or good at; strong point; forte: ～生 student with special skills (in sports, etc)

特点 tèdiǎn　distinguishing or unique feature; characteristic; trait

特定 tèdìng ❶ specially designated or appointed: ～人选 specially appointed candidate ❷ specific; specified; given: ～的生活环境 specified or given environment

特工 tègōng　secret service (agent): ～人员 secret service personnel; special agent; spy

特技 tèjì　stunt; trick; special effects: ～飞行 stunt flying; aerobatics / ～摄影 trick photography / ～演员 stunt man or woman

特价 tèjià　special offer; bargain price; sale: ～书 sale book / ～部 bargain counter

特快 tèkuài ❶ express: ～专递 express mail service (EMS) ❷ (short for 特别快车) (special) express; express train

特派 tèpài　specially appointed: ～员 commissioner (of a government, etc) / ～记者 special correspondent; accredited journalist

特权 tèquán　privilege; prerogative; perquisite: ～地位 privileged status / ～思想 idea that one is entitled to privileges; "special privilege" mentality

特色 tèsè　characteristic; distinctive feature or quality: 有中国～的社会主义 socialism with Chinese characteristics

特赦 tèshè　special pardon or amnesty: ～令 decree of special pardon or amnesty

特殊 tèshū　special; particular; exceptional: ～化 become privileged; seek privileges / ～性 particularity; peculi-

arity; specific characteristic / ～条件 specific or exceptional condition

特务 tèwù ❶ special task or duties ❷ (tèwu) special or secret agent; spy

特写 tèxiě ❶ feature (article or story): 新闻～ news features ❷ close-up: ～镜头 close-up (shot)

特许 tèxǔ　special permission: ～进口 import under special license; licensed import / ～经营商店 franchise store

特异 tèyì ❶ exceptionally good; excellent; superfine ❷ peculiar; distinctive: ～功能 extrasensory perception (ESP)

特约 tèyuē　engage by special arrangement; invite specially: ～记者 special correspondent / ～演员 guest actor or actress

特征 tèzhēng　characteristic; feature; trait

tēng

煺 tēng　heat up (cold food, etc) by steaming or baking

téng

疼 téng ❶ also "疼痛" ache; pain; hurt ❷ also "疼爱" love dearly; be fond of; dote on

腾 téng ❶ gallop; jump; bound: ～越 jump over ❷ rise; ascend; soar: ～贵 (of prices) shoot up; soar; skyrocket / ～空 soar; rise high into the air / ～～ soaring; seething; ablaze ❸ make room; release; vacate: ～退 vacate (a house, etc) and return it to the owner / ～出时间 try to make time (for sth); find time ❹ used after a verb to denote repeated action: 倒～ do sth over and over again

腾飞 téngfēi ❶ fly about; soar ❷ (undergo) rapid development; (make a) take-off

腾云驾雾 téngyún-jiàwù ❶ levitate; speed across the sky ❷ feel giddy or dizzy; be totally at sea

誉(謄) téng transcribe; copy out；～录 also "誊写" transcribe; copy out

藤(籐) téng ❶ vine ❷ cane; rattan：～编 (do) rattan basketwork or work

tī

体(體) tī see also tǐ

体己 tīji also "梯己" ❶ also "体己钱" private savings (as distinct from family income, etc) ❷ intimate; confidential：～话 confidences / ～人 confidant

剔 tī ❶ clean with a pointed tool; pick ❷ pick out and reject; get rid of：～除糟粕 get rid of the dross

剔透 tītòu bright and limpid; transparent

梯 tī ❶ ladder; steps; stairs：～子 stepladder; ladder ❷ equipment which functions as a ladder or stairs；电～ lift; elevator ❸ anything shaped like a staircase; terraced：～田 terraced fields; terraces / ～队〈军〉echelon (formation); echelon or line of successors

梯形 tīxíng 〈数〉trapezoid; trapezium

锑 tī 〈化〉antimony (Sb)

踢 tī kick; play (football)：～踏舞 step or tap dance / ～皮球 kick a ball；〈喻〉pass the buck (to and fro)

tí

提 tí ❶ carry (in hand with arm hanging down)：～包 handbag; (shopping) bag; valise ❷ move upward; raise; promote：～价 increase or raise prices / ～神 invigorate; refresh; give a lift / ～速 speed up / ～味 make (food, etc) more appetizing (by adding condiments); season ❸ move up (a date); advance：～前 "提早"的 (sth) in advance or ahead of time; move up (a date); advance ❹ speak of; put forward; submit：～法 way sth is put; formulation; wording / ～亲 make a proposal of marriage (on behalf of a family) / ～问 ask or put a question; quiz / ～请注意 call attention (to) ❺ draw; take out; withdraw：～款 draw or withdraw money (from a bank) / ～单 also "提货单" bill of lading (B/L) ❻ bring or take out from prison; summon：～审 bring (a prisoner, etc) before the court; bring to trial; fetch for interrogation ❼ also "挑" rising stroke (in Chinese characters) see also dī

提案 tí'àn motion; proposal; draft resolution：～审查委员会 motions (examination) committee

提拔 tíbá promote; raise；被～为经理 be promoted to manager

提倡 tíchàng advocate; promote; encourage

提成 tíchéng deduct or take a percentage (from a sum of money, etc); take a cut

提出 tíchū put forward; raise; set (forth)：～辞职 tender one's resignation / ～异议 object (to sth); take exception to / ～严格的要求 set strict demands

提纲 tígāng outline；讨论～ outline for discussion

提纲挈领 tígāng-qièlǐng concentrate or focus on the main points; bring out the essentials; give the gist

提高 tígāo raise; lift; improve：～警惕 enhance or heighten one's vigilance / ～认识 deepen one's understanding

提供 tígōng　provide; supply; offer: ~证据 furnish evidence / ~优质服务 offer quality service

提交 tíjiāo　submit; refer: ~表决 put (sth) to the vote

提炼 tíliàn　extract and purify; abstract: refine (crude oil)

提名 tímíng　nominate: ~奖 nomination

提起 tíqǐ　❶ mention; speak of; bring up ❷ arouse; boost; brace up: ~精神 brace oneself up ❸ put forward; initiate; institute: ~公诉 initiate a public prosecution

提挈 tíqiè　〈书〉❶ take with one; lead; command ❷ guide and support: ~后辈 give guidance and help to younger people

提琴 tíqín　any instrument of the violin family; fiddle: ~手 violinist; fiddler

提取 tíqǔ　❶ draw; pick up; collect: ~货物 pick up goods; take delivery of goods ❷ extract (metal from ore); abstract; recover

提升 tíshēng　❶ promote ❷ hoist; elevate: ~机 hoist; elevator

提示 tíshì　point out; prompt: ~要点 indicate the main points; brief sb on the key points

提携 tíxié　❶ lead (a child, etc) by the hand; guide and support ❷ 〈书〉 join hands; cooperate: 互相~ help each other (in getting promotions); work together

提心吊胆 tíxīn-diàodǎn　have one's heart in one's mouth; be on tenterhooks; be in constant fear

提醒 tíxǐng　remind; alert; warn: ~大家注意 call everybody's attention (to sth)

提要 tíyào　❶ sum up the main points; wrap up; synopsize ❷ summary; abstract; synopsis

提议 tíyì　❶ propose; suggest; move ❷ proposal; motion

啼 tí　❶ cry; weep aloud: ~哭 cry; wail / ~饥号寒 cry from hunger and cold; wail in hunger and cold / ~笑皆非 not know whether to laugh or cry; find (sth) both laughable and irritating ❷ (of birds) crow; caw; (of beasts) howl

题 tí　❶ topic; subject; title: ~库 examination question bank ❷ also "题写" write; inscribe

题材 tícái　subject matter; topic; theme: ~新颖 original in the choice of subject (matter)

题词 tící　❶ write words of encouragement, appreciation or commemoration ❷ inscription; dedication

题解 tíjiě　❶ explanatory note on the title or background of an article ❷ key to exercises or problems

题名 tímíng　❶ inscribe one's name; autograph: ~留念 give one's autograph as a memento ❷ name of a title

题目 tímù　❶ title; subject; topic ❷ exercise problem; examination question

题字 tízì　❶ write; inscribe ❷ inscription

醍 tí

醍醐灌顶 tíhúguàndǐng　〈喻〉be filled with wisdom; be enlightened; suddenly feel refreshed

蹄 tí　hoof: ~筋 tendons of beef, mutton or pork

tǐ

体(體) tǐ　❶ (part of the) body; limb; physique: ~检 physical examination; health check-up / ~能 physical strength (as displayed in sports); stamina ❷ posture; carriage; bearing / ~形 (bodily) form; physical shape / ~型 type of build; figure / ~质 physique; constitution / ~重 (body) weight ❷ (state of a) substance; body; bulk ❸ style; form; ～裁 type of literature; genre / ～例 stylistic rules and layout; style ❹ personally do or experience (sth); put oneself in another's position; ～恤 understand and sympathize; concern oneself with; show solicitude for ❺ system; regime; ～系 system; set-up; network

体操 tǐcāo gymnastics; ～运动员 gymnast

体察 tǐchá experience and observe; be understanding and sympathetic

体格 tǐgé ❶ physique; build; constitution ❷ bodily form; build; figure; ～匀称 of proportional build

体会 tǐhuì know or learn from experience; realize; 个人～ personal experience or understanding

体积 tǐjī volume; bulk; size; ～大 bulky; large

体力 tǐlì physical or bodily strength; physical power; ～劳动 physical or manual labour

体谅 tǐliàng show understanding and sympathy; make allowances (for)

体面 tǐmiàn ❶ dignity; prestige; face; 有失～ (of sth) be a loss of face; (of sb) lose face ❷ honourable; creditable; respectable ❸ good-looking; smart; presentable

体魄 tǐpò physique; physical health; ～强健 have a tough constitution; be sturdy

体坛 tǐtán sports circles or world

体贴 tǐtiē show consideration; give every care; ～入微 look after (sb) with great care; be extremely considerate or thoughtful (of sb)

体统 tǐtǒng decorum; propriety; decency; 成何～！How disgraceful!

体味 tǐwèi savour; chew; appreciate; ～人情冷暖 experience the inconstancy of human relationships

体温 tǐwēn (body) temperature; 量～ take one's temperature / ～计 (clinical) thermometer

体无完肤 tǐwúwánfū be a mass of bruises; 〈喻〉be revised or changed beyond recognition; be scathingly refuted

体现 tǐxiàn embody; manifest; give expression to; ～全貌 reflect the complete picture

体验 tǐyàn learn through personal experience or practice; experience; ～生活 observe and learn from real life

体育 tǐyù ❶ physical culture or education (PE); physical exercise or training ❷ sports; ～场 stadium; sports ground / ～馆 gymnasium; gym / ～道德 sportsmanship

体制 tǐzhì ❶ system (of organization); set-up; regime; ～改革 structural or institutional reform; restructuring ❷ 〈书〉(of literary works) form; pattern; genre

tì

屉（屜） tì also "屉子" ❶ food steamer with several trays; steamer tray ❷〈方〉drawer

剃 tì shave; ～刀 razor / ～度〈宗教〉tonsure / ～光头 have one's head shaved; 〈喻〉lay an egg; fail miserably

倜 tì

倜傥 tìtǎng 〈书〉free and easy of manner; unconventional

涕 tì ❶ tear ❷ mucus of the nose; snivel

惕 tì cautious; watchful

替 tì ❶ take the place of; replace; substitute for; ～罪羊 also "替死鬼" scapegoat; fall guy; whipping boy / ～补队员 substitute (player); alternate; understudy ❷ for; on behalf of; ～父报仇 avenge one's father

❸〈书〉decline; fall

替代 tìdài substitute (for); replace; supersede:不可～ irreplaceable / ～品 substitute (for sth); ersatz / ～能源 alternative energy

替换 tìhuàn replace; substitute for; take the place of:～的衣服 a change of clothes

替身 tìshēn ❶ substitute; replacement; stand-in: ～母亲 surrogate mother ❷ scapegoat; fall guy; whipping boy

嚏 tì 〈书〉sneeze:～喷 sneeze

tiān

天 tiān ❶ sky; heaven:～价 sky-high price — incredibly high price / ～穹〈书〉vault of heaven; firmament / ～蓝色 sky blue; azure / ～高皇帝远〈俗〉be beyond the reach of law and government; when the cat's away, the mice will play ❷ overhead: ～窗〈建筑〉skylight / ～线 antenna; aerial / ～花板 ceiling ❸ day; time of day:正午～ high noon ❹ season:冬～ winter ❺ weather:下雪～ snowy weather / ～不作美 Heaven is not co-operative — the weather is not helpful (to one's plans); the weather lets one down / ～要下雨,娘要嫁人〈俗〉if it threatens to rain and your mother wishes to remarry — so be it; there's no use worrying about sth inevitable / ～有不测风云,人有旦夕祸福.〈谚〉Man's fortune is as unpredictable as the weather. ❻ natural; inborn; inherent:～敌 natural enemy / ～堑 natural moat; chasm; gift / ～险 natural barrier or obstacle / ～灾人祸 natural calamities and man-made misfortunes; natural and man-made disasters ❼ Heaven; God: ～赐 sent by Heaven or God; Heaven-ordained / ～骄(short for 天之骄子)

God's favoured son; unusually lucky person / ～命 God's will; mandate of heaven; fate / ～仙 goddess; fairy maiden; beauty / ～意〈迷信〉will of Heaven; God's will / ～子 Son of Heaven — the emperor / ～府之国(usu used in reference to Sichuan Province) land of abundance or plenty / ～无绝人之路 Heaven never drives a man to the wall; every cloud has a silver lining / ～网恢恢,疏而不漏.〈谚〉God's mill grinds slow but sure. or Justice has a long arm.

天边 tiānbiān also "天际" ❶ ends of the earth; remotest places:远在～ far, far away ❷ (over the) horizon

天才 tiāncái (person of) genius; talent; gift:～教育 genius education

天成 tiānchéng (as if) produced by heaven; springing from nature; natural:～佳偶 perfect match or marriage made by Heaven

天地 tiāndì ❶ heaven and earth; world; universe:～良心 also "天理良心" in my soul of souls; in all honest truth; in all fairness ❷ field of activity; sphere; world; 儿童～ children's world ❸ scene; situation; plight:落到这般～ come to such a (sorry) pass

天⋯地⋯ tiān⋯dì⋯ inserted into a bi-syllabic word or used to join words similar in meaning for emphasis:天长地久 enduring as heaven and earth; everlasting and unchanging / 天翻地覆 heaven and earth turning upside down; earth-shaking / 天高地厚 (usu used after 不知) immensity of the universe; complexity of things / 天昏地暗 dark all round / 〈喻〉chaos and darkness / 天经地义 principle of heaven and earth; unalterable truth / 天罗地网 inescapable net (of law, etc); tight encirclement / 天造地设 created by nature; heavenly; ideal / 天诛地灭 be destroyed by heaven and earth; stand condemned by God; may Heaven strike one dead / 天不怕，地不怕 fear nothing at all; be dauntless

天鹅 tiān'é　*also* "鹄" swan: ~绒 velvet

天方夜谭 Tiānfāng Yètán　*The Thousand and One Nights*; sth simply incredible: 〈喻〉 cock and bull story

天分 tiānfèn　*also* "天资" natural gift; talent: 很有~ quite gifted; very talented

天赋 tiānfù　❶ endowed by nature; inherent; innate: ~人权 inalienable rights of man ❷ *see* "天分"

天干 tiāngān ten Heavenly Stems *see also* "干支" gānzhī

天国 tiānguó　❶〈宗教〉(kingdom of) heaven ❷ utopia; paradise

天花 tiānhuā　*also* "痘"〈医〉smallpox

天花乱坠 tiānhuāluànzhuì　(speak so eloquently that) it rains flowers; give an exaggerated account of sth

天皇 tiānhuáng　❶ God of Heaven ❷ Son of Heaven — emperor ❸ emperor of Japan; mikado; tenno

天机 tiānjī　God's design; secret of providence: ~不可泄露〈俗〉one must not reveal the design of God; one must not give away a crucial secret

天井 tiānjǐng　❶ courtyard (enclosed by housing or walls); patio ❷ uncovered skylight in a traditional house

天空 tiānkōng　sky; heavens: ~景色 skyscape

天籁 tiānlài　〈书〉sounds of nature: ~俱寂。Tranquillity reigned.

天理 tiānlǐ　❶ heavenly principles — ethics as propounded by the Song Confucianists ❷ (plain) justice: ~难容 justice would not tolerate this; heaven forbid

天良 tiānliáng　conscience: ~发现 be stung by conscience; one's better nature asserts itself / ~未泯 retain a shred of conscience; be not totally lost to conscience

天伦 tiānlún　〈书〉natural bonds and ethical relationships between members of a family: ~之乐 family love and happiness; (esp) happiness of a family living together

天南地北 tiānnán-dìběi　*also* "天南海北" ❶ *also* "天各一方" (of a family or friends) be far apart; live in different corners of the country or world ❷ from different places or areas; from all over ❸ (chat about) a wide range of things; everything under the sun

天年 tiānnián　natural span of life; one's natural life: 安享~ spend one's last years in peace

天平 tiānpíng　balance; scales

天气 tiānqì　❶ weather: ~预报 weather forecast ❷ (point of) time: ~不早了。It's getting late.

天桥 tiānqiáo　platform bridge; overpass; overhead walkway or crosswalk: 过街~ pedestrians' overpass (across a street)

天然 tiānrán　natural: ~气 natural gas / ~免疫 *also* "自然免疫" congenital or native immunity

天壤之别 tiānrǎngzhībié　*also* "天渊之别" as far apart as heaven and earth; worlds or poles apart; world of difference

天人 tiānrén　〈书〉❶ (way of) heaven and man: ~感应 correspondence between man and heaven; communication or interaction between man and nature / ~合一 theory that man is an integral part of nature; harmony of man with nature ❷ "heavenly person" — genius or beauty

天日 tiānrì　sky and sun; light: 难见~ can hardly see the light of day again; can hardly see the injustice redressed or regain one's freedom

天色 tiānsè　colour of the sky; time of the day; weather: ~微明。The sky is

faintly light with the dawn. / 看～要起
风了。It seems the wind is rising.

天生 tiānshēng　born; inborn; inher-
ent：～桥 also "天然桥"〈地〉natural
bridge / ～尤物 born siren; sex kit-
ten / ～的一对 ideal couple

天时 tiānshí　❶ season; climate;
weather：～不正 perverse or abnormal
weather　❷ timeliness; opportunity：～、
地利、人和 good timing, geographical
convenience and harmonious human relations; favourable climatic, geographical and human conditions　❸ time：～尚
早。It's still early.

天使 tiānshǐ　〈宗教〉angel

天书 tiānshū　❶〈迷信〉book or epis-
tle from heaven　❷ abstruse or illegible
writing

天堂 tiāntáng　heaven; paradise; ideal
life；人间～ paradise on earth

天体 tiāntǐ　celestial body; star：～力
学 celestial mechanics

天庭 tiāntíng　❶ middle of the fore-
head：～饱满 (have a) full forehead　❷
abode of deities; heavenly court;〈旧〉
royal court or residence

天外 tiānwài　❶ beyond the horizon
or earth; in outer space; extraterres-
trial：～来客 visitor from outer space;
ET / ～有天〈谚〉there is always another heaven beyond this one — there
is no limit to the universe; able as you
are, there is always someone abler　❷
highest and farthest place; sky of the
skies；魂飞～ one's soul flitting away
to nowhere; be scared to death

天王星 tiānwángxīng　〈天文〉Uranus

天文 tiānwén　astronomy：～馆 plane-
tarium / ～台 (astronomical) observatory / ～数字 astronomical or enormous figure

天下 tiānxià　❶ land under heaven;
country; world：～大事 world affairs;
major events in the country / ～无双
unparalleled in the world; peerless;

unique / ～为公 the world for all — a
legendary utopia / ～乌鸦一般黑〈俗〉
all crows are black — evil people are
the same all over the world; in every
country dogs bite　❷ rule; domination;
state power：打～ fight for state power / 人民的～ government or rule by
the people

天象 tiānxiàng　❶ astronomical or celestial phenomena　❷ changes of wind
and cloud

天性 tiānxìng　natural instinct; na-
ture：～宽厚 be generous and tolerant
by nature

天涯 tiānyá　end of the world; remotest place on earth：～比邻 (of friends)
be close to each other though physically
far apart / ～海角 ends of the earth;
remotest corners of the earth / ～咫尺。
It is but a small world.

天衣无缝 tiānyīwúfèng　seamless
heavenly robe — (usu of literary work,
etc) perfect; flawless

天真 tiānzhēn　❶ innocent; simple
and unaffected; artless：～无邪 innocent and pure　❷ naive; childish：～的
想法 naive idea

天职 tiānzhí　bounden duty; mission

天主教 Tiānzhǔjiào　Catholicism：～徒
Catholic

添 tiān　add; get or give more; in-
crease：～彩 add honour to; do
credit to / ～丁〈旧〉have a baby (esp
a boy) born into the family / ～乱〈口〉
increase the confusion or chaos; add to
the trouble / ～置 acquire; buy / ～加
剂 additive / ～油加醋 also "添枝加
叶" garble a story by adding trimmings
to it; embellish a story / ～砖加瓦 do
what little one can; do one's bit

tián

田 tián　(cultivated) land; farmland; field (of ores, etc)：煤

coal field / ～产 (farm-)land property / ～赋〈旧〉land tax / ～埂 low bank of earth between fields; ridge / ～鸡 (popular name for 青蛙) frog / ～螺〈动物〉river snail / ～野 (large tract of) fields and open country

田地 tiándì ❶ field; farmland; crop land ❷ wretched situation; (sorry) plight

田径 tiánjìng 〈体〉track and field; ～运动 track and field sports; athletics

田园 tiányuán fields and gardens; countryside; ～诗 idyll; pastoral poetry / ～生活 idyllic or pastoral life

恬 tián 〈书〉❶ quiet; tranquil; peaceful; ～淡 quiet; tranquil; indifferent to fame or gain / ～静 quiet; serene; peaceful / ～适 quiet and comfortable ❷ not care at all; be indifferent; ～不知耻 have no sense of shame; be shameless

甜 tián ❶ sweet; honeyed; ～点 sweet pastry; dessert / ～瓜 musk melon / ～润 (of voice, etc) sweet and mellow; sweet and pleasant / ～食 sweet food; sweetmeats; dessert / ～酸苦辣 sweet, sour, bitter and hot — all kinds of flavours; all the sweets and bitters of life ❷ (of sleep) sound

甜菜 tiáncài beet; beetroot; ～糖 beet sugar

甜美 tiánměi ❶ sweet; luscious ❷ pleasant; refreshing; ～的爱情 sweet love

甜蜜 tiánmì sweet; happy; 甜言蜜语〈贬〉sweet words and honeyed phrases; sweet talk

甜水 tiánshuǐ ❶ fresh or sweet water; ～井 fresh or sweet water well ❷ happiness and comfort; 生活在～里 live a happy and comfortable life

甜丝丝 tiánsīsī ❶ pleasantly sweet ❷ also "甜滋滋" pleased; gratified; happy

甜头 tiántou ❶ sweetish taste; pleasant flavour ❷ (as an inducement) benefit; sop; 尝到～ draw benefit from sth; appreciate the good of sth

填 tián ❶ fill; stuff; supplement; ～料 packing; stuffing; filling / ～平 fill and level up / ～写 fill in; write / ～鸭式教学法 cramming method of teaching ❷ write; fill in or out (a form, etc); ～字游戏 crossword puzzle

填充 tiánchōng ❶ fill up; stuff ❷ fill in the blanks (as in a test paper); ～测试 cloze test

填词 tiáncí compose a poem to a tune of ci (词); write words to a melody

填空 tiánkòng ❶ fill a vacant position; fill a vacancy; ～补缺 fill vacancies and supply deficiencies ❷ see "填充❷"

tiǎn

忝 tiǎn 〈书〉〈谦〉be unworthy of the honour; ～列门墙 have the honour to be a student of sb's

殄 tiǎn (usu 殄灭)〈书〉extirpate; exterminate

觍 tiǎn ❶ (usu 觍颜)〈书〉ashamed ❷ brazen; ～着脸 brazen it out

腆 tiǎn 〈口〉protrude; stick or thrust out (one's belly, etc)

舔 tiǎn lick; lap; ～干净 lick (sth) clean / ～屁股〈粗〉lick sb's ass; fawn (on sb) servilely

tiāo

佻 tiāo also "佻薄"〈书〉frivolous; flippant

挑 tiāo ❶ choose; select; pick ❷ find (fault); pick (holes); be fastidious; ～眼〈方〉be fastidious (about formalities, etc); find fault / ～

刺儿 nit-pick; be captious ❸ carry on the shoulder with a pole; shoulder: ～重担 shoulder a heavy load; assume heavy responsibilities ❹ load carried on a shoulder pole: ～子 load carried on a shoulder pole: 〈喻〉responsibility
see also tiǎo

挑拣 tiāojiǎn　pick (and choose): 挑三拣四 *also* "挑肥拣瘦" pick and choose; be choosy

挑食 tiāoshí　*also* "挑嘴" have a partiality for certain kinds of food; be particular or choosy about what one eats

挑剔 tiāotī　nit-pick; be captious or fastidious: 无可～ beyond criticism; faultless

挑选 tiāoxuǎn　choose; select; opt for

挑 tiāo　〈书〉❶ be heir to; 兼～ be heir to both one's father and uncle ❷ move into the ancestral shrine: 不～之祖 founding father who is forever esteemed (though not in the ancestral shrine)

tiáo

条(條) tiáo　❶ twig ❷ long narrow piece; strip; slip: ～案 long narrow table / ～凳 bench / ～幅 vertically-hung scroll; scroll / ～形码 *also* "条码" bar code ❸ long and slender in pattern or shape; stripe; streak: ～纹布 striped cloth ❹ item; article; clause; ～款 clause; article; provision / ～令 〈军〉regulations / ～文 article; clause ❺ order: ～贯分明 〈书〉clear and systematic ❻〈量〉*used with* **a)** *sth narrow and long*: 两～河 two rivers **b)** *itemized or abstract nouns*: 几～新闻 several pieces or items of news

条分缕析 tiáofēn-lǚxī　analyse point by point; make a careful and detailed analysis

条件 tiáojiàn　❶ condition; factor; circumstance: ～反射 〈生理〉conditioned reflex ❷ requirement; prerequisite; condition: 在对等～下 on condition of reciprocity; on a reciprocal basis / 不附带任何～ with no strings attached ❸ situation; state; condition: 身体～ physical condition; health

条理 tiáolǐ　proper arrangement; systematic presentation; orderliness: ～分明 well-organized; methodical

条例 tiáolì　regulations; rules; ordinances

条目 tiáomù　❶ clauses and subclauses (in a formal document) ❷ entry (in a dictionary)

条条 tiáotiáo　❶ rules and regulations; conventions: ～框框 〈贬〉conventions and restrictions; all kinds of taboos ❷ vertical lines of leadership or organization ❸ main points (of theory or knowledge); tenets: 书本上的～ abstractions from books; dogma

条约 tiáoyuē　treaty; pact; covenant

条子 tiáozi　❶ strip (of cloth, etc) ❷ brief informal note

tiáo

迢 tiáo

迢迢 tiáotiáo　far away; remote: 千里～ come from a thousand *li* away

调 tiáo　❶ suit well; fit in perfectly; be harmonious ❷ mix; regulate; adjust; ～控 regulate and control / ～试 (conduct a) preliminary or shakedown test; trial run ❸ mediate; reconcile; arbitrate: ～停 mediate; intervene; act as an intermediary ❹ tease; provoke; instigate: ～情 flirt; dally / ～唆 incite; abet; instigate
see also diào

调羹 tiáogēng　spoon

调和 tiáohé　❶ be or put in harmonious proportion; regulate; blend: 色彩～ harmonious or well-matched colours ❷ mediate; reconcile: 从中～ mediate; act as a mediator ❸ (usu used in the negative) compromise; make concessions;不可 ~ admitting of no compromise; irreconcilable

调剂 tiáojì adjust; regulate; ~ 余缺 adjust surpluses and deficiencies / ~生活 enliven or enrich one's life; relax

调教 tiáojiào ❶ teach (a child, etc); train; discipline ❷ tame (an animal, etc); break in

调节 tiáojié regulate; adjust; control; ~ 器 regulator; adjuster / ~ 税 regulatory tax

调解 tiáojiě mediate; arbitrate; make peace;~ 人 mediator; peacemaker

调侃 tiáokǎn ridicule; mock; banter

调理 tiáolǐ ❶ nurse (a patient, etc) ❷ take care of; look after ❸ see "调教"

调配 tiáopèi mix; blend;~ 几味草药 prepare a few doses of herbal medicine see also diàopèi

调皮 tiáopí ❶ naughty; mischievous; unruly; ~ 捣蛋 mischievous; troublesome; recalcitrant ❷ tricky; smart-alecky

调频 tiáopín ❶ adjust frequency (of a receiver) or output (of a generator) ❷ (short for 频率调制) frequency modulation (FM);~ 收音机 FM receiver

调味 tiáowèi flavour; dress; season; ~ 品 also "调料" condiment; flavouring; seasoning

调戏 tiáoxì take liberties with (a woman); dally with; assail (a woman) with obscenities

调笑 tiáoxiào make fun of; poke fun at; tease

调养 tiáoyǎng also "调摄" take good care of oneself (after an illness); nurse oneself back to health; recuperate

调整 tiáozhěng readjust; regulate; revise;~ 人力 redistribute manpower; realign staff

调制 tiáozhì ❶ mix; blend and make; concoct; ~ 鸡尾酒 prepare a

cocktail ❷ 〈信息〉modulation;~ 解调器 modulator-demodulator (MODEM)

筶 tiáo

筶帚 tiáozhou whisk broom

鬈 tiáo 〈书〉child's hanging hair;~ 龄 childhood

tiǎo

挑 tiǎo ❶ pick, push or hold up with a pole or stick; raise; lift;~ 大拇哥 give the thumbs up ❷ poke; prick;~ 灯心 trim the lamp-wick ❸ (in embroidery) cross-stitch ❹ stir up; instigate; foment;~ 动 arouse; foment; incite / ~ 唆 incite; abet; instigate / ~ 起争端 provoke a dispute ❺ rising stroke (in Chinese characters) see also tiāo

挑拨 tiǎobō instigate; incite; stir up trouble;~ 离间 sow dissension; stir up trouble; drive a wedge (between people)

挑大梁 tiǎodàliáng (as of an actor or actress) play the leading or key role; shoulder a major responsibility; be a mainstay

挑逗 tiǎodòu provoke; tease; dally; ~ 寻衅 pick a quarrel

挑明 tiǎomíng bring into the open; lay open or bare;~ 关系 publicize a relationship

挑头 tiǎotóu be the first (to do sth); take the lead or initiative

挑衅 tiǎoxìn provoke;~ 者 provocateur / ~ 行为 provocative act

挑战 tiǎozhàn challenge (to battle or contest); throw down the gauntlet;~ 书 (letter of) challenge

tiào

眺 tiào (usu 眺望) look into the distance from a high place

粜(糶) tiào sell (grain)

跳 tiào ❶ jump; leap; spring：～高〈体〉high jump / ～马〈体〉vaulting horse; horse-vaulting / ～绳 rope skipping / ～进黄河洗不清〈俗〉even if one jumped into the Yellow River, one could not wash oneself clean — there's nothing one can do to clear one's name ❷ move up and down; beat; pulsate：急得~脚 stamp (one's foot) with impatience ❸ skip (over); make omissions：～级 also "跳班"(of pupils) skip a grade / ～两行 skip or jump two lines

跳板 tiàobǎn ❶ gangplank; gangway ❷〈体〉springboard; diving board ❸〈喻〉stepping stone (to sth)

跳槽 tiàocáo drop one job, etc, for another; job-hop; jilt (a lover)

跳梁 tiàoliáng also "跳踉" jump up and down; perform antics; be rampant：～小丑 buffoon who performs antics; contemptible scoundrel

跳棋 tiàoqí Chinese chequers; halma

跳伞 tiàosǎn parachute; bail out：～运动 parachute-jumping / ～运动员 parachutist; parachuter

跳水 tiàoshuǐ ❶〈体〉dive：～运动员 diver ❷〈喻〉(of prices) nosedive; plummet

跳舞 tiàowǔ ❶ dance ❷ ballroom dancing

跳远 tiàoyuǎn 〈体〉long or broad jump：立定～ standing long jump / 三级～ hop, step and jump

跳跃 tiàoyuè ❶ jump; leap; bound：～式发展 develop by leaps and bounds ❷ (of flame, etc) flicker

跳蚤 tiàozao flea：～市场 flea market

tiē

帖 tiē ❶ (usu 服帖) submissive; pliant; obedient ❷ (usu 妥帖) proper; steady; secure
see also tiě; tiè

贴 tiē ❶ paste; stick; attach：～布告 put up a notice / 往自己脸上～金 put feathers in one's own cap; blow one's own trumpet ❷ cling to; keep, press or nestle closely to：～题 relevant; pertinent; to the point ❸ subsidize; help (out) financially：～钱 give sb money to help him or her out ❹〈量〉used of medicated plaster：一～膏药 a piece of medicated plaster ❺ see "帖" tiě

贴补 tiēbǔ ❶ subsidize; help (out) financially：～家用 help pay family expenses ❷ eke out by drawing on one's savings

贴近 tiējìn ❶ press or get close to; nestle up against ❷ intimate (with); close (to)

贴切 tiēqiè (of words) apt; fitting; appropriate

贴身 tiēshēn ❶ next to the skin：～内衣 underwear; underclothes ❷ (of clothes, etc) fit nicely; be a good fit ❸ personal：～保镖 personal bodyguard

贴心 tiēxīn also "贴己" intimate; close：～话 words spoken in confidence; confidences / ～人 trusted companion; confidant(e)

tiě

帖 tiě ❶ invitation：下～ send an invitation ❷〈旧〉(used for betrothal, etc) age card ❸ (brief) note; card ❹〈方〉〈量〉(used of herbal medicine) dose; draught
see also tiē; tiè

铁(鐵) tiě ❶ iron; ferrum (Fe)：～饼〈体〉discus (throw) / ～灰(色) dark grey / ～匠 blacksmith; ironsmith / ～器 ironware / ～青 (of one's look) ashen; livid; ghastly pale / ～皮箱子 iron-plated case ❷ hard or strong as iron：～拳 iron or mailed fist；powerful attack／～饭碗 iron rice bowl — secure job／～公鸡 stingy person；miser／～算盘 meticulous calculation；competent accountant；shrewd person／～哥们儿（口）sworn or close friend；faithful pal or crony ❸ harsh；stern；cruel；～蹄 iron heel — rule by force；tyrannical rule／～面无私 impartial and incorruptible；just and stern／～石心肠 be hard-hearted；have a heart of stone ❹ ironclad；indisputable；unalterable：～案 ironclad case／～(了)心 steel one's heart；be unshakable or adamant in one's determination／～板钉钉 ironclad；absolutely certain；adamant／～的纪律 iron discipline

铁杵磨成针 tiěchǔmóchéngzhēn an iron pestle can be ground down to a needle；perseverance will prevail；little strokes fell great oaks

铁窗 tiěchuāng ❶ window with iron grating ❷ prison (bars)：～生涯 life behind bars；prison life

铁杆 tiěgǎn ❶ reliable (friend)；loyal (follower) ❷ stubborn；inveterate；dyed-in-the-wool：～汉奸 out-and-out traitor

铁路 tiělù also "铁道" railway；railroad：～线 railway line／～运输 railway or rail transportation

铁人 tiěrén 〈喻〉man with an iron will：～三项〈体〉triathlon

铁树开花 tiěshùkāihuā like (sago) cycas in blossom — something seldom seen or hardly possible

铁腕 tiěwàn iron hand：～人物 iron-handed person；strong man

铁血 tiěxuè ❶ iron-willed and ready to sacrifice oneself：～男儿 strong-willed and valiant man ❷ harsh and ruthless：～政策 blood-and-iron policy

铁证 tiězhèng ironclad proof；irrefutable evidence：～如山 irrefutable，con-clusive proof；ironclad evidence

tiè

帖 tiè book of models (of hand-writing or painting) for learners to copy　see also tiē；tiě

tīng

厅（廳） tīng ❶ hall：～堂 hall；chamber ❷ office：办公～ general office ❸ department under a provincial government：财政～ department of finance

汀 tīng 〈书〉low，level land along a river；spit of land：～线 line track (of a seashore)

听（聽） tīng ❶ listen；hear：～写 dictation／～众 audience；listeners／～得见 (of sth) be audible；(of sb) can hear／～而不闻 listen but hear not；turn a deaf ear to；remain indifferent to ❷ heed；obey：～从 obey；follow；comply with／～喝（口）at sb's disposal or service；at sb's beck and call ❸〈书〉administer；manage：～政 (of a monarch or regent) hold court；administer affairs of state ❹ let be；allow：～便 as one pleases；please yourself／～其自然 let things take their own course；let matters slide ❺ tin；can：～装 canned；tinned

听候 tīnghòu wait for (a decision，etc)；be pending：～调遣 be ready to do sb's bidding

听话 tīnghuà heed what an elder or a superior says；be obedient or well behaved：不要哭了，～！Stop crying and be a good child！

听觉 tīngjué 〈生理〉sense of hearing；audition：～不灵 (have) poor hearing；be hard of hearing

听力 tīnglì ❶ hearing ❷ aural or listening comprehension

听凭 tīngpíng allow; let (sb do as he pleases); ～处理 leave everything to sb's discretion

听取 tīngqǔ listen to; ～反映 solicit comments

听任 tīngrèn 〈书〉allow (sth bad); let (sb do as he pleases); ～宰割 place oneself at sb's mercy / 听之任之 let (bad practices, etc) go unchecked; shut one's eyes to (unhealthy tendencies, etc)

听说 tīngshuō ❶ listening and speaking (in language learning) ❷ be told; hear (of sth); it is said

听天由命 tīngtiānyóumìng submit to the will of Heaven; resign oneself to one's fate; trust to luck

听筒 tīngtǒng ❶ (telephone) receiver ❷ 〈电〉headphone; earphone ❸ also "听诊器"〈医〉stethoscope

听信 tīngxìn ❶ wait for information ❷ believe what one hears

听证 tīngzhèng hear (the evidence of litigants); 举行～会 hold a hearing

烃(烴) tīng 〈化〉hydrocarbon

tíng

廷 tíng court of a monarch

亭 tíng ❶ pavilion; kiosk ❷ stall; booth; kiosk ❸ 〈书〉just right; well-proportioned

亭亭 tíngtíng also "婷婷"〈书〉tall and erect; upright; ～玉立 (of a girl or tree) stand gracefully tall and erect; be slim and graceful

庭 tíng ❶ hall ❷ front courtyard or yard; ～院 also "庭除" courtyard ❸ law court; ～审 try; interrogate

停 tíng ❶ stop; cease; halt; ～办 stop working; cease operation;

close down / ～电 power cut or failure; blackout / ～飞 (of aircraft) be grounded / ～火 ceasefire / ～赛 (of a match, etc) stop; (of an athlete, etc) be temporarily disqualified from contests / ～薪留职 suspend one's position with one's salary suspended; obtain an indefinite leave of absence ❷ stop over; stay ❸ ready; settled; ～妥 all set; well arranged; all in order ❹ part (of a total); portion; 三～儿中的两～儿 two thirds

停泊 tíngbó anchor; berth; ～处 berth; anchorage

停车 tíngchē ❶ stop; pull up ❷ park; ～场 car park; parking lot or area ❸ (of a machine) stall; stop working

停当 tíngdang ready; settled; 收拾～ put everything in order; finish packing

停顿 tíngdùn ❶ stop; halt; be at a standstill ❷ pause (in speaking)

停放 tíngfàng park (a vehicle); place

停机 tíngjī ❶ (of a film, TV play, etc) finish shooting ❷ (of an airplane) park; ～坪 (aircraft) parking area or apron; tarmac

停靠 tíngkào (of a train) stop; (of a ship) berth; ～港 port of call

停留 tíngliú ❶ stay for a time; stop; lay over ❷ remain; stagnate

停业 tíngyè ❶ suspend business; close temporarily ❷ wind up a business; go out of business; close down

停战 tíngzhàn armistice; truce; ceasefire; ～协议 armistice; truce agreement

停职 tíngzhí suspend sb from his or her duties; ～检查 be temporarily relieved of one's post to make a self-criticism

停止 tíngzhǐ stop; cease; halt; ～供应 cut off the supply

停滞 tíngzhì also "停滞不前" stagnate; be at a standstill; bog down

霆 tíng thunderbolt; lightning

tǐng

挺 tǐng ❶ hard and straight; erect; stiff: ~立 stand upright or erect ❷ straighten up; stick out; protrude: ~身而出 step forward bravely; rise courageously; come out boldly ❸ endure; bear; hold or stick out: 有病硬 ~着 brave it out when ill ❹ very; rather; quite ❺〈量〉*used of machine guns*: 一~机枪 a machine gun

挺拔 tǐngbá ❶ tall and straight; towering ❷ steady and forceful; powerful

挺进 tǐngjìn （of troops）drive on; press ahead; push forward

铤

铤 tǐng

铤而走险 tǐng'érzǒuxiǎn risk danger in desperation; make a reckless move

艇

艇 tǐng （light）boat; skiff; （light）naval vessel

tōng

通 tōng ❶ open; through; leading to: ~车 (of a railway or highway) be open to traffic; be commissioned; (of a place) have transport service / ~兑 circulate and be convertible / ~关 go through the customs / ~票 through ticket / ~都大邑 big city; metropolis / ~衢大道 thoroughfare; highway ❷ connect; link; communicate: ~敌 collude or collaborate secretly with the enemy / ~好〈书〉(of nations) have friendly relations / ~婚 be related by marriage; intermarry / ~奸 commit adultery; have illicit sexual intercourse / ~邮 (accessible by) postal communication ❸ notify; inform; tell ❹ know or understand thoroughly; be well versed in: ~今博古 conversant with things past and present; erudite

and informed ❺（usu 通顺）logical; coherent; correct: 文字不~ ungrammatical and incoherent writing ❻ general; common; entire: ~病 common failing or defect; prevalent problem / ~例 general rule; usual practice / ~史 comprehensive or general history / ~则 general rule / ~观全局 take a comprehensive or an overall view of the situation / ~身上下 all over the body *see also* tòng

通报 tōngbào ❶ cite or announce in a dispatch or circular; circulate a notice or dispatch: ~表扬 cite (sb) for commendation in an official dispatch; circulate a notice of commendation ❷ (usu used in academia) bulletin; journal ❸ make known; report; inform: 通名报姓 introduce oneself

通才 tōngcái all-round or versatile person; generalist: ~教育 liberal or general education

通常 tōngcháng general; common; usual

通畅 tōngchàng ❶ unobstructed; free; clear: 呼吸~ easy breathing ❷ (of writing, etc) easy and smooth; fluent

通称 tōngchēng ❶ be generally known as (sth) or called (sth) ❷ general term; popular name

通达 tōngdá understanding; sensible: 通情达理 showing good sense; sensible; reasonable / 通权达变 be flexible and untrammelled by conventions; adapt oneself to circumstances; act as the occasion requires

通道 tōngdào ❶ thoroughfare; road ❷ aisle; passageway

通电 tōngdiàn ❶ set up an electric circuit; electrify: 这个村子最近~了。Electricity reached the village recently. ❷ send a circular telegram; publish an open telegram

通读 tōngdú ❶ read over or

through; read from cover to cover ❷ understand (what one reads); comprehend

通风 tōngfēng ❶ ventilate; be well ventilated; ～口 (air) vent ❷ (usu 通风报信) divulge (secret) information (to); tip off

通告 tōnggào give public notice; announce (in a circular, etc); 张贴～ put up a notice

通共 tōnggòng in all; altogether; all told

通过 tōngguò ❶ pass (through a place, etc); cross; traverse ❷ adopt (resolution, etc); pass; carry ❸ by means of; by; through; ～谈判 by or through negotiations ❸ ask the consent or approval of (superiors, etc)

通红 tōnghóng also tònghóng very red; red through and through; ～的太阳 glowing sun

通货 tōnghuò 〈经〉currency; current money; ～紧缩 (shortened as 通缩) deflation (of currency) / ～膨胀 (shortened as 通胀) inflation

通缉 tōngjī order the arrest (of sb); list as wanted; ～令 order for arrest (of sb)

通力 tōnglì (usu 通力合作) make a concerted effort (to do sth); pitch in (for sth) together; fully cooperate (in doing sth)

通令 tōnglìng (issue a) circular or general order

通论 tōnglùn ❶ well-rounded argument; convincing thesis ❷ general survey (on); introduction (to)

通明 tōngmíng well-illuminated; brightly lit; 灯火～ ablaze with lights

通盘 tōngpán overall; all-round; comprehensive; ～考虑 take the overall situation into account; consider from every possible angle

通气 tōngqì ❶ aerate (water in a pond, etc); ventilate (a place) ❷ be in

touch or communication (with each other); keep (each other) informed

通融 tōngróng ❶ stretch rules or get around regulations to accommodate sb; make an exception in sb's favour ❷ accommodate (sb) with a short-term loan; lend

通商 tōngshāng (of nations) have trade relations; ～口岸 trading or open port

通俗 tōngsú popular; common; easy; ～化 popularize / ～歌曲 popular or pop song / ～易懂 easy to understand

通通 tōngtōng also "通统"; "统统" all; entirely; wholly

通宵 tōngxiāo also "通宵达旦" all or whole night; throughout the night; 玩个～ make a night of it (playing cards, etc)

通晓 tōngxiǎo thoroughly understand; be well versed in; be proficient in

通信 tōngxìn ❶ communicate by letter; correspond; ～录 address book ❷ send a message; contact; communicate; ～员 messenger; orderly / ～卫星 communication satellite

通行 tōngxíng ❶ pass or go through; ～权 right of way / ～费 transit duty; toll / ～证 pass; permit; (as in a war) safe conduct / ～无阻 and unobstructed; accessible to the public ❷ current; common; general

通讯 tōngxùn ❶ (tele-)communication ❷ correspondence; reportage; news report or dispatch; ～社 news agency; news or press service / ～员 reporter; (press) correspondent

通用 tōngyòng ❶ in common use; current; general; ～软件〈信息〉common or general-purpose software ❷ interchangeable

通知 tōngzhī ❶ notify; inform; advise ❷ notice; circular; message

嗵 tōng 〈象声〉thump; thud:他的心～～直跳。His heart was thumping.

tóng

同（仝） tóng ❶ same; identical; similar:～辈 of the same generation; peer / ～上 (used in filling out a form, etc) ditto; *idem* / ～宗 of the same clan; having common ancestry / ～义词 synonym / ～音词 homophone; homonym / ～工～酬 equal pay for equal work / ～声传译 simultaneous interpretation ❷ share; do together; have in common:～班 be in or of the same class; classmate / ～伴 companion / ～类 (people or things) of the same kind; similar / ～僚〈旧〉fellow official; colleague / ～病相怜 fellow sufferers commiserate with each other; be in the same boat / ～仇敌忾 share a bitter hatred of the enemy; be filled with a common hatred for the enemy / ～甘共苦 go through thick and thin together; share weal and woe; share comforts and hardships ❸ with:～专家商量 consult the experts ❹ as...as; like; as:～哥哥一般高 as tall as one's elder brother ❺〈连〉and; as well as;纸～笔 paper and pen

同胞 tóngbāo ❶ born of the same parents:～兄弟 full brothers ❷ fellow countryman; compatriot

同步 tóngbù coordinate in time or progress; synchronize:～建设 synchronized construction / ～卫星 synchronous or geostationary satellite

同窗 tóngchuāng ❶ study under the same teacher; study in the same school or class ❷ fellow student; schoolmate; classmate

同床 tóngchuáng share the same bed:～共枕 *also* "同衾共枕" be bedfellows or sex partners / ～异梦 be strange bedfellows; hide different purposes behind the semblance of accord

同党 tóngdǎng ❶ belong to the same party or organization ❷ member of the same party or organization; confederate; accomplice

同道 tóngdào ❶ person of the same ideal or conviction; person of the same trade or occupation ❷ *see* "同行❸"

同等 tóngděng of the same class, rank, or status; on an equal basis or footing:～地位 equal in status; on an equal footing / ～学力 have the same educational level (as a regular college graduate, etc)

同感 tónggǎn same feeling or impression; consensus:颇有～ feel very much the same

同归于尽 tóngguīyújìn die or perish together; end in common ruin

同行 tóngháng ❶ be of the same trade or occupation ❷ colleague ❸ (tóngxíng) *also* "同道"; "同路" take the same route; travel together

同化 tónghuà assimilate:民族～政策 policy of national assimilation

同伙 tónghuǒ ❶ work in partnership; collude (in doing evil) ❷ partner; confederate; fellow gangster

同居 tóngjū live together; (esp) cohabit; shack up (together)

同流合污 tóngliú-héwū go along with an evil trend; associate with a vile person; wallow in the mire with sb

同盟 tóngméng ❶ allied; joint:～国 allied nation; ally / ～罢工 joint strike ❷ alliance; league

同谋 tóngmóu ❶ conspire (with sb) ❷ *also* "同谋犯" co-conspirator; confederate; accomplice

同年 tóngnián ❶ in the same year ❷ *also* "同龄"; "同庚" of the same age; contemporary

同情 tóngqíng sympathize with; show

sympathy for：～心 sympathy；compassion

同时 tóngshí ❶ at the same time；meanwhile；in the meantime ❷ moreover；besides；in addition

同事 tóngshì ❶ work in the same place；work together ❷ also "同人"；"同仁" colleague；fellow worker

同室操戈 tóngshìcāogē internal or fratricidal strife；internecine feud

同位素 tóngwèisù 〈化〉isotope；放射性～ radioisotope

同喜 tóngxǐ 〈套〉thank you for your congratulations

同乡 tóngxiāng person from the same village，town or province；fellow villager，townsman or provincial：大 ～ fellow provincial / 小 ～ fellow townsman

同心 tóngxīn ❶ with one heart；of like mind and spirit：～同德 be of one heart and one mind；be dedicated to the same cause / ～协力 also "同心戮力" work together with one heart；make concerted efforts ❷ concentric；homocentric：～圆 〈数〉concentric circles

同性 tóngxìng ❶ of the same sex ❷ of the same nature or character；like

同性恋 tóngxìngliàn homosexuality：～者 homosexual / 男～者 gay / 女～者 lesbian

同学 tóngxué ❶ be in the same school ❷ fellow student；schoolmate；classmate ❸ form of address used in speaking to a student：～们，请安静。Students，please be quiet.

同样 tóngyàng ❶ same；equal；similar ❷ similarly；by the same token

同一 tóngyī ❶ same；identical ❷ also "同一性" 〈哲〉identity；unity

同意 tóngyì agree（with or to）；consent（to）

同志 tóngzhì（often used as a form of address on the Chinese mainland）comrade

同舟共济 tóngzhōugòngjì people in the same boat should help each other；pull together in times of trouble；pool one's efforts and help each other out

彤 tóng 〈书〉red：～云 red clouds；dark clouds（as before a snow）

茼 tóng

茼蒿 tónghāo 〈植〉crown-daisy

桐 tóng 〈植〉❶（usu 泡桐）paulownia ❷ tung tree：～油 tung oil ❸（usu 梧桐）phoenix tree

铜 tóng copper（Cu）：～臭 stink of money / ～匠 coppersmith / ～牌〈体〉bronze medal / ～器 bronze，brass or copper ware / ～钱 copper coin / ～像 bronze statue / ～墙铁壁 bastion of iron；impregnable fortress；tower of strength

童（❸ 僮） tóng ❶ child：～工 child labourer or labour / ～话 children's or nursery story；fairy tale / ～年 childhood / ～趣 childish delight；innocent playfulness（as of a child）/ ～谣 children's rhyme or song；nursery rhyme / ～养媳〈旧〉child bride / ～子军 boy scout / ～叟无欺 cheat neither the old nor the young；be honest with all customers / ～心未泯 retain a childlike heart；keep traces of childlike innocence or playfulness / ～言无忌 children say what they think；children and fools speak the truth ❷ virgin：～女 virgin girl / ～贞（esp of a woman）virginity；chastity ❸ 〈旧〉pageboy ❹ bare；bald；barren：～山濯濯 bare and barren hills

酮 tóng 〈化〉ketone

瞳 tóng

瞳瞳 tóngtóng 〈书〉❶ brilliance of the rising sun ❷（of eyes）glisten；glimmer；flash

瞳 tóng　also "瞳孔"; "瞳人" pupil (of the eye)

tǒng

统 tǒng　❶ continuum or order of interrelated things; system; genealogy ❷ all; entirely; together: ～共 altogether; in all / ～管 unified management; centralized control / ～观全局 considering the overall situation; taken as a whole ❸ lead; command; control; ～领 command; lead; commander

统筹 tǒngchóu　make overall plans; plan as a whole; coordinate in an overall manner: ～安排 make a comprehensive arrangement (of sth)

统计 tǒngjì　❶ statistics: ～学 statistics / ～数字 statistical figures; statistics ❷ add up; count

统帅 tǒngshuài　❶ commander-in-chief; commander ❷ see "统率"

统率 tǒngshuài　also "统帅" command; lead; ～全军 lead the whole force; be in overall command

统辖 tǒngxiá　have under one's jurisdiction; exercise control over

统一 tǒngyī　unify; unite; integrate; ～体 entity; unity / ～大业 great cause of reunification / ～考试 (shortened as 统考) uniform or unified examination / ～行动 coordinate actions; act in unison / ～认识 reach common understanding or consensus / ～战线 (shortened as 统战) united front / ～的多民族国家 unitary multinational state

统治 tǒngzhì　❶ rule; control; ～者 ruler / ～阶级 ruling class ❷ dominate

捅 tǒng　❶ poke; stab; push (with one's hand or elbow): ～娄子 also "捅漏子"〈口〉make a mess (of sth); make a blunder; get into trouble / ～马蜂窝〈口〉stir up a hornet's nest; bring a hornet's nest about one's ears

❷ disclose (a secret, etc); leak; give away

桶 tǒng　bucket; pail; barrel

筒 tǒng　❶ section of thick bamboo ❷ thick tube-shaped object: 枪～ barrel of a gun / ～裙 straight skirt

tòng

恸(慟) tòng　〈书〉❶ deep sorrow; grief; agony ❷ cry out loud; wail: ～哭 wail; cry one's heart out

通 tòng　〈量〉referring to action: 发了一～议论 make a torrent of comments　see also tōng

痛 tòng　❶ ache; pain: 牙～ (have a) toothache / 触及～处 touch sb's sore spot; touch sb on the raw / 我的脚很～. My foot hurts badly. ❷ sadness; grief; sorrow: ～楚 pain; agony; distress / ～不欲生 grieve to the extent of wishing to die; be overwhelmed with sorrow ❸ extremely; thoroughly; bitterly: ～斥 make a stinging attack on; scathingly denounce / 打～ beat soundly / ～哭 cry or weep bitterly; wail / ～骂 scold severely; curse roundly; give a good scolding / ～饮 drink one's fill; drink to one's heart's content

痛定思痛 tòngdìngsītòng　recall a painful experience (as a reminder or warning); draw a lesson from a bitter experience; bring home a painful lesson

痛改前非 tònggǎiqiánfēi　earnestly repent and reform oneself; sincerely mend one's way; make a clean break with one's (past) misdeeds

痛感 tònggǎn　❶ keenly feel; be keenly aware (of sth) ❷ sense of pain

痛恨 tònghèn　hate bitterly; utterly loathe

痛苦 tòngkǔ pain; agony; distress; ～万分 (of sth) be very distressing; (of sb) suffer infinite agony

痛快 tòngkuài ❶ happy; delighted; gratified ❷ to one's heart's content; to one's great satisfaction; ～淋漓 unrestrained and forceful; vigorous ❸ frank and direct; forthright; straightforward

痛切 tòngqiè with great agony; most sorrowfully; keenly

痛惜 tòngxī deeply regret; feel remorse for; deplore

痛心 tòngxīn distressed; saddened; grieved; ～疾首 with bitter hatred; with great resentment

痛痒 tòngyǎng ❶ sufferings; hardships; difficulties ❷ importance; consequence; 无关～ of no consequence; of little account

tōu

偷 tōu ❶ steal; pilfer; pinch; ～工减料 scamp work and stint material; jerry-build; 〈俗〉go for wool and come back shorn ❷ stealthily; secretly; surreptitiously; ～渡 steal across (a guarded river, etc); ～看 look secretly; peep; peek; ～猎 poach; ～情 carry on a clandestine (usu extra-marital) love affair; ～听 listen in (on sb); eavesdrop; ～袭 (make a) sneak attack or raid; surprise attack; ～税漏税 evade taxes ❸ take (time) off; find (time); ～闲 snatch a moment of leisure; find time ❹ seek temporary ease; muddle along; ～安 seek temporary ease; (of a regime, etc) drag out a precarious existence; ～生 drag out an ignoble existence

偷换 tōuhuàn supersede surreptitiously; substitute stealthily; replace secretly; 偷梁换柱 cheat by substituting sth (usu inferior) for sth else; 偷天换日

commit a gigantic fraud

偷空 tōukòng take time off (to do sth); snatch a moment; ～打个盹 snatch a doze

偷懒 tōulǎn be unwilling to exert oneself; loaf on the job; be lazy

偷窃 tōuqiè also "偷盗" steal; pilfer

偷偷 tōutōu stealthily; covertly; surreptitiously; ～溜走 slink or sneak away; ～摸摸 furtively; on the sly

tóu

头(頭) tóu ❶ head; ～发 hair (on the human head); ～巾 scarf; kerchief; ～盔 (steel) helmet; ～颅 head; ～盖骨 also "头骨"〈生理〉cranium; skull; ～破血流 badly battered; 〈喻〉thoroughly beaten; ～重脚轻 top-heavy; dizzy ❷ hair (style); ～髻 hair bun or coil ❸ top; tip; end; 两～尖尖 with sharp points at both ends ❹ beginning; end; remnant; 开个好～ make a good beginning; 粉笔～儿 chalk stub or stump ❺ chief; leader; boss; ～head leader; chief; commander; ～目〈贬〉ringleader; chieftain; ～～儿〈口〉boss; head; chief; ～面人物 prominent figure; bigwig; big shot ❻ side; aspect; 两～讨好 try to please both sides ❼ number one; first; ～号 number or size one; first-rate; top quality; ～版 front page (of a newspaper) ❽ previous; before; in front; ～里 in front; ahead; beforehand; ～天 day before; yesterday; ～春节 before the Spring Festival ❾〈量〉a) used with domestic animals; 十～牛 ten head of cattle b) used with garlic; 两～蒜 two bulbs of garlic ❿ (tou) suffix forming a noun a) used with a noun; 骨～bone b) used with a verb; 接～头 contact c) used with an adjective; 准～儿 accuracy ⓫ (tou) suffix of a noun of *locality*；里～ inside

头等 tóuděng first-class; first-rate：～奖 first prize / ～大事 matter of prime importance; major event

头昏 tóuhūn dizzy; giddy：～眼花 have one's head swimming and one's eyes blurred; be seeing stars

头脑 tóunǎo ❶ brains; mind：～清楚 have a clear mind; be clear-headed / 有商业～ have a head for business; have a business sense ❷ see "头绪" ❸ (口) chief; chieftain; leader：头头脑脑 (various) leaders; bosses (of all kinds)

头皮 tóupí ❶ scalp ❷ *also* "头屑" dandruff; scurf

头痛 tóutòng *also* "头疼" (have a) headache：～脑热 headache and slight fever; slight ailment / 让人～的事情 knotty or thorny problem; headache

头头是道 tóutóushìdào clear and logical; closely reasoned and well argued；讲得～ argue convincingly

头衔 tóuxián title

头绪 tóuxù main thread (of sth complicated); clue：毫无～ have no clues to follow; be in a complete mess

投 tóu ❶ throw; toss; fling：～弹 drop a bomb; throw a hand grenade / ～河 throw or drown oneself in a river / ～篮〈体〉shoot (a basket) / ～射 throw; cast; project (a ray of light, etc) / ～掷 throw; fling; hurl / ～石问路 cast a stone to find out whether one should proceed; send up a trial balloon ❷ put in; invest：～料 feed material ❸ project; cast：～映 reflect; mirror ❹ send; dispatch; deliver：～寄 send by mail; post ❺ go to; enter; join：～敌 defect to the enemy / ～考 sign up for an examination / ～医 seek medical advice; go to a doctor ❻ fit in or agree with; cater to：～其所好 cater to sb's tastes ❼ approaching; before：～暮 towards dusk

投案 tóu'àn give oneself up to the po-

lice：～自首 surrender oneself to the police and confess one's crime

投保 tóubǎo buy insurance; insure：～单 insurance policy / ～金额 sum insured

投奔 tóubèn ❶ *also* "投靠" go to (a friend, etc) for shelter or help ❷ go and join (an organization, etc)

投笔从戎 tóubǐcóngróng throw aside the writing brush and join the army; give up academic pursuits for a military career

投标 tóubiāo submit a tender; enter a bid; bid (for a project)：～人 bidder; tenderer

投产 tóuchǎn go into operation; put into production; commission

投诚 tóuchéng surrender (to the just side); cross or come over

投递 tóudì deliver：～员 *also* "邮递员" postman; mailman

投放 tóufàng ❶ throw or put in ❷ put (money) into circulation; put (goods) on the market：～大量资金 invest heavily (in sth)

投稿 tóugǎo submit a piece of writing for publication; contribute (to a newspaper or magazine)：～人 contributor

投合 tóuhé ❶ see "投缘" ❷ cater to (sb's needs, etc)

投机 tóujī ❶ see "投缘" ❷ speculate; profiteer：～商 speculator; profiteer / ～倒把 engage in speculation and profiteering / ～分子 opportunist; careerist / ～取巧 gain advantage by trickery; be opportunistic

投井下石 tóujǐngxiàshí *also* "落井下石" hit a person when he's down

投票 tóupiào vote; cast a vote：～权 right to vote; suffrage / ～箱 ballot box / ～站 polling booth or station; the polls / ～否决 vote down / ～通过 vote through

投入 tóurù ❶ throw or put into：～训练 throw oneself into training ❷ do sth with concentration; be engrossed (in sth) ❸ input; investment; ～产出比 〈经〉input-output ratio

投身 tóushēn throw oneself; plunge; ～教育事业 dedicate oneself to educational work

投鼠忌器 tóushǔjìqì hesitate to take action against an evildoer for fear of harming good people involved

投诉 tóusù complain: ～信 letter of complaint

投宿 tóusù seek temporary lodging; put up for the night

投胎 tóutāi (迷信) be reincarnated

投桃报李 tóutáo-bàolǐ repay a favour; exchange favours; be reciprocal

投降 tóuxiáng surrender; capitulate; give oneself up

投影 tóuyǐng ❶ projection: ～机 overhead projector / ～电视 also "背投电视" projection television ❷ shadow ❸ reflection

投缘 tóuyuán congenial; agreeable: 两人十分～。The two of them hit it off well.

投资 tóuzī invest; put in (money, etc): ～办学 make an investment in education / ～银行 investment bank

骰 tóu also "骰子" 〈方〉dice

tòu

透 tòu ❶ penetrate; pass through; seep or leak through: ～光 let in light ❷ tell secretly; leak; give away: ～漏机密 let out or betray a secret ❸ thoroughly; in a penetrating way; clearly: 看～ understand thoroughly; see through / ～辟 penetrating; incisive; thorough / ～心儿凉 chill (sb) to the bone ❹ to saturation; to the extreme; completely: ～顶 〈贬〉thoroughly; absolutely; extremely / ～雨 saturating or soaking rain; soaker

❺ appear; look; show: 小伙子～着机灵。The lad has a smart look.

透彻 tòuchè penetrating; thoroughgoing; thorough: 讲～ explain (sth) clearly; drive (a point) home

透风 tòufēng ❶ let in air; aerate; ventilate ❷ air (sth) ❸ divulge a secret; leak; tip sb off

透露 tòulù divulge; leak; disclose: ～风声 leak or disclose information / 权威人士～ according to authoritative sources

透明 tòumíng transparent: ～度 transparency

透气 tòuqì ❶ let air in or through; aerate; ventilate: ～性 (of a fabric) air permeability ❷ breathe freely; breathe in fresh air ❸ see 透风❷

透视 tòushì ❶ perspective ❷ 〈医〉fluoroscopy; X-ray examination: 肺部～ have one's chest X-rayed ❸ see clearly; see through

透析 tòuxī ❶ 〈医〉dialysis ❷ (give a) penetrating analysis (of sth)

透支 tòuzhī ❶ overdraw; make an overdraft ❷ overspend; have or run a deficit ❸ draw one's salary in advance; anticipate one's pay

tū

凸 tū protruding; bulging; convex: ～面镜 〈理〉convex mirror

秃 tū ❶ bald; bare: ～顶 get bald; bald (head) / ～鹫 (cinereous) vulture ❷ barren (hill, etc); bare (tree, etc); blunt; unpointed: ～笔 bald writing brush; poor writing ability ❸ incomplete; deficient; unsatisfactory: 煞尾太～ a bit lame at the end

突 tū ❶ dash forward; charge; sprint: ～围 break through a ring of encirclement ❷ all of a sudden; abruptly; unexpected: ～变 sudden or abrupt change; 〈哲〉leap / ～袭 (make

a) surprise attack / ～飞猛进 advance by leaps and bounds; forge ahead rapidly ❸ projecting; protruding; sticking out

突出 tūchū ❶ charge out of; break through ❷ protruding; prominent; outstanding：～的特点 salient feature ❸ give prominence to; stress; emphasize；～主题 bring the main theme into bold relief

突发 tūfā erupt; burst or break out：心脏病～ (have a) heart attack / ～事件 unexpected incident; emergency

突击 tūjī ❶ make a sudden and violent attack; assault：～队 assault team; shock brigade or team; ad hoc team for an urgent task ❷ make a rush; do a crash job；～任务 rush job; shock work

突破 tūpò break through; surmount; overcome：～口 also "突破点"〈军〉breakthrough point; point of penetration / ～防线 break through the (opponent's) defence

突起 tūqǐ ❶ break out; suddenly appear：狂风～。A strong wind sprang up. ❷ rise high; tower

突然 tūrán suddenly; abruptly; unexpectedly：～停止 stop short / ～事变 eventuality; contingency

突如其来 tūrúqílái arise suddenly; come all of a sudden

突突 tūtū〈象声〉used of short, continuous sounds：心～地跳。My heart went pit-a-pat.

突兀 tūwù ❶ lofty; towering ❷ sudden; abrupt; unexpected

tú

图（圖） tú ❶ picture; drawing; chart；～案 pattern; design / ～表 chart; diagram; graph / ～钉 drawing pin; thumbtack / ～景 scene (in a picture, etc); view; prospect / ～例 legend (of a map,

etc)；key / ～形 graph; (geometric) figure / ～样 pattern; design; draft / ～章 seal; stamp / ～纸 blueprint; drawing / ～文电视 teletext ❷ scheme; seek; be after：别有所～ have different plans; have one's own axe to grind

图画 túhuà drawing; picture; painting

图解 tújiě ❶ diagram; graph; figure ❷〈数〉graphic solution：～法 graphic method

图谋 túmóu ❶ plot; scheme; conspire：～不轨 hatch a sinister plot; engage in underhand activities ❷ plan; stratagem; trap

图片 túpiàn picture; photograph：～社 picture service / ～说明 caption

图书 túshū books：～馆 library / ～资料 books and reference materials

图腾 túténg totem：～崇拜 totem worship; totemism

图像 túxiàng picture; image：～识别 pattern or image recognition

荼 tú

荼毒 túdú〈书〉inflict great suffering on; torment：～生灵 plunge the people into the depth of suffering

徒 tú ❶ on foot：～步旅行 travel on foot; hike ❷ bare; empty：～手 barehanded; unarmed ❸ merely; just; only：～有虚名 also "徒有其名" have an undeserved reputation ❹ in vain; to no avail; futile：～费唇舌 waste one's breath ❺ (usu 徒弟) apprentice; pupil; disciple：～工 apprentice (worker) / ～子～孙〈贬〉hangers-on and their spawn; gang of followers ❻ (of a religion) believer; follower ❼〈贬〉person; fellow; member of a clique

徒劳 túláo (make a) useless or futile effort; (work) in vain：～无功 also "徒劳无益" make a futile effort; work to no avail

徒然 túrán ❶ futile; in vain; to no avail; ～耗费时间 waste one's time ❷ only; merely; simply

徒刑 túxíng 〈法〉imprisonment; (prison) sentence;无期～ life sentence or imprisonment

途 tú way; road; route; ～经 by way of; via / ～径 way; path; avenue / ～中 on the way; en route

涂(塗) tú ❶ spread; apply; smear; ～料 coating; paint / ～脂抹粉 apply powder and paint; embellish; whitewash ❷ scribble; daub; scrawl; ～改 alter; modify; change / ～抹 daub; paint; scrawl / 鸦 scrawl; graffiti; 〈谦〉poor handwriting / ～乙〈书〉prune (an essay, etc); delete and alter ❸ blot or cross out; erase; ～去一行 delete a line ❹ 〈书〉mud; slush

涂饰 túshì ❶ cover with paint, lacquer, etc ❷ daub (plaster, etc) on a wall; 〈喻〉whitewash

涂炭 tútàn 〈书〉❶ mud and ashes — utter misery; severe suffering ❷ make (people) suffer

屠 tú slaughter (animals for food); massacre; butcher; ～场 slaughterhouse; abattoir / ～城 massacre the inhabitants of a captured city / ～刀 butcher's knife / ～夫 butcher; ruthless despot or ruler / ～户 (as a trade) butcher / ～杀 slaughter; massacre; kill indiscriminately / ～宰 butcher; slaughter

tǔ

土 tǔ ❶ soil; earth; dust; ～路 dirt road / 面如～色 turn deadly pale ❷ land; ground; territory; ～葬 burial (in the ground) ❸ local; native; indigenous;～话 also "土语" local dialect / ～皇帝 local tyrant or despot / ～特产 local speciality or specialty / ～

豪劣绅 local tyrants and evil gentry; despotic landlords / ～生～长 born and brought up on one's native soil; native ❹ home-made; folk;～布 hand-woven or homespun cloth / ～洋结合 combine indigenous and foreign methods; combine traditional and modern methods ❺ unrefined; unenlightened; crude; ～包子〈贬〉clodhopper; (country) bumpkin / ～头～脑 cloddish; unsophisticated

土崩瓦解 tǔbēng-wǎjiě disintegrate; crumble; fall to pieces

土地 tǔdì ❶ land; soil; ～改革 (shortened to 土改) land or agrarian reform ❷ territory; area ❸ (tǔdi) also "土地爷" local god of the land; village god

土豆 tǔdòu potato; 炸～片 crisps; (US) chips / 炸～条 chips; (US) French fries

土方 tǔfāng ❶ earthwork; cubic metre of earth ❷〈中医〉folk recipe or prescription; home remedy

土匪 tǔfěi bandit; brigand

土木 tǔmù building; construction; ～〈建筑〉工程 civil engineering

土气 tǔqì also "土里土气" rustic (style); uncouth (bearing); cloddish (manner);穿着～ dressed like a bumpkin

土壤 tǔrǎng soil;～肥力 soil fertility; 孕育战争的～ soil for war; hotbed of war

土星 tǔxīng 〈天文〉Saturn

土著 tǔzhù aboriginal; aborigine;～居民 original or indigenous inhabitants

吐 tǔ ❶ spit; ～痰 spit; expectorate / ～故纳新 exhale the old and inhale the new; get rid of the stale and take in the fresh ❷ emit; send out; put forth; ～穗〈农〉earing or heading (of cereal plants) ❸ say; tell; pour out; ～露心扉 unbosom oneself; pour out one's heart / ～字清楚 clear

articulation
see also tù

钍

钍 tǔ thorium (Th)

tù

吐

吐 tù ❶ spit; vomit; throw up: ~
血 spit blood / ~沫 saliva; spittle; spit ❷ give up unwillingly; disgorge: ~赃 disgorge ill-gotten gain
see also tǔ

兔(兎)

兔(兎) tù hare; rabbit: ~唇
〈医〉harelip; cleft lip /
~崽子〈粗〉brat; bastard / ~死狐悲
the fox mourns the death of the hare —
like grieves for like / ~子尾巴长不了
〈贬〉sth won't last long; sb's days are
numbered

tuān

湍

湍 tuān （usu 湍流）〈书〉swift
current; rapids; torrents: ~急
(of a current) swift; rapid

tuán

团(團)

团(團) tuán ❶ round; circu-
lar: ~扇 moon-shaped
or round fan / ~鱼 soft-shelled turtle
❷ roundish mass (esp) dumpling: 纸
~儿 paper crumpled up into a ball ❸
roll (into a ball) ❹ unite; assemble;
conglomerate: ~拜 (during a festival)
mutual greetings or congratulations in a
group ❺ group; organization ❻ (short
for 共产主义青年团) (the Communist)
Youth League: ~支部 (Youth) League
branch ❼ 〈军〉regiment: ~长 regimental commander ❽ 〈量〉*used of
roundish mass, or sometimes sth abstract*: 一~乱麻 a mass of entangled
flax yarn; a mess

团队 tuánduì group; corps; team: ~

精神 esprit de corps; team spirit / ~
协作 teamwork

团粉 tuánfěn cooking starch

团伙 tuánhuǒ gang; ring: ~犯罪
gang crime

团结 tuánjié unite; rally: ~一致 unite
as one / ~就是力量。Unity is
strength.

团聚 tuánjù ❶ reunite: 合家~ family
reunion ❷ gather; assemble

团体 tuántǐ organization; group;
team: ~票 group ticket / ~冠军 team
title

团团 tuántuán round and round; all
round: ~转 go round and round; move
in a circle / ~围住 surround completely; encircle; cluster round

团员 tuányuán ❶ member of a group
or delegation ❷ member of the Communist Youth League; League member

团圆 tuányuán ❶ reunion: ~饭 family reunion dinner ❷ round; circular: ~
脸 round face

tuī

推

推 tuī ❶ push; shove; thrust: ~
倒 push over; overturn; overthrow / ~拿〈中医〉massage / ~土机
bulldozer / (with a tool) cut; plane;
mow: ~头〈口〉cut sb's hair (with
clippers); have a haircut ❸ push forward; promote; advance: ~向高潮
push to a climax / ~出最新产品 promote latest products ❹ infer; deduce;
extend: ~论 inference; deduction;
corollary / ~求 find out (from what is
known); inquire / ~本溯源 *also* "推
本穷源" trace the origin; ascertain the
cause; get to the bottom ❺ decline;
shift; shirk: ~辞 *also* "推却" decline;
refuse; turn down / ~三阻四 make all
sorts of excuses; give (sb) the run-
around ❻ put off; delay; postpone: ~
延 *also* "推迟" put off; postpone ❼

hold in esteem; praise highly; ～重 think highly of; hold in esteem ❽ elect; choose; recommend; ～选 elect; choose

推波助澜 tuībō-zhùlán make a stormy sea stormier; add fuel to the fire; pour oil on the flames

推测 tuīcè *also* "推想" infer; conjecture; guess

推陈出新 tuīchén-chūxīn weed through the old to bring forth the new; bring forth the new from the old

推崇 tuīchóng hold in esteem; praise highly; extol; ～备至 be full of praise (for sb)

推动 tuīdòng push forward; promote; give impetus to; ～力 motive or driving force

推断 tuīduàn infer; deduce; 根据已知事实 ～ draw inferences from known facts

推翻 tuīfān ❶ overthrow (a regime, etc); overturn; topple ❷ repudiate (a decision, etc); cancel; reverse

推广 tuīguǎng popularize; spread; extend; 推而广之 by logical extension; by the same token; likewise

推己及人 tuījǐjírén put oneself in the place of another; do onto others as you would be done by; empathize

推荐 tuījiàn recommend; ～人 recommender; reference

推进 tuījìn ❶ push or carry forward; promote; give impetus to ❷ 〈军〉 move or push forward; drive

推举 tuījǔ choose; recommend; elect (a representative, etc)

推理 tuīlǐ reason; infer; ratiocinate; ～小说 ratiocinative novel

推敲 tuīqiāo weigh (one's words); deliberate; 经得起 ～ can stand close scrutiny

推让 tuīràng decline (a favour, etc) out of modesty; yield; submit

推算 tuīsuàn calculate; estimate;

reckon

推托 tuītuō offer as an excuse (for not doing sth); plead; 借故 ～ find an excuse to decline; beg off

推脱 tuītuō evade; dodge; shirk; ～责任 evade or shirk responsibility; shift blame onto others

推诿 tuīwěi *also* "推委" shift (blame, etc); pass the buck; 互相 ～ shift responsibility onto each other; pass the buck around

推销 tuīxiāo promote sales; market; sell; ～术 marketing technique; salesmanship / ～员 salesman

推卸 tuīxiè shirk (responsibility, etc); evade; shift off

推心置腹 tuīxīnzhìfù open one's heart (to sb); place full confidence (in sb); confide in (sb)

推行 tuīxíng carry out; pursue (a policy); introduce (sth new)

推移 tuīyí (of time) elapse; pass; (of a situation, etc) develop

tuí

颓 tuí ❶ collapse; crumble; become dilapidated or ruined; ～垣断壁 crumbling walls and ruined houses — a scene of decay or devastation; debris ❷ decline; decay; ～败 decline; decay; become corrupt / ～废 decadent; dissipated; degenerate ❸ dejected; dispirited; ～丧 dejected; crestfallen; listless / ～唐 dejected; dispirited; disconsolate

tuǐ

腿 tuǐ ❶ leg; ～肚子 calf (of the leg) ❷ leg-like support; leg; 床 ～ legs of a bed ❸ ham; 云 ～ Yunnan ham

腿脚 tuǐjiǎo legs and feet; ability to walk; ～不便 have difficulty walking /

~利落 move briskly; be nimble

tuì

退 tuì ❶ (make a) move backwards; withdraw; retreat: ~兵 retreat; withdraw one's troops; repulse (the enemy) / ~潮 ebb (tide) / ~烧 also "退热" bring down or allay a fever; (of a person's temperature) come down ❷ retire or withdraw from; leave; adjourn: ~场 leave (an arena, etc); exit / ~庭 adjourn the court / ~位 give up the throne; abdicate / ~席 leave a banquet or a meeting; walk out / ~学 leave school; discontinue one's schooling; drop out / ~隐 (旧) (of an official) retire from public life; go into retirement / ~居二线 retreat to the second line of work; give up an active post but remain as adviser / ~出历史舞台 step down from the stage of history ❸ decline; return; cancel: ~还 also "退回" return; send back / ~货 return merchandise / ~票 return a ticket; get a refund for a ticket / ~钱 refund; reimburse

退避 tuìbì withdraw and keep off; keep out of the way; yield: ~三舍 give way (to sb) to avoid a conflict; keep a good distance (from sb); avoid like a plague

退步 tuìbù ❶ lag or fall behind; retrogress ❷ make a concession; give in; give way ❸ room for manoeuvre; leeway: 留个~ leave some leeway; keep other options open

退耕 tuìgēng let cultivated land revert to its natural state; stop cultivating (land): ~还林 reforest cultivated land

退化 tuìhuà ❶ degenerate; retrograde; retrogress: 机能~ functional retrogradation ❷ worsen; become worse

退路 tuìlù ❶ route or line of retreat

退 ❷ see "退步❸"

退却 tuìquè ❶ (军) retreat; withdraw ❷ hang or shrink back; flinch

退让 tuìràng ❶ step back or aside; make way ❷ make a concession; yield; give in

退缩 tuìsuō shrink back; flinch; cower

退休 tuìxiū retire: ~金 retirement pay; pension / ~人员 retiree; pensioner; the retired

退役 tuìyì ❶ also "退伍" retire from active military service:~军人 demobilized soldier; ex-serviceman; veteran ❷ (of outdated weapons) be taken out of service; be decommissioned ❸ (esp of athletes) retire

蜕 tuì ❶ also "蜕皮" slough off; exuviate ❷ exuviae; slough; 蝉~ cicada exuviae ❸ also "蜕毛" (of birds) moult

蜕变 tuìbiàn ❶ (理) decay ❷ change qualitatively; transmute; degenerate

蜕化 tuìhuà ❶ slough off; exuviate ❷ also "蜕化变质" degenerate

煺 tuì scald (a pig, chicken, etc) in order to remove hairs or feathers

褪 tuì ❶ take off (clothes); shed (feathers) ❷ also "褪色"; "退色" fade

tūn

吞 tūn ❶ swallow; devour; gulp down: ~噬 devour; gobble up; engulf / ~咽 swallow ❷ seize; take (illegal) possession of; annex: ~并 annex; take over; gobble up

吞没 tūnmò ❶ embezzle or misappropriate (public money, etc) ❷ (of floods, etc) swallow up; submerge; engulf

吞吐 tūntǔ ❶ (of a port, etc) take in and send out in large quantities; handle：～量 handling capacity; volume of freight handled ❷ hesitate in speech; hum and ha：吞吞吐吐 mutter and mumble; speak hesitantly

tún

屯 tún ❶ gather; collect; store up：～聚 assemble（troops）; gather together ❷（usu 屯兵）station or quarter（troops）❸（often used in place names）village

囤 tún store up; hoard：～积居奇 hoard and corner; profiteer by hoarding　see also dùn

臀 tún buttock; rump：～部 buttocks /～围 hipline

tuō

托（❹-❻**託**） tuō ❶ hold in the palm; support with the hand or palm; hold up：～盘（serving）tray ❷ sth serving as a support：～子 base; stand; support ❸ serve as a foil; set off：～儿〈方〉decoy; come-on ❹ leave to the care of; entrust：～儿所 nursery; kindergarten; childcare centre ❺ give as a pretext; plead：～病 pleading illness; on the pretext of illness /～词 also "托辞" find a pretext; use a subterfuge; make an excuse /～故退席 leave a banquet or meeting on a pretext ❻ ask; count upon; rely on：～人情 ask sb to help arrange sth; seek the good offices of sb

托福 tuōfú ❶〈套〉thanks to you：托您老的福，我们都平安。Thank you for your concern, Sir. We are all safe and sound. ❷ TOEFL（Test of English as a Foreign Language）

托付 tuōfù entrust; commit to sb's care：把孩子～给邻居 leave one's child to the care of one's neighbour

托管 tuōguǎn trusteeship：～国 trust-

ee /～领土 trust territory

托拉斯 tuōlāsī〈经〉trust：反～法 antitrust law

托梦 tuōmèng〈迷信〉(as of a ghost) appear in one's dream and make a request or a revelation

托名 tuōmíng use sb else's name for one's own purpose; do sth in sb else's name：～行骗 practise fraud in sb else's name

托运 tuōyùn consign（goods, etc）for shipment; check（baggage）

拖 tuō ❶ pull; tug; drag：～把 also "拖布"; "墩布" mop; swab 儿 also "拖斗" trailer /～船 tugboat; tug; towboat /～儿带女 also "拖家带口" have one's children with one; be burdened with a family /～人下水 drag sb into crime, debauchery, etc, with one; corrupt sb /～着根辫子 wear a pigtail down one's back ❷ delay; postpone; procrastinate：～堂（of a teacher）not dismiss the class on time; drag on the class /～时间 dilly-dally; play for time

拖后腿 tuōhòutuǐ hinder or impede sb; hold sb back; be a drag on

拖拉 tuōlā ❶ also "拖沓" dilatory; slow; sluggish：作风～ sluggish style of work ❷ see "拖延"

拖拉机 tuōlājī tractor：手扶～ walking tractor /轮带式～ wheeled tractor /履带式～ tracked or caterpillar tractor

拖累 tuōlěi encumber; burden; implicate：受孩子～ be tied down by children

拖泥带水 tuōní-dàishuǐ messy; sloppy; slovenly：说话～ speak in a roundabout way

拖欠 tuōqiàn be behind in payment; be in arrears（with rent, etc）

拖鞋 tuōxié slippers

拖延 tuōyán delay; postpone; procrastinate：～战术 delaying or stalling tactics

脱 tuō ❶ shed; take or cast off; de-;～毛 shed hair or feathers; moult; depilate (furs, etc) /～帽 take off one's hat /～皮 slough off or shed skin; exuviate /～色 decolorize; fade /～衣舞 striptease /～脂奶 skim milk; non-fat milk /～氧核糖核酸 deoxyribonucleic acid (DNA) ❷ escape from; extricate oneself from; get out of:～轨 derail /～贫 get rid of or eradicate poverty; become prosperous /～缰之马 (like a) runaway horse ❸ miss out (words); omit; elide:这里～了一行。One line is missing here.

脱产 tuōchǎn be released from work (to do sth):～培训 off-job training /半～学习 study for half the time

脱钩 tuōgōu be separated or disconnected from; cut one's ties with; delink (one thing from another)

脱节 tuōjié come apart; be split or disjointed; be out of line:理论与实践～ Theory is divorced from practice.

脱口 tuōkǒu say sth unguardedly; blurt out:～秀 talk show /～而出 say unwittingly; blurt out; let slip

脱离 tuōlí cut or free oneself from; break away from:～群众 cut oneself off from the masses /～危险 be out of danger; escape from peril /～夫妻关系 be divorced (from sb)

脱落 tuōluò ❶ drop; fall off or away; come off ❷ (of words, etc) be omitted or missing

脱身 tuōshēn get away; get free; extricate oneself;～而走 give sb the slip; escape secretly

脱手 tuōshǒu ❶ slip out of the hand; let go; let slip ❷ get off one's hands; dispose of; sell

脱水 tuōshuǐ dehydration; 〈医〉loss of body fluids:～蔬菜 dehydrated vegetable

脱俗 tuōsú free from vulgarity; refined

脱胎 tuōtāi emerge from the womb of; be born out of; be derived from;～换骨 thoroughly remould oneself; undergo a radical transformation

脱位 tuōwèi also "脱白"〈医〉dislocation:关节～ joint dislocation

脱险 tuōxiǎn escape or be out of danger;侥幸～ have a narrow escape

脱销 tuōxiāo out of stock; sold out

脱颖而出 tuōyǐng'érchū (of talented person) rise from obscurity; become prominent; come to the fore

tuó

驮 tuó carry or bear on the back　see also duò

陀 tuó

陀螺 tuóluó spinning top:抽～ whip a top

坨 tuó ❶ (of food made of flour) stick together ❷ lump; heap

驼 tuó ❶ camel:～峰 hump (of a camel) /～色 light tan ❷ (usu 驼背) hunchbacked; humpbacked

砣(❶铊) tuó ❶ movable or sliding weight of a balance or steelyard ❷ stone roller

鸵 tuó

鸵鸟 tuóniǎo ostrich:～政策 ostrich policy; ostrichism

tuǒ

妥 tuǒ ❶ appropriate; suitable; proper:～当 appropriate; proper; suitable /～善 perfect; well-arranged; proper /～帖 fit and proper; appropriate; fitting ❷ (often used after a verb) ready; settled; finished:货已购～。The goods have been purchased.

妥协 tuǒxié come to terms; compromise：达成～ reach a compromise

椭（橢） tuǒ ellipse：～圆〈数〉ellipse；oval；ellipsoid

tuò

拓 tuò open up；develop；reclaim：～荒 open up virgin soil；reclaim wasteland / ～宽 broaden；extend / ～

展 expand；extend；develop *see also* tà

唾 tuò ❶ saliva；spittle：～液 *also* "唾沫" saliva；spittle ❷ spit；expectorate；show one's contempt（by spitting）：～骂 spit on and curse；spurn / ～弃 contemn；spurn；treat with contempt / ～手可得（get or win）with hands down；as easy as pie

W

wā

挖 wā dig; excavate; cut out: ~墙脚〈口〉undermine the foundation (of sth); cut the ground from under sb's feet / ~土机 excavator; steam shovel / ~出奸细 ferret out a spy / ~空心思〈贬〉rack or cudgel one's brains

挖苦 wāku speak sarcastically or ironically; taunt: ~话 sarcastic remark; ironic thrust

哇 wā ❶〈象声〉sound of crying, etc.: ~~地哭 cry loudly / 老鸦~~叫。Crows were cawing noisily. ❷〈叹〉used for emphasis: ~，好大的火! Wow, what a fire! see also wa

哇啦 wālā also "哇喇"〈象声〉din; uproar: ~~地乱吵 raise an uproar / ~~地说个不停 chatter on loudly

洼（窪） wā ❶〈low-lying; hollow; depressed: ~陷 depressed; sunken ❷ also "洼地" depression; low-lying area

蛙 wā frog: ~泳〈体〉(do the) breaststroke; frog style or stroke

wá

娃 wá ❶ baby; child: 女~儿 baby girl ❷〈方〉newborn animal: 狗~ puppy

wǎ

瓦 wǎ ❶ tile: ~房 tile-roofed house / ~匠 also "瓦工" bricklayer; tiler ❷ made of baked clay; earthen: ~罐 earthen jar ❸（short for 瓦特）〈电〉watt

瓦解 wǎjiě (cause to) fall apart; crumble; disintegrate

瓦蓝 wǎlán azure; bright blue; sky-blue

瓦砾 wǎlì rubble; debris

瓦斯 wǎsī gas: ~爆炸 gas explosion

wà

瓦 wà cover (a roof) with tiles; tile see also wǎ

袜（襪） wà socks; stockings; hose: 连裤~ pantyhose; tights / ~带 suspenders; garters / ~套 (ankle) socks

wa

哇 wa〈助〉variant of 啊 after words ending phonetically in u or ɑo: 多好~! Wonderful! see also wā

wāi

歪 wāi ❶ askew; tilted; slanting: ~扭 twisted; crooked / ~正

着 hit the mark by a fluke; win success by mere chance ❷ improper; unethical; evil: ～才 perverted genius or talent / ～道 crooked path; evil way of life; wicked idea or trick / ～理 lame argument; false reasoning; sophistry / ～风邪气 harmful trends and sinister practices

歪门邪道 wāimén-xiédào　crooked ways or means; dishonest practices: 搞 ～ be up to sth crooked

歪曲 wāiqū ❶ distort; misrepresent; twist ❷ *also* "歪斜" crooked; askew; aslant: 面部 ～ distorted face

wǎi

崴 wǎi　sprain; twist: ～ 了脚 sprain one's ankle

wài

外 wài ❶ outer; outside: ～ 观 outward appearance; exterior / ～壳 case; shell; husk / ～貌 appearance; looks / ～层空间 outer space ❷ other (than one's own): ～出 be not in; be not at home / ～逃 flee to some other place; flee the country / ～乡人 person from another part of the country; non-local ❸ foreign; external; alien: ～币 foreign currency / ～宾 foreign guest or visitor / ～电 dispatch from a foreign news agency / ～患 foreign aggression / ～文 *also* "外语" foreign language / ～侮 foreign or external aggression / ～债 external or foreign debt / ～星人 extraterrestrial being (ET) ❹ (relatives) of one's mother, sister or daughter: ～公 *also* "外祖父" maternal grandfather; grandpa / ～婆 *also* "外祖母" maternal grandmother; grandma / ～戚 ⟨史⟩ king's or emperor's in-law (on his mother's or wife's

side) / ～孙 daughter's son; grandson / ～甥女 sister's daughter; niece ❺ not of the same family, organization, etc; not closely related: 不是 ～ 人 no outsider; one of us ❻ besides; in addition; beyond: 百里之 ～ beyond a hundred *li*; over a hundred *li* away / ～加 additional; extra; plus ❼ unofficial: ～号 nickname / ～史 unofficial history; anecdotal account / ～传 unofficial biography or history

外表 wàibiǎo　(outward) appearance; exterior; surface: ～粗糙 have a rough surface; look coarse

外部 wàibù ❶ outside; external; extraneous: ～条件 external conditions ❷ exterior; outer; surface: ～形状 exterior shape

外道 wàidao　stand on ceremony; treat (sb) ceremoniously

外国 wàiguó　foreign (country): ～人 foreigner; alien / ～侨民 foreign national

外行 wàiháng ❶ lay; uninitiated; nonprofessional: ～话 lay language ❷ layman; novice; nonprofessional

外汇 wàihuì　foreign exchange or currency: ～储备 foreign exchange reserve

外籍 wàijí　(of) foreign nationality: ～华人 foreign national of Chinese origin / ～专家 foreign expert

外交 wàijiāo　diplomacy; foreign affairs: ～官 diplomat / ～关系 diplomatic relations / ～政策 foreign policy

外界 wàijiè　of the external or outside world; outside: ～舆论 public opinion

外科 wàikē　⟨医⟩ surgical department: ～手术 surgical operation / ～医生 surgeon

外快 wàikuài　extra profit or earnings

外来 wàilái　outside; foreign; extraneous: ～户 household or person from another place; non-native / ～语 word of foreign origin; foreign word; loanword

外露 wàilù　show (one's feelings, etc); display; be an extrovert

外面 wàimiàn　❶ appearance; exterior; surface; ~儿光 (have a) deceptively smooth appearance; (be) slick on the outward ❷ (wàimian) *also* "外边" outside; out; ~有人等你。Someone is waiting for you outside.

外贸 wàimào　(short for 对外贸易) foreign or external trade; ~经营权 power or authorization to engage in foreign trade

外…内… wài…nèi…　*also* "外…中…" outwardly … but inwardly …; ~强中干 outwardly strong but inwardly weak; fierce of mien but faint of heart / 外柔内刚 outwardly gentle but inwardly tough; iron fist in a velvet glove / 外松内紧 relaxed in appearance but alert in reality

外勤 wàiqín　❶ work done in the field (not in the office nor at headquarters); 跑~ do fieldwork ❷ field personnel; fieldworker

外事 wàishì　❶ foreign or external affairs; ~活动 public function concerning foreigners; ~办公室 (shortened as 外办) foreign affairs office; (at a school) international programme ❷ affairs outside one's family or personal circle; 不问~ not care about outside affairs

外套 wàitào　❶ overcoat; coat; outer garment

外围 wàiwéi　periphery; ~组织 peripheral organization / 扫清~ wipe out peripheral obstacles; 〈喻〉 pave the way (for sth)

外线 wàixiàn　❶ 〈军〉 exterior lines ❷ outside (telephone) connections; 拨~ dial an outside number

外向 wàixiàng　❶ extroversion; 性格~的人 extrovert ❷ export-oriented (economy, etc)

外心 wàixīn　(harbour) unfaithful or disloyal intentions (about one's husband or wife, or one's country or company, etc)

外延 wàiyán　denotation; extension; ~意义 denotative meaning

外衣 wàiyī　❶ coat; jacket; outer garment ❷ outward show; appearance; façade; 披着合法的~ behind a façade of legitimacy

外遇 wàiyù　(have an) extra-marital affair

外援 wàiyuán　❶ foreign aid; outside help; external assistance ❷ 〈体〉 foreign player

外在 wàizài　external; outside; extrinsic

外资 wàizī　foreign capital or investment; ~企业 (shortened as 外企) foreign-invested or -funded enterprise; foreign enterprise

外族 wàizú　❶ relative on mother's or wife's side ❷ (person) not of the same clan ❸ foreigner; alien

wān

弯(彎) wān　❶ curved; crooked; ~路 winding road or path; detour / ~曲 (of road, river, etc) winding; meandering; zigzag ❷ bend; ~弓〈书〉 draw or bend a bow / ~腰 bend over

剜 wān　cut, gouge or scoop out; ~肉补疮 *also* "挖肉补疮" cut out good flesh to patch up an ulcer — resort to a remedy worse than the ailment; rob Peter to pay Paul

湾(灣) wān　❶ bend in a stream; 水~ river bend ❷ gulf; bay; estuary ❸ (cast) anchor; moor (a boat, etc)

蜿 wān

蜿蜒 wānyán　❶ (of snake, etc) wriggle ❷ wind; zigzag; meander; 山路~ winding mountain path

豌

豌 wān　also "豌豆" pea

wán

丸 wán ❶ ball；pellet：鱼～子 fish-ball ❷ pill；bolus：～剂 pill / ～药 pill or bolus of Chinese medicine

纨 wán 〈书〉fine silk fabric：～袴子弟 profligate son of the rich；playboy

完 wán ❶ intact；entire；whole：～好 intact；whole；in good condition / ～人 perfect man / ～胜 win a total victory（over sb）；rout ❷ exhaust；finish；use up：米吃～了 run out of rice ❸ end；finish；be over or through：～工 complete a project；finish doing sth / ～结 end；conclude；finish / ～婚 also "完姻"〈书〉consummate a marriage；get married ❹ pay（tax）

完备 wánbèi all；complete；perfect：设施～ have all necessary facilities

完毕 wánbì finish；complete；end：准备～。Everything is ready.

完璧归赵 wánbìguīzhào return sth to its owner in perfect condition

完成 wánchéng accomplish；complete；fulfil

完蛋 wándàn be done for；be ruined or finished：快要～了 be on one's last legs

完满 wánmǎn successful；perfect：～结束 come to a successful close

完美 wánměi perfect；consummate；superb：～无缺 perfect；impeccable；flawless

完全 wánquán complete；entire；full：～相同 identical

完善 wánshàn ❶ perfect；ideal；consummate：装备～ well-equipped ❷ make perfect；improve：～管理 perfect or improve management

完事 wánshì finish；be done；come to an end：～大吉 get it over and done with

完整 wánzhěng complete；entire；intact：结构～ well-organized / ～地保存 preserve（sth）intact

玩 wán ❶ play；have fun；amuse or enjoy oneself：～要 play；frolic；have fun / ～物 plaything；toy / ～得开心 have a good time ❷ play（a game or an instrument）：～儿票 perform（Chinese opera，etc）as an amateur / ～儿不转〈口〉cannot manage；find sth too much for one ❸ use；employ；resort to（tricks，etc）❹ trifle or toy with；treat lightly：～忽职守（commit）dereliction of duty ❺ enjoy；appreciate；find pleasure in：～赏 enjoy；admire；take pleasure or delight in / ～物丧志 lose one's lofty aspirations for sensuous pleasures；blunt the edge of one's determination in sensuous luxury ❻ curio

玩火 wánhuǒ play with fire：～自焚 whoever plays with fire shall perish by it

玩具 wánjù toy；plaything：～熊 teddy bear / ～手枪 toy pistol

玩弄 wánnòng ❶ play or juggle with；show off：～词句 indulge in rhetoric ❷ play fast and loose with；dally or trifle with：～女性 womanize ❸ resort to（tricks，etc）；engage in；employ：～权术 play politics

玩偶 wán'ǒu doll；toy figurine；〈喻〉plaything

玩儿命 wánrmìng 〈口〉gamble or play with one's life；do things recklessly：～干活儿 work recklessly（ie at the expense of one's health）

玩儿完 wánrwán 〈口〉the jig is up；the fun is over；（of sb）be done for

玩世不恭 wánshìbùgōng defy all ethical values；disdain worldly affairs；be cynical

玩味 wánwèi ponder；chew the cud；ruminate：颇耐～ well worth pondering

玩笑 wánxiào　joke; jest: 开～ tell or crack a joke

玩意儿 wányìr　*also* "玩艺儿"〈口〉❶ toy; plaything ❷ (of acrobatics, etc) (item of) performance; trick ❸ thing; creature: 真不是个～ (of sb) be an utter scoundrel

顽 wán ❶ stupid; foolish; dense ❷ stubborn; persistent: ～敌 stubborn enemy; inveterate foe / ～疾 stubborn, chronic disease; persistent trouble / ～抗 put up a stubborn resistance ❸ naughty; mischievous: ～童 naughty child; urchin ❹ *see* "玩❶-❸" wán

顽固 wángù ❶ obstinate; stubborn; headstrong: ～不化 incorrigibly obstinate; dyed in the wool ❷ bitterly opposed to change or progress; bigoted: diehard: ～分子 diehard (element) ❸ (of disease) chronic and hard to cure

顽劣 wánliè　stubborn and wicked; (of a child) naughty and unruly

顽皮 wánpí　(usu of a child) naughty; mischievous

顽强 wánqiáng　indomitable; staunch; tenacious

顽症 wánzhèng ❶ stubborn, chronic disease; persistent ailment ❷〈喻〉sth hard to deal with; hard nut to crack

烷 wán　*also* "烷烃"〈化〉alkane

wǎn

宛 wǎn ❶ winding; circuitous; tortuous ❷〈书〉as if; just like: ～然在目 as if before one's very eyes / ～如一条玉带 just like a jade belt

宛转 wǎnzhuǎn ❶ *see* "宛❶" ❷ *also* "辗转" toss about; pass through (many places) ❸ *see* "婉转" wǎnzhuǎn

莞 wǎn

莞尔 wǎn'ěr　〈书〉smile: ～一笑 give a winsome smile

挽(❶❸**輓**) wǎn ❶ draw; hold; pull: ～弓 draw a bow / ～着裤腿 with one's trouser legs rolled up ❷ reverse; retrieve ❸ elegize (the deceased) 〈书〉～词 *also* "挽辞" elegiac words; elegy / ～歌 dirge; elegy / ～联 elegiac couplet ❹ *see* "绾" wǎn

挽回 wǎnhuí ❶ retrieve; recover; redeem: 无可～ beyond retrieval; irretrievable / ～面子 save face / ～名誉 redeem or recover one's reputation ❷ take back; recover (rights, etc)

挽救 wǎnjiù　save; rescue; deliver: ～民族危亡 save the nation from subjugation

挽留 wǎnliú　urge sb to stay

晚 wǎn ❶ evening; night (time): ～安〈套〉good night / ～场 *also* "夜场" evening show or performance / ～饭 supper; dinner / ～会 evening entertainment; soirée; evening party / ～霞 sunset glow / ～礼服 black tie; full evening dress ❷ far on in time; late: ～婚 marrying at a mature age; late marriage / ～秋 late autumn; late-autumn crop / ～熟〈农〉late-maturing / ～育 late childbirth ❸ succeeding; junior: ～辈 younger generation; (sb's) junior ❹〈谦〉yours humbly: ～生〈书〉I, your humble pupil

晚点 wǎndiǎn　(of a train, plane, etc) late; behind schedule; delayed: ～运行 run behind schedule / ～15 分钟 be fifteen minutes late

晚节 wǎnjié ❶ integrity or honour in one's later years: ～不终 ruin one's integrity in one's later years ❷〈书〉remaining years (of a person or dynasty); sunset of life

晚景 wǎnjǐng ❶ evening scene ❷ *also* "晚境" life or circumstances in old age: ～凄凉 lead a miserable, dreary life in one's old age

晚年 wǎnnián　old age；one's later or remaining years

晚期 wǎnqī　later period；(of disease, etc) terminal stage：～作品 one's later works

惋 wǎn　〈书〉heave a sigh；sigh；～伤 sigh with sorrow；lament

惋惜 wǎnxī　feel sorry；sympathize；～错过了机会 sorry for having missed an opportunity

婉 wǎn　❶ mild；restrained；tactful：～劝 plead (with sb) tactfully / ～顺 (of women) gentle and agreeable；meek　❷〈书〉lovely；graceful；elegant：～容 lovely features；graceful manners

婉辞 wǎncí　❶ also "婉词" gentle or courteous words；euphemism：～推却 decline courteously　❷ also "婉拒"；"婉谢" graciously decline；politely refuse

婉丽 wǎnlì　〈书〉❶ beautiful；lovely　❷ (of poems) graceful：清新～ fresh and graceful

婉言 wǎnyán　gentle remarks；tactful expressions：～劝阻 try to dissuade tactfully

婉约 wǎnyuē　〈书〉subtle and restrained；～其辞 use restrained language；speak or write with restraint

婉转 wǎnzhuǎn　also "宛转" ❶ mild and indirect；tactful；gentle　❷ (of sound, etc) sweet and agreeable

绾 wǎn　coil up：头上一个发髻 coil or tie up one's hair

皖 Wǎn　another name for Anhui (安徽)

碗 wǎn　❶ bowl：～橱 cupboard　❷ bowl-like vessel or object：轴一儿 axle-bowl

wàn

万(萬) wàn　❶ ten thousand；十一～ hundred thousand / ～里挑一 one in ten thousand　❷ very

great number；myriad；all；～物 also "万类" all creatures / ～花筒 kaleidoscope / ～死不辞 willing to risk a thousand deaths (for a cause, etc) / ～象更新 everything looks fresh and gay；everything takes on a new look / ～应灵药 elixir for all ills；panacea　❸ absolutely；extremely；under all circumstances：～全 completely safe；surefire (plan, etc) / ～幸 extremely lucky or fortunate (in surviving a disaster, etc) / ～无此理 cannot be true under any circumstances

万般 wànbān　❶ all kinds　❷ exceedingly；extremely：～无奈 have no alternative whatever (but to do sth)

万不得已 wànbùdéyǐ　only when it is absolutely necessary；as a last resort：～的办法 last-ditch plan；last resort

万恶 wàn'è　❶ absolutely vicious：～不赦 vicious beyond redemption；iniquitous　❷ all evil

万方 wànfāng　❶ all parts (of the country or world)：～同庆 (of a festival) be celebrated everywhere　❷ see "万千"

万分 wànfēn　also "万状" very much；exceedingly；extremely

万古 wàngǔ　throughout the ages；for ever and ever；～长青 remain fresh forever；be everlasting / ～流芳 leave a good name in history

万家灯火 wànjiādēnghuǒ　lamps and candles of a myriad households (as of a city)；lights twinkling in numerous houses

万劫不复 wànjiébùfù　beyond redemption；doomed forever

万金油 wànjīnyóu　❶ Tiger Balm (for treating various minor ailments)　❷ Jack of all trades (and master of none)

万籁 wànlài　all kinds of (nature's) sounds：～俱寂 all is quiet；silence reigns everywhere

万里 wànlǐ　ten thousand *li*; very long; boundless;～长城 Great Wall /～长空 boundless sky /～长征 Long March (1934-1935); very long journey

万马 wànmǎ　*used in the following idioms*:～奔腾 like ten thousand horses galloping ahead; going full steam ahead /～齐喑 ten thousand horses stand muted; apathy reigns supreme

万能 wànnéng　❶ omnipotent; all powerful ❷ universal; all-purpose; versatile;～胶 all-purpose adhesive /～钥匙 master key; pass-key

万千 wànqiān　also "万方"; "万端" myriad; numerous; multifarious:仪态～ graceful in all aspects

万人 wànrén　numerous people; all and sundry:～坑 mass grave /～空巷。The whole town turns out (to celebrate, etc).

万事 wànshì　all things; everything:～大吉 everything is just fine; all's well and propitious /～俱备,只欠东风。Everything is ready, except for one crucial factor.

万岁 wànsuì　❶ long live:世界和平～! Long live world peace! ❷ also "万岁爷" (term of deference to the emperor) His majesty; Your majesty

万万 wànwàn　❶ hundred million:千千～ millions upon millions ❷ absolutely (not); on no account:～不可失信 absolutely must not break one's promise

万无一失 wànwúyīshī　have every chance of success; run no risk at all; be perfectly safe

万一 wànyī　❶ one ten-thousandth; minutest portion ❷ contingency; emergency; eventuality:不怕一万,就怕～。(俗) One should always prepare for the worst even if it is unlikely to happen. ❸〈连〉(just) in case; if by any chance:～他不来呢? What if he doesn't come?

万众 wànzhòng　millions of people; the masses;～一心 (millions of people) united as one; all of one heart and mind

腕 wàn　❶ wrist;～力 wrist strength or power;〈喻〉ability (to get things done); finesse

腕儿 wànr　also "大腕儿"〈口〉star (actor, anchor, etc); mainstay (in a theatrical troupe, etc)

蔓 wàn　tendrilled vine:瓜～儿 melon vine　*see also* mán; màn

wāng

汪 wāng　❶ (of water) deep and wide:～洋大海 boundless ocean ❷ (of liquids) collect; gather; accumulate:眼里～着泪水 eyes brimming with tears ❸〈量〉*used for liquid*:一～清水 a pool of clear water

汪汪 wāngwāng　❶ brimming with water or tears:两眼泪～(with) tearful eyes ❷〈象声〉(of a dog) bark; yap; bow-wow

wáng

亡 wáng　❶ flee; escape; run away ❷ lose; be lost;～佚 lost; missing ❸ die; pass away; perish;～故 pass away; die /～灵 also "亡魂" soul of a deceased person; ghost /～友 deceased friend ❹ fall; subjugate

亡国 wángguó　have one's nation subjugated;～奴 slave of a foreign conqueror; vanquished people /～灭种 suffer national subjugation and extermination

亡命 wángmìng　❶ flee; escape; go into exile;～他乡 flee one's hometown ❷ desperate; reckless:～之徒 desperado

亡羊补牢 wángyángbǔláo　mend the fold after a sheep is lost; take belated action;～,犹未为晚。Better late than never.

王 wáng ❶ king; monarch; prince:~储 crown prince / ~妃 princess; consort of a prince / ~府 residence of a prince / ~宫 (imperial or royal) palace / ~后 queen; queen consort / ~位 throne / ~子 prince / ~公大臣 princes, dukes and ministers / ~孙公子 descendent of a noble family ❷ head; chief; king:~浆 royal jelly ❸ best; strongest:~水〈化〉aqua regia

王八 wángba ❶ (popular term for 乌龟 or 鳖) turtle; tortoise:~蛋〈粗〉bastard; son of a bitch ❷〈粗〉cuckold ❸〈旧〉pimp; pander

王朝 wángcháo dynasty; reign (of a monarch); royal or imperial court

王法 wángfǎ law of the land; law:目无~ lawless; defying the law

王国 wángguó kingdom;〈喻〉realm; domain:数学的~ domain of mathematics

王牌 wángpái trump card; ace:~军 elite troops; ace or crack force

王室 wángshì ❶ royal family:~宗亲 relative of a royal family ❷ royal or imperial court

王爷 wángye 〈旧〉(reverent term of address for a prince) Your or His Highness

wǎng

网(網) wǎng ❶ net (for fishing, etc); net-like object:~兜 string bag / ~眼 mesh ❷ network:交通~ network of transport ❸〈信息〉network; web; (esp) Internet:~吧 Internet café; cyberbar / ~迷 also "网虫" Internet buff or geek; web enthusiast / ~民 netizen; network population / ~页 web page / ~站 web station / ~址 Internet address; website ❹ catch with a net; net ❺ cover or enclose as with a net; enmesh

网点 wǎngdiǎn network:商业~ commercial network; trading establishments; outlets

网开一面 wǎngkāiyīmiàn leave one side of the net open — give (sb) a way out; be lenient or merciful

网罗 wǎngluó ❶ fishing net; bird trap ❷ enlist the services of; recruit:~人才 scout for talent

网络 wǎngluò ❶ system; network:邮政~ postal network ❷〈信息〉network; web; cyber:~化 networking / ~终端 network terminal / ~出入口 portal / ~服务器 network server / 浏览器 web browser

网球 wǎngqiú tennis:~拍 tennis racket / ~场 tennis court

网上 wǎngshàng 〈信息〉on-line:~购物 shopping on Internet; on-line shopping / ~冲浪 surf the net; net surfing

枉 wǎng ❶ crooked; warped; wrong ❷ twist; bend; pervert:~法 pervert the law ❸ treat unjustly; wrong (sb):~杀无辜 kill an innocent person wantonly ❹ in vain; to no avail; uselessly:~然 futile; useless / 不~此行。The trip was not made in vain.

枉费 wǎngfèi waste; try in vain; be of no avail:~心机 rack one's brains in vain; scheme to no avail

枉自 wǎngzì in vain; for nothing; no purpose:~费力 work hard at sth in vain

罔 wǎng 〈书〉❶ deceive ❷ no; not:药石~效 beyond medical cure

往 wǎng ❶ go:寒来暑~ as summer goes and winter comes; as time passes ❷ in the direction of; towards:~外走 go out / ~下说 go on (talking) ❸ former; past; previous:~年 in former years; previously / ~日 in former days; in the past

往常 wǎngcháng as before; as usual;

比～晚 later than usual

往返 wǎngfǎn　travel to and fro; go back and forth; ～票 round-trip ticket

往复 wǎngfù ❶ move back and forth; repeat oneself; 四时～ cycle of four seasons *also*「往还」❷ contact; intercourse; exchange (of correspondence, etc)

往后 wǎnghòu ❶ from now on; later on; in the future ❷ backwards; back

往来 wǎnglái ❶ come and go ❷ contact; exchange; dealings; 友好～ friendly exchanges / ～账 current account

往事 wǎngshì　past events; ～不堪回首 can't bear to look back

往往 wǎngwǎng　often; frequently; usually

往昔 wǎngxī　*also*「往时」in former times; in those days; 一如～ as before

惘 wǎng　feel frustrated; be in a trance; ～然若失 feel lost; be listless

wàng

妄 wàng ❶ absurd; ridiculous; ～念 fanciful or absurd idea; wild fancy ❷ presumptuously; excessively; rashly; ～称 claim presumptuously / ～为 take reckless action; commit an outrage / ～加评论 make indiscreet or rash comments

妄图 wàngtú　try in vain; make a futile attempt

妄想 wàngxiǎng　vain hope; futile attempt; wishful thinking; ～狂〈医〉paranoia; paranoid / ～统治世界 vainly hope to dominate the whole world

妄自菲薄 wàngzìfěibó　belittle or humble oneself unduly; have a sense of inferiority

妄自尊大 wàngzìzūndà　be overweening or overbearing; be self-important or arrogant

忘 wàng　forget; neglect; (of sth) escape one's memory; ～本 forget one's origin or past (suffering, etc) / ～性大 be forgetful; have a poor memory

忘恩负义 wàng'ēnfùyì　be ungrateful; bite the hand that feeds one

忘乎所以 wànghūsuǒyǐ　forget oneself; get swollen-headed; 兴之所起，～ be carried away by one's impulse; let one's enthusiasm get the better of one

忘怀 wànghuái　forget; dismiss from one's mind; 难以～ unable to dismiss from one's mind; (of sth) unforgettable

忘记 wàngjì ❶ forget; cannot recall or remember ❷ overlook (duties, etc); neglect; lose sight of

忘年交 wàngniánjiāo　friendship between people of different generations; good friends despite great disparity in age

忘情 wàngqíng ❶ be unruffled by emotion; be detached or indifferent; 不能～ remain sentimentally attached ❷ let oneself go; enjoy with abandon; ～地歌唱 sing to one's heart's content

忘却 wàngquè　*also*「忘掉」forget; fail to remember

忘我 wàngwǒ　be selfless; ～地劳动 toil selflessly; work untiringly

忘形 wàngxíng　be beside oneself (with glee, etc); forget oneself; be puffed up

旺 wàng　flourishing; vigorous; abundant; ～季 peak period; busy season / ～盛 exuberant; vibrant; vigorous / ～销 sell well / 火很～ roaring fire; raging flames

望 wàng ❶ look or gaze (into the distance); ～而却步 shrink back at the sight (of sth dangerous or difficult); recoil; flinch / ～而生畏 be terrified or awed by the sight; look with fear; stand in awe ❷ call on; pay a visit; visit ❸ hope; expect; look forward to; ~子成龙 long to see one's children succeed in life; hope one's children will make the grade ❹ reputation; fame; prestige; ~族 distinguished or prominent family ❺ to; towards; ~东走 go eastwards / ~ 观众招手 wave to the audience ❻ （usu 望月）full moon; （usu 望日）day of the full moon (15th, sometimes 16th, of a lunar month)

望尘莫及 wàngchénmòjí fall way behind; be far too inferior

望穿秋水 wàngchuānqiūshuǐ *also* "望眼欲穿" gaze with eager expectation; look forward with impatient expectancy

望风 wàngfēng ❶ be on the lookout (for people doing sth secret); keep watch ❷ at the sight of; ~而逃 flee at the mere sight or rumour / ~披靡 (of a demoralized army) flee pell-mell at the mere sight of the enemy; flee at sight

望梅止渴 wàngméizhǐkě look at plums to quench thirst — console oneself with false hopes; feed on fancies

望文生义 wàngwénshēngyì take the words at their face value; interpret without real understanding

望洋兴叹 wàngyángxīngtàn bemoan one's inadequacy in the face of a great task; feel powerless and frustrated before sth difficult or expensive

望远镜 wàngyuǎnjìng telescope; 小~ opera glasses

wēi

危 wēi ❶ danger; hazard; peril; ~房 house in dangerous state; ramshackle or crumbling house / ~言耸听 say sth frightening to produce a great sensation; make a sensational or an alarmist statement / ~在旦夕 be in imminent danger; be on the verge of

death or destruction; (of one's fate) hang by a thread / ~重病人 serious or critical cases ❷ endanger; jeopardize; imperil ❸ 〈书〉 high; precipitous; sheer; ~峰 precipitous peak ❹ 〈书〉 proper; erect; upright; ~坐 sit bolt upright

危害 wēihài harm; endanger; jeopardize; ~性 harm; perniciousness

危机 wēijī crisis; ~感 sense of crisis / ~四伏 beset with crises

危急 wēijí critical; precarious; 情况~ be faced with imminent danger / ~关头 (in) time of great danger; (at a) critical juncture

危难 wēinàn danger and disaster; ~之中见真情。A true friend is best found in adversity.

危亡 wēiwáng danger of extinction or destruction

危险 wēixiǎn dangerous; perilous; risky; ~品 dangerous goods or articles / ~信号 danger signal

威 wēi ❶ impressive strength; mighty force; prowess; ~猛 powerful and valiant / ~名 prestige or fame (based upon one's prowess) / ~势 (of sb) power and influence; (of sth) force and momentum / ~望 prestige ❷ by force; by sheer strength; ~逼 compel or threaten by force; coerce / ~吓 intimidate; browbeat; bully

威风 wēifēng ❶ power and prestige; awe-inspiring bearing or manners; 要~ throw one's weight about / ~凛凛 have an awe-inspiring bearing or a commanding presence; be majestic-looking ❷ imposing; impressive; awe-inspiring

威力 wēilì (formidable) power; force; might; 发挥政策~ fully tap the potential of a policy; give full play to a policy

威慑 wēishè deter; ~力量 deterrent (force) / ~政策 policy of deterrence

威士忌 wēishìjì whisky

威武 wēiwǔ　might; force; power: ～不屈 not submit to force / ～雄壮 full of power and grandeur; mighty and magnificent

威胁 wēixié　threaten; menace; intimidate: ～利诱 combine threats with inducements; use both the carrot and the stick

威信 wēixìn　prestige; popularity: ～扫地 have one's prestige swept into the dust; be completely discredited

威严 wēiyán　dignified; imposing; awe-inspiring: 保持尊长的～ keep an elder's dignity

透 wēi

逶迤 wēiyí　also "委蛇"〈书〉winding; meandering

偎 wēi (usu 偎依) snuggle or cuddle up to; lean close to: ～在怀里 nestle in one's arms

微 wēi ❶ minute; slight; micro-: ～风 (gentle) breeze / ～电脑 also "微机" micro-computer; personal computer (PC) / ～电子 microelectronics / ～粒子 micro-particle / ～生物 microorganism; microbe / ～处理机〈信息〉microprocessor / ～量元素 trace element; microelement / 略表～忱〈书〉as a (slight) token of one's sincere gratitude ❷ one millionth part; micro-: ～米 micron ❸ profound; abstruse; esoteric

微波 wēibō　microwave: ～炉 microwave oven / ～通信 microwave communication

微薄 wēibó　little; meagre; scanty

微不足道 wēibùzúdào　not worth mentioning; insignificant; negligible

微词 wēicí　also "微辞"〈书〉complaint; covert criticism

微服 wēifú　〈书〉in plain clothes; incognito: ～私访 (of officials) travel incognito on a fact-finding mission

微观 wēiguān　microcosmic; microscopic; micro-: ～经济 microeconomy /

～世界 microcosmos; microcosm; micro-world

微乎其微 wēihūqíwēi　very little; insignificant; negligible

微积分 wēijīfēn　〈数〉(differential and integral) calculus

微贱 wēijiàn　humble; lowly; obscure: 出身～ be of humble origin

微妙 wēimiào　delicate; sensitive; subtle

微弱 wēiruò　faint; feeble; weak: ～多数 (by a) slender or narrow majority

微缩 wēisuō　microform: ～景观 miniature scenery / ～软片 microfiche

微调 wēitiáo　adjust slightly; fine-tune: 工资～ slight raise of salary

微小 wēixiǎo　little; tiny; slight

微笑 wēixiào　smile: ～服务 smiling service

微型 wēixíng　miniature; mini-: ～汽车 minicar; mini; subcompact / ～小说 mini-novel; one-page novel

煨 wēi ❶ cook over a slow fire; stew; simmer ❷ roast (potatoes, etc) in fresh cinders

巍 wēi　towering; soaring; lofty: ～然屹立 stand lofty and firm; tower majestically / ～峨的群山 lofty mountains

wéi

韦(韋) wéi

韦编三绝 wéibiānsānjué　〈喻〉study diligently; be an avid reader

为(爲) wéi ❶ do; act; perform: ～非作歹 do evil; commit outrages ❷ serve or act as; take as: ～人师表 be an exemplary teacher; be a model of virtue and learning / 以团结～重 value solidarity above everything else ❸ become; turn: 转忧～喜. Worry turns into joy. ❹ be; mean; make: ～限 be within the limit of; be no more than / ～数可观 be considerable in number or quantity ❺ *used together with 所 to introduce the agent*:～风雪所阻 be held up by a snowstorm; be snowed up ❻〈副〉a) *used after certain monosyllabic adjectives to form adverbs indicating extent, scope, etc*:广～流传 spread far and wide b) *used after certain monosyllabic adverbs to strengthen the tone*:更～重要 even more important ❼ *used before a monosyllabic word to form a verb*:～害 harm; hurt / ～患 bring disaster or trouble; be a curse or burden / ～生 earn one's living (by sth) / ～伍 associate or mix (with sb); keep company

see also wèi

为富不仁 wéifùbùrén rich and cruel; wealthy and heartless

为难 wéinán ❶ be embarrassed; feel awkward or uneasy ❷ make things difficult for (sb)

为人 wéirén be; behave; conduct:～处世 the way one conducts oneself in society / ～正派 be a decent man

为时 wéishí ❶ *also* "为期" last:～一周 last a week ❷ in terms of time:～过早 premature; too early or soon; far ahead of time

为首 wéishǒu headed or led by; with sb as the leader:～分子 leading member; ringleader

为所欲为 wéisuǒyùwéi do as one pleases; have one's own way

为止 wéizhǐ till; up to:迄今～ to this day; so far; up to now

圩 wéi dike; embankment *see also* xū

圩子 wéizi *also* "围子" protective embankment round low-lying fields; defensive wall round a village:土～ fortified village

违（違） wéi ❶ go or be against; disobey; vio-

late:～犯 violate; infringe; break / ～令 disobey orders; act in defiance of orders / ～宪 against the constitution; unconstitutional / ～禁品 contraband (goods) ❷ part with; leave

违法 wéifǎ break or violate the law; be illegal:～分子 lawbreaker / ～乱纪 violate the law and discipline; commit malfeasance

违反 wéifǎn *also* "违背" violate; go against; run counter to:～良心 go against one's conscience / ～合同 break a contract

违和 wéihé〈婉〉have a minor ailment; be indisposed

违抗 wéikàng disobey; defy:～领导 defy the higher-ups; be insubordinate

违心 wéixīn against one's conscience; contrary to one's conviction:～之论 insincere talk; untruthful statement

违约 wéiyuē ❶ break a contract; violate a treaty, etc:～责任 liability for breach of contract ❷ go back on one's word; break an appointment

违章 wéizhāng break rules and regulations:～操作 operate contrary to the instructions or regulations / ～建筑 unauthorized construction

围（圍） wéi ❶ enclose; surround; besiege:～捕 surround and catch; round up / ～攻 besiege and attack; launch convergent attacks on;〈喻〉jointly speak or write against / ～歼 surround and annihilate / ～巾 "围脖儿" scarf; muffler / ～墙 enclosing wall; enclosure / ～裙 apron ❷〈量〉a) length of two hand spans (with thumb and index finger stretched):腰大十～ waist of twenty hand spans b) what one can hold with both arms stretched:树大五～ tree as thick as ten arm spans

围观 wéiguān surround and watch; 引起～ draw a curious crowd

围剿 wéijiǎo encircle and suppress; 文

化～ cultural suppression

围困 wéikùn　besiege; hem in; pin down

围拢 wéilǒng　crowd around; close in on; converge on

围棋 wéiqí　*weiqi* — encirclement chess; go

围绕 wéirào　❶ round; around：～太阳转 revolve round the sun ❷ centre on (a theme, etc); revolve round a (question, etc)

闱(闈) wéi　❶ palace side gate ❷ hall of the imperial (civil service) examination：入～ be selected as a candidate

桅 wéi　(usu 桅杆) mast

唯 wéi　only; solely; alone：～此为大. This alone is the most important. *see also* wěi

唯物 wéiwù　〈哲〉take matter as primary; adopt a materialist approach：～论 *also* "唯物主义" materialism / ～辩证法 materialist dialectics

唯心 wéixīn　〈哲〉take consciousness as primary; adopt an idealist approach：～论 *also* "唯心主义" idealism

帷 wéi　*also* "帏" curtain：～帐 bed curtain; mosquito net / ～幕 *also* "帷幔" heavy curtain (for the stage, etc) / ～幄〈书〉army tent

惟 wéi　❶ only; solely; alone：～有 only; solely / ～命是从 *also* "唯命是听" always do as one is told; be always ready to take orders / ～我独尊 *also* "唯我独尊" overweening; extremely conceited ❷ but; only that：雨虽止，～路仍泥泞. The rain has stopped but the road is still muddy.

惟独 wéidú　*also* "唯独" only; alone

惟恐 wéikǒng　*also* "唯恐" fear nothing but…; desire … only：～天下不乱 desire to see the world plunged into turmoil; be always ready to stir up trouble

惟利是图 wéilìshìtú　*also* "唯利是图" seek nothing but profit; put profit before everything else

惟妙惟肖 wéimiào-wéixiào　*see* "维妙惟肖" wéimiào-wéixiào

惟一 wéiyī　*also* "唯一" only; sole; unique

维 wéi　❶ bind; tie up; hold together ❷ keep; maintain; uphold：～权 uphold or defend one's rights ❸ dimension：三～空间 three-dimensional space

维持 wéichí　❶ keep; maintain; preserve：～生命 keep alive; preserve life ❷ protect; safeguard; support：亏他暗中～ thanks to his secret support

维和 wéihé　(short for 维持和平) peace-keeping：～部队 peace-keeping force

维护 wéihù　safeguard; preserve; defend

维妙维肖 wéimiào-wéixiào　*also* "维妙惟肖" remarkably true to life; absolutely lifelike; vivid

维生素 wéishēngsù　(formerly 维他命) vitamin

维吾尔 Wéiwú'ěr　Uygur：～语 Uygur language / ～族 *also* "维族" Uygur, ethnic group living in the Xinjiang Uygur Autonomous Region

维系 wéixì　hold together; keep up; maintain：～人心 keep up popular morale

维新 wéixīn　reform; modernization：～派 reformist; reformer

维修 wéixiū　service; maintain：～费 maintenance cost or charge; upkeep

wěi

伟(偉) wěi　❶ great：～大 great; lofty; mighty / ～绩 great feat; outstanding exploit; brilliant achievement ❷〈书〉strong and handsome：～岸 big and tall

伪(偽) wěi ❶ false; fake; bogus;～钞 counterfeit or fake banknote /～劣 counterfeit and inferior; fake and shoddy /～证〈法〉 false witness, testimony or evidence; (commit) perjury /～君子 hypocrite /～科学 pseudo-science ❷ puppet; quisling;～军 quisling army; puppet troops

伪善 wěishàn　hypocrisy;～的嘴脸 true features as a hypocrite

伪造 wěizào　fake; forge; counterfeit;～历史 falsify history; fabricate past record /～账目 doctor accounts; cook the books

伪装 wěizhuāng ❶ pretend; feign; disguise;～革命 pretend to be revolutionary ❷ disguise; guise; mask;剥去～ strip off sb's mask ❸〈军〉camouflage

苇(葦) wěi　reed;～荡 also "芦荡" reed marsh /～席 reed mat

尾 wěi ❶ tail; rear;～灯 tail or rear light (of a car, etc); stern light (of a ship) /～气 (tail) exhaust ❷ end;～期 final phase; last or final stage ❸ remaining part; remainder; remnant;～欠 balance due; remainder of a debt or levy /～数 last numeral of a multi-digit figure; odd amount in addition to the round number ❹〈量〉used of fish;数一～金鱼 several goldfish　see also yǐ

尾巴 wěiba ❶ tail; tail-like part;～翘上了天〈喻〉be very cocky; be overweening ❷ remaining part of sth;不留～ leave no loose ends ❸ person who shadows sb or follows sb round; tail; appendage

尾大不掉 wěidàbùdiào　the tail wagging the dog; (of an organization) too cumbersome to be effective

尾声 wěishēng ❶〈戏〉coda;〈乐〉epilogue ❷ end; ending (as of a literary work);将近～ be drawing to a close

尾随 wěisuí　tail (behind sb); tag along after; follow at sb's heels

纬(緯) wěi ❶ weft; woof;～纱 woof /～线 weft;〈地〉parallel ❷ also "纬度"〈地〉latitude

委 wěi ❶ entrust; assign; appoint;～派 appoint; dispatch; send /～以重任 entrust sb with an important task ❷ throw away; discard; cast aside;～弃 cast aside; discard; give up ❸ see "逶" wěi ❹ (short for 委员会 or 委员) committee; committee member ❺ indirect; circuitous; roundabout;～婉 mild and roundabout; tactful ❻ listless; depressed; dejected;～顿 tired; weary; listless ❼〈书〉actually; indeed; certainly;～实难办。It's indeed a hard nut to crack.

委决 wěijué　decide; make up one's mind;～不下 be hesitant and unable to reach a decision

委靡 wěimǐ　also "萎靡" listless; lethargic; dispirited;～不振 dejected and apathetic; lethargic

委曲求全 wěiqūqiúquán　stoop to compromise; compromise for the general interest

委屈 wěiqu ❶ feel wronged or aggrieved; nurse a grievance;倾吐心中的～ pour out one's grievances ❷ put (sb) to great inconvenience; do (sb) wrong;这件事可真～你了。I'm sorry you've had to go through all this.

委任 wěirèn　appoint (sb to an office or as sth);～状 certificate of appointment; commission

委身 wěishēn〈书〉❶ stoop (to do sth); put oneself at sb's disposal ❷ (of a woman) give oneself to; marry

委托 wěituō　entrust; trust; commission;～人 trustor /～书 trust deed; power of attorney /被～人 trustee

委员 wěiyuán　member of a committee; committee member;～会 commit-

逶 wěi *also* "委" shift; shirk; transfer: ～过于人 shift blame onto sb else

娓 wěi

娓娓 wěiwěi （talk）tirelessly; （speak）interestingly: ～动听 sound pleasing and attractive; be very pleasant to the ear

萎 wěi ❶ wither; wilt; fade:～谢 wither; wilt; fade ❷ decline: 气儿～了 become deflated or flat

萎靡 wěimǐ *see* "委靡" wěimǐ

萎缩 wěisuō ❶（of flowers, etc）wither; shrivel; shrink ❷ dejected; listless; 神情～ in low spirits; dispirited ❸（经）shrink; sag; contract ❹（医）atrophy:～性胃炎 atrophic gastritis; gastrotropia

唯 wěi （书）yea　*see also* wéi

唯唯喏喏 wěiwěinuònuò　be a yes man; be servile

猥 wěi ❶ numerous; multifarious; miscellaneous:～杂 miscellaneous ❷ base; lascivious; salacious:～辞 *also* "猥词" obscene language; salacious words / ～琐 *also* "委琐" wretched; miserable

猥亵 wěixiè ❶ lewd; obscene; salacious: 言行～ obscene in words and conduct ❷ act indecently towards（a female）; take liberties with; harass

瘘 wěi （中医）paralysis

wèi

卫（衛） wèi defend; guard; protect:～兵 guard; bodyguard / ～队 bodyguards; armed escort / ～护 defend; protect; guard / ～道士〈贬〉apologist / ～冕成功

（体）succeed in defending one's championship

卫生 wèishēng ❶ hygienic; sanitary:～间 toilet; rest room / ～纸 toilet paper ❷ hygiene; sanitation:讲～ pay attention to hygiene / ～室 clinic / ～院 （township or county）hospital

卫戍 wèishù　garrison:～部队 garrison force

卫星 wèixīng ❶〈天文〉satellite; moon ❷ sth that has the function of a satellite:～城市 satellite town or city ❸ artificial or man-made satellite:～导航 satellite navigation / ～电话 satphone / ～电视（shortened as 卫视）satellite TV

为（爲） wèi ❶〈书〉be on the side of; help; protect:～人到底 see sb through if you really want to help him or her ❷ on behalf of; for the benefit of; in the interest of:～国捐躯 give up one's life or die for one's country / ～虎作伥 help a villain in evildoing; be in the service of a tyrant / ～民请命 plead in the name of the people; serve or pose as a spokesman of the people ❸ for（the sake of）; on account of:～何 for what reason; why ❹ to; into:～渊驱鱼 从丛驱雀 drive people to the enemy's side; play into the enemy's hands　*see also* wéi

为了 wèile　for; for the sake of; in order to:～方便读者 for readers' convenience

为人作嫁 wèirénzuòjià make bridal clothes for sb else to wear; toil for others without reaping any reward in return

为什么 wèishénme　why; why is it that; how come:～不早说？Why didn't you say it sooner?

未 wèi （副）❶ not yet:～成年 under age; minor / ～亡人〈旧〉widow;（used by a widow）I / ～竟之

志 unaccomplished ideal or ambition / ～老先衰 prematurely senile; old before one's time / 防范于～然 prevent sth from happening ❷ not; no: ～卜先知 have foresight; need no crystal ball to see / ～敢苟同 beg to differ; disagree / ～能免俗 be unable to rise above convention; bow to conventional practice / ～置可否 be non-committal ❸ 8th of the Earthly Branches　see also "干支" gānzhī

未必 wèibì　may not; not necessarily

未曾 wèicéng　not; never: 这点我～想到 It had never occurred to me.

未尝 wèicháng　❶ see "未曾" ❷ also "未始" used before a negative to denote a mild affirmative: ～不可 by no means impossible

未婚 wèihūn　unmarried; single: ～夫 fiancé / ～妻 fiancée / ～母亲 single mother

未可 wèikě　should in no case; must not: ～小视 should in no case be underestimated / ～厚非 give no cause for much criticism; be not altogether inexcusable

未来 wèilái　❶ coming; approaching: ～几天 (in the) next few days ❷ future; tomorrow

未免 wèimiǎn　used to indicate mild disagreement or negation: 这～会使он难堪。 This would most probably embarrass him.

未遂 wèisuì　unfulfilled; abortive: ～政变 abortive coup d'état / 行刺～ attempted assassination

未雨绸缪 wèiyǔchóumóu　repair the house before it rains; save for a rainy day; take preventive measures

未知数 wèizhīshù　❶ 〈数〉 unknown number ❷ unknown; not sure; uncertain

位 wèi　❶ place; location; seat: 各就各～。〈体〉On your marks! ❷ position; rank; status: ～极人臣 rise to the highest official position (under a monarch) ❸ throne: 退～ abdicate the throne ❹ 〈数〉 place; figure; 〈信息〉 bit: 个～ unit's place / 十～ ten's place / 六～ six-digit number ❺ 〈量〉 used in deferential reference to people: 几～? How many? / 各～女士。 Ladies!

位次 wèicì　❶ status or rank (in a hierarchy); position or place (on a list, etc) ❷ order of seats; seating arrangement: ～卡 place card

位于 wèiyú　be located or situated; lie

位置 wèizhi　❶ also "位子" seat; place; location: 按指定～入席 take one's designated seat ❷ position; place: 占有重要～ hold an important position ❸ also "位子" post; position; job

味 wèi　❶ taste; flavour: ～觉 sense of taste / ～同嚼蜡 taste like tallow or wax; be as dry as dust ❷ smell; scent; odour ❸ implication; significance; sense ❹ distinguish the flavour of; reflect on: 细～ ponder carefully ❺ 〈量〉 ingredient; 〈中医〉 这方子共有八～药。 This prescription specifies eight ingredients.

味道 wèidao　❶ taste; flavour: ～鲜美 taste delicious ❷ interest; sense: 有～ (of writing, etc) be interesting ❸ 〈方〉 odour; smell

味精 wèijīng　also "味素" monosodium glutamate (MSG); gourmet powder

畏 wèi　❶ fear; dread: ～避 avoid out of fear; shrink or flinch from / ～怯 timid; timorous; cowardly / ～首～尾 be full of misgivings; be overcautious / ～之如虎 stand in mortal fear (of sth or sb) / 视为～途 regard as a dangerous road to take; be afraid to undertake sth ❷ admire; awe: ～友 friend who inspires both awe and respect; revered friend

畏惧 wèijù　fear; dread; be afraid: 无

所～ be fearless

畏难 wèinán be scared of difficulty：正视现实而不～ face the facts squarely without fear

畏缩 wèisuō recoil；flinch；cringe；不前 *also* "畏葸不前" recoil in fear；cower；hang back

畏罪 wèizuì dread punishment for one's crime：～自杀 commit suicide for fear of punishment

胃 wèi stomach；～癌 stomach cancer；gastric carcinoma / ～病 stomach trouble；gastric disease / ～酸 hydrochloric acid in gastric juice / ～痛 stomachache / ～炎 gastritis / ～液 gastric juice / ～溃疡 gastric ulcer / ～镜检查 gastroscopy

胃口 wèikǒu ❶ appetite：～欠佳 have a poor appetite ❷ liking；fancy；对～ to one's liking ❸〈喻〉ambition；appetite：～很大 have a wild ambition

谓 wèi ❶〈书〉say；或～ people say；it is said ❷ call；name；mean：何～人造卫星? What is meant by man-made satellite?

谓语 wèiyǔ〈语言〉predicate

尉 wèi *also* "尉官"〈军〉junior officer

遗 wèi〈书〉offer as a gift；make a present of：～之以书 make a present of books *see also* yí

喂（❷❸餧） wèi ❶〈叹〉hello；hi；hey ❷ give food to；feed：～养 breed；raise；keep ❸ spoon-feed；feed：～奶 feed milk；breastfeed；suckle

猬 wèi〈动物〉hedgehog

蔚 wèi〈书〉❶ luxuriant；grand；magnificent：～为大国 great country in all its magnificence / ～为大观 present a splendid sight；offer a spectacular view ❷ colourful；beautiful

蔚蓝 wèilán azure；sky blue

蔚然 wèirán exuberant；flourishing；

～成林 grow into an exuberant wood / ～成风 become common practice；be the prevailing trend

慰 wèi ❶ console；soothe；comfort：～勉 comfort and encourage ❷ feel relieved：得信甚～。I was relieved to receive your letter.

慰藉 wèijiè〈书〉consolation；comfort：感到～ feel comforted or gratified

慰劳 wèiláo bring gifts in recognition of service rendered：～品 gifts (for those who have rendered service)

慰留 wèiliú (try to) persuade sb to stay

慰问 wèiwèn express sympathy and solicitude；show gratitude and appreciation；extend regards or greetings：～团 group sent to convey regards and appreciation / ～信 letter of sympathy；sympathy note

wēn

温 wēn ❶ warm；lukewarm；tepid：～水 lukewarm or warm water / ～泉 hot spring ❷ temperature：～差 difference in temperature；range of temperature ❸ warm up；heat up (to a moderate degree)：～酒 warm up wine ❹ gentle；meek；tender：～厚 gentle and kind；good-natured ❺ (usu 温习) review；restudy

温饱 wēnbǎo have enough to eat and wear：～型 having or providing just enough to eat and wear

温床 wēnchuáng〈农〉〈喻〉hotbed；breeding ground (for evils, etc)

温存 wēncún ❶ (to a person of the opposite sex) be attentive；give tender attention：～备至 be gentle and attentive；shower attentions (on sb) ❷ kind；gentle；tender

温带 wēndài temperate zone：～气候 temperate climate

温度 wēndù temperature：～计 *also*

"温度表" thermometer

温故知新 wēngùzhīxīn gain new insights through reviewing old material; recalling the past helps one understand the present

温和 wēnhé ❶ (of weather) temperate; mild; moderate ❷ (of temperament, etc) gentle; mild; moderate;～派 moderates ❸ (wēnhuo) (of food, water, etc) lukewarm; warm

温暖 wēnnuǎn mild; warm;～如春 mild as spring /～人心 heart-warming

温情 wēnqíng tender affection;～脉脉 full of tender feeling /～主义 (贬) undue leniency or soft-heartedness; sentimentalism

温柔 wēnróu gentle (and soft); sweet;～一笑 give a sweet smile

温室 wēnshì hothouse; greenhouse; conservatory;～效应 greenhouse effect

温顺 wēnshùn docile; meek; tame

温吞 wēntūn (of liquid, etc) lukewarm; tepid;～水 lukewarm water; 〈喻〉staid or phlegmatic temper

温文尔雅 wēnwén'ěryǎ (of manner, etc) gentle and cultivated; cultured; refined

温馨 wēnxīn mild and fragrant; warm and cosy;～的友情 warm friendship

瘟 wēn ❶ (中医) acute communicable disease;～病 seasonal epidemic /～神 god of plague /～疫 pestilence; plague ❷ lackadaisical; dull; insipid;～头～脑 muddle-headed; dull and confused

wén

文 wén ❶ script; language; inscription;外～ foreign language ❷ literary writing; document;～案 also "文档" official documents; files; archives /～本 text; version (of a treaty, etc) /～风 style of writing /～豪 literary giant; great writer /～集

collected works /～房四宝 four treasures of the study — writing brush, ink stick, ink slab and paper /～如其人 the style is the man; like author, like book /～山会海 mountains of documents and seas of meetings; endless documents and meetings /这句话太～。This sentence is too bookish. ❸ culture; civilization; art;～工团 art troupe; song and dance ensemble ❹ also "文科" liberal arts; humanities;～学士 bachelor of arts (BA) ❺ 〈旧〉etiquette; formal ritual; 虚～ empty form; dead letter ❻ civilian; civil;～职 civilian post /～治武功 statecraft and military exploits ❼ soft; mild; refined;～火 slow fire; gentle heat /～静 gentle and quiet /～戏 Chinese opera focusing on singing and acting /～弱书生 frail-looking intellectual ❽ tattoo;～身 tattoo ❾ (usu 文饰) cover up; paint out; explain away;～过饰非 conceal mistakes and gloss over wrongs; cover up one's errors ❿ 〈量〉used of ancient coins;一～钱 a farthing

文笔 wénbǐ style of writing;～优美 write beautifully

文不对题 wénbùduìtí irrelevant to the subject; beside the point; wide of the mark

文采 wéncǎi ❶ rich and bright colours;～斑斓 multi-coloured ❷ literary grace or gift; elegant diction; 缺少～ lacking in literary grace

文辞 wéncí also "文词" ❶ diction; language;～华丽 flowery language; ornate diction ❷ articles and essays; writing

文牍 wéndú official documents and correspondence;～主义 red tape

文法 wénfǎ grammar;～不通 grammatically incorrect; wrong in grammar

文稿 wéngǎo manuscript; draft; 草拟～ draft a document

文告 wéngào proclamation; bulletin;

statement

文革 Wéngé （short for 文化大革命）Cultural Revolution (1966 - 1976)

文官 wénguān　civil official or servant；～政府 civil government / ～制度 civil service (system)

文化 wénhuà ❶ civilization；culture：～宫 palace of culture；cultural palace / ～馆 cultural centre / ～人 man of letters；literati；intellectual / ～冲击 culture shock ❷〈考古〉ancient culture or civilization：～层 cultural stratum ❸ education；schooling；literacy：学～ learn to read and write / 没有～ illiterate / ～程度 *also* "文化水平" educational level

文件 wénjiàn ❶ official documents and correspondence；papers；file：～夹 file (folder) ❷ article or work concerning political studies，etc；document：～汇编 compilation of documents ❸〈信息〉file：～服务器 file server

文教 wénjiào （short for 文化教育）culture and education：～界 cultural and educational circles

文具 wénjù　stationery：～店 stationer's；stationery shop

文库 wénkù　series of books issued in a single format by a publisher；library.

文理 wénlǐ ❶ unity and coherence in writing：～通顺 be logical and coherent；make smooth reading ❷ liberal arts and science

文盲 wénmáng　illiterate (person)：半～ semi-illiterate / 扫除～ wipe out illiteracy

文秘 wénmì　secretary：～专业 discipline of secretarial work

文明 wénmíng ❶ civilization ❷ civilized；civil；civic：～公约 pact on civic virtues / ～生产 run production in a civilized and efficient way ❸ modern；western：～结婚 modern-style marriage

文墨 wénmò　writing；literacy：粗通～ be barely literate

文凭 wénpíng　diploma：混～ muddle along to get a diploma；wangle a diploma

文气 wénqì ❶ force or cohesion of writing：～贯通 cohesive writing ❷ (wénqi) gentle and reserved

文人 wénrén　man of letters；scholar：～墨客 literati

文史 wénshǐ　literature and history：～馆 research institute of culture and history / ～资料 historical accounts of past events

文书 wénshū ❶ documents；official dispatches ❷ scribe；copyist；secretary

文思 wénsī （creative) flow of ideas or train of thought in writing：～敏捷 have a ready pen；wield a facile pen

文坛 wéntán　literary world，arena，or circles；world of letters

文体 wéntǐ ❶ type of writing；literary form；genre ❷ (short for 文娱体育) recreation and sports

文武 wénwǔ ❶ civil accomplishments and military prowess：～双全 be well versed both in civil and military affairs；be adept with both pen and sword ❷〈书〉civil and military means：peaceful and coercive methods：～并用 use both persuasion and coercion ❸〈书〉ministers and generals；civil and military officials

文物 wénwù　cultural or historical relic

文献 wénxiàn　document；literature：～记录片 documentary (film) / ～检索中心 document retrieval centre

文选 wénxuǎn　selected works；literary selections

文学 wénxué　literature：～家 writer；man of letters / ～语言 standard speech or language；literary language

文雅 wényǎ　elegant；graceful；cultured：谈吐～ talk in refined taste

文言 wényán　classical Chinese：～文 writings in classical Chinese；classical style of writing

文艺 wényì （short for 文学艺术）art and literature；～复兴〈史〉Renaissance／～节目 programme of entertainment；theatrical item or performance／～批评 art and literary criticism

文娱 wényú cultural recreation；entertainment；～活动 recreational activities

文摘 wénzhāi extract from articles or books；abstract；digest

文章 wénzhāng ❶ essay；article；writings ❷ hidden or implied meaning；implication：其中大有～。There is much more to it than meets the eye. ❸ way （of doing sth）；room （for improvement，etc）：大有～可做 there is much room for improvement；there is much to be done

文质彬彬 wénzhìbīnbīn suave；urbane；quiet and scholarly

文绉绉 wénzhōuzhōu genteel；bookish：说话～的 talk like a book

文字 wénzì ❶ characters；script；written language：表意～ ideography；ideogram／～处理系统〈信息〉word-processing system ❷ writing；wording：～狱〈史〉literary inquisition／～简练 written in a concise style／～游戏 play on words；juggle with terms

纹 wén ❶ （of a fabric or utensil） pattern：～饰 engraved or painted patterns ❷ line；vein；grain：～理 veins；grain／～路 lines；grain

纹丝不动 wénsībùdòng absolutely still or motionless

闻 wén ❶ hear：～所未闻 unheard-of ❷ news；story；anecdote：奇～ strange story ❸〈书〉well-known；renowned；famous：～人 well-known figure；eminent person；celebrity ❹ repute；reputation：令～ good repute ❺ smell：～见一股烧焦的味道 smell sth burning

闻风 wénfēng hear the news：～而动 take action as soon as one hears about

the matter／～丧胆 become panic-stricken at the news

闻名 wénmíng ❶ be familiar with sb's name；know sb by repute ❷ well-known；celebrated；famous

蚊 wén （usu 蚊子）mosquito：～香 mosquito-repellent incense／～帐 mosquito net／电～香 electric mosquito repellent

wěn

刎 wěn cut one's throat：～颈之交 friends who are ready to die for each other；tested friends

吻 wěn ❶ lips；muzzle or snout （of an animal）❷ touch by the lips；kiss：～别 kiss sb goodbye

吻合 wěnhé be identical；fit perfectly；tally （with）

紊 wěn dishevelled；disorderly；confused

紊乱 wěnluàn disorder；chaos；confusion：思想～ confused thoughts

稳（穩） wěn ❶ steady；steadfast；calm：坐～ sit tight／～步 with steady steps；steadily／～如泰山 as stable as Mount Tai；rock-firm ❷ sure；certain：～获 sure or certain to get （sth）；have full assurance of （success）❸ stabilize；calm；put at ease：～住阵脚 hold one's position；secure a foothold

稳操胜券 wěncāoshèngquàn also "稳操胜算" be sure to win；be certain of victory；have full assurance of success

稳当 wěndang ❶ reliable；dependable；secure：办事～ be reliable in doing things ❷ steady；sure；stable：走路～ walk steadily

稳定 wěndìng stable；steady；calm：社会～ social stability／～情绪 calm down／～物价 stabilize prices／～增长 grow steadily／～的职业 stable or secure job

稳固 wěngù firm; solid; stable:政权 ~ stable government / ~ 经济基础 consolidate the economic foundation

稳健 wěnjiàn ❶ firm; stable; steady:~的步子 steady steps ❷ steady; prudent; reliable:措施 ~ (take) prudent measures

稳妥 wěntuǒ safe; reliable; trustworthy:~可靠 safe and reliable

稳扎稳打 wěnzhā-wěndǎ make steady progress and strike sure blows; go about things steadily and surely

稳重 wěnzhòng steady; discreet; prudent:为人 ~ conduct oneself with discretion

wèn

问 wèn ❶ ask; inquire:~话 ask; question / ~询 inquiry:~ 长 ~ 短 ask about this and that; make solicitous inquiries / ~卷调查 investigation by questionnaire ❷ ask or inquire after:~安 (usu to elders) pay one's respects; wish sb good health / ~ 好 send one's regards; say hello; extend greetings ❸ interrogate; question; examine:~案 try or hear a case; try or interrogate a suspect ❹ hold responsible; intervene:惟你是~. I'll hold you responsible for it.

问道于盲 wèndàoyúmáng ask the way from a blind person — seek advice from one who can offer none; seek enlightenment from an ignoramus

问鼎 wèndǐng ❶ intend to seize (state) power ❷ try to win a championship

问号 wènhào question or interrogation mark (?); (喻) unknown factor; unsettled problem

问候 wènhòu send one's regards; extend greetings:~信 letter of greetings

问津 wènjīn 〈书〉 (used usu in the negative) make inquiries; show inter-

est:不敢 ~ dare not even ask (about sth); give (sb or sth) a wide berth

问世 wènshì (of a book) be published; (of a product) be available in the market; come out

问事 wènshì ❶ inquire:~处 information desk; inquiry office ❷ attend to business; concern oneself with work

问题 wèntí ❶ question:~ 单 questionnaire ❷ problem; issue; matter:~ 儿童 problem child ❸ crucial point; key:如今有了计划,~是怎样落实. Now that we've got a plan, the thing is how to carry it out. ❹ trouble; mishap; something wrong:出 ~ run into trouble; go wrong

问心无愧 wènxīnwúkuì feel at ease upon self-inspection; have a clear conscience

问讯 wènxùn ❶ inquire; ask:~处 information office; inquiry desk ❷ interrogate; question

问罪 wènzuì denounce; condemn:大 兴~之师 denounce sb publicly for his crimes or serious errors

璺 wèn crack (on glassware or earthenware)

wēng

翁 wēng ❶ old man:~媪 elderly couple / ~仲 carved stone figure (usu in front of a tomb) ❷ father:尊 ~ your father ❸ husband's father; father-in-law (of a woman):~ 姑 husband's parents; parents-in-law (of a woman) ❹ wife's father:~ 婿 father-in-law and son-in-law

嗡 wēng 〈象声〉 buzz; hum; drone

wèng

瓮(甕) wèng earthen jar:~ 中捉鳖 catch a turtle in

a jar — be sure of success; (of sth) be a walkover

瓮声瓮气 wèngshēng-wèngqì　in a low muffled voice or sound

蕹 wèng

蕹菜 wèngcài　also "空心菜" water spinach

wō

莴(萵) wō

莴苣 wōjù　lettuce
莴笋 wōsǔn　asparagus lettuce

倭 Wō 〈史〉Japan; ～寇 Japanese pirates

倭瓜 wōguā　pumpkin; cushaw

涡(渦) wō whirlpool; maelstrom; eddy; ～流 also "涡旋" whirlpool; vortex; eddy

涡轮 wōlún　turbine; ～机 also "透平机" turbine / ～发电机 turbo-generator

喔 wō 〈象声〉used of cock's crow; ～～叫 cock-a-doodle-doo

窝(窩) wō ❶ nest; ～里斗 〈口〉〈喻〉internecine strife; infighting ❷ lair; den; haunt; 贼～ thieves' den / ～点 lair; den; hideout ❸ hollow (part); pit; 山～儿 mountain hollow ❹ harbour; shelter; shield; ～家 also "窝主" fence / ～赃 harbour loot or contraband ❺ huddle or curl up; stay still; bottle up; ～气 lacking fresh air; stuffy ❻ bend; 用铁丝～一个衣架 bend wire into a coat hanger ❼ 〈量〉litter; brood; 一～小鸭 a brood of ducklings

窝藏 wōcáng　conceal; harbour; shelter (criminals, etc)

窝工 wōgōng　enforced idleness (due to poor organization, etc); hold-up in work; 窝了半天工。Work was held up for half a day.

窝火 wōhuǒ　also "窝气" simmer with

rage; be forced to bottle up one's anger; 你说～不～? Isn't this vexing?

窝囊 wōnang　❶ helplessly vexed or exasperated; 受～气 be helplessly annoyed ❷ weak and cowardly; hopelessly stupid; ～废 cowardly weakling; good-for-nothing

窝棚 wōpeng　shack; shed; shanty

窝头 wōtóu　also "窝窝头" steamed bread of coarse grain; (esp) corn bun

蜗(蝸) wō (usu 蜗牛) snail; ～居 〈书〉〈谦〉humble abode / ～行牛步 move at a snail's pace

踒 wō sprain (ankle, etc)

wǒ

我 wǒ ❶ I; me; my; ～见 my (personal) view ❷ we; us; our; 亡～之心 intention to subjugate our country ❸ self; one; ～行～素 do whatever one pleases; go one's own way no matter what others may say / ～字当头 (have a) me-first mentality

我们 wǒmen　❶ we; us; our ❷ 〈口〉I; me; my; ～那口子 my wife or husband

wò

沃 wò ❶ 〈书〉irrigate; pour (water, etc) ❷ fertile; rich; ～野 rich fields

卧(臥) wò ❶ lie; ～倒 lie down; drop to the ground / ～佛 reclining Buddha / ～轨 lie on the rails to stop the train or commit suicide) / ～病在床 be laid up in bed; be bedridden ❷ (of animals or birds) crouch; sit ❸ for sleeping in; ～具 bedding / ～室 also "卧房" bedroom ❹ (short for 卧铺) sleeping berth

卧车 wòchē　❶ (of a train) sleeping

carriage; sleeper ❷ car; sedan

卧床 wòchuáng　lie in bed; ～休息 (have) bed rest / ～不起 be very ill

卧底 wòdǐ　serve as a planted agent; 派人～ have agents planted (among the enemy)

卧薪尝胆 wòxīnchángdǎn　endure all possible hardships (to strengthen one's resolve)

碰 wò　flat stone or iron rammer with ropes attached at the sides; 打～ tamp (earth) with a rammer

握 wò　take in one's hand; hold; grasp; ～力 gripping power; grip / ～紧拳头 clench one's fist / 手～大权 wield great power

握手 wòshǒu　shake or clasp hands; ～告别 (shortened as 握别) part with a handshake / ～言欢 have a congenial handshake; bury the hatchet

斡 wò

斡旋 wòxuán　mediate (between two parties); use one's good offices

龌 wò

龌龊 wòchuò　❶ unclean; dirty; filthy ❷ (of behaviour, etc) base; sordid

wū

乌(烏) wū　❶〈动物〉crow ❷ black; dark; ～发 glossy black hair / ～黑 pitch-black; jet-black / ～亮 glossy black ❸〈书〉(used in a rhetorical question) what; how; ～能苟活? How can I live on in shame?

乌龟 wūguī　❶ tortoise; ～壳 tortoise shell ❷ cuckold

乌合之众 wūhézhīzhòng　disorderly or motley crowd; rabble; mob

乌龙 wūlóng　also "乌龙球"〈体〉own goal; 自摆～ kick the ball into one's own goal

乌龙茶 wūlóngchá　oolong tea

乌七八糟 wūqībāzāo　also "污七八糟" ❶ in a horrible mess; in great disorder; all in a jumble ❷ (of words, ideas, etc) obscene; dirty; salacious

乌纱帽 wūshāmào　〈旧〉black gauze hat for an official; 〈喻〉official post

乌托邦 wūtuōbāng　Utopia; utopian fancy

乌鸦 wūyā　crow; ～嘴 terrible gossip

乌烟瘴气 wūyān-zhàngqì　foul or pestilential atmosphere; 闹得～ kick up a horrible rumpus

乌有 wūyǒu　〈书〉nothing; naught; fiction; 化为～ come to nothing or naught

乌云 wūyún　❶ black or dark cloud; 〈喻〉depressing or sinister situation; 战争的～ dark clouds of war / 他头蒙上了一层～。His mind clouded over. ❷〈喻〉women's black hair

乌贼 wūzéi　also "墨鱼"; "墨斗鱼" cuttlefish; inkfish

污 wū　❶ dirty; filthy; foul; ～垢 dirt; filth / ～名 bad name / ～渍 stain; smear ❷ corrupt; dishonest; ～吏 corrupt or dishonest official ❸ defile; vilify; smear; ～损 smear and damage; vandalize

污点 wūdiǎn　❶ stain; spot ❷ blemish; defect; 历史～ blemish in one's record

污秽 wūhuì　〈书〉dirty; filthy; foul; 满身～ dirty or filthy all over / 思想～ dirty or filthy mind

污蔑 wūmiè　see "诬蔑" wūmiè

污七八糟 wūqībāzāo　see "乌七八糟" wūqībāzāo

污染 wūrǎn　pollute; contaminate; ～物 pollutant; contaminant / ～源 source of pollution / ～社会风气 debase social morals

污辱 wūrǔ　❶ see "侮辱" wǔrǔ ❷ sully; tarnish (reputation, etc)

污水 wūshuǐ　polluted or waste water;

sewage; slops;生活～ domestic sewage / ～处理 sewage disposal or treatment

污浊 wūzhuó　dirty; muddy; filthy;污泥浊水 mud and sludge; filth and mire

巫 wū　shaman; witch; wizard;～婆 also "女巫" witch; sorceress / ～师 also "巫士" wizard; sorcerer / ～术 witchcraft; sorcery / ～医 witch doctor

呜（嗚）wū　〈象声〉hoot; toot;～～大鼻 blubber noisily / 汽笛～～叫. A horn hooted.

呜呼 wūhū　also "乌呼" ❶〈书〉〈叹〉alas; alack;～! 其心何毒! Alas! What a venomous person! ❷ die;—命～ give up the ghost; kick the bucket

呜咽 wūyè　〈书〉❶ sob; whimper ❷ (of wind, etc) mourn; wail; weep

钨（鎢）wū　tungsten; wolfram (W)

诬 wū　accuse falsely; slander;～害 injure by spreading false reports; calumniate; frame / ～赖 falsely incriminate or accuse

诬告 wūgào　falsely accuse or charge; trump up a charge against;～罪〈法〉crime of false charge / ～案件 trumped-up case; frame-up

诬蔑 wūmiè　also "污蔑" slander; defame; smear; ～好人 sling mud at a good person / 竭尽～之能事 stop at nothing in spreading lies and slanders

诬陷 wūxiàn　produce false evidence against; frame a case against; frame;～不实之词 slanders and false charges

屋 wū　❶ house;～顶 roof; house-top / ～檐 eaves / ～上架屋〈喻〉house over another house — redundant or overlapping organizations; unnecessary duplication ❷ room

wú

无（無）wú　❶ not having; without; ～ 故 without cause or reason / ～礼 impolite; impu-

dent; rude / ～味 tasteless; insipid / ～畏 dauntless; courageous / ～伴奏 without （instrumental） accompaniment; unaccompanied / ～底洞〈喻〉bottomless pit / ～神论 atheism / ～价之宝 priceless treasure; invaluable asset / ～米之炊 cook a meal without rice; make bricks without straw / ～冕之王 king without a crown — person without a title but very influential / ～期徒刑 life imprisonment / ～绳电话 cordless （phone） / ～息贷款 interest-free loan / ～偿付能力〈经〉insolvent / ～党派人士 nonparty personage; Independent ❷ regardless or irrespective of; no matter whether, what, etc;国～大小, 一律平等. All nations, big or small, are equal. ❸ do not; must not; may not;～忘国耻. Do not forget humiliations to our country.

无比 wúbǐ　incomparable; unparalleled; exceeding;激动～ extremely excited / ～幸福 height of happiness

无边 wúbiān　also "无边无际" boundless; limitless; vast

无病呻吟 wúbìngshēnyín　moan and groan without being ill; pine and whine without cause; adopt an affected pose

无补 wúbǔ　of no help or avail;于事～ of no avail; to no （useful） purpose

无不 wúbù　without exception; invariably; all

无…不… wú…bù…　*used to join an object with its verb for emphasis*;无恶不作 stop at no evil; commit all manner of crimes / 无话不谈 keep no secrets （from sb or each other）; be in sb's or each other's confidence / 无坚不摧 carry all before one; be ever-victorious; be all-conquering / 无孔不入〈贬〉never missing any opportunity; all-pervasive / 无奇不有 there is no lack of strange things; extraordinary things abound / 无微不至 meticulously; with great care; in every possible way

无产阶级 wúchǎn jiējí proletariat：～专政 dictatorship of the proletariat

无常 wúcháng ❶ variable; changeable; fickle：天气变化～。The weather is unpredictable. ❷〈迷信〉*Wuchang*, a ghost supposed to summon and take away a person's soul upon death ❸〈婉〉pass away; die

无偿 wúcháng unpaid; free; gratuitous：～劳动 unpaid labour / ～献血 donate blood gratis / ～调用 commandeer

无耻 wúchǐ shameless; brazen; impudent：～之尤 brazen in the extreme

无出其右 wúchūqíyòu second to none; peerless

无从 wúcóng have no way (of doing sth); be unable (to do sth)：～谈起 not know where to start

无敌 wúdí unmatched; invincible：天下～ unmatched anywhere in the world

无地自容 wúdìzìróng wish that one could sink through the ground (for shame); feel utterly ashamed

无的放矢 wúdìfàngshǐ shoot at random; be totally irrelevant：～的空谈 irrelevant; idle talk

无动于衷 wúdòngyúzhōng unmoved; indifferent; impassive

无独有偶 wúdú-yǒu'ǒu there is another to match it (in stupidity, etc); things never come singly but in pairs

无度 wúdù immoderate; inordinate; excessive：挥霍～ squander wantonly; be excessively extravagant

无端 wúduān without rhyme or reason; groundless：～受罚 be punished or fined for no fault of one's own

无法 wúfǎ unable; incapable; powerless：～辨认 beyond recognition; unidentifiable

无妨 wúfáng ❶ also "无碍" there is no harm (in doing sth) ❷ also "不妨" have no reason not to; may or might as well：有意见～直说。Feel free to speak out if you have anything on your mind.

无非 wúfēi nothing but; no more than; merely

无风不起浪 wúfēngbùqǐlàng〈俗〉there are no waves without wind; there is no smoke without fire

无公害 wúgōnghài pollution or nuisance free：～工艺 nuisanceless technology / ～蔬菜 pollution-free vegetable

无辜 wúgū innocent; guiltless：株连～ implicate the innocent (in a criminal case)

无关 wúguān have nothing to do (with); be irrelevant (to)：～大局 not affecting the overall situation; of little consequence; insignificant / ～痛痒 unimportant; irrelevant; pointless

无官一身轻 wúguānyīshēnqīng〈俗〉out of office, out of cares; feel carefree without official duties

无轨 wúguǐ (short for 无轨电车)〈口〉trolleybus：103 路～ trolleybus No 103

无害 wúhài harmless; innocuous：～气体 innocuous gas / ～通过〈法〉innocent passage

无核 wúhé ❶ non-nuclear; nuclear-free：～化 denuclearize; make nuclear free / ～国家 non-nuclear country; non-nuclear-weapon state ❷ seedless; stoneless：～葡萄干 seedless raisins

无机 wújī〈化〉inorganic; mineral：～物 inorganic matter; mineral

无稽 wújī unfounded; fantastic; absurd：～之谈 unfounded rumour; sheer nonsense

无几 wújǐ few; little; hardly any：所剩～。There is little left. / 相差～ The difference is negligible.

无济于事 wújìyúshì of no avail; to no effect

无精打采 wújīngdǎcǎi listless; lack adaisical; downcast：～地回到家中 come back home in low spirits

无可 wúkě no; not; beyond：～非议

beyond reproach; above criticism; blameless / 无(I have) no comment(to make) / ~厚非 give no cause for much criticism(though not without faults) / ~奈何 have no choice; be helpless / ~置疑 beyond doubt; indubitable; unquestionable / ~无不可(of sth) make no difference; (of sb) not care one way or the other

无···可··· wú···kě··· *used to join an object with its verb for emphatic negation*: 无计可施 at one's wit's end; at the end of one's tether / 无家可归 homeless; displaced

无愧 wúkuì have a clear conscience; feel no qualms; be worthy of (sth); ~于英雄的称号 deserve the title of hero

无赖 wúlài ❶ shameless; brazen: 耍~ act shamelessly; brazen it out ❷ hooligan; scoundrel

无理 wúlǐ ❶ unreasonable; unwarranted; unjustifiable: ~取闹 kick up a row for no reason at all; be deliberately provocative / ~搅三分 wrangle without justification; put on a semblance of reasonableness though in the wrong ❷〈数〉irrational: ~式 irrational expression

无力 wúlì ❶ beyond one's power; powerless; unable: ~应付 powerless or unable to cope (with) ❷ lack strength; feel weak: 四肢~ feel weak in one's limbs

无聊 wúliáo ❶ bored; dull: 闲得~ idle and bored ❷ senseless; silly; vulgar: ~的话 silly talk; nonsense

无论 wúlùn no matter (who, how, etc); -ever; regardless (of): ~如何 whatever happens; in any case; under any circumstances / ~何时何地 whenever and wherever

无名 wúmíng ❶ nameless; anonymous: ~氏 anonymous person or writer / ~指 ring or third finger / ~高地 unnamed hill ❷ unknown to the world; ~

小卒 nobody; small potato / ~英雄 unsung hero; unknown soldier ❸ indefinable; inexpressible; indescribable: ~火 also "无明火" inexplicable anger

无奈 wúnài ❶ cannot but; have no alternative or choice but; ~ have no option (but to do sth) / 这也是~的事。That cannot be helped. ❷ also "无如" unfortunately; but

无能 wúnéng incompetent; inept; incapable: ~为力 be incapable of doing anything to help; be powerless (to do sth) / ~之辈 incompetent people

无巧不成书 wúqiǎobùchéngshū 〈俗〉it is coincidence that makes a story; what a coincidence; as luck would have it

无情 wúqíng ❶ unfeeling; heartless: ~无义 heartless and faithless ❷ merciless; ruthless: ~的嘲讽 bitter satire

无穷 wúqióng infinite; limitless; boundless: ~小〈数〉infinitely small; infinitesimal / ~无尽 infinite; endless; inexhaustible

无人 wúrén ❶ unmanned: ~宇宙飞船 unmanned spaceship / ~驾驶飞机 pilotless plane ❷ without population; not populated: ~区 depopulated zone; no man's land ❸ self-service: ~售书处 self-service book stall

无伤大雅 wúshāngdàyǎ involve no major principle; not matter much; be immaterial

无上 wúshàng supreme; paramount; highest: ~荣光 highest honour

无声 wúshēng noiseless; still; silent: ~片 also "默片" silent film / ~手枪 pistol with a silencer / ~无臭 unknown; little known; obscure

无事 wúshì for nothing; out of nothing: ~生非 create trouble out of nothing; stir up unnecessary trouble / ~不登三宝殿〈俗〉never go to the temple for nothing; call on sb only when one needs his help

无视 wúshì ignore; disregard; defy; ～法纪 defy law and discipline

无数 wúshù ❶ innumerable; untold; countless; 死伤～ (suffer) countless casualties ❷ not know for certain; not be sure; be uncertain

无私 wúsī selfless; unselfish; disinterested

无所 wúsuǒ ❶ used to indicate negation in a phrase; ～事事 be occupied with nothing; idle away one's time / ～适从 not know which way to turn; be at a loss what to do / ～作为 attempt nothing and accomplish nothing; be in a state of apathy or helplessness ❷ used with 不 to indicate emphatic affirmation: ～不包 all-embracing; all-inclusive / ～不能 omnipotent; capable of everything / ～不为 stop at nothing; commit all kinds of evils / ～不知 know everything; be omniscient / ～不用其极 go to any lengths; resort to every conceivable means

无所谓 wúsuǒwèi ❶ cannot be designated as; not deserve the name of; not make much of ❷ care nothing; not take seriously; be indifferent

无妄之灾 wúwàngzhīzāi uncalled-for calamity: 他忽遭雷击,真是～。As luck would have it, he was struck by lightning.

无为 wúwéi (as a Taoist concept of life) do nothing; let things take their own course; ～而治 govern by doing nothing against nature; rule by laissezfaire

无谓 wúwèi meaningless; pointless; senseless

无…无… wú…wú… ❶ used before two parallel characters, similar or identical in meaning, to achieve emphasis: 无法无天 defy laws human or divine; be absolutely outrageous / 无尽无休 ceaseless; infinite / 无拘无束 unconstrained; unrestrained / 无时无刻 all the time; at every moment; unceasingly / 无影无踪 disappear without a trace; melt into thin air / 无忧无虑 free from care or anxieties; carefree / 无缘无故 without rhyme or reason; for no reason at all ❷ used before two parallel characters contrasting in meaning to show the range of effect: 无冬无夏 be it winter or summer; all the year round; throughout the year / 无日无夜 day and night; round the clock

无限 wúxiàn infinite; boundless; unlimited; 前途～ (have) boundless prospects / ～的创造力 inexhaustible creative power

无线 wúxiàn wireless; radio: ～电 radio; radio set / ～电话 radiotelephone / ～电台 radio station / ～广播 radio broadcast

无效 wúxiào of or to no avail; invalid; null and void: 过期～ (become) invalid upon expiration / ～合同 invalid contract / ～劳动 ineffectual work; useless labour

无懈可击 wúxièkějī leaving no room for criticism; unassailable; impregnable

无心 wúxīn ❶ not in the mood for; not inclined to; ～开玩笑 be in no joking mood ❷ also "无意" unintentionally; unwittingly; inadvertently

无形 wúxíng ❶ invisible; intangible; incorporeal; ～财产 incorporeal or intangible property / ～贸易 invisible trade ❷ also "无形中" imperceptibly; unnoticeably; virtually

无须 wúxū also "无需" need not; be not necessary; not have to

无言以对 wúyányǐduì not know what to say in reply: 他问得我～。His questions left me with no reply.

无恙 wúyàng 〈书〉in good health; well; safe: 别来～? I trust everything has been fine with you since we last met.

无业 wúyè jobless; unemployed; ～游民 jobless riff-raff; vagrant

无疑 wúyí beyond doubt; certainly; undoubtedly; 确认 ～ ascertain beyond any shadow of doubt

无以复加 wúyǐfùjiā could not be more...; be in the extreme; 手段之残忍，～。The means adopted couldn't be more cruel.

无意 wúyì ❶ not intend (to do sth); have no intention (to do sth); not be inclined; ～干涉 have no intention to intervene ❷ see "无心❷"

无庸 wúyōng see "毋庸" wúyōng

无用 wúyòng useless; of no avail; no good; ～功〈理〉useless work / ～之辈 good-for-nothing

无与伦比 wúyǔlúnbǐ unique; incomparable; unparalleled

无缘 wúyuán be destined not to; have no chance to; not have the good fortune (of doing sth); ～相识 not have had the pleasure of making sb's acquaintance

无政府主义 wúzhèngfǔzhǔyì anarchism; ～者 anarchist / ～状态 anarchy; chaos

无知 wúzhī ignorant; ～之辈 ignoramus

无中生有 wúzhōngshēngyǒu create sth out of nothing; fabricate out of thin air; be fictitious

无足轻重 wúzúqīngzhòng of little importance or consequence; trivial; insignificant; ～的人 nobody; small potato; peanuts

无罪 wúzuì innocent; not guilty; ～释放 set free with a verdict of "not guilty"; release upon acquittal / ～推定〈法〉presumption of innocence

毋 wú 〈书〉no; not; ～妄言。Do not lie.

毋宁 wúníng also "无宁"〈副〉rather... than...; 与其坐而论道，～起而行动。Let us act instead of talking idly

about principle.

毋庸 wúyōng also "无庸" need not; be unnecessary; ～讳言 to be frank; (there is) no need for reticence / ～置疑 beyond all doubt; doubtless; undoubtedly

芜(蕪) wú 〈书〉❶ (land) overgrown with weeds ❷〈喻〉mixed and disorderly; superfluous; useless; ～杂 (usu of writings) mixed and disorderly; confused

吾 wú 〈书〉I; we; ～辈 I; we; us

吴 Wú region covering southern Jiangsu and northern Zhejiang; ～语 Wu dialect

梧 wú also "梧桐"〈植〉Chinese parasol (tree)

蜈 wú

蜈蚣 wúgōng 〈动物〉centipede

wǔ

五 wǔ five; ～味 five flavours — sweet, sour, bitter, pungent and salty; all sorts of flavours / ～角星 five-pointed star / ～角大楼 (US Department of Defense) the Pentagon / ～分钟热度 short-lived enthusiasm; (like a) flash in the pan / ～天工作制 five-day (working) week

五彩 wǔcǎi also "五色" ❶ five colours — blue, yellow, red, white and black ❷ multicoloured; ～缤纷 blazing with colour; colourful

五大三粗 wǔdà-sāncū tall and brawny

五代 Wǔdài Five Dynasties, 907-960 (Later Liang 后梁, 907-923; Later Tang 后唐, 923-936; Later Jin 后晋, 936-946; Later Han 后汉, 947-950; and Later Zhou 后周, 951-960)

五帝 Wǔdì see "三皇五帝" Sānhuáng-

Wǔdì

五分制 wǔfēnzhì five-grade marking system, using 5, 4, 3, 2 and 1 to represent respectively "excellent", "good", "fair", "poor" or "fail", and "very poor"

五更 wǔgēng ❶ five watches of the night (from dusk to dawn) ❷ fifth watch — just before dawn

五谷 wǔgǔ five cereals — rice, two kinds of millet, wheat and beans, food crops in general：～丰登 abundant harvest of all food crops / ～杂粮（all kinds of) food grains

五官 wǔguān ❶ five sense organs — ears, eyes, mouth, nose and body ❷ facial features：～端正 have regular features

五光十色 wǔguāng-shísè of all hues and colours; of all kinds; multifarious

五湖四海 wǔhú-sìhǎi five lakes and four seas — all corners of the land：来自～ hail from all over the country

五花八门 wǔhuā-bāmén multifarious; kaleidoscopic; of all sorts

五花肉 wǔhuāròu streaky pork

五金 wǔjīn ❶ five metals — gold, silver, copper, iron and tin ❷ metals; hardware：小～ metal fittings (such as nails, bolts, etc) / ～店 hardware store

五经 Wǔjīng see "四书五经" Sìshū-Wǔjīng

五马分尸 wǔmǎfēnshī also "五牛分尸"〈史〉capital punishment by tying the victim's head and each of his limbs to a horse and driving the five horses in different directions to tear him to pieces；〈喻〉tear or break sth to pieces; divide up

五十步笑百步 wǔshíbùxiàobǎibù one who retreats fifty paces laughs at one who retreats a hundred; the pot calls the kettle black

五体投地 wǔtǐtóudì prostrate oneself on the ground (in admiration); be knocked out with admiration

五线谱 wǔxiànpǔ 〈乐〉staff; stave

五香 wǔxiāng five spices — prickly ash, star aniseed, cinnamon, clove and fennel; spices in general：～豆 spiced beans / ～豆腐干 spicy bean cheese

五星 wǔxīng five stars：～红旗 Five-Star Red Flag, national flag of the PRC / ～上将 (US) five-star general / ～宾馆 five-star hotel

五行 wǔxíng five elements (water 水, fire 火, wood 木, metal 金, and earth 土) — a theory used by ancient Chinese philosophers to explain the origin of the world, by physicians of traditional Chinese medicine to make pathological diagnoses, and by superstitious people in fortune-telling：～相克. The five elements subdue one another (in the order of water, fire, metal, wood, earth, and water again). / ～相生. The five elements promote one another (in the order of wood, fire, earth, metal, water, and wood again).

五颜六色 wǔyán-liùsè of various colours; multicoloured; colourful

五一 Wǔ-Yī May 1; May Day：～劳动节 (shortened as 五一) Labour Day; May 1

五音 wǔyīn 〈乐〉five notes of the ancient pentatonic scale：～不全 have a poor ear and voice; be a poor singer

五月 wǔyuè ❶ May ❷ fifth lunar month; fifth moon：～节

五岳 Wǔyuè 〈史〉Five Sacred Mountains, ie Mount Tai (东岳泰山), Mount Hua (西岳华山), Mount Heng (南岳衡山), Mount Heng (北岳恒山), and Mount Song (中岳嵩山)

五脏 wǔzàng five internal organs — heart, liver, spleen, lungs and kidneys：～六腑 all the internal organs of the human body; vital organs

五洲 wǔzhōu whole world; everywhere in the world; the world over

午 wǔ ❶ 7th of the Earthly Branches *see also* "干支" gānzhī ❷ noon; midday；～饭 lunch／～间 noon; midday；～觉 *also* "午觉" (take an) afternoon nap; noontime snooze; siesta／～休 noon break; midday rest; lunch hour／～宴 feast at noon; luncheon／～夜 midnight

伍 wǔ ❶ army：入～ join the army; enlist ❷ company：相与为～ keep company with sb ❸ five (used for the numeral 五 to avoid mistakes or alterations)

忤 (**牾**) wǔ 〈书〉 contradict; go against; run counter to：～逆 unfilial; disobedient (to one's parents)

妩 (**嫵**) wǔ

妩媚 wǔmèi (of a flower, woman, etc) lovely; attractive; charming

武 wǔ ❶ military; of martial arts or acrobatics；～将 military officer; general／～警 (short for 武装警察) armed police／～力 military strength; force／～生 (戏) actor playing a martial role／～戏 military piece; piece full of acrobatic fighting／～林高手 master of martial arts ❷ bold and powerful; valiant; fierce：～火 intense or high heat (in cooking, etc)

武昌鱼 wǔchāngyú blunt-snout bream

武打 wǔdǎ acrobatic or kung fu fighting：～片 martial arts or kung fu movie

武断 wǔduàn ❶ make an arbitrary decision or assertion ❷ arbitrary

武功 wǔgōng *also* "武工" *wushu* or acrobatic skill：～深厚 well versed in acrobatic skill or *wushu*

武官 wǔguān ❶ military officer ❷ military attaché：海军～ naval attaché

武力 wǔlì ❶ armed force; military strength：放弃使用～ or 以～相威胁 give up use or threat of force ❷ (brute) force

武器 wǔqì ❶ weapon; arms：～装备 weaponry ❷ sth used as a weapon：思想～ ideological weapon

武士 wǔshì ❶ palace guard ❷ man of prowess; warrior：～俑 warrior (burial) figure ❸ (Japan) samurai：～道 bushido

武术 wǔshù *wushu*; martial arts; kung fu：练～ learn or practise martial arts

武侠 wǔxiá chivalrous swordsman：～小说 martial arts fiction; kung fu novel

武艺 wǔyì *wushu*, martial arts, or kung fu skill：～高强 adept in *wushu* skills

武装 wǔzhuāng ❶ arms; military equipment; battle outfit or gear：全副～ (in) full battle gear; armed to the teeth／～斗争 armed struggle／～力量 armed forces; military power／用先进装备～部队 arm the troops with state-of-the-art weaponry ❷ armed forces

侮 wǔ ❶ insult; humiliate; bully：～慢 slight; treat disrespectfully; humiliate ❷ *also* "外侮" foreign invasion and oppression

侮蔑 wǔmiè be scornful; treat with contempt：并无～之意 (carry) no suggestion of contempt

侮辱 wǔrǔ *also* "污辱" insult; humiliate; affront：～名誉 be an insult to sb's reputation

捂 wǔ cover; muffle; hide：～汗 be heavily dressed or covered in bed in order to sweat (out a cold, etc)／～盖子 keep the lid on; cover up the truth

舞 wǔ ❶ dance (with sb or sth); move about as if in a dance：～伴 (dancing) partner／～会 dance; ball／～剑 (perform) swordplay／～剧

dance drama; ballet / ～曲 dance (music) / ～厅 also "舞场" (commercial) dance hall / ～狮子 (perform the) lion dance ❷ flourish; wield; play with; ～棍弄棒 brandish a club — practise *wushu* (in certain basic skills)

舞弊 wǔbì　embezzlement; fraudulent practice: 考试～ cheat in an examination

舞蹈 wǔdǎo　dance; ～家 dancer / ～编导 choreographer

舞动 wǔdòng　wave; shake; brandish; 在风中～ (of a flag, etc) flutter in the breeze

舞台 wǔtái　stage: 政治～ (喻) political arena or stage / ～布景 (stage) scenery; décor / ～美术 (shortened as 舞美) stage art; stagecraft / ～生涯 stage career

舞文弄墨 wǔwén-nòngmò ❶ pervert the law by playing with legal phraseology ❷ engage in phrase-mongering

wù

勿 wù　(usu used in imperative sentences) no; not: 切～上当! Beware of swindlers! / 请～打扰。Do not disturb.

戊 wù　5th of the Heavenly Stems　*see also* "干支" gānzhī

务(務) wù ❶ task; affair; business: 要～ important affair ❷ apply oneself to; be engaged in; go in for: ～农 go in for farming; be a farmer; work in the fields ❸ must; be sure to: ～求 also "务使" be sure to have sth done; ensure / ～请准时出席。Be sure to be present on time.

务必 wùbì　also "务须" must; be sure to; be imperative: ～吃透文件的精神实质。It is essential to grasp the spirit of the document.

务实 wùshí　deal with concrete or practical matters: ～精神 spirit of realism;

pragmatism / 重在～。The important thing is to solve specific problems.

务虚 wùxū　discuss principles or ideological guidelines; discuss matters from a plane of principle: 理论～会 meeting to discuss theoretical and cognitive problems / 先～, 后务实。Discuss principles before concrete matters.

坞(塢) wù ❶ depressed place; hollow: 山～ valley; col ❷ structure tall on all sides, which keeps out the wind: 竹～ bamboo shelter

物 wù ❶ thing; material; creature: ～力 material resources / ～证 material evidence / ～主 owner (of property or of sth stolen) / ～尽其用 put things to best use; make full use of what one has / ～美价廉 of excellent quality and reasonable price; cheap and fine / ～～交换 barter ❷ outside world as distinct from oneself; people other than oneself: ～议 criticism from others ❸ content; essence; substance

物产 wùchǎn　product; produce: ～丰富 plentiful in products

物极必反 wùjíbìfǎn　things turn into their opposites when they reach the extreme; no extremes will hold long

物价 wùjià　(commodity) price: ～补贴 subsidy to make up for price increases / ～政策 pricing policy / ～指数 price index / ～飞涨。Prices soar.

物件 wùjiàn　object; thing; article: ～小 trinket

物理 wùlǐ　physics: ～疗法 (shortened as 理疗) physical therapy; physiotherapy

物流 wùliú　flow of goods; logistics: ～公司 logistics company / ～管理 management of goods flow

物品 wùpǐn　article; goods; product: 贵重～ valuables / 零星～ sundries; odds and ends / 私人～ personal belongings or effects / 违禁～ contraban

物色 wùsè　look for; recruit; seek

物体 wùtǐ　body; substance; object

物业 wùyè　real estate; property / ~费用 real estate service charge / ~公司 real estate management company / ~管理 property management

物以类聚 wùyǐlèijù　like attracts like; birds of a feather flock together

物以稀为贵 wùyǐxīwéiguì　when a thing is rare, it becomes precious; scarcity enhances value

物质 wùzhì ❶ matter; substance / ~不灭定律 law of the conservation of matter ❷ material; ~刺激 material incentive / ~文明 material civilization

物种 wùzhǒng　species; ~群 species population

物资 wùzī　goods and materials; 出口~ goods for export / ~分配 distribution of materials / ~丰富 rich supply of commodities

误 wù ❶ mistake; error; ~判 (of a judge, referee, etc) pass wrong judgement; give a wrong verdict / ~杀 kill by mistake or accident; 〈法〉(commit) manslaughter / ~信 wrongly believe; be misled / ~人歧途 go astray; be misled ❷ miss; delay; ~工 cause delay in work; be late for, or absent from work / ~期 miss the deadline; exceed the time limit ❸ harm; damage; ~国 damage national interests; harm the country / ~事 bungle or spoil matters (through delay, oversight, etc) / ~人子弟 lead young people astray; mislead the younger generation

误差 wùchā　error; tolerance; ~范围 range of error

误导 wùdǎo　mislead; lead astray

误点 wùdiǎn　late; overdue; behind time or schedule

误会 wùhuì　misunderstand; misinterpret; misconstrue; 消除~ remove misunderstanding

误解 wùjiě　misread; misunderstand; miscomprehend; 纯属~ sheer misunderstanding

误区 wùqū　"area of error" — long-standing mistaken idea or concept; 走出~ get rid of a long-standing misconception

误诊 wùzhěn ❶ make or give a wrong diagnosis; 把肺炎~为感冒 diagnose pneumonia as a common cold ❷ miss the chance for timely diagnosis and treatment

恶(惡) wù　dislike; loathe; detest; ~寒〈中医〉aversion to cold　see also ě; è

悟 wù　realize; become aware; awaken; ~道 comprehend the way of truth / ~性 power of understanding; comprehension; aptitude (for understanding or mastering sth)

晤 wù　meet; encounter; interview; ~面 meet; see (sb) / ~谈 meet and talk; have a talk or discussion; interview

焐 wù　warm up; keep warm; ~酒 warm up wine

痦 wù

痦子 wùzi　naevus; mole

骛 wù 〈书〉❶ move about freely and quickly ❷ go after; seek for; pursue; 外~ also "旁骛" be distracted by sth irrelevant; be inattentive

雾(霧) wù ❶ fog; mist; ~霭〈书〉mist; haze / ~气 fog; mist; vapour / ~凇 also "树挂" rime / ~茫茫 foggy; misty; hazy / ~里看花 see flowers in a mist; see hazily; have a hazy idea or impression ❷ fine spray; 喷~器 sprayer

寤 wù 〈书〉❶ wake up; ~寐以求 crave day and night ❷ see "悟"

X

xī

夕 xī ❶ sunset; dusk: ~照 glow of the setting sun; evening glow ❷ evening; night

夕阳 xīyáng ❶ setting sun: ~产业 sunset or fading industry / ~西下。 The sun sets in the west. ❷〈喻〉old age; one's later years

兮 xī 〈书〉〈助〉*used like 啊 or 呀 in modern Chinese*: 风萧萧~易水寒。The wind moans and sighs while the water in the Yi River chills.

西 xī ❶ west; 晒 (of a room, etc) facing west / ~亚 West Asia / ~半球 Western Hemisphere / ~电东送 transmission of electricity from west to east China ❷〈书〉the Occident; the West: ~餐 Western or European food / ~学 Western learning / ~医 (doctor of) Western medicine / ~装 *also* "西服" Western-style clothes

西北 xīběi ❶ north-west ❷ (Xīběi) north-west China; the North-West

西部 xībù ❶ west ❷ (Xībù) West of China or the US: ~片 (US) western; Wild West or cowboy movie / ~大开发 large-scale development of the West (of China)

西方 xīfāng ❶ west ❷ (Xīfāng) the West; the Occident: ~国家 Western countries ❸ *see* "西天❷"

西风 xīfēng ❶ west or autumn wind ❷ Western style, practice or culture

西瓜 xīguā watermelon

西汉 Xīhàn Western Han Dynasty (206 BC-25 AD)

西红柿 xīhóngshì (popular term for 番茄) tomato: ~酱 tomato sauce; ketchup

西葫芦 xīhúlu 〈植〉pumpkin; summer squash

西化 xīhuà *also* "欧化" westernize: 全盘~ total westernization

西晋 Xījìn Western Jin Dynasty (265-316)

西兰花 xīlánhuā (popularly known as 绿菜花) broccoli

西南 xīnán ❶ south-west ❷ (Xīnán) south-west China; the South-West

西施 Xīshī *also* "西子" name of a famous beauty in the late Spring and Autumn Period; beautiful woman; beauty

西天 xītiān ❶ (ancient Buddhist name for) India ❷ *also* "极乐世界" Western Paradise: 上~ go west; die

西西 xīxī *also* "毫升" (of liquid) cc (cubic centimetre)

西夏 Xīxià Western Xia Dynasty (1038-1227)

西洋 Xīyáng 〈旧〉❶ the West; the Occident: ~景 *also* "西洋镜" peep show; hanky-panky; trickery / ~参 *also* "花旗参"〈中药〉American ginseng ❷ Western Seas, ie seas and lands west of the South China Sea

西周 Xīzhōu Western Zhou Dynasty (1046 BC-771 BC)

吸 xī ❶ inhale; breathe in; draw: ~烟斗 draw at one's pipe; smoke a pipe ❷ absorb; suck up;

straw (for sipping liquid); suction or sucker pipe / ～力 suction; attraction / ～纳 accept; adopt / ～吮 suck; absorb / ～尘器 vacuum (cleaner) / ～血鬼 bloodsucker; vampire ❸ attract; draw to oneself; ～铁石 loadstone; lodestone; magnet

吸毒 xīdú （short for 吸食毒品）use or take drugs;～者 drug addict / ～成瘾 be addicted to drugs

吸取 xīqǔ absorb; draw; assimilate; ～教训 learn one's lesson

吸收 xīshōu ❶ absorb; assimilate; take in; ～障碍〈医〉malabsorption ❷ recruit; enrol; admit (members, etc)

吸烟 xīyān smoke;～区 smoking area

吸引 xīyǐn attract; draw; fascinate;～力 attraction; fascination

汐 xī tide during the night; night tide

希 xī ❶ hope; wish; ～冀〈书〉yearn for; aspire after; desire / ～图 harbour the intention of; try or attempt to / 敬～指教. Your advice is hereby earnestly solicited. ❷ see "稀❶" 的 "xī"

希罕 xīhan see "稀罕" xīhan

希奇 xīqí see "稀奇" xīqí

希望 xīwàng ❶ hope; wish; ～工程 Project Hope / ～落空 have one's hopes shattered ❷ person or thing that is likely to bring success

昔 xī past; former; ～日 also "昔时"(in) past or bygone days; (in) former times

析 xī ❶ divide; separate; ～产 divide property ❷ analyse; dissect; ～义 expound the meaning (of a word)

矽 xī (old name for 硅)〈化〉silicon (Si)

唏 xī 〈书〉sigh;～嘘 sob

牺（犠） xī

牺牲 xīshēng ❶ 〈史〉beast slaugh-

tered for sacrifice; sacrifice: ～品〈喻〉sacrifice; prey; victim ❷ lay down one's life; die ❸ give up (one's own interests, etc); sacrifice (sb's interests, etc)

息 xī ❶ breath:一一尚存 there's breath left in one; one is still alive ❷ news ❸ cease; stop; end;～怒 cease to be angry; calm one's anger ❹ rest; break; 小～ have a short rest; take a short break ❺ grow; breed; multiply ❻ interest;付～ pay interest / ～金 interest (money)

息肉 xīròu also "瘜肉"〈医〉polyp; polypus

息事宁人 xīshì-níngrén ❶ patch up a quarrel and reconcile the parties concerned; pour oil on troubled waters ❷ make concessions to avoid trouble; pacify sb by meeting him or her halfway; gloss things over to stay on good terms; 抱着～的态度 adopt a conciliatory attitude

息息相关 xīxīxiāngguān also "息息相通" be closely related or bound up

息影 xīyǐng ❶ 〈书〉live in retirement; go into seclusion ❷ (of an actor or actress) retire from the film world

奚 xī

奚落 xīluò taunt; ridicule; jeer or scoff at

硒 xī 〈化〉selenium (Se)

欷 xī

欷歔 xīxū also "唏嘘"〈书〉sob:～不止 keep on sobbing

悉 xī ❶ all; entirely; ～力 do one's utmost; go all out; spare no effort / ～听尊便. Do as you please. ❷ know; understand; learn:来函悉～. Your letter has come to hand.

悉数 xīshù 〈书〉(each and) all:～归公 turn in everything to the state

悉心 xīxīn　devote all one's attention; exercise the greatest care; ～照料 look after with the utmost care; take the utmost care of

烯 xī　〈化〉alkene

浙 xī

浙沥 xīlì　〈象声〉(as of wind, rain or falling leaves) rustle; patter

惜 xī ❶ value; cherish; appreciate; ～墨如金 regard one's ink as if it were gold; be extremely prudent about one's writing, calligraphy, or painting ❷ regret; pity; feel sorry for; ～败 (in a game) lose by a narrow margin / ～老怜贫 care for the aged and sympathize with the poor ❸ stint; spare; grudge; ～别 be reluctant to part; hate to see sb go; find it hard to take leave (of sb) / ～力 be sparing of one's energy; spare one's efforts

晰 xī　clear; distinct; explicit

稀 xī ❶ rare; scarce; uncommon; ～客 rare visitor / ～缺 scarce; lacking; in short supply / ～世之宝 rare treasure ❷ sparse; thinly scattered ❸ diluted; watery; thin;～薄 (of air, etc) rarefied; thin / ～饭 gruel; porridge /～泥 thin mud; slime /～汤 寡水 (as of gruel, soup, etc) watery and tasteless

稀罕 xīhan　also "希罕" ❶ rare; unusual; uncommon ❷ value as a rarity; treasure; cherish; 我才不～你的臭钱 呢。 I couldn't care less about your lousy money.

稀烂 xīlàn ❶ completely mashed; pulpy; 炖得～ stew to a pulp ❷ also "稀巴烂" smashed to pieces; broken to smithereens

稀里糊涂 xīlihútú ❶ not knowing what is what; at sea; muddle-headed ❷ careless; casual; ～地混日子 muddle along carelessly

稀里哗啦 xīlihuālā　〈口〉❶〈象声〉patter; crash; 雨～下了起来。 The rain began pouring down. ❷ smashed to pieces; in total disorder

稀奇 xīqí　also "希奇" rare; peculiar; curious; ～古怪 curious and bizarre; fantastic

稀少 xīshǎo　also "希少" few; rare; scarce;人烟～ sparsely populated

稀释 xīshì　dilute; attenuate; 〈化〉diluent; thinner

稀疏 xīshū　(of hair, etc) thin; sparse; few and far between

稀松 xīsōng ❶ lax; sloppy; poor ❷ also "稀松平常" unimportant; trifling; trivial

稀土 xītǔ　rare earth;～元素 also "稀 土金属"〈化〉rare earth element or metal

稀稀拉拉 xīxi-lālā　also "稀稀落落" sparse; scattered; ～的掌声 sporadic applause

稀有 xīyǒu　also "希有" rare; uncommon;～金属〈化〉rare metal

翕 xī　〈书〉fold; close; furl;～动 (as of lips, etc) open and close alternately

犀 xī　also "犀牛" rhinoceros;～角 rhinoceros horn

犀利 xīlì　keen; sharp; trenchant;～ 笔触 trenchant pen; incisive style

晳 xī　(usu 白晳)〈书〉light-complexioned; fair-skinned

锡 xī ❶ tin (Sn);～箔 tinfoil paper / ～匠 tinsmith / ～纸 tinfoil; silver paper /〈书〉bestow; grant

溪 xī　also "溪流" stream; brook; rivulet

熙 xī　〈书〉❶ brightness; light ❷ happy and content ❸ prosperous; flourishing

熙熙攘攘 xīxī-rǎngrǎng　bustle about; bustle with activity; 街上行人～。 The street was a sea of pedestrians.

蜥 xī　also "蜥蜴" lizard

僖 xī　〈书〉happy and joyous

熄 xī　extinguish (a fire); put out (a light); ～灯 turn off a light / ～火 (of an engine, etc) go dead; put out (a fire) / ～灭 extinguish; put out; (of a fire, etc) go out

嘻 xī　〈象声〉sound of laughing: ～～一笑 giggle (at sb)

嘻嘻哈哈 xīxī-hāhā　laughing and joking; happy-go-lucky: 这可不是～的事。This is no joking matter.

膝 xī　knee: ～盖 knee; kneecap / ～关节 knee joint

膝下 xīxià　❶ respectful term of address for one's parents, etc, in letter-writing: 父母大人～ my beloved parents ❷ used to indicate whether one has children: ～犹虚 have no child yet

嬉 xī　〈书〉play; have fun: ～戏 play; sport; frolic

嬉皮士 xīpíshì　hippie

嬉皮笑脸 xīpí-xiàoliǎn　also "嘻皮笑脸" grin cheekily; smile and grimace; be comically cheerful

嬉笑 xīxiào　laugh and play; frolic: ～怒骂 mirth, laughter, anger and curses — (earthy depictions of) various moods of life

熹 xī　〈书〉brightness; dawn; daybreak: 晨光～微 pale light of dawn

窸 xī

窸窣 xīsū　〈象声〉rustle

蹊 xī　〈书〉footpath: 另辟～径 look for another way; seek a different solution or shortcut　see also qī

蟋 xī

蟋蟀 xīshuài　also "蛐蛐儿"〈动物〉cricket: 斗～ (have a) cricket fight

曦 xī　〈书〉sunlight (usu in early morning): ～光 sunlight

xí

习(習) xí　❶ study; learn; practise: ～题 exercise (in school work); sum / ～作 exercise in composition, painting, etc / ～字帖 copybook; calligraphy model ❷ be accustomed or used to; be familiar with: ～染〈书〉contract (a bad habit); get into (evil ways) / ～以为常 be accustomed or used to; be in or get into the habit of ❸ habit; custom: convention: ～俗 custom; practice; convention / ～语 idiom

习惯 xíguàn　❶ be accustomed or used to; be familiar with: ～成自然 Habit is second nature. ❷ habit; custom; convention: ～法 common or customary law / ～势力 force of habit

习气 xíqì　bad habit or practice: 官僚～ (practices of) bureaucracy

习习 xíxí　(of wind) blow gently

习性 xíxìng　habits and characteristics; temperament: 生活～ habits and characteristics (as of an animal); way of life

席(❶蓆) xí　❶ mat: ～棚 (temporary) mat shed / ～地而坐 sit on the ground or floor (as if on a mat) ❷ seat; place; box: 记者～ seats for the press / ～次 order of seats; seating arrangement; one's seat as arranged ❸ also "席位" seat in parliament, etc ❹ feast; banquet; dinner: ～间 at or during a feast ❺〈量〉一～话 a talk

席不暇暖 xíbùxiánnuǎn　not sit long enough to warm the seat; be in a tearing hurry; be as busy as a bee

席卷 xíjuǎn　roll up like a mat; sweep across: ～而逃 make a clean sweep and decamp; make off with everything one can lay hands on / ～天下 conquer the whole country in a sweep

席梦思 xímèngsī inner-spring mattress; spring bed

袭(襲) xí ❶ raid; attack; ～取 take by surprise / ～扰 make harassing attacks; harass ❷ follow the pattern of; carry on as before; copy; ～封〈史〉inherit a rank or title / ～用故技 use the old tactics; repeat an old trick ❸〈书〉〈量〉suit; dress; 一～棉衣 a suit of cotton-padded clothes

袭击 xíjī spring an attack on; attack by surprise; raid; 遭到洪水～ be hit by floods

媳 xí daughter-in-law

媳妇 xífù ❶ also "儿媳妇儿" daughter-in-law; son's wife ❷ wife of a junior relative; 兄弟～ wife of one's younger brother; sister-in-law

媳妇儿 xífur 〈方〉❶ wife; 娶～ (of a man) take a wife; get married ❷ young married woman

檄 xí (usu 檄文) official summons or call to arms; official proclamation (denouncing a traitor, etc)

xǐ

洗 xǐ ❶ wash; bathe; clean; ～脑〈喻〉brainwashing; indoctrination / ～钱 money laundering / ～浴 take a bath / ～灌 wash; cleanse / ～发剂 shampoo / ～脸盆 washbasin; washbowl / ～染店 laundering and dyeing shop / 把录音～掉 erase a recording ❷〈宗教〉baptize ❸ redress; remedy; right; ～雪 wipe out (a disgrace); redress (a wrong) ❹ kill and loot; sack; ～劫 loot; ransack; sack ❺ develop (film); ～印 develop and print; process / ～相片 have photos printed

❻ shuffle; 重新～牌 reshuffle (cards, cabinet, etc)

洗尘 xǐchén give a dinner of welcome (to a visitor from afar)

洗涤 xǐdí wash; rinse; cleanse; ～剂 detergent

洗耳恭听 xǐ'ěrgōngtīng lend an attentive ear; listen with respectful attention; be all ears

洗礼 xǐlǐ 〈宗教〉〈喻〉baptism; 施～ administer baptism (to sb) / 经受炮火的～ receive the baptism of fire; go through the test of war

洗练 xǐliàn (of writing, etc) neat; succinct; terse

洗手 xǐshǒu ❶ (as of a gangster, etc) stop doing evil; ～不干 reform oneself and hang up one's axe ❷ wash one's hands of sth; give up (a vocation, hobby, etc) ❸〈婉〉go to the lavatory; use the restroom; ～间 lavatory; toilet; bathroom

洗刷 xǐshuā ❶ wash and brush; scrub ❷ wash off; remove; clear oneself of (guilt, etc); ～自己 vindicate oneself

洗心革面 xǐxīn-gémiàn turn over a new leaf; start one's life afresh; reform oneself thoroughly

洗衣 xǐyī wash clothes; do one's washing; ～板 washboard / ～店 laundry / ～粉 washing powder / ～机 washing machine; washer

洗澡 xǐzǎo have or take a bath; bath; ～间 bathhouse; bathroom / ～盆 bathtub

玺(璽) xǐ imperial or royal seal

铣 xǐ milling; ～床 milling machine see also xiǎn

徙 xǐ ❶ move (from one place to another); migrate ❷〈书〉be transferred (to another post, etc)

喜 xǐ ❶ happy; joyful; pleased; ～人 gratifying; heartening / ～

洋洋 beaming with pleasure or joy; radiant ❷ happy event (esp a wedding, etc); auspicious occasion; ~酒 (wine drunk at a) wedding feast / ~讯 happy or good news; glad tidings ❷ ~雨 seasonable or welcome rain / 双~临门 be blessed with double happiness ❸ pregnancy; 害~ be pregnant; show symptoms of pregnancy ❹ like; like; ~新厌旧 be fickle in one's affection ❺ (as of some plant or food) be prone to; agree with; require; ~光 photophilous

喜爱 xǐ'ài love; be fond of; be keen on; ~交际 love company; be sociable

喜不自胜 xǐbùzìshèng be unable to restrain oneself for joy; be delighted beyond measure; be overjoyed

喜出望外 xǐchūwàngwài be overjoyed (at unexpected good news, etc); be pleasantly surprised

喜好 xǐhào like; be fond of; be keen on; 个人~ personal preferences

喜欢 xǐhuan ❶ like; love; be fond of; 讨某人~ win sb's favour; make sb happy ❷ happy; delighted; elated

喜剧 xǐjù comedy; ~小品 comedy skit / ~演员 comedian

喜马拉雅山脉 Xǐmǎlāyǎ Shānmài Himalayan Mountains; Himalayas

喜怒 xǐnù happiness or anger — varying moods; ~无常 subject to changing moods; volatile; capricious / ~哀乐不形于色 never show one's feelings; be inscrutable

喜庆 xǐqìng (occasion or event) calling for celebration or jubilation; ~气氛 atmosphere of rejoicing and festivity

喜鹊 xǐque also "鹊"〈动物〉magpie

喜事 xǐshì ❶ happy event; joyous occasion; glad tidings ❷ wedding; 办~ hold a wedding ceremony

喜闻乐见 xǐwén-lèjiàn love to see and hear; love; 青年人~的作品 works that young people love; works that are popular among the young

喜笑颜开 xǐxiàoyánkāi (of one's face) light up with happiness; be wreathed in smiles; beam with pleasure

喜形于色 xǐxíngyúsè be visibly pleased; be radiant with joy

喜悦 xǐyuè delightful; happy; joyous

屟 xǐ〈书〉shoes; slippers; sandals

禧 xǐ happiness; jubilation; 年~ season's greetings; Happy New Year

xì

戏(戲) xì ❶ play; sport; have fun ❷ make fun of; joke with; ~称 call (sb) jokingly; joking nickname / ~谑 banter; crack jokes / ~说 (render a) free, usu playful version (of history, etc) ❸ drama; opera; play; show; ~路 ability to act different types of characters / ~迷 theatre-goer; theatre fan / ~院 theatre

戏法 xìfǎ juggling; sleight of hand; magic; 变~ juggle; conjure; perform a trick

戏剧 xìjù drama; play; theatre; ~家 playwright; dramatist / ~性 dramatic

戏曲 xìqǔ traditional opera; ~片 documentary film of a traditional opera; film adaptation of a traditional opera

戏耍 xìshuǎ ❶ also "戏弄" play tricks on; make fun of; tease ❷ play; amuse oneself; idle about

戏言 xìyán joke; playful words; humorous remarks; ~天下事 joke about everything under the sun

系(❸❼係、❸–❻繫) xì ❶ system; series; line; ~谱 pedigree; genealogy ❷ department; faculty; 中文~ Chinese department ❸ relate to; rely on; ~词 (in logic) copula;〈语言〉link verb / 成败所~ success or failure hinges on this; stand or fall by this ❹ be concerned; feel solicitous: ~念〈书〉 be concerned or anxious about ❺ tie (up); fasten: ~马 tether a horse ❻ take into custody; jail: ~狱 be put in prison ❼〈书〉be:~确~实情。It is indeed the truth.

see also jì

系列 xìliè　series; set: ~片 serial / ~产品 set of products; serial products

系统 xìtǒng　system; set-up; 党、政~ Party and government set-ups / ~化 systematize / ~工程（project of）systems or systematic engineering

细 xì ❶ thin; slender; fine: ~沙 fine sand / ~纱 spun yarn ❷（of a voice）thin and soft; gentle: ~声~气 in a gentle, quiet voice; soft-spoken ❸ fine; exquisite; delicate; ~粮 fine grains（wheat, rice, etc）/ ~雨 drizzle; fine rain ❹ careful; meticulous; detailed: ~活 job requiring fine workmanship or meticulous care; fine and delicate work / ~说 narrate in detail / ~则 detailed rules and regulations; by-laws / ~嚼慢咽 chew one's food well before swallowing it; eat one's meal slowly ❺ minute; trivial; trifling: ~碎 small and broken; in fine scraps / ~小 very small; tiny; trivial / ~枝末节 petty details; non-essentials

细胞 xìbāo　cell: ~核 nucleus

细节 xìjié　details; specifics; particulars

细菌 xìjūn　bacterium; germ: ~战 germ warfare / ~感染 bacterial infection

细密 xìmì ❶ fine and closely woven; close: 质地~的大理石 marble of close texture ❷ with great precision and care; meticulous; detailed: 观察~ be observant

细嫩 xìnèn　fine; delicate; tender: 细皮嫩肉 delicate skin and soft flesh — be fragile or delicate

细腻 xìnì ❶（of skin, etc）fine and smooth; delicate ❷ exquisite; minute: 感情~ of fine sentiments / 刻画~ depict to a nicety

细软 xìruǎn ❶ jewellery; expensive clothing and other valuables ❷ soft and slender

细水长流 xìshuǐchángliú ❶ plan for the long term to avoid running short ❷ go about little by little without let-up; work persistently

细微 xìwēi　tiny; slight; subtle: ~之处 niceties; subtleties

细心 xìxīn　meticulous; careful; attentive: ~照顾 care for（sb）tenderly; take meticulous care of

细致 xìzhì ❶ careful; meticulous; painstaking ❷ fine; exquisite; delicate

阋（鬩） xì〈书〉quarrel; fight

隙 xì ❶ crack; chink; crevice ❷ gap; interval: 农~ interval between busy seasons in farming ❸ loophole; opening; opportunity: 可乘之~ opening to take advantage of ❹ discord; rift; grudge: 与人有~ have a quarrel with sb; bear sb a grudge

xiā

呷 xiā〈方〉sip; drink: ~一口酒 take a sip of wine

虾（蝦） xiā　shrimp: ~米 dried, shelled shrimps;〈方〉small shrimps / ~仁 shelled fresh shrimps; shrimp meat / ~子 shrimp roe or eggs / ~兵蟹将 numerous（but ineffectual）followers or troops

瞎 xiā ❶ blind: ~了左眼 blind in the left eye / ~猫逮住死耗子〈俗〉get sth by sheer luck / ~子点灯白费蜡〈俗〉（like lighting a candle for a blind man）it's sheer waste ❷ groundlessly; foolishly; to no avail: ~

扯 talk irresponsibly; gossip; waffle / 〜忙 fuss about nothing; be all fuss and feathers / 〜蒙 (make a) wild guess / 〜闹 mess about; fool around; play rough house / 〜指挥 give arbitrary and impracticable directions; command at whim; 睁眼说一话 tell a barefaced lie; lie blazingly ❸〈口〉(of things) fail (to meet the expectation); 〜炮 unexploded shell or firecracker; dud / 〜账 bad debt

xiá

匣 xiá *also* "匣子" small box or case; casket

侠(俠) xiá *also* "侠客" person adept in martial arts and given to chivalrous conduct; chivalrous swordsman; 〜义 with a strong sense of justice and ready to help the weak; chivalrous

狎 xiá be improperly familiar; indulge in flirtations or intimacies; 〜妓 visit a brothel; have fun with a prostitute / 〜昵 be improperly familiar

峡(峽) xiá gorge; 〜谷 gorge; canyon

狭(狹) xiá narrow; 〜长 long and narrow / 〜小 narrow and small; cramped / 〜义 narrow sense

狭隘 xiá'ài ❶ narrow (road, etc) ❷ narrow-minded; illiberal; 心胸〜 narrow-minded; parochial

狭路相逢 xiálùxiāngféng (of enemies) meet face to face on a narrow path — come into unavoidable confrontation; confront each other face to face

狭窄 xiázhǎi ❶ narrow; cramped (room, etc) ❷ see "狭隘 ❷"

遐 xiá 〈书〉❶ far; distant; remote; 〜迩闻名 be known far and near; enjoy great renown ❷ lasting; durable; long; 〜想 reverie; daydream;

(wild) fancy

瑕 xiá flaw (in a piece of jade); defect; drawback; shortcoming; 〜疵 flaw; defect; blemish / 〜不掩瑜 small defects cannot obscure virtues; drawbacks do not overshadow achievements

暇 xiá free time; spare moment; leisure; 无〜 be too busy (to do sth)

辖 xiá ❶ linchpin ❷ have jurisdiction over; have under one's command; govern; 〜区 area or district under one's jurisdiction / 〜制 restrain; check; control

霞 xiá rosy clouds; morning or evening glow; 〜光 rays of morning or evening sunlight

黠 xiá 〈书〉sly; crafty; cunning; 〜慧 intelligent and crafty; smart and cunning

xià

下 xià ❶ below; under; underneath; 〜层 lower levels or strata; grass-roots level / 〜方 below; underneath / 〜列 listed or mentioned below; following; ensuing / 〜肢〈生理〉lower limbs; legs ❷ lower; inferior; poor; 〜品 low-grade (stuff); inferior (work) / 〜作 low; mean; indecent / 〜里巴人 popular (art); lowbrow (literature) ❸ next; latter; later; 〜旬 last ten-day period of a month / 〜午 afternoon / 〜辈子 next life / 〜不为例 not be taken as a precedent; must not happen again / 〜〜星期 week after the next ❹ go down or downward; (of rain, etc) fall; get off; 〜跌 fall; drop; go down / 〜网〈信息〉(go) offline / 〜载〈信息〉download / 〜半旗 fly a flag at half mast (as a sign of mourning) / 〜坡路 downhill path or journey; decline; deteriorate ❺ go (down) to：～地 go to the fields；get out of bed；leave a sick bed **⑤** (of gods，etc) descend to the (mortal) world / ～馆子 go and eat in a restaurant；eat out / ～基层 go to the grass roots **⑥** issue；deliver；send；～令 give orders；order；instruct / ～达任务 assign a task **⑦** exit；leave (off)；finish (work，etc)：～学 finish school / ～火线 leave the battlefield **⑧** put in；cast：～注 (in gambling，etc) place a bet；lay down a stake；stake (sth) **⑨** take away or off；unload；dismantle；～某人的枪 take away sb's gun；disarm sb **⑩** apply；use：～筷 start eating；help oneself / ～力 exert oneself；make efforts / ～药 prescribe medicine；put in poison / ～毒手 strike a vicious blow (at sb)；lay murderous hands (on sb) / ～功夫 put in time and energy；take pains **⑪** capture；seize；take：连～三城 capture three cities in succession；defeat three adversaries in a row **⑫** give in；yield：各不相～。Neither side would give in. **⑬** *used after a noun to indicate* **a**) *subordination，circumstances，extent，etc*：名～ under sb's name **b**) *particular time or season*：节～ during a holiday or festival **⑭** *used after a verb to indicate* **a**) *downward motion*：跳～卡车 jump off a truck **b**) *room or space*：坐不～五个人 cannot seat 5 people **c**) *completion or consequence of an action*：备～几种方案 get ready several plans **⑮** *used after a numeral to indicate orientation or position*：四～无人 with nobody around **⑯** play (board) games：～棋 play chess；have a game of chess **⑰** form (an opinion)；draw (a conclusion)；give (a definition)：～保证 make a pledge **⑱** (of animals) give birth to；lay：～蛋 lay eggs **⑲** (usu in the negative) less than：不～十次 no less than ten times **⑳** 〈量〉*used to indicate repetition of ac-*

tion：敲了两～门 give a couple of knocks on the door **㉑** *used after "下" or "几" to indicate one's ability or skill*：他真有两～！He really can show you a thing or two！

【下巴】xiàba **❶** lower jaw **❷** *also* "下颏儿" chin

【下班】xiàbān come or go off work；knock off：下早班 come off morning shift

【下半】xiàbàn second or latter half；～时 *also* "下半场" second half (of a game) / ～辈子 latter half of one's life；one's remaining years

【下笔】xiàbǐ put pen to paper；begin to write or paint：～如有神 write with inspiration；write quickly and powerfully

【下不来】xiàbulái **❶** (of fever，price，etc) refuse to come down **❷** cannot accomplish or succeed；没有 100 万元 not be able to buy sth for less than one million yuan **❸** feel awkward or embarrassed：让人脸上～ make sb embarrassed

【下策】xiàcè bad plan；unwise move；worst option or alternative：不得已出此～ have no alternative but to resort to this

【下场】xiàchǎng **❶** 〈戏〉 go off stage；〈体〉 leave the playing field；exit **❷** (xiàchang) 〈贬〉 end；fate：不会有好～ come to no good end

【下沉】xiàchén (of a ship，etc) sink；(of land，etc) subside；submerge

【下饭】xiàfàn (of a dish of food) go (well) with rice

【下放】xiàfàng **❶** transfer to a lower level；devolve (power) **❷** send (cadres，etc) to do manual labour or work at the grass-roots level

【下风】xiàfēng **❶** leeward；downwind：站在～处 stand to leeward **❷** inferior or disadvantageous position；处于～ be at a disadvantage

【下岗】xiàgǎng **❶** come or go off (sentry) duty ❷ (as of a worker) be removed from a post; be made redundant; be laid off：～人员再就业 re-employment of laid-off personnel

下跪 xiàguì　kneel down; be on bended knees：～求饶 beg for mercy on bended knees

下海 xiàhǎi　❶ go to sea; put out to sea; (of fishermen) go fishing in the sea ❷ (of an amateur) turn career performer ❸ (of people from other walks of life) go in for business; become a businessman

下级 xiàjí　lower level; subordinate：～军官 lower-ranking or junior officer

下贱 xiàjiàn　❶ low; humble：出身～ be of low birth ❷〈粗〉mean; low-down; obscene：～货 lowly girl; slut

下降 xiàjiàng　descend; fall; decline：威信～ declining prestige

下酒 xiàjiǔ　❶ drink wine (with sth); (of dishes) go well with wine：～菜 dish that goes well with wine

下课 xiàkè　❶ dismiss or finish class; class is over ❷ (of a coach, etc) be dismissed or sacked; resign

下来 xiàlái　❶ come down；部里要～人检查工作。Some people from the ministry are coming to inspect the work here. ❷ (of crops, etc) be harvested ❸ (xialai) used after a verb to indicate a) downward direction or movement from far to near：从舞台上走～ come off the stage　b) continuation from past to present or from start to finish：坚持～ persist to the end　c) completion or result of an action：雨一时停不～。The rain won't stop for a while yet. ❹ (xialai) used after certain adjectives to indicate increasing degree：天色暗了～。It got darker.

下流 xiàliú　❶ see “下游❶”❷ low; base; obscene：～话 salacious remarks; obscene language; obscenities

下落 xiàluò　❶ whereabouts：～不明 of unknown whereabouts ❷ drop; fall; decline

下马 xiàmǎ　❶ get off or dismount from a horse：～威 severity shown (by an official) in assuming office; (make a) show of strength at first contact ❷ discontinue (a project, etc)

下毛毛雨 xiàmáomaoyǔ　❶ drizzle ❷ break (bad news, etc) little by little; criticize or scold gently

下面 xiàmian　also “下边”；“下头” ❶ below; under; beneath ❷ immediately after; next; following：～该谁了？Who's next? ❸ lower level; subordinate：～的群众 people at the grassroots

下情 xiàqíng　❶ conditions at the lower levels; circumstances and sentiments of the common people or one's subordinates：～上达 make the situation at the lower levels known to the higher authorities; report the circumstances and sentiments of the common people to the higher-ups ❷〈谦〉my situation or circumstances; my state of mind

下去 xiàqù　❶ go down; get off; descend；～调查一下 go down to the grass roots to investigate ❷ (xiaqu) used after a verb to indicate a) descending motion or movement from near to afar：洪水退了～。The flood receded. b) continuation：说～ go on (speaking) ❸ (xiaqu) used after certain adjectives to indicate an increasing degree：天气还得热～。It'll get still hotter.

下身 xiàshēn　❶ lower part of the body：上身长，～短 (have) a long torso and short legs ❷ private parts ❸ trousers; pants

下市 xiàshì　❶ go or be off season ❷ close shop ❸ also “下牌”〈经〉(of a company) be taken off the stock market; be delisted

下手 xiàshǒu ❶ put one's hand to (a job, etc); set about：下不去手 cannot bear to do (sth cruel, etc)；flinch (before sth hard, etc) ❷ *also* "下首" right-hand (seat)：坐在我的~ sit next to me ❸〈口〉assistant；helper：给人打~ act as sb's assistant；assist sb

下水 xiàshuǐ ❶ (cause a ship, etc to) move into the water；be launched：~典礼 launching ceremony ❷ (of fabrics, etc) be soaked in water；be washed ❸ engage in evil-doing；fall into evil ways ❹ down a river；downstream ❺ (xiàshui) (cooked as food) offal；entrails

下水道 xiàshuǐdào sewer；drain：~系统 sewer system；sewerage

下榻 xiàtà〈书〉stay (at a place during a trip)；find accommodation

下台 xiàtái ❶ step down from the stage or platform ❷ hand over power；leave office；赶~ drive (sb) out of office；throw out ❸ (usu in the negative) get out of a sorry plight or an embarrassing situation：下不了台 be unable to back down with grace；be on the spot

下文 xiàwén ❶ what comes later in an article or book：~将进一步说明。More about this later. ❷ later development；outcome；result：不见~。Nothing's been heard of it.

下限 xiàxiàn lower limit；prescribed minimum；floor (level)

下泻 xiàxiè ❶ *also* "下泄" (of water) flow downward ❷ (have) loose bowels；(suffer from) diarrhoea

下野 xiàyě (as of a ruler or politician) fall from power；retire from the political arena；被迫~ be forced to step down

下议院 xiàyìyuàn *also* "下院" lower house or chamber (of a parliament)；(UK) House of Commons

下意识 xiàyìshí subconscious：~地重复了一句 repeat a sentence without thinking

下游 xiàyóu ❶ lower reaches (of a river) ❷ backward position；lagging behind：暂处~ lag behind for the time being ❸〈经〉downstream：~产品 downstream product

吓(嚇) xià frighten；scare；intimidate：~唬 frighten；scare；bluff；~人 terrifying；appalling；frightening *see also* hè

夏 xià ❶ summer：~季 summer / ~粮 summer grain crops / ~收 summer harvesting or harvest / ~时制 summer time (ST) / (Xià) Xia Dynasty (2070 BC–1600 BC) ❸ ancient name for China：~历 traditional Chinese calendar；lunar calendar

夏令 xiàlìng ❶ summer；summertime：~营 summer camp ❷ summer weather

夏至 xiàzhì Summer Solstice, 10th seasonal division point *see also* "节气" jiéqì

罅 xià〈书〉crack；chink；crevice：~隙 crevice；cleft；fissure

xiān

仙(僊) xiān celestial being；immortal；fairy：~丹 immortality pill；elixir of life / ~鹤 (as in fairy tales) white crane or stork raised by immortals；〈口〉red-crowned crane；stork / ~境 fairyland；wonderland；paradise / ~女 young female immortal；fairy maiden / ~人 immortal；celestial being / ~逝〈婉〉pass away

仙人掌 xiānrénzhǎng〔植〕cactus；球状~ *also* "仙人球" bulbous cactus

先 xiān ❶ early；earlier；before：~导 lead the way；be in the van / ~例 precedent / ~期 earlier on；in advance / ~前 in the past；before；previously / ~睹为快 consider it a pleasure to be among the first to read or watch (sth) / ～公后私 subordinate one's personal interests to public interests / ～见之明 ability to anticipate what is coming; prophetic vision; foresight / ～下手为强, 后下手遭殃. He who strikes first prevails; he who strikes late fails. ❷ older generation; ancestor; forefather ❸〈敬〉deceased; late; ～父 my late father / ～烈 martyr / ～哲 great thinker of the past

先辈 xiānbèi ❶ older or earlier generation ❷ ancestors; forefathers; forerunners

先发制人 xiānfāzhìrén gain the initiative by striking first; steal a march on one's rival; forestall the enemy: ～的攻击 pre-emptive strike

先锋 xiānfēng pioneer; van (guard); ～队 vanguard

先河 xiānhé source; precedent; forerunner: 开我国话剧的～ break a path for China's modern drama

先后 xiānhòu ❶ early or late; priority (order): 分清～缓急 put things in priority order ❷ in succession; one after another

先进 xiānjìn advanced: ～事迹 meritorious or exemplary deed / ～工作者 advanced or model worker

先决 xiānjué prerequisite: ～条件 prerequisite; precondition

先来后到 xiānlái-hòudào in the order of arrival; first come, first served

先礼后兵 xiānlǐ-hòubīng a gentleman first and a warrior second; words before blows; using peaceful means before resorting to force

先遣 xiānqiǎn sent in advance: ～队 advance party or detachment

先秦 Xiānqín before Qin Dynasty; pre-Qin (usu 770 BC-221 BC)

先驱 xiānqū also "先驱者" pioneer; forerunner; trailblazer

先人 xiānrén ❶ ancestor; forefather ❷ late father (usu of sb else)

先入为主 xiānrùwéizhǔ first impressions are strongest; preconceived ideas keep a strong hold; be prejudiced or biased: 凡事不可～. You should always be on your guard against any bias.

先声夺人 xiānshēngduórén forestall one's opponent by a show of strength; overawe others by displaying one's prowess; seize the initiative

先生 xiānsheng ❶ teacher: 王～的课 Mr Wang's class ❷ mister (Mr); gentleman; sir: 主席～! Mr Chairman! ❸ husband ❹〈方〉doctor ❺ used to refer to people engaged in certain trades or as a title: 风水～ geomancer / 足球～ Mr Football

先天 xiāntiān ❶ congenital; inbred; inborn: ～性缺陷 birth defect / ～性心脏病 congenital heart disease ❷〈哲〉a priori; innate

先行 xiānxíng ❶ go ahead of the rest; start off before the others; precede; ～者 pioneer; forerunner ❷ beforehand; earlier; in advance: ～通知 inform in advance ❸ also "先行官" commander of an advance unit or vanguard

先斩后奏 xiānzhǎn-hòuzòu act first and report afterwards; do sth without prior approval (from one's superiors)

先兆 xiānzhào omen; portent; sign

先知 xiānzhī ❶ person of foresight: ～先觉 person of foresight or vision; having foresight ❷〈宗教〉prophet

纤(纖) xiān fine; tiny; minute: ～巧 delicate; exquisite / ～弱 slender and fragile; delicate / ～细 slim; slender; fine / ～尘不染 be not soiled by a particle of dust; be spotlessly clean or meticulously upright / ～悉无遗 with no detail unnoticed or omitted; down to the minutest detail see also qiàn

纤维 xiānwéi fibre; staple: ～板〈建筑〉fibreboard; fibrous slab / ～素 cellulose

氙 xiān 〈化〉xenon (Xe)：～灯 xenon lamp

籼(秈) xiān

籼稻 xiāndào long-grained non-glutinous rice；*indica* rice

掀 xiān ❶ lift (a cover, etc)；open up；turn over ❷ convulse；rock；shake：～动 move；set in motion；unleash

掀起 xiānqǐ ❶ lift；raise ❷ surge (up)；cause to surge：暴风～漫天黄沙。The windstorm blew yellow sand all over the sky. ❸ launch (a movement, etc)；start；set off (mass fervour, etc)

锨 xiān (usu 铁锨) shovel；spade

鲜 xiān ❶ fresh；new：～花 (fresh) flowers / ～嫩 fresh and tender ❷ bright(-coloured)：～红 bright red；scarlet ❸ delicious；tasty：～脆 fresh and crisp ❹ delicacy；aquatic food；时～ vegetables or fruits just in season
see also xiǎn

鲜活 xiānhuó ❶ (of fish, etc) fresh (and alive) ❷ vivid；lively：～的个性 lively personality

鲜美 xiānměi ❶ delicious；tasty ❷ 〈书〉fresh and beautiful

鲜明 xiānmíng ❶ (of colour) bright；shiny ❷ clear-cut；sharp；distinct：爱憎～ unequivocal about what one loves and what one hates

鲜血 xiānxuè blood：～淋漓 dripping with blood

鲜艳 xiānyàn bright- or gaily-coloured；bright and beautiful：～夺目 dazzlingly beautiful；resplendent

xián

闲(閒) xián ❶ unoccupied；idle；leisurely：～逛 saunter；stroll；loaf / ～居 stay at home idle / ～适 leisurely and comfortable；easy and carefree / ～谈 *also* "闲聊" chat；gossip / ～不住 refuse to be idle；always keep oneself occupied / 没～心 be in no mood for jokes ❷ not in use；unoccupied；lying idle：～房 vacant house or room / ～钱 (口) spare money ❸ spare time；leisure：～暇 *also* "闲空"；"闲工夫" free or spare time；leisure ❹ irrelevant；random；idle：～杂人员 people without fixed duties；redundant staff；irrelevant people / 看～书 do light reading；read for amusement

闲话 xiánhuà ❶ digression；cackle：～少说！Cut the cackle! ❷ complaint；gossip：说人～ gossip about others ❸ 〈书〉talk casually；chat

闲气 xiánqì anger about trifles；uncalled-for abuse：生～ be angry over a trifle / 受～ take uncalled-for abuse

闲情逸致 xiánqíng-yìzhì cultivated pleasures of a leisurely life；leisurely，carefree mood (for sth)

闲人 xiánrén ❶ idle or unoccupied person；idler ❷ person not concerned：～免进。No admittance except on business.

闲散 xiánsǎn ❶ free and leisurely；at a loose end ❷ scattered and unused；idle：～资金 idle capital

闲事 xiánshì ❶ matter not of one's concern；other people's business：爱管～ love to poke one's nose into other people's business；be a busybody ❷ unimportant matter；trifle

闲言碎语 xiányán-suìyǔ ❶ unrelated trivia；digressions ❷ groundless accusations or complaints (usu behind people's backs)；gossip：背地里散布～ gossip behind sb's back

闲置 xiánzhì leave unused or idle；gather dust：～设备 idle equipment

贤(賢) xián ❶ able and virtuous (person)；worthy

or wise (man)：～惠 also "贤慧" (of a woman) virtuous and kind; kind and understanding; kind-hearted / ～明 wise and able; capable and intelligent; sagacious / ～人 person of virtue; wise man / ～内助 good or understanding wife / ～妻良母 (traditional ideal of womanhood) understanding wife and loving mother / 社会～达 prominent public figures or personages ❷〈敬〉 used to refer to people of the same or younger generation：～弟 (term of respect for one's younger brother or a man younger than oneself) my worthy brother

弦(❷**絃**) xián ❶ bowstring ❷ string of a musical instrument; chord：～乐队 string orchestra or band / ～乐器 stringed instrument / ～外之音〈喻〉overtones; implication; innuendo ❸ spring (of a watch, etc)：给闹钟上～ wind up an alarm clock ❹〈数〉chord; hypotenuse

咸(❷**鹹**) xián ❶〈书〉all; both：老少～宜 good for old and young alike ❷ salted; salty：～菜 salted vegetables; pickles / ～淡 degree of saltiness / ～肉 salted meat; bacon / ～水湖 saltwater lake

涎 xián saliva：～水〈方〉saliva / ～皮赖脸 brazen-faced; shameless and loathsome; cheeky

娴(**嫻**) xián ❶ refined; elegant：～雅 (of a woman) refined; graceful; elegant / 娴顺～静 meek and gentle ❷ (usu 娴熟) adept; skilled; well-versed

衔(**啣**) xián ❶ hold in the mouth ❷ cherish; harbour; bear：～冤 nurse a bitter sense of injustice; suffer a wrong or miscarriage of justice ❸〈书〉accept (instructions or orders)：～命组阁 be authorized to form a cabinet ❹ connect; link：～接 link up; connect; join

舷 xián side of a ship or plane; board：右～ starboard / 左～ port / ～窗 porthole / ～梯 (of a ship, etc) gangway (ladder)；(of a plane) ramp

痫(**癇**) xián also "癲癇"〈医〉epilepsy

嫌 xián ❶ suspicion：有贪赃之～ be suspected of corruption ❷ ill will; hard feeling; grudge：消释前～ remove previous ill will; bury the hatchet / ～隙 also "嫌怨" ill feeling; animosity; grudge ❸ dislike; loathe; complain：讨人～ get oneself disliked; be unpopular / ～烦 not want to take the trouble; regard as too much bother / ～贵 consider (sth) too expensive; regard (the price) as too high

嫌弃 xiánqì dislike and shun; cold-shoulder

嫌恶 xiánwù abhor; detest; loathe：令人～ loathsome; detestable

嫌疑 xiányí suspicion：有偷盗～ be suspected of theft / ～人 also "嫌(疑)犯" suspect

xiǎn

显(**顯**) xiǎn ❶ evident; obvious; prominent：～得 look; seem; appear / ～而易见 obvious; as plain as daylight ❷ show (off); reveal; display：～现 reveal oneself; emerge; show (up) / ～效 show or produce an effect：～身手 display one's talent; distinguish oneself / ～微镜 microscope / ～像管 (信息) cathode ray tube (CRT); picture tube ❸ illustrious and influential：～达 (usu of an official) illustrious and influential; famous and powerful / ～学〈书〉famous school of thought or subject of learning ❹〈书〉〈敬〉(of one's parents, etc) deceased; late：～妣 my late mother

显贵 xiǎnguì ❶ of high position; influential ❷ eminent personage; bigwig

显赫 xiǎnhè eminent; illustrious; influential; ～一时 high and mighty for a time

显露 xiǎnlù become visible; appear; reveal; ～头角 make one's mark; show promise

显然 xiǎnrán obvious; evident; clear

显示 xiǎnshì show; display; demonstrate; ～器〈信息〉monitor

显眼 xiǎnyǎn eye-catching; conspicuous; showy; 打扮得太～ be too loudly dressed

显要 xiǎnyào prominent and important; powerful and influential; ～位置 (in a) prominent place / 身居～ occupy a powerful and influential position / 政界～ bigwigs in the political arena; the high and mighty

显耀 xiǎnyào ❶ powerful and prestigious; powerful and illustrious ❷ vaunt; show off

显著 xiǎnzhù conspicuous; marked; prominent; 疗效～ have conspicuous curative effects / ～不同 clearly different

险（險） xiǎn ❶ place difficult of access; ～隘 strategic pass; defile / ～要（place) strategically located and difficult to approach ❷ danger; peril; risk; ～境 dangerous situation; perilous plight / ～峻 dangerously steep; precipitous / ～情 dangerous situation; danger / ～兆 harbinger of danger; dangerous omen ❸ sinister; perfidious; vicious; ～诈 sinister and sly ❹ by a hair's breadth; almost; nearly; ～胜 win by a narrow margin / ～些送命 narrowly escape from death; be nearly killed / ～遭不测 barely escape an accident or a trap; have a narrow escape / 好～啊! What a near thing!

险恶 xiǎn'è ❶ dangerous; treacherous; ominous; 处境～ find oneself in mortal danger ❷ sinister; vicious; malicious; 用心～ have a sinister intention

险象 xiǎnxiàng dangerous sign or symptom; ～环生 dangerous symptoms appear one after another; be exposed to danger on all sides

险阻 xiǎnzǔ （of roads) dangerous and difficult; 〈喻〉dangers and difficulties

蚬 xiǎn 〈动物〉a kind of freshwater bivalves

铣 xiǎn see also xǐ

铣铁 xiǎntiě cast iron

跣 xiǎn （usu 跣足）〈书〉barefooted

鲜（尟） xiǎn little; rare; ～见 rarely seen; rare / ～为人知 little known see also xiān

藓 xiǎn 〈植〉moss

燹 xiǎn 〈书〉fire or flames (of war); 兵～ ravages of war

xiàn

苋 xiàn （usu 苋菜）〈植〉(three-coloured) amaranth

县（縣） xiàn county; (Japan) prefecture; ～城 county seat or town / ～长 head of a county; county magistrate / ～志 county annals or records

现 xiàn ❶ present(-day); current; existing; ～今 nowadays; at present; these days / ～状 current situation; present state of affairs; status quo / ～官不如～管.〈俗〉He who has immediate jurisdiction over you is the highest existing official. ❷ as the occasion arises; impromptu; extempore; ～炒～卖 sell what one has just made ready; use what one has just learned / ～宰的活鱼 live fish that has just been killed (for the occasion) ❸ on hand; ready (money); available: ～存 extant; on hand; in stock / ～房 spot housing / ～金 also "现款"; "现钱" ready money; cash ❹ show; reveal; appear: ～丑 also "现眼" make a fool of oneself; bring shame on oneself; be disgraced / ～形 reveal one's true nature or form; show one's true colours; be exposed

现场 xiànchǎng ❶ scene (of an accident or crime) ❷ site; spot: ～会 on-the-spot meeting / ～直播 live (broadcast)

现成 xiànchéng ready-made: ～饭 food ready for the table; unearned gain / 等～儿的 expect to have sth ready for one without working for it

现代 xiàndài ❶ modern times; contemporary age: ～史 modern history ❷ modern; present-day; contemporary: ～化 modernize / ～派 modernist (school); avant-garde

现货 xiànhuò merchandise on hand; spot commodity; spots: ～价格 spot price / ～市场 spot market

现任 xiànrèn ❶ hold the office of ❷ also "现职" currently in office; present; incumbent

现身说法 xiànshēn-shuōfǎ draw a moral from one's own experience; use one's own experience as an object lesson

现实 xiànshí ❶ reality; actuality ❷ real; realistic; factual: ～主义 realism

现世 xiànshì ❶〈宗教〉this life or world ❷ lose face; be discredited; bring shame on oneself: ～宝 living disgrace; ne'er-do-well; good-for-nothing

现象 xiànxiàng appearance (of things); phenomenon: 透过～看实质 grasp the essence through the appearance

现行 xiànxíng ❶ currently in effect; in force; in operation: ～法 law in effect ❷ (of a criminal) active

现役 xiànyì active service or duty: 服～ be on active service / ～军人 soldier in active service; serviceman

现在 xiànzài now; at present; for the time being: ～为止 up until now; to the present

限 xiàn ❶ limit; prescribe; confine: 以此为～ set a limit at this / ～额 norm; limit; quota / ～价 set or prescribe a price ❷ (usu 门限)〈书〉 threshold

限定 xiàndìng set a limit to; prescribe; confine: 在～的时间内 within the prescribed time (limit)

限度 xiàndù limit; limitation: 降低到最低～ reduce to a minimum

限量 xiànliàng ❶ limit the quantity; set the bounds: 前途不可～ have boundless or unlimited prospects ❷ see "限度"

限令 xiànlìng order sb to do sth within a time limit: ～24 小时内离境 order sb to leave the country within 24 hours; give sb 24 hours' notice to leave the country

限期 xiànqī (set a) time limit or deadline: ～报到 report for duty by the specified time / 延长～ extend the time limit

限制 xiànzhì restrict; confine; limit: ～性措施 restrictive measure / 时速～ speed limit / 由于篇幅的～ owing to the limitation of space; due to limited space

线(綫、線) xiàn ❶ (cotton) thread; string; (metal) wire: ～圈 coil / ～绳 cotton rope / ～手套 knit cotton gloves / ～轴儿 reel or spool (of thread); bobbin / ～装书 thread-bound book ❷〈数〉line: ～性代数 linear algebra ❸ sth shaped like or imagined as a line or thread: ～香 slender stick of incense / 国界～ demarcation line between two countries ❹ clue; lead; thread: ～人

inner connection; informer; spy **⑤** 〈量〉*used after* 一 *to indicate a tiny amount*：一一光明 a gleam of light

线路 xiànlù　line; route; circuit：地铁 ~ subway line / ~图 circuit diagram; plan of wiring

线索 xiànsuǒ　clue; lead; thread：破案 ~ clue for solving a case / 故事的~ thread of a story

线条 xiàntiáo　**①** (in art) line **②** lines (of an artifact, etc); figure (of a person, etc); outline

宪（憲） xiàn　**①**〈书〉statute; law：~章 charter **②** constitution：~兵 military police; gendarme / ~法 constitution; charter / ~政 constitutional government; constitutionalism

陷 xiàn　**①** get stuck or bogged down; sink into：~坑 pitfall; pit / ~进事务堆里 get bogged down in everyday routine; be up to one's neck with daily chores **②** sink; cave in：眼眶深~ sunken eyes **③** frame; set up：设 ~ lay a trap (for sb) **④** (of a city, etc) be captured or taken; fall **⑤** defect; flaw; deficiency

陷害 xiànhài　frame; set up; make a false charge against：政治~ political frame-up

陷阱 xiànjǐng　pitfall; trap; snare：落入~ fall into a trap

陷落 xiànluò　**①** subside; sink; cave in **②** *see* "陷入 **①**" **③** (of territory) fall; be captured：~敌手 fall into enemy hands

陷入 xiànrù　**①** sink into; land (oneself) in; come to; ~僵局 come to a deadlock; land in an impasse **②** be immersed or lost in; be deep in：~对往事的追忆 be immersed in reveries of the past

陷于 xiànyú　sink or fall into; be bogged down in：~孤立 find oneself isolated

馅 xiàn　filling; stuffing：肉~儿饼 meat pie / 饺子~儿 stuffing for *jiaozi*

羡 xiàn　admire; envy; covet：~妒 admire and envy / ~慕 admire; envy

献（獻） xiàn　**①** offer; present; donate：~宝 present a treasure；〈喻〉offer a valuable piece of advice or experience / ~血 donate one's blood / ~花圈 lay a wreath / ~计~策 offer or give advice; make suggestions **②** show; display：~丑〈谦〉show one's incompetence or inadequacy; make a fool of oneself / ~技 *also* "献艺" display one's feat or skill; perform

献词 xiàncí　*also* "献辞" congratulatory message (on a particular occasion)

献礼 xiànlǐ　present a gift; offer a present (for a solemn occasion)

献媚 xiànmèi　try to ingratiate oneself (with sb); fawn; toady：~的丑态 disgusting ingratiation

献身 xiànshēn　devote oneself (to); lay down one's life (for)：~精神 spirit of selfless devotion

腺 xiàn　gland：汗~ sweat gland

霰 xiàn　graupel

xiāng

乡（鄉） xiāng　**①** country; countryside; village：~村 village; country; rural area **②** native place; home village or town; birthplace：~愁 homesickness; nostalgia / ~情 affection for one's home town or village / ~音 accent of one's native place; local dialect **③** township — rural administrative unit under county or district

乡里 xiānglǐ　**①** native village or

town:荣归～ return in glory to one's native place ❷ *see* "乡亲❶"

乡亲 xiāngqīn ❶ *also* "乡里（乡亲）" person from one's native village or town; fellow villager or townsman ❷ local people; villagers; folks

乡土 xiāngtǔ native land; home village; locality:～观念 provincialism /～气息 local colour or flavour /～文学 local-colour literature

乡下 xiāngxia 〈口〉village; country; countryside:～人 country folk; villager; country cousin

乡镇 xiāngzhèn villages and towns; small towns; township:～企业 township enterprise

相 xiāng ❶ each other; one another; mutually:～爱 love each other /～等 be equal /～容 be compatible with each other /～安无事 coexist without trouble; live in peace with each other /～辅～成 supplement or complement each other /～距咫尺 be but a step to; be close by /～约同行 make an appointment to go together /血肉～连 be linked like flesh and blood / 意见～左 fail to agree; not see eye to eye / 互不～让. Neither would give in. ❷ *used to indicate an action one does to the other*:好言～劝 offer well-meant advice / 实不～瞒 to tell you the truth / 有一事～烦.〈套〉I have to trouble you about sth. ❸ *see and evaluate in person*; choose (for oneself or for sb close to oneself):～亲 see and size up a prospective mate (for oneself or for one's son or daughter) *see also* xiàng

相比 xiāngbǐ compare; contrast:～之下 compared with sb or sth; in contrast with sb or sth

相差 xiāngchà differ:～悬殊 widely different; poles apart

相称 xiāngchèn match; suit; fit:和身份不～ not worthy of or compatible

with one's status

相持 xiāngchí confront each other with neither side yielding:～不下 be locked in a stalemate

相处 xiāngchǔ get along (with one another); 和睦～ live in peace and harmony; get along well

相传 xiāngchuán ❶ legend has it; long be current (among the people):～已久的神话 myth of long standing ❷ pass on from one to another; 世代～ handed down from generation to generation

相当 xiāngdāng ❶ match; correspond to; be equal to:实力～ be matched in power or strength ❷ suitable; proper; fit:他当队长倒是很～. He is the right man to be team leader. ❸ quite; fairly; rather

相得益彰 xiāngdéyìzhāng each supplements and enriches the other; each brings out the best in the other

相抵 xiāngdǐ ❶ offset; balance; counterbalance:收支～ make both ends meet; break even ❷ (of opinions, etc) conflict with or go against each other

相对 xiāngduì ❶〈书〉face to face; opposite:～无言 face each other in silence ❷ opposed to each other:词义～ opposite in meaning ❸ relative:～论〈理〉(theory of) relativity /～而言 relatively or comparatively speaking /～真理〈哲〉relative truth

相反 xiāngfǎn ❶ opposite; opposed; contrary:～相成 be both opposite and complementary to each other; oppose and yet complement each other ❷ on the contrary; just the opposite

相仿 xiāngfǎng similar; more or less the same

相逢 xiāngféng meet (by chance); run into; come across

相符 xiāngfú conform to; agree with; correspond to:与事实～ conform to or tally with the facts

相干 xiānggān　(often used in negative or interrogative sentences) have to do with; be concerned with: 与她毫不 ～ have absolutely nothing to do with her

相关 xiāngguān　related; interrelated; concerned; 密切～ have a lot to do (with); be closely related (to) / ～学科 allied disciplines or subjects

相好 xiānghǎo　❶ be friends; be on intimate terms ❷ have a love affair ❸ lover: 早年的～ old flame

相互 xiānghù　mutual; reciprocal; each other; ～关系 interrelationship; mutual relations / ～学习 learn from each other

相继 xiāngjì　in succession; one after another

相见 xiāngjiàn　meet; see each other: ～恨晚 regret not being able to meet sooner

相交 xiāngjiāo　❶ cross; intersect ❷ be or make friends; ～多年的朋友 friend of many years' standing

相近 xiāngjìn　close; near; similar: 比分～ close score / 年龄～ similar in age

相敬如宾 xiāngjìngrúbīn　(of husband and wife) treat each other with respect due to a guest; be courteous to each other as to a guest

相配 xiāngpèi　be well matched (as in a marriage); match each other

相扑 xiāngpū　〈体〉❶ (ancient game of) wrestling ❷ (Japanese) sumo wrestling: ～运动员 sumo wrestler; sumoist

相濡以沫 xiāngrúyǐmò　help and comfort each other in time of adversity or crisis

相识 xiāngshí　❶ be acquainted with each other ❷ acquaintance

相思 xiāngsī　yearning between lovers: 单～ one-sided or unrequited love / ～病 lovesickness

相似 xiāngsì　also "相像" resemble; parallel; be similar or alike: 外表～ be similar in appearance; look alike

相提并论 xiāngtí-bìnglùn　mention in the same breath; lump together; place on a par

相通 xiāngtōng　(of rooms, etc) communicate; (of sentiments, etc) connected or linked

相同 xiāngtóng　identical; same; (in) common; 持～的观点 hold identical views; share the same views

相投 xiāngtóu　be congenial or compatible; agree with each other: 情趣～ be temperamentally compatible; have congenial tastes and interests

相信 xiāngxìn　believe; trust; be convinced: 令人难以～ incredible

相形 xiāngxíng　by contrast; by comparison: ～见绌 prove inferior by contrast; pale into insignificance

相依 xiāngyī　mutually dependent; interdependent; ～为命 depend on each other for survival

相宜 xiāngyí　suitable; fitting; appropriate

相应 xiāngyìng　corresponding; relevant; appropriate; ～的措施 appropriate measures / ～地变化工作方法 modify one's working methods accordingly

相映 xiāngyìng　set each other off; form a contrast; ～成趣 set each other off and form a pleasant contrast

香 xiāng　❶ fragrant; scented; aromatic; ～菜 coriander; cilantro / ～草〈植〉sweetgrass; vanilla / ～肠 sausage / ～菇 also "香菰"; "香蕈" mushroom / ～瓜 muskmelon / ～气 sweet smell; pleasant scent; fragrance / ～水 perfume; scent / ～味 fragrance; scent; aroma / ～油 sesame oil / ～皂 perfumed or scented soap; toilet soap ❷ (of food) savoury; appetizing; delicious ❸ (eat) with relish; (sleep) soundly ❹ in vogue; popular; welcome: 吃～ be popular ❺ perfume; (esp) incense; joss stick; ～案 long table for incense burners; incense altar / ～客 pilgrim / ～炉 incense burner; censer ❻ *used as a complimentary attribute*，*esp of women*：～消玉殒 the fragrance vanishes and the jade perishes — a beauty passes away

香槟 xiāngbīn　champagne

香波 xiāngbō　shampoo：去头屑～ anti-dandruff shampoo

香醇 xiāngchún　(of wine, tea, etc) fragrant and mellow; rich; pure

香火 xiānghuǒ　❶ joss sticks and candles burning at a temple：～很盛 full of devotees ❷ temple attendant ❸ *see* "香烟❷"

香蕉 xiāngjiāo　banana：～水〈化〉banana oil / ～苹果 (a variety of apple) Delicious

香料 xiāngliào　❶ perfume ❷ spice

香甜 xiāngtián　❶ fragrant and sweet ❷ (sleep) soundly

香烟 xiāngyān　❶ *also* "香火" incense smoke ❷ *also* "香火" ceremony to burn incense for one's ancestors：断了～〈喻〉have one's family line discontinued; have no male heir ❸ *also* "纸烟"；"卷烟" cigarette：一条～ a carton of cigarettes

香艳 xiāngyàn　(of poetry or other writing) sensual; voluptuous; sexy

厢(廂) xiāng　❶ *also* "厢房" (usu of a one-storeyed compound house) wing; wing-room ❷ compartment (of a train); box (in a theatre)

湘 Xiāng　another name for Hunan (湖南)：～菜 Hunan cuisine; Hunanese food

箱 xiāng　❶ box; case; trunk：～底 (at the) bottom of a chest or case; valuables stowed away at the bottom of the chest; nest egg ❷ box-like thing：～式货车 boxcar; box van

襄 xiāng　〈书〉assist; aid; help：～理 (at a banks, etc) assistant

manager / 鼎力～助〈敬〉do one's best to help; spare no effort to help

镶 xiāng　inlay; edge; border：～边 rim; edge; border / ～牙 put in a false tooth

镶嵌 xiāngqiàn　inlay; set; mount：画 mosaic

xiáng

详 xiáng　❶ detailed; minute：～密 elaborate; scrupulous; meticulous / ～情 details; specifics; particulars ❷ explain in detail; elaborate：另～ to be explained elsewhere / 内～ (on an envelope, etc) see inside ❸ clear：不～ unknown

详尽 xiángjìn　detailed; exhaustive; thorough：～的计划 elaborate plan

详明 xiángmíng　full and clear：记叙～ make detailed and clear records

详细 xiángxì　detailed; exhaustive; minute：～讨论 discuss (sth) in detail

降 xiáng　❶ surrender; capitulate; show the white flag：～服 yield; surrender ❷ subdue; vanquish; tame：～伏劣马 break in an intractable horse / 一物～一物。〈俗〉Everything has its vanquisher.

see also jiàng

祥 xiáng　auspicious; propitious; lucky：～瑞 auspicious sign; propitious omen / ～兆 good omen

祥和 xiánghé　❶ auspicious and peaceful ❷ kind; gentle; benign：神情～ wear a benign expression

翔 xiáng　circle in the air; fly

翔实 xiángshí　*also* "详实" full and accurate; detailed and thorough

xiǎng

享 xiǎng　❶ enjoy; share：～福 enjoy a happy life; be in clover；

live in ease and comfort；～誉 enjoy fame；be renowned ❷ see "飨" xiǎng

享乐 xiǎnglè　enjoy a life of pleasure；indulge in creature comforts：～主义 hedonism；pleasure-seeking

享年 xiǎngnián　〈敬〉die at or live to the age of：～八十有四 die at the age of 84

享受 xiǎngshòu　enjoy；贪图～ abandon oneself to ease and comfort／一种难得的艺术～ a rare artistic treat

享用 xiǎngyòng　enjoy（food or the use of sth）

享有 xiǎngyǒu　enjoy（rights，fame，etc）：～盛名 enjoy great renown；be renowned

 响（響） xiǎng ❶ echo；re-sound：～彻云霄 resound or reverberate through the skies；echo to the clouds ❷ sound；ring；fire：～锣 beat or sound a gong ❸ loud；noisy：～器 Chinese percussion instruments／打～指 snap the fingers ❹ also "响声" sound；noise

响当当 xiǎngdāngdāng　so good as to pass the stiffest test；worthy of the name；outstanding：～的人物 outstanding personage；quite a figure

响动 xiǎngdong　sound of sth astir；noise

响亮 xiǎngliàng　loud and clear；ringing；sonorous：声音～ resounding voice

响尾蛇 xiǎngwěishé　rattlesnake

响应 xiǎngyìng　respond；reply；answer：群起～ rise in response（to a call，etc）

饷 xiǎng ❶〈书〉entertain（with food and drink）❷〈旧〉（usu of soldiers，policemen，etc）pay：发～ issue pay

飨（饗） xiǎng 〈书〉treat to food and drink；entertain：以～观众 for the benefit of the audience

想 xiǎng ❶ think；reflect；mull over：～通 straighten out one's

thinking；think（sth）through or out；clarify in one's mind／～不开 take things too seriously；take a matter to heart／～来～去 give sth a good deal of thought；turn sth over and over in one's mind／～不到他也会说这样的话！Fancy him saying such things! ❷ suppose；consider；think：我～他会同意。I suppose he will agree. ❸ want；would like；intend to：你～要哪件上衣？Which jacket do you want? ❹ remember with longing；pine for；miss：～家 be homesick；yearn for one's family

想必 xiǎngbì　presumably；most probably；most likely：这电话～是他打来的。The call must be from him.

想当然 xiǎngdāngrán　assume as a matter of course；take for granted：不要～地下判断。Don't pass a judgement on sheer assumption.

想法 xiǎngfǎ ❶ think of a way；try：想方设法 do everything possible；try by hook or by crook ❷（xiǎngfa）idea；opinion；view：按他的～ in his view；to his mind

想见 xiǎngjiàn　see；infer；gather：由此可以～… one can see from this…

想来 xiǎnglái　it may be assumed that；presumably；supposedly：这事～不错。This seems alright.

想念 xiǎngniàn　recall with longing；long to see again；miss

想入非非 xiǎngrùfēifēi　indulge in fantasy；allow one's fancy to run wild；have maggots in one's head

想头 xiǎngtou　〈口〉❶ idea；notion ❷ hope：这事看来没～了。This appears to be quite hopeless now.

想望 xiǎngwàng　hope；long；desire：～当律师 long to be a lawyer

想像 xiǎngxiàng　also "想象" imagine；fancy；visualize：～力 imaginative power；imagination／不可～ unimaginable；unthinkable

鲞（鯗） xiǎng also "鲞鱼" dried fish

xiàng

向（❶-❸嚮） xiàng ❶ direction; orientation; trend: ~导 (act as a) guide; show (sb) the way ❷ face; turn towards: ~阳 be exposed to the sun; face the sun; (of a room, etc) face south / ~隅〈书〉face a corner — feel very isolated or frustrated / ~钱看 money-oriented; money-grubbing / ~日葵 also "葵花"〈植〉sunflower / ~心力〈理〉centripetal force ❸〈书〉approaching; near; close to; ~晚 towards evening; at dusk ❹ side with; favour; be partial to: 人心~背 popular support or opposition; will of the people ❺〈介〉indicating direction of an action: ~右看齐! (word of command) Eyes right! ❻ formerly; all along; always: ~有研究 have been doing research all along

向来 xiànglái always; all along; invariably: ~不守信 never keep one's promise

向上 xiàngshàng ❶ upwards; up: ~爬 climb up;〈喻〉be intent on personal advancement; climb up the social ladder ❷ move forward; advance; improve: 努力~ strive for improvement

向往 xiàngwǎng yearn or long for; look forward to

向着 xiàngzhe ❶ turn towards; face: ~东方站立 stand eastward ❷〈口〉take sb's part; side with; favour: 别总~他。Don't always favour him.

项 xiàng ❶ nape (of the neck): ~链 also "项练" necklace ❷ category; item; sum (of money): 逐~讨论 discuss (sth) item by item ❸〈数〉term: 同类~ like term

项背 xiàngbèi one's back: 不可望其~ be a far cry from sb; not fit to hold a candle to sb

项目 xiàngmù item; project; 经营~ item of business / ~融资 project financing

巷 xiàng narrow street; lane; alley: ~战 street or house-to-house fighting; urban warfare see also hàng

相 xiàng ❶ look;〈理〉phase (position): 可怜~ (wear a) pitiful look / 三~电动机 three-phase motor ❷ image; picture; photo: ~册 photo album / ~片 photograph; photo ❸ look at and appraise; examine the physiognomy of: ~面 practise physiognomy; read sb's fortune in his or her face ❹ assist; help: ~夫教子 assist one's husband and bring up the children ❺ prime or chief minister; chancellor; minister (in some countries) see also xiāng

相机 xiàngjī ❶ watch for an opportunity; bide one's time: ~行事 act according to circumstances; do as one sees fit ❷ camera

相貌 xiàngmào looks; bearing; appearance: ~堂堂 have a dignified appearance; have a majestic bearing

相声 xiàngsheng 〈戏〉comic dialogue; crosstalk

象 xiàng ❶ elephant: ~鼻 trunk; proboscis ❷ also "相" elephant or chancellor, one of the pieces in Chinese chess ❸ appearance; look; image ❹ imitate; mimic: ~声词〈语言〉onomatopoeia; mimetic word

象棋 xiàngqí (Chinese) chess: 国际~ chess

象形 xiàngxíng 〈语言〉pictographic characters or pictographs; hieroglyphs: ~文字 pictograph; hieroglyph

象牙 xiàngyá elephant's tusk; ivory: ~塔 ivory tower — aloofness from practical life

象征 xiàngzhēng symbol; emblem;

token：～性 symbolic；emblematic／～光明 symbolize light

像 xiàng ❶ likeness (of sb)；portrait；〈理〉image：～章 badge or button with sb's likeness on it／虚～ virtual image／石膏～ plastic statue ❷ resemble；take after；look like：长得～父亲 take after one's father；be a chip off the old block／一回是儿 just like the real thing；in a decent manner；for real ❸ look as if；appear；seem：屋里～是有人来过. It seems that someone has been in the room. ❹ such as；for example；like

像话 xiànghuà reasonable；proper；right：太不～ most unseemly；simply outrageous

像样 xiàngyàng also "像样子" up to the mark；presentable；decent：字写得挺～ write a good hand

橡 xiàng ❶ also "橡树"oak；～实 also "橡子"acorn ❷ also "橡胶树" rubber tree：～胶 rubber／～皮 rubber；eraser

xiāo

枭（梟） xiāo ❶ a kind of owl ❷〈书〉fierce and brave；fierce and ambitious：～将 brave general／～雄 fierce and ambitious chief；capable but unscrupulous leader ❸〈史〉hang (severed heads)：～首示众 cut off sb's head and hang it up as a warning to all

削 xiāo pare or peel with a knife；cut；whittle：～梨 peel a pear／～球（体）cut；chop (in ping-pong)／～铅笔 sharpen a pencil see also xuē

骁（驍） xiāo〈书〉valiant；brave：～将 valiant general／～勇 valiant；brave

逍 xiāo

逍遥 xiāoyáo free and unfettered；carefree：～自在 take life easy；be leisurely and carefree／～法外 go unpunished (by law)；go scot-free；be at large

消 xiāo ❶ disappear；vanish；melt：～散 (of fog, smell, etc) scatter and disappear；dissipate；vanish／暑热～退 abating of summer heat ❷ eliminate；dispel；remove：～愁 allay cares；dispel worries／～减 decrease；lessen；reduce／～气 cool or calm down；be mollified／～肿 reduce or remove a swelling；〈喻〉trim；downsize ❸ pass the time in a leisurely way；idle away (the time)：～暑 take a summer holiday／～夜 (have a) midnight snack ❹ (after 不, 只, 何, etc) need；require；take：不～说 needless to say；it goes without saying；no doubt

消沉 xiāochén in low spirits；downhearted；depressed

消除 xiāochú also "消释"；"消解" eliminate；dispel；get rid of：～隔阂 clear up a misunderstanding

消毒 xiāodú ❶ disinfect；sterilize；pasteurize：～柜 disinfecting cabinet／～牛奶 sterilized or pasteurized milk ❷ decontaminate；dispel pernicious influence

消防 xiāofáng fire fighting or prevention：～车 fire engine or truck／～队 fire brigade／～水龙 fire hose

消费 xiāofèi consume：～品 consumer goods／～信贷 consumer credit／～需求 consumer demand；demand of consumption

消耗 xiāohào ❶ consume；use up：～精力 consume one's energy ❷ expend；deplete；wear down：～战 war of attrition

消化 xiāohuà ❶ digest：～不良 indigestion；dyspepsia／～系统 digestive system ❷〈喻〉digest (what one learns)；absorb

消极 xiāojí ❶ negative：起～作用 exert a negative influence；play a negative role ❷ passive; inactive; negative: ～情绪 inactivity; lethargy; low spirits

消灭 xiāomiè ❶ perish; die out; become extinct ❷ exterminate; annihilate; eradicate: ～贫困 root out poverty

消磨 xiāomó ❶ wear down; fritter away; blunt: ～锐气 wear down one's drive; blunt one's enthusiasm ❷ while or idle away; kill (time)

消遣 xiāoqiǎn ❶ relax or divert oneself; while away the time ❷ pastime; distraction; diversion

消融 xiāoróng also "消溶" (of ice, snow, etc) thaw; melt

消失 xiāoshī disappear; vanish; fade away

消逝 xiāoshì die or fade away; vanish; elapse: 随着岁月的 ～ with the passage or lapse of time

消受 xiāoshòu ❶ (often used in the negative) enjoy: 无福 ～ not have the luck to enjoy (sth) ❷ endure; bear; stand

消瘦 xiāoshòu become thin or emaciated

消亡 xiāowáng wither away; die out; be extinct

消息 xiāoxi ❶ news; information; report: ～ 灵通人士 well-informed source ❷ tidings; news; word

消闲 xiāoxián ❶ kill (leisure) time; idle away the hours: ～的好去处 good resort to spend one's leisure ❷ at leisure; carefree: ～自在 leisurely and carefree; free from trammels

消炎 xiāoyán 〈医〉diminish or allay inflammation: ～片 anti-inflammation pill

消音 xiāoyīn also "消声" noise elimination or reduction: ～器 silencer; muffler

宵 xiāo night

宵禁 xiāojìn curfew: 解除～ lift a curfew

萧(蕭) xiāo deserted and miserable; desolate; dreary: ～索 bleak and chilly; desolate

萧墙 xiāoqiáng 〈书〉screen wall inside the gate of a Chinese house: ～之祸 trouble arising at home; internal strife

萧瑟 xiāosè ❶ rustle in the air; sough: ～秋风 sighing autumn wind ❷ bleak; melancholy; desolate: 秋景～ bleak autumn scene

萧条 xiāotiáo ❶ desolate; bleak ❷ 〈经〉slump; depression: 经济～ economic depression; slump

萧萧 xiāoxiāo 〈书〉〈象声〉sound of wind soughing or of horses neighing

硝 xiāo nitre; saltpetre: ～酸 also "硝镪水"〈化〉hydrogen nitrate; nitric acid / ～化甘油〈化〉nitroglycerine

硝烟 xiāoyān smoke of gunpowder: ～弥漫 be enveloped in smoke (of gunpowder)

销 xiāo ❶ melt (metal): ～兵 destroy arms ❷ cancel; annul; cross out: ～案 close a case / ～账 cancel or remove from an account; write off an account or debt ❸ put on sale; sell; market ❹ pay out; expend; spend ❺ pin: ～子 pin; peg; dowel ❻ fasten with a latch: ～上门 latch the door; put on the latch

销毁 xiāohuǐ destroy (by melting or burning)

销魂 xiāohún also "消魂" be overwhelmed with sorrow or joy; be extremely happy and satisfied

销路 xiāolù sale; market; outlet: 打开～ find markets (for sth) / ～不佳 sell poorly; have a dull market

销声匿迹 xiāoshēng-nìjì keep silent and lie low; disappear from the scene; stay in oblivion

销售 xiāoshòu market; sales: ～量 sales volume / ～淡季 period of slack sales; slack season

销赃 xiāozāng　❶ disposal of stolen goods or spoils　❷ destroy stolen goods;~灭迹 destroy evidence by getting rid of stolen goods

箫（簫） xiāo *xiao*, a vertical bamboo flute

潇（瀟） xiāo 〈书〉(of water) deep and clear

潇洒 xiāosǎ *also* "萧洒" natural and elegant; free and unconventional;~自如 free and elegant; with easy grace

潇潇 xiāoxiāo　❶ whistling (of wind) and pattering (of rain)　❷ drizzly:春雨 ~ drizzling spring rain

霄 xiāo clouds; sky; heaven;~壤 之别 as far apart as heaven and earth; poles apart; world of difference / 气冲一汉 have one's spirit soaring to the firmament; be in a towering rage

嚣 xiāo clamour; hubbub; din;~ 声一杂 a babel of crowd

嚣张 xiāozhāng　rampant; audacious; aggressive:~一时 run rampant for a time; be high and mighty for a while

xiáo

渞（殽） xiáo confuse; mix;~ 乱 confuse; disturb; confound

xiǎo

小 xiǎo　❶ small; little; minor;~巴 *also* "小面包(车)"〈口〉minibus / ~报 tabloid; tab / ~结 brief summing-up; (preliminary) summary / ~楷 regular script in small characters / ~我 self; ego; individual / ~酌 〈书〉drinks with snacks; informal dinner / ~百货 small articles of daily use; sundries / ~标题 sub-heading; subhead; subtitle / ~册子 pamphlet;

booklet; brochure / ~气候 microclimate; 〈喻〉specific political or economic climate / ~人物 small potato; nobody; nonentity / ~恩~惠 petty favours; sops ❷ for a short while; for a little time:~睡 (have a) catnap; nap; doze / ~别重逢 meet again after a short interval ❸ a little; a bit; slightly:~试锋芒 display only a small part of one's talent; show the tip of an iceberg ❹ a little less than; almost:~半 less than half; lesser or smaller part / ~一百 a little less than a hundred ❺ 〈谦〉I; me; my:~儿 my son ❻ young; younger; youngest;~蜜〈贬〉girl secretary cum mistress; young sweetheart (of an older married man) / ~名 *also* "乳名" pet name (for a child); childhood name / ~两口〈口〉 young couple / ~时候〈口〉childhood; early youth / ~白脸儿〈贬〉handsome young man (usu with effeminate features) ❼ *used before a surname to refer to a young person*, *or before a given name to refer to a child*:~马 Young Ma

小报告 xiǎobàogào　〈贬〉backbiting report; complaint behind sb's back;打 ~ backbite; snitch

小辈 xiǎobèi　younger member (of a family, profession, etc); junior:小字 辈 youngsters; younger generation

小本经营 xiǎoběnjīngyíng　run a small business; do business in a small way:~起家 start (business) on a shoestring

小便 xiǎobiàn　❶ pass water; pee; piss ❷ penis; vulva

小辫子 xiǎobiànzi　❶ *also* "小辫儿" short braid; pigtail ❷ mistake or shortcoming that may be exploited; vulnerable point; handle:抓住一整人 exploit sb's mistakes or shortcomings to give him or her a hard time

小菜 xiǎocài　❶ side dish; hors

d'oeuvres ❷ *also* "小菜一碟" easy job; no big deal ❸〈方〉meat, fish or vegetables as distinguished from rice or other staples; dishes

小产 xiǎochǎn （have a）miscarriage; abortion；（of animals）slink

小炒 xiǎochǎo individually stir-fried dish; à la carte dish

小车 xiǎochē ❶ wheelbarrow; handbarrow; handcart; pushcart ❷ sedan (car)

小吃 xiǎochī ❶ small and cheap dishes（in a restaurant）❷ snacks; refreshments ❸（esp in Western-style food）cold dish; hors d'oeuvre

小丑 xiǎochǒu ❶ clown; buffoon ❷ villain; mean person

小聪明 xiǎocōngming 〈贬〉cleverness in trivial matters; petty shrewdness or trick；要～ try to be smart in a petty way; play a petty trick

小打小闹 xiǎodǎ-xiǎonào （do sth）in dribs and drabs; on a small scale; in a piecemeal manner

小道 xiǎodào ❶ path; trail；羊肠～ winding trail ❷ grapevine; bush telegraph；～儿消息 grapevine（news）; back-alley news; hearsay

小调 xiǎodiào ❶ popular tune; ditty ❷〈乐〉minor；C～协奏曲 concerto in C minor

小动作 xiǎodòngzuò petty action or trick; manoeuvre；搞～ play a petty trick；（of a child in class）get fidgety

小肚鸡肠 xiǎodù-jīcháng petty-minded; narrow-minded

小儿 xiǎo'ér ❶ child; infant；黄毛～ chit of a child / 麻痹症〈医〉infantile paralysis；犬～〈谦〉my son

小儿科 xiǎo'érkē ❶〈医〉（department of）pediatrics；～医生 pediatrician ❷ kid's stuff; easy mark; petty stuff；干这点事还不是～！Why, that's just as easy as pie.

小贩 xiǎofàn pedlar; vendor; hawk-

er；小商～ small tradespeople and pedlars

小费 xiǎofèi *also* "小账" tip; gratuity；给～（give a）tip; tip

小工 xiǎogōng unskilled labourer；打～ do odd jobs; be a labourer

小广播 xiǎoguǎngbō ❶ gossip; rumour; grapevine（news）；爱听～ indulge in gossip; gorge oneself on rumours ❷ rumour-monger; gossip

小鬼 xiǎoguǐ ❶〈迷信〉little devil that runs errands for the King of Hell; imp; goblin ❷（term of endearment in addressing a child or youngster）"little devil"; lad; kid

小孩儿 xiǎoháir 〈口〉❶ *also* "小孩子" child; kid；耍～脾气 behave childishly; be pettish ❷ sons and daughters（usu not yet grown up）; children

小寒 xiǎohán Slight Cold, 23rd seasonal division point *see also* "节气" jiéqì

小号 xiǎohào ❶（of clothing, etc）small size（S）❷〈乐〉trumpet; clarion

小伙子 xiǎohuǒzi 〈口〉young man or fellow; youngster; lad

小集团 xiǎojítuán clique; faction；搞～ set up a faction; form a clique

小家碧玉 xiǎojiābìyù pretty girl of humble birth; daughter of a humble family

小家子气 xiǎojiāziqì unease or nervousness（in public）typical of people of low birth; petty or vulgar behaviour; narrow-mindedness；言谈举止有点～ have something petty or vulgar about one's speech and behaviour

小脚 xiǎojiǎo bound feet（of women in former times）；裹～ having one's feet bound; foot-binding

小节 xiǎojié ❶ small matter; trifle；生活～ matters concerning one's personal life only ❷〈乐〉bar; measure

小姐 xiǎojiě ❶ unmarried young lady; miss；王～ Miss Wang ❷ respectful term of address for a young woman：导游～ miss guide；tourist guide / ～，结账。Waitress, bill, please.

小九九 xiǎojiǔjiǔ ❶ also "九九歌" multiplication table ❷（喻）calculation；scheming；谁有他或者她的～Who doesn't have his or her own own calculations?

小看 xiǎokàn also "小瞧" look down upon；slight；belittle；不可～ not to be slighted

小康 xiǎokāng comfortably off；comparatively or moderately well-off；～水平 comparatively well-off standard of living；comfortable life

小麦 xiǎomài wheat；春～ spring wheat

小卖部 xiǎomàibù ❶ shop attached to a hotel, factory, etc；retail department ❷ buffet；snack counter

小满 xiǎomǎn Grain Budding, 8th seasonal division point see also "节气" jiéqì

小米 xiǎomǐ millet；黏～ glutinous millet

小脑 xiǎonǎo 〈生理〉cerebellum

小年 xiǎonián ❶ lunar year of which the last month has 29 days ❷ Preliminary Eve — 23rd or 24th of the last month of the lunar year ❸〈农〉off-year：苹果～ off-year for the apple crop

小朋友 xiǎopéngyǒu ❶ term of address used by an adult to a child：～，几岁了？How old are you, kiddie? ❷ children

小品 xiǎopǐn short, simple literary or artistic creation；essay；skit：演～ put on a skit / ～文 (familiar) essay

小气 xiǎoqi stingy；miserly；mean：～鬼 miser；skinflint；penny pincher

小巧 xiǎoqiǎo small and nimble；small and ingenious；～玲珑 small and exquisite；petite

小区 xiǎoqū plot；（housing）estate；

居民～ residential community / ～建设 housing estate development

小圈子 xiǎoquānzi ❶ narrow confining environment ❷ small circle or set of people；coterie：搞～ confine oneself to a small set；form a coterie

小人 xiǎorén ❶〈旧〉person of low position；〈谦〉your humble servant — I ❷ base or low person；mean person；villain：～得志 small man swollen with success；villain holding sway

小生 xiǎoshēng 〈戏〉young man's role

小时 xiǎoshí hour：～工 maid or labourer paid by the hour / ～工资 hourly pay or wage

小市民 xiǎoshìmín ❶ urban petty bourgeois ❷ philistine：～作风 philistinism

小暑 xiǎoshǔ Slight Heat, 11th seasonal division point see also "节气" jiéqì

小数 xiǎoshù ❶〈数〉decimal number or fraction；decimal：～点 decimal point ❷ small (in) number；small sum

小说 xiǎoshuō novel；fiction；story：小～ also "微型小说" miniature story (usu about 1,000 words long)；short-short story

小算盘 xiǎosuànpan selfish calculations；petty niggling：打～ think of one's selfish interests；be calculating

小提琴 xiǎotíqín violin；fiddle：～手 violinist

小题大做 xiǎotídàzuò make a fuss over a trifle；make a mountain out of a molehill；have a tempest in a teacup

小偷 xiǎotōu petty or sneak thief；pilferer；pickpocket：～小摸 petty theft；pilfering

小巫见大巫 xiǎowūjiàndàwū feel or be dwarfed；pale into insignificance by comparison

小媳妇 xiǎoxífu ❶ young (married) woman ❷ person whom anyone can vent his or her spite upon; whipping boy

小小不言 xiǎoxiǎobùyán 〈口〉too insignificant to mention; too trivial to talk about;～的事 triviality; trifle

小写 xiǎoxiě ❶ ordinary form of a Chinese numeral; Arabic numeral;～金额 amount in Arabic numerals ❷ small letter;～字母 small letter

小心 xiǎoxīn watch out for; take care; be careful or cautious;～翼翼 with utmost care; with extreme caution; gingerly /～为妙。One cannot be too careful.

小心眼儿 xiǎoxīnyǎnr ❶ narrow-minded; petty ❷ petty calculation or scheming;要～ exercise one's wits in a petty manner; be calculating

小型 xiǎoxíng small; small-scale; miniature;～化 miniaturize

小性儿 xiǎoxìngr 〈方〉petty anger; childish temper; petulance;使～ throw a tantrum; be petulant

小学 xiǎoxué primary or elementary school;～生 (primary school) pupil; schoolboy or schoolgirl

小雪 xiǎoxuě Slight Snow, 20th seasonal division point　*see also* "节气" jiéqì

小夜曲 xiǎoyèqǔ 〈乐〉serenade

小意思 xiǎoyìsi ❶〈谦〉small token (of kindly feelings); small gift; souvenir ❷ (sth) not worth mentioning; insignificant; negligible

小月 xiǎoyuè ❶ solar month of 30 days ❷ lunar month of 29 days

小子 xiǎozi 〈口〉❶ boy ❷〈贬〉bloke; fellow; guy

小卒 xiǎozú ❶ private (in an army); cipher; man of no consequence:无名～ mere nobody; cipher ❷ (in chess) pawn

小组 xiǎozǔ group:～会 group meeting /～循环赛〈体〉group round robin

晓（曉） xiǎo ❶ dawn; day-break ❷ know:〈口〉know; be aware of /粗～文字 know how to read and write; be barely literate ❸ let (sb) know; inform; tell:～谕〈书〉give explicit instructions or directions /～以利害 explain to sb where his or her interests lie; warn sb of possible consequences

xiào

孝 xiào ❶ filial piety:～道 code of supporting and waiting on one's parents; filial piety / 尽～心 do one's filial duties (to one's parents); show one's filial love ❷ mourning period or dress;带～ be in mourning (dress)

孝敬 xiàojìng ❶ be obedient and respectful to (parents, etc) ❷ give presents (to one's elders or superiors)

孝顺 xiàoshùn show filial obedience or piety; be filial

孝子 xiàozǐ ❶ filial or dutiful son ❷ bereaved son; son in mourning

肖 xiào resemble; be similar or like:长相酷～ bear a striking resemblance (to sb)

肖像 xiàoxiàng portrait; portraiture:～权〈法〉right of personal portrait; portraiture right

校 xiào ❶ school:～风 ethos of a school; school spirit /～花〈旧〉campus queen; school belle /～徽 school badge /～历 school calendar /～庆 anniversary of the founding of a school /～长 (of primary or secondary school) headmaster; principal; (of university or college) president; chancellor ❷ field officer:上～ colonel　*see also* jiào

校友 xiàoyǒu alumnus; alumna;～会 alumni association

校园 xiàoyuán campus; school yard:～网〈信息〉campus network /～歌曲

campus song

哮 xiào ❶ heavy breathing; wheeze; cough; ～喘 have (a fit of) asthma; cough and gasp for breath ❷ roar; howl; yell

笑 xiào ❶ smile; laugh; ～剧 *also* "闹剧" farce / ～料 laughing stock / ～声 laugh; laughter / ～星 comic star / ～眯眯 smilingly; with a smile / ～盈盈 smiling happily ❷ ridicule; laugh at; deride; ～掉大牙 (make people) laugh their heads off; be utterly ridiculous

笑柄 xiàobǐng laughing stock; butt (of ridicule); joke; 传为 ～ become a standing joke

笑话 xiàohua ❶ joke; jest; pleasantry; 闹 ～ make a fool of oneself; make a ridiculous mistake / ～百出 make all kinds of foolish mistakes ❷ laugh at; deride; ridicule

笑里藏刀 xiàolǐcángdāo hide murderous intent behind one's smiles; smile treacherously; have an iron hand in a velvet glove

笑面虎 xiàomiànhǔ outwardly kind but inwardly cruel person; wicked person wearing a hypocritical smile; wolf in sheep's clothing

笑纳 xiàonà 〈套〉 kindly accept (what is offered as a gift)

笑容 xiàoróng smiling expression; smile; ～ 可掬 be radiant with smiles; wear a charming smile

笑谈 xiàotán ❶ *see* "笑柄" ❷ joke; jest ❸ laugh and talk; chat smilingly

笑逐颜开 xiàozhúyánkāi beam with smiles; be wreathed in smiles

效(②傚、③効) xiào ❶ effect; result; efficiency; 用 ～ effectiveness; utility; usefulness ❷ imitate; follow the example of; follow suit; 仿 ～ imitate; copy; follow / ～颦 copy blindly; imitate servilely; play the ape ❸ devote or

dedicate (oneself); render (a service); ～命 go all out to serve (one's country, etc); be ready to die for (a cause, etc) / ～忠国家 devote oneself heart and soul to the motherland

效法 xiàofǎ follow the example of; learn from; emulate

效果 xiàoguǒ ❶ effect; result; ～显著 bring about a striking effect; prove highly effective ❷ 〈戏〉 sound and lighting effects

效劳 xiàoláo work for; serve; 为国 ～ serve one's own country / 效犬马之劳 serve sb faithfully

效力 xiàolì ❶ render one's service to; serve ❷ effect; force; avail; 发挥 ～ produce effects; prove effective

效率 xiàolǜ productivity; efficiency; ～低 inefficient

效益 xiàoyì result; benefit; 经济 ～ economic results or returns

效应 xiàoyìng ❶ (physical or chemical) effect; 热 ～ heat effect; thermal results ❷ effect; result; 名牌 ～ famous brand effect

啸(嘯) xiào ❶ (of people) whistle; 一 声 长 ～ (give) a long whistle ❷ (of birds or animals) scream; roar; howl; 虎 ～ roar of a tiger ❸ sound of some natural phenomena

啸聚 xiàojù 〈书〉 band together; gang up; ～山林 (of bandits, etc) form a band and take to the hills; go to the greenwood

xiē

些 xiē 〈量〉 ❶ *indicating an indefinite quantity*; 前 ～年 several years ago ❷ *used after an adjective or a verb as a modifier of degree*; 简单 ～ a little simpler; a bit easier

些微 xiēwēi slightly; a little; a bit; 有点儿凉 a little chilly / ～淡了点 (of

food) lack a pinch of salt

些许 xiēxǔ a little; a bit：略知～
know a little (about sth) / ～小事 a
mere trifle

撅 xiē drive (a wedge, etc.)：～个
楔子 drive a wedge (into a wall,
etc)

楔 xiē (usu 楔子) wedge; (wood-
en or bamboo) peg：～形文字〈考
古〉cuneiform

歇 xiē ❶ rest; stop (work, etc);
quit：～脚 also "歇腿" take a
break while walking; stop for a rest /
～凉 relax in a cool place; enjoy the
cool / ～手 stop doing sth; break off
❷〈方〉go to bed

歇顶 xiēdǐng also "谢顶" (get) thin
on top; (go) bald

歇工 xiēgōng ❶ stop work; knock
off ❷ (of an enterprise) close down;
(of a project) be suspended

歇后语 xiēhòuyǔ two-part allegorical
saying

歇斯底里 xiēsīdǐlǐ ❶〈医〉hysteria
❷ morbidly emotional; hysterical

歇息 xiēxī ❶ have a rest ❷ go to
sleep; put up for the night

蝎（蠍） xiē also "蝎子" scor-
pion

蝎虎 xiēhǔ also "蝎虎子"; "壁虎"
gecko; house lizard

xié

协（協） xié ❶ harmonize;
concert; coordinate：～
力 combine efforts; make a concerted
effort / ～和各方 harmonize all the
parties concerned ❷ cooperate; aid;
assist：～查 help to investigate; assist
in an investigation / ～办单位 co-
sponsor (of an event)

协定 xiédìng ❶ agreement; convention; accord ❷ reach an agreement (on
sth); agree on：～配额 agreed or bilat-

eral quota

协会 xiéhuì association; society

协商 xiéshāng consult; discuss; talk
things over：～会议 consultative conference

协调 xiétiáo coordinate; harmonize;
be in tune with：发挥～作用 play a co-
ordinating role; act as coordinator

协同 xiétóng work in concert or coordination; cooperate：～作战 fight in coordination

协议 xiéyì ❶ agree; consult：达成～
reach agreement / ～离婚〈法〉divorce
by agreement; consensual divorce ❷
〈信息〉protocol

协助 xiézhù assist; help

协奏曲 xiézòuqǔ 　〈乐〉concerto：钢琴
～ piano concerto

协作 xiézuò cooperate; collaborate：～
精神 spirit of cooperation

邪 xié ❶ evil; heretic：～教 (evil)
cult; heretic sect / ～念 evil
thought; wicked or lascivious intention / ～气 perverse trend; evil influence / ～说 heresy; fallacy / 引上～路
lead astray ❷ irregular; abnormal;
strange：热得～了 abnormally hot ❸
〈中医〉unhealthy environmental influence that causes disease; miasma ❹
〈迷信〉evil spirits; 驱～ exorcise evil
spirits

邪恶 xié'è evil (people); wicked;
sinister

邪乎 xiéhu 　〈口〉❶ abnormal;
extraordinary; extreme：闹腾得～ make
a terrible row ❷ excessive; strange;
fantastic：说得～ give an excessively
exaggerated version (of sth); spin a
fantastic yarn

邪门 xiémén ❶ evil idea; sinister in-
tention：～歪道 dishonest practices or
methods; evil or illegal doings ❷ (usu
邪门儿)〈方〉abnormal; strange; odd

胁（脅、脋） xié ❶ flank;
side of the hu-

man body from the armpit to the hip; 左 ~ left side ❷ compel; coerce; force; ~ 迫 intimidate; coerce; force

胁从 xiécóng （be an）accomplice under duress; ~分子 accomplice under duress; reluctant follower

挟（挾） xié ❶ hold under the arm; ~ 带 carry or bring along forcibly ❷ coerce; compel; force sb to submit; 以性命相 ~ threaten sb with death ❸ bear; harbour; ~ 嫌 〈书〉bear a grudge

挟持 xiéchí ❶ seize sb（on both sides）by the arms ❷ hold under duress; abduct; kidnap

挟制 xiézhì also "胁制" coerce（by force or by taking advantage of sb's weakness）; have sb under one's thumb

偕 xié together with; accompanied by; in the company of; ~ 老（of husband and wife）grow old together / ~ 同 accompany; go together with

斜 xié oblique; slanting; askew; ~ 睨 squint（contemptuously）at; look sideways at / ~ 坡 slope / ~ 体 italics / ~ 线 oblique line / ~ 阳 setting sun / ~ 对面 also "斜对过" diagonally or across from / ~ 纹布 twill; drill / 走上 ~ 路 take the wrong path; go astray

斜视 xiéshì ❶ also "斜眼"〈医〉strabismus ❷ look sideways or askance; cast a sidelong glance

谐 xié ❶ harmony; accord; agreement; 关系~ 的 harmonious relations ❷ humorous; ~ 谑 poke fun; banter; jest / ~ 趣横生 be full of humour

谐调 xiétiáo harmonious; well-balanced; 色彩~ well-matched colours

谐音 xiéyīn ❶ homophonic; homonymic; ~现象 homophony ❷ euphony; harmony of sound

颉 xié

颉颃 xiéháng 〈书〉compare; rival; 与名家相~ be equally matched with famous masters

携（攜） xié ❶ carry; take or bring along; ~ 带家眷 bring one's family along / ~款外逃 flee abroad with embezzled funds ❷ take or hold by the hand; ~手 hand in hand; together

鞋 xié shoes; ~带 shoelace; shoe-string / ~底 sole（of a shoe）/ ~ 垫 shoe-pad; insole / ~ 油 shoe polish

撷 xié 〈书〉pick; pluck; ~ 取 pick; pluck; select / ~ 英 select the very best

xiě

写（寫） xiě ❶ write; ~字台（writing）desk ❷ compose; write; ~ 稿 write; contribute / ~ 日记 keep a diary; make an entry in one's diary / ~ 作技巧 writing technique ❸ describe; portray; depict ❹ paint; sketch; draw; ~ 意画 freehand brushwork painting

写生 xiěshēng paint or draw from life or nature; 静物~ still-life painting

写实 xiěshí write or paint realistically; ~文学 realistic literature

写照 xiězhào portray; characterize; 栩栩如生的 ~ vivid, true-to-life portrayal

写真 xiězhēn ❶ paint or portray（a person）; portrait ❷ describe sth as it is

写字楼 xiězìlóu office（building）: ~ 招租 office space to let

血 xiě colloquial variant of xuè see also "血" xuè

血淋淋 xiělīnlīn dripping with blood; bloody; atrocious; ~的教训 lesson paid for in blood

血丝 xiěsī trace of blood; 布满 ~ 的眼 blood-shot eyes

xiè

泄（洩） xiè ❶ let out; discharge; release; ～ 洪 discharge or release floodwater ❷ divulge; leak; disclose; ～ 底 reveal or divulge the bottom line; let the cat out of the bag / ～ 密 divulge or leak a secret; disclose confidential information ❸ give vent to; vent; ～ 愤 give vent to one's spite or resentment

泄漏 xièlòu ❶ (of gases or liquids) leak; discharge *also* "泄露" let out; disclose; reveal

泄气 xièqì ❶ *also* "泄劲" lose heart; feel frustrated; be disheartened; ～ 话 discouraging remarks; disheartening remarks ❷ 〈口〉 pathetic; piteous; 输得真～! What a pathetic defeat!

泻（瀉） xiè ❶ flow swiftly; rush down; pour out ❷ loose bowels; diarrhoea; (as in cattle) scour; ～ 肚 loose bowels; diarrhoea; ～ 药 antidiarrhoeal

卸 xiè ❶ unload; discharge; unhitch (draught animals, etc); ～ 货 unload (cargo) / ～ 包袱 be rid of a burden ❷ remove; take off; dismantle; ～ 妆 remove one's make-up; take off one's formal dress and ornaments / ～ 磨杀驴 〈俗〉 kill the donkey the moment it leaves the millstone — give sb the boot as soon as he has done his job ❸ lay down; shirk; ～ 肩 remove one's burden; shirk one's responsibility; pass the buck / ～ 任 be relieved of one's office

屑 xiè ❶ bits; scraps; crumbs; 木 ～ bits of wood; filings / 面包 ～ breadcrumbs ❷ (mostly used in the negative) consider worthwhile; deign; 不 ～ 计较 disdain to bother (about sth); consider it beneath one to fuss

械 xiè ❶ tool; device; instrument ❷ weapon; arms; ～ 斗 (of groups of people) fight with weapons ❸ 〈书〉 fetters; shackles

亵（褻） xiè ❶ treat with irreverence; be disrespectful; ～ 渎 blaspheme; desecrate; profane / ～ 慢 treat lightly; show disrespect ❷ lewd; obscene; indecent; ～ 语 dirty words; obscenities

谢 xiè ❶ thank; ～ 词 *also* "谢辞" thank-you speech / ～ ～ thanks; thank you / ～ 天 ～ 地 thank Heavens; count oneself lucky / 聊表 ～ 意 *also* "聊表谢忱" as a token of one's gratitude ❷ make an apology; apologize; ～ 罪 apologize for an offence; offer an apology ❸ decline; refuse; ～ 却 decline politely ❹ (of flowers, etc) wither

谢绝 xièjué refuse or decline with thanks; ～ 参观 (of a place, etc) not open to visitors

谢客 xièkè ❶ decline to receive visitors; close one's door to guests ❷ thank visitors or guests for their company

谢幕 xièmù (answer a) curtain call; ～ 七次 take seven curtain calls

谢世 xièshì 〈书〉 depart this life; pass away; die

解 xiè get the point; be clear about; see; ～ 开其中奥妙 get wise to the secret / 使尽浑身 ～ 数 use all one's skills; do all one is capable of *see also* jiě; jiè

榭 xiè pavilion or house on a terrace

邂 xiè

邂逅 xièhòu 〈书〉 meet by chance; run into

瀣 xiè ❶ (of plaster, porridge, etc) become thinner or watery ❷ dilute

懈 xiè slack; lax; remiss; ～ 怠 slack; sluggish; careless

蟹 xiè crab；~黄 ovary and digestive glands of a crab (eaten as a delicacy)

xīn

心 xīn ❶〈生理〉heart：~房 atrium；〈喻〉inner heart / ~率 heart rate / ~室 ventricle / ~电图 electrocardiogram / ~绞痛 angina pectoris / ~肌梗（塞）myocardial infarction；heart attack / ~血管病 cardiovascular disease ❷ heart；mind；feeling：~服 genuinely convinced；acknowledge or admire from the bottom of one's heart / ~焦 anxious；troubled；worried / ~声 inner voice；heartfelt wish；aspiration / ~算 mental arithmetic or calculation / ~碎 heartbroken / ~细 careful；meticulous / ~上人 person of one's heart；heart-throb / ~潮澎湃 feel an upsurge of emotions / ~慈面软 kind-hearted and merciful / ~想事成 get what one longs for / ~中有数 have a clear idea (of sth)；know one's own mind / 暖人~田 warm sb's heart ❸ heart；centre；core：江~ middle of a river / 白菜~ heart of a cabbage

心爱 xīn'ài love；treasure；cherish：~的人 one's beloved；loved one

心安理得 xīn'ān-lǐdé have a good or an easy conscience；have no qualms of conscience

心病 xīnbìng ❶ mental anguish；worry；anxiety：~还得心药治。The cure of an anguished heart is happiness. ❷ secret cause of remorse；sore point；hang-up

心不在焉 xīnbùzàiyān absent-minded；inattentive；wool-gathering

心肠 xīncháng ❶ intention；mind；heart：~狠毒 be evil-minded ❷ feeling；emotion；heart：~软 also "心软" have a soft or tender heart；be lenient

❸ see "心思❸"

心驰神往 xīnchí-shénwǎng yearn after (a place) as if one's mind were already there；be so excited by sth as to take mental possession of it

心胆俱裂 xīndǎnjùliè be frightened out of one's wits；be panic-stricken

心得 xīndé what one has learned from work，study，etc：交流~ compare notes on what one has learned

心地 xīndì ❶ mind；character；nature：~狭窄 narrow-minded ❷ state of mind；mood：~轻松 be relaxed in mood

心动 xīndòng ❶ also "心跳" heartbeat ❷ have one's desire or enthusiasm aroused；be tempted or stirred

心烦意乱 xīnfán-yìluàn be confused and worried；be terribly upset

心浮气躁 xīnfú-qìzào be restless and fretful；be unsettled and short-tempered

心腹 xīnfù ❶ trusted；reliable：~之交 bosom friend ❷ trusted subordinate or follower；henchman ❸ deep in one's heart；secret；confidential：说~话 confide in sb；exchange confidences / ~之患 cancer in one's vital organs；grave hidden trouble or danger

心甘 xīngān willing；ready：~情愿 be most willing to；do sth gladly

心肝 xīngān ❶ heart；conscience：毫无~ be heartless；be dead to all feelings ❷ (used as an endearment) darling；deary

心寒 xīnhán be bitterly disappointed or disenchanted：令人~ disappointing；disenchanting

心黑 xīnhēi ❶ evil；venomous：~手辣 also "心狠手辣" cruel and evil；vicious and merciless ❷ greedy；predatory

心花怒放 xīnhuānùfàng burst with joy；be ecstatic or elated

心怀 xīnhuái ❶ harbour；cherish；

bear；～叵测 harbour sinister motives ❷ feeling；mood；intention：抒发～ give voice to one's feelings ❸ nature；state of mind：～坦白 candid by nature

心慌 xīnhuāng ❶ be flustered or jittery；get nervous：～意乱 be fidgety and flustered；be alarmed and confused；be all in a flutter ❷ 〈方〉(of the heart) palpitate

心灰意懒 xīnhuī-yìlǎn also "心灰意冷" be disheartened or downhearted；be dispirited；lose heart completely

心机 xīnjī thinking；calculating；scheming：费尽～ try one's utmost；spare no pains

心急 xīnjí impatient；anxious；short-tempered：～如焚 also "心急火燎" be burning with impatience；be consumed by anxiety；get the jitters

心计 xīnjì calculation；cunning；scheming：有～ be calculating / 要～ try to be smart (with sb)

心迹 xīnjì true state of mind；heart：剖白～ lay bare one's true feelings；bare one's heart

心惊肉跳 xīnjīng-ròutiào feel nervous and jumpy；be filled with apprehension；shake in one's boots

心境 xīnjìng state or frame of mind；mood：～苦闷 be in a gloomy mood；feel low

心坎 xīnkǎn bottom of one's heart；说到人家的～儿上 strike a chord in sb's heart

心口 xīnkǒu ❶ pit of the stomach：～堵得慌 feel suffocated；feel a tightness in the chest ❷ mind and mouth — what one thinks and what one says：～如一 say what one thinks；be frank and unreserved；speak one's mind

心宽 xīnkuān be broad-minded；take things easy：～体胖 also "心广体胖" be carefree and well-nourished；be fit and happy

心旷神怡 xīnkuàng-shényí refreshed

in mind and heart；relaxed and happy；carefree and joyous

心理 xīnlǐ psychology；mentality：～素质 psychological quality / ～医生 psychologist

心力 xīnlì mental and physical efforts：～交瘁 be exhausted both mentally and physically / ～衰竭〈医〉heart failure

心里 xīnlǐ ❶ in the heart：～不舒服 feel uncomfortable ❷ in (the) mind；at heart：～话 what is on one's mind；one's innermost thoughts and feelings / ～打鼓 feel uneasy；be on pins and needles

心灵 xīnlíng ❶ clever；intelligent；quick-witted：～手巧 be clever and deft ❷ heart；soul；mind：～感应 telepathy / ～深处 in the innermost depths of one's heart；deep in one's heart

心领 xīnlǐng ❶ understand；comprehend：～神会 understand tacitly；readily take a hint ❷ 〈套〉used to express one's thanks，esp when declining a gift or invitation：你的好意，我～了。I appreciate your kindness.

心乱如麻 xīnluànrúmá have one's mind as confused as a tangled skein；be utterly confused and disconcerted

心满意足 xīnmǎn-yìzú be perfectly content；be completely satisfied

心明眼亮 xīnmíng-yǎnliàng be sharp-eyed and clear-headed；be discerning

心目 xīnmù mind；view：年轻人～中的偶像 idol in the eyes of the young

心平气和 xīnpíng-qìhé even-tempered and good-humoured；unruffled；calm

心情 xīnqíng frame or state of mind；mood；spirit：～沉重 one's mind is weighed down (with sorrow, etc)；have a heavy heart

心曲 xīnqū what is on one's mind；倾诉～ pour out one's secret concerns；give vent to one's pent-up feelings

心神 xīnshén (state of) mind：～恍惚 be absent-minded；be distrait / ～不定

anxious and distracted

心事 xīnshì　load on one's mind; preoccupation; worry; ～重重 weighed down with care; preoccupied with worry

心术 xīnshù ❶〈贬〉intention; design; ～不正 harbour evil intentions ❷ see "心计"

心思 xīnsi ❶ idea; thought; mind; 想～ be lost in thought or contemplation ❷ thinking; 颇费～ take a lot of hard thinking ❸ state of mind or mood for doing sth; inclination; 干什么都没～ be in no mood for anything

心酸 xīnsuān　be sorrowful; feel sad; ～落泪 shed tears in grief

心态 xīntài　psychology; mentality; mental attitude

心疼 xīnténg ❶ love (dearly) ❷ feel painful; be tormented or distressed; grudge; ～花钱 be loath to spend money

心头 xīntóu　mind; heart; 涌上～ surge to one's mind; occur to one / ～肉 darling of one's heart; best loved one; most treasured possession

心无二用 xīnwú'èryòng　one cannot keep one's mind on two things at the same time; he who pursues two hares catches neither

心心相印 xīnxīnxiāngyìn　have heartto-heart communion with each other; show mutual understanding and attraction

心胸 xīnxiōng ❶ breadth of mind; ～豁达 have a generous heart; be broadminded ❷ aspiration; ambition; 很有～的小伙儿 young fellow of great aspirations

心虚 xīnxū ❶ afraid of being found out; with a guilty conscience; nervous ❷ lacking in self-confidence; timorous; diffident

心绪 xīnxù　(calm or disturbed) state of mind; mood; ～不宁 in a disturbed state of mind; flustered

心血 xīnxuè　painstaking care or effort; 花费～ take painstaking effort (in doing sth)

心血来潮 xīnxuèláicháo　be prompted by a sudden impulse; be carried away by a whim; ～，忘乎所以 lose one's head in a moment of excitement

心眼儿 xīnyǎnr ❶ heart; mind; 打～里高兴 warm the cockles of one's heart ❷ intention; heart; 没安好～ be up to no good ❸ intelligence; wit; 缺～ slow-witted / 留个～ be on one's guard (against sb or sth) ❹ baseless doubts; unfounded misgivings; ～太多 be oversensitive ❺ breadth or narrowness of mind; (lack of) tolerance; ～小 have a petty mind; be narrow-minded

心意 xīnyì ❶ regard; kindly feelings; 领人～ appreciate sb's kind regard / 一点儿～ a token of one's gratitude ❷ meaning; aim; intention; 按自己的～来生活 live as one wishes

心有余而力不足 xīnyǒuyú'érlìbùzú be unable to do what one wants very much to; one's ability falls short of one's wish

心有余悸 xīnyǒuyújì　one's heart still flutters with fear; have a lingering fear

心猿意马 xīnyuán-yìmǎ　restless and whimsical; of several minds

心愿 xīnyuàn　cherished desire; wish; dream; 了却平生～ have one's lifelong wish fulfilled

心悦诚服 xīnyuèchéngfú　admire from the bottom of one's heart; be completely convinced

心脏 xīnzàng〈生理〉❶ heart; ～病 heart disease ❷ centre; heart; ～地带 heartland

心照不宣 xīnzhàobùxuān　understand each other without speaking a word; have a tacit mutual understanding

心直口快 xīnzhí-kǒukuài　be frank and outspoken; be plain-spoken and

straightforward

心醉 xīnzuì charmed; enchanted; fascinated; 令人～ charming; enchanting

芯 xīn rush pith; 灯～ wick (for a lamp) *see also* xìn

芯片 xīnpiàn *also* "集成电路块"〈信息〉microchip; chip

辛 xīn ❶ (as in flavour) hot; pungent ❷ hard; difficult; laborious;～劳 toil; pains ❸ bitter; distressing; painful;～酸 sad; bitter; painful ❹ 8th of the Heavenly Stems *see also* "干支" gānzhī

辛苦 xīnkǔ ❶ hard; toilsome; laborious; 不辞～ spare no pains; make painstaking efforts /～费 (lobbying) commission; service charge; tip ❷〈套〉*used to ask sb to do sth*; 这事又得～您了。I'm afraid we'll have to trouble you again.

辛辣 xīnlà pungent; bitter; incisive; 气味～ have a pungent smell /～的讽刺 bitter irony; biting sarcasm; scathing satire

辛勤 xīnqín industrious; assiduous; hardworking

欣 xīn glad; happy; joyful;～然〈书〉joyfully; gladly; with pleasure /～慰 gratified; satisfied /～幸 be glad and thankful /～逢盛世 happy to live in a prosperous age

欣赏 xīnshǎng ❶ enjoy; admire;～名家手笔 admire the work of a master ❷ appreciate; value: 自我～ self-appreciation; self-glorification

欣喜 xīnxǐ elated; joyful; happy;～若狂 be wild with joy; go into raptures

欣欣向荣 xīnxīnxiàngróng thriving; flourishing; prosperous

锌 xīn〈化〉zinc (Zn)

新 xīn ❶ new; fresh; modern;～交 new friend or acquaintance /～绿 fresh green of early spring /～式 new type or style; modern; up-to-

date /～手 new or green hand; novice; rookie /～意 new idea or meaning; originality /～老交替 succession of the older by the younger generation; replacement of the old by the new /～瓶装旧酒 old wine in a new bottle — same old stuff with a new label /～石器时代 Neolithic Age; New Stone Age /另结～欢 acquire a new sweetheart ❷ recently; newly:～来 乍到 newly arrived ❸ newly or recently married:～房 bridal or wedding chamber /～郎 bridegroom /～娘 bride

新潮 xīncháo ❶ new trend or tendency ❷ modish; fashionable; avant-garde;～作家 avant-garde writer

新陈代谢 xīnchéndàixiè metabolism;〈喻〉the new superseding the old

新春 xīnchūn ❶ Lunar New Year's Day;～佳节 (on the) happy occasion of the Spring Festival ❷ early spring;～伊始 beginning of the year

新婚 xīnhūn newly-married;～夫妇 newly-married couple; newly-weds

新教 Xīnjiào〈宗〉(of Christianity) Protestantism;～徒 Protestant

新近 xīnjìn recently; of late;～发生的事情 recent event or development

新年 xīnnián New Year;～好! Happy New Year!

新奇 xīnqí new and strange; novel;～事物 novelty

新人 xīnrén ❶ people of a new type; reformed person ❷ new face or recruit; new talent ❸ newly-wed, esp the bride

新任 xīnrèn ❶ newly-appointed ❷ new appointment or post

新锐 xīnruì ❶ novel and sharp; new and vigorous ❷ avant-garde ❸ trendsetter; new star; promising young talent

新生 xīnshēng ❶ newborn; newly born;～力量 newly emerging force; new force or blood / 重获～ receive a new lease of life ❷ new student; freshman

新闻 xīnwén ❶ news：~片 newsreel；news film / ~记者 newsman；reporter；journalist / ~发布会 press conference；news briefing ❷ sth new；new development

新禧 xīnxǐ new year greetings：恭贺~！Happy New Year！

新鲜 xīnxiān ❶ fresh ❷ new；original；novel，~事物 something new；novelty

新兴 xīnxīng new and developing；newly emerging；burgeoning：~公司 start-up / ~行业 emergent industry

新星 xīnxīng ❶〈天文〉nova ❷〈喻〉new or rising star：歌坛~ new singing star

新秀 xīnxiù rising star：羽坛~ rising badminton star

新颖 xīnyǐng new；original；novel：~性 novelty

新月 xīnyuè ❶ crescent：一弯~ crescent moon ❷ also "朔月"〈天文〉new moon

歆 xīn〈书〉envy；admire；adore：令人~羡 enviable；admirable

薪 xīn ❶ firewood；faggot ❷ salary：~水 also "薪金"；"薪俸" salary；pay

馨 xīn〈书〉strong and pervasive fragrance

馨香 xīnxiāng〈书〉❶ fragrance；aroma ❷ smell of burning incense

xìn

芯 xìn see also xīn

芯子 xìnzi ❶ fuse；wick：爆竹~ fuse of a firecracker ❷ forked tongue（of a snake）

信 xìn ❶ true；truthful；reliable：~史 true or authentic history；reliable historical account ❷ believe；trust：~物 token of pledge；keepsake / ~不过 distrust / ~以为真 take as valid；accept as true ❸ profess faith in；embrace；believe in：~教 believe in a religion；be religious / ~条 article of creed or faith；precept；tenet / ~徒 believer；disciple；devotee ❹ at will；at random；casually：~步 walk in a leisurely and aimless manner；stroll；roam / ~手拈来 have（words，material，etc）at one's fingertips and write with facility ❺ letter；mail：~访 letters and visits（by the public）/ ~封 envelope / ~函 letter；mail；correspondence / ~汇 mail transfer（M/T）；postal（money）order / ~笺 letter or writing paper ❻ message；news；word：~鸽 carrier pigeon；homer / ~使 courier；messenger；emissary / 口~儿 oral or verbal message ❼ see "芯" xìn ❽ arsenic：~石 white arsenic

信贷 xìndài credit：~额度 line of credit / ~紧缩 credit crunch or squeeze

信风 xìnfēng also "贸易风" trade（wind）：~带 trade wind zone

信奉 xìnfèng believe in；profess：~基督教 profess Christianity；be a Christian

信服 xìnfú have implicit faith（in sb）；accept completely；be convinced：令人~ convincing

信号 xìnhào ❶ sign；signal：~弹 signal flare ❷〈电〉signal：~失真 signal distortion

信件 xìnjiàn letters，printed matter，etc；mail：往来~ outgoing and incoming mail；correspondence

信口 xìnkǒu blurt out one's thoughts：~雌黄 make irresponsible remarks；talk sheer nonsense / ~开河 talk off the top of one's head；shoot one's mouth off

信赖 xìnlài trust；believe in；have faith in：值得~ trustworthy

信念 xìnniàn faith；belief；conviction

信任 xìnrèn trust；confidence：~投票 vote of confidence / ~危机 credibility

crisis

信誓旦旦 xìnshìdàndàn pledge or promise in all sincerity and seriousness; vow solemnly

信守 xìnshǒu keep faith; abide by; stick to; ~ 不渝 be unswervingly faithful; abide by consistently

信托 xìntuō ❶ trust; entrust ❷ 〈经〉 trust; ~ 基金 trust fund / ~ 商店 commission shop; second-hand goods shop

信息 xìnxī ❶ message; news; word; 传递 ~ carry a message; pass on word ❷ information; ~ 化 informatization / ~ 爆炸 information explosion / ~ 技术 information technology (IT) / ~ 高速公路 information superhighway

信箱 xìnxiāng ❶ postbox; mailbox ❷ post-office box (POB) ❸ letter box

信心 xìnxīn confidence; faith; 充满 ~ brim with confidence

信仰 xìnyǎng belief; faith; conviction; ~ 危机 crisis in belief; credibility crisis / ~ 自由 freedom of conscience / 不同政治 ~ 的人 people of different political persuasions

信义 xìnyì good faith; honour; 重 ~ stand upon one's honour; act in good faith

信用 xìnyòng ❶ credibility; credit; honour; 讲 ~ 的人 man of his word; man of honour ❷ credit; ~ 卡 credit card / ~ 评估 also "信用评级" credit rating or evaluation ❸ 〈书〉 trust and appoint

信誉 xìnyù prestige; credit; reputation; 商业 ~ business reputation

衅（釁） xìn quarrel; row; dispute

xīng

兴（興） xīng ❶ （make） flourish; promote; become or make popular; ~ 隆 (of business, etc) prosperous; thriving; flour-

ishing / ~ 盛 also "兴旺" thriving; flourishing; in the ascendant / ~ 衰 also "兴亡" prosperity and adversity; rise and fall; fate (of a nation, etc) ❷ begin; start; found; ~ 办 set up; start; initiate / ~ 建 build; construct / ~ 修 start construction (on a large project); build ❸ get up; rise; 晨 ~ get up in the morning ❹ (usually used in the negative) allow; let; permit; 不 ~ 打人。You must not rough people up. ❺ (usu 兴许) 〈方〉 probably; maybe; perhaps

see also xìng

兴奋 xīngfèn ❶ excited; elated; ~ 点 hotspot ❷ 〈生理〉 excitation; ~ 剂 stimulant; analeptic; dope

兴风作浪 xīngfēng-zuòlàng stir up or make trouble; fan the flames of disorder

兴利除弊 xīnglì-chúbì promote what is beneficial and abolish what is harmful; start good practices and weed out corrupt ones

兴起 xīngqǐ ❶ rise; spring up; be on the upsurge ❷ 〈书〉 spring to action (on stimulus)

兴师动众 xīngshī-dòngzhòng drag in a great number of people (to do sth)

星 xīng ❶ star; any heavenly body; sth like a star; ~ 辰 stars; constellations / ~ 光 starlight / ~ 空 starlit or starry sky / ~ 球 celestial or heavenly body / ~ 系 〈天文〉 galaxy / ~ 象 configuration and movement of the stars (as basis for astrology) / ~ 云（天文）nebula / ~ 座（天文）constellation / ~ 际航行 interplanetary or space flight ❷ famous performer; star; 笑 ~ famous comedian ❸ bit; piece; particle

星斗 xīngdǒu stars; (esp) the Big Dipper; 满天 ~ star-studded sky / 星移斗转 also "星转斗移" the stars change their positions in the sky; the seasons change; time passes

星火 xīnghuǒ ❶ spark ❷ shooting star; meteor

星级 xīngjí star (as used in the ranking of hotels): 五 ~ 宾 馆 five-star hotel

星罗棋布 xīngluó-qíbù be scattered all over: 大小湖泊 ~ (of a region, etc) be dotted or studded with lakes big and small

星期 xīngqī also "礼拜" ❶ week: 上 ~ last week ❷ used to denote day of the week: ~ 一 Monday (Mon) / ~ 二 Tuesday (Tues) / ~ 三 Wednesday (Wed) / ~ 四 Thursday (Thur) / ~ 五 Friday (Fri) / ~ 六 Saturday (Sat) ❸ also "星期日" Sunday (Sun)

星星 xīngxing ❶ tiny spot; a bit: ~ 点点 tiny spots; bits and pieces; fragments ❷ (xīngxing) 〈口〉star

星子 xīngzi bits; pieces: 吐沫 ~ spittle; flying bits of saliva

猩 xīng

猩红 xīnghóng scarlet; blood-red: ~ 热〈医〉scarlet fever

猩猩 xīngxing orangutan: 大 ~ gorilla / 黑 ~ chimpanzee

惺 xīng 〈书〉❶ intelligent; clever: ~ ~ 惜 ~ ~ the clever appreciate each other; like attracts like ❷ come to one's senses; be sober: ~ 松 also "惺松" bleary-eyed

惺惺作态 xīngxīngzuòtài be affected; pretend; simulate (friendship, etc)

腥 xīng ❶ raw meat or fish (as food): 荤 ~ dishes of meat or fish ❷ having the smell of fish, seafood, etc; rank: ~ 臭 stinking; reeking / ~ 气 (having the) smell of fish, seafood, etc; rank or stinking (smell) / ~ 味儿 rank smell of fish / ~ 风血雨 foul wind and rain of blood — scene of ruthless massacre; reign of terror

xíng

刑 xíng ❶ punishment; sentence: ~ 场 execution ground / ~ 罚 penalty; punishment / ~ 律 criminal law ❷ torture; corporal punishment: ~ 具 instruments of torture or punishment; handcuffs and fetters

刑法 xíngfǎ ❶ penal code; criminal law ❷ (xíngfa) corporal punishment; torture: 动 ~ administer corporal punishment; resort to torture

刑事 xíngshì 〈法〉criminal; penal: ~ 犯 criminal (offender) / ~ 法 庭 (shortened as 刑庭) criminal court or tribunal / ~ 警察 (shortened as 刑警) criminal police or policeman / ~ 责任 criminal responsibility

刑讯 xíngxùn question or interrogate by torture: ~ 逼供 extort a confession by torture; subject (sb) to torture to obtain a confession

行 xíng ❶ go; walk; travel: ~ 期 date of departure / ~ 人 pedestrian; passer-by / ~ 装 outfit for a journey; travelling gear; luggage ❷ transitory; temporary; makeshift: ~ 宫 provisional palace for the emperor's stay away from the capital ❸ be current; prevail; circulate: ~ 时 (of a thing) be fashionable; be in vogue; (of a person) be in the ascendant ❹ do; practise; implement: ~ 贿 offer bribes / ~ 礼 salute; greet / ~ 骗 practise deception; swindle; cheat / ~ 窃 commit theft; steal / ~ 善 do good deeds or works; be charitable / ~ 刑 carry out a death sentence; execute / ~ 不通 unworkable; impracticable / ~ 方 便 make things easy (for sb); do a favour / ~ 之有效 effective; effectual ❺ used before a two-character verb as part of the modifier: 即 ~ 查复 check and reply promptly ❻ behaviour; conduct; deed;

～若无事 behave as if nothing had happened; behave with perfect composure or total indifference ❼ will do; be all right;走着去也～。It's all right if we walk there. ❽ able; capable; competent;搞公关～ be good at PR ❾〈书〉presently; shortly; soon
see also háng

行程 xíngchéng ❶ distance of travel; travel route;～万里 (make a) 10,000 *li* or extremely long journey ❷ itinerary (for travel); course; process

行刺 xíngcì assassinate;～未遂 fail in one's attempt to assassinate; attempt an assassination (without success)

行动 xíngdòng ❶ move or get about;～不便 have difficulty getting about ❷ act; operate; move;～纲领 programme of action

行将 xíngjiāng〈书〉soon; about to; on the point of;～就木 be near one's death; have one foot in the grave; one's days are numbered

行径 xíngjìng〈贬〉act; move;野蛮～ barbarous action; barbarity

行军 xíngjūn (of troops) march;急～ (make a) forced march /～床 camp bed or cot

行李 xíngli luggage; baggage;～架 luggage or baggage rack /～卷儿 bedroll; bedding roll or pack /～寄存处 left-luggage office; checkroom

行色 xíngsè manner, style or circumstances of departure;～匆匆 set out on one's journey in a great hurry

行尸走肉 xíngshī-zǒuròu walking corpse; zombie; utterly worthless person

行使 xíngshǐ exercise; perform; use;～职权 perform one's official functions

行驶 xíngshǐ (of a vehicle, ship, etc) drive; sail; ply;安全～ safe driving (of a vehicle)

行事 xíngshì ❶ behave or conduct oneself ❷ do things; act;看人～ act

differently with different people

行书 xíngshū (of Chinese calligraphy) running script or hand

行头 xíngtou ❶ actor's costumes and paraphernalia ❷〈谑〉clothing

行为 xíngwéi behaviour; conduct; act;～规范 code of conduct; behavioural norm

行文 xíngwén ❶ style or manner of writing;～简洁 succinctly written ❷ send an official communication

行销 xíngxiāo be on sale;～全球 marketed or on sale all over the world

行星 xíngxīng〈天文〉planet;小～ asteroid; planetoid

行凶 xíngxiōng commit physical assault; commit an act of violence;～杀人 commit murder or manslaughter

行医 xíngyī practise medicine (usu on one's own)

行云流水 xíngyún-liúshuǐ (write, sing, etc) with natural grace and fluency

行政 xíngzhèng administration; the executive;～区 administrative area or region /～部门 administrative department; the executive branch; the administration /～处分 administrative or disciplinary sanction /～拘留〈法〉administrative detention /～长官 administrative or chief executive /～职务 administrative function or post

行踪 xíngzōng *also* "行迹" whereabouts; track; trace;～诡秘 be of mysterious or uncertain whereabouts

饧(餳) xíng (of candy, dough, etc) become sticky and soft ❶

形 xíng ❶ form; appearance; shape;～似 be similar or resemble in form or appearance ❷ body; entity;～同虚设 exist in name only ❸ manifest; express;～诸笔墨 put down in black and white ❹ compare; contrast

形成 xíngchéng　form; take shape; shape up; ～强烈反差 form a sharp contrast

形而上学 xíng'érshàngxué　*also* "玄学"〈哲〉❶ metaphysics ❷ static, isolated and one-sided approach to things of the world

形迹 xíngjì　(of a person) movements and look; ～可疑 suspicious-looking ❷ sign; trace; mark; 不留～ leave no trace ❸ etiquette; formality; 不拘～ without formality; not standing on ceremony

形容 xíngróng　❶〈书〉look; appearance; countenance; ～憔悴 wan-looking; gaunt; haggard ❷ describe; 无法～ beyond description / ～词〈语言〉adjective

形声 xíngshēng　*also* "谐声"〈语言〉pictophonetic method of word-formation, accounting for some 80% of Chinese characters

形式 xíngshì　form; mode; shape; 表现～ mode of expression / ～逻辑 formal logic / ～主义 formalism

形势 xíngshì　❶ terrain; topography ❷ state of affairs; situation; circumstances; ～严峻 grim situation; trying circumstances

形态 xíngtài　❶ form; shape; pattern; ～万千 multifarious in form; myriads of forms; multiform ❷ morphology

形体 xíngtǐ　❶ figure; physique; body ❷ form and structure; 汉字的～特点 formal features of Chinese characters

形象 xíngxiàng　❶ image; figure; form; ～设计师 image designer ❷ literary or artistic image; imagery; ～思维 *also* "艺术思维" thinking in (terms of) images ❸ vivid; graphic; expressive

形形色色 xíngxíng-sèsè　of every colour and hue; of many varieties; of all shades or forms

形影 xíngyǐng　❶ body and shadow; object and reflection; ～不离 inseparable as body and shadow; always together / 形单影只 all on one's own; solitary ❷ shadow

形状 xíngzhuàng　shape; form; appearance; ～差不多 look quite alike

型 xíng　❶ mould (for casting) ❷ model; type; variety; ～号 model; type / 中～企业 medium-size enterprise

xǐng

省 xǐng　❶ *also* "省察" examine oneself critically; introspect ❷ visit (esp one's parents or elders); ～亲 visit one's family and relatives / ～视 visit (a patient, etc); find out about (condition of the people, etc) ❸ come to realize; become conscious or aware; ～悟〈书〉come to realize the truth, etc; wake up to reality
see also shěng

醒 xǐng　❶ regain consciousness; sober up; come to; ～酒 (of sth) dispel the effect of alcohol; (of sb) sober up ❷ wake up; awaken; be awake ❸ clear in mind; alert; aware; ～悟 come to oneself; come to see the truth; wake up to reality ❹ striking to the eye; eye-catching; conspicuous; ～目 eye-catching; striking; conspicuous

擤 xǐng　blow (one's nose)

xìng

兴(興) xìng　passion or appetite (for sth); mood or desire (to do sth); interest; ～冲冲 in high spirits; with joy and excitement / ～头上 in the thick of one's enthusiasm / ～高采烈 with great joy; in high spirits; jubilant　*see also* xīng

兴趣 xìngqù　interest；饶有～ (of sth) interesting；(of sb) interested (in sth)

兴味 xìngwèi　interest；relish；～盎然 with great relish or interest / ～索然 be fed up；lose all interest

兴致 xìngzhì　interest；agreeable mood (for sth)；～勃勃 full of enthusiasm；in high spirits；elated

杏 xìng　〈植〉apricot；almond；～黄 apricot (yellow) / ～仁 apricot kernel；almond / ～核儿 apricot stone

幸(⑤倖) xìng　❶ good fortune；happiness；～事 good fortune；blessing ❷ rejoice；be happy；喜～ rejoice ❸〈书〉I hope；I trust；～勿推却。Pray do not refuse. ❹ fortuitously；fortunately；luckily；～而 luckily；fortunately / ～会〈套〉be lucky enough or have the honour to meet ❺〈书〉favour ❻〈旧〉(of a monarch) come to；arrive at

幸存 xìngcún　(fortunately) survive；～者 survivor

幸福 xìngfú　❶ happiness；welfare；well-being ❷ happy；blissful

幸亏 xìngkuī　also "幸好"〈副〉fortunately；luckily

幸免 xìngmiǎn　escape by sheer luck；have a narrow escape；～于难 survive a disaster or escape death by sheer chance

幸运 xìngyùn　❶ good fortune；unexpected luck ❷ fortunate；very gratifying

幸灾乐祸 xìngzāi-lèhuò　gloat over another's misfortune；revel in sb's discomfiture；show malicious joy

性 xìng　❶ also "性子" nature；character；temperament；～急 impatient；impetuous；short-tempered ❷ noun- or adjective-forming suffix denoting an abstract quality；可塑～ plasticity ❸ sex；gender；～爱 sexual love / ～病 sexually transmitted disease (STD)；venereal disease (VD) /

～感 sex appeal；sexiness / ～交 (have) sexual intercourse；coitus；sex / ～欲 sexual desire or urge / ～高潮〈生理〉orgasm / ～教育 sex education / ～器官 sexual organs；genitals / ～骚扰 sexual harassment / ～生活 sexual life；sex ❹〈语言〉gender：中～名词 neuter noun

性别 xìngbié　sexual distinction；sex；gender；～歧视 sexism；sex discrimination

性格 xìnggé　also "性情" disposition；character；temperament；～孤僻 be of retiring or uncommunicative disposition；be unsociable

性命 xìngmìng　life；～交关 also "性命攸关" (matter) of life and death；of crucial importance

性能 xìngnéng　function (of a machine, etc)；performance；property

性质 xìngzhì　quality；nature；property

性子 xìngzi　❶ temper ❷ (of medicine or liquor) strength；potency

姓 xìng　family or clan name；surname；～名 surname and given name；full name / ～氏 surname

悻 xìng

悻悻 xìngxìng　angry；enraged；resentful；～而去 go away angrily；leave in a huff

xiōng

凶(❸-❺兇) xiōng　❶ inauspicious；unlucky；ominous；～兆 ill omen；evil boding / ～多吉少 bode ill rather than well；be fraught with grim possibilities ❷ crop failure；famine；～年 year of famine ❸ fierce；menacing；ferocious；～暴 brutally fierce；ferocious / ～悍 ferocious and tough；fierce and ruthless / ～猛 (of beast, wind, etc) fierce；violent；

ferocious / ～相 ferocious features;
fierce look ❹ terrible; violent; fearful;
吵得很～ have a terrible row ❺ relating to violence or murder;～案 murder
(case); homicide / ～犯 homicide or
murder suspect / ～器 tool or weapon
used for criminal purposes / ～杀 homicide; murder / ～手 murderer; killer;
assassin

凶残 xiōngcán ❶ savage and cruel;
brutal and ruthless ❷〈书〉savage and
cruel person

凶恶 xiōng'è fierce; vicious; fiendish;凶神恶煞 evil spirit; devil; fiend

凶狠 xiōnghěn ❶ fierce and malicious; ferocious and ruthless ❷ forceful; vigorous;扣球～ smash forcefully

凶险 xiōngxiǎn ❶ in a very dangerous state; precarious; critical;病情～
be critically ill ❷ ferocious and sinister; fiendish and insidious

兄 xiōng ❶ elder brother; elder
male relative of one's own generation;～嫂 elder brother and his wife
❷ courteous form of address between
men;老～ (familiar form of address between male friends) brother; man

兄弟 xiōngdi ❶ (xiōngdì) (like)
brothers; brethren; ～民族 brotherly
nationalities ❷ younger brother ❸ familiar form of address for a man
younger than oneself ❹〈谦〉your
humble servant, I

兄长 xiōngzhǎng respectful form of
address for an elder brother or a male
friend older than oneself;请～多指教。
Kindly give us your advice.

匈 xiōng

匈奴 Xiōngnú Xiongnu or Hun,
ancient nomadic people living in north
China

洶(洶) xiōng rush of water;
tumult;～涌 surging;
tempestuous; turbulent

洶洶 xiōngxiōng 〈书〉❶ sound of
roaring waves ❷ violent; fierce; truculent;气势～ blustering and truculent
also "讻讻"〈书〉turbulent; tumultuous

胸 xiōng ❶ chest; breast; thorax;～部 chest; thorax / ～口
pit of the stomach; chest / ～脯 chest;
bust; breast / ～围 (of human body)
chest measurement; bust / ～罩 brassiere; bra / ～针 brooch / ～膜炎
pleurisy / 挺起～膛 throw out one's
chest ❷ mind; heart;～无城府 simple
and candid; artless / ～中有数 also
"心中有数" have a good idea of how
things stand; know what's what

胸怀 xiōnghuái ❶ have in mind;
cherish;～大志 cherish lofty ambitions; be ambitious ❷ heart; mind;～
坦荡 open-hearted; frank; candid ❸
chest; bosom

胸襟 xiōngjīn ❶ (breadth of) mind;
～开阔 broad- or large-minded ❷
mood; state of mind; sentiments;抒写
～ describe one's feelings ❸ upper
front part of a jacket

胸无点墨 xiōngwúdiǎnmò completely
illiterate; uneducated

胸有成竹 xiōngyǒuchéngzhú also "成
竹在胸" have a well-thought-out plan,
stratagem, etc, in mind; be well
prepared (for an eventuality, etc)

xióng

雄 xióng ❶ male; ～鸡 cock;
rooster / ～狮 (male) lion ❷ imposing; powerful; mighty; ～浑 (of
writing, etc) vigorous and firm;
powerful; forceful / ～健 robust; virile;
vigorous / ～师 powerful army / ～图
lofty aspiration; great ambition; grand
design / ～文 powerful writing; great
works; masterpiece / ～才大略 of
great talent and bold vision ❸ person

or state having great power and influence

雄辩 xióngbiàn convincing argument; eloquence；～家 eloquent speaker; orator / ～地证明 convincingly prove (sth)

雄风 xióngfēng heroic carriage; bold or gallant appearance；重振～ reassert one's power or influence

雄厚 xiónghòu rich; huge; abundant (capital, etc)

雄赳赳 xióngjiūjiū valiantly; gallantly；～，气昂昂 valorously and spiritedly; full of mettle

雄伟 xióngwěi ❶ grand; imposing; magnificent ❷ (of a person) tall and strong; stalwart

雄心 xióngxīn noble ambition; lofty aspiration；～勃勃 extremely ambitious; full of ambitions

雄壮 xióngzhuàng ❶ full of power and grandeur; imposing; magnificent ❷ stalwart; robust；身材～ of sturdy build

熊 xióng ❶ bear：～掌 bear's paw (as a rare delicacy) ❷〈方〉rebuke; upbraid; scold ❸〈方〉impotent; timid; faint-hearted；～包 chicken-heart; good-for-nothing

熊猫 xióngmāo also "猫熊" panda：大～ giant panda / 小～ lesser panda

熊市 xióngshì〈经〉bear or bearish market

熊熊 xióngxióng flaming; ablaze; raging；～烈火 raging flames; conflagration

xiū

休 xiū ❶ stop; end; cease：～兵〈书〉stop fighting; end hostilities / ～会 adjourn; recess / ～庭 adjourn the court / ～学 be temporarily absent from school; suspend schooling ❷ rest; repose：～眠 dormancy / ～憩

〈书〉have or take a rest; repose / ～整 (of troops) rest and reorganize ❸〈旧〉divorce one's wife and send her home ❹ don't；~怪 blame not / ～想 don't think or imagine (sth); stop dreaming ❺〈书〉good fortune; rejoicing：~戚与共 share weal and woe; stay together through thick and thin

休假 xiūjià have a holiday or vacation; (of soldiers, etc) be on leave or furlough：休病假 be on sick leave / 休年假 have one's annual vacation

休克 xiūkè〈医〉shock：~疗法 shock treatment or therapy

休息 xiūxī have or take a rest; rest：~日 day off / ~室 lounge; lobby

休闲 xiūxián ❶ be not working; have leisure：~服 leisure clothing; casual wear / ~鞋 leisure shoes ❷〈农〉lie fallow：~地 fallow land

休养 xiūyǎng ❶ recuperate; convalesce：~所 rest home; sanatorium ❷ (of economy, etc) recover; rehabilitate：~生息 (of a nation) recuperate and multiply; rest and rehabilitate

休业 xiūyè ❶ suspend or close business：今日~。Closed for the day. ❷ (of a short-term course, etc) end; wind up

休止 xiūzhǐ end; stop; cease：~符〈乐〉rest

咻

咻咻 xiūxiū〈象声〉❶ *used for the sound of breathing*：发出～的鼻息 breathe noisily ❷ *used to describe the cry of some birds and animals*：小鸭～。The ducklings were cheeping.

修 xiū also "脩" ❶ embellish; decorate; adorn：～润 (of writings) polish; touch up ❷ repair; fix; overhaul：~补 mend; repair; revamp / ~浚 dredge (a canal, etc) / ~配 make repairs and supply replacements ❸ write; compile：～史〈书〉

write or compile history / ～书〈书〉write a letter or book ❹ study; learn; cultivate: ～心养性 cultivate one's mind and improve one's character; cultivate oneself / ～业期满 finish schooling / ～身、齐家、治国、平天下。(Confucian motto) Cultivate yourself, put your family in order, run the local government well, and bring peace to the entire country. ❺〈宗教〉try to attain immortality through self-cultivation, etc; ～炼 give oneself up to austere religious discipline, esp Buddhist or Taoist control of mind and body / ～女 (Roman Catholic or Greek Orthodox) nun; sister / ～行 practise Buddhism or Taoism ❻ build; construct: ～建 build; construct; erect / ～路 build a road ❼ trim; pare; prune: ～剪 trim or prune (a tree, fingernails, etc); clip / ～脚 pedicure ❽ (usu 修长)〈书〉long; tall and slim

修辞 xiūcí 〈语言〉rhetoric

修道 xiūdào 〈宗教〉cultivate oneself according to a religious doctrine: ～士 also "修士" monk / ～院 monastery (for men); convent (for women)

修订 xiūdìng revise: ～本 revised edition

修复 xiūfù restore (relations, etc); renovate (sth ancient); repair

修改 xiūgǎi revise; amend; modify

修好 xiūhǎo ❶〈书〉promote friendly relations (between states) ❷ do good (deeds)

修理 xiūlǐ ❶ repair; mend; fix ❷ trim (flowers, etc); prune; pare

修葺 xiūqì also "修缮" repair; refurbish; renovate: ～一新 take on a new look after renovation; have a facelift

修饰 xiūshì ❶ decorate; adorn; embellish: ～门面 window-dressing ❷ make up and dress up ❸ polish (a piece of writing); modify; qualify: ～语〈语言〉modifier

修养 xiūyǎng ❶ accomplishment; understanding; mastery: 很有艺术～ be of high artistic accomplishment ❷ self-cultivation: 缺少～ lacking in self-cultivation; boorish

修整 xiūzhěng ❶ repair and maintain; recondition (a building, etc) ❷ prune; trim

修正 xiūzhèng ❶ modify; revise; correct: ～案 amendment ❷ adulterate (Marxism-Leninism); revise: ～主义 revisionism

羞 xiū ❶ shy; coy; bashful: ～怯 shy; timid; sheepish / ～涩 bashful; diffident; embarrassed / ～答答 coy; shy; bashful ❷ feel ashamed or mortified: ～愤 ashamed and indignant / ～愧 also ashamed; abashed; discomfited / ～耻之心 sense of shame / ～与为伍 be ashamed to be seen in sb's company; consider it beneath one to associate with sb ❸ see "馐" xiū

羞辱 xiūrǔ shame; disgrace; humiliation: 蒙受～ suffer disgrace or humiliation / ～某人 put sb to shame

馐 xiū 〈书〉delicacy; choice food; dainty: 珍～ rare delicacy

xiǔ

朽 xiǔ ❶ (mostly of wood) rotten; decayed: ～木 rotten wood or tree; useless person ❷ senile: ～迈〈书〉old and weak; senile; decrepit

宿 xiǔ 〈量〉used for nights: 住了一一 stay for one night　see also sù; xiù

xiù

秀 xiù ❶ (of grain crops) put forth flowers or ears ❷ elegant; beautiful; pretty and delicate: ～美 beautiful; pretty / ～美 graceful; delicate; elegant / ～外慧中 (of women) be endowed with both beauty and intelligence; be both pretty and bright ❸ clever; smart; intelligent; 内～ intelligent without showing it; inwardly smart ❹ excellent (person); superb; outstanding (talent); 新～ new talent

秀才 xiùcái ❶ *xiucai*, who passed the imperial examination at the county level in the Ming and Qing dynasties ❷ scholar; skilful writer

秀气 xiùqi ❶ (of features, etc) delicate; graceful; elegant ❷ (of speech and manners) refined; gentle; urbane ❸ (of articles of use) delicate and well-made; superb; exquisite

秀色 xiùsè prettiness; beauty; ～可餐 (of an attractive woman or beautiful scenery) feast to the eye; beauty to feast one's eyes on

岫 xiù 〈书〉❶ cave; cavern ❷ mountain (peak)

臭 xiù ❶ odour; smell; 乳～ smell of milk — be childish ❷ *see* "嗅"
xiù　*see also* chòu

袖 xiù ❶ sleeve; ～口 cuff (of a sleeve); wristband / ～套 oversleeve / ～章 sleeve badge; brassard; armband ❷ tuck or hide inside the sleeve; ～手旁观 look on with folded arms; stand by unconcerned; remain an indifferent spectator

袖珍 xiùzhēn pocket(-size); miniature; ～字典 pocket dictionary

绣（繡） xiù embroider

绣花 xiùhuā embroider; do embroidery; ～针 embroidery needle / ～枕头 pillow with an embroidered case; outwardly attractive but worthless person

宿 xiù constellation　*see also* sù; xiǔ

锈（鏽） xiù ❶ rust; 〈农〉 rust (disease) ❷ become rusty

嗅 xiù scent; smell; sniff; ～觉 sense of smell; scent

溴 xiù 〈化〉 bromine (Br)

xū

圩 xū *also* "圩场" 〈方〉 country fair　*see also* wéi

戌 xū 11th of the Earthly Branches　*see also* "干支" gānzhī

吁 xū 〈书〉 sigh; ～～直喘 breathe heavily; pant / 长～一声 utter or heave a long sigh　*see also* yù

须（❷❸鬚） xū ❶ must; have to; ～要认真对待 must be taken seriously ❷ beard; mustache; ～眉 〈书〉 beard and eyebrows; man ❸ *also* "须子" 〈动物〉 feeler; 〈植〉 tassel; ～根 fibrous root

须臾 xūyú 〈书〉 moment; minute; instant

须知 xūzhī ❶ points for attention; guide; notice; 考试～ information for examinees ❷ one should know; it must be borne in mind

胥 xū 〈书〉❶ *also* "胥吏" petty official ❷ all; each and every

虚 xū ❶ empty; void; vacant; ～掩 (of door, etc) unlocked or unlatched; (of jacket, etc) not buttoned up / ～位以待 leave a seat vacant for; reserve a seat for ❷ diffident; timid; cowardly; ～怯 be ashamed and afraid at heart; have a guilty conscience ❸ false; deceitful; nominal; ～度 spend (time) in vain; idle away / ～惊 (have a) false alarm / ～名 undeserved reputation; false fame / ～岁 nominal age (by the tradition of considering a baby one year old at birth and adding a year each lunar new year) / ～线 dotted line; 〈数〉 imaginary line / ～职 nominal position; sinecure / ～套子 mere formalities；conventionalities／～情假意 false display of affection；insincerity／～有其表 look impressive but lack real worth；be striking only in appearance ❹ humble；unassuming；modest；～怀若谷 have a receptive mind；be extremely open-minded or modest ❺ weak；feeble；in poor health：～汗 abnormal sweating due to general debility；deficiency sweat／～胖 puffiness／～脱〈医〉collapse；prostration ❻ general or guiding principle；theory

虚报 xūbào　make a false report：～开支 pad the expenses／～年龄 lie about one's age

虚词 xūcí　❶ also "虚字"〈语言〉function or form word ❷ also "虚辞"〈书〉exaggeration；empty words

虚浮 xūfú　(of style of work, etc) impractical；shallow；superficial

虚构 xūgòu　fabricate；concoct；make up：纯属～ mere fiction；sheer fabrication

虚幻 xūhuàn　unreal；illusory；imaginary：～的感觉 hallucination

虚假 xūjiǎ　false；sham；hypocritical

虚夸 xūkuā　exaggerative；pompous；boastful

虚拟 xūnǐ　❶ hypothetical；subjunctive：〈信息〉virtual：～现实 virtual reality／～语气〈语言〉subjunctive mood ❷ invented；assumed；fictitious

虚荣 xūróng　vanity：～心 vanity；vainglory

虚弱 xūruò　❶ in poor health；frail；weak ❷ (of national strength, etc) weak；feeble

虚实 xūshí　❶ false or true — actual situation；things as they are：虚虚实实 combine the true and the false；use feints and ambushes ❷ general principles and specific matters；～并举 pay attention to both theory and practical work

虚伪 xūwěi　sham；false；hypocritical

虚无 xūwú　nihility；emptiness；nothingness：～缥缈 purely imaginary；fanciful；illusory／～主义 nihilism

虚心 xūxīn　open-minded；unassuming；modest

虚与委蛇 xūyǔwěiyí　treat courteously but insincerely；feign politeness and compliance

虚张声势 xūzhāngshēngshì　make an empty show of strength；bluff and bluster；be swashbuckling

墟 xū　❶ ruins：废～ ruins ❷ see "圩" xū

需 xū　❶ need；require；demand：～求〈经〉demand；requirement；need ❷ necessities；needs

需要 xūyào　❶ require；need；demand；call for；demand：～立即解决 call for prompt solution ❷ needs

嘘 xū　❶ breathe out slowly：～气 exhale slowly／～寒问暖 inquire after sb's well-being；be solicitous about sb's health；show great concern for sb ❷ utter a sigh；sigh：～唏 also "欷歔"〈书〉sob ❸ (of cooking fire, steam, etc) scald；burn ❹ hiss；boo：～下台 boo (sb) off the stage／～，轻点儿声。Hush! Don't make so much noise.
see also shī

xú

徐 xú　〈书〉slowly；gently：～图 seek to achieve gradually／～行 walk leisurely

xǔ

许 xǔ　❶ praise；commend：推～ recommend ❷ make a promise；promise：～婚 consent to the marriage of one's daughter；(of a girl) agree to marry／～诺 make a promise；promise; pledge / ～愿 make a vow (to a god); make a resolution (to oneself); promise (sb) a reward ❸ *also* "许配" betroth; be betrothed or engaged to; 尚未～人 (of a girl) not yet engaged ❹ allow; permit; consent; ～可 permit; allow; approve / 只～成功, 不～失败。 There must be success, and no failure. ❺ perhaps; probably; maybe; ～是要下雨吧。 It's probably going to rain. ❻ *expressing extent or amount:* ～多 many; much; a lot / ～久 for a long time; for ages ❼〈书〉about; approximately; 二十～ about twenty ❽〈书〉place; 何～人? Where is the person from? or Who is this man?

诩
xǔ 〈书〉brag; boast; blow one's own horn; 以专家自～ style oneself an expert

栩
xǔ
栩栩如生 xǔxǔrúshēng lifelike; lively; vivid

xù

旭
xù 〈书〉brilliance of the rising sun; ～日东升 sun rising in the eastern sky — symbol of youth and vigour

序
xù ❶ order; sequence; ～号 serial or sequence number / ～列 order; alignment; array / ～数词 ordinal number ❷〈书〉arrange in order; order; ～次 arrange (books, etc) in serial order ❸ initial; opening; introductory; ～论 introductory chapter; introduction / ～幕 opening scene in a play; prelude / ～曲 overture; prelude (to an event, etc) / ～言 *also* "序文"; "叙言" preface; foreword

叙（敍、敘）
xù ❶ talk; chitchat; chat; ～别 have a farewell talk; bid farewell (to sb) / ～旧 talk about the old days;

reminisce about the past / ～谈 chat; chitchat ❷ give an account of; narrate; relate; 自～ account of oneself; autobiographic note or statement / ～述 narrate; recount; relate / ～事诗 narrative poem ❸ assess; evaluate; appraise; ～功 assess contributions or services rendered / 按才～用 employ people according to their capabilities ❹ *see* "序"

恤（卹）
xù ❶〈书〉worry; misgiving; apprehension ❷ pity; sympathize; commiserate ❸ give relief; compensate; ～金 pension for a disabled person or the family of the deceased

畜
xù raise (domestic animals); breed; rear; ～牧 animal husbandry; stock farming / ～产品 animal or livestock product *see also* chù

酗
xù
酗酒 xùjiǔ be given to heavy drinking; be alcoholic

勖
xù 〈书〉encourage; ～勉 have added; give repeated encouragement

绪
xù ❶ beginning of a matter; ～论 *also* "绪言" (of works) introduction ❷〈书〉remnants; ～余 remainder ❸ mental or emotional state; mood; 情～ mood ❹〈书〉task; cause; undertaking; 遗～ unfinished task

续（續）
xù ❶ continue; renew; extend; ～编 *also* "续编" continuation (of a book); sequel / ～假 extend one's leave of absence / ～借 renew (a library book) / ～聘 continue to engage (sb); continue the employment (of sb) / ～弦 remarry after the death of one's wife; second wife (after the death of the first one) ❷ add; increase; supply more; ～茶 add more tea

絮
xù ❶ (cotton) wadding; padding ❷ sth resembling cotton; 柳

~ willow catkins ❸ wad or pad (as with cotton) ❹ long-winded; loquacious; garrulous; ~ 叨 talk in a long-winded or garrulous way / ~语〈书〉talk or chatter endlessly; prattle on and on

婿（壻） xù ❶ son-in-law ❷ husband

蓄 xù ❶ store or save up: ~洪 flood storage / ~积 store or save up / ~水 retain or store water / ~电池 storage battery; accumulator ❷ (cause to) grow; ~养 keep and feed; raise (animals); build up (energy) / ~须 grow a beard ❸ harbour; cherish; entertain (ideas)

蓄谋 xùmóu 〈贬〉plan in advance; premeditate: ~反叛 harbour plans for an insurrection

蓄意 xùyì 〈贬〉premeditated; calculated; deliberate: ~寻衅 pick a fight (with sb)

煦 xù 〈书〉warm; balmy

xuān

轩 xuān ❶〈书〉high; lofty; 难分~轾 hard to tell who or which is superior; about equal ❷ small room or veranda with windows; open corridor or pavilion: 茶~ tea room

轩昂 xuān'áng ❶ dignified; impressive; imposing: 志气~ aim high in life; aspire to great success ❷〈书〉tall and big

轩然 xuānrán ❶ (of laughter) loud and uncontrolled ❷ rising high; towering: ~大波 great disturbance; mighty uproar

宣 xuān ❶ announce; declare; proclaim: ~读 read out (in public); announce / ~明 make clear; clarify / ~示 express in public; make known ❷ summon into the presence of the emperor by an imperial edict: ~召 summon (sb) by an imperial edict; summon to court ❸ see "宣泄❶"

宣布 xuānbù announce; declare; proclaim: ~会议结束 declare a meeting closed

宣称 xuānchēng assert; claim; profess

宣传 xuānchuán promote; publicize; disseminate: ~画 also "招贴画" (picture) poster / ~品 publicity or promotion material / ~机器〈贬〉propaganda machine

宣告 xuāngào declare; proclaim; announce: ~破产 declare bankruptcy; go bankrupt / ~死亡 declare (sb) dead

宣判 xuānpàn 〈法〉pronounce or deliver judgement: ~无罪 pronounce (sb) not guilty; acquit (sb) of a charge

宣誓 xuānshì take or swear an oath; make a vow or pledge: ~就任总统 take one's oath of office as president; be sworn in as president

宣泄 xuānxiè ❶ drain or lead off (liquids): ~不畅 (of floodwater) cannot drain off ❷ get sth off one's chest; unbosom oneself; reveal: ~不满情绪 give vent to one's dissatisfaction ❸〈书〉reveal; let out (a secret, etc)

宣言 xuānyán ❶ declaration; proclamation; manifesto: 《共产党~》 *Communist Manifesto* ❷ see "宣告"

宣扬 xuānyáng publicize; propagate; advertise: 大肆~ make or raise a big fanfare (about sth)

宣战 xuānzhàn declare or proclaim war; 〈喻〉battle or struggle (against)

宣纸 xuānzhǐ Xuan paper, a high quality paper esp good for traditional Chinese painting and calligraphy

萱 xuān ❶ also "萱草" yellow or tawny day lily ❷ also "萱堂"〈书〉〈敬〉(your) mother

揎 xuān roll up sleeves: ~拳捋袖 roll up one's sleeves and raise

one's fists (to fight)

喧(誼) xuān noisy; clamorous; uproarious; ~ 嚷 (raise a) clamour, hubbub or racket / ~ 扰 harass by noise and disturbance; raise a racket or tumult / ~ 天 fill the air with resounding noise / ~ 嚣 noisy; clamorous; tumultuous

喧宾夺主 xuānbīnduózhǔ a noisy guest usurps the host's role; the secondary supercedes the primary; steal the show

喧哗 xuānhuá make (confused) noise; hubbub; uproar; 请勿~！Please keep quiet.

喧闹 xuānnào noisy and exciting; bustling (market, etc)

喧腾 xuānténg noise and excitement; uproar; 锣鼓 ~ deafening sound of gongs and drums

暄 xuān ❶〈书〉genial warmth (as of the sun) ❷ also "喧腾" 〈方〉fluffy; soft

煊 xuān see "喧❶" xuān

煊赫 xuānhè 〈书〉of great renown and influence; illustrious; celebrated

儇 xuān

儇薄 xuānbó also "嬛佻"〈书〉(clever but) frivolous

xuán

玄 xuān ❶ black; dark; ~ 服 black gown ❷ profound; subtle; abstruse; ~ 奥 abstruse; profound; recondite / ~ 远〈书〉profound and far-reaching; abstruse; remote ❸ mysterious; far-fetched; incredible; ~ 乎〈口〉inscrutable; mysterious; subtle / ~ 机 mysteries of the universe; profound secret; ingenious principle of action / ~ 想 fantasy; fancy; illusion / ~ 之又 ~ mystery of mysteries; ex-

tremely abstruse; unfathomable

玄妙 xuánmiào mysteriously wonderful; abstruse; ~ 莫测 too mysterious to comprehend; inscrutable

玄孙 xuánsūn great-great-grandson

玄虚 xuánxū deceitful trick; occult; mystery; 故 弄 ~ purposely make a mystery of simple things; be deliberately mystifying

悬(懸) xuán ❶ hang; suspend; ~ 垂 (of objects) hang down / ~ 吊 suspend; dangle; hang in midair / ~ 浮 be suspended or float (in the air, etc) / ~ 梯 hanging ladder / ~ 心 〈喻〉be consumed by worry and anxiety; worry; feel anxious ❷ unresolved; unsettled; outstanding; ~ 而 未 决 outstanding; unsettled ❸ imagine; ~ 想 imagine; conjecture; fancy ❹ far apart; ~ 隔 far apart; be widely separated ❺ also "悬乎"〈方〉dangerous; precarious; perilous

悬案 xuán'àn ❶ unsettled law case; pending lawsuit ❷ outstanding issue

悬挂 xuánguà hang; suspend; fly (a flag)

悬空 xuánkōng hang in the air; suspend in midair;〈喻〉uncertain; unsettled;这笔资金还~着。The funding is still up in the air.

悬念 xuánniàn ❶〈书〉be concerned or worried about (sb who is elsewhere); think of (sb in absence) ❷ suspense; ~ 大师 master of suspense

悬赏 xuánshǎng offer or post a reward (for sth)

悬殊 xuánshū vast difference; great disparity; wide gap; 贫富 ~。The rich and the poor are poles apart.

悬崖 xuányá overhanging or steep cliff; precipice; ~ 勒马 rein in at the brink of a precipice; pull back before it is too late

旋 xuán ❶ revolve; circle; spin; ~ 绕 curl up; wind around / ~

钮 knob ❷ return; go or come back; ～
里 〈书〉 return to one's hometown ❸
〈书〉 soon; quickly; ～即 shortly or
soon afterwards; immediately
see also xuàn

旋律 xuánlǜ 〈乐〉melody; 主～ keynote; (main) theme

旋涡 xuánwō *also* "漩涡" whirlpool;
eddy; vortex

旋踵 xuánzhǒng 〈书〉turn round on
one's heel; 〈喻〉flinch; 〈喻〉in an instant; ～而至 arrive immediately afterwards

旋转 xuánzhuàn revolve; rotate;
whirl; ～餐厅 revolving restaurant /
木马 merry-go-round / ～乾坤 reverse
the course of events; effect a drastic
change

漩 xuán whirlpool; eddy

xuǎn

选（選） xuǎn ❶ choose; se-
lect; pick; ～本 anthol-
ogy / ～段 selected passage / ～辑 selected edition / ～手 athlete or player
selected for a competition; contestant /
～题 chosen subject; selected topic /
～种 〈农〉seed selection / ～美比赛
beauty contest ❷ elect; ～民 (individual) voter; elector; (collective) elector-
ate / ～票 vote; ballot / ～区 electoral
district or ward; constituency / ～代表
elect sb as representative ❸ person
elected; thing chosen; 佳～ good choice
or selection ❹ selections; anthology;
作品～ selected works

选拔 xuǎnbá select; choose; scout; ～
赛 〈体〉(selective) trials

选材 xuǎncái choose qualified personnel; select (suitable) material

选集 xuǎnjí selected works or writings; selections; anthology

选举 xuǎnjǔ elect; 差额～ competitive

or multiple choice election / 等额～
one-candidate election / ～权 right to
vote; franchise; suffrage

选派 xuǎnpài select and send; detail;
～留学生 select students for studying
overseas

选修 xuǎnxiū take as an elective
course; ～课 elective or optional course

选择 xuǎnzé select; choose; pick; ～
题 multiple-choice test

烜 xuǎn 〈书〉grand; magnificent;
～赫一时 have great renown and
influence for a time

癣 xuǎn tinea; ringworm

xuàn

券 xuàn *also* "拱券" arch; ～门
arch entrance　*see also* quàn

泫 xuàn 〈书〉fall in drops; drip;
～然泪下 tears trickling down
the cheeks

炫 xuàn 〈书〉❶ daze; dazzle;
blaze; ～目 dazzling ❷ show off;
display; ～示 make a show of; show
off; display

炫耀 xuànyào ❶ shine; illuminate ❷
make a display of; flaunt; vaunt

绚 xuàn gorgeous; (of colour)
prismatic; ～烂 brilliant; splendid; gorgeous / ～丽 bright and colourful; gorgeous; magnificent

眩 xuàn ❶ dizzy; giddy; ～晕 diz-
ziness; giddiness; 〈医〉vertigo
❷〈书〉dazzled; bewildered; ～于物质
享受 obsessed with material comforts;
indulge in worldly pleasures

旋（❷❸镟） xuàn ❶ whirl;
～风 whirlwind;
cyclone ❷ turn on a lathe; ～床 *also*
"车床" (turning) lathe ❸ ～子 *also* "旋子"
hot water container for warming wine
❹ at the time when sth is needed; at
the last moment; ～用～买 buy sth

when you need it; buy for immediate use

see also xuán

渲 xuàn

渲染 xuànrǎn ❶ wash (a drawing) with water-colours; apply colours (to a drawing) ❷ play up; exaggerate; pile it on

楦 xuàn

❶ *also* "楦子" (shoe) last; (hat) block ❷ shape with a last or block 〈方〉 stuff; fill up

xuē

削 xuē

(used only in compound words) cut; pare; whittle: ～价 cut prices; lower or reduce the price / ～肩 drooping or sloping shoulders / ～减 cut or whittle down; reduce; slash / ～平〈书〉 suppress; wipe out; eliminate / ～弱 weaken; sap; undermine / ～足适履 cut the feet to fit the shoes; mechanically copy regardless of specific conditions　*see also* xiāo

靴 xuē *also* "靴子" boots

xué

穴 xué ❶ cave; hole; den: ～居 live in caves ❷ (pit for) grave ❸ 〈中医〉 acupuncture point: ～位 *also* "穴道" acupuncture point

学(學) xué ❶ study; learn: ～步 (usu of babies) learn to walk; grope forward / ～费 tuition (fee); education expenses / ～分 credit / ～年 academic or school year / ～期 (school) term; semester / ～时 class hour; period / ～员 student; trainee / ～长〈敬〉 former schoolmate / ～以致用 study for the purpose of application; study sth in order to apply it ❷ imitate; mimic; copy:

～坏 follow bad examples; succumb to evil; pick up bad habits ❸ learning; knowledge; scholarship: ～阀 scholar-tyrant / ～会 learned or professional society; institute / ～界 academic or educational circles / ～派 school (of thought) / ～者 *also* "学人" scholar; man of learning; learned person / ～无止境 knowledge knows no bounds; there is no limit to knowledge ❹ subject of study; field or branch of learning: 汉～ Chinese studies; Sinology ❺ school; college; university: ～报 learned or university journal / ～潮 student strike; campus upheaval / ～前教育 preschool education

学风 xuéfēng style of study; academic atmosphere: ～严谨 meticulous and rigorous in academic work

学府 xuéfǔ institution or seat of learning: 高等～ institution of tertiary education or higher learning

学籍 xuéjí status as a student; name on the school roll: 开除～ throw (sb) out of school; expel (sb) from school / ～管理 administration of student records; registrar's work

学究 xuéjiū scholar; pedant: ～气 pedantry

学科 xuékē ❶ branch of learning; field of study; discipline: ～带头人 leading scholar in a branch of learning / 跨～研究 interdisciplinary research ❷ course; subject

学力 xuélì knowledge or educational level; academic attainments: 具有同等～ with the same educational level (as a school graduate, etc)

学历 xuélì record of formal schooling or education: 具有大学本科～ be a university graduate

学龄 xuélíng school age: ～儿童 children of school age; school-age children / ～前儿童 pre-school children

学名 xuémíng ❶ registered name at

X

school; formal name used at school ❷ scientific name (eg Latin name for plants, etc)

学舌 xuéshé ❶ mechanically repeat other people's words; parrot ❷〈口〉pass on rumours; gossip

学生 xuéshēng student; pupil; disciple:～会 student union or association /～票 ticket at student discount /～证 student ID or card

学识 xuéshí learning; knowledge; scholarly attainments:～过人 surpass others in knowledge; be unusually learned

学士 xuéshì ❶ scholar ❷ bachelor:法～ Bachelor of Laws (LLB) / 理～ Bachelor of Science (BS) / 文～ Bachelor of Arts (BA)

学术 xuéshù academic learning; science:～交流 academic exchanges /刊物 learned journal; academic publication /～论文 research or scientific paper; thesis

学说 xuéshuō theory; doctrine; teachings

学徒 xuétú ❶ serve one's apprenticeship ❷ apprentice; trainee

学位 xuéwèi (academic) degree:攻读～ study for or do a degree /～点 degree-conferring institution /～论文 academic dissertation /～证书 diploma

学问 xuéwen ❶ branch of learning ❷ learning; knowledge; scholarship:～家 man of learning

学习 xuéxí ❶ study; learn:～班 (studying) class ❷ learn from; follow the example of; emulate

学校 xuéxiào school; educational institution

学业 xuéyè studies; school work:～有成 be academically accomplished

学院 xuéyuàn college; academy; institute

学制 xuézhì educational or school system:～四年 4-year's schooling

学子 xuézǐ 〈书〉student; scholar:海外～ students studying overseas

踅 xué pace up and down; walk to and fro; turn back half way:～摸〈口〉look or scout for

嗹 xué 〈方〉laugh:发～ make one laugh; be facetious

嗹头 xuétóu 〈方〉❶ words or acts meant to amuse people or to elicit laughter ❷ tricks; gimmicks ❸ funny; farcical

xuě

雪 xuě ❶ snow:～崩 (snow) avalanche; snow-slide /～盲〈医〉snow blindness /～片 snowflake /～橇 sled; sledge; sleigh /～山 snow-capped mountain /～线〈地〉snow line ❷ snow-like:～白 white as snow; snow-white /～糕 ice lolly; popsicle ❸ wipe out (a humiliation, etc); avenge (a wrong, etc):～冤 clear (sb) of a false charge; redress a wrong

雪花 xuěhuā snowflake:～膏 vanishing cream

雪茄 xuějiā also "雪茄烟" cigar

雪里红 xuělǐhóng also "雪里蕻"〈植〉potherb mustard

雪亮 xuěliàng bright as snow; shiny (knife, etc); sharp (eyes, etc)

雪人 xuěrén ❶ human-like figure made of snow; snowman:堆～ make a snowman ❷ abominable snowman; Yeti; Bigfoot

雪上加霜 xuěshàngjiāshuāng add to the miseries of sb who is already unfortunate enough; rub salt into sb's wounds

雪中送炭 xuězhōngsòngtàn send charcoal in snowy weather — provide timely help; bring comfort to those in trouble

鳕 xué 〈动物〉cod

xuè

血 xuè ❶ blood；～癌 also "白血病" blood cancer；leukaemia／～案 homicide or murder case／～红 blood red／～迹 also "血斑"；"血渍" bloodstain／～库 blood bank／～泊 pool of blood；bloodbath／～清 serum／～书 letter written in one's own blood (expressing determination)；／～栓 thrombus／～洗 drench in bloodbath／～样 sample or specimen／～型 blood group or type／～脂 blood fat／～小板 (blood) platelet／～海深仇 huge debt of blood；intense and inveterate hatred ❷ related by blood；～亲 blood relations；consanguinity ❸ zeal；ardour；courage

see also xiě

血本 xuèběn principal；original capital；～无归 cannot even recover one's capital；lose every cent invested

血管 xuèguǎn 〈生理〉blood vessel；～瘤 angioma／～硬化 vascular sclerosis

血汗 xuèhàn blood and sweat；sweat of one's brow；～钱 money earned by onerous toil

血口喷人 xuèkǒupēnrén maliciously attack；venomously slander

血泪 xuèlèi blood and tears；tears of blood

血气 xuèqì ❶ sap；vitality；vigour；～方刚 full of sap or mettle；of hot blood ❷ *see* "血性"

血肉 xuèròu ❶ blood and muscle；～之躯 human body；flesh and blood；mortal flesh ❷ extremely close relationship；～相连 as close as flesh and blood

血色 xuèsè redness of the skin；colour：面无～ have little colour in the cheeks；look pale or pallid

血糖 xuètáng 〈医〉blood sugar；～低

hypoglycemia／～高 hyperglycemia

血统 xuètǒng blood relationship or lineage；extraction：中国～的外国人 foreign nationals of Chinese descent

血腥 xuèxīng reeking of blood；blood-thirsty；sanguinary；～屠杀 cold-blooded massacre

血性 xuèxìng upright and courageous；～男儿 brave and righteous man

血压 xuèyā 〈生理〉blood pressure；低～ low blood pressure；hypotension／高～ high blood pressure；hypertension

血液 xuèyè 〈生理〉blood；～病 blood disease／～新 fresh blood；lifeline；backbone force

血缘 xuèyuán ties of blood；consanguinity；relationship by birth；～关系 blood relationship；consanguineity

血债 xuèzhài debt of blood；～累累 owe a mountain of blood debts；commit a string of murders

血战 xuèzhàn ❶ bloody or extremely fierce battle ❷ wage desperate struggle；～到底 fight to the last drop of one's blood；fight to the bitter end

谑 xuè 〈书〉joke；banter；tease

xūn

勋（勳） xūn ❶ meritorious service；exploit；achievement；～业 〈书〉meritorious service；great achievement ❷ *also* "勋章" medal；decoration

勋爵 xūnjué ❶ 〈史〉title of nobility conferred for meritorious service ❷ (UK) Lord

埙（壎） xūn ancient Chinese wind instrument，made of clay with one to six holes and shaped like an egg

熏（❶❷燻） xūn ❶ smoke；fumigate；臭气～天。It stinks to high heaven. ❷ treat (fish, etc) with smoke; smoke; ～肉 smoked meat / ～制 fumigate (with jasmine, etc); cure (meat, etc) by smoke; smoke ❸ pleasantly warm; genial;～风〈书〉warm southerly breeze *see also* xùn

熏染 xūnrǎn exert a gradual, corrupting influence on; corrupt

熏陶 xūntáo exert a gradual, uplifting influence on; foster; nurture

薰 xūn ❶〈书〉a kind of sweet grass; fragrance (of flowers, etc) ❷ *see* "熏❷"

醺 xūn drunk;醉～～ dead drunk; blotto

xún

旬 xún ❶ period of ten days;上～ first ten days of a month / ～刊 publication appearing once every ten days ❷ period of ten years in age;七～老人 old man of seventy

寻(尋) xún ❶ look for; search; seek; ～问 seek; explore; inquire / ～事 seek a quarrel; pick a fight / ～味 chew over (meaning of sth); ruminate; mull or think over / ～开心〈方〉make fun (of sb); joke (about sb or sth) / ～花问柳 frequent houses of ill fame or prostitution; visit brothels; go whoring ❷ ancient measure of length, equal to about eight chi (尺)

寻常 xúncháng ordinary; common; usual;～事 commonplace

寻访 xúnfǎng look for; try to find; inquire about; 寻亲访友 call on relatives and friends / 寻幽访胜 search for and visit secluded places of quiet beauty

寻根 xúngēn ❶ trace sth to its source; get to the bottom of things ❷ find the roots of one's family

寻呼 xúnhū beep-page; ～机 pager; beeper / ～台 beep-paging station

寻欢作乐 xúnhuān-zuòlè seek pleasure and make merry; indulge in sensual pleasures

寻觅 xúnmì try to find; seek; look for

寻求 xúnqiú seek; pursue; search for

寻死 xúnsǐ *also* "寻短见" (try to) commit suicide; try to kill oneself;～觅活 threaten to commit suicide

寻思 xúnsi meditate; ponder; contemplate

寻衅 xúnxìn pick a quarrel; provoke; ～滋事 kick up a row and make trouble

寻找 xúnzhǎo seek; search; look for; ～出路 try to find a way out

巡(巡) xún ❶ patrol; inspect; make one's rounds;～幸〈书〉(of a monarch) go on an inspection tour; tour / ～弋 (of warships) cruise; ply the waters / ～边员〈体〉linesman / ～洋舰〈军〉cruiser ❷〈量〉round of drinks:酒过三～ (when) the wine has gone round three times

巡查 xúnchá go on a tour of inspection; make one's rounds

巡航 xúnháng cruise; ～导弹 cruise missile

巡回 xúnhuí tour; go the rounds; make a circuit;～大使 roving ambassador / ～演出 performing tour

巡警 xúnjǐng ❶〈旧〉policeman ❷ patrolling police or policeman

巡礼 xúnlǐ ❶ visit a sacred land; make a pilgrimage ❷ tour; tour

巡逻 xúnluó go on patrol; patrol; ～队 patrol (party) / ～艇 patrol boat

巡视 xúnshì ❶ make an inspection tour; tour;～员 inspector ❷ look around

巡游 xúnyóu ❶ saunter; stroll ❷ (of police) patrol

询 xún *also* "询问" ask; inquire; consult

荨(蕁) xún *see also* qián

荨麻疹 xúnmázhěn *also* "风疹块"〈医〉nettle rash

浔(潯) xún 〈书〉waterside; water margin；江～ river bank

循 xún follow; abide by; act in accordance with；～例 follow the usual practice; act in accordance with precedents／～序渐进 proceed in an orderly and gradual way

循规蹈矩 xúnguī-dǎojǔ observe rules and follow orders docilely; conform to convention; toe the line

循环 xúnhuán circulate; cycle；～赛〈体〉round robin／～水 circulating water／～利用 cycling utilization／～小数〈数〉recurring decimal

循循善诱 xúnxúnshànyòu be good at giving systematic guidance; teach with skill and patience

鲟(鱘) xún 〈动物〉sturgeon

训 xùn ❶ lecture; instruct; train；～话 (give an) admonitory talk to subordinates／～令 instructions; orders; directive／～示 (give) instructions ❷ teachings; motto; example：遗～ teachings of the deceased ❸ explanation of words：～诂 interpretation of ancient texts; textual exegesis

训斥 xùnchì reprimand; rebuke; scold

训诫 xùnjiè ❶ admonish (subordinates, etc); advise ❷ 〈法〉rebuke; reprimand

训练 xùnliàn train; drill；～有素 well-trained

讯 xùn ❶ (usu 讯问) ask; inquire；〈法〉interrogate ❷ message; dispatch; news：简～ news in brief／～号 signal (sent by electro-magnetic wave, etc)／～息 message; wire signal

汛 xùn seasonal flood or high water；～期 flood or high-water season／～情 information on the flood situation

迅 xùn fast; swift；～即 immediately; at once／～疾 swift; rapid／～捷 fast; agile; quick／～猛 sudden and violent／～速 rapid; fast／～雷不及掩耳 as sudden or quick as a flash of lightning

驯 xùn ❶ tame and docile; gentle; obedient：～良 tractable; docile; tame／～顺 submissive; tame and docile ❷ tame; domesticate；～化 domesticate; tame

驯服 xùnfú ❶ docile; meek; tame ❷ tame; subdue; break in

驯鹿 xùnlù also "四不象" reindeer

驯养 xùnyǎng raise and train (animals); domesticate；～员 trainer; keeper

徇(狥) xùn ❶ comply with; give in to; submit or yield to；～情枉法 bend the law for the benefit of one's relatives or friends／～私舞弊 serve one's selfish interests by engaging in irregularities; resort to fraudulent practices for personal gain ❷ see "殉❷" xùn

逊(遜) xùn ❶ 〈书〉(of a monarch) abdicate；～位 abdicate one's throne ❷ unassuming; modest：～顺 self-effacing; unassuming; modest and docile ❸ 〈书〉inferior：～色 inferior; disappointing／稍～一筹 a shade inferior

殉 xùn ❶ also "殉葬" be buried alive with the dead ❷ sacrifice one's life for; die for：～国 die for one's country; give one's life for the country／～难 die for a just cause; die a martyr／～情 die or commit suicide for love／～职 die in line of duty

熏 xùn 〈方〉be poisoned or suffocated by coal gas　see also xūn

蕈 xùn 〈植〉gill fungus

Y

yā

丫 yā ❶ *also* "桠" (usu 枝丫 or 枝桠) bifurcation (at top end); fork (of a tree); branch ❷ (usu 小丫) 〈方〉 little girl

丫头 yātou ❶ girl ❷ *also* "丫鬟" slave or servant girl

压(壓) yā ❶ press; crush; hold or weigh down: ~垮 crush by pressure / ~价 force prices down; demand price reduction / ~实 (make) compact; ram ❷ bring pressure to bear on; force; overwhelm: 技~群芳 have incomparable skills / 以势~人 co-erce people with one's power / ~卷之作 one's best work or masterpiece ❸ keep under control; hold down or back: ~住火 hold back one's anger; control one's tem-per ❹ approach; get closer; near: ~境 press on to the border ❺ pigeonhole; shelve; hold up: ~船 hold up cargo ships in harbour / ~库 overstock ❻ take a risk on sth; stake: ~宝 *also* "押宝" gambling game played with dice under a bowl; stake; wager
see also yà

压倒 yādǎo overwhelm; overpower; subdue: ~多数 overwhelming majority / ~一切的任务 overriding task

压低 yādī lower; force down (prices, etc): ~声音说话 speak in a lower voice

压服 yāfú force to submit; coerce into submission: 压而不服 would not submit to coercion

压惊 yājīng help sb get over a shock (by entertaining)

压力 yālì ❶ 〈理〉 pressure: ~锅 pressure cooker ❷ pressure; strain; stress: 施加~ put pressure on; bring pressure to bear on / ~大的工作 stressful work

压迫 yāpò ❶ oppress; repress: ~者 oppressor ❷ 〈医〉 constrict: 有~感 feel a constriction (in the chest, etc)

压岁钱 yāsuìqián money given to a child as a lunar New Year gift

压缩 yāsuō ❶ compress; compact; condense: ~饼干 ship biscuit; hardtack ❷ reduce; cut down on: ~编制 reduce staff; downsize

压抑 yāyì constrain; inhibit; contain

压榨 yāzhà ❶ press; squeeze ❷ ex-ploit; fleece; bleed white

压阵 yāzhèn ❶ bring up the rear ❷ *also* "压场" keep order; keep things under control

压制 yāzhì ❶ suppress; stifle; repress: ~积极性 restrain or dampen sb's enthusiasm ❷ press: ~板 pressboard

压轴戏 yāzhòuxì *also* "压场戏"; "压台戏" last and best item on a theatrical programme; grand finale

呀 yā ❶ 〈叹〉 *indicating surprise*: ~, 车晚点了! Oh, the train is late. ❷ 〈象声〉 creak: ~的一声门开了。The door squeaked open.
see also ya

押 yā ❶ give (property, etc) as se-curity; mortgage; pawn: ~金 de-posit; security (money) / 一笔款 give mortgage loan ❷ detain (a suspect, etc); take away; take into custody ❸ accompany as an escort; escort; ~送 escort (a prisoner, etc to a place); escort (goods) in transport ❹ signature; mark made in place of signature

押解 yājiè ❶ take (a criminal, etc) away under escort; escort; ~出境 deport under escort ❷ also "押运" escort (goods) in transport; transport (goods) under escort

押韵 yāyùn also "压韵" rhyme

鸦 yā crow; ~雀无声 Silence reigns.

鸦片 yāpiàn also "雅片" opium; 吸~ smoke opium / ~鬼 opium addict

鸭 yā duck; 公~ drake / 小~ duckling / ~绒 duck's down; eiderdown / ~舌帽 peaked cap

鸭蛋 yādàn ❶ duck's egg; ~脸 oval face / ~青 pale blue ❷〈口〉(as a score) zero; 得了个~ get a zero; lay an egg

yá

牙 yá ❶ tooth; 剔~ pick one's teeth / ~床 also "牙龈"〈生理〉gum / ~膏 toothpaste / ~垢 dental calculus; tartar / ~签 toothpick / ~刷 toothbrush / ~痛 toothache ❷ ivory; ~雕 ivory carving ❸ sth shaped like a tooth; ~轮 gear (wheel)

牙碜 yáchen ❶ (of food) gritty ❷ (of language) vulgar; coarse

牙科 yákē〈医〉(department of) dentistry; ~医生 dentist; dental surgeon / ~诊所 dental clinic

牙口 yákou ❶ age of a draught animal as shown by the number of its teeth ❷ condition of an old person's teeth; 人老了，~不济了。I'm getting old and my teeth are no good.

牙牙 yáyá〈象声〉(of a baby) babble; ~学语 learn to speak

伢 yá (usu 伢崽 or 伢子)〈方〉child; kid

芽 yá ❶ bud; sprout; shoot ❷ sth resembling a bud or sprout; 肉~〈医〉granulation

蚜 yá also "蚜虫" aphid; aphis

崖 yá precipice; cliff; crag; ~壁 precipice; cliff; escarpment

涯 yá ❶ shore; bank; ~岸 embankment ❷ margin; bound; limit; 无边无~ boundless

睚 yá

睚眦必报 yázìbìbào seek revenge for the smallest grievance — be utterly narrow-minded and revengeful

衙 yá (usu 衙门) yamen, government office in dynastic China; ~内〈旧〉child of a high official / ~役 yamen runner

yǎ

哑(啞) yǎ ❶ mute; dumb; ~剧 dumb show; mime / ~铃〈体〉dumbbell ❷ (of voice) hoarse; husky; 把嗓子喊~了 shout oneself hoarse ❸ (usu 哑弹) (of shell, etc) dud

哑巴 yǎba dumb person; mute; 吃~亏 sustain an unmentionable loss or wrong / ~吃黄连，有苦说不出〈俗〉have to suffer in silence

哑口无言 yǎkǒuwúyán be left without an argument; be tongue-tied; be rendered speechless

哑谜 yǎmí puzzling remark; enigma; riddle; 打~ speak enigmatically; keep people guessing

哑然 yǎrán ❶〈书〉quiet; still; silent ❷ be struck dumb with amazement; ~失惊 be dumbfounded ❸ sound of laughing; laugh; ~失笑 be unable to suppress a laugh; cannot help laughing

哑语 yǎyǔ　sign language：打～ communicate by signs

雅 yǎ ❶ 〈书〉standard；proper；correct：～言 standard language ❷ refined；polished；elegant：～趣 good taste / ～士 refined scholar；person of refined taste ❸ 〈敬〉your：～教 your esteemed advice ❹ 〈书〉acquaintance；friendship：同窗之～ friendship of classmates ❺ 〈书〉usually；customarily：～爱丹青 take to painting；be keen on painting ❻ 〈书〉very；extremely：～以为美 consider sth very beautiful

雅观 yǎguān　(often used in the negative) refined (in manner, etc)；tasteful：很不～ unseemly；unsightly；boorish

雅号 yǎhào ❶ elegant name；〈敬〉your, his or her name ❷ 〈谑〉nickname

雅量 yǎliàng ❶ large-mindedness；magnanimity；generosity：有～ be broadminded ❷ great capacity for liquor

雅俗共赏 yǎsúgòngshǎng　(of a work of art, etc) be enjoyed by both highbrows and lowbrows；suit both refined and popular tastes

雅兴 yǎxìng　aesthetic mood or pretensions：无下棋之～ be in no mood to play chess

雅正 yǎzhèng ❶ 〈书〉standard；correct；appropriate (diction, etc) ❷ upright；honest；virtuous ❸ 〈套〉used when giving one's works as a gift：某某先生～ To Mr So and So with the compliments of the author

雅致 yǎzhì　refined；elegant；tasteful：陈设～ furnished in good taste

雅座 yǎzuò　private room (in a restaurant, etc)

yà

轧 yà ❶ flatten with a roller；roll or run over：～棉花 gin cotton ❷ squeeze or push out ❸ 〈象声〉(of a machine) click

see also zhá

亚（亞） yà ❶ inferior；second；sub-：～军 (in a sports contest) second place；runner-up / ～健康〈医〉sub-health / ～热带 subtropical zone；subtropics / 不～于任何人 not inferior to any one；second to none ❷ (Yà) (short for 亚洲) Asia：～运会 Asian Games

亚麻 yàmá 〈植〉flax：～布 linen (cloth)

亚马孙河 Yàmǎsūnhé　Amazon River, in South America

压（壓） yà　see also yā

压根儿 yàgēnr　(usu used in the negative) from the start；totally；altogether：～没这回事 It's sheer fabrication.

讶 yà 〈书〉be surprised, astonished or amazed

氩（氬） yà 〈化〉argon (Ar)

揠 yà

揠苗助长 yàmiáozhùzhǎng　see "拔苗助长" bámiáozhùzhǎng

ya

呀 ya 〈助〉variant of 啊, used after a word ending in a, e, i, o or ü：快点去～! Hurry up!　see also yā

yān

咽 yān 〈生理〉pharynx：～炎 pharyngitis　see also yàn；yè

咽喉 yānhóu ❶ pharynx and larynx；throat ❷ vital passage；key point：～要道 junction of strategic importance

恹（懨） yān

恹恹 yānyān 〈书〉weak and weary through illness; tired and ill; ～欲睡 feel sleepy from infirmity; be weak and drowsy

殷 yān (usu 殷红)〈书〉blackish or dark red　*see also* yīn

胭(臙) yān

胭脂 yānzhi　rouge:往脸上擦～ rouge one's cheeks

烟(煙、❹菸) yān ❶ smoke; ～筒 *also* "烟囱" chimney; funnel; stovepipe / ～消云散 vanish like smoke; melt into thin air ❷ mist; vapour: ～霭〈书〉mist and clouds / ～雾 smoke; mist; smog / ～雨 misty rain / ～波浩淼 vast expanse of mist-covered waters ❸ (of eyes) be irritated by smoke ❹ tobacco; cigarette: ～草 tobacco / ～袋 small-bowled, long-stemmed pipe / ～民 smoker; smoking population / ～丝 cut or pipe tobacco / ～头 *also* "烟蒂" cigarette end or stub / ～灰缸 ashtray ❺ (usu 大烟) opium ❻ *also* "烟子" soot

烟尘 yānchén ❶ smoke and dust ❷ beacon-fire and battle-dust — war

烟斗 yāndǒu (tobacco) pipe: ～嘴 bit (of a smoking pipe); mouthpiece

烟鬼 yānguǐ ❶ opium addict ❷ heavy or chain smoker

烟花 yānhuā ❶〈书〉beautiful scenery in spring ❷〈旧〉prostitute: ～街 streetwalker; prostitute / ～巷 red-light lane or district ❸ *see* "烟火❸"

烟火 yānhuǒ ❶ smoke and fire: 严禁～。Smoking and fire are strictly forbidden. ❷ cooked food: 不食人间～ not eat anything of this world; not belong to this world ❸ (yānhuo) *also* "烟花"; "焰火" fireworks: 放～ set off fireworks

烟幕 yānmù smokescreen: 放～ put up a smokescreen / ～弹 smoke shell or bomb; 〈喻〉smokescreen

烟瘾 yānyǐn craving for tobacco: ～大 be a heavy smoker

焉 yān 〈书〉❶ here; this ❷ (often used in a rhetorical question) how; why: ～能不去? How can I not go there? ❸〈助〉used to round off a sentence: 吾行将就木～。I already have one foot in the grave.

阉 yān ❶ castrate; spay: ～割 castrate; spay / 〈喻〉emasculate ❷ (usu 阉党 or 阉人)〈书〉〈贬〉eunuch

淹 yān ❶ flood; inundate; submerge: ～没 submerge; inundate / ～死 drown ❷ tingle or smart from sweat ❸〈书〉wide; extensive: 学问～博 erudite; very learned

腌(醃) yān preserve in salt, sugar, etc; salt; pickle: ～肉 salted meat; bacon / ～黄瓜 pickled cucumber

湮 yān 〈书〉❶ (usu 湮没) be consigned to oblivion; be neglected or forgotten ❷ silt up

嫣 yān 〈书〉pretty; beautiful; handsome: ～然一笑 give a charming or sweet smile

燕 Yān (northern) Hebei; ～京 old name for Beijing (北京) *see also* yàn

yán

延 yán ❶ prolong; extend; lengthen; ～绵 be continuous; stretch long and unbroken / ～年益寿 (of a tonic, etc) prolong life; contribute to longevity ❷ postpone; put off: ～迟 delay; postpone; defer / ～期 extend; postpone; put off ❸〈书〉engage; employ: ～师 hire a teacher

延长 yáncháng lengthen; prolong; extend

延缓 yánhuǎn postpone; put off; slow down

延聘 yánpìn ❶ also "延请"〈书〉engage; employ ❷ prolong or extend the employment of (sb)：～一年 be employed for another year (beyond retirement, etc)

延伸 yánshēn stretch; extend; lengthen

延误 yánwù incur loss through delay; miss：～时机 miss an opportunity through delay

延续 yánxù continue; prolong; last：～性 continuity

芫 yán

芫荽 yánsuī 〈植〉coriander

严(嚴)

yán ❶ tight：～丝合缝 fit together perfectly; dovetail;〈喻〉be watertight / ～守机密 keep a secret closely ❷ strict; rigorous：～办 deal with (sb) strictly; punish (sb) with severity / ～防 take strict precautions (against); be on full alert (for) / ～令 also "严命" order rigorously or strictly / ～打斗争 (launch a) campaign to crack down on crime / ～以律己，宽以待人 be strict with oneself and lenient with others ❸ heavy; severe; extreme：～冬 severe winter / ～寒 icy cold; bitter cold

严惩 yánchéng mete out severe punishment; punish severely：～不贷 punish without mercy

严词 yáncí in strong terms; in stern words：～拒绝 sternly rebuff; categorically reject

严格 yángé ❶ strict; rigorous; stringent：～要求自己 be strict with oneself ❷ enforce rigorously; regulate strictly：～物价管理 strictly regulate commodity prices

严谨 yánjǐn ❶ careful and prudent; circumspect; scrupulous ❷ meticulous; precise and exact; 措词～ precise and measured wording

严峻 yánjùn ❶ stern; rigorous;

grim：面容～ look stern; wear a stern expression ❷ grave; serious; severe

严酷 yánkù ❶ harsh; bitter; grim：～的考验 grim test ❷ cruel; merciless ruthless

严厉 yánlì stern; harsh; severe

严密 yánmì ❶ compact; well-knit ❷ tight; close; meticulous ❸ make compact; tighten：～规章制度 tighten up the rules and regulations

严明 yánmíng ❶ strict and impartial ❷ rigorously enforce：～纪律 enforce discipline strictly

严实 yánshí ❶ tight; close：把瓶子盖～ cap a bottle tight / (hide sth) in safety

严肃 yánsù ❶ (of expression, etc) serious; stern; grave ❷ (of manner, etc) strict; exacting; severe ❸ tighten up; enforce strictly

严刑 yánxíng cruel or harsh punishment; torture：～峻法 draconian law / ～拷打 subject sb to torture

严阵以待 yánzhènyǐdài be fully prepared for any eventuality：～的战士 soldiers in combat readiness

严整 yánzhěng ❶ in neat formation under strict discipline ❷ meticulous; scrupulous

严正 yánzhèng solemn and just; stern and principled：～抗议 (lodge a) stern protest (with sb against sth)

严重 yánzhòng serious; grave; severe：～障碍 formidable obstacle / ～急性呼吸综合征 (commonly called 非典〈医〉severe acute respiratory syndrom (SARS)

言 yán ❶ speech; remark; word

～简意赅 brief and to the point concise and thorough / ～外之意 also "言下之意" what is actually meant implication / ～为心声 words are the voice of the mind; what the heart thinks the tongue speaks / ～之无物 (of speech or writing) lacking in sub stance; devoid of content / ～多必失。He who talks much is bound to err. ❷ say; talk; speak; ～不由衷 speak insincerely; speak tongue in cheek / ～而无信 fail to keep faith; break one's word / ～过其实 overstate; blow up; make a mountain out of a molehill / ～之成理 also "言之有理" sound reasonable; speak in a convincing way ❸ character; word; 万～书 petition of ten thousand words

言传 yánchuán express or explain in words; teach or instruct verbally; ～身教 teach by precept and example / 难以～ indescribable; beyond words

言辞 yáncí also "言词" words; remarks; speech; 不善～ not good at expressing oneself / ～犀利 use sharp words; speak daggers

言归于好 yánguīyúhǎo become reconciled; make it up (with sb)

言归正传 yánguīzhèngzhuàn to come back to our story; to return to the subject

言和 yánhé make peace; bury the hatchet; 握手～ shake hands in reconciliation; shake hands and make it up

言论 yánlùn opinion on public affairs; ～自由 freedom of speech

言情 yánqíng (of works) romantic; sentimental; ～小说 romantic fiction; sentimental novel

言谈 yántán the way one speaks; what one says; ～举止 speech and bearing

言听计从 yántīng-jìcóng act upon whatever sb says; always follow sb's advice

言行 yánxíng words and deeds; speech and action; 言出必行 be as good as one's word; keep one's promise / ～不一。One's deeds do not match one's words.

言语 yányǔ ❶ spoken language; speech; ～不清 mumble indistinctly ❷ (yányu) 〈方〉speak; answer; 不爱～ quiet; reticent

妍 yán 〈书〉beautiful; enchanting; 不辨～媸 unable to tell what is beautiful and what is ugly

岩(巖) yán ❶ rock; ～洞 grotto / ～浆〈地〉magma / ～石 rock ❷ rock cliff; crag; ～画 cliff carving; rock painting

炎 yán ❶ scorching; extremely hot; ～热 (of weather) scorching; blazing; sweltering / ～暑 hot or sultry summer; summer heat ❷ inflammation; ～症 inflammation ❸ 〈喻〉power; influence; 世态～凉 snobberies of the world ❹ (Yán) (usu 炎帝) Yandi or Red Emperor, regarded as one of the original ancestors of the Chinese nation; ～黄子孙 descendants of Yandi and Huangdi; the Chinese nation

沿 yán ❶ along; ～岸 along the bank or coast; littoral / ～途 along the road; on the way ❷ follow or conform to (tradition, etc); ～例办理 act according to precedents; follow established practice ❸ edge; brim; border; 缸～儿 edge of a jar ❹ trim (with tape, ribbon, etc)

沿革 yángé course of change and development; evolution

沿海 yánhǎi along the coast; coastal; offshore; ～岛屿 offshore island / ～国家 littoral state

沿袭 yánxí carry on as before; continue; follow; ～陈规 keep to the beaten track; follow convention

沿用 yányòng continue to use or employ (an old method, etc)

研 yán ❶ grind; rub; pestle; ～磨 grind; pestle; polish / ～墨 rub an ink stick on an inkslab ❷ study; research; ～读 read intensively; study assiduously / ～发 research and develop (R & D) / ～习 study

研究 yánjiū ❶ study; research; ～生

postgraduate (student); graduate student / ～员 research fellow; researcher / ～院 research institute; academy; graduate school ❷ consider; study; deliberate on (problems, etc)

研讨 yántǎo　deliberate; discuss; ～会 workshop; seminar; symposium

研制 yánzhì　research and manufacture; develop

盐(鹽) yán salt; 精～ refined
salt / ～卤 bittern / ～水 salt solution; brine / ～酸 〈化〉hydrochloric acid / ～碱地 saline-alkali soil

阎 yán

阎王 Yánwang　❶ also "阎罗"; "阎王爷" 〈宗教〉Yama; King of Hell; 见～ kick the bucket; die ❷ extremely cruel person, usu referring to a local tyrant; ～账 〈口〉usury; shark's loan

筵 yán also "筵席" banquet; feast

颜 yán ❶ face; look; countenance; ～容枯槁 look haggard ❷ decency; face; 无～见人 feel too ashamed to see anyone ❸ dye; colour; ～料 pigment; colour; dyestuff

颜面 yánmiàn　❶ face ❷ decency; face; ～扫地 lose face completely; be thoroughly discredited

颜色 yánsè　❶ colour; hue ❷ 〈书〉countenance; complexion ❸ facial expression ❹ look worn or action taken to warn or punish sb; 给他们点～看。 Teach them a lesson. ❺ (yánshai) 〈口〉pigment; dyestuff

檐(簷) yán ❶ eaves
ledge; brim; 帽～ visor of a cap; brim of a hat

yǎn

奄 yǎn 〈书〉❶ (usu 奄有) cover;
overspread ❷ (usu 奄忽) sud-

denly; all of a sudden

奄奄 yǎnyǎn　feeble breathing; ～一息 at one's last gasp; on one's last legs

俨(儼) yǎn 〈书〉❶ majestic;
serious; dignified ❷ (usu 俨如) just as; like

俨然 yǎnrán　〈书〉❶ (of look, etc) solemn; majestic; dignified ❷ neatly arranged; in apple-pie order ❸ just as; like; ～是位行家 behave like an expert

衍 yǎn 〈书〉❶ spread out; de-
velop; unfold; ～变 also "衍化" develop; evolve ❷ redundant; superfluous; ～文 redundant word (due to misprinting or miscopying)

衍生 yǎnshēng　❶ derive; evolve; ～物 〈化〉derivative ❷ multiply; produce

掩 yǎn ❶ cover; conceal; hide; ～
藏 cover up; hide; conceal / ～埋 bury / ～人耳目 deceive the public; fool people ❷ close; shut (door, etc) ❸ 〈方〉get (one's fingers, etc) caught in the door, etc ❹ (usu 掩杀 or 掩袭) 〈书〉attack by surprise

掩蔽 yǎnbì　cover; camouflage; ～物 cover; screen

掩耳盗铃 yǎn'ěr dàolíng　practise self-deception (in wrongdoing); bury one's head in the sand like an ostrich

掩盖 yǎngài　❶ cover; overspread ❷ hide; conceal; cover up (a crime, etc)

掩护 yǎnhù　screen; shield; cover; ～火力 covering fire

掩饰 yǎnshì　cover up; gloss over; conceal

掩映 yǎnyìng　set off (one another)

眼 yǎn ❶ eye; ～底 〈生理〉eye
ground / ～尖 be sharp-eyed; have sharp eyes / ～泪 tears / ～生 look unfamiliar / ～药 eyedrops; eye ointment / ～睫毛 eyelash / ～里没人 look down upon everyone else / ～冒金星 see stars / 明手快 also "眼疾手快" quick of eye and deft of hand; agile / ～见为实。〈俗〉Seeing is believing. ❷

small hole:扎个～儿 punch a hole ❸ key point; crux ❹ unaccented beat in traditional Chinese music ❺〈量〉used of a well or cave-dwelling:打一～井 sink a well

眼巴巴 yǎnbābā ❶ (of expectation) eager; anxious ❷ also "眼睁睁" unable to do anything to help; helpless

眼馋 yǎnchán eye covetously; covet; envy

眼福 yǎnfú fortune to see sth rare or beautiful:大饱～ feast one's eyes (on sth); have an eyeful (of sth)

眼高手低 yǎngāo-shǒudī have high standards but little ability; be fastidious but incompetent

眼光 yǎnguāng ❶ eye:投以期待的～ eye (sb) with expectation ❷ sight; foresight; vision:～短浅 shortsighted ❸ viewpoint; standpoint; outlook:把～放远点 see things in a broader perspective

眼红 yǎnhóng ❶ covetous; envious; jealous ❷ with flaming eyes; furious

眼花 yǎnhuā have dim eyesight or blurred vision:～缭乱 dazed; dazzled

眼界 yǎnjiè field of vision or view; outlook

眼睛 yǎnjing eye:～向下 look towards the grassroots; concern oneself with the common people

眼镜 yǎnjìng glasses; spectacles:配～ have one's glasses made / ～店 optician's

眼镜蛇 yǎnjìngshé cobra

眼看 yǎnkàn ❶ soon; in no time:～就要天亮了. It's almost daybreak. ❷ watch helplessly; look on indifferently:～着不管 stand by and look on

眼科 yǎnkē (department of) ophthalmology; eye department:～医生 ophthalmologist; oculist; eye-doctor

眼力 yǎnlì ❶ eyesight; vision ❷ judgement; discernment; perceptiveness:有～ have an eye (for sth); be good at judgement; be discerning

眼皮 yǎnpí eyelid:单～ single-edged eyelid / ～底下 right before one's eyes; under one's nose / ～子浅 shortsighted; easily pleased; shallow

眼前 yǎnqián ❶ before one's eyes ❷ at the present time; at the moment; now:～利益 immediate interests

眼圈 yǎnquān also "眼眶" rim of the eye; eye socket; orbit:～发黑 have livid rings round one's eyes / ～红了 be about to cry; be on the verge of tears

眼热 yǎnrè covet; envy:让人～的高工资 attractive high salary

眼色 yǎnsè meaningful glance; wink:使～ also "递眼色" wink at sb; tip sb the wink / 看人～ take one's cue from sb; be at sb's beck and call

眼神 yǎnshén ❶ expression in one's eyes ❷〈方〉eyesight; sight

眼下 yǎnxià at present; right now

眼线 yǎnxiàn ❶ eye-line ❷ scout-cum-guide; informer; snitch

眼中钉 yǎnzhōngdīng thorn in one's side; eyesore

眼拙 yǎnzhuō 〈套〉used when one forgets seeing sb before:恕我～，您贵姓? Please forgive me for my poor memory. May I know your name?

偃 yǎn 〈书〉❶ fall on one's back; lie down ❷ desist; stop; cease:～旗息鼓 stop fighting; cease to criticize or attack (sb); be on a secret (and silent) march

演 yǎn ❶ develop; evolve:～化 develop; evolve / ～进 gradual progress; evolution ❷ elaborate; deduce ❸ drill, practise or calculate (according to a set pattern, etc):～兵场 drill ground ❹ perform; play; act:～唱 sing (in a performance); act a part in traditional opera / ～员 actor or actress; performer; player

演变 yǎnbiàn change; develop; evolve

演播 yǎnbō　televise or broadcast (performances, etc): ～室 (television) studio

演出 yǎnchū　perform; show; put on (a show): 首次～ first performance; première / ～单位 producer

演讲 yǎnjiǎng　also "演说" (give a) lecture; (make or deliver a) speech: ～家 public speaker; elocutionist / ～技巧 public-speaking technique

演示 yǎnshì　demonstrate: 用～方法进行教学 teach through demonstration

演算 yǎnsuàn　make or perform mathematical calculations: ～习题 do sums

演习 yǎnxí　manoeuvre; exercise; drill: 消防～ fire drill

演戏 yǎnxì　❶ put on a play; act in a play ❷ play-act; pretend

演义 yǎnyì　(historical) novel or romance

演艺 yǎnyì　performing arts: ～界 circle of performing artists

演绎 yǎnyì　deduction: ～法 deductive method; deduction ❷ evolve; develop; bring forth

演奏 yǎnzòu　play (a musical instrument) in a performance

魇(魘) yǎn　(have a) nightmare

魇(魘) yǎn

魇鼠 yǎnshǔ　〈动物〉〈喻〉mole

yàn

厌(厭) yàn　❶ be satisfied or satiated: 学而不～ have an insatiable desire to learn ❷ be bored of; be bored or disgusted with; detest: ～恨 bitterly detest; loathe; abhor / ～世 be sick of life; be world-weary / ～战 be war-weary

厌烦 yànfán　be sick of; be bored with: ～的心情 boredom

厌倦 yànjuàn　be weary or tired of: ～的情绪 ennui

厌食 yànshí　❶ loss of appetite ❷ also "厌食症" 〈医〉anorexia

厌恶 yànwù　detest; abhor; loathe

砚 yàn　also "砚台"; "砚池" inkstone; inkslab

咽(嚥) yàn　❶ swallow; devour: ～气 breathe one's last; die / 一口一下去 swallow at one gulp ❷ hold back; check: ～不下这口气 be unable to swallow an insult, etc

see also yān; yè

艳(艷、豔) yàn　❶ bright; fresh and attractive; gorgeous: ～丽 bright-coloured; gorgeous; flowery / 一如桃李 (of a woman) gorgeously beautiful ❷ amorous; romantic: ～福 (of a man) fortune to win the favour of a beauty / ～史 love story; amorous adventure / ～情小说 love novel; amorous fiction; erotica

艳羡 yànxiàn　〈书〉very much envy: 不胜～ be green with envy

艳阳 yànyáng　❶ radiant sun ❷ also "艳阳天" bright sunny skies; bright spring day

晏 yàn　❶ behind time; late: ～起 get up late ❷ ease and comfort

唁 yàn　extend condolences: ～电 telegram or message of condolence

宴 yàn　❶ entertain at dinner; fete ❷ also "宴席" feast; banquet; spread ❸ ease and comfort

宴会 yànhuì　banquet; feast; dinner party: ～厅 banquet hall

宴请 yànqǐng　entertain at a banquet; fete: ～宾客 entertain or fete guests

验(驗、騐) yàn　❶ examine; check; test: ～光 have one's eyesight measured / ～尸 〈法〉(hold a) postmortem; autopsy / ～血 (have a) blood test / ～电

正身 identify the criminal (before execution) ❷ prove effective; produce the expected result;～方〈中医〉proved recipe; ready prescription / 屡试屡～ prove effective in every test

验收 yànshōu　accept sth as up to standard after a check; check and accept

验算 yànsuàn　〈数〉check computations;～公式 check formula

验证 yànzhèng　test and verify; 得到～ be verified

谚 yàn　also "谚语" proverb; saying; saw

堰 yàn　weir; dam; barrage

雁(鴈)　yàn　wild goose;～行 orderly ranks of wild geese in flight / ～过拔毛〈喻〉catch every chance to seek gain; fleece whomever possible

焰(燄)　yàn　flame; blaze

焰火 yànhuǒ　see "烟火❸" yānhuo

酽(釅)　yàn　(of tea, etc) thick; strong

燕　yàn　swallow;～窝 edible bird's nest / ～尾服 swallow-tailed coat; tails　see also Yān

燕麦 yànmài　oats;～片 oatmeal

赝(贋)　yàn　〈书〉counterfeit; spurious; fake;～品 art forgery; fake relic

yāng

央　yāng ❶ entreat; beg; earnestly ask;～求 also "央告" beg; entreat; implore / ～人说情 ask sb to put in a good word for one ❷ centre;～行 central bank (of a country) ❸〈书〉end; finish; 夜未～ night is not over yet — in the small hours

泱　yāng

泱泱 yāngyāng　〈书〉❶ (of waters) vast ❷ great; magnificent;～大国 great country

殃　yāng　(bring) disaster; (spell) calamity;～及无辜 spell calamity for innocent people

秧　yāng ❶ seedling; sprout; (esp) rice seedling;～田 (rice) seedling bed ❷ vine; stem; 瓜～ melon vines ❸ (of some domestic animals) young; 鱼～ young fish; fry

秧歌 yāngge　yangge, a popular rural folk dance; 扭～ do the yangge dance

yáng

扬(揚、颺)　yáng ❶ raise; hoist;～尘 raise dust; blowing or shifting dust / ～帆 set sail / ～声器 loudspeaker / ～眉吐气 hold one's head high; feel happy and proud ❷ fly upward; flutter;～升 (of prices, etc) soar; skyrocket ❸ spread; publicize; make known;～威海外 show one's might overseas

扬长避短 yángcháng-bìduǎn　avoid one's weaknesses while exploiting one's strengths; make the best use of advantages and fight shy of disadvantages

扬长而去 yángcháng'érqù　swagger off; stalk off

扬场 yángcháng　〈农〉winnow;～机 winnowing machine; winnower

扬名 yángmíng　make a name for oneself; win renown

扬弃 yángqì　❶〈哲〉sublate; develop what is useful and discard what is not ❷ abandon; discard

扬汤止沸 yángtāngzhǐfèi　try to stop water from boiling by scooping it up and pouring it back — adopt a halfway solution; take ineffective measures

扬言 yángyán　prate; boast; threaten (to take action)

决　yāng

扬扬 yángyáng　also "洋洋" with great self-satisfaction; complacently; triumphantly; ～得意 proud and happy; as pleased or proud as Punch

羊 yáng sheep; goat; ～羔 lamb / ～毫 writing brush made of goat's hair / ～圈 sheepfold; sheep pen / 绒 cashmere / ～肠小道 narrow winding trail; meandering footpath

羊角风 yángjiǎofēng　also "羊痫风" (popular term for 癫痫) epilepsy

羊毛 yángmáo sheep's wool; fleece; 剪～ shear a sheep / ～衫 woollen sweater / ～出在羊身上〈俗〉you pay for what you get; there is no free lunch

羊皮 yángpí sheepskin; ～纸 parchment / 披着～的狼 wolf in sheep's clothing

羊肉 yángròu mutton; ～串 mutton cubes roasted on a skewer; shish kebab

羊水 yángshuǐ〈生理〉aminiotic fluid

阳(陽) yáng ❶ (in traditional philosophy) *yang*, the masculine or positive principle in nature ❷ sun; ～光 sunlight; sunshine / ～历 solar calendar / ～伞 parasol; sunshade / ～台 balcony; sun porch ❸ south of a hill or north of a river ❹ in relief; convex; ～文 character cut in relief ❺ open; overt; outward; ～奉阴违 agree in public but oppose in private; feign compliance ❻ of this world or life; ～间 in this (human) world ❼〈理〉positive; ～极〈电〉positive pole; positive electrode; anode ❽ male genitals; ～痿〈医〉erectile dysfunction (ED); sexual impotence

阳春 yángchūn (warm) spring (season); ～白雪 highbrow art and literature

阳刚 yánggāng masculinity; virility; ～之美 beauty of manly virility

阳关道 yángguāndào　also "阳关大道" broad road; thoroughfare; 你走你的～, 我走我的独木桥〈俗〉You go your way; I'll go mine.

阳平 yángpíng〈语言〉second tone in modern standard Chinese　see also "四声" sìshēng

阳性 yángxìng ❶〈医〉positive; 呈～反应 test positive (for sth) ❷〈语言〉masculine gender

杨(楊) yáng poplar; ～柳 (poplar and) willow

杨梅 yángméi ❶〈植〉red bayberry ❷〈方〉strawberry

佯 yáng pretend; feign; sham; ～攻〈军〉feign an attack; make a feint / ～死 sham dead; feign death; play possum / ～言〈书〉claim falsely; lie / ～作不知 pretend not to know; feign ignorance

疡(瘍) yáng ❶〈书〉sore ❷ ulcer

洋 yáng ❶ vast; abundant ❷ ocean; ～流 ocean current ❸ foreign; imported; Western; ～房 Western-style house / ～为中用 make foreign things serve China; adapt foreign things to Chinese use ❹ modern; ～办法 modern methods ❺ (usu 洋钱 or 大洋)〈旧〉silver dollar

洋白菜 yángbáicài　also "圆白菜" (popular term for 结球甘蓝) cabbage

洋葱 yángcōng　also "葱头" onion

洋泾浜 yángjīngbāng pidgin (English)

洋奴 yángnú flunkey of imperialism; worshipper of everything foreign; ～思想 slavish mentality towards foreigners and foreign things; fetish of everything foreign

洋气 yángqì ❶ foreign flavour; Western style ❷ foreign; outlandish; stylish; 洋里～〈贬〉in a flashy foreign style

洋洋 yángyáng ❶ abundant; copious; ～大观 of great variety and richness; spectacular; magnificent / ～洒洒 (of an article or a talk) fluent; voluminous; great in scale or momentum ❷ see "扬扬" yángyáng

洋溢 yángyì　brim or overflow with; be full of：豪情～ full of lofty sentiments

yǎng

仰 yǎng　❶ look up; face upward：～视 raise one's eyes; look up / ～泳〈体〉(do the) backstroke / ～天长叹 throw up one's head and sigh deeply; lament loudly / ～卧起坐〈体〉sit-ups ❷ admire; revere; look up to：～慕 admire; hold in high esteem ❸ rely or depend on：～赖 rely or depend on / ～望 look up (to)：respectfully seek guidance or advice from / ～仗 count on; look to sb for support / ～人鼻息 be slavishly dependent on sb; be at sb's beck and call

养(養) yǎng　❶ support; keep; provide for：～家 糊口 support a family; have a family to provide for ❷ raise; keep; grow：～蜂 bee-keeping; apiculture / ～花 grow flowers ❸ give birth to：～儿方知父母恩。〈俗〉You don't fully appreciate your parents' love and care for you until you have a child yourself. ❹ adoptive; foster：～女 adopted or foster daughter ❺ form; cultivate; refine：～神 repose or cultivate one's nature or natural character ❻ nourish; recuperate; keep in good condition：～病 rest and recuperate / ～分 nutrient / ～护 maintain (roads, etc)；conserve / ～料 nourishment; nutriment ❼ foster; support：以工～农 foster agriculture by industry

养活 yǎnghuo　support; keep; feed ❷ give birth to and rear

养精蓄锐 yǎngjīng-xùruì　conserve energy and build up strength; store up (one's) energy

养老 yǎnglǎo　❶ provide for the aged (esp one's parents)：～金 old-age pension / ～院 home for the aged / ～保险 endowment insurance ❷ live out one's life in retirement

养生 yǎngshēng　preserve one's health; keep in good health：～之道 way to stay healthy

养痈成患 yǎngyōngchénghuàn　also "养痈遗患" a boil neglected becomes the bane of one's life; appeasement means no end of trouble

养育 yǎngyù　bring up; rear：报答父母之恩 repay one's parents for their loving care

养殖 yǎngzhí　breed; cultivate：～场 (breeding) farm / ～业 breeding and farming industry

养尊处优 yǎngzūn-chǔyōu　enjoy a high position and a life of ease and comfort; live in clover

氧 yǎng　(usu 氧气)〈化〉oxygen (O)：～吧 oxygen bar (for oxygen therapy) / ～化 oxidize; oxidate

痒(癢) yǎng　itch; tickle：浑身发～ feel itchy or itch all over

yàng

怏 yàng

怏怏 yàngyàng　disgruntled; morose：～不得志 sullen with frustration

样(樣) yàng　❶ shape; appearance; expression：长得跟母亲一个～儿 take after one's mother ❷ sample; model; pattern：～机 prototype (plane or machine) / ～片 (of a film) rushes; work print; sample film / ～图 master drawing ❸〈量〉kind; type; variety：～～俱全 all available

样板 yàngbǎn　❶ sample plate; template ❷ model; example：树～ set an example

样本 yàngběn　sample (book); specimen; 服装～ dress pattern book

样品 yàngpǐn　sample (product); specimen; 符合～规格 come up to sample; comply with sample

样式 yàngshì　pattern; style; fashion; 流行的～ latest fashions / ～别致 (of) novel design

样子 yàngzi　❶ appearance; expression; shape; 显出不高兴的～ look unhappy / 看～要下雨. It looks like rain. ❷ sample; model; pattern; 时装～ fashion pattern

恙 yàng　〈书〉ailment; illness; indisposition

漾 yàng　❶ ripple ❷ brim over; overflow; 脸上～出笑容 brim with a smile

yāo

幺 yāo　❶ (used orally for the numeral 一) one ❷〈方〉youngest; ～妹 youngest sister

夭 yāo　❶ die young; ～折 die young; come to a premature end ❷〈书〉luxuriant; exuberant

吆 yāo

吆喝 yāohe　shout; hawk (wares); loudly urge (on) an animal

吆五喝六 yāowǔ-hèliù　shout when playing dice; 〈方〉be domineering or overbearing

约 yāo　weigh; ～斤葡萄 weigh out half a kilo of grapes (for a customer); (of a customer) buy half a kilo of grapes　see also yuē

妖 yāo　❶ monster; demon; evil spirit; ～怪 monster; devil; demon / ～精 evil spirit; seductress / ～孽〈书〉thing associated with evil or misfortune; evil spirit; evildoer / ～术 black magic; witchcraft; sorcery / 魔鬼怪 monsters of every description / ～言惑众 spread fallacies to hoodwink the public; stir up public feeling by sophistry ❷ (of a woman) coquettish; seductive; ～媚 seductively charming; bewitching / ～艳 pretty and flirtatious / ～里～气 coquettish or sexy in an evil way ❸ (usu 妖娆) charming; enchanting

要 yāo　❶ (usu 要求) demand; claim; ask ❷ force; compel; coerce; ～挟 coerce or threaten by taking advantage of sb's weakness; blackmail　see also yào

腰 yāo　❶ waist; small of the back; ～包 purse; pocket; wallet / ～带 waistband; belt; girdle / ～鼓 waist drum (dance) / ～围 waistline ❷ pocket; purse; wallet; ～缠万贯 roll in money; be very rich ❸ middle; 拦～切断 cut in the middle; cut in half ❹ waist-like terrain; 海～ strait

腰板儿 yāobǎnr　❶ waist and back; 挺直～ straighten one's back ❷ physique; 硬朗 hale and hearty

腰杆子 yāogǎnzi　❶ see "腰板儿❶" ❷ backing; support; ～硬 have strong backing

腰果 yāoguǒ　cashew

腰身 yāoshēn　waistline (of a person); waist (measurement); girth; 收～ take in the waist of a dress

腰子 yāozi　(popular term for 肾) kidney

邀 yāo　❶ invite; ask; request; ～集 invite or ask a group of people to meet; call together ❷〈书〉gain; seek; ～功 also "要功" claim credit for non-existent or sb else's achievements / ～买人心 seek popularity; buy popular support ❸ (usu 邀击 or 邀截) intercept

邀请 yāoqǐng　invite (for specific purposes); ～国 host country / ～赛 invitational tournament

yáo

爻 yáo　lines which form the eight trigrams (八卦)：阳～ whole line ("—")／阴～ broken line "- -")

尧(堯) Yáo

尧舜 Yáo-Shùn　Yao and Shun, legendary model rulers of remote antiquity；〈喻〉sages；人皆可为～. Everybody can become a Yao or Shun — human nature is virtuous.

肴(餚) yáo　meat and fish dishes；～馔〈书〉courses at a banquet；sumptuous food

窑(窰) yáo　❶ kiln：砖～ brick kiln ❷ (usu small and manually operated) pit：煤～ coal pit ❸ cave dwelling：～洞 cave dwelling ❹〈方〉brothel：～姐儿 whore；prostitute／逛～子 visit a brothel；go whoring

谣 yáo　❶ ballad；rhyme ❷ rumour；hearsay：传 as it is rumoured；according to hearsay；rumour／～言 rumour；hearsay；gossip

摇 yáo　shake；wave；rock：～撼 rock or shake violently；shake to the roots or foundation／～奖 lottery／～椅 rocking chair／～身一变 change into another form at an instant／～尾乞怜 wag one's tail ingratiatingly；beg like a dog for mercy

摇摆 yáobǎi　sway；swing；waver：～舞 rock and roll；rock'n'roll／～不定 swing to and fro；chop and change；waver

摇荡 yáodàng　shake；rock；sway：随波～ sway on the waves

摇动 yáodòng　wave；shake；sway：彩旗～ wave coloured flags／随风～ sway or flutter in the wind

摇滚乐 yáogǔnyuè　big beat；rock'n'roll (music)

摇晃 yáohuàng　shake；sway；rock：～的桌子 shaky or rickety table／摇摇晃晃地站起身来 stagger to one's feet

摇篮 yáolán　cradle：～曲 lullaby；cradle song／中华文明的～ cradle of Chinese civilization

摇旗呐喊 yáoqínàhǎn　cheer or root (for sb)；boost (sb's) morale；drum up support (for sb)

摇钱树 yáoqiánshù　legendary money tree；〈喻〉milch or cash cow

摇头 yáotóu　shake one's head：～丸 Ecstasy (pill)，a narcotic／～晃脑 look very much pleased with oneself；assume an air of self-conceit

摇摇欲坠 yáoyáoyùzhuì　teetering on the verge of collapse；tottering；crumbling

摇曳 yáoyè　flicker；sway：树影～ swaying shadows of trees

遥 yáo　distant；remote；faraway：～测 remote monitoring or metering；telemetry／～望 look into the distance；look far／～相呼应 echo each other at a distance；coordinate with each other from afar

遥感 yáogǎn　〈信息〉remote sensing：～器 remote sensor

遥控 yáokòng　〈信息〉remote control；telecontrol／～飞行器 remotely piloted vehicle

遥想 yáoxiǎng　❶ think back；recollect；recall ❷ think of the future；envisage

遥遥 yáoyáo　❶ far distant or away；remote：～领先 be far ahead ❷ by a long time；far into the future：～无期 not in the foreseeable future

遥远 yáoyuǎn　distant；remote：相距～ far apart from each other／～的往事 time-honoured events；far-back memories

瑶 yáo　〈书〉❶ precious jade ❷ precious；wonderful：～浆 good wine

yǎo

杳 yǎo 〈书〉too far away to be readily accessible：～如黄鹤 also "杳无踪影" disappear without a trace; vanish into thin air / ～无音信 have absolutely no news about sb; (of sb) disappear for good and all

咬 yǎo ❶ bite; gnaw; snap at：～定 insist; assert / ～耳朵〈口〉whisper (in sb's ear) / ～紧牙关 grit or clench one's teeth; bite the bullet / ～牙切齿 clench or gnash one's teeth (in hatred) ❷ (of a dog) bark ❸ incriminate or implicate (sb innocent)：乱～好人 implicate innocent people indiscriminately ❹ pronounce; enunciate; articulate：～字儿清楚 have clear pronunciation; be articulate ❺ (usu 咬文嚼字) be fastidious or nitpicking (about the use of words) ❻ (usu 咬住) follow closely; close in; advance on：双方比分～得很紧。It's a close game.

窅 yǎo ladle out; scoop up：～子 dipper; ladle; scoop

窈 yǎo

窈窕 yǎotiǎo 〈书〉(of a girl) gentle and graceful：～淑女 graceful fair maiden

yào

药(藥) yào ❶ medicine; drug; remedy：～草 medicinal herb / ～典 pharmacopoeia / ～粉 also "药面" medicinal powder / ～膏 ointment; salve; plaster / ～酒 medicinal liquor / ～棉 absorbent cotton / ～片 (medicinal) tablet / ～膳 food cooked with medicinal herbs; medicated diet / ～丸 pill; bolus / ～罐子 pot for decocting herbal medicine；〈喻〉chronic patient; perennial invalid / ～剂师 pharmacist; druggist; chemist ❷ used of certain chemicals：火～ gunpowder ❸ 〈书〉cure with medicine：不～而愈 recover without medical treatment ❹ kill with poison：～蟑螂 poison cockroaches

药店 yàodiàn ❶ also "药房" drugstore; chemist's shop; pharmacy ❷ also "药铺" herbal medicine shop

药方 yàofāng prescription：开～ write out a prescription

药力 yàolì efficacy of a drug or medicine：充分发挥～ make the most of a drug

药品 yàopǐn medicines and chemical reagents：家庭备用～ family pharmacy

药石 yàoshí remedies：～之言 words that work like medicine; salutary advice / ～罔效。All medical treatment was in vain.

药物 yàowù medicines; pharmaceuticals; medicaments / ～过敏 drug allergy / ～牙膏 medicated toothpaste

药性 yàoxìng property of a medicine：～平和 mild medicine

要 yào ❶ important; significant; essential：～隘 strategic pass / ～案 major case / ～道 main artery or highway; thoroughfare / ～略 outline; summary; synopsis / ～人 very important person (VIP); bigwig / ～塞 fort; fortress; fortification / ～闻 important news; front-page story / ～员 high official ❷ want; ask for; demand：～价 ask or charge a price; demand or attach conditions / ～债 demand payment of a debt ❸ must; should; have to：～尊重老人。We must show respect for the old. ❹ require; need; take：～不得 no good; of no use; intolerable / 不～脸 shameless; impudent / ～多长时间？How long does it take? ❺ be going to; be about to：～过年了。The New Year is drawing near. ❻ if; suppose; in case：他～不同意怎么办？What if he doesn't agree? ❼ *used to indicate an estimation or a choice in comparison*：第二个方案～切实可行些。The second plan is more practicable.

see also yāo

要不 yàobù *also* "要不然" ❶ otherwise; or (else)：快走，～就晚了。Hurry up, or we'll be late. ❷ *also* "要么""要末" (either...) or...；～去看戏，～去听音乐。Let's go to a play or a concert.

要不是 yàobushì if it were not for; but for; without：～这场大雾，飞机就按时起飞了。But for the heavy fog, the plane would have taken off on time.

要点 yàodiǎn ❶ *also* "要旨" main points; essentials; gist ❷ key stronghold：战略～ strategic position

要饭 yàofàn beg (for food or money)：～的 beggar

要害 yàohài vital part (of one's body)；〈喻〉crucial or strategic point; crux：～部门 key department / 问题的～ crux of the matter

要好 yàohǎo ❶ be on good terms; be friends ❷ be eager to improve oneself; want to do well

要津 yàojīn ❶ *also* "要冲" important communication hub ❷ *also* "要职"〈书〉important post：位居～ occupy a key post

要紧 yàojǐn ❶ vital; important; essential ❷ serious; critical：他的病～吗？Is he very ill?

要领 yàolǐng ❶ main points; gist ❷ basic requirements (of an exercise or a skill); knack; essentials：掌握～ get the knack or hang of sth

要命 yàomìng ❶ cost one's life; drive one to one's death; kill；这是～的病。It's a fatal disease. ❷ *also* "要死" to an extreme degree; extremely; terribly：挤得～ packed like sardines ❸ nuisance：真～，我的表又慢了。What a nuisance! My watch is slow again.

要强 yàoqiáng be eager to excel in whatever one does; be anxious to outdo others

要是 yàoshi if; suppose; in case：～你有兴趣的话，咱们一起去。We can go together if you're interested.

要素 yàosù essential factor; crucial component; key element：成功的～ key factors of success

要言不烦 yàoyánbùfán concise and succinct in speech or in writing; terse

钥(鑰) yào

钥匙 yàoshi key：配～ have a key made (to fit a lock) / ～环 key ring

耀 yào

❶ shine; radiate; illuminate：～斑〈天文〉solar flare / ～眼 (of light) dazzling; blinding ❷ vaunt; show off; boast of：～武扬威 make a show of one's strength; show off one's prowess; swagger about ❸ (usu 荣耀) glory; honour; credit

yē

耶 yē

耶稣 Yēsū Jesus：～基督 Jesus Christ / ～诞辰 *also* "圣诞节" Christmas

掖 yē

tuck in or up; thrust in between：～好被子 tuck (sb) up

椰 yē

also "椰子" coconut (palm); coco：～蓉 coconut mash / ～汁 *also* "椰奶" coconut milk

噎 yē

❶ choke; be choked (as by wind or smoke) ❷ 〈方〉render (sb) speechless by saying sth blunt or rude; choke (sb) off

yé

爷(爺) yé

❶〈方〉father or grandfather ❷ respectful form of address for a man of the elder generation：大～ uncle ❸〈旧〉

form of address for an official or rich man：老～ lord; master; sir ❹ form of address for god：老天～ (King of) Heaven

爷们 yémen 〈方〉❶ man; menfolk ❷ husband; hubby

爷爷 yéye (paternal) grandfather; grandpa (also used as a respectful form of address for an old man)：王～ Grandpa Wang

揶 yé

揶揄 yéyú 〈书〉mock; ridicule; deride

也 yě

也 yě〈副〉❶ also; too; either：你不开口，我～不开口。If you don't speak, I shan't speak either. ❷ (used in pairs) both…and…; either…or…; as well as：他的个儿～高，力气～大。He's both tall and strong. ❸ used to indicate concession or resignation：我看一只好如此了。I'm afraid we'll have to leave it at that. ❹ often used together with 一点，连, etc for emphasis：这话一点～不错。There's nothing at all wrong with this remark. ❺〈书〉〈助〉used to indicate judgement, explanation, a question or a pause：来何疾～? How come it arrived so quickly? / 荀况者，赵人～。Xun Kuang was a native of the state of Zhao.

也罢 yěbà 〈助〉❶ used to indicate tolerance or resignation：他不同意～，不必勉强。It's alright if he doesn't agree. Don't force him. ❷ whether…or…; no matter whether：花～，鸟～，什么都引不起他的兴趣。Flowers or birds, nothing can arouse his interest.

也好 yěhǎo 〈助〉used to indicate agreement or approval：你讲一讲～。免得发生误会。It would be best for

you to give an explanation so as to avoid any misunderstanding. ❷ see "也罢❷"

也许 yěxǔ 〈副〉perhaps; maybe; probably

冶 yě

冶 yě ❶ smelt (metal)：～金 metallurgy / ～炼 smelt ❷〈书〉(of a woman) be coquettishly or seductively dressed；～容 seductive dress or make-up; bewitching or seductive appearance

野 yě

野 yě ❶ open country; wild land：～餐 picnic / ～炊 cook in the open; cook out / ～火 wildfire; prairie or bush fire / ～营 camp; bivouac / 富有～趣 full of idyllic or pastoral appeal ❷ not in power; out of office; unofficial：～史 unofficial history ❸ wild; uncultivated; undomesticated：～菜 edible wild herbs / ～人 savage; barbarian；〈喻〉boor / ～兽 wild beast or animal / ～兔 hare / ～味 game (as food) / ～种〈粗〉bastard / ～猪 wild boar ❹ rude; rough; wild：撒～ behave rudely ❺ unrestrained; unruly; undisciplined：～性 wild nature; unruliness / 把心玩儿～了 can't take one's mind off play

野鸡 yějī ❶ (popular term for 雉) pheasant ❷ street girl; streetwalker ❸ irregular; unlicensed：～大学 unlicensed university; diploma mill

野蛮 yěmán ❶ uncivilized; barbarian; savage：～人 savage; barbarian ❷ atrocious; barbarous; brutal：～行径 barbarous act

野生 yěshēng wild; uncultivated：～生物保护区 wildlife sanctuary or preserve

野外 yěwài open country; field：～作业 field operation

野心 yěxīn audacious or wild ambition; careerism：～家 careerist / ～勃勃 be overweeningly ambitious; burn with wild ambition; be thirsty for power

野战 yězhàn 〈军〉(conduct) field operations：～军 field army

yè

业(業) yè ❶ business; industry; occupation：～界 business circles or community / ～外人士 people from outside the industry or profession; outsiders ❷ (course of) study：～师 my (former) teacher / ～精于勤。Scholarship comes from diligence. ❸ estate; property：～主 owner of an estate, etc；proprietor ❹ (of Buddhism) karma; (usu evil or sinful) deed：～海 sea of sin; iniquity ❺ engage in; go in for：～商 engage in commerce; be in business ❻ (usu 业已) already; before now

业绩 yèjì ❶ outstanding achievement; exploit ❷ performance：～考核 performance evaluation

业务 yèwù vocational or professional work; business：～能力 professional competence

业余 yèyú ❶ sparetime; leisure：～爱好 hobby / ～兼职 sparetime job; moonlighting ❷ amateur (writer, etc)；nonprofessional

叶(葉) yè ❶ leaf; blade; foliage：～片 (leaf) blade / ～绿素〈植〉chlorophyll / ～落归根 falling leaves settle on their roots; a person residing away from his ancestral home eventually returns to it ❷ leaf-like thing：肺～ lobe of the lung ❸ see "页" ❹ part of a historical period；19世纪初～ early in the 18th century；(in the) early 1800's

叶公好龙 Yègōnghàolóng Lord Ye's love of dragons — professed love of what one does not really understand or even fears

页(頁) yè ❶ leaf; sheet; sth like a sheet；增～ supplementary sheet / ～码 page number / ～岩〈地〉shale ❷ 〈喻〉page：光辉的一～ a glorious page

曳 yè drag; haul; pull；～引 tow; tug; pull

夜(亱) yè night; evening：～班 night shift or duty / ～景 night scene; nocturnal sight / ～盲 night blindness / ～市 night fair or market; business at night / ～晚 night / ～宵 also "夜消" midnight snacks / ～校 night or evening school / ～战 night fighting; work at night / ～光表 luminous watch / ～总会 nightclub / ～阑人静 in the still of night / ～以继日 day and night; round the clock

夜叉 yèchā yaksha, an evil spirit；〈喻〉hideous and ferocious person；母～ hideous woman; termagant (woman)

夜长梦多 yècháng-mèngduō when night is long, dreams are many; a long delay may mean trouble；这事要抓紧办, 免得～。We must get it done without delay, or else something untoward may happen.

夜郎自大 yèlángzìdà conceit stemming from pure ignorance; parochial arrogance：有点成绩就一起来 become conceited after some success

夜猫子 yèmāozi 〈方〉❶ owl ❷ person who likes staying up late; night owl

夜幕 yèmù gathering darkness; night：在一中消失 disappear into the darkness

夜色 yèsè night scene; darkness; dusk；趁着～ under cover of night

夜莺 yèyīng 〈动物〉nightingale

咽 yè (of sound) obstructed and low; muffled　see also yān

yàn

液 yè liquid; fluid; juice：～氢 liquid hydrogen / ～体 liquid / ～压 hydraulic pressure

液化 yèhuà liquefy：～天然气 liquefied natural gas (LNG)

液晶 yèjīng 〈理〉liquid crystal；～显示 liquid crystal display (LCD) / ～显示器 LCD monitor

谒 yè also "谒见"〈书〉call on (a superior or elder)；pay homage to；pay one's respects to

腋 yè also "腋窝" armpit；～臭 underarm odour；bromhidrosis

靥(靨) yè dimple；笑～ dimple；smiling face

yī

一 yī ❶ one；a；～等 first-class；first-rate；top-notch / ～刹那 in an instant；in a flash；in the twinkling of an eye / ～元论〈哲〉monism / ～臂之力 (lend a) helping hand；help / ～国两制 one country, two systems / ～决雌雄 fight it out；wage a decisive battle / ～念之差 wrong decision made in a moment of weakness；momentary slip / ～盘散沙 (like) a sheet of loose sand；in a state of disunity or disarray / ～炮打响 (of a literary work, performance, etc) become an instant success / ～笑置之 dismiss with a laugh or smile；laugh (sth) off / ～语道破 lay bare the truth with one penetrating remark；hit the nail on the head / ～夫一妻制 monogyny；monogamy / ～衣带水的邻邦 close neighbours separated only by a strip of water ❷ concentrated；wholehearted：～门心思 lost or engrossed (in doing sth) ❸ (one and the) same；equal：～色 of the same colour or hue / ～色 of the same type；uniform / ～模一样 exactly alike；as like as two peas / ～如既往 (same) as before；just as in the past；as usual or always / ～鼻孔出气 collude with one another；be cheek by jowl (with sb) ❹ another；also；otherwise：～名 also "又名" be also known as (sth) ❺ whole；entire：～生 also "一辈子" all one's life；throughout one's life；as long as one lives / ～场空 all in vain；futile；to no avail / ～肚子牢骚 be full of complaints；brim with grievances / ～瓶子不响，半瓶子晃荡〈俗〉the smatterer chatters away, whereas the wise man remains silent；he who knows least boasts most ❻ used to indicate an action taken just for once or of short duration **a)** between reduplicated (often monosyllabic) verbs：看～看 take a look **b)** after a verb and before a classifier：白跑～趟 make a fruitless trip **c)** before a noun followed by a verb：～锅端 eliminate or wipe out completely；give all one has / ～棍子打死 finish off with one blow；completely negate ❼ used before a verb, etc to indicate an action leading to the following consequence：～吐为快 have to get it off one's chest；find it necessary to speak up ❽ once；now that：～经 as soon as；the moment；once / ～失足成千古恨 one false move brings everlasting grief；the error of a moment becomes the regret of a lifetime ❾〈书〉〈助〉used for emphasis：～反常态 be not one's usual self；act out of character

一把手 yībǎshǒu ❶ party to an undertaking；(important) member：咱们搭伙干，你也算～。We'll count you in and pool our efforts. ❷ also "一把好手" good hand；past master；able person：里里外外～ be adept at everything one does, both inside and outside the house ❸ first in command；number one man

一把抓 yībǎzhuā ❶ take everything into one's own hands；attend to everything oneself ❷ grasp all indiscriminately；try to tackle all problems at once with no priority

一败涂地 yībàitúdì fall to the ground；suffer a crushing defeat；be ruined completely

一般 yībān ❶ same as; just like; as …as…;不跟孩子～见识 not lower oneself to the same level as a child ❷ one kind;别有一滋味在心头 (with) a kind of indescribable taste in one's heart ❸ general; usual; common;～化 generalization / ～规律 universal or general rule / ～来说 generally speaking

一板一眼 yībǎn-yīyǎn following a prescribed pattern (in speech or action); meticulous and methodical

一半 yībàn (one) half; in part;各得～ go halves

一…半… yī…bàn… *used before similar or related words, meaning not much or long*;一官半职 some position or other; minor official post / 一时半会儿 (usu used in the negative) a short time; a little while / 一知半解 (have a) smattering of knowledge; scanty or half-baked knowledge

一本万利 yīběnwànlì make huge profits out of a small capital; be extremely profitable

一本正经 yīběnzhèngjīng in all seriousness; in real earnest;～的面孔 serious expression

一笔 yībǐ (at) one or every stroke;～带过 touch upon lightly; mention in passing / ～勾销 write off or cancel at one stroke

一边 yībiān ❶ one side;～倒 lean to one side; be partial (to sb); enjoy overwhelming superiority / 理屈的～儿 party in the wrong ❷ by the side of;站在～不说话 stand silent on the side ❸ *used in duplicates to indicate two actions taking place at the same time*;孩子们一唱，～跳。The children sang as they danced.

一表人才 yībiǎoréncái be handsome; have an impressive or striking appearance

一并 yībìng along with sb or sth else; in the lump;～答复 make a comprehensive reply (to a number of questions)

一…不… yī…bù… ❶ *used before antonymous verbs to indicate irreversible action or condition*;一病不起 take to one's bed and never leave it again; fall ill never to recover / 一蹶不振 collapse after one setback; be unable to recover after one defeat or failure ❷ *used before a noun and a verb for emphasis*;一动不动 not move an inch; be perfectly still

一步一个脚印儿 yībùyīgèjiǎoyìnr work steadily and make solid progress; do solid work;地干工作 do one's job in a down-to-earth manner

一倡百和 yīchàng-bǎihè *also* "一唱百和";"一呼百应" (of a suggestion, etc) meet with general approval; (of a call) receive warm response

一唱一和 yīchàng-yīhè 〈贬〉sing a duet with sb; echo each other; collude with each other

一尘不染 yīchénbùrǎn ❶ (of a person) pure-minded or -hearted; free from corruption ❷ (of an environment) not soiled by a speck of dust; spotlessly clean

一成不变 yīchéngbùbiàn (be) fixed and immutable; stick in a rut

一筹莫展 yīchóumòzhǎn can find no way out; be at one's wits' end; be at a loss

一触即发 yīchùjífā may be triggered at any moment; be on the verge of breaking out; be explosive;战事～。War is imminent.

一锤 yīchuí *also* "一槌" (at) one stroke of the hammer or gong;～定音 set the tune with one beat of the gong — say the last word; make the final decision / ～子买卖 "once-for-all" deal (regardless of consequences)

一次 yīcì ❶ once; one;～成功 succeed at one stroke ❷ primary;〈数〉

linear；～能源 *also* "初级能源" primary energy（resources）/ ～ 方程 linear equation

一次性 yīcìxìng　only once：～减价 one-off sale / ～用品 throwaways / ～针管 disposable syringes

一旦 yīdàn　❶ in a single day；in a very short time　❷ some day；once

一刀 yīdāo　❶ at one blow or stroke；～切 *also* "一刀齐" cut it even at one stroke；impose uniformity（in all cases）；allow no flexibility / ～两断 sever at one blow；make a clean break

一点儿 yīdiǎnr　❶ a bit；a little；somewhat：有 ～ 甜 somewhat sweet / 一丁点儿〈方〉a wee bit；a tiny bit　❷（usu used in the negative）the least bit：～意见也没有 have no objection at all

一定 yīdìng　❶ fixed；specified；definite：～之规 fixed pattern；set rule；fixed idea or way of doing things　❷ definitely；inevitably；necessarily：你～是搞错了。You must have got it wrong. ❸ be bound to；be sure to；resolutely　❹ given；particular；certain：从～意义上说 in a sense　❺ fair；considerable；due：达到～水平 reach a fairly high level

一度 yīdù　❶ period of time；spell　❷ once；for a time：～脱销 be out of stock for some time

一……而…… yī……ér……　*used before verbs to indicate a result coming immediately after an action*：一蹴而就 accomplish in one move；reach the goal with one leap；succeed overnight / 一哄而散 break up in a hubbub；scatter in a rush；disperse helter-skelter / 一挥而就 flourish the pen and it's done；finish a piece of writing or a painting at one go / 一扫而光 make a clean sweep of；finish off / 一拥而上 rush up in a crowd；gather round at once

一二 yī'èr　one or two；just a few；just a little；略知～ know a little（about sth）

一……二…… yī……èr……　❶ *used each before an element of a disyllabic adjective, verb, etc, for emphasis*：一干二净 wholly；thoroughly；completely / 一看二帮 watch and help / 一清二白 perfectly clear or clean；blameless　❷ *used to join two similar or different words*：一来二去 in the course of contacts；by and by / 一穷二白 poor and blank；both impoverished and ignorant / 一不做，二不休 carry sth through at all cost once you've started it；in for a penny, in for a pound / 一回生，二回熟 first time strangers, second time acquaintances；ill at ease the first time, at home the second；get to know in due time

一发千钧 yīfàqiānjūn　*also* "千钧一发" hang by a thread；be in imminent danger：在 这 ～ 之际 at this critical juncture

一帆风顺 yīfānfēngshùn　plain or smooth sailing；smooth and successful career

一风吹 yīfēngchuī　❶ scatter to the winds；dismiss（charges，etc）altogether；write off　❷ have one prevailing or dominant trend

一概 yīgài　〈副〉one and all；without exception；totally：不能 ～ 而论 not to be lumped together；must not generalize about sth

一个 yīge　（used in idioms）just one；one only：～劲儿 *also* "一股劲儿" at a stretch；without stop；persistently / ～心眼儿 of one mind；devoted；stubborn / ～巴掌拍不响〈俗〉it takes two to make a quarrel；it takes two to tango

一共 yīgòng　altogether；in all；all told

一鼓作气 yīgǔzuòqì　do sth at one go；press on to the finish（without letup）；get sth done in one vigorous effort

一贯 yīguàn　consistently；steadily；all along

一会儿 yīhuìr ❶ (in) a little while; (in) a moment ❷ *used before a pair of antonyms to indicate alternating circumstances*: ~哭~笑 cry one moment and laugh the next

一技之长 yījìzhīcháng proficiency in a particular line or field; professional skill; speciality

一家之言 yījiāzhīyán distinctive point of view or theory; particular school of thought; style of one's own: 成~ establish one's own school, theory or style

一见 yījiàn at first sight: ~钟情 *also* "一见倾心" fall in love at first sight / ~如故 feel like old friends at the first meeting; take to each other immediately

一箭 yījiàn an arrow shot; a stone's throw: ~双雕 shoot two hawks with one arrow; kill two birds with one stone / ~之仇 loss or defeat to be avenged

一…就… yī…jiù… *used to indicate one action closely following the other*: 一点就通 *also* "一点就透" take a hint immediately / 我一到家,天就下起雨来了。The moment I got home it began to rain.

一举 yījǔ at one stroke; at the first try: ~成名 become famous overnight; achieve instant fame / ~两得 serve two purposes at once; kill two birds with one stone

一孔之见 yīkǒngzhījiàn peephole view; limited or one-sided view

一口 yīkǒu ❶ (of accent and intonation) pure: 操~京腔 speak a pure Beijing accent ❷ with certainty; readily; outright: ~咬定 assert emphatically; state categorically; insist ❸ one mouthful; one stroke: 吃不成个胖子 (俗) you can't build up your body on one mouthful; nothing can be accomplished with one single effort

一口气 yīkǒuqì ❶ one breath; 只要还有~ as long as there's breath left in one ❷ in one breath; without a break; at one go

一块石头落地 yīkuàishítouluòdì have a load (taken) off one's mind; set one's mind at rest; feel relieved

一览 yīlǎn ❶ general survey; bird's-eye view; overview: ~表 checklist; chart; table ❷ clearly; completely: ~无余 take in everything at a glance

一揽子 yīlǎnzi wholesale; package: ~交易 package deal

一劳永逸 yīláoyǒngyì gain lasting repose by one (supreme) effort; get sth done once for all; achieve a permanent solution (to a problem)

一连 yīlián in a row; successively; running: ~三次 three times in a row

一了百了 yīliǎobǎiliǎo all troubles end when the main trouble ends; death ends all one's troubles; death pays all debts

一鳞半爪 yīlín-bànzhǎo *also* "东鳞西爪" odd bits; scraps; fragments: ~的知识 fragmentary knowledge; smattering of knowledge

一流 yīliú ❶ of the same kind; of the kind: 属于大款~人物 one of the nouveaux riches ❷ first-rate; top-grade; first-class: ~文学作品 first-rate literary works

一路 yīlù ❶ all the way; throughout the journey: ~领先 take the lead all the way / ~顺风 (be) plain sailing; (have a) pleasant journey; (have) good trip ❷ of the same kind; of like kind: ~货色 *also* "一路货" same stuff; one of a kind; birds of a feather ❸ go the same way; take the same road ❹ continuously; always: ~上扬 (of prices, etc) continue to soar; keep going up

一律 yīlǜ ❶ same; identical; uniform: 强求~ impose rigid uniformity ❷ all; each and all; without exception;

法律面前～平等 equal before the law

一落千丈 yīluòqiānzhàng experience a disastrous decline or drastic fall; have a big comedown: 情绪～ plummet in spirits; be crestfallen

一马当先 yīmǎdāngxiān be in the forefront; take the lead

一马平川 yīmǎpíngchuān wide expanse of flat land

一脉相承 yīmàixiāngchéng also "一脉相传" come down in one continuous line; can be traced to the same origin; be in the same stream

一毛不拔 yīmáobùbá unwilling to give up even a hair — very stingy or miserly; close-fisted

一面 yīmiàn ❶ one side, aspect or field; one party: ～之词 statement of only one of the parties; one side of the story ❷ (used in duplication) at the same time; simultaneously: ～听～作笔记 take notes while listening ❸〔书〕have met once; ～之交 have met just once; be casually acquainted

一鸣惊人 yīmíngjīngrén (of an obscure person) amaze the world with a single brilliant feat; set the Thames on fire

一命呜呼 yīmìngwūhū also "一命归天" die; kick the bucket; give up the ghost

一目 yīmù (used in idioms) at one glance: ～了然 see clearly at a glance; (of sth) be as plain as the nose on sb's face / ～十行 take in ten lines at a glance — read very rapidly

一年 yīnián one year; the whole year: ～半载 in a year or so; in about a year / ～到头 throughout the year; all (the) year round

一诺千金 yīnuòqiānjīn promise that is worth a thousand pieces of gold; solemn promise: ～的人 man of his word

一拍即合 yīpāijíhé hit it off readily; chime or fit in easily

一瞥 yīpiē ❶ (quick) glance: 投以忧郁的～ cast (sb) a melancholy glance ❷ (often used in a title) glimpse; brief survey

一贫如洗 yīpínrúxǐ also "一文不名" penniless; utterly destitute

一暴十寒 yīpù-shíhán work hard for one day and be idle for ten — work by fits and starts; lack in perseverance

一起 yīqǐ also "一块儿" ❶ in the same place; 在～工作 work in the same place / 说不到～ speak at cross-purposes; not see eye to eye ❷ also "一齐" together; simultaneously; in company

一气 yīqì ❶ at one go; without a break; at a stretch; ～呵成 (of an essay, etc) form a coherent whole; make smooth reading ❷〈贬〉spell; fit: 胡说～ tell cock-and-bull stories; shoot off one's mouth ❸ a fit of anger: ～之下 in a fit of pique; in an outburst of anger

一钱不值 yīqiánbùzhí also "一文不值" not worth a penny; utterly worthless; mere trash: 把书贬得～ condemn a book as not worth the paper it is printed on

一窍不通 yīqiàobùtōng know nothing about; have no knowledge of; be completely ignorant of

一切 yīqiè all; every: ～向钱看 put money above all else; be money-oriented / ～的～ each and every thing; all in all

一丘之貉 yīqiūzhīhé 〈贬〉jackals from the same lair; birds of a feather; tarred with the same brush

一日 yīrì a day; one day: ～千里 at a tremendous pace; with giant strides; by leaps and bounds / ～三秋 (short for 一日不见, 如隔三秋) a day's separation seems as long as three years; miss sb very much

一身 yīshēn ❶ all over the body: ～债 be head over heels in debt; be up to one's neck in debt ❷ suit (of clothes):

~休闲服 be casually dressed ❸ by oneself; alone; ~二任 hold two jobs concurrently; serve in a dual capacity

一时 yīshí ❶ (for a) period of time; 盛极一时 be all the rage for the time ❷ temporary; momentary; offhand; ~半刻 also "一时半会儿" a short time; a little while / ~冲动 (be) caught by an impulse; (act) on the spur of the moment ❸ now ..., now ...; one moment ..., the next ...; ~晴, ~雨. One moment it's clear, the next it rains.

一视同仁 yīshìtóngrén treat all alike; regard all as equals

一手 yīshǒu ❶ by or in one hand; ~交钱, ~交货 cash on delivery; COD ❷ single-handed; all by oneself; all alone; ~包办 keep everything in one's own hands; take sole control of; monopolize / ~遮天 abuse one's power to hide the truth; hoodwink the public ❸ proficiency; skill; trick; ~好字 (write a) good hand

一丝 yīsī a tiny bit; a trace; ~不苟 scrupulous about every detail; conscientious and meticulous / ~不挂 not have a stitch on; be stark-naked / ~笑容 (wear) a faint smile

一塌糊涂 yītāhútu in an awful or terrible state; in a muddle; messy; 吵得~ kick up a terrible row

一天 yītiān ❶ one day; ~工作八小时 work eight hours a day ❷ daytime; ~到晚 from morning till night; all day long ❸ also "有一天" one day (in the past)

一头 yītóu ❶ of several things happening at the same time; 他一走, 一说。He talked as he walked. ❷ directly; straightaway; 打开车门, 他一钻了进来。As I opened the car door, he climbed in. ❸ suddenly; all of a sudden; headlong; ~碰见他 run into him ❹ one end; side or aspect; 顾了这一~, 顾不上那~ cannot attend to both sides

at once ❺ a head; 你的点子比我高~。 Your idea is superior to mine.

一团 yītuán one mass; all over; completely; ~和气 keep on good terms with everybody (at the expense of principle); curry favour with people all round / ~乱麻 like a mass of tangled flax — totally confused; in a complete mess; in a turmoil

一网打尽 yīwǎngdǎjìn catch the whole lot in a dragnet; net the whole lot; make a clean sweep

一往情深 yīwǎngqíngshēn be passionately devoted; be deeply attached; be head over heels in love

一往无前 yīwǎngwúqián press forward with indomitable will; forge ahead relentlessly; ~的献身精神 indomitable spirit of dedication

一望无际 yīwàngwújì stretch as far as the eye can see; stretch to the horizon; ~的原野 vast expanse of open country

一味 yīwèi purely; stubbornly; persistently; ~追求名利 seek nothing but fame and wealth

一无 yīwú not in the least; not at all; ~是处 without a single redeeming virtue; devoid of any merit / ~所有 not have a thing to one's name; be stony broke / ~所知 be completely in the dark; be absolutely ignorant (of sth)

一五一十 yīwǔ-yīshí ❶ count carefully ❷ (narrate) systematically and in full detail; from first to last

一下 yīxià also "一下子" ❶ used after a verb, indicating an act or an attempt; 看~ have a look for a short while; all at once; suddenly ❷ in a short while; ~进了三个球 score three goals in a short while

一线 yīxiàn ❶ war front; front line; ~工人 worker at the production line ❷ a ray or gleam of; ~生机 a slim chance of survival; a gleam of hope in despair

一相情愿 yīxiāngqíngyuàn also "一

厢情愿" wishful thinking

一向 yīxiàng ❶ earlier on; of late: 这 ~ lately ❷ consistently; all along; always: ~ 爱好音乐 be a music lover all along

一些 yīxiē ❶ a number or amount of; certain; some ❷ tiny bit; few; little: 就这么 ~ 钱了. This is all the money left. ❸ used after an adjective, a verb, etc to indicate a slight change in degree: 快 ~! Faster!

一心 yīxīn ❶ wholeheartedly; earnestly; heart and soul: ~ 想发财 be bent on making a fortune / ~ 不能二用 one cannot apply oneself to two jobs at once; one cannot spin and reel at the same time ❷ of one mind; with one heart: ~ 一德 be of one heart and one mind

一行 yīxíng people travelling together; party; team: 大使及其 ~ the ambassador and his party

一言 yīyán one word; a single word: ~ 堂 what I say goes; person who won't tolerate dissenting views; dictatorial style of work / ~ 不发 not say a word; remain silent / ~ 九鼎 (say the) decisive word; words that carry great weight / ~ 难尽 you cannot explain the matter in a few words; it is a long story / ~ 以蔽之 to sum up in a word; in short / ~ 既出, 驷马难追 what is said cannot be unsaid; will never go back on one's word

一样 yīyàng same; equally; alike: ~ 的货色 same stuff; birds of a feather / 像白昼 ~ 明亮 as bright as day

一叶知秋 yīyèzhīqiū the falling of one leaf heralds the coming of autumn; a straw shows which way the wind blows; a small sign can point to a great trend

一一 yīyī one by one; one after another: ~ 解释 explain one by one / ~ 记在心里 remember everything or every detail

一……一…… yī…yī… ❶ used before similar nouns to indicate the whole of sth or a small amount: 一点一滴 every little bit; (not) a bit / 一举一动 every single action; (not) a single action ❷ used before different nouns to indicate a) contrast: 一龙一猪 dragon and pig — two persons between whom there is no comparison b) relationship: 一本一利 capital and profit; profit proportionate to the capital ❸ used before verbs to indicate sequence: 一惊一乍 fuss and fluster ❹ used before related verbs to indicate coordination or alternation: 一张一弛 tension alternating with relaxation ❺ used before opposite nouns of direction or antonymous adjectives to indicate contrary positions or situations: 一前一后 one in front, one following

一意孤行 yīyìgūxíng cling obstinately to one's course; act willfully

一应 yīyīng all; every: ~ 俱全. Everything needed is available.

一元化 yīyuánhuà ❶ also "一体化" integrate; centralize: 经济 ~ economic integration ❷ unified: ~ 管理 unified management

一再 yīzài time and again; again and again; repeatedly

一……再…… yī…zài… used before the same replicated verb to indicate repetition: 一忍再忍 hold one's temper again and again; try hard to keep one's temper

一早 yīzǎo also "一大早" 〈口〉 early in the morning: 明天 ~ first thing tomorrow morning

一朝 yīzhāo once; in one day: ~ 一夕 in a single day; overnight / ~ 被蛇咬, 十年怕井绳 〈俗〉 once bitten, twice shy; a burnt child dreads the fire

一针见血 yīzhēnjiànxiě get to the truth with a single pertinent remark;

hit the nail on the head:这批评~。The criticism hit home.

一直 yīzhí ❶ straight：～走 go straight ahead；keep straight on ❷ continuously；always：我们～是好朋友。We've been good friends all along. ❸ all the way:从老人~到小孩，没有不喜欢他的。Everyone likes him, old and young.

一纸空文 yīzhǐkōngwén a mere scrap of paper；not worth the paper it is written on

一致 yīzhì ❶ identical；unanimous；consistent:根本利益～ share fundamental interests ❷ work together；act in unison:～行动 take concerted action

一掷千金 yīzhìqiānjīn spend one's money extravagantly；throw away money like dirt；spend money like water

一字 yīzì ❶ a (single) word；one word:～千金 one word is worth a thousand pieces of gold — excellent literary work or calligraphy ❷ like the character 一；a (long) line or row:摆开～长蛇阵 form a single-line battle array；string out in a long line

伊 yī ❶〈书〉〈助〉used to introduce a phrase or sentence:～于胡底? Where will it all end? ❷ he；she

伊甸园 yīdiànyuán (of Christianity) Garden of Eden；Paradise

伊始 yīshǐ 〈书〉beginning:上任～ upon assuming office

伊斯兰 Yīsīlán Islam;~教 Islam;Islamism / ～国家 Islamic country / ~教徒 Moslem；Muslim

衣 yī ❶ clothes；garment；dress:～柜 wardrobe / ～架 coat hanger；clothes tree or stand / ～料 dress material / ～物 clothing and other articles of daily use；personal effects / ～帽间 cloakroom / ～锦还乡 return home after making good / ～衫褴褛 shabbily dressed；dressed in rags / ~

食住行 food，clothing，shelter and transport — basic necessities of life ❷ coating；covering:琴～ piano cover

衣钵 yībō Buddhist monk's mantle and alms bowl which he hands down to his disciple；legacy:～相传 pass one's mantle on to a successor；hand down the legacy

衣服 yīfu also "衣裳" clothing；clothes；dress

衣冠 yīguān hat and clothes；dress；attire:～楚楚 immaculately dressed / ～禽兽 beast in human attire；brute

衣着 yīzhuó clothing，headgear and footwear:～朴素 be plainly dressed

医（醫） yī ❶ doctor (of medicine)；medical practitioner:～德 medical ethics / ～生 doctor；physician；surgeon / ～术 medical skill；art of healing / ～嘱 (on) doctor's advice or orders ❷ medical science or service；medicine:～科 medical education in general；medicine ❸ treat；cure；heal

医护 yīhù cure and nurse；provide medical service:～人员 doctors and nurses；medical staff

医疗 yīliáo medical treatment:～保险 medical insurance / ～事故 faulty medical or surgical treatment；malpractice

医生 yīshēng (qualified) doctor:主任～ chief physician or surgeon

医务 yīwù medical matters:～工作 medical work

医学 yīxué medical science；medicine:～界 medical circles

医药 yīyào medicine:～费 medical expenses or costs

医院 yīyuàn hospital:专科～ specialized hospital

医治 yīzhì cure；treat；heal:～无效 (of a patient) fail to respond to treatment

依 yī ❶ depend or rely on；count on；look to:～恃权势 rely on

one's power and position / 无所一托 have nothing or nobody to count on ❷ *also* "依从" obey; comply with; yield to ❸ according to; in the light of; on the basis of；～次 in proper order; one after another; successively；～此 the rest may be inferred (from this); infer by analogy / ～样葫芦 *also* "依样画葫芦" draw a gourd according to the model — copy mechanically

依存 yīcún depend on sb or sth for existence；相互～的关系 interdependence

依法 yīfǎ ❶ according to fixed rule；～炮制 prepare herbal medicine by the prescribed method — follow a set pattern; follow suit ❷ according to law；～惩办 punish according to law; mete out punishment in accordance with the law

依附 yīfù ❶ be attached to; cling to ❷ depend or rely on; become an appendage to；～权贵 cotton to the powers that be

依旧 yījiù as before; as usual; as of old；～忙碌 (as) busy as ever / 风景～。The scenery remains the same.

依据 yījù ❶ basis; grounds; foundation；以事实为～ on the basis of facts ❷ according to; on the basis of; in line with；～先例 act in the light of precedent; go by precedent

依靠 yīkào ❶ rely or depend on; count on ❷ sb or sth to fall back on; support; backing

依赖 yīlài ❶ depend on; cling to；～性 dependence ❷（usu 相互依赖）be interdependent

依恋 yīliàn be reluctant to leave; feel regret at separation；～之情 sentimental attachment (to sb or sth)

依然 yīrán still; as before; as usual；～如故 remain as before; stay unchanged

依偎 yīwēi snuggle up to; nestle up against; lean close to

依稀 yīxī vaguely; faintly; dimly

依依 yīyī ❶〈书〉(of branch or twig) frail and gentle, swaying in the wind ❷ reluctant to part；～不舍 be reluctant to part; cannot bear to leave

依仗 yīzhàng count on; rely or depend on；～人多 count on the advantage of having more people; rely on one's numerical superiority

依照 yīzhào according to; in the light of; on the basis of

咿 yī

咿呀 yīyā ❶〈象声〉squeak; creak；桨声～ squeak of oars in oarlocks ❷ prattle; babble；～学语的婴儿 babbling baby

铱 yī〈化〉iridium (Ir)；～金笔 iridium-point pen

壹 yī one (used for the numeral 一 on cheques, banknotes, etc.) to prevent mistakes or alterations

揖 yī〈书〉(make a) bow with hands clasped；～别 bid farewell by bowing; say goodbye (to) / 作个～ make a bow

漪 yī〈书〉ripples；～澜 ripples and billows

噫 yī〈叹〉❶〈书〉alas ❷ why; how come；～，他今天怎么来了? How come he came here today?

yí

仪（儀） yí ❶ appearance; bearing; looks；～容 looks; appearance ❷ ceremony; rite; protocol；～式 ceremony; rite; function ❸ present; gift ❹〈书〉admire; yearn for; look forward to；心～已久 have long admired sb ❺（usu 仪器）apparatus; instrument

仪表 yíbiǎo ❶ appearance; looks; bearing；～堂堂 dignified in appearance; impressive-looking; imposing ❷

meter (on a plane, etc)

仪态 yítài 〈书〉bearing; deportment; carriage: ~万方 *also* "仪态万千" (as of a beauty) appear in all one's glory

仪仗 yízhàng　weapons, flags, etc carried by guards (at state ceremonies, etc); flags, slogans, banners, etc carried in the front of a procession: ~队 guard of honour

夷 yí 〈书〉❶ level; smooth; safe: 化险为~ turn danger into safety; head off a disaster ❷ raze; level; wipe out: ~为平地 level to the ground; raze ❸ (usu 东夷) 〈史〉tribes in the east of China; barbarians ❹ 〈旧〉foreign country; foreigner

饴 yí maltose: 高粱~ sorghum candy / ~糖 maltose; malt sugar

怡 yí 〈书〉be happy or joyful: ~然 happy; contented; satisfied

宜 yí ❶ suitable; appropriate; desirable: 少儿不~ not suitable for children ❷ should; ought to (esp used in the negative): ~早不~晚 better early than late

宜人 yírén　pleasant; delightful; attractive: 景色~ charming scenery

咦 yí 〈叹〉(indicating surprise) well; why: ~! 你还在这儿! Well, so you are still here!

贻 yí ❶ send sb a gift; make sb a present of sth ❷ bequeath; leave behind: ~笑大方 make a laughing stock of oneself before connoisseurs; incur the ridicule of experts

贻害 yíhài　leave a legacy of trouble: ~无穷 cause no end of trouble; entail untold harm

贻误 yíwù　adversely affect; miss; bungle: ~战机 bungle the chance of winning a battle; forfeit a chance for combat

姨 yí ❶ mother's sister; maternal aunt: ~表 maternal cousin / ~夫 *also* "姨父" husband of one's maternal aunt; uncle ❷ wife's sister; sister-in-law: 小~子 wife's younger sister

姨太太 yítàitai　*also* "姨太"; "姨娘" 〈口〉concubine

胰 yí (usu 胰腺) 〈生理〉pancreas: ~岛素 insulin

移 yí ❶ move; remove; shift: ~居 move; migrate; emigrate / ~栽 〈农〉transplant / ~情别恋 shift one's affection to sb else / ~山倒海 remove mountains and drain seas; make tremendous effort to conquer or transform nature ❷ change; alter; transform: ~风易俗 transform established social traditions; change prevailing customs and habits

移动 yídòng　move; shift: ~电话 mobile or cellular phone / ~通信 mobile service

移花接木 yíhuā-jiēmù　graft (one twig on another); 〈喻〉stealthily substitute or replace one thing for another

移交 yíjiāo ❶ turn or hand over; transfer ❷ hand over one's job to a successor

移民 yímín ❶ migrate; emigrate; immigrate: 申请~ apply for an immigrant visa / 向边远地区~ settle or relocate people in remote areas / ~点 settlement / ~局 immigration service ❷ emigrant; immigrant

移植 yízhí 〈植〉〈医〉transplant; graft: 皮肤~ skin graft / 心脏~ heart transplanting

遗 yí ❶ (usu 遗失) lose ❷ (usu 遗忘) omit; forget ❸ sth lost or omitted ❹ leave behind or over; keep back: ~风 tradition left over from the past / ~恨 lasting regret; remorse / ~迹 (historical) ruins; remains; vestiges / ~址 ruins; relics / ~臭万年 go down in history as a byword of infamy; earn eternal notoriety ❺ leave at death; bequeath: ~稿 posthumous

manuscript / ～孤 orphan / ～孀 widow; relict / ～体 *also* "遗骸" remains (of the dead) / ～愿 unfulfilled wish of the deceased; last wish / ～赠 bequeath (at death) / ～腹子 posthumous child ❻ involuntarily discharge (urine, etc) / ～精 (seminal) emission / ～尿 bed-wetting
see also wèi

遗产 yíchǎn ❶ inheritance; legacy: ～税 estate tax; inheritance tax; succession duty ❷〈喻〉legacy; heritage: 历史～ legacy of history

遗传 yíchuán heredity; inheritance: ～学 genetics / ～工程 *also* "基因工程" genetic engineering / ～基因 hereditary gene

遗憾 yíhàn ❶ deep regret; remorse: 终生的～ lifelong regret ❷ regret; deplore: 你不能来，实在～。It's really a pity that you can't come.

遗老 yílǎo ❶ surviving adherent of an overthrown dynasty; old diehard: ～遗少 old fogies and young diehards ❷〈书〉old people who have witnessed important social changes

遗留 yíliú leave behind; hand down: 历史～的问题 issue left over by history; legacy from the past

遗漏 yílòu fail to do sth; omit; leave out

遗弃 yíqì abandon; forsake; desert: 被～的女婴 abandoned baby girl

遗容 yíróng ❶ looks of the deceased; remains ❷ portrait of the deceased

遗书 yíshū ❶ (usu used in book titles) posthumous papers ❷ letter or note left by sb immediately before death ❸〈书〉books that have been lost; books no longer extant or available

遗嘱 yízhǔ will; testament: 立～ make a will / 未立～〈法〉(die) intestate or will-less

颐 yí ❶ cheek: ～指气使 order people about by facial expressions; be extremely arrogant ❷ keep

fit; take care of; preserve: ～养天年 take care of oneself so as to enjoy one's natural span of life

疑 yí ❶ doubt; disbelieve; suspect: ～忌 be suspicious; distrust / ～神～鬼 be even afraid of one's own shadow; be unreasonably suspicious / ～似病例 suspected case ❷ doubtful; suspicious; uncertain: ～案 doubtful case; open question; mystery / ～点 doubtful or questionable point / ～犯 suspect (in a case) / ～念 doubts; misgivings / 布下～阵 lay a deceptive trap

疑惑 yíhuò feel puzzled; be doubtful: ～不解 feel doubtful

疑惧 yíjù apprehensions; misgivings: ～不安 be assailed with misgivings

疑虑 yílǜ misgivings; doubts; uncertainties: 解除～ clear one's mind of doubt; free sb from misgivings

疑难 yínán difficult; thorny; knotty: ～杂症 cases hard to diagnose and cure; difficult and complicated cases

疑团 yítuán doubts and suspicions

疑问 yíwèn query; question; doubt: 毫无～ beyond doubt / ～句〈语言〉interrogative sentence

疑心 yíxīn ❶ suspicion: ～病 suspicious frame of mind; paranoia ❷ suspect; wonder

疑义 yíyì doubt; doubtful point: 大家对他的能力没有～。No one doubted his ability.

疑云 yíyún suspicion clouding one's mind; doubt: 驱散～ dispel suspicion

yǐ

乙 yǐ ❶ 2nd of the Heavenly Stems *see also* "干支" gānzhī ❷ second; sth meaning second in order: ～等 second grade; grade Ⅱ / ～醇 *also* "酒精"〈化〉ethanol; alcohol / ～醚〈化〉ether / ～烯〈化〉ethylene:

ethane / ～型肝炎（shortened as 乙肝）hepatitis B

已 yǐ ❶ stop; cease; end; 叹息不～ keep sighing ❷ already; ～故 deceased; late / ～经 already / ～然 already; be already so; have long been the case / ～往 before; previously; in the past / ～决犯〈法〉convicted prisoner; convict / ～知数〈数〉known number ❸〈书〉thereafter; later on; afterwards ❹〈书〉too; excessively; 极 extremely; to the nth degree

以 yǐ ❶ use; take; ～暴易暴 replace one tyranny by another / ～德报怨 return good for evil; repay ingratitude with kindness / ～毒攻毒 combat poison with poison; set a thief to catch a thief / ～礼相待 treat (sb) with due respect; be polite or courteous (to people) / ～理服人 convince people by reasoning / ～权谋私 abuse one's power for personal gains; seek personal benefit by taking advantage of one's power and position / ～牙还牙 tit for tat; pay sb back in his own coin / ～英雄为榜样 take a hero as one's role model; model oneself upon a hero / ～小人之心，度君子之腹 gauge the heart of a gentleman with one's own mean measure / ～其人之道，还治其人之身 do unto him as he does unto others; pay sb back in his own coin ❷ according to; in order of: ～此类推 deduce the rest from this; infer on the analogy of this / ～次购票 book tickets one by one ❸ because of; for; by: ～貌取人 judge people by appearances / 不～言举人 not promote or recommend a person just by what he says ❹ in order to; so as to; for: ～观后效 (lighten a punishment and) see if the offender mends his ways / ～防万一 ready for any eventuality; (just) in case / ～求一逞 in an attempt to fulfil one's ambition; in a (desperate) bid for success / ～资参

考 as a reference ❺〈书〉〈连〉used in the same way as 而: 水阔～深。The river is wide and deep. ❻ used before monosyllabic words of locality to indicate the limits of time, place, direction or number: 长江～南 south of the Yangtze River / 权限～内 within one's competence or authority

以便 yǐbiàn so that; in order to; for the purpose of: 备好材料～开工 get materials ready so as to begin a project

以点带面 yǐdiǎndàimiàn fan out from a point to an area; spread the experience gained at selected units to an entire area

以讹传讹 yǐ'échuán'é spread an erroneous message; pass on a rumour; propagate a falsehood or an error

以工代赈 yǐgōngdàizhèn provide jobs (usu in public works) as a form of relief; provide work-relief: ～工程 work-relief project

以后 yǐhòu after; afterwards; since

以及 yǐjí〈连〉as well as; along with; in addition: 电视机～其他家电 television sets as well as other home appliances

以己度人 yǐjǐduórén judge others by oneself; put oneself in sb else's shoes; measure others' corn by one's own bushel

以假乱真 yǐjiǎluànzhēn mix the spurious with the genuine; create confusion by passing off the fake as the real thing: 赝品达到了～的程度。The imitation was so good that it was difficult to tell it from the real thing.

以儆效尤 yǐjǐngxiàoyóu punish sb as a warning to others; make an example of sb

以来 yǐlái since: 建国～ since the founding of the People's Republic

以邻为壑 yǐlínwéihè shift one's troubles onto others; benefit oneself at the expense of others

以卵投石 yǐluǎntóushí　also "以卵击石" throw an egg against a rock — overrate oneself and court defeat by pitting oneself against sb far stronger

以免 yǐmiǎn 〈连〉in order to avoid or prevent; lest

以偏概全 yǐpiāngàiquán　regard the part as the whole; be lopsided; adopt a one-sided approach

以前 yǐqián　before; ago; previously — 三年～ three years ago

以上 yǐshàng ❶ more than; over; above: 十人～ over ten peo- ple; ten people or more ❷ above; foregoing; above-mentioned: ～观点 the above ideas

以身 yǐshēn　oneself; in person: ～试法 defy or challenge the law personally / ～殉职 die at one's post; die in harness / ～作则 set an example with one's own conduct; set a personal example

以退为进 yǐtuìwéijìn　retreat in order to advance; fall back so as to move forward; make concessions to gain advantages

以往 yǐwǎng　before; formerly; previously: ～的经历 previous experience

以为 yǐwéi　think; believe; consider: 不～然 not think so; take exception (to sth)

以下 yǐxià ❶ below; under: 25 岁～ under 25 (years of age) ❷ the following: ～是详细的行动计划. The following is a detailed plan of action.

以一当十 yǐyīdāngshí　pit one against ten; fight courageously; work efficiently

以逸待劳 yǐyìdàiláo　be rested and ready to meet a tired-out opponent; wait at one's ease for an exhausted enemy

以至 yǐzhì　also "以至于" 〈连〉 ❶ down to; up to: 从沿海城市～内地农村 from coastal cities to inland rural areas ❷ to such an extent as to…; so…

that…; even: 他专心看书，～没听到敲门声. He was so engrossed in his reading that he didn't hear the knocks at the door.

以致 yǐzhì 〈连〉so that; consequently; as a result: 由于疏忽大意～出了严重事故. A serious accident happened as a result of carelessness.

尾 yǐ ❶ (usu 马尾) hairs on a horsetail ❷ spikelets on a cricket's tail: 三～儿 female cricket (with three spikelets on its tail)
see also wěi

矣 yǐ 〈书〉〈助〉❶ used at the end of a sentence like 了: 俱往～. All is over now. ❷ used in exclamation: 甚～, 汝之不惠! How stupid you are!

迤 yǐ stretch or extend towards: ～逦 winding; tortuous; meandering

蚁(蟻) yǐ ant: ～巢 ant nest / ～后 gyne; ant queen

倚 yǐ ❶ lean on or against; rest on or against ❷ rely or depend on; count on: ～仗 bank or count on / ～老卖老 show self-importance for being aged; flaunt one's seniority / ～势凌人 use one's power and influence to bully others ❸ 〈书〉biased; prejudiced; partial: 中立不～ remain neutral; be unbiased; stay impartial

倚靠 yǐkào ❶ lean on or against; rest on or against ❷ rely or depend on; count on

倚重 yǐzhòng　value and trust: ～助手 lean heavily on one's assistants / 过于～技巧 attach too much importance to technique

椅 yǐ　chair: ～背 back of a chair

旖 yǐ

旖旎 yǐnǐ 〈书〉charming and gentle; enchanting

yì

亿（億） yì ❶ hundred million：～万富翁 billionaire；multi-millionaire ❷ vast numbers

义（義） yì ❶ just；righteous；fair：～举 magnanimous act undertaken for the public good；righteous deed／～卖 sale for charity or other worthy causes；charity bazaar／～师 also "义军" righteous army (against tyranny, etc)／～士 person who upholds the cause of justice；noble-minded or chivalrous person／～演 benefit or charity performance／～诊 free medical consultation (for some worthy cause) ❷ affection or sense of duty involved in a relationship；loyalty；faith：～犬 faithful dog ❸ adopted；adoptive：～父 adoptive father／～子 adopted son ❹ artificial；false：～齿〈医〉false tooth；denture／～肢〈医〉artificial limb ❺ meaning；sense；significance：～项 item of an entry (in a dictionary)

义不容辞 yìbùróngcí be duty-bound；have an bounden duty；(of sth) be incumbent (on sb)

义愤 yìfèn righteous or moral indignation：～填膺 be filled with (righteous) indignation

义气 yìqi code of brotherhood；personal loyalty：重～ set store by personal loyalty／为人～ be loyal to one's friends

义无反顾 yìwúfǎngù honour permits no turning back；be duty-bound not to retreat；(do sth) without the least reservation or hesitation

义务 yìwù ❶ duty；obligation：～兵 compulsory serviceman；conscript／～教育 compulsory education ❷ voluntary；gratuitous；free (of charge)：～劳动 voluntary or volunteer labour

义勇军 yìyǒngjūn (army of) volunteers：～进行曲 March of the Volunteers (national anthem of China)

义正词严 yìzhèng-cíyán speak sternly out of a sense of justice；speak in all seriousness

艺（藝） yì ❶ skill；technique：～高人胆大 boldness of execution stems from superb skill；great skill engenders bravery ❷ art；performing art：～名 stage name／～苑 realm of art and literature；art and literary circles

艺人 yìrén ❶ actor or artist (in traditional opera, acrobatics, etc) ❷ artisan；handicraftsman

艺术 yìshù ❶ art：～家 artist／～品 work of art／～性 artistic quality；artistry／～体操 also "韵律体操" artistic or rhythmic gymnastics ❷ skill；art；craft：教学～ teaching skills；art of teaching ❸ artistic；tasteful；stylish

刈 yì〈书〉mow；cut down

忆（憶） yì recall；recollect：～苦思甜 recall past sorrows and savour present joys；contrast past misery with present happiness

议（議） yì ❶ opinion；view；proposal ❷ discuss；deliberate；negotiate：～案 proposal；motion；bill／～和 negotiate peace／～价 negotiated price／～题 subject under discussion；topic for discussion／～政 deliberate on political and governmental affairs ❸ comment；remark；debate

议程 yìchéng agenda；order of business；order of the day

议定书 yìdìngshū protocol：经济合作～ protocol of economic cooperation

议会 yìhuì also "国会" (UK) Parliament; (US) Congress; (France) National Assembly; (Japan) Diet; (Germany) Reichstag; (Russia) Duma

议论 yìlùn　talk; deliberate; discuss; ～文 argumentative writing; argumentation / ～纷纷 give rise to much discussion; be widely discussed

议事 yìshì　discuss official business; ～规则 rules of procedures / ～日程 agenda; order of the day

议员 yìyuán　member of a legislative assembly; (UK) Member of Parliament (MP); (US) Congressman; (Japan) Dietman

议院 yìyuàn　legislative assembly; (UK) parliament; congress; 上～ Upper House; (UK) House of Lords / 下～ Lower House; (UK) House of Commons

议长 yìzhǎng　Speaker (of a legislative body); president

屹 yì〈书〉towering like a mountain peak; ～立 stand towering like a giant / ～然不动 firm and unshakable

亦 yì〈书〉also; too; as well as; ～庄～谐 both solemn and witty; serious and comical at the same time; serio-comic / ～步～趋 ape sb at every step; imitate sb's every move; follow slavishly

异(異) yì ❶ not the same; different; dissimilar; ～读 variant pronunciation / ～议 disagreement; objection; dissent / ～乎寻常 out of the ordinary; unusual; extraordinary ❷ strange; unusual; extraordinary; ～兽 strange animal / 大放～彩 blossom in radiant brilliance ❸ surprising; astonishing; odd; 深以为～ regard as most unusual; (of sth) strike one as very odd ❹ other; another; alien; 他日〈书〉some other day; (in) former days; (in) bygone times / ～教徒 pagan; heathen / 怀有～心 harbour

disloyalty ❺ separate; part; divide

异常 yìcháng ❶ unusual; abnormal; odd ❷ extremely; exceedingly; particularly

异端 yìduān　unorthodox belief; heterodoxy; heresy; ～邪说 heretical beliefs; unorthodox opinions

异国 yìguó　foreign country or land; ～情调 exotic flavour; the exotic

异化 yìhuà　alienation; dissimilation

异己 yìjǐ　dissident; alien; ～分子 dissident; alien element

异军突起 yìjūntūqǐ　a new force emerges all of a sudden; (of sth new) become all the rage

异同 yìtóng　similar and dissimilar; 比较二者的～ compare the similarities and differences between the two / 异口同声 with one voice; in unison / 异曲同工 be different in approach but equally satisfactory in result; achieve the same goal through different means

异物 yìwù ❶ foreign matter or body; 气管～ foreign body in the trachea ❷〈书〉dead person ❸〈书〉strange article; sth bizarre

异乡 yìxiāng　foreign or strange land; ～人 person from elsewhere; stranger; alien

异想天开 yìxiǎngtiānkāi　indulge in the wildest fantasy; have a most bizarre idea

异性 yìxìng ❶ opposite sex; ～间的往来 contacts between the sexes ❷ different or dissimilar in nature

异样 yìyàng ❶ different; 看上去没有～ look the same ❷ unusual; peculiar; odd; 用～的眼光看人 look at sb with curious eyes

异族 yìzú　different race or nation; ～通婚 mixed marriage

抑 yì ❶ press down; suppress; restrain; ～强扶弱 restrain the powerful and help the weak; curb the strong and assist the weak ❷ also "

或"〈书〉or ❸〈书〉yet; but ❹〈书〉besides; moreover

抑扬顿挫 yì-yáng-dùn-cuò　with a rising and falling rhythm; in measured tones; in cadence

抑 yì　dejected; depressed; gloomy; ~症〈医〉depression

抑制 yìzhì　❶〈生理〉inhibition ❷ restrain; curb; check; ~怒火 restrain or hold one's temper

呓(囈) yì　talk in one's sleep; ~语 talk in one's sleep; delirious utterances; ravings

邑 yì　❶ city ❷ county

佚 yì　see "逸" yì

役 yì　❶ labour ❷ military service; ~龄 enlistment or conscription age ❸ work; use; ~使 work (domestic animals); use ❹〈旧〉servant ❺ battle; campaign

译(譯) yì　translate; interpret; ~本 translation (of a book); version / ~名 translated term or name / ~文 translated text; translation / ~音 transliteration / ~员 interpreter / ~者 translator / ~注 translate and annotate / ~著 also "译作" works of translation / ~制片 dubbed film

易 yì　❶ easy; ~拉罐 pop-top or ring-pull can / ~燃物 combustible; inflammable; flammable / ~如反掌 as easy as pie; duck soup; piece of cake ❷ amiable ❸ change; alter; ~手 (of land, power, etc) change hands ❹ exchange; ~货贸易 barter (trade)

诣 yì　❶〈书〉〈敬〉(call on); visit; ~烈士墓 pay respects to the tomb of a martyr ❷ (academic or technical) attainments

驿(驛) yì　〈史〉post station (now usu used in place names); ~道 post road / ~站 post station

绎(繹) yì　〈书〉unravel; sort out

轶 yì　see "逸❹❺" yì

疫 yì　epidemic disease; pestilence; ~苗〈医〉vaccine / ~情 information about and appraisal of an epidemic; epidemic situation

弈 yì　〈书〉weiqi or go, a board game; ~林 community of chess players; chess circles ❷ play chess; 对~ play chess against each other

奕 yì　〈书〉grand; magnificent; ~~ radiating power and vitality

益 yì　❶ good; benefit; advantage / ~处 benefit; profit; advantage / ~鸟 beneficial or useful bird / ~友 friend and mentor; helpful friend ❷ increase; add to; ~智 enhance intelligence ❸ (usu 益发 or 益加) all the more; still more; increasingly

悒 yì　〈书〉sad; worried; in low spirits; ~闷 distress; anxiety

谊 yì　friendship; 师生之~ friendly relationship between teacher and student

逸 yì　❶ ease; leisure; rest; ~乐 comfort and pleasure; leisure and joy ❷ escape; flee; run away ❸ live in seclusion or solitude; ~民 hermit; recluse ❹ be lost; ~散 (of gas, etc) be lost; evaporate; dissipate / ~事 anecdote (esp about a famous person) / ~文 ancient essay no longer extant / ~闻 anecdote; hearsay ❺ surpass; excel; ~群 excel all others; be preeminent

翌 yì　〈书〉(in time) next; ~日 next day

肄 yì　study; ~业 study in school or at college

裔 yì　〈书〉❶ descendants; posterity; 华~美国人 American of Chinese descent or origin; Chinese American ❷ distant land

意 yì ❶ meaning; idea：～念 idea；thought / ～象 image；imagery / ～蕴 inner meaning; implication / ～在言外 the meaning is implied; there is more than meets the eye ❷ wish; desire; intention：～旨 intention; wish; will / ～中人 person one is in love with; person of one's heart ❸ anticipate; expect：～表 beyond one's expectation; unexpected / ～想 imagine; expect; anticipate

意会 yìhuì understand what's implied; sense：只可～，不可言传 can be sensed, but not explained in words

意见 yìjiàn ❶ idea; view; opinion：～箱 suggestion box ❷ objection; criticism; complaint：闹～ quarrel with each other

意境 yìjìng artistic mood or conception：～恢弘 magnificently conceived

意料 yìliào anticipate; expect：～之中 as expected

意气 yìqì ❶ will and spirit：～风发 high-spirited and vigorous; full of daring and vigour ❷ temperament：～相投 be congenial in temperament; see eye to eye ❸ personal feelings or prejudice：～用事 act on impulse or whim; be swayed by personal feelings

意识 yìshí ❶ consciousness：～流 stream of consciousness / ～形态〈哲〉ideology / 爱国～ patriotism; patriotic feelings ❷ (often used together with 到) be conscious or aware of; awake to; realize

意思 yìsi ❶ meaning; idea; implication ❷ opinion; intention; desire ❸ (show one's) appreciation; token of gratitude, etc：买些东西～一下。Let's buy something to express our appreciation. ❹ interest; fun：没～的电影 boring movie

意图 yìtú intention; intent：摸清他的～ find out what he is after

意外 yìwài ❶ unexpected; unanticipated; unforeseen：～风险 emergency risk ❷ accident; mishap; bad luck

意味 yìwèi ❶ meaning; significance; implication：～深长 profound in significance; pregnant with meaning; highly significant / 这～着什么? What does this imply? ❷ interest; overtone; flavour

意向 yìxiàng intention; purpose：～书 letter of intent

意义 yìyì meaning; sense; significance：～深远 be of far-reaching importance

意译 yìyì ❶ free translation (v. literal translation) ❷ semantic translation (v. transliteration)

意愿 yìyuàn wish; longing; desire

意志 yìzhì will：～消沉 be in broken or low spirits; be depressed or demoralized

溢 yì ❶ overflow; spill：～出 spill over; overflow / ～于言表 show in one's words and expression; come through in overtones ❷ excessive; exaggerated：～美之词 excessive praise

缢 yì 〈书〉hang：～杀 strangle to death; kill by strangling

瘗 yì 〈书〉bury; inter

毅 yì firm; resolute; steadfast：～力 willpower; will; stamina / ～然 resolutely; firmly

熠 yì

熠熠 yìyì 〈书〉radiant; brilliant：光彩～ brilliant splendour

薏 yì

薏米 yìmǐ also "薏仁米"; "苡仁" seed of Job's tears

翳 yì ❶〈书〉cover; screen：荫～ be shaded or hidden by foliage ❷〈医〉slight corneal opacity; nebula

臆 yì ❶ (usu 胸臆) chest ❷ subjectively：～测 conjecture; surmise; speculation / ～断 assume; suppose, speculate / ～想 supposition; assumption / ～造 fabricate (a story, etc); invent; concoct

翼 yì ❶ wing of a bird, etc ❷ side; flank; ～侧〈军〉flank ❸〈书〉assist (a ruler); aid

癔 yì

癔病 yìbìng　*also* "歇斯底里"〈医〉hysteria

懿 yì 〈书〉exemplary; ～旨 edict of an empress or empress dowager

yīn

因 yīn ❶〈书〉follow; carry on; ～袭陈规 stick to or follow outmoded rules ❷〈书〉on the basis of; in accordance with; in the light of; ～材施教 teach a person according to his or her aptitude; suit the instruction to the student's level ❸ cause; reason; grounds; ～由 reason; cause ❹ because (of); due to; as a result of; ～祸得福 profit by adversity / ～小失大 save a little only to lose a lot; be penny wise and pound foolish

因此 yīncǐ for this reason; therefore; consequently

因地制宜 yīndìzhìyí do what is appropriate in the light of local circumstances; suit measures to local conditions; act according to circumstances

因而 yīn'ér as a result; thus; therefore

因果 yīnguǒ ❶ cause and effect; 互为～ interact as both cause and effect / ～律 law of causation ❷〈宗教〉karma; destiny; preordained fate; ～报应 retribution for sin

因陋就简 yīnlòu-jiùjiǎn make do with whatever is available; do things as simply and thriftily as possible

因人 yīnrén *used in idioms*; ～成事 achieve sth with the help of others; rely on others for success / ～而异 differ from person to person; vary with each individual / ～设事 create a job to accommodate a person

因势利导 yīnshìlìdǎo make the best use of a situation and guide sth along in the light of its general trend; adroitly suit action to circumstances; take the tide at the flood

因素 yīnsù ❶ element; component; 积极～ positive element ❷ cause or circumstance that brings about success or failure; factor; 决定性～ decisive factor; determinant

因特网 yīntèwǎng *also* "国际互联网" Internet; ～服务提供者 ISP (Internet service provider) / ～内容经营者 ICP (Internet content provider)

因为 yīnwèi because (of); for; as

因循 yīnxún ❶ continue to follow (old customs, etc); stick to; ～守旧 stick to old ways; stay in the old rut; follow the beaten track ❷ procrastinate; delay; ～延误 procrastinate until it is too late

因噎废食 yīnyēfèishí give up eating for fear of choking — refrain from doing sth necessary for fear of a slight risk; throw out the baby with the bathwater

因应 yīnyìng adjust to; meet; deal with; ～变局 adjust to changes; deal with an eventuality

因缘 yīnyuán ❶〈宗教〉principal and subsidiary causes; cause ❷ predestined relationship

因子 yīnzǐ *also* "因式"〈数〉factor; divisor。

阴（陰） yīn ❶ *see* "阴历❶" ❷ moon; ～历 lunar calendar; traditional Chinese calendar ❸（of weather）overcast; cloudy; gloomy; ～天 overcast sky; cloudy day / ～雨 overcast and rainy / ～云 dark clouds ❹ shade: ～干 dry in the shade / ～影 shadow; shade ❺ north of a hill; south of a river ❻ in intaglio; hidden; secret: ～文 characters cut in intaglio / ～一套, 阳一套 act one way in public and another in private; double-deal ❼ sinister; perfidious; foul: ～笑 sinister smile or grin ❽ of the nether world: ～曹 *also* "阴间"; "阴司" nether world; Hades / ～宅 tomb; grave / ～魂不散 the ghost lingers on; the evil influence remains ❾〈理〉negative: ～电 negative electricity or charge / ～极〈电〉negative electrode; negative pole; cathode / ～离子 negative ion; anion ❿ (usu 阴部)〈生理〉private parts (esp of the female); pudenda: ～道 vagina / ～茎 penis; phallus / ～毛 pubic hair; pubes

阴暗 yīn'àn　dim; dark; gloomy: ～面〈喻〉dark or seamy side of things; unhealthy things in life

阴沉 yīnchén　overcast; gloomy; somber: 面色～ be grim-faced; look glum / 阴沉沉的天 gloomy or overcast sky

阴错阳差 yīncuò-yángchā　mistake or error due to a strange combination of circumstances; accidental mistake or error

阴德 yīndé　*also* "阴骘" good deed to the credit of the doer in the next world: 广积～ accumulate credit in the next world

阴风 yīnfēng　❶ chill wind ❷ evil or ill wind; 扇～ fan the winds of evil; stir up trouble

阴沟 yīngōu　covered drain; sewer; sewerage: ～里翻船 capsize in a drain — fail where failure is least expected

阴冷 yīnlěng　❶ (of weather) cold and gloomy ❷ sombre; cold; glum: 性格～ of a cold and glum nature

阴凉 yīnliáng　shady and cool: ～儿 cool shade

阴霾 yīnmái　haze: 战争的～ (under the) shadow of war

阴谋 yīnmóu　conspiracy; plot; underhand scheme: ～家 conspirator; intriguer; schemer / ～诡计 conspiracy; schemes and intrigues

阴平 yīnpíng　〈语言〉first tone in modern standard Chinese　*see also* "四声" sìshēng

阴森 yīnsēn　gloomy and horrid; ghastly; gruesome

阴私 yīnsī　secret not to be divulged; shameful secret; skeleton in the cupboard

阴险 yīnxiǎn　sinister; insidious; treacherous: ～毒辣 sinister and vicious; insidious and ruthless

阴性 yīnxìng　❶〈医〉negative: 化验结果为～ test negative (for sth) ❷〈语言〉feminine gender

阴阳 yīnyáng　❶ (in traditional philosophy) *Yin and Yang*, opposite principles or forces existing in nature and human affairs: 阴盛阳衰〈中医〉*Yin* rises while *Yang* declines; 〈喻〉the female is more powerful or numerous than the male ❷ ancient theory on the functioning of celestial bodies such as the sun and the moon: ～历 lunisolar calendar ❸ astrology, divination, geomancy, etc: ～生 *also* "阴阳家"; "阴阳先生" geomancer

阴阳怪气 yīnyángguàiqì　eccentric; cynical; (usu purposefully) equivocal: 净说些～的话 always speak enigmatically

阴郁 yīnyù　gloomy; dismal; depressed

茵 yīn　mattress: ～～ (of grass, etc) lush and thick

荫(蔭) yīn　shade (of a tree): ～蔽 shade; cover; be shaded or hidden　*see also* yìn

音 yīn　❶ sound; voice; tone: ～标〈语言〉phonetic symbol or transcription / ～叉 tuning fork / ～调

tone; pitch / ～符〈乐〉(musical) note / ～高〈乐〉pitch / ～阶〈乐〉scale / ～节〈语言〉syllable / ～量 sound volume / ～律 also "乐律"〈乐〉temperament / ～色 also "音质" tone colour; timbre / ～速〈理〉speed of sound; sound velocity / ～箱 sound box; speaker / ～译 also "译音" transliteration / ～域〈乐〉range; compass; gamut / ～讯 news; word; ～信 also "音讯" news; mail

音儿 yīnr 〈方〉❶ voice ❷ implication; 听话听～ listen for the meaning behind sb's words

音容 yīnróng 〈书〉voice and look of sb; likeness of sb; ～宛在 could recall sb's voice and look as if sb were still alive

音响 yīnxiǎng ❶ sound; acoustics; ～设备 sound or acoustic equipment / ～效果 sound effects; acoustics ❷ (short for 组合音响) hi-fi (stereo component) system

音像 yīnxiàng　audio and video; ～制品 audio and video products

音乐 yīnyuè　music; ～会 concert / ～家 musician / ～剧 musical (comedy) / ～厅 concert hall / ～电视 music TV (MTV) / ～学院 conservatory of music; music school

洇 yīn　(of ink) spread and sink in; run (on paper)

姻 yīn ❶ marriage; ～亲 relation by marriage / ～缘 predestined marital relationship; match made by Heaven ❷ relation by marriage; ～兄 brother-in-law

氤 yīn

氤氲 yīnyūn 〈书〉(of smoke, mist, etc) dense; thick

殷 yīn ❶ rich; plentiful; abundant; ～实 well-to-do; well-off; substantial ❷ eager; ardent; cordial; ～切 earnest; ardent; eager ❸ (Yīn) Yin Dynasty, the later period of Shang

(商) Dynasty
see also yān

殷勤 yīnqín　*also* "慇懃" keen to please; eagerly attentive; solicitous; 献～ try to please sb; shower attentions upon sb / ～接待 show solicitous hospitality

堙 yīn 〈书〉❶ mound ❷ block or stop up; ～没良田 (of desert, etc) lay waste once-fertile land

暗(瘖) yīn 〈书〉❶ (usu 喑哑) (of voice) hoarse; husky ❷ silent; mute

yín

吟 yín ❶ intone; recite; chant; ～诗 recite or compose poetry / ～诵 chant; recite / ～咏 recite with a cadence; intone; chant ❷ song as a type of classical poetry ❸ 〈书〉groan; lament; sigh

垠 yín 〈书〉boundary; limit

猌 yín

猌猌 yínyín 〈书〉(of a dog) yap; yelp

银 yín ❶ silver (Ag); ～婚 silver wedding; 25th wedding anniversary / ～楼 silverware shop; jewellery or jeweller's shop / ～牌 silver medal; second place / ～器 silverware; silver (work) ❷ relating to money; ～两 also "银子" silver (as currency); money / ～钱 money / ～圆 also "银元"; "银洋" silver dollar ❸ silver-coloured; ～白 silvery white / ～灰 silver (grey)

银耳 yín'ěr　*also* "白木耳" tremella

银根 yíngēn　supply in money market; money supply; ～紧 tight money / 放松～ relax money supply

银行 yínháng　bank; ～法 banking law / ～家 banker / ～卡 bank credit card / 存折 bankbook

银河 yínhé　*also* "银汉"; "天河"

Milky Way；～系〈天文〉Milky Way system；the Galaxy

银幕 yínmù （motion-picture）screen；搬上～ make（a novel，etc）into a film

银屏 yínpíng （television）screen；重上～ return to the TV screen

银杏 yínxìng 〈植〉ginkgo

银鱼 yínyú 〈动物〉whitebait

淫 yín ❶ excessive；extreme；～雨 *also* "霪雨" too much or excessive rain / ～威 despotic power；abuse of power ❷ indulgent；licentious；～荡 loose（in morals）；lascivious；lewd / ～欲 sexual desire；lust ❸ adulterous；promiscuous；dissolute；～妇 wanton woman；adulteress / ～乱 sexually promiscuous；loose in sexual relations ❹ （of words，etc）lewd；obscene；pornographic；～秽 obscene；pornographic；salacious / ～书 pornographic book；pornography

寅 yín 3rd of the Earthly Branches；～吃卯粮 eat one's corn in the blade；spend on deficit　*see also* "干支" gānzhī

夤 yín 〈书〉❶ hold in respectful awe；ingratiate oneself；～缘 advance one's career by fawning on bigwigs；make use of one's connections to climb up ❷ deep；～夜 late at night；in the dead of the night

yǐn

引 yǐn ❶ pull；stretch；extend；～弓 pull or draw a bow / ～吭高歌 sing at the top of one's voice；sing heartily ❷ lead；draw；induce；～见 introduce；present / ～路 guide；lead（the way）/ ～火烧身 bring trouble on oneself；make self-criticism to encourage criticism from others / ～狼入室 open the door to a dangerous foe / ～蛇出洞 draw a snake out of its hole — induce sb to reveal his or her true colours

❸ leave；～退 quit or leave office；resign / ～辞 resign one's position（to avoid suspicion，etc）❹ cause；arouse；trigger；～逗 tease；lure；entice / ～发 initiate；set off（a fire，etc）；arouse （imagination，etc）/ ～人注目 eye-catching；noticeable；conspicuous ❺ quote；cite；～号 quotation marks（" "）；quotes / ～述 quote；cite / ～文 quoted passage；quotation / ～证 quote or cite as evidence / ～经据典 quote the classics or authoritative works

引爆 yǐnbào ignite；detonate；～装置 detonating device；detonator；igniter

引导 yǐndǎo ❶ lead；pilot；show round ❷ guide；善于～学生 give students proper guidance

引渡 yǐndù 〈法〉extradite；～条约 extradition treaty

引而不发 yǐn'érbùfā enlighten people through guidance；be skilful at guidance or control；bide one's time fully prepared

引荐 yǐnjiàn （introduce and）recommend；～人 recommender

引进 yǐnjìn ❶ *see* "引荐" ❷ introduce；import；absorb；～技术 import or introduce technology / ～外资 absorb foreign investment

引咎 yǐnjiù 〈书〉acknowledge one's mistake；take the blame；～辞职 take the blame and resign

引力 yǐnlì 〈理〉gravitation；gravitational force；attraction，～场 gravitational field

引起 yǐnqǐ set or touch off；bring about；arouse

引擎 yǐnqíng engine；双～飞机 twin-engine plane

引人入胜 yǐnrénrùshèng thrilling；fascinating；enchanting

引申 yǐnshēn extend（the meaning of a word or a phrase）；～义 extended meaning

引水 yǐnshuǐ ❶ draw or channel water:~工程 water diversion works or project **②** also "引航" pilot a ship into harbour:~员 pilot

引信 yǐnxìn also "信管" detonator; fuse

引言 yǐnyán foreword; introduction; opening remarks

引以为戒 yǐnyǐwéijiè learn a lesson from a previous error; learn from sb's mistake; take warning

引用 yǐnyòng **①** quote; cite; invoke **②** recommend; employ; appoint:~私人 employ one's own people

引诱 yǐnyòu lead astray; entice; seduce:~青少年犯罪 entice youngsters into crime

引子 yǐnzi **①** 〈戏〉opening lines of an actor or actress **②** introductory part of some music **③** (of speech or writing) introductory remarks **④** 〈中药〉ingredient added to enhance the efficacy of medicine

饮 yǐn **①** drink; drink wine or other liquor:一~而尽 gulp down; drink off / ~弹而亡〈书〉be killed by a bullet **②** sth to drink; drink:~料 also "饮品" drink; beverage **③** nurse; bottle up; bite down hard (usu hatred):~恨终身 die with a deep grievance in one's heart

see also yìn

饮泣 yǐnqì 〈书〉weep in silence; weep silent tears:~吞声 swallow one's tears; choke back one's sobs

饮食 yǐnshí **①** food and drink; diet:~店 eating house; eatery / ~业 catering trade / ~结构 (pattern of one's) diet / ~卫生 dietetic hygiene; healthful food and drink **②** drink and eat:~男女 food, drink and sex — basic needs or desires of life

饮水 yǐnshuǐ **①** also "饮用水" drinking or potable water; water for cooking:~机 water dispenser **②** drink water:~思源 when you drink water, think of its source — never forget where one's happiness comes from; feel grateful

饮誉 yǐnyù enjoy fame; be acclaimed; win praise:~海内外 win worldwide fame

饮鸩止渴 yǐnzhènzhǐkě drink poison to quench thirst — seek temporary relief regardless of the consequences

隐（隱） yǐn **①** hide (from view); conceal:~伏 lie hidden or low; hide; lurk / ~含 imply; contain vaguely / ~士 hermit; recluse / ~姓埋名 conceal or hide one's identity; live incognito **②** latent; hidden; secret:~疾 shameful disease (such as VD) / ~情 fact or reason one wishes to hide; unmentionable secret / ~痛 secret anguish; dull pain / ~忧 secret worry or anxiety / ~衷 feelings one wishes to keep to oneself; inner feelings

隐蔽 yǐnbì **①** take cover; conceal; hide:~的敌人 hidden enemies **②** serving for concealment; cryptic; hidden:~色 cryptic colour / ~地形 hidden terrain

隐藏 yǐncáng hide; conceal; keep or remain under cover:~在暗处 lurk in the shadows

隐患 yǐnhuàn hidden trouble; lurking danger; snake in the grass

隐讳 yǐnhuì cover up; hide; avoid mentioning:毫不~ withhold nothing; be perfectly candid

隐晦 yǐnhuì obscure; veiled; ambiguous:~曲折 (of a statement, etc) obscure and roundabout

隐居 yǐnjū withdraw from society and live in seclusion; be a hermit

隐瞒 yǐnmán hide; conceal; hold back:~真相 withhold or suppress the truth; keep the lid over sth

隐秘 yǐnmì **①** hidden; concealed **②** secret:内心的~ inner secret

隐匿 yǐnnì 〈书〉hide; conceal; lie

low：～罪〈法〉misprision / ～证据 suppress evidence

隐忍 yǐnrěn　bear patiently；endure silently；forbear；～苟活 swallow the humiliation and live on

隐私 yǐnsī　private matter；personal secret；privacy：～权 privacy (rights)

隐退 yǐntuì ❶ (of night, etc) recede；fade away；disappear ❷ live in seclusion；retire from political life

隐形 yǐnxíng ❶ hidden；covert；invisible：～收入 invisible or off-payroll income / ～眼镜 contact lens ❷〈军〉stealth：～飞机 stealth aircraft

隐性 yǐnxìng　recessive：～基因 recessive gene

隐隐 yǐnyǐn　faint；indistinct；dull：～绰绰 vague；dim；indistinct / ～作痛 hurt faintly；give a dull pain

隐语 yǐnyǔ ❶ insinuating or enigmatic language；deliberately vague remark ❷ argot；cant

隐喻 yǐnyù　also "暗喻"〈语言〉metaphor

隐约 yǐnyuē　indistinct；faint；vague：～其词 use ambiguous language；equivocate

瘾（癮） yǐn　addiction；habitual craving；passion：有～ be addicted (to sth)；be keen (on sth) / 犯烟～ have an urge to smoke；crave a cigarette / ～头 addiction；obsession；strong interest / ～君子 dope addict；doper；heavy smoker

yìn

印 yìn ❶ seal；chop：～鉴 specimen seal impression (for checking) / ～泥 red ink paste used for seals / ～台 ink pad；stamp pad / ～信 official seal / ～章 seal；chop；signet ❷ mark；print；stamp：带有时代的～记 be marked with the characteristics of the times ❸ print；engrave：～次 impression (of a book) /

发 print and distribute；issue and circulate / ～制 print (plates, etc) / ～染厂 printing and dyeing mill / ～照片 print a photo；have a print made ❹ tally (with sth)；conform；accord：～证 confirm；verify；corroborate

印地语 Yìndìyǔ　Hindi

印第安人 Yìndì'ānrén　(American) Indian；Native American

印度 Yìndù　India：～教 Hinduism / ～人 Indian / ～洋 Indian Ocean

印花 yìnhuā ❶ printing：～布 printed calico；cotton print；prints ❷ (revenue) stamp：～税 stamp tax or duty

印刷 yìnshuā　printing：～厂 printing house；press；print shop / ～品 printed matter / ～术 (art of) printing / ～体 block letter；print hand / ～错误 printing mistake；misprint；typographic error

印堂 yìntáng　part of the forehead between the eyebrows

印象 yìnxiàng　impression：留下深刻～ leave a deep impression (on sb) / ～不好 be unfavourably impressed (by sb)；have a poor impression (of sb)

印子 yìnzi ❶ mark；print；trace：手～ handprint ❷ (usu 印子钱) loan at exorbitant interest；usury

饮 yìn　water (an animal)　see also yǐn

荫（蔭） yìn ❶ shady and damp ❷〈书〉shelter；protect：～庇 protection by one's elders or ancestors　see also yīn

窨 yìn　cellar；basement：～井〈建筑〉inspection well or shaft

yīng

应（應） yīng ❶ answer；respond：无人～门。Nobody answered the door. ❷ promise；agree；accept：～允 agree；assent; approve ❸ should; ought to be due;～尽的义务 duty incumbent on one; one's bounden duty

see also yìng

应得 yīngdé　deserve; merit; be due (to sb); 罪有～ deserve the punishment / ～的奖赏 due reward

应该 yīnggāi　*also* "应当" should; ought to; must; 这事太不～. That is much too much.

应有 yīngyǒu　due; deserved; proper; ～尽有 have everything that one expects to find

英 yīng ❶〈书〉blossom; bloom; petal; 落～ fallen petals ❷ outstanding (person); hero; man of valour; ～豪 *also* "英杰" heroes; men of great bravery; outstanding figures / ～名 illustrious or great name / ～模 heroes and model workers ❸ (Yīng) (short for 英国) Britain; England; ～镑 pound sterling / ～尺 (formerly also 呎) foot / ～寸 (formerly also 吋) inch / ～里 (formerly also 哩) mile / ～亩 acre / ～文 *also* "英语" English (language) / ～国人 a Briton; the English; the British / ～联邦 British Commonwealth (of Nations) / ～伦三岛 British Isles

英才 yīngcái ❶ (usu of sb young) talented person; person of outstanding ability ❷ talent; wisdom

英俊 yīngjùn ❶ eminently talented; outstanding; brilliant; ～有为 brilliant and promising ❷ handsome and spirited; good-looking and bright

英烈 yīngliè ❶ courageous and unyielding; indomitable ❷ martyr who died heroically

英灵 yīnglíng　*also* "英魂" spirit of the brave departed; spirit of a martyr

英明 yīngmíng　wise; sagacious; brilliant

英年 yīngnián　prime of life; youthful years; youth; ～早逝 die in one's prime

英雄 yīngxióng　hero; 女～ heroine / ～本色 (action or conduct) befitting a hero / ～所见略同 heroes share the same thought; great minds think alike

英勇 yīngyǒng　heroic; brave; valiant

英姿 yīngzī　heroic bearing; ～飒爽 valorous and heroic (in bearing); bright and brave

莺（鶯） yīng〈动物〉warbler; oriole

婴 yīng　baby; infant; ～儿车 baby carriage; pram; stroller / ～儿床 crib; cot; cradle

嘤 yīng〈书〉〈象声〉(as of birds) chirp

罂 yīng

罂粟 yīngsù〈植〉poppy

缨 yīng ❶ ribbon or band used to fasten a hat ❷ tassel; 红～枪 red-tasselled spear ❸ sth shaped like a tassel; 萝卜～ radish leaves

樱 yīng ❶ (usu 樱桃) cherry ❷ (usu 樱花) oriental cherry; cherry blossom

鹦 yīng

鹦鹉 yīngwǔ　*also* "鹦哥"〈动物〉parrot; ～学舌 repeat the words of others like a parrot; parrot

膺 yīng〈书〉❶ chest; breast ❷ bear; shoulder; receive; 荣～要职 be honoured to assume a post of great responsibility ❸ (usu 膺惩) send a punitive expedition against; attack

鹰 yīng　hawk; eagle; ～派〈喻〉hawk / ～犬 lackey; running dog; hired thug / ～钩鼻子 aquiline nose

yíng

迎 yíng ❶ meet; greet; receive; 远～ go over a long distance to meet sb / ～新 see the New Year in; welcome new arrivals ❷ go or move towards; meet face to face; ～面 head-on; face to face; in one's face / ～着风浪前进 forge ahead in the teeth of winds and waves

迎春 yíngchūn ❶ greet the spring; ～会 party to usher in the spring ❷ also "迎春花"〈植〉winter jasmine

迎风 yíngfēng ❶ facing or against the wind; ～而立 stand against the wind ❷ in, down or with the wind; ～招展 flutter in the wind

迎合 yínghé　make a special effort to please; cater or pander to

迎接 yíngjiē ❶ also "迎迓" receive; welcome; greet (a guest, etc) ❷ meet (a challenge, etc); face (difficulties, etc)

迎刃而解 yíngrèn'érjiě　(of a problem) be readily solved; be readily done or resolved

迎头 yíngtóu　head-on; straight; directly; ～赶上 catch up with the foremost; catch up at the double / ～痛击 deal a head-on blow; attack head-on

迎战 yíngzhàn　meet (an approaching enemy) head-on; take on (a rival in competition, etc)

茎（莖） yíng　〈书〉grave; cemetery

荧（熒） yíng　〈书〉glimmering; gleaming; dim (light); 众星～～ sparkling stars

荧光 yíngguāng　〈书〉fluorescence; fluorescent light; ～灯 fluorescent lamp

荧屏 yíngpíng ❶ also "荧光屏" fluorescent screen; screen (of a television, monitor, etc) ❷ television; ～新星 new TV star

盈 yíng ❶ fill; pack; throng; ～溢 brim or overflow (with enthusiasm, etc) ❷ surplus; gain; ～亏 waxing and waning (of the moon); profit and loss (of an enterprise) / ～利 also "赢利"(gain) profit / ～余 also "赢

余" surplus; gain; profit

莹（瑩） yíng ❶〈书〉jade-like stone ❷ lustrous and transparent;泪水～～ glittering tears

萤（螢） yíng　also "萤火虫" firefly; glowworm

营（營） yíng ❶ seek (profit, etc); pursue;非～利机构 non-profit institution ❷ operate; manage; run; ～建 construct; build / ～运 (of trains, etc) operate; run ❸ camp; barracks; ～地 campsite; camping ground / ～房 barracks / ～火 campfire ❹〈军〉battalion

营救 yíngjiù　rescue; save; succour

营垒 yínglěi ❶ barracks and enclosing walls ❷〈喻〉camp; bloc

营生 yíngshēng ❶ make or eke out a living ❷ (yíngsheng)〈方〉job; occupation; line of business

营私 yíngsī　seek private gain; pursue selfish ends; feather one's nest; ～舞弊 engage in malpractice for selfish ends; practise graft

营销 yíngxiāo　marketing;～员 salesman / ～策略 marketing strategy

营养 yíngyǎng　nutrition; nourishment; aliment; ～品 nutriment; nutrient; tonic / ～师 nutritionist; dietitian / ～不良 malnutrition; undernourishment

营业 yíngyè　do business;～额 turnover; volume of business / ～税 business tax; turnover tax; transactions tax / ～员 shop assistant / ～范围 scope of business operation / ～时间 business hours

营造 yíngzào ❶ build; construct; ～商 builder (as a businessman) / ～学术氛围 build up an academic ethos ❷ plant (trees); afforest

萦（縈） yíng　〈书〉entwine; entangle; encompass; ～怀 occupy one's mind; absorb one's attention / ～回 also "萦绕" go round

and round; hover; linger

楹 yíng　principal column of a hall; pillar;～联 couplet written on a scroll and hung on a pillar

蝇(蠅) yíng　housefly; fly;～拍 flyswatter; flyflap /～头小利 petty profits /～营狗苟 shamelessly seek personal gain; drag out an ignoble existence

赢 yíng　❶ win; beat; defeat;～家 winner ❷ gain or obtain (profit, etc);～得 win; gain; earn /～利 also "盈利" (gain) profit

瀛 yíng　〈书〉sea; ocean: 东～ East China Sea;〈喻〉Japan

yǐng

颖 yǐng　〈书〉❶ glume; grain husk ❷ tip (of a writing brush, etc); point ❸ clever; bright:～慧 clever; intelligent /～悟 bright; smart

影 yǐng　❶ shadow; reflection; image ❷ trace; vestige; vague impression;～绰绰 vaguely; dimly; indistinctly ❸ photograph; picture:～集 photo or picture album ❹ motion picture; film; movie:～后 movie queen; most popular female movie star /～迷 film or movie fan /～片 film; picture /～评 film review /～坛 film circles; filmdom /～院 cinema; movie theatre /～视界 also "影视圈" film and TV circles ❺ trace; copy; photograph;～印 photo-offset printing; photo-offset process

影壁 yǐngbì　❶ inside screen wall (facing the gate inside a traditional Chinese courtyard) ❷ also "照壁" outside screen wall facing the gate of a house ❸ wall with carved murals

影碟 yǐngdié　VCR (videocassette recorder) or video disc;～机 VCR player

影射 yǐngshè　also "隐射" allude to; hint obliquely at; insinuate;～攻击 attack by innuendo

影响 yǐngxiǎng　affect; influence; impact;～情绪 dampen one's spirits or enthusiasm

影子 yǐngzi　❶ shadow; reflection; image:～戏 shadow play /～内阁 shadow cabinet ❷ trace; vestige; vague impression:没～的事 sth totally groundless; cock-and-bull story

瘿 yǐng　❶〈中医〉goitre ❷ also "虫瘿" gall

yìng

应(應) yìng　❶ answer; reply; respond:～诉〈法〉(of the accused) respond to charges; take up self-defence ❷ comply with; grant; accept:～募 also "应招" join up; enlist /～诺 assent; agree; undertake /～聘 accept an offer (of a job) or invitation (to do sth) /～邀 be invited; (do sth) at sb's invitation; on invitation /～战 meet an invading enemy; accept or take up a challenge ❸ suit; conform to; accord with:～运而生 arise at the right moment; emerge as the times require ❹ deal or cope with; meet:～敌 deal with one's enemy or opponent; meet an enemy in battle

see also yīng

应变 yìngbiàn　meet an emergency or a contingency;～措施 emergency measure

应承 yìngchéng　agree (to do sth); consent; accept (an order, etc)

应酬 yìngchou　❶ socialize; entertain;～多 have a lot of entertaining to do ❷ dinner party

应答 yìngdá　also "应对" reply; answer:～如流 respond readily and promptly; answer readily and fluently

应付 yìngfù　❶ deal or cope with; treat; handle:～自如 cope with or handle a situation with ease; be equal to the occasion ❷ do (sth) perfunctorily; go through the motions; make do；～人 give sb the run-around

应急 yìngjí　meet an urgent need; meet an emergency or a contingency；～计划 exigency plan; crash programme

应接不暇 yìngjiēbùxiá　have not a moment's leisure in one's work; have more visitors or business than one can attend to

应景 yìngjǐng　❶ do sth after a fashion; act for the sake of politeness, etc; go through the motions：喝两盅应个景儿 drink a cup or two to suit the occasion ❷ in season; for the occasion：～文章 sth written or done for the occasion

应力 yìnglì　〈理〉stress; tension

应声 yìngshēng　appear right away when called; happen right at the sound of sth.：～虫 yesman; echo／～而至 appear right on call

应时 yìngshí　❶ seasonable; in season：～瓜果 fruits of the season ❷ at once; promptly; immediately

应试 yìngshì　sit for or take an examination：～教育 examination-oriented education

应验 yìngyàn　come true; be confirmed or fulfilled

应用 yìngyòng　❶ use; employ; apply ❷ applied：～文 practical writing (as in official documents, etc)／～科学 applied sciences／软件 application software

应征 yìngzhēng　❶ be recruited; enlist; join up：～入伍 join the army; enlist ❷ respond to a call for contribution of articles

映 yìng　reflect; mirror; shine；～象 reflection; impression; image／～照 *also* "映射" shine upon; shed or cast light on

映衬 yìngchèn　❶ set off；相互～ match each other well ❷ contrast; antithesis

硬 yìng　❶ hard; stiff; tough：～币 hard cash; coin; specie／～度 hardness／～化 hardening；〈医〉sclerosis；(of ideas) rigid; ossified／～木 hardwood／～盘〈信息〉hard (magnetic) disk／～水 hard water／～卧 hard sleeping berth (on a train)／～席 *also* "硬座" hard seat (on a train)／～邦邦 very hard; stiff; clumsy／～通货 hard currency／～纸板 hardboard; cardboard／～着陆 (make a) hard landing／～笔书法 calligraphy by hard-tipped pen ❷ strong; tough; inflexible：～汉 tough guy; macho man; man of iron will／～仗 tough battle; formidable task／～指标 inflexible target, goal or requirement; mandatory quota or criterion ❸ manage with effort：～撑 *also* "硬挺" endure with all one's will; hold out with all one's might／～说 assert; allege／～着头皮 toughen one's scalp; brace or force oneself (to do sth against one's will) ❹ good; able; capable：笔头儿～ write a powerful hand／～功夫 high proficiency; great skill

硬骨头 yìnggǔtou　❶ person of indomitable will ❷ hard nut; difficult task；啃～ crack a hard nut; work at a difficult task

硬件 yìngjiàn　hardware；〈喻〉physical equipment：～工程师〈信息〉hardware engineer

硬朗 yìnglang　(of an elderly person) hale and hearty; sturdy

硬碰硬 yìngpèngyìng　❶ meet force with force; match strength with strength; confront the tough with toughness ❷ (of a job) demanding painstaking work or real skill; exacting

硬伤 yìngshāng　❶ damage or injury caused by outside force ❷ rudimentary and conspicuous mistake (in a manuscript, etc)

硬性 yìngxìng rigid; stiff; hard:～规定 hard and fast rule

yō

哟 yō 〈叹〉*used at the beginning of a sentence to express slight surprise or acclamation*:～，你又瘦了。Oh! You've become even thinner than before. *see also* yo

yo

哟 yo 〈助〉*used at the end of a sentence to urge sb on, etc*:快点来～! Come over here, quick! *see also* yō

yōng

佣(傭) yōng ❶ hire; employ ❷ servant:～工 hired labourer; servant
see also yòng

拥(擁) yōng ❶ (usu 拥抱) clasp or hold in one's arms; embrace; hug:～有 own; have; possess ❷ surround; gather (around); crowd:～挤 crowd; throng; push and squeeze / 道路～塞 congested or jammed roads ❸ support; uphold:～戴 support; hold in esteem / ～护 support; back; be for

痈(癰) yōng 〈医〉carbuncle; large boil:～疽 ulcer

邕 Yōng another name for Nanning (南宁), capital of Guangxi (广西)

庸 yōng ❶ commonplace; mediocre; inferior:～才 mediocre person; mediocrity / ～碌 mediocre and unambitious / ～医 quack; charlatan / ～人自扰 worry about imagined troubles; make much fuss about nothing ❷ 〈书〉(used in the negative) need:无～

细述。There is no need to go into details.

庸俗 yōngsú vulgar; coarse; philistine:～化 vulgarize; debase / ～唯物主义 〈哲〉vulgar materialism

雍 yōng 〈书〉harmony:～容 graceful and poised; refined and self-possessed

慵 yōng 〈书〉weary; lethargic; languid:～惰 lazy; languid

壅 yōng ❶ 〈书〉stop up; obstruct:～塞 clog up; jam; congest ❷ heap (soil or fertilizer) over and around the roots (of trees, etc)

臃 yōng 〈书〉swollen:～肿 too fat to move freely; cumbersome; 〈喻〉overstaffed

鳙 yōng *also* "鳙鱼"; "胖头鱼" variegated carp; bighead

yǒng

永 yǒng perpetually; forever; for all time:～别 *also* "永诀" part forever; be separated by death / ～存 everlasting / ～垂青史 go down in history

永垂不朽 yǒngchuíbùxiǔ be immortal; live forever:人民英雄～! Eternal glory to the people's heroes!

永恒 yǒnghéng eternal; perpetual; permanent:～的主题 timeless theme

永久 yǒngjiǔ permanent; everlasting; eternal:～居留 permanent residency

永生 yǒngshēng ❶ eternal life; immortality ❷ throughout one's life; lifelong:～永世 all one's life; for ever and ever

永远 yǒngyuǎn always; forever; once and for all

甬 Yǒng another name for Ningbo (宁波) of Zhejiang (浙江)

甬道 yǒngdào ❶ *also* "甬路" paved path leading to a main hall or a tomb ❷ corridor; passageway

咏（詠） yǒng ❶ chant; recite; intone; ～唱 chant (a poem) ❷ express or narrate in poetic form; ～怀 express one's sentiments and aspirations in poetic form; 歌以～志 chant a poem to express one's aspirations

咏叹 yǒngtàn sing; intone; chant; ～调〈乐〉aria; operatic solo

泳 yǒng swim; ～池 swimming pool / ～道 (swimming) lane / ～坛 swimming circles / ～装 swimming suit (for women)

俑 yǒng figurine (for burial with the dead); tomb figure

勇 yǒng brave; valiant; courageous; ～士 person of great courage and strength; warrior / ～往直前 march forward courageously; advance bravely / ～于负责 be bold in shouldering responsibilities

勇敢 yǒnggǎn brave; courageous; valorous

勇猛 yǒngměng courageous and powerful; full of valour and vigour; ～善战 brave and skilful in battle

勇气 yǒngqì nerve; courage; mettle; 鼓起～ pick or pluck up one's courage

涌（湧） yǒng (of water, etc) gush; surge; emerge; ～动 roll; surge / ～现 emerge in large numbers; come to the fore; come forth / ～进会场 surge or swarm into a meeting hall

蛹 yǒng pupa; chrysalis

踊（踴） yǒng leap or jump up

踊跃 yǒngyuè ❶ leap; jump; ～欢呼 leap and cheer ❷ falling over each other (to do sth); keenly; enthusiastically; ～参加 participate enthusiastically

yòng

用 yòng ❶ use; utilize; apply; ～法 use; usage; application / ～刑 torture; put (sb) to torture / ～非所长 fail to make use of sb's or one's strengths / ～毛笔写字 write with a brush / 无～武之地 find no scope for one's abilities ❷ expense; spending; outlay; ～度 expenditure; spending; outlay / ～费 expense; charge; cost ❸ use; usefulness; utility; 何～之有! What's the use of it! ❹ (used in the negative) need; have to; ～不了这么多钱。There is no need for so much money. / ～不着跟他生气 It is not worthwhile to be angry with him. / 不～客气。Don't stand on ceremony. ❺〈敬〉eat; drink; have; ～饭 have a meal; eat

用兵 yòngbīng employ military forces; resort to arms; ～如神 direct military operations with miraculous skill; be a past master in the art of war

用场 yòngchǎng use; application; 派上～ be put to use; come in handy

用处 yòngchu use; utility; good; 大有～ can be put to good use; be very useful

用功 yònggōng hardworking; diligent; studious

用户 yònghù user; consumer; ～终端〈信息〉user terminal / ～识别卡 SIM (subscriber identity module) card

用具 yòngjù utensil; implement; tool

用力 yònglì also "用劲" use one's strength; exert oneself; put one's shoulder to the wheel

用品 yòngpǐn articles for use; 日常～ articles for daily use; daily necessities

用人 yòngrén ❶ employ people; make use of personnel; ～不当 employ or use people inappropriately; fail to choose the right person for a job / ～单位 employing unit; employer ❷ (yòngren)〈旧〉servant

用事 yòngshì ❶〈书〉be in power ❷〈贬〉act (in a certain way); conduct oneself

用途 yòngtú use; application; purpose

用心 yòngxīn ❶ diligently; attentively; with concentration ❷ motive; purpose; intention: ～良苦 have bethought oneself (over sth) really hard

用意 yòngyì intention; aim; purpose: 你～何在？ What are you up to?

用语 yòngyǔ ❶ choice of words; wording; diction ❷ phraseology; terminology; term: 法律～ legal parlance

佣 yòng commission: ～金 commission; brokerage; middleman's fee *see also* yōng

yōu

优（優） yōu ❶ good; excellent: ～等 top-notch; first-rate; excellent ❷ plentiful; affluent: ～裕 well-off; affluent; abundant / ～游自得〈书〉live a leisurely and contented life ❸ give preferential treatment; favour: ～抚 give special care and preferential treatment (to disabled servicemen, etc) / ～遇有加 give (sb) exceedingly good treatment; treat (sb) generously ❹ *also* "优伶"〈旧〉actor or actress

优待 yōudài give special or preferential treatment: ～券 complimentary ticket

优点 yōudiǎn merit; strong point; forte: 发扬～ give play to one's strengths

优厚 yōuhòu munificent; generous; liberal: 条件～ liberal terms

优化 yōuhuà optimize; ～组合 optimization or optimal grouping / ～产品结构 optimize product mix

优惠 yōuhuì preferential; favourable: ～券 coupon (for buying sth at reduced price, etc) / ～贷款 loan on preferential terms; soft loan

优良 yōuliáng fine; good; superior

优美 yōuměi graceful; elegant; fine: 风景～ beautiful scenery

优柔寡断 yōuróuguǎduàn irresolute (and hesitant); indecisive

优生 yōushēng healthy birth: ～优育 giving birth to healthy babies and bringing them up in a sound way; healthy birth and sound care

优胜 yōushèng winning; superior; excellent: ～奖 excellence award / ～劣败 *also* "优胜劣汰" the good prevailing over the bad; survival of the fittest

优势 yōushì superiority; advantage; dominant position: 局部～ local or partial superiority / 空中～ air supremacy

优先 yōuxiān have priority; take or have precedence: ～权 priority; preference

优秀 yōuxiù excellent; outstanding; splendid

优雅 yōuyǎ elegant; graceful; exquisite

优异 yōuyì exceedingly good; superb; outstanding

优越 yōuyuè superior; favourable; advantageous: ～感 sense of superiority; superiority complex / ～性 superiority; advantage

优质 yōuzhì high quality or grade; top-notch: ～产品 quality product

忧（憂） yōu worry; concern oneself; be sad or depressed: 为国分～ share the woes of the nation / ～愁 sad; worried; depressed / ～愤 worried and indignant / ～虑 worried; anxious; concerned / 伤~ distressed; upset; laden with grief / ～国～民 concern oneself with one's country and people

忧患 yōuhuàn suffering; misery; hardship: ～意识 sense of urgency (about danger, etc); sense of crisis

忧心 yōuxīn worry; concern; anxiety: ～忡忡 heavy-hearted; care-laden; laden with anxieties / ～如焚 burning with anxiety; extremely worried

忧郁 yōuyù melancholy; heavy-heart-ed; dejected: ~症〈医〉melancholia

呦 yōu〈叹〉*used to express surprise*, *etc*: ~! 电视机也坏了？Why, the television no longer works.

幽 yōu ❶ deep and remote; secluded; dim: ~暗 dim; shadowy; gloomy / ~谷 deep and secluded valley / ~居 live as a hermit; live in seclusion / ~趣 elegant taste (as of a hermit); delightful serenity or delights of seclusion / ~深 *also* "幽邃" (of forests, etc) deep and serene; secluded and tranquil ❷ secret; hidden; covert: ~愤 hidden grief; pent-up resentment / ~会 (lovers') secret meeting; rendezvous; tryst / ~怨 hidden bitterness (as of a young girl disappointed in love) ❸ quiet; tranquil; serene: ~情 profound and undefinable sentiments; exquisite feelings ❹ imprison; place in confinement: ~禁 incarcerate; put under house arrest; imprison ❺ (of the) nether world: ~灵 *also* "幽魂" ghost; spectre

幽静 yōujìng quiet and secluded; tranquil; peaceful

幽默 yōumò humour: ~感 sense of humour

幽思 yōusī ❶ be lost in reverie; ponder; meditate ❷ innermost thoughts and feelings; hidden sentiments: ~绵绵 brimming with subtle sentiments

幽雅 yōuyǎ tranquil and elegant; (of a place) quiet and tastefully laid out

幽幽 yōuyōu〈书〉❶ (of sound, light, etc) faint; feeble; weak ❷ looming in the distance; remote and latent: ~乡情 deep, latent nostalgia

悠 yōu ❶ remote in time or space; long; far: ~长 long; long-drawn-out; protracted / ~远 long ago; far-distant; remote ❷ leisurely; with

ease; unhurried: ~闲 *also* "幽闲" leisurely and carefree / ~着点儿，别累着了。〈方〉Take it easy, and don't overwork yourself. ❸〈口〉swing; sway: ~荡 swing to and fro; sway back and forth

悠久 yōujiǔ long; long-standing; age-old: 历史~ of a long history; age-old

悠然 yōurán easy and carefree: ~自得 be carefree and content / ~神往 (of one's thoughts) be carried away (to the remote past or a distant place)

悠扬 yōuyáng (of music, etc) rising and falling; in harmony; melodious

悠悠 yōuyōu ❶ long; remote; infinite: ~岁月 long years ❷ leisurely; unhurriedly: ~自得 carefree and content ❸〈书〉numerous; myriad; a multitude: ~万物 myriads of things

yóu

尤 yóu ❶ remarkable; conspicuous; outstanding: ~物〈书〉extraordinary or outstanding thing; rarity; beauty ❷ (usu 尤其) particularly; especially; in particular: ~为不满 particularly dissatisfied ❸ fault; error; wrongdoing ❹ have a grudge against; resent; blame

由 yóu ❶ cause; reason; grounds: ~头 pretext; excuse ❷ follow; obey: 信不信~你 believe it or not ❸ (starting) from; (passing) by; owing or due to: ~浅入深 from the easy to the difficult; from the elementary to the profound ❹ (up) to: 会议~你主持 It is up to you to chair the meeting. ❺ by means of; through: ~三部分组成 composed of three parts

由不得 yóubude ❶ not be up to (sb); be beyond (sb's) control; not admit of (sth) ❷ cannot help; cannot but: ~笑了 cannot help laughing; laugh involuntarily

由此 yóucǐ from this; as a result：～及彼 from this to that；from one to the other / ～可见 thus it can be seen; it is therefore clear

由来 yóulái ❶ from the inception; up to now：～已久 long-standing; time-honoured ❷ cause; source; reason

由于 yóuyú owing or thanks to; because of：～众所周知的原因 owing to causes known to all

由衷 yóuzhōng from the bottom of one's heart; heart-felt：～之言 words from the bottom of one's heart / 感到～的高兴 heartily rejoice

邮（郵） yóu ❶ post; mail：～包 (postal) parcel / ～差〈旧〉postman / ～船 (ocean) liner; packet ship / ～戳 postmark / ～费 postage / ～购 buy by mail order; purchase by postal order / ～汇 remit by post / ～寄 send by post; post / ～局 also "邮政局" post office / ～票 (postage) stamp / ～亭 postal kiosk; newsagent / ～筒 pillar box; postbox; mailbox / ～箱 postbox; mailbox ❷ stamps; philately：～展 philatelic exhibition; stamp show

邮递 yóudì postal or mail delivery：～员 postman; mailman

邮电 yóudiàn post and telecommunications：～局 post and telecommunication office

邮件 yóujiàn postal matter; post; mail：挂号～ registered mail / 航空～ air mail / 快递～ express mail

邮政 yóuzhèng postal service：～编码 (shortened as 邮编) postcode; zip (code) / ～储蓄 postal savings (deposit) / ～汇票 postal (money) order / ～信箱 post-office box (P/OB)

邮资 yóuzī postage：～已付 postage paid; postpaid

犹（猶） yóu 〈书〉❶ (usu 犹如) just as; like; as if ❷ still; even：话～未了。The words

were hardly finished.

犹大 Yóudà Judas; traitor

犹太 Yóutài Jew; Jewish：～人 Jewish (people); Jew / ～教 Judaism; Jewish religion

犹豫 yóuyù also "犹疑" hesitate; vacillate; be irresolute：～不决 hesitate; remain undecided; be of two minds

油 yóu ❶ oil; fat; grease：～布 oilcloth; oilskin; tarpaulin / ～灯 oil lamp / ～管 oil pipe / ～井 oil well / ～库 oil depot; tank farm / ～耗 (of a car, etc) consumption of petrol, etc / ～画 oil painting / ～轮 also "油船" (oil) tanker / ～墨 printing ink / ～污 greasy dirt or filth / ～烟 soot / ～渣 dregs of fat / ～渍 greasy filth; oil stain / ～老虎 oil or gas guzzler / ～作物 oil bearing or oilseed crop ❷ apply tung oil or varnish; paint (furniture, etc) ❸ be stained with oil or grease：～乎乎 oily; greasy ❹ oily; slick; glib

油饼 yóubǐng ❶ also "油枯" soya bean or groundnut dregs after oil been extracted; oil cakes ❷ oil-fried dough cake

油彩 yóucǎi greasepaint; paint：～太厚 be too thickly painted

油菜 yóucài ❶ also "芸薹" rape：～籽 rapeseed ❷ green rape

油茶 yóuchá ❶〈植〉tea-oil tree; oil-tea camellia ❷ gruel of sweetened, fried flour

油光 yóuguāng glossy; shiny; varnished：～水滑 extremely shiny and smooth

油滑 yóuhuá slick; slippery; foxy：～头滑脑 (of manner) slick; flippant / 油腔滑调 (of speech) glib; unctuous; flippant

油矿 yóukuàng ❶ oil deposit ❷ also "油田" oilfield：～工人 oilfield worker

油绿 yóulǜ glossy dark green

油门 yóumén ❶ throttle：开大～ turn

the throttle up ❷〈口〉accelerator：踩 ~ step on the accelerator

油腻 yóunì ❶ oily；greasy ❷ greasy food

油漆 yóuqī ❶ paint；varnish：~未干！ Wet paint！ ❷ cover with paint；paint

油然 yóurán ❶ spontaneously；unwittingly：~而生 (of a feeling) rise of itself；rush or well up ❷ densely；profusely

油水 yóushui ❶ grease；oil ❷ profit；gain：捞 ~ make some gain；pick up some crumbs

油酥 yóusū short；crisp；flaky：~点心 shortbread

油条 yóutiáo ❶ deep-fried twisted dough stick ❷ also "油子" sly guy；fox；老~ foxy old hand；old fox

油头粉面 yóutóu-fěnmiàn coquettish or dandified in appearance

油汪汪 yóuwāngwāng ❶ dripping with oil；greasy ❷ glossy；shiny：~的麦苗儿 shiny green wheat seedlings

油印 yóuyìn mimeograph：~机 mimeograph

油炸 yóuzhá deep-fry：~ 土豆片 French fries；chips

柚 yóu

柚木 yóumù〈植〉teak　see also yòu

疣 yóu （commonly known as 瘊子）〈医〉wart

莜 yóu

莜麦 yóumài also "油麦"〈植〉naked or raw oats

铀 yóu〈化〉uranium (U)：~弹〈军〉U-bomb

蚰 yóu

蚰蜒 yóuyán〈动物〉common house centipede

鱿 yóu

鱿鱼 yóuyú squid

游（❷-❹ 遊） yóu ❶ swim：~水 swim；畅~

长江 have a good swim in the Yangtze ❷ stroll or rove about；travel；tour：~船 also "游舫" pleasure boat / ~记 travel notes；travels / ~人 also "游客" visitor (to a park, etc)；sightseer；tourist / ~艇 yacht；pleasure boat / ~兴 interest in going on an excursion；enthusiasm or mood for sightseeing / ~街示众 parade sb through the streets to expose him to the public / ~山玩水 tour mountains and rivers；travel from one scenic spot to another ❸〈书〉associate (with sb) ❹ roving；migrating；unsettled：~民 hobo；tramp；vagrant / ~侠〈旧〉roving brave；knight-errant ❺ part of a river；reach：黄河中 ~ middle reaches of the Yellow River

游荡 yóudàng ❶ loaf about；idle；loiter ❷ stroll；saunter ❸ (of a boat, etc) float

游击 yóujī (wage) guerrilla warfare：~队 guerrilla force or detachment / ~战 guerrilla war or warfare

游览 yóulǎn go sightseeing；tour；visit：~车 tour bus；tourist coach or bus

游乐 yóulè amusement；recreation：~场 amusement or recreational park / ~园 pleasure ground；recreational garden；amusement park

游离 yóulí ❶〈化〉free：~态 free state ❷ dissociate；drift away：~于集体之外 be aloof from the collective；be detached from the group

游历 yóulì travel for pleasure；tour；travel

游牧 yóumù move about in quest of pasture；rove about as a nomad：~部落 nomadic tribe

游刃有余 yóurèn-yǒuyú do a job with skill and ease；accomplish sth effortlessly；be more than competent

游手好闲 yóushǒuhàoxián idle about; loaf; ～之徒 loafer

游说 yóushuì go about selling an idea or drumming up support; canvas; lobby

游玩 yóuwán ❶ amuse oneself; have fun; play ❷ go sightseeing; visit

游戏 yóuxì ❶ pastime; game; ～机 (short for 电子游戏机) video game player / ～规则 rules of the game ❷ play; have fun

游行 yóuxíng parade; march; demonstration

游移 yóuyí ❶ move back and forth ❷ (of attitude, policy, etc) waver; hesitate; vacillate; ～不决 be hesitant and indecisive

游弋 yóuyì cruise; patrol; 军舰在海上～。Warships were plying the sea.

游艺 yóuyì entertainment; recreation; ～节目 programme of theatrical and other performances

游泳 yóuyǒng swim; ～池 swimming pool / ～馆 natatorium; enclosed swimming pool / ～裤 bathing or swimming trunks / ～帽 bathing or swimming cap / ～衣 swimsuit; swimming or bathing suit

游子 yóuzǐ 〈书〉person who has been away from his home or country for a long time; 海外～ overseas Chinese

yǒu

友 yǒu ❶ friend; ～人 friend / ～情 friendly sentiments; friendship / ～邦 friendly nation ❷ intimate; close; friendly; ～爱 friendly affection; fraternal love / ～善〈书〉friendly; genial; amicable

友好 yǒuhǎo ❶ (close) friend; 身前～ friends of the deceased ❷ friendly; amiable; amicable; ～城市 cities of friendship; sister or twin cities

友谊 yǒuyì friendship; ～赛 friendly (match)

有 yǒu ❶ have; own; possess; ～愧 feel guilty; feel qualms (about sth) / ～喜〈口〉be pregnant / ～罪 be guilty (of an offence) / ～的是 (of sb) have plenty of (of sth) be in abundance; there is no lack of / ～分量 weighty; significant / ～空儿 have time; be free / ～价证券 (negotiable) securities / ～期徒刑〈法〉set term of imprisonment / ～识之士 person with breadth of vision; person of discernment or insight / ～章可循 have rules to go by; be governed by existing rules / ～其父,必～其子 like father, like son; chip of the old block / ～福同享,～祸同当 share weal and woe; stick together through thick and thin / ～志者事竟成.〈谚〉Where there is a will there is a way. / ～则改之, 无则加勉。Correct mistakes if you have made any, and guard against them if you have not. ❷ used to indicate existence or occurrence of sth; 这事还～商量儿。There is still room for discussion on the matter. ❸ used for estimation or comparison; 她～你高吗? Is she as tall as you are? ❹ some (people, time, or place); certain; ～时 sometimes; at times; from time to time / ～人赞成、～人反对。Some are for it; others are against it. ❺ used before certain verbs to form polite formulae; ～扰 thanks for your hospitality

有碍 yǒu'ài hinder; obstruct; affect (adversely); ～风化 adversely affect morals and manners / ～观瞻 offend the eye; be an eyesore

有案可稽 yǒu'ànkějī also "有案可查" be on record; be documented

有板有眼 yǒubǎn-yǒuyǎn rhythmical; measured; orderly; 说起话来～ speak in a well-measured manner

有偿 yǒucháng compensated with payment; ～服务 paid service / ～使用

(make) compensated use (of sth); use for a fee

有待 yǒudài　remain (to be done); await; ~解决 have yet to be resolved; be pending

有底 yǒudǐ　know what's what; be fully prepared for what is coming; 心里~ know how things stand and feel confident

有的放矢 yǒudìfàngshǐ　have a definite object in view; do sth with a definite purpose in mind

有点 yǒudiǎn　❶ some; a small amount; a little ❷〈副〉(usu used of sth unfavourable) somewhat; rather; a bit; ~不舒服 be a bit under the weather

有方 yǒufāng　with the proper method; in the right way; methodically; 指导~ give proper guidance

有关 yǒuguān　have sth to do with; relate to; concern; ~当局 authorities concerned; competent or relevant authorities

有鬼 yǒuguǐ　there is sth fishy; have a guilty conscience; 感到其中~ smell a rat

有过之无不及 yǒuguòzhīwúbùjí (mostly used in a bad sense) go even farther than; outdo

有害 yǒuhài　harmful; injurious; detrimental

有机 yǒujī　❶〈化〉organic; ~体 organism / ~物 organic matter ❷〈喻〉organic; intrinsic; ~组成部分 component part

有劲 yǒujìn　❶ have great physical strength; strong ❷ with keen interest; interesting

有口 yǒukǒu　❶ on every tongue; ~皆碑 be praised by everyone; win universal commendation ❷ though having a tongue; ~难辩 find it difficult to defend or vindicate oneself

有赖 yǒulài　rely or rest on; ~于双方

的诚意 rely on the sincerity of the two sides

有劳 yǒuláo　〈套〉thanks for the effort; ~你带个话儿。Would you please be so kind as to take a message for me?

有理 yǒulǐ　❶ reasonable; justified; in the right ❷〈数〉rational; ~数 rational number

有力 yǒulì　strong; powerful; vigorous

有利 yǒulì　advantageous; favourable; profitable; ~时机 opportune time; favourable opportunity / ~可图 have good prospects of gain; stand to profit; (of sth) be profitable

有门儿 yǒuménr　❶ begin to find a solution; be hopeful (of success); 看样子, 这事~了! It looks as if there is hope of getting it done. ❷ get the hang (of sth)

有名 yǒumíng　well-known; famous; celebrated

有名无实 yǒumíng-wúshí　in name but not in reality; merely nominal; titular; ~的领导人 titular leader; figurehead

有目共睹 yǒumùgòngdǔ　be there for all to see; be obvious to all; be as clear as day

有钱 yǒuqián　rich; affluent; wealthy; ~能使鬼推磨〈俗〉money makes the mare go; money talks

有情 yǒuqíng　be in love; be feeling; ~人终成眷属 lovers are destined to be married; Jack shall have Jill, all shall be well

有求必应 yǒuqiúbìyìng　comply with every request; be always ready to help

有趣 yǒuqù　interesting; amusing; fascinating

有如 yǒurú　just as; be like; as if; 好得~同胞兄弟 as intimate as brothers

有色 yǒusè　coloured; ~人种 coloured race / ~金属 nonferrous metal / ~眼镜 coloured spectacles; 〈喻〉prejudice

有神论 yǒushénlùn　theism; ~者

theist

有生力量 yǒushēng lìliàng ❶ effective (troop or personnel) strength; effectives ❷ troops; army

有恃无恐 yǒushìwúkǒng be secure in the knowledge that one has strong backing; be emboldened by powerful support; fear nothing with sb at one's back;有了证据更觉得～了 become all the bolder with evidence in one's hands

有数 yǒushù ❶ know exactly how things stand; know the score ❷ not many; only a few

有所 yǒusuǒ to some extent; some; somewhat;～保留 have reservations / 你～不知。There are some things you don't know.

有条不紊 yǒutiáobùwěn in apple-pie order; methodical; systematical

有望 yǒuwàng hopeful (of doing sth);康复～。There is hope of recovery.

有为 yǒuwéi full of promise; promising;年轻～ young and promising

有…无… yǒu…wú… ❶ used to indicate that the former but not the latter;有口无心 be sharp-tongued but mean no malice; be blunt and tactless / 有气无力 listless; feeble; faint and weak / 有眼无珠 have eyes but see not; be undiscerning / 有勇无谋 be more brave than wise; be foolhardy ❷ used to emphasize that there is only the former;有去无还 gone never to return / 有增无减 ever-increasing; ever-growing; ever-expanding ❸ used to indicate that with the former there is no danger of the latter;有备无患 where there is precaution, there is no danger; preparedness averts peril; be prepared against all eventualities ❹ used to mean that sth may or may not exist;有意无意 wittingly or unwittingly; consciously or unconsciously; by accident or design

有限 yǒuxiàn ❶ limited; finite;～公司 limited (-liability) company ❷ not many; not high in degree;能力～ meagre in ability; not very capable

有线 yǒuxiàn wired;～电话 line or wire telephony / ～电视 closed-circuit television; cable TV

有效 yǒuxiào effective; authentic; valid;～期 period of validity; time of efficacy

有些 yǒuxiē ❶ some; part ❷ some; not much; not many ❸ to some extent; somewhat; rather;～累 a bit tired

有心 yǒuxīn ❶ have a mind to; be bent on;～人 person bent on achieving sth; determined and conscientious person ❷ intentionally; purposely; by design

有形 yǒuxíng tangible; visible;～贸易 visible trade / ～资产 tangible assets; tangibles

有幸 yǒuxìng have the luck or pleasure (of doing sth); be fortunate enough (to do sth)

有言在先 yǒuyánzàixiān make it clear beforehand; caution in advance; forewarn

有眼不识泰山 yǒuyǎnbùshítàishān fail to recognize a person of eminence in his presence; entertain an angel unawares

有益 yǒuyì profitable; beneficial; valuable;～于国家 be of value to the country

有意 yǒuyì ❶ see "有心" ❷ also "有意思" be attracted (sexually); take a fancy (to sb)

有意识 yǒuyìshí consciously;～让对方犯错误 deliberately lead the other party astray

有意思 yǒuyìsi ❶ significant; meaningful ❷ interesting; amusing; enjoyable ❸ see "有意❷"

有…有… yǒu…yǒu… ❶ used before nouns or verbs opposite or contrastive *in meaning to indicate that both are present*：有来有往 give and take；be reciprocal / 有始有终 manage sth from beginning to end；carry sth through ❷ *used for emphasis before words with the same or similar meaning*：有情有义 affectionate and true；true and loyal / 有声有色 full of sound and colour；vivid and dramatic；spirited / 有说有笑 talk and laugh；be merry / 有条有理 methodical；orderly / 有血有肉 true to life；vivid；lifelike / 有鼻子有眼儿 describe every detail vividly；show or portray to the life

有余 yǒuyú ❶ have a surplus；be more than enough：聪明～，温厚不足 be more intelligent than gentle and kind ❷ more than；-odd：30～ over thirty

有缘 yǒuyuán （usu used in a good sense）be predestined or fated；be bonded with；have an affinity for（each other）

有朝一日 yǒuzhāoyīrì some day；one day

有助于 yǒuzhùyú contribute to（sth）；be conducive to（sth）；help（to do sth）

酉 yǒu 10th of the Earthly Branches *see also* "干支" gānzhī

莠 yǒu 〈书〉bad（people）：不分良～ not distinguish between the bad and the good

黝 yǒu black；dark：～黯 *also* "黝暗" dim；dark / ～黑 dark；swarthy

yòu

又 yòu 〈副〉❶ *indicating repetition or continuation*：看了～看 look（at sth）again and again / 一天～一天 day after day ❷ *indicating simultaneous existence of several conditions or qualities*：～打～拉 strike and stroke alternately；combine reward with threat；employ a carrot-and-stick policy / ～惊～喜 be both startled and delighted；be pleasantly surprised ❸ furthermore；moreover；besides：～及 postscript（PS）/ ～名 alias；assumed name ❹ *indicating addition of an odd number to a whole*：三～二分之一 three and a half ❺ *used often in parallel to indicate two contradictory things*：～要马儿跑，～要马儿不吃草〈俗〉expect the horse to run fast but not graze it；try to eat one's cake and have it ❻ *used for emphasis*：你～不是不知道。It's not as if you don't know.

右 yòu ❶ right（side）：～边 *also* "右面" right or right-hand side；right / 向～拐 turn right ❷ west（of a river or mountain）❸ right side；side of precedence：无出其～ second to none ❹ conservative；the Right

右派 yòupài the Right；right wing：～分子 rightist / ～人士 right-wingers

右倾 yòuqīng Right deviation：～思想 Right-deviationist thinking / ～机会主义 Right opportunism

右手 yòushǒu ❶ right hand ❷ *also* "右首" right-hand side；right

右翼 yòuyì ❶〈军〉right flank or wing ❷ Right；right-wing

幼 yòu ❶ young；minor；under age：～虫 larva / ～雏 young bird；nestling / ～苗 seedling；saplings / ～年 childhood；infancy / ～芽 young shoot；bud / ～子 youngest or baby son ❷ children；the young

幼儿 yòu'ér child；infant：～园 kindergarten；nursery school / ～教育 preschool education

幼小 yòuxiǎo immature：～的心灵 immature mind

幼稚 yòuzhì ❶ young；juvenile；infantile：～工业〈经〉infant industry ❷ childish；puerile；naive

佑（祐） yòu help；protect；bless：～护 protect；defend

柚 yòu also "柚子" fruit of Rangoon teak, commonly known as shaddock or pomelo　see also yóu

囿 yòu 〈书〉❶ animal farm or park ❷ limited; constrained; hampered; ～于成见 be blinded by prejudice; be biased

宥 yòu 〈书〉excuse; forgive: 务祈见～ Please accept my sincere apologies.

诱 yòu ❶ guide; direct; induce: ～劝 inveigle; lure ❷ lure; tempt; seduce: ～逼 also "诱诮" cajole and coerce; entice and threaten / ～饵 bait / ～供 trap or coax sb into (making a) confession / ～拐 abduct; kidnap / ～奸 seduce / ～骗 inveigle; cajole; trap / ～杀 trap and kill / ～降 lure into capitulation / ～敌深入 lure the enemy in deep / 景色～人. The scenery is captivating.

诱导 yòudǎo　guide; lead; induce: 善于～ be good at guidance

诱发 yòufā ❶ inspire; induce: ～联想 inspire association ❷ bring out (sth potential or latent); cause to happen; induce

诱惑 yòuhuò ❶ entice; seduce; lure ❷ attract; captivate; allure; ～力 tempting force

诱因 yòuyīn　immediate cause; cause (of a disease)

釉 yòu　glaze; ～陶 glazed pottery / ～质 also "珐琅质" 〈生理〉enamel

鼬 yòu 〈动〉weasel: 黄～ brown weasel

yū

迂 yū ❶ go round; take a detour; wind one's way: ～缓 dilatory; sluggish / ～曲 tortuous; winding ❷ given to outworn rules and ideas; pe-

dantic; impractical: ～见 impractical, pedantic view / ～阔 high-sounding and impractical / ～夫子 pedant

迂腐 yūfǔ　given to outworn rules and ideas; pedantic: ～无用 doltish and useless

迂回 yūhuí ❶ circuitous; tortuous; roundabout ❷ 〈军〉outflank: ～战术 outflanking tactics

淤(❸瘀) yū ❶ silt up: ～积 silt up; deposit; (of anger, etc) pent-up / ～塞 (of a river, etc) silt up; be blocked or choked with silt / ～滞 retarded with silt; silted ❷ (usu 淤泥) silt; sediment; mud ❸ stasis: ～血 extravasated blood

yú

于(於) yú ❶ used to introduce a) time or place: ～6 时 30 分到达 arrive at 6:30 b) object or direction: 趋～寒冷 tend to be cold; become cold c) aspect, cause or purpose: ～心不忍 not have the heart to; cannot bear to d) source or starting point: 出～好心 out of good will e) comparison: 多～20 more than twenty; exceed twenty f) agent of action: 见笑～人 be laughed at by others ❷ used as a suffix a) after a verb: 属～ belong to b) after an adjective: 敢～斗争 dare to fight

于今 yújīn ❶ up to the present; by now: 重庆一别，～八年. It is eight years since we parted in Chongqing. ❷ nowadays; today; now: ～为烈 stronger than ever before

于是 yúshì　also "于是乎" hence; therefore; as a result

予 yú 〈书〉I; me: ～取～求 take whatever one wants — take freely; make unlimited or exorbitant demands　see also yǔ

余(❶-❸餘) yú ❶ surplus; spare; remain-

Y

ing:~党 remnants (of an overthrown clique, etc); remaining cohorts / ~毒 residual poison; pernicious vestige; evil influence / ~额 remaining sum; balance / ~晖 *also* "余辉" last rays of the setting sun; afterglow / ~留 left (over); remaining / ~孽 remnant evil force; surviving supporter of an evil cause / ~震〈地〉aftershock ❷ more than; odd; over:20一 5 over twenty days ❸ after; later than; beyond:悲愤之~ when sobered down after sorrow ❹〈书〉I; me

余波 yúbō repercussions; aftermath:~未平。The repercussions are still felt.

余地 yúdì leeway; latitude; room:留有~ allow some leeway (for)

余悸 yújì lingering fear; 心有~。 One's heart is still throbbing with fear.

余热 yúrè ❶ surplus heat; waste or residual heat ❷〈喻〉energy of retirees:贡献~ make continued contributions in retirement

余生 yúshēng ❶ one's remaining years; remainder of one's life ❷ survival:劫后~ survive a holocaust

余味 yúwèi agreeable aftertaste; pleasant impression:~无穷 leave a lasting and pleasant impression or aftertaste

余暇 yúxiá spare time; leisure (time)

余兴 yúxìng ❶ lingering interest ❷ entertainment after the main event

余音 yúyīn lingering (pleasant) sound:~绕梁,三日不绝。Echoes of the songs kept reverberating in the air for a long time afterwards.

鱼(魚) yú fish; ~翅 shark's fin / ~刺 fishbone / ~ 饵 bait / ~竿 fishing rod / ~鳞 (fish) scale / ~苗 fish fry / ~群 shoal or school of fish / ~鲜 fish and shellfish as food / ~汛 *also* "鱼讯" fishing season / ~肚白 pale; greyish white / ~

肝油 cod-liver oil / ~米之乡 land of fish and rice; land of milk and honey; land of abundance / ~水情深 as close as water and fish; of profound friendship

鱼贯 yúguàn one following the other; in single file: ~ 而入 enter in single file; file in

鱼雷 yúléi〈军〉torpedo:~艇 torpedo or mosquito boat; patrol torpedo boat (PT boat)

鱼龙混杂 yúlónghùnzá the genuine mixed with the false; good and bad jumbled together

鱼目混珠 yúmùhùnzhū palm off the bad as the good; pass off the sham as the genuine

鱼肉 yúròu ❶ flesh of fish; fish and meat:~丸子 fishball ❷ oppress; victimize:~乡里 tyrannize the locality

鱼死网破 yúsǐ-wǎngpò〈喻〉the fish dies and the nets gets torn — end up in common ruin; fight like the Kilkenny cats

鱼游釜中 yúyóufǔzhōng like fish swimming in a cooking pot — on the verge of death; in a perilous situation

鱼跃 yúyuè ❶ (like) fish leaping out of water ❷〈体〉fish dive:~救球 (make a) diving save

鱼子 yúzǐ roe; fish eggs:~酱 caviar

竽 yú *yu*, ancient Chinese wind-pipe

谀 yú〈书〉fawn (on sb); curry favour (with sb); flatter:~辞 flattering remarks; flattery

娱 yú give pleasure to; entertain; amuse:~悦 please; make happy; give pleasure

娱乐 yúlè amusement; entertainment; recreation:~场 amusement park / 好好一一番 enjoy oneself heartily; have a good time

渔 yú ❶ fishing; ~ 场 fishing ground; fishery / ~ 歌 fisherman's song / ～具 also "鱼具" fishing gear or tackle / ～民 fisherman; fishing population / ～政 fishery administration ❷ take sth one has no right to

渔猎 yúliè reap unfair gains; profit at others' expense:从中～ exploit a situation to benefit oneself; cash in on other people's efforts

渔猎 yúliè ❶ fishing and hunting ❷〈书〉plunder; pursue:～女色 also "渔色"(of a man) seek carnal pleasure; womanize

渔人之利 yúrénzhīlì fisherman's gains — profit seized by a third party:坐收～ quietly reap third party profit from a fight between others

渔业 yúyè fishery:～区 fishing zone; fishery limits

隅 yú ❶ corner; nook ❷ outlying area; border:海～ seaboard

揄 yú

揄扬 yúyáng〈书〉❶ praise:极口～ praise or extol to the sky; speak highly of ❷ propagate; advocate:～大义 publicize a just cause

喁 yú

喁喁 yúyú〈书〉❶ echo; parrot ❷ talk in an undertone; whisper:～私语 talk privately in a low voice

逾 yú ❶ surpass; exceed; go beyond:～分 beyond the limit; excessive /～期 exceed the time limit; be overdue / 年～花甲 be over 60 years of age ❷ even more:悲痛～甚 even more grieved

逾越 yúyuè exceed; go beyond; surmount:～常规 depart from the usual practice; go against convention /～权限 overstep one's authority; go beyond one's competence

腴 yú (usu 腴润)(of a person) fat; plump; rounded out ❷ fertile

渝 yú ❶ change one's faith, etc.:至死不～ remain staunch unto death ❷ (Yú) another name for Chongqing（重庆）

愉 yú pleased; happy; delighted:面露不～ look displeased or annoyed

愉快 yúkuài happy; joyful; cheerful:过得非常～ have a very good time

愉悦 yúyuè joyful; cheerful; in high spirits:心情～ (with) a joyful heart; delighted; cheerful

瑜 yú ❶〈书〉(splendour or luster of) beautiful jade;〈喻〉virtue:瑕～互见 have defects as well as merits; have both strengths and weaknesses

瑜伽 yújiā also "瑜珈" yoga

榆 yú〈植〉elm:～木脑袋 blockhead; foolish, brainless person

虞 yú〈书〉❶ speculate; suppose; expect ❷ anxiety; misgiving; worry:无饥寒之～ not have to worry about food and clothing ❸ deceive; cheat; dupe:无贰无～ be neither disloyal nor deceitful

愚 yú ❶ foolish; doltish; stupid:～钝 slow-witted; dull; stupid /～人 fool; dolt /～妄 ignorant but arrogant; stupid but conceited /～不可及 stupid in the extreme; hopelessly stupid ❷ make a fool of; fool:～民政策 obscurantist policy; obscurantism ❸〈谦〉humble:～见 in my humble opinion; as far as I can see

愚笨 yúbèn foolish; stupid; slow-witted

愚蠢 yúchǔn stupid; foolish; silly

愚公移山 Yúgōngyíshān the Foolish Old Man who removed the mountains — (symbol of the) spirit of perseverance

愚昧 yúmèi ignorant; foolish:～无知 foolish and ignorant; unenlightened; benighted

愚弄 yúnòng　dupe; make a fool of; deceive

舆 yú　〈书〉❶ cart; coach; carriage ❷ palanquin; sedan chair ❸ land; area; territory ❹ public; popular: ～情 public sentiment; popular feeling

舆论 yúlùn　public opinion: 左右～ manipulate public opinion ／ ～界 the media; press circles ／ ～工具 mass media; the media

yǔ

与(與) yǔ　❶ give; offer; grant: ～人方便，自己方便。〈俗〉He who helps others helps himself. ❷〈书〉associate with; be in friendly contact with: 朝夕～共 be in friendly contact with; 朝夕～共 be together from morning till night; be closely associated ❸〈书〉praise; commend; assist: ～人为善 sincerely help people to improve; have good intentions towards people ❹ with; against: ～时俱进 march with or keep abreast of the times ／ ～众不同 out of the ordinary; different from the common run; unconventional ❺ and; together with　*see also* yù

与虎谋皮 yǔhǔmóupí　expect sb to act against his or her own interests; attempt the impossible

与其 yǔqí　(usu used with 毋宁 or 不如) (would rather …) than; rather than: ～多而杂，不如少而精。Less but better rather than more but inferior.

与日俱增 yǔrìjùzēng　grow with each passing day; increase steadily

与世 yǔshì　(used in idioms) with or from the world: ～长辞 depart from the world for ever; pass away ／ ～无争 stand aloof from worldly strife; hold oneself aloof from the world

予 yǔ　give; grant; bestow: ～人口实 give sb a handle; give cause

for gossip ／ ～以批评 subject (sb) to criticism; criticize (sb)　*see also* yú

屿(嶼) yǔ　small island; islet

宇 yǔ　❶ eaves; house: 屋～ house; building ❷ space; universe; world: 名扬～内 be famous the world over ❸ manner; bearing; temperament

宇航 yǔháng　space navigation; astronavigation: ～服 space suit ／ ～员 spaceman; (US) astronaut; (Russian) cosmonaut

宇宙 yǔzhòu　❶ universe; space; cosmos: ～飞船 spaceship; spacecraft ❷ world: ～观 *also* "世界观" world view

羽 yǔ　❶ feather; plume ❷ wing ❸〈量〉*used of birds*: 一～信鸽 a carrier pigeon

羽毛 yǔmáo　❶ feather; plume: ～球 badminton; shuttlecock ／ ～丰满 full-fledged; mature ❷〈喻〉reputation: 爱惜～ cherish one's reputation

羽绒 yǔróng　eiderdown; down: ～服 down-padded anorak

羽翼 yǔyì　❶ wing ❷〈贬〉assistant; supporter: 广收～ canvass for support extensively

雨 yǔ　rain: ～点 raindrop ／ ～季 rainy season; monsoon (season) ／ ～具 rain gear; rainwear ／ ～量 rainfall; precipitation ／ ～林 rainforest ／ ～鞋 rain shoes; galoshes ／ ～过天晴 the rain passes off and the sky clears up; after gloom comes brightness

雨后春笋 yǔhòuchūnsǔn　spring up like bamboo shoots after a spring rain; grow like mushrooms

雨露 yǔlù　❶ rain and dew ❷ favour; bounty

雨水 yǔshuǐ　❶ rainwater; rain ❷ Rain Water, 2nd seasonal division point　*see also* "节气" jiéqì

语 yǔ　❶ language; tongue; words: ～病 faulty wording ／ ～

词 words and phrases / ～调 intonation; voice / ～法 grammar / ～感 (instinctive) feel for the language / ～汇 vocabulary / ～录 quotation / ～塞 tongue-tied; speechless / ～态〈语言〉voice / ～序〈语言〉word order / ～义 meaning of a word; semantic meaning / ～音 speech sounds; pronunciation / ～意深长 very meaningful ❷ speak; say; 不言不～ keep silent ❸ adage; proverb; saying ❹ sign; signal; 手～ sign language

语气 yǔqì ❶ tone; manner of speaking; ～冷淡 (speak) in a cold tone ❷〈语言〉mood

语体 yǔtǐ 〈语言〉type of writing; variety of language; style; 书面～ written style / ～文 also "白话文" vernacular (writing)

语文 yǔwén ❶ language; ～课 Chinese / ～水平 language proficiency ❷ language and literature

语无伦次 yǔwúlúncì speak incoherently or illogically; talk in a confused manner

语焉不详 yǔyānbùxiáng not go into detail; not elaborate; not be clear

语言 yǔyán (spoken) language; discourse; ～美 beauty of one's verbal expressions; courtesy in speech / ～学 linguistics; philology / ～简练 concise language / ～实验室 language lab

语重心长 yǔzhòng-xīncháng sincere words and earnest wishes; (say sth) in all earnestness

yù

与(與) yù join or participate in; ～会 participate in a conference; attend a meeting / ～闻 be let into (a secret, etc); have the knowledge of an insider　*see also* yǔ

玉 yù ❶ jade; jade-like stone; ～雕 jade carving or sculpture / ～碎 die a heroic death (like a broken piece of jade) / ～玺 imperial jade seal / ～不琢，不成器〈谚〉jade cannot be made into anything without being cut and polished — one cannot be useful without being educated ❷ pure; fair; beautiful; ～液琼浆 top-quality wine ❸〈敬〉your; his; her; ～体 your health

玉帛 yùbó 〈书〉jade objects and silk fabrics (used as gifts in ancient times); wealth; 化干戈为～ turn hostility into friendship

玉成 yùchéng 〈敬〉kindly help make a success of (sth); please assist in accomplishing (sth)

玉皇大帝 Yùhuáng Dàdì *also* "玉帝" Jade Emperor of Heaven, the supreme deity of Taoism

玉洁冰清 yùjié-bīngqīng pure as jade and chaste as ice; pure and virtuous

玉兰 yùlán 〈植〉*yulan* magnolia

玉米 yùmǐ (popular term for 玉蜀黍) maize; (Indian) corn; ～面 maize flour; cornmeal

玉石 yùshí jade (and stone); ～俱焚 jade and stone are burned together — everything is destroyed, be it good or bad

驭 yù ❶ drive (a carriage, etc) ❷〈书〉command; control; govern

芋 yù ❶ *also* "芋头"〈植〉taro; dasheen ❷ similar tuber crop; 洋～ potato

吁(籲) yù appeal; plead; call; ～请 appeal and request; petition　*see also* xū

妪(嫗) yù 〈书〉old woman; 老～ crone

郁(❶❷鬱) yù ❶ (of plants) teeming; luxuriant; lush ❷ (of sorrow, anger, etc) pent-up; gloomy; depressed; ～积 *also* "郁结" (of anger, etc) smouldering; pent-up / ～悒不乐〈书〉feel low; be down-hearted ❸ of powerful or strong fragrance; strongly fragrant: 香气 ~ 馥〈书〉heavy perfume; strong scent

郁金香 yùjīnxiāng 〈植〉tulip

郁闷 yùmèn gloomy; depressed: ~ 无聊 be depressed and cheerless; have a thin time

郁郁 yùyù 〈书〉❶ high literary grace; great literary talent: 文采 ~ overflowing with literary elegance ❷ (of plants) lush and green; luxuriant; verdant: ~ 葱葱 also "郁郁苍苍" lush and green ❸ gloomy; depressed: ~ 寡欢 joyless and melancholy; depressed and unhappy

育 yù ❶ give birth to; bear: ~ 龄 childbearing age ❷ rear; raise; grow: ~ 林 afforestation; tree-planting / ~ 苗 grow seedlings / ~ 种〈农〉breeding / ~ 婴堂〈旧〉orphanage; foundling hospital ❸ educate; cultivate

狱(獄) yù ❶ prison; jail: ~ 吏 prison warder or warden; jailer ❷ lawsuit; case

浴 yù have a bath; bathe: ~ 池 common bathing pool; public bathhouse or bath / ~ 缸 (ceramic) bathtub; bath / ~ 巾 bath towel / ~ 盆 (wooden) bathtub / ~ 血奋战 fight a bloody war / 天然 ~ 场 natural bathing resort

预 yù ❶ in advance; beforehand: ~ 案 plan against a possible development; contingency plan / ~ 报 forecast; prediction / ~ 热 preheating / ~ 赛〈体〉preliminary (contest or heat) / ~ 售 advance booking (of tickets, etc) or sale (of housing, etc) / ~ 习 prepare (lessons) before class; preview / ~ 选 primaries; straw vote / ~ 演 preview (of a show) / ~ 约 make an appointment / ~ 兆 omen; sign; harbinger / ~ 产期〈医〉expected date of childbirth ❷ see "与" yù

预备 yùbèi prepare; get ready: ~ 役

〈军〉reserve duty / ~ 党员 probationary Party member / ~ 会议 preparatory meeting

预测 yùcè predict; foresee; forecast: 市场 ~ market prediction or forecasting

预订 yùdìng reserve or book (a ticket, etc); place an order for; subscribe to

预定 yùdìng fix or arrange in advance; predetermine; schedule

预防 yùfáng take precautions against (a flood, etc); guard against; prevent: ~ 为主 give priority to precaution measures; prevention first / ~ 注射 also "预防接种" preventive inoculation; vaccination

预感 yùgǎn (have a) premonition; presentiment

预告 yùgào ❶ announce in advance; herald ❷ advance notice: 电影 ~ movie announcement

预计 yùjì calculate in advance; estimate; anticipate

预见 yùjiàn ❶ foresee; foretell; predict: 在可以 ~ 的将来 in the foreseeable future ❷ foresight; prevision: ~ 性 foresight; farsightedness

预警 yùjǐng forewarning; early warning: ~ 机〈军〉early-warning plane

预料 yùliào also "预想" expect; predict; anticipate: 超出 ~ more than expected; beyond one's expectations

预谋 yùmóu premeditate; plan beforehand; prearrange: 有 ~ 的行为 deliberate or premeditated action

预期 yùqī expect; envisage; anticipate: 达到 ~ 的目的 attain the anticipated objective(s)

预审 yùshěn ❶ antecedent trial; preliminary hearing ❷ questioning during investigation; inquiry

预示 yùshì foretell; presage; forebode

预算 yùsuàn budget: 编制 ~ work out a budget / ~ 赤字 budget deficit / ~ 年度 budget year

预先 yùxiān beforehand; in advance; pre-: ～付款 pay in advance; advance payment; pre-payment

预言 yùyán prophesy; predict; foretell: ～家 prophet / 科学～ scientific prediction or prophecy

预支 yùzhī pay or get in advance: ～费用 prepaid expenses / 一三个月工资 (draw) an advance of three months' salary

域 yù ❶ land within certain boundaries; area; region: ～外 outside the country ❷ domain; sphere; range: ～名〈信息〉domain name (DN)

欲(❶慾) yù ❶ desire; lust: ～火 strong (sexual) desire; carnal lust / ～望 wish; desire; lust ❷ want; wish; yearn: ～哭无泪 have no tears to shed though in deep sorrow / ～加之罪,何患无辞 if you are out to condemn sb, you can always trump up a charge; give a dog a bad name and hang him ❸ need; should: 胆～大而心～细. One should be both bold and prudent. ❹ about to; on the point of:东方～晓. Day is breaking in the east.

欲罢不能 yùbàbùnéng try to stop but cannot; be unable to rein in even though one wants to

欲盖弥彰 yùgàimízhāng the more one tries to hide, the more one is exposed; try to cover up a misdeed only to make it more conspicuous

欲壑难填 yùhènántián greed is like a valley that can never be filled; avarice knows no bounds

欲擒故纵 yùqíngùzòng leave sb at large the better to apprehend him; give sb enough line or rope

欲速则不达 yùsùzébùdá more haste, less speed; haste makes waste

阈 yù 〈书〉doorsill; threshold; limits: 听～〈理〉audibility or aural threshold

谕 yù decree; instruct; order: ～旨 imperial decree or edict

遇 yù ❶ meet; encounter: ～到 also "遇见" meet; run into; come across / ～害 be murdered / ～救 be rescued / ～事 when anything crops up; when confronted with a problem / ～雨 be caught in a rain ❷ treat; receive: ～我甚厚 treat me very generously ❸ chance; opportunity

遇刺 yùcì be attacked by an assassin; ～身亡 be assassinated / 幸免～ escape an attempt on one's life

遇难 yùnàn ❶ be killed in an accident; be murdered ❷ be in trouble; face danger: ～成祥 misfortune turned into good luck

遇险 yùxiǎn meet with a mishap; be in danger or distress: ～信号 distress signal; GMDSS; 〈旧〉SOS

喻 yù ❶ explain; tell; inform: ～之以理 explain by reasoning ❷ understand; know; be aware of:不言而～ it goes without saying ❸ analogy; figure of speech: ～义 allegorical or metaphorical meaning

御(❸禦) yù ❶ drive; ride; 〈旧〉control: ～者 carriage driver / ～下 control one's subordinates ❷ related to the emperor or king; imperial; royal: ～玺 imperial seal; (UK) privy seal / ～林军 imperial or imperial guards; 〈喻〉elite (armed) forces / ～驾亲征 (of an emperor) command an expedition personally; 〈谦〉do sth in person ❸ defend (against sb); resist; keep out: ～寒 keep out the cold; keep warm

御用 yùyòng employed by the emperor; 〈贬〉hired; in the pay of sb; ～报刊 hired or paid press / ～文人 scribbler hired by the imperial court; hack writer

寓 yù ❶ inhabit; reside; dwell: ～公 retired official, etc, in exile

Y

unemployed gentleman away from home / ～所 residence; abode; dwelling / ～居海外 make one's home in an alien land ❷ imply; place; contain;～意 implied meaning; moral; message / ～教于乐(carry on) education through entertainment; edutainment ❸ residence; dwelling place;王～ Wangs' residence

寓言 yùyán ❶ parable; allegory;～诗 allegorical poem ❷ fable;《伊索～》Aesop's Fables

裕 yù ❶ abundant; plentiful; ample;～如 effortless; with ease; affluent ❷〈书〉enrich; make affluent; 富国～民 enrich the nation

愈(❶癒) yù ❶ be cured; heal; recover; ～合〈医〉heal up / 病～出院 leave hospital after recovery ❷ be better than; overtake; surpass ❸ the more … the more …; more and more;～加 also "愈发" increasingly; even more; all the more / ～演～烈 become increasingly fierce or intense; go from bad to worse / ～早～好。The sooner the better.

誉(譽) yù ❶ reputation; renown; fame;～满全球 of world renown; world-famous ❷ praise; commend; extol; ～不绝口 be full of praise; praise or extol to the skies

熨 yù see also yùn

熨帖 yùtiē ❶(of wording) appropriate; fitting; proper ❷(of mood) calm; peaceful; quiet ❸ settled; well done

豫 yù ❶〈书〉pleased; happy; glad;心中不～ be displeased ❷〈书〉comfort; contentment; 逸～亡身。Over-indulgence spells ruin. ❸ see "预❶" yù ❹(Yù) another name for Henan (河南) / ～剧 also "河南梆子" Henan opera

鹬 yù〈动物〉sandpiper; snipe;～蚌相争，渔人得利。When the

snipe and the clam grapple, it's the fisherman who stands to benefit. or Two dogs fight for a bone, and a third runs away with it.

鬻 yù〈书〉sell;卖儿～女 sell one's children for survival

yuān

鸢 yuān (popularly known as 老鹰) kite; hawk

鸳 yuān mandarin duck;～侣 loving couple; husband and wife

鸳鸯 yuānyāng ❶ mandarin ducks;〈喻〉loving couple ❷ forming a pair; for couples;～剑 paired swords / ～座 love seat (in a cinema, etc) / ～火锅 double hot pot

冤(寃) yuān ❶ wrong; grievance; injustice;～案 wrong verdict; injustice; wrong / ～情 true facts about an injustice / ～沉海底。The injustice will remain unredressed for ever. ❷ hatred; enmity; feud;～仇 enmity; rancour; feud / ～孽 enmity and sin / ～～相报。Reprisal breeds reprisal. ❸ see "冤枉❸" ❹〈方〉kid; fool;～大头 foolish spender; sucker / 别～人! Don't kid me!

冤家 yuānjia ❶ enemy; foe;～路窄。Foes are fated to meet on a narrow path. / ～宜解不宜结。The knot of hatred should be untied, not tightened. ❷ one's destined love; sweetheart or lover in a love-hate relationship;不是～不聚头。Enemies and lovers are destined to meet.

冤屈 yuānqū wrong; treat unjustly;～好人 wrong an innocent person / 洗雪～ redress an injustice

冤枉 yuānwang ❶ unfair; unjust; wrong;～官司 unjust verdict; uncalled-for lawsuit or wrong ❷ see "冤屈" ❸ not worthwhile; for nothing; in vain; 花～钱 spend money in vain; (of sth) be a sheer waste of money / 受～气 be treated unjustly; be the target of much unfair criticism / 走～路 make a vain trip; follow a lengthy route

冤狱 yuānyù　unjust charge or verdict; miscarriage of justice: 制造～ frame (sth) up; frame (sb)

渊(淵) yuān　❶ deep pool ❷ (usu 渊深) deep; profound: ～博 broad and profound; erudite

渊薮 yuānsǒu　〈喻〉haunt; den; lair: 罪恶～ breeding ground of crime; sink of iniquity

渊源 yuānyuán　origin; source: 历史～ historical origins (of sth)

yuán

元 yuán　❶ first; initial; primary: ～旦 New Year's Day / ～月 first lunar month; January ❷ arch; chief; principal: ～首 head of state; 〈书〉monarch / ～凶 prime culprit; arch-criminal / ～勋 man of outstanding merit; founding father ❸ basic; essential; fundamental: ～音 〈语言〉vowel ❹ unit; component: ～件 element; component; cell ❺ yuan, basic unit of money ❻ (Yuán) Yuan Dynasty (1206-1368)

元老 yuánlǎo　senior or elder statesman; founding member

元气 yuánqì　vitality; vigour: ～大伤 have one's constitution undermined or vitality sapped

元帅 yuánshuài　〈军〉marshal; 大～ generalissimo

元素 yuánsù　element; essential factor: ～周期表 periodic table of elements

元宵 yuánxiāo　❶ 15th night of the 1st lunar month: ～节 also "灯节" Lantern Festival ❷ (glutinous) rice dumpling

园(園) yuán　❶ garden; plot; plantation: ～地 (garden) plot; 〈喻〉field; domain / ～丁 gardener; 〈喻〉teacher / ～林 garden; park / ～艺 gardening; horticulture ❷ place of recreation, etc; park: 高科技～区 hi-tech park

员 yuán　❶ person engaged in a certain field of activity: ～工 staff; personnel / 推销～ (travelling) salesman ❷ member; 队～ team member ❸〈量〉used of generals: 一～猛将 a valiant general; a vigorous man

垣 yuán　〈书〉❶ wall ❷ town; city: 省～ provincial capital

原 yuán　❶ primary; initial; original: ～版 original edition; (film, etc) in the original / ～稿 original manuscript; master copy / ～籍 ancestral home; domicile of origin; native place / ～貌 original look or state / ～配 also "元配" first wife; wife by first marriage / ～文 original; original or source text / ～型 prototype / ～意 original meaning or intention / ～著 original (work) / ～动力 motive power or force / ～班人马 old cast or staff; original team ❷ unprocessed; crude; raw: ～油 crude (oil) / ～材料 raw and unprocessed materials ❸ excuse; forgive; pardon: 情有可～ excusable; pardonable ❹ plain; level; open country: ～野 open country; champaign

原本 yuánběn　❶ original manuscript; master copy ❷ first or original edition; the original ❸ originally; formerly

原创 yuánchuàng　create; invent; originate: ～设计 original design / 富有～性 full of originality; very creative

原地 yuándì　(in) the same place: ～不动 remain where one is; stay put / ～踏步 mark time; make no headway

原封 yuánfēng　with the seal unbroken; intact: ～不动 be left intact; remain untouched

原告 yuángào　〈法〉plaintiff (for civil cases); prosecutor (for criminal cases)

原教旨主义 yuánjiàozhǐzhǔyì fundamentalism：~分子 fundamentalist

原来 yuánlái ❶ also "原先" original; former：~的样子 former look or state / 她~住这里，最近才搬走。She lived here until recently. ❷ so; as it turns out to be：~如此。So, that's how it is. or I see.

原理 yuánlǐ principle; theory; tenet

原谅 yuánliàng excuse; forgive; pardon：不可~ inexcusable; unforgivable

原始 yuánshǐ ❶ primary; original; firsthand：~材料 firsthand material or information; primary data ❷ primeval; primitive：~积累 primitive accumulation / ~社会 primitive society

原委 yuánwěi whole story; all the details：诉述~ give a full account of sth

原形 yuánxíng 〈贬〉original shape; true features：~毕露 be revealed for what one is; show one's true colours

原因 yuányīn cause; grounds; reason：由于这个~ on this account

原原本本 yuányuán-běnběn whole story; everything

原则 yuánzé principle：坚持~ stick to principle; live up to one's principles / ~上 in principle / ~立场 principled stand

原装 yuánzhuāng ❶ factory-packed (in the country of origin) ❷ original packing

原状 yuánzhuàng original state; status quo ante：保持~ leave sth in the original state; leave sth intact

原子 yuánzǐ atom：~弹 A-bomb; atom or atomic bomb / ~核 atomic nucleus / ~能 atomic energy

圆 yuán ❶ round; circular; spherical：~顶 dome / ~号 〈乐〉(French) horn / ~柱 column；〈数〉cylinder / ~括号 parenthesis ("()") / ~桌会议 round-table conference ❷ 〈数〉circle：半~ semicircle / ~周 circumference; periphery / ~锥 circular

cone; taper ❸ tactful; satisfactory：~熟 skilful; tactful; flexible / ~通 flexible; conciliatory; accommodating ❹ justify; make complete or perfect：~谎 make a lie sound plausible; explain a lie away ❺ also "元" yuan, basic unit of currency ❻ also "元" coin：银~ silver dollar

圆场 yuánchǎng （usu 打圆场）smooth things over; mediate; help to effect a compromise：说几句~话 say a few conciliatory words

圆规 yuánguī (pair of) compasses

圆滑 yuánhuá smooth and wily; slick and sly; tactful

圆寂 yuánjì （of Buddhism）achieve *Parinirvana*; pass away

圆满 yuánmǎn satisfactory; perfect：~结束 come or bring to a successful conclusion / ~的方案 flawless plan

圆梦 yuánmèng ❶ 〈迷信〉have one's dream read ❷ have one's dream fulfilled or realized：圆了上大学的梦 realize one's long-cherished desire to go to college

圆润 yuánrùn ❶ （of voice）mellow and full; sweet and melodious ❷ （of handwriting, etc）fluent; smooth

圆舞曲 yuánwǔqǔ 〈乐〉waltz

圆珠笔 yuánzhūbǐ ball-point pen; ball-pen：~芯 ball-pen refiller

鼋（黿） yuán also "鼋鱼"；"鳖" soft-shelled turtle

援 yuán ❶ pull by hand; hold ❷ quote; cite：~例 follow or cite a precedent ❸ help; aid; rescue：~军 also "援军" reinforcements; relief troops / ~建 provide aid in construction / ~款 financial assistance; relief money

援救 yuánjiù rescue; help; save

援引 yuányǐn ❶ also "援用" cite; invoke; quote：~法律规定 invoke a legal provision ❷ recommend or appoint sb out of favouritism

援助 yuánzhù help；aid；assist：经济 ～ economic aid

缘 yuán ❶ reason；～由 *also* "原由" reason；cause ❷〈书〉because；for；why；～何发怒？What are you angry for？ ❸ predestined relationship or affinity；happy fate or chance ❹〈书〉along：～溪而行 walk along a stream ❺（usu 边缘）rim；brink；edge

缘分 yuánfèn fate or chance that brings people together；predestined affinity or relationship：有～ be brought together by fate

缘故 yuángù *also* "原故" cause；reason；motive：不解其中～ not know the whys and the wherefores (of sth)

缘木求鱼 yuánmùqiúyú climb a tree to catch fish — adopt a wrong and fruitless approach；try to get blood out of a turnip

缘起 yuánqǐ ❶ cause；origin ❷ account of the cause or origin of sth：成立学会的～ account of the founding of the Association

猿 yuán ape：～猴 apes and monkeys／～人 ape-man

源 yuán ❶（usu 源头）water source；fountainhead ❷ source；cause；root：货～ source of supplies

源流 yuánliú source and course；origin and development：追溯～ trace sth back to its source or origin

源泉 yuánquán well-spring；fountainhead：力量的～ source of strength

源源 yuányuán in a steady stream；steadily；continuously：～不绝 in an endless flow；continuously；incessantly

源远流长 yuányuǎn-liúcháng distant source and long stream；〈喻〉having a long history；of long standing

辕 yuán ❶ shafts (of a cart, etc) ❷〈旧〉outer gate of a government office or barracks；〈喻〉government office

yuǎn

远（遠） yuǎn ❶（of time and space）far；distant；remote：～处 *also* "远方"（in the）distance；（at a）distant place／～东 Far East／～古 remote antiquity／～航（make a）long voyage／～郊 outer suburbs；exurbs／～道而来 come a long way；come from afar／～涉重洋 *also* "远渡重洋" come or go across a vast ocean；travel across the high seas／～在天边 though seemingly far away／～水不解近渴。〈俗〉Distant water cannot quench present thirst. ❷（of blood relationship）distant；remote；not intimate：～祖 remote ancestor／～房兄弟 distant cousin／～亲不如近邻。〈俗〉A close neighbour means more than a distant relative. ❸（of differences）by far：～～超过 far exceed

远程 yuǎnchéng long-range；long-distance：～导弹 long-range missile／～访问（信息）remote access／～教育（信息）distance or remote learning

远大 yuǎndà long-range；broad；lofty；ambitious：目光～ be farsighted；have a broad vision／～前程（have a）bright future；（show）great promise

远见 yuǎnjiàn foresight；far-sightedness；vision：～卓识 foresight and sagacity

远近 yuǎnjìn ❶ distance ❷ far and near；far and wide；everywhere：～驰名 known far and wide

远景 yuǎnjǐng ❶ distant view；（in a movie）long shot ❷ long-range perspective；prospect：～规划 long-range plan

远虑 yuǎnlǜ foresight；long view：人无～，必有近忧。One who fails to see far ahead will face danger close at hand. or He who doesn't plan for the future will find trouble at his doorstep.

远洋 yuǎnyáng　(of an) ocean;～船队 oceangoing fleet / ～渔业 deep-sea or pelagic fishing

远征 yuǎnzhēng　expedition;～军 expeditionary army

远走高飞 yuǎnzǒu-gāofēi　soar high and fly far; flee to faraway places

远足 yuǎnzú　excursion; hike; walking tour

yuàn

苑 yuàn　〈书〉❶ enclosed ground for keeping animals, etc; garden; park ❷ centre (of art and literature, etc)

怨 yuàn　❶ resentment; hatred; grudge;～愤 discontent; indignation / ～偶〈书〉unhappy couple ❷ blame; resent; curse;～言 complaint; grumble

怨恨 yuànhèn　bear a grudge against; resent; hate;满心的～ full of hatred

怨气 yuànqì　grievance; complaint; resentment;～冲天 towering resentment

怨声载道 yuànshēngzàidào　complaints (of the people) fill the streets; complaints are heard everywhere

怨天尤人 yuàntiān-yóurén　blame God and man; find fault with everyone and everything

院 yuàn　❶ (usu 院子 or 院落) yard; courtyard; compound;～墙 wall surrounding a house; courtyard wall ❷ used for certain government institutions or public places:～校 colleges and universities / 中国科学～～士 academician or member of the Chinese Academy of Sciences

愿（❶-❸願） yuàn　❶ wish; hope; desire:一切如～。 Everything has been as wished. / ～天下有情人终成眷属。

May all lovers unite in marriage! ❷ be willing or ready; be glad;～效犬马之劳〈书〉willing to do what little one can; ready to render one's service ❸ vow; declare solemnly;许下～心 make a vow (before Buddha or a god) ❹ 〈书〉honest and prudent

愿望 yuànwàng　wish; hope; desire:良好的～ best of wishes; good intention

愿意 yuànyì　❶ be willing; be ready ❷ wish; want; hope

yuē

日 yuē　〈书〉❶ say:子～… Confucius said… ❷ call; name:名之～暑 call it sundial

约 yuē　❶ make an appointment; agree; arrange;～见 make an appointment (with sb. or to see sb) ❷ ask or invite (in advance); engage;～请 invite; ask ❸ pact; agreement; appointment; 有～在先 have a prior agreement or appointment ❹ check; restrict; restrain;～制 restrain; contain; keep within bounds ❺ simple; brief; succinct;～而详 succinct but full ❻ about; around; or so;～计 come approximately to / ～莫 also "约摸" about; roughly ❼ also "约分" reduce (a fraction)

see also yāo

约定 yuēdìng　agree; appoint; arrange;～俗成 established by popular usage; accepted through common practice

约法三章 yuēfǎsānzhāng　make or agree on a few simple rules to be observed by all concerned

约会 yuēhuì　(make an) appointment or engagement; (of a couple) date;和女孩子～ date a girl

约略 yuēlüè　❶ rough; approximate;～知道一些 have a rough idea (of sth)；know a bit (about sth) ❷ vaguely；dimly；～可见 dimly visible

约束 yuēshù　keep within bounds；restrain；constrain：～力 binding force／觉得受～ feel constrained

yuè

月 yuè ❶ moon：～饼 moon cake／～光 moonlight；moonshine；moonbeam／～亮 moon／～夜 moonlit or moonlight night／～牙儿 also "月芽儿" crescent (moon)；new moon／～白风清 quiet moonlit night ❷ month；monthly：～刊 monthly (magazine)／～票 monthly ticket／～息 also "月利" monthly interest ❸ (full-)moon shaped；round：～门 also "月亮门" moon(-shaped) gate

月白 yuèbái　also "月白色" bluish white；pale blue

月份 yuèfèn　month：～牌〈口〉calendar

月季 yuèjì〈植〉Chinese rose

月经 yuèjīng〈生理〉menstruation；menses；(monthly) period：～不调 (have) irregular menstruation

月球 yuèqiú〈天文〉moon：～探测 lunar exploration

月食 yuèshí　also "月蚀"〈天文〉lunar eclipse：月偏食 partial lunar eclipse／月全食 total lunar eclipse

月台 yuètái ❶ open air platform ❷ also "站台" railway platform：～票 platform ticket

月下老人 yuèxià lǎorén　also "月老" god who unites man and woman in marriage；matchmaker；go-between

月子 yuèzi ❶ month of confinement after childbirth：坐～ be in confinement ❷ time of childbirth；confinement

乐(樂) yuè music：～池 orchestra (pit)／～队 band；orchestra／～谱 music score；(sheet) music／～器 (musical) instrument／～曲 (musical) composition；(a piece of) music ❷ 团 philharmonic society or orchestra／～音 musical sound；tone／～章〈乐〉movement　see also lè

乐府 yuèfǔ ❶〈史〉official conservatory set up in the Han Dynasty for the collection of folk songs and ballads ❷ folk songs or ballads in the Han style

岳(❶嶽) yuè ❶ high mountain ❷ wife's parents：～父 also "岳丈" wife's father；father-in-law

阅 yuè ❶ read；scan；peruse：～卷 mark or grade (examination) papers ❷ review；inspect：～操 inspect or watch a military drill ❸ experience；undergo；pass through：～世很深〈书〉have seen a great deal of life；be worldly-wise

阅兵 yuèbīng　review or inspect troops：～式 military parade

阅读 yuèdú　read：～能力 reading ability

阅览 yuèlǎn　read；browse：～室 reading room

阅历 yuèlì ❶ see, hear or do for oneself：出去～一番 go out and experience life ❷ experience：增长～ enrich one's experience；gain experience

悦 yuè happy；glad；pleased：～耳 pleasing to the ear；sweet／～目 pleasing to the eye；attractive；good-looking／令人～服 win one's hearty acclaim；be thoroughly convincing

跃(躍) yuè jump；leap；spring：～进 jump or leap forward；make big strides／～居世界首位 leap to first place in the world；leap to lead the world／～～欲试 be eager to have a go；be anxious to have a try；itch for action

越 yuè ❶ get or jump over；cross：～过 cross；traverse；surmount (obstacles, etc)／～境 cross the border illegally; sneak into or out of a country / ～洋电缆 transoceanic cable ❷ exceed; pass; overstep: ～权 exceed or go beyond one's powers; overstep one's authority ❸ (of voice or emotion) be at a high pitch; vigorous: 情绪激～ be excited ❹ used in duplicates to indicate increasing degree: ～多～好。The more, the better. ❺ (Yuè) eastern Zhejiang centring round Shaoxing (绍兴): ～剧 Shaoxing opera

越冬 yuèdōng　live through the winter; overwinter: ～作物 winter or over-wintering crop

越发 yuèfā　also "越加" ❶ even or still more; all the more ❷ (used after 越 or 越是) the more… the more…: 工作越(是)忙，～要细心。The busier the work, the more careful one should be.

越轨 yuèguǐ　go beyond the limits; exceed the bounds; transgress: 行为～ commit an indiscretion or a transgression; act improperly

越级 yuèjí　❶ skip a rank or grade: ～提拔 promote sb more than one grade at one time ❷ bypass the immediate leadership: ～上告 go (over sb's head) to the higher-ups with one's complaints

越野 yuèyě　cross-country: ～车 cross-country or offroad vehicle / ～赛 cross-country race; (of vehicles) offroad racing

越狱 yuèyù　escape from prison; break jail: ～犯 prison breaker; escaped convict / ～行动 prison-break

越俎代疱 yuèzǔdàipáo　take sb else's job into one's own hands; exceed one's mandate and meddle in sb else's business; act outside one's area of responsibility

粤 Yuè　another name for Guangdong (广东): ～菜 Guangdong food; Cantonese cuisine / ～语 Guangdong dialect; Cantonese

yūn

晕 yūn　❶ dizzy; giddy; faint: ～头转向 confused and disorientated; muddled / ～～忽忽 in a daze; dizzy; giddy ❷ swoon; faint; pass out: ～倒 fall (down) in a faint; pass out / ～厥〈医〉syncope; faint
see also yùn

yún

云(❷❸雲) yún　❶ say; utter: 不知所～ not understand what sb says; find (sth) unintelligible ❷ cloud: ～彩 cloud / ～层 cloud layer / ～霞 rosy or pink clouds; rose-tinted clouds / ～海茫茫 boundless sea of clouds / ～泥之别〈喻〉(of social status, etc) as far apart as cloud and mud; poles apart ❸ (Yún) short for Yunnan (云南): ～贵高原 Yunnan-Guizhou Plateau

云集 yúnjí　come together from various places; gather; converge

云梯 yúntī　scaling ladder

云雾 yúnwù　cloud and mist; mist: 云山雾罩 as if enveloped in (cloud and) mist; rambling; confusing / 云消雾散 *also* "烟消云散"〈喻〉cease to exist; vanish into thin air

云霄 yúnxiāo *also* "云天": sky: 直上～ rise or fly right towards the sky

云烟 yúnyān　❶ cloud and smoke; mist and smoke: 犹如过眼～ like a fleeting cloud; transient ❷ Yunnan tobacco or cigarettes

云游 yúnyóu　(of a Buddhist monk or Taoist priest) roam; wander: ～四方 roam from place to place

云雨 yúnyǔ　〈旧〉make love; have sex

匀 yún　❶ even; equitable: ～净 even; in proportion; uniform / ～整 neat and well spaced; tidy and even /

~速运动〈理〉uniform motion ❷ even up; divide evenly: 把两份苹果一~一 divide two portions of apples evenly ❸ take from sth and give to sb; spare: 把药品一点点给他们用。Let's give them some of our medicine.

匀称 yúnchèn　well-proportioned; well-balanced; even: 排列~ evenly arranged / 五官~ (have) regular features

芸(蕓) yún　also "芸薹"〈植〉(oil-bearing) rape

芸豆 yúndòu　also "云豆" kidney bean

芸芸 yúnyún〈书〉large amounts or numbers; many; numerous: 万物~ myriads of things / ~众生 (of Buddhism) all living things; all mortal beings

绘 yún

绘绘 yúnyún　numerous and disorderly; myriad and confused

耘 yún　weed: ~田 weed the fields

yǔn

允 yǔn ❶ consent; grant; permit: ~从 consent, agree ❷ just; fair; impartial; 平~ fair and just; equitable

允当 yǔndàng　proper; suitable; appropriate: 难易~ just the right degree of difficulty

允诺 yǔnnuò　commit oneself (to sth); promise; undertake: 欣然~ readily consent

允许 yǔnxǔ　allow; permit; agree: 情况~的话 if circumstances permit

陨 yǔn　fall from the sky or outer space: ~星〈天文〉meteorite

陨落 yǔnluò　(of a heavenly body, etc) fall from the sky or outer space: 巨星~。A giant star fell from the sky. or A great man passed away.

陨灭 yǔnmiè ❶ fall from outer space and burn up ❷ also "殒灭"〈书〉die; be killed; perish

陨石 yǔnshí〈天文〉stony meteorite; aerolite: ~雨 meteorite shower

殒 yǔn　(usu 殒命)〈书〉perish; die; pass away

yùn

孕 yùn　pregnant: 不~ unable to conceive; sterile / ~妇 pregnant woman / ~期 pregnancy; gestation

孕育 yùnyù　be pregnant or fraught with; breed: ~着无限生机 be full of vigour

运(運) yùn ❶ motion; movement ❷ transport; haul; carry: ~费 transport expenses; freight / ~力 means of transport / ~送 transport; carry; ship ❸ use; wield; utilize: ~思敏捷 be quick at writing ❹ luck; fortune; destiny: 交~ have a stroke of luck; be in luck

运笔 yùnbǐ　wield a pen; write or paint with a brush: ~如飞 write furiously fast

运筹 yùnchóu　devise strategies; plan: ~学 operational or operations research / ~帷幄 plan strategies and command operations

运动 yùndòng ❶ motion; movement: ~战 mobile war / ~神经〈生理〉motor nerve ❷ sports; exercise; athletics: ~场 sports ground; playground; stadium / ~会 sports or athletic meet; games / ~员 sportsman or sportswoman; athlete; player / ~项目 (sports) events and games ❸ movement; campaign; drive: 扫盲~ anti-illiteracy campaign ❹ (yùndong) arrange things through pull; canvass; drum up: ~有关人士 canvass the parties concerned

运河 yùnhé　canal: 大~ Grand Canal

运气 yùnqì　fate; luck; fortune: ~不

好 have hard luck / 他今天真～! How lucky he is today!

运输 yùnshū　transport; carriage; conveyance:～机 transport or cargo plane / ～量 freight volume / ～业 transport service; carrying trade; transportation / ～工具 means of transport; conveyance

运算 yùnsuàn　〈数〉operate; calculate;～能力 operation capacity; calculating ability / 每秒钟～次数 calculations per second

运行 yùnxíng　move; be in motion or operation;列车～表 train schedule

运营 yùnyíng　❶ (of vehicles or ships) open to service; go into operation;投入～ put into commission or operation / ～范围 range of service ❷ operate; run; be in operation:～成本 operation cost

运用 yùnyòng　apply; use; wield:～自如 use or handle with skill; have a perfect command (of sth)

运载 yùnzài　load and deliver; carry:～工具 means of delivery; carrier / ～火箭 carrier rocket

运转 yùnzhuǎn　❶ move in a circular orbit; revolve; turn round ❷ operate; run; work

运作 yùnzuò　implement; operate; carry through:～方式 way to implement or operate; mode of implementation or operation

晕 yùn　❶ dizzy; faint; sick:～场 have stage fright / ～车 be carsick / ～船 be seasick ❷ haze or halo round some colour or light:日～ solar halo / 脸上的红～ blush on one's face *see also* yūn

酝（醖）yùn

酝酿 yùnniàng　brew; ferment; deliberate (upon sth):～人选 consider and discuss candidates

愠 yùn　〈书〉angry; annoyed; irritated:面带～色 appear angry; look irritated

韵（韻）yùn　❶ beautiful or sweet sound; sound pleasant to the ear:～调悠扬 sweet tune ❷ *also* "韵母"〈语言〉vowel of a Chinese syllable ❸ rhyme:～文 verse ❹ appeal; charm:～致淡雅 natural and graceful bearing

韵律 yùnlǜ　❶ metre and rhyme scheme in verse; prosody ❷ rhythm:～体操 rhythmic gymnastics

韵事 yùnshì　romantic or anecdotic event; love affair

韵味 yùnwèi　❶ meaning implied by sound and rhythm; implicit richness:～十足 impregnated with meaning ❷ charm; interest; appeal

蕴 yùn　〈书〉❶ contain; hold in store;～藉 restrained; well-controlled; refined / ～结心头 pent-up ❷ profoundness:精～ profound content; essentials

蕴藏 yùncáng　contain; store; hold in store:～着丰富的石油 rich in oil resources

蕴涵 yùnhán　*also* "蕴含"〈书〉contain; entail:～极深 have a profound message; have deep implications

熨 yùn　iron; press:～斗 flat iron; iron / ～衣板 ironing board　*see also* yù

Z

zā

扎（紥、紮） zā tie; bind; fasten: ～辫子 plait one's hair　*see also* zhā

匝 zā〈书〉❶ circle; circumference: 绕树两～ circle a tree twice ❷ surround; encircle ❸ whole; full: ～地 all around; everywhere

咂 zā ❶ sip; suck: ～一口茶 take a sip of tea ❷（usu 咂嘴）smack one's lips（in admiration, agreement, etc）❸ taste or savour carefully

zá

杂（雜） zá ❶ varied; mixed; sundry: ～家 eclectic; jack-of-all-trades / ～面 *also* "杂合面" flour made from various coarse cereals and beans; noodles made from such flour / ～色 variegated; varicoloured / ～事 sundry or trivial matters / ～物 odds and ends / ～项 sundry or miscellaneous items（in an account）/ ～八 mixed; motley; assorted / ～食动物 omnivorous animal ❷ extra; irregular: ～草 weeds; rank grass / ～费 sundry fees or charges; extras; incidentals / ～念 distracting thoughts; selfish considerations / ～质 impurities ❸ mix; combine; mingle: ～居（of two or more ethnic groups）live together

杂拌儿 zábànr ❶ mixed sweetmeats; assorted preserved fruits; ～糖 assorted candies ❷ mixture; medley

杂感 zágǎn sundry impressions; random thoughts or remarks; writing about these

杂烩 záhuì mixed stew; hotchpotch; 〈喻〉mixture: 东拼西凑的大～ scissors-and-paste article

杂货 záhuò sundry goods; groceries; general merchandise: ～店 grocery; the grocer's

杂记 zájì ❶ miscellanies（as a type of literature）❷ jottings; notes

杂技 zájì acrobatics: ～团 acrobatic troupe / ～演员 acrobat

杂交 zájiāo hybridize; cross(-breed): ～玉米 hybrid or cross-bred maize / ～育种 cross-breeding

杂粮 záliáng coarse cereals or food grains（maize, barley, etc）

杂乱 záluàn *also* "杂沓" untidy; confused; disorderly: ～无章 disorderly and unsystematic; jumbled

杂牌 zápái less known or inferior brand: ～货 goods of inferior brands / ～军 miscellaneous troops; troops of miscellaneous allegiances

杂耍 záshuǎ variety show; vaudeville

杂碎 zásui chopped cooked entrails of sheep, oxen, etc

杂文 záwén （satirical）essay: ～家 essayist

杂音 záyīn ❶ noise ❷〈电〉static ❸〈医〉souffle; murmur: 心脏～ heart murmur; cardiac souffle

杂志 zázhì magazine: 过期～ back numbers

杂种 zázhǒng ❶ hybrid; cross-breed ❷〈粗〉bastard; son of a bitch

砸 zá ❶ pound; crush; tamp: ~地基 tamp the foundations solid ❷ break; shatter; smash: ~锅〈方〉fall through; come a cropper / ~饭碗 get the sack / ~牌子 smash the signboard — mar the reputation of a firm, etc ❸〈方〉fail; fall through; be bungled: 考~了 blow an exam

zǎ

咋 zǎ 〈方〉what; how; why: 他~样了? How is he now?　*see also* zé; zhā

zāi

灾(災) zāi ❶ calamity; disaster; catastrophe: ~害 (natural) disaster; calamity / ~荒 famine (due to crop failure) / ~祸 disaster; calamity; misfortune / ~民 victims of a natural calamity; afflicted people / ~难 suffering; disaster; catastrophe / ~情 damage caused by a disaster / ~区 disaster or afflicted area ❷ personal misfortune or ill luck; mishap: ~殃 suffering; misfortune; disaster / ~星〈迷信〉unlucky star; misfortune

哉 zāi 〈书〉❶ for exclamation: 快~! What a delight! ❷ used to express doubt or to form a rhetorical question: 何足道~! It is really not worth mentioning!

栽 zāi ❶ also "栽种" plant; grow: ~秧 transplant seedlings ❷ insert; stick; impose: ~赃 plant stolen or contraband goods (on sb); frame (sb) / ~罪名 trump up a charge (against sb); frame (sb) ❸ young plant; seedling: 桃~ peach seedlings ❹ tumble; topple; fall: ~跟头 tum-

ble; fall; come a cropper / ~了一跤 trip and fall / 认~〈方〉admit defeat

栽培 zāipéi ❶ cultivate; grow (plants, etc) ❷ foster; train; educate ❸ help advance sb's career; support and encourage: 多谢您的~。Thank you for your help and support.

zǎi

仔 zǎi　see "崽" zǒi　see also zǐ

载 zǎi ❶ year: 三年五~ three to five years ❷ put down in writing; enter (in a register); record: 据报 ~ according to the newspapers / ~入史册 go down in the annals of history　*see also* zài

宰 zǎi ❶ be in charge of; head: ~相 (in a monarchy) prime minister; chancellor ❷ also "宰杀" slaughter; kill (a pig, etc) ❸ (usu 宰人) rip (sb) off; overcharge: fleece

宰割 zǎigē ❶ slaughter and cut up ❷ oppress and exploit; ride roughshod over: 任人~ allow oneself to be trampled upon

崽 zǎi 〈方〉❶ son ❷ young man: 打工~ young manual worker ❸ young animal; whelp: 猪~ piglet

崽子 zǎizi 〈粗〉whelp; brat; bastard: 狗~! Son of a bitch! / 小兔~! You brat!

zài

再 zài ❶ again; once more; another time: ~版 second edition or impression / ~次 also "再度" once more or again; one more time / ~婚 remarry; marry again / ~现 (of a past event) reappear; be reproduced / ~保险〈经〉reinsurance / ~就业 (of laid-off workers) find jobs again; be re-employed / ~投资 reinvest; plough back (profits as investment) / 断肢～植 re-attaching a severed limb; replantation of a limb ❷ to a greater extent or degree: 音量～大点儿 (turn it up) a little louder ❸ 〈副〉 *used to indicate* a) *possible consequence*: ～不快点就要迟到了。We'll be late if we don't hurry up. b) *sequence of two actions*: 把情况了解清楚～下结论 find out all about a matter before drawing conclusions c) *additional information*: 在座的编辑、记者，～就是实习的学生。Present are editors and reporters, as well as student interns. ❹ (often followed by 也 for emphasis) however; no matter how: ～贵也得买 We'll have to buy it whatever the expense. ❺ 〈书〉continue; return: 良机难～。Opportunity knocks but once.

再见 zàijiàn *also* "再会" goodbye; see you again; au revoir

再接再厉 zàijiē-zàilì make persistent or redoubled efforts; work ceaselessly and unremittingly; advance from strength to strength

再三 zàisān over and over again; time and again; repeatedly

再生 zàishēng ❶ revive; rise again: ～父母 second parent (who saves one's life); great benefactor ❷ reprocess; recycle; regenerate: ～林 regenerated or re-grown forest / ～纸 recycled paper / ～资源 renewable resources

再说 zàishuō ❶ talk about sth some other time; put sth off for the time being ❷ *also* "再则"; "再者" besides; moreover: 现在找他太晚了，～他也不一定在家。It's too late to go and see him now; besides, he may not be at home.

在 zài ❶ exist; be living: ～世 living; alive ❷ find oneself (in a place); be; belong to: ～场 on the scene or spot; present / ～朝 hold office in court; be in power or office / ～

家 be at home; be in / ～线〈信息〉online / ～座 be present (at a meeting, etc); participate ❸ consist in; rest with; rely on: 贵～坚持。The most important thing is perseverance. ❹ 〈助〉 *used together with* 所 *for emphasis*: ～所不辞 will not decline under any circumstances / ～所难免 can hardly avoid; be unavoidable ❺ *indicating time, place, condition, scope, etc*: 记～心上 keep in mind / ～他看来 in his opinion; as he sees it ❻ 〈副〉 *indicating an action in progress*: ～逃犯 escaped convict; criminal at large or on the run / ～建工程 project under construction

在行 zàiháng be a professional; be expert at sth; know the ropes: 开车她十分～。Driving is very much in her line.

在乎 zàihu ❶ *see* "在于" ❷ care (about); mind; take to heart: 不～别人的态度 not care what other people think

在即 zàijí near at hand; before long; shortly

在劫难逃 zàijiénántáo it is impossible to escape one's doom; what is destined cannot be avoided: 看来你我真是～了!〈谑〉It seems we're both in for it.

在理 zàilǐ stand to reason; be reasonable or sensible

在望 zàiwàng ❶ be in sight; come in view: 隐隐～ dimly visible ❷ be in the offing; be round the corner: 丰收～ A bumper harvest is in the offing.

在位 zàiwèi ❶ be on the throne; reign ❷ *see* "在职"

在下 zàixià 〈旧〉〈谦〉I: 容～申述理由。Please allow me to give an explanation.

在先 zàixiān ❶ (implying a change) formerly; before ❷ earlier on; before sth takes place: 有言～ make clear beforehand; have agreed before

在押 zàiyā 〈法〉under detention; in

custody; ～犯 criminal in custody; prisoner

在野 zàiyě　out of office; in opposition; ～党 party not in office; opposition party

在意 zàiyì　pay attention to; care
about; mind: 没 ～ not take notice (of
sth); not notice

在于 zàiyú　❶ lie in; rest with: 生命
～运动。The secret of life lies in constant motion. ❷ be determined by; depend on: 去不去 ～你自己。It's up to
you to decide whether you'll go or not.

在职 zàizhí　be on the job; be employed; be at one's post: ～培训 in-
service or on-the-job training / ～期间
during one's tenure of office

载 zài　❶ carry; bring; be loaded
with: ～荷 load / ～体 carrier /
～誉归来 come back with flying colours / ～人飞行器 manned craft ❷ (of
a road, etc) be filled with: 风雪一途。
The snowstorm blocked the road. ❸
〈书〉and; moreover; at the same time:
～歌～舞 singing and dancing joyously
see also zǎi

载重 zàizhòng　load; carrying capacity: ～量 (of a ship, etc) loading
or deadweight capacity / ～ 汽 车
heavy(-duty) truck or lorry

zān

糌 zān

糌粑 zānba　*zanba*, or roasted *qingke*
barley flour, a staple of Tibetans

簪 zān　❶ *also* "簪子" hair clasp;
hairpin ❷ wear (flowers, etc) in
one's hair

zán

咱（喒、偺）zán　❶ we (in-
cluding both the

speaker and the person or persons spoken to): ～大伙儿一条心。We are all
of one heart and one mind. ❷〈方〉I

咱们 zánmen　❶ *see* "咱❶" ❷ *used to
mean oneself or the person addressed*:
不哭, ～乖。You be a good boy and
stop crying. ～买不起, 看看还不行
吗。Can't I just have a look, even
though I can't afford it?

zǎn

攒 zǎn　accumulate; collect; save:
～钱买书 save up to buy books;
save up for books　*see also* cuán

zàn

暂 zàn　❶（usu 暂短）transient;
brief ❷ for the time being; for
the moment; momentarily: ～ 定 set
tentatively / ～缓 put off; postpone;
suspend

暂且 zànqiě　temporarily; for the time
being; for the moment: 这事 ～ 搁一
搁。Let's put the matter aside for the
time being.

暂时 zànshí　temporary; for the time
being: ～代理 act (as …) / ～的工作
temporary work

暂停 zàntíng　❶ suspend; discontinue
for the time being ❷〈体〉timeout

暂行 zànxíng　provisional; temporary: ～条例 interim regulations

赞（賛、讚）zàn　❶ sup-
port; aid; as-
sist ❷ praise; laud; eulogize: ～歌
paean; hymn / ～颂 laud; eulogize;
sing the praises of / ～叹 marvel at;
gasp in admiration / ～誉 praise; commend; acclaim / ～不绝口 be full of
praise; praise unceasingly; shower
praises

赞成 zànchéng　❶ approve of; agree
with; favour: ～ 票 affirmative vote;

vote of assent ❷〈书〉help accomplish; ~其事 help accomplish the task

赞美 zànměi eulogize; extol; praise; ~诗〈宗教〉hymn; psalm; chant

赞赏 zànshǎng think highly of; appreciate; admire; 表示~ express one's appreciation (for sth)

赞同 zàntóng approve of; accept; endorse; 我~你的意见。I go along with you on this point.

赞许 zànxǔ praise; commend; approve of; ~的微笑 approving smile

赞扬 zànyáng speak highly of; pay tribute to; commend; ~孩子的进步 praise children for their progress

赞助 zànzhù support; assistance; aid; 拉~ canvass for contributions or sponsors / ~者 sponsor

zāng

赃(臟) zāng stolen goods; embezzled money; spoils; ~官 corrupt official / ~物 stolen or embezzled goods; booty; spoils

脏(髒) zāng dirty; filthy; unclean; ~弹〈军〉dirty bomb / ~话 dirty words; obscene language / ~水 filthy water; slops; sewage / ~字 four-letter word
see also zàng

臧 zāng

臧否 zāngpǐ 〈书〉pass judgement on; appraise; ~人物 comment on the merits and demerits of people; pass judgement on people

zàng

脏(臟) zàng *also* "脏腑"; "脏器" internal organs of the body; viscera

葬 zàng bury; inter; ~地 burial ground; grave / ~礼 funeral

(rites) / ~送 ruin; wreck / ~身火海 perish in (a sea of) flames

藏 zàng ❶ storage; depository ❷ Buddhist or Taoist scriptures ❸ (Zàng) (short for 西藏) Tibet; ~语 Tibetan language / ~学 Tibetology / ~族 Tibetan (ethnic group)
see also cáng

藏蓝 zànglán purplish blue

藏青 zàngqīng dark blue

zāo

遭 zāo ❶ meet with (disaster, etc); sustain; suffer; ~难 suffer a misfortune; be killed in an accident, etc / ~殃 suffer (disaster or misfortune) / ~灾 suffer a disaster; be hit by a natural calamity / ~罪 suffer (hardships, tortures, etc) / 惨~毒手 be killed in cold blood ❷〈量〉time; turn; round; 来回走了好几~ walk back and forth several times

遭到 zāodào (usu used before bi-syllabic verbs) suffer; sustain; be; ~冷落 be left out in the cold; be given the cold shoulder

遭受 zāoshòu suffer; undergo; sustain; ~台风袭击 be hit or struck by a typhoon

遭遇 zāoyù ❶ come across; encounter; run into; ~战〈军〉encounter; meeting engagement; skirmish / ~不幸 have bad luck; meet with adversity ❷ *also* "遭际" experience; (hapless) fate; (hard) lot

糟 zāo ❶ (distillers' or brewers') grains; ~糠之妻 wife who shared her husband's hard lot ❷ pickle with grains or in wine; ~鱼 pickled fish ❸ rotten; worn out; ~木头 rotten wood ❹ in a wretched state; in a mess; 身体~ in poor health; frail / ~心 vexed; annoyed; depressed / ~了! 赶不上火车了! Blast! We'll miss the train!

糟糕 zāogāo　unlucky; bad; terrible; ～透顶 as bad as bad can be; most unlucky / ～，我把开会的事忘了！My goodness! I forgot all about the meeting.

糟粕 zāopò　dross; dregs: 弃其一，取其精华 discard the dross and assimilate the essence

糟蹋 zāotà　also "糟踏" "糟践" ❶ waste; ruin; damage: ～人才 waste talents ❷ insult; trample on: 你怎么随便～人? How can you talk about others in such dreadful terms? ❸ violate (a woman); ravish; rape

záo

凿(鑿) záo　❶ also "凿子" chisel ❷ bore a hole; chisel; dig: ～井 dig a well; sink a shaft or pit ❸〈书〉certain; authentic; irrefutable: ～空 farfetched; implausible / ～～有据 with indisputable evidence

zǎo

早 zǎo　❶ morning: ～餐 also "早饭" breakfast / ～场 morning show (at a cinema, etc) / ～晨 also "早上" morning / ～点 (light) breakfast / ～市 morning fair or market ❷ former; early; earlier (than scheduled or expected): ～产 premature birth / ～恋 puppy or calf love / ～先 formerly; previously; before / ～～儿〈口〉as soon as possible; well in advance / 他～已毕业。He graduated long ago. ❸ used before a verb to indicate supposition and / or regret: ～知今日，悔不当初 had I known it, I wouldn't have done it; if only I knew ❹ also "早安" "早上好" ("word of greeting") good morning

早年 zǎonián　❶ many years ago; in the past ❷ in one's early years

早期 zǎoqī　early stage or phase: ～症状〈医〉incipient or early symptoms

早日 zǎorì　❶ at an early date; early; soon: ～归来 return as soon as possible ❷ in the past; former: 恢复～的光彩 regain or restore one's former lustre

早熟 zǎoshú　❶ also "早慧"〈生理〉precocity: ～儿童 precocious children ❷ early-ripe; early-maturing (variety, etc)

早晚 zǎowǎn　❶ morning and evening ❷ sooner or later; one of these days: 你～会后悔的。You will regret it sooner or later. ❸ time: 这～他许是到上海了。He may have arrived in Shanghai by this time. ❹〈方〉some time in the future; some day

枣(棗) zǎo　jujube; (Chinese) date: ～红 purplish red; claret / ～泥 jujube paste

蚤 zǎo　flea

澡 zǎo　bath: ～盆 bathtub / ～堂 public baths; bathhouse

藻 zǎo　❶ algae; aquatic plants ❷ literary adornment: ～饰〈书〉embellish; adorn (in writing)

zào

皂 zào　❶ black: ～白难辨 not distinguish black from white; confound right and wrong ❷ soap: ～片 soap flakes

灶(竈) zào　❶ kitchen range; cooking stove: ～具 cooking utensils / ～台 top of a kitchen range ❷ kitchen; mess; canteen ❸ (usu 灶王爷 or 灶神) kitchen god

造 zào　❶ make; build; create: ～成 cause; give rise to; bring about / ～假 make a fake or counterfeit / ～价 cost of construction or manufacture / 〜林 afforestation / 〜孽 also "作孽"〈宗教〉do evil; commit a sin / 〜势 build up momentum (for sb or sth); promote / 〜假账 cook accounts / 〜物 主〈宗教〉God; the Creator ❷ one of the two parties to a legal agreement or lawsuit; 甲〜 party A ❸ crop; 一年三 〜 three crops a year ❹〈书〉go to; arrive at; reach; 〜访 pay a visit (at sb's house); call on ❺ achievements; accomplishments ❻ train; educate; cultivate; 可〜之才 person of promise

造次 zàocì〈书〉❶ hurried; hasty; 〜 之间 in a hurry; in a moment of haste ❷ rash; imprudent; 不可〜。Don't be impetuous.

造反 zàofǎn　rise in rebellion; rebel; revolt; 〜者 rebel

造福 zàofú　bring benefit to; do good for; 为人民〜 work for the well-being of the people

造化 zàohuà ❶〈书〉the Creator; Nature ❷〈zàohua〉fortune; good luck; 你可是〜不浅哪! How lucky you are!

造就 zàojiù ❶ create; train; bring up ❷ also "造诣" (academic, etc) achievements; attainments

造型 zàoxíng ❶ modelling; mould-making; 〜艺术 plastic arts ❷ model; mould; form; 独特〜 unique in shape

造谣 zàoyáo　cook up a story; spread a rumour; 〜生事 start a rumour to create disturbances; stir up trouble by rumour-mongering

造作 zàozuo　affected; unnatural; artificial; 举止〜 be affected in manner

噪 zào ❶ (of birds, insects etc) chirp ❷ make an uproar; clam-our; 〜音 also "噪声" noise; din ❸ become well known; 声名大〜 gain great fame

燥 zào　dry; 〜热 hot and dry

躁 zào　rash; impetuous; impul-sive; 脾气〜 be impetuous or hot-tempered / 〜动 move restlessly or agitatedly; be jittery or fretful

zé

则 zé ❶ (usu 准则) standard; norm; criterion ❷ rule; decree; regulation; 守〜 rules of conduct ❸ 〈量〉item (of news); paragraph or piece (of writing); 一〜新闻 an item of news ❹〈书〉〈连〉used to indicate a) sequence of actions; 歌毕，〜掌声四 起。The song was greeted by loud ap-plause. b) cause and effect, condi-tion, etc; 唇亡〜齿寒。If the lips are gone, the teeth will be exposed to the cold. c) contrast; 其事虽易为，其理一 难明。While the work is easy to do, the reason is hard to explain. d) tran-sition; 今〜不然。Things are different now. e) concession; 少〜少，聊胜于 无。Though not enough, it is better than nothing. ❺ used together with 一，二，三 to enumerate causes or rea-sons; 他没有考上大学，一〜基础差，二〜复习时间短⋯。He failed the college entrance examination because, first, he lacked a good grounding in the subjects; second, he didn't have enough time for revision⋯ ❻〈书〉be; 此〜意料中之事也! That is only to be expected! ❼ make; do; 〜声 make a sound; speak

责 zé ❶ duty; obligation; respon-sibility; 为国效劳，人人有〜。Everyone has a duty to his country. ❷ demand; exact; require; 〜人宽，己 严 be strict with oneself and generous towards others ❸ interrogate; question closely; call to account; 〜问 ask re-provingly; sternly call (sb) to account ❹ criticize; reproach; blame; 〜难 censure; reproach; reproach; blame ❺ also "责 罚" punish; penalize

责备 zébèi　reproach; blame; reprimand：~的目光 reproachful look

责成 zéchéng　*also* "责令" instruct or order（sb.to do sth）；enjoin

责怪 zéguài　blame；reproach：这事不能~他。He is not to blame for this.

责骂 zémà　scold；rebuke；dress down：挨了一顿~ get a scolding or dressing-down

责任 zérèn　❶ duty；obligation；responsibility：~感 *also* "责任心" sense of responsibility or duty / ~制 system of job responsibility；responsibility system / ~编辑（shortened as 责编）editor in charge；project editor ❷ responsibility for a wrong or failure；blame：推卸~ shirk responsibility；shift the blame onto others；pass the buck

责无旁贷 zéwúpángdài　（of sth）be one's unshirkable responsibility；（of sb）be duty-bound

择（擇） zé　select；choose；pick：~偶 choose one's spouse / ~业 select a job；choose an occupation / ~吉日开张 choose an auspicious day to start a business / ~善而从 choose and embrace what is good；accept what is sound and reasonable / ~优录取 enroll only those who are outstanding；employ on the basis of competitive selection　*see also* zhái

咋 zé　〈书〉bite：~舌 be tongue-tied（with remorse or fear）；refrain from speech　*see also* zǎ；zhā

泽（澤） zé　❶ pool；pond；swamp：~国〈书〉land of rivers and lakes；flooded area ❷ wet；moist；damp ❸ lustre（of metals，pearls，etc）❹〈书〉favour；largesse；beneficence：~流后世。One's benevolence reaches down to later generations.

啧 zé　click of the tongue：~~赞叹 be profuse in one's praise / ~有烦言。There are a lot of complaints.

zè

仄 zè　❶ narrow；cramped：人多地~（with）too many people and too little land ❷ uneasy；sorry：歉~ sorry；apologetic ❸（usu 仄声）〈语言〉oblique tones in classical Chinese，as distinct from the level tones（平声）

zéi

贼 zéi　❶ thief；burglar：〈喻〉vermin：~人 thief；robber；evildoer / ~窝 thieves' den / ~喊捉~ a thief crying "Stop thief" / ~去关门 neglect to lock the door until the burglar has gone；take action only after the harm is done ❷ wicked；crooked；evil：~眉鼠眼 wear a thievish expression；look like a sly fox / ~头~脑 thievish；stealthy；furtive ❸〈方〉sly；cunning：~心不死 cannot suppress evil thoughts；refuse to give up one's sinister intentions or designs ❹〈方〉extremely；terribly；disagreeably：~冷 terribly cold

zěn

怎 zěn　why；what；how：这事该~办？What's to be done about it？

怎么 zěnme　❶ *inquiring about cause，condition，etc*：水~不热？Why isn't the water hot enough？❷ *indicating nature，condition or manner*：你愿意~干就~干吧。Do as you please. ❸ *used in the negative to indicate inadequacy*：我不~了解他。I don't know him well enough. ❹ *used at the beginning of a sentence to indicate surprise，usu followed by a pause*：~，你想不认账？What？You want to deny your debt？

怎么着 zěnmezhe　❶ *inquiring about*

an action or a state：我们去游泳，你～？We are going swimming. What about you？ ❷ indicating an action or a state of affairs：我愿意～就～，不用你管。I'll do as I please, and that is none of your business. ❸ see "怎么❹"

怎样 zěnyàng also "怎么样" ❶ inquiring about nature, condition, manner, volition, etc：情况进展～？How is everything going？❷ see "怎么❹"
❸ euphemistic formula for negation：这幅画画得不～。This painting is not particularly good. / 你能把他～？What can you do about him？

zèn

谮 zèn 〈书〉slander；calumniate；～言 calumny；defamation

zēng

曾 zēng relationship between great-grandchildren and great-grand-parents：～孙 great-grandson / ～祖（paternal）great-grandfather　see also céng

增 zēng increase；enhance；grow：～产 increase production / ～幅 range or margin of increase；rate of growth / ～刊 supplement（to a periodical，etc）；supplementary issue / ～删 additions and deletions；alterations / ～收节支 increase revenue and reduce expenditure / 为国～光 do credit or add glory to one's country / 骨质～生〈医〉calcium deposits；condensing osteitis

增补 zēngbǔ add；supplement；augment；～本 enlarged edition

增订 zēngdìng ❶ revise and enlarge（a book）；expand and improve ❷ subscribe to（more newspapers, magazines，etc）

增加 zēngjiā increase；augment；raise：～工资 get a raise（in pay）/ ～

信心 enhance one's confidence；become more confident

增进 zēngjìn enhance；promote；further：～了解 further or strengthen understanding

增强 zēngqiáng make strong or stronger；strengthen；enhance：～体质 build up one's health

增添 zēngtiān add；increase；augment：～麻烦 add to（sb's）trouble；put（sb）to much trouble

增援 zēngyuán reinforce：～前线 send reinforcements to the battle front

增长 zēngzhǎng increase；enhance；grow：～率 rate of growth or increase；growth rate / ～见识 enrich one's knowledge and experience

增值 zēngzhí 〈经〉rise or increase in value；appreciate：欧元～ appreciation of euro / ～税 value added tax（VAT）

增殖 zēngzhí ❶ proliferate；multiply：细胞～ proliferation of cells ❷ breed；reproduce；propagate：～财富 increase wealth

憎 zēng hate；loathe；abhor：～恨 hate；loathe；detest / ～恶 detest；abhor；abominate

zèng

锃 zèng （of utensils，etc）polished：～亮 shiny

赠 zèng send as a gift；give as a present：～答〈书〉present each other with gifts, poems, etc / ～票（give sb a）complimentary ticket / ～品 gift；giveaway / ～券 free coupon / ～送 present as a gift；give as a present / ～言 words of advice or encouragement at parting / ～阅本 complimentary copy

zhā

扎（❸紮、❸紥） zhā ❶ prick；needle into：～手 prick the hand；〈喻〉thorny；ticklish／～针〈中医〉receive acupuncture treatment／～耳朵眼儿 pierce the earlobes (for earrings) ❷〈方〉plunge；dive；get (into sth) ：～猛子 dive (into water) ❸ (of troops) be stationed or quartered：～营 pitch a camp；camp

see also zā

扎堆 zhāduī　gather together (in a group, etc)：～儿聊天 chat in a group

扎根 zhāgēn　take or strike root：～边疆 settle in the border areas

扎啤 zhāpí　draught beer

扎实 zhāshí　❶ sturdy；strong；robust：身子板儿～ have a strong physique ❷ solid；firm；sound：学问～ have sound scholarship／～地做几件事 do a few things in real earnest

扎眼 zhāyǎn　❶ dazzling；loud；garish：打扮～ be loudly dressed ❷ offensively conspicuous；very showy

咋

zhā　*see also* zǎ；zé

咋呼 zhāhu　*also* "咋唬"〈方〉❶ shout loudly；大声～ shout at the top of one's voice ❷ bluster；show off (one's authority, etc)：这姑娘有点～。The girl's a bit obstreperous.

喳

zhā　〈象声〉sound of birds：喜鹊～～叫。Magpies were twittering.　*see also* chā

渣

zhā　❶ dregs；sediment；residue：～滓 *also* "渣子" dregs；residue；scum ❷ broken bits：点心～ crumbs or scraps of pastry

zhá

札(❸剳)

zhá　❶〈考古〉thin pieces of wood used for writing ❷〈书〉letter ❸ notes：～记 reading notes or commentary

轧

zhá　roll (steel)：～钢 steel rolling　*see also* yà

闸

zhá　❶ *also* "闸门" floodgate；sluice (gate) ❷ dam up water；brake：松～ take off the brake ❸〈口〉electric switch：合～ close a switch／～盒 fuse box

炸

zhá　❶ fry (in deep fat or oil)；deep-fry：～酱面 noodles served with fried bean plaster／～土豆条 French fries；chips ❷〈方〉dip (vegetables, etc) in boiling water；scald (as a way of cooking)

see also zhà

铡

zhá　❶ *also* "铡刀" hay cutter；fodder chopper ❷ cut up or chop with a hay cutter

zhǎ

拃

zhǎ　❶ measure by stretching one's hand across in one span ❷〈量〉(hand) span：三～宽 three spans wide

眨

zhǎ　blink；wink；bat (the eyes)：～巴〈方〉blink／～眼 wink；blink；(in a) twinkling

zhà

乍

zhà　❶ (at) first；for the first time：一～看 at first glance ❷ suddenly；abruptly：风～起。A sudden breeze rose.

诈

zhà　❶ cheat；swindle；deceive：～取 obtain by cheating；swindle sb out of sth ❷ pretend；feign；fake：～死 feign death；play possum／～降 pretend to capitulate；feign surrender ❸ bluff sb into giving information；draw (sb) out：～唬 bluff；bluster

诈骗 zhàpiàn　defraud (sb of sth)；swindle (sb out of sth)：～犯 swindler／～罪 crime of fraud

栅

zhà　(usu 栅栏) railings；palisade；bars

炸 zhà ❶ (of a balloon, etc) explode; break; burst ❷ blow up (a house, etc); blast; bomb: ～弹 bomb / ～药 explosive (charge); dynamite; TNT ❸〈口〉explode with anger; flare up ❹〈方〉scamper; scurry away; flee in terror: ～窝 (of birds, etc) flee from nest in fright; (of a crowd of people) be thrown into confusion or disarray

see also zhá

痄 zhà

痄腮 zhàsai 〈中医〉mumps

蚱 zhà

蚱蜢 zhàměng grasshopper

榨(搾) zhà press; extract; squeeze out: ～果汁机 juice extractor

榨菜 zhàcài (hot pickled) mustard tuber

榨取 zhàqǔ ❶ *see* "榨" ❷ extort; squeeze: ～民脂民膏 batten on the flesh and blood of the people

zhāi

斋(齋) zhāi ❶ (usu 斋戒)〈宗教〉wear clean clothes and abstain from meat, wine, etc to show one's piety (to gods or ancestors); fast: ～月 (of Islam) Ramadan, 9th month of the Muslim year; month of fast ❷ vegetarian diet adopted by Buddhists and Taoists: ～饭 food that monks obtain by begging; vegetarian meal in a monastery ❸ give alms (to a monk, etc) ❹ room or house: 书～ study

摘 zhāi ❶ pick; pluck; take off: ～除〈医〉remove; excise / ～取 pick; pluck / ～帽子 remove the (political) label ❷ select; pick out; make extracts from: ～编 select and edit; extract and compile / ～抄 extract and copy; make extracts; cull / ～录 make extracts or excerpts; extract / ～由 key extracts (of a document); résumé ❸ *also* "摘借" borrow money when in urgent need

摘要 zhāiyào ❶ make a summary or an abstract: ～记录 jot down the main points / ～刊登 carry a summary (in a newspaper or magazine) ❷ summary; abstract

摘引 zhāiyǐn quote: ～名人语录 cite quotations from a celebrity

zhái

宅 zhái residence; dwelling; house: ～基 foundations of a house; house site / ～门 gate of an old-style big house / ～family living in such a mansion / ～院 house with a courtyard / ～子〈口〉residence; house

择(擇) zhái select; choose; pick: ～菜 trim vegetables for cooking / ～席 be unable to sleep well in a new place　*see also* zé

zhǎi

窄 zhǎi ❶ narrow: ～小 narrow (and small); cramped ❷ petty; small-minded: 心眼儿 narrow-minded ❸ hard up; badly off; on the rocks

zhài

债 zhài debt: ～户 debtor / ～款 loan; debt / ～主 creditor / ～台高筑 be heavily in debt; be up to one's ears in debt; be debt-ridden

债权 zhàiquán creditor's right;〈法〉obligatory right: ～国 creditor nation / ～人 creditor; lender

债券 zhàiquàn bond; debenture: 赎回到期～ redeem bonds for payment /

～持有人 bond holder

债务 zhàiwù　debt; liabilities; amount due; 偿还～ pay back a debt; meet one's debt / ～国 debtor nation / ～人 debtor

寨 zhài　also "砦" ❶ stockade; fence ❷ camp; 偷营劫～ raid an enemy camp ❸ mountain stronghold; ～主〈旧〉brigand chief ❹ also "寨子" stockaded village; fenced hamlet

zhān

占 zhān　practise divination; divine; ～卜 practise divination; divine / ～卦 divine by means of the Eight Trigrams（八卦）/ ～星 divine by astrology; cast a horoscope　*see also* zhàn

沾（❶❷霑） zhān ❶ moisten; wet; damp; 汗水～湿 wet with sweat ❷ be stained or soiled with; ～满了泥 covered with mud stains ❸ touch; ～手 touch with one's hand; have a hand (in sth) ❹ gain by association with sb or sth; benefit from some sort of relationship; 利益均～ have an equal share of the benefit; share the benefit equally

沾边 zhānbiān ❶ touch on; have sth to do with; 此事与他毫不～。He has nothing at all to do with this. ❷ (of words, etc) be relevant or pertinent; to the point

沾光 zhānguāng　benefit from association with sb or sth; cash in on one's connection with sb; gain from sb's support or influence

沾亲带故 zhānqīn-dàigù　have ties of kinship or friendship (with sb); be related (to sb) somehow or other

沾染 zhānrǎn　contract (bad habits, etc); be infected with; be contaminated by

沾沾自喜 zhānzhānzìxǐ　be pleased with oneself; feel complacent; be self-satisfied

毡（氈、氊） zhān　felt; ～房 yurt / ～靴 felt boots / ～子 felt (rug or blanket)

粘 zhān　glue; stick; paste; ～信封 seal up an envelope　*see also* nián

粘连 zhānlián　〈医〉adhesion; 肠～ intestinal adhesion

粘贴 zhāntiē　glue; paste; stick; ～布告 put up a notice

谵 zhān　〈书〉rave; rant; be delirious; ～妄〈医〉delirium / ～语 delirious or wild talk; ranting and raving

瞻 zhān　look up or forward; ～念 look ahead; think of / ～望 look forward; look far ahead

瞻前顾后 zhānqián-gùhòu ❶ look ahead and behind; consider carefully; weigh the pros and cons ❷ be overcautious and hesitate; shilly-shally

瞻仰 zhānyǎng　look at with reverence; pay tribute to; ～遗容 pay one's last respects to sb's remains

zhǎn

斩 zhǎn ❶ chop; cut; kill; ～获 kill or capture;〈体〉gain (titles, etc) / ～首 behead; decapitate / ～草除根 destroy root and branch / ～尽杀绝 exterminate ruthlessly; wipe out ❷〈方〉fleece; blackmail; ～客 fleece customers

斩钉截铁 zhǎndīng-jiétiě　firm and decisive; categorical; final; ～地表示 state in categorical terms; speak with finality

盏（盞） zhǎn ❶ small cup; ～ tea cup ❷〈量〉两～电灯 two electric lamps

展 zhǎn ❶ open up; spread out; stretch; ~翅 unfold the wings; get ready for flight / ~眉舒目 stretch the eyes and relax the brows; beam with joy ❷ put to good use; give free play to; display: 一~身手 show one's capabilities ❸ put off; postpone; prolong; ~缓 put off; postpone; extend ❹ exhibit; show: ~播 arrange and broadcast (television programmes, etc) / ~出 put on display; exhibit; (of sth) be on show / ~品 exhibit; item on display / ~室 exhibition room; showroom / ~台 also "展位" showcase; booth; display counter

展开 zhǎnkāi ❶ spread out; open up; unfold; ~地毯 roll out a carpet / ~谈问题 elaborate on a question ❷ launch; set off: ~攻势 mount an offensive / ~学术争鸣 conduct an academic debate

展览 zhǎnlǎn display; exhibit; show: 花卉~ flower show / ~馆 exhibition centre or hall / ~会 exhibition

展期 zhǎnqī ❶ extend a time limit; postpone;〈经〉roll over (debt, etc) ❷ exhibition time or period

展示 zhǎnshì put on display; show; reveal: ~证据 show evidence / ~历史的本来面目 present historical facts as they actually occurred

展望 zhǎnwàng ❶ look into the distance; look to the future; look ahead ❷ forecast; prospect; vista: 21 世纪~ 21st century in prospect

展现 zhǎnxiàn unfold before one's eyes; appear; show: ~才华 show one's talent; display one's abilities

展销 zhǎnxiāo display and sell (goods, etc): ~会 commodities fair; sales exhibition

崭 zhǎn 〈书〉rise high; towering (over): ~露头角 begin to distinguish oneself; stand out conspicuously; cut a striking figure

崭新 zhǎnxīn brand new; wholly new

辗 zhǎn

辗转 zhǎnzhuǎn also "展转" ❶ toss about (in bed); toss and turn: ~难眠 toss and turn (in bed); be unable to go to sleep; lie in bed wide awake ❷ pass through many hands or places: ~流传 spread from place to place

zhàn

占（佔） zhàn ❶ take possession of; occupy; seize: ~着茅坑不拉屎〈俗〉hold on to a post without doing a stroke of work and refuse to let anyone else take over; be a dog in the manger ❷ constitute; hold; make up: ~先 take the lead; get ahead (of sb) / ~上风 get the upper hand; have the edge (over sb); turn the tables (on sb) / ~绝对优势 hold an overwhelming advantage; hold all the trumps / ~人口的 70% account for or make up 70 per cent of the population. *see also* zhān

占据 zhànjù occupy; seize; hold: ~电台 seize a radio station / ~领导位置 hold a leading position

占理 zhànlǐ make sense; be sensible or reasonable: 说话~ be reasonable in one's argument

占领 zhànlǐng capture; seize; occupy: ~国 occupation power

占便宜 zhàn piányi ❶ take undue advantage; profit at the expense of others: 占了便宜卖乖 show off one's smartness after gaining an advantage ❷ have the edge (over sb); be advantageous or favourable

占用 zhànyòng occupy: ~公款 use public money for one's own end

占有 zhànyǒu ❶ take possession of; own; have: ~市场 capture a market / ~第一手材料 have first-hand informa-

Z

栈(棧) zhàn ❶ shed; pen; fold ❷ (usu 栈道) plank road built along the face of a cliff; viaduct; ～桥 landing stage (at a port); loading bridge (at a railway station) ❸ warehouse; ～房 warehouse; storehouse

战(戰) zhàn ❶ war; warfare; combat; ～报 war communiqué or bulletin; battlefield report / ～场 battleground; battlefront; theatre of operations / ～犯 war criminal / ～俘 prisoner of war (POW) / ～果 fruits of victory; success in combat or contest / ～壕 trench; entrenchment / ～时 wartime / ～事 war; battle; hostilities / ～役 campaign; battle / ～利品 spoils of war; war trophy or booty / ～地记者 war correspondent / ～功赫赫 win great distinction in war; achieve miraculous feats in war ❷ fight; battle; ～天斗地 fight heaven and earth; combat nature; brave the elements ❸ tremble; shiver; shudder; ～栗 also "颤栗"; "战抖" shake; tremble; shiver

战败 zhànbài ❶ suffer a defeat; be defeated; lose (a battle or war); ～国 conquered or vanquished nation; defeated country ❷ triumph over; vanquish; beat

战备 zhànbèi war preparedness or preparations; combat readiness; ～状态 alert posture; combat readiness against war

战斗 zhàndòu ❶ battle; combat; hostilities; ～机 fighter (plane) / ～力 combat effectiveness; fighting capacity ❷ fight; struggle; ～性 militancy

战国 Zhànguó (period of) Warring States (475 BC-221 BC); ～七雄 Seven Major Powers during the period of Warring States, ie Qi (齐), Chu (楚),

Yan (燕), Zhao (赵), Han (韩), Wei (魏) and Qin (秦)

战火 zhànhuǒ flames of war; ～纷飞 (with) flames of war raging far and wide

战机 zhànjī ❶ opportunity for combat ❷ fighter (plane)

战绩 zhànjì military or contest achievements; ～平平 score mediocre (military or contest) achievements

战局 zhànjú war situation; 扭转～ turn the tables on the enemy

战乱 zhànluàn chaos caused by war; war turmoil; 连年～ successive years of war

战略 zhànlüè strategy; ～家 strategist / ～部署 strategic plans or deployments / ～核武器 strategic nuclear weapons / ～上藐视敌人，战术上重视敌人。Despise the enemy strategically and take full account of him tactically.

战区 zhànqū war zone; theatre of operations or war; ～导弹防御系统 (US) Theater Missile Defense (TMD)

战胜 zhànshèng triumph over; defeat; vanquish; ～国 victorious nation; victor / ～疾病 triumph over disease; cure one's illness

战士 zhànshì ❶ soldier; man ❷ champion (of a cause, etc); warrior; fighter

战术 zhànshù (military) tactics; ～武器 tactical weapons

战无不胜 zhànwúbùshèng ever-victorious; all-conquering

战线 zhànxiàn battle line; front; 在各条～上 in every field of endeavour; on all fronts

战友 zhànyǒu comrade-in-arms; battle companion

战战兢兢 zhànzhàn-jīngjīng ❶ shivering with fear; with fear and trepidation ❷ with caution; gingerly; overcautious

战争 zhànzhēng war; warfare; ～狂 war mania or maniac / ～贩子 warmonger / ～罪行 war crime

站 zhàn ❶ stand; get up; be on one's feet; ～队 line up; fall in; stand in line / ～岗 stand guard; stand sentinel or sentry / ～立 stand (up); rise; be on one's feet / ～柜台 serve behind the counter (as a shop assistant) / ～在人民的立场上 uphold the stand of the people ❷ stop; come to a halt; ～台 also "月台" railway platform / 车～ (bus, etc) station; stop ❸ centre for rendering certain services: 文化～ cultural centre

站稳 zhànwěn ❶ be at or come to a standstill; keep one's footing ❷〈喻〉stand firm; take a firm stand; ～脚跟 gain a firm foothold / ～立场 take a firm stand

站住 zhànzhù ❶ stand; halt ❷ stop firmly on one's feet; keep one's footing ❸ stand or hold one's ground; consolidate one's position: 他在城里总算～了。He finally gained a foothold in the city. ❹ (of an argument, etc) hold water; be valid or tenable

绽 zhàn split; tear; burst: ～放 (of flowers, etc) come into bloom; break out into blossom / ～裂 split; break; burst / ～露 appear; become visible / ～线 (of clothing) split at the seams

湛 zhàn ❶ profound; thorough; deep ❷ crystal clear; limpid: ～蓝 azure (blue)

颤 zhàn shake; tremble; shiver: ～抖 tremble from head to foot / ～栗 also "战栗" shake; tremble; shiver　see also chàn

蘸 zhàn dip in (ink, sauce, etc): ～水钢笔 (dip) pen

zhāng

张(張) zhāng ❶ open; spread; draw (a bow, etc): ～弛 tension and relaxation ❷ lay on; display: ～贴 post (a poster, etc) / ～灯结彩 hang up lanterns and silk festoons; (of a place) be decorated with lanterns and colourful streamers ❸ magnify; exaggerate; run rampant: ～狂 rampant; insolent; impudent ❹ look; glance: ～望 peep; peer; look around ❺〈量〉a) of paper, tickets, etc: 一～报纸 a piece of newspaper b) of beds, tables, etc: 一～沙发 a sofa c) of human faces, etc: 一～利嘴 a sharp tongue d) of bows, ploughs, etc: 一～弓 a bow

张冠李戴 zhāngguānlǐdài attribute sth to the wrong person; confuse one thing with another; get things mixed up

张皇失措 zhānghuángshīcuò be in a flurry of alarm; lose one's nerve; be scared stiff

张口结舌 zhāngkǒu-jiéshé be agape and tongue-tied; be at a loss for words

张罗 zhāngluo ❶ take care of; get busy about; attend to: ～后事 make arrangements for sb's funeral ❷ raise (funds); collect (money, etc) ❸ greet and entertain (guests); wait on (customers, etc)

张牙舞爪 zhāngyá-wǔzhǎo make threatening gestures; act arrogantly and ferociously; swagger and bluster

张扬 zhāngyáng come out into the open; make widely known; make public: 大肆～ give enormous publicity to

章 zhāng ❶ chapter; section; clause: ～节 chapters (and sections) / ～回小说 traditional novel with chapters and chapter titles in couplets ❷ rules; regulations; charter: 照～处理 handle according to rules ❸ order; orderliness ❹ (usu 奏章) memorial to the throne ❺ seal; signet; stamp: 私～ private seal ❻ badge; insignia; medal

章程 zhāngchéng ❶ rules; regu-

Z

lations; constitution: 按～办事 act according to rules ❷ (zhāngcheng) solution; way: 自有～ have one's own way (of doing sth); know one's own mind (about sth)

章法 zhāngfǎ ❶ organization and structure of a piece of writing or painting; art of composition or painting: 不拘～ have no regard for the conventions of composition ❷ order; method; way: 乱了～ be thrown off balance

章鱼 zhāngyú octopus

獐 zhāng (usu 獐子) river deer; Chinese water deer: ～头鼠目 with hideous features and shifty eyes; repulsively ugly and sly-looking

彰 zhāng ❶ obvious; evident; conspicuous: ～明较著 conspicuous; outstanding ❷ cite (in dispatches); commend

彰显 zhāngxiǎn ❶ evident; prominent; conspicuous ❷ make evident or clear; demonstrate clearly

樟 zhāng camphor tree: ～脑 camphor / ～木 camphor-wood

蟑 zhāng

蟑螂 zhāngláng cockroach; roach

zhǎng

长(長) zhǎng ❶ older (generation); elder; senior: ～辈 senior member of a family; person of the elder generation / ～者 (venerable) elder ❷ eldest; oldest: ～孙 eldest son's eldest son; eldest grandson ❸ chief; head; leader: ～官 senior officer or official; commanding officer ❹ grow; develop: ～膘 (of a domestic animal) fatten; flesh out;〈谑〉(of people) get fat / ～个儿 (of a child, etc) grow taller / ～大成人 be grown up ❺ boost; enhance; increase: ～才干 enhance one's abilities

see also cháng

长进 zhǎngjìn progress; improvement: 大有～ make much progress; improve a lot

长老 zhǎnglǎo ❶〈书〉elderly person; elder ❷ (respectful form of address for a monk) elder ❸〈宗教〉local religious leader; elder

长势 zhǎngshì the way a crop is growing; growth: ～旺盛 grow luxuriantly

长相 zhǎngxiàng 〈口〉looks; features; countenance: ～一模一样 look as like as two peas

涨(漲) zhǎng (of water, prices, etc) rise; go up: ～潮 rising or flood tide / ～幅 (of prices, etc) range of rise / ～价 rise or hike in price　see also zhàng

掌 zhǎng ❶ palm (of the human hand); pad (of certain animals' feet); sole (of foot or shoe): ～鞋 mend the sole of a shoe / ～心 centre or hollow of the palm; sphere of control / ～上电脑 handheld computer; palm-top / ～上明珠 apple of one's eye — beloved daughter / 给马钉～(子) shoe a horse ❷ strike with the palm of the hand; slap: ～嘴 slap sb on the face ❸ hold in one's hand; take charge of; control or wield; ～控 control; have in one's hand / ～权 power; exercise control / ～勺儿 do the cooking; prepare a meal

掌舵 zhǎngduò ❶ operate the rudder; steer a boat;〈喻〉be at the helm　also "掌舵人" helmsman; steersman

掌故 zhǎnggù anecdote; tale

掌管 zhǎngguǎn take charge of; run; administer: ～人事 be in charge of personnel matters

掌柜 zhǎngguì also "掌柜的" ❶ shopkeeper; manager (of a shop) ❷〈方〉husband; hubby: 内～ missus; wife

掌声 zhǎngshēng　clapping; applause: ～雷动 burst into thunderous applause
掌握 zhǎngwò ❶ grasp; master; learn thoroughly: 熟练～英语口语 speak English fluently ❷ have in hand; take charge of; control: ～政权 be in power

zhàng

丈 zhàng ❶ zhang, a unit of length (= 3⅓ metres): ～二和尚，摸不着头脑 cannot make head or tail of it; be all at sea (about sth) ❷ also "丈量" measure (land) ❸ form of address for certain male relatives by marriage: 姨～ husband of mother's sister; uncle
丈夫 zhàngfū ❶ man; ～气概 manliness ❷ (zhàngfu) husband
丈母 zhàngmu　also "丈母娘" wife's mother; mother-in-law
丈人 zhàngren　wife's father; father-in-law

仗 zhàng ❶ fight; battle; war ❷ 〈书〉hold (a weapon): ～剑而行 walk sword in hand ❸ rely or depend on; on the strength of: ～势欺人 abuse one's power and bully people; play the bully on the strength of one's power or connections
仗义 zhàngyì ❶ uphold justice: ～执言 speak out to uphold justice ❷ be loyal or generous (to friends); etc): ～疏财 be generous in helping the poor or needy

杖 zhàng ❶ cane; stick; club ❷ rod or staff used for a specific purpose: 擀面～ rolling pin

帐(帳) zhàng ❶ curtain; tent; canopy: ～幕 tent / ～篷 tent / ～子 bed-curtain; mosquito net ❷ see "账" zhàng

账(賬) zhàng ❶ account: ～单 bill; account; check /

～号 account number / ～目 items of an account; accounts ❷ (usu 账簿 or 账本) account book: ～面利润 book profit ❸ debt; credit: 要～ demand payment of debt
账户 zhànghù　account: 开～ open an account (with a bank, etc) / 结清～ close an account

胀(脹) zhàng ❶ grow in size; expand; distend: 热～冷缩 expand when heated and contract when cooled ❷ swell; be bloated: 肚子～ feel bloated in the stomach

涨(漲) zhàng ❶ swell after absorbing water, etc: be swelled by a rush of blood; redden: 脑子发～ feel one's head swimming / ～红了脸 (of one's face) go red; flush ❸ (of weights and measures, etc) be more, longer, etc than expected: 钱花～了 spend more than one plans for
see also zhǎng

障 zhàng ❶ hinder; impede; obstruct: ～眼法 also "遮眼法" cover-up; camouflage; disguise ❷ screen; barrier; block
障碍 zhàng'ài ❶ hinder; block; obstruct: ～物 obstacle; hindrance; barrier ❷ obstacle; barrier; impediment: ～赛跑 obstacle race; steeplechase

幛 zhàng　also "幛子" large, oblong sheet of silk with an inscription (presented at a wedding, funeral, etc)

嶂 zhàng　screen-like mountain peak

瘴 zhàng　also "瘴气" miasma

zhāo

招 zhāo ❶ beckon; gesture: ～魂〈迷信〉call back the spirit of the dead; 〈喻〉try to revive / ～手 beckon; wave / ～之即来 come at sb's beck and call ❷ recruit; invite; attract: ～

Z

考 recruit or enrol by public examination / ～募 recruit; enrol; enlist / ～引 draw; attract; induce / ～女婿 find a husband for one's daughter (and have him live in one's house after marriage) / ～兵买马 raise or enlarge an army;〈喻〉recruit personnel / ～商引资 attract business and investments (from overseas, etc) ❸ offend; provoke; cause; ～事 bring trouble on oneself; court trouble ❹ confess; admit; own up; ～供 confess (one's crime) / ～认 plead guilty ❺ see "着" zhāo

招安 zhāo'ān 〈史〉offer amnesty to rebels and enlist their service; 受～ (of rebels) accept amnesty and pledge loyalty to the ruler

招标 zhāobiāo invite tenders, bids, or public bidding; ～制 public bidding system / ～采购 purchase by bidding or tender

招待 zhāodài give or hold a reception; entertain; serve (customers); ～会 reception / ～券 complimentary ticket / ～所 guesthouse; hostel

招呼 zhāohu ❶ call; shout ❷ (usu 打招呼) hail; greet; say hello to ❸ ask; tell; notify; ～旅客上车 ask the passengers to get aboard ❹ take care of; look after; attend to

招集 zhāojí muster or gather (people); convene (a meeting, etc)

招架 zhāojià ward off blows; hold one's own; 只有～之功，毫无还手之力 be able only to parry attacks with no strength left to hit back

招揽 zhāolǎn also "招徕" solicit (customers, business, etc); canvass

招领 zhāolǐng announce the finding of lost property; 失物～ (lost and) found

招牌 zhāopai shop sign; signboard; pretence; 砸～ ruin one's reputation

招聘 zhāopìn engage by public notice; invite applications for a job; ～广告 employment advertisement; job ad

招惹 zhāorě ❶ invite; incur; court; ～是非 court trouble ❷〈方〉(mostly used in the negative) tease; provoke

招生 zhāoshēng enrol new students; recruit students; ～简章 school admission brochure / ～办公室 admission office

招收 zhāoshōu enrol; recruit; take in

招贴 zhāotiē poster; placard; bill; ～画 picture poster or placard

招摇 zhāoyáo act ostentatiously; show off; ～过市 blatantly seek the limelight; strive for publicity / ～撞骗 bluster and swindle

招展 zhāozhǎn move to and fro; flutter; wave; 随风～ (of flags, etc) flap or flutter in the wind

招致 zhāozhì ❶ recruit (talents, etc); seek and employ ❷ result in (sth bad); incur; lead to

招租 zhāozū solicit or attract lodgers; to let; 房屋～ house to let

昭 zhāo ❶ clear; evident; obvious; ～彰 clear; manifest; obvious ❷〈书〉show; demonstrate; ～示 make clear to all; declare publicly; proclaim

昭然 zhāorán obvious; manifest; very clear; ～若揭 all too obvious; clear as daylight

昭雪 zhāoxuě exonerate; rehabilitate; redress

昭著 zhāozhù clear; evident; manifest; 军功～ have signal military exploits to one's credit

着 zhāo also "招" ❶ move in chess; 支～儿 (watch a game of chess and) give advice to a player; kibitz ❷ trick; device; tactic; 实在没～了 be at one's wits' end

see also zháo; zhe; zhuó

着数 zhāoshù also "招数" ❶ move in

chess ❷ movement in *wushu* (武术)：
~利落 be nimble in *wushu* movements
❸ trick; device: 使尽了~ exhaust all
one's devices; be at the end of one's
tether

朝 zhāo ❶（early）morning;
dawn: ~露〈书〉(like) morning
dew — short-lived; ephemeral / ~霞
morning glow; rosy dawn / ~思暮想
long for sth day and night; pine for sth /
~阳产业 sunrise industry ❷ day: 今
~ today

see also cháo

朝气 zhāoqì ❶ youthful spirit; vim and
vigour; vitality: ~蓬勃 burst with
youthful spirit; be full of vigour and vitality

朝三暮四 zhāosān-mùsì blow hot
and cold; play fast and loose; chop and
change

朝夕 zhāoxī ❶ morning and evening;
day and night; constantly: ~思念
think about sb day and night ❷ shortly; very short time: 只争~ seize every
minute / 朝不保夕 not know in the
morning what may happen in the evening; be in a precarious condition / 朝令
夕改 issue an order in the morning and
rescind it in the evening; make changes
in policy at will

zháo

着 zháo ❶ touch; contact: ~边
touch on the subject, etc; be relevant ❷ feel; suffer: ~慌 panic; become flustered or jittery / ~急 worry;
feel anxious / ~凉 catch a cold or chill /
~魔 be bewitched, entranced or possessed / ~迷 be fascinated or enchanted ❸ burn: ~火 catch fire; be in
flames ❹ *used after a verb to indicate
the result of the action*: 谜语猜~了
guess a riddle right ❺〈方〉fall asleep

see also zhāo; zhe; zhuó

zhǎo

爪 zhǎo claw; talon: ~牙 flun-
keys; underlings *see also* zhuǎ

找 zhǎo ❶ look or hunt for; try to
discover: ~死 court death / ~
寻 try to find; look for; seek / ~辙
〈方〉find a solution or an excuse; seek a
way out; use a pretext / ~对象 seek a
partner in marriage ❷ make up; give
change: ~补 make up a deficiency;
add / ~齐 make uniform or complete;
even up; make up a deficiency / 少~钱
give short change

找茬儿 zhǎochár *also*"找碴儿"find
fault; pick holes; nit-pick

找事 zhǎoshì ❶ look or hunt for a
job; seek employment ❷ kick up a
row; pick a quarrel ❸ (of a child, etc)
add to the trouble

沼 zhǎo natural pond: ~气 marsh
gas; biogas; methane / ~泽
marsh; swamp; bog

zhào

召 zhào call together; gather;
summon: ~回 recall (diplomats,
products, etc); ~开 hold (a meeting,
etc); convene; convoke

召唤 zhàohuàn call; summon: 时代
的~ call of the times

召集 zhàojí call together; convene;
assemble: ~人 convener

召见 zhàojiàn ❶ call in (a subordinate) officially; give an audience to ❷
summon (a foreign envoy) to an interview

兆 zhào ❶ *also*"兆头"sign;
omen; portent ❷ augur; portend;
foretell: 瑞雪~丰年 A timely snow
promises a good harvest. ❸ million;
mega-: ~赫〈电〉megahertz（MHz）;
megacycles per second ❹ million mil-

lion; trillion

诏 zhào ❶ 〈书〉instruct; admonish; exhort *also* "诏书" imperial edict

笊

笊篱 zhàolí bamboo, wicker or wire strainer

照 zhào ❶ shine; illuminate; light up: ～射 shine; illuminate; irradiate ❷ reflect; mirror: ～镜子 look in the mirror; 〈喻〉examine oneself ❸ take a picture; photograph; shoot: ～片(儿) photo; photograph; picture / ～排 photo-type setting; photo-composition ❹ licence; permit: 无～经营 trade or operate without a licence; interlope ❺ take care of; look after; attend to: ～管 look after; care for; be in charge of ❻ (usu 知照) inform; notify ❼ (usu 对照) compare; contrast; check (against sth else) ❽ in the direction of; towards: ～那边看 look in that direction ❾ according to; in conformity with: ～办 act accordingly / ～登 publish (letters, etc) without alteration / ～旧 as before; as of old / ～例 as a rule; in general; usually / ～本宜科 read entirely from a prepared text; echo what a book says / ～葫芦画瓢 *also* "照猫画虎" mechanically imitate or copy; ape

照常 zhàocháng as usual; as scheduled: ～营业 (carry on) business as usual

照抄 zhàochāo ❶ copy word for word; copy verbatim ❷ *also* "照搬" indiscriminately imitate; blindly copy

照发 zhàofā ❶ approve (a document, etc) for distribution ❷ (of salary, etc) be paid as usual

照顾 zhàogù ❶ take into account; show consideration for; allow for: ～全局 take the overall situation into account / ～他的困难 give consideration

to his difficulties ❷ look after; care for; attend to ❸ (of a customer) patronize; shop at

照会 zhàohuì ❶ present, deliver, or address a note to (a foreign mission, etc) ❷ note: 答复～ note of reply

照料 zhàoliào *also* "照看" care for; attend to; keep an eye on

照面儿 zhàomiànr ❶ (usu 打个照面儿) encounter; run into; come across ❷ (mostly in the negative) put in an appearance; show or turn up; meet: 不敢～ dare not show up

照明 zhàomíng illumination; lighting: ～弹 flare; star shell / ～设备 lighting equipment

照相 zhàoxiàng *also* "照像" take a picture or photo; photograph: ～簿 photo album / ～馆 photo studio / ～机 *also* "相机" camera

照样 zhàoyàng ❶ after a pattern or model: ～儿复制一份 make a copy from the original ❷ in the same way; all the same; as before

照耀 zhàoyào shine; irradiate; illuminate

照应 zhàoyìng ❶ coordinate; correlate: 前后～ be well organized ❷ (zhàoying) *see* "照料"

罩 zhào ❶ cover; envelop; overspread: 毛衣外面～件外套 wear a jacket over one's sweater ❷ *also* "罩子" cover; shade; hood ❸ *also* "罩衣" outer garment; dust-coat: overall ❹ small cage or coop for raising chickens

肇 zhào ❶ cause (trouble, etc); lead to: ～事 cause or make trouble; stir up a disturbance ❷ 〈书〉begin; commence; initiate: ～端 beginning; origin

zhē

折 zhē 〈口〉❶ roll over; turn over and over: ～跟头 turn a somersault; loop the loop ❷ pour (hot water, etc) back and forth between two containers

see also shé; zhé

折腾 zhēteng 〈口〉❶ turn from side to side; toss and turn ❷ do sth again and again; mess or tamper with ❸ cause physical or mental suffering; torment: 这病真~人。The disease is such a torment.

蜇 zhē ❶ (of a wasp, etc) sting ❷ (of pungent smell, etc) cause sharp pain; (of eyes; etc) smart

遮 zhē ❶ cover (up); hide; screen: ~丑 hide one's shame; gloss over one's blemish or weakness / ~阴 (provide) shade / ~眼法 cover-up; camouflage ❷ hinder; obstruct; impede: ~拦 block; obstruct; hinder

遮蔽 zhēbì cover; shelter; block: ~严寒 shelter (sb) from the severe cold / 遮天蔽日 (of dust-storm, etc) block out the sun

遮挡 zhēdǎng keep out; shelter; cover: ~风沙 keep out wind and dust / 毫无~ without cover or shelter

遮盖 zhēgài ❶ cover; spread over: 遮天盖地 (of sand, etc) blot out the sky and cover up the earth — be overwhelming ❷ conceal; hide; cover up (a crime, etc)

遮羞 zhēxiū cover one's private parts; cover up one's embarrassment or shame: ~布 loincloth; fig leaf;〈喻〉disguise

遮掩 zhēyǎn ❶ cover; envelop; block ❷ cover up; conceal; gloss over: ~错误 gloss over a mistake

遮阳 zhēyáng sunshade: ~帽 sun hat or helmet / ~伞 parasol

zhé

折(❹❿**摺**) zhé ❶ break; snap; fracture;

~桂 pick the laurel;〈喻〉pass an imperial examination / ~成两截 snap or break in half / ~戟沉沙 suffer a disastrous defeat ❷ be deprived of; lose: ~寿〈迷信〉reduce one's lifetime ❸ bend; turn; change direction: ~回 *also* "折返" turn back / ~腰〈书〉bend or humble oneself; bow; cringe ❹ fold: ~扇 folding fan / ~纸 paper-folding; origami ❺ be filled with admiration; be won over; be convinced; 心~ admire from the bottom of one's heart; be thoroughly convinced ❻ convert or change into; amount to: ~账 pay a debt in kind (with sth) / ~算为欧元 convert into euros ❼ discount; rebate; 打七~ give 30% discount; charge 70% of the original price ❽ (of traditional opera) act; ~子戏 scene or excerpt from a traditional opera; highlight from an opera ❾ turning stroke (in Chinese characters) ❿ book or booklet used for keeping accounts, etc: 存~ deposit book; bankbook

see also shé; zhé

折叠 zhédié fold: ~伞 folding umbrella / ~椅 *also* "折椅" folding, foldaway, or collapsible chair

折服 zhéfú ❶ subdue (a rival, etc); bring sb to his knees ❷ win over; fill with admiration: 令人~ compel admiration; be convincing

折合 zhéhé ❶ convert (one currency, etc) into (another) ❷ amount to; be equal to

折价 zhéjià ❶ evaluate in terms of money: ~赔偿 pay compensation (for sth) at the market price ❷ reduce the price: ~处理 sell at reduced prices

折旧 zhéjiù 〈经〉depreciation: ~费 depreciation charge / ~率 rate of depreciation

折扣 zhékòu discount; rebate: 打~ (sell) at a discount;〈喻〉(do sth) in a reduced form

折磨 zhémó　cause physical or mental suffering; torment; torture

折射 zhéshè　❶〈理〉refraction; ～波 refracted wave　❷ reveal; reflect

折中 zhézhōng　*also* "折衷" aim at the golden mean; try to be impartial; compromise; ～方案 compromise proposal or solution / ～调和 take a middle course; mediate by glossing over differences / ～主义 eclecticism

哲 zhé　❶ intelligent; wise; sagacious; ～理 philosophical wisdom; philosophy / ～人〈书〉philosopher; sage / ～学 philosophy　❷ wise man; sage

辄(輒) zhé　〈书〉❶ always; often; regularly　❷ as soon as; soon after

蛰(蟄) zhé　〈书〉hibernate; ～伏 (of animals) dormancy; hibernation / ～居 live in seclusion or solitude

谪(謫) zhé　〈书〉❶〈史〉banish (a high official) from the court; exile; ～居 live in exile　❷ (of an immortal, etc) be banished from Heaven　❸ blame; rebuke; censure; 众口交～ be subject to public censure

辙 zhé　❶ track of a wheel; rut; direction of traffic　❷ rhyme (of a song, etc); 合～押韵 be in rhyme　❸〈方〉way; idea; wit; 没～了 be at one's wit's end

zhě

者 zhě　❶ *used as a noun-forming suffix*; 强～ the strong; top dog / 演出～ performer / 社会主义～ socialist　❷〈书〉*used after such numerals as* 二、三 *or* 数 *to refer to things mentioned above*; 两～必须并重。Both should be equally stressed.　❸〈书〉*indicating a rhetorical pause*; 光

阴～，百代之过客。Time is a passer-by that never stops for any generation.

锗 zhě　〈化〉germanium (Ge)

赭 zhě　burnt ochre; reddish brown

褶 zhě　(usu 褶子) pleat; crease; wrinkle; ～皱 wrinkle (in the skin);〈地〉fold

zhè

这(這) zhè　(colloquially *also* zhèi) this; these; ～般 so; such; like this / ～边 this side; this way; here / ～次 this time; present; current / ～些 *also* "这些个" these / ～会儿〈口〉right now; at the moment / ～山望着那山高〈俗〉it is always the other mountain that looks higher; the grass is greener on the other side of the fence; never feel satisfied with what one's got　❷ now; then; 他～才明白事情的真相。Only then did he realize the truth.

这个 zhège　❶ this (one); ～人 this guy　❷〈口〉*used in exclamations*; 大伙儿～乐啊! How happy everybody was!

这么 zhème　so; such; this way; ～点儿 such a tiny bit / ～多人 so many people / ～着不行。This won't do.

这儿 zhèr　〈口〉❶ *also* "这里" (over) here; ～的风景 the scenery here / 到～来。Come over here.　❷ then; now; 从～以后 since then; from now on

这样 zhèyàng　such; of this kind; like this; ～的问题 such problems / ～那样 this or that; one kind or another; all kinds or sorts

浙 Zhè　short for Zhejiang (浙江)

蔗 zhè　sugarcane; ～糖 cane sugar; sucrose

鹧 zhè

鹧鸪 zhègū 〈动物〉francolin；partridge

zhe

着 zhe 〈助〉❶ *used after a verb to indicate* a) *an action in progress*：他们正开～会呢。They are having a meeting. b) *a state*：天气冷～呢。It's freezing cold. ❷ *used to give force to a verb or an adjective*：你仔细听～。Just listen. ❸ *used in forming a preposition*：顺～ along

see also zhāo；zháo；zhuó

zhēn

贞 zhēn ❶ loyal；staunch；faithful ❷ 〈旧〉(of a woman) chastity or virginity：～洁 chaste / ～烈 so chaste as to die rather than lose one's chastity ❸ *also* "贞卜"〈书〉divination

贞节 zhēnjié *also* "贞操" ❶ moral integrity；loyalty：～之士 man of integrity ❷ virginity (of an unmarried woman)；chastity (of a widow)

针 zhēn ❶ needle；anything like a needle：毛线～ knitting needle / ～织品 knit goods；knitwear ❷ stitch：缝两～ put a couple of stitches (in a jacket, etc) / ～脚 (line of) stitches ❸ injection；inoculation；shot：～剂 injection ❹ acupuncture：～灸 acupuncture and moxibustion / ～麻 (short for 针刺麻醉) acupuncture anaesthesia / ～刺疗法 acupuncture treatment

针砭 zhēnbiān criticise；refute：～朝政 criticise the handling of state affairs

针对 zhēnduì be aimed at；be targeted on；be directed against：缺乏～性 without a clear aim

针锋相对 zhēnfēngxiāngduì (give) tit for tat；measure for measure；(act) in direct opposition (to)

针线 zhēnxiàn needlework；needlecraft：～包 sewing kit / ～活儿 needlework；sewing

侦 zhēn investigate；scout；detect：～查 investigate (a crime) / ～缉 track down and arrest / ～破 investigate and crack；break (a criminal case)

侦察 zhēnchá 〈军〉reconnoitre；scout：～兵 scout / ～机 reconnaissance plane；scout

侦探 zhēntàn ❶ do detective work；spy：～小说 detective story ❷ detective；spy：私家～ private detective

珍 zhēn ❶ treasure；riches：宝～ jewellery；treasure；riches ❷ treasured；precious；rare：～本 rare edition or book / ～贵 precious；valuable；rare / ～品 treasure；(喻) gem / ～馐 *also* "珍羞" delicacies；dainties / ～禽异兽 rare birds and (unusual) animals / ～稀物种 rare species ❸ value highly；set great store by：～爱生命 treasure or cherish life

珍藏 zhēncáng ❶ collect；amass and treasure：～本 collection edition or copy ❷ rare and valuable collected articles；such a collection

珍奇 zhēnqí rare (and curious)：～花木 rare flowers and trees

珍视 zhēnshì prize；value；set store by

珍惜 zhēnxī treasure；cherish；value

珍重 zhēnzhòng ❶ cherish；treasure；value highly ❷ take care of or look after oneself：多加～！Please take good care of yourself!

珍珠 zhēnzhū *also* "真珠" pearl：养殖～ cultured pearl

帧 zhēn 〈量〉*of paintings and calligraphy, etc*：一～画 a painting

胗 zhēn gizzard：鸭～肝儿 duck's gizzard and liver

真 zhēn ❶ true；real；genuine：～品 *also* "真迹" genuine piece；authentic work / ～丝 pure silk / ～面目 true features / ～善美 the true, the good and the beautiful / ～刀－枪 the real thing；(in) real earnest / ～假莫辨 unable to distinguish between the true and the false / ～知灼见 correct and deep understanding；profound insight；penetrating judgement / ～金不怕火炼〈谚〉a good anvil does not fear the hammer；a person of integrity or the real thing can stand any test ❷ really；truly；indeed：～麻烦您了。Sorry to have put you to so much trouble. ❸ clearly；distinctly；unmistakably：听得～ hear clearly ❹ also "真书"；"楷书" (in Chinese calligraphy) regular script ❺〈书〉nature；natural state：返朴归～ recover one's original simplicity；go back to nature

真诚 zhēnchéng　sincere；true；honest：～的心意 sincerity

真谛 zhēndì　true meaning；essence：生活的～ essence of life

真格的 zhēngéde　〈方〉serious；real；true：动～ mean business / 说～ seriously (speaking)

真菌 zhēnjūn　fungus

真空 zhēnkōng　vacuum：填～ fill a vacuum / ～管 vacuum tube or valve / ～包装 vacuum packing / ～地带〈军〉no man's land

真理 zhēnlǐ　truth：捍卫～ uphold truth

真皮 zhēnpí　❶〈生理〉derma；corium ❷ real or genuine leather

真切 zhēnqiè　❶ distinct；clear；graphic：记不～ cannot remember clearly ❷ sincere；genuine：情意～ genuine feeling

真情 zhēnqíng　❶ real or true situation；actual circumstances；facts ❷ also "真情实意" genuine feelings；real sentiments

真人 zhēnrén　❶ true man (who has attained immortality through practising Taoism)：～不露相。〈喻〉A true mas-

ter never shows off his attainments. ❷ real people；～真事 real people and real events；real story

真实 zhēnshí　real；true；authentic：～性 authenticity；truthfulness / 真才实学 real ability and learning；genuine knowledge or competence / 真名实姓 real name / 真凭实据 hard or factual evidence；ironclad or conclusive proof / 真枪实弹 live ammunition

真相 zhēnxiàng　also "真象" real situation；actual state of affairs；truth：～大白 the truth is out；the facts are clear now

真心 zhēnxīn　heartfelt；wholehearted；sincere：～相爱 be truly in love (with each other)

真正 zhēnzhèng　❶ real；true；genuine ❷ really；truly；genuinely

真挚 zhēnzhì　sincere；genuine；cordial

真主 Zhēnzhǔ　also "安拉" (of Islam) Allah

砧 zhēn　hammering block；anvil：～板 chopping block or board

蓁 zhēn

蓁蓁 zhēnzhēn　〈书〉❶ luxuriant；exuberant；profuse ❷ also "榛榛" growing thickly or densely；densely-wooded

斟 zhēn　pour (wine or tea)：自～ 自饮 help oneself to the wine

斟酌 zhēnzhuó　turn over in one's mind；consider；deliberate：～处理 settle after due consideration；handle at one's discretion / ～用词 weigh one's words

甄 zhēn　〈书〉draw a distinction；discriminate；examine：～选 also "甄拔" select

甄别 zhēnbié　❶ distinguish；screen；examine：～史料 identify historical data ❷ test and assess：～干部 test and assess cadres

榛 zhēn　also "榛子"〈植〉hazel；hazelnut

箴 zhēn 〈书〉advise; exhort; admonish; ~言 admonition; exhortation; maxim

臻 zhēn 〈书〉attain (a higher level); become (better): 日~繁荣 become more and more prosperous; boom day by day

zhěn

诊 zhěn examine (a patient): ~疗 make a diagnosis and give treatment / ~脉 also "号脉" feel the pulse / ~室 consulting room / ~所 also "诊疗所" clinic / ~治 make a diagnosis and give treatment

诊断 zhěnduàn diagnose: ~书 medical certificate

枕 zhěn ❶ (usu 枕头) pillow: ~巾 towel used to cover a pillow / ~套 also "枕头套" pillowcase; pillow slip ❷ rest one's head on: ~藉〈书〉lie or fall down together higgledy-piggledy / ~戈待旦 wait for daybreak with one's head pillowed on one's weapon; be on the alert

轸 zhěn 〈书〉sorrowful; grieved: ~悼 grieve or mourn over sb's death / ~念 sorrowfully cherish sb's memory

畛 zhěn

畛域 zhěnyù 〈书〉boundary: 不分~ regardless of distinctions

疹 zhěn bleb; rash: 热~ heat rash / ~子〈口〉(the) measles

缜 zhěn

缜密 zhěnmì careful; detailed; meticulous: 文思~ meticulous writing

zhèn

阵 zhèn ❶ battle array or formation; position; front (lines): ~亡 fall in battle; be killed in action / ~线〈喻〉front; alignment ❷ period of time; some time: ~痛 labour pains; birth pangs; 〈喻〉throes / ~雨 shower / 那~儿 at the time ❸ 〈量〉used of sth that happens abruptly and lasts a short time: 一~风 a gust of wind / 一~欢呼 a burst of cheers

阵地 zhèndì position; front: ~战 〈军〉positional warfare / 思想~ ideological front

阵脚 zhènjiǎo ❶ front line ❷ position; situation; circumstances: 压住~ secure one's position; hold one's own / 大乱 be thrown into confusion

阵容 zhènróng ❶ battle array or formation ❷ lineup: ~整齐 well-balanced cast

阵势 zhènshì ❶ battle array; combat dispositions ❷ circumstances; scene; situation: 看这~要下雨了。It looks like rain.

阵营 zhènyíng camp: 民主~ democratic camp

鸩(酖) zhèn ❶ poisoned wine ❷ 〈书〉(try to) kill with poisoned wine

振 zhèn ❶ shake; flutter; flap: ~臂 raise one's arm / ~笔疾书 write with flying strokes; wield one's pen furiously ❷ (usu 振动) vibrate: ~荡〈理〉vibrate; 〈电〉oscillate ❸ rise with force and spirit; brace up; boost: 精神为之一~ be braced up; become fresh with energy

振奋 zhènfèn ❶ rise with force and spirit; rouse oneself; be high-spirited: 群情~。Everyone is exhilarated. ❷ encourage; inspire; stimulate: ~士气 boost the morale

振兴 zhènxīng promote; invigorate; vitalize: ~中华 achieve China's rejuvenation; invigorate China

振振有词 zhènzhènyǒucí also "振振有辞" speak glibly (to justify oneself, etc); speak fluently and plausibly

振作 zhènzuò pull oneself together; bestir oneself; display vigour

朕 zhèn ❶ (used by an emperor to refer to himself) we ❷ 〈书〉sign; omen; 〈兆 sign; omen

赈 zhèn bring relief to; relieve; aid; ~济 relieve; aid / ~ 灾 relieve the people in a disaster area

震 zhèn ❶ shake; quake; shock; ~ 颤 tremble; quiver; vibrate / ~ 源〈地〉focus (of an earthquake); seismic origin or focus / ~ 中〈地〉epicentre ❷ be shocked; be greatly excited; 感到 ~ 惊 be astonished or stunned ❸ see 八卦 bāguà

震荡 zhèndàng shake; quake; reverberate; 社会 ~ social upheaval

震动 zhèndòng ❶ shake; quake; tremble ❷ shock (people); astonish; excite

震耳欲聋 zhèn'ěryùlóng deafening; thunderous

震撼 zhènhàn shake; shake; stir; ~ 全球 earthshaking

震级 zhènjí 〈地〉(earthquake) magnitude; ~ 为里氏 6.4 级。The quake reads 6.4 on the Richter scale.

震惊 zhènjīng stun; amaze; astonish

震怒 zhènnù be furious, enraged or infuriated

震慑 zhènshè frighten; awe; intimidate; 起~作用 be terrifying or intimidating

镇 zhèn ❶ press or force down; suppress; ease; ~ 咳 ease the cough ❷ calm; tranquil; stable ❸ keep peace by force; garrison; ~ 守 garrison; guard (a place of strategic importance) ❹ garrison post; 边防重 ~ key frontier post ❺ township; 乡 ~ townships and villages ❻ relatively large (market) town ❼ cool (beer or other beverage) with cold water or ice; ice

镇定 zhèndìng ❶ (in an emergency,

etc) calm and collected; composed; ~ 自若 be perfectly calm and collected; be self-possessed ❷ calm down

镇静 zhènjìng ❶ unruffled; calm; composed ❷ calm down; ~ 剂 sedative; tranquillizer

镇压 zhènyā ❶ suppress; quell; put down ❷ execute (a criminal)

zhēng

正 zhēng (usu 正月) first month of the lunar year; first moon
see also zhèng

争 zhēng ❶ contend; compete; vie; ~ 鸣 contend (over academic issues); 〈喻〉express differences freely / ~ 抢 contend or vie (with sb) for; scramble for (the ball, etc) / ~ 霸世界 contend for world supremacy; strive to dominate the world / ~ 风吃醋 be jealous (of a rival in love) / ~ 强好胜 be emulative; be up on things ❷ argue; dispute; wrangle; ~ 端 dispute; conflict; controversy / 意气之 ~ dispute caused by personal grudges

争辩 zhēngbiàn argue; dispute; debate; 无可 ~ beyond dispute; indisputable

争吵 zhēngchǎo quarrel; bicker; squabble

争斗 zhēngdòu ❶ fight; struggle ❷ contend; oppose; 好 ~ contentious / 争奇斗艳 compete or contend for beauty and fascination

争夺 zhēngduó fight, struggle or vie for; 争分夺秒 seize every minute and second; race against time / ~ 权夺利 scramble for power and wealth

争光 zhēngguāng win honour (for); do credit (to)

争论 zhēnglùn dispute; debate; 的焦点 focus of a dispute; matter at issue

争气 zhēngqì make a good showing; win honour (for); bring credit (to)

争取 zhēngqǔ　strive for; win over; ~多数 try to win over the majority; ~主动 make efforts to seize the initiative

争先 zhēngxiān　try to get ahead of the others; strive to be the first to do sth; ~恐后 strive to be the first and fear to lag behind; fall over each other (to do sth)

争议 zhēngyì　dispute; debate; controversy; 有~的问题 controversial issue

争执 zhēngzhí　take issue with; dispute; quarrel; ~不下 each holds on to his position; each sticks to his guns

征(❸-❻**徵**) zhēng　❶ make a long journey; ~途 also "征程" journey; path; course ❷ go on an expedition; ~伐 go on a punitive expedition (against sb) / ~战 go on an expedition or a campaign ❸ levy (troops or taxes); draft; collect; ~购 (of a state) requisition by purchase ❹ solicit; ask for; ~募 enlist; recruit / ~聘 advertise a vacancy; invite applications for a job; advertise for / ~文 solicit articles or contributions (on a chosen subject) / ~询 consult; seek the opinion of ❺ evidence; proof; 信而有~ reliable and borne out by evidence; proven ❻ sign; portent; phenomenon; ~候 sign; indication / ~象 symptom; sign / ~兆 sign; omen; portent

征兵 zhēngbīng　conscript; draft; call up; ~制 conscription system; compulsory military service

征调 zhēngdiào　requisition (materials, etc); draft; call up (people, etc)

征服 zhēngfú　conquer; vanquish; subjugate; ~观众 captivate the audience / ~江河 tame rivers

征婚 zhēnghūn　seek a marriage partner publicly; ~启事 lonely hearts ad

征集 zhēngjí　❶ solicit or seek (comments, etc) publicly; gather or collect (relics, etc) through public channels ❷ see "征调"

征求 zhēngqiú　solicit; invite; ask for; ~订户 also "征订" solicit subscriptions (to a newspaper, etc) / ~专家意见 consult the experts

征收 zhēngshōu　levy (taxes, etc); collect; requisition (land, etc)

征用 zhēngyòng　requisition; commandeer; take over for use; ~补偿 compensation for requisitioned property

征召 zhēngzhào　❶ recruit; enlist; call up 〈书〉appoint sb to an office; call upon sb to serve

怔 zhēng　〈书〉terror-stricken; panicky; ~忡〈中医〉palpitation / ~忪 be seized with terror; be scared or panic-stricken

挣 zhēng

挣扎 zhēngzhá　struggle; battle; ~着站起来 struggle to one's feet　see also zhèng

峥 zhēng

峥嵘 zhēngróng　❶ towering; soaring; lofty and steep ❷ outstanding; remarkable; extraordinary; ~岁月 eventful years; memorable times

狰 zhēng

狰狞 zhēngníng　sinister; hideous; ferocious

症(**癥**) zhēng

症结 zhēngjié　〈中医〉lump in the abdomen;〈喻〉crux; core; 问题的~ crux of the matter　see also zhèng

睁 zhēng　open (the eyes); ~眼睛 illiterate (person) / ~只眼, 闭只眼 look on the other side; turn a blind eye (to sth); wink at sth

铮 zhēng

铮铮 zhēngzhēng ❶〈象声〉clang; clank ❷ outstanding; well-known: ～铁汉 upright man worthy of his name

筝 zhēng ❶ Chinese zither with 21 or 25 strings ❷ (usu 风筝) kite

蒸 zhēng ❶ (usu 蒸发) evaporate: ～腾 (of steam) rising ❷ steam: ～饺 steamed dumpling / ～笼 steamer

蒸馏 zhēngliú 〈理〉distillation: ～水 distilled water

蒸气 zhēngqì also "水蒸气" vapour

蒸汽 zhēngqì steam: ～机 steam engine / ～浴 also "蒸气浴" sauna; steam bath

蒸蒸日上 zhēngzhēngrìshàng prosper day by day; make rapid progress; be thriving

zhěng

拯 zhěng (usu 拯救) save; rescue; free

整 zhěng ❶ whole; complete; entire: ～个 whole; entire; full / ～块 whole piece of material / ～数〈数〉integer; whole number / ～天 whole day; all day (long) ❷ in good order; orderly; tidy: 衣冠不～ untidily dressed ❸ put in order; straighten; rectify: ～编 reorganize; restructure / ～队 dress the ranks; line up / ～休 (of troops, etc) reorganize and rest / ～流器〈电〉rectifier / 把床铺一～一 tidy up one's bed ❹ fix; repair; make: 把桌子一干净。Clear up the table. ❺ punish; castigate; make suffer: ～人 make sb suffer; make things difficult for sb

整饬 zhěngchì ❶ put in order; rectify; strengthen: ～军纪 strengthen military discipline ❷ orderly; neat; tidy: 服式～ neatly dressed

整顿 zhěngdùn rectify; consolidate; reorganize: ～企业 reorganize or over-haul an enterprise / ～市场 put a market in order

整合 zhěnghé integrate; consolidate; unify: ～系统〈信息〉integrated system / ～不同意见 unify or coordinate differing views

整洁 zhěngjié clean and tidy; orderly; trim

整理 zhěnglǐ straighten or sort out; arrange: ～思路 straighten out one's thinking / ～房间 tidy up a room

整齐 zhěngqí ❶ orderly; neat; tidy: 步调～ keep in step / ～划一 uniform; alike ❷ even; level; regular: 水平～ of even level / ～的节奏 regular rhythms

整容 zhěngróng face-lift; ～术 plastic surgery; face-lifting

整体 zhěngtǐ whole; totality; entirety: ～观念 concept of viewing the situation as a whole or in its totality / ～规划 overall planning

整形 zhěngxíng 〈医〉plastic: ～外科 plastic surgery; plastics / ～医生 plastic surgeon

整修 zhěngxiū rebuild; renovate; recondition: ～危房 renovate a dilapidated house

整治 zhěngzhì ❶ renovate; repair; recondition ❷ punish; fix; make to suffer: ～无照摊贩 punish unlicensed vendors ❸ do; perform; work at: ～菜肴 prepare dishes

整装 zhěngzhuāng pack one's things; get one's things ready (for a trip): ～待发 all packed up and ready to set out

zhèng

正 zhèng ❶ straight; upright; perpendicular: ～西 due west / ～眼看人 look sb in the face; look squarely at sb ❷ (of time) sharp; on time; punctually: ～点 (of trains, etc) on time or schedule / ～午 (high) noon

❸ front; obverse; right (side): ～手〈体〉forehand ❹ upright; impartial; honest: ～人君子 man of high principle; gentleman ❺ correct; right; proper: ～道 right way or path; truth; law / ～理 correct principle; valid reason; truth / ～事 one's proper business ❻ (of colour or flavour) pure; right: ～红 pure red / ～味儿 (of food, etc) taste right ❼ regular; normal; official: ～版 official or legal copy (of a book, etc) / ～剧 serious drama / ～楷 regular script / ～品 also "正牌" quality product; certified goods / ～史 official history books written in biographical style ❽ chief; main; principal: ～门 main entrance / ～文 main body (of a book, etc); text / ～职 (of a unit) principal; chief / ～选队员 regular player; member of the first team ❾ positive; 〈数〉plus: ～电 positive electricity / ～数 positive number ❿ set right; correct; rectify: ～骨〈中医〉bone-setting / ～人先～己。Those who wish to make others upright must be upright themselves. ⓫ just; exactly; precisely: ～合我意。Suits me fine. ⓬〈副〉used to indicate an action in progress: ～在 be in the process (of doing sth); be doing / 我～听广播呢。I'm listening to the radio.

see also zhēng

正本清源 zhèngběn-qīngyuán tackle a problem at its root; radically reform; thoroughly overhaul

正比 zhèngbǐ ❶ direct proportion: 成～ be directly proportional (to sth) ❷ also "正比例" direct ratio

正常 zhèngcháng normal; usual; regular: ～化 normalize / ～贸易关系 (formerly 最惠国待遇) normal trade relations (NTR)

正大光明 zhèngdàguāngmíng open and aboveboard; frank and honest

正当 zhèngdāng ❶ just when; just as;

just the time for: ～年 in the prime of life; in one's prime ❷ 〈zhèngdàng〉proper; appropriate; legitimate: ～防卫 justifiable defence / ～权益 legitimate and lawful rights and interests ❸〈zhèngdàng〉(of a person's character) upright; honest

正法 zhèngfǎ execute (a criminal): 立即～ execute the criminal immediately; carry out summary execution

正方 zhèngfāng ❶ square: ～体 cube / ～形 square ❷ (of debaters) positive side; pros

正告 zhènggào earnestly admonish; sternly warn

正规 zhèngguī standard; regular; proper: ～军 regular army / ～教育 formal education

正轨 zhèngguǐ right track; correct path: 走上～ get on to the right track

正果 zhèngguǒ 〈宗教〉consummation: 修成～ attain consummation and become a Buddha; 〈喻〉obtain academic achievements

正好 zhènghǎo ❶ (of time, size, number, etc) just right ❷ also "正巧" happen or chance to; it (so) happens that: 那时我～出差在外。I happened to be away on business at the time.

正襟危坐 zhèngjīnwēizuò straighten one's clothes and sit properly; sit bolt upright; be all seriousness

正经 zhèngjīng ❶ decent; honest; respectable: ～人 honest person; regular guy ❷ serious; proper; right: ～八百〈方〉serious; earnest ❸ formal; standard: ～货 standard goods ❹〈方〉truly; indeed; very much so

正面 zhèngmiàn ❶ front; face; façade: ～图 front view / ～战场 frontline battlefield ❷ obverse or right side; 钱币的～ obverse side of a coin; heads ❸ positive: ～人物 positive character ❹ straightforward; direct; open: ～冲突 head-on conflict or clash

正派 zhèngpài　upright; honest; decent：～家 honest or decent family

正气 zhèngqì　❶ healthy trend; moral ... ❷ unyielding integrity; moral cour... ～凛然 awe-inspiring probity

正确 zhèngquè　correct; right; proper：正...correctness; soundness; validity

正式 zhèngshì　formal; official; regular：...党员 full member of a party / ～访问 ...cial visit / ～文本 official text / ～职 ...regular occupation

正视 zhèngshì　look in the face; look ...arely at; face up to：～现实 face (up ...reality / ～自己的缺点 acknowledge ...'s shortcomings

正题 zhèngtí　subject or topic of a talk or ...say; main theme：不要离开～。Don't ...gress.

正统 zhèngtǒng　❶ legitimism：按～ ...ccording to legitimism ❷ orthodox：～思...想 orthodox thinking

正颜厉色 zhèngyán-lìsè　put on a stern ...countenance; be serious and severe

正义 zhèngyì　❶ justice：～感 sense of justice ❷ just; righteous：～的斗争 just struggle

正直 zhèngzhí　open and aboveboard; upright; fair-minded：～的学者 honest scholar

正中 zhèngzhōng　also "正当中" middle; centre：大厅～ centre of a hall

正中下怀 zhèngzhōngxiàhuái　fit in exactly with one's desire; be just what one wants; be precisely to one's liking or taste

正宗 zhèngzōng　❶ orthodox school：儒学～ orthodox Confucianism ❷ authentic：～川菜 authentic Sichuan-style cooking

证（證）zhèng

证　zhèng　❶ testify to; prove; demonstrate：～词〈法〉testimony / ～件 credentials; papers; certificate / ～书 certificate; testimonial; credentials / ～章 badge / ～婚人 chief witness at a wedding ceremony ❷ certificate; card

证据 zhèngjù　proof; evidence; testimony：～确凿 irrefutable evidence; ironclad proof

证明 zhèngmíng　❶ prove; uphold; testify：经实践～ verified through practice ❷ certificate; identification; testimonial

证券 zhèngquàn　bond; securities：～商 stock-broker; securities dealer / ～市场 securities or stock market / ～指数 stock exchange index

证人 zhèngren　witness：～席 witness-box; witness stand

证实 zhèngshí　confirm; verify; establish

郑（鄭）Zhèng

郑重 zhèngzhòng　serious; solemn; earnest：～其事 solemnly; seriously; in earnest / ～宣布 solemnly declare

诤 zhèng

诤　zhèng　〈书〉criticise frankly; expostulate; remonstrate：～言 frank criticism; forthright admonition or remonstration / ～友 friend who will give forthright admonition or expostulation

政 zhèng

政　zhèng　❶ politics; political affairs; government：～党 political party / ～见 political view / ～客 politician / ～令 government decree or order / ～审（short for 政治审查）examine sb's political record; be vetted for one's political background / ～坛 political arena / ～体 system or form of government / ～协（short for 政治协商会议）political consultative conference / ～要 prominent political figure; VIP / ～企分开 separation of the functions of enterprises from those of the government; detachment of enterprises from the government / ～通人和 good government and harmonious people ❷ administrative affairs of certain government departments ❸ affairs of a family or an organization ·

政变 zhèngbiàn　coup (d'état)

政策 zhèngcè　policy：按～办事 act in accordance with relevant policies

政府 zhèngfǔ　government：～部门 government departments / ～行为 act of the government

政绩 zhèngjì　achievements in one's political career；～不佳 have little credit to claim in one's political career

政界 zhèngjiè　political or government circles；～人士 political figures

政局 zhèngjú　political situation or scene；～动荡 turbulent political scene

政论 zhènglùn　political comment；～家 political essayist or commentator / ～文 political essay

政权 zhèngquán　❶ political or state power；regime；夺取～ seize state power ❷ organs of political power；state organs；～交接 transfer of government

政委 zhèngwěi　（short for 政治委员） political commissar

政务 zhèngwù　administrative affairs；government affairs or administration；～繁忙 be busy with administrative affairs

政治 zhèngzhì　politics；political affairs；～犯 political prisoner / ～家 statesman / ～局 Political Bureau；Politburo (of a party) / ～学 political science / ～避难 political refuge or asylum / ～面目 political affiliation or background

挣 zhèng　❶ struggle to get free；try to shake off；～脱 throw off；break away from / ～命 struggle to save one's life；work desperately / ～钱 earn or make money / ～碗饭吃 make a living；earn one's bread
see also zhēng

症 zhèng　disease；malady；illness；～候 disease；symptom / ～状 symptom　*see also* zhēng

zhī

之 zhī　❶ 〈书〉go to；由京～宁 leave Beijing for Nanjing ❷ *used in place of a person or thing as an object*；学而时习～ learn and constantly review what one has learned ❸ *used without specific ref-*

erence；生死与～ live and die together ❹ this；that；～后 after or behind this；later；thereafter / ～前 before this；ago；prior to；/ ～外 apart from this；besides；beyond ❺ *used like* 的：米麦～类 rice，wheat，or the like / 某某～流〈贬〉So-and-So and his ilk ❻ *used between the subject and the predicative to render a subordinate phrase*；皮～不存，毛将焉附？ With the hide gone，what can the hair attach itself to?

之乎者也 zhī-hū-zhě-yě　literary jargon；pedantic terms；archaisms

之间 zhījiān　❶ between；among；春夏～ between spring and summer ❷ *used after certain bi-syllabic verbs or adverbs to indicate transience*；眨眼～ in the twinkling of an eye / 忽然～ all of a sudden

支 zhī　❶ prop up；set or put up；support；～床 set up a bed / ～点〈理〉fulcrum / ～架 support；stand；trestle / ～前 support the front ❷ send away；put sb off；order about；～派 order；send；dispatch / 把人～开 send sb away with some excuse ❸ pay out or draw (money) / ～付 pay / ～取 draw；receive ❹ branch；offshoot；～脉 offshoot (of a mountain range) / ～线 branch line；feeder (line) ❺ 〈量〉a) *of army units*；一～军队 an army contingent b) *of songs*；一～民歌 a folk song c) *of watts*；25～光 25 watts d) *textile counts*；100～纱 100-count yarn e) *for long，thin，inflexible objects*；一～铅笔 a pencil ❻ *see* "干支" gānzhī

支部 zhībù　(of a political party or organization，esp CPC or Chinese Communist Youth League) branch；cell；～书记 (shortened as 支书) secretary of a (Party or League) branch

支撑 zhīchēng　❶ prop or hold up；sustain；support ❷ be barely able to support (one's family，etc)；shore up (a tottering regime, etc）; maintain: ～门面 keep up appearances

支持 zhīchí ❶ hold out; bear up; sustain: 累得～不住了 too tired to hold out any longer ❷ support; back; be in favour of: ～率 rate of support (for a politician, etc) / ～软件〈信息〉support software

支出 zhīchū　pay（money）; spend; expend: ～大于收入。The expenses exceed the income.

支离破碎 zhīlí-pòsuì　broken up; fragmented; (of argument) full of scattered and incoherent details

支流 zhīliú ❶ tributary; branch（of a river, etc）❷ minor aspects; non-essentials

支配 zhīpèi ❶ allocate; arrange ❷ control; determine; govern

支票 zhīpiào　cheque; check: ～簿 chequebook

支气管 zhīqìguǎn　bronchus: ～炎 bronchitis

支使 zhīshi ❶ order or boss（sb）about ❷ send away; put off

支吾 zhīwú　hedge; equivocate: ～其词 speak equivocally; hum and haw

支应 zhīyìng ❶ manage; handle; deal with: ～差事 do an (official) errand ❷ supply: ～粮草 supply rations and fodder ❸ care for; wait on; attend to: ～门户 look after a place

支援 zhīyuán　support; assist; help

支柱 zhīzhù ❶ pillar; prop ❷〈喻〉pillar; mainstay: ～产业 pillar industry

只（隻） zhī ❶ isolated; single; one only: ～身 alone; solitarily; all by oneself / ～言片语（usu in the negative) a word or two ❷〈量〉a) for one of a pair: 一～鞋 one shoe b) for certain animals, birds: 一～猫 one cat c) for certain containers: 四～皮箱 four leather suitcases d) for small boats, etc: 一～筏子 a raft
see also zhǐ

汁 zhī　juice: 柠檬～ lemon juice / 牛肉～ beef extract

芝 zhī〈植〉glossy ganoderma

芝麻 zhīma　sesame（seed）: ～酱 also "芝麻酱" sesame paste / ～油 also "香油" sesame oil / ～官〈贬〉petty government official

吱 zhī〈象声〉creak: ～地一声停住 creak to a stop　see also zī

枝 zhī ❶ branch; twig: ～杈 also "枝条";"枝桠" branch; twig / ～繁叶茂 (of trees) with luxuriant foliage and spreading branches ❷〈量〉a) of flowers with stems: 一～樱花 a spray of cherry blossoms b) of stick-like things: 一～步枪 a rifle

枝节 zhījié ❶ branches and knots; side issue; minor aspect: ～问题 side issue; trivial matter; trifle ❷ unexpected complications

枝蔓 zhīmàn　branches and tendrils; complicated and confused; involved and jumbled; 不枝不蔓 (of writing, etc) neat and straightforward

知 zhī ❶ know; be aware（of）: ～悉 know; learn（of）; be informed of / ～根～底 know（sb or sth）through and through / ～过必改 correct one's mistake without fail when one becomes aware of it / ～法犯法 knowingly break the law / ～冷～热 feel for sb as for oneself; be very considerate / ～难而退 beat a retreat in the face of difficulties; shrink back from difficulties / ～遇之恩 indebtedness to a superior for his appreciation and recognition of one's talents / ～无不言,言无不尽 say all one knows and say it without reserve ❷ inform; notify; tell: ～会〈口〉notify orally / ～照 send word to; inform; tell ❸ knowledge; learning ❹〈书〉intimate friend: ～交 bosom or intimate friend / ～音 person who is deeply appreciative of one; alter ego ❺〈旧〉administer; be in charge of: ～县

〈史〉county magistrate

知道 zhīdào　know; realize; be aware of: ～窍门 know the ropes

知己 zhījǐ　❶ on intimate terms; under standing ❷ bosom friend

知觉 zhījué　❶ perception ❷ consciousness: 失去～ lose consciousness; pass out; go into a coma

知了 zhīliǎo　(another name for 蝉)〈动物〉cicada

知名 zhīmíng　famous; renowned; celebrated: ～人士 well-known figure; celebrity / 提高～度 make better known

知情 zhīqíng　❶ know the inside story; have inside information: ～人 person in the know; person who knows clues to a case / ～不报 failure to report information about a felon or felony;〈法〉misprision ❷ feel grateful for sb's kindness to one

知趣 zhīqù　also "识趣" behave properly in a delicate situation; show good sense; be tactful

知人善任 zhīrén-shànrèn　(of a leader) know one's subordinates well enough to put them where they can give full play to their abilities; know how to judge and use people

知识 zhīshi　knowledge: ～产权 intellectual property right (IPR) / ～产业 knowledge industry / ～分子 educated person; intellectual; the intelligentsia / 经济 knowledge(-based) economy / ～渊博 have encyclopedic knowledge; be knowledgeable or learned / ～密集型 knowledge-intensive

知心 zhīxīn　heart-to-heart; intimate: ～话 words from the heart; confidences / ～人 intimate friend; confidant

知足 zhīzú　be content with what one has: ～常乐 happy is he who is content; contentment is happiness

肢 zhī　limb: 假～ artificial limb / 前～ forelimbs (of an animal or insect) / 上～ upper limbs; arms

肢解 zhījiě　also "支解" member (a deceased per country, etc)

肢体 zhītǐ　❶ limbs ❷ li～健壮 healthy body

织（織） zhī　weave darning; ～布 weave (cloth)
锦缎" brocade

脂 zhī　fat; grease fat; grease;〈喻〉fru rouge

脂肪 zhīfáng　fat; 植物～～酸

脂肪 zhīfáng　fatty liver / ～酸

脂粉 zhīfěn　rouge and powder; cosmetics: ～气 (of literature, etc) womanliness; femininity; effeminacy / ～钱 (women's) pocket money

蜘 zhī

蜘蛛 zhīzhū　spider: ～网 spider-web; cobweb

zhí

执（執） zhí　❶ hold; grip; grasp: ～笔 do the actual writing; put on paper ❷ take charge of; carry out; execute: ～导 direct (a film, etc) / ～教 teach; be a teacher / ～勤 (of policemen, etc) be on duty / ～刑 execute a punishment (esp capital punishment) ❸ stick or adhere to; persist in ❹〈书〉catch; seize; capture ❺ written acknowledgement; 收～ receipt ❻〈书〉intimate friend; 父～ father's good friend

执法 zhífǎ　enforce laws and decrees; ～机关 law enforcement agency / ～如山 enforce the law strictly; uphold the law firmly

执迷不悟 zhímíbùwù　be perverse; persist in pursuing a wrong course; refuse to mend one's ways

执牛耳 zhíniú'ěr　be the acknowledged

he leading position; rule the

obstate; pigheaded; self-

carry out; execute; im-
计划 carry out or execute a
席 executive or presiding

sist on; persist in; be bent
tubbornly refuse to comply

be in control of; control;
事 be in charge of personnel
权 hold the reins of govern-
political power
licence; permit
g be in power; wield state
er at the helm of state; ~党 ruling party
also "执者" ❶ inflexible;
事 be fussy about trifles ❷
ngingly; be persevering; ~地
ersevere in the pursuit of truth
❶ straight; direct; ~拨〈通
direct dialing / ~播 (TV or
broadcast);〈农〉direct seeding /
ngstop; direct / ~属 dir-
r; directly affiliated to / ~译
slation / ~流电 direct current
辖市 municipality directly un-
entral Government / ~奔家里
aight for home ❷ vertical; upright; perpendicular; ~立 stand erect or
upright; ~挺挺 straight and stiff; bolt
upright; ramrod straight ❸ straighten;
~起身子 straighten up; straighten one's
back ❹ just; upright; ~朴 upright and
simple; honest and sincere ❺ candid;
frank; straightforward; ~白 say plainly;
tell straight /~性子 straightforward
(person); downright; blunt ❻ vertical
stroke (in Chinese characters) ❼ continuously; straight; 逗得大伙儿~乐 set
everybody laughing ❽ just; simply;
exactly; 说得~像真的一样 speak of sth

as if it were real

直肠 zhícháng 〈生理〉rectum

直到 zhídào *also* "直至" until; up to;
up till; ~半夜才回家 not return home
until midnight

直观 zhíguān directly perceived through
the senses; audio-visual; ~教具 aids to
object teaching; audio-visual aids

直角 zhíjiǎo 〈数〉right angle; ~三角
形 right(-angled) triangle

直接 zhíjiē direct; straight; immediate; ~税 direct tax /~三通 direct
links in trade, mail and air and shipping
services

直截了当 zhíjiéliǎodàng blunt;
point-blank; straightforward; 说话~
not mince words; talk turkey

直径 zhíjìng 〈数〉diameter; ~3 米
three metres in diameter

直觉 zhíjué intuition; 凭~感到 feel
(it) in one's bones; by intuitive knowledge

直升机 zhíshēngjī (commonly known
as 直升飞机) helicopter; chopper

直抒 zhíshū express freely; state
frankly; ~胸臆 pour out one's heart;
speak one's heart plainly

直率 zhíshuài outspoken; candid;
straightforward; ~地谈出自己的意见
give (sb) a piece of one's mind (about
sth)

直爽 zhíshuǎng frank; candid; outspoken; 性格~ frank by nature

直系 zhíxì lineal; ~后代 lineal descendant / ~亲属 directly-related family
members

直线 zhíxiàn ❶ straight line; ~距离
straight-line or crow-fly distance ❷ linear; rectilinear; direct; ~电话 direct-
dial telephone / ~思维 linear thinking
❸ steep; sharp; ~上升 shoot up;
soar

直销 zhíxiāo direct sale by producers;
direct marketing or placement; 厂家~
factory sales

直言不讳 zhíyánbùhuì　speak bluntly; call a spade a spade; not mince words

侄（姪） zhí　brother's son; nephew; ～子 also "侄儿" brother's son; ～女 brother's daughter; niece

值 zhí　❶ value; worth; price ❷ cost; be worth or worthwhile; ～当〈方〉worthwhile; worth it / ～10 元 be worth 10 yuan ❸ happen or chance to; during; ～此国家危急之秋 at this time of national crisis ❹ be on duty; take one's turn at sth; ～夜 on night duty; on the night watch

值班 zhíbān　be on duty or shift; ～室 duty room / ～员 person on duty; duty officer

值得 zhídé　❶ be worth the money; 买得～ a good buy; worth the price ❷ be of value; be worthwhile; ～一试。It's worth trying.

值钱 zhíqián　valuable; expensive; ～货 expensive goods; valuables

值勤 zhíqín　(of policemen, etc) be on (point) duty; ～巡逻 be on patrol

值日 zhírì　be on duty for the day; be one's turn to be on duty; ～表 rota; duty roster / ～生 student on duty (for the day)

职（職） zhí　❶ duty; job; 分 bounden duty ❷ position; post; office; 在～ on the job; at the post / ～员 clerk; office worker; staff member ❸ be in charge of; administer; manage; ～掌政务 be in charge of state affairs

职称 zhíchēng　professional title or rank; ～评审委员会 committee for evaluation of professional titles; academic promotion committee

职工 zhígōng　workers and staff members; employees; staff; ～持股 employee ownership of stock

职能 zhínéng　function; ～部门 functional departments

职权 zhíquán　powers or authority of office; functions and powers; ～范围 scope of functions and powers; terms of reference

职守 zhíshǒu　post; duty; 忠于～ be faithful in the discharge of one's duties

职务 zhíwù　post; position; job; ～发明 invention made during service; service invention / ～犯罪 crime committed through abuse of position; in-service crime; career crime / ～津贴 duty allowance

职业 zhíyè　job; profession; occupation; ～病 occupational disease / ～保障 job security / ～道德 professional or work ethics / ～妇女 career woman / ～教育 vocational education / ～介绍所 employment agency; job centre; hiring hall / ～运动员 professional (athlete)

职责 zhízé　duty; obligation; responsibility; ～不清 lack of clear-cut job responsibility; vague delimitation of responsibilities and duties

植 zhí　❶ plant; grow; ～被 vegetation / ～根〈喻〉take or strike root; be rooted (in) / ～皮（skin）grafting / ～树造林 afforestation ❷ set up; build; establish

植物 zhíwù　plant; vegetable; phyto-; ～人 vegetable / ～油 vegetable oil / ～园 botanical garden

殖 zhí　breed; multiply; propagate

殖民 zhímín　colonize; establish a colony; ～地 colony / ～国家 colonialist power / ～统治 colonial rule / ～主义 colonialism

摭 zhí　(usu 摭拾)〈书〉pick up; collect

踯（躑） zhí

踯躅 zhízhú　〈书〉walk to and fro; loiter about; tramp

zhǐ

止 zhǐ ❶ stop; halt; cease; ～境 limit; boundary / 泪流不～. Tears keep rolling down. ❷ prohibit; check; hold back / ～渴 quench or satisfy one's thirst / ～血 stop or stanch bleeding / ～痛药 anodyne; analgesic; pain-killer / ～咳糖浆 cough syrup ❸ to; till; until; 到目前为为 to date; up to now ❹ only; sole

止步 zhǐbù halt; stop; go no further; ～不前 stand still; mark time; make no headway / 游人～. No visitors. or Out of bounds for tourists.

止息 zhǐxī cease; stop; subside; 永无～ unceasing; ceaseless

只(衹) zhǐ ❶ only; merely; ～说不做 all talk and no action / ～见树木,不见森林 can't see the wood for the trees; grasp only the details, but not the overall picture / ～知其一,不知其二 know only one aspect of a matter, but be ignorant of the other; see only one side of the picture ❷ all that there is; only; ～得 *also* "只好" have no choice but to; be compelled to; have to
see also zhī

只不过 zhǐbùguò only; just; nothing but; ～擦破点皮, 没事儿的. It's only a scratch, nothing serious.

只读 zhǐdú 〈信息〉read-only; ～光盘 CD-ROM / ～存储器 read-only memory (ROM)

只顾 zhǐgù ❶ be absorbed or engrossed in ❷ pay attention only to; care only for

只管 zhǐguǎn ❶ do by all means; feel free to; 有什么问题～问. Please feel free to ask any question. ❷ *see* "只顾 ❷"

只是 zhǐshì ❶ merely; only; nothing but; 这～托词. It's merely a pretext.

❷ invariably; simply; 随我怎么问,他～摇头,不回答. For all my questions he simply shook his head and refused to say a thing. ❸ but; only; however; 这书不错,～太贵了. This is a good book, only it's too expensive.

只要 zhǐyào so long as; provided; if; ～功夫深,铁杵磨成针〈谚〉perseverance spells success; many strokes fell great oaks

只有 zhǐyǒu only; alone; 眼下也～这样做了. That's the only thing we can do under the circumstances.

旨 zhǐ ❶〈书〉delicious; delectable ❷ purport; purpose; ～在加强合作 aim at strengthening cooperation ❸ intention; wish; (royal) decree; ～令 (royal) order; edict; decree / ～意 intention; intent

址 zhǐ site; location; 新～ new site or address

抵 zhǐ

抵掌 zhǐzhǎng 〈书〉clap (one's hands to show pleasure); ～而谈 have a heart-to-heart or cordial chat

纸 zhǐ ❶ paper; ～板 paperboard; cardboard / ～币 paper money; (bank) note / ～浆 (paper) pulp / ～巾 paper towel; kleenex / ～牌 playing cards / ～钱〈迷信〉money made in the form of coins and burned as offering to the dead / ～烟 cigarette / ～张 (sheets of) paper / ～老虎 paper tiger (outwardly strong but inwardly weak) ❷〈量〉sheet; 一～家书 a letter from home

纸包不住火 zhǐbāobuzhùhuǒ you can't wrap fire in paper — there is no hiding the facts; truth will out

纸上谈兵 zhǐshàngtánbīng talk about military strategy on paper — be an armchair strategist; talk about generalities without getting down to brass tacks

纸醉金迷 zhǐzuì-jīnmí (a life of) luxury and dissipation: 过着~的生活 lead a life of debauchery; wallow in the flesh-pots

指 zhǐ ❶ finger; ~法 fingering (on the piano, etc) / ~环（finger）ring / ~尖 finger tip / ~纹 fingerprint / ~印 fingerprint; fingermark ❷ finger-breadth; 两一宽 two finger-breadths wide ❸ point (to); ~路牌 road-sign; signpost; guidepost / ~路明灯（喻）beacon or guiding light ❹ (of hair) stand; bristle; 令人发~ make one's blood boil; make one bristle with indignation ❺ direct; point out; ~拨 give directions or advice / ~斥 reprove; reprimand; condemn / ~出 point out; state clearly / ~明 indicate clearly; point out / ~认 (as a witness) identify; recognize; point out ❻ refer to; 这话不是~你的。That wasn't directed against you. ❼ depend or rely on; count on; ~靠 depend or rely on; look to (for help) / ~不定 not sure; perhaps; maybe / 这个家就~着你了。We depend on you to support the family.

指标 zhǐbiāo target; quota; index; 进口~ import quota / 质量~ quality index

指导 zhǐdǎo guide; direct; instruct; ~员 political instructor (of a PLA company); instructor (for young pioneers, etc) / ~价格 guided or guidance price / ~思想 guiding principle / 技术~ technical adviser

指点 zhǐdiǎn ❶ instruct; give directions or advice; ~迷津 show sb how to get on the right path ❷ point one's finger at; pick on

指定 zhǐdìng appoint; assign; name; ~继承人 designated heir / ~一个日期 appoint a date

指挥 zhǐhuī ❶ command; direct; conduct; ~棒 baton / ~部 command;

headquarters / ~员 commander (in the army); one who is in charge (of a project, etc) / ~若定 be perfectly calm and collected in directing a battle; give competent leadership ❷ commander; director; conductor

指甲 zhǐjia nail; 修~ trim nails; manicure / ~锉 nail file / ~刀 nail clippers / ~油 nail polish / ~盖儿〈口〉fingernail

指教 zhǐjiào instruct; teach;〈套〉give advice or comments

指控 zhǐkòng accuse (sb of sth); charge (sb with sth)

指令 zhǐlìng ❶ instruct; order; direct; ~性计划 mandatory planning or plan ❷ (written) instructions or directives (from above) ❸〈通信〉instruction; command; order; ~系统 instruction repertoire

指鹿为马 zhǐlùwéimǎ call a stag a horse — deliberately distort facts; confuse right and wrong

指名 zhǐmíng mention by name; name; ~道姓 name names / ~批评 criticize sb by name

指南 zhǐnán guide; guidebook; 行动的~ guide to action / ~针 compass

指派 zhǐpài appoint; assign; designate; ~她当组长 appoint her (to be) group leader

指日可待 zhǐrìkědài can be realized very soon; be just round the corner

指桑骂槐 zhǐsāngmàhuái also "指鸡骂狗" point at one but abuse another; attack by innuendo

指使 zhǐshǐ instigate; incite (sb to do sth); 幕后~者 person behind the scenes; hidden instigator

指示 zhǐshì ❶ indicate; show; ~灯 pilot lamp ❷ instruct; direct (sb to do sth) ❸ instruction; directive; order

指手画脚 zhǐshǒu-huàjiǎo ❶ make animated gestures; gesticulate profusely ❷ issue orders right and left; criti-

this and condemn that; carp and cavil (at sb)

指数 zhǐshù ❶〈数〉exponent ❷ index (number): 综合~ composite index

指望 zhǐwang ❶ look forward to; count on; expect ❷ hope: 没有~ beyond hope; hopeless

指要 zhǐyào also "旨要"〈书〉main idea; gist

指引 zhǐyǐn point (the way); lead; guide: ~航向 chart the course

指责 zhǐzé censure; criticize; reproach

指摘 zhǐzhāi nitpick; pick faults and criticize: 无可~ above reproach

指针 zhǐzhēn ❶ (needle) indicator; pointer ❷ guiding principle; guideline

指正 zhǐzhèng point out and correct mistakes:〈套〉make comments or criticisms: 不对之处务请~。Please feel free to point out our errors.

咫 zhǐ

咫尺 zhǐchǐ〈书〉very close or near: ~天涯 a short distance away, and yet poles apart — see little of each other though living nearby

趾 zhǐ ❶ toe ❷ foot: ~高气扬 strut about and give oneself airs; be on one's high horse; be haughty

酯 zhǐ〈化〉ester

zhì

至 zhì ❶ reaching; to; until: ~此 at this point; until now; to such an extent / ~今 so far; up to now; to date ❷ extremely; very; most: ~宝 priceless or invaluable treasure / ~诚 with complete sincerity; in real earnest / ~迟 at (the) latest; no later than / ~少 at (the) least; not less or fewer than / ~高无上 highest; supreme; paramount / ~关紧要 most import-

ant; imperative; of utmost importance / ~理名言 famous dictum; golden saying; well-known truth

至交 zhìjiāo closest or best friend; bosom friend

至亲 zhìqīn next of kin; closest relative: ~好友 close relatives and good friends; kith and kin

至上 zhìshàng supreme; highest: 顾客~。Customers first.

至于 zhìyú ❶ go as far as to; go to such an extent: 不~公然说谎 wouldn't go so far as to tell a barefaced lie ❷ as for; as to

志(❷-❹誌) zhì ❶ will; ambition; ideal: ~向 aspiration; dream; ambition / ~士仁 people of high ideals and integrity / ~在必得 be determined to win; be bent on getting / ~在四方 be ready to go far away from home in pursuit of a great career ❷ remember; keep in mind; record: ~哀 express mourning / ~喜 serve as celebration or congratulation ❸ records; chronicles; annals ❹ mark; sign: 立碑为~ erect a tablet as a marker

志大才疏 zhìdà-cáishū have lofty aspirations but little talent; aim at more than one can achieve

志气 zhìqì aspiration; ambition; ideal: 有~ aspiring; ambitious

志趣 zhìqù (aspiration and) interest; inclination: ~相投 have similar inclinations

志同道合 zhìtóng-dàohé cherish the same ideals and take the same course; be devoted to a common cause; be of like mind

志愿 zhìyuàn ❶ aspiration; wish; ideal ❷ volunteer; do sth of one's own accord: ~兵 volunteer (soldier) / ~者 volunteer

帜(幟) zhì flag; streamer; banner

制(❶製) zhì ❶ make; manufacture: ～假 make fake goods / ～品 products; wares; goods / ～糖 refine sugar / ～图 map-making; drafting; drawing ❷ work out; draw up; formulate: ～宪 draw up a constitution ❸ check; control; command: ～衡 checks and balances / ～高点〈军〉commanding height or point / ～空权〈军〉control of the air; air domination or supremacy / ～敌于死命 have the enemy by the throat; spell death to the enemy ❹ system: 联邦～ federal system

制裁 zhìcái impose sanctions (on); punish: 解除～ lift sanctions (against)

制导 zhìdǎo guide (a missile, etc): ～系统 guidance system / 激光～炸弹 laser-guided bomb

制订 zhìdìng work out; formulate; draw up (a plan, etc)

制定 zhìdìng lay down (rules, etc); draw up; make (a policy, etc)

制动 zhìdòng brake: 紧急～ (apply the) emergency brake / ～器 brake

制度 zhìdù ❶ rules; regulations; institution: ～化 institutionalize ❷ system; institution: 社会～ social system or order

制服 zhìfú ❶ also "制伏" check (sth); subdue (sb); bring under control ❷ uniform

制冷 zhìlěng refrigerate: ～剂 refrigerant / ～系统 refrigerating system

制式 zhìshì ❶ service pattern: ～军服 regulation uniform ❷ system; format: ～转换 conversion of system / 多～电视机 multi-system TV set

制约 zhìyuē restrict; restrain; limit

制造 zhìzào ❶ make; manufacture; produce: 中国～ made in China / ～业 manufacturing industry ❷ create; fabricate: ～分裂 foment splits / ～矛盾 sow dissension / ～谣言 invent rumours

制止 zhìzhǐ check; ban; stop

制作 zhìzuò make; manufacture: 精心～ make (sth) with meticulous care

质(質) zhì ❶ nature; substance; quality: ～变 qualitative change ❷ simple; natural; plain: ～直〈书〉simple and honest / ～言之 in plain words; frankly speaking ❸ ask; question: ～询 inquire about; question ❹〈书〉pawn; pledge; security: ～押 mortgage; pledge

质地 zhìdì ❶ quality of a material; texture: ～美 of superb texture ❷ character; nature: 这孩子～并不差. The child is not really inferior by nature.

质感 zhìgǎn (of works of art) sense of reality: 表现不同物体的～ give a life-like portrayal of various objects

质量 zhìliàng ❶〈理〉mass: ～比 mass ratio ❷ quality: 教学～ quality of teaching / ～差 of poor quality; inferior / ～管理 quality management or control

质朴 zhìpǔ simple and unadorned; natural; plain

质问 zhìwèn question; interrogate

质疑 zhìyí call in question; question: ～问难 raise doubts and difficult questions for discussion; seek solutions to thorny problems

质子 zhìzǐ〈理〉proton

炙 zhì broil; grill; roast: ～烤 broil; grill / ～热 scorching or burning hot / ～手可热 burning to the touch;〈喻〉showing one's power arrogantly; very influential

治 zhì ❶ rule; govern; control: ～国安民 run the country well and ensure peace and security for the people / ～山～水 tame rivers and mountains / ～外法权 extraterritoriality ❷ stability; order; peace: ～世〈书〉times of peace and prosperity ❸〈旧〉seat of a local government: 县～ county seat ❹ treat (a disease); heal (a wound, etc); cure: ~本 effect a permanent cure; tackle a problem, etc at its root / ~标 effect a temporary cure; alleviate the symptoms of an illness / ~愈率 (医) cure rate / ~病救人 cure the sickness to save the patient; help sb mend his or her ways ❺ eliminate; stamp out; ~蝗 wipe out locusts / ~贫 eliminate or get rid of poverty ❻ punish: ~罪 bring to justice; punish ❼ study; research: ~史 specialize in history / ~学谨严 be scrupulous or meticulous in one's scholarly work

治安 zhì'ān　law and order; public order: 扰乱~ disturb peace and order

治理 zhìlǐ ❶ administer; rule; govern: ~整顿 improve the economic environment and rectify the economic order; improve management and performance ❷ harness (nature, etc); tame; bring under control

治疗 zhìliáo　treat; cure: 住院~ be hospitalized / ~无效 (of a patient) fail to respond to treatment

治丧 zhìsāng　make funeral arrangements: ~委员会 funeral committee

治装 zhìzhuāng　〈书〉purchase things (esp clothes) necessary for a long journey; pack for a journey: ~费 clothing allowance (as for an official going abroad)

栉(櫛) zhì　〈书〉❶ comb: ~比鳞次 (of buildings, etc) be close together (like comb teeth or fish scales) ❷ comb (hair): ~风沐雨 be combed by the wind and washed by the rain — brave the elements (travelling or working)

峙 zhì　〈书〉stand erect; rise aloft; tower: ~立 stand towering; tower aloft

桎 zhì　〈书〉fetters: ~梏 fetters and handcuffs; chains; shackles

挚(摯) zhì　〈书〉sincere; earnest; heartfelt: ~爱 love sincerely / ~友 close or bosom friend

致(緻) zhì ❶ send; extend; deliver: ~哀 pay one's respects to the deceased / ~贺 extend one's congratulations / ~谢 express one's thanks; extend thanks (to sb) ❷ concentrate; devote ❸ achieve; bring about; cause: ~残 cause disability; become disabled; be crippled / ~富 become rich; acquire wealth / ~癌物质 (医) carcinogen; carcinogenic substance / 因伤~死 die of a wound; be fatally wounded ❹ manner or style that attracts attention or arouses interest; interest: 曲折有~ intricate and interesting ❺ fine; delicate; exquisite: ~密 fine and close; compact

致辞 zhìcí　also "致词" make an address; deliver a speech: 致答辞 make a speech in reply

致敬 zhìjìng　salute; pay homage or tribute to: ~电 message of greetings

致力 zhìlì　dedicate or devote oneself; be devoted to

致命 zhìmìng　lethal; fatal; mortal: ~伤 mortal or fatal wound / ~弱点 Achilles' heel / ~的打击 deadly blow

致使 zhìshǐ　cause; lead to; result in: 他没有及时就医,~病情恶化。His condition worsened for lack of timely treatment.

致意 zhìyì　send one's regards; present one's compliments; extend one's greetings: 微笑~ greet (sb) with a smile

秩 zhì　〈书〉❶ order ❷ official salary or rank ❸ decade: 年已七~ 70 years of age

秩序 zhìxù　order; sequence: ~井然 in apple-pie order

掷(擲) zhì　throw; cast; fling: ~还〈套〉please

return (sth) / ~ 标枪〈体〉javelin throw / ~ 骰子 cast the dice; play dice / ~ 地有声〈喻〉(of writings, etc) sonorous and forceful; full of heroic and lofty sentiments

痔 zhì also "痔疮"〈医〉haemorrhoids; piles

窒 zhì 〈书〉stop up; block; obstruct：~ 碍 have obstacles; be blocked / ~ 息 stifle; choke; suffocate

蛭 zhì (usu 水蛭) leech

智 zhì wisdom; intelligence; resourcefulness：~ 残 also "智障" mentally-retarded / ~ 齿〈生理〉wisdom tooth / ~ 取 capture (a fort, etc) by stratagem / ~ 商 (short for 智力商数) intelligence quotient (IQ) / ~ 育 intellectual education; mental development / ~ 勇双全 be both brave and intelligent; combine wisdom and courage / ~ 者千虑，必有一失〈谚〉even the wise are not always free from error; nobody is infallible

智多星 zhìduōxīng resourceful person; mastermind; wizard

智慧 zhìhuì wisdom; sagacity; intelligence

智力 zhìlì intelligence; intellect：~ 测验 intelligence test / ~ 超群 be extraordinarily intelligent / ~ 竞赛 intelligence or knowledge contest; intelligence quiz (game)

智谋 zhìmóu wit; resourcefulness：有 ~ resourceful; full of ideas

智囊 zhìnáng brain truster：~ 团 think tank; brain trust

智能 zhìnéng ❶ intellect and ability; intellectual power：~ 犯罪 intelligent crime ❷ (of things) smart; intelligent：~ 卡〈经〉smart card / ~ 机器人 intelligent or smart robot

痣 zhì nevus; mole

滞（滯） zhì stagnant; sluggish; be at a standstill：~ 洪 flood detention / ~ 缓 slow; tardy; sluggish / ~ 留 be held up; (of vehicle, etc) wait on demurrage / ~ 销 also "滞背" (of goods, etc) unsalable; unmarketable / ~ 纳金 fine for delaying payment; overdue fine

滞后 zhìhòu lag behind：~ 消费 lagged consumption

置 zhì ❶ place; set; put：~ 放 place; put / ~ 身事外 keep aloof from sth; take no part in sth; refuse to get involved in sth / ~ 不予一评 make no comment / 难以~信 hard to believe; incredible ❷ set up; form; establish; install：~ 景 set up (stage) scenery ❸ buy; purchase：~ 产 purchase real estate; buy property / ~ 办嫁妆 make purchases for a dowry

置辩 zhìbiàn 〈书〉(usu used in the negative) argue; justify：无须 ~。There's no need to debate the point.

置换 zhìhuàn ❶〈化〉displacement; substitution;〈数〉permutation ❷ replace; substitute; switch：土地 ~ relocate by yielding one's old venue for a price

置若罔闻 zhìruòwǎngwén turn a deaf ear to; ignore

置疑 zhìyí (usu used in the negative) doubt：毫不 ~ show no shadow of a doubt; have not the slightest doubt

置之 zhìzhī (used in certain idioms) put sb or sth：~ 不理 close one's eyes to; brush aside; pay no heed to / ~ 度外 give no thought to; think nothing of; disregard / ~ 脑后 dismiss from one's mind; ignore and forget / ~ 死地而后快 not feel content unless sb is got rid of; be satisfied with nothing less than the ruin of sb

雉 zhì ❶ pheasant ❷ parapet section of a city wall：~ 堞 crenellation; battlement

稚 zhì　young; childish; ~拙 (of art, etc) simple and unsophisticated / ~子〈书〉child

稚嫩 zhìnèn ❶ young and delicate; ~的童音 child's tender voice ❷ immature; puerile

稚气 zhìqì childishness; ~未泯 retain a childish heart; retain traces of childish innocence or playfulness

踬(躓) zhì 〈书〉trip; stumble; suffer a setback

zhōng

中 zhōng ❶ (at the) centre; (in the) middle; ~部 central section; middle part / ~东 Middle East / ~非 Central Africa ❷ (Zhōng) China; ~餐 Chinese cuisine or food / ~文 Chinese (language) / ~日关系 Sino-Japanese relations ❸ in; among; amid; 城~ in the city ❹ between two ends or extremes; medium; impartial; ~波 (通信) medium wave / ~层 middle level / ~程 intermediate or medium (range) / ~饭 midday meal; lunch / ~锋 (basketball) centre; (of soccer, etc) centre forward / ~号 medium size (M) / ~年 middle age; middle life / ~午 noon; midday / ~指 middle finger / ~产阶级 middle class / ~道而废 be abandoned halfway ❺ suitable or fit for; good for; ~听 pleasant to the ear; to one's liking ❻ 〈方〉all right; okay; ~不~? Is it okay? ❼ in the process or course of; 在研究~ under study

see also zhòng

中饱 zhōngbǎo　profit from money entrusted to one's care; line one's pockets with money under one's care; misappropriate; ~私囊 divert public money to one's private purse

中辍 zhōngchuò　stop in the middle (of doing sth); give up halfway; 学业~ discontinue one's studies; drop out of school

中等 zhōngděng ❶ (of education) secondary; intermediate; ~教育 secondary (school) education / ~专科学校 (shortened as 中专) secondary technical school; polytechnic school ❷ medium; average; middling; ~城市 medium-sized city / ~身材 (of) medium height / ~发达国家 moderately developed country

中断 zhōngduàn　suspend; break off; hold up; ~供应 cut off supplies / ~外交关系 suspend diplomatic relations

中共 Zhōnggòng (short for 中国共产党) CPC (Communist Party of China); ~中央 CPC Central Committee

中古 zhōnggǔ ❶ middle ancient times (in Chinese history, from the 3rd to the 10th century) ❷ *also* "中世纪" Middle Ages (from the fall of the Rome in 476 to the fall of Constantinople in 1453); medieval times

中国 Zhōngguó　China; ~化 Sinicize; Sinify / ~热 China fever or craze / ~人 Chinese / ~通 China expert or hand; Sinologist / ~学 Sinology; Chinese studies / ~象棋 Chinese chess / ~国民党 Nationalist Party of China; the Kuomingtang

中和 zhōnghé 〈化〉〈喻〉neutralize; ~剂 neutralizer

中华 Zhōnghuá　China; ~鲟 Chinese paddlefish / ~民国 Republic of China (1912-1949) / ~民族 Chinese nation / 大~经济圈 greater China economic zone / ~人民共和国 the People's Republic of China (1949-)

中级 zhōngjí ❶ middle rank; mid-level; intermediate; ~职称 professional titles of middle rank / ~人民法院 intermediate people's court

中坚 zhōngjiān　nucleus; backbone; mainstay; 社会~ salt of the earth / ~分子 backbone elements

中间 zhōngjiān ❶ in; among; amid; 混在人群～ hide oneself in a crowd ❷ (at the) centre; (in the) middle; 广场～ at the centre of a square ❸ between two ends or extremes; medium; intermediate; ～派 middle elements; middle-of-the-roaders / ～商 middleman; intermediary / ～道路 middle road

中将 zhōngjiàng 〈军〉(in the army and air force) lieutenant general; (in the navy) vice admiral

中介 zhōngjiè intermediary; medium; ～人 also "中介"; "中人" middleman; intermediary; go-between / ～服务 intermediary service

中立 zhōnglì neutral; ～国 neutral state / 严守～ observe one's neutral status strictly; be strictly neutral

中流 zhōngliú ❶ midstream; ～砥柱 firm rock in midstream; tower of strength; mainstay ❷ middle; middling; ～水平 (of) middling level

中落 zhōngluò decline (in the course of development); sink; ebb; 家道～。The family is on the decline.

中期 zhōngqī ❶ middle period; ～报告 interim report / ～选举 (US) midterm election ❷ medium term; ～贷款 medium-term loan / ～预报 mid-range forecast

中秋 Zhōngqiū also "中秋节" Mid-Autumn Festival (15th day of the 8th lunar month); Moon Festival

中山装 zhōngshānzhuāng modern Chinese tunic suit (named after Sun Yet-sen, called "Mao suit" in the West)

中枢 zhōngshū centre; 领导～ leading centre; central leadership / 交通～ communication hub / ～神经 nervous centralis

中途 zhōngtú halfway; midway; ～港 port of call / ～退场 leave before a meeting is over; walk out

中外 zhōngwài China and foreign; at home and abroad; 名震～ renowned at home and abroad / ～合资企业 Chinese-foreign joint venture

中尉 zhōngwèi (in the army and air force) first lieutenant; (in the navy) lieutenant junior grade

中校 zhōngxiào (in the army and air force) lieutenant colonel; (in the navy) commander

中心 zhōngxīn ❶ middle or central position; 镇～ in the centre of the town ❷ main; key; ～人物 key figure; central character / ～思想 main idea; gist ❸ centre; core; 政治～ political centre / ～城市 central or core city

中兴 zhōngxīng resurgence; 国运～ resurgence of a nation

中性 zhōngxìng ❶ neutral; ～词 neutral word / ～纸 neutral paper ❷ (语言)neuter; ～名词 neuter noun

中学 zhōngxué ❶ secondary, middle or high school ❷ (zhōngxué) (late Qing dynasty term) Chinese (traditional) learning; ～为体,西学为用 take Chinese learning as the base, and Western learning for application

中央 zhōngyāng ❶ centre; middle; 广场～ in the middle of a square / ～空调 central air conditioning; centrally air-conditioned / ～处理机(信息)central processing unit (CPU); central processor / ～商务区 central business district (CBD) ❷ highest leading body (of a state, party, etc); central authorities; ～集权 centralization of power / ～委员 member of the Central Committee (of the CPC) / ～银行 central bank / ～各部委 Ministries and Commissions under the State Council / ～情报局 (US) Central Intelligence Agency (CIA)

中药 zhōngyào traditional Chinese medicine; ～ traditional Chinese pharmacy / 中草药 Chinese herbal medicine / 中成药 prepared Chinese

Z

medicine

中医 zhōngyī ❶ traditional Chinese medical science; ~学院 college of traditional Chinese medicine ❷ doctor or practitioner of traditional Chinese medicine

中庸 zhōngyōng ❶ golden mean (of the Confucian school); ~之道 doctrine of the mean; golden mean ❷ (Zhōngyōng) see "四书五经" Sìshū Wǔjīng ❸ 〈书〉mediocre; average; middling; ~之辈 person of mediocre abilities; mediocrity

中用 zhōngyòng be of use; be helpful; 中看不~用 be pleasant to the eye but of little use; (of a person) handsome but good for nothing

中游 zhōngyóu ❶ middle reaches (of a river) ❷ state of being middling; mediocre; so-so; 不甘~ not resigned to the middling state; not content to remain mediocre

中原 Zhōngyuán Central Plains (ie the middle and lower reaches of the Yellow River); (used as a general reference) China; ~逐鹿 fight for domination in the country; fight for the throne

中允 zhōngyǔn also "公允" 〈书〉fair-minded; equitable; impartial

中止 zhōngzhǐ discontinue; suspend; cut short; ~谈判 cut short or break off negotiations / ~营业 wind up operations

中转 zhōngzhuǎn ❶ change trains ❷ 〈经〉entrepôt; transit shipment; ~站 transfer station / ~货物 goods to be transhipped / ~贸易 entrepôt trade

中子 zhōngzǐ neutron; ~弹 neutron bomb

忠 zhōng loyal; faithful; devoted; ~臣 loyal court official / ~骨 loyal bones; remains of a martyr / ~肝义胆 faithful and gallant; daring and patriotic / ~言逆耳 candid advice grates on the ear; honest exhortations may be unpleasant to the ear / ~于职守 be devoted to one's duty

忠诚 zhōngchéng loyal; faithful; staunch; ~待人 treat people with warmth and sincerity / ~教育事业 be devoted to education

忠告 zhōnggào sincerely advise; exhort; admonish; 不听~ reject sincere advice; turn a deaf ear to exhortations

忠厚 zhōnghòu honest and tolerant; sincere and kindhearted

忠良 zhōngliáng loyal and honest; faithful and staunch; ~之士 loyal and upright person / 陷害~ frame a loyal and virtuous man

忠烈 zhōngliè ❶ lay down one's life out of loyalty to the country; ~之臣 loyal court official who remains faithful to the last ❷ martyr

忠实 zhōngshí true; faithful; trustworthy; ~可靠 honest and reliable; trustworthy / ~原文 be faithful to the original

忠心 zhōngxīn loyalty; dedication; devotion; 表~ pledge one's loyalty / ~耿耿 loyal and devoted; faithful and steadfast

忠贞 zhōngzhēn loyal and staunch; ~不渝 also "忠贞不二" unswervingly loyal; steadfast and unyielding

终 zhōng ❶ end; close; finish; ~场 (at the) end of a game, show or an exam ❷ die; 80 而~ die at 80 ❸ eventually; in the end; after all; ~成功 be sure to succeed eventually ❹ whole; entire; all; ~日 all day (long)

终点 zhōngdiǎn ❶ end point; destination; ~站 terminus; terminal ❷ 〈体〉finish; ~线 finishing line or tape

终端 zhōngduān terminal; end; 汉字~ 〈信息〉Chinese language terminal / ~用户 end-user

终归 zhōngguī also "终究" eventually; in the end; after all; 孩子~是孩子

Children will be children.

终极 zhōngjí　final; ultimate: ～关怀 ultimate concern / ～目标 final aim

终结 zhōngjié ❶ end; final stage come to an end; 事情远未～。The matter is far from being resolved.

终了 zhōngliǎo　end (of a period): 战斗～ at the end of fighting

终南捷径 zhōngnánjiéjìng　shortcut to high office or success; royal road to fame

终年 zhōngnián ❶ all the year round; throughout the year ❷ age at which one dies: ～90 die at the age of ninety

终身 zhōngshēn ❶ lifelong; throughout one's life: ～制 lifelong tenure / ～大事 event of lifelong significance (usu meaning marriage) / ～监禁 life imprisonment ❷ marriage: 私定～ arrange one's own marriage (without asking for permission of one's parents)

终审 zhōngshěn 〈法〉last instance; final judgement: ～权 power of final adjudication / ～法院 court of last instance / ～判决 final adjudication; final or last judgement

终生 zhōngshēng　one's lifetime; all one's life: ～难忘的教训 not forget the lesson to the end of one's days

终于 zhōngyú　at (long) last; in the end; eventually

终止 zhōngzhǐ　stop; put an end to; terminate: ～合同 terminate a contract / ～日期 closing date; expiry date

盅 zhōng　handleless cup: 茶～ tea cup

钟（❶❸鐘、❷鍾） zhōng ❶ bell: ～楼 bell tower; belfry; clock tower ❷ clock: ～表 clocks and watches; timepieces ❸ time (as measured in hours and minutes): 三个～头〈口〉three hours ❹ concentrate (one's affections, etc); focus on: ～灵毓秀。The concentration of the best of the land nurtures the best of talents.

钟爱 zhōng'ài　love dearly; cherish: 倍受的～小女儿 darling baby daughter

钟点 zhōngdiǎn 〈口〉❶ time for sth to be done or to happen; appointed time: 还不到～。It's not time yet. ❷ hour: ～工 hourly worker (usu a domestic paid by the hour)

钟鼎文 zhōngdǐngwén　also "金文" (language used in) inscriptions on ancient bronze objects

钟情 zhōngqíng　be deeply in love; be captivated: ～于她 fall for her

钟乳石 zhōngrǔshí　also "石钟乳" stalactite

衷 zhōng　inner heart or feeling: 初～ original intention or idea / ～肠〈书〉heartfelt words or feelings / ～曲〈书〉heartfelt emotion; inmost feelings / 倾吐～情 pour out one's inner feelings; open one's heart (to sb)

衷心 zhōngxīn　heartfelt; wholeheartedly; from the bottom of one's heart: ～祝愿 sincerely wish

zhǒng

肿（腫） zhǒng　swell; be swollen: ～块 tumour; mass / ～瘤 tumour / ～胀 swelling; swollen

种（種） zhǒng ❶ seed; strain; species: 菜～ vegetable seeds / 剧～ type of drama, esp of traditional opera / ～畜 breeding or stud stock / ～群 population ❷ race: 黄～ yellow race ❸ guts; grit; pluck: 有～ have guts ❹〈量〉kind; sort; type: 15～灯具 fifteen kinds of lights

see also zhòng

种类 zhǒnglèi　kind; variety; category: ～繁多 a great variety (of sth)

种种 zhǒngzhǒng　all sorts of; a variety of; various: ～困难 all kinds of difficulties

种子 zhǒngzi　seed：仇恨的～ seeds of hatred / ～田 seed-breeding field / ～基金〈经〉seed money / ～选手〈体〉seeded player；seed

种族 zhǒngzú　race；ethnicity：～隔离 racial segregation / ～灭绝 genocide / ～歧视 racial discrimination / ～清洗 ethnic cleansing / ～主义 racism；racialism

冢（塚） zhǒng　tomb；grave

踵 zhǒng　〈书〉❶ heel：不旋～ without turning one's heels — in an instant ❷ call in person：～门相告 call personally to pass the news ❸ follow closely：～至 arrive on the heels of another / ～武前贤 follow the example of past sages

zhòng

中 zhòng　❶ hit；fit exactly；win：～奖 win a prize in a lottery；draw a winning ticket / ～选 be chosen or selected / 一语～的 hit the nail squarely on the head with one's remark ❷ fall into；sustain；suffer：～弹 be struck by a bullet；get shot / ～风 (be seized with) apoplexy；(have a) stroke / ～计 walk into a trap；play into sb's hands / ～魔 be bewitched or possessed / ～暑 (suffer) heatstroke；sunstroke / ～煤气 be gassed
see also zhōng

中毒 zhòngdú　poisoning；toxication：铅～ lead poisoning / 思想～ be poisoned in mind

中肯 zhòngkěn　(of remarks) sincere and pertinent：十分～ very much to the point

中伤 zhòngshāng　slander；vilify；calumniate：造谣～ spread slanderous rumours

中意 zhòngyì　be to one's taste or liking；catch one's fancy

仲 zhòng　❶ (of the three months in a season) second：～夏 second month of summer ❷ (of brothers) second in order of birth：～父 father's younger brother

仲裁 zhòngcái　arbitrate：～人 arbitrator / ～法庭 court of arbitration

众（衆） zhòng　❶ many；numerous；innumerable：～寡悬殊 great disparity in numerical strength；(against) overwhelming odds / ～矢之的 target of each and all；object of angry public criticism ❷ large number of people；crowd；multitude：～怒难犯 you cannot afford to incur public wrath；it is dangerous to arouse the people's anger / ～所周知 as everyone knows；as is well known；it is common knowledge / ～说纷纭。Opinions differ.

众多 zhòngduō　many；numerous；multitudinous：人口～ be populous；have a large population

众口 zhòngkǒu　*used in the following idioms associated with a multitude of people*：～难调 it is difficult to cater to all tastes；one man's meat is another man's poison；tastes differ / ～铄金 public clamour can confound right and wrong；if you throw enough mud, some of it will stick / ～一词 unanimous in opinion；with one voice

众目睽睽 zhòngmùkuíkuí　under the watchful eyes of the people；with all eyes centred on one；in the public eye

众叛亲离 zhòngpàn-qīnlí　be opposed by the public and deserted by one's followers；face utter isolation

众人 zhòngrén　everybody：～拾柴火焰高。〈俗〉The fire burns high when everybody brings wood to it.

众望 zhòngwàng　people's expectations；popular trust：～所归 enjoy popular confidence or trust；command public respect and support

众议院 zhòngyìyuàn （US, Australia, Japan, etc) House of Representatives; (Italy, Mexico, Chile, etc) Chamber of Deputies: ～议员 also "众议员" representative (in a Congress); Congressman or Congresswoman

众志成城 zhòngzhìchéngchéng unity is strength; unity is the path to victory

种(種) zhòng sow; grow; cultivate: ～菜 grow vegetables / ～地 till land; go in for farming / ～瓜得瓜,～豆得豆 you must reap what you have sown; as you sow, so will you reap　see also zhǒng

种痘 zhòngdòu also "种牛痘" (give or receive) vaccination (against smallpox)

种植 zhòngzhí plant; grow; cultivate: ～业 planting industry / ～园 plantation

重 zhòng ❶ weight: 你有多～? How much do you weigh? ❷ heavy; weighty; considerable in amount or value: ～兵 large number of troops; huge forces / ～担 heavy burden; difficult task; great responsibility / ～活 heavy work / ～奖 (offer) rich or ample rewards / ～氢〈化〉heavy hydrogen; deuterium / ～水〈化〉heavy water; deuterium oxide / ～工业 heavy industry / ～武器 heavy weapons / ～型卡车 heavy-duty truck / ～于泰山 weightier than Mount Tai — of great significance / 话说得太～ put it too strongly / ～赏之下,必有勇夫。〈谚〉A handsome reward will make the brave come forward. ❸ deep; serious; severe: ～办 severely punish; hand out a severe sentence / ～病 serious disease / ～伤 serious wound; severe injury / ～孝 in deep mourning ❹ important: ～臣〈书〉high court official (charged with heavy responsibilities) / ～地 place of importance (out of bounds to the general public) / ～任 important

task or post ❺ lay stress on; place importance to; hold in esteem: ～男轻女 value men and boys above women and girls; regard men as superior to women ❻ prudent; discreet

see also chóng

重创 zhòngchuāng wound badly; inflict grievous losses or casualties on; maul (heavily): 身受～ be seriously wounded or injured

重大 zhòngdà great; major; tremendous: ～案件 major or important case / ～损失 heavy or grievous losses

重点 zhòngdiǎn focal point; key; priority: ～工程 major or priority project / ～学校 key school or university / ～护理病房 intensive care unit (ICU)

重读 zhòngdú 〈语言〉stress: 非～音节 unstressed syllable

重力 zhònglì 〈理〉gravity; gravitational force

重利 zhònglì ❶ high or exorbitant interest: ～盘剥 practise usury ❷ huge profit: 牟取～ seek excessive profits ❸ 〈书〉value material gains: ～轻义 place material gains above what is right

重量 zhòngliàng weight: ～级〈体〉〈喻〉heavyweight

重视 zhòngshì attach importance to; set store by; lay stress on: ～用户意见 value customers' opinions

重听 zhòngtīng hard of hearing

重头 zhòngtóu important part; focus: ～戏 opera or drama requiring great exertion in the performance; 〈喻〉important part or focus of an activity

重心 zhòngxīn ❶ 〈理〉centre of gravity ❷ focus; crux: 工作～ focus of work

重要 zhòngyào important; significant; major: ～性 importance / ～人物 important person; VIP; prominent figure

重音 zhòngyīn 〈语言〉stress; 〈语言〉〈乐〉accent

Z

重用 zhòngyòng   assign (sb) to a key post; put (sb) in a key position

重罪 zhòngzuì 〈法〉felony; ～犯 felon; ～轻判 under punishment (for a felony)

zhōu

舟 zhōu 〈书〉boat; ～桥 pontoon (bridge) / ～楫往来 travel by boat

州 zhōu ❶〈史〉administrative division; prefecture ❷ (US) state

诌(謅) zhōu   spin (a yarn); cook up; 瞎～ make up a wild story; talk irresponsibly

周(❶-❻週、❼啁) zhōu ❶ circumference; perimeter; circuit; ～边 neighbouring; surrounding / ～长 circumference; perimeter; girth ❷ circle; go round; ～游 travel or journey round; tour / ～而复始 go round and begin again; move in cycles ❸ all; whole; ～身温暖 be warm all over ❹ thoughtful; considerate; attentive; 考虑不～ not be thoughtful enough / 煞费一章 take great pains; go to a lot of trouble ❺ period of time (esp week); ～刊 weekly (publication); weekly supplement (of a newspaper, etc) / ～末 weekend ❻〈电〉cycle; 兆～ megacycle ❼ help out (the needy); assist; relieve; ～济灾民 relieve victims of a disaster; send relief to people in an afflicted area ❽ (Zhōu) Zhou Dynasty (1046 BC-256 BC)

周到 zhōudào   thoughtful; solicitous; attentive; 照顾～ take good care of; be attentive to

周密 zhōumì   meticulous; thorough; well-conceived; 推理～ meticulous reasoning

周年 zhōunián   anniversary; 50～纪念 (golden) jubilee / 100～纪念 centenary

周期 zhōuqī   cycle; (cycle) period;

duration; 现金周转～ cycle of cash flow / ～表〈化〉periodic table (of elements) / ～性危机 periodic o cyclical crises

周全 zhōuquán ❶ circumspect; thou ough; comprehensive; 计划～ pla everything to the last detail ❷ help s attain sth; assist; 这事就全靠您一了 We count on you in this.

周岁 zhōusuì   one full year of life; ～eighteen years old / 给孩子过～ cele brate a child's first birthday

周围 zhōuwéi   round; around; abou 大楼～ around a building

周详 zhōuxiáng   careful; thorough comprehensive

周旋 zhōuxuán ❶ (of a big bird, etc circle; wheel; spiral ❷ mix (with) fraternize; socialize; 善于～ be a goo mixer / ～了几句 exchange a few con pliments (with sb) ❸ engage (an ene my); deal or contend with (a rival, etc)

周折 zhōuzhé   twists and turns; trou ble; setbacks; 颇费～ cause a lot o trouble; take much effort

周转 zhōuzhuǎn ❶〈经〉turnover; 一量 (volume of) turnover / ～资 working, circulating or revolving fun ❷ be adequate to meet the need; ～ 开 be short (of); be cash-strapped

洲 zhōu ❶ continent; ～际 inter continental / 亚～ Asia ❷ islet a river; sandbar

啁 zhōu

啁啾 zhōujiū 〈书〉〈象声〉(of birds chirp; twitter; warble

粥 zhōu   gruel; porridge; conge ～少僧多 many monks, litt porridge — not enough to go round

zhóu

妯 zhóu

妯娌 zhóulǐ　wives of brothers; sisters-in-law

轴 zhóu ❶ axle; shaft: 轮～ wheel axle / ～承 bearing ❷ axis; pivot: 地～ earth's axis / ～心 axis ❸ spool; roller; rod: 画～ roller for a scroll of Chinese painting / ～线 spool of thread

zhǒu

肘 zhǒu ❶ elbow: ～腋〈书〉elbow and armpit;〈喻〉(of trouble, etc) very close ❷ (usu 肘子) upper part of a leg of pork

帚(箒) zhǒu　broom

zhòu

咒(呪) zhòu ❶ incantation: ～语 incantation; spell ❷ curse; swear; damn: ～骂 utter curses against; swear; abuse ❸ oath: 起个～ take an oath

宙 zhòu ❶ time (conceived as past, present and future) ❷ eon; aeon (first division of geologic time)

绉(縐) zhòu (usu 绉纱) crepe; crape: ～纹纸 crepe paper

胄 zhòu ❶〈书〉descendants or offspring (of monarchs or aristocrats) ❷ helmet: 甲～ armour and helmet

昼(晝) zhòu daylight; daytime; day: ～夜 day and night; round the clock; all the time

皱(皺) zhòu wrinkle; crease: ～巴巴 full of wrinkles; crumpled; rumpled / ～眉头 knit or contract one's brows; frown

皱纹 zhòuwén　wrinkles; lines: 眼角～ crow's feet

骤 zhòu ❶ (of a horse) trot: 驰～ gallop ❷ rapid; hurried: ～雨

torrential rain ❸ sudden; abrupt: ～然 all of a sudden; suddenly; abruptly / ～不及防 be taken by surprise

zhū

朱(❷硃) zhū ❶ vermilion; bright red: ～笔 writing brush dipped in red ink / ～红 vermilion; bright red / ～鹮〈动物〉red ibis / ～门 red-lacquered gates of wealthy people's mansions / ～文 characters on a seal carved in relief ❷ (usu 朱砂) cinnabar; vermilion

侏 zhū

侏儒 zhūrú　dwarf; midget; pygmy: ～症〈医〉dwarfism

诛 zhū 〈书〉❶ put (a criminal) to death; execute: ～戮无辜 kill or slaughter the innocent ❷ condemn; punish: ～心之论 exposure of sb's ulterior motives; incisive criticism ❸ ask for; extort; blackmail: ～求无已 make endless extortions

珠 zhū ❶ pearl: ～光宝气 adorned with brilliant jewels and pearls; richly bejewelled ❷ bead: ～帘 bead curtain / ～算 calculation with or counting by the abacus

珠宝 zhūbǎo　pearls and jewels; jewellery: ～店 jeweller's (shop)

珠玑 zhūjī 〈书〉pearl;〈喻〉excellent writing; exquisite diction

珠江 Zhū Jiāng　Zhujiang or Pearl River

珠联璧合 zhūlián-bìhé (constitute an) excellent combination; (form a) perfect pair

珠穆朗玛峰 Zhūmùlǎngmǎfēng (shortened as 珠峰) Mount Qomolangma (known in the West as Mt Everest)

株 zhū ❶ base of a tree; stump ❷ (individual) plant: ～距〈农〉spacing in a row (of plants) ❸〈量〉of *plants and trees*：三～桃树 three peach trees

株连 zhūlián   involve; incriminate; implicate (innocent people)

株守 zhūshǒu   〈书〉hold on to without letting go; cling stubbornly to

诸 zhū ❶ all; numerous; various; ～多〈书〉(used with sth abstract) plenty of; a good deal; lots of / ～君〈套〉ladies and gentlemen / ～子百家 various schools of thought and their exponents (from pre-Qin times to the early Han Dynasty) / ～事顺遂。Everything goes smoothly. ❷〈书〉*mixed pronunciation of* 之于 *or* 之乎：投～渤海 throw (sth) into the Bohai Sea

诸葛 Zhūgě   short for Zhuge Liang (诸葛亮), incarnation of wisdom and resourcefulness：小～ latter-day Zhuge Liang - person as resourceful as Zhuge Liang / 诸葛亮会 meeting to pool wisdom; brain-storming session

诸侯 zhūhóu   enfeoffed dukes or princes; 〈谑〉leaders of provinces or regions

诸如 zhūrú   such as; for example：～此类 things like that; and what not; and so on and so forth

诸位 zhūwèi   polite term for addressing a number of people：～好！Hello, everybody! / ～女士先生！Ladies and Gentlemen!

铢 zhū   tiny unit of weight：～积寸累 accumulate bit by bit; build up gradually

猪（豬） zhū   pig; hog：～圈 pigsty; pigpen / ～苗 *also* "猪仔" piglet; shoat / ～排 pork chop / ～皮 pigskin; hogskin / ～肉 pork / ～食 pigwash; pig feed; swill / ～蹄 *also* "猪爪" pig's foot; trotter / ～油 lard / ～鬃 (hog) bristles

蛛 zhū   spider：～网 spider web; cobweb / ～丝马迹 clues;

traces; tracks

zhú

竹 zhú   bamboo：～板 bamboo clappers / ～帛〈考古〉bamboo slips and silk (used for writing); 〈喻〉ancient records, esp history books / ～简〈考古〉bamboo slip (used for writing) / ～笋 bamboo shoots / ～篮打水一场空 make a futile effort; (of sth) come to nothing

逐 zhú ❶ pursue; seek; chase：～水草而居 migrate from place to place in search of water and grass ❷ expel; oust; drive out：～出家门 drive (one's son, etc) out of one's home / 下～客令 ask an unwelcome guest to leave; show sb the door ❸ one by one; in turn：～个 *also* "逐一" one by one; one after another / ～日 day by day; every day; daily / ～字～句 word for word; line by line verbatim

逐步 zhúbù   step by step; gradually; progressively：～放开 relax control gradually; decontrol progressively / ～升级 escalate

逐渐 zhújiàn   gradually; steadily; by degrees：天气～转暖。It's getting warmer and warmer.

逐鹿 zhúlù   〈书〉fight for the crown; bid for state power；〈喻〉compete for a championship or prize

烛（燭） zhú ❶ candle：～光 candle; candlelight ❷ (common name for 瓦特) watt：40～灯泡 40-watt bulb

zhǔ

主 zhǔ ❶ host; owner; master：一家之～ head of the house; master of the house / ～队〈体〉home or host team / ～妇 housewife; hostess / ～场比赛〈体〉home game ❷ person or party concerned; ~ 顾 customer; client; patron ❸〈宗教〉God; Lord; Allah ❹ principal; chief; main: ~板〈信息〉motherboard / ~编 chief editor or compiler; editor in chief /~宾 guest of honour / ~调 main theme; keynote / ~犯〈法〉prime culprit; principal / ~干〈植〉trunk;〈喻〉mainstay; backbone / ~谋〈be〉chief plotter or instigator / ~食 staple food / ~线 main thread (of a literary work, etc); motif / ~修 specialize (in a particular field of study); major / ~页〈信息〉homepage / ~旨 purport; substance; gist / ~动脉〈生理〉aorta / ~旋律〈乐〉〈喻〉theme; main idea; basic concept / ~次不分 confuse the principal with the secondary; get one's priorities wrong ❺ be in charge of; preside over; manage: ~刀 be the operating surgeon; operate / ~婚 preside over a wedding ceremony; officiate at a wedding ❻ advocate; favour: ~和 advocate peace; favour a peaceful settlement / ~和派 peace party; doves / ~战派 war party; war hawks ❼ foretell; indicate; signify: ~吉 an auspicious sign ❽ definite view or judgement; 心中无~ at a loss (as to) what to do / ~见 one's own judgement; definite opinion ❾ (usu 神主) memorial tablet (of the deceased)

主办 zhǔbàn sponsor; direct: ~单位 sponsor

主持 zhǔchí ❶ preside over (a meeting, etc); chair; host: ~人 host or hostess (of a programme, etc); master of ceremonies (at a function); (TV, etc) anchor ❷ take charge of; be responsible for; direct: ~日常工作 be in charge of day-to-day work ❸ uphold; champion; stand for: ~公道 uphold justice; stand for fair play

主导 zhǔdǎo ❶ guiding; leading; ruling: ~思想 ruling ideas; dominant ideology / 起~作用 play a leading

role; serve as the prime mover ❷ leading factor

主动 zhǔdòng initiative; 掌握~ seize the initiative; have the initiative in one's hands / ~语态〈语言〉active voice / ~作出让步 offer a concession

主攻 zhǔgōng 〈军〉main attack: ~手〈体〉ace striker; spiker / ~部队 main attack force / ~方向 main direction of attack

主观 zhǔguān subjective: ~愿望 subjective desire; wishful thinking / ~主义 subjectivism / ~能动性〈哲〉subjective initiative; dynamism

主管 zhǔguǎn ❶ be in charge of or responsible for: ~当局 competent or appropriate authorities ❷ person in charge; executive

主机 zhǔjī ❶ main engine; principal machine: ~组 main set ❷〈信息〉mainframe; host computer ❸〈军〉lead plane; leader

主教 zhǔjiào 〈宗教〉bishop: 大~ archbishop / 红衣~ also "枢机主教" cardinal / ~辖区 diocese

主角 zhǔjué leading role; star part; lead: 男~ leading actor / 演~ star (in a film, etc); play the lead / 唱~〈喻〉play a leading role

主力 zhǔlì main force; mainstay: ~军 main or principal force / ~队员〈体〉top player or mainstay of a team

主流 zhǔliú main current or trend; mainstream; essential aspect: ~媒体 mainstream or mainline media / 分清~和支流 distinguish between the principal and secondary aspects; see (sth) in proper perspective

主权 zhǔquán sovereign rights; sovereignty: 领土~ territorial sovereignty / ~国家 sovereign state

主人 zhǔrén ❶ host or hostess ❷ (used by the employee) master or mistress ❸ owner; master: 国家的~ masters of a country

Z

主人翁 zhǔrénwēng ❶ master (of one's own country, society, etc) ❷ *also* "主人公" hero or heroine (in a literary work); protagonist

主任 zhǔrèn head; director (of a department, etc); chairman (of a committee, etc)

主使 zhǔshǐ instigate; incite; abet; 受人～ at sb's instigation

主事 zhǔshì be in charge; ～的人 person in charge

主题 zhǔtí theme; subject; motif; ～歌 theme song / ～公园 theme park

主体 zhǔtǐ ❶ main body; main or principal part; ～工程 principal part of a project ❷〈哲〉〈法〉subject

主席 zhǔxí chairman or chairperson (of a meeting, etc); president (of an organization or a state); ～台 rostrum; platform / ～团 presidium

主心骨 zhǔxīngǔ ❶ backbone; mainstay; pillar ❷ ideas of one's own; 没～ not know one's own mind; be indecisive

主要 zhǔyào major; primary; principal; ～矛盾 principal contradiction

主义 zhǔyì doctrine; -ism

主意 zhǔyi ❶ decision; judgement; definite view; 有～ know one's own mind / 拿定～ make up one's mind; make a decision ❷ idea; way; plan; 出～ give advice

主语 zhǔyǔ〈语言〉subject

主宰 zhǔzǎi dominate; govern; control; ～自己的命运 decide one's own destiny; have one's fate in one's own hands

主张 zhǔzhāng ❶ hold; favour; advocate ❷ view; stand; proposition

主治 zhǔzhì ❶ (of medicine) be for (a disease); (of a doctor) be in charge; ～医生 doctor in charge of a case; physician-in-charge / ～医师 (as a professional title) physician or surgeon in charge

拄 zhǔ lean on (a stick, etc); ～杖而行 walk with a cane

煮 zhǔ boil; stew; cook; ～面条 cook noodles / ～豆燃萁 (engage in) fraternal persecution; fratricidal strife / ～鹤焚琴 destroy sth exquisite in a philistine manner; spoil the fun boorishly

属(屬) zhǔ〈书〉❶ join; connect; combine ❷ centre (one's attention, etc) upon; concentrate on; ～意 fix one's mind (on); have the inclination (to do sth); favour *see also* shǔ

嘱(囑) zhǔ ❶ exhort; advise; urge; 叮嘱 urge; exhort; tell ❷ entrust; ask; tell; ～托 entrust; ask / ～依～而行 do as told

瞩(矚) zhǔ fasten one's look on; look steadily; gaze

瞩目 zhǔmù fix one's eyes upon; rivet one's attention on; 万众～ be the focus of public attention / 引人～ arrest people's attention; eye-catching

瞩望 zhǔwàng〈书〉❶ look steadily; gaze ❷ *also* "属望" hope; look forward to; earnestly expect

zhù

伫(佇、竚) zhù (usu 伫立)〈书〉stand for a long time

苎(苧) zhù

苎麻 zhùmá〈植〉ramie

助 zhù help; assist; aid; ～词〈语言〉auxiliary or function word / ～攻〈军〉(make a) holding or secondary attack;〈体〉assist in attack / ～教 (of a college faculty) assistant teacher; (US) (teaching) assistant; helper; aide / ～产士 midwife / ～听器 audi-phone; hearing aid; aid / ～学金 (student) grant; grant-in-aid / ～人为乐 take delight in helping others / ～纣为虐 help a tyrant do evil; hold a candle for the devil / ～人一臂之力 lend or give sb a (helping) hand

助理 zhùlǐ assistant: 部长～ assistant minister / ～工程师 assistant engineer

助威 zhùwēi boost the morale (of sb); cheer; root (for sb)

助兴 zhùxìng add to the fun; make things more lively; liven things up

助长 zhùzhǎng （贬）abet; foster; foment: ～不正之风 encourage a malpractice

住 zhù ❶ live; stay; reside: ～处 also "住所" residence; lodging; accommodation / ～户 household; resident / ～读生 also "住校生" resident student; boarder ❷ stop; end; cease: ～口 also "住嘴" stop talking; shut up; keep quiet / ～手 stay one's hand; stop (doing sth) ❸ used after some verbs as a complement indicating a halt, stillness, fastness, etc: 接～! Catch it!

住持 zhùchí （宗教）(Buddhist or Taoist) abbot

住房 zhùfáng housing; lodgings; accommodation: ～津贴 housing subsidy; accommodation allowance / ～公积金 public accumulation fund for housing

住宿 zhùsù stay; put up; accommodate

住院 zhùyuàn be hospitalized: ～部 in-patient department / ～处 admission office (in a hospital) / ～费 hospitalization expenses

住宅 zhùzhái residence; dwelling; housing: ～区 residential quarters / 小区 residential sub-area; housing estate

住址 zhùzhǐ address: 这封信～写错了。The letter is wrongly addressed.

贮（貯） zhù store; save; lay aside: ～存 keep (in storage); store / ～运 store and ship

贮藏 zhùcáng ❶ store up; lay in ❷ (mineral) deposit; reserve: 矿产～丰富 be rich in mineral resources

注（❹❺註） zhù ❶ pour: ～入 pour (sth) into; (of a river, etc) empty into (the sea) / ～资 increase registered capital ❷ pay full attention; concentrate ❸ stake (as in gambling) ❹ explain with notes; annotate: ～脚 footnote / ～疏《书》(provide) notes and commentaries ∠～音〈语言〉phonetic notation ❺ put on record; record; register

注册 zhùcè register: 新生报到～ registration of new students / ～商标 registered trademark / ～会计师 certified public accountant

注定 zhùdìng be doomed, fated or destined (to destruction, etc)

注解 zhùjiě also "注释" ❶ explain with notes; annotate: ～本 annotated version ❷ (explanatory) note; annotation

注明 zhùmíng give clear indication of; label: ～有毒 be labelled poisonous / 未～日期 bear no date; be undated

注目 zhùmù fix one's eyes (on); take a steady look (at): ～礼 salute with eyes

注射 zhùshè 〈医〉inject; give an injection: ～器 syringe / ～葡萄糖 give (sb) a glucose injection

注视 zhùshì look attentively at; gaze at; closely watch: ～远方 stare into the distance / ～局势的发展 follow the development of the situation

注销 zhùxiāo cancel; annul; write off: ～户口 cancel sb's household registration / ～欠款 write off a debt

注意 zhùyì pay attention to; take notice of; be careful about: ～力 attention / ～事项 points for attention; matters requiring attention / ～,汽车来了! Watch out! There is a car coming.

注重 zhùzhòng　lay stress on; stress; emphasize; ~ 实际 be pragmatic; be concerned with practical results

驻 zhù ❶ stop; halt; stay; ~ 足 make a temporary stay; halt; stop ❷ be stationed or posted; ~ 军 station troops; troops stationed (at a place); garrison / ~ 守 *also* "驻防" garrison; defend / ~ 扎 (of troops) be stationed or quartered / ~ 在国 state to which a diplomatic envoy is accredited; country of residence / ~ 外工作 overseas postings

驻地 zhùdì ❶ place where troops or fieldworkers are stationed; 边防军 ~ frontier guard station ❷ seat (of a local administrative organ); 省府 ~ seat of the provincial government; provincial capital

驻颜 zhùyán　remain youthful in appearance; ~ 有术 have a recipe for maintaining youthful appearance; be able to preserve one's youthful looks

柱 zhù　pillar; column; column-like thing; ~ 石 pillar; mainstay; tower of strength / ~ 子 post; pillar / 冰 ~ icicle

炷 zhù 〈书〉❶ wick (of an oil lamp) ❷ burn (a joss stick) ❸ (量); 三~香 three burning joss sticks

祝 zhù ❶ offer good wishes; wish; ~ 词 *also* "祝辞" congratulatory speech; prayers at sacrificial rites / ~ 祷 wish and pray / ~ 捷 celebrate a victory / ~ 寿 congratulate (an elderly person) on his or her birthday; offer birthday congratulations / ~ 你生日快乐! Happy birthday to you! / ~ 你早日康复。I wish you a speedy recovery!

祝福 zhùfú ❶ bless; wish; 最美好的 ~ best wishes or blessings ❷ 〈旧〉 New Year's sacrifice

祝贺 zhùhè　congratulate; felicitate; ~ 获奖 congratulate sb on winning a prize / ~ 新年 extend New Year greet-ings

祝酒 zhùjiǔ　drink a toast; toast; 向贵宾 ~ toast the distinguished guests / 致 ~ 词 propose a toast

祝愿 zhùyuàn　wish; ~ 你们幸福。I wish you happiness. or May you live in happiness.

疰 zhù

疰夏 zhùxià 〈中医〉(usu of children) summer indisposition (characterized by loss of appetite and weight in summer, etc)

著 zhù ❶ marked; conspicuous; outstanding; ~ 称 be celebrated or noted (for sth); be famous / ~ 名 famous; well-known; celebrated ❷ show; prove; 颇~成效 prove highly effective ❸ write; compose; ~ 者 author; writer / ~ 书立说 write a book to expound a theory; produce scholarly works ❹ work; book; 新~ new book

著述 zhùshù ❶ write; compile ❷ writings; work; ~ 等身 have written so much that one's works can be piled up to one's height — be a prolific writer

著作 zhùzuò ❶ write; ~ 权 copyright / ~ 人 author; writer ❷ work; writings

蛀 zhù ❶ (usu 蛀虫) insect that eats or feeds on books, clothes, wood, etc; moth;〈喻〉vermin ❷ (of moths, etc) eat into; bore through; ~ 蚀 worm-eaten;〈喻〉eroded

铸(鑄) zhù ❶ cast; found; ~ 币 coin; specie / ~ 件 cast; casting / ~ 造 casting; founding ❷ make; cause; ~ 成大错 make a grievous mistake

筑(❶築) zhù ❶ build; construct; ~ 路 road-building ❷ zhu, an ancient 13-stringed instrument played with a light bamboo stick; 击 ~ play the *zhu*

(Zhù) another name for Guiyang (贵阳), capital of Guizhou Province

箸(筯) zhù 〈书〉chopsticks

zhuā

抓 zhuā ❶ grab; grasp; seize: ~获 catch; seize; capture / ~权 grab power / ~辫子 seize on sb's fault or error; capitalize on sb's vulnerable point / ~工夫 find time (to do sth) / ~苗头 watch out for the first signs or symptoms of a trend / ~住机遇 seize an opportunity ❷ scratch: ~痒 scratch an itch; relieve the itching ❸ arrest; press-gang: ~兵 press-gang conscripts / ~捕 arrest; catch; apprehend / ~差 press sb into service; get sb to do sth ❹ lay stress on; take charge of: ~人事 be in charge of personnel matters / ~总儿〈口〉assume overall command or responsibility / ~点带面 concentrate on selected units to draw experience for overall work ❺ grip or hold attention: ~住观众 hold the attention of the audience; enthral the audience

抓耳挠腮 zhuā'ěr-náosāi tweak one's ears and scratch one's cheeks: 急得～ scratch one's head out of anxiety

抓紧 zhuājǐn keep a firm grasp on; pay close attention to: ~时间 make the best use of one's time; lose no time (in doing sth)

抓阄儿 zhuājiūr draw or cast lots (to decide sth)

抓瞎 zhuāxiā 〈口〉be at a loss what to do; be in a rush and muddle; be thrown off balance

抓药 zhuāyào（of Chinese herbal medicine) have a prescription filled or made up; (of a pharmacy) fill or make up a prescription

zhuǎ

爪 zhuǎ ❶ claw; talon; paw ❷ foot or base (of certain utensils): 三～儿铁锅 three-footed iron pot
see also zhǎo

zhuāi

拽 zhuāi 〈方〉❶ fling; cast; throw ❷ disabled or injured in the arm
see also zhuài

zhuǎi

转(轉) zhuǎi *also* "转文" 〈方〉talk like a book
see also zhuǎn; zhuàn

跩 zhuǎi 〈方〉waddle: 走路一～一～的 waddle along

zhuài

拽 zhuài pull; drag; haul: ~人的袖子 pull sb by the sleeve *see also* zhuāi

zhuān

专(專) zhuān ❶ concentrate on; specialize in: ~长 special skill; specialized knowledge; expertise / ~场 show of a particular variety or for a special audience; special performance / ~程 (make a) special trip / ~攻 specialize in; be a specialist of / ~人 person specially assigned to a task or job / ~著 monograph; treatise / ~诚拜访 call on or visit (sb) specially / ~款～用 fund to be used for a specified purpose only ❷ monopolize: ~权 monopolize power / ~擅 〈书〉usurp authority; act presumptuously

专案 zhuān'àn special case for investigation；~组 special group for the investigation of a case

专断 zhuānduàn make arbitrary decisions；act peremptorily；~独行 act wilfully on one's own

专横 zhuānhèng tyrannical；imperious；domineering；~跋扈 arrogant and despotic

专家 zhuānjiā expert；specialist；~门诊 outpatient service by specialists

专科 zhuānkē ❶ speciality；special field of study；~医生 (medical) specialist ❷ college for professional training；vocational training school

专栏 zhuānlán special column (in a newspaper, etc)；~作家 columnist

专利 zhuānlì patent；~品 patented product or article；〈喻〉exclusive preserve / ~权 patent (right)

专门 zhuānmén ❶ special；specialized；~机构 special organ；specialized agency / ~人才 people with professional skill；professional talent ❷〈口〉frequently；habitually；~讲风凉话 be given to making sarcastic comments

专名 zhuānmíng （short for 专有名词）〈语言〉proper noun

专题 zhuāntí special subject or topic；~报道 special coverage or report / ~讨论会 seminar

专心 zhuānxīn concentrate on；be engrossed；~致志 single-minded；completely absorbed

专业 zhuānyè ❶ special field of study；specialized subject；discipline；~课 specialized course / ~设置 specialities offered ❷ specialized trade or profession；special vocation or line；~户 household or person specialized in a particular economic undertaking；specialized household / ~技术 professional skill / ~作家 professional writer / ~化程度 level of specialization

专一 zhuānyī concentrating on one

aim or purpose；single-minded：心思~ （give sth) undivided attention

专营 zhuānyíng also "专卖" monopoly；sale through exclusive agencies：盐的~ salt monopoly

专用 zhuānyòng special （purpose)；~列车 special train / ~软件 special-purpose software

专政 zhuānzhèng dictatorship；~对象 object or target of dictatorship / ~机关 organ of dictatorship

专职 zhuānzhí ❶ also "专责" sole duty；specific responsibility ❷ also "专任" full-time；regular；~人员 full-time personnel；regulars

专制 zhuānzhì autocracy；~君主 autocrat / ~政府 autocratic government / ~主义 despotism；authoritarianism

专注 zhuānzhù focus on；be absorbed in；devote oneself to：神情~ with concentrated or rapt attention

砖（磚） zhuān ❶ brick；~坯 unfired brick / ~木结构〈建筑〉post and panel structure ❷ brick-like thing：~茶 brick tea

zhuān

转（轉） zhuǎn ❶ turn；shift；change：~产 （of an enterprise, etc) convert production from one commodity to another；change the line of production / ~车 change buses or trains；transfer to another bus or train / ~会 transfer to another (sports) club / ~学 (of a student) transfer to another school / ~义〈语言〉transferred meaning；figurative sense / ~危为安 turn danger into safety；turn the corner；pull through a crisis / ~战南北 fight north and south ❷ pass on；forward；transfer；~告 pass on a message；convey / ~交 pass on；send (through sb else) / ~述 tell or report sth as told by another；retell /

~载 reprint (sth that has been published elsewhere); carry / ~赠 *also* "转送" make a present of sth given to one / ~租 sublet; sublease

see also zhuǎi; zhuàn

转变 zhuǎnbiàn change; transform; ~态度 change one's attitude or outlook

转播 zhuǎnbō (of radio or TV broadcast) relay (a programme, etc); ~台 relay station

转达 zhuǎndá pass on; convey; forward; ~意见 convey or forward sb's suggestions / ~问候 give (sb) one's regards

转动 zhuǎndòng turn (round and round); move; rotate; ~眼珠 goggle or roll one's eyes *see also* zhuàndòng

转关系 zhuǎnguānxi transfer the registration of (a certain status, etc); 转户口关系 report to the local authorities for change of domicile / 转组织关系 transfer the registration of one's (Party or League) membership (from one unit to another)

转轨 zhuǎnguǐ change the existing structure, etc; make a paradigm shift; ~经济 transition economy / 向技术密集型~ change to technology-intensive production

转化 zhuǎnhuà change; turn; transform; 向有利方面~ change for the better; take a favourable turn / 把坏事~为好事 turn bad into good things; turn bane into boon

转换 zhuǎnhuàn switch; change; convert; ~频道 switch to another channel

转机 zhuǎnjī ❶ turn for the better; favourable turn; turning point ❷ change planes

转基因 zhuǎnjīyīn transgenic; ~技术 transgenic technology / ~食品 genetically-engineered, -modified or -altered food

转嫁 zhuǎnjià shift; transfer; ~罪责 lay the blame on sb else

转口 zhuǎnkǒu transit; ~港 transit port; entrepôt; ~贸易 entrepôt or transit trade

转让 zhuǎnràng transfer (the ownership of sth); make over; 可~票据 transferable instrument

转入 zhuǎnrù change over to; switch or shift to; ~地下 go underground / ~正题 come to the main theme; get down to brass tacks

转身 zhuǎnshēn ❶ (of a person) turn; turn round; face about ❷ *also* "转脸" in no time; in a wink

转手 zhuǎnshǒu ❶ do sth through a third party; (ask sb to) pass on ❷ resell; ~倒卖 resell at a higher price

转瞬 zhuǎnshùn *also* "转眼" in the twinkling of an eye; in a flash; ~即逝 vanish or disappear in a flash

转弯 zhuǎnwān ❶ make a turn; turn; ~抹角 (of a road, etc) be full of twists and turns; zigzag; (of a person) beat about the bush ❷ change one's view or stand

转向 zhuǎnxiàng ❶ change direction; turn; veer; 把脸~观众 turn towards the audience ❷ 〈贬〉change one's political orientation

see also zhuànxiàng

转型 zhuǎnxíng ❶ (of a factory, etc) convert from one type of product to another; change the line of production ❷ fundamental change; transformation; 社会~期 period of social transformation

转业 zhuǎnyè (of military personnel) be transferred to civilian work; be demobilized; ~军人 demobilized serviceman

转移 zhuǎnyí ❶ shift; divert; evacuate; ~视线 distract or divert sb's attention ❷ change; shift; ~话题 shift the conversation to another topic / 不以人的意志为~ independent of man's will

转运 zhuǎnyùn ❶ have a turn or change of luck; luck turns in one's favour ❷ transfer; transport; forward; ～站 transfer or staging post

转账 zhuǎnzhàng transfer accounts: ～结算 transfer and settlement of accounts / ～支票 check only for account

转折 zhuǎnzhé ❶ turn or shift in the course of events; ～点 also "转换点" turning point ❷ transition (of an essay)

转正 zhuǎnzhèng ❶ (of a probationary Party member) become a full member ❷ (of a temporary worker) become a regular worker

zhuàn

传(傳) zhuàn ❶ commentaries on classics ❷ biography; ～略 brief biography; biographical sketch / ～记文学 biographical literature ❸ novel or story written in historical style: 春香～ The Story of Chun Xiang
see also chuán

转(轉) zhuàn ❶ rotate; revolve; spin; ～炉 converter (in steel-making) / ～门 revolving door / ～盘 rotary; roundabout; (US) traffic circle / ～速 rotation speed / ～台 revolving stage; Lazy Susan (on a table) / ～椅 swivel chair; merry-go-round ❷ turn round (sth); move about; 绕着湖～两圈 walk twice round a lake ❸ 〈量〉revolution: 每分钟6000～ 6,000 rpm
see also zhuǎi; zhuǎn

转动 zhuàndòng turn; revolve; rotate: 顺时针方向～ rotate clockwise
see also zhuǎndòng

转弯子 zhuànwānzi beat about the bush; speak in a roundabout way

转向 zhuànxiàng lose one's bearings; get lost; be confused　*see also*

zhuǎnxiàng

转悠 zhuànyou *also* "转游"〈口〉❶ (of eyes, etc) roll; turn; move from side to side ❷ take a leisurely walk; stroll; saunter

唛(囀) zhuàn 〈书〉(of birds) twitter; chirp; sing

赚 zhuàn ❶ make (a profit, etc); gain; earn: ～钱 make money; net a profit / ～外快 moonlight for profit; 没～头儿 unprofitable ❸ profitable; worthwhile
see also zuàn

撰 zhuàn write; compose: ～述 write; compose; writings

篆 zhuàn ❶ (usu 篆书 or 篆字) seal character (ancient style of Chinese calligraphy) ❷ write seal characters ❸ (official, etc) seal: ～刻 seal cutting

馔 zhuàn 〈书〉food: 美～ delicious food; delicacies

zhuāng

妆(妝、粧) zhuāng ❶ make up; wear make-up ❷ woman's personal adornments or ornaments: ～饰 adorn; embellish; dress up ❸ trousseau; dowry: ～奁 dressing case; trousseau; dowry

庄(莊) zhuāng ❶ village: ～户人 peasant; farmer ❷ manor; estate: ～园 manor; estate ❸ place of business: 茶～ tea shop ❹ (in gambling) banker: 做～ be the banker; 〈经〉sway stock prices / ～家 banker (in gambling); 〈经〉investor who tries to sway stock prices ❺ serious; sober; solemn

庄稼 zhuāngjia crops: ～地 crop land; farmland; fields / ～汉 farmer; peasant / ～活儿 farm work

庄严 zhuāngyán solemn; stately: ～宣告 solemnly declare

庄重 zhuāngzhòng serious; grave; solemn: 神色～ wear a solemn expression; look grave

桩(椿) zhuāng ❶ also "桩子" stake; pile; post ❷ 〈量〉一～丑闻 a scandal

装(裝) zhuāng ❶ dress up; deck (out); act: ～殓 dress and lay a corpse in a coffin / ～卖药的 deck oneself out as a medicine pedlar ❷ clothing; dress; stage make-up and costume ❸ pretend; feign; make believe: ～病 malinger; feign illness / ～蒜〈口〉pretend not to know; fake ignorance / ～疯卖傻 feign madness and act like an idiot; play the fool ❹ load; pack; fill: ～船 load a ship / ～货 load cargo / ～箱 pack a box / ～载量 loading capacity ❺ install; fit; assemble: ～电话 have a telephone installed ❻ binding; bookbinding: ～裱 mount (a picture, etc)

装扮 zhuāngbàn ❶ dress up; deck; act: ～入时 be fashionably dressed / ～反面人物 act the part of a villain ❷ disguise; masquerade; pretend: ～成局外人 make believe that one is an outsider

装备 zhuāngbèi equip; furnish; fit out: 先进～ state-of-art equipment / ～精良 well-equipped

装点 zhuāngdiǎn decorate; adorn; deck

装订 zhuāngdìng binding; bookbinding: 皮面～ bound in leather / ～成册 bind in a volume; bind together into book form

装潢 zhuānghuáng mount (a picture, etc); decorate; adorn: ～别致 uniquely decorated / ～门面 also "装门面" put up a façade; do window dressing; keep up appearances

装甲 zhuāngjiǎ armour: ～兵 armoured force or troops / ～车 armoured vehicle

装模作样 zhuāngmú-zuòyàng behave affectedly; put on a show; attitudinize

装配 zhuāngpèi assemble; fit (together): ～线 assembly or assembling line

装腔作势 zhuāngqiāng-zuòshì strike a pose; be affected or pretentious

装饰 zhuāngshì decorate; adorn; ornament: ～品 ornament; decoration / ～艺术 decorative art

装束 zhuāngshù ❶ dress; clothes; attire: ～大方 be tastefully attired ❷ 〈书〉pack for a journey: ～停当 be packed

装修 zhuāngxiū fix up; fit up (a house, etc): 室内～ interior decorating

装帧 zhuāngzhēn binding and layout (of a book, etc): ～新颖 distinctively bound

装置 zhuāngzhì install; equip; fit: 自动化～ automatic device / ～天线 install an antenna

zhuǎng

奘 zhuǎng 〈方〉big and thick; stout; robust

zhuàng

壮(壯) zhuàng ❶ strong; robust: ～健 healthy and strong; robust / ～劳力 able-bodied adult or labourer ❷ magnificent; splendid; grand: ～举 magnificent feat; great exploit or undertaking ❸ strengthen; improve; make better: ～胆 boost sb's courage; embolden / ～门面 lend impressiveness or grandeur (to a scene); add or lend lustre (to sth) ❹ (Zhuàng) (usu 壮族) Zhuang ethnic group, distributed over Guangxi, Yunnan and Guangdong

壮大 zhuàngdà ❶ become or make strong; strengthen; expand: ～经济实

力 increase or enhance economic power ❷ strong; robust

壮丁 zhuàngdīng 〈旧〉 able-bodied man (subject to conscription): 抓～ press-gang conscripts

壮工 zhuànggōng unskilled labourer

壮观 zhuàngguān magnificent sight; grand spectacle

壮阔 zhuàngkuò immense; magnificent; grand: 规模～ of grand scale

壮丽 zhuànglì magnificent; splendid; glorious: ～的诗篇 splendid poem / ～的事业 glorious undertaking

壮烈 zhuàngliè heroic; brave and noble-minded: ～牺牲 die a hero's death; die a martyr

壮年 zhuàngnián one's thirties or forties: 正当～ be in the prime of life

壮士 zhuàngshì heroic man; hero; warrior: ～断腕 behave like a warrior cutting off his own wrist (to save the arm); cut one's losses determinedly

壮实 zhuàngshi strong and vigorous; sturdy; robust: ～得像头牛 be as strong as a horse

壮行 zhuàngxíng enable (sb) to depart in style; give (sb) a big send-off

壮志 zhuàngzhì noble ideals; high aspirations: ～凌云 have lofty or soaring aspirations

状（狀） zhuàng ❶ shape; form; appearance: 呈衰老～ look old and feeble ❷ state of affairs; condition ❸ account; written complaint; lawsuit: ～纸 official form for filing a complaint / ～子 written complaint; indictment ❹ certificate

状况 zhuàngkuàng condition; situation; state (of affairs): 生活～ living conditions

状态 zhuàngtài state; condition: 最佳～ best condition; top form

状语 zhuàngyǔ 〈语言〉 adverbial (modifier)

状元 zhuàngyuán ❶ Number One Scholar, candidate who came out first in the highest imperial examination ❷ very best (in any field); top-notch: 高考～ number one in the college-entrance examinations

撞 zhuàng ❶ strike; knock down; collide: ～钟 strike a bell / 汽车～人了。A car knocked somebody down. ❷ (usu 撞见) meet by chance; run or bump into; come across ❸ probe; try: ～运气 try one's luck ❹ barge; dash; rush

撞车 zhuàngchē ❶ collision of vehicles ❷ clash; contradict: 两个会～了。The two meetings clash in timing.

撞击 zhuàngjī collide; strike; dash against: 新旧观念的～ clash between old and new ideas

幢 zhuàng 〈方〉〈量〉 used of buildings: 一～五层楼房 a five-storeyed building

戆 zhuàng (usu 戆直)〈书〉 blunt and tactless; simple and honest
see also gàng

zhuī

追 zhuī ❶ chase; pursue; run or go after: pursue and capture - ～风〈喻〉follow the fashion or trend / ～星族 star chaser; groupie / ～名逐利 seek fame and wealth ❷ trace; look into; try to find out: *see also* "追还" recover (lost property, etc) / ～缴 cause to disgorge (loot, etc); recover / ～问 question closely; examine minutely / ～债 press for or demand payment of a debt ❸ bring back to mind; recall: ～思 recall; reminisce; look back on ❹ after the event; retroactively; posthumously: ～记 award or cite posthumously / ～授 confer or award (a title, etc) posthumously

追查 zhuīchá investigate; find out;

追悼 zhuīdào　mourn over（sb's death）；～会 memorial meeting

追赶 zhuīgǎn　run after；chase；pursue：～世界先进水平 try to catch up with the world advanced level

追悔 zhuīhuǐ　repentance；regret；remorse：～莫及 it is too late to repent；（of sb）show tardy repentance

追击 zhuījī　pursue and attack；follow up：乘胜～ follow up a victory with hot pursuit

追加 zhuījiā　add to（the original amount）；supplement：～经费（allocate）additional funds / ～预算（make a）supplementary budget

追究 zhuījiū　look into；find out；get to the root of（a matter, etc）：～责任 ascertain responsibility（for an accident, etc）；prosecute（sb）for his or her liability / 追根究底 get to the bottom（of sth）；go into the whys and wherefores

追求 zhuīqiú　❶ seek（truth, etc）；pursue；go after ❷ woo（a girl, etc）；court；run after

追认 zhuīrèn　❶ subsequently confirm or endorse；recognize retroactively ❷ admit or confer after death：被～为中共党员 be posthumously admitted as a member of the CPC

追溯 zhuīsù　trace back to；date from：追本溯源 trace（sth）back to the source；get at the root（of sth）

追随 zhuīsuí　follow；adhere to：～者 follower；adherent / ～左右 follow（sb）closely；be a close follower

追叙 zhuīxù　tell about the past；recount or narrate what happened earlier；flashback

追忆 zhuīyì　call（past memories, etc）to mind；recall；look back

追逐 zhuīzhú　❶ chase；pursue：～嬉戏 have fun chasing one another ❷ seek；quest；go after：追名逐利 hanker after fame and gain

追踪 zhuīzōng　track（escaped criminal, etc）；trace；trail：～报道 follow-up report

椎 zhuī　also "椎骨"〈生理〉vertebra

锥 zhuī　❶ awl；awl-like thing；cone ❷ bore；drill：～个眼儿 make a hole with an awl

zhuì

坠（墜）zhuì　❶ fall；tumble；drop：～毁 fall and smash；（of a plane, etc）crash / ～落（of sth heavy）fall；drop ❷ weigh down；droop ❸ also "坠子" weight；hanging object：耳～ ear pendant

缀 zhuì　❶ sew；stitch：～上几针 put in a few stitches ❷ put（words）together；compose；write：～辑 edit；compile ❸ adorn；decorate：～满繁星的天空 star-studded sky

惴 zhuì　〈书〉be anxious and afraid：～～不安 anxious and fearful；alarmed and on tenterhooks；ill at ease

缒 zhuì　let down（with a rope）

赘 zhuì　superfluous；redundant；repetitious：～述 give unnecessary details；be repetitious

赘言 zhuìyán　❶ say more than is needed；be superfluous ❷ also "赘词" superfluous words

赘疣 zhuìyóu　also "赘瘤"；"瘊子" ❶ wart ❷ anything superfluous or useless；superfluity

zhūn

肫 zhūn　gizzard（of a fowl）

谆 zhūn　sincerely；earnestly and tirelessly：～～教诲 instruct earnestly / ～～善诱 teach and guide untiringly

zhǔn

准(**②⑥準**)　zhǔn ❶ allow; permit; grant; ～假一个月 grant (sb) a month's leave ❷ standard; criterion; yardstick: ～绳 criterion; norm; yardstick ❸ in line with; follow: ～此办理 handle (sth) in the same manner ❹ accurate; exact; precise: ～点 on the dot; on time / ～话 *also* "准信" definite information; exact commitment / ～时 punctual; on time; on schedule ～谱儿 certainty; sure thing ❺ definitely; surely; certainly: 这办法一行。This will definitely work. ❻ quasi-; para-: ～将 (in certain foreign armies) brigadier (general); (in navies) commodore / ～尉 warrant officer / ～军事组织 paramilitary organization

准保 zhǔnbǎo　*also* "准定" certainly; undoubtedly; for sure: ～不行 certainly won't do / ～按时送到 guarantee delivery on time

准备 zhǔnbèi ❶ prepare; get ready: 作两手～ prepare for both eventualities / ～活动〈体〉warming-up or limbering-up (exercise) ❷ think (of doing); intend (to do); plan

准确 zhǔnquè　accurate; precise; exact: ～无误 with unerring accuracy; exactly right

准儿 zhǔnr　〈口〉certain; sure; positive: 心里有～ feel sure; know what one is doing / 没～ 他今天不来了。Perhaps he won't come today.

准头 zhǔntou　〈口〉accuracy; precision: 有～ be accurate or reliable

准星 zhǔnxīng ❶ zero point on a steelyard; 〈喻〉definite idea or norm: 他说话没～。His words are not reliable. ❷ front sight (of a gun)

准许 zhǔnxǔ　grant (a request, etc);

allow; permit

准予 zhǔnyǔ　(as in a document) grant; approve; allow: ～放行 allow (sb or sth) to pass

准则 zhǔnzé　norm; standard; code: 道德～ moral code; morality

zhuō

拙　zhuō ❶ clumsy; awkward: ～劣 clumsy and inferior; poor ❷ 〈谦〉my: ～见 my (humble) opinion / ～荆〈书〉my wife

捉　zhuō ❶ clutch; hold firmly; grab: ～笔 hold or wield a pen ❷ catch; seize; capture: ～奸 catch adulterers in the act

捉刀 zhuōdāo　ghostwrite (for sb): ～人 ghostwriter

捉襟见肘 zhuōjīnjiànzhǒu　have too many difficulties to cope with; in straitened circumstances: 入不敷出，～ be hard put to it to make both ends meet

捉迷藏 zhuōmícáng ❶ (play) hide-and-seek; blind-man's bluff ❷ 〈喻〉play hide-and-seek; beat about the bush; hedge

捉摸 zhuōmō　ascertain; conjecture; fathom: 难以～ difficult to fathom; unpredictable; elusive

捉拿 zhuōná　arrest; apprehend; catch: ～归案 bring to justice

捉弄 zhuōnòng　tease; make fun of; play pranks on

桌　zhuō ❶ table; desk: ～布 tablecloth / 摆到～面儿上来 put (all the cards) on the table; bring (problems) out into the open ❷ 〈量〉*of a feast, etc*: 五～客人 five tables of guests

zhuó

灼　zhuó ❶ burn; sear; scorch: ～热 scorching hot; 〈喻〉passionate;

fervent ❷ bright; shining; luminous; ~见 penetrating insight; profound idea

苗 zhuó

苗壮 zhuózhuàng　vigorous; sturdy; ~成长 grow healthily and vigorously

卓 zhuó

❶ tall and upright; ~立 stand upright or erect ❷ remarkable; outstanding; eminent; ~见 excellent view; brilliant idea / ~然不同 standing; remarkable / ~识 outstanding insight; wise judgement; vision / ~尔不群 stand head and shoulders above others; be pre-eminent or outstanding

卓绝 zhuójué　unsurpassed; of the highest degree; 英勇~ extremely brave

卓有成效 zhuóyǒuchéngxiào　highly effective; very fruitful or successful.

卓越 zhuóyuè　outstanding; remarkable; brilliant

卓著 zhuózhù　distinguished (service, etc); illustrious (exploits, etc); eminent

斫 zhuó　〈书〉chop; hack; cut

浊(濁) zhuó

❶ muddy; murky; turbid; ~流 muddy stream;〈喻〉forces of darkness and decadence ❷ (of voices) deep and thick; ~音 voiced sound ❸ chaotic; confused; disorderly; ~世〈书〉corrupted world; turbulent times;〈宗教〉mortal world

酌 zhuó

❶ pour out (wine); drink; 自斟自~ drink alone; enjoy a glass of wine by oneself ❷ 〈书〉meal with wine or spirits; 小~ light meal ❸ weigh and consider; mull over; ~办 do as one thinks fit; act according to one's judgement / ~定 make a decision as one sees fit; use one's discretion

酌量 zhuóliáng　give due consideration; use one's judgement; ~购买 buy at one's discretion

酌情 zhuóqíng　take into consideration the circumstances; use one's discretion; ~处理 settle a matter as one sees fit; deal with matters on the merits of each case

啄 zhuó　peck; ~木鸟 woodpecker

着 zhuó

❶ wear (clothes); be dressed; ~装 put on (clothes, headgear, etc); dress ❷ touch; contact; ~陆 (of a plane, etc) land; touch down ❸ attach; apply; use; ~笔 set pen to paper; begin to write or paint / ~色 apply colour; colour ❹ whereabouts; assured source; 衣食无~ have nothing to eat or wear ❺ send; dispatch; ~人前去 send sb there ❻ 〈旧〉used in documents, indicating an imperative tone of voice; ~即缉拿凶手。The criminal must be brought to justice immediately.

see also zhāo; zháo; zhe

着力 zhuólì　make an effort; exert oneself; ~描写 take great pains to describe; concentrate one's efforts on depicting

着落 zhuóluò　whereabouts; assured source

着墨 zhuómò　describe in writing; paint; ~不多 be only sketchily depicted

着实 zhuóshí ❶ indeed; really; truly; ~难办 truly hard to do; a real hard nut to crack ❷ sharply; severely; ~数落了他一顿 give him a good scolding

着手 zhuóshǒu　put one's hand to; set about; begin; 从调查事实~ start with finding out the facts

着想 zhuóxiǎng　consider; think about; 从长远利益~ for the sake of long-term interests

着眼 zhuóyǎn　view from the angle of; have in mind; take as the basis; ~点 focus of attention; point of departure / ~于未来 have one's eyes on the future

着意 zhuóyì ❶ exert oneself; strive;

~准备 take great pains with the preparation ❷ take seriously; mind

着重 zhuózhòng　stress; emphasize; underline; ~号 mark of emphasis / ~解决住房问题 make a special effort to solve the housing problem

琢 zhuó　chisel; cut; carve　*see also* zuó

琢磨 zhuómó　❶ carve and polish (jade, etc) ❷ (of literary works) polish; refine
see also zuómó

擢 zhuó　〈书〉❶ pull out; extract; ~发难数 countless; innumerable ❷ (usu 擢升) advance in rank; raise; promote

濯 zhuó　〈书〉wash

濯濯 zhuózhuó　〈书〉(of mountains) bare; bald; denuded; 童山~ bare hills

镯 zhuó　(usu 镯子) bracelet

zī

吱(嗞) zī　〈象声〉(of small animals) squeak; (of small birds) chirp; cheep; ~声〈方〉utter a sound; speak　*see also* zhī

孜 zī

孜孜 zīzī　*also* "孳孳" diligent; industrious; hardworking; ~不倦 tireless; indefatigable

咨(❶諮) zī　❶ consult; seek advice; take counsel ❷ (usu 咨文) report delivered by head of government on state affairs

咨询 zīxún　consult; seek advice (from); hold counsel (with); 提供法律~ provide legal advice / ~服务 consulting service / ~公司 consultancy (company)

姿 zī　❶ looks; countenance; appearance; ~容 looks; appear-

ance / ~色 (of a woman) good looks ❷ gesture; carriage; posture; 坐~ (in a) sitting posture

姿势 zīshì　gesture; posture; carriage; ~优美 carry oneself gracefully / 摆好~拍照 pose for a photo

姿态 zītài　❶ posture; bearing; deportment ❷ attitude; pose; gesture; 做出~ make a gesture; strike a pose

兹 zī　❶ this; ~事体大 This is no small matter. ❷ now; at present; ~公布名单如下。Below is the list.

赀 zī　❶ *also* "訾" (usu in the negative) reckon; calculate; estimate; 所费不~ incur a considerable expense ❷ *see* "资❶"

资 zī　❶ asset; money; expense; ~财 capital and goods; assets / ~不抵债 unable to pay one's debt with all one's assets; insolvent / ~方 与劳方 capital and labour ❷ provide; supply; support; ~敌 aid or support the enemy / 以~借鉴 serve as an example ❸ *also* "资质" natural ability; endowment; aptitude ❹ qualifications; seniority; record of service; ~望 seniority and prestige / ~深教授 senior professor

资本 zīběn　❶ capital; ~家 capitalist / ~市场 capital market / ~项目 capital account / ~主义 capitalism / ~密集型 capital-intensive ❷ sth to capitalize on; capital; 讨价还价的~ bargaining chip or counter

资产 zīchǎn　❶ property; estate; capital; ~阶级 capitalist (class); bourgeoisie ❷〈经〉assets; ~重组 reorganization of assets / ~负债表 statement of assets and liabilities; balance sheet / 国有~流失 loss of state property or assets

资格 zīgé　❶ qualifications; 取消~ disqualify (sb from sth) / ~赛〈体〉qualification match; qualifier / ~审查

委员会 credentials committee ❷ seniority: 老~的政治家 senior or veteran statesman

资金 zījīn　fund; capital: ~流动 cash flow; flow of capital

资历 zīlì　qualifications; record of service; seniority: ~浅 lacking in qualifications and experience; junior

资料 zīliào　❶ means: 劳动~ means of labour ❷ data; material; information: ~室 reference room / ~处理 data processing

资信 zīxìn　credit: ~等级 credit rating / ~可靠 creditworthy / ~评估 credit evaluation

资讯 zīxùn　〈方〉information; data *see also* "信息" xìnxī

资源 zīyuán　(natural) resources: ~丰富 rich in resources

资助 zīzhù　aid financially; sponsor: ~者 sponsor / 寻求~ solicit financial aid; seek sponsors

辐

辐重 zīzhòng　〈军〉impedimenta; baggage and other supplies of an army

孳

zī (usu 孳生) multiply; propagate; breed

滋

zī　❶ grow; multiply; breed: ~蔓〈书〉(of weeds or evils) grow and spread / ~事 make trouble; provoke a dispute ❷ increase; become more: 贪取~甚 be more corrupt and greedy than ever ❸〈方〉spurt (water, etc); spout; burst

滋补 zībǔ　nourishing; nutritious: ~身体 build up one's health

滋扰 zīrǎo　harass; stir up trouble

滋润 zīrùn　❶ moist; humid ❷ moisten; nourish: ~皮肤 nourish skin ❸〈方〉happy and comfortable

滋生 zīshēng　❶ also "孳生" breed; propagate; multiply ❷ bring; cause; create: ~事端 stir up or create trouble; raise a disturbance

滋味 zīwèi　taste; savour; flavour: 心中不是~ feel upset or bad / 品尝菜看的~ taste or sample a dish

滋养 zīyǎng　❶ nourish: ~品 nourishing food; nutriment; nourishment ❷ nutriment; nourishment

滋长 zīzhǎng　grow; develop; engender: ~骄傲情绪 become conceited

赵

赵趄 zījū　〈书〉❶ walk with difficulty; lumber along ❷ hesitate to advance; falter: ~不前 hesitate to act; hang back

锱

锱铢必较 zīzhūbìjiào　haggle over every penny; dispute over trivialities

龇

zī〈口〉bare; show: ~牙咧嘴 bare one's teeth; look ferocious; contort one's face in pain

髭

zī moustache: ~须 moustache; whiskers

zǐ

子

zǐ　❶ son; child; progeny: ~女 sons and daughters; children / ~嗣 also "子息" son; male offspring ❷ person: 士~ scholar ❸ title of respect for a man, esp one that founds a school of thought: 孔~ Confucius ❹ (in ancient times) you ❺ *see* "籽" zǐ ❻ egg: 下~儿 lay eggs ❼ *see* "仔" zǐ ❽ subsidiary; subordinate; derivative: ~金 interest (derived from principal) / ~公司 sub-company; subsidiary ❾ sth small and hard; small coin: 石头~儿 small stone; pebble ❿ 1st of the Earthly Branches *see also* "干支" gānzhī ⓫ (usu 子时) period of the day from 11 p.m. to 1 a.m.: ~夜 midnight ⓬ (usu 子爵) viscount ⓭〈量〉一~挂面 a bundle of fine dried noodles / 一~毛线 a hank of knitting wool ⓮ (zi) used after a noun, adjective or verb to make a noun: 矮～ short person; shorty; dwarf ⓑ（zi）used after a classifier as a suffix: 敲了几下～门 give a few knocks at the door

子弹 zǐdàn bullet; cartridge: ～带 cartridge belt; bandoleer

子弟 zǐdì younger generation; children: ～兵 the people's own army / ～学校（affiliated to a factory, etc）school for children of the staff

子宫 zǐgōng 〈生理〉uterus; womb: ～颈 cervix (of womb)

子孙 zǐsūn children and children's children; descendants: ～后代 descendants; posterity / ～满堂（have a）family of many children

子午线 zǐwǔxiàn meridian (line): 本初～ prime meridian

子虚乌有 zǐxū-wūyǒu groundless; fictitious; non-existent: 纯属～ pure fiction

仔 zǐ also "子"（usu of domestic animals or fowl）young; small; tender: ～畜 young or newborn animal / ～鸡 chick see also zǎi

仔细 zǐxì also "子细" ❶ careful; meticulous; attentive: ～查 (make a) look or watch out; take care: ～小偷儿! Look out for pickpockets! ❸〈方〉frugal; thrifty; economical: 日子过得～ be frugal of one's expenses; live frugally

姊 zǐ（elder）sister: ～妹（elder and younger）sisters

籽 zǐ also "子" seed: ～粒〈农〉seed; grain; kernel / ～棉 unginned cotton / 结～儿 bear seed; go to seed

梓 zǐ ❶〈植〉Chinese catalpa: ～里〈书〉hometown; native place ❷ cut blocks for printing: 付～ send to the printers

紫 zǐ purple; violet; dark red: ～菜〈植〉laver / ～红 purplish red / ～檀〈植〉red sandalwood; padauk / ～竹 also "黑竹"〈植〉black bamboo / ～禁城 Forbidden City (in Beijing) / ～荆花 bauhinia / ～罗兰〈植〉violet / ～砂壶 boccaro teapot / ～外线 also "紫外光"〈理〉ultraviolet ray / ～药水 also "龙胆紫" gentian violet / ～云英 also "红花草"〈植〉Chinese milk vetch

訾 zǐ〈书〉slander; smear; calumniate: ～毁 vilify; defame / ～议 find fault with; disparage

滓 zǐ sediment; dregs; lees

zì

自 zì ❶ self; oneself; one's own: ～爱（proper）respect for oneself; self-respect / ～查（make a）self-examination / ～嘲 laugh at oneself; self-ridicule / ～称 style oneself; claim to be; profess / ～焚 burn oneself to death; self-immolation / ～馁 lose heart or confidence; be disheartened or discouraged / ～谦 modest; self-effacing /～述 give an account of oneself / ～习（of students）study by oneself / ～缢 also "自经"〈书〉hang oneself / ～鸣钟 chime clock / ～产—销 produce and market on one's own; market one's own products / ～来水笔 fountain pen / ～谋出路 find one's own means of livelihood; search for a job or solution oneself / ～强不息 strive unceasingly to become stronger; work hard to improve oneself / ～取灭亡 court or invite destruction; work for one's own doom / ～认晦气 look upon bad luck with resignation; grin and bear it / ～视过高 think too highly of oneself; be self-important / ～讨苦吃 bring trouble upon oneself / ～寻烦恼 torture oneself with unpleasant thoughts; worry oneself for no reason at all / ～言～语 speak one's thoughts aloud; think aloud ❷ naturally; cer tainly; as a matter of course; ~不待言 it goes without saying; be self-evident ❸ from; since; ~小 also "自幼" from childhood; as a child / ~古以来 from time immemorial; since ancient times / ~上而下 from top to bottom; from above / ~始至终 from beginning to end; from start to finish; all through

自拔 zìbá rid oneself (of pain or evil-doing); free or extricate oneself

自白 zìbái ❶ make clear one's meaning or position; vindicate oneself ❷ also "自供" confession; ~书 also "自供状" written confession

自暴自弃 zìbào-zìqì give oneself up for lost; abandon oneself as hopeless

自卑 zìbēi feel inferior (to others); look down upon oneself; ~感 sense of inferiority; inferiority complex

自惭形秽 zìcánxínghuì have a sense of inferiority or inadequacy; feel ashamed of one's unworthiness; feel small

自成一家 zìchéngyìjiā also "自成一体" (as in art and literature) have a style of one's own; be unique in one's style

自吹自擂 zìchuī-zìléi blow one's own trumpet; brag

自从 zìcóng also "自打" since; ~五月以来 since May

自大 zìdà self-important; arrogant; conceited; ~狂 megalomania / 自高~ arrogant; conceited; full of vainglory

自得 zìdé ❶ enjoy or appreciate in one's own way; ~其乐 enjoy (sth) in one's own way; be happy and content with one's lot ❷ self-satisfied; complacent; contented; 洋洋~ complacent; smug

自动 zìdòng ❶ voluntary; of one's own accord; ~离职 quit a job without permission; take French leave ❷ automatic; automated; ~化 automation / ~步枪 automatic rifle / ~扶梯 escal-

ator / ~铅笔 propelling pencil / ~柜员机 also "自动取款机" ATM; automated teller (machine) / ~生产线 automated production line / ~售货机 vending machine / ~寻的导弹 homing missile

自发 zìfā spontaneous; ~性 spontaneity / ~性罢工 wildcat strike

自费 zìfèi at one's own expense; ~生 self-funded or self-financed student / ~留学 study abroad at one's own expense

自负 zìfù ❶ hold oneself responsible; ~盈亏 (of an enterprise) assume sole responsibility for profits and losses; be held economically responsible ❷ be conceited; be puffed up; pride oneself (on sth)

自告奋勇 zìgàofènyǒng volunteer to undertake (a difficult task); offer to do (sth difficult)

自顾不暇 zìgùbùxiá be unable even to shift for oneself (much less look after others); have trouble even in taking care of oneself

自豪 zìháo be proud of; take pride in; ~感 sense of pride

自己 zìjǐ ❶ oneself; ~跟~过不去 (too) hard on oneself ❷ related to oneself; one's own; ~人 one of us; people of one's own circle

自给 zìjǐ self-sufficient; self-supporting; self-contained; ~率 degree of self-sufficiency / ~自足 self-sufficiency; autarky

自尽 zìjìn commit suicide; kill oneself; take one's own life

自疚 zìjiù guilty conscience; compunction; 深感~ have a bad conscience; feel compunctious

自居 zìjū 〈贬〉 consider oneself to be; call oneself; pose as; 以老资格~ flaunt one's seniority

自决 zìjué make one's own decision; determine for oneself; 民族~权 right

Z

自觉 zìjué ❶ realize; be aware of: ～理亏 know where one is in the wrong ❷ on one's own initiative; consciously: ～性 (political) consciousness; readiness (to do one's duty, etc) / ～自愿 of one's own volition; voluntarily; willingly

自愧不如 zìkuìbùrú also "自愧弗如" feel inadequate; be ashamed of one's inferiority

自来水 zìláishuǐ running or tap water: ～厂 waterworks

自理 zìlǐ ❶ provide for oneself: 费用～ pay one's own expenses ❷ take care of oneself

自力更生 zìlìgēngshēng depend on oneself; rely on one's own efforts: ～，艰苦奋斗 self-reliance and hard work

自立 zìlì stand on one's own feet; earn one's own bread; be self-supporting: ～门户 live apart from one's family; break away from (a larger group, etc); become independent

自量 zìliàng (properly) rate one's own ability or strength: 自不量力 overestimate one's strength; overrate oneself

自流 zìliú ❶ (of water, etc) flow spontaneously or by itself: ～井 artesian well / ～排水 free-draining ❷ drift along; run or take its course; (of a person) do as one pleases

自律 zìlǜ 〈书〉self-discipline: ～甚严 be very strict with oneself; be highly self-disciplined

自满 zìmǎn self-satisfied; smug; complacent

自鸣得意 zìmíngdéyì be very pleased with oneself; feel smug (about oneself); preen oneself

自命 zìmìng claim; consider oneself; regard oneself as: ～不凡 consider oneself head and shoulders above the ordinary run; think no end of oneself; be self-important

自欺欺人 zìqīqīrén deceive oneself as well as others; practise self-deception

自然 zìrán ❶ natural world; nature: ～界 natural world; nature / ～规律 natural law; law of nature / ～科学 natural science ❷ natural; in the natural course of events; ～而然 naturally; spontaneously; of oneself / ～经济 natural economy / ～死亡 natural death ❸ of course; certainly; naturally ❹ (zìran) at ease; unaffected; natural

自如 zìrú 〈书〉smoothly; freely; with ease: 行动～ move about freely

自若 zìruò 〈书〉self-possessed; composed; calm and at ease

自杀 zìshā commit suicide; kill oneself: ～爆炸 suicide bombing

自身 zìshēn one's own; oneself: ～难保 cannot even protect oneself

自生自灭 zìshēng-zìmiè (of sth) emerge of itself and perish of itself; take its course

自食 zìshí used in certain idioms: ～其果 eat one's own bitter fruit; reap what one has sown / ～其力 earn one's own living; live on one's own toil / ～其言 go back on one's own word; break one's word

自恃 zìshì 〈书〉❶ over-confident and complacent ❷ rely, count or depend on: ～有后台 rely on sb's backing; count on one's powerful connections

自首 zìshǒu ❶ (of a criminal) surrender oneself; give oneself up ❷ make a political recantation; capitulate to the enemy: ～变节分子 renegade; turncoat

自私 zìsī egoistic; selfish; self-centred: ～自利 selfish; egoistic

自卫 zìwèi defending oneself; self-defence: 奋起～ rise in self-defence / ～能力 capacity to defend oneself

自刎 zìwěn also "自刭" cut one's throat; commit suicide thus

自我 zìwǒ self; oneself: ～介绍 self-introduction / ～批评 self-criticism /

～欣赏 self-admiration; narcissism

自相 zìxiāng each other; to oneself: **～残杀** seek to destroy each other; dog eats dog / **～矛盾** contradict oneself; be self-contradictory ·

自新 zìxīn turn over a new leaf; make a fresh start; begin life anew

自信 zìxìn be self-confident: **过于～** be overconfident; be cocksure / **缺乏～** lack self-confidence; be diffident

自行 zìxíng ❶ by oneself: **～其是** act as one thinks fit; go one's own way ❷ of oneself; of one's own accord or free will: **～消失** disappear of itself

自行车 zìxíngchē bicycle; bike; **～赛** cycle racing; cycling

自诩 zìxǔ 〈书〉praise oneself; boast; brag

自选 zìxuǎn ❶〈体〉free; optional: **～动作** optional exercise ❷ (of a store, etc) self-service: **～商场** self-service market; supermarket

自学 zìxué study on one's own; teach oneself: **～成才** become educated through self-study; be self-taught / **～考试** self-study examination

自以为是 zìyǐwéishì consider oneself always in the right; be cocksure and impervious to criticism; be opinionated

自由 zìyóu ❶ freedom; liberty: **个人～** personal freedom; individual freedom ❷ free; unrestricted; unrestrained: **～港** free (trade) port / **～化** liberalization / **～诗** free verse / **～泳** freestyle; crawl / **～泛滥** (of sth bad) spread unchecked; run wild; run rampant / **～放任** let things go their own way; allow unrestrained freedom; laissez-faire / **～恋爱** free choice of marriage partner; free courtship / **～散漫** lax in discipline; slack / **～体操** floor exercise; callisthenics / **～主义** liberalism; indiscipline; lack of principle / **～职业者** professional / **～撰稿人** freelance

自圆其说 zìyuánqíshuō make one's statement sound plausible; justify oneself

自怨自艾 zìyuàn-zìyì be full of remorse and self-reproach

自愿 zìyuàn of one's own free will; voluntarily: **～退出** opt out / **～互利** voluntary participation and mutual benefit

自在 zìzài ❶ free; untrammeled; unrestrained: **自由～** leisurely and carefree; happy-go-lucky; free and easy ❷ (zizai) comfortable; at ease: **很不～** rather ill at ease

自知之明 zìzhīzhīmíng self-knowledge; wisdom of knowing one's own limitations: **人贵有～.** A man's virtue lies in taking a proper measure of himself.

自治 zìzhì autonomy; self-government: **～区** autonomous region / **～权** (right to) autonomy

自制 zìzhì ❶ made by oneself; self-made ❷ control or constrain oneself: **～力** self-control; self-restraint

自重 zìzhòng ❶ behave with dignity: **请～!** Mind your conduct, please! ❷〈书〉enhance one's influence or position: **拥兵～** extend one's influence with military power ❸ (as of a vehicle) dead weight

自主 zìzhǔ decide for oneself; keep the initiative in one's own hands: **～权** power to make one's own decisions; decision-making or autonomous power / **～经营** have full authority for management

自助 zìzhù self-service: **～餐** buffet (meal) / **～餐厅** buffet (restaurant) / **～商店** self-service shop

自传 zìzhuàn autobiography: **～体小说** autobiographical novel

自转 zìzhuàn 〈天文〉rotation (of the earth, etc)

自尊 zìzūn respect or esteem oneself: **～心** (sense of) self-respect; self-

Z

esteem

自作 zìzuò ❶ fancy or imagine oneself to be：～聪明 fancy oneself smart；think oneself clever ❷ do sth (by) oneself：～主张 act on one's own；make a decision without approval／～自受 suffer the consequence of what one does；lie in the bed one has made；stew in one's own juice

字 zì ❶ word；character：～典 dictionary；lexicon／～条 brief note／～珠玑 every word a gem；exquisite writing ❷ pronunciation (of a word or character)：～正腔圆 (as of opera singers) pronounce every word correctly and in a sweet, mellow voice；be perfect in articulation ❸ form of a written or printed character；style of handwriting：～帖 copybook (for calligraphy)；models of calligraphy ❹ script；writing；calligraphy：～画 calligraphy and painting ❺ receipt；voucher；written pledge：～据 written pledge such as receipt, IOU, contract, etc ❻ another name derived from the meaning of one's original name：杜甫～子美。Du Fu styled himself Zimei. ❼〈俗〉number shown on an electric meter, water meter, etc ❽〈书〉(of a girl) be betrothed or engaged：未～ not yet betrothed

字调 zìdiào also "声调"〈语言〉tones of Chinese characters see also "四声" sìshēng

字符 zìfú 〈信息〉character：～串 character string／～识别 character reading or recognition

字号 zìhao (name of a) shop：京城的老～ old, reputable shop in the capital

字迹 zìjì handwriting；writing：～潦草 sloppy handwriting

字节 zìjié 〈信息〉byte：兆～ megabyte

字句 zìjù words and expressions；writing：～不通 ungrammatical and in-

coherent writing／字斟句酌 pick one's words with great care；weigh every word

字里行间 zìlǐ-hángjiān (read) between the lines；(show) by implication

字面 zìmiàn literal：～上的解释 literal interpretation

字母 zìmǔ letters of an alphabet；letter：～表 alphabet／按～顺序排列 be in alphabetical order；be arranged alphabetically

字幕 zìmù captions (of films) etc；subtitles

字体 zìtǐ ❶ typeface；script ❷ style of calligraphy ❸ handwriting；writing：～工整 neat handwriting

字眼 zìyǎn turn of expression；wording；diction：抠～儿 find fault with the wording；be word-catching or -splitting

字纸篓 zìzhǐlǒu wastepaper basket

恣 zì be self-indulgent；throw off all restraint：～睢〈书〉reckless；wanton；unbridled／～情享乐 indulge oneself as much as one likes；enjoy to one's heart's content

恣肆 zìsì 〈书〉❶ unrestrained；wilful；self-indulgent：骄横～ arrogant and wilful ❷ (of speech, etc) forceful and unrestrained；free and natural

恣意 zìyì wanton；unbridled；wilful：～妄为 behave unscrupulously；act wilfully

渍 zì ❶ soak；steep；ret：汗水把白衬衣～黄了。The white shirt has yellowed with sweat. ❷ (usu 渍涝) floodwater on low-lying land；water-logging ❸ be soiled or stained：油～ sludge；grease

zōng

宗 zōng ❶ ancestry：～庙 ancestral temple or shrine of a ruling house／～谱 family tree；genealogy ❷ clan：～室 imperial or royal clan／～族

patriarchal clan; clansman ❸ faction; sect; school; ~匠 great master (of an academic school, etc) ❹ hold in esteem; model (one's work) on; follow; ~仰〈书〉hold in esteem; revere ❺ aim; purpose; objective: 万变不离其 ~ remain essentially the same despite all apparent changes ❻〈量〉大 ~ 贷 款 a large loan / 一 ~ 刑事案件 a criminal case

宗法 zōngfǎ ❶ (patriarchal) clan rules and regulations: ~ 制度 patriarchal clan system ❷ follow; model on; take as example

宗教 zōngjiào religion: 笃信 ~ be profoundly religious / ~ 信仰 religious belief

宗派 zōngpài faction; sect: ~ 斗争 factional strife / ~ 主义 sectarianism

宗师 zōngshī master of great learning and integrity

宗旨 zōngzhǐ aim; purpose: 以振兴 教育为 ~ aim at vitalizing education

综 zōng sum up; put together; combine: ~ 计 sum or add up / ~ 观全局 size up the overall situation / ~ 上所述 to sum up; to put it in a nutshell / 新闻 ~ 述 news roundup or wrap-up

综合 zōnghé ❶ synthesize; summarize ❷ synthetic; comprehensive; integrated: ~ 征〈医〉syndrome / ~ 报道 news roundup / ~ 大学 (comprehensive) university / ~ 国力 overall national strength / ~ 利用 comprehensive utilization; multipurpose use

棕（椶） zōng ❶ palm; palm fibre; coir: ~ 榈 also "棕树" palm / ~ 绳 coir rope ❷ also "棕色" brown

踪（蹤） zōng also "踪迹" track; trace; footprint

踪影 zōngyǐng trace; shadow; sign: ~ 全无 disappear without a trace; vanish into thin air

鬃 zōng (hog) bristle; mane (of a horse)

zǒng

总（總） zǒng ❶ gather; put together; sum up: ~ 而言之 in brief; to sum up; all in all ❷ general; overall; total: ~ 裁 president (of a company or political party) / ~ 称 general term or reference / ~ 额 total (amount); gross amount / ~ 攻〈军〉general offensive / ~ 数 also "总和" aggregate (number); (sum) total / ~ 动员 general or total mobilization / ~ 需求 aggregate demand ❸ chief; leading; general: ~ 部 general headquarters / ~ 纲 general programme or principles / ~ 机〈通信〉telephone exchange; switchboard / ~ 编辑 (shortened as 总编) editor-in-chief / ~ 公司 head office (of a corporation); parent company; (controlling) corporation / ~ 经理 general manager; president / ~ 书记 general secretary; secretary-general / ~ 司令 commander-in-chief / ~ 参谋长 chief of general staff / ~ 工程师 chief engineer ❹ without exception; always; invariably: 他 ~ 是迟到。 He is always late. ❺ anyway; eventually; sooner or later: ~ 归 eventually; anyhow; at any rate / 问题 ~ 得解决。 The problem must be solved. ❻ at least; surely: 她出国 ~ 该有十年了吧。 It must be ten years since she went abroad.

总督 zǒngdū ❶ governor-general (of one or more provinces, in the Qing Dynasty) ❷ viceroy; governor (in British colonies) ❸ governor-general (in some Commonwealth countries)

总共 zǒnggòng altogether; in all; in toto

总管 zǒngguǎn ❶ (person) in full or general charge (of sth): 人力资源 ~

human resources manager ❷ 〈旧〉butler (of a rich family)

总汇 zǒnghuì ❶ (of streams) come or flow together; ～入海 converge and empty into the sea / 力量的～ aggregation of strength ❷ (often used as name of a shop) emporium; town; 服装～ clothing town

总集 zǒngjí collection of writings or poems by many authors or poets; anthology

总计 zǒngjì ❶ 〈数〉grand total ❷ total; amount to; add up to

总监 zǒngjiān inspector general; chief inspector; 税务～ Tax Inspector General / 财务～ (of a company) CFO (Chief Financial Officer)

总角 zǒngjiǎo 〈书〉〈喻〉childhood; ～之交 childhood friend

总结 zǒngjié sum up; summarize; ～会 summing-up meeting / ～报告 final or concluding report / 做～ make a summary; give a summing-up

总揽 zǒnglǎn assume overall responsibility; take full charge; ～大权 exercise overall authority; assume full power

总理 zǒnglǐ ❶ premier; prime minister; (of Germany) chancellor ❷ (of some political parties) chairman ❸ 〈书〉assume overall responsibility; ～其事 take full charge of sth

总算 zǒngsuàn ❶ at last; eventually; finally; 风～停了。The wind subsided at last. ❷ all things considered; by and large; on the whole

总体 zǒngtǐ general; overall; total; ～战 total or general war / ～设计 overall or master design

总统 zǒngtǒng president (of a republic); ～府 presidential palace / ～制 presidential system

总务 zǒngwù general affairs or services; ～处 general affairs division

总之 zǒngzhī generally speaking; in short; in a word

zòng

纵（縱） zòng ❶ vertical; from north to south; from front to back; ～队 column; file / ～向 vertical; from top to bottom; from front to back / ～剖面 also "纵切面"; "纵断面" vertical section; longitudinal profile ❷ release; set free; free; ～敌贻患 court future trouble by setting one's enemy free ❸ indulge; let loose; do freely; ～酒 drink to excess; be addicted to drinking / ～声 at the top of one's voice; as loudly as one can / ～目远眺 look as far as the eye can see; gaze into the distance / ～谈时事 talk freely about current affairs ❹ also "纵身" throw oneself (forward or upward); jump; leap ❺ 〈书〉even if; (even) though; ～使 also "纵令" even if; even though / ～死不悔 refuse to repent even to the end of one's life

纵横 zònghéng ❶ vertically and horizontally; in length and breadth; ～交错 (of rivers, etc) crisscross / ～捭阖 〈喻〉manoeuvre among various states, groups, etc; scheme artfully ❷ with great ease; fluently; freely; 笔意～ write fluently ❸ (of an army) move about freely and quickly; sweep through (through vast areas)

纵虎归山 zònghǔguīshān also "放虎归山" set a tiger free — cause future calamity; have no end of future trouble

纵火 zònghuǒ set fire (to houses, etc); commit arson; ～案 case of arson / ～犯 arsonist

纵览 zònglǎn look far and wide; make a comprehensive survey; ～古今 also "纵观古今" take a panoramic view of both ancient and modern times

纵情 zòngqíng to one's heart's content; as much as one likes; ～大笑 laugh as much as one likes; give oneself over to laughter / ～痛哭 weep one's fill

纵然 zòngrán　even though; even if; no matter whether: ～他不支持, 我们也要干到底。We'll stick to the end even if he refuses to support us.

纵容 zòngróng　connive or wink at; indulge: ～非法活动 wink at unlawful activities / ～自己的孩子 pamper one's child

纵深 zòngshēn　〈军〉〈喻〉depth: 向～推进 push in deep / 改革要不断向～发展。It is imperative to deepen the reform continuously.

粽 zòng

粽子 zòngzi　pyramid-shaped dumpling made of glutinous rice wrapped in bamboo or reed leaves

zǒu

走 zǒu　❶ walk; go; travel: ～失 get lost; be missing / ～极端 go to extremes / ～着瞧 wait and see / ～南闯北 travel extensively; be much travelled ❷ run; rush about: ～马上任 take office; assume a post ❸ move; operate; wield: ～笔〈书〉write swiftly / ～低 (of prices, etc) move downward; decline / ～俏 (of goods, etc) sell well; be salable / 该你～(棋)了。It is your turn to make the next move. / 我的表不～了。My watch has stopped. ❹ leave; go away: 〈婉〉die ❺ call on; visit: ～亲戚 call on or visit relatives ❻ through; by; from: ～正门 go through the main gate ❼ leak; reveal; let out: 车胎～气了。The tyre went flat. ❽ be different from the original; lose shape, flavour, etc: ～色 lose colour; discolour; fade / ～调儿 out of tune; not at the correct musical pitch

走板 zǒubǎn　❶ (in singing traditional Chinese opera) be or go off the beat ❷

also "走题" speak beside the point; wander from the subject; be wide of the mark

走动 zǒudòng　❶ move or get about; stretch one's legs: 来回～ walk to and fro ❷ socialize; visit each other: 两家人不常～。The two families seldom call on each other.

走读 zǒudú　attend a day school: ～生 day or nonresident student

走访 zǒufǎng　❶ have an interview with; interview ❷ go and see; call on; visit

走钢丝 zǒugāngsī　❶ wire-walking; tightrope walking: 表演～ perform on the tightrope ❷〈喻〉walk a tightrope; walk on thin ice

走狗 zǒugǒu　running dog; lackey; flunkey

走过场 zǒuguòchǎng　❶ (in traditional opera) go from one end of the stage to the other without stopping ❷ also "走形式" do sth as a mere formality; go through the motions

走红 zǒuhóng　❶ see "走运" ❷ be in favour or demand; be popular

走后门 zǒuhòumén　get in by the back door; secure advantages through pull or connections: ～现象 backdoor dealings

走火 zǒuhuǒ　❶ (of firearms) go off accidentally ❷〈电〉sparking (of wires, etc) ❸〈喻〉go too far in what one says; put sth too strongly

走廊 zǒuláng　❶ corridor; passage; passageway ❷〈喻〉corridor: 空中～ air corridor

走漏 zǒulòu　also "走露" divulge; let or leak out: ～风声 leak information; let out a secret

走路 zǒulù　❶ walk; go on foot: 走错路 take a wrong path; go astray / 走老路 follow a set routine; move in a rut / 走弯路 make a detour; follow a zigzag course / 走下坡路 go downhill; go from bad to worse ❷ see "走人"

走马看花 zǒumǎkànhuā　*also* "走马观花" look at flowers while riding on horseback — gain a superficial understanding through cursory observation：～地看风景 snatch a glance of the landscape

走人 zǒurén　〈口〉(of a person) leave；depart；get away：叫他卷铺盖～。Tell him to pack off. or Send him packing.

走神儿 zǒushénr　absent-minded；inattentive；wool-gathering

走势 zǒushì　❶ see "走向 ❶" ❷ trend；tendency

走私 zǒusī　smuggle：～犯 smuggler / ～团伙 smuggling ring

走投无路 zǒutóuwúlù　have no way out；be driven to a tight corner；come to the end of one's tether

走向 zǒuxiàng　❶ run；trend；alignment：边界～ alignment or run of a boundary line ❷ move towards；head for；be on the way to：～世界 step onto the world arena；become a world player；open to the outside world / ～衰落 be on the decline

走穴 zǒuxué　(of performers) moonlight

走样 zǒuyàng　lose shape；be out of form；deviate from the original model：把作者的意思说～了 misinterpret or misrepresent the author

走运 zǒuyùn　have a stroke of luck；be lucky or fortunate：不～ have bad or tough or hard luck；be off one's luck

走卒 zǒuzú　pawn；cat's paw；flunkey

走嘴 zǒuzuǐ　*also* "说走嘴" make a slip of the tongue；blurt sth out；let slip an inadvertent remark

zòu

奏 zòu　❶ play；strike up；perform (on a musical instrument)：～乐 play music；strike up a tune / ～鸣曲 〈乐〉sonata ❷ achieve；attain；produce：～捷 win a battle；score a victory；be triumphant / ～效 prove effective；achieve the intended result ❸ present a memorial to an emperor：～章 *also* "奏疏" memorial to the throne

揍 zòu　❶〈口〉beat；hit ❷〈方〉break；smash：把瓶子给～了 smash a bottle

zū

租 zū　❶ rent；hire；lease：～户 tenant (of housing)；leaseholder；hirer (of sth) / ～约 lease / ～用场地 hire a venue ❷ rent or hire out；lease：～佃 (of a landlord) rent out land to tenants ❸ rent：～金 *also* "租钱" rent；rental / ～子 〈口〉(land or ground) rent

租界 zūjiè　〈史〉(foreign) concession or settlement：法～ French Concession (in pre-WWII Shanghai, etc)

租借 zūjiè　❶ rent；hire；lease：～地 leased territory；leasehold / ～人 lessee；tenant；hirer ❷ rent or hire out；lease

租赁 zūlìn　rent or hire；rent or hire out；lease：～业 leasing trade / ～公司 leasing company / ～经营 lease operation or management

zú

足 zú　❶ foot；leg；leg-shaped support of a utensil ❷ adequate；sufficient；full：劲头很～ be full of energy / ～赤 pure gold / ～见 it serves to show；one can well imagine；obviously / 不～月 (of a baby) born prematurely / ～～睡了三天 sleep for a good three days ❸ deserve；merit；be worth：何～挂齿 nothing to speak of；not worth mentioning

足够 zúgòu　adequate；enough；sufficient：有～的思想准备 be fully prepared mentally／有您这句话就～了。Your words are good enough for me. or I'm contented with what you've said.

足迹 zújì　footprint；trace；track：～遍全国 have been to every corner of the country

足球 zúqiú　soccer；football：～场（football）field；pitch／～运动员footballer；football player

足坛 zútán　football circles；world of soccer：～名将 famous football player

足下 zúxià　（used mostly in letters）respectful form of address between friends：烦～代劳。Will you please do this for me?

足智多谋 zúzhì-duōmóu　wise and resourceful；shrewd and full of stratagems

卒 zú ❶ soldier；private；(in Chinese chess) pawn ❷〈旧〉servant；attendant：役～ servant；flunkey ❸〈书〉finish；end；wind up：～岁 pass a year／～业 graduate；complete one's studies／～成帝业 finally win the imperial throne ❹ die：病～ die of illness

族 zú ❶ clan：～谱 family or genealogical tree；genealogy／～人 clansman／～长 clan elder；head of a clan ❷ nationality；race；ethnic group：回～ Hui ethnic group／～群（ethnic）group；community ❸ class or group of things or people with common features：工薪～ salaried people

镞 zú　also "箭镞"〈书〉arrowhead

zǔ

诅 zǔ　curse；swear：～咒 call down evil，misfortune，etc upon sb；curse

阻 zǔ　block；hinder；obstruct：～断 block；cut off／～截 check；

intercept／～难 put obstacles in sb's way；stand in the way／山河～隔 separated or cut off by rivers and mountains

阻碍 zǔ'ài ❶ hinder；impede；block：～交通 block or hold up the traffic ❷ obstacle；hindrance；impediment：毫无～ without a hitch

阻挡 zǔdǎng　stop；block；obstruct：不可～ not to be blocked；unstoppable

阻击 zǔjī　〈军〉block；check；intercept：～战 blocking action

阻拦 zǔlán　stop；obstruct；bar the way：～行人横穿马路 stop pedestrians from jay-walking

阻力 zǔlì ❶ obstruction；hindrance；resistance：冲破重重～ break through one obstacle after another ❷〈理〉resistance；pullback；drag：空气～ air resistance

阻挠 zǔnáo　stand in the way；create obstacles；hinder

阻塞 zǔsè　(of traffic，road，etc) block；jam；clog

阻止 zǔzhǐ　stop；prevent；hold back：～人们交往 bar people from associating with each other

组 zǔ ❶ organize；build；form：～稿（of editors）commission authors to write on specific topics；solicit contributions／～阁 form or set up a cabinet；〈喻〉form a leading body／～建 set up；establish（an organization，etc）／～团出访 organize a delegation for a foreign tour ❷ group；team ❸ (of literary works，etc) suite；series：～曲〈乐〉suite／.～诗 series of poems

组成 zǔchéng　form；compose；constitute：～部分 component (part)；ingredient／由 20 人～ consist of twenty people

组合 zǔhé　make up；combine；compose：词的～ combination of words／～家具 composite or combination furniture／～音响 hi-fi（stereo component system)

组织 zǔzhī ❶ organize; form: ～货源 find new sources of goods / ～能力 organizational ability / ～委员会（shortened as 组委会）organizing committee ❷ organization; organized system: ～法 organic law / ～观念 sense of organization / ★关系 membership credentials; organizational affiliation / ～生活 cell meeting of an organization ❸〈生理〉〈医〉tissue: 神经～ nerve or nervous tissue

组装 zǔzhuāng　assemble; ～图 assembly drawing / ～生产线 assembly line

俎 zǔ ❶ utensil for sacrificial ox or sheep ❷ chopping block: ～上肉〈书〉meat on the chopping block — helpless victim

祖 zǔ ❶ grand-: ～父（paternal）grandfather / ～母（paternal）grandmother ❷ ancestor: ～辈 forefathers; ancestors; ancestry / ～坟 ancestral grave / ～业 ancestral estate; great achievements of one's ancestors / ～宗 also ～上"forefathers; ancestry; forebears / ～传秘方 secret recipe handed down in the family ❸ founder; originator: ～师 founder of a school of learning or a religious sect; originator of a secret society or a trade

祖国 zǔguó　motherland; fatherland; homeland: ～统一大业 great cause of national reunification

祖籍 zǔjí　original family home; ancestral home; land of one's forefathers: ～山东 be of Shandong origin

祖先 zǔxiān ❶ ancestors; ancestry; forefathers ❷ ancient organisms from which present-day living things or beings are evolved: 人类的～是类人猿。Man descended from anthropoid ape.

祖祖辈辈 zǔzǔ-bèibèi　from generation to generation; generation after generation; for generations

zuān

钻（鑽） zuān ❶ drill; bore (a hole, etc) ❷ get or sneak into; make one's way into: ～到水里 disappear into the water ❸ make a thorough study of; study intensively; dig into: ～书本 bury oneself in books; dig into books ❹ curry favour with sb in authority: ～门子〈口〉fawn on the powers that be
see also zuàn

钻空子 zuānkòngzi　take advantage of a loophole; exploit an opening: 让人钻了空子 give sb a handle against one

钻牛角尖 zuānniújiǎojiān ❶ waste time and effort studying sth insignificant or insoluble; split hairs ❷ get oneself into a dead end and refuse to acknowledge it

钻探 zuāntàn　(exploration) drilling: ～设备 drilling equipment / ～石油 drill for oil

钻研 zuānyán　dig into; study intensively: ～业务 dig into one's vocational work; work hard to improve one's professional skill

钻营 zuānyíng　fawn on sb in authority for personal gain; use pull to attain one's end

zuǎn

纂 zuǎn　compile; edit: ～辑 sort out and edit

zuàn

钻（鑽） zuàn ❶ drill; auger: ～机 (drilling) rig / ～头 bit (of a drill); drill bit ❷ *also* "钻石" diamond; jewel: ～戒 diamond ring
see also zuān

赚攥 zuàn 〈方〉deceive; hoax; kid see also zhuàn
zuàn grip; grasp; hold; ～拳 clench one's fist

zuǐ

嘴 zuǐ ❶ mouth; sth shaped or functioning like a mouth; ～唇 lip / 壶～ spout of a teapot ❷ used to describe a feature or trait associated with the function of the mouth; ～笨 clumsy at speech; inarticulate / ～馋 fond of good food; gluttonous / ～刁 particular about food / ～紧 also "嘴严" tight-lipped; close-mouthed; discreet / ～快 also "嘴松" loose-tongued; blabbing / ～甜 smooth-tongued; honey-lipped / ～硬 be reluctant or unwilling to admit error or defeat

嘴巴 zuǐba （area around the）mouth; 打～ slap sb's face; box sb's ears

嘴脸 zuǐliǎn 〈贬〉looks; features; countenance: 成天没个好～ pull a long face all day long

zuì

最 zuì ❶ most; least: ～爱 best loved; darling of one's heart / ～多 (at) most; maximum / ～北边 farthest to the north; northernmost / ～里头 innermost / ～下面 at the very bottom; bottommost / ～惠国待遇 most-favoured-nation （MFN） treatment; MFN trading status / ～不发达国家 least developed country （LDC） / ～能说明问题 can best illustrate the point ❷ topmost: 世界之～ best of the world

最初 zuìchū initial; first; earliest; ～几天 (on the) first few days / ～她并不同意。She didn't agree at first.

最低 zuìdī lowest; minimum; ～工资

minimum wage

最高 zuìgāo highest; tallest; best; ～纲领 maximum programme / ～统帅 supreme commander / ～限价 ceiling price

最好 zuìhǎo ❶ best; top-notch; first-rate; ～的服务 first-class service ❷ had better or best; it would be best: 你～三思而行。You'd better think twice before you act.

最后 zuìhòu lastly; finally; ultimately: ～定稿 final version / ～通牒 ultimatum

最佳 zuìjiā best; optimal; optimum: ～方案 optimization programme; optimum solution / ～影片奖 Best Movie Award / 处于～(竞技)状态 be in top form

最近 zuìjìn ❶ lately; recently; of late: ～几个月 (in the) last few months ❷ soon; in the near future

最优 zuìyōu optimum; optimal; best; ～化〈数〉optimization / ～选择 optimum selection; best choice

最终 zuìzhōng last; final; ultimate: ～产品 end product / ～目的 ultimate aim / ～取得胜利 win final victory; triumph in the end

罪 zuì ❶ guilt; offence; crime; ～证 evidence of a crime; proof of one's guilt / ～状 charge in an indictment; (fact about a) crime / ～该万死 be guilty of a crime for which one deserves ten thousand deaths / ～魁祸首 arch-criminal; chief culprit / 有应得 receive well-deserved punishment ❷ (usu 罪咎) fault; failing; blame ❸ suffering; hardship; pain ❹ put the blame on; blame; ～己 blame oneself (for a mistake, etc)

罪不容诛 zuìbùróngzhū even death cannot atone for the offence; commit a heinous crime which even capital punishment cannot expiate

罪恶 zuì'è crime; guilt; evil; ～滔天 be guilty of towering or heinous crimes /

~的阴谋 evil plot; sinister scheme / 罪大恶极 guilty of the most atrocious crimes

罪犯 zuìfàn criminal; offender; culprit

罪过 zuìguo ❶ fault; offence; sin ❷ 〈谦〉 *used of an undeserved honour*, *etc*: 让您这样破费，真是~! It gives me a guilty conscience to let you go to such expense.

罪名 zuìmíng accusation; charge: 以间谍~被捕 be arrested on an espionage charge

罪孽 zuìniè wrongdoing that brings retribution; sin: ~深重 be steeped in iniquity

罪人 zuìrén guilty person; sinner; offender: 历史~ person condemned by history / 民族的~ a traitor to one's nation

罪行 zuìxíng crime; guilt; offence: 交待全部~ make a clean breast of one's crimes

罪责 zuìzé responsibility for an offence; culpability: ~难逃 can hardly get away with one's culpability; will not escape punishment for one's crime

蕞

蕞尔小国 zuì'érxiǎoguó 〈书〉small country; tiny state

醉

醉 zuì ❶ drunk; intoxicated; inebriated: ~鬼 drunkard; soak; inebriate / ~态 state of being drunk; drunkenness / ~意 signs or feeling of being drunk / ~醺醺 drunk; intoxicated; tipsy / ~翁之意不在酒 have other things in mind; have another axe to grind ❷ be drunk with; indulge in: ~心 be preoccupied with; be wrapped up or immersed in / ~生梦死 dream one's life away; lead a befuddled life / 春意~人 enchanting springtime ❸ (of certain food) soaked or steeped in liquor: ~虾 (as a cold dish) liquor-soaked shrimps

zūn

尊 zūn ❶ of a senior generation or rank; senior; elder: ~卑有序 proper regard for precedence; proper order of seniority ❷ esteem; respect; honour: ~老爱幼 respect the old and cherish the young ❸ 〈敬〉 honour: ~意 your opinion / ~姓大名 your name ❹ 〈量〉: 一~大炮 an artillery piece ❺ *also* "樽" ancient wine vessel

尊称 zūnchēng ❶ address or call (sb) respectfully ❷ respectful form of address; honorific title

尊崇 zūnchóng esteem; revere; venerate

尊贵 zūnguì honourable; respected; distinguished: ~的客人 honoured or distinguished guest

尊敬 zūnjìng ❶ respect; esteem; honour: 令人~ be worthy of respect / ~长辈 be respectful to one's elders ❷ honourable; respected; distinguished: ~的来宾们 distinguished guests

尊容 zūnróng (often used to show contempt) sb's looks or appearance: 瞧你那副~! See what a spectacle you are!

尊严 zūnyán dignity; integrity; honour: 民族~ national pride

尊长 zūnzhǎng elders and betters: 目无~ have no regard for one's elders and betters

尊重 zūnzhòng ❶ respect; revere; recognize: ~事实 face the facts / ~知识，~人才 esteem knowledge and talent ❷ (of behaviour) dignified; serious: 请你放~些! Please behave yourself!

遵 zūn abide by; adhere to; follow: ~命〈敬〉obey your command; comply with your wish / ~行 act on; abide by; follow / ~纪守法 observe law and discipline

遵从 zūncóng　follow; comply with; defer to; 判决 accept a verdict

遵守 zūnshǒu　abide by; comply with; honour: ～诺言 keep one's promise; honour one's commitment / ～交通规则 observe traffic rules

遵循 zūnxún　follow; observe; abide by: ～宪法 abide by the constitution

遵照 zūnzhào　comply with; conform to; act in compliance with (instructions from above, etc)

鳟 zūn　also "鳟鱼" trout; 虹～ rainbow trout

zǔn

撙 zǔn　save: ～节 practise economy; save; retrench

zuō

作 zuō　(usu 作坊)(handicraft) workshop　see also zuò

嘬 zuō　〈方〉suck (milk, etc)

zuó

昨 zuó　❶ yesterday: ～天 also "昨日" yesterday / ～夜 last night ❷ in the past; formerly: 今是而～非 right today but wrong in the past

琢 zuó　see also zhuó

琢磨 zuómo　❶ turn over in one's mind; mull over; ponder: ～出个办法 figure out a way ❷ guess; suppose; think: 我～他不会来了。 I guess he's not coming.
see also zhuómó

zuǒ

左 zuǒ　❶ left (side): ～边 also "左侧"; "左面" (on the) left or left-hand side; left / ～手 left hand (side) / ～撇子 left-hander; southpaw / ～券在握 have victory in the bag; be sure to win ❷ eccentric; heretical; erroneous: ～脾气 also "左性子" (person) of obdurate temperament; stubborn; pig-headed / ～道旁门 heresy; heretical sect; heterodox school ❸ contrary; opposite; different: 观点相～ hold different views; be at variance ❹ progressive; radical; left: 极～ ultra-left

左近 zuǒjìn　in the neighbourhood; round the corner; nearby

左派 zuǒpài　the left; left wing; leftist: ～分子 leftist; left-winger; lefty / ～政党 party of the left

左倾 zuǒqīng　❶ left-leaning; progressive ❷ "left" deviation: ～错误 "left" mistake

左袒 zuǒtǎn　〈书〉side with; be partial to

左翼 zuǒyì　left wing; the left; 〈军〉 left flank: ～分子 left-winger / ～作家 left-wing writer

左右 zuǒyòu　❶ left and right; one way or another: ～逢源 gain advantage from both sides; be able to achieve success one way or another; conduct oneself in a slick way / ～为难 (find oneself) between the devil and the deep blue sea; in a dilemma ❷ those in close attendance; attendants; retinue: ～手 right-hand man; chief aide; valuable assistant / 屏退～ order one's attendants to leave ❸ control; manipulate; influence: 为人～ be under sb's sway; fall under sb's influence ❹ (used after a numeral) around; or so: 10 天～ ten days or so; around ten days ❺ 〈方〉 anyway; anyhow; in any case

左…右… zuǒ…yòu…　used before two similar words for emphasis: 左膀右臂 right-hand man; capable lieutenant / 左顾右盼 glance right and left;

Z

look around / 左邻右舍（next door）neighbours / 左思右想 turn (sth) over in one's mind; ponder

佐 zuǒ assist; help; ~餐 go with rice or bread / ~理国事 assist (a ruler) with state affairs

佐证 zuǒzhèng also "左证" evidence; proof

撮 zuǒ 〈量〉used for a bunch of hair: 一~白毛 a tuft of white hair　see also cuō

zuò

作 zuò ❶ rise; get up; come or bring up: 日出而~ get up at sunrise / 枪声大~。Heavy fighting broke out. ❷ do; make; ~答 answer; reply / ~报告 make a speech or report; give a talk / ~假账 falsify accounts; cook the books / ~结论 reach a conclusion; pass a verdict / ~法自毙 fall into one's own trap; be hoist with one's own petard ❸ write; compose: ~词 write words (for a song) / ~家 writer / ~曲 write music; compose ❹ writings; work: 不朽之~ immortal or monumental work / ~品 works (of art and literature) ❺ pretend; feign; affect: ~态 affect; put on a pose; strike an attitude / 故～惊讶 put on a show of surprise; pretend surprise ❻ act or take as; be; become: ~ 保 be sb's guarantor; stand surety for sb; go bail for sb / ~陪 help entertain the guest of honour; be invited to keep the chief guest company / ~中 act as a middleman; be an intermediary / ~ 表率 serve as an example ❼ feel; have: 浑身~痒 itch all over
see also zuó

作案 zuò'àn commit a crime or an offence; carry out criminal activities: ~时被捕 be caught red-handed

作罢 zuòbà drop; cancel; give up

作弊 zuòbì practise fraud; cheat (in an examination, etc); 通同～ work together to cheat; practise fraud as partners

作壁上观 zuòbìshàngguān stand by and watch; be an onlooker

作别 zuòbié 〈书〉bid farewell; say adieu; take one's leave (of)

作对 zuòduì ❶ set oneself against (sb); be antagonistic to; oppose ❷ also "成双作对" make a pair; join in a marriage

作恶 zuò'è do evil; ~多端 do all sorts of evil; commit numerous crimes

作法 zuòfǎ ❶ (as of a Taoist priest) resort to magic art ❷ technique of writing; art of composition ❸ also "做法" way of doing things; practice; approach

作废 zuòfèi become invalid; be annulled or invalidated

作风 zuòfēng style (of work); style (of doing things): ～正派 be honest and upright; be open and aboveboard

作梗 zuògěng obstruct; hinder; create difficulties

作古 zuògǔ 〈书〉〈婉〉pass away; depart this life

作怪 zuòguài make mischief; stir up trouble: 兴妖～ conjure up a host of demons to create trouble; make trouble

作假 zuòjiǎ also "作伪" ❶ fake (relics, etc); forge; falsify ❷ behave affectedly; be unnatural or coy

作价 zuòjià fix a price for sth; appraise; evaluate: ～变卖 sell at a price

作茧自缚 zuòjiǎnzìfù get enmeshed in a web of one's own spinning; put a noose around one's own neck; work against oneself

作践 zuòjian ❶ spoil; ruin; waste: ～自己 wear oneself down (wilfully) ❷ humiliate; insult; violate (a woman)

作客 zuòkè ❶〈书〉sojourn: ～异乡

sojourn in a strange place or an alien land ❷ be a guest; visit; call on: 欢迎来北京～! Welcome to (visit) Beijing!

作乐 zuòlè make merry; have a good time; enjoy oneself: 饮酒～ drink wine and make merry; have a good time drinking

作料 zuòliào *also* "佐料" condiments; seasoning

作乱 zuòluàn stage a rebellion; incite a revolt

作美 zuòměi (often used in the negative) help; cooperate: 老天不～。The weather is not cooperative.

作难 zuònán ❶ feel embarrassed; be at a loss: 对不起, 让你～了。I'm sorry to have put you in this awkward situation. ❷ embarrass; make things difficult for

作孽 zuòniè do evil; commit a sin: 这样对待孩子真是～! It is sinful to treat a child like this.

作弄 zuònòng make a fool of; poke fun at; play tricks on

作呕 zuò'ǒu feel sick or nausea; feel like vomiting: 令人～ sickening; disgusting

作数 zuòshù (of sth) be valid; count; hold: 说话～ mean what one says

作祟 zuòsuì (of ghosts, etc) haunt (a place, etc); do mischief; create trouble: 这都是虚荣心心～。All this trouble is caused by vanity.

作威作福 zuòwēi-zuòfú ride roughshod over others; lord it over the people; play the tyrant

作为 zuòwéi ❶ conduct; action ❷ accomplish; do sth worthwhile: 有所～ achieve sth ❸ regard or treat as: take for: 把别人～挡箭牌 use sb as a shield ❹ as: ～老师的责任 one's responsibilities as a teacher

作文 zuòwén (write a) composition: ～讲评 comment on students' compositions

作物 zuòwù crop: 单一～经济 single-crop economy

作息 zuòxī work and rest: ～时间表 daily (work) schedule

作业 zuòyè ❶ school assignment or homework ❷ work; operation; production: 深海～ deep sea operation / ～班 work team

作揖 zuòyī make a bow with hands folded in front

作用 zuòyòng ❶ act on; affect: ～力〈理〉acting force / ～范围 sphere of action / 反～力 reacting force ❷ effect; role; function: 起积极～ play a positive role

作战 zuòzhàn fight (a battle); conduct operations: ～部署 operational preparations / ～指挥部 operational headquarters

作者 zuòzhě author; writer: ～不详 by an anonymous author; of unknown authorship

作证 zuòzhèng (of sth) serve as proof or evidence; (of sb) testify; bear witness (to sth)

坐 zuò ❶ sit; be seated; take a seat: ～等 sit (back) and wait / ～牢 be in jail; be imprisoned / ～探 hidden enemy agent; mole / ～而论道 sit back and indulge in empty talk; be a phrasemonger / ～失良机 let slip a golden opportunity (through inaction) / ～西朝东 (of a building, etc) face east ❷ travel by (train, etc): ～船 travel by boat; take a boat ❸ (a pan, etc) on a fire ❹ (of a gun, etc) recoil; (of a building) sink (back); sag ❺ (of a tree, etc) bear (fruit) ❻ result in or develop into a disease: ～下了腰疼病 gradually get lumbago ❼ (usu 坐罪)〈书〉be punished or condemned; ～实 verify; confirm; prove (a charge, etc) ❽〈书〉because of; owing to; on account of: ～此解职 be dismissed on this account

坐班 zuòbān　have (stipulated) office hours

坐吃山空 zuòchīshānkōng　remain idle and eat away a whole fortune; spend without earning; (of savings, etc) be eaten away without replenishment

坐次 zuòcì　also "座次" seating arrangement or order: 排～ arrange the seating order / ～表 seating chart

坐地分赃 zuòdìfēnzāng　(of a ringleader, etc) take a share of the spoils without participating personally in the robbery; divide or split the loot

坐观成败 zuòguānchéngbài　sit back and watch a fight on the sidelines; wait to see what will come of another's venture

坐井观天 zuòjǐngguāntiān　observe the sky from the bottom of a well — have a very narrow view or limited outlook

坐蜡 zuòlà　〈方〉be in a tight spot; land in a predicament: 让人～ put sb in a tight spot; get sb into hot water

坐冷板凳 zuòlěngbǎndèng　❶ hold an unimportant post and be ignored ❷ be kept waiting on the sidelines; be left to cool one's heels; be given the cold shoulder

坐立不安 zuòlìbù'ān　be restless or fidgety; be on pins and needles

坐落 zuòluò　(of a building, etc) be established in a place; be situated or located

坐山观虎斗 zuòshānguānhǔdòu　sit atop a mountain to watch the tigers fight — watch in safety while others fight it out (and reap the spoils when both sides are exhausted)

坐视 zuòshì　sit by and watch; look on with folded arms: ～不救 watch idly by without lending a helping hand

坐收渔利 zuòshōuyúlì　(short for 坐收渔人之利) reap advantages from a conflict without participating; profit from others' tussle; reap third party profit

坐位 zuòwèi　also "座位" ❶ place (to sit); seat: 排～ make seating arrangements ❷ thing to sit on; seat

坐卧不宁 zuòwòbùníng　also "坐卧不安" be unable to sit or sleep at ease; be on tenterhooks; be agitated

坐享其成 zuòxiǎngqíchéng　sit idle and enjoy the fruits of others' work; reap where one has not sown

坐以待毙 zuòyǐdàibì　anticipate certain death without putting up a struggle; await one's doom hands down

坐月子 zuòyuèzi　〈口〉be in confinement (after giving birth)

坐镇 zuòzhèn　(of a commander) personally attend to garrison duty; assume personal command; 〈喻〉(of sb important) be present personally

柞

柞 zuò　〈植〉oak

柞蚕 zuòcán　tussah: ～丝 tussah silk

座

座 zuò　❶ seat; place: ～钟 desk clock / ～上客 guest of honour; honoured guest / 上～儿 (of a play, theatre, etc) be a box-office success ❷ stand; base; pedestal ❸ (short for 星座) constellation: 天琴～ Lyra ❹〈旧〉〈敬〉form of address for a high-ranking official based on his position: 处～〈谑〉Honourable Divisional Chief ❺〈量〉used of sth large and solid: 一～城堡 a castle

座舱 zuòcāng　❶ (of a passenger plane) cabin ❷ (of a fighter) cockpit

座次 zuòcì　see "坐次" zuòcì

座机 zuòjī　private or special plane: 总统～ presidential plane

座谈 zuòtán　have an informal discussion (on sth): ～会 forum; symposium; informal discussion

座位 zuòwèi　see "坐位" zuòwèi

座无虚席 zuòwúxūxí　have a full or packed house; be packed

座右铭 zuòyòumíng motto；maxim

做 zuò ❶ make；manufacture；produce：～鞋 make shoes / ～圈套 set a trap ❷ write；compose ❸ do；undertake；engage in：～爱 make love；have sex / ～操 do exercises；work out / ～饭 do cooking；prepare a meal / ～买卖 also "做生意" do business；be engaged in trade / ～头发 do one's hair (usu at hairdresser's) ❹ hold (a celebration)：～寿 celebrate a birthday (usu of an elderly person)；give a birthday party ❺ be；become：～媒 be a matchmaker or go-between / ～好人 try to get along with everybody indiscriminately；play the good guy / ～朋友 make friends (with sb)；be friends ❻ be used as；serve as ❼ pretend；feign：～戏 do sth for appearance sake；～样子 make a show；go through the motions

做伴 zuòbàn keep sb company：有你～太好了。I am very glad to have your company.

做东 zuòdōng play the host；act as host：这次我～。This is my treat.

做法 zuòfǎ see "作法❸" zuòfǎ

做工 zuògōng ❶ do manual work ❷ workmanship：～差 of poor workmanship ❸ charge for the making of sth

做绝 zuòjué push (things) to the outside limit；leave no leeway for manoeuvre；pass the point of no return：坏事～ commit every kind of villainy

做客 zuòkè be a guest：欢迎来我家～。You are welcome to my house.

做梦 zuòmèng ❶ have a dream；dream：～也没想到的机会 undreamed-of opportunity ❷ day-dream；have a pipe dream

做人 zuòrén ❶ behave；conduct oneself；get along with people：不会～ not know how to behave tactfully in society ❷ be a person of integrity

做人情 zuòrénqíng do (sb) a special favour：把人家的东西拿去～ make a gift of what belongs to sb else

做声 zuòshēng make a sound (as when speaking, etc)：不～ keep mum or silent

做事 zuòshì ❶ handle affairs；act：～认真 be conscientious in everything one does ❷ work；be employed；have a job

做手脚 zuòshǒujiǎo juggle (things)；rig (sth)

做文章 zuòwénzhāng ❶ write an essay ❷ make an issue of；make a fuss over；capitalize on：抓住件事～ seize upon sth and make an issue of it

做戏 zuòxì ❶ act；perform ❷ put on a show；play-act

做贼心虚 zuòzéixīnxū have a guilty conscience；feel guilty

做主 zuòzhǔ ❶ decide；have the final say ❷ back (sb) up；support

做作 zuòzuo unnatural；affected；artificial：表情～ wear an unnatural expression

英文字母开头的词语
Words or Expressions Beginning with English Letters

A 股 short for A 种股票；A-shares, *renminbi*-denominated shares issued domestically for Chinese natural and artificial persons, and qualified foreign investors

AA 制 Dutch treat; going Dutch

A 型血 blood type A

AB 型血 blood type AB

ADSL asymmetrical digital subscriber line（非对称数字用户线路）

AIDS *see* "艾滋病" àizībìng

AM *also* "调幅" amplitude modulation

APC *also* "复方阿司匹林" compound aspirin

ATM 机 *also* "自动取款机"；"自动柜员机" automated teller machine; ATM

B 超 ultrasonic diagnosis B; ultrasonic diagnostic apparatus B; 做～ have or make an ultrasonic B check

B 股 short for B 种股票；B-shares, *renminbi*-valued shares issued domestically in US or HK dollars for overseas investors and Chinese nationals alike

B 型血 blood type B

BBS 〈信息〉bulletin board system（电子公告牌系统）；bulletin board service（电子公告牌服务）

BP 机 *also* "寻呼机"；"呼机" beeper; pager

CAD 技术 *also* "计算机辅助设计技术" CAD（computer-aided design）technology

CBD 区 *also* "中央商务区" Central Business District（of a city）

CD *also* "激光唱盘"compact disc

CD-ROM *also* "只读光盘" compact disc read-only memory

CDMA *also* "码分多址" code division multiple access；～手机 CDMA mobile phone

CEO *also* "首席执行官" Chief Executive Officer

CPU *also* "中央处理器"〈信息〉central processing unit

CT computerized tomography（计算机体层成像）；computerized

tomograph （计算机体层成像仪）：做～ have or make a CT check / ～机 computerized tomograph; CT apparatus

DIY do it yourself（自己动手做）

DNA deoxyribonucleic acid；～测定 DNA profiling / ～芯片 also "基因芯片"〈医〉DNA chip

DOS also "磁盘操作系统" disk operating system

DVD 机 DVD（digital versatile disc）player

E-mail also "电子邮件" electronic mail

EMS 业务 EMS（express mail service）business

F-1 赛车 Formula One racing（car）；F-1 racing

FAX also "传真" short for facsimile：发～ send a fax / ～机 fax machine

FM also "调频" frequency modulation

GDP also "国内生产总值" gross domestic product

GNP also "国民生产总值" gross national product

GPS also "全球定位系统" Global Positioning System

GRE （US） graduate record examinations（研究生入学资格考试）

GSM Global System for Mobile Communication（全球移动通信系统）：～手机 GSM mobile phone

H 股 short for H 种股票；H-shares, shares issued in hard currencies by state-owned Chinese corporations to raise funds in Hong Kong

hi-fi high-fidelity（高保真度）：～音响 hi-fi system

HIV 病毒 also "艾滋病病毒" HIV （human immunodeficiency virus）

IC 卡 IC（integrated circuit）card

ICU also "重症监护病房" intensive care unit

Internet see "因特网" yīntèwǎng

IP International Protocol （for Internet）：～卡 IP card / ～地址 IP address / ～电话 Internet telephone（call）

IQ also "智商" intelligence quotient

ISDN also "综合业务数字网"（popularly called 一线通）integrated services digital network

ISO 系列标准 ISO（International Standards Organization）serial standards（for quality control）

IT 产业 also "信息技术产业" IT （information technology）industry

K 金 carat gold；14～ 14 carat gold（58.3% gold）/ 18～ 18 carat gold（75% gold）

KTV karaoke-TV room （in a hotel, club, etc）

LD 唱机　LD (laser disc) player

MBA　*also* "工商管理硕士" master of business administration

MP3　MPEG 1 audio layer 3（一种常用的数字音频压缩格式）

MPA　*also* "公共管理硕士" master of public administration

MTV 节目　MTV (music television) programme

O 型血　blood type O

PC 机　*also* "个人电脑" personal computer (PC)

pH 值　pH (value)

RMB　short for "*renminbi*"（人民币）

SARS　*see* "非典" fēidiǎn

SIM 卡　*also* "用户身份识别卡" SIM (subscriber identification module) card

SOHO　small office home office（小型家居办公室）

SOS　(officially replaced by GMDSS) signal used to ask for rescue or help in an emergency：～儿童村 SOS children's village, special philanthropic institution for taking in and looking after orphans and homeless children

T 型台　catwalk (as in fashion shows)

T 恤衫　T-shirt

VCD 机　VCD (video compact disc) player

VIP　very important person（要人；贵宾）

WC　water closet（盥洗室；厕所）

WWW　*also* "万维网" World Wide Web

X 光　*also* "X 射线"；"爱克斯光" X-ray

附　录
Appendices

1. 中国历史年代简表

A Brief Chronology of Chinese History

五帝时代 Period of the Five Legendary Rulers c. 2600 BC - 2070 BC		黄帝 Huangdi (or Yellow Emperor） 颛顼 Zhuanxu 帝喾 Diku (or Emperor Ku) 唐尧 Yao (of Tang) 虞舜 Shun (of Yu)
夏 Xia Dynasty		c. 2070 BC - c. 1600 BC
商 Shang Dynasty		c. 1600 BC - 1046 BC
西周 Western Zhou Dynasty		1046 BC - 771 BC
东周 Eastern Zhou Dynasty 770 BC - 256 BC	春秋 Spring and Autumn Period	770 BC - 476 BC
	战国 Warring States Period	475 BC - 221 BC
秦 Qin Dynasty		221 BC - 206 BC
汉 Han Dynasty 206 BC - 220 AD	西汉 Western Han	206 BC - 25 AD
	东汉 Eastern Han	25 - 220
三国 Three Kingdoms 220 - 280	魏 Wei	220 - 265
	蜀汉 Shu Han	221 - 263
	吴 Wu	222 - 280
晋 Jin Dynasty 265 - 420	西晋 Western Jin	265 - 316
	东晋 Eastern Jin	317 - 420

		宋 Song (420 - 479)
南北朝 Northern and Southern Dynasties 420 - 589	南朝 Southern Dynasties	齐 Qi (479 - 502)
		梁 Liang (502 - 557)
		陈 Chen (557 - 589)
	北朝 Northern Dynasties	北魏 Northern Wei (386 - 534)
		东魏 Eastern Wei (534 - 550)
		北齐 Northern Qi (550 - 577)
		西魏 Western Wei (535 - 556)
		北周 Northern Zhou (557 - 581)
隋　Sui Dynasty		581 - 618
唐　Tang Dynasty		618 - 907
五代 Five Dynasties (907 - 960)	后梁 Later Liang (907 - 923)	
	后唐 Later Tang (923 - 936)	
	后晋 Later Jin (936 - 946)	
	后汉 Later Han (947 - 950)	
	后周 Later Zhou (951 - 960)	
宋　Song Dynasty 960 - 1279	北宋 Northern Song	960 - 1127
	南宋 Southern Song	1127 - 1279
辽　Liao (or Qidan, or Chitan)		916 - 1125 (est. 907)
金　Jin		1115 - 1234
西夏　Xixia (or Tangut)		1038 - 1227
元　Yuan Dynasty		1279 - 1368 (est. 1206)
明　Ming Dynasty		1368 - 1644
清　Qing Dynasty		1644 - 1911 (est. 1616)
中华民国　Republic of China		1912 - 1949
中华人民共和国　People's Republic of China		1949 -

2. 中国各民族
Ethnic Groups in China

中 文 in Chinese	汉语拼音 in Pinyin	英 文 in English	中 文 in Chinese	汉语拼音 in Pinyin	英 文 in English
阿昌族	Achang	Achang	傈僳族	Lisu	Lisu
白 族	Bai	Bai	珞巴族	Luoba	Lhoba
保安族	Bao'an	Bonan	满 族	Man	Manchu
布朗族	Bulang	Blang	毛南族	Maonan	Maonan
布依族	Buyi	Bouyei	门巴族	Menba	Monba
朝鲜族	Chaoxian	Korean	蒙古族	Menggu	Mongol
达斡尔族	Dawo'er	Daur	苗 族	Miao	Miao
傣 族	Dai	Dai	仫佬族	Mulao	Mulam
德昂族	De'ang	De'ang	纳西族	Naxi	Naxi
东乡族	Dongxiang	Dongxiang	怒 族	Nu	Nu
侗 族	Dong	Dong	普米族	Pumi	Primi
独龙族	Dulong	Derung	羌 族	Qiang	Qiang
俄罗斯族	Eluosi	Russian	撒拉族	Sala	Salar
鄂伦春族	Elunchun	Oroqen	畲 族	She	She
鄂温克族	Ewenke	Ewenki	水 族	Shui	Sui
高山族	Gaoshan	Gaoshan	塔吉克族	Tajike	Tajik
仡佬族	Gelao	Gelao	塔塔尔族	Tata'er	Tatar
哈尼族	Hani	Hani	土 族	Tu	Tu
哈萨克族	Hasake	Kazak	土家族	Tujia	Tujia
汉 族	Han	Han	佤 族	Wa	Va
赫哲族	Hezhe	Hezhen	维吾尔族	Weiwu'er	Uygur
回 族	Hui	Hui	乌孜别克族	Wuzibieke	Uzbek
基诺族	Jinuo	Jino	锡伯族	Xibo	Xibe
京 族	Jing	Gin	瑶 族	Yao	Yao
景颇族	Jingpo	Jingpo	彝 族	Yi	Yi
柯尔克孜族	Ke'erkezi	Kirgiz	裕固族	Yugu	Yugur
拉祜族	Lahu	Lahu	藏 族	Zang	Tibetan
黎 族	Li	Li	壮 族	Zhuang	Zhuang

3. 中国行政区划和省、区首府

China's Administrative Divisions and Provincial or Regional Capitals

直辖市
Municipalities Directly under the Central Government

北京(京)	Beijing (Jing)
上海(沪)	Shanghai (Hu)
天津(津)	Tianjin (Jin)
重庆(渝)	Chongqing (Yu)

省、自治区及其首府
Provinces, Autonomous Regions and Their Capitals

河北省(冀)	Hebei Province (Ji)
石家庄	Shijiazhuang
山西省(晋)	Shanxi Province (Jin)
太原	Taiyuan
内蒙古自治区(内蒙)	Nei Mongol or Inner Mongolia Autonomous Region (Nei Mongol)
呼和浩特	Hohhot
辽宁省(辽)	Liaoning Province (Liao)
沈阳	Shenyang
吉林省(吉)	Jilin Province (Ji)
长春	Changchun
黑龙江省(黑)	Heilongjiang Province (Hei)
哈尔滨	Harbin
江苏省(苏)	Jiangsu Province (Su)
南京	Nanjing
浙江省(浙)	Zhejiang Province (Zhe)

杭州	Hangzhou
安徽省(皖)	Anhui Province (Wan)
合肥	Hefei
福建省(闽)	Fujian Province (Min)
福州	Fuzhou
江西省(赣)	Jiangxi Province (Gan)
南昌	Nanchang
山东省(鲁)	Shandong Province (Lu)
济南	Jinan
河南省(豫)	Henan Province (Yu)
郑州	Zhengzhou
湖北省(鄂)	Hubei Province (E)
武汉	Wuhan
湖南省(湘)	Hunan Province (Xiang)
长沙	Changsha
广东省(粤)	Guangdong Province (Yue)
广州	Guangzhou
广西壮族自治区(桂)	Guangxi Zhuang Autonomous Region (Gui)
南宁	Nanning
海南省(琼)	Hainan Province (Qiong)
海口	Haikou
四川省(川或蜀)	Sichuan Province (Chuan or Shu)
成都	Chengdu
贵州省(黔或贵)	Guizhou Province (Qian or Gui)
贵阳	Guiyang
云南省(滇或云)	Yunnan Province (Dian or Yun)
昆明	Kunming
西藏自治区(藏)	Xizang or Tibet Autonomous Region (Zang)
拉萨	Lhasa
陕西省(陕或秦)	Shaanxi Province (Shan or Qin)
西安	Xi'an
甘肃省(甘或陇)	Gansu Province (Gan or Long)
兰州	Lanzhou
青海省(青)	Qinghai Province (Qing)
西宁	Xining
宁夏回族自治区(宁)	Ningxia Hui Autonomous Region (Ning)
银川	Yinchuan
新疆维吾尔自治区(新)	Xinjiang Uygur Autonomous Region (Xin)

乌鲁木齐	Urumqi
台湾省(台)	Taiwan Province (Tai)
台北	Taipei

特 别 行 政 区
Special Administrative Regions

| 香港(港) | Hong Kong Special Administrative Region (HKSAR) |
| 澳门(澳) | Macao Special Administrative Region (MSAR) |

图书在版编目(CIP)数据

新时代汉英小词典/潘绍中主编. —北京:商务印书
馆,2003
ISBN 7-100-03758-1

I. 新... II. 潘... III. ①英语—词典②词典—汉、
英— IV. H316

中国版本图书馆 CIP 数据核字(2003)第 021263 号

XĪNSHÍDÀI HÀNYĪNG XIǍOCÍDIǍN
新时代汉英小词典
潘绍中 主编

商 务 印 书 馆 出 版
(北京王府井大街36号 邮政编码100710)
商 务 印 书 馆 发 行
河北三河市艺苑印刷厂印刷
ISBN 7-100-03758-1/H·951

2003年9月第1版   开本 850×1270 1/64
2003年9月第1次印刷   印张 16⅝ 插页 1
印数 50 000 册

定价:28.00元